Lecture Notes in Computer Science 14372

Founding Editors

Gerhard Goos
Juris Hartmanis

Editorial Board Members

Elisa Bertino, *Purdue University, West Lafayette, IN, USA*
Wen Gao, *Peking University, Beijing, China*
Bernhard Steffen ⓘ, *TU Dortmund University, Dortmund, Germany*
Moti Yung ⓘ, *Columbia University, New York, NY, USA*

The series Lecture Notes in Computer Science (LNCS), including its subseries Lecture Notes in Artificial Intelligence (LNAI) and Lecture Notes in Bioinformatics (LNBI), has established itself as a medium for the publication of new developments in computer science and information technology research, teaching, and education.

LNCS enjoys close cooperation with the computer science R & D community, the series counts many renowned academics among its volume editors and paper authors, and collaborates with prestigious societies. Its mission is to serve this international community by providing an invaluable service, mainly focused on the publication of conference and workshop proceedings and postproceedings. LNCS commenced publication in 1973.

Guy Rothblum · Hoeteck Wee
Editors

Theory of Cryptography

21st International Conference, TCC 2023
Taipei, Taiwan, November 29 – December 2, 2023
Proceedings, Part IV

 Springer

Editors
Guy Rothblum 🆔
Apple
Cupertino, CA, USA

Hoeteck Wee
NTT Research
Sunnyvale, CA, USA

ISSN 0302-9743 ISSN 1611-3349 (electronic)
Lecture Notes in Computer Science
ISBN 978-3-031-48623-4 ISBN 978-3-031-48624-1 (eBook)
https://doi.org/10.1007/978-3-031-48624-1

This Springer imprint is published by the registered company Springer Nature Switzerland AG
The registered company address is: Gewerbestrasse 11, 6330 Cham, Switzerland

Paper in this product is recyclable.

Preface

The 21st Theory of Cryptography Conference (TCC 2023) was held during November 29 – December 2, 2023, at Academia Sinica in Taipei, Taiwan. It was sponsored by the International Association for Cryptologic Research (IACR). The general chairs of the conference were Kai-Min Chung and Bo-Yin Yang.

The conference received 168 submissions, of which the Program Committee (PC) selected 68 for presentation giving an acceptance rate of 40%. Each submission was reviewed by at least three PC members in a single-blind process. The 39 PC members (including PC chairs), all top researchers in our field, were helped by 195 external reviewers, who were consulted when appropriate. These proceedings consist of the revised versions of the 68 accepted papers. The revisions were not reviewed, and the authors bear full responsibility for the content of their papers.

We are extremely grateful to Kevin McCurley for providing fast and reliable technical support for the HotCRP review software. We also thank Kay McKelly for her help with the conference website.

This was the ninth year that TCC presented the Test of Time Award to an outstanding paper that was published at TCC at least eight years ago, making a significant contribution to the theory of cryptography, preferably with influence also in other areas of cryptography, theory, and beyond. This year, the Test of Time Award Committee selected the following paper, published at TCC 2007: "Multi-authority Attribute Based Encryption" by Melissa Chase. The award committee recognized this paper for "the first attribute-based encryption scheme in which no small subset of authorities can compromise user privacy, inspiring further work in decentralized functional encryption." The author was invited to deliver a talk at TCC 2023.

This year, TCC awarded a Best Young Researcher Award for the best paper authored solely by young researchers. The award was given to the paper "Memory Checking for Parallel RAMs" by Surya Mathialagan.

We are greatly indebted to the many people who were involved in making TCC 2023 a success. First of all, a big thanks to the most important contributors: all the authors who submitted fantastic papers to the conference. Next, we would like to thank the PC members for their hard work, dedication, and diligence in reviewing and selecting the papers. We are also thankful to the external reviewers for their volunteered hard work and investment in reviewing papers and answering questions. For running the conference itself, we are very grateful to the general chairs, Kai-Min Chung and Bo-Yin Yang, as well as the staff at Academia Sinica (Institute of Information Science and Research Center of Information Technology Innovation). For help with these proceedings, we thank the team at Springer. We appreciate the sponsorship from IACR, Hackers in Taiwan, Quantum Safe Migration Center (QSMC), NTT Research and BTQ. Finally, we are thankful to

Tal Malkin and the TCC Steering Committee as well as the entire thriving and vibrant TCC community.

October 2023   Guy Rothblum
                                                     Hoeteck Wee

Organization

General Chairs

Kai-Min Chung   Academia Sinica, Taiwan
Bo-Yin Yang   Academia Sinica, Taiwan

Program Committee Chairs

Guy N. Rothblum   Apple, USA and Weizmann Institute, Israel
Hoeteck Wee   NTT Research, USA and ENS, France

Steering Committee

Jesper Buus Nielsen   Aarhus University, Denmark
Krzysztof Pietrzak   Institute of Science and Technology, Austria
Huijia (Rachel) Lin   University of Washington, USA
Yuval Ishai   Technion, Israel
Tal Malkin   Columbia University, USA
Manoj M. Prabhakaran   IIT Bombay, India
Salil Vadhan   Harvard University, USA

Program Committee

Prabhanjan Ananth   UCSB, USA
Christian Badertscher   Input Output, Switzerland
Chris Brzuska   Aalto University, Finland
Ran Canetti   Boston University, USA
Nico Döttling   CISPA, Germany
Rosario Gennaro   CUNY and Protocol Labs, USA
Aarushi Goel   NTT Research, USA
Siyao Guo   NYU Shanghai, China
Shai Halevi   AWS, USA
Pavel Hubáček   Czech Academy of Sciences and Charles
     University, Czech Republic
Yuval Ishai   Technion, Israel

Aayush Jain	CMU, USA
Zhengzhong Jin	MIT, USA
Yael Kalai	Microsoft Research and MIT, USA
Chethan Kamath	Tel Aviv University, Israel
Bhavana Kanukurthi	IISc, India
Jiahui Liu	MIT, USA
Mohammad Mahmoody	University of Virginia, USA
Giulio Malavolta	Bocconi University, Italy and Max Planck Institute for Security and Privacy, Germany
Peihan Miao	Brown University, USA
Eran Omri	Ariel University, Israel
Claudio Orlandi	Aarhus, Denmark
João Ribeiro	NOVA LINCS and NOVA University Lisbon, Portugal
Doreen Riepel	UC San Diego, USA
Carla Ràfols	Universitat Pompeu Fabra, Spain
Luisa Siniscalchi	Technical University of Denmark, Denmark
Naomi Sirkin	Drexel University, USA
Nicholas Spooner	University of Warwick, USA
Akshayaram Srinivasan	University of Toronto, Canada
Stefano Tessaro	University of Washington, USA
Eliad Tsfadia	Georgetown University, USA
Mingyuan Wang	UC Berkeley, USA
Shota Yamada	AIST, Japan
Takashi Yamakawa	NTT Social Informatics Laboratories, Japan
Kevin Yeo	Google and Columbia University, USA
Eylon Yogev	Bar-Ilan University, Israel
Mark Zhandry	NTT Research, USA

Additional Reviewers

Damiano Abram	Benedikt Auerbach
Hamza Abusalah	Renas Bacho
Abtin Afshar	Saikrishna Badrinarayanan
Siddharth Agarwal	Chen Bai
Divesh Aggarwal	Laasya Bangalore
Shweta Agrawal	Khashayar Barooti
Martin Albrecht	James Bartusek
Nicolas Alhaddad	Balthazar Bauer
Bar Alon	Shany Ben-David
Benny Applebaum	Fabrice Benhamouda
Gal Arnon	Jean-François Biasse

Alexander Bienstock
Olivier Blazy
Jeremiah Blocki
Andrej Bogdanov
Madalina Bolboceanu
Jonathan Bootle
Pedro Branco
Jesper Buus Nielsen
Alper Çakan
Matteo Campanelli
Shujiao Cao
Jeffrey Champion
Megan Chen
Arka Rai Choudhuri
Valerio Cini
Henry Corrigan-Gibbs
Geoffroy Couteau
Elizabeth Crites
Hongrui Cui
Marcel Dall'Agnol
Quang Dao
Pratish Datta
Koen de Boer
Leo Decastro
Giovanni Deligios
Lalita Devadas
Jack Doerner
Jelle Don
Leo Ducas
Jesko Dujmovic
Julien Duman
Antonio Faonio
Oriol Farràs
Danilo Francati
Cody Freitag
Phillip Gajland
Chaya Ganesh
Rachit Garg
Gayathri Garimella
Romain Gay
Peter Gaži
Ashrujit Ghoshal
Emanuele Giunta
Rishab Goyal
Yanqi Gu

Ziyi Guan
Jiaxin Guan
Aditya Gulati
Iftach Haitner
Mohammad Hajiabadi
Mathias Hall-Andersen
Shuai Han
Dominik Hartmann
Aditya Hegde
Alexandra Henzinger
Shuichi Hirahara
Taiga Hiroka
Charlotte Hoffmann
Alex Hoover
Yao-Ching Hsieh
Zihan Hu
James Hulett
Joseph Jaeger
Fatih Kaleoglu
Ari Karchmer
Shuichi Katsumata
Jonathan Katz
Fuyuki Kitagawa
Ohad Klein
Karen Klein
Michael Klooß
Dimitris Kolonelos
Ilan Komargodski
Yashvanth Kondi
Venkata Koppula
Alexis Korb
Sabrina Kunzweiler
Thijs Laarhoven
Jonas Lehmann
Baiyu Li
Xiao Liang
Yao-Ting Lin
Wei-Kai Lin
Yanyi Liu
Qipeng Liu
Tianren Liu
Zeyu Liu
Chen-Da Liu Zhang
Julian Loss
Paul Lou

Steve Lu
Ji Luo
Fermi Ma
Nir Magrafta
Monosij Maitra
Christian Majenz
Alexander May
Noam Mazor
Bart Mennink
Hart Montgomery
Tamer Mour
Alice Murphy
Anne Müller
Mikito Nanashima
Varun Narayanan
Hai Nguyen
Olga Nissenbaum
Sai Lakshmi Bhavana Obbattu
Maciej Obremski
Kazuma Ohara
Aurel Page
Mahak Pancholi
Guillermo Pascual Perez
Anat Paskin-Cherniavsky
Shravani Patil
Sikhar Patranabis
Chris Peikert
Zach Pepin
Krzysztof Pietrzak
Guru Vamsi Policharla
Alexander Poremba
Alex Poremba
Ludo Pulles
Wei Qi
Luowen Qian
Willy Quach
Divya Ravi
Nicolas Resch
Leah Namisa Rosenbloom
Lior Rotem
Ron Rothblum
Lance Roy

Yusuke Sakai
Pratik Sarkar
Sruthi Sekar
Joon Young Seo
Akash Shah
Devika Sharma
Laura Shea
Sina Shiehian
Kazumasa Shinagawa
Omri Shmueli
Jad Silbak
Pratik Soni
Sriram Sridhar
Akira Takahashi
Ben Terner
Junichi Tomida
Max Tromanhauser
Rotem Tsabary
Yiannis Tselekounis
Nikhil Vanjani
Prashant Vasudevan
Marloes Venema
Muthuramakrishnan Venkitasubramaniam
Hendrik Waldner
Michael Walter
Zhedong Wang
Gaven Watson
Weiqiang Wen
Daniel Wichs
David Wu
Ke Wu
Zhiye Xie
Tiancheng Xie
Anshu Yadav
Michelle Yeo
Runzhi Zeng
Jiaheng Zhang
Rachel Zhang
Cong Zhang
Chenzhi Zhu
Jincheng Zhuang
Vassilis Zikas

Contents – Part IV

Group-Based Cryptography

Byzantine Agreement, Consensus and Composability

Lattices

Rigorous Foundations for Dual Attacks in Coding Theory

Charles Meyer-Hilfiger[(✉)] and Jean-Pierre Tillich

Project COSMIQ, Inria de Paris, Paris, France
{charles.meyer-hilfiger,jean-pierre.tillich}@inria.fr

Abstract. Dual attacks aiming at decoding generic linear codes have been found recently to outperform for certain parameters information set decoding techniques which have been for 60 years the dominant tool for solving this problem and choosing the parameters of code-based cryptosystems. However, the analysis of the complexity of these dual attacks relies on some unproven assumptions that are not even fully backed up with experimental evidence. These dual attacks can actually be viewed as the code-based analogue of dual attacks in lattice based cryptography. Here too, dual attacks have been found out those past years to be strong competitors to primal attacks and a controversy has emerged whether similar heuristics made for instance on the independence of certain random variables really hold. We will show that the dual attacks in coding theory can be studied by providing in a first step a simple alternative expression of the fundamental quantity used in these dual attacks. We then show that this expression can be studied without relying on independence assumptions whatsoever. This study leads us to discover that there is indeed a problem with the latest and most powerful dual attack proposed in [CDMT22] and that for the parameters chosen in this algorithm there are indeed false candidates which are produced and which are not predicted by the analysis provided there which relies on independence assumptions. We then suggest a slight modification of this algorithm consisting in a further verification step, analyze it thoroughly, provide experimental evidence that our analysis is accurate and show that the complexity claims made in [CDMT22] are indeed valid for this modified algorithm. This approach provides a simple methodology for studying rigorously dual attacks which could turn out to be useful for further developing the subject.

1 Introduction

1.1 The Decoding Problem and Methods for Solving It

Code-based cryptography is based on the hardness of decoding generic linear codes which in the binary case corresponds to

Problem 1 (decoding a linear code). *Let $\mathscr{C}$ be a binary linear code over $\mathbb{F}_2$ of dimension k and length n, i.e. a subspace of $\mathbb{F}_2^n$ of dimension k. We are given $\mathbf{y} = \mathbf{c} + \mathbf{e}$ where $\mathbf{c} \in \mathscr{C}$ and $\mathbf{e}$ is an error vector of Hamming weight $|\mathbf{e}| = t$ and we wish to recover $\mathbf{c}$ and $\mathbf{e}$.*

© International Association for Cryptologic Research 2023
G. Rothblum and H. Wee (Eds.): TCC 2023, LNCS 14372, pp. 3–32, 2023.
https://doi.org/10.1007/978-3-031-48624-1_1

Equivalently, this problem can also be viewed as solving an underdetermined linear system with a weight constraint. Indeed, we can associate to a subspace $\mathscr{C}$ of dimension k of $\mathbb{F}_2^n$ a binary $(n-k) \times n$ matrix $\mathbf{H}$ (also called a *parity-check* matrix of the code) whose kernel defines $\mathscr{C}$, namely $\mathscr{C} = \{\mathbf{x} \in \mathbb{F}_2^n : \mathbf{Hx}^{\mathsf{T}} = \mathbf{0}\}$. The decoding problem is equivalent to find an $\mathbf{e}$ of Hamming weight t such that $\mathbf{He}^{\mathsf{T}} = \mathbf{s}^{\mathsf{T}}$ where $\mathbf{s}$ is the *syndrome* of $\mathbf{y}$ with respect to $\mathbf{H}$, *i.e.* $\mathbf{s}^{\mathsf{T}} = \mathbf{Hy}^{\mathsf{T}}$. This can be verified by observing that if there exists $\mathbf{c} \in \mathscr{C}$ and $\mathbf{e}$ such that $\mathbf{y} = \mathbf{c} + \mathbf{e}$ then $\mathbf{Hy}^{\mathsf{T}} = \mathbf{H}(\mathbf{c} + \mathbf{e})^{\mathsf{T}} = \mathbf{Hc}^{\mathsf{T}} + \mathbf{He}^{\mathsf{T}} = \mathbf{He}^{\mathsf{T}}$.

This problem has been studied for many years [Pra62, Ste88, Dum91, Bar97, FS09, BLP11, MMT11, BJMM12, MO15, BM17] and until recently the best way to solve this problem has been based on variations/improvements on the information set decoding (ISD) algorithm of [Pra62]. They are basically all of exponential complexity in the codelength n for a fixed code rate $R \stackrel{\triangle}{=} \frac{k}{n}$, and error rate $\tau \stackrel{\triangle}{=} \frac{t}{n}$: correcting t errors in a binary linear code of length n with the aforementioned algorithms has a cost of $2^{\alpha n(1+o(1))}$ where $\alpha = \alpha(R, \tau)$ is a constant depending on the algorithm which is used. All the efforts that have been spent on this problem have only managed to decrease slightly this exponent α. This exponent is the key for estimating the security level of any code-based cryptosystem. This was the case until [CDMT22] found a way to improve greatly another decoding strategy, statistical decoding [Jab01], and this despite the fact that this strategy is far from being competitive as shown in [Ove06, DT17a]. Indeed, [CDMT22] showed that when performing a modification of statistical decoding already suggested in [DT17b, §8], there is a dramatic improvement which allows to beat significantly the best ISD algorithms in the low rate regime (say $R < 0.3$). Basically the idea is to split the support in two pieces and reduce decoding to an LPN problem that is solved with standard Fourier techniques.

1.2   Reduction to LPN

It can be argued that [CDMT22] is more than just a variation of the original statistical decoding algorithm, it is also a rather different way of approaching the decoding problem. As in [Jab01] the first step consists in producing low-weight parity-check equations, i.e. vectors that are in the row span of a parity-check matrix of the code and that are of low Hamming weight. But the way these parity-check equations are used is different (and even their form is different as we will explain shortly). Basically they are used to *reduce* the decoding problem to an LPN problem with as many samples (or oracle calls) as there are parity-check equations. Recall that the LPN problem is defined as follows

Problem 2 (LPN problem). *Let $\mathbf{s} \in \mathbb{F}_2^s$ be a secret vector and let $\tau \in [0, 1]$ be a parameter. Let $\mathcal{O}_{\mathbf{s}, \tau}(\cdot)$ be an oracle which, on a call, output:*

$$(\mathbf{a}, \langle \mathbf{s}, \mathbf{a} \rangle + e)$$

where $\mathbf{a}$ is uniformly distributed on $\mathbb{F}_2^s$ and e is distributed according to a Bernoulli of parameter τ. Moreover $\mathbf{a}$ and e are independent. We have access to $\mathcal{O}_{\mathbf{s}, \tau}(\cdot)$ and want to find $\mathbf{s}$.

The notation $\langle \mathbf{x}, \mathbf{y} \rangle$ stands for the scalar product $\sum_{i=1}^{n} x_i y_i$ performed over $\mathbb{F}_2$ between two binary vectors $\mathbf{x} = (x_i)_{1 \leq i \leq n}$ and $\mathbf{y} = (y_i)_{1 \leq i \leq n}$. The idea behind the reduction comes by noticing that given $\mathbf{y} = \mathbf{c} + \mathbf{e}$ the noisy codeword we wish to decode and $\mathbf{h} \in \mathscr{C}^{\perp}$ a parity-check of $\mathscr{C}$ we have that

$$\langle \mathbf{y}, \mathbf{h} \rangle = \langle \mathbf{e}, \mathbf{h} \rangle.$$

Now, by considering $\mathscr{P}$ and $\mathscr{N}$ two complementary parts of the positions we can write that

$$\langle \mathbf{y}, \mathbf{h} \rangle = \langle \mathbf{e}, \mathbf{h} \rangle = \langle \mathbf{e}_{\mathscr{P}}, \mathbf{h}_{\mathscr{P}} \rangle + \langle \mathbf{e}_{\mathscr{N}}, \mathbf{h}_{\mathscr{N}} \rangle$$

where $\mathbf{x}_{\mathscr{I}}$ denotes for a vector $\mathbf{x} = (x_i)_{1 \leq i \leq n}$ and a subset $\mathscr{I}$ of indices the vector $(x_i)_{i \in \mathscr{I}}$. And thus $\langle \mathbf{y}, \mathbf{h} \rangle$ can be seen as an LPN sample given as follows:

$$(\mathbf{a}, \langle \mathbf{a}, \mathbf{s} \rangle + e) \quad \text{with} \quad \begin{cases} \mathbf{a} \overset{\triangle}{=} \mathbf{h}_{\mathscr{P}} \\ \mathbf{s} \overset{\triangle}{=} \mathbf{e}_{\mathscr{P}} \\ e \overset{\triangle}{=} \langle \mathbf{e}_{\mathscr{N}}, \mathbf{h}_{\mathscr{N}} \rangle \end{cases} \tag{1.1}$$

where $\mathbf{e}_{\mathscr{P}}$ is the secret of our LPN problem, the samples come from $\mathbf{h}_{\mathscr{P}}$ and the noise is given by $\langle \mathbf{e}_{\mathscr{N}}, \mathbf{h}_{\mathscr{N}} \rangle$. We expect that the noise term $e = \langle \mathbf{e}_{\mathscr{N}}, \mathbf{h}_{\mathscr{N}} \rangle = \sum_{i \in \mathscr{N}} \mathbf{e}_i \mathbf{h}_i$ is more biased toward zero as $w \overset{\triangle}{=} |\mathbf{h}_{\mathscr{N}}|$ and $|\mathbf{e}_{\mathscr{N}}|$ decreases so that we need less samples to solve the LPN problem.

The idea of RLPN is to compute a set $\mathscr{H}$ of N parity checks of $\mathscr{C}$ of weight w on $\mathscr{N}$ to get N LPN samples and then solve the LPN problem to recover $\mathbf{e}_{\mathscr{P}}$. To that extent, [CDMT22] makes the assumption that the samples (1.1) match exactly the framework of the LPN Problem 2.

1.3   Dual Attacks and a Controversy

Statistical decoding [Jab01] or its variant, namely RLPN decoding, fall both into the category of what can be called a *dual attack* which means here a decoding algorithm that computes in a first step low weight codewords in the dual code (i.e. the vector space spanned by the rows of a parity-check matrix of the code) and then computes the inner products of the received word $\mathbf{y}$ with those parity-check to infer some information about the error $\mathbf{e}$. These methods can be viewed as the coding theoretic analogue of the dual attacks in lattice based cryptography [MR09] and like in coding theory were shown after a sequence of improvements [Alb17, EJK20, GJ21, MAT22] to be able of being competitive with primal attacks, and the crucial improvement came from similar techniques, namely by a splitting strategy. However, it was noticed in [CDMT22, §3.4] that the i.i.d. Bernoulli model implied by the LPN model for the $\langle \mathbf{e}_{\mathscr{N}}, \mathbf{h}_{\mathscr{N}} \rangle$'s is not always accurate but it was conjectured there that the discrepancy between this ideal model and experiments was not severe enough to impact the asymptotic analysis of the decoding based on this model. In lattice based cryptography, the dual attacks were strongly questioned recently in [DP23] by showing that similar assumptions made for analyzing dual attacks were in contradiction with some theorems in certain regimes or with well-tested heuristics in some other regimes. This raises the issue of really having a theoretical analysis of dual attacks on which we can rely on, not only to have faith on the predictions made with it on dual attacks in code or lattice-based cryptography but also to develop the topic.

It should be noted that this work has already begun in [CDMT22, Prop. 3.1], where the basic assumption of statistical decoding is proved. Indeed, the very first task is to estimate the "noise" term $\langle \mathbf{e}_{\mathcal{N}}, \mathbf{h}_{\mathcal{N}} \rangle$, or simply $\langle \mathbf{e}, \mathbf{h} \rangle$ where $\mathbf{e}$ is of a certain weight and $\mathbf{h}$ a parity-check equation of some weight too. The estimation of the bias $\varepsilon \overset{\triangle}{=} \mathrm{bias}(\langle \mathbf{e}, \mathbf{h} \rangle)$ is crucial, the reason being that $1/\varepsilon^2$ is the quantity that governs the complexity of statistical decoding (we need to collect that many samples in order to distinguish random scalar products from scalar products of this form). We have used here the following notation for a binary random variable X:

$$\mathrm{bias}(X) \overset{\triangle}{=} \mathbb{P}(X = 0) - \mathbb{P}(X = 1).$$

In [Jab01, Ove06, DT17b] this was done by assuming that $\mathrm{bias}(\langle \mathbf{e}, \mathbf{h} \rangle)$ is the same as the bias of $\langle \mathbf{e}, \mathbf{h}' \rangle$ where $\mathbf{h}'$ is uniformly distributed among the words of the same weight as $\mathbf{h}$. The point is that the bias of the latter can be computed by using Krawtchouk polynomials (see Sect. 2.3)

$$\mathrm{bias}(\langle \mathbf{e}, \mathbf{h}' \rangle) = \frac{K_w^{(n)}(|\mathbf{e}|)}{\binom{n}{w}}, \tag{1.2}$$

where $| \cdot |$ stands for the Hamming weight and $w = |\mathbf{h}'|$. [CDMT22, Prop. 3.1] proved that for a random code $\mathscr{C}$ we typically have $\mathrm{bias}(\langle \mathbf{e}, \mathbf{h} \rangle) = \mathrm{bias}(\langle \mathbf{e}, \mathbf{h}' \rangle)(1 + o(1))$ as soon as the number of parity-check equations of weight w is large enough, namely it requires that this quantity is of the form $\omega(1/\varepsilon^2)$.

1.4   Our Contribution

A Formula for the Bias. If we simplify a little bit, a Krawtchouk polynomial is essentially decreasing in the weight $|\mathbf{e}|$[1] and therefore decoding by using a bunch of scalar products $\langle \mathbf{h}, \mathbf{y} \rangle$ is really finding the $\mathbf{x} \in \mathbb{F}_2^s$ such that the $\langle \mathbf{h}, \mathbf{y} \rangle + \langle \mathbf{h}_{\mathscr{P}}, \mathbf{x} \rangle$'s take the value 0 the most often. Indeed, if $\mathbf{x} = \mathbf{e}_{\mathscr{P}}$ then $\langle \mathbf{h}, \mathbf{y} \rangle + \langle \mathbf{h}_{\mathscr{P}}, \mathbf{x} \rangle = \langle \mathbf{h}, \mathbf{y} \rangle + \langle \mathbf{h}_{\mathscr{P}}, \mathbf{e} \rangle = \langle \mathbf{h}_{\mathcal{N}}, \mathbf{e}_{\mathcal{N}} \rangle$ by using that $\langle \mathbf{e}, \mathbf{h} \rangle = \langle \mathbf{e}_{\mathscr{P}}, \mathbf{h}_{\mathscr{P}} \rangle + \langle \mathbf{e}_{\mathcal{N}}, \mathbf{h}_{\mathcal{N}} \rangle$. In such a case, we could expect that $\langle \mathbf{h}_{\mathcal{N}}, \mathbf{e}_{\mathcal{N}} \rangle$ is biased towards 0. For the wrong choice of $\mathbf{x}$, we expect that $\langle \mathbf{h}, \mathbf{y} \rangle + \langle \mathbf{h}_{\mathscr{P}}, \mathbf{x} \rangle$ behaves essentially like a Bernoulli random variable of parameter $\frac{1}{2}$ which is independent from $\langle \mathbf{h}_{\mathcal{N}}, \mathbf{e}_{\mathcal{N}} \rangle$. In a nutshell, the RLPN decoder of [CDMT22] is based

---

[1] It is decreasing in the interval $[0, n/2 - \sqrt{w(n-w)}]$ and then even if there are fluctuations (the polynomial has zeros) it behaves like $\mathrm{poly}(n) \sin(\alpha) e^{\beta n}$ with an exponent β which is decreasing with $t = |\mathbf{e}|$ and where Proposition 2 shows that there are nearby weights t' and w' for t and w respectively for which the exponential term captures the behavior of $K_{w'}(t')$.

on this heuristic together with a fast Fourier transform trick which allows to compute the weights of the vectors $\mathbf{v}(\mathbf{x}) = (\langle \mathbf{h}, \mathbf{y} \rangle + \langle \mathbf{h}_{\mathscr{P}}, \mathbf{x} \rangle)_{\mathbf{h} \in \mathscr{H}}$ all at once for all $\mathbf{x} \in \mathbb{F}_2^s$ where $\mathscr{H}$ is the set of parity-checks we use for decoding. The analysis of the decoder in [CDMT22] uses basically the aforementioned heuristic on the behavior of the $\mathbf{v}(\mathbf{x})$'s.

However, we have found that we have to be more careful than this for the model of the random variable bias($\langle \mathbf{h}, \mathbf{y} \rangle + \langle \mathbf{h}_{\mathscr{P}}, \mathbf{x} \rangle$) when $\mathbf{h}$ is chosen uniformly at random among the parity-check equations of weight w on $\mathscr{N}$. Our first contribution is indeed to give a general proposition which allows to get a clear picture about the bias of these random variables

Proposition 1. *Let $\mathscr{C}$ be an $[n, k]$-linear code. Let $\mathbf{y} = \mathbf{c} + \mathbf{e}$ be the noisy codeword we want to decode. Let $\mathscr{P}$ and $\mathscr{N}$ be two complementary subsets of $[\![1, n]\!]$ of size s and $n - s$ respectively and such that the restriction $\mathscr{C}_{\mathscr{P}}$ of the codewords of $\mathscr{C}$ to $\mathscr{P}$ has full dimension s. Then there is a unique linear map $\mathbf{R}$ such that $\mathbf{h}_{\mathscr{P}}^{\top} = \mathbf{R}\mathbf{h}_{\mathscr{N}}^{\top}$ for any parity-check $\mathbf{h}$. Let $\mathbf{x}$ be a vector of $\mathbb{F}_2^s$ and let $\mathbf{h}$ be sampled uniformly at random among the set $\mathscr{H}_{\mathscr{N}}(w)$ of parity-checks of $\mathscr{C}$ that are of weight w on $\mathscr{N}$. We have*

$$\text{bias}\left(\langle \mathbf{y}, \mathbf{h} \rangle + \langle \mathbf{x}, \mathbf{h}_{\mathscr{P}} \rangle\right) = \frac{1}{2^{k-s}|\mathscr{H}_{\mathscr{N}}(w)|} \sum_{\mathbf{c}^{\mathscr{N}} \in \mathscr{C}^{\mathscr{N}}} K_w^{(n-s)}\left(|(\mathbf{x} + \mathbf{e}_{\mathscr{P}})\mathbf{R} + \mathbf{e}_{\mathscr{N}} + \mathbf{c}^{\mathscr{N}}|\right),$$

$$(1.3)$$

where $\mathscr{C}^{\mathscr{N}}$ is $\mathscr{C}$ shortened in $[\![1, n]\!] \setminus \mathscr{N} = \mathscr{P}$, i.e. $\mathscr{C}^{\mathscr{N}} = \{\mathbf{c}_{\mathscr{N}} : \mathbf{c} \in \mathscr{C}, \ \mathbf{c}_{\mathscr{P}} = \mathbf{0}\}$.

A simple corollary of this result (by taking $\mathscr{P} = \emptyset$) is also that

Corollary 1. *Let $\mathscr{C}$ be an $[n, k]$-linear code. Let w be an integer in $[\![0, n]\!]$ and let $\mathbf{e}$ be a vector of $\mathbb{F}_2^n$ sampled uniformly at random among the set $\mathscr{H}(w)$ of parity-checks of $\mathscr{C}$ of weight w. Then*

$$\text{bias}\left(\langle \mathbf{e}, \mathbf{h} \rangle\right) = \frac{1}{2^k |\mathscr{H}(w)|} \sum_{\mathbf{c} \in \mathscr{C}} K_w^{(n)}\left(|\mathbf{c} + \mathbf{e}|\right). \qquad (1.4)$$

This gives a formula of the bias used in standard statistical decoding which holds for *all codes* and not only for *most* codes as is the case of the aforementioned Proposition 3.1 in [CDMT22]. An analysis of this sum for random codes allows to easily recover this proposition as $2^k |\mathscr{H}(w)| \approx \binom{n}{w}$ and the sum is easily seen to be dominated by the term $K_w^{(n)}(|\mathbf{e}|)$ in this case. The nice thing about this corollary is that it allows in principle to get a handle on this bias for more specific class of codes.

Analysis of RLPN Decoding and a Simple Correction. Proposition 1 is instrumental in analyzing the RLPN decoder of [CDMT22]. We will show that the heuristic made for the behavior of $\mathbf{v}(\mathbf{x})$ does not hold, and for the choice of parameters made in the RLPN decoder, with overwhelming probability there exists a bunch of $\mathbf{x}$ in $\mathbb{F}_2^s$ such that $\langle \mathbf{h}, \mathbf{y} \rangle + \langle \mathbf{h}_{\mathscr{P}}, \mathbf{x} \rangle$ is more biased toward zero than $\langle \mathbf{e}_{\mathscr{N}}, \mathbf{h}_{\mathscr{N}} \rangle$, the error term associated to the secret vector $\mathbf{e}_{\mathscr{P}}$ we wish to recover. In such a case, $\mathbf{e}_{\mathscr{P}}$ is not the solution to the LPN problem anymore. This shows that the RLPN decoding algorithm does not work as expected in [CDMT22]. Fortunately the set of $\mathbf{x}$ for which $\langle \mathbf{h}, \mathbf{y} \rangle + \langle \mathbf{h}_{\mathscr{P}}, \mathbf{x} \rangle$ is more biased toward zero than $\langle \mathbf{e}_{\mathscr{N}}, \mathbf{h}_{\mathscr{N}} \rangle$ can be bounded rigorously by using Proposition 1 and turns out to be moderate enough that a simple correction of the RLPN decoder works. It suffices to keep all candidates $\mathbf{x}$ whose bias($\langle \mathbf{h}, \mathbf{y} \rangle + \langle \mathbf{h}_{\mathscr{P}}, \mathbf{x} \rangle$) is above a certain threshold for which we also expect to keep $\mathbf{e}_{\mathscr{P}}$ and check if the candidate is correct by decoding a code in which s positions are removed (those belonging to $\mathscr{P}$) and for which the s positions of the error on which we bet (corresponding to $\mathbf{x}$) allow to decrease by s the dimension of the code. This problem is much easier to solve than the original decoding problem. It can for instance be solved by simple ISD algorithms. This variant of the RLPN decoder can be analyzed rigorously thanks to the aforementioned bound on the number of candidates. It turns out that for the parameters chosen in the RLPN decoder of [CDMT22], at least in the region where it beats the best ISD decoding algorithms, the number of those candidates times the complexity of an ISD solver on the reduced problem is not more than producing the set of parity-checks of weight w on $\mathscr{N}$ and computing the set of candidates by the fast Fourier technique used in [CDMT22]. From this we actually infer that the complexity result given in [CDMT22] actually holds for this variant of the RLPN decoder.

2   Notation and Preliminaries

2.1   Notation

Set, Vector and Matrix Notation. $[\![a, b]\!]$ indicates the closed integer interval between a and b. $\mathbb{F}_2$ is the binary field. $|E|$ is the cardinality of a finite set E. Vectors are indicated by lowercase bold letters $\mathbf{x}$ and matrices by uppercase bold letters $\mathbf{A}$. For a vector $\mathbf{x} = (x_i)_{1 \leq i \leq n}$ and $\mathcal{I} \subset [\![1, n]\!]$, $\mathbf{x}_{\mathcal{I}}$ is given by $\mathbf{x}_{\mathcal{I}} = (x_i)_{i \in \mathcal{I}}$ and $|\mathbf{x}|$ stands for the Hamming weight of $\mathbf{x}$. $\mathcal{S}_w^n \overset{\triangle}{=} \{\mathbf{x} \in \mathbb{F}_2^n \ : \ |\mathbf{x}| = w\}$ is the Hamming sphere of weight w of $\mathbb{F}_2^n$.

Probability and Entropy. When $\mathcal{D}$ is a probability distribution we write that $\mathbf{X} \sim \mathcal{D}$ to specify that $\mathbf{X}$ is distributed according to $\mathcal{D}$. More simply, when $\mathscr{H}$ is a set we write that $\mathbf{h} \hookleftarrow \mathscr{H}$ to specify that $\mathbf{h}$ is a random variable uniformly distributed over $\mathscr{H}$. Let $h_2(x) \overset{\triangle}{=} -x \log_2(x) - (1 - x) \log_2(1 - x)$ be the binary entropy and h_2^{-1} its inverse on $[0, \frac{1}{2}]$.

Fourier Transform. Let $f : \mathbb{F}_2^n \to \mathbb{R}$ be a function. We define the Fourier transform $\widehat{f} : \mathbb{F}_2^n \to \mathbb{R}$ of f as $\widehat{f}(\mathbf{x}) = \sum_{\mathbf{u} \in \mathbb{F}_2^n} f(\mathbf{u}) (-1)^{\langle \mathbf{x}, \mathbf{u} \rangle}$.

Landau and Asymptotic Notation. For real valued functions defined over $\mathbb{R}$ or $\mathbb{N}$ we define $o(), O(), \Omega(), \Theta()$, in the usual way. We write that $f = \omega(g)$ when f dominates g asymptotically; that is when $\lim_{x \to \infty} \frac{|f(x)|}{g(x)} = \infty$. We use the less common notation $\widetilde{O}()$, where $f = \widetilde{O}(g)$ means that $f(x) = O\left(g(x) \log^k g(x)\right)$ for some k. We will use this for functions which have an exponential behaviour, say $g(x) = e^{\alpha x}$, in which case $f(x) = \widetilde{O}(g(x))$ means that $f(x) = O(P(x)g(x))$ where P is a polynomial in x. We write that $f(n) = \text{poly}(n) \, g(n)$ when there exist two reals d_1 and d_2 such that $g(n) \, n^{d_2} < f(n) < g(n) \, n^{d_1}$.

2.2 Linear Codes

Definition 1. *(Binary linear code and dual code) A binary linear code $\mathscr{C}$ of length n and dimension k is a linear subspace of $\mathbb{F}_2^n$ of dimension k. We say that $\mathscr{C}$ is an $[n, k]$ linear code. We call $R = \frac{k}{n}$ the rate of the code. We denote by $\mathscr{C}^\perp$ the subspace of the vectors orthogonal to $\mathscr{C}$, i.e. $\mathscr{C}^\perp \overset{\triangle}{=} \{\mathbf{d} \in \mathbb{F}_2^n : \langle \mathbf{c}, \mathbf{d} \rangle = 0, \forall \mathbf{c} \in \mathscr{C}\}$.*

We will also use the following notions of

Definition 2. *(punctured code) For a code $\mathscr{C}$ and a subset $\mathcal{I}$ of code positions, we denote by $\mathscr{C}_\mathcal{I}$ the punctured code obtained from $\mathscr{C}$ by keeping only the positions in I, i.e.:*

$$\mathscr{C}_\mathcal{I} = \{\mathbf{c}_\mathcal{I} : \mathbf{c} \in \mathscr{C}\}.$$

Definition 3. *(shortened code) For a code $\mathscr{C}$ and a subset I of code positions, we denote by $\mathscr{C}^\mathcal{I}$ the shortened code obtained as follows:*

$$\mathscr{C}^\mathcal{I} = \{\mathbf{c}_\mathcal{I} : \mathbf{c} \in \mathscr{C} \text{ such that } \mathbf{c}_{[\![1,n]\!]\setminus\mathcal{I}} = \mathbf{0}\}.$$

It is readily seen that for any code $\mathscr{C}$ and any subset of positions $\mathscr{I}$ we have

$$(\mathscr{C}_\mathscr{I})^\perp = (\mathscr{C}^\perp)^\mathscr{I} \quad \text{and} \quad (\mathscr{C}^\mathscr{I})^\perp = (\mathscr{C}^\perp)_\mathscr{I}. \tag{2.1}$$

2.3 Krawtchouk Polynomial

We recall here some properties about Krawtchouk polynomial that will be useful in the article. Many useful properties can be found in [KS21, §2.2]

Definition 4. *(Krawtchouk polynomial) We define the Krawtchouk polynomial $K_w^{(n)}$ of degree w and of order n as $K_w^{(n)}(X) \overset{\triangle}{=} \sum_{j=0}^w (-1)^j \binom{X}{j}\binom{n-X}{w-j}$.*

The following fact is well known, it gives an alternate expression of the Krawtchouk polynomial (see for instance [vL99, Lemma 5.3.1]) :

Fact 3. *For any $\mathbf{a} \in \mathbb{F}_2^n$,*

$$K_w^{(n)}(|\mathbf{x}|) = \sum_{\mathbf{y} \in \mathbb{F}_2^n : |\mathbf{y}| = w} (-1)^{\langle \mathbf{x}, \mathbf{y} \rangle}. \tag{2.2}$$

We recall here the summary of some known results about Krawtchouk polynomials made in [CDMT22].

Proposition 2. *[CDMT22, Prop. 3.5, Prop. 3.6]*

1. *Value at 0. For all $0 \leq w \leq n$, $K_w^{(n)}(0) = \binom{n}{w}$.*
2. *Reciprocity. For all $0 \leq t, w \leq n$, $\binom{n}{t} K_w^{(n)}(t) = \binom{n}{w} K_t^{(n)}(w)$.*
3. *Roots. The polynomials $K_w^{(n)}$ have w distinct roots which lie in the interval $\left[n/2 - \sqrt{w(n-w)}, n/2 + \sqrt{w(n-w)} \right]$. The distance between roots is at least 2 and at most $o(n)$.*
4. *Magnitude in and out the root region. Let τ and ω be two reals in $[0,1]$. Let $\omega^{\perp} \triangleq \frac{1}{2} - \sqrt{\omega(1-\omega)}$, and let $z \triangleq \frac{1 - 2\tau - \sqrt{D}}{2(1-\omega)}$ where $D \triangleq (1-2\tau)^2 - 4\omega(1-\omega)$. Define*

$$\widetilde{\kappa}(\tau, \omega) \triangleq \begin{cases} \tau \log_2(1-z) + (1-\tau)\log_2(1+z) - \omega \log_2 z & \text{if } \tau \in [0, \omega^{\perp}] \\ \frac{1 - h(\tau) + h(\omega)}{2} & \text{otherwise.} \end{cases}$$

   - *4.1. If $\tau \leq \frac{1}{2} - \sqrt{\omega(1-\omega)}$, then for all t and w such that $\lim_{n \to \infty} \frac{t}{n} = \tau$ and $\lim_{n \to \infty} \frac{w}{n} = \omega$ we have $K_w^{(n)}(t) = 2^{n(\widetilde{\kappa}(\tau, \omega) + o(1))}$.*
   - *4.2. If $\tau > \frac{1}{2} - \sqrt{\omega(1-\omega)}$, then there exists $t(n)$ and $w(n)$ such that $\lim_{n \to \infty} \frac{t}{n} = \tau$, $\lim_{n \to \infty} \frac{w}{n} = \omega$ and $\left| K_w^{(n)}(t) \right| = 2^{n(\widetilde{\kappa}(\tau, \omega) + o(1))}$.*

3   An Expression for the Bias of $\langle \mathbf{y}, \mathbf{h} \rangle + \langle \mathbf{x}, \mathbf{h}_{\mathscr{P}} \rangle$

In this section, we give the basic tool for studying the fundamental quantity manipulated by the RLPN algorithm, namely the bias $\langle \mathbf{y}, \mathbf{h} \rangle + \langle \mathbf{x}, \mathbf{h}_{\mathscr{P}} \rangle$. Let us first rewrite this expression as a scalar product of a vector depending on $\mathbf{x}$ and $\mathbf{e}$ with the restriction $\mathbf{h}_{\mathscr{N}}$ of $\mathbf{h}$ to $\mathscr{N}$. This is given by

Lemma 1. *Let $\mathscr{C}$ be an $[n, k]$, $\mathbf{c} \in \mathscr{C}$ and $\mathbf{y} = \mathbf{c} + \mathbf{e}$ be a noisy codeword. Let $\mathscr{P}$ and $\mathscr{N}$ be complementary subsets of $[\![1, n]\!]$ of size s and $n - s$ respectively and suppose that $\dim \mathscr{C}_{\mathscr{P}} = s$. Then there exists a unique linear map $\mathbf{R} : \mathbb{F}_2^{n-s} \to \mathbb{F}_2^s$ such that for all $\mathbf{h} \in \mathscr{C}^{\perp}$:*

$$\mathbf{h}_{\mathscr{P}}^{\mathsf{T}} = \mathbf{R}\, \mathbf{h}_{\mathscr{N}}^{\mathsf{T}}. \tag{3.1}$$

Moreover, we have that for all $\mathbf{h} \in \mathscr{C}^{\perp}$ and $\mathbf{x} \in \mathbb{F}_2^s$:

$$\langle \mathbf{y}, \mathbf{h} \rangle + \langle \mathbf{x}, \mathbf{h}_{\mathscr{P}} \rangle = \langle \mathbf{x}\mathbf{R} + \mathbf{e}_{\mathscr{P}}\mathbf{R} + \mathbf{e}_{\mathscr{N}}, \mathbf{h}_{\mathscr{N}} \rangle. \tag{3.2}$$

Proof. First, let us show (3.1). Suppose w.l.o.g. that $\mathscr{P} = [\![1, s]\!]$ and $\mathscr{N} = [\![s+1, n]\!]$. Let $\mathbf{G} \in \mathbb{F}_2^{k \times n}$ be a generator matrix of $\mathscr{C}$. Because $\mathscr{C}_{\mathscr{P}}$ is of dimension s there exists an invertible $\mathbf{J} \in \mathbb{F}_2^{k \times k}$ such that

$$\mathbf{J}\mathbf{G} = \begin{pmatrix} \mathrm{Id}_s & \mathbf{R} \\ \mathbf{0}_{k-s} & \mathbf{R}' \end{pmatrix}$$

where $\mathbf{R} \in \mathbb{F}_2^{s \times (n-s)}$ and $\mathbf{R}' \in \mathbb{F}_2^{(k-s) \times (n-s)}$. $\mathbf{J}\mathbf{G}$ is another generator matrix for $\mathscr{C}$. Therefore for any $\mathbf{h} \in \mathscr{C}^{\perp}$ we have $\mathbf{J}\mathbf{G}\mathbf{h}^{\mathsf{T}} = 0$. Since $\mathbf{J}\mathbf{G}\mathbf{h}^{\mathsf{T}} = \mathbf{h}_{\mathscr{P}}^{\mathsf{T}} + \mathbf{R}\mathbf{h}_{\mathscr{N}}^{\mathsf{T}}$, this gives (3.1). It is readily seen that $\mathbf{R}$ seen as a linear map is unique.

Now, let us prove (3.2). Recall that $\langle \mathbf{y}, \mathbf{h} \rangle = \langle \mathbf{e}_{\mathscr{P}}, \mathbf{h}_{\mathscr{P}} \rangle + \langle \mathbf{e}_{\mathscr{N}}, \mathbf{h}_{\mathscr{N}} \rangle$. Thus

$$
\begin{aligned}
\langle \mathbf{y}, \mathbf{h} \rangle + \langle \mathbf{x}, \mathbf{h}_{\mathscr{P}} \rangle &= \langle \mathbf{e}_{\mathscr{P}} + \mathbf{x}, \mathbf{h}_{\mathscr{P}} \rangle + \langle \mathbf{e}_{\mathscr{N}}, \mathbf{h}_{\mathscr{N}} \rangle \\
&= \langle \mathbf{e}_{\mathscr{P}} + \mathbf{x}, \left(\mathbf{R}\,\mathbf{h}_{\mathscr{N}}{}^{\mathsf{T}} \right)^{\mathsf{T}} \rangle + \langle \mathbf{e}_{\mathscr{N}}, \mathbf{h}_{\mathscr{N}} \rangle \quad \text{(Using (3.1))} \\
&= \langle (\mathbf{e}_{\mathscr{P}} + \mathbf{x})\,\mathbf{R}, \mathbf{h}_{\mathscr{N}} \rangle + \langle \mathbf{e}_{\mathscr{N}}, \mathbf{h}_{\mathscr{N}} \rangle \\
&= \langle (\mathbf{e}_{\mathscr{P}} + \mathbf{x})\,\mathbf{R} + \mathbf{e}_{\mathscr{N}}, \mathbf{h}_{\mathscr{N}} \rangle.
\end{aligned}
$$

$\square$

The RLPN decoder of [CDMT22] produces in its first step many parity-check equations of weight w on $\mathscr{N}$ by using standard techniques for producing low-weight codewords in a code. More elaborate techniques actually produce parity-check equations which have unbalanced weights, say $\mathscr{N}$ is partitioned into two sets $\mathscr{N}_1$ and $\mathscr{N}_2$ and $\mathbf{h}$ is of weight w_i on $\mathscr{N}_i$ for $i \in \{1,2\}$ and $w = w_1 + w_2$. Generally if we are looking for parity-check equations of an $[n,k]$ code $\mathscr{C}$, we look for codewords in the dual $\mathscr{C}^{\perp}$ which is of dimension $n - k$, we generally choose $\mathscr{N}_2$ of size slightly larger than $n - k$, say $|\mathscr{N}_2| = n - k + \ell$ and try to minimize the weight w_2 as much as we can on this part, whereas the rest of the parity on $\mathscr{N}$ (i.e. the $\mathscr{N}_1$ part) is just computed linearly from the $\mathbf{h}_{\mathscr{N}_2}$ and is of weight w_2 close to $|\mathscr{N}_1|/2$ (see picture below).

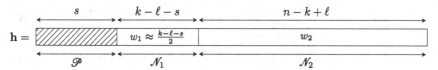

Our main tool for studying the RLPN decoder is now the following expression of the bias by using Lemma 1 and duality with the Poisson formula

Proposition 3. *Let $\mathscr{C}$ be an $[n,k]$ code. Let $\mathbf{y} = \mathbf{c} + \mathbf{e}$ be a noisy codeword (where $\mathbf{c} \in \mathscr{C}$). Let $\mathscr{P}$, $\mathscr{N}_1$ and $\mathscr{N}_2$ be fixed complementary subsets of $[\![1,n]\!]$ of size s, $k - \ell - s$ and $n - k + \ell$ respectively and such that $\dim \mathscr{C}_{\mathscr{P}} = s$. We denote $\mathscr{N} \stackrel{\triangle}{=} \mathscr{N}_1 \cup \mathscr{N}_2$. Then there exists a unique linear map $\mathbf{R} : \mathbb{F}_2^{n-s} \to \mathbb{F}_2^s$ such that for all $\mathbf{h} \in \mathscr{C}^{\perp}$, we have $\mathbf{h}_{\mathscr{P}}{}^{\mathsf{T}} = \mathbf{R}\,\mathbf{h}_{\mathscr{N}}{}^{\mathsf{T}}$. Let $\mathbf{x}$ be a fixed vector of $\mathbb{F}_2^s$ and let $\mathbf{h}$ be a vector sampled uniformly at random among the set $\widetilde{\mathscr{H}}$ of parity-checks of $\mathscr{C}$ that are of weight w_1 on $\mathscr{N}_1$ and w_2 on $\mathscr{N}_2$. We have that:*

$$
\operatorname{bias}\left(\langle \mathbf{y}, \mathbf{h} \rangle + \langle \mathbf{x}, \mathbf{h}_{\mathscr{P}} \rangle \right) = \frac{1}{2^{k-s}\,|\widetilde{\mathscr{H}}|} \sum_{\mathbf{c}^{\mathscr{N}} \in \mathscr{C}^{\mathscr{N}}} K_{w_1}^{(k-\ell-s)}(|\mathbf{c}_1|)\,K_{w_2}^{(n-k+\ell)}(|\mathbf{c}_2|), \quad (3.3)
$$

where $\mathbf{c}_1 \stackrel{\triangle}{=} \left((\mathbf{x} + \mathbf{e}_{\mathscr{P}})\mathbf{R} + \mathbf{e}_{\mathscr{N}} + \mathbf{c}^{\mathscr{N}} \right)_{\mathscr{N}_1}$ and $\mathbf{c}_2 \stackrel{\triangle}{=} \left((\mathbf{x} + \mathbf{e}_{\mathscr{P}})\mathbf{R} + \mathbf{e}_{\mathscr{N}} + \mathbf{c}^{\mathscr{N}} \right)_{\mathscr{N}_2}$.

Proof. Let us notice that

$$
\text{bias}\left(\langle \mathbf{y}, \mathbf{h} \rangle + \langle \mathbf{x}, \mathbf{h}_{\mathscr{P}} \rangle\right) = \frac{1}{|\widetilde{\mathscr{H}}|} \sum_{\mathbf{h} \in \widetilde{\mathscr{H}}} (-1)^{\langle \mathbf{y}, \mathbf{h} \rangle + \langle \mathbf{x}, \mathbf{h}_{\mathscr{P}} \rangle}
$$

$$
= \frac{1}{|\widetilde{\mathscr{H}}|} \sum_{\mathbf{h}_{\mathcal{N}} : \mathbf{h} \in \widetilde{\mathscr{H}}} (-1)^{\langle (\mathbf{x}+\mathbf{e}_{\mathscr{P}})\mathbf{R}+\mathbf{e}_{\mathcal{N}} , \mathbf{h}_{\mathcal{N}} \rangle} \quad \text{(by Lemma 1)}
$$

$$
= \frac{1}{|\widetilde{\mathscr{H}}|} \sum_{\mathbf{h}_{\mathcal{N}} \in (\mathscr{C}^{\perp})_{\mathcal{N}}} f(\mathbf{h}_{\mathcal{N}})
$$

where $f(\mathbf{z}) \overset{\triangle}{=} (-1)^{\langle (\mathbf{x}+\mathbf{e}_{\mathscr{P}})\mathbf{R}+\mathbf{e}_{\mathcal{N}} , \mathbf{z} \rangle} \mathbf{1}_{\{|\mathbf{z}_{\mathcal{N}_1}|=w_1, \, |\mathbf{z}_{\mathcal{N}_2}|=w_2\}}.$

Thanks to (2.1), we have that $(\mathscr{C}^{\perp})_{\mathcal{N}} = (\mathscr{C}^{\mathcal{N}})^{\perp}$. By using the Poisson formula (see [MS86, Lemma 2, Ch. 5. §2]), together with $\dim(\mathscr{C}^{\mathcal{N}}) = k - s$, we get

$$
\frac{1}{|\widetilde{\mathscr{H}}|} \sum_{\mathbf{h}_{\mathcal{N}} \in (\mathscr{C}^{\mathcal{N}})^{\perp}} f(\mathbf{h}_{\mathcal{N}}) = \frac{1}{2^{k-s}|\widetilde{\mathscr{H}}|} \sum_{\mathbf{c}^{\mathcal{N}} \in \mathscr{C}^{\mathcal{N}}} \widehat{f}(\mathbf{c}^{\mathcal{N}}). \tag{3.4}
$$

Let $g(\mathbf{z}_{\mathcal{N}}) \overset{\triangle}{=} \mathbf{1}_{\{|\mathbf{z}_{\mathcal{N}_1}|=w_1, \, |\mathbf{z}_{\mathcal{N}_2}|=w_2\}}$. We have

$$
\widehat{g}(\mathbf{u}_{\mathcal{N}}) = \sum_{\mathbf{z}_{\mathcal{N}} : |\mathbf{z}_{\mathcal{N}_1}|=w_1, \, |\mathbf{z}_{\mathcal{N}_2}|=w_2} (-1)^{\langle \mathbf{u}_{\mathcal{N}_1}, \mathbf{z}_{\mathcal{N}_1} \rangle + \langle \mathbf{u}_{\mathcal{N}_2}, \mathbf{z}_{\mathcal{N}_2} \rangle} \tag{3.5}
$$

$$
= \sum_{\mathbf{z}_{\mathcal{N}_1} \in \mathcal{S}_{w_1}^{k-\ell-s}} (-1)^{\langle \mathbf{u}_{\mathcal{N}_1}, \mathbf{z}_{\mathcal{N}_1} \rangle} \sum_{\mathbf{z}_{\mathcal{N}_2} \in \mathcal{S}_{w_2}^{n-k+\ell}} (-1)^{\langle \mathbf{u}_{\mathcal{N}_2}, \mathbf{z}_{\mathcal{N}_2} \rangle} \tag{3.6}
$$

$$
= K_{w_1}^{(k-\ell-s)}(|\mathbf{u}_{\mathcal{N}_1}|) K_{w_2}^{(n-k+\ell)}(|\mathbf{u}_{\mathcal{N}_2}|) \quad \text{(by (3))}. \tag{3.7}
$$

We finish the proof by noticing that from the definition of f we have

$$
\widehat{f}(\mathbf{c}^{\mathcal{N}}) = \widehat{g}(\mathbf{c}^{\mathcal{N}} + (\mathbf{x} + \mathbf{e}_{\mathscr{P}})\mathbf{R} + \mathbf{e}_{\mathcal{N}}).
$$

$\square$

Proposition 1 is a special case of this proposition when $\mathcal{N}_2 = \mathcal{N}$ and $\mathcal{N}_1 = \emptyset$.

4   A Corrected RLPN Algorithm

As we show in Sect. 5, the RLPN decoding algorithm proposed in [CDMT22] together with the choice of parameters made there has exponentially many candidates that pass the same test as the right candidate $\mathbf{e}_{\mathscr{P}}$. As already explained in the introduction, there is a very simple way to tackle this issue by simply continuing as if a candidate is the right one. If it is the right candidate, further decoding will succeed and if not, decoding will fail. This leads to the following algorithm.

Algorithm 4.1. corrected RLPN decoder

Input: $\mathbf{y}$, t, $\mathscr{C}$ an $[n, k]$-code
Parameters: s, w_1, w_2, u_1, u_2
Output: e such that $|\mathbf{e}| = t$ and $\mathbf{y} - \mathbf{e} \in \mathscr{C}$.

1: **function** RLPNDECODE($\mathbf{y}$, $\mathscr{C}$, t)
2:     **while** True **do**
3:         $(\mathscr{P}, \mathscr{N}_1, \mathscr{N}_2) \xleftarrow{\$} \{\mathscr{P} \sqcup \mathscr{N}_1 \sqcup \mathscr{N}_2 = [\![1, n]\!] \text{ s.t } \#\mathscr{P} = s, \#\mathscr{N}_1 = k - \ell - s, \#\mathscr{N}_2 = n - k + \ell\}$

4:         $\mathscr{H} \leftarrow \text{CREATE}(N, w_1, \mathscr{N}_1, w_2, \mathscr{N}_2)$
5:         $\widehat{f_{\mathbf{y}, \mathscr{H}}} \leftarrow \text{FFT}(f_{\mathbf{y}, \mathscr{H}})$
6:         $\mathcal{S} \leftarrow \{\mathbf{x} \in \mathcal{S}^s_{t-u} : \widehat{f_{\mathbf{y}, \mathscr{H}}}(\mathbf{x}) > \frac{\delta}{2} N\}$ $\triangleright \, \delta = \frac{K_{w_1}^{(k-\ell-s)}(u_1)}{\binom{k-\ell-s}{w_1}} \frac{K_{w_2}^{(n-k+\ell)}(u_2)}{\binom{n-k+\ell}{w_2}}.$
7:         **if** $|\mathcal{S}| < N_{\text{candi}}^{\max}$ **then**
8:             **for** $\mathbf{x} \in \mathcal{S}$ **do**
9:                 $\mathbf{e}' \leftarrow \text{SOLVE-SUBPROBLEM}(\mathscr{C}, \mathscr{N}_1 \cup \mathscr{N}_2, \mathbf{y}, \mathbf{x}, u)$
10:                 **if** $\mathbf{e}' \neq \perp$ **then**
11:                     **return** e such that $\mathbf{e}_{\mathscr{P}} = \mathbf{x}$ and $\mathbf{e}_{\mathscr{N}} = \mathbf{e}'$
12:                 **end if**
13:             **end for**
14:         **end if**
15:     **end while**
16:     **return** $\perp$ $\triangleright$ If no solution found return "fail".
17: **end function**

This algorithm contains the following ingredients:

- Line 2. An outer loop repeated until the solution is found. Each time new complementary subsets $\mathscr{P}, \mathscr{N}_1$ and $\mathscr{N}_2$ of $[\![1, n]\!]$ are chosen with the hope of having $\mathbf{e}_{\mathscr{N}_1}$ and $\mathbf{e}_{\mathscr{N}_2}$ of unusually low weight u_1 and u_2 respectively.
- Line 4. A routine CREATE($N, w_1, \mathscr{N}_1, w_2, \mathscr{N}_2$) creating a set $\mathscr{H}$ of parity-check equations uniformly sampled among the $\mathbf{h} \in \mathscr{C}^\perp$ such that $|\mathbf{h}_{\mathscr{N}_1}| = w_1$ and $|\mathbf{h}_{\mathscr{N}_2}| = w_2$. We do not specify how this function is realized here: this is explained in [CDMT22, §4, §5]. In practice w_1 is chosen as $\frac{k-\ell-s}{2} + o(n)$ (and so is u_1) where the term in $o(n)$ is such that 4.2 of Proposition 2 applies.
- Line 5. A routine $\text{FFT}(f_{\mathbf{y}, \mathscr{H}})$ that computes the fast Fourier transform $\widehat{f_{\mathbf{y}, \mathscr{H}}}$ of the function $f_{\mathbf{y}, \mathscr{H}}$ from $\mathbb{F}_2^s$ to $\mathbb{R}$ defined as $f_{\mathbf{y}, \mathscr{H}}(\mathbf{a}) = \sum_{\substack{\mathbf{h} \in \mathscr{H} \\ \mathbf{h}_{\mathscr{P}} = \mathbf{a}}} (-1)^{\langle \mathbf{y}, \mathbf{h} \rangle}$ (and 0 if there is no such $\mathbf{h}$).
- Line 6. We compute a set of candidates $\mathcal{S} = \{\mathbf{x} \in \mathcal{S}^s_{t-u_1-u_2} : \widehat{f_{\mathbf{y}, \mathscr{H}}}(\mathbf{x}) > \frac{\delta}{2} N\}$. We expect that if $|\mathbf{e}_{\mathscr{N}_1}| = u_1$ and $|\mathbf{e}_{\mathscr{N}_2}| = u_2$ then $\mathbf{e}_{\mathscr{P}} \in \mathcal{S}$. This set of candidates will also contain other vectors which are false positives.
- A routine SOLVE-SUBPROBLEM($\mathscr{C}, \mathscr{N}, \mathbf{y}, \mathbf{x}, u$) that allows us to verify if a candidate $\mathbf{x} \in \mathcal{S}$ is a false positive or $\mathbf{e}_{\mathscr{P}}$. This routine solves a decoding problem on the code $\mathscr{C}$ shortened on $\mathscr{N}$, namely $\mathscr{C}^{\mathscr{N}}$. More specifically, supposing without loss of generality that $\mathscr{P} = [\![1, s]\!]$, $\mathscr{N} = \mathscr{N}_1 \cup \mathscr{N}_2 = [\![s + 1, n]\!]$ and $\mathscr{C}_{\mathscr{P}}$ is of full rank dimension s we can compute $\mathbf{G}$ a generator matrix of $\mathscr{C}$ of the form $\mathbf{G} = \begin{pmatrix} \text{Id}_s & \mathbf{R} \\ 0_{k-s} & \mathbf{R}' \end{pmatrix}$ by applying a partial Gaussian elimination on a generator matrix of $\mathscr{C}$. Then SOLVE-SUBPROBLEM($\mathscr{C}, \mathscr{N}, \mathbf{y}, \mathbf{x}, u$) decodes

at distance u the word $\mathbf{y}' \overset{\triangle}{=} \mathbf{y}_{\mathcal{N}} - (\mathbf{y}_{\mathcal{P}} - \mathbf{x})\mathbf{R}$ onto the code $\mathscr{C}^{\mathcal{N}}$ of generator matrix $\mathbf{R}'$. This routine is expected to return $\mathbf{e}_{\mathcal{N}}$ if $\mathbf{x} = \mathbf{e}_{\mathcal{P}}$ and to fail (return $\perp$) in case $\mathbf{x} \neq \mathbf{e}_{\mathcal{P}}$.

There are two changes with respect to RLPN:

- Line 6, 8. Originally RLPN took $\mathbf{x} \in \mathbb{F}_2^s$ that maximizes $\widehat{f_{\mathbf{y},\mathscr{H}}}(\mathbf{x})$ and checked if $\mathbf{x}$ met the threshold $\widehat{f_{\mathbf{y},\mathscr{H}}}(\mathbf{x}) > \frac{\delta}{2}N$. If the threshold was met, then it asserted that $\mathbf{x}$ equals $\mathbf{e}_{\mathcal{P}}$. In the corrected RLPN we (i) only consider the vectors of $\mathbb{F}_2^s$ of weight $t - u$, (ii) compute the set $\mathcal{S}$ of all vectors $\mathbf{x} \in \mathbb{F}_2^s$ of weight $t - u$ such that $\widehat{f_{\mathbf{y},\mathscr{H}}}(\mathbf{x}) > \frac{\delta}{2}N$. We then solve the resulting decoding problem on $\mathscr{C}^{\mathcal{N}}$ for each $\mathbf{x} \in \mathcal{S}$. Notice here that it can happen, depending on the parameters that $\mathcal{S}$ is of exponential size.
- Line 7. We discard $\mathcal{S}$ if it is bigger than $N_{\text{candi}}^{\max}$. This number is chosen to be of order $\max\left(\widetilde{O}(\mathbb{E}[\mathcal{S}]), 1\right)$ so that a proportion $1 - o(1)$ of iterations passes the test and a proportion $o(1)$ of iterations is discarded. This allows us to bound the number of calls made to SOLVE-SUBPROBLEM. This step is mainly useful for the proof of complexity of the algorithm in Sect. 5.

This algorithm is easily transformed into its simplified and less efficient counterpart spliting the vectors in two parts $\mathcal{P}$ and $\mathcal{N}$ ([CDMT22, §3]). More precisely the "simplified" corrected RLPN is taking $\ell = k - s$ leading to $\mathcal{N}_1 = \emptyset$, $w_1 = 0$, $u_1 = 0$. To simplify notation we define $\mathcal{N} \overset{\triangle}{=} \mathcal{N}_2$, $w \overset{\triangle}{=} w_2$, $u \overset{\triangle}{=} u_2$. Thus in this simplified version we compute parity-checks $\mathbf{h} \in \mathscr{C}^{\perp}$ with this shape:

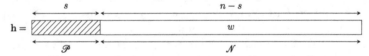

and make the bet that the error vector $\mathbf{e}$ (of weight t) has this shape:

5   Analysis of Corrected RLPN When the Support is Split in Two Parts

Algorithm 4.1 is analyzed here in its simplest form, namely when the support is split in two parts $\mathcal{P}$ and $\mathcal{N}$. In all this section, we call $\widetilde{\mathscr{H}}$ the set of all parity-checks of weight w on $\mathcal{N}$, as such the set $\mathscr{H}$ (Line 4 of Algorithm 4.1) is a random subset of $\widetilde{\mathscr{H}}$ of size N elements, i.e. we use the following notation

Notation 4.

$$\widetilde{\mathscr{H}} \overset{\triangle}{=} \{\mathbf{h} \in \mathscr{C}^{\perp} : |\mathbf{h}_{\mathscr{N}}| = w\} \tag{5.1}$$

$$N \overset{\triangle}{=} |\mathscr{H}| \quad \text{(number of parity-check equations used in Alg. 4.1)}, \tag{5.2}$$

$$\delta \overset{\triangle}{=} \frac{K_w^{(n-s)}(u)}{\binom{n-s}{w}}. \tag{5.3}$$

By noticing that $\left(\mathscr{C}^{\perp}\right)_{\mathscr{N}}$ is an $[n-s, n-k]$-linear code we have the following useful fact regarding the distribution of the size of $\widetilde{\mathscr{H}}$ when $\mathscr{C}$ is a random $[n,k]$-linear code.

Fact 5. *[Bar97, Lem. 1.1, §1.3]*

$$\mathbb{E}_{\mathscr{C}}\left(|\widetilde{\mathscr{H}}|\right) = \frac{\binom{n-s}{w}}{2^{k-s}}, \tag{5.4}$$

$$\mathbf{Var}_{\mathscr{C}}\left(|\widetilde{\mathscr{H}}|\right) \leq \frac{\binom{n-s}{w}}{2^{k-s}}. \tag{5.5}$$

We assume from now on that the parameters meet the RLPN constraints so that the algorithm of [CDMT22] works, namely that k, w, s, u and N verify:

Parameter constraint 6. *The expected size of $\widetilde{\mathscr{H}}$ (the number of parity-checks of weight w on $\mathscr{N}$) and N verify*

$$\frac{\binom{n-s}{w}}{2^{k-s}} = \frac{f(n)}{\delta^2} \quad \text{where } f(n) = \omega(n^5), \tag{5.6}$$

$$N = \frac{g(n)}{\delta^2} \quad \text{where } g(n) = \omega(n). \tag{5.7}$$

Remark 1. Note that (5.6) is just slightly stronger than the constraint given in the original analysis [CDMT22, Prop. 3.9] where the right-hand term is $\frac{\omega(n)}{\delta^2}$. This is needed here in Proposition 5 in the complexity analysis.

5.1 Correctness of Algorithm 4.1

In this section we show that we expect to find the error $\mathbf{e}$ of weight t when the bet on $\mathbf{e}_{\mathscr{N}}$ is valid, *i.e.* $|\mathbf{e}_{\mathscr{N}}| = u$. In this case, we show that we expect with high probability that $\mathbf{e}_{\mathscr{P}} \in S$. Then, calling SOLVE-SUBPROBLEM on $\mathbf{e}_{\mathscr{P}}$ returns the rest of the secret vector $\mathbf{e}_{\mathscr{N}}$. It is readily seen that the probability over the choice of $\mathscr{P}$ and $\mathscr{N}$ complementary in $[\![1, n]\!]$ of size s and $n-s$ respectively that the bet is valid is given by $P_{\text{Succ}} = \frac{\binom{s}{t-u}\binom{n-s}{u}}{\binom{n}{t}}$. More formally,

Proposition 4. *(Correctness) After at most $N_{\text{iter}} = \omega\left(\frac{\binom{s}{t-u}\binom{n-s}{u}}{\binom{n}{t}}\right)$ executions of the outer loop (Line 2) of Algorithm 4.1, the algorithm outputs with probability $1-o(1)$ over the choices of $\mathscr{C}$ and $\mathscr{H}$, an $\mathbf{e} \in \mathbb{F}_2^n$ of weight t such that $\mathbf{y} - \mathbf{e} \in \mathscr{C}$.*

It is essentially the same proof as in [CDMT22] but without using any assumptions. The proof is given in §C.1 of the appendix.

5.2   Complexity Analysis of Algorithm 4.1

This subsection gives the complexity analysis of the corrected RLPN algorithm when applied to a random $[n, k]$-code $\mathscr{C}$.

Estimating the Expected Number of Candidates. The key part of this analysis relies on estimating the size of $\mathcal{S}$ defined by

$$\mathcal{S} \stackrel{\triangle}{=} \{\mathbf{x} \in \mathcal{S}^s_{t-u} : \widehat{f_{\mathbf{y},\mathscr{H}}}(\mathbf{x}) > \frac{\delta}{2}N\}.$$

The final formula for the upper-bound of $\mathbb{E}_{\mathscr{C},\mathscr{H}}(|\mathcal{S}|)$ is given in Proposition 5. We give here an outline of the proof.

Step 1. Firstly, by definition $\widehat{f_{\mathbf{y},\mathscr{H}}}(\mathbf{x}) \stackrel{\triangle}{=} \sum_{\mathbf{h} \in \mathscr{H}} (-1)^{\langle \mathbf{y},\mathbf{h} \rangle + \langle \mathbf{x}, \mathbf{h}_{\mathscr{P}} \rangle}$ and $N \stackrel{\triangle}{=} |\mathscr{H}|$ thus it is readily seen that we have the following fact

Fact 7.

$$\widehat{f_{\mathbf{y},\mathscr{H}}}(\mathbf{x}) = N \operatorname{bias}_{\mathbf{h} \hookleftarrow \mathscr{H}}(\langle \mathbf{y}, \mathbf{h} \rangle + \langle \mathbf{x}, \mathbf{h}_{\mathscr{P}} \rangle).$$

Notice how the distribution of $\operatorname{bias}_{\mathbf{h} \hookleftarrow \mathscr{H}}(\langle \mathbf{y}, \mathbf{h} \rangle + \langle \mathbf{x}, \mathbf{h}_{\mathscr{P}} \rangle)$ is independent of $\mathbf{x}$ as long as $\mathbf{x} \neq \mathbf{e}_{\mathscr{P}}$ thus we can write using the linearity of the expectation that

$$\mathbb{E}_{\mathscr{C},\mathscr{H}}(|\mathcal{S} \setminus \{\mathbf{e}_{\mathscr{P}}\}|) \leq \binom{s}{t-u} \mathbb{P}_{\mathscr{C},\mathscr{H}}\left(\widehat{f_{\mathbf{y},\mathscr{H}}}(\mathbf{x}) > N\delta/2\right)$$

$$= \binom{s}{t-u} \mathbb{P}_{\mathscr{C},\mathscr{H}}(\operatorname{bias}_{\mathbf{h} \hookleftarrow \mathscr{H}}(\langle \mathbf{y}, \mathbf{h} \rangle + \langle \mathbf{x}, \mathbf{h}_{\mathscr{P}} \rangle) > \delta/2).$$

We then relate $\mathbb{P}_{\mathscr{C},\mathscr{H}}(\operatorname{bias}_{\mathbf{h} \hookleftarrow \mathscr{H}}(\langle \mathbf{y}, \mathbf{h} \rangle + \langle \mathbf{x}, \mathbf{h}_{\mathscr{P}} \rangle) > \delta/2)$ with the probability that the bias is above $\delta/4$ when we choose $\mathbf{h}$ uniformly at random among the whole set $\widetilde{\mathscr{H}}$ of parity-check equations to get

$$\mathbb{E}_{\mathscr{C},\mathscr{H}}(|\mathcal{S} \setminus \{\mathbf{e}_{\mathscr{P}}\}|) \leq \binom{s}{t-u} O\left(\mathbb{P}_{\mathscr{C}}\left(\operatorname{bias}_{\mathbf{h} \hookleftarrow \widetilde{\mathscr{H}}}(\langle \mathbf{y}, \mathbf{h} \rangle + \langle \mathbf{x}, \mathbf{h}_{\mathscr{P}} \rangle) > \frac{\delta}{4}\right)\right).$$

$$(5.8)$$

Step 2. The point is now that Proposition 1 can be invoked to get

$$\operatorname{bias}_{\mathbf{h} \hookleftarrow \widetilde{\mathscr{H}}}(\langle \mathbf{y}, \mathbf{h} \rangle + \langle \mathbf{x}, \mathbf{h}_{\mathscr{P}} \rangle) = \frac{1}{2^{k-s}|\widetilde{\mathscr{H}}|} \sum_{i=0}^{n-s} N_i K_w^{(n-s)}(i) \qquad (5.9)$$

where N_i is the number of codewords in the code $(\mathbf{x} + \mathbf{e}_{\mathscr{P}})\mathbf{R} + \mathbf{e}_{\mathscr{N}} + \mathscr{C}^{\mathscr{N}}$ of weight i. The crucial argument is now used, it is a centering trick based on the fact that $\sum_{i=0}^{n-s} \bar{N}_i K_w^{(n-s)}(i) = 0$ where $\bar{N}_i \stackrel{\triangle}{=} \mathbb{E}(N_i)$. This is used to upper-bound the probability appearing in (5.8) by

$$O(n) \max_{i=0\ldots n-s} \mathbb{P}_{\mathscr{C}}\left(|N_i - \mathbb{E}_{\mathscr{C}}(N_i)| > \left|\frac{K_w^{(n-s)}(u)}{K_w^{(n-s)}(i)}\right| \frac{1}{\Theta(n)}\right).$$

Step 3. We then bound the previous probability by distinguishing two cases for $i \in [\![0, n-s]\!]$:

(i) when i is not too big compared to u $(i < u + o(n))$ the previous probability is upper-bounded by $\mathbb{E}_{\mathscr{C}}\left(N_i\right) = \frac{\binom{n-s}{i}}{2^{n-k}}$;

(ii) otherwise the previous probability is bounded by some $2^{-\omega(n)}$.

Unfortunately, the known tail bounds about the weight enumerators of a random code will be insufficient to prove our result.

Thus, to make our analysis tractable we will model the weight enumerators as Poisson variables, namely:

Assumption 8.

$$N_i \sim \text{Poisson}\left(\frac{\binom{n-s}{i}}{2^{n-k}}\right).$$

Experimental results concerning the validity of this assumption can be found in Appendix D: we show there that the distribution of bias$_{\mathbf{h} \mapsto \mathscr{H}}\left(\langle \mathbf{y}, \mathbf{h} \rangle + \langle \mathbf{x}, \mathbf{h}_{\mathscr{P}} \rangle\right)$ does not change under Assumption 8.

Assumption 8 is only used in Lemma 6 of Appendix §C.3 to upper bound $\mathbb{P}\left(|N_i - \mathbb{E}_{\mathscr{C}}\left(N_i\right)| > \omega(n)\sqrt{\text{Var}_{\mathscr{C}}\left(N_i\right)}\right)$ by some $2^{-\omega(n)}$ for large i's. As such, a more minimalistic assumption bounding the previous probability would in fact be sufficient to prove our result. All in all, we prove the following proposition giving an upper bound on $\mathbb{E}\left(|\mathcal{S}|\right)$.

Proposition 5. *We have under Assumption 8 that:*

$$\mathbb{E}_{\mathscr{C}, \mathscr{H}}\left(|\mathcal{S} \setminus \{\mathbf{e}_{\mathscr{P}}\}|\right) = \tilde{O}\left(\binom{s}{t-u}\frac{\binom{n-s}{u}}{2^{n-k}}\right). \tag{5.10}$$

This proposition is proved in Appendix §C.3. Note that there is also in Appendix §C.2 a simple lower bound on this quantity which is of the right order and which gives an insight where this bound comes from.

Complexity of the Algorithm. The complexity of this variant of RLPN decoding follows on the spot from the formula of the complexity of the original RLPN algorithm [CDMT22, Prop. 3.10]) where we add an extra cost (Line 10 to 14) per iteration which is equal to $|\mathcal{S}|$ times the cost of a call to SOLVE-SUBPROBLEM. From this we readily deduce that the original RLPN original complexity claims hold as long as

Proposition 6. *Let* $T_{solve\text{-}subproblem}(n-s, k-s, u)$ *be the complexity of* SOLVE-SUBPROBLEM *for decoding* u *errors in an* $[n-s, k-s]$ *linear code. Suppose that*

$$\max\left(\binom{s}{t-u}\frac{\binom{n-s}{u}}{2^{n-k}}, 1\right) T_{solve\text{-}subproblem}\left(n-s, k-s, u\right) \leq \tilde{O}(2^s) \tag{5.11}$$

Then, under Model 8, the expected complexity of the corrected RLPN algorithm is a $\tilde{O}()$ *of the RLPN claimed complexity made in [CDMT22, Prop 3.10].*

The original asymptotic parameters[2] of RLPN [CDMT22, §4.1] satisfy for all rates the asymptotic counterpart of (5.11) when SOLVE-SUBPROBLEM uses Dumer's decoder [Dum91] recalled in Appendix B. This can be verified from the supplementary material GitHub page[3]. We give in Appendix §C.4 further results about the complexity of Algorithm 4.1.

6   Concluding Remarks

We have provided here tools for removing all the independence assumptions used for analyzing the most recent (and powerful) dual attack in coding theory [CDMT22]. Even if this decoder does not work as predicted in [CDMT22] we provide here an analysis of the number of candidates in $\mathcal{S}$ provided by the slightly modified Algorithm 4.1 which shows that under a very mild assumption on the N_i's (Assumption 8) the original complexity claims are indeed valid for the modified algorithm. Assumption 8 is only used to show large deviation results for the number of codewords N_i of weight i in a random code. Proving rigourous tail bounds on N_i would then give a complete proof of the complexity of Algorithm 4.1. It is also clear that the fundamental tool, the duality result (Proposition 1) carries over straightforwardly for studying dual attacks in lattice based cryptography and so does part of our approach which removed independence assumptions.

Acknowledgement. We would like to express our thanks to Thomas Debris-Alazard for the insightful discussions. The work of C. Meyer-Hilfiger was funded by the French Agence de l'innovation de défense and by Inria. The work of J-P. Tillich was funded by the French Agence Nationale de la Recherche through the France 2023 ANR project ANR-22-PETQ-0008 PQ-TLS.

Appendix

A   Complexity of [Dum86] to Compute Low Weight Parity-Checks

We give here the asymptotic complexity of one of the method devised in [CDMT22, §4.1] to produce low weight parity-checks.

Proposition 7. *Asymptotic complexity of Dumer's [Dum86] method to compute low weight parity-checks. Let* $R \overset{\triangle}{=} \lim_{n \to \infty} \frac{k}{n}, \omega \overset{\triangle}{=} \lim_{n \to \infty} \frac{w}{n}$. *The asymptotic time and space complexities of Dumer's [Dum86] method to compute and store* $2^{n\,(h_2(\omega) - R + o(1))}$ *parity-checks are in* $2^{n\,(\alpha + o(1))}$ *where* $\alpha \overset{\triangle}{=} \max\left(\frac{h(\omega)}{2}, h_2(\omega) - R\right)$.

---

[2] https://github.com/tillich/RLPNdecoding/blob/master/supplementaryMaterial/RLPN_Dumer89.csv.

[3] https://github.com/meyer-hilfiger/Rigorous-Foundations-for-Dual-Attacks-in-Coding-Theory.

B   [Dum91] ISD Decoder

Proposition 8 (Asymptotic time complexity of ISD Decoder [Dum91]).
*Let $R \overset{\triangle}{=} \lim\limits_{n\to\infty} \frac{k}{n}, \tau \overset{\triangle}{=} \lim\limits_{n\to\infty} \frac{t}{n}$ and suppose that $\tau \le h_2^{-1}(1-R)$. Let ℓ and w be two
(implicit) parameters of the algorithm and define $\lambda \overset{\triangle}{=} \lim\limits_{n\to\infty} \frac{\ell}{n}, \omega \overset{\triangle}{=} \lim\limits_{n\to\infty} \frac{w}{n}$. The
time and space complexities of [Dum91] decoder to decode a word at distance t
in an $[n,k]$ linear code are given by $2^{n\,(\alpha+o(1))}$ and $2^{n\,(\beta+o(1))}$ respectively where*

$$\alpha \overset{\triangle}{=} \pi + \max\left(\frac{R+\lambda}{2} h_2\left(\frac{\omega}{R+\lambda}\right), (R+\lambda) h_2\left(\frac{\omega}{R+\lambda}\right) - \lambda\right), \tag{B.1}$$

$$\pi \overset{\triangle}{=} h_2(\tau) - (1-R-\lambda)h_2\left(\frac{\tau-\omega}{1-R-\lambda}\right) - (R+\lambda)h_2\left(\frac{\omega}{R+\lambda}\right), \tag{B.2}$$

$$\beta \overset{\triangle}{=} \frac{R+\lambda}{2} h_2\left(\frac{\omega}{R+\lambda}\right). \tag{B.3}$$

Moreover λ and ω must verify the following constraints:

$$0 \le \lambda \le 1-R, \qquad \max(R+\lambda+\tau-1, 0) \le \omega \le \min(\tau, R+\lambda).$$

C   Proofs and Results Corresponding to Section 5

C.1   Proof of Proposition 4

The aim of this subsection is to prove

Proposition 4. *(Correctness) After at most $N_{\text{iter}} = \omega\left(\frac{\binom{s}{t-u}\binom{n-s}{u}}{\binom{n}{t}}\right)$ executions
of the outer loop (Line 2) of Algorithm 4.1, the algorithm outputs with probability
$1-o(1)$ over the choices of $\mathscr{C}$ and $\mathscr{H}$, an $\mathbf{e} \in \mathbb{F}_2^n$ of weight t such that $\mathbf{y}-\mathbf{e} \in \mathscr{C}$.*

It is readily seen that when $N_{\text{iter}} = \omega\left(\frac{\binom{s}{t-u}\binom{n-s}{u}}{\binom{n}{t}}\right)$ there exists, with proba-
bility $1-o(1)$, an iteration such that $|\mathbf{e}_{\mathscr{N}}| = u$. Let us consider such an iteration
and show that $\mathbf{e}_{\mathscr{P}} \in S$ with high probability. Recall that

$$S \overset{\triangle}{=} \{\mathbf{x} \in S_{t-u}^s : \widehat{f_{\mathbf{y},\mathscr{H}}}(\mathbf{x}) > \frac{\delta}{2}N\}$$

and that from Fact 7 we have that

$$\widehat{f_{\mathbf{y},\mathscr{H}}}(\mathbf{x}) = N \, \text{bias}_{\mathbf{h}\hookleftarrow\mathscr{H}}(\langle\mathbf{y},\mathbf{h}\rangle + \langle\mathbf{x},\mathbf{h}_{\mathscr{P}}\rangle).$$

Now, using the fact that

$$\langle\mathbf{y},\mathbf{h}\rangle + \langle\mathbf{e}_{\mathscr{P}},\mathbf{h}_{\mathscr{P}}\rangle = \langle\mathbf{e}_{\mathscr{N}},\mathbf{h}_{\mathscr{N}}\rangle,$$

we only have to lower bound the term

$$\mathbb{P}_{\mathscr{C},\mathscr{H}}\left(\text{bias}_{\mathbf{h}\hookleftarrow\mathscr{H}}\left(\langle\mathbf{e}_{\mathscr{N}},\mathbf{h}_{\mathscr{N}}\rangle\right) > \frac{\delta}{2}\right)$$

to lower bound the probability that $\mathbf{e}_{\mathscr{P}}$ belong to $\mathcal{S}$. The only known results we have regarding the bias of $\langle\mathbf{e}_{\mathscr{N}},\mathbf{h}_{\mathscr{N}}\rangle$ is when $\mathbf{h}$ is sampled in $\widetilde{\mathscr{H}}$ (see [CDMT22, Prop. 3.1] and Proposition 1). But, because $\mathscr{H}$ is a random subset of N (where N is lower bounded in Parameter constraint 6) elements of the set $\widetilde{\mathscr{H}}$, the distribution of $\text{bias}_{\mathbf{h}\hookleftarrow\mathscr{H}}\left(\langle\mathbf{e}_{\mathscr{N}},\mathbf{h}_{\mathscr{N}}\rangle\right)$ is relatively close to the distribution of $\text{bias}_{\mathbf{h}\hookleftarrow\widetilde{\mathscr{H}}}(\langle\mathbf{e}_{\mathscr{N}},\mathbf{h}_{\mathscr{N}}\rangle)$. Namely, we have:

Lemma 2. *For any constant $c > 0$:*

$$\mathbb{P}_{\mathscr{C},\mathscr{H}}\left(\left|\text{bias}_{\mathbf{h}\hookleftarrow\mathscr{H}}\left(\langle\mathbf{e}_{\mathscr{N}},\mathbf{h}_{\mathscr{N}}\rangle\right) - \text{bias}_{\mathbf{h}\hookleftarrow\widetilde{\mathscr{H}}}(\langle\mathbf{e}_{\mathscr{N}},\mathbf{h}_{\mathscr{N}}\rangle)\right| \geq \delta\,c\right) \leq 2^{-\omega(n)}$$

Proof. The proof is available in the eprint version of the paper.   □

And thus, as a corollary we get the following lower bound on our probability:

Corollary 2. *We have that*

$$\mathbb{P}_{\mathscr{C},\mathscr{H}}\left(\text{bias}_{\mathbf{h}\hookleftarrow\mathscr{H}}\left(\langle\mathbf{e}_{\mathscr{N}},\mathbf{h}_{\mathscr{N}}\rangle\right) > \frac{\delta}{2}\right) \geq (1 - e^{-\omega(n)})\,\mathbb{P}_{\mathscr{C}}\left(\text{bias}_{\mathbf{h}\hookleftarrow\widetilde{\mathscr{H}}}(\langle\mathbf{e}_{\mathscr{N}},\mathbf{h}_{\mathscr{N}}\rangle) > \frac{\delta}{1.5}\right).$$

Now, recall that we supposed that the iteration considered is such that $|\mathbf{e}_{\mathscr{N}}| = u$. Moreover, from Condition (5.7) in Parameter constraint 6 we have that $N = \omega(\frac{n}{\delta^2})$. Thus, a direct application of Proposition [CDMT22, Prop. 3.1] gives us that with probability $1 - o(1)$ over the choice of $\mathscr{C}$, we have

$$\text{bias}_{\mathbf{h}\hookleftarrow\widetilde{\mathscr{H}}}(\langle\mathbf{e}_{\mathscr{N}},\mathbf{h}_{\mathscr{N}}\rangle) = \delta\,(1 + o(1)).$$

And thus we have that:

$$\mathbb{P}_{\mathscr{C}}\left(\text{bias}_{\mathbf{h}\hookleftarrow\widetilde{\mathscr{H}}}(\langle\mathbf{e}_{\mathscr{N}},\mathbf{h}_{\mathscr{N}}\rangle) > \frac{\delta}{1.5}\right) = 1 - o(1).$$

This concludes the proof that $\mathbf{e}_{\mathscr{P}}$ belongs to $\mathcal{S}$ with probability $1 - o(1)$ which in turns proves the correctness of Proposition 4.

C.2   A Simple Lower Bound

It turns out that we could easily compute a lower bound on the size of $\mathcal{S}$ using Lemma 1 altogether with a slight adaptation of Proposition [CDMT22, Prop. 3.1]. Indeed, recall that in Lemma 1 we proved that for a parity-check $\mathbf{h}$:

$$\langle\mathbf{y},\mathbf{h}\rangle + \langle\mathbf{x},\mathbf{h}_{\mathscr{P}}\rangle = \langle(\mathbf{x}+\mathbf{e}_{\mathscr{P}})\mathbf{R}+\mathbf{e}_{\mathscr{N}},\mathbf{h}_{\mathscr{N}}\rangle, \tag{C.1}$$

$$= \langle(\mathbf{x}+\mathbf{e}_{\mathscr{P}})\mathbf{R}+\mathbf{e}_{\mathscr{N}}+\mathbf{c}^{\mathscr{N}},\mathbf{h}_{\mathscr{N}}\rangle, \quad \forall\mathbf{c}^{\mathscr{N}}\in\mathscr{C}^{\mathscr{N}}, \tag{C.2}$$

where in the last line we used the fact that $\mathbf{h}_{\mathcal{N}} \in \left(\mathscr{C}^{\mathcal{N}}\right)^{\perp}$. Thus if there exists $\mathbf{c}^{\mathcal{N}} \in \mathscr{C}^{\mathcal{H}}$ such that

$$\left|(\mathbf{x} + \mathbf{e}_{\mathscr{P}})\mathbf{R} + \mathbf{e}_{\mathcal{N}} + \mathbf{c}^{\mathcal{N}}\right| \le u. \tag{C.3}$$

then with high probability

$$\mathrm{bias}_{\mathbf{h} \hookleftarrow \widetilde{\mathscr{H}}}\left(\langle(\mathbf{x} + \mathbf{e}_{\mathscr{P}})\mathbf{R} + \mathbf{e}_{\mathcal{N}} + \mathbf{c}^{\mathcal{N}}, \mathbf{h}_{\mathcal{N}}\rangle\right) \ge \delta(1 + o(1)).$$

As a matter of fact, from Parameter constraint 6 we have that $N = \omega\left(\frac{n}{\delta^2}\right)$, and, because $K_w^{(n-s)}$ is decreasing in this range, we can use a slight adaptation of Proposition [CDMT22, Prop. 3.1] to show this point. And thus with high probability $\mathbf{x} \in \mathcal{S}$. We can give a lower bound on the number of $\mathbf{x}$ verifying Condition (C.3) by counting the number of codewords of weight lower than u in the following code:

$$\{(\mathbf{x} + \mathbf{e}_{\mathscr{P}})\mathbf{R} + \mathbf{e}_{\mathcal{N}} + \mathbf{c}^{\mathcal{N}} : (\mathbf{x}, \mathbf{c}^{\mathcal{N}}) \in \mathcal{S}_{t-u}^s \times \mathscr{C}^{\mathcal{N}}\}.$$

This is a random code of length $n - s$ and with a maximum size of $\left|\mathcal{S}_{t-u}^s\right| \left|\mathscr{C}^{\mathcal{N}}\right|$. Thus we expect that there are at most

$$\tilde{O}\left(\left|\mathcal{S}_{t-u}^s\right| \left|\mathscr{C}^{\mathcal{N}}\right| \frac{\binom{n-s}{u}}{2^{n-s}}\right) = \tilde{O}\left(\binom{s}{t-u} \frac{\binom{n-s}{u}}{2^{n-k}}\right)$$

codewords of weight lower than u in the previous code, giving us a lower bound on the expected size of $\mathcal{S}$. This lower-bound actually matches up to polynomial terms the upper-bound appearing in Proposition 5.

C.3   Proof of Proposition 5

Let us first recall Proposition 5

Proposition 5. *We have under Assumption 8 that:*

$$\mathbb{E}_{\mathscr{C}, \mathscr{H}}\left(|\mathcal{S} \setminus \{\mathbf{e}_{\mathscr{P}}\}|\right) = \tilde{O}\left(\binom{s}{t-u} \frac{\binom{n-s}{u}}{2^{n-k}}\right). \tag{5.10}$$

To ease up our analysis, we will suppose in the following that the predicate $P\left(\widetilde{\mathscr{H}}\right)$ defined as:

$$P\left(\widetilde{\mathscr{H}}\right) : " \left|\widetilde{\mathscr{H}}\right| \ge \frac{\mathbb{E}_{\mathscr{C}}\left(\left|\widetilde{\mathscr{H}}\right|\right)}{2} " \tag{C.4}$$

is true and we will only compute the value of $\mathbb{E}_{\mathscr{C}, \mathscr{H}}\left(|\mathcal{S}| \mid P\left(\widetilde{\mathscr{H}}\right)\right)$. We can show using the Bienaymé-Tchebychev inequality that $P\left(\widetilde{\mathscr{H}}\right)$ is true with probability $1 - o(1)$. However, contrary to the previous supposition that $\mathscr{C}_{\mathscr{P}}$ is of full rank dimension s, in general, we have no way of verifying in polynomial time if $P\left(\widetilde{\mathcal{H}}\right)$ is true or not, thus we cannot just simply restart the algorithm from Line 2 if it is not true. The strategy we adopt is to bound the complexity of each iteration of corrected RLPN regardless of the value of the predicate $P\left(\widetilde{\mathcal{H}}\right)$, this is done by discarding the iterations that are such that the size of $\mathcal{S}$ is greater than a certain threshold (Line 7 of Algorithm 4.1). The correctness of our algorithm is not impacted by this as the probability that $P\left(\widetilde{\mathcal{H}}\right)$ is verified is in $1 - o(1)$ and the threshold will be chosen such that, when $P\left(\widetilde{\mathcal{H}}\right)$ is verified the set $\mathcal{S}$ meets the threshold with probability $1 - o(1)$. More specifically, the threshold $N_{\text{candi}}^{\max}$ is chosen as

$$n\, \mathbb{E}_{\mathscr{C},\mathscr{H}}\left(|\mathcal{S}| \,\Big|\, P\left(\widetilde{\mathcal{H}}\right)\right),$$

and, we can show using Markov inequality that this treshold is met with probability $1 - o(1)$ for the iterations such that $P\left(\widetilde{\mathcal{H}}\right)$ is true. Thus in what follows we will only compute the value of $\mathbb{E}_{\mathscr{C},\mathscr{H}}\left(|\mathcal{S}| \,\Big|\, P\left(\widetilde{\mathcal{H}}\right)\right)$ and, to simplify notation we just write it as $\mathbb{E}_{\mathscr{C},\mathscr{H}}\left(|\mathcal{S}|\right)$. We are ready now to prove Proposition 5.

Step 1. It is readily seen that by linearity of the expected value and from the fact that the distribution of $\text{bias}_{\mathbf{h} \hookrightarrow \mathscr{H}}\left(\langle \mathbf{y}, \mathbf{h} \rangle + \langle \mathbf{x}, \mathbf{h}_{\mathscr{P}} \rangle\right) > \frac{\delta}{2}$ does not depend on $\mathbf{x}$ as long as $\mathbf{x} \neq \mathbf{e}_{\mathscr{P}}$ we have

Fact 9.

$$\mathbb{E}_{\mathscr{C},\mathscr{H}}\left(|\mathcal{S} \setminus \{\mathbf{e}_{\mathscr{P}}\}|\right) \leq \binom{s}{t-u}\, \mathbb{P}_{\mathscr{C},\mathscr{H}}\left(\text{bias}_{\mathbf{h} \hookrightarrow \mathscr{H}}\left(\langle \mathbf{y}, \mathbf{h} \rangle + \langle \mathbf{x}, \mathbf{h}_{\mathscr{P}} \rangle\right) > \frac{\delta}{2}\right).$$

The only known results we have regarding the bias is when $\mathbf{h}$ is sampled in $\widetilde{\mathcal{H}}$ (see [CDMT22, Prop. 3.1] and Proposition 1). But we have the following slight generalization of Lemma 2 which essentially tells us that the distribution of the bias when $\mathbf{h}$ is sampled in $\mathscr{H}$ is close to the bias when $\mathbf{h}$ is sampled in $\widetilde{\mathcal{H}}$.

Lemma 3. *For any constant $c > 0$:*

$$\mathbb{P}_{\mathscr{C},\mathscr{H}}\left(\left|\text{bias}_{\mathbf{h} \hookrightarrow \mathscr{H}}\left(\langle \mathbf{y}, \mathbf{h} \rangle + \langle \mathbf{x}, \mathbf{h}_{\mathscr{P}} \rangle\right) - \text{bias}_{\mathbf{h} \hookrightarrow \widetilde{\mathcal{H}}}\left(\langle \mathbf{y}, \mathbf{h} \rangle + \langle \mathbf{x}, \mathbf{h}_{\mathscr{P}} \rangle\right)\right| \geq \delta c\right) \leq 2^{-\omega(n)}.$$

As a direct corollary we get the following bound

Corollary 3. *We have that*

$$\mathbb{P}_{\mathscr{C},\mathscr{H}}\left(\text{bias}_{\mathbf{h} \hookrightarrow \mathscr{H}}\left(\langle \mathbf{y}, \mathbf{h} \rangle + \langle \mathbf{x}, \mathbf{h}_{\mathscr{P}} \rangle\right) > \frac{\delta}{2}\right) = O\left(\mathbb{P}_{\mathscr{C}}\left(\text{bias}_{\mathbf{h} \hookrightarrow \widetilde{\mathcal{H}}}\left(\langle \mathbf{y}, \mathbf{h} \rangle + \langle \mathbf{x}, \mathbf{h}_{\mathscr{P}} \rangle\right) > \frac{\delta}{4}\right)\right).$$

Step 2. Thus we are now interested in upper bounding $\mathbb{P}_{\mathscr{C}}\left(\text{bias}_{\mathbf{h}\hookleftarrow\widetilde{\mathscr{H}}}(\langle\mathbf{y},\mathbf{h}\rangle+\langle\mathbf{x},\mathbf{h}_{\mathscr{P}}\rangle)>\frac{\delta}{4}\right)$. A first step is given in the next Lemma 4. This lemma uses the fact that we can write using Proposition 1 the former bias as

$$\text{bias}_{\mathbf{h}\hookleftarrow\widetilde{\mathscr{H}}}(\langle\mathbf{y},\mathbf{h}\rangle+\langle\mathbf{x},\mathbf{h}_{\mathscr{P}}\rangle)=\frac{1}{2^{k-s}\left|\widetilde{\mathscr{H}}\right|}\sum_{i=0}^{n-s}N_i\left(\mathscr{C}^{\mathscr{N}}+(\mathbf{x}+\mathbf{e}_{\mathscr{P}})\mathbf{R}+\mathbf{e}_{\mathscr{N}}\right)K_w^{(n-s)}(i)$$

where $N_i()$ is the number of codeword of weight i in a code, namely:

$$N_i\left(\mathscr{C}^{\mathscr{N}}+(\mathbf{x}+\mathbf{e}_{\mathscr{P}})\mathbf{R}+\mathbf{e}_{\mathscr{N}}\right)\triangleq\left|\left(\mathscr{C}^{\mathscr{N}}+(\mathbf{x}+\mathbf{e}_{\mathscr{P}})\mathbf{R}+\mathbf{e}_{\mathscr{N}}\right)\bigcap S_i^{n-s}\right|.$$

We define, for simplicity:

Notation 10.

$$N_i\triangleq N_i\left(\mathscr{C}^{\mathscr{N}}+(\mathbf{x}+\mathbf{e}_{\mathscr{P}})\mathbf{R}+\mathbf{e}_{\mathscr{N}}\right),\tag{C.5}$$

$$\bar{N}_i\triangleq\mathbb{E}_{\mathscr{C}}\left(N_i\right).\tag{C.6}$$

Recall that $\mathscr{C}^{\mathscr{N}}+(\mathbf{x}+\mathbf{e}_{\mathscr{P}})\mathbf{R}+\mathbf{e}_{\mathscr{N}}$ is a coset of the $[n-s,k-s]$ linear code $\mathscr{C}^{\mathscr{N}}$ thus it is readily seen that we have

Fact 11. *[Bar97, Lem. 1.1, §1.3]*

$$\bar{N}_i=\frac{\binom{n-s}{i}}{2^{n-k}},\tag{C.7}$$

$$\mathbf{Var}_{\mathscr{C}}\left(N_i\right)\leq\frac{\binom{n-s}{i}}{2^{n-k}}.\tag{C.8}$$

The following lemma essentially says that we can study only the dominant term in the previous sum to bound the tail distribution of the bias. The key trick will be to use Krawtchouk polynomials orthogonality with the measure $\mu(i)=\binom{n-s}{i}$ so that we gain a factor $\bar{N}_iK_w^{(n-s)}(i)$ in our expressions

Lemma 4. *We have that*

$$\mathbb{P}_{\mathscr{C}}\left(\text{bias}_{\mathbf{h}\hookleftarrow\widetilde{\mathscr{H}}}(\langle\mathbf{y},\mathbf{h}\rangle-\langle\mathbf{x},\mathbf{h}_{\mathscr{P}}\rangle)>\frac{\delta}{4}\right)\leq$$

$$n\max_{i=0...n-s}\mathbb{P}_{\mathscr{C}}\left(\left|N_i-\bar{N}_i\right|>\left|\frac{K_w^{(n-s)}(u)}{K_w^{(n-s)}(i)}\right|\frac{1}{8(n-s+1)}\right)$$

Proof. By using Proposition 1 we derive that

$$\text{bias}_{\mathbf{h}\hookleftarrow\widetilde{\mathscr{H}}}(\langle\mathbf{y},\mathbf{h}\rangle-\langle\mathbf{x},\mathbf{h}_{\mathscr{P}}\rangle)=\frac{1}{2^{k-s}\left|\widetilde{\mathscr{H}}\right|}\sum_{i=0}^{n-s}N_i\,K_w^{(n-s)}(i).$$

From the orthogonality of Krawtchouk polynomials relatively to the measure $\mu(i) = \binom{n-s}{i}$ [MS86, Ch. 5. §7. Theorem 16] we have:

$$\sum_{i=0}^{n-s} \binom{n-s}{i} K_w^{(n-s)}(i) = 0.$$

And thus, altogether with Fact 11 we have that

$$\frac{1}{2^{k-s}|\widetilde{\mathscr{H}}|} \sum_{i=0}^{n-s} \bar{N}_i\, K_w^{(n-s)}(i) = 0.$$

And thus,

$$\frac{1}{2^{k-s}|\widetilde{\mathscr{H}}|} \sum_{i=0}^{n-s} N_i\, K_w^{(n-s)}(i) = \frac{1}{2^{k-s}|\widetilde{\mathscr{H}}|} \sum_{i=0}^{n-s} (N_i - \bar{N}_i)\, K_w^{(n-s)}(i). \qquad (C.9)$$

Moreover, the event

$$\frac{1}{2^{k-s}|\widetilde{\mathscr{H}}|} \sum_{i=0}^{n-s} (N_i - \bar{N}_i)\, K_w^{(n-s)}(i) > \frac{\delta}{4}$$

implies that it exists $i \in [\![0, n-s]\!]$ such that

$$\frac{1}{2^{k-s}|\widetilde{\mathscr{H}}|} (N_i - \bar{N}_i)\, K_w^{(n-s)}(i) > \frac{\delta}{4(n-s+1)}. \qquad (C.10)$$

Thus we get:

$$\mathbb{P}_{\mathscr{C}} \left(\frac{1}{2^{k-s}|\widetilde{\mathscr{H}}|} \sum_{i=0}^{n-s} (N_i - \bar{N}_i)\, K_w^{(n-s)}(i) > \frac{\delta}{4} \right)$$

$$\leq \mathbb{P}_{\mathscr{C}} \left(\bigvee_{i=0}^{n-s} \left(\frac{1}{2^{k-s}|\widetilde{\mathscr{H}}|} (N_i - \bar{N}_i)\, K_w^{(n-s)}(i) > \frac{\delta}{4(n-s+1)} \right) \right) \quad \text{(using } C.10)$$

$$\leq \sum_{i=0}^{n-s} \mathbb{P}_{\mathscr{C}} \left(\frac{1}{2^{k-s}|\widetilde{\mathscr{H}}|} (N_i - \bar{N}_i)\, K_w^{(n-s)}(i) > \frac{\delta}{4(n-s+1)} \right) \quad \text{(union bound)}$$

$$\leq (n-s+1) \max_{i=0\ldots(n-s)} \mathbb{P}_{\mathscr{C}} \left(\frac{1}{2^{k-s}|\widetilde{\mathscr{H}}|} (N_i - \bar{N}_i)\, K_w^{(n-s)}(i) > \frac{\delta}{4(n-s+1)} \right)$$

$$\leq (n-s+1) \max_{i=0\ldots(n-s)} \mathbb{P}_{\mathscr{C}} \left(|N_i - \bar{N}_i| > \left| \frac{\delta\, 2^{k-s}\, |\widetilde{\mathscr{H}}|}{K_w^{(n-s)}(i)} \right| \frac{1}{4(n-s+1)} \right)$$

Now we get our result using the fact that $\delta = \frac{K_w^{(n-s)}(u)}{\binom{n-s}{w}}$ (Equation (5.3) of Parameter constraint 6) altogether with the fact that we supposed in (C.4) that $|\widetilde{\mathscr{H}}| > \frac{1}{2} \mathbb{E}_{\mathscr{C}}\left(|\widetilde{\mathscr{H}}|\right)$ and that from Fact 5 we have that $\mathbb{E}_{\mathscr{C}}\left(|\widetilde{\mathscr{H}}|\right) = \frac{\binom{n-s}{w}}{2^{k-s}}$. $\qquad \square$

Step 3. In this step we want to upper bound

$$\mathbb{P}_{\mathscr{C}}\left(\left|N_i - \bar{N}_i\right| > \left|\frac{K_w^{(n-s)}(u)}{K_w^{(n-s)}(i)}\right| \frac{1}{8(n-s+1)}\right)$$

First we give a useful lemma which essentially tells us that the right term in the probability is always greater than $\sqrt{\mathbf{Var}_{\mathscr{C}}(N_i)} = \sqrt{\bar{N}_i}$.

Lemma 5. *We have that*

$$\bar{N}_i\, f(n) < \left(\frac{K_w^{(n-s)}(u)}{K_w^{(n-s)}(i)}\right)^2$$

Proof. The proof is available in the eprint version of the paper.   □

We want to obtain an exponential bound on the previous probability

$$\mathbb{P}_{\mathscr{C}}\left(\left|N_i - \bar{N}_i\right| > \left|\frac{K_w^{(n-s)}(u)}{K_w^{(n-s)}(i)}\right| \frac{1}{8(n-s+1)}\right).$$

But, very few results are known about the N_i's, or, more generally the weight distribution of a random affine code. The first two moments of N_i are known with Fact 11. Some higher moments are studied in [LM19, BEL10], but in general, there is no known expressions for all the higher moments of the weight distribution of a random linear code. Furthermore, up to our knowledge no exponential tail bound on $N_i - \bar{N}_i$ exists. Thus, we are left to bound the previous probability using only the expected value and the variance of N_i by using Bienaymé-Tchebychev second order bound (which is the best bound we can get for a generic random variable using only its first two moments) which is given by:

$$\mathbb{P}_{\mathscr{C}}\left(\left|N_i - \bar{N}_i\right| > p(n)\sqrt{\mathbf{Var}(N_i)}\right) \le \frac{1}{p(n)^2}$$

Now the problem is that the previous Lemma 5 is tight for some $i \approx \frac{n-s}{2}$, namely we have:

$$\bar{N}_i\, f(n) = \text{poly}(n) \left(\frac{K_w^{(n-s)}(u)}{K_w^{(n-s)}(i)}\right)^2 \tag{C.11}$$

And thus if f is big enough we have that

$$\left|\frac{K_w^{(n-s)}(u)}{K_w^{(n-s)}(i)}\right| \frac{1}{8(n-s+1)} = \text{poly}(n)\sqrt{\mathbf{Var}(N_i)}.$$

As a result we can only get a polynomial bound using the Bienaymé-Tchebychev inequality. The fact that equation (C.11) holds can be seen with the fact that Krawtchouk polynomials attain their ℓ_2 norm [KS21, Prop. 2.15] (regarding the measure $\mu(i) = \frac{\binom{n-s}{i}}{2^{n-s}}$), up to a polynomial factor for certain i close to $(n-s)/2$, namely we have

$$\left(K_w^{(n-s)}(i)\right)^2 = \text{poly}(n)\binom{n-s}{w}2^{n-s}.$$

All in all, to be able to use tighter bounds, we decide to model in Assumption 8 the weight distributions N_i as Poisson variables of parameters

$$\mathbb{E}(N_i) = \frac{\binom{n-s}{i}}{2^{n-k}}.$$

We ran extensive experimentations to show that the distribution of the bias remains unchanged is we replace the weight distribution N_i by the former model. See Sect. D for the experimental results. We are now ready to give the two following tail bounds for $N_i - \bar{N}_i$. We first give a bound for the i's that are relatively small compared to u, namely when $i < u + O(\log n)$ (which corresponds to the case $\text{poly}(n)\, K_w^{(n-s)}(u) < K_w^{(n-s)}(i)$). Then, we prove a second bound using our model for the i's that are relatively big compared to u (which corresponds to the case $\text{poly}(n)\, K_w^{(n-s)}(u) > K_w^{(n-s)}(i)$).

Lemma 6. *Define* $\epsilon \stackrel{\triangle}{=} 1/4$. *We have:*

$$If \quad \left|\frac{K_w^{(n-s)}(u)}{K_w^{(n-s)}(i)}\right| \leq n^{2+\epsilon} \quad then \quad \mathbb{P}_{\mathscr{C}}\left(|N_i - \bar{N}_i| > \left|\frac{K_w^{(n-s)}(u)}{K_w^{(n-s)}(i)}\right| \frac{1}{8(n-s+1)}\right) \leq \frac{\binom{n-s}{i}}{2^{n-k}}.$$

$$(C.12)$$

Moreover, under Assumption 8 we have:

$$If \quad \left|\frac{K_w^{(n-s)}(u)}{K_w^{(n-s)}(i)}\right| > n^{2+\epsilon} \quad then \quad \mathbb{P}_{\mathscr{C}}\left(|N_i - \bar{N}_i| > \left|\frac{K_w^{(n-s)}(u)}{K_w^{(n-s)}(i)}\right| \frac{1}{8(n-s+1)}\right) \leq 2^{-\omega(n)}.$$

$$(C.13)$$

Proof. The proof is available in the eprint version of the paper.

Lemma 7. *We have under Assumption 8 that:*

$$\mathbb{P}_{\mathscr{C}}\left(bias_{\mathbf{h} \hookleftarrow \widetilde{\mathscr{H}}}(\langle \mathbf{y}, \mathbf{h}\rangle - \langle \mathbf{x}, \mathbf{h}_{\mathscr{P}}\rangle) > \frac{\delta}{4}\right) \leq \tilde{O}\left(\frac{\binom{n-s}{u}}{2^{n-k}}\right) \quad (C.14)$$

Proof. The proof is available in the eprint version of the paper. □

And thus, Fact 9 altogether with Lemma 7 proves Proposition 5 which gives the expected size of $\mathcal{S}$.

C.4 Further Results on the Complexity of Algorithm 4.1

Let us give here the complexity of Algorithm 4.1 when the support is split in two parts $\mathscr{P}$ and $\mathscr{N}$.

Proposition 9. *The expected space and time complexities of the "2-split" version of Algorithm 4.1 to decode an* $[n, k]$-*linear code at distance* t *are given by*

Time: $\tilde{O}\left(\dfrac{T_{eq} + T_{FFT}}{P_{succ}}\right) + \tilde{O}\left(\max\left(1, \dfrac{S}{P_{succ}}\right) T'(n-s, k-s, u)\right),$

Space: $O(S_{eq} + 2^s + S').$

Where

- $P_{succ} = \frac{\binom{s}{t-u}\binom{n-s}{u}}{\binom{n}{t}}$ is the probability over $\mathcal{N}$ that $|\mathbf{e}_{\mathcal{N}}| = u$,
- S_{eq}, T_{eq} are respectively the space and time complexities of $\text{CREATE}(N,w,\mathscr{P})$ for computing N parity-checks of weight w on $\mathcal{N}$,
- $T_{\text{FFT}} = O(2^s)$ is the time complexity of the fast Fourier Transform,
- $S = \tilde{O}\left(\binom{s}{t-u}\frac{\binom{n-s}{u}}{2^{n-k}}\right)$ is the average number of candidates in the set S
- S', T' are respectively the space and time complexities of SOLVE-SUBPROBLEM to decode an $[n-s, k-s]$ code at distance u.

and where N the number of LPN samples and the parameters s, u and w are such that:

$$N < \frac{\binom{n-s}{w}}{2^{k-s}} \quad and \quad N = \omega\left(n^5 \left(\frac{\binom{n-s}{w}}{K_w^{(n-s)}(u)}\right)^2\right).$$

Notice here that the only change in the complexity of Algorithm 4.1 compared to the original RLPN algorithm (Proposition 3.10 of [CDMT22]) is that we added a term

$$\tilde{O}\left(\max\left(1, \frac{S}{P_{succ}}\right) T'(n-s, k-s, u)\right)$$

in the complexity. We now give the asymptotic complexity of the corrected RLPN algorithm. Note that the techniques used to compute low-weight parity-checks [Dum86, CDMT22] compute in fact all the parity checks of weight w on $\mathcal{N}$. Thus, to simplify the next proposition we will simply replace the parameter N by the expected number of parity-checks of weight w on $\mathcal{N}$ that is $\frac{\binom{n-s}{w}}{2^{k-s}}$.

Proposition 10. *Define*

$$R \overset{\triangle}{=} \lim_{n\to\infty} \frac{k}{n}, \quad \tau \overset{\triangle}{=} \lim_{n\to\infty} \frac{t}{n}, \quad \sigma \overset{\triangle}{=} \lim_{n\to\infty} \frac{s}{n}, \quad w \overset{\triangle}{=} \lim_{n\to\infty} \frac{w}{n}, \quad \mu \overset{\triangle}{=} \lim_{n\to\infty} \frac{u}{n}.$$

The number of LPN samples N is chosen to be equal to the total number of parity-checks of weight w on $\mathcal{N}$, namely $N = 2^{n\,(\nu_{eq}+o(1))}$ where $\nu_{eq} \overset{\triangle}{=} (1-\sigma)\,h_2\left(\frac{w}{1-\sigma}\right)$ $-(R-\sigma)$. Then, the time complexity of the RLPN-decoder to decode an $[n,k]$-linear code at distance t is given by $2^{n\,(\alpha+o(1))}$ and the space complexity is $2^{n\,(\alpha_{\text{space}}+o(1))}$ where

$$\alpha \overset{\triangle}{=} \max\Bigg((1-\sigma)\gamma\left(\frac{R-\sigma}{1-\sigma}, \frac{w}{1-\sigma}\right) + \pi, \sigma + \pi, \max\left(\chi + \pi, 0\right)$$

$$+(1-\sigma)\alpha'\left(\frac{R-\sigma}{1-\sigma}, \frac{\mu}{1-\sigma}\right)\Bigg),$$

$$\pi \overset{\triangle}{=} h(\tau) - \sigma h\left(\frac{\tau-\mu}{\sigma}\right) - (1-\sigma)h\left(\frac{\mu}{1-\sigma}\right),$$

$$\chi \overset{\triangle}{=} \sigma h\left(\frac{\tau-\mu}{\sigma}\right) + (1-\sigma)h\left(\frac{\mu}{1-\sigma}\right) - (1-R),$$

$$\alpha_{\text{space}} \overset{\triangle}{=} \max\left((1-\sigma)\alpha'_{\text{space}}\left(\frac{R-\sigma}{1-\sigma}, \frac{\mu}{1-\sigma}\right), (1-\sigma)\gamma_{\text{space}}\left(\frac{R-\sigma}{1-\sigma}, \frac{w}{1-\sigma}\right)\right).$$

And where

- *the time complexity of* CREATE *to compute all parity-checks of relative weight τ' of a code of rate R' and length n' is given by $2^{n'\,\gamma(R',\tau')}$ and the space complexity is $2^{n'\,\gamma_{\mathrm{space}}(R',\tau')}$.*
- *The time complexity of* SOLVE-SUBPROBLEM *to decode a code of rate R' and length n' at relative distance τ' is given by $2^{n'\,\alpha'(R',\tau')}$. Its space complexity is $2^{n'\,\alpha'_{\mathrm{space}}(R',\tau')}$.*

Moreover, σ, μ, and ω are non-negative and such that

$$\sigma \leq R, \quad \tau - \sigma \leq \mu \leq \tau, \quad \omega \leq 1 - \sigma,$$

$$\nu_{\mathrm{eq}} \geq 2\,(1-\sigma)\left(h_2\left(\frac{\omega}{1-\sigma}\right) - \widetilde{\kappa}\left(\frac{\omega}{1-\sigma}, \frac{\mu}{1-\sigma}\right)\right),$$

where $\widetilde{\kappa}$ is the function defined in Proposition 2.

The only added term here compared to the original RLPN asymptotic complexity exponent is

$$\max\left(\chi + \pi, 0\right) + (1-\sigma)\alpha'\left(\frac{R-\sigma}{1-\sigma}, \frac{\mu}{1-\sigma}\right).$$

For simplicity, we make the choice here to use [Dum91] ISD-decoder as the routine SOLVE-SUBPROBLEM to solve the relevant decoding problem. Thus, we simply replace α' in Proposition 10 by the asymptotic complexity of [Dum91] ISD-decoder given in Proposition 8 of Sect. B. One could use [Dum86] to compute parity-checks and thus replace γ by the exponent given in Proposition 7 or use some more involved methods as described in [CDMT22, §5].

D   Experimental Results Regarding the Poisson Model

In this section we give experimental evidence for our claims which rely on the Poisson Model 8. Specifically, we show that the experimental distribution of the bias of $\langle \mathbf{y}, \mathbf{h} \rangle + \langle \mathbf{x}, \mathbf{h}_{\mathscr{P}} \rangle$ coincides with the theoretical distribution of the random variable X obtained by replacing the N_i's in Proposition 3:

$$\mathrm{bias}_{\mathbf{h} \hookleftarrow \widetilde{\mathscr{H}}}(\langle \mathbf{y}, \mathbf{h} \rangle + \langle \mathbf{x}, \mathbf{h}_{\mathscr{P}} \rangle)$$

$$= \frac{1}{2^{k-s}\left|\widetilde{\mathscr{H}}\right|} \sum_{i=0}^{n} N_i\left(\mathscr{C}^{\mathscr{N}} + (\mathbf{x} + \mathbf{e}_{\mathscr{P}})\mathbf{R} + \mathbf{e}_{\mathscr{N}}\right) K_w^{(n-s)}(i)$$

by independent Poisson variables $\widetilde{N}_i$ of parameter $\mathbb{E}_{\mathscr{C}}\left(\left|N_i\left(\mathscr{C}^{\mathscr{N}} + (\mathbf{x} + \mathbf{e}_{\mathscr{P}})\mathbf{R} + \mathbf{e}_{\mathscr{N}}\right)\right|\right) = \frac{\binom{n-s}{i}}{2^{n-k}}$. That is

$$X \triangleq \frac{1}{2^{k-s}\left|\widetilde{\mathscr{H}}\right|} \sum_{i=0}^{n} \widetilde{N}_i K_w^{(n-s)}(i). \tag{D.1}$$

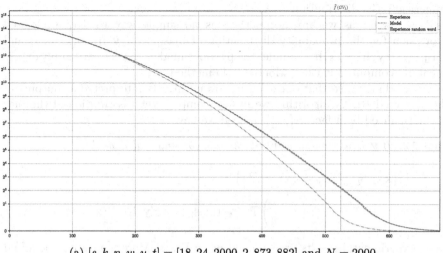

(a) $[s, k, n, w, u, t] = [18, 24, 2000, 2, 873, 882]$ and $N = 2000$

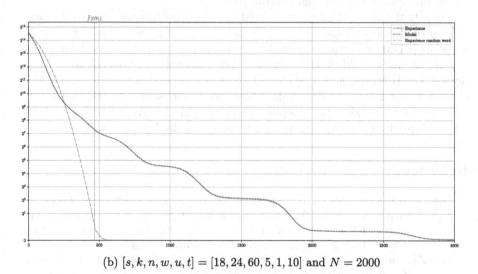

(b) $[s, k, n, w, u, t] = [18, 24, 60, 5, 1, 10]$ and $N = 2000$

Fig. 1. Expected size of the set $\{\mathbf{x} \in \mathcal{S}_{t-u}^{s} : \widehat{f_{\mathbf{y}, \mathscr{H}}} (\mathbf{x}) \geq T\}$ as a function of T for two different parameters.

- ———— Experimentally in corrected RLPN.
- ─ ─ ─ ─ Theoretically under the independent Poisson Model (D.1).
- ⋯⋯⋯ Theoretically under LPN model, that is, if we supposed that the LPN samples produced by RLPN followed exactly the framework of Problem 2.

We define $\widehat{f}(GV_1) \triangleq N - 2\, d_{\mathrm{GV}} \left(N, \log_2 \left(\binom{s}{t-u} \right) \right)$ corresponding to the highest theoretical Fourier coefficient under the LPN model.

The independence assumption on the $\widetilde{N}_i$'s was just made to be able to compute numerically the distribution of X.

Now, as far as we are aware, there is no simple way to derive a closed expression for the probability distribution of $\mathrm{bias}_{\mathbf{h} \hookleftarrow \widetilde{\mathscr{H}}}(\langle \mathbf{y}, \mathbf{h} \rangle + \langle \mathbf{x}, \mathbf{h}_{\mathscr{P}} \rangle)$ and $\mathrm{bias}_{\mathbf{h} \hookleftarrow \mathscr{H}}(\langle \mathbf{y}, \mathbf{h} \rangle + \langle \mathbf{x}, \mathbf{h}_{\mathscr{P}} \rangle)$ under the previous model. As such, we simply experimentally computed it using Monte-Carlo method.

As a side note, so that our quantity are intuitively interpreted as outputs of the corrected RLPN algorithm we in fact compare the distribution of the bias but normalized by a factor $\binom{s}{t-u}$, indeed we have:

Fact 12. *If* $\mathbf{y}$ *is a random word of* $\mathbb{F}_2^n$ *then for any real* T *we have*

$$
\mathbb{E}_{\mathscr{C}} \left(\left| \left\{ \mathbf{x} \in \mathcal{S}_{t-u}^s : \widehat{f_{\mathbf{y}, \mathscr{H}}}(\mathbf{x}) \geq T \right\} \right| \right)
$$
$$
= \binom{s}{t-u} \mathbb{P}_{\mathscr{C}, \mathscr{H}}\left(\mathrm{bias}_{\mathbf{h} \hookleftarrow \mathscr{H}}(\langle \mathbf{y}, \mathbf{h} \rangle + \langle \mathbf{x}, \mathbf{h}_{\mathscr{P}} \rangle) \geq T \right).
$$

Some experimental results are summed up in Fig. 1. More figures can be found in the supplementary material GitHub page[4].

Note that the parameters considered are such that we have unusually large Fourier coefficients compared to what we would expect if the original LPN model made in [CDMT22] was to hold. It is readily seen that if the LPN model of [CDMT22] was to hold the full curve in red should roughly match the green dash-dotted one. However, as [CDMT22, §3.4] already noticed, and as we also notice here, it is not the case. The dashed blue curve represents the tail coefficients given by Fact 12 under this independent Poisson Model. We see that our model very well predicts the experimental distribution of the Fourier coefficients.

References

[Alb17] Albrecht, M.R.: On dual lattice attacks against small-secret LWE and parameter choices in HElib and SEAL. In: Coron, J.-S., Nielsen, J.B. (eds.) EUROCRYPT 2017. LNCS, vol. 10211, pp. 103–129. Springer, Cham (2017). https://doi.org/10.1007/978-3-319-56614-6_4

[Bar97] Barg, A.: Complexity issues in coding theory. Electronic Colloquium on Computational Complexity, October 1997

[BEL10] Blinovsky, V., Erez, U., Litsyn, S.: Weight distribution moments of random linear/coset codes. Des. Codes Crypt. **57**, 127–138 (2010)

[BJMM12] Becker, A., Joux, A., May, A., Meurer, A.: Decoding random binary linear codes in $2^{n/20}$: how $1+1 = 0$ improves information set decoding. In: Pointcheval, D., Johansson, T. (eds.) EUROCRYPT 2012. LNCS, vol. 7237, pp. 520–536. Springer, Heidelberg (2012). https://doi.org/10.1007/978-3-642-29011-4_31

---

[4] https://github.com/meyer-hilfiger/Rigorous-Foundations-for-Dual-Attacks-in-Coding-Theory.

[BLP11]   Bernstein, D.J., Lange, T., Peters, C.: Smaller decoding exponents: ball-collision decoding. In: Rogaway, P. (ed.) CRYPTO 2011. LNCS, vol. 6841, pp. 743–760. Springer, Heidelberg (2011). https://doi.org/10.1007/978-3-642-22792-9_42

[BM17]   Both, L., May, A.: Optimizing BJMM with nearest neighbors: full decoding in $2^{2/21n}$ and McEliece security. In: WCC Workshop on Coding and Cryptography, September 2017

[CDMT22]   Carrier, K., Debris-Alazard, T., Meyer-Hilfiger, C., Tillich, J.P.: Statistical decoding 2.0: reducing decoding to LPN. In: Agrawal, S., Lin, D. (eds.) Advances in Cryptology – ASIACRYPT 2022. ASIACRYPT 2022. LNCS, vol. 13794, pp. 477–507. Springer, Cham (2022). https://doi.org/10.1007/978-3-031-22972-5_17

[DP23]   Ducas, L., Pulles, L.N.: Does the dual-sieve attack on learning with errors even work? IACR Cryptol. ePrint Arch., p. 302 (2023)

[DT17a]   Debris-Alazard, T., Tillich, J.P.: Statistical decoding. In: Proceedings of the IEEE International Symposium on Information Theory - ISIT 2017, pp. 1798–1802, Aachen, Germany, June 2017

[DT17b]   Debris-Alazard, T., Tillich, J.P.: Statistical decoding. preprint, January 2017. arXiv:1701.07416

[Dum86]   Dumer, I.: On syndrome decoding of linear codes. In: Proceedings of the 9th All-Union Symposium on Redundancy in Information Systems, abstracts of papers (in Russian), Part 2, pp. 157–159, Leningrad (1986)

[Dum91]   Dumer, I.: On minimum distance decoding of linear codes. In: Proceedings of the 5th Joint Soviet-Swedish International Workshop Information Theory, pp. 50–52, Moscow (1991)

[EJK20]   Espitau, T., Joux, A., Kharchenko, N.: On a dual/hybrid approach to small secret LWE. In: Bhargavan, K., Oswald, E., Prabhakaran, M. (eds.) INDOCRYPT 2020. LNCS, vol. 12578, pp. 440–462. Springer, Cham (2020). https://doi.org/10.1007/978-3-030-65277-7_20

[FS09]   Finiasz, M., Sendrier, N.: Security bounds for the design of code-based cryptosystems. In: Matsui, M. (ed.) ASIACRYPT 2009. LNCS, vol. 5912, pp. 88–105. Springer, Heidelberg (2009). https://doi.org/10.1007/978-3-642-10366-7_6

[GJ21]   Guo, Q., Johansson, T.: Faster dual lattice attacks for solving LWE with applications to CRYSTALS. In: Tibouchi, M., Wang, H. (eds.) ASIACRYPT 2021. LNCS, vol. 13093, pp. 33–62. Springer, Cham (2021). https://doi.org/10.1007/978-3-030-92068-5_2

[Jab01]   Jabri, A.A.: A statistical decoding algorithm for general linear block codes. In: Honary, B. (ed.) Cryptography and Coding 2001. LNCS, vol. 2260, pp. 1–8. Springer, Heidelberg (2001). https://doi.org/10.1007/3-540-45325-3_1

[KS21]   Kirshner, N., Samorodnitsky, A.: A moment ratio bound for polynomials and some extremal properties of Krawchouk polynomials and hamming spheres. IEEE Trans. Inform. Theory $67(6)$, 3509–3541 (2021)

[LM19]   Linial, N., Mosheiff, J.: On the weight distribution of random binary linear codes. Random Struct. Algorithms 56, 5–36 (2019)

[MAT22]   MATZOV. Report on the Security of LWE: Improved Dual Lattice Attack, April 2022

[MMT11]   May, A., Meurer, A., Thomae, E.: Decoding random linear codes in $\tilde{O}(2^{0.054n})$. In: Lee, D.H., Wang, X. (eds.) ASIACRYPT 2011. LNCS, vol. 7073, pp. 107–124. Springer, Heidelberg (2011). https://doi.org/10.1007/978-3-642-25385-0_6

[MO15] May, A., Ozerov, I.: On computing nearest neighbors with applications to decoding of binary linear codes. In: Oswald, E., Fischlin, M. (eds.) EURO-CRYPT 2015. LNCS, vol. 9056, pp. 203–228. Springer, Heidelberg (2015). https://doi.org/10.1007/978-3-662-46800-5_9

[MR09] Micciancio, D., Regev, O.: Lattice-based cryptography. In: Bernstein, D.J., Buchmann, J., Dahmen, E. (eds.) Post-Quantum Cryptography, pp. 147–191. Springer, Berlin, Heidelberg (2009). https://doi.org/10.1007/978-3-540-88702-7_5

[MS86] MacWilliams, F.J., Sloane, N.J.A.: The Theory of Error-Correcting Codes, 5th edn. North-Holland, Amsterdam (1986)

[Ove06] Overbeck, R.: Statistical decoding revisited. In: Batten, L.M., Safavi-Naini, R. (eds.) ACISP 2006. LNCS, vol. 4058, pp. 283–294. Springer, Heidelberg (2006). https://doi.org/10.1007/11780656_24

[Pra62] Prange, E.: The use of information sets in decoding cyclic codes. IRE Trans. Inf. Theory 8(5), 5–9 (1962)

[Ste88] Stern, J.: A method for finding codewords of small weight. In: Cohen, G., Wolfmann, J. (eds.) Coding Theory 1988. LNCS, vol. 388, pp. 106–113. Springer, Heidelberg (1989). https://doi.org/10.1007/BFb0019850

[vL99] Van Lint, J.H.: Introduction to Coding Theory, 3rd edn. In: Graduate Texts in Mathematics. Springer, Berlin, Heidelberg (1999). https://doi.org/10.1007/978-3-642-58575-3

On the Multi-user Security of LWE-Based NIKE

Roman Langrehr[✉][iD]

ETH Zurich, Zürich, Switzerland
roman.langrehr@inf.ethz.ch

Abstract. Non-interactive key exchange (NIKE) schemes like the Diffie-Hellman key exchange are a widespread building block in several cryptographic protocols. Since the Diffie-Hellman key exchange is not post-quantum secure, it is important to investigate post-quantum alternatives.

We analyze the security of the LWE-based NIKE by Ding et al. (ePrint 2012) and Peikert (PQCrypt 2014) in a multi-user setting where the same public key is used to generate shared keys with multiple other users. The Diffie-Hellman key exchange achieves this security notion. The mentioned LWE-based NIKE scheme comes with an inherent correctness error (Guo et al., PKC 2020), and this has significant implications for the multi-user security, necessitating a closer examination.

Single-user security generically implies multi-user security when all users generate their keys honestly for NIKE schemes with negligible correctness error. However, the LWE-based NIKE requires a super-polynomial modulus to achieve a negligible correctness error, which makes the scheme less efficient. We show that

- generically, single-user security does not imply multi-user security when the correctness error is non-negligible, but despite this
- the LWE-based NIKE with polynomial modulus is multi-user secure for honest users when the number of users is fixed in advance. This result takes advantage of the leakage-resilience properties of LWE.

We then turn to a stronger model of multi-user security that allows adversarially generated public keys. For this model, we consider a variant of the LWE-based NIKE where each public key is equipped with a NIZKPoK of the secret key. Adding NIZKPoKs is a standard technique for this stronger model and Hesse et al. (Crypto 2018) showed that this is sufficient to achieve security in the stronger multi-user security model for perfectly correct NIKEs (which the LWE-based NIKE is not). We show that

- for certain parameters that include all parameters with polynomial modulus, the LWE-based NIKE can be efficiently attacked with adversarially generated public keys, despite the use of NIZKPoKs, but
- for suitable parameters (that require a super-polynomial modulus), this security notion is achieved by the LWE-based NIKE with NIZKPoKs.

This stronger security notion has been previously achieved for LWE-based NIKE only in the QROM, while all our results are in the standard model.

G. Rothblum and H. Wee (Eds.): TCC 2023, LNCS 14372, pp. 33–62, 2023.
https://doi.org/10.1007/978-3-031-48624-1_2

1   Introduction

Non-interactive Key Exchange. Non-interactive key exchange (NIKE) schemes allow every pair of users to compute a common shared key, that is hidden to everybody else, using a public-key infrastructure. The first NIKE scheme was presented in the seminal work by Diffie and Hellman [19]. There, public keys are group elements g^{x_i} of a suitable prime-order group with a fixed generator g and the corresponding secret key is the discrete log x_i. The shared key for two users with public keys g^{x_i} and g^{x_j} is $K_{i,j} = g^{x_i \cdot x_j}$ and can be computed using x_i as $K_{i,j} = (g^{x_j})^{x_i}$ and similarly with x_j as $K_{i,j} = (g^{x_i})^{x_j}$. For an outsider who only sees the public keys g^{x_i} and g^{x_j}, the shared key $K_{i,j}$ is indistinguishable from a uniformly random group element by the Decisional Diffie-Hellman assumption.

The notion of a NIKE was only formalized much later by Cash, Kiltz, and Shoup [15] and further analyzed by Freire, Hofheinz, Kiltz, and Paterson [23]. NIKE schemes are a useful building block, especially when minimizing communication costs, for example, for wireless channels [14] or interactive key exchange [9]. Another interesting application of NIKE is deniable authentication [21], however this requires the NIKE to be perfectly correct and thus cannot be instantiated with the LWE-based NIKE considered in this work.

Although the Diffie-Hellman NIKE is very simple and efficient, it unfortunately is not secure against quantum computers. With the recent breaking [16,36,44] of SIDH [30], there are now, to the best of our knowledge, essentially two NIKE schemes that promise to achieve post-quantum security. The first is CSIDH [17], which, like SIDH, is based on isogenies, but is not affected by the attacks on SIDH. The other is the LWE-based NIKE introduced by Ding, Xie, and Lin [20] and Peikert [40]. This work is about the latter scheme.

NIKE from LWE. In the LWE-based NIKE from [20,40] there are two different types of users, which we will call left and right users. A shared key can be computed only between a left and a right user. This can be easily converted to a full-fledged NIKE by generating for every user a left and a right key and deciding, based on some fixed rule, which user uses his left key and which user uses his right key for the shared key computation.

The users share a common random matrix $\mathbf{A} \in \mathbb{Z}_q^{n \times n}$. Now each user samples a short vector $\mathbf{s}_i \in \mathbb{Z}_q^n$ (any short distribution with sufficient min-entropy will do), which will be its secret key, and an error vector $\mathbf{e}_i \in \mathbb{Z}^n$ whose entries are sampled according to a discrete Gaussian distribution. For a left user, the public key is $\mathsf{pk}_{L,i} = \mathbf{s}_i^\top \mathbf{A} + \mathbf{e}_i^\top$. For a right user, the public key is $\mathsf{pk}_{R,i} = \mathbf{A}\mathbf{s}_i + \mathbf{e}_i$. Now, a left user i and a right user j can both compute approximations of $\mathbf{s}_i^\top \mathbf{A}\mathbf{s}_j$: The left user can do so by sampling $e' \in \mathbb{Z}$ according to a discrete Gaussian distribution and computing $\mathbf{s}_i^\top \mathsf{pk}_{R,j} + e' = \mathbf{s}_i^\top \mathbf{A}\mathbf{s}_j + \underbrace{\mathbf{s}_i^\top \mathbf{e}_j + e'}_{\text{short}}$. Similarly, the right user can sample $e'' \in \mathbb{Z}$ according to a discrete Gaussian distribution and compute $\mathsf{pk}_{L,i}\mathbf{s}_j + e'' = \mathbf{s}_i^\top \mathbf{A}\mathbf{s}_j + \underbrace{\mathbf{e}_i^\top \mathbf{s}_j}_{\text{short}} + e''$. The additional error terms e' and e'' are necessary to prove security.[1]

By rounding these preliminary shared keys to, e.g., one bit, both users can obtain the same shared key with high probability. When a super-polynomial modulus-to-noise ratio is used, they will get the same bit with overwhelming probability, but with a polynomial modulus-to-noise ratio, there will be a non-negligible probability for not obtaining the same bit. Guo, Kamath, Rosen, and Sotiraki [26] showed that this is unavoidable for a large class of LWE-based NIKE schemes, even when multiple LWE samples are used per user.

Since LWE with polynomial modulus-to-noise ratio is more efficient due to the smaller modulus and is a qualitatively weaker assumption than LWE with super-polynomial modulus-to-noise ratio (it has better reductions to worst-case lattice problems [13,41,43]), it is still desirable to use a polynomial modulus-to-noise ratio when a small but non-negligible error probability is tolerable. This is the case, for example, in scenarios where interaction is possible but costly, such as [9,14].

Most of this work focuses on the polynomial modulus-to-noise ratio.

Security Models for NIKE. To study the security of a NIKE scheme, [15] introduced several security notions. We recall three of them which we use in this work.

The first notion is light security. Here, the adversary gets two public keys (here, a left public key and a right public key) and has to distinguish the shared key corresponding to these two public keys from a uniformly random key. This security notion captures scenarios where each public/secret key pair is used only for one shared key computation. However, for scalability and ease of use, it is often desirable to use the same key pair to compute shared keys with many other users.

The second notion we consider is adaptive HKR (honest key registration) security. It captures such scenarios, at least when all users generate their keys honestly. It is defined with a security game where the adversary can make adaptively the following operations via oracles:

- register a user and obtain their public key
- extract a user's secret key
- reveal the shared key of a pair of users (the adversary can specify which user contributes the secret key)
- (once) get challenged by either obtaining a real shared key (as in a reveal query) or a random shared key

---

[1] Using the learning with rounding assumption, the error terms e' and e'' could be avoided to prove "light security" (defined later). However, for the more advanced security notions considered in this work, rounding alone is not sufficient. Also, for super-polynomial modulus-to-noise ratio, the rounding can be omitted for light and adaptive HKR security because it has only negligible probability of changing the shared key.

The goal of the adversary is to guess whether he gets real or random shared keys in the challenge without making any query that makes this trivial (extracting the secret key of one challenge user or using the reveal oracle on the pair of challenge users).

The third and strongest security notion is adaptive DKR (dishonest key registration) security, where the adversary can do the same operations as in the adaptive HKR security game but additionally it can register users with adversarially chosen public keys. These users can be used to obtain shared keys with honest users (e.g., a challenge user) in the reveal oracle. The honest user's secret key is used here to compute the shared key.

In [23] it was shown that light security implies adaptive security, but this reduction requires that the NIKE scheme has a negligible correctness error. The reduction works by guessing both challenge users and using the public keys from the light security game as their public keys. Since it does not know the secret keys of the challenge users, the reduction answers reveal queries with one challenge user always with the secret key of the other, non-challenge user (here we rely on the negligible correctness error). The challenge query is answered with the purported shared key from the light security game. So far, this security model has been used directly only in the context of tight security (since the above reduction is not tight) [4,27,28], but we think it is also important to consider this notion for NIKE schemes with non-negligible correctness error, like the LWE-based construction with polynomial modulus-to-noise ratio.

In [27] it was furthermore shown that any adaptive HKR secure NIKE scheme with perfect correctness can be made adaptive DKR secure by equipping public keys with a non-interactive zero-knowledge proof of knowledge (NIZKPoK) of the secret key. Due to the requirement of perfect correctness, their transformation is not immediately applicable to the LWE-based NIKE schemes (no matter the modulus-to-noise ratio).

The original works on LWE-based NIKE only proved light security [20,40]. A very recent work [24] showed that a variant of the LWE-based NIKE with super-polynomial modulus is adaptively DKR secure in the (quantum) random oracle model. Informally speaking, they achieved this by showing that the NIZKPoK approach of [27] can be applied even to NIKE schemes achieving only statistical correctness when we can guarantee that the correctness error is negligible even for adversarially generated public/secret key pairs (possibly depending on the other public key). They achieve this by adding a random offset to the unrounded shared keys that is obtained by querying the random oracle on the public keys and identities of the two users. This approach seems not to carry over to the standard model and cannot be applied to a polynomial modulus-to-noise ratio because this would require a polynomial bound on the number of (Q)ROM queries.

1.1 Our Results and Open Questions

This work analyzes the security notions achieved by the LWE-based NIKE of [20,40], depending on the parameters.

Adaptive HKR Security with Polynomial Modulus-to-Noise Ratio. A natural approach to prove adaptive HKR security for the LWE-based NIKE with polynomial modulus-to-noise ratio would be to generalize the generic result of [23] to NIKE with non-negligible correctness error. We show that this is unfortunately impossible. Namely, in the full version we give a separation between light and adaptive HKR security by constructing a NIKE scheme with correctness error $p(\lambda) \in [0, 1]$, for any efficiently computable function p, which achieves light security, but has an attacker against adaptive HKR security with advantage $\approx p(\lambda)$. This attacker only needs to register one additional user (apart from the two users for the challenge).

The main result of this work is that, fortunately, for suitable parameters (that still have a polynomial modulus-to-noise ratio), the LWE-based NIKE scheme can achieve adaptive HKR security. However, the parameters we need depend on the number of users N that the adversary registers in the security game. Thus, we only achieve adaptive HKR security for an (arbitrary) a priori bounded number of users. We call this N-bounded adaptive HKR security. An interesting open problem is whether the NIKE can also achieve adaptive HKR security for an unbounded number of users. We show some barriers that need to be overcome to prove this.

Adaptive DKR Security. We then turn to adaptive DKR security. In this setting, we consider the NIKE where all public keys are equipped with a NIZKPoK of the secret key. We first show that when the noise that is added to the unrounded shared keys is of polynomial size, the scheme is not DKR secure by providing an attacker. The authors of [24] conjectured that their scheme is secure without the use of a (Q)ROM. However, the provided attack can break their scheme in time $\mathcal{O}(\sqrt{q/B_e})$ (in particular, the attack is independent of the LWE dimension) if the QROM is omitted and in polynomial time if the rounding function is additionally slightly changed. Especially since the particularities of the rounding function are irrelevant in their proof, the attack also shows barriers to prove DKR security without the QROM for the original rounding function.

We then show that when the noise added to the unrounded shared keys is super-polynomially larger than the size of the public keys and the size of the LWE secret, the scheme achieves adaptive DKR secure via the transformation of [27]. This requires a super-polynomial modulus-to-noise ratio. An interesting open problem is whether there is a different way to construct a NIKE from LWE with polynomial modulus-to-noise ratio that achieves adaptive DKR security.

Table 1 summarizes the results of this work.

1.2   Technical Overview

We briefly recall the security proof of light security for the LWE-based NIKE. Let us assume without loss of generality that the challenge shared key is computed with the left user's secret key $\mathbf{s}_L^\star$. We need to show that $\mathbf{s}_L^\star \cdot \mathsf{pk}_R^\star$ looks random to an adversary that knows the public key of the left user $(\mathbf{s}_L^\star)^\top \mathbf{A} + (\mathbf{e}_L^\star)^\top$ and the right user's public key $\mathsf{pk}_R^\star = \mathbf{A}\mathbf{s}_R^\star + \mathbf{e}_R^\star$. The proof proceeds with

Table 1. The security notions achieved by LWE-based NIKE. The highlighted results are from this work. In the adaptive DKR security column, poly. and super-poly. refer to the size of noise added to the unrounded shared keys. ✓ means that this security notion is achieved and ✗ means that there is an attack.

modulus-to-noise ratio	light security	adaptive HKR security	adaptive DKR security (with NIZKPoK)
polynomial	✓	✓ (bounded) ? (unbounded)	✗
super-polynomial	✓	✓	✗ poly. ✓ super-poly. ✓ with (Q)ROM [24]

a two-step hybrid argument. In the first step, $\mathsf{pk}_R^\star$ is replaced by a uniformly random value chosen from $\mathbb{Z}_q^n$, which is justified by the LWE assumption (with n samples). In the next and final step, we switch the left user's public key and the challenge shared key to uniformly random. To do this, we need $n+1$ samples $\mathbf{b} = (\mathbf{s}_L^\star)^\top (\mathbf{A}|\mathbf{v}) + (\mathbf{e}_L^\star)^\top$. The reduction uses $\mathbf{v}$ as the public key for the right user and the leftmost n entries of $\mathbf{b}$ as the public key for the left user. The rightmost entry $\mathbf{b}$ is then the shared key between these users. Since $\mathbf{b}$ is computationally indistinguishable from a uniformly random vector, light security follows.

Bounded HKR Security for LWE-NIKE. To prove adaptive HKR security, we first have to make one minor change to the NIKE scheme. Namely, we need to make the shared key generation algorithm deterministic, to avoid that the adversary can learn multiple shared keys for the same pair of users with the same user contributing its secret key. We do this by adding a key for a pseudorandom function (PRF) to each user's secret key. In the shared key algorithm, the randomness is now replaced by the output of the PRF evaluated on the other user's identity (or public key).

The reduction then begins by guessing which of the users registered by the adversary will be used for the challenge query, just as in the generic reduction of [23]. Without loss of generality we assume again that the challenge shared key is computed with the left challenge user's secret key. The difficulty here is that the secret keys of the challenge users are also used in reveal shared key queries to reveal the shared key with other users. In [23] these queries are answered using the other, non-challenge user's secret key. Here, however, the reduction can not directly use the other user's secret key to compute this shared key because it will differ with noticeable probability.

Trick 1: Using Leakage. The first trick we use to be able to answer these reveal queries is to use leakage about the challenge user's secret key and noise to correct for the other user's secret key being used. Concretely, when the right challenge user with public key $\mathsf{pk}_R^\star = \mathbf{A}\mathbf{s}_R^\star + \mathbf{e}_R^\star$ computes the shared key with another left user with public key $\mathsf{pk}_L = \mathbf{s}_L^\top \mathbf{A} + \mathbf{e}_L^\top$ the right user gets as unrounded shared key $s_L^\top As_R^\star + e_L^\top s_R^\star + e'$ while the left user gets $s_L^\top As_R^\star + s_L^\top e_R^\star + e''$. where e and e'' is a noise that is identically distributed in both cases. When the reduction gets the leakage $e_L^\top s_R^\star$ and $s_L^\top e_R^\star$, it can use the leakage to compute the shared key from the right user's perspective given the shared key from the left user's perspective, which the reduction can compute without the right user's secret key.

In [10,13] it is shown that LWE (with short secrets) is hard even given arbitrary leakage of the secret s, as long as enough min-entropy remains in s. We use this result to justify the leakage of $e_L^\top s_R^\star$.

Leakage about the error was first considered in [13] under the name extended LWE. There, the leakage is an inner product of the error with a uniformly random binary vector. This result is applicable in our setting (when the secret distribution is a binary distribution), but unfortunately it is not clear how to generalize this result to multiple hints. Thus, we can allow only one user apart from the challenge users. A later work considered a version with multiple hints [1], where you get the inner product of the LWE error with a matrix Z, but that matrix has a special structure that makes their result not applicable to our problem. Instead, we use a recent result [22] showing that LWE holds even when several *noisy* hints about the LWE secret are provided. Concretely, they show that the LWE holds even given $Ze + e'$ for a short matrix Z, the LWE error vector e and some new noise e' sampled according to a discrete Gaussian distribution. This works well with our LWE-based NIKE because we already have a noise term added to the shared keys that can be used for this result.

This allows us to show security for any number of users N, as long as this number is fixed in advance (before selecting the concrete parameters for the scheme). The drawback of this approach is that we have to increase the noise size and therefore the correctness error (if the modulus stays fixed) to support a larger number of users. Concretely, the noise in the shared key grows with $\mathcal{O}(\sqrt{N})$ and there is an inherent barrier to do better than this: Note that our reduction so far has not taken advantage of the rounding (the rounding is done only to achieve correctness). Thus, the reduction would still work when the adversary gets access to the unrounded shared keys in the reveal shared key queries. In this experiment, the adversary can query a shared key between a non-challenge user and a challenge user once with the challenge user's secret key and once with the other user's secret key and thus learn their difference

$$e_L^\top s_R^\star - s_L^\top e_R^\star + e' - e''.$$

The adversary can do this for many users to obtain a system of noisy linear equations of the secret $(s_R^\star | e_R^\star)$. Importantly, unlike in LWE, in these equations all components are so small that, with overwhelming probability, these equations hold over the integers $\mathbb{Z}$ and not only in $\mathbb{Z}_q$. Such systems of equations can be solved efficiently, given only logarithmically more equations than information-theoretically necessary to determine the secret [6]. This lower bound matches our result asymptotically (up to the logarithmic factor).

Trick 2: Make Use of the Rounding. We next present how we can bypass the above barrier by using the rounding function in the security proof. The high-level idea for this is very simple: When an unrounded shared key is far enough away from a rounding boundary, the reduction can ensure that the rounded shared key is the same, regardless of which user's secret key is used for the computation. In this way, the reduction does not need the leakage terms in many cases. See Fig. 1 for an illustration.

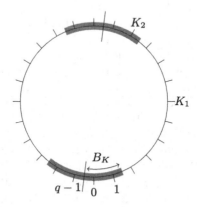

Fig. 1. Illustration of Trick 2. Here, the unrounded shared keys are rounded to one bit. The rounding boundaries are at 0 and $(q - 1)/2$. B_K denotes the maximum value by which the unrounded shared keys of one pair of users can differ. When an unrounded shared key is outside the red area, such as K_1, it does not matter which user's secret key is used to compute the shared key, because the rounded result will be the same. However, if the shared key lies in the red zone, such as K_2, it can make a difference which secret key is used. (Color figure online)

Realizing this idea is delicate because it is crucial that the leakage about the LWE secret is independent of the LWE matrix $\mathbf{A}$. Even with just one bit of leakage about $\mathbf{s}$ which depends on $\mathbf{A}$, we could break LWE.[2] However, whether an unrounded shared key is close to a rounding boundary or not clearly depends on $\mathbf{A}$.

We exploit that the leakage about the error vectors, in contrast to the LWE secret, can depend on $\mathbf{A}$. Concretely, the result of [22] shows that for suitable parameters

$$(\mathbf{e}_1, \mathbf{Z}\mathbf{e}_1 + \mathbf{e}_2) \approx_s (\mathbf{e}' + \mathbf{f}_1, \mathbf{f}_2),$$

where $\mathbf{Z}$ is any short matrix, $\mathbf{e}'$ is a noise term with a distribution suitable for the LWE assumption, $\mathbf{e}_1$ is distributed as the noise we add to the public keys, and

---

[2] The leakage bit can be the most significant bit of the first entry of $\mathbf{s}^\top \mathbf{A}$. This is very likely to agree with the most significant bit of the first entry of $\mathbf{s}^\top \mathbf{A} + \mathbf{e}^\top$ since $\mathbf{e}$ is short, but only agrees with probability $1/2$ with the most significant bit of a uniformly random vector.

e_2 is distributed as the noise we add to the unrounded shared keys. The vectors $\mathbf{f}_1$ and $\mathbf{f}_2$ are correlated, but independent of $\mathbf{e}'$. They can be efficiently sampled given $\mathbf{Z}$ (and the parameters for the noise terms). This can be used to reduce the hardness of LWE with error leakage to the hardness of plain LWE as follows: Given an LWE instance $(\mathbf{A}, \mathbf{b})$ where $\mathbf{b}$ is uniformly random or $\mathbf{b} = \mathbf{s}^\top \mathbf{A} + \mathbf{e}^\top$ where $\mathbf{e}$ has the same distribution as $\mathbf{e}'$ from the statement above. The reduction can now compute a matrix $\mathbf{Z}$ (possibly dependent on $\mathbf{A}$ and $\mathbf{b}$) and use it to sample $(\mathbf{f}_1, \mathbf{f}_2)$. The new LWE challenge is $(\mathbf{A}, \mathbf{b} + \mathbf{f}_1^\top)$ with leakage $\mathbf{f}_2$. Note that $\mathbf{b} + \mathbf{f}_1^\top$ is uniformly random if $\mathbf{b}$ was uniformly random, or an LWE sample (with higher noise) if $\mathbf{b}$ was an LWE sample.

We next explain how we use this to switch the right challenge key from real to random with less leakage. The switch for the left challenge key and shared key works analogously. For this reduction, we use a parameter k that determines the leakage sizes. If k is at least super-logarithmic in the security parameter, the number of users N can be increased by increasing the modulus linearly.

The reduction starts by sampling k error vectors $\mathbf{e}_{L,1}, \ldots, \mathbf{e}_{L,k}$ for public keys. These are used to define the leakage function for the LWE secret. This is then sent to the leakage resilient LWE challenger to get the LWE instance $(\mathbf{A}, \mathbf{b})$ with leakage about the secret $\mathbf{s}_R^\star$ (namely $\mathbf{e}_{L,i}^\top \mathbf{s}_R^\star$ for all $i \in [k]$). The public key for the right challenge user will be $\mathbf{b} + \mathbf{f}_1^\top$, but the reduction does not know $\mathbf{f}_1$ at this point, because it would have to specify the error leakage matrix $\mathbf{Z}$ before. However, $\mathbf{f}_1$ will be short, and we can use $\mathbf{b}$ as an approximation of the right challenge user's public key. The reduction then samples for all left non-challenge users the secret key $\mathbf{s}_L$ and computes $\mathbf{s}_L^\top \mathbf{b}$. If this is close to a rounding barrier, the reduction has to use the leakage to simulate a reveal query between this user and the challenge user. In this case, the reduction uses one of the pre-sampled error vectors $\mathbf{e}_{L,i}$ for this user and adds the secret $\mathbf{s}_L$ of this user (as a row vector) to the error leakage matrix $\mathbf{Z}$. If this case occurs more than k times, the reduction aborts. If $\mathbf{s}_L^\top \mathbf{b}$ is far from a rounding barrier, the reduction samples a fresh error vector $\mathbf{e}$ for this user. When this has been done for all users, the matrix $\mathbf{Z}$ is complete and the reduction can now sample $(\mathbf{f}_1, \mathbf{f}_2)$. It then uses $\mathbf{b} + \mathbf{f}_1$ as a public key for the right challenge user. The error leakage $\mathbf{f}_2$, together with the leakage about the LWE secret obtained before, can be used as in Trick 1 to simulate unrounded shared keys that are supposed to be computed with the right challenge user's secret key by using the left user's secret key instead and correcting the error that occurred by this change for a part of the left non-challenge users. For the other non-challenge users we have the guarantee that the error that occurred by this change disappears by the rounding operation.

Since the security proof here relies crucially on the rounding operation, it is important that only the output of the rounding function is used in subsequent protocols. Therefore, the key reconciliation mechanism of [20, 40], a protocol that can correct the LWE-NIKE correctness error simply by interactively sending one bit, cannot be used here directly. But we show that this protocol can, in fact, be used by using the two least significant bits of the rounding result. That is, by rounding to three bits, we can get a one-bit shared key along with the necessary auxiliary information for the interactive reconciliation procedure.

Limitations for Unbound Adaptive HKR Security. At the end of the description of Trick 1, we showed that an adversary can learn noisy linear equations about a challenge user's secret key by taking the differences of unrounded shared keys computed with the challenge user's secret key and the other user's secret key. This attack can still be applied when the adversary gets only the rounded shared keys, but now the adversary will learn a certain interval where the inner product $(s_R^\star | e_R^\star) a_i$ lies for several short vectors a_i. This can be turned into an integer linear program (ILP) where $(s_R^\star | e_R^\star)$ is one solution. In all our results, we use parameters such that the solution space of this ILP is still exponentially large, and thus the ILP is not useful. However, if the number of users is unbounded, the adversary can obtain enough inequalities for the ILP to (likely) have a unique solution. Since ILP is an NP-complete problem, this does not immediately yield an efficient attack. But it seems that this makes proving security difficult and requires new techniques.

DKR Insecurity of LWE-NIKE with NIZKPoK. We then analyze the security of the LWE NIKE in the DKR security model. We show how to turn the above attack idea with the ILP into an efficient attack with dishonest key registration queries. With dishonest key registrations, the adversary can essentially control the vectors a_i. In particular, the adversary can make all a_i unit vectors, so that this $2n$ dimensional ILP can be solved by solving $2n$ 1-dimensional ILPs, which can be done efficiently.

The difficulty herewith is to ensure that the ILP has one unique solution. Essentially, we show that this attack works as long as the noise added to the shared keys is of polynomial size, capturing all (useful) parameter settings for polynomial modulus-to-noise ratio and some parameters for super-polynomial modulus-to-noise ratio.

DKR Security by Smudging. We show that despite the above attack, the LWE NIKE is DKR secure when the noise added to the unrounded shared keys is super-polynomially larger than the size of the public keys and the size of the LWE secret, because it "smudges" the problematic terms $e_L^\top s_R^\star$ and $s_L^\top e_R^\star$. Thus, the distribution of the shared key is now statistically independent of which user's secret key was used, even if one key pair is adversarially generated. This is sufficient to reduce adaptive DKR security to adaptive HKR security by equipping public keys with NIZKPoKs, as in [27].

Ring LWE. All our results generalize to the ring and module LWE setting. Therefore, we present our results in the technical part with module LWE, which contains unstructured LWE (LWE in $\mathbb{Z}_q$) and ring LWE as special cases.

1.3 Roadmap

In Sect. 2 we recall the basic definitions and results of previous work. In Sect. 2.4, we also included a brief survey of papers on the leakage resilience of unstructured, ring, and module LWE. The separation of light and adaptive HKR security for NIKE with non-negligible correctness error is postponed to the full version. In Sect. 3 we prove bounded adaptive HKR security for the LWE-based NIKE with polynomial modulus-to-noise ratio. In the full version we describe an attacker against DKR security (in the presence of NIZKPoKs) when the noise added to the unrounded shared keys is of polynomial size and we prove DKR security with NIZKPoKs when this noise is of super-polynomial size.

2 Preliminaries

We use $\mathbb{N}_0$ for the set of natural numbers with zero and $\mathbb{N}_+$ for the set of natural numbers without zero. For strings a, b we use $a\|b$ to denote the concatenation of a and b.

We use $x \xleftarrow{\$} S$ to denote the process of sampling an element x from a set S uniformly at random. For a probability distribution $\mathcal{D}$, we write $x \leftarrow \mathcal{D}$ to denote that the random variable x is distributed according to $\mathcal{D}$. For a (probabilistic) algorithm $\mathcal{A}$ we write $x \leftarrow \mathcal{A}(b)$ to denote the random variable x outputted by $\mathcal{A}$ on input b. When we want to make the random coins used for sampling explicit, we write $x \xleftarrow{\$}_r S$, $x \leftarrow_r \mathcal{D}$, or $x \leftarrow_r \mathcal{A}(b)$ where r is a string of sufficiently many (uniformly random) bits.

Definition 1 (Statistical distance). *The statistical distance between two random variables X and Y is defined as*

$$\mathsf{SD}(X, Y) := \frac{1}{2} \sum_x |\Pr[X = x] - \Pr[Y = x]|.$$

2.1 Linear Algebra

Every real matrix $\mathbf{M} \in \mathbb{R}^{n \times m}$ can be written as $\mathbf{M} = \mathbf{U}\mathbf{D}\mathbf{V}^\top$ where $\mathbf{U} \in \mathbb{R}^{n \times n}$, $\mathbf{V} \in \mathbb{R}^{m \times m}$ is a orthogonal matrix and $\mathbf{D} \in \mathbb{R}^{n \times m}$ is an upper diagonal matrix (singular value decomposition). The entries of $\mathbf{D}$ are called the singular values of $\mathbf{M}$ and we denote the smallest singular value by $\sigma_{\min}(\mathbf{M})$ and the largest singular value by $\sigma_{\max}(\mathbf{M})$. The largest singular value $\sigma_{\max}(\mathbf{M})$ is equal to the Euclidean spectral norm $\|\mathbf{M}\|_2 := \max_{\|\mathbf{x}\|_2=1} \|\mathbf{A}\mathbf{x}\|_2$.

If $\mathbf{\Sigma} \in \mathbb{R}^{n \times n}$ is a symmetric positive-definite matrix, its singular value decomposition is of the form $\mathbf{\Sigma} = \mathbf{U}\mathbf{D}\mathbf{U}^\top$ where $\mathbf{U} \in \mathbb{R}^{n \times n}$ is an orthogonal matrix and $\mathbf{D} \in \mathbb{R}^{n \times n}$ is a diagonal matrix. Let $\sqrt{\mathbf{D}} \in \mathbb{R}^{n \times n}$ be the matrix obtained by applying the square root function component-wise to all entries of $\mathbf{D}$. With this, we define $\sqrt{\mathbf{\Sigma}} = \mathbf{U}\sqrt{\mathbf{D}}\mathbf{U}^\top$.

We will use the following bound for the largest singular value of a short matrix.

Lemma 1. *Let $\mathbf{M} \in [-B, B]^{n \times m}$ for $B > 0$. Then $\sigma_{\max}(\mathbf{M}) \leq B\sqrt{n}$.*

Proof.

$$\sigma_{\max}(\mathbf{M}) = \|\mathbf{M}\|_2 = \max_{\|\mathbf{x}\|_2=1} \|\mathbf{A}\mathbf{x}\|_2 \le B\sqrt{n}$$

The last step uses the fact that $\mathbf{A}\mathbf{x}$ is an n-dimensional vector with entries in $[-B, B]$.   □

2.2   Discrete Gaussian Distribution

Let $\mathbf{\Sigma} \in \mathbb{R}^{n \times n}$ be a symmetric positive-definite matrix. Then the *Gaussian function* on $\mathbb{R}^n$ is defined as $\rho_{\sqrt{\mathbf{\Sigma}}}(\mathbf{x}) := \exp(-\pi \mathbf{x}^\top \mathbf{\Sigma}^{-1} \mathbf{x})$. The function extends to sets in the usual way. That is, for any countable set $A \subseteq \mathbb{R}^n$, $\rho_{\sqrt{\mathbf{\Sigma}}}(A) := \sum_{\mathbf{x} \in A} \rho_{\sqrt{\mathbf{\Sigma}}}(\mathbf{x})$.

Moreover, for every countable set $A \subseteq \mathbb{R}^n$ and any $\mathbf{x} \in A$, the *discrete Gaussian function* is defined by $\rho_{A, \sqrt{\mathbf{\Sigma}}}(\mathbf{x}) := \frac{\rho_{\sqrt{\mathbf{\Sigma}}}(\mathbf{x})}{\rho_{\sqrt{\mathbf{\Sigma}}}(A)}$ and we denote the corresponding *discrete Gaussian distribution* as $\mathcal{D}_{A, \sqrt{\mathbf{\Sigma}}}$.

If $\mathbf{\Sigma} = \sigma^2 \cdot \mathbf{I}_n$, where $\mathbf{I}_n$ is the $n \times n$ identity matrix, we denote the Gaussian function by ρ_σ, the discrete Gaussian function by $\rho_{A,\sigma}$ and the discrete Gaussian distribution by $\mathcal{D}_{A,\sigma}$ for short.

2.3   Lattices

A lattice $\mathbf{\Lambda} \subseteq \mathbb{R}^n$ is a set of all integer linear combinations of a set of k linear independent vectors of $\mathbb{R}^n$, the basis of $\mathbf{\Lambda}$. We call k the rank of the lattice. The dual of a lattice $\mathbf{\Lambda}$ is $\mathbf{\Lambda}^* := \{\mathbf{w} \in \mathbb{R}^n \mid \forall \mathbf{v} \in \mathbf{\Lambda} : \langle \mathbf{v}, \mathbf{w} \rangle \in \mathbb{Z}\}$

In this work, we will be dealing with lattices of the form $\mathcal{R}^n$ where $\mathcal{R}$ is a ring that becomes a lattice through a fixed embedding (injective ring homomorphism[3]) $\psi : \mathcal{R} \to \mathbb{R}^d$. We extend ψ componentwise to vectors and matrices over $\mathcal{R}$. In this work, we will always implicitly assume that rings come with such an embedding. Typically, $\mathcal{R}$ will be $\mathbb{Z}[\zeta]$ where ζ is an element of order ℓ (i.e., an ℓ-th root of unity), the ring of algebraic integers of the cyclotomic number field $\mathbb{Q}(\zeta)$. The minimal polynomial of ζ has degree $d := \phi(\ell)$ (where ϕ is Euler's totient function) and we will also call this the degree of the ring.

For this ring, we will use the canonical embedding that is defined as follows: Every number field $\mathbb{Q}(\zeta)$ of degree d has a d embedding in $\mathbb{C}$ denoted by $\sigma_i : \mathbb{Q}(\zeta) \to \mathbb{C}$, each of them sending ζ to one of the primitive d-th roots of $\mathbb{C}$. For a suitable ordering of these embeddings and suitable $s_1, s_2 \in \mathbb{N}_0$ satisfying $d = s_1 + 2s_2$ we get that the following is a ring-homomorphism called the canonical embedding:

$$\sigma : \mathbb{Q}(\zeta) \to H := \{(x_1, \ldots, x_d) \in \mathbb{R}^{s_1} \times \mathbb{C}^{s_2} \mid \forall i \in [s_2] : x_{s_1+i} = \overline{x_{s_1+s_2+i}}\}$$
$$x \mapsto (\sigma_1(x), \ldots, \sigma_d(x))$$

There exists an inner product space isomorphism $\Theta : H \to \mathbb{R}^d$. With this we get the embedding $\psi := (\Theta \circ \sigma)\big|_{\mathbb{Z}[\zeta]}$.

---

[3] Here, $\mathbb{R}^d$ is a ring with component-wise addition and multiplication.

The embedding also induces a norm on the ring elements $\mathbf{r} \in \mathcal{R}^n$: For $p \in \mathbb{N}_+ \cup \{\infty\}$ we define $\|\mathbf{r}\|_p := \|\psi(\mathbf{r})\|_p$.

To bound the norm of a product, we have to take into account the ring expansion factor.

Definition 2 (Ring expansion factor). *The ring expansion factor $\gamma_\mathcal{R}$ of a ring is* $\max_{a,b \in \mathcal{R} \setminus \{0\}} \frac{\|a \cdot b\|_2}{\|a\|_2 \cdot \|b\|_2}$.

When working with $\mathcal{R} = \mathbb{Z}$, the ring expansion factor is obviously $\gamma_\mathbb{Z} = 1$. For prime-power cyclotomics it is $\gamma_\mathcal{R} \leq 2d$ and for power-of-two cyclotomics it is $\gamma_\mathcal{R} \leq d$ [2].

For a symmetric positive-definite matrix $\boldsymbol{\Sigma} \in \mathbb{R}^{dn \times dn}$ we write $\mathcal{D}_{\mathcal{R}^n, \sqrt{\boldsymbol{\Sigma}}}$ for the distribution that samples $\mathbf{r} \in \mathcal{R}^n$ with probability $\rho_{\psi(\mathcal{R})^n, \sqrt{\boldsymbol{\Sigma}}}(\psi(\mathbf{r}))$.

For $q \in \mathbb{N}_+$ we write $\mathcal{R}_q := \mathcal{R}/q\mathcal{R}$.

We recall the definition of the smoothing parameter for lattices.

Definition 3 ([39]). *Let $\boldsymbol{\Lambda}$ be a lattice, and $\varepsilon > 0$. Then $\eta_\varepsilon(\boldsymbol{\Lambda}) := \min\{s > 0 \mid \rho_{1/s}(\boldsymbol{\Lambda}^* \setminus \{\mathbf{0}\}) \leq \varepsilon\}$.*

For an invertible matrix $\mathbf{M} \in \mathbb{R}^{n \times n}$ and a lattice $\boldsymbol{\Lambda} \subseteq \mathbb{R}^n$, we write $\mathbf{M} \geq \eta_\varepsilon(\boldsymbol{\Lambda})$ iff $1 \geq \eta_\varepsilon(\boldsymbol{\Lambda}\mathbf{M}^{-1})$.

We use the following tail-bound for (possibly non-spherical) discrete Gaussian distributions.

Lemma 2. *For any $k > 1$, $n \in \mathbb{N}_+$ and any symmetric positive definite matrix $\boldsymbol{\Sigma} \in \mathbb{R}^{n \times n}$*

$$\Pr_{\mathbf{z} \leftarrow \mathcal{D}_{\mathbb{Z}^n, \sqrt{\boldsymbol{\Sigma}}}} [\|\mathbf{z}\|_2 > k\sqrt{\sigma_{\mathsf{max}}(\boldsymbol{\Sigma})n/2\pi}] < k^n e^{n(1-k^2)/2}.$$

The proof follows the outline of the proof of [33, Lemma 4.4 (3)].

Proof. We apply [5, Lemma 1.5], that for all lattices $\boldsymbol{\Lambda} \in \mathbb{R}^n$ and any $c \geq 1/\sqrt{2\pi}$

$$\sum_{\mathbf{z} \in \boldsymbol{\Lambda}, \|\mathbf{z}\|_2 > c\sqrt{n}} \exp(-\pi\|\mathbf{z}\|_2^2) < \left(c\sqrt{2\pi e}e^{-\pi c^2}\right)^n \sum_{\mathbf{z} \in \boldsymbol{\Lambda}} e^{-\pi\|\mathbf{z}\|_2^2},$$

to the lattice $\boldsymbol{\Lambda} = \sqrt{\boldsymbol{\Sigma}}^{-1}\mathbb{Z}^n$ to get the following:

$$\sum_{\mathbf{z} \in \sqrt{\boldsymbol{\Sigma}}^{-1}\mathbb{Z}^n, \mathbf{z}^\top\mathbf{z} > c^2 n} \exp(-\pi\mathbf{z}^\top\mathbf{z}) < \left(c\sqrt{2\pi e}e^{-\pi c^2}\right)^n \sum_{\mathbf{z} \in \sqrt{\boldsymbol{\Sigma}}^{-1}\mathbb{Z}^n} e^{-\pi\mathbf{z}^\top\mathbf{z}}.$$

Now we substitute $\mathbf{x} := \sqrt{\boldsymbol{\Sigma}}\mathbf{z}$ to get

$$\sum_{\mathbf{x} \in \mathbb{Z}^n, \mathbf{x}^\top\boldsymbol{\Sigma}^{-1}\mathbf{x} > c^2 n} \exp(-\pi\mathbf{x}^\top\boldsymbol{\Sigma}^{-1}\mathbf{x}) < \left(c\sqrt{2\pi e}e^{-\pi c^2}\right)^n \sum_{\mathbf{x} \in \mathbb{Z}^n} e^{-\pi\mathbf{x}^\top\boldsymbol{\Sigma}^{-1}\mathbf{x}}. \quad (1)$$

Next we use $\mathbf{x}^\top \sigma_{\mathsf{max}}(\boldsymbol{\Sigma})^{-1}\mathbf{I}_n\mathbf{x} = \mathbf{x}^\top \sigma_{\mathsf{min}}(\boldsymbol{\Sigma}^{-1})\mathbf{I}_n\mathbf{x} \le \mathbf{x}^\top\boldsymbol{\Sigma}^{-1}\mathbf{x}$ to get

$$
\sum_{\mathbf{x}\in\mathbb{Z}^n,\mathbf{x}^\top\sigma_{\mathsf{max}}(\boldsymbol{\Sigma})^{-1}\mathbf{I}_n\mathbf{x}>c^2 n} \exp(-\pi\mathbf{x}^\top\boldsymbol{\Sigma}^{-1}\mathbf{x}) \le \sum_{\mathbf{x}\in\mathbb{Z}^n,\mathbf{x}^\top\boldsymbol{\Sigma}^{-1}\mathbf{x}>c^2 n} \exp(-\pi\mathbf{x}^\top\boldsymbol{\Sigma}^{-1}\mathbf{x})
$$

$$
\overset{(1)}{<} \left(c\sqrt{2\pi e}e^{-\pi c^2}\right)^n \sum_{\mathbf{x}\in\mathbb{Z}^n} e^{-\pi\mathbf{x}^\top\boldsymbol{\Sigma}^{-1}\mathbf{x}}
$$

which can be rearranged to

$$
\sum_{\mathbf{x}\in\mathbb{Z}^n,\mathbf{x}^\top\mathbf{x}>c^2\sigma_{\mathsf{max}}(\boldsymbol{\Sigma})n} \rho_{\mathbb{Z}^n,\sqrt{\boldsymbol{\Sigma}}}(\mathbf{x}) < \left(c\sqrt{2\pi e}e^{-\pi c^2}\right)^n = (c\sqrt{2\pi})^n e^{(1/2-\pi c^2)n}.
$$

The lemma follows by setting $c = k/\sqrt{2\pi}$. □

2.4   (Module) Learning with Errors

We will use the module learning with errors problem (M-LWE) in this work. This includes the interesting special cases of unstructured LWE and ring LWE (R-LWE).

Definition 4 (M-LWE assumption with leakage). *The* $(\mathcal{R}, n, m, q, \mathcal{S}, \mathcal{E}, \mathcal{L})$-LWE *assumption for a ring* $\mathcal{R}$ *of degree* d, $n, m, q \in \mathbb{N}_+$, *the secret distribution* $\mathcal{S}$ *on* $\mathcal{R}_q^n$ *and the error distribution* $\mathcal{E}$ *on* $\mathcal{R}_q^m$ *and an (efficiently decidable) set of allowed (efficiently computable) leakage functions* $\mathcal{L}$ *states that for every PPT adversary* $\mathcal{A} = (\mathcal{A}_1, \mathcal{A}_2)$,

$$
\mathsf{Adv}^{\mathsf{lwe}}_{\mathcal{R},n,m,q,\mathcal{S},\mathcal{E},\mathcal{L}}(\mathcal{A}) := \Pr[\mathcal{A}_2(\mathbf{A}, \mathbf{s}^\top\mathbf{A} + \mathbf{e}^\top, \mathsf{st}, \ell) - \mathcal{A}_2(\mathbf{A}, \mathbf{z}, \mathsf{st}, \ell)]
$$

is negligible in $d \cdot n$, *where the probability is taken over* $\mathbf{A} \leftarrow \mathcal{R}_q^{n\times m}$, $\mathbf{s} \leftarrow \mathcal{S}$, $\mathbf{e} \leftarrow \mathcal{E}$, $(\mathsf{st}, f) \leftarrow \mathcal{A}_1(1^\lambda)$, *and the internal randomness of* $\mathcal{A}_2$ *for* $\ell := f(\mathbf{s})$ *if* $f \in \mathcal{L}$ *and* $\ell := \varepsilon$ *otherwise.*

In this paper, we require that the error distribution is a discrete Gaussian distribution ($\mathcal{E} = \mathcal{D}_{\mathcal{R}^n,\boldsymbol{\Sigma}}$). To build a NIKE scheme, we also require that $\mathcal{S}$ outputs only short vectors, e.g., binary or discrete Gaussian vectors.

Unstructured LWE. The case of $d = 1$, that is, where, without loss of generality, $\mathcal{R} = \mathbb{Z}$, is called (unstructured) LWE and was introduced by [43].

For standard LWE, where $\mathcal{S}$ is the uniform distribution on $\mathbb{Z}_q^n$, Regev [43] showed that for n growing polynomially in the security parameter and $\mathcal{E} = \mathcal{D}_{\mathbb{Z}_q^n,\sigma}$ with $\sigma > \max\{2\sqrt{n}, q/2^{n^c}\}$ for a constant $c \in (0,1)$ the hardness of LWE can be reduced quantumly to hard worst-case lattice problems, namely approximating the decision version of the shortest vector problem (GapSVP) and the shortest independent vector problem (SIVP) within $\widetilde{\mathcal{O}}(n2^{n^c})$. Later works also gave classical reductions for $q \ge 2^{n/2}$ consisting of small primes [41] and polynomial moduli [13].

This gives strong indication that the LWE assumption holds for both polynomial and super-polynomial modulus(q)-to-noise(σ) ratios, while the former is preferable because it has qualitatively better reductions to lattice problems and arithmetic with polynomial moduli is more efficient than for super-polynomial moduli.

The work [3] first showed the hardness of LWE with a short secret distribution, namely a discrete Gaussian distribution, as used for the error, can be reduced to standard LWE. The work [25] then showed that the LWE with binary secret and leakage about the secret (as long as enough min-entropy remains in the secret) is implied by standard LWE in the super-polynomial modulus-to-noise ratio regime. The follow-ups [13,38] showed that LWE with a polynomial modulus-to-noise ratio and a binary secret (and leakage in [13]) is implied by LWE with uniform secrets. Finally, the work [10] showed the hardness of LWE with "noise lossy" distributions, which include all short distributions with enough min-entropy, with a reduction to standard LWE. The result can be easily extended to capture also leakage about the secret as long as enough min-entropy remains in the secret. In particular, their result holds even with polynomial modulus-to-noise ratio. The reductions of both [25] and [10] are not dimension-preserving. The work [18] presents a framework for incorporating (noisy) linear leakage about the LWE secret (and error) into attacks on LWE.

Ring LWE. Ring LWE refers to the special case where $n = 1$. The problem was introduced in [34,35] to improve the concrete efficiency of LWE-based schemes.

The work [11] analyzed the hardness of the search variant for ring LWE for entropic secret distributions, and again their result can easily be extended to the leakage setting. They show the hardness of search ring LWE for entropic secret distributions based on the Decisional Small Polynomial Ratio (DSPR) problem. Their result requires that the min-entropy of the secret distributions is at least $d \log(\gamma \mathsf{poly}(d)) + \omega(\log \lambda)$, where γ is the standard deviation of the Gaussian distribution used in the DSPR problem. This excludes the use of binary secrets but can be satisfied by somewhat short distributions that are sufficient for our purposes. Their result also requires a certain non-degeneracy property that is proven only for power-of-two cyclotomic rings, but they conjecture that it holds for the ring of algebraic integer over all number fields.

Unfortunately, our NIKE construction relies on the hardness of the decisional (ring) LWE problem, so this result cannot be directly applied here.[4] The result of [32], which we describe in the next paragraph, implies a hardness result for decisional entropic ring LWE.

Many hardness results for ring LWE naturally require the non-spherical discrete Gaussian error distributions [11,34,35,42] and converting to spherical Gaussians comes at a price [42]. Thus in this work we present our results for possibly non-spherical discrete Gaussians.

---

[4] There exist search-to-decision reductions for (ring/module) LWE, but those reductions do not preserve the secret distributions and thus cannot be applied in the leaky/entropic secret regime.

Module LWE. Module LWE was introduced in [12,31] to interpolate between ring and module LWE.

For module LWE, there are two hardness results for entropic secret distributions (which again can easily be restated as results about leakage resilience). The first result [32] comes in a flavor similar to [10]: They show hardness of module LWE for all short secret distributions with enough min-entropy, including binary distributions, via a reduction to module LWE that is not dimension-preserving.

The second result [7] comes in the flavor of [11]: They show hardness of the search variant (thus, this result is not directly applicable for our construction) of module LWE for secret distributions with enough min-entropy (again, the entropy requirement here excludes binary distributions but can be satisfied by somewhat short distributions) with a dimension-preserving reduction to the module NTRU.

2.5   Noisy Hints

We recall (a special case of) a theorem of [22] showing that noisy hints about the LWE error can be simulated, for suitable parameters, without knowing the error (at the cost of increasing the error size).

Lemma 3 ([22, Theorem 2, simplified]). *Let $\mathcal{R}$ be a ring of degree d, m, $k \in \mathbb{N}_+$, $\mathbf{Z} \in \mathbb{R}^{k \times m}$ and $\varepsilon > 0$. Let $\boldsymbol{\Sigma}_0 \in \mathbb{R}^{dm \times dm}, \mathbf{T}_0 \in \mathbb{R}^{dk \times dk}$ and $s, t \geq 2\sqrt{2}$ such that*

$$\sqrt{\boldsymbol{\Sigma}_0} \geq \eta_\varepsilon(\mathcal{R}^m), \qquad \sqrt{\mathbf{T}_0} \geq \eta_\varepsilon(\mathcal{R}^k), \text{ and}$$

$$t^2 \sigma_{\min}(\mathbf{T}_0) \geq \frac{(s^2 + 1)(s^2 + 2)}{s^2} \sigma_{\max}(\boldsymbol{\Sigma}_0) \sigma_{\max}(\psi(\mathbf{Z}))^2.$$

Then, for $\boldsymbol{\Sigma} := (s^2 + 1)\boldsymbol{\Sigma}_0$, $\mathbf{T} := (t^2 + 1)\mathbf{T}_0$, and $\overline{\boldsymbol{\Sigma}} := s^2/4 \cdot \boldsymbol{\Sigma}_0$ there exists an efficiently sampable distribution $\mathcal{F}$ on $\mathcal{R}^m \times \mathcal{R}^k$ such that for $\mathbf{e}_1 \leftarrow \mathcal{D}_{\mathcal{R}^m, \sqrt{\boldsymbol{\Sigma}}}$, $\mathbf{e}_2 \leftarrow \mathcal{D}_{\mathcal{R}^k, \sqrt{\mathbf{T}}}$, $\mathbf{e} \leftarrow \mathcal{D}_{\mathcal{R}^m, \sqrt{\overline{\boldsymbol{\Sigma}}}}$, and $(\mathbf{f}_1, \mathbf{f}_2) \leftarrow \mathcal{F}$ we have

$$\mathsf{SD}((\mathbf{e}_1, \mathbf{Z}\mathbf{e}_1 + \mathbf{e}_2), (\mathbf{e} + \mathbf{f}_1, \mathbf{f}_2)) \leq 22\varepsilon$$

2.6   Non-interactive Key Exchange (NIKE)

For the purpose of this paper, we introduce the notion of an asymmetric NIKE. In contrast to a standard NIKE, this distinguishes between "left" and "right" users. A shared key can be computed only between a left and a right user. This is more convenient to work with in the LWE setting, where left and right keys are computed differently. An asymmetric NIKE implies a standard NIKE as introduced in [15] by generating for every user a left and a right key and deciding based on a canonical rule (e.g., based on the lexicographic order of their identities) which user takes the left role and which user takes the right role in the shared key computation. All security notions considered in this work carry over to their standard NIKE counterparts under this transformation.

Definition 5 (NIKE). *An asymmetric NIKE scheme with identity space $\mathcal{IDS}$ and shared key space $\mathcal{K}$ (with $|\mathcal{IDS}|, |\mathcal{K}| \geq 2$) consists of the following five PPT algorithms:*

- Setup *inputs the unary encoded security parameter 1^λ and samples public parameters* pp,
- KeyGenL *inputs the parameters* pp *and an identity* $\mathrm{id}_L \in \mathcal{IDS}$ *and samples a left key pair* $(\mathrm{pk}_L, \mathrm{sk}_L) \in \mathcal{LPK} \times \mathcal{LSK}$,
- KeyGenR *inputs the parameters* pp *and an identity* $\mathrm{id}_R \in \mathcal{IDS}$ *and samples a right key pair* $(\mathrm{pk}_R, \mathrm{sk}_R) \in \mathcal{RPK} \times \mathcal{RSK}$,
- SharedKeyL *inputs the parameters* pp, *an identity* id_R *with its corresponding right public key* pk_R *and another identity* id_L *with its corresponding left secret key* sk_L *and outputs a shared key K or the failure symbol $\perp$.*
- SharedKeyR *inputs the parameters* pp, *an identity* id_L *with its corresponding left public key* pk_L *and another identity* id_R *with its corresponding right secret key* sk_R *and outputs a shared key K or the failure symbol $\perp$.*

The standard definition of NIKE is obtained by requiring KeyGenL = KeyGenR and SharedKeyL = SharedKeyR.

Definition 6 (Correctness). *We say that a NIKE* NIKE = (Setup, KeyGenL, KeyGenR, SharedKeyL, SharedKeyR) *for identity space $\mathcal{IDS}$ has correctness error $\varepsilon_{\mathsf{corr}}$, if for all $\lambda \in \mathbb{N}_+$ and all $\mathrm{id}_L, \mathrm{id}_R \in \mathcal{IDS}$ with $\mathrm{id}_L \neq \mathrm{id}_R$ for*

- pp $\leftarrow$ Setup(1^λ),
- $(\mathrm{pk}_L, \mathrm{sk}_L) \leftarrow$ KeyGenL$(\mathrm{pp}, \mathrm{id}_L)$,
- $(\mathrm{pk}_R, \mathrm{sk}_R) \leftarrow$ KeyGenR$(\mathrm{pp}, \mathrm{id}_R)$,
- $K_L \leftarrow$ SharedKeyL$(\mathrm{pp}, \mathrm{id}_R, \mathrm{pk}_R, \mathrm{id}_L, \mathrm{sk}_L)$, *and*
- $K_R \leftarrow$ SharedKeyR$(\mathrm{pp}, \mathrm{id}_L, \mathrm{pk}_L, \mathrm{id}_R, \mathrm{sk}_R)$

$$\Pr[K_L = K_R \neq \perp] \geq 1 - \varepsilon_{\mathsf{corr}}(\lambda),$$

where the probability is taken over the randomness used to sample pp, $(\mathrm{pk}_L, \mathrm{sk}_L)$, $(\mathrm{pk}_R, \mathrm{sk}_R)$, K_L *and* K_R.

A NIKE is statistically correct *if $\varepsilon_{\mathsf{corr}}$ is negligible and* perfectly correct *iff $\varepsilon_{\mathsf{corr}} = 0$.*

In this work, we consider three variants of security for NIKE. The weakest notion is light security. Here, the adversary can register only two users $\mathrm{id}_L^\star, \mathrm{id}_R^\star$ and use them for the challenge. This security notion captures scenarios where each public key is used only to compute a single shared key.

The next stronger notion is adaptive HKR (honest key registration) security, which allows an adversary to adaptively register an arbitrary number of users, corrupt users, and reveal shared keys between two users. For simplicity we still allow only one challenge query, but the more realistic notion with multiple challenge queries is implied by the single-challenge notion via a standard hybrid argument. This notion captures multi-user scenarios where a public key can be used to generate shared keys with many other users. However, it assumes that all users generate their public and secret key honestly.

The more realistic and stronger notion is adaptive DKR (dishonest key registration), which additionally allows the adversary to reveal shared keys between honest users and public keys of his choice.

Definition 7 (Security). *An asymmetric NIKE* NIKE *is lightly, (N-user) adaptively HKR, or DKR secure if for all PPT adversaries $\mathcal{A}$*

$$\mathsf{Adv}_{\mathsf{NIKE},\mathcal{I}}^{\mathcal{A},\mathrm{xxx}}(\lambda) := 2|\Pr[\mathsf{Exp}_{\mathcal{A},\mathsf{NIKE}}^{\mathrm{xxx}}(\lambda) \Rightarrow 1] - 1/2|$$

is negligible for xxx = light, xxx = N-user-adaptive-HKR, xxx = adaptive-HKR *or* xxx = adaptive-DKR, *respectively. The games* $\mathsf{Exp}_{\mathcal{A},\mathsf{NIKE}}^{\mathrm{xxx}}$ *are defined in Fig. 2.*

Table 2. The following table indicates how often the adversary is allowed to query each of the oracles in the light, (N-user) adaptive HKR, and adaptive DKR security game. The symbol "∞" stands for arbitrary many allowed queries. In all games, a $\mathcal{O}_{\mathsf{testL}}$ or a $\mathcal{O}_{\mathsf{testR}}$ query is allowed.

	$\mathcal{O}_{\mathsf{regHL}}$	$\mathcal{O}_{\mathsf{regHR}}$	$\mathcal{O}_{\mathsf{extrL}}$	$\mathcal{O}_{\mathsf{extrR}}$	$\mathcal{O}_{\mathsf{regDL}}$	$\mathcal{O}_{\mathsf{regDR}}$	$\mathcal{O}_{\mathsf{revL}}$	$\mathcal{O}_{\mathsf{revL}}$	$\mathcal{O}_{\mathsf{testL}}$	$\mathcal{O}_{\mathsf{testR}}$
light	1	1	0	0	0	0	0	0	1	
N-user adpt. HKR	N	N	∞	∞	0	0	∞	∞	1	
adaptive HKR	∞	∞	∞	∞	0	0	∞	∞	1	
adaptive DKR	∞	∞	∞	∞	∞	∞	∞	∞	1	

2.7   Pseudorandom Function (PRF)

Definition 8. *A PRF for domain $\mathcal{D}$ and range $\mathcal{E}$ consists of two PPT algorithms*

- Gen(1^λ) *inputs the unary encoded security parameter and outputs a PRF key k and*
- PRF(k, x) *inputs a PRF key k and $x \in \mathcal{D}$ and outputs $y \in \mathcal{E}$.*

Definition 9. *A PRF is* pseudorandom *if for every PPT adversary $\mathcal{A}$*

$$\mathsf{Adv}_{\mathcal{A},\mathsf{PRF}}^{\mathsf{prf}}(\lambda) := |\Pr_{k \leftarrow \mathsf{Gen}(1^\lambda)}[\mathcal{A}^{\mathsf{PRF}(k,\cdot)}(1^\lambda) = 1] - \Pr_{\mathsf{RF} \xleftarrow{\$} \mathcal{E}^{\mathcal{D}}}[\mathcal{A}^{\mathsf{RF}(\cdot)}(1^\lambda) = 1]|.$$

Here, $\mathcal{E}^{\mathcal{D}}$ denotes the set of all functions from $\mathcal{D}$ to $\mathcal{E}$.

3   Security for Multiple Users

In this section, we present an LWE-based NIKE that achieves N-user adaptive HKR security for any polynomial number of users N. The price for a higher number of users is either an increase in the correctness error or an increase in the modulus (without increasing the absolute error size). Compared to the LWE-based NIKEs in previous works, the only difference in this construction is that we

$\mathrm{Exp}_{\mathcal{A},\mathrm{NIKE}}^{\mathrm{light}/(N\text{-user-})\mathrm{adaptive\text{-}HKR}/\mathrm{adaptive\text{-}DKR}}(\lambda)$:	$\mathcal{O}_{\mathrm{regDL}}(\mathrm{id}_L \in \mathcal{IDS}, \mathrm{pk}_L \in \mathcal{PK})$:

$\mathrm{Exp}_{\mathcal{A},\mathrm{NIKE}}^{\mathrm{light}/(N\text{-user-})\mathrm{adaptive\text{-}HKR}/\mathrm{adaptive\text{-}DKR}}(\lambda)$:

$\mathrm{pp} \leftarrow \mathsf{Setup}(1^\lambda)$
$Q_{\mathrm{extrL}} := \emptyset;\ Q_{\mathrm{extrR}} := \emptyset$
$Q_{\mathrm{rev}} := \emptyset;\ Q_{\mathrm{test}} := \emptyset$
$\mathsf{lpks} : \mathcal{IDS} \dashrightarrow \mathcal{LPK}$
$\mathsf{rpks} : \mathcal{IDS} \dashrightarrow \mathcal{RPK}$
$\mathsf{lsks} : \mathcal{IDS} \dashrightarrow \mathcal{LSK}$
$\mathsf{rsks} : \mathcal{IDS} \dashrightarrow \mathcal{RSK}$
$b \xleftarrow{\$} \{0,1\}$
$b^\star \leftarrow \mathcal{A}(\mathrm{pp})$
if $Q_{\mathrm{rev}} \cap Q_{\mathrm{test}} = \emptyset \wedge \nexists(\mathrm{id}_1, \mathrm{id}_2) \in Q_{\mathrm{test}}$:
$\mathrm{id}_1 \in Q_{\mathrm{extrL}} \vee \mathrm{id}_2 \in Q_{\mathrm{extrR}}$ **then**
$\quad$ **return** $b \overset{?}{=} b^\star$
else
$\quad$ **return** $b' \xleftarrow{\$} \{0,1\}$

$\underline{\mathcal{O}_{\mathrm{regHL}}(\mathrm{id}_L \in \mathcal{IDS})}$:

if $\mathsf{lpks}(\mathrm{id}_L) \neq \bot$ **then return** $\bot$
$(\mathrm{pk}_L, \mathrm{sk}_L) \leftarrow \mathsf{KeyGenL}(\mathrm{pp}, \mathrm{id}_L)$
$\mathsf{lpks}(\mathrm{id}_L) := \mathrm{pk}_L;\ \mathsf{lsks}(\mathrm{id}_L) := \mathrm{sk}_L$
return pk_L

$\underline{\mathcal{O}_{\mathrm{regHR}}(\mathrm{id}_R \in \mathcal{IDS})}$:

if $\mathsf{rpks}(\mathrm{id}_R) \neq \bot$ **then return** $\bot$
$(\mathrm{pk}_R, \mathrm{sk}_R) \leftarrow \mathsf{KeyGenR}(\mathrm{pp}, \mathrm{id}_R)$
$\mathsf{rpks}(\mathrm{id}_R) := \mathrm{pk}_R;\ \mathsf{rsks}(\mathrm{id}_R) := \mathrm{sk}_R$
return pk_R

$\underline{\mathcal{O}_{\mathrm{extrL}}(\mathrm{id}_L \in \mathcal{IDS})}$:

if $\mathsf{lsks}(\mathrm{id}_L) \neq \bot$ **then**
$\quad Q_{\mathrm{extrL}} := Q_{\mathrm{extrL}} \cup \{\mathrm{id}_L\}$
$\quad$ **return** $\mathsf{lsks}(\mathrm{id}_L)$
else return $\bot$

$\underline{\mathcal{O}_{\mathrm{extrR}}(\mathrm{id}_R \in \mathcal{IDS})}$:

if $\mathsf{rsks}(\mathrm{id}_R) \neq \bot$ **then**
$\quad Q_{\mathrm{extrR}} := Q_{\mathrm{extrR}} \cup \{\mathrm{id}_R\}$
$\quad$ **return** $\mathsf{rsks}(\mathrm{id}_R)$
else return $\bot$

$\underline{\mathcal{O}_{\mathrm{regDL}}(\mathrm{id}_L \in \mathcal{IDS}, \mathrm{pk}_L \in \mathcal{PK})}$:

if $\mathsf{lpks}(\mathrm{id}_L) \neq \bot$ **then return** $\bot$
$\mathsf{lpks}(\mathrm{id}_L) := \mathrm{pk}_L$
return OK

$\underline{\mathcal{O}_{\mathrm{regDR}}(\mathrm{id}_R \in \mathcal{IDS}, \mathrm{pk}_R \in \mathcal{PK})}$:

if $\mathsf{rpks}(\mathrm{id}_R) \neq \bot$ **then return** $\bot$
$\mathsf{rpks}(\mathrm{id}_R) := \mathrm{pk}_R$
return OK

$\underline{\mathcal{O}_{\mathrm{revL}}(\mathrm{id}_R \in \mathcal{IDS}, \mathrm{id}_L \in \mathcal{IDS})}$:

if $\mathsf{rpks}(\mathrm{id}_R) \neq \bot \wedge \mathsf{lsks}(\mathrm{id}_L) \neq \bot$ **then**
$\quad Q_{\mathrm{rev}} := Q_{\mathrm{rev}} \cup \{(\mathrm{id}_L, \mathrm{id}_R)\}$
$\quad \mathrm{pk}_R := \mathsf{rpks}(\mathrm{id}_R);\ \mathrm{sk}_L := \mathsf{lsks}(\mathrm{id}_L)$
$\quad$ **ret.** $\mathsf{SharedKeyL}(\mathrm{pp}, \mathrm{id}_R, \mathrm{pk}_R, \mathrm{id}_L, \mathrm{sk}_L)$
else return $\bot$

$\underline{\mathcal{O}_{\mathrm{revR}}(\mathrm{id}_L \in \mathcal{IDS}, \mathrm{id}_R \in \mathcal{IDS})}$:

if $\mathsf{lpks}(\mathrm{id}_L) \neq \bot \wedge \mathsf{rsks}(\mathrm{id}_R) \neq \bot$ **then**
$\quad Q_{\mathrm{rev}} := Q_{\mathrm{rev}} \cup \{(\mathrm{id}_L, \mathrm{id}_R)\}$
$\quad \mathrm{pk}_L := \mathsf{lpks}(\mathrm{id}_L);\ \mathrm{sk}_R := \mathsf{rsks}(\mathrm{id}_R)$
$\quad$ **ret.** $\mathsf{SharedKeyR}(\mathrm{pp}, \mathrm{id}_L, \mathrm{pk}_L, \mathrm{id}_R, \mathrm{sk}_R)$
else return $\bot$

$\underline{\mathcal{O}_{\mathrm{testL}}(\mathrm{id}_R^\star \in \mathcal{IDS}, \mathrm{id}_L^\star \in \mathcal{IDS})}$:

if $\mathsf{rsks}(\mathrm{id}_R^\star) \neq \bot \wedge \mathsf{lsks}(\mathrm{id}_L^\star) \neq \bot$ **then**
$\quad Q_{\mathrm{test}} := Q_{\mathrm{test}} \cup \{(\mathrm{id}_L^\star, \mathrm{id}_R^\star)\}$
$\quad \mathrm{pk}_R^\star := \mathsf{rpks}(\mathrm{id}_R^\star);\ \mathrm{sk}_L^\star := \mathsf{lsks}(\mathrm{id}_L^\star)$
$\quad K_0^\star \leftarrow \mathsf{SharedKeyL}(\mathrm{pp}, \mathrm{id}_R^\star, \mathrm{pk}_R^\star, \mathrm{id}_L^\star, \mathrm{sk}_L^\star)$
$\quad K_1^\star \xleftarrow{\$} \mathcal{K}$
$\quad$ **return** $K_b^\star$
else return $\bot$

$\underline{\mathcal{O}_{\mathrm{testR}}(\mathrm{id}_L^\star \in \mathcal{IDS}, \mathrm{id}_R^\star \in \mathcal{IDS})}$:

if $\mathsf{lsks}(\mathrm{id}_L^\star) \neq \bot \wedge \mathsf{rsks}(\mathrm{id}_R^\star) \neq \bot$ **then**
$\quad Q_{\mathrm{test}} := Q_{\mathrm{test}} \cup \{(\mathrm{id}_L^\star, \mathrm{id}_R^\star)\}$
$\quad \mathrm{pk}_L^\star := \mathsf{lpks}(\mathrm{id}_L^\star);\ \mathrm{sk}_R^\star := \mathsf{rsks}(\mathrm{id}_R^\star)$
$\quad K_0^\star \leftarrow \mathsf{SharedKeyR}(\mathrm{pp}, \mathrm{id}_L^\star, \mathrm{pk}_L^\star, \mathrm{id}_R^\star, \mathrm{sk}_R^\star)$
$\quad K_1^\star \xleftarrow{\$} \mathcal{K}$
$\quad$ **return** $K_b^\star$
else return $\bot$

Fig. 2. Experiment for light, N-user adaptive HKR, and adaptive DKR security of an asymmetric NIKE scheme $\mathsf{NIKE} = (\mathsf{Setup}, \mathsf{KeyGenL}, \mathsf{KeyGenR}, \mathsf{SharedKeyL}, \mathsf{SharedKeyR})$ with identity space $\mathcal{IDS}$. $\mathcal{LPK}$ and $\mathcal{RPK}$ denote the left and right public key spaces, and $\mathcal{LSK}$ and $\mathcal{RSK}$ denote the left and right secret key spaces, respectively. The adversary $\mathcal{A}$ has access to the oracles as indicated in Table 2. The partial maps lpks, rpks, lsks, and rsks are initially totally undefined.

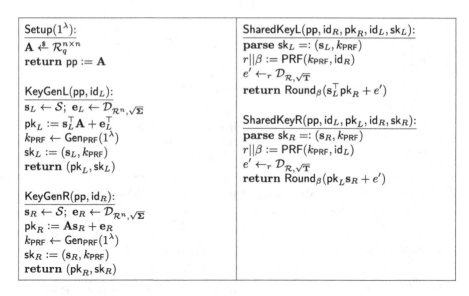

Fig. 3. The LWE based NIKE we consider in this section. It is identical to previous works except for the use of a PRF.

make the SharedKey algorithm deterministic by generating all the randomness used for the shared key generation with a PRF whose seed is stored in the user's secret key. This is necessary to avoid duplicated shared key queries for the same (ordered) pair of users. Alternatively, a user could keep a state of all already generated shared keys.

The NIKE scheme is shown in Fig. 3. It requires a PRF $\mathsf{PRF} = (\mathsf{Gen}_{\mathsf{PRF}}, \mathsf{PRF})$ with domain $\mathcal{D} = \mathcal{IDS}$ and range $\{0,1\}^{\alpha+\rho}$ where α is the number of random bits required for sampling from discrete Gaussian $\mathcal{D}_{\mathcal{R},\sqrt{\mathbf{T}}}$ and ρ determines the shared key space (see below). The LWE secret distribution $\mathcal{S}$ can be any short distribution on $\mathcal{R}^n$. Let $B_{\mathbf{s}} > 0$ be a bound on the size of $\mathcal{S}$, i.e., for all $\mathbf{s}$ in the range of $\mathcal{S}$ we have $\|\mathbf{s}\|_\infty < B_{\mathbf{s}}$. We also put the following mild requirement on the distribution $\mathcal{S}$: For all $k \in \mathbb{N}_+$ (growing polynomial in the security parameter), $\mathbf{s}, \mathbf{s}_1, \ldots, \mathbf{s}_k \leftarrow \mathcal{S}$, $\mathbf{A} \leftarrow \mathcal{R}_q^{n\times n}$, and $u_1, \ldots, u_k \leftarrow \mathcal{R}_q$ we have

$$\mathsf{SD}((\mathbf{s}^\top \mathbf{A}\mathbf{s}_1, \ldots, \mathbf{s}^\top \mathbf{A}\mathbf{s}_k), (u_1, \ldots, u_k)) \leq \varepsilon_{\mathsf{lohl}}(\lambda) \tag{2}$$

for a negligible function $\varepsilon_{\mathsf{lohl}}$. This is true for any distribution $\mathcal{S}$ with sufficient min-entropy if $\mathcal{R} = \mathbb{Z}$ by the left-over hash lemma [29] and for any cyclotomic ring $\mathcal{R}$ by a ring version of the left-over hash lemma [37], [8, Lemma 7].

In this NIKE, the shared key is obtained by rounding a ring element. When two users compute their shared key, they will get close (but rarely identical) unrounded shared keys. The purpose of the rounding procedure is to obtain a shared key that agrees with high probability, but in this work it will also play an important role in the security reduction. Let $d' \leq d$ be a parameter controlling the size of the shared key.[5] To define the rounding function (for $\beta \in \{0,1\}^\rho$), let q' be the unique integer with $q' \in [q - 2^\rho + 1, q]$ and $2^q \mid q'$. Then we define

$$\mathsf{Round}_\beta : \mathcal{R}_q \to (\{0,1\}^\rho)^{d'}$$
$$r \mapsto (\mathsf{round}_\beta(\mathbf{x}_1), \ldots, \mathsf{round}_\beta(\mathbf{x}_{d'})) \text{ where } \mathbf{x} = \psi(r)$$
$$\mathsf{round}_\beta : \{0, \ldots, q-1\} \to \{0,1\}^\rho$$
$$x \mapsto \begin{cases} x \operatorname{div} \frac{q'}{2^\rho} & \text{if } x < q' \\ \beta & \text{otherwise} \end{cases}$$

where the coefficients of $\mathcal{R}_q$ (under the fixed embedding ψ) are interpreted as integers in $\{0, \ldots, q\}$. This definition of the rounding function satisfies two properties that are important for the NIKE construction:

- For uniformly random input $r \in \mathcal{R}_q$ and uniformly random β, $\mathsf{Round}_\beta(r)$ is uniformly random in $(\{0,1\}^\rho)^d$.
- "Close" inputs lead as often as possible to the same output.

The latter property is analyzed more formally in the correctness theorem for this NIKE.

Theorem 1 (Correctness). *The NIKE scheme presented in Fig. 3 has correctness error*

$$\varepsilon_{\mathsf{corr}}(\lambda) \le \frac{2^\rho(4nB_\mathbf{s}\sqrt{nd\sigma_{\max}(\mathbf{\Sigma})/\pi} + 4\sqrt{(n+1)d\sigma_{\max}(\mathbf{T})/2\pi} + 1)}{q}$$
$$+ 2\sqrt{2}^{nd}e^{-nd/2} + 2\sqrt{n+1}^d e^{-nd/2} + \varepsilon_{\mathsf{lohl}}(\lambda) + \mathsf{Adv}^{\mathsf{prf}}_{\mathcal{A},\mathsf{PRF}}(\lambda).$$

Proof For this analysis we assume that the randomness used in the shared key generation algorithm is truly random and not generated with a PRF. This changes the correctness error at most by $\mathsf{Adv}^{\mathsf{prf}}_{\mathcal{A},\mathsf{PRF}}(\lambda)$.

Let $\mathbf{A} \xleftarrow{\$} \mathcal{R}_q^{n \times n}, \mathbf{s}_L, \mathbf{s}_R \leftarrow \mathcal{S}$; $\mathbf{e}_L, \mathbf{e}_R \leftarrow \mathcal{D}_{\mathcal{R}^n, \sqrt{\Sigma}}$, and $e'_L, e'_R \leftarrow \mathcal{D}_{\mathcal{R}, \sqrt{\mathbf{T}}}$. When a user with left public key $\mathbf{s}_L^\top \mathbf{A} + \mathbf{e}_L^\top$ and a user with right public key $\mathsf{pk}_R := \mathbf{A}\mathbf{s}_R + \mathbf{e}_R$ compute the shared key between them, the unrounded keys are

$$r_L := \mathbf{s}_L^\top(\mathbf{A}\mathbf{s}_R + \mathbf{e}_R) + e'_L \quad \text{and} \quad r_R := (\mathbf{s}_L^\top \mathbf{A} + \mathbf{e}_L^\top)\mathbf{s}_R + e'_R$$

and thus the ∞-norm of their difference is

$$\|r_L - r_R\|_\infty = \|\mathbf{s}_L^\top \mathbf{e}_R + e'_L - \mathbf{e}_L^\top \mathbf{s}_R - e'_R\|_\infty$$
$$\le n \cdot \|\mathbf{s}_L\|_\infty \cdot \|\mathbf{e}_R\|_\infty + \|e'_L\|_\infty + n \cdot \|\mathbf{e}_L\|_\infty \cdot \|\mathbf{s}_R\|_\infty + \|e'_R\|_\infty.$$
$$\le n \cdot \|\mathbf{s}_L\|_\infty \cdot \|\mathbf{e}_R\|_2 + \|e'_L\|_2 + n \cdot \|\mathbf{e}_L\|_2 \cdot \|\mathbf{s}_R\|_\infty + \|e'_R\|_2.$$
$$\overset{(*)}{\le} 2nB_\mathbf{s}\sqrt{2nd\sigma_{\max}(\mathbf{\Sigma})/2\pi} + 2\sqrt{(n+1)d\sigma_{\max}(\mathbf{T})/2\pi} =: B_K.$$

---

[5] With ring/module LWE it might be desirable to use a higher ring degree than the number of bits needed for the shared key.

where the inequality marked with $(*)$ holds with probability at least $2\sqrt{2}^{nd}e^{-nd/2} + 2\sqrt{n+1}^d e^{-nd/2}$ (which is negligible in nd) by applying Lemma 2 with $k = \sqrt{2}$ to bound $\|e_R\|_2$ and $\|e_L\|_2$ and applying the same lemma with $k = \sqrt{n+1}$ to bound $\|e'_L\|_2$ and $\|e'_R\|_2$.

The round$_\beta$ procedure splits the set $\{0, \ldots, q-1\}$ into 2^ρ intervals and rounds two values to the same bits if they lie inside the same interval. A correctness error can only occur if the unrounded shared key of the left user is within distance B_K from an interval boundary or greater than or equal to q' (in which case the rounding function returns the random value β). Since $s_L^\top \mathbf{A} s_R$ and thus also the unrounded shared key is $\varepsilon_{\mathsf{lohl}}(\lambda)$ close to uniformly random by Eq. (2), this can happen at most with probability $2^\rho(2B_K + 1)/q + \varepsilon_{\mathsf{lohl}}(\lambda)$.

Combining these results proves the theorem. $\qquad\square$

In the security analysis, we introduce another parameter k that controls the number of users N such that the NIKE is still N-user adaptive HKR secure. We can always have $N = k + 1$ many users, but by increasing the modulus (i.e., decreasing the correctness error), we can allow more users. Increasing the parameter k also increases the leakage about the LWE secret (and thus ultimately nd) as well as the noise and thus the correctness error. For the N-user adaptive HKR secure of the NIKE we have the following requirements on the parameters:

- $\varepsilon > 0$ is negligible.
- The matrices $\mathbf{\Sigma} \in \mathbb{R}^{nd \times nd}$, $\mathbf{T} \in \mathbb{R}^{d \times d}$, and $\overline{\mathbf{\Sigma}} \in \mathbb{R}^{nd \times nd}$ meet the requirements of Lemma 3 for every hint matrix $\mathbf{Z} \in \mathcal{R}_q^{k \times n}$ with $\|\mathbf{Z}\|_\infty \leq B_\mathbf{s}$. That is, there exist $s, t \in \mathbb{R}$ with
  - $s, t \geq 2\sqrt{2}$
  - $\sqrt{\Sigma_0} \geq \eta_\varepsilon(\mathcal{R}^n)$ and $\sqrt{\mathbf{T_0}} \geq \eta_\varepsilon(\mathcal{R}^k)$
  - $t^2\sigma_{\min}(\mathbf{T_0}) \geq \frac{(s^2+1)(s^2+2)}{s^2}\sigma_{\max}(\Sigma_0)B_\mathbf{s}^2 k$ (using Lemma 1)
- The $(\mathcal{R}, n, n+1, q, \mathcal{S}, \mathcal{D}_{\mathcal{R}_q^{n+1}, \sqrt{\widehat{\mathbf{\Sigma}}}}, \mathcal{L})$-LWE assumption holds for

$$\mathcal{L} = \left\{ f : \mathcal{R}_q^n \to \mathcal{R}_q^k \;\middle|\; \mathbf{Y} \in \mathcal{R}_q^{k \times n} \right\} \quad \text{and} \quad \widehat{\mathbf{\Sigma}} = \begin{pmatrix} \mathbf{\Sigma} & 0 \\ 0 & \mathbf{T} \end{pmatrix} \in \mathbb{R}^{(n+1)d \times (n+1)d}.$$
$$s \mapsto \mathbf{Y}s$$

- $k \geq N - 1$ or $k \in \Omega((\mu + 1) \cdot \mathsf{superlog}(\lambda))$ for a super-logarithmic function superlog and for

$$\mu := \frac{(N-1)2^\rho(4nB_\mathbf{s}\sqrt{\frac{nd\sigma_{\max}(\mathbf{\Sigma})}{\pi}} + 2\sqrt{\frac{(n+1)d\sigma_{\max}(\mathbf{T})}{2\pi}}) + 1)}{q} \leq N\varepsilon_{\mathsf{corr}}(\lambda)$$

Theorem 2 (Security). *The NIKE* NIKE *in Fig. 3 is N-user adaptive HKR secure if all the requirements mentioned for the above parameters are satisfied. More precisely, for every PPT adversary $\mathcal{A}$ against the N-user adaptive HKR security of* NIKE *there exist PPT adversaries $\mathcal{B}, \mathcal{C}$ (with approximately the same* *run time) such that*

$$\mathsf{Adv}_{\mathcal{A},\mathsf{NIKE}}^{N\text{-user-adaptive-HKR}}(\lambda) \leq 4N^2 \Bigg(\mathsf{Adv}_{\mathcal{R},n,n+1,q,\mathcal{S},\mathcal{D}_{\mathcal{R}_q^{n+1}},\sqrt{\Sigma},\mathcal{L}}^{\mathsf{lwe}}(\mathcal{B}) + \mathsf{Adv}_{\mathcal{C},\mathsf{PRF}}^{\mathsf{prf}}(\lambda) $$

$$+ 22\varepsilon + \begin{cases} 0 & \text{if } k \geq N-1 \\ (*) & \text{otherwise} \end{cases} \Bigg)$$

$$(*) = N(2\sqrt{2}^{nd}e^{-nd/2} + 2\sqrt{n+1}^d e^{-nd/2}) + \varepsilon_{\mathsf{lohl}}(\lambda) + \exp(-\frac{k^2/\mu - 2k + 1/\mu}{1 + k/\mu})$$

Proof. We prove security in a weaker model where the adversary has to specify the index of the $\mathcal{O}_{\mathsf{regHL}}$ and the $\mathcal{O}_{\mathsf{regHR}}$ before making any queries and otherwise proceeds as the N-user adaptive HKR security game. Security in this model implies N-user adaptive HKR security via a standard guessing argument with a security loss of N^2.

We also assume that the adversary makes a $\mathcal{O}_{\mathsf{testL}}$ query and not a $\mathcal{O}_{\mathsf{testR}}$ query. By switching "left" and "right" in the proof, we can get a proof that works for a $\mathcal{O}_{\mathsf{testR}}$ query, and by guessing which of the two cases occurs, we get a proof for the real N-user adaptive HKR security with loss 2.

The proof proceeds via a hybrid argument with the following games. The full version contains a pseudocode description of all games.

- G_0 is the real N-user adaptive HKR security game with the restrictions mentioned above.
- G_1 proceeds as G_0, but for both challenge users a truly random function (computed on the fly) is used instead of the PRF to generate the randomness in the SharedKeyL and SharedKeyR algorithm. We will use RF_L for the random function replacing the PRF with the left challenge user's secret key and RF_R for the random function replacing the PRF with the right challenge user's secret key. In the following, we will use $\overline{\mathsf{RF}}_L(\mathsf{id})$ and $\overline{\mathsf{RF}}_R(\mathsf{id})$ to denote the first part of the output of the random function that is used to generate the random coins for the discrete Gaussian sampling algorithm, and $\underline{\mathsf{RF}}_L(\mathsf{id})$ and $\underline{\mathsf{RF}}_R(\mathsf{id})$ for the second part that is used for the rounding function.
- G_2 changes conceptually how the unrounded shared keys in $\mathcal{O}_{\mathsf{revR}}$ queries with the right challenge user are computed: Let $\mathsf{pk}_R^\star := \mathbf{A}\mathsf{s}_R^\star + \mathbf{e}_R^\star$ be the right challenge user's public key. In an $\mathcal{O}_{\mathsf{revR}}$ query with the right challenge user and a left user id with public key $\mathsf{pk}_L = \mathsf{s}_L^\top\mathbf{A} + \mathbf{e}_L^\top$ and $e' \leftarrow_{\overline{\mathsf{RF}}_R(\mathsf{id})} \mathcal{D}_{\mathcal{R},\sqrt{\mathbf{T}}}$ the shared key is computed as $\mathsf{s}_L^\top\mathsf{pk}_R^\star - \mathsf{s}_L^\top\mathbf{e}_R^\star + \mathbf{e}_L^\top\mathsf{s}_R^\star + e'$. For conceptual simplicity, the reduction here stores the error vectors for each user.
- In G_3 the right challenge user's public key $\mathsf{pk}_R^\star$ is replaced by a uniformly random value. In that game there is still a secret key and an error vector sampled for the right challenge user to answer $\mathcal{O}_{\mathsf{revR}}$ as in G_2, but this secret key and error vector are independent of the public key.
- G_4 makes changes analogous to G_2 to the computation of the unrounded shared keys in $\mathcal{O}_{\mathsf{revL}}$ queries with the left challenge user. Let $\mathsf{pk}_L^\star := (\mathsf{s}_L^\star)^\top\mathbf{A} + (\mathbf{e}_L^\star)^\top$

be the left challenge user's public key. In a $\mathcal{O}_{\mathsf{revL}}$ query with the left challenge user and a right user id with public key $\mathsf{pk}_R = \mathbf{A}\mathsf{s}_R + \mathsf{e}_R$ and $e' \xleftarrow{\;\;\;\;} \mathcal{D}_{\mathcal{R},\sqrt{\mathbf{T}}}$ the shared key is computed as $\mathsf{pk}_L^\star \mathsf{s}_R - (\mathsf{e}_L^\star)^\top \mathsf{s}_R + (\mathsf{s}_L^\star)^\top \mathsf{e}_R + e'$.

- In G_5 the left challenge user's public key is uniformly random. Similarly to G_3, there is still an independent secret key and error vector generated to answer $\mathcal{O}_{\mathsf{revL}}$ queries as in G_4. Furthermore, in this hybrid, the $\mathcal{O}_{\mathsf{testL}}$ query will always be answered with a uniform random key.

Lemma 4 ($\mathsf{G}_0 \leadsto \mathsf{G}_1$). *For every PPT adversary $\mathcal{A}$ there exists a PPT adversary $\mathcal{C}$ with*

$$\left|\Pr[\mathsf{G}_0^{\mathcal{A}} \Rightarrow 1] - \Pr[\mathsf{G}_1^{\mathcal{A}} \Rightarrow 1]\right| \leq 2\mathsf{Adv}_{\mathcal{C},\mathsf{PRF}}^{\mathsf{prf}}(\lambda)$$

Proof. Since the left and right challenge user may not be corrupted, their PRF key is never exposed. Thus, an adversary who is able to distinguish G_0 and G_1 can be reduced straightforwardly to an adversary breaking at least one of the two instances of the PRF security game. □

Lemma 5 ($\mathsf{G}_1 \leadsto \mathsf{G}_2$)

$$\Pr[\mathsf{G}_1^{\mathcal{A}} \Rightarrow 1] = \Pr[\mathsf{G}_2^{\mathcal{A}} \Rightarrow 1]$$

Proof. The games G_1 and G_2 are identical. Let $\mathsf{pk}_R^\star := \mathbf{A}\mathsf{s}_R^\star + \mathsf{e}_R^\star$ be the right challenge user's public key. In a $\mathcal{O}_{\mathsf{revR}}$ query with a left user id with public key $\mathsf{pk}_L = \mathsf{s}_L^\top \mathbf{A} + \mathsf{e}_L^\top$ and $e' \xleftarrow{\;\;\;\;} \mathcal{D}_{\mathcal{R},\sqrt{\mathbf{T}}}$ the shared key is computed in G_2 as

$$\mathsf{s}_L^\top \mathsf{pk}_R^\star - \mathsf{s}_L^\top \mathsf{e}_R^\star + \mathsf{e}_L^\top \mathsf{s}_R^\star + e' = \mathsf{s}_L^\top (\mathbf{A}\mathsf{s}_R^\star + \mathsf{e}_R^\star) - \mathsf{s}_L^\top \mathsf{e}_R^\star + \mathsf{e}_L^\top \mathsf{s}_R^\star + e'$$
$$= \mathsf{s}_L^\top \mathbf{A}\mathsf{s}_R^\star + \mathsf{e}_L^\top \mathsf{s}_R^\star + e' = \mathsf{pk}_L \mathsf{s}_R^\star + e'$$

which matches how this shared key is computed in G_1. □

Lemma 6 ($\mathsf{G}_2 \leadsto \mathsf{G}_3$). *For every PPT adversary $\mathcal{A}$ there exists a PPT adversary $\mathcal{B}$ with*

$$\left|\Pr[\mathsf{G}_2^{\mathcal{A}} \Rightarrow 1] - \Pr[\mathsf{G}_3^{\mathcal{A}} \Rightarrow 1]\right| \leq \mathsf{Adv}_{\mathcal{R},n,n,q,\mathcal{S},\mathcal{D}_{\mathcal{R}^n,\sqrt{\mathbf{\Sigma}}},\mathcal{L}}^{\mathsf{lwe}}(\mathcal{B}) + 22\varepsilon$$

$$+ \begin{cases} 0 & \text{if } k \geq N-1 \\ (*) & \text{otherwise} \end{cases}$$

$$(*) = N(2\sqrt{2}^{nd}e^{-nd/2} + 2\sqrt{n+1}^{d}e^{-nd/2}) + \varepsilon_{\mathsf{lohl}}(\lambda) + \exp\left(-\frac{k^2/\mu - 2k + 1/\mu}{1 + k/\mu}\right)$$

Proof. We build a reduction for this game transition as follows: the reduction samples in the beginning $\mathsf{e}_{L,1}, \ldots, \mathsf{e}_{L,k} \leftarrow \mathcal{D}_{\mathcal{R}^n,\sqrt{\mathbf{\Sigma}}}$ and defines $f(\mathsf{s}) := (\mathsf{e}_{L,1} | \cdots | \mathsf{e}_{L,k})^\top \mathsf{s}$. It then sends f to the $(\mathcal{R}, n, n, q, \mathcal{S}, \mathcal{D}_{\mathcal{R}^n,\sqrt{\mathbf{\Sigma}}}, \mathcal{L})$-LWE challenger to get back $(\mathbf{A}, \mathbf{b}, \ell)$ where $\mathbf{b} = (\mathsf{s}_R^\star)^\top \mathbf{A} + (\mathsf{e}_R^\star)^\top$ for $\mathsf{s}_R^\star \leftarrow \mathcal{S}$ and $\mathsf{e}_R^\star \leftarrow \mathcal{D}_{\mathcal{R}^n,\sqrt{\mathbf{\Sigma}}}$ or $\mathbf{b} \xleftarrow{\$} \mathcal{R}_q^n$ and $\ell = f(\mathsf{s}_R^\star)$.

The reduction sends $\mathsf{pp} := \mathbf{A}^\top$ to the adversary. The reduction then pre-generates $N-1$ public/secret key pairs for the left non-challenge user as follows. Initially, it sets $i := 1$. Now it samples $N-1$ times $\mathbf{s}_L \leftarrow \mathcal{S}$.

Case A: If $\mathbf{b} \cdot \mathbf{s}_L$ is within distance

$$2nB_{\mathbf{s}}\sqrt{2nd\sigma_{\mathsf{max}}(\mathbf{\Sigma})/2\pi} + \sqrt{(n+1)d\sigma_{\mathsf{max}}(\mathbf{T})/2\pi} =: B_{\mathsf{dz}}$$

of an interval boundary of the rounding function or larger than or equal to q' (we will refer to this as the danger zone), the reduction sets $\mathbf{s}_{L,i} := \mathbf{s}_L$ and stores for this user as public key $\mathsf{pk}_{L,i} := \mathbf{s}_{L,i}^\top \mathbf{A} + \mathbf{e}_{L,i}^\top$ and $\mathbf{s}_{L,i}$ as secret key $i \leq k$. If $i > k$, the reduction aborts. Each time case A has occurred, the reduction increments finally i by 1.

Case B: If $\mathbf{b} \cdot \mathbf{s}_L$ is outside the danger zone, the reduction proceeds normally to generate the key, that is, it samples $\mathbf{e}_L \leftarrow \mathcal{D}_{\mathcal{R}^n, \sqrt{\Sigma}}$ and stores $\mathbf{s}_L^\top \mathbf{A} + \mathbf{e}_L^\top$ as public key and $\mathbf{s}_L$ as secret key.

For all left users with a case B public key, no correctness error with the right challenge user will occur (with overwhelming probability). For those users with a case A public key, a correctness error might occur, but the reduction can detect this knowing $\mathbf{s}_L^\top \mathbf{e}_R^\star$ and $\mathbf{e}_L^\top \mathbf{s}_R^\star$. The latter term is known to the reduction by the leakage. If $k \geq N-1$, the reduction can pick case A for all key pairs for simplicity. We next describe the steps the reduction takes to also learn the former term.

Let $\mathbf{Z} := (\mathbf{s}_{L,1} | \cdots | \mathbf{s}_{L,k})^\top$ (if less than k left user have a case A public key, set $\mathbf{s}_{L,i} = \mathbf{0}$ for the remaining indices $i \leq k$). Now let $\mathcal{F}$ be the distribution from Lemma 3 when using this lemma with $\sqrt{\Sigma}$ for the distribution of $\mathbf{e}_1$, $\sqrt{\mathbf{T}}$ for the distribution of $\mathbf{e}_2$ and $\sqrt{\Sigma}$ for the distribution of $\mathbf{e}$ and $\mathbf{Z}$ as the hint matrix. The reduction then samples $(\mathbf{f}_1, \mathbf{f}_2) \leftarrow \mathcal{F}$.

In the registration query for the right challenge user, the reduction returns $\mathbf{b}^\top + \mathbf{f}_1$ as public key. For each left user registration query, except for the left challenge user, the reduction returns one of the pre-generated left public keys. The registration queries for the right non-challenge user and the left challenge user, as well as all $\mathcal{O}_{\mathsf{extrL}}$ and $\mathcal{O}_{\mathsf{extrR}}$ queries are answered honestly.

When the reduction performs a $\mathcal{O}_{\mathsf{revR}}$ with the right challenge user and a left user with a case B public/secret key, the reduction returns $\mathsf{Round}_0(\mathbf{s}_L^\top \mathsf{pk}_R^\star)$. where $\mathbf{s}_L^\top$ is the left user's secret key. When the left user id_L is the i-th user with a case A public/secret key, the reduction returns $\mathsf{Round}_{\overline{\mathsf{RF}_R(\mathsf{id}_L)}}(\mathbf{s}_L^\top \mathsf{pk}_R^\star - (\mathbf{f}_2)_i + \ell_i)$. All other $\mathcal{O}_{\mathsf{revR}}$, all $\mathcal{O}_{\mathsf{revL}}$, and the $\mathcal{O}_{\mathsf{testL}}$ query do not need the right challenge user's secret key and are answered honestly by the reduction.

Analysis. Left users with a case A public/secret key pair have an unrounded shared key with the right challenge user outside of the danger zone, i.e., a correctness error can occur at most with the negligible probability $2\sqrt{2}^{nd}e^{-nd/2} + 2\sqrt{n+1}^d e^{-nd/2}$ and thus, with overwhelming probability, the shared key computed by the reduction is identical to the shared key as computed in G_2 or G_3. For left users with a case B public/secret key, observe that $(\mathbf{f}_2)_i = \mathbf{s}_L^\top(\mathbf{e}_R^\star + \mathbf{f}_1) - e'$ is distributed as $\mathcal{D}_{\mathcal{R}, \sqrt{\mathbf{T}}}$ with probability at least $1-22\varepsilon$ by Lemma 3 and $\ell_i = \mathbf{e}_L^\top \mathbf{s}_R^\star$. Thus, when the reduction does not abort, it simulates the game G_2 if it receives a real LWE challenge and G_3 if it receives a random LWE challenge.

If $k \geq N - 1$, the reduction never aborts. Otherwise, we use that the probability that a left user has an unrounded shared key in the danger zone with the right challenge user is at most $p := 2^\rho (2B_{\mathsf{dz}} + 1)q$ and this is independent for each left user except with probability $\varepsilon_{\mathsf{lohl}}(\lambda)$ by Eq. (2). Let X be the random variable denoting the number of case A left users. Then the expected value of X is $\mu := (N - 1)/p$. With the Chernoff bound for Bernoulli distributions, we get the following bound on the probability that X exceeds k:

$$\Pr[X \geq k] \leq \exp\left(-\frac{(k/\mu - 1)^2 \mu}{1 + k/\mu}\right) = \exp\left(-\frac{k^2/\mu - 2k + 1/\mu}{1 + k/\mu}\right) \tag{3}$$

which is negligible if $k \in \Omega((\mu + 1) \cdot \mathsf{superlog}(\lambda))$ for a super-logarithmic function superlog. $\qquad \square$

Lemma 7 ($G_3 \rightsquigarrow G_4$)

$$\Pr[G_3^{\mathcal{A}} \Rightarrow 1] = \Pr[G_4^{\mathcal{A}} \Rightarrow 1]$$

The proof is analogous to Lemma 5, just with the roles of left and right swapped.

Lemma 8 ($G_4 \rightsquigarrow G_5$). *For every PPT adversary $\mathcal{A}$ there exists a PPT adversary $\mathcal{B}$ with*

$$\left|\Pr[G_4^{\mathcal{A}} \Rightarrow 1] - \Pr[G_5^{\mathcal{A}} \Rightarrow 1]\right| \leq \mathsf{Adv}^{\mathsf{lwe}}_{\mathcal{R}, n, n+1, q, \mathcal{S}, \mathcal{D}_{\mathcal{R}_q^{n+1}, \sqrt{\Sigma}}, \mathcal{L}}(\mathcal{A}) + 22\varepsilon$$

$$+ \begin{cases} 0 & \text{if } k \geq N - 1 \\ (*) & \text{otherwise} \end{cases}$$

$$(*) = N(2\sqrt{2}^{nd} e^{-nd/2} + 2\sqrt{n+1}^d e^{-nd/2}) + \varepsilon_{\mathsf{lohl}}(\lambda) + \exp\left(-\frac{k^2/\mu - 2k + 1/\mu}{1 + k/\mu}\right)$$

The reduction for this transition is in large parts similar to the proof for Lemma 6. Here, we describe only the differences in detail.

Proof. The reduction sends a function f distributed as in Lemma 6 to the $(\mathcal{R}, n, n+1, q, \mathcal{S}, \mathcal{D}_{\mathcal{R}^n, \sqrt{\Sigma}}, \mathcal{L})$-LWE challenger to get back $(\mathbf{A}, \mathbf{b}, \ell)$ where $\mathbf{b} = (\mathbf{s}_L^\star)^\top \mathbf{A} + (\mathbf{e}_L^\star)^\top$ for $\mathbf{s}_L^\star \leftarrow \mathcal{S}$ and $\mathbf{e}_L^\star \leftarrow \mathcal{D}_{\mathcal{R}^n, \sqrt{\Sigma}}$ or $\mathbf{b} \xleftarrow{\$} \mathcal{R}_q^n$ and $\ell = f(\mathbf{s}_L^\star)$. Let $\overline{\mathbf{A}} \in \mathcal{R}_q^{n \times n}$ be the top $n \times n$ matrix of $\mathbf{A}$ and let $\underline{\mathbf{A}} \in \mathcal{R}_q^{1 \times n}$ be the bottom row of $\mathbf{A}$. Similarly, let $\overline{\mathbf{b}} \in \mathcal{R}_q^n$ be the top n entries of $\mathbf{b}$ and $\underline{\mathbf{b}} \in \mathcal{R}_q$ the last entry of $\mathbf{b}$.

The reduction sends $\mathsf{pp} := \overline{\mathbf{A}}$ to the adversary. The reduction then pre-generates $N - 1$ public/secret key pairs for the right non-challenge user as in Lemma 6, except for using $\overline{\mathbf{b}}$ instead of $\mathbf{b}$ and thereby generates the matrix $\mathbf{Z} \in \mathcal{R}_q^{n \times n}$ whose row vectors are the LWE secrets of right (non-challenge) users whose unrounded shared key with the left challenge user lies in the danger zone. It uses this matrix to obtain the distribution $\mathcal{F}$ from Lemma 3. The reduction then samples $(\mathbf{f}_1, \mathbf{f}_2) \leftarrow \mathcal{F}$.

The reduction uses $\underline{\mathbf{A}}^\top$ as the public key for the right challenge user $\mathrm{id}_R^\star$ and $\overline{\mathbf{b}} + \mathbf{f}_1$ as the public key for the left challenge user. The public keys for left non-challenge users are generated honestly and the right non-challenge users the pre-generated keys are used. All $\mathcal{O}_{\mathsf{extrL}}$ and $\mathcal{O}_{\mathsf{extrR}}$ queries are answered honestly. All $\mathcal{O}_{\mathsf{revR}}$ queries and those $\mathcal{O}_{\mathsf{revL}}$ queries that do not involve the left challenge user are answered as in G_4. The $\mathcal{O}_{\mathsf{revL}}$ with the left challenge user are answered using the right user's secret key and potentially using the leakage ℓ about the left challenge user's secret and the hints $\mathbf{f}_2$ about the left challenge user's error to correct for the other secret key being used, analogously to Lemma 6.

For the challenge shared key, the reduction returns $\mathsf{Round}_\beta(\underline{\mathbf{b}})$ where $\beta = \underline{\mathsf{RF}}_L(\mathrm{id}_R^\star)$.

The reduction analysis is identical to the one for Lemma 6, except for the challenge query. For that, observe that if the reduction received a real LWE challenge, then $\underline{\mathbf{b}} = (\mathbf{s}_L^\star)^\top \underline{\mathbf{A}}^\top + (\underline{\mathbf{e}}_L^\star)^\top$ where $(\underline{\mathbf{e}}_L^\star)^\top$ is the last entry of $\mathbf{e}_L^\star$ which is distributed as $\mathcal{D}_{\mathcal{R}, \sqrt{\mathbf{T}}}$. The reduction simulates G_4 in this case. If the reduction received a random LWE challenge, then $\underline{\mathbf{b}}$ is uniformly random and, since β is uniformly random, too, the output of $\mathsf{Round}_\beta(\underline{\mathbf{b}})$ is uniformly random. Thus, the reduction simulates G_5 in this case. $\qquad\square$

Lemma 9 (Adv. in G_5)

$$\Pr[\mathsf{G}_5^{\mathcal{A}} \Rightarrow 1] = 1/2$$

Proof. In G_5, the adversary's view is independent of the challenge bit, and therefore every adversary will win the game with probability exactly $1/2$. $\qquad\square$

Proof. Combining Lemmata 4–9 completes the proof of Theorem 2. $\qquad\square$

3.1   Reconciliation

In [20, 40] a protocol is shown that can correct potential errors in the shared key resulting from the LWE-based NIKE interactively by sending 1 bit. We show that this approach also works on already rounded keys, which becomes necessary in our work, since rounding is essential for the security proof. This "uses up" the two least significant bits of the shared key, so for a one bit shared key we now need to round it to three bits.

We require for the reconciliation mechanism that $2^\rho \mid q$ (to avoid the case where the shared key is just (pseudo)random) and $\rho \geq 3$. Let K_{12} and K_{21} be the rounded shared keys of a pair of users id_1 and id_2, where K_{12} was computed with the secret key of id_1 and K_{21} was computed with the secret key of id_2. The idea is that K_{12} and K_{21}, interpreted as numbers in $\mathbb{Z}_{2^\rho}$, can differ at most by 1 for suitable noise sizes. Either of the users can now send the second least significant bit of his shared key as a signal to the other user. If this matches the second least significant bit of his shared key, the first $\rho - 2$ bits of their shared key are identical as well. Otherwise, the signal-receiving user looks at the least significant bit. If this is 1, he obtains the same shared key as the other user by adding 1 to his shared key. On the other hand, if this bit is 0, he has to subtract 1 from his shared key. In all cases, the user can then use the $\rho - 2$ most significant bits as the shared key.

Acknowledgments. I would like to thank my supervisor Dennis Hofheinz for feedback on my ideas and an early draft of this paper. I also want to thank the reviewers of TCC 2023 for their suggestions.

References

1. Agrawal, S., Libert, B., Stehlé, D.: Fully secure functional encryption for inner products, from standard assumptions. In: Robshaw, M., Katz, J. (eds.) CRYPTO 2016, Part III. LNCS, vol. 9816, pp. 333–362. Springer, Cham (2016). https://doi.org/10.1007/978-3-662-53015-3_12

2. Albrecht, M.R., Lai, R.W.F.: Subtractive sets over cyclotomic rings - limits of Schnorr-like arguments over lattices. In: Malkin, T., Peikert, C. (eds.) CRYPTO 2021, Part II. LNCS, vol. 12826, pp. 519–548. Springer, Cham (2021). https://doi.org/10.1007/978-3-030-84245-1_18

3. Applebaum, B., Cash, D., Peikert, C., Sahai, A.: Fast cryptographic primitives and circular-secure encryption based on hard learning problems. In: Halevi, S. (ed.) CRYPTO 2009. LNCS, vol. 5677, pp. 595–618. Springer, Heidelberg (2009). https://doi.org/10.1007/978-3-642-03356-8_35

4. Bader, C., Jager, T., Li, Y., Schäge, S.: On the impossibility of tight cryptographic reductions. In: Fischlin, M., Coron, J.S. (eds.) EUROCRYPT 2016, Part II. LNCS, vol. 9666, pp. 273–304. Springer, Cham (2016). https://doi.org/10.1007/978-3-662-49896-5_10

5. Banaszczyk, W.: New bounds in some transference theorems in the geometry of numbers. Mathematische Annalen **296**(4), 625–636 (1993)

6. Bootle, J., Delaplace, C., Espitau, T., Fouque, P.-A., Tibouchi, M.: LWE without modular reduction and improved side-channel attacks against BLISS. In: Peyrin, T., Galbraith, S. (eds.) ASIACRYPT 2018, Part I. LNCS, vol. 11272, pp. 494–524. Springer, Cham (2018). https://doi.org/10.1007/978-3-030-03326-2_17

7. Boudgoust, K., Jeudy, C., Roux-Langlois, A., Wen, W.: Entropic hardness of Module-LWE from Module-NTRU. In: Isobe, T., Sarkar, S. (eds.) INDOCRYPT 2022. LNCS, vol. 13774, pp. 78–99. Springer, Cham (2022). https://doi.org/10.1007/978-3-031-22912-1_4

8. Boudgoust, K., Jeudy, C., Roux-Langlois, A., Wen, W.: Towards classical hardness of Module-LWE: the linear rank case. In: Moriai, S., Wang, H. (eds.) ASIACRYPT 2020, Part II. LNCS, vol. 12492, pp. 289–317. Springer, Cham (2020). https://doi.org/10.1007/978-3-030-64834-3_10

9. Boyd, C., Mao, W., Paterson, K.G.: Key agreement using statically keyed authenticators. In: Jakobsson, M., Yung, M., Zhou, J. (eds.) ACNS 2004. LNCS, vol. 3089, pp. 248–262. Springer, Heidelberg (2004). https://doi.org/10.1007/978-3-540-24852-1_18

10. Brakerski, Z., Döttling, N.: Hardness of LWE on general entropic distributions. In: Canteaut, A., Ishai, Y. (eds.) EUROCRYPT 2020, Part II. LNCS, vol. 12106, pp. 551–575. Springer, Cham (2020). https://doi.org/10.1007/978-3-030-45724-2_19

11. Brakerski, Z., Döttling, N.: Lossiness and entropic hardness for Ring-LWE. In: Pass, R., Pietrzak, K. (eds.) TCC 2020, Part I. LNCS, vol. 12550, pp. 1–27. Springer, Cham (2020). https://doi.org/10.1007/978-3-030-64375-1_1

12. Brakerski, Z., Gentry, C., Vaikuntanathan, V.: (Leveled) fully homomorphic encryption without bootstrapping. In: ITCS 2012, pp. 309–325 (2012). https://doi.org/10.1145/2090236.2090262

13. Brakerski, Z., Langlois, A., Peikert, C., Regev, O., Stehlé, D.: Classical hardness of learning with errors. In: 45th ACM STOC, pp. 575–584 (2013). https://doi.org/10.1145/2488608.2488680
14. Capar, C., Goeckel, D., Paterson, K.G., Quaglia, E.A., Towsley, D., Zafer, M.: Signal-flow-based analysis of wireless security protocols. Inf. Comput. **226**, 37–56 (2013). https://doi.org/10.1016/j.ic.2013.03.004
15. Cash, D., Kiltz, E., Shoup, V.: The Twin Diffie-Hellman problem and applications. In: Smart, N. (ed.) EUROCRYPT 2008. LNCS, vol. 4965, pp. 127–145. Springer, Heidelberg (2008). https://doi.org/10.1007/978-3-540-78967-3_8
16. Castryck, W., Decru, T.: An efficient key recovery attack on SIDH. In: Hazay, C., Stam, M. (eds.) EUROCRYPT 2023, Part V, vol. 14008, pp. 423–447. Springer, Cham (2023). https://doi.org/10.1007/978-3-031-30589-4_15
17. Castryck, W., Lange, T., Martindale, C., Panny, L., Renes, J.: CSIDH: an efficient post-quantum commutative group action. In: Peyrin, T., Galbraith, S. (eds.) ASIACRYPT 2018. LNCS, vol. 11274, pp. 395–427. Springer, Cham (2018). https://doi.org/10.1007/978-3-030-03332-3_15
18. Dachman-Soled, D., Ducas, L., Gong, H., Rossi, M.: LWE with side information: attacks and concrete security estimation. In: Micciancio, D., Ristenpart, T. (eds.) CRYPTO 2020, Part II. LNCS, vol. 12171, pp. 329–358. Springer, Cham (2020). https://doi.org/10.1007/978-3-030-56880-1_12
19. Diffie, W., Hellman, M.E.: New directions in cryptography. IEEE Trans. Inf. Theory **22**(6), 644–654 (1976). https://doi.org/10.1109/TIT.1976.1055638
20. Ding, J., Xie, X., Lin, X.: A simple provably secure key exchange scheme based on the learning with errors problem. Cryptology ePrint Archive, Report 2012/688 (2012)
21. Dodis, Y., Katz, J., Smith, A., Walfish, S.: Composability and on-line deniability of authentication. In: Reingold, O. (ed.) TCC 2009. LNCS, vol. 5444, pp. 146–162. Springer, Heidelberg (2009). https://doi.org/10.1007/978-3-642-00457-5_10
22. Döttling, N., Kolonelos, D., Lai, R.W.F., Lin, C., Malavolta, G., Rahimi, A.: Efficient Laconic cryptography from learning with errors. In: Hazay, C., Stam, M. (eds.) EUROCRYPT 2023, Part III. LNCS, vol. 14006, pp. 417–446. Springer, Cham (2023). https://doi.org/10.1007/978-3-031-30620-4_14
23. Freire, E.S.V., Hofheinz, D., Kiltz, E., Paterson, K.G.: Non-interactive key exchange. In: Kurosawa, K., Hanaoka, G. (eds.) PKC 2013. LNCS, vol. 7778, pp. 254–271. Springer, Heidelberg (2013). https://doi.org/10.1007/978-3-642-36362-7_17
24. Gajland, P., de Kock, B., Quaresma, M., Malavolta, G., Schwabe, P.: Swoosh: practical lattice-based non-interactive key exchange. Cryptology ePrint Archive, Report 2023/271 (2023)
25. Goldwasser, S., Kalai, Y.T., Peikert, C., Vaikuntanathan, V.: Robustness of the learning with errors assumption. In: Innovations in Computer Science - ICS 2010, Tsinghua University, Beijing, China, 5–7 January 2010, Proceedings, pp. 230–240 (2010)
26. Guo, S., Kamath, P., Rosen, A., Sotiraki, K.: Limits on the efficiency of (Ring) LWE based non-interactive key exchange. In: Kiayias, A., Kohlweiss, M., Wallden, P., Zikas, V. (eds.) PKC 2020, Part I. LNCS, vol. 12110, pp. 374–395. Springer, Cham (2020). https://doi.org/10.1007/978-3-030-45374-9_13
27. Hesse, J., Hofheinz, D., Kohl, L.: On tightly secure non-interactive key exchange. In: Shacham, H., Boldyreva, A. (eds.) CRYPTO 2018, Part II. LNCS, vol. 10992, pp. 65–94. Springer, Cham (2018). https://doi.org/10.1007/978-3-319-96881-0_3

28. Hesse, J., Hofheinz, D., Kohl, L., Langrehr, R.: Towards tight adaptive security of non-interactive key exchange. In: Nissim, K., Waters, B. (eds.) TCC 2021, Part III. LNCS, vol. 13044, pp. 286–316. Springer, Cham (2021). https://doi.org/10.1007/978-3-030-90456-2_10
29. Impagliazzo, R., Levin, L.A., Luby, M.: Pseudo-random generation from one-way functions (Extended Abstracts). In: 21st ACM STOC, pp. 12–24 (1989). https://doi.org/10.1145/73007.73009
30. Jao, D., De Feo, L.: Towards quantum-resistant cryptosystems from supersingular elliptic curve isogenies. In: Yang, B.-Y. (ed.) PQCrypto 2011. LNCS, vol. 7071, pp. 19–34. Springer, Heidelberg (2011). https://doi.org/10.1007/978-3-642-25405-5_2
31. Langlois, A., Stehlé, D.: Worst-case to average-case reductions for module lattices. Des. Codes Cryptogr. **75**(3), 565–599 (2015). https://doi.org/10.1007/s10623-014-9938-4
32. Lin, H., Wang, M., Zhuang, J., Wang, Y.: Hardness of Module-LWE and Ring-LWE on general entropic distributions. Cryptology ePrint Archive, Report 2020/1238 (2020)
33. Lyubashevsky, V.: Lattice signatures without trapdoors. In: Pointcheval, D., Johansson, T. (eds.) EUROCRYPT 2012. LNCS, vol. 7237, pp. 738–755. Springer, Heidelberg (2012). https://doi.org/10.1007/978-3-642-29011-4_43
34. Lyubashevsky, V., Peikert, C., Regev, O.: A toolkit for Ring-LWE cryptography. In: Johansson, T., Nguyen, P.Q. (eds.) EUROCRYPT 2013. LNCS, vol. 7881, pp. 35–54. Springer, Heidelberg (2013). https://doi.org/10.1007/978-3-642-38348-9_3
35. Lyubashevsky, V., Peikert, C., Regev, O.: On ideal lattices and learning with errors over rings. In: Gilbert, H. (ed.) EUROCRYPT 2010. LNCS, vol. 6110, pp. 1–23. Springer, Heidelberg (2010). https://doi.org/10.1007/978-3-642-13190-5_1
36. Maino, L., Martindale, C., Panny, L., Pope, G., Wesolowski, B.: A direct key recovery attack on SIDH. In: Hazay, C., Stam, M. (eds.) EUROCRYPT 2023, Part V, vol. 14008, pp. 448–471. Springer, Cham (2023). https://doi.org/10.1007/978-3-031-30589-4_16
37. Micciancio, D.: Generalized compact knapsacks, cyclic lattices, and efficient one-way functions. Comput. Complex. **16**(4), 365–411 (2007). https://doi.org/10.1007/s00037-007-0234-9
38. Micciancio, D.: On the hardness of learning with errors with binary secrets. Theory Comput. **14**(1), 1–17 (2018)
39. Micciancio, D., Regev, O.: Worst-case to average-case reductions based on Gaussian measures. In: 45th FOCS 2004, pp. 372–381 (2004). https://doi.org/10.1109/FOCS.2004.72
40. Peikert, C.: Lattice cryptography for the internet. In: Mosca, M. (ed.) PQCrypto 2014. LNCS, vol. 8772, pp. 197–219. Springer, Cham (2014). https://doi.org/10.1007/978-3-319-11659-4_12
41. Peikert, C.: Public-key cryptosystems from the worst-case shortest vector problem: extended abstract. In: 41st ACM STOC 2009, pp. 333–342 (2009). https://doi.org/10.1145/1536414.1536461
42. Peikert, C., Regev, O., Stephens-Davidowitz, N.: Pseudorandomness of Ring-LWE for any ring and modulus. In: 49th ACM STOC 2017, pp. 461–473 (2017). https://doi.org/10.1145/3055399.3055489
43. Regev, O.: On lattices, learning with errors, random linear codes, and cryptography. In: 37th ACM STOC 2005, pp. 84–93 (2005). https://doi.org/10.1145/1060590.1060603
44. Robert, D.: Breaking SIDH in polynomial time. In: Hazay, C., Stam, M. (eds.) EUROCRYPT 2023, Part V. LNCS, vol. 14008, pp. 472–503. Springer, Cham (2023). https://doi.org/10.1007/978-3-031-30589-4_17

Ideal-SVP is Hard for Small-Norm Uniform Prime Ideals

Joël Felderhoff[1]([✉]), Alice Pellet-Mary[2], Damien Stehlé[3],
and Benjamin Wesolowski[4]

[1] Inria Lyon, Lyon, France, ENS de Lyon and LIP, UMR 5668, Lyon, France
joel.felderhoff@ens-lyon.fr
[2] Univ. Bordeaux, CNRS, Inria, Bordeaux INP, IMB, Talence, France
alice.pellet-mary@math.u-bordeaux.fr
[3] ENS de Lyon and CryptoLab, Inc., Lyon, France
damien.stehle@cryptolab.co.kr
[4] ENS de Lyon, CNRS, UMPA, UMR 5669, Lyon, France
benjamin.wesolowski@ens-lyon.fr

Abstract. The presumed hardness of the Shortest Vector Problem for ideal lattices (Ideal-SVP) has been a fruitful assumption to understand other assumptions on algebraic lattices and as a security foundation of cryptosystems. Gentry [CRYPTO'10] proved that Ideal-SVP enjoys a worst-case to average-case reduction, where the average-case distribution is the uniform distribution over the set of *inverses of prime ideals* of small algebraic norm (below $d^{O(d)}$ for cyclotomic fields, where d refers to the field degree). De Boer et al. [CRYPTO'20] obtained another random self-reducibility result for an average-case distribution involving *integral ideals* of norm $2^{O(d^2)}$.

In this work, we show that Ideal-SVP for the uniform distribution over inverses of small-norm prime ideals reduces to Ideal-SVP for the uniform distribution over small-norm prime ideals. Combined with Gentry's reduction, this leads to a worst-case to average-case reduction for the uniform distribution over the set of *small-norm prime ideals*. Using the reduction from Pellet-Mary and Stehlé [ASIACRYPT'21], this notably leads to the first distribution over NTRU instances with a polynomial modulus whose hardness is supported by a worst-case lattice problem.

1 Introduction

Lattice-based cryptography is built upon on the hardness of a variety of computational problems related to the shortest vector problem (SVP), consisting in finding a shortest non-zero vector in a Euclidean lattice, possibly up to some approximation factor. As generic lattices typically lead to poor performance, cryptographic schemes often use so-called algebraic variants. The case of *ideal lattices* has attracted particular attention since the introduction of Ring-SIS [Mic02,LM06,PR06] and Ring-LWE [SSTX09,LPR10,PRS17]. These problems have both enabled the construction of very efficient cryptosystems, and are known to be at least as hard as finding short non-zero vectors in ideal lattices.

© International Association for Cryptologic Research 2023
G. Rothblum and H. Wee (Eds.): TCC 2023, LNCS 14372, pp. 63–92, 2023.
https://doi.org/10.1007/978-3-031-48624-1_3

Let $K = \mathbb{Q}[X]/P(X)$ be a number field of degree d (i.e., $P(X) \in \mathbb{Z}[X]$ is an irreducible polynomial of degree d) and let $\mathcal{O}_K$ be its ring of integers. As K is naturally a Hermitian vector space (via the canonical embedding $\sigma : K \to \mathbb{C}^d$), any ideal in $\mathcal{O}_K$ is a Euclidean lattice. Such ideals, with the associated lattice structure, are *ideal lattices*. In this work, we focus on the id-HSVP problem (ideal Hermite Shortest Vector Problem), an approximate version of SVP for ideal lattices consisting in finding a non-zero-vector in the ideal lattice whose norm is within a given factor of the root determinant. Note that id-HSVP and SVP for ideal lattices are equivalent up to some small parameter losses.

In cryptographic applications, it is typically insufficient for a computational problem to be hard in the worst case: one needs instances to be hard *on average* for some distribution with non-trivial entropy. Such a guarantee can be provided by proving worst-case to average-case reductions: if there is an algorithm which performs well on random instances of problem A with non-negligible probability (i.e., for the average case), then there is an algorithm which performs well for any instance of problem B (i.e., for the worst case). When the two problems are the same (up to the approximation factor), we may refer to this property as random self-reducibility. Note that self-reducibility is associated not only to a problem, but also to a distribution on the instances, and the choice of distribution may be of critical importance.

The first random self-reducibility result for id-HSVP was proven by Gentry [Gen09a, Gen10], for supporting the security of the first fully homomorphic encryption scheme [Gen09a, Gen09b]. Gentry proved that id-HSVP in the worst case reduces to id-HSVP for *the inverse of a uniformly chosen prime ideal among those with algebraic norm in a prescribed interval* $[A, B]$. Note that Gentry states this result in terms of the Bounded Distance Decoding problem for the prime ideals themselves (not their inverses) – the two formulations are equivalent thanks to Regev's quantum reduction from SIVP in a lattice L to BDD in the dual lattice $L^\vee$ [Reg05]. Gentry's reduction enables interval boundaries A and B that have a bounded ratio and can be chosen as small as $\Delta_K^{O(1)} \cdot d^{O(d)}$, where Δ_K and d respectively refer to the field discriminant and degree.[1] A weaker result is proved in [Gen10], but it can be boosted as detailed in [Gen09a]. This reduction requires an ideal-factoring oracle (which can be implemented in quantum polynomial time using Shor's algorithm [Sho94]) but is otherwise polynomial-time, and introduces a loss in the approximation factor that is bounded as $\Delta_K^{O(1/d)} \cdot d^{O(1)}$.

A different average-case distribution is considered in [BDPW20]. The space of all ideal lattices, up to isometries, is itself an arithmetic-geometric object, the Arakelov class group, and comes with a natural notion of "uniform distribution". Mathematically, this distribution is convenient because of the rich theory surrounding it. Computationally, one cannot work directly with it: first because it is continuous, and second because we do not have a canonical way of representing the isometry class of a lattice. Thanks to an appropriate rounding procedure, de Boer et al. [BDPW20] introduced a distribution on ideals of

---

[1] For the sake of simplicity, we assume for the introduction that we are given a basis of the ring of integers $\mathcal{O}_K$ whose vectors have norms $\leq \Delta_K^{O(1/d)} \cdot d^{O(1)}$.

norm $\Delta_K^{O(1)} \cdot 2^{O(d^2)}$ that mimics this continuous distribution and proved the self-reducibility of id-HSVP for this distribution.[2] This reduction is polynomial and also incurs an approximation factor loss of $\Delta_K^{O(1/d)} \cdot d^{O(1)}$. Note that the ideals of this distribution have much larger norms than those of Gentry's reduction. This unfortunately leads to cryptographic instances of larger sizes. In [PS21], the authors observed that the algebraic norm reached by the reduction from de Boer et al. can be decreased, but at the expense of a super-polynomial running-time.

The above discussion raises the following question:

Can we reduce id-HSVP in the worst-case to id-HSVP for uniform prime ideals of norms bounded as $\Delta_K^{O(1)} \cdot d^{O(d)}$, in time polynomial in $\Delta_K^{1/d}$ and d?

Contributions. We describe a new quantum self-reduction for id-HSVP. We prove that if $\mathcal{W}$ is a set of ideals and $\mathcal{W}^{-1}$ is the set of inverses of the ideals of $\mathcal{W}$, then solving id-HSVP for the uniform distribution over $\mathcal{W}^{-1}$ reduces to solving id-HSVP for the uniform distribution over $\mathcal{W}$ and to solving id-HSVP for a uniform ideal within those having their norms in a prescribed interval. Both the cost of the reduction and the loss in the approximation factor are polynomially bounded in the degree d and the root-discriminant $\Delta_K^{1/d}$ of the number field. The precise statement is provided in Theorem 5.1.

When specialized with $\mathcal{W}$ chosen as the set of prime ideals of algebraic norm $\Delta_K^{O(1)} \cdot d^{O(d)}$, our reduction implies that solving id-HSVP for the inverse of uniform primes ideals is no harder than solving it for uniform prime ideals (still for those of algebraic norm $\Delta_K^{O(1)} \cdot d^{O(d)}$). The success probability of this reduction is proportional to the proportion of prime ideals among all integral ideals of norm bounded by some $A = \text{poly}(\Delta_K)$. Combined with Gentry's reduction [Gen09a], our work implies the random self-reducibility of id-HSVP for the uniform distribution over prime ideals. As Gentry's original reduction considers the bounded distance decoding problem, we present an adaptation to the shortest vector problem in the extended version of this work. Note that the polynomial dependency in the proportion of prime ideals may have a considerable impact on the cost of this reduction (there exists number fields for which the proportion of prime ideals is exponentially small in the degree).

This new reduction, along with the Karp reduction of [PS21], gives a new distribution over NTRU instances with modulus polynomial in d and $\Delta_K^{1/d}$ whose difficulty relies on the worst-case problem id-HSVP. To our knowledge this is the first time a distribution over NTRU instance with polynomial modulus is based on a worst-case problem, even though this distribution needs a factoring oracle to be sampled from.

Technical Overview. We now give an overview of the average-case to average-case reduction for id-HSVP. Let $\mathcal{W}$ be a set of fractional ideals represented by

---

[2] The bound on the norm is obtained by combining Lemma 4.1 and Theorem 4.5 from [BDPW20].

their Hermite Normal Form. The goal of our reduction is to find (with non-negligible probability) a short non-zero vector in a given uniform element of $\mathcal{W}^{-1}$, given access to two oracles: $\mathcal{O}_\mathcal{W}$ which solves id-HSVP with non-negligible probability for a uniform element of $\mathcal{W}$, and $\mathcal{O}_\mathcal{I}$ which solves it with non-negligible probability for a uniform integral ideal with norm between A and $4A$, for $A = \Delta_K^{O(1/d)} \cdot d^{O(1)}$. In everything that follows we assume that we have a factoring oracle (for integers, or equivalently, for integral ideals). Such an oracle can be instantiated in quantum polynomial time with Shor's algorithm, or in sub-exponential time with the number field sieve algorithm.

Before diving into our contribution, let us explain a key idea developed in [Boe22, Chap. 6]. By *ideal of norm 1*, we mean a (replete) ideal[3] of the form $I/\mathcal{N}(I)^{1/d}$. The space of ideals of norm 1 has a natural notion of uniformity. Let B_r denote the ℓ_∞ ball of radius r. In [Boe22, Th. 6.21], it is proved that if J is sampled uniformly in the set of ideals of norm 1, and x is uniform in $B_r \cap J$, then the integral ideal $x \cdot J^{-1}$ is almost uniform in the set of integral ideals of norm less than r^d.

Now, our reduction follows the following structure. We are given a uniform $I \in \mathcal{W}$, and tasked with finding a short non-zero vector $v_{I^{-1}} \in I^{-1}$.

1. Find a short non-zero vector $v_I \in I$ with the oracle $\mathcal{O}_\mathcal{W}$.
2. Generate a uniform norm-1 ideal I', together with a short non-zero vector $v_{I'} \in I'$. The ideal $J = I' \cdot I/\mathcal{N}(I)^{1/d}$ is also uniform in the space of ideals of norm 1, and we can compute a short basis $\mathbf{B}_J$ of J thanks to the short non-zero vectors v_I and $v_{I'}$.
3. Sample $x \in B_r \cap J$; this uses our knowledge of the good basis $\mathbf{B}_J$. Hopefully, the integral ideal $\mathfrak{b} = x \cdot J^{-1}$ is almost uniform in the set of integral ideals of bounded norm.
4. Find a short non-zero vector $v_\mathfrak{b} \in \mathfrak{b}$ with the oracle $\mathcal{O}_\mathcal{I}$.
5. Return the vector $v_{I^{-1}} = x^{-1} \cdot v_{I'} \cdot v_\mathfrak{b} \cdot \mathcal{N}(I)^{-1/d} \in I^{-1}$.

One can check that $v_{I^{-1}} \in I^{-1}$, but is it short? Its factors are short by construction, except possibly x^{-1}. Indeed, the element x itself is bounded (it is in the set B_r), but its inverse may not be. To circumvent this issue, we would like to replace the ℓ_∞ ball B_r with another shape X which contains only *balanced* vectors (i.e., close to a vector of the form $\lambda \cdot (1, \ldots, 1)$), so that for any short $x \in X$, we have that x^{-1} is small. We prove that the result of [Boe22] holds for general sets X satisfying certain conditions. We consider a new shape $\mathcal{B}_{A,B}^\eta$ (see Fig. 1 and Definition 4.1) that verifies the conditions, and contains only balanced elements. Now, replacing B_r with $\mathcal{B}_{A,B}^\eta$ in Step 3, we sample an element x such that x^{-1} is small, hence all the factors of $v_{I^{-1}}$ are small, and $v_{I^{-1}}$ is indeed a solution to id-HSVP in I^{-1}.

While Step 3 constitutes the main difficulty of the reduction, and the technical core of our paper, let us briefly comment on Step 2. We need to sample a uniform norm-1 ideal I', together with a short non-zero vector $v_{I'} \in I'$.

---

[3] A replete ideal is a subset of $K_\mathbb{R} := K \otimes_\mathbb{Q} \mathbb{R}$ of the form $\alpha \cdot I$ where $I \subseteq \mathcal{O}_K$ is an integral ideal of $\mathcal{O}_K$ and $\alpha \in K_\mathbb{R}^\times$ is invertible. More details can be found in the preliminaries.

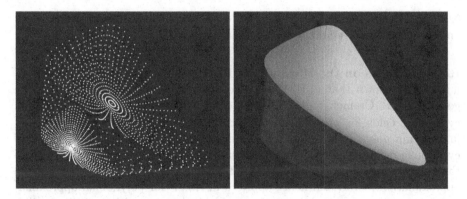

Fig. 1. A plot of $\mathcal{B}^{\eta}_{A,B}$ intersected with the subspace $K_{\mathbb{R}}^{+} := \{x \in K_{\mathbb{R}} \mid \sigma_i(x) \in \mathbb{R}_{>0}$ for all $i\}$. Here we have $(d_{\mathbb{R}}, d_{\mathbb{C}}) = (3,0), A = 20, B = 40$ and $\eta = \exp(1)$.

In [BDPW20], it is proven that if an ideal $\mathfrak{p}$ is sampled uniformly in the set of prime ideals with norm less than $(d^d \cdot \Delta_K)^c$ for some constant c, then, up to a small Gaussian factor, the ideal $\mathfrak{p}/\mathcal{N}(\mathfrak{p})^{1/d}$ is close to uniform in the set of norm-1 ideals. It is therefore sufficient to generate such a prime ideal $\mathfrak{p}$ together with a short element $v_{\mathfrak{p}} \in \mathfrak{p}$. The technique is extracted from [Gen09a, Chap. 17], and requires a factoring oracle. It first samples a small element $x \in \mathcal{O}_K$ with the Gaussian distribution. It then factors $(x) = \mathfrak{p}_1^{e_1} \cdot \ldots \cdot \mathfrak{p}_k^{e_k}$ and uniformly selects one of the factors $\mathfrak{p}_i$. Finalizing with a rejection sampling step, it can be proved that the chosen $\mathfrak{p}$ is almost uniform in the set of primes of norm $\lesssim \mathcal{N}(x)$.

We now have a reduction from id-HSVP for inverses of ideal of a set $\mathcal{W}$, to id-HSVP for ideals of $\mathcal{W}$ and id-HSVP for a uniform ideal of norm in some interval $[A, 4A]$ for A as small as $\Delta_K^{O(1))} \cdot d^{O(d)}$. This gives a trivial reduction from id-HSVP for a uniform ideal to id-HSVP for an uniform prime ideal, with a success probability decrease of a factor $O(1/\tilde{\rho}_A)$, where $1/\tilde{\rho}_A$ is the proportion of prime ideals among the set of all integral ideals of norm $\leq A$. We can now combine this last reduction with our main result (taking $\mathcal{W}$ to be the set of prime ideals of norm in $[A, 4A]$) in order to reduce id-HSVP for inverses of prime ideals to id-HSVP for prime ideals. This, combined with the worst-case to average-case reduction of [Gen09a] gives a worst-case to average-case reduction for id-HSVP where the average-case is the uniform distribution over prime ideals of norm in $[A, 4A]$.

Finally, note that a reduction from id-HSVP to NTRU was recently given in [PS21]. It transforms an integral ideal I into an NTRU instance of modulus polynomial larger than $\mathcal{N}(I)^{1/d}$. Our self-reduction (in contrast with the one from [Gen09a]) applies to integral ideals and can be composed with the one from [PS21]. The distribution of NTRU instances obtained by sampling a uniform prime ideal of norm in $[A, 4A]$ and applying [PS21, Alg. 4.1] is at least as difficult to solve as worst-case id-HSVP. By setting $A = \Delta_K^{O(1)} \cdot d^{O(d)}$, we obtain an NTRU modulus bounded as $\Delta_K^{O(1/d)} \cdot d^{O(1)}$. Note that "overstretched

NTRU" attacks [ABD16, CJL16, KF17] do not apply for this distribution as, among others, they require a much larger modulus.

Related Works on the Hardness of Id-HSVP. On the upper bound front, it has been shown that id-HSVP is susceptible to better algorithms than the generic HSVP. Cramer et al. [CDPR16] described an algorithm for id-HSVP in cyclotomic fields for principal ideals with an approximation factor $\exp \widetilde{O}(\sqrt{d})$ in quantum polynomial time. It was later generalized to all ideals [CDW17] of cyclotomic fields and (with pre-processing) to all number fields [PHS19]. Note that in the present work, all our reductions feature polynomial losses on the approximation factor, and hence apply to id-HSVP for polynomial approximation factors, a regime that is not impacted by these algorithms. Still, families of easy instances for id-HSVP have been identified even for polynomial approximation factors [PXWC21, PML21, BEP22], specifically ideals stabilized by many field automorphisms. While these families are very sparse, their existence further motivates the study of different distributions of id-HSVP instances.

2   Preliminaries

In this section we state some technical results, the proof of those are available in the extended version of this work.

The notation ln will refer to the base-e logarithm. For any function $f : X \to \mathbb{R}$ and $S \subseteq X$ with S countable, we define $f(S) := \sum_{x \in S} f(x)$.

We will let $\mathcal{G}(\mathbf{c}, s)$ denote the continuous Gaussian distribution of center $\mathbf{c}$ and of standard deviation s on some vector spaces that will always be specified.

We will use both the statistical distance and Rényi divergence between distributions. Let D_1, D_2 be distributions over a countable set X. Their statistical distance is $\mathrm{SD}(D_1, D_2) = \sum_{x \in X} |D_1(x) - D_2(x)| / 2$. For any event $E \subseteq X$, we have $D_2(E) \geq D_1(E) - \mathrm{SD}(D_1, D_2)$. If $\mathrm{Supp}(D_1) \subseteq \mathrm{Supp}(D_2)$, their Rényi divergence of infinite order is $\mathrm{RD}_\infty(D_1 \parallel D_2) = \max_{x \in \mathrm{Supp}(D_1)} D_1(x)/D_2(x)$. For any event $E \subseteq \mathrm{Supp}(D_1)$, we have $D_2(E) \geq D_1(E)/\mathrm{RD}_\infty(D_1 \parallel D_2)$.

When using oracles with a non-zero probability of failing, we assume without loss of generality that either the oracle returns a valid result or $\perp$ (as in our cases, the validity of the output can always be checked efficiently).

2.1   Lattices

Let $n \geq 1$. A lattice in $\mathbb{R}^n$ is a discrete additive subgroup of $\mathbb{R}^n$ of the form $L = \sum_{1 \leq i \leq k} \mathbf{b}_i \cdot \mathbb{Z}$ for some linearly independent $\mathbf{b}_i \in \mathbb{R}^n$ that are said to form a basis of L. A lattice is said to be full rank if any of its bases is full-rank in $\mathbb{R}^n$. If L is a lattice, we define its covering radius as $\mu(L) = \inf_{x \in \mathbb{R}^n} \mathrm{dist}(x, \mathcal{L})$ and its volume as $\mathrm{vol}(L) = \sqrt{\det(\mathbf{B} \cdot \mathbf{B}^T)}$, where $\mathbf{B} = (\mathbf{b}_1 \| \dots \| \mathbf{b}_k)$ (this quantity is independent of the choice of basis $(\mathbf{b}_1 \| \dots \| \mathbf{b}_k)$ of L). For any basis $(\mathbf{b}_1, \dots, \mathbf{b}_k) \in \mathbb{R}^{n \times k}$ of a lattice, we define $\|\mathbf{B}\| = \max_i \|\mathbf{b}_i\|_2$ and let $(\mathbf{b}_1^\star, \dots, \mathbf{b}_k^\star)$ denote its Gram-Schmidt vectors.

2.2 Algebraic Number Theory

We present here the number theoretic objects we will use throughout this work. For an in-depth introduction to the field, the reader is referred to [Coh96, Neu13]. Let K be a number field of degree $d \geq 2$ and discriminant Δ_K. Let $\mathcal{O}_K$ be its ring of integers.

Ideals. An ideal $\mathfrak{a} \subseteq \mathcal{O}_K$ is called an *integral* ideal. A *fractional ideal* of K is a discrete subset of K of the form $(x) = x\mathfrak{a}$, where $x \in K$ and $\mathfrak{a}$ is an integral ideal. Equivalently, a fractional ideal is a finitely generated $\mathcal{O}_K$-submodule of K. A fractional ideal of the form $x \cdot \mathcal{O}_K$ is called *principal*. In this work, we will take the convention that gothic letters (such as $\mathfrak{a}, \mathfrak{b}, \mathfrak{p}$) correspond to integral ideals, while upper-case letters (such as I, J) refer to ideals that are not necessarily integral.

For any fractional ideals I, J, we define the product $I \cdot J$ as the ideal generated by all products $a \cdot b$ for $a \in I, b \in J$ and the inverse I^{-1} as the ideal $I^{-1} = \{x \in K, xI \subseteq \mathcal{O}_K\}$. An integral ideal $\mathfrak{p}$ is said to be prime if there do not exist $\mathfrak{a}$ and $\mathfrak{b}$ integral and distinct from $\mathfrak{p}$ such that $\mathfrak{p} = \mathfrak{a}\mathfrak{b}$. These properties give the set of fractional ideals a group structure, the quotient group of fractional ideals of K by principal ideals is the class group of K, it is denoted Cl_K and is finite. We define the algebraic norm of an integral ideal $\mathfrak{a}$ by $\mathcal{N}(\mathfrak{a}) = [\mathcal{O}_K : \mathfrak{a}]$. We have $\mathcal{N}(\mathfrak{a}\mathfrak{b}) = \mathcal{N}(\mathfrak{a})\mathcal{N}(\mathfrak{b})$ for all integral ideals $\mathfrak{a}$ and $\mathfrak{b}$. If I is a fractional ideal, there exists an integer N such that $N \cdot I$ is integral, and we define $\mathcal{N}(I) = \mathcal{N}(N \cdot I)/N^d$ (this is independent of the choice of N). The multiplicativity property of the norm carries over to fractional ideals. For any set $\mathcal{W}$ of fractional ideals we define $\mathcal{W}^{-1} = \{I^{-1}, I \in \mathcal{W}\}$. For any $2 \leq A \leq B$, we define $\mathcal{I}_{A,B}$ the set of integral ideal with norm in $[A, B]$ and $\mathcal{P}_{A,B}$ the set of prime ideals with norm in $[A, B]$.

Embedding and Ideal Lattices. The canonical embedding $\sigma : K \to \mathbb{C}^d$ is defined as $x \mapsto (\sigma_1(x), \ldots, \sigma_d(x))$, where the σ_i's are the complex embeddings of K, ordered so the $d_\mathbb{R}$ ones with values in $\mathbb{R}$ come first, and $\sigma_i = \overline{\sigma_{d_\mathbb{C}+i}}$ for all $d_\mathbb{R} < i \leq d_\mathbb{R} + d_\mathbb{C}$ (note that $d = d_\mathbb{R} + 2d_\mathbb{C}$). We define $K_\mathbb{R} = K \otimes_\mathbb{Q} \mathbb{R}$, which is a ring containing K. The complex embeddings σ_i and the canonical embedding σ are extended to $K_\mathbb{R}$, and we have that $\sigma(K_\mathbb{R})$ is the set of $\mathbf{x} \in \mathbb{C}^d$ such that $x_i \in \mathbb{R}$ for $1 \leq i \leq d_\mathbb{R}$ and $x_{d_\mathbb{C}+i} = \overline{x_i}$ for $d_\mathbb{R} < i \leq d_\mathbb{R} + d_\mathbb{C}$. This is a real vector space of dimension d and a ring where addition and multiplication are performed coordinate-wise. The canonical embedding allows us to view any element x of K (and of $K_\mathbb{R}$) as a vector in $\mathbb{C}^d$, and to define $\|x\| = \|\sigma(x)\|$. The (absolute) algebraic norm of $x \in K_\mathbb{R}$ is defined as $\mathcal{N}(x) = \prod_{1 \leq i \leq d} |\sigma_i(x)|$. We have $\mathcal{N}(x \cdot \mathcal{O}_K) = \mathcal{N}(x)$.

We define $K_\mathbb{R}^0$ the set of norm-1 elements of $K_\mathbb{R}$. A replete ideal is a subset of $K_\mathbb{R}$ of the form $x \cdot \mathfrak{a}$, where $\mathfrak{a}$ is an integral ideal and $x \in K_\mathbb{R}^\times$ is invertible (we exclude divisors of zero). With this notation, if $\mathfrak{a}$ is principal, we call $x \cdot \mathfrak{a}$ a principal replete ideal. Multiplication and inversion are extended to the set of replete ideals by $(x \cdot \mathfrak{a}) \cdot (y \cdot \mathfrak{b}) = (xy) \cdot (\mathfrak{a}\mathfrak{b})$ and $(x \cdot \mathfrak{a})^{-1} = x^{-1} \cdot \mathfrak{a}^{-1}$. If we remove the zero ideal, then this set is a (multiplicative) group. We also extend the algebraic norm to replete ideals by $\mathcal{N}(x \cdot \mathfrak{a}) = \mathcal{N}(x) \cdot \mathcal{N}(\mathfrak{a})$.

Every non-zero replete ideal $x\mathfrak{a}$ corresponds to a full-rank lattice $\sigma(x\mathfrak{a})$. By abuse of notation, we identify $x\mathfrak{a}$ and $\sigma(x\mathfrak{a})$. We have $\mathrm{vol}(x\mathfrak{a}) = \sqrt{\Delta_K} \cdot \mathcal{N}(x\mathfrak{a})$, and the covering radius in ℓ_∞ norm of $x\mathfrak{a}$ is bounded from above by:

$$\mu_\infty(x\mathfrak{a}) \leq d \cdot \lambda_d^{(\infty)}(x\mathfrak{a}) \leq d \cdot \lambda_1^{(\infty)}(x\mathfrak{a}) \cdot \lambda_d^\infty(\mathcal{O}_K) \leq d \cdot \Delta_K^{3/(2d)} \cdot \mathcal{N}(x\mathfrak{a})^{1/d}, \quad (1)$$

where we bounded $\lambda_1(x\mathfrak{a})$ by $\Delta_K^{1/(2d)} \cdot \mathcal{N}(x\mathfrak{a})^{1/d}$ using Minkowski's theorem and $\lambda_d^\infty(\mathcal{O}_K)$ by $\Delta_K^{1/d}$ using [BST+20, Th. 3.1] (adapted to the ℓ_∞ norm in [Boe22, Th. A.4]). For an (integral / fractional / replete) ideal, we call the corresponding image an (integral / fractional / replete) ideal lattices (with respect to K). We define idLat^0 as the set of replete ideal lattices of norm 1. This is a compact subgroup of idLat, and it admits a uniform distribution $\mathcal{U}(\mathrm{idLat}^0)$.

Lemma 2.1. *Let J be a replete ideal, then*

$$\Pr_{I \leftarrow \mathcal{U}(\mathrm{idLat}^0)} \left(\exists x \in K_\mathbb{R}^\times : J = I \cdot (x) \right) = \frac{1}{|\mathrm{Cl}_K|}$$

We define the logarithmic embedding of $K_\mathbb{R}$, by taking the natural logarithm of every embedding of an element:

$$\mathrm{Ln} : K_\mathbb{R}^\times \longrightarrow \mathrm{Ln}(K_\mathbb{R}) = \mathbb{R}^d$$
$$x \longmapsto (\ln|\sigma_i(x)|)_i$$

The following lemma is a standard result on the logarithmic embedding. The first statement is a rewriting of the equality $\mathrm{Ln}(x) = 0$ and the second one is a consequence of Dirichlet's unit theorem.

Lemma 2.2. *The function Ln has kernel $\{x \in K_\mathbb{R}^\times : \forall i, |x_i| = 1\}$, whose intersection with $\mathcal{O}_K$ is the set μ_K of roots of unity of K.*

By relying on random walks in the Arakelov class group of K, de Boer et al. [BDPW20] proposed an efficient algorithm to sample from $\mathcal{U}(\mathrm{idLat}^0)$. We give here a simplified version of this result borrowed from [FPS22], for a single-step random walk.

Lemma 2.3 ([FPS22, Le. 2.4]). *Let $A \geq 2$, and D the distribution over idLat^0 of*

$$I = u \cdot \mathrm{Exp}(\zeta) \cdot \mathfrak{p} \cdot \mathcal{N}(\mathfrak{p})^{-1/d},$$

for $\mathfrak{p}$ uniform in $\mathcal{P}_{0,A}$, u uniform in $\{x \in K_\mathbb{R}^\times : \forall i \leq d, |x_i| = 1\}$ and ζ sampled according to $\mathcal{G}(0, d^{-3/2})$ in $\mathrm{span}(\mathrm{Ln}(\mathcal{O}_K^\times))$ conditioned on $\|\zeta\| \leq 1/d$. Then there exists an absolute constant $c > 1$ such that if $A \geq (d^d \cdot \Delta_K)^c$, then

$$\mathrm{SD}(D, \mathcal{U}(\mathrm{idLat}^0)) = 2^{-\Omega(d)}.$$

Balanced Elements. For the reductions presented in this article, it will some-times be convenient to use balanced elements of $K_\mathbb{R}$, i.e., elements whose ℓ_∞ norm and the one of their inverse are not far from the geometric mean of their coordinates: in other terms they do not have an exceptionally small or large coordinate in comparison to the others. This property is convenient as it implies that multiplying an ideal by one of these elements will not change its geometry significantly, in particular if x is balanced and v is small in the ideal $x \cdot I$, then $x^{-1} \cdot v$ will be small in I. The formal definition is as follows.

Definition 2.4. *Let $\eta > 1$. An element x in $K_\mathbb{R}$ is said to be η-balanced if*

$$\|x\|_\infty \leq \eta \cdot |\mathcal{N}(x)|^{\frac{1}{d}} \quad and \quad \|x^{-1}\|_\infty \leq \eta \cdot |\mathcal{N}(x)|^{-\frac{1}{d}}.$$

Density of Prime Ideals. For any $A \geq 1$, we let $\tilde{\rho}_A$ denote the inverse of the proportion of prime ideals among all integral ideals of K of norm $\leq A$, i.e.,

$$\tilde{\rho}_A := \frac{|\{\mathfrak{a} \subset \mathcal{O}_K \,|\, \mathcal{N}(\mathfrak{a}) \leq A\}|}{|\{\mathfrak{p} \subset \mathcal{O}_K \text{ prime} \,|\, \mathcal{N}(\mathfrak{p}) \leq A\}|}.$$

In this article, we will be interested in $\tilde{\rho}_A$ for values of A of the order of poly(Δ_K). Unfortunately, we are not aware of estimates for $\tilde{\rho}_A$ when A is this "small". However, it is known that when the number field K is fixed and A tends to infinity, it holds that

$$\tilde{\rho}_A \underset{A \to \infty}{\sim} \rho_K \cdot \ln(A),$$

where ρ_K is the residue of the Dedekind zeta function at 1. This comes from the fact that $|\{\mathfrak{p} \subset \mathcal{O}_K \text{ prime} \,|\, \mathcal{N}(\mathfrak{p}) \leq A\}| \sim A/\ln(A)$ (see [BS96, Th. 8.7.4]), and that $|\{\mathfrak{a} \subset \mathcal{O}_K \,|\, \mathcal{N}(\mathfrak{a}) \leq A\}| \sim \rho_K \cdot A$ (see [Web08]). The quantity ρ_K is known to be poly$(\log \Delta_K)$ for some number fields such as cyclotomic fields (under ERH, see [Boe22, Th. A.5]), but there also exist families of fields in which ρ_K is exponential in the degree and $\Delta_K^{1/(2d)}$ (e.g., for some multi-quadratic number fields).

2.3   Algorithmic Problems

Representing Field Elements and Ideals. We assume that we know a $\mathbb{Z}$-basis $\mathbf{B}_{\mathcal{O}_K}$ of $\mathcal{O}_K$, and that it is LLL-reduced with respect to the geometry induced by σ (in some cases, a much better basis could be known). We define $\delta_K := \|\mathbf{B}_{\mathcal{O}_K}\|$. Since $\mathbf{B}_{\mathcal{O}_K}$ is LLL-reduced, we have that $\delta_K \leq 2^d \cdot \lambda_d(\mathcal{O}_K) = O(2^d \cdot \Delta_K^{1/d})$ from [BST+20, Th. 3.1], which implies that $\log \delta_K = O(\log \Delta_K)$.

Elements of K will be represented as vectors of $\mathbb{Q}^d$, corresponding to their coordinates in the basis $\mathbf{B}_K$. Fractional ideals of K will be represented by a $\mathbb{Z}$-basis, i.e., d elements of K generating the ideal (each element being represented as a vector of $\mathbb{Q}^d$ as described above). The bases we obtain for a fractional ideal I are in $\mathbb{Q}^{d \times d}$, so they admit a Hermite Normal Form (HNF), which provides a canonical representation for I. When replete ideals are used in algorithms, they will be represented by an arbitrary basis with size polynomial in the log of their norm and in $\log \Delta_K$ (with a polynomial number of bits of precision).

Algorithmic Problems in Ideals. In this article, we will consider the Hermite shortest vector problem in ideals, as well as related algorithmic problems.

Definition 2.5. *Let $\gamma \geq 1$. The ideal Hermite Shortest Vector Problem* id-HSVP$_\gamma$ *asks, given as input a fractional ideal I represented by its HNF basis, to find a non-zero element $x \in I$ such that $\|x\| \leq \gamma \cdot \mathrm{vol}(I)^{1/d}$. For a finite set X of fractional ideals, the average-case variant X-avg-id-HSVP$_\gamma$ asks to solve* id-HSVP$_\gamma$ *when the input ideal I is uniformly sampled in X. The success probability of an algorithm $\mathcal{A}$ when solving X-avg-id-HSVP$_\gamma$ is defined as*

$$\Pr_{I \hookleftarrow X}\left[x \in I \text{ and } \|x\| \leq \gamma \cdot \mathrm{vol}(I)^{1/d} \mid \mathcal{A}(I) = x \right],$$

where the randomness is taken over the choice of I and the possible internal randomness of $\mathcal{A}$.

The problem inv-HSVP$_\gamma$ *is* id-HSVP$_\gamma$ *restricted to inverses of integral ideal lattices.*

The problems inv-HSVP$_\gamma$ and id-HSVP$_\gamma$ are equivalent under Karp reductions, without any loss in the approximation factor, as shown in the following lemma (the other direction follows from the definition).

Lemma 2.6 (Folklore). *For any $\gamma \geq 1$, there is a Karp polynomial-time reduction from* id-HSVP$_\gamma$ *to* inv-HSVP$_\gamma$.

2.4   Algorithms on Ideals

We will often manipulate ideals and their basis. We will use the following results on how to derive a short basis from a full-rank set of vectors.

Lemma 2.7 (Corollary of [MG02, Le. 7.1]). *There exists a polynomial time algorithm that takes as input a basis $\mathbf{B}$ of an n-dimensional lattice L and a set of n linearly independent vectors $\mathbf{s}_1, \cdots, \mathbf{s}_n \in L$ and outputs a new basis $\mathbf{C}$ of L such that $\|\mathbf{C}^\star\| \leq \max_i \|\mathbf{s}_i^*\|$ and $\|\mathbf{C}\| \leq \sqrt{n} \cdot \max_i \|\mathbf{s}_i\|$.*

We will use Lemma 2.7 to perform arithmetic over ideals while bounding the sizes of the outputs.

Lemma 2.8. *There exist polynomial-time algorithms* InvertIdeal, Reduce-Ideal *and* MultiplyIdeals *with the following specifications.*

- InvertIdeal *takes as input an integral ideal $\mathfrak{a}$ and outputs a basis $\mathbf{B}$ of $\mathfrak{a}^{-1}$ such that $\|\mathbf{B}^\star\| \leq \delta_K$ and $\|\mathbf{B}\| \leq \sqrt{d} \cdot \delta_K$.*
- ReduceIdeal *takes as input a basis $\mathbf{B}$ of an ideal $I \subset K_\mathbb{R}$ and a vector $v \in I \setminus \{0\}$ and returns a basis $\mathbf{B}_I$ of I such that $\|\mathbf{B}_I^\star\| \leq \delta_K \cdot \|v\|$ and $\|\mathbf{B}_I\| \leq \sqrt{d} \cdot \delta_K \cdot \|v\|$.*
- MultiplyIdeals *takes as input bases $\mathbf{B}_I$ and $\mathbf{B}_J$ of two ideals $I, J \subseteq K_\mathbb{R}$ and output $\mathbf{B}_{IJ}$ a basis of $I \cdot J$ such that $\|\mathbf{B}_{IJ}^\star\| \leq \|\mathbf{B}_I\| \cdot \|\mathbf{B}_J\|$ and $\|\mathbf{B}_{IJ}\| \leq \sqrt{d} \cdot \|\mathbf{B}_I\| \cdot \|\mathbf{B}_J\|$.*

For $I = \mathcal{O}_K$, the following lemma states that one can quantumly and efficiently sample a random prime ideal together with a short element in it, hence the name. We give a proof based on [PS21] but note that a similar statement was already given as [Gen09a, Th. 16.3.4, Le. 17.2.1] (see also [Gen10, Se. 3.3]).

Lemma 2.9 (Adapted from [PS21, Lemma C.1]). *There exists an algorithm* SampleWithTrap *that on input integers* $2 \leq A < B$*, a real* $\varepsilon \in (0,1)$ *and a basis* $\mathbf{B}_I$ *of a fractional ideal* I*, samples a pair* $(\mathfrak{p}, w)$ *such that*

1. *the distribution of* $\mathfrak{p}$ *is within statistical distance* ε *from the uniform distribution over* $\mathcal{P}_{A,B}$*;*
2. *the element* w *belongs to* $I \cdot \mathfrak{p} \setminus \{0\}$*;*
3. *we have* $\|w\| \leq 2\sqrt{4d + \ln(24B/\varepsilon)} \cdot s$ *with* $s = \max\left(s_{sample}, s_{smooth}\right)$ *and*
   - $s_{sample} = \sqrt{d} \cdot \|\mathbf{B}_I^\star\|$*.*
   - $s_{smooth} = (\Delta_K \cdot B \cdot \mathcal{N}(I))^{1/d} \cdot \sqrt{\ln(24B/\varepsilon)}$*.*

Furthermore, if the algorithm is given access to an oracle factoring integral ideals of norm smaller than $(2\sqrt{4d + \ln(24B/\varepsilon)} \cdot s)^d \cdot \mathcal{N}(I)^{-1}$*, then the algorithm runs in expected time polynomial in* $B/|\mathcal{P}_{A,B}|, B/A, \log \Delta_K, \log B, \log(1/\varepsilon)$ *and in the size of* I*.*

Note that we will use this result with $\varepsilon = \exp(-d)$ in order to simplify computations and subsequently omit this input.

Factoring Ideals. Factoring an integral ideal $\mathfrak{a}$ in $\mathcal{O}_K$ can be done by factoring the algebraic norm $\mathcal{N}(\mathfrak{a})$ of $\mathfrak{a}$ over the integers; computing, for all the prime factors $p \mid \mathcal{N}(\mathfrak{a})$, the set of prime ideals whose norm is a power of p (there are at most d of those); and testing for each of these prime if they divide $\mathfrak{a}$. Factoring $\mathcal{N}(\mathfrak{a})$ can be performed quantumly in time polynomial in $\log \mathcal{N}(\mathfrak{a})$ (using Shor's algorithm [Sho94]). Computing the set of prime ideals of norm a given prime integer p can be performed classically in time polynomial in $\log p$ and $\log \Delta_K$ using Buchmann-Lenstra's algorithm [BL94], described in details in [Coh96, Sec. 6.2.5]. Finally, testing whether a prime ideal $\mathfrak{p}$ divides $\mathfrak{a}$ can be done in time polynomial in the bit-sizes of $\mathfrak{p}$ and $\mathfrak{a}$. Overall, factoring ideals can be done in quantum-polynomial time (using Shor's algorithm) or in classical sub-exponential time (using the Number Field Sieve).

2.5 Worst-Case to Average-Case Reduction for Inverse of Primes

In [Gen09a, Ch. 16 & 17], Gentry described a self-reduction for a variant of the bounded distance decoding problem, from worst-case ideals to prime ideals taken uniformly at random with their norm in some interval $[A, B]$ (for a suitable choice of A and B). This reduction can be adapted to the shortest vector problem (instead of the bounded distance decoding problem), but it requires to take the inverse of the ideals, implying that the average-case distribution we obtain is over the inverses of prime ideals uniformly chosen in the interval $[A, B]$. Below, we state the result of Gentry's reduction adapted to SVP, whose proof is available in the extended version of this work.

Theorem 2.10 (Adapted from [Gen09a, Ch. 16 & 17]). *There exist some* $C_{1,K} = \text{poly}(\Delta_K^{1/d}, \log \Delta_K, \delta_K)$ *and* $C_{2,K} = \text{poly}(\log \Delta_K, \delta_K)$ *such that the following holds. Let* $\gamma_{avg} \in [1, 2^d]$, $A \geq C_{1,K}^d \cdot \gamma_{avg}^d$ *satisfying* $A \leq (\Delta_K)^{d^{O(1)}}$ *and* $\gamma = A^{1/d} \cdot C_{2,K}$. *Then*

$$\text{id-HSVP}_\gamma \quad \text{reduces to} \quad \mathcal{P}_{A,4A}^{-1}\text{-avg-id-HSVP}_{\gamma_{avg}}.$$

The reduction is probabilistic and, assuming it has access to an oracle factoring integral ideals whose norms have bit-size $\text{poly}(\log \Delta_K)$, *it runs in expected time polynomial in its input size,* $\log \Delta_K$ *and* $1/\delta$, *where* δ *is the success probability of the* $\mathcal{P}_{A,4A}^{-1}\text{-avg-id-HSVP}_{\gamma_{avg}}$ *oracle.*[4]

3   Self-reducibility of id-HSVP to Inverses

Let $\mathcal{W}$ be a set of fractional ideals. In this section, we provide a framework for reducing id-HSVP for the uniform distribution over $\mathcal{W}$ to id-HSVP for the uniform distribution over $\mathcal{W}^{-1} = \{I^{-1} : I \in \mathcal{W}\}$. The reduction, provided in Theorem 3.4 relies on three oracles (beyond the one for id-HSVP for $\mathcal{U}(\mathcal{W})$). The first one factors integral ideals, and can be instantiated with a quantum polynomial-time algorithm. The second one samples from $I \cap X$, where I is an arbitrary norm-1 replete ideal and X is a well-chosen set: this oracle will be instantiated in Sect. 4. The last one finds short non-zero vectors in integral ideals uniformly distributed within those having their norms in a prescribed interval. Overall, this will lead to a quantum polynomial-time reduction from $\mathcal{W}^{-1}$-avg-id-HSVP to $\mathcal{W}$-avg-id-HSVP and $\mathcal{I}_{A,4A}$-avg-id-HSVP for a well-chosen A.

The reduction is built in several steps. First, we show how to map a uniform norm-1 replete ideal to an integral ideal uniform among those with norms in $[A, 4A]$, using a new approach introduced in [Boe22, Sec. 6]. This is parametrized by a set X that will be instantiated in Sect. 4. The second step gives a way to randomize an arbitrary ideal to an integral ideal uniform among those with norms in $[A, 4A]$, along with a hint that allows to map a short vector of the resulting ideal to a short vector in the inverse of the input ideal. Finally, this allows to describe the reduction.

3.1   From a Uniform Norm-1 Ideal to a Uniform Integral Ideal

In this subsection, we present a way to sample uniformly among integral ideals whose norms belong to a prescribed interval. Given a compact set X verifying certain properties, our sampler takes as input a uniform ideal $I \in \text{idLat}^0$, samples a point uniformly in $I \cap X$ and output $(x) \cdot I^{-1} \subseteq \mathcal{O}_K$. It holds that if X is well-designed, then the output distribution is close to the uniform distribution

---

[4] The choice of $4A$ for the upper bound on the norm of the ideals is not a strict requirement of this theorem. We instantiated the theorem with this value in order to simplify its statement.

over the set of integral ideals in terms of Rényi divergence. Our sampler generalizes [Boe22, Th. 6.9], where the set X is assumed to be the ℓ_∞ ball. This new degree of freedom will allow us (in Sect. 4) to choose a set X whose points are balanced, which will be essential for the proof of Theroem 5.1. Note that we do not use the Arakelov ray divisor formalism to state our results: those of [Boe22, Sec. 6] are stated with respect to a modulus $\mathfrak{m} \subseteq \mathcal{O}_K$ and here we take $\mathfrak{m} = \mathcal{O}_K$.

Definition 3.1. *Let $X \subset K_\mathbb{R}$. We say that X is compact and invariant by complex rotations if the following hold:*

- *$\sigma(X)$ is a compact subset of $\mathbb{C}^d$;*
- *for any $\zeta = (\zeta_1, \ldots, \zeta_d) \in \sigma(K_\mathbb{R})$ with $|\zeta_1| = \cdots = |\zeta_d| = 1$, it holds that $\sigma^{-1}(\zeta) \cdot X = \{\sigma^{-1}(\zeta) \cdot x \mid x \in X\} \subseteq X$.*

We consider the `IdealRound` algorithm (Algorithm 3.1), whose output distribution generalizes the distribution presented in [Boe22, Th. 6.9]. It is parametrized by an arbitrary compact set $X \subset K_\mathbb{R}$, takes as input a norm-1 replete ideal (i.e., an element of idLat^0) and returns an integral ideal. We define $\mathcal{D}_{\text{Ideal}}(X)$ as the distribution $\texttt{IdealRound}_X(\mathcal{U}(\text{idLat}^0))$. For the moment, we are not interested in the efficiency of $\texttt{IdealRound}_X$, but only in the relationship between $\mathcal{D}_{\text{Ideal}}(X)$ and the uniform distribution over ideals with norms belonging to an interval. This is the purpose of the following result.

Algorithm 3.1 `IdealRound`

Input: $I \in \text{idLat}^0$.
Parameter: $X \subset K_\mathbb{R}$ compact.
Output: An integral ideal $\mathfrak{a}$.
 1: Sample $x \leftarrow \mathcal{U}(I \cap X)$.
 2: Return $\mathfrak{a} = (x) \cdot I^{-1}$.

Lemma 3.2. *For any $t \in \mathbb{R}$, let $H_t = \{x \in \text{Ln}\, K_\mathbb{R} \mid \sum_i x_i = t\}$. Let X be a compact subset of $K_\mathbb{R}$ invariant by complex rotations (as per Definition 3.1) and $B > A > 2$. Assume that:*

- *There exist some real numbers $C \geq 1$ and $C' > 0$ such that we have $|I \cap X| \in C' \cdot [1, C]$ for any $I \in \text{idLat}^0$;*
- *there exists $C'' \in \mathbb{R}$ such that for any $t \in [\ln(A), \ln(B)]$ we have*

$$\text{vol}\left(\text{Ln}(X) \bigcap H_t\right) = C'';$$

- *for any $t \notin [\ln(A), \ln(B)]$, we have $\text{vol}(\text{Ln}(X) \cap H_t) = 0$.*

Then the support of $\mathcal{D}_{\text{Ideal}}(X)$ is contained in $\mathcal{I}_{A,B}$ and

$$\text{RD}_\infty(\mathcal{U}(\mathcal{I}_{A,B}) \parallel \mathcal{D}_{\text{Ideal}}(X)) \leq C.$$

We now comment the conditions of Lemma 3.2. The second and third conditions state that, when embedded in $\mathrm{Ln}(K_{\mathbb{R}})$ the set $\mathrm{Ln}(X)$ should be contained between the two hyperplanes $H_{\log(A)}$ and $H_{\log(B)}$, and that between those hyperplanes, the slices $\mathrm{Ln}(X) \cap H_t$ should have constant volume. Those conditions will yield the bounds on the norm of the output ideal. The first condition states that for any norm-1 replete ideal I, the number of points in $X \cap I$ should be non-zero and almost independent of I. Conditions 1 and 2 will imply the near-uniformity of the output distribution. The proof below is adapted from [Boe22, Th. 6.9].

Proof. Fix an integral ideal $\mathfrak{b}$ and a norm-1 replete ideal I. We are going to compute bounds on

$$p_{I,\mathfrak{b}} = \Pr_{x} \left((x) \cdot I^{-1} = \mathfrak{b} \right) = \Pr_{x} \left((x) = I \cdot \mathfrak{b} \right) = \Pr_{x} \left(x \text{ generates } I \cdot \mathfrak{b} \right),$$

where the randomness is over $x \leftarrow \mathcal{U}(I \cap X)$. For an ideal J, we define $G_J = \{x \in K_{\mathbb{R}} : (x) = J\}$ as the set of generators of J (if J is not principal, it is the empty set). Note that $G_{I\cdot\mathfrak{b}} = \{x \in K_{\mathbb{R}} : (x) = I \cdot \mathfrak{b}\} \subseteq I$. We have

$$p_{I,\mathfrak{b}} = \frac{|G_{I\cdot\mathfrak{b}} \cap X|}{|I \cap X|} \in \left|G_{I\cdot\mathfrak{b}} \bigcap X\right| \cdot C'^{-1} \cdot [C^{-1}, 1],$$

where the inclusion follows from the first assumption of the lemma. For any I that is not in the class of $\mathfrak{b}^{-1}$ modulo principal ideals, we have that $G_{I\cdot\mathfrak{b}}$ is empty, since $I \cdot \mathfrak{b}$ is not principal. Let $[\mathfrak{b}^{-1}]^0$ be the set of all norm-1 replete ideals of the form $(\alpha) \cdot \mathfrak{b}^{-1}$ for some $\alpha \in K_{\mathbb{R}}$ (i.e., the coset of $\mathfrak{b}^{-1}$ in idLat^0 modulo principal ideals). Let $I_0 = \mathcal{N}(\mathfrak{b})^{1/d} \cdot \mathfrak{b}^{-1}$, which belongs to $[\mathfrak{b}^{-1}]^0$. There is a bijection between $K_{\mathbb{R}}^0/\mathcal{O}_K^{\times}$ and $[\mathfrak{b}^{-1}]^0$ given by $u \mapsto (u) \cdot I_0$. This implies that

$$\underset{I \leftarrow \mathcal{U}(\mathrm{idLat}^0)}{\mathbb{E}} \left(\left|G_{I\cdot\mathfrak{b}} \bigcap X\right| \right) = \underset{I \leftarrow \mathcal{U}(\mathrm{idLat}^0)}{\Pr} (I \in [\mathfrak{b}^{-1}]^0) \cdot \underset{u}{\mathbb{E}} \left(\left|G_{\mathcal{N}(\mathfrak{b})^{1/d}\cdot(u)} \bigcap X\right| \right)$$

$$= \frac{1}{|\mathrm{Cl}_K|} \cdot \underset{u}{\mathbb{E}} \left(\left|G_{\mathcal{N}(\mathfrak{b})^{1/d}\cdot(u)} \bigcap X\right| \right),$$

where $u \leftarrow \mathcal{U}(K_{\mathbb{R}}^0/\mathcal{O}_K^{\times})$ and the second equality comes from Lemma 2.1. Let μ_K be the set of roots of unity in K. Using the fact that the Ln function is $|\mu_K|$-to-1 when its input is restricted to generators of a principal replete ideal I, and that X is invariant by complex rotations, we have:

$$\forall I \in \mathrm{idLat}^0 : \left|G_I \bigcap X\right| = |\mu_K| \cdot \left|\mathrm{Ln}(G_I) \bigcap \mathrm{Ln}(X)\right|.$$

In our context, this implies that for any $u \in K_{\mathbb{R}}^0$,

$$\left|G_{\mathcal{N}(\mathfrak{b})^{1/d}\cdot(u)} \bigcap X\right| = |\mu_K| \cdot \left|\mathrm{Ln}(X) \bigcap \left\{\mathrm{Ln}(x) : x = v \cdot u \cdot \mathcal{N}(\mathfrak{b})^{1/d}, v \in \mathcal{O}_K^{\times}\right\}\right|$$

$$= |\mu_K| \cdot \left|\mathrm{Ln}(X) \bigcap (\Lambda_K + \mathrm{Ln}(u) + \mathrm{Ln}(\mathcal{N}(\mathfrak{b})^{1/d}))\right|$$

$$= |\mu_K| \cdot \left|(\mathrm{Ln}(X) - \mathrm{Ln}(\mathcal{N}(\mathfrak{b})^{1/d})) \bigcap (\Lambda_K + \mathrm{Ln}(u))\right|,$$

where $\Lambda_K = \mathrm{Ln}\,\mathcal{O}_K^{\times}$. Note that Λ_K is full rank in H_0, and that $\mathrm{Ln}(u) \in H_0$ for any $u \in K_{\mathbb{R}}^0$. Moreover, the vector $\mathrm{Ln}(u)$ is uniform in H_0/Λ_K when u is uniform in $K_{\mathbb{R}}^0/\mathcal{O}_K^{\times}$. We are hence considering a uniform lattice shift and, for any measurable set $\mathcal{S} \subseteq H_0$, we have:

$$\underset{u}{\mathbb{E}}\Big(\big|(\Lambda_K + \mathrm{Ln}(u))\bigcap \mathcal{S}\big|\Big) = \frac{\mathrm{Vol}(\mathcal{S})}{\mathrm{Vol}(\Lambda_K)}.$$

Applying this to the set $\mathcal{S} = (\mathrm{Ln}(X) - \mathrm{Ln}(\mathcal{N}(\mathfrak{b})^{1/d})) \cap H_0$, we obtain

$$\underset{u}{\mathbb{E}}\left(\Big|G_{\mathcal{N}(\mathfrak{b})^{1/d}\cdot(u)}\bigcap X\Big|\right) = |\mu_K| \cdot \frac{\mathrm{Vol}((\mathrm{Ln}(X) - \mathrm{Ln}(\mathcal{N}(\mathfrak{b})^{1/d}))\bigcap H_0)}{\mathrm{Vol}(\Lambda_K)}.$$

Observe that by definition of H_t for $t \in \mathbb{R}$, it holds that

$$(\mathrm{Ln}(X) - \mathrm{Ln}(\mathcal{N}(\mathfrak{b})^{1/d}))\bigcap H_0 = \Big(\mathrm{Ln}(X)\bigcap H_{\ln \mathcal{N}(\mathfrak{b})}\Big) - \mathrm{Ln}(\mathcal{N}(\mathfrak{b})^{1/d}).$$

Since shifting by $\mathrm{Ln}(\mathcal{N}(\mathfrak{b})^{1/d})$ does not change the volume, we obtain

$$\underset{u}{\mathbb{E}}\left(\Big|G_{\mathcal{N}(\mathfrak{b})^{1/d}\cdot(u)}\bigcap X\Big|\right) = |\mu_K| \cdot \frac{\mathrm{Vol}(\mathrm{Ln}(X)\bigcap H_{\ln \mathcal{N}(\mathfrak{b})})}{\mathrm{Vol}(\Lambda_K)}.$$

Recall from the second and third assumptions that

$$\mathrm{Vol}\Big(\mathrm{Ln}(X)\bigcap H_{\ln \mathcal{N}(\mathfrak{b})}\Big) = \begin{cases} C'' & \text{if } \ln \mathcal{N}(\mathfrak{b}) \in [\ln A, \ln B], \\ 0 & \text{otherwise.} \end{cases}$$

Let $p = C'' \cdot |\mu_K| / (C' \cdot |\mathrm{Cl}_K| \cdot \mathrm{Vol}(\Lambda_K))$. Combining everything, this proves that

$$p_{\mathfrak{b}} := \underset{I \leftarrow \mathcal{U}(\mathrm{idLat}^0)}{\mathbb{E}}(p_{\mathfrak{b},I}) \in \begin{cases} p \cdot [C^{-1}, 1] & \text{if } \mathcal{N}(\mathfrak{b}) \in [A, B], \\ \{0\} & \text{otherwise.} \end{cases}$$

Observe that $p_{\mathfrak{b}}$ is equal to $\mathcal{D}_{\mathrm{Ideal}}(X)(\mathfrak{b})$, the probability of the ideal $\mathfrak{b}$ for the distribution $\mathcal{D}_{\mathrm{Ideal}}(X)$. The equation above then means that $\mathcal{D}_{\mathrm{Ideal}}(X)$ outputs ideals with norm in $[A, B]$ with probability essentially equal to p (up to a factor C), and other ideals with probability 0. We quantify this using the Rényi divergence. As $1 = \sum_{\mathfrak{b} \in \mathcal{I}_{A,B}} p_{\mathfrak{b}} \in p \cdot |\mathcal{I}_{A,B}| \cdot [C^{-1}, 1]$, we have that $p \in |\mathcal{I}_{A,B}|^{-1} \cdot [1, C]$, and hence:

$$\forall \mathfrak{b} \in \mathcal{I}_{A,B}: \quad \frac{p_{\mathfrak{b}}}{\mathcal{U}(\mathcal{I}_{A,B})(\mathfrak{b})} \in [C^{-1}, C],$$

hence $\mathrm{RD}_{\infty}(\mathcal{U}(\mathcal{I}_{A,B}) \,\|\, \mathcal{D}_{\mathrm{Ideal}}(X)) \leq C$, which complete the proof. $\qquad \square$

3.2   From an Arbitrary Ideal to a Uniform Integral Ideal

Below, we give an algorithm, $\texttt{RandomizeIdeal}_{A,X}$ (see Algorithm 3.2), which on input an arbitrary ideal I, returns a uniform integral ideal $\mathfrak{b}$ and a short non-zero vector $y \in \mathfrak{b}^{-1} \cdot I^{-1}$. The algorithm is parametrized by an integer A and a set X satisfying the conditions of Lemma 3.2. $\mathtt{RandomizeIdeal}_{A,X}$ starts by sampling a uniform norm-1 ideal J, i.e., with distribution equal to $\mathcal{U}(\mathrm{idLat}^0)$, along with a small element v_J in it, using the $\mathtt{SampleWithTrap}$ algorithm. Since $\mathcal{U}(\mathrm{idLat}^0)$ is the Haar distribution on a compact group, the ideal $I' = J \cdot (I/\mathcal{N}(I)^{1/d})$ is also uniform. We then use $\mathtt{IdealRound}$ to map $\mathcal{U}(\mathrm{idLat}^0)$ to the uniform distribution over integral ideals with norms in $[A, 4A]$. In more details, a uniform point x in $I' \cap X$ is sampled and Lemma 3.2 implies that $\mathfrak{b} := x \cdot I'^{-1}$ is almost uniform, and $v_J \cdot x^{-1}$ is a small element in $\mathfrak{b}^{-1} \cdot \mathcal{N}(I)^{1/d} \cdot I^{-1}$ if x is balanced. We note that Steps 7 and 8 below are exactly the $\mathtt{IdealRound}$ algorithm applied to the ideal I'. However, we cannot call this algorithm in a black-box way, as we need to know the intermediate value x for Step 9 of the algorithm.

Algorithm 3.2 $\mathtt{RandomizeIdeal}$

Input: A basis $\mathbf{B}_I$ of an ideal I.
Parameters: A integer and $X \subset K_{\mathbb{R}} \setminus \{0\}$ compact.
Oracles: $\mathcal{F}$ for factoring integral ideals, $\mathcal{S}$ for sampling from $\mathcal{U}(I \cap X)$ for $I \in \mathrm{idLat}^0$.
Output: $\mathfrak{b}$ an integral ideal, $y \in \mathfrak{b}^{-1} \cdot I^{-1} \setminus \{0\}$.
1: Sample $(\mathfrak{q}, v_{\mathfrak{q}}) \leftarrow \mathtt{SampleWithTrap}_{A,4A}(\mathbf{B}_{\mathcal{O}_K})$, using $\mathcal{F}$.
2: Sample $\zeta \leftarrow \mathcal{G}(0, d^{-3/2})$ in $\mathrm{span}(\mathrm{Ln}(\mathcal{O}_K^{\times}))$ conditioned on $\|\zeta\| \leq 1/d$.
3: Sample u uniform in $\{x \in K_{\mathbb{R}}^{\times} : \forall i \leq d, |x_i| = 1\}$.
4: Let $J = u \cdot \mathrm{Exp}(\zeta) \cdot \mathcal{N}(\mathfrak{q})^{-1/d} \cdot \mathfrak{q}$ and $v_J = u \cdot \exp(\zeta) \cdot \mathcal{N}(\mathfrak{q})^{-1/d} \cdot v_{\mathfrak{q}}$.
5: Compute $\mathbf{B}_J = \mathtt{ReduceIdeal}(J, v_J)$.
6: Let $I' = J \cdot I \cdot \mathcal{N}(I)^{-1/d}$ and $\mathbf{B}_{I'} = \mathtt{MultiplyIdeals}(\mathbf{B}_J, \mathcal{N}(I)^{-1/d} \cdot \mathbf{B}_I)$.
7: Sample $x \leftarrow \mathcal{U}(I' \cap X)$, using $\mathcal{S}$.
8: Let $\mathfrak{b} = x \cdot I'^{-1}$.
9: Let $y = x^{-1} \cdot \mathcal{N}(I)^{-1/d} \cdot v_J$.
10: Return $(\mathfrak{b}, y)$.

Lemma 3.3. *Let $A \geq \max(\delta_K^d, d^d \Delta_K^c)$ for c as in Lemma 2.3. Let X be a compact subset of $K_{\mathbb{R}} \setminus \{0\}$ whose elements are η-balanced for some $\eta > 1$ and satisfy the assumptions of Lemma 3.2 for A and $B = 4A$. Assume that $|\mathcal{P}_{0,A}| / |\mathcal{P}_{0,4A}| \leq c'$ for some $c' < 1$. On input a basis $\mathbf{B}_I$ of an ideal I, $\mathtt{RandomizeIdeal}_{A,X}$ runs in time polynomial in $\log A$, $\log \Delta_K$, $A/|\mathcal{P}_{A,4A}|$ and the size of its input, and returns $(\mathfrak{b}, y)$ satisfying*

$$\mathfrak{b} \in \mathcal{I}_{A,4A},$$
$$y \in \mathfrak{b}^{-1} I^{-1} \setminus \{0\},$$
$$\|y\| \leq 85 \cdot d \cdot \eta \cdot \Delta_K^{1/d} \cdot \mathcal{N}(I\mathfrak{b})^{-1/d}.$$

Finally, if D and $\mathcal{U}$ respectively denote the distribution of $\mathfrak{b}$ and the uniform distribution over $\mathcal{I}_{A,4A}$, then the following holds for any event $E \subseteq \mathcal{I}_{A,4A}$:

$$D(E) \geq \frac{\mathcal{U}(E)}{\Theta(1)} - 2^{-\Omega(d)}.$$

$$D_1 \xrightarrow{\text{SD}=2^{-\Omega(d)}} D_2 \xrightarrow{\text{RD}_\infty=O(1)} D_3 \xleftarrow{\text{SD}=2^{-\Omega(d)}} D_4$$

IdealRound$(\cdot) \downarrow$ $\downarrow$ $\downarrow$ $\downarrow$

$$D = \widetilde{D}_1 \xrightarrow{\text{SD}=2^{-\Omega(d)}} \widetilde{D}_2 \xrightarrow{\text{RD}_\infty=O(1)} \widetilde{D}_3 \xleftarrow{\text{SD}=2^{-\Omega(d)}} \widetilde{D}_4 \xrightarrow{\text{RD}_\infty=O(1)} \mathcal{U}(\mathcal{I}_{A,4A})$$

Fig. 2. Relations between the distributions of the proof of Lemma 3.3.

Proof. We first bound the Euclidean norms of the variables occurring during the execution of the algorithm. By Lemma 2.9 and the assumption that $A \geq \delta_K^d$, we have that $0 < \|v_{\mathfrak{q}}\| \leq 51 \cdot d \cdot (A\Delta_K)^{1/d}$. Now, note that $\|u\|_\infty = 1$, $\|\exp(\zeta)\|_\infty \leq \exp(1/2)$ and $\mathcal{N}(\mathfrak{q})^{-1/d} \leq A^{-1/d}$. We then have $\|v_J\| \leq 85 \cdot d \cdot \Delta_K^{1/d}$ (and $v_J \neq 0$). Then, by Lemma 2.8, we have $0 < \|\mathbf{B}_J\| \leq 85 \cdot d^{1.5} \cdot \delta_K \cdot \Delta_K^{1/d}$ and

$$\|\mathbf{B}_{I'}\| \leq 85 \cdot d^2 \cdot \delta_K \cdot \Delta_K^{1/d} \cdot \mathcal{N}(I)^{-1/d} \cdot \|\mathbf{B}_I\|.$$

As elements of X are non-zero and η-balanced, we have that $\|x^{-1}\|_\infty \leq \eta \cdot \mathcal{N}(x)^{-1/d}$. Also, note that since $\mathcal{N}(I') = 1$, we have $\mathcal{N}(\mathfrak{b}) = \mathcal{N}(x)$. As a result, we obtain that $y \neq 0$ and:

$$\|y\| \leq \mathcal{N}(I)^{-1/d} \cdot \|x^{-1}\|_\infty \cdot \|v_J\|$$
$$\leq \mathcal{N}(I)^{-1/d} \cdot \eta \cdot \mathcal{N}(x)^{-1/d} \cdot 85 \cdot d \cdot \Delta_K^{1/d}$$
$$= 85 \cdot d \cdot \eta \cdot \Delta_K^{1/d} \cdot \mathcal{N}(I\mathfrak{b})^{-1/d}.$$

The latter and the fact that $\mathcal{N}(\mathfrak{b}) = \mathcal{N}(x)$ belongs to $[A, 4A]$ (by assumption on X) provide the first statement on the output.

The previous computations show that every quantity manipulated by the algorithm has size polynomial in $\log A$, $\log \Delta_K$ and the bit-size of the input. Note that SampleWithTrap$_{A,4A}$ runs in polynomial time in $A/|\mathcal{P}_{A,4A}|$. The overall running time is then polynomial in $\log A$, $\log \Delta_K$, $A/|\mathcal{P}_{A,4A}|$ and the size of the input.

We now analyze the distribution of $\mathfrak{b}$. For this purpose, we define the following distributions (see also Fig. 2):

- D_1 is the distribution of J at Step 4;
- D_2 is the distribution $u \cdot \exp(\zeta) \cdot \mathfrak{q} \cdot \mathcal{N}(\mathfrak{q})^{-1/d}$ where $\mathfrak{q}$ is uniform in $\mathcal{P}_{A,4A}$, and u, ζ are sampled as in Steps 2 and 3;
- D_3 is the same as D_2 but with $\mathfrak{q}$ uniform in $\mathcal{P}_{0,4A}$;
- D_4 is $\mathcal{U}(\text{idLat}^0)$.

Note that we have the following relationships between the D_i's:

- $\text{SD}(D_1, D_2) = 2^{-\Omega(d)}$, thanks to Lemma 2.9 and the data processing inequality;
- $\text{RD}_\infty(D_3 \| D_2) = \Theta(1)$, thanks to the assumption on $|\mathcal{P}_{0,A}| / |\mathcal{P}_{0,4A}|$;
- $\text{SD}(D_3, D_4) = 2^{-\Omega(d)}$ thanks to Lemma 2.3.

We also define $\widetilde{D_i}$ (for $i \leq 4$) as the distribution of $\mathfrak{b}$ obtained by sampling J from D_i, setting $I' = J \cdot I \cdot \mathcal{N}(I)^{-1/d}$, sampling x from $\mathcal{U}(I' \cap X)$ and returning $x \cdot I'^{-1}$. Note that $\widetilde{D_1}$ is D and that $\widetilde{D_4}$ is $\mathcal{D}_{\mathrm{Ideal}}(X)$. Indeed, as $\mathcal{U}(\mathrm{idLat}^0)$ is invariant by multiplication by a fixed norm-1 replete ideal, the ideal $I' = J \cdot I \cdot \mathcal{N}(I)^{-1/d}$ is then distributed from $\mathcal{U}(\mathrm{idLat}^0)$. The data-processing inequalities of the statistical distance and Rényi divergence imply that the above relations also hold for $\widetilde{D_i}$ in place of D_i, for all i. Furthermore, by choice of X, the Rényi divergence from $\mathcal{U}(\mathcal{I}_{A,4A})$ to $\widetilde{D_4}$ is equal to $\Theta(1)$.

Using the probability preservation properties of the statistical distance and Rényi divergence, we obtain that for any event $E \subseteq \mathcal{I}_{A,4A}$, we have:

$$\widetilde{D_1}(E) \geq \frac{\mathcal{U}(E) - 2^{-\Omega(d)}}{\Theta(1)} - 2^{-\Omega(d)} = \frac{\mathcal{U}(E)}{\Theta(1)} - 2^{-\Omega(d)}$$

which completes the proof. $\qquad\square$

3.3 From Ideal to Their Inverses

Let $\mathcal{W}$ be a set of fractional ideals. Below, we reduce $\mathcal{W}^{-1}$-avg-id-HSVP to $\mathcal{W}$-avg-id-HSVP and $\mathcal{I}_{A,4A}$-avg-id-HSVP for some appropriate integer A and approximation factors. Recall that $\mathcal{W}^{-1}$ refers to the set $\{I^{-1}, I \in \mathcal{W}\}$.

The reduction is described as an algorithm, $\texttt{InverseToIntegral}_{A,X}^{\mathcal{W}}$ (Algorithm 3.3), which takes as input the inverse I^{-1} of an integral ideal $I \in \mathcal{W}$ and returns a short non-zero element of I^{-1}. It is parametrized by an integer A and a compact set X satisfying the conditions of Lemma 3.2. It relies on four oracles: oracle $\mathcal{O}_{\mathcal{W}}$ for solving $\mathcal{W}$-avg-id-HSVP, oracle $\mathcal{O}_{\mathcal{I}}$ for $\mathcal{I}_{A,4A}$-avg-id-HSVP, oracle $\mathcal{F}$ for factoring integral ideals; and oracle $\mathcal{S}$ for sampling from $I \cap X$ for $I \in \mathrm{idLat}^0$. Recall that $\mathcal{F}$ can be instantiated as a quantum polynomial time algorithm. An instantiation of oracle $\mathcal{S}$ will be provided in Sect. 4, based on the design of a nice set X for Lemma 3.2. The reduction first uses $\mathcal{O}_{\mathcal{W}}$ on the inverse I of its input, which gives a short non-zero vector $v_I \in I$. Then $\texttt{RandomizeIdeal}_{A,X}$ (introduced in the previous subsection) is invoked to randomize I into a uniform integral ideal $\mathfrak{b}$ with norm in $[A, 4A]$. $\texttt{RandomizeIdeal}_{A,X}$ also returns a short non-zero $y_{(I\mathfrak{b})^{-1}}$ in $(I\mathfrak{b})^{-1}$. Then $\mathcal{O}_{\mathcal{I}}$ is invoked on $\mathfrak{b}$ and returns a short non-zero $v_{\mathfrak{b}}$ in $\mathfrak{b}$. The reduction finally outputs $v_{\mathfrak{b}} \cdot y_{(I\mathfrak{b})^{-1}} \in I^{-1}$ that is short and non-zero. The proof of Theorem 3.4 is available in the extended version of this work.

The astute reader will notice that, in the above description, the vector v_I and hence the oracle $\mathcal{O}_{\mathcal{W}}$ do not seem to be used in the subsequent steps. In fact, we will be able to instantiate $\mathcal{S}$ only if given a short basis of I (see Lemma 4.9). The approximation factor reached by $\mathcal{O}_{\mathcal{W}}$ will lead to a lower bound condition on A: the smaller the approximation factor, the smaller the lower bound on A.

Algorithm 3.3 InverseToIntegral$^{\mathcal{W}}$

Input: I^{-1} with $I \in \mathcal{W}$.
Parameters: A integer and $X \subset K_{\mathbb{R}} \setminus \{0\}$ compact.
Oracles: $\mathcal{O}_{\mathcal{W}}$ for $\mathcal{W}$-avg-id-HSVP$_{\gamma_{\mathcal{W}}}$, $\mathcal{O}_{\mathcal{I}}$ for $\mathcal{I}_{A,4A}$-avg-id-HSVP$_{\gamma_{\mathcal{I}}}$,
  $\mathcal{F}$ for factoring integral ideals and $\mathcal{S}$ for sampling from $\mathcal{U}(I \cap X)$ for $I \in$ idLat^0.
Output: $x \in I^{-1} \setminus \{0\}$.

1: Compute $v_I \leftarrow \mathcal{O}_{\mathcal{W}}(I)$.
2: If $v_I = \perp$, then return $\perp$.
3: Compute $\mathbf{B}_I = \texttt{ReduceIdeal}(I, v_I)$.
4: Sample $(\mathfrak{b}, y_{(I\mathfrak{b})^{-1}}) \leftarrow \texttt{RandomizeIdeal}_{A,X}(\mathbf{B}_I)$, using $\mathcal{F}$ and $\mathcal{S}$.
5: Compute $v_{\mathfrak{b}} \leftarrow \mathcal{O}_{\mathcal{I}}(\mathfrak{b})$.
6: If $v_{\mathfrak{b}} = \perp$, then return $\perp$.
7: Return $v_{\mathfrak{b}} \cdot y_{(I\mathfrak{b})^{-1}}$.

Theorem 3.4. *Let $\mathcal{W}$ be a finite set of fractional ideals. Let $\gamma_{\mathcal{W}}, \gamma_{\mathcal{I}} \geq 1$ and $A \geq \max(\delta_K^d, d^d \Delta_K^c)$ for c as in Lemma 2.3. Let X be a compact subset of $K_{\mathbb{R}} \setminus \{0\}$ whose elements are η-balanced for some $\eta > 1$ and satisfy the assumptions of Lemma 3.2 for A and $B = 4A$. Assume that $|\mathcal{P}_{0,A}| / |\mathcal{P}_{0,4A}| \leq c'$ for some constant $c' < 1$. Let $\mathcal{O}_{\mathcal{W}}$ an oracle for $\mathcal{W}$-avg-id-HSVP$_{\gamma_{\mathcal{W}}}$ with success probability $\varepsilon_{\mathcal{W}}$ and $\mathcal{O}_{\mathcal{I}}$ an oracle for $\mathcal{I}_{A,4A}$-avg-id-HSVP$_{\gamma_{\mathcal{I}}}$ with success probability $\varepsilon_{\mathcal{I}}$.*

When given access to $\mathcal{O}_{\mathcal{W}}, \mathcal{O}_{\mathcal{I}}$, an integral ideal-factoring oracle $\mathcal{F}$ and an oracle $\mathcal{S}$ for sampling from $\mathcal{U}(I \cap X)$ for $I \in$ idLat^0, InverseToIntegral$_{A,X}^{\mathcal{W}}$ runs in expected time polynomial in $\log A, \log \Delta_K, A/|\mathcal{P}_{A,4A}|$ and the size of its input. Further, if its input I is such that I is distributed from $\mathcal{U}(\mathcal{W})$, it outputs $x \neq \perp$ with probability $\geq \varepsilon_{\mathcal{I}} \cdot (\varepsilon_{\mathcal{W}}/\Theta(1) - 2^{-\Omega(d)})$. If $x \neq \perp$, then we have

$$x \in I^{-1} \setminus \{0\} \quad and \quad \|x\| \leq \gamma' \cdot \mathrm{Vol}(I^{-1})^{1/d},$$

for $\gamma' = 85 \cdot \gamma_{\mathcal{I}} \cdot \Delta_K^{1/d} \cdot d \cdot \eta$.

Proof. Assume first that neither v_I nor $v_{\mathfrak{b}}$ is equal to $\perp$. As the assumptions of Lemma 3.3 are satisfied, we have $y_{(I\mathfrak{b})^{-1}} \in (I\mathfrak{b})^{-1} \setminus \{0\}$ and

$$\|y_{(I\mathfrak{b})^{-1}}\| \leq 85 \cdot d \cdot \eta \cdot \Delta_K^{1/d} \cdot \mathcal{N}(I\mathfrak{b})^{-1/d}.$$

Now, by assumption, we have that $v_{\mathfrak{b}} \in \mathfrak{b} \setminus \{0\}$ satisfies $\|v_{\mathfrak{b}}\| \leq \gamma_{\mathcal{I}} \cdot \Delta_K^{1/(2d)} \cdot \mathcal{N}(\mathfrak{b})^{1/d}$. We then obtain that $x = v_{\mathfrak{b}} \cdot y_{(I\mathfrak{b})^{-1}} \in I^{-1}$ is non-zero and satisfies:

$$\|x\| \leq \|v_{\mathfrak{b}}\| \cdot \|y_{(I\mathfrak{b})^{-1}}\| \leq \gamma_{\mathcal{I}} \cdot \Delta_K^{3/(2d)} \cdot 85 \cdot d \cdot \eta \cdot \mathcal{N}(I)^{-1/d}.$$

Towards completing the proof, not that the algorithm succeeds if and only if neither v_I nor $v_{\mathfrak{b}}$ is equal to $\perp$. The probability that v_I is not $\perp$ is exactly $\varepsilon_{\mathcal{I}}$. Using Lemma 3.3 with the event E set to $\mathcal{O}_{\mathcal{I}}(\mathfrak{b})$ succeeding, we obtain that $v_{\mathfrak{b}}$ is not $\perp$ with probability $\geq \varepsilon_{\mathcal{W}}/\Theta(1) - 2^{-\Omega(d)}$. Note that the second probability is over the internal randomness of RandomizeIdeal$_{A,X}(\mathbf{B}_I)$. $\square$

4   The Sampling Set

Lemma 3.2 states that if a compact X satisfies a certain number of conditions, then the output distribution of $\mathtt{IdealRound}_X$ resembles the uniform distribution over integral ideals whose norms belong to a prescribed interval. In this subsection, we show that the set $\mathcal{B}^{\eta}_{A,B}$ defined below satisfies those constraints. We will later also use the fact that its elements are η-balanced. An instantiation of the set $\mathcal{B}^{\eta}_{A,B}$ can be visualized in Fig. 1.

Definition 4.1. *Let $B > A > 0$ and $\eta > 1$. We define the set:*

$$\mathcal{B}^{\eta}_{A,B} = \left\{ x \in K^{\times}_{\mathbb{R}} \,\middle|\, \mathcal{N}(x) \in [A, B], \; \left\| \mathrm{Ln}\left(\frac{x}{\mathcal{N}(x)^{1/d}} \right) \right\|_2 \le \ln(\eta) \right\}.$$

The purpose of this section is to prove the following theorem.

Theorem 4.2. *Let $A, B, \eta, \delta > 0$ satisfying $A^{1/d} \ge d^3 \cdot \eta \cdot \max(\Delta_K^{3/(2d)}, \delta)$, $B/A \ge 4$ and $\eta \ge \mathrm{e}$. The set $\mathcal{B}^{\eta}_{A,B}$ is compact and invariant by complex rotations, satisfies the conditions of Lemma 3.2 and its elements are η-balanced. Further, there exists an algorithm $\mathtt{SampleUniform}^{\eta}_{A,B}$ that, given as input a basis $\mathbf{B}_I$ of a norm-1 replete ideal satisfying $\|\mathbf{B}^{\star}_I\| \le \delta$, samples uniformly in $I \cap \mathcal{B}^{\eta}_{A,B}$ and whose expected running time is polynomial in $\log B$, d and B/A.*

4.1   Volume of the Set $\mathcal{B}^{\eta}_{A,B}$

Before proving that the assumptions of Lemma 3.2 are satisfied by $\mathcal{B}^{\eta}_{A,B}$, we first study its volume and its approximate invariance under translation.

Lemma 4.3. *For any $B > A > 0$ and $\eta > 1$, we have*

$$\mathrm{Vol}\left(\mathcal{B}^{\eta}_{A,B}\right) = \frac{2^{d_{\mathbb{R}}} \cdot (2\sqrt{2}\pi)^{d_{\mathbb{C}}} \cdot V_{d_{\mathbb{R}}+d_{\mathbb{C}}-1}}{\sqrt{d}} \cdot (B - A) \cdot (\ln \eta)^{d_{\mathbb{R}}+d_{\mathbb{C}}-1},$$

where V_n is the volume of the n-dimensional unit ℓ_2 hyperball for any $n \ge 1$.

The computation of the volume proceeds by a change of variable, between $\mathbb{R}^d$ and $\sigma(K_{\mathbb{R}})$. The relevant aspect of the volume formula for the present work is the linear dependency in $(B - A) \cdot (\ln \eta)^{d_{\mathbb{R}}+d_{\mathbb{C}}-1}$.

The proof of Lemma 4.3 gives us the volume of the set $\mathcal{B}^{\eta}_{A,B}$, but it also a way to sample uniformly in it.

Lemma 4.4. *There exists a probabilistic algorithm that samples from $\mathcal{U}(\mathcal{B}^{\eta}_{A,B})$ for any $B > A > 0$ and $\eta > 1$. The expected running time of this algorithm is polynomial in $\log B$, d (the degree of K) and B/A.*

4.2 Properties of the Set $\mathcal{B}^{\eta}_{A,B}$

The goal of this subsection is to prove that the set $\mathcal{B}^{\eta}_{A,B}$ satisfies the properties needed to apply Lemma 3.2.

Lemma 4.5. *For any $B > A > 0$ and $\eta > 1$, the set $\mathcal{B}^{\eta}_{A,B}$ is compact, invariant by complex rotations and its elements are η-balanced.*

Proof. Compactness follows from the fact that $\mathcal{B}^{\eta}_{A,B}$ is closed and contained in the ball in infinity norm with radius $\eta \cdot B^{1/d}$. Invariance by complex rotations follows from the fact that both $\mathcal{N}(\cdot)$ and $\mathrm{Ln}(\cdot)$ are invariant by complex rotations (i.e., we have $\mathcal{N}(\zeta x) = \mathcal{N}(x)$ and $\mathrm{Ln}(\zeta x) = \mathrm{Ln}(x)$ if $x \in K_{\mathbb{R}}$ and $\zeta \in K_{\mathbb{R}}$ is such that $|\sigma_i(\zeta)| = 1$ for all i's). Let $x \in \mathcal{B}^{\eta}_{A,B}$, we have that

$$\left\| \frac{x}{\mathcal{N}(x)^{1/d}} \right\|_{\infty} = \exp\left(\left\| \mathrm{Ln}\left(\frac{x}{\mathcal{N}(x)^{1/d}} \right) \right\|_{\infty} \right) \leq \exp\left(\left\| \mathrm{Ln}(\frac{x}{\mathcal{N}(x)^{1/d}}) \right\|_2 \right) \leq \eta.$$

The same holds for $\mathcal{N}(x)^{1/d}/x$ since $\left\| \mathrm{Ln}\left(x/\mathcal{N}(x)^{1/d} \right) \right\|_{\infty} = \left\| \mathrm{Ln}\left(\mathcal{N}(x)^{1/d}/x \right) \right\|_{\infty}$, which proves that x is η-balanced. □

We now prove that the slices $\mathrm{Ln}(\mathcal{B}^{\eta}_{A,B}) \cap H_t$ are empty when $t \notin [\ln A, \ln B]$ and have constant volume otherwise.

Lemma 4.6. *Let $B > A > 0$ and $\eta > 1$. For $t \in \mathbb{R}$, we define $H_t = \{x \in \mathrm{Ln}\,K_{\mathbb{R}} | \sum_i x_i = t\}$. Then $\mathrm{Ln}(\mathcal{B}^{\eta}_{A,B}) \cap H_t = \emptyset$ for $t \notin [\ln A, \ln B]$, and the volume of $\mathrm{Ln}(\mathcal{B}^{\eta}_{A,B}) \cap H_t$ is constant for $t \notin [\ln A, \ln B]$.*

Proof. By definition of $\mathcal{B}^{\eta}_{A,B}$, we have that

$$\mathrm{Ln}\left(\mathcal{B}^{\eta}_{A,B} \right) = \left\{ \mathbf{x} \in \mathrm{Ln}(K_{\mathbb{R}}) : \sum_{i \leq d} x_i \in [\ln A, \ln B], \left\| x - \left(\sum_{i \leq d} x_i \right) \cdot 1_d \right\|_2 \leq \ln \eta \right\},$$

where 1_d refers to the d-dimensional all-1 vector. The intersection with H_t is the empty set if $t \notin [\ln A, \ln B]$. Otherwise, it is the ball centered in $t \cdot 1$ with radius $\ln(\eta)$, whose volume do not depend on t. □

At this stage, only the first condition of Lemma 3.2 remains to be proved. We start by an auxiliary lemma, where we prove that if we shift the set $\mathcal{B}^{\eta}_{A,B}$ by some small vector, then the resulting set is included in another slightly larger set $\mathcal{B}^{\eta'}_{A',B'}$. The parameter f in the lemma below quantifies how small the shift vector needs to be, as a function of the parameters A and η. For the rest of the article, one can think of f as being of the order of $\mathrm{poly}(d)$.

Lemma 4.7. *Let $B > A > 0, \eta > 1$ and $v \in K_{\mathbb{R}}$. Assume that $A^{1/d} \geq \eta \cdot f \cdot \|v\|_{\infty}$ for some $f > 1$. Then*

$$\mathcal{B}^{\eta}_{A,B} + v \subset \mathcal{B}^{\eta'}_{A',B'}$$

with $A' = A \cdot (1 - 1/f)^d$, $B' = B \cdot (1 + 1/f)^d$ and $\eta' = \eta \cdot \exp(2\sqrt{d}/(f - 1))$.

Proof. Let $x \in \mathcal{B}^{\eta}_{A,B}$, we are going to show that $x + v \in \mathcal{B}^{\eta'}_{A',B'}$. The definition of $\mathcal{B}^{\eta}_{A,B}$ and the fact that $A^{1/d} \geq \eta \cdot f \cdot \|v\|_{\infty}$ imply that we have, for every i,

$$\frac{|v_i|}{|x_i|} \leq \frac{\|v\|_{\infty}}{|x_i|} \leq \frac{\|v\|_{\infty} \cdot \eta}{\mathcal{N}(x)^{1/d}} \leq \frac{\|v\|_{\infty} \cdot \eta}{A^{1/d}} \leq \frac{1}{f}.$$

The triangle inequality then gives that $|x_i + v_i| > 0$ for all i, and hence that $x + v \in K^{\times}_{\mathbb{R}}$. Further, note that

$$\frac{\mathcal{N}(x+v)}{\mathcal{N}(x)} = \prod_i \left| \frac{x_i + v_i}{x_i} \right| = \prod_i \left| 1 + \frac{v_i}{x_i} \right|.$$

Since $|v_i/x_i| \leq 1/f$ holds for all i, this implies that $\mathcal{N}(x+v)/\mathcal{N}(x) \in [(1 - 1/f)^d, (1 + 1/f)^d]$, which in turn shows that $\mathcal{N}(x+v) \in [A', B']$.

Towards completing the proof, note that

$$\left\| \text{Ln} \left(\frac{x+v}{\mathcal{N}(x+v)^{1/d}} \right) - \text{Ln} \left(\frac{x}{\mathcal{N}(x)^{1/d}} \right) \right\| = \left\| \text{Ln} \left(1 + \frac{v}{x} \right) - \frac{1}{d} \ln \left(\frac{\mathcal{N}(x+v)}{\mathcal{N}(x)} \right) \cdot \mathbf{1} \right\|$$

$$\leq \left\| \text{Ln} \left(1 + \frac{v}{x} \right) \right\| + \frac{1}{\sqrt{d}} \cdot \left| \ln \left(\frac{\mathcal{N}(x+v)}{\mathcal{N}(x)} \right) \right|$$

$$\leq \sqrt{d} \cdot \frac{\|v/x\|_{\infty}}{1 - \|v/x\|_{\infty}} + \sqrt{d} \cdot \frac{1/f}{1 - 1/f}$$

$$\leq \frac{2\sqrt{d}}{f-1},$$

where we used the fact that

$$|\ln(1+y)| = \max \left(\ln(1+y), \ln \left(1 + \frac{-y}{1+y} \right) \right) \leq \frac{|y|}{1 - |y|},$$

for any $y \in (-1, 1)$. This implies that

$$\left\| \text{Ln} \left(\frac{x+v}{\mathcal{N}(x+v)^{1/d}} \right) \right\| \leq \ln(\eta) + \frac{2\sqrt{d}}{f-1} = \ln(\eta').$$

We conclude that $x + v$ belongs to $\mathcal{B}^{\eta'}_{A',B'}$.   □

We are now ready to prove that the first condition of Lemma 3.2 is satisfied. To count the number of points of the ideal lattice I that belong to $\mathcal{B}^{\eta}_{A,B}$, we tile the space with shifts of a fundamental domain of the lattice (concretely, the Voronoi cell for the ℓ_{∞} norm). Using Lemma 4.7, we show that the union of Voronoi cells corresponding to elements of $I \cap \mathcal{B}^{\eta}_{A,B}$ contains a smaller version $\mathcal{B}^{\eta_0}_{A_0,B_0}$ of the set, and is contained in a larger version $\mathcal{B}^{\eta_1}_{A_1,B_1}$. By carefully choosing parameters, we can ensure that the ratio of volumes of these two sets is bounded from above by a constant. In the lemma statement, note that C' is independent of the ideal I, but may depend on the other parameters, such as A, B, η and K. This proof is an adaptation of [Boe22, Le. 6.13] with $\mathcal{B}^{\eta}_{A,B}$ instead of the ℓ_{∞} ball.

Lemma 4.8. *Let A, B, η verifying $A^{1/d} \geq \eta \cdot d^3 \cdot \Delta_K^{3/(2d)}$, $B/A \geq 4$ and $\eta \geq e$. There exists $C' > 0$ such that for any replete ideal $I \in \mathrm{idLat}^0$, we have*

$$\left| I \bigcap \mathcal{B}_{A,B}^\eta \right| \in C' \cdot [1, 340].$$

Proof. Let I be a norm-1 ideal, and let $V_\infty(I)$ be its ℓ_∞-norm Voronoi cell, i.e., $V_\infty(I) = \{y \in K_\mathbb{R} : \forall x \in I \setminus \{0\}, \|y + x\|_\infty \geq \|y\|_\infty\}$. We let $\mu_\infty(I)$ denote the (ℓ_∞-norm) radius of $V_\infty(I)$. By (1), we have that $\mu_\infty(I) \leq d \cdot \Delta_K^{3/(2d)}$. As a consequence, Lemma 4.7 instantiated with $f = d^2$ gives that since $A^{1/d} \geq \eta \cdot d^3 \cdot \Delta_K^{3/(2d)}$

$$\mathcal{B}_{A,B}^\eta + V_\infty(I) \subset \mathcal{B}_{A_1,B_1}^{\eta_1},$$

with $A_1 = A \cdot (1 - 1/d^2)^d$, $B_1 = B \cdot (1 + 1/d^2)^d$ and $\eta_1 = \eta \cdot \exp(2\sqrt{d}/(d^2 - 1))$. Recall that we assumed that $d \geq 2$ in all the article, so that we have $f > 1$ as needed for Lemma 4.7.

Let $A_0 = A \cdot (1 - 1/d^2)^{-d}$, $B_0 = B \cdot (1 + 1/d^2)^{-d}$ and $\eta_0 = \eta \cdot \exp(-2\sqrt{d}/(d^2 - 1))$. From the lower bound on η (and $d \geq 2$), one can check that $\eta_0 > 1$. Moreover, we have that $B_0/A_0 \geq 1/3 \cdot B/A \geq 4/3$ and hence that $B_0 > A_0$. Finally, from $A_0 \geq A$ and $\eta_0 \leq \eta$, we obtain that $A_0^{1/d} \geq \eta_0 \cdot f \cdot \mu_\infty(I)$ with $f = d^2$. This implies that we can apply Lemma 4.7 again on A_0, B_0, η_0 and $f = d^2$ and we obtain:

$$\mathcal{B}_{A_0,B_0}^{\eta_0} + V_\infty(I) \subset \mathcal{B}_{A,B}^\eta.$$

Note that for any $x \in \mathcal{B}_{A_0,B_0}^{\eta_0}$, there exists some (not necessarily unique) $\ell_x \in I$ such that $x - \ell_x \in V_\infty(I)$. This implies that $\ell_x \in (\mathcal{B}_{A_0,B_0}^{\eta_0} + V_\infty(I)) \cap I$. Therefore, we have

$$\mathcal{B}_{A_0,B_0}^{\eta_0} \subseteq \bigcup_{\ell \in (\mathcal{B}_{A_0,B_0}^{\eta_0} + V_\infty(I)) \cap I} \ell + V_\infty(I) \subseteq \bigcup_{\ell \in \mathcal{B}_{A,B}^\eta \cap I} \ell + V_\infty(I).$$

The above union is made of sets that are disjoints except for volume-0 intersections, so we have

$$\mathrm{Vol}(\mathcal{B}_{A_0,B_0}^{\eta_0}) \leq \mathrm{Vol}\left(\bigcup_{\ell \in \mathcal{B}_{A,B}^\eta \cap I} \ell + V_\infty(I) \right) = \left| \mathcal{B}_{A,B}^\eta \bigcap I \right| \cdot \mathrm{Vol}(V_\infty(I))$$

$$= \left| \mathcal{B}_{A,B}^\eta \bigcap I \right| \cdot \sqrt{\Delta_K}.$$

Similarly, we have:

$$\left| \mathcal{B}_{A,B}^\eta \bigcap I \right| \cdot \sqrt{\Delta_K} \leq \mathrm{Vol}(\mathcal{B}_{A_1,B_1}^{\eta_1}).$$

This gives us

$$\left| \mathcal{B}_{A,B}^\eta \bigcap I \right| \in C' \cdot \left[1, \frac{\mathrm{Vol}(\mathcal{B}_{A_1,B_1}^{\eta_1})}{\mathrm{Vol}(\mathcal{B}_{A_0,B_0}^{\eta_0})} \right],$$

where $C' = \text{Vol}(\mathcal{B}^{\eta_0}_{A_0,B_0})/\sqrt{\Delta_K} > 0$. It remains to bound the right boundary of the interval. By using Lemma 4.3, we obtain that

$$\frac{\text{Vol}(\mathcal{B}^{\eta_1}_{A_1,B_1})}{\text{Vol}(\mathcal{B}^{\eta_0}_{A_0,B_0})} = \frac{(B_1 - A_1) \cdot (\ln \eta_1)^{d_\mathbb{R}+d_\mathbb{C}-1}}{(B_0 - A_0) \cdot (\ln \eta_0)^{d_\mathbb{R}+d_\mathbb{C}-1}} \leq \frac{B_1 - A_1}{B_0 - A_0} \cdot \left(\frac{\ln \eta_1}{\ln \eta_0}\right)^{d-1}.$$

Recall that we have already seen that $B_0/A_0 \geq 4/3$. This implies that

$$\frac{B_1 - A_1}{B_0 - A_0} \leq \frac{B_1}{B_0 - A_0} = \left(1 + \frac{1}{d^2}\right)^{2d} \cdot \frac{1}{1 - (A_0/B_0)} \leq \frac{5}{2} \cdot \frac{1}{1 - 3/4} = 10.$$

Using the fact that $\ln \eta \geq 1$, we also have:

$$\left(\frac{\ln \eta_1}{\ln \eta_0}\right)^{d-1} = \left(\frac{\ln \eta + 2\sqrt{d}/(d^2 - 1)}{\ln \eta - 2\sqrt{d}/(d^2 - 1)}\right)^{d-1} \leq \left(\frac{1 + 2\sqrt{d}/(d^2 - 1)}{1 - 2\sqrt{d}/(d^2 - 1)}\right)^{d-1} \leq 34.$$

This completes the proof.   □

4.3   Sampling Uniform Ideal Elements in $\mathcal{B}^{\eta}_{A,B}$

We now show how to uniformly sample in $I \cap \mathcal{B}^{\eta}_{A,B}$, where I is a norm-1 ideal. For this purpose, $\texttt{SampleUniform}^{\eta}_{A,B}$ (Algorithm 4.1) uniformly samples in a larger $\mathcal{B}^{\eta_1}_{A_1,B_1}$ (using Lemma 4.4) and deterministically round to I using Babai's nearest plane algorithm [Bab86, Th. 3.1]. The sample is kept if it belongs to $\mathcal{B}^{\eta}_{A,B}$.

Algorithm 4.1 $\texttt{SampleUniform}^{\eta}_{A,B}$

Input: $\mathbf{B}_I$ a basis of an ideal $I \in \text{idLat}^0$.
Output: $x \in I \cap \mathcal{B}^{\eta}_{A,B}$.

1: Let $A_1 = A \cdot (1 - 1/d^2)^d$, $B_1 = B \cdot (1 + 1/d^2)^d$ and $\eta_1 = \eta \cdot \exp(2\sqrt{d}/(d^2 - 1))$.
2: **repeat**
3:     Sample $y \leftarrow \mathcal{U}(\mathcal{B}^{\eta'}_{A',B'})$.
4:     Run Babai's nearest plane algorithm on $(\mathbf{B}_I, y)$; let $x \in I$ be the output.
5: **until** $x \in \mathcal{B}^{\eta}_{A,B}$.
6: Return x.

Lemma 4.9. *Let A, B, η with $B/A \geq 4$ and $\eta \geq e$. Let $I \in \text{idLat}^0$ given by a basis $\mathbf{B}_I$ and $\delta = \|\mathbf{B}_I^\star\|$. Assume that $A^{1/d} \geq d^{2.5} \cdot \eta \cdot \delta$. Then $\texttt{SampleUniform}^{\eta}_{A,B}$ samples uniformly in $I \cap \mathcal{B}^{\eta}_{A,B}$ and its expected running time is polynomial in $\log B$, d and B/A.*

Proof. Let $\mathcal{P}(\mathbf{B}_I) = \mathbf{B}_I^\star \cdot (-1/2, 1/2]^d$ be the rounding cell of Babai's nearest plane algorithm. In order to prove that the output distribution is uniform, it suffices to prove that for any point $x \in I \cap \mathcal{B}^{\eta}_{A,B}$, we have $\mathcal{P}(\mathbf{B}_I) + x \subset \mathcal{B}^{\eta_1}_{A_1,B_1}$.

The definition of the nearest-plane algorithm's rounding cell implies that the ℓ_∞ norm of vectors in $\mathcal{P}(\mathbf{B}_I)$ is at most $\sqrt{d}\delta$. The definitions of A_1, B_1, η_1 and Lemma 4.7 (with $f = d^2$) allow us to conclude.

The running time follows from Lemma 4.4 and from bounding the probability that after Step 4, we have $x \notin \mathcal{B}^\eta_{A,B}$. This occurs if $y \notin \cup_{x \in \mathcal{B}^\eta_{A,B} \cap I} (x + \mathcal{P}(\mathbf{B}_I))$. As in the proof of Lemma 4.8, we have that:

$$\mathcal{B}^{\eta_0}_{A_0,B_0} \subset \sum_{x \in \mathcal{B}^\eta_{A,B} \cap I} x + \mathcal{P}(\mathbf{B}_I),$$

where $A_0 = A \cdot (1 + 1/d^2)^d$, $B_0 = B \cdot (1 - 1/d^2)^d$ and $\eta_0 = \eta \cdot \exp(-2\sqrt{d}/(d^2 - 1))$. The probability of exiting the loop is then bounded from below by

$$\frac{\mathrm{Vol}(\mathcal{B}^{\eta_0}_{A_0,B_0})}{\mathrm{Vol}(\mathcal{B}^{\eta_1}_{A_1,B_1})} \geq \frac{B_0 - A_0}{B_1 - A_1} \cdot \frac{(\ln \eta_0)^{d-1}}{(\ln \eta_1)^{d-1}} \geq \Omega(1),$$

where the inequalities are as in the proof of Lemma 4.8. $\square$

5 Wrapping up

We combine Theorems 3.4 and 4.2 to obtain the main result from this work. To simplify the statement, we instantiate the integral ideal-factoring oracle with a quantum polynomial-time algorithm, and use the Extended Riemann Hypothesis. The latter allows us to bound $|\mathcal{P}_{0,A}| / |\mathcal{P}_{0,4A}|$ by a constant that is < 1 when $A \geq (\log \Delta_K)^{\Omega(1)}$ and $A/|\mathcal{P}_{A,4A}|$ by $O(\ln A)$ (see [BS96, Th. 8.7.4]).

Theorem 5.1 (ERH). *There exists $C_K = (d\delta_K \Delta_K^{1/d})^{O(1)}$ such that the following holds. Let $\mathcal{W}$ be a finite set of fractional ideals. Let $\gamma_\mathcal{W}, \gamma_\mathcal{I} \geq 1$ and A with $A^{1/d} \geq C_K \cdot \gamma_\mathcal{W}$. Let $\mathcal{O}_\mathcal{W}$ an oracle for $\mathcal{W}$-avg-id-HSVP$_{\gamma_\mathcal{W}}$ with success probability $\varepsilon_\mathcal{W}$ and $\mathcal{O}_\mathcal{I}$ an oracle for $\mathcal{I}_{A,4A}$-avg-id-HSVP$_{\gamma_\mathcal{I}}$ with success probability $\varepsilon_\mathcal{I}$.*

There exists a quantum algorithm making one call to $\mathcal{O}_\mathcal{W}$ and one call to $\mathcal{O}_\mathcal{I}$ whose running time is polynomial in $\log A$, $\log \Delta_K$ and the size of its input, such that the following holds. Given as input $I \sim \mathcal{U}(\mathcal{W})$, it outputs $x \in I^{-1} \setminus \{0\}$ with probability $\geq \varepsilon_\mathcal{I} \cdot (\varepsilon_\mathcal{W}/\Theta(1) - 2^{-\Omega(d)})$ such that

$$\|x\| \leq \gamma' \cdot \mathrm{Vol}(I^{-1})^{1/d} \quad \text{with} \quad \gamma' = 232 \cdot d \cdot \Delta_K^{1/d} \cdot \gamma_\mathcal{I}.$$

As a corollary, we obtain a quantum reduction from $\mathcal{I}_{A,4A}^{-1}$-avg-id-HSVP$_{\gamma'}$ to $\mathcal{I}_{A,4A}$-avg-id-HSVP$_\gamma$ and from $\mathcal{P}_{A,4A}^{-1}$-avg-id-HSVP$_{\gamma'}$ to $\mathcal{P}_{A,4A}$-avg-id-HSVP$_\gamma$ if $A^{1/d} \geq (d\delta_K \Delta_K^{1/d})^{\Omega(1)} \cdot \gamma$ and $\gamma' = O(d\Delta_K^{1/d}) \cdot \gamma$. Note that in the case of prime ideals, the success probability decreases with $\tilde{\rho}_A$ (the inverse of the proportion of prime ideals among all ideals of norm $\leq A$), which may or may not be small depending on the choice of the field K. This dependency arises from hoping that a uniform integral ideal is prime.

Corollary 5.2 (ERH). *There exists* $C_K = (d\delta_K \Delta_K^{1/d})^{O(1)}$ *such that the following holds. Let* $\gamma \geq 1$ *and* A *with* $A^{1/d} \geq C_K \cdot \gamma$. *Let* $\mathcal{O}$ *an oracle for* $\mathcal{I}_{A,4A}$-*avg-id-HSVP*$_\gamma$ *with success probability* $\varepsilon \geq 2^{-\Omega(d)}$.

There exists a quantum algorithm making two calls to $\mathcal{O}$ *whose running time is polynomial in* $\log A$, $\log \Delta_K$ *and the size of its input, such that, given as input* $\mathfrak{a} \sim \mathcal{U}(\mathcal{I}_{A,4A})$, *it outputs* $x \in \mathfrak{a}^{-1} \setminus \{0\}$ *with probability* $\Omega(\varepsilon^2)$ *with*

$$\|x\| \leq \gamma' \cdot \mathrm{Vol}(\mathfrak{a}^{-1})^{1/d} \quad \text{with} \quad \gamma' = 232 \cdot d \cdot \Delta_K^{1/d} \cdot \gamma.$$

Corollary 5.3 (ERH). *There exists* $C_K = (d\delta_K \Delta_K^{1/d})^{O(1)}$ *such that the following holds. Let* $\gamma \geq 1$ *and* A *with* $A^{1/d} \geq C_K \cdot \gamma$. *Let* $\mathcal{O}$ *an oracle for* $\mathcal{P}_{A,4A}$-*avg-id-HSVP*$_\gamma$ *with success probability* $\varepsilon \geq 2^{-\Omega(d)}$.

There exists a quantum algorithm making two calls to $\mathcal{O}$ *whose running time is polynomial in* $\log A$, $\log \Delta_K$ *and the size of its input, such that, given as input* $\mathfrak{p} \sim \mathcal{U}(\mathcal{P}_{A,4A})$, *it outputs* $x \in \mathfrak{p}^{-1} \setminus \{0\}$ *with probability* $\Omega(\varepsilon^2/\tilde{\rho}_A)$ *with*

$$\|x\| \leq \gamma' \cdot \mathrm{Vol}(\mathfrak{p}^{-1})^{1/d} \quad \text{with} \quad \gamma' = 232 \cdot d \cdot \Delta_K^{1/d} \cdot \gamma.$$

Combining Corollary 5.3 with Theorem 2.10, we obtain a quantum worst-case to average-case reduction for ideal-HSVP, where the average-case distribution is the uniform distribution over prime ideals with norm in some interval $[A, 4A]$.

Corollary 5.4 (ERH). *Let* $\gamma \geq 1$. *There exists some* $\gamma' = \gamma \cdot \mathrm{poly}(\Delta_K^{1/d}$, $\log \Delta_K, \delta_K)$ *and* $A = \gamma^d \cdot \mathrm{poly}(\Delta_K, (\log \Delta_K)^d, \delta_K^d)$ *such that*

$$\text{id-HSVP}_{\gamma'} \quad \text{reduces to} \quad \mathcal{P}_{A,4A}\text{-avg-id-HSVP}_\gamma.$$

The reduction is quantum and runs in expected time polynomial in its input size, $\log \Delta_K$, $1/\tilde{\rho}_A$ *and* $1/\varepsilon$, *where* ε *is the success probability of the oracle solving* $\mathcal{P}_{A,4A}$-*avg-id-HSVP*$_\gamma$.

6 NTRU with Polynomial Modulus

The main result of this section is Corollary 6.3. It gives a distribution over NTRU instances with small modulus q that is hard on average, under the worst-case id-HSVP hardness assumption. For a full description of this result, see the extended version of this paper.

Definition 6.1 ([PS21, Def. 3.1 and 3.4]). *Let* $\gamma \geq \gamma' \geq 1$ *be real numbers. Let* $q \geq 2$ *be an integer.*

- *A* (γ, q)-*NTRU instance is an element* $h \in \mathcal{O}_K/q\mathcal{O}_K$ *such that there exists* $(f, g) \in \mathcal{O}_K \setminus \{(0,0)\}$ *verifying* $f = h \cdot g \bmod q$ *and* $\|f\|, \|g\| \leq \sqrt{q}/\gamma$.

- *The* (γ, γ', q)-*NTRU problem asks, given a* (γ, q)-*NTRU instance* h, *to find* $(f, g) \in \mathcal{O}_K \setminus \{(0,0)\}$ *verifying* $f = h \cdot g \bmod q$ *and* $\|f\|, \|g\| \leq \sqrt{q}/\gamma'$.

- *Let D be a distribution over (γ, q)-NTRU instances. The (D, γ, γ', q)-NTRU problem asks to solve (γ, γ', q)-NTRU for an instance sampled from D, with non-negligible probability (over the choice of the instance and the internal randomness of the algorithm).*

Note that in this work we are only interested in the vector version of NTRU from [PS21]. We let `IdealToNTRU` denote [PS21, Alg. 4.1]. It takes as input a basis of an integral ideal $\mathfrak{a}$ and a modulus q and outputs an instance of (γ, q)-NTRU whose solution is related to a short non-zero vector of $\mathfrak{a}$. The following result is a consequence of [PS21, Le. 4.3], whose proof is very similar to [PS21, Th. 4.1]. We provide a proof for the sake of completeness.

Theorem 6.2 (Adapted from [PS21, Th. 4.1]). *Let $\gamma \geq \gamma' \geq 1$ be real numbers, $q \geq 2$ be an integer, and*

$$N = \frac{1}{2^{d+2}} \cdot \left(\frac{\sqrt{q}}{\gamma \cdot d^{1.5} \cdot \delta_K \cdot \Delta_K^{1/(2d)}} \right)^d .$$

Let $\mathfrak{a}$ be an integral ideal of norm in $[N, 2^{d+2} \cdot N]$ and $h = \text{IdealToNTRU}(\mathfrak{a}, q)$. Then h is a (γ, q)-NTRU instance. If (f, g) is a solution to (γ, γ', q)-NTRU on instance h, then g is a solution to γ_{HSVP}-id-HSVP for instance $\mathfrak{a}$, where $\gamma_{\text{HSVP}} = \gamma/\gamma' \cdot 4d^{1.5} \cdot \delta_K$.

Further, `IdealToNTRU` runs in time polynomial in its input size and in $\log \Delta_K$.

Note that the statement is void if $2^{d+2} \cdot N < 1$ (no integral ideal has norm in $(0, 1)$): an extra parameter constraint is implicitly required for it to be meaningful.

For $A, q \geq 2$, we define $D_{\text{NTRU}}^{A,q} = \text{IdealToNTRU}(\mathcal{U}(\mathcal{P}_{A,4A}), q)$. Theorem 6.2 implies a polynomial-time reduction from $\mathcal{I}_{A,4A}$-avg-id-HSVP to $(D_{\text{NTRU}}^{A,q}, \gamma, \gamma', q)$-NTRU for well chosen γ, γ', A and q. Combining Corollary 5.4 and Theorem 6.2 give the following result.

Corollary 6.3 (ERH). *Let $\gamma \geq \gamma' \geq 1$. There exists an integer $q = (\gamma^4/\gamma'^2) \cdot \text{poly}(\Delta_K^{1/d}, \log \Delta_K, \delta_K)$, and real numbers $\gamma_{\text{HSVP}} = (\gamma/\gamma') \cdot \text{poly}(\Delta_K^{1/d}, \log \Delta_K, \delta_K)$ and $A = (\gamma/\gamma')^d \cdot \text{poly}(\Delta_K, (\log \Delta_K)^d, \delta_K^d)$ such that*

$$\text{id-HSVP}_{\gamma_{\text{HSVP}}} \quad \text{reduces to} \quad (D_{\text{NTRU}}^{A,q}, \gamma, \gamma', q)\text{-NTRU}.$$

The reduction is quantum and runs in expected time polynomial in its input size, $\log q$, $\log \Delta_K$, $1/\tilde{\rho}_A$ and $1/\varepsilon$, where ε is the success probability of the oracle solving $(D_{\text{NTRU}}^{A,q}, \gamma, \gamma', q)$-NTRU.

Proof. Without loss of generality, we can assume that $\gamma/\gamma' \leq 2^d$, since otherwise we have a polynomial time algorithm solving id-HSVP$_{\gamma_{\text{HSVP}}}$ for $\gamma_{\text{HSVP}} = \gamma/\gamma'$. Let $\Gamma = (\gamma/\gamma') \cdot 4d^{1.5} \cdot \delta_K$. Let $A = \Gamma^d \cdot \text{poly}(\Delta_K, (\log \Delta_K)^d, \delta_K^d)$ be as in Corollary 5.4, with "$\gamma = \Gamma$". Similarly, let $\gamma_{\text{HSVP}} = \Gamma \cdot \text{poly}(\Delta_K^{1/d}, \log \Delta_K, \delta_K)$ be the quantity γ' from Corollary 5.4, with "$\gamma = \Gamma$". Finally, let $X = \gamma \cdot 2 \cdot (4A)^{1/d}$.

$d^{1.5} \cdot \delta_K \cdot \Delta_K^{1/(2d)}$ and $q = \lfloor X^2 \rfloor$. Note that $q \geq X^2/4$. Note that $\gamma_{\mathrm{HSVP}} = (\gamma/\gamma') \cdot$
$\mathrm{poly}(\Delta_K^{1/d}, \log \Delta_K, \delta_K)$ and that $q = (\gamma^4/\gamma'^2) \cdot \mathrm{poly}(\Delta_K^{1/d}, \log \Delta_K, \delta_K)$.

Let $N = \frac{1}{2^{d+2}} \cdot \left(\frac{\sqrt{q}}{\gamma \cdot d^{1.5} \cdot \delta_K \cdot \Delta_K^{1/(2d)}} \right)^d$ be as in Theorem 6.2. Using the fact that
$X/2 \leq \sqrt{q} \leq X$ and the definition of X, we have that $[A, 4A] \subseteq [N, 2^{d+2} \cdot N]$.
Hence, the support of the distribution $\mathcal{U}(\mathcal{P}_{A,4A})$ is contained in the set of integral
ideals with norm in $[N, 2^{d+2} \cdot N]$.

Recall that $D_{\mathrm{NTRU}}^{A,q}$ is the distribution $\texttt{IdealToNTRU}(\mathcal{U}(\mathcal{P}_{A,4A}), q)$. By Theorem 6.2, there is a reduction from $\mathcal{P}_{A,4A}$-avg-id-HSVP$_\Gamma$ to $(D_{\mathrm{NTRU}}^{A,q}, \gamma, \gamma', q)$-
NTRU, which runs in time polynomial in $\log q$, $\log \Delta_K$ and $\log A = \mathrm{poly}(\log \Delta_K)$
(since $\gamma/\gamma' \leq 2^d$) and preserves the success probability of the algorithm. Moreover, from Corollary 5.4, id-HSVP$_{\gamma_{\mathrm{HSVP}}}$ reduces to $\mathcal{P}_{A,4A}$-avg-id-HSVP$_\Gamma$, which
is quantum and runs in expected time polynomial in its input size, $\log \Delta_K$, $1/\tilde{\rho}_A$
and $1/\varepsilon$. Combining both reductions gives the desired result. $\square$

Note that the distribution $D_{\mathrm{NTRU}}^{A,q}$ can be sampled from along with a trapdoor
by running $\texttt{SampleWithTrap}$ with appropriate parameters (in order to generate
an ideal from $\mathcal{U}(\mathcal{P}_{A,4A})$ together with a short non-zero vector in it), and then
running the $\texttt{IdealToNTRU}$ algorithm. This, however, requires an access to a factoring oracle (for the $\texttt{SampleWithTrap}$ algorithm). Finding a classical algorithm
to efficiently sample from $D_{\mathrm{NTRU}}^{A,q}$ with a trapdoor is an interesting open problem.

Acknowledgments. The authors thank Koen de Boer, Guillaume Hanrot, Aurel Page
and Noah Stephens-Davidowitz for helpful discussions. Joël Felderhoff is funded by the
Direction Générale de l'Armement (Pôle de Recherche CYBER). The authors were
supported by the CHARM ANR-NSF grant (ANR-21-CE94-0003) and by the PEPR
quantique France 2030 programme (ANR-22-PETQ-0008).

References

[ABD16] Albrecht, M., Bai, S., Ducas, L.: A subfield lattice attack on overstretched
NTRU assumptions. In: Robshaw, M., Katz, J. (eds.) CRYPTO 2016.
LNCS, vol. 9814, pp. 153–178. Springer, Heidelberg (2016). https://doi.
org/10.1007/978-3-662-53018-4_6

[Bab86] Babai, L.: On Lovász' lattice reduction and the nearest lattice point problem. Combinatorica (1986)

[BDPW20] de Boer, K., Ducas, L., Pellet-Mary, A., Wesolowski, B.: Random self-reducibility of ideal-SVP via Arakelov random walks. In: Micciancio, D.,
Ristenpart, T. (eds.) CRYPTO 2020. LNCS, vol. 12171, pp. 243–273.
Springer, Cham (2020). https://doi.org/10.1007/978-3-030-56880-1_9

[BEP22] Boudgoust, K., Gachon, E., Pellet-Mary, A.: Some easy instances of Ideal-SVP and implications on the partial Vandermonde knapsack problem.
In: Dodis, Y., Shrimpton, T. (eds.) CRYPTO 2022, vol. 13508. Springer,
Cham (2022). https://doi.org/10.1007/978-3-031-15979-4_17

[BL94] Buchmann, J.A., Lenstra, H.W.: Computing maximal orders and factoring over $\mathbb{Z}_p$. Preprint (1994)

[Boe22] de Boer, K.: Random Walks on Arakelov Class Groups. Ph.D. thesis, Leiden University (2022). Available on request from the author

[BS96] Bach, E., Shallit, J.O.: Algorithmic Number Theory: Efficient Algorithms. MIT Press (1996)

[BST+20] Bhargava, M., Shankar, A., Taniguchi, T., Thorne, F., Tsimerman, J., Zhao, Y.: Bounds on 2-torsion in class groups of number fields and integral points on elliptic curves. J. AMS (2020)

[CDPR16] Cramer, R., Ducas, L., Peikert, C., Regev, O.: Recovering short generators of principal ideals in cyclotomic rings. In: Fischlin, M., Coron, J.-S. (eds.) EUROCRYPT 2016. LNCS, vol. 9666, pp. 559–585. Springer, Heidelberg (2016). https://doi.org/10.1007/978-3-662-49896-5_20

[CDW17] Cramer, R., Ducas, L., Wesolowski, B.: Short stickelberger class relations and application to ideal-SVP. In: Coron, J.-S., Nielsen, J.B. (eds.) EUROCRYPT 2017. LNCS, vol. 10210, pp. 324–348. Springer, Cham (2017). https://doi.org/10.1007/978-3-319-56620-7_12

[CJL16] Cheon, J.H., Jeong, J., Lee, C.: An algorithm for NTRU problems and cryptanalysis of the GGH multilinear map without a low-level encoding of zero. LMS J. Comput. Math. (2016)

[Coh96] Cohen, H.: A Course in Computational Algebraic Number Theory. Springer, Cham (1996)

[FPS22] Felderhoff, J., Pellet-Mary, A., Stehlé, D.: On module unique-SVP and NTRU. In: Agrawal, S., Lin, D. (eds.) ASIACRYPT 2022. LNCS, vol. 13793, pp. 709–740. Springer, Cham (2022). https://doi.org/10.1007/978-3-031-22969-5_24

[Gen09a] Gentry, C.: A Fully Homomorphic Encryption Scheme. Ph.D. thesis, Stanford University (2009)

[Gen09b] Gentry, C.: Fully homomorphic encryption using ideal lattices. In: STOC (2009)

[Gen10] Gentry, C.: Toward basing fully homomorphic encryption on worst-case hardness. In: Rabin, T. (ed.) CRYPTO 2010. LNCS, vol. 6223, pp. 116–137. Springer, Heidelberg (2010). https://doi.org/10.1007/978-3-642-14623-7_7

[KF17] Kirchner, P., Fouque, P.-A.: revisiting lattice attacks on overstretched NTRU parameters. In: Coron, J.-S., Nielsen, J.B. (eds.) EUROCRYPT 2017. LNCS, vol. 10210, pp. 3–26. Springer, Cham (2017). https://doi.org/10.1007/978-3-319-56620-7_1

[LM06] Lyubashevsky, V., Micciancio, D.: Generalized compact knapsacks are collision resistant. In: ICALP (2006)

[LPR10] Lyubashevsky, V., Peikert, C., Regev, O.: On ideal lattices and learning with errors over rings. In: Gilbert, H. (ed.) EUROCRYPT 2010. LNCS, vol. 6110, pp. 1–23. Springer, Heidelberg (2010). https://doi.org/10.1007/978-3-642-13190-5_1

[MG02] Micciancio, D., Goldwasser, S.: Complexity of Lattice Problems: A Cryptographic Perspective. Springer, New York (2002). https://doi.org/10.1007/978-1-4615-0897-7

[Mic02] Micciancio, D.: Generalized compact knapsacks, cyclic lattices, and efficient one-way functions from worst-case complexity assumptions. In: FOCS (2002)

[Neu13] Neukirch, J.: Algebraic Number Theory. Springer (2013)

[PHS19] Pellet-Mary, A., Hanrot, G., Stehlé, D.: Approx-SVP in ideal lattices with pre-processing. In: Ishai, Y., Rijmen, V. (eds.) EUROCRYPT 2019. LNCS, vol. 11477, pp. 685–716. Springer, Cham (2019). https://doi.org/10.1007/978-3-030-17656-3_24

[PML21] Porter, C., Mendelsohn, A., Ling, C.: Subfield algorithms for Ideal- and Module-SVP based on the decomposition group. IACR Cryptol. ePrint Arch. (2021)

[PR06] Peikert, C., Rosen, A.: Efficient collision-resistant hashing from worst-case assumptions on cyclic lattices. In: TCC (2006)

[PRS17] Peikert, C., Regev, O., Stephens-Davidowitz, N.: Pseudorandomness of ring-LWE for any ring and modulus. In: STOC (2017)

[PS21] Pellet-Mary, A., Stehlé, D.: On the hardness of the NTRU problem. In: Tibouchi, M., Wang, H. (eds.) ASIACRYPT 2021. LNCS, vol. 13090, pp. 3–35. Springer, Cham (2021). https://doi.org/10.1007/978-3-030-92062-3_1

[PXWC21] Pan, Y., Xu, J., Wadleigh, N., Cheng, Q.: On the ideal shortest vector problem over random rational primes. In: Canteaut, A., Standaert, F.-X. (eds.) EUROCRYPT 2021. LNCS, vol. 12696, pp. 559–583. Springer, Cham (2021). https://doi.org/10.1007/978-3-030-77870-5_20

[Reg05] Regev, O.: On lattices, learning with errors, random linear codes, and cryptography. In: STOC (2005)

[Sho94] Shor, P.W.: Algorithms for quantum computation: discrete logarithms and factoring. In: FOCS (1994)

[SSTX09] Stehlé, D., Steinfeld, R., Tanaka, K., Xagawa, K.: Efficient public key encryption based on ideal lattices. In: Matsui, M. (ed.) ASIACRYPT 2009. LNCS, vol. 5912, pp. 617–635. Springer, Heidelberg (2009). https://doi.org/10.1007/978-3-642-10366-7_36

[Web08] Weber, H.: Lehrbuch der algebra, vol. ii. Vieweg und Sohn, Braunschweig (1908)

Revocable Cryptography from Learning with Errors

Prabhanjan Ananth[1], Alexander Poremba[2(✉)] [iD],
and Vinod Vaikuntanathan[3] [iD]

[1] UC Santa Barbara, Santa Barbara, USA
prabhanjan@cs.ucsb.edu
[2] California Institute of Technology, Pasadena, USA
aporemba@caltech.edu
[3] Massachusetts Institute of Technology, Cambridge, USA
vinodv@mit.edu

Abstract. Quantum cryptography leverages unique properties of quantum information in order to construct cryptographic primitives that are oftentimes impossible classically. In this work, we build on the no-cloning principle of quantum mechanics and design cryptographic schemes with *key revocation capabilities*. We consider schemes where secret keys are represented as quantum states with the guarantee that, once the secret key is successfully revoked from a user, they no longer have the ability to perform the same functionality as before.

We define and construct several fundamental cryptographic primitives with *key-revocation capabilities*, namely pseudorandom functions, secret-key and public-key encryption, and even fully homomorphic encryption, assuming the quantum sub-exponential hardness of the learning with errors problem. Central to all our constructions is our method of making the Dual-Regev encryption (Gentry, Peikert and Vaikuntanathan, STOC 2008) scheme revocable.

1 Introduction

Quantum computing presents exciting new opportunities for cryptography, using remarkable properties of quantum information to construct cryptographic primitives that are unattainable classically. At the heart of quantum cryptography lies the *no-cloning principle* [30,57] of quantum information which stipulates that it is fundamentally impossible to copy an unknown quantum state. Indeed, Wiesner [56] in his seminal work from the 1970s used the no-cloning principle to construct a quantum money scheme, wherein quantum states are used to construct banknotes that can be verified to be authentic (using a secret key) but cannot be counterfeited. Ever since this watershed moment, and especially so in the recent years, a wide variety of primitives referred to as *unclonable* primitives have been studied and constructed in the context of encryption [21,23,36,38], digital signatures [46] and pseudorandom functions [27].

Full version at https://eprint.iacr.org/2023/325.

ⓒ International Association for Cryptologic Research 2023
G. Rothblum and H. Wee (Eds.): TCC 2023, LNCS 14372, pp. 93–122, 2023.
https://doi.org/10.1007/978-3-031-48624-1_4

Our Work: Revocable Cryptography. Delegation and revocation of privilege are problems of great importance in cryptography. Indeed, the problem of revocation in the context of digital signatures and certificates in the classical world is a thorny problem [50,52]. In this work, we undertake a systematic study of *revocable (quantum) cryptography* which allows us to delegate and revoke privileges in the context of several fundamental cryptographic primitives. This continues a recent line of work in quantum cryptography dealing with revoking (or certifiably deleting) states such as quantum ciphertexts or simple quantum programs [11,14,21,36,39,48,54]. In this framework, revocation is to be understood from the perspective of the recipient of the quantum state; namely, the recipient can certify the loss of certain privileges by producing a certificate (either classical or quantum) which can be verified by another party.

As a motivating example, consider the setting of an employee at a company who takes a vacation and wishes to authorize a colleague to perform certain tasks on her behalf, tasks that involve handling sensitive data. Since the sensitive data is (required to be) encrypted, the employee must necessarily share her decryption keys with her colleague. When she returns from vacation, she would like to have her decryption key back; naturally, one would like to ensure that her colleague should not be able to decrypt future ciphertexts (which are encrypted under the same public key) once the key is "returned". Evidently, if the decryption key is a classical object, this is impossible to achieve as the key can be copied at will.

In revocable (quantum) cryptography, we associate a cryptographic functionality, such as decryption using a secret key, with a quantum state in such a way that a user can compute this functionality if and only if they are in possession of the quantum state. We then design a revocation algorithm which enables the user to certifiably return the quantum state to the owner. Security requires that once the user returns the state (via our revocation algorithm), they should not have the ability to evaluate the functionality (e.g. decrypt ciphertexts) anymore. We refer to this new security notion as *revocation security.*

Another, possibly non-obvious, application is to detecting malware attacks. Consider a malicious party who hacks into an electronic device and manages to steal a user's decryption keys. If cryptographic keys are represented by classical bits, it is inherently challenging to detect such attacks that compromise user keys. For all we know, the intruder could have stolen the user's decryption keys without leaving a trace. Indeed, a few years ago, decryption keys which were used to protect cell-phone communications [41] were successfully stolen by spies without being detected.[1] With revocable cryptography, a malicious user successfully stealing a user key would invariably revoke the decryption capability from the user. This latter event can be detected.

Our Results in a Nutshell. We construct revocable cryptographic objects under standard cryptographic assumptions. Our first main result constructs a key-revocable public-key encryption scheme, and our second main result constructs a key-revocable pseudorandom function. We obtain several corollaries and exten-

---

[1] The attack would indeed have gone undetected but for the Snowden revelations.

sions, including key-revocable secret-key encryption and key-revocable fully homomorphic encryption. In all these primitives, secret keys are represented as quantum states that retain the functionality of the original secret keys. We design revocation procedures and guarantee that once a user successfully passes the procedure, they cannot compute the functionality any more.

All our constructions are secure under the quantum subexponential hardness of learning with errors [49]—provided that revocation succeeds with high probability. At the heart of all of our contributions lies our result which shows that the Dual-Regev public-key encryption scheme of [34] satisfies revocation security.

Related Notions. There are several recent notions in quantum cryptography that are related to revocability. Of particular relevance is the stronger notion of copy-protection introduced by Aaronson [1]. Breaking the revocable security of a task gives the adversary a way to make two copies of a (possibly different) state both of which are capable of computing the same functionality. Thus, copy-protection is a stronger notion. However, the only known constructions of copy-protection schemes [27,46] rely on the heavy hammer of *post-quantum secure* indistinguishability obfuscation for which there are no known constructions based on well-studied assumptions. Our constructions, in contrast, rely on the post-quantum hardness of the standard learning with errors problem. A different related notion is the significantly weaker definition of secure software leasing [11] which guarantees that once the quantum state computing a functionality is returned, the *honest evaluation algorithm* cannot compute the original functionality. Yet another orthogonal notion is that of certifiably deleting *ciphertexts*, originating from the works of Unruh [54] and Broadbent and Islam [21]. In contrast, our goal is to delegate and revoke *cryptographic capabilities* enabled by private keys. For detailed comparisons, we refer the reader to Sect. 1.5.

1.1 Our Contributions in More Detail

We present our results in more detail below. First, we introduce the notion of key-revocable public-key encryption. Our main result is that the Dual-Regev public-key encryption scheme [34] satisfies revocation security. After that, we study revocation security in the context of fully homomorphic encryption and pseudorandom functions.

Key-Revocable Public-Key Encryption. We consider public-key encryption schemes where the decryption key, modeled as a quantum state, can be delegated to a third party and can later be revoked [36]. The syntax of a key-revocable public-key scheme (Definition 1) is as follows:

- KeyGen(1^λ): this is a setup procedure which outputs a public key PK, a master secret key MSK and a decryption key ρ_{SK}. While the master secret key is typically a classical string, the decryption key is modeled as a quantum state. (The use cases of MSK and ρ_{SK} are different, as will be evident below.)

- Enc(PK, x): this is the regular classical encryption algorithm which outputs a ciphertext CT.
- Dec(ρ_{SK}, CT): this is a quantum algorithm which takes as input the quantum decryption key ρ_{SK} and a classical ciphertext, and produces a plaintext.
- Revoke(PK, MSK, σ): this is the revocation procedure that outputs Valid or Invalid. If σ equals the decryption key ρ_{SK}, then Revoke outputs Valid with high probability.

After the decryption key is returned, we require that the sender loses its ability to decrypt ciphertexts. This is formalized as follows (see Definition 2): conditioned on revocation being successful, no adversary can distinguish whether it is given an encryption of a message versus the uniform distribution over the ciphertext space with advantage better than $\mathsf{negl}(\lambda)$. Moreover, we require that revocation succeeds with a probability negligibly close to 1 (more on this later). We prove the following.

Theorem 1 (Informal). *Assuming that the* LWE *and* SIS *problems with subexponential modulus are hard against quantum adversaries running in subexponential time, there exists a key-revocable public-key encryption scheme.*

Due to the quantum reduction from SIS to LWE [51], the two assumptions are, in some sense, equivalent. Therefore, we can in principle rely on the subexponential hardness of LWE alone.

Our work improves upon prior works, which either use post-quantum secure indistinguishability obfuscation [27,36] or consider the weaker private-key setting [44].

Key-Revocable Public-Key Encryption with Classical Revocation. Our previous notion of key-revocable encryption schemes models the key as a quantum state which can later be "returned." One may therefore reasonably ask whether it is possible to achieve a classical notion of revocation, similar to the idea of deletion certificates in the context of quantum encryption [14,21,39,40,48]. Rather then return a quantum decryption key, the recipient would simply apply an appropriate measurement (as specified by a procedure Delete), and output a classical certificate which can be verified using Revoke. We also consider key-revocable public-key encryption scheme with classical revocation hich has the same syntax as a regular key-revocable public-key scheme, except that revocation process occurs via the following two procedures:

- Delete(ρ_{SK}): this takes as input a quantum decryption key ρ_{SK}, and produces a classical revocation certificate π.
- Revoke(PK, MSK, π): this takes as input the (classical) master secret key MSK and a (classical) certificate π, and outputs Valid or Invalid. If π is the output of Delete(ρ_{SK}), then Revoke outputs Valid with high probability.

Our notion of security is essentially the same as for a regular key-revocable public-key encryption scheme where revocation is quantum. We prove the following in the full version of the paper.

Theorem 2 (Informal). *Assuming that the* LWE *and* SIS *problems with subexponential modulus are hard against quantum adversaries running in subexponential time, there exists a key-revocable public-key encryption scheme with classical revocation.*

The assumptions required for the theorem are essentially the same as for our previous Dual-Regev scheme.

Key-Revocable Fully Homomorphic Encryption. We go beyond the traditional public-key setting and design the first *fully homomorphic encryption* (FHE) scheme [20,33] with key-revocation capabilities. Our construction is based on a variant of the (leveled) FHE scheme of Gentry, Sahai and Waters [35], which we extend to a key-revocable encryption scheme using Gaussian superpositions. The syntax of a key-revocable FHE scheme is the same as in the key-revocable public-key setting from before (Definition 1), except for the additional algorithm Eval which is the same as in a regular FHE scheme. We prove the following in the full version of the paper.

Theorem 3 (Informal). *Assuming that the* LWE *and* SIS *problems with subexponential modulus are hard against quantum adversaries running in subexponential time, there exists a key-revocable (leveled) fully homomorphic encryption scheme.*

We prove the theorem by invoking the security of our key-revocable Dual-Regev public-key encryption scheme in Sect. 3. Similar to the case of revocable PKE with classical revocation, we can also consider revocable FHE with classical revocation, which can be achieved based on the same assumptions as above.

(Key-)Revocable Pseudorandom Functions. We consider other cryptographic primitives with key-revocation capabilities that go beyond decryption functionalities; specifically, we introduce the notion of *key-revocable* pseudorandom functions (PRFs) with the following syntax:

- $\mathsf{Gen}(1^\lambda)$: outputs a PRF key k, a quantum key ρ_k and a master key MSK.
- $\mathsf{PRF}(k; x)$: on key k and input x, output a value y. This is deterministic.
- $\mathsf{Eval}(\rho_k, x)$: on input a state ρ_k and an input x, output a value y.
- $\mathsf{Revoke}(\mathsf{MSK}, \sigma)$: on input a verification key MSK and state σ, outputs Valid or Invalid.

After the quantum key ρ_k is successfully returned, we require that the sender loses its ability to evaluate the PRF. This is formalized as follows: no efficient adversary can simultaneously pass the revocation phase and succeed in distinguishing the output of a pseudorandom function on a random challenge input x^* versus uniform with advantage better than $\mathsf{negl}(\lambda)$. In fact, we consider a more general definition where the adversary receives many challenge inputs instead of just one.

We give the first construction of key-revocable pseudorandom functions (PRFs) from standard assumptions. Previous schemes implicit in [27] either require indistinguishability obfuscation, or considered weaker notions of revocable PRFs in the form of *secure software leasing* [11,45], which merely prevents the possiblity of *honestly* evaluating the PRF once the key is revoked.

Since in the context of pseudorandom functions, it is clear what is being revoked, we instead simply call the notion revocable pseudorandom functions. We prove the following in the full version of the paper.

Theorem 4 (Informal). *Assuming that the* LWE *and* SIS *problems with subexponential modulus are hard against quantum adversaries running in subexponential time, there exist key-revocable pseudorandom functions.*

Revocable pseudorandom functions immediately give us key-revocable (manytime secure) secret-key encryption schemes. We also revocable PRFs with classical revocation can be achieved based on the same assumptions as above.

Inverse Polynomial Revocation Based on SDRE *Conjectures.* In all the results above, we assume that the probability of revocation is negligibly close to 1. Even in this restrictive setting, our proofs turn out to be highly non-trivial and require careful use of a diverse set of techniques! Moreover, to date, no constructions of key-revocable PRFs or FHE were known based on assumptions weaker than post-quantum iO.

A natural question to explore is whether we can achieve the following stronger security notion of revocable public-key encryption: if the adversary successfully revokes with inverse polynomial probability then semantic security of revocable PKE still holds. If we can achieve this stronger notion of revocable PKE then we would also achieve the corresponding stronger notions of revocable PRFs and FHE based on the same computational assumptions.

In the full version, we show how to achieve all of our results based on a conjecture, that we call *Simultaneous Dual-Regev Extraction* (SDRE) conjecture. Informally, the conjecture states that if Dual-Regev PKE is not key-revocable then there exists a QPT adversary who given a Gaussian superposition $|\psi_{\mathbf{y}}\rangle$ of short preimages mapping a random matrix $\mathbf{A}$ to a vector $\mathbf{y}$ can simultaneously produce $|\psi_{\mathbf{y}}\rangle$ and a short vector in the support of $|\psi_{\mathbf{y}}\rangle$ with non-negligible probability. In more detail, the qSDRE conjecture states the following: suppose the Dual-Regev PKE is not key-revocable (according to the above stronger definition) then there exists a QPT adversary $\mathcal{A} = (\mathcal{A}_1, \mathcal{A}_2)$ such that:

- $\mathcal{A}_1$ is given $(\mathbf{A}, \mathbf{y}, |\psi_{\mathbf{y}}\rangle)$, where $\mathbf{A} \xleftarrow{\$} \mathbb{Z}_q^{n \times m}$ and $|\psi_{\mathbf{y}}\rangle$ is a Gaussian superposition of all the short vectors mapping $\mathbf{A}$ to $\mathbf{y}$. It produces a bipartite state on two registers R and AUX.
- A projective measurement on R is applied that projects onto the state $|\psi_{\mathbf{y}}\rangle\langle\psi_{\mathbf{y}}|$, and $\mathcal{A}_2$ is run on AUX. We require that the (simultaneous) probability that the projective measurement succeeds and $\mathcal{A}_2$ outputs a short preimage mapping $\mathbf{A}$ to $\mathbf{y}$ should be inverse polynomial.

The difficulty in proving the conjecture lies in the fact that one needs to invoke the LWE assumption with respect to $\mathcal{A}_2$ who holds AUX, while at the same time guaranteeing that an inefficient projective measurement succeeds on a separate register R. We leave proving (or refuting) the above conjecture to future works.

We also consider another variant of the above conjecture where $\mathcal{A}_1$ is instead given $|\psi_{\mathbf{y}}^{\mathbf{v}}\rangle$, which is essentially $|\psi_{\mathbf{y}}\rangle$, except that a phase of $\omega_q^{\langle \mathbf{x}, \lfloor \frac{q}{\nu} \rfloor \cdot \mathbf{v}\rangle}$ is planted for the term $|\mathbf{x}\rangle$ in the superposition. $\mathcal{A}_2$ is expected to output $\mathsf{CT} \approx \mathbf{S}^\mathsf{T}\mathbf{A} + \lfloor \frac{q}{\nu} \rfloor \cdot \mathbf{v}^\mathsf{T}$, for some $\mathbf{S} \in \mathbb{Z}_q^n$, on the register R. We refer to this conjecture as cSDRE (i.e., 'c' stands for classical revocation).

Discussion: Unclonable Cryptography from LWE. Over the years, the existence of many fundamental cryptographic primitives such as pseudorandom functions [13], fully homomorphic encryption [20], attribute-based encryption [18] and succinct argument systems [26] have been based on the existence of learning with errors. In fact, as far as we know, there are only a few foundational primitives remaining (indistinguishability obfuscation is one such example) whose existence is not (yet) known to be based on learning with errors.

The situation is quite different in the world of unclonable cryptography. Most of the prominent results have information-theoretic guarantees but restricted functionalities [21,23] or are based on the existence of post-quantum indistinguishability obfuscation [27,58]. While there are works [45] that do propose lattice-based constructions of unclonable primitives, there are still many primitives, such as quantum money and quantum copy-protection, whose feasibility we would like to establish based on the post-quantum hardness of the learning with errors (or other such relatively well-studied assumptions). We hope that our work presents a new toolkit towards building more unclonable primitives from LWE.

Independent and Concurrent Work. Independently and concurrently[2], Agrawal et al. [5] explored the notion of public-key encryption with secure leasing which is related to key-revocable public-key encryption. We highlight the differences below:

- *Advanced notions*: We obtain key-revocable *fully homomorphic encryption* and key-revocable *pseudorandom functions* which are unique to our work. They explore other notions of advanced encryption with secure leasing including attribute-based encryption and functional encryption, which are not explored in our work.
- *Security definition*: We consider the stronger notion of classical revocation[3] whereas they consider quantum revocation.
- *Public-key encryption*: They achieve a generic construction based on any post-quantum secure public-key encryption[4] whereas our notion is based on the post-quantum hardness of the learning with errors problem or the SDRE conjecture. Their construction of revocable public-key encryption involves many complex abstractions whereas our construction is based on the versatile Dual-Regev public-key encryption scheme.

---

[2] Both of our works were posted online around the same time.

[3] The stronger notion was updated in our paper subsequent to posting of our and their work.

[4] Their construction achieves the stronger definition where the revocation only needs to succeed with inverse polynomial probability.

1.2 Overview

We now give a technical overview of our constructions and their high level proof ideas. We begin with the key-revocable public-key encryption construction. A natural idea would be to start with Regev's public-key encryption scheme [49] and to then upgrade the construction in order to make it revocable. However, natural attempts to associate an unclonable quantum state with the decryption key fail and thus, we instead consider the Dual-Regev public-key encryption scheme and make it key-revocable. We describe the scheme below.

Key-Revocable Dual-Regev Public-Key Encryption. Our first construction is based on the *Dual-Regev* public-key encryption scheme [34] and makes use of Gaussian superpositions which serve as a quantum decryption key. We give an overview of Construction 1 below.

- KeyGen(1^n): sample a matrix $\mathbf{A} \in \mathbb{Z}_q^{n \times m}$ along with a *short trapdoor basis* $\mathsf{td}_{\mathbf{A}}$. To generate the decryption key, we employ the following procedure[5]: Using the matrix $\mathbf{A}$ as input, first create a Gaussian superposition of short vectors in $\mathbb{Z}^m \cap (-\frac{q}{2}, \frac{q}{2}]^m$, denoted by[6]

$$|\psi\rangle = \sum_{\mathbf{x} \in \mathbb{Z}_q^m} \rho_\sigma(\mathbf{x}) |\mathbf{x}\rangle \otimes |\mathbf{A} \cdot \mathbf{x} \ (\mathrm{mod}\ q)\rangle$$

where $\rho_\sigma(\mathbf{x}) = \exp(-\pi \|\mathbf{x}\|^2 / \sigma^2)$ is the Gaussian measure, for some $\sigma > 0$. Next, measure the second register which partially collapses the superposition and results in the *coset state*

$$|\psi_{\mathbf{y}}\rangle = \sum_{\substack{\mathbf{x} \in \mathbb{Z}_q^m: \\ \mathbf{Ax} = \mathbf{y} \ (\mathrm{mod}\ q)}} \rho_\sigma(\mathbf{x}) |\mathbf{x}\rangle$$

for some outcome $\mathbf{y} \in \mathbb{Z}_q^n$. Finally, we let $|\psi_{\mathbf{y}}\rangle$ be the decryption key ρ_{SK}, $(\mathbf{A}, \mathbf{y})$ be the public key PK, and we let the trapdoor $\mathsf{td}_{\mathbf{A}}$ serve as the master secret key MSK.

- Enc(PK, μ) is identical to Dual-Regev encryption. To encrypt a bit $\mu \in \{0, 1\}$, sample a random string $\mathbf{s} \xleftarrow{\$} \mathbb{Z}_q^n$ together with discrete Gaussian errors $\mathbf{e} \in \mathbb{Z}^m$ and $e' \in \mathbb{Z}$, and output the (classical) ciphertext CT given by

$$\mathsf{CT} = (\mathbf{s}^\mathsf{T}\mathbf{A} + \mathbf{e}^\mathsf{T}, \mathbf{s}^\mathsf{T}\mathbf{y} + e' + \mu \cdot \lfloor \tfrac{q}{2} \rfloor) \ \in \mathbb{Z}_q^m \times \mathbb{Z}_q.$$

- Dec($\rho_{\mathsf{SK}}, \mathsf{CT}$): to decrypt a ciphertext CT using the decryption key $\rho_{\mathsf{SK}} = |\psi_{\mathbf{y}}\rangle$, first apply the unitary $U : |\mathbf{x}\rangle |0\rangle \to |\mathbf{x}\rangle |\mathsf{CT} \cdot (-\mathbf{x}, 1)^\mathsf{T}\rangle$ on input $|\psi_{\mathbf{y}}\rangle |0\rangle$, and then measure the second register in the computational basis. Because $|\psi_{\mathbf{y}}\rangle$ is

---

[5] In the full version of the paper, this is formalized as the procedure GenGauss.
[6] Note that the state is not normalized for convenience.

a superposition of short vectors $\mathbf{x}$ subject to $\mathbf{A} \cdot \mathbf{x} = \mathbf{y} \pmod{q}$, we obtain an approximation of $\mu \cdot \lfloor \frac{q}{2} \rfloor$ from which we can recover μ.[7]

- Revoke($\mathsf{PK}, \mathsf{MSK}, \rho$): to verify the returned state ρ given as input the public key $(\mathbf{A}, \mathbf{y})$ and master secret key $\mathsf{td}_\mathbf{A}$, apply the projective measurement $\{|\psi_\mathbf{y}\rangle\langle\psi_\mathbf{y}|, I - |\psi_\mathbf{y}\rangle\langle\psi_\mathbf{y}|\}$ onto ρ. Output Valid, if the measurement succeeds, and output Invalid, otherwise.

Implementing Revocation, Efficiently. Note that performing a projective measurement onto a fixed Gaussian state $|\psi_\mathbf{y}\rangle$ is, in general, computationally infeasible. In fact, if it were to be possible to efficiently perform this projection using $(\mathbf{A}, \mathbf{y})$ alone, then one could easily use such a procedure to solve the short integer solution (SIS) problem. Fortunately, we additionally have the trapdoor for $\mathbf{A}$ at our disposal in order to perform such a projection.

One of our contributions is to design a *quantum discrete Gaussian sampler for q-ary lattices*[8] which, given as input $(\mathbf{A}, \mathbf{y}, \mathsf{td}_\mathbf{A}, \sigma)$, implements a unitary that efficiently prepares the Gaussian superposition $|\psi_\mathbf{y}\rangle$ from scratch with access to the trapdoor $\mathsf{td}_\mathbf{A}$. At a high level, our Gaussian sampler (formally stated in the full version) can be alternately thought of as an explicit quantum reduction from the *inhomogenous* SIS problem [6] to the search variant of the LWE problem.

Insight: Reduction to SIS. Our goal is to use the state returned by the adversary and to leverage the indistinguishability guarantee in order to break some computational problem. It should seem suspicious whether such a reduction is even possible: after all the adversary is returning the state we gave them! *How could this possibly help?* Our main insight lies in the following observation: while the adversary does eventually return the state we give them, the only way it can later succeed in breaking the semantic security of dual Regev PKE is if it retains useful information about the state. If we could somehow extract this information from the adversary, then using the extracted information alongside the returned state, we could hope to break some computational assumption. For instance, suppose we can extract a short vector $\mathbf{x}$ such that $\mathbf{A} \cdot \mathbf{x} = \mathbf{y} \pmod{q}$. By measuring the state returned by the adversary, we could then hope to get a second short vector $\mathbf{x}'$ such that $\mathbf{A} \cdot \mathbf{x}' = \mathbf{y} \pmod{q}$, and from this, we can recover a short solution in the kernel of $\mathbf{A} \in \mathbb{Z}_q^{n \times m}$.

Even if, for a moment, we disregard the issue of being able to extract $\mathbf{x}$ from the adversary, there are still some important missing steps in the above proof template:

- Firstly, measuring the returned state should give a vector different from $\mathbf{x}$ with non-negligible probability. In order to prove this, we need to argue that the squared ampltidue of every term is bounded away from 1. In the full version, we prove this statement holds as long as $\mathbf{A}$ is full rank.

---

[7] For appropriate choices of parameters, decryption via rounding succeeds at outputting μ with overwhelming probability and hence we can invoke the "almost as good as new" lemma [2] to recover the original state $|\psi_\mathbf{y}\rangle$.

[8] In the full version of the paper, this is formalized as the procedure QSampGauss.

- Secondly, the reduction to SIS would only get as input $\mathbf{A}$ and not a trapdoor for $\mathbf{A}$. This means that it will no longer be possible for the reduction to actually check whether the state returned by the adversary is valid. We observe that, instead of first verifying whether the returned state is valid and then measuring in the computational basis, we can in fact skip verification and immediately go ahead and measure the state in the computational basis; this is implicit in the analysis in the proof the distinct pair extraction lemma (see full version).
- Finally, the adversary could have entangled the returned state with its residual state in such a way that measuring the returned state always yields the same vector $\mathbf{x}$ as the one extracted from the adversary. In the same analysis in the proof of the distinct pair extraction lemma, we prove that, even if the adversary entangles its state with the returned state, with non-negligible probability we get two distinct short vectors mapping $\mathbf{A}$ to $\mathbf{y}$.

All that is left is to argue that it is possible to extract $\mathbf{x}$ from the adversary while simultaneously verifying whether the returned state is correct or not. To show that we can indeed extract another short pre-image from the adversary's quantum side information, we make use of what we call a *simultaneous search-to-decision reduction with quantum auxiliary input* for the Dual-Regev scheme.

Main Contribution: Simultaneous Search-to-Decision Reduction with Quantum Advice. Informally, our theorem says the following: any successful Dual-Regev distinguisher with access to quantum side information AUX (which depends on the decryption key) can be converted into a successful extractor that finds a key on input AUX – even conditioned on Revoke succeeding on a seperate register R. We now present some intuition behind our proof.

Suppose there exists a successful Dual-Regev distinguisher $\mathcal{D}$ (as part of the adversary $\mathcal{A}$) that, given quantum auxiliary information AUX, can distinguish between $(\mathbf{s}^\mathsf{T}\mathbf{A} + \mathbf{e}^\mathsf{T}, \mathbf{s}^\mathsf{T}\mathbf{y} + e')$ and uniform $(\mathbf{u}, r) \in \mathbb{Z}_q^m \times \mathbb{Z}_q$ with advantage ϵ.

Ignoring Register R: For now, let us ignore the fact that Revoke is simultaneously applied on system R. Inspired by techniques from the *leakage resilience* literature [31], we now make the following observation. Letting $\mathbf{y} = \mathbf{A} \cdot \mathbf{x}_0 \pmod{q}$, for some Gaussian vector $\mathbf{x}_0$ with distribution proportional to $\rho_\sigma(\mathbf{x}_0)$, the former sample can be written as $(\mathbf{s}^\mathsf{T}\mathbf{A}+\mathbf{e}^\mathsf{T}, (\mathbf{s}^\mathsf{T}\mathbf{A}+\mathbf{e}^\mathsf{T}) \cdot \mathbf{x}_0 + e')$. Here, we assume a *noise flooding* regime in which the noise magnitude of e' is significantly larger than that of $\mathbf{e}^\mathsf{T} \cdot \mathbf{x}_0$. Because the distributions are statistically close, the distinguisher $\mathcal{D}$ must succeed at distinguishing the sample from uniform with probability negligibly close to ϵ. Finally, we invoke the LWE assumption and claim that the same distinguishing advantage persists, even if we replace $(\mathbf{s}^\mathsf{T}\mathbf{A} + \mathbf{e}^\mathsf{T})$ with a random string $\mathbf{u} \in \mathbb{Z}_q^m$. Here, we rely on the fact that the underlying LWE sample is, in some sense, independent of the auxiliary input AUX handed to the distinguisher $\mathcal{D}$. To show that this is the case, we need to argue that the reduction can generate the appropriate inputs to $\mathcal{D}$ on input $\mathbf{A}$; in particular it should be able to generate the auxiliary input AUX (which depends on a state $|\psi_\mathbf{y}\rangle$), while simultaneously producing a Gaussian vector $\mathbf{x}_0$ such that $\mathbf{A} \cdot \mathbf{x}_0 = \mathbf{y} \pmod{q}$.

Note that this seems to violate the SIS assumption, since the ability to produce both a superposition $|\psi_{\mathbf{y}}\rangle$ of pre-images and a single pre-image $\mathbf{x}_0$ would allow one to obtain a collision for $\mathbf{y}$.

Invoking Gaussian-Collapsing: To overcome this issue, we ask the reduction to generate the quantum auxiliary input in a different way; rather than computing AUX as a function of $|\psi_{\mathbf{y}}\rangle$, we compute it as a function of $|\mathbf{x}_0\rangle$, where $\mathbf{x}_0$ results from *collapsing* the state $|\psi_{\mathbf{y}}\rangle$ via a measurement in the computational basis. By invoking the *Gaussian collapsing property* [48], we can show that the auxiliary information computed using $|\psi_{\mathbf{y}}\rangle$ is computationally indistinguishable from the auxiliary information computed using $|\mathbf{x}_0\rangle$. Once we invoke the collapsed version of $|\psi_{\mathbf{y}}\rangle$, we can carry out the reduction and conclude that $\mathcal{D}$ can distinguish between the samples $(\mathbf{u}, \mathbf{u}^\mathsf{T}\mathbf{x}_0)$ and $(\mathbf{u}, r)$, where $\mathbf{u}$ and r are random and $\mathbf{x}_0$ is Gaussian, with advantage negligibly close to ϵ.[9] Notice that $\mathcal{D}$ now resembles a so-called *Goldreich-Levin* distinguisher [37].

Reduction to Goldreich-Levin: Assuming the existence of a quantum Goldreich-Levin theorem for the field $\mathbb{Z}_q$, one could then convert $\mathcal{D}$ into an extractor that extracts $\mathbf{x}_0$ with high probability. Prior to our work, a quantum Goldreich-Levin theorem was only known for $\mathbb{Z}_2$ [4,27]. In particular, it is unclear how to extend prior work towards higher order fields $\mathbb{Z}_q$ because the interference pattern in the analysis of the quantum extractor does not seem to generalize beyond the case when $q = 2$. Fortunately, we can rely on the *classical* Goldreich-Levin theorem for finite fields due to Dodis et al. [31], as well as recent work by Bitansky, Brakerski and Kalai. [17] which shows that a large class of classical reductions can be generically converted into a quantum reductions. This allows us to obtain the first quantum Goldreich-Levin theorem for large fields, which we prove formally in the full version. Specifically, we can show that a distinguisher $\mathcal{D}$ that, given auxiliary input AUX, can distinguish between $(\mathbf{u}, \mathbf{u}^\mathsf{T}\mathbf{x}_0)$ and $(\mathbf{u}, r)$ with advantage ε can be converted into a quantum extractor that can extract $\mathbf{x}_0$ given AUX in time $\mathrm{poly}(1/\varepsilon, q)$ with probability $\mathrm{poly}(\varepsilon, 1/q)$.

Incorporating the Revoked Register R: To complete the security proof behind our key-revocable Dual-Regev scheme, we need to show something *stronger*; namely, we need to argue that the Goldreich-Levin extractor succeeds on input AUX – even conditioned on the fact that Revoke outputs Valid when applied on a separate register R (which may be entangled with AUX). We can consider two cases based on the security definition.

– Revocation succeeds with probability negligibly close to 1: in this case, applying the revocation or not does not make a difference since the state before applying revocation is negligibly close (in trace distance) to the state after applying revocation. Thus, the analysis is essentially the same as the setting where we ignore the register R.

---

[9] Technically, $\mathcal{D}$ can distinguish between $(\mathbf{u}, \mathbf{u}^\mathsf{T}\mathbf{x}_0 + e')$ and $(\mathbf{u}, r)$ for a Gaussian error e'. However, by defining a distinguisher $\tilde{\mathcal{D}}$ that first shifts $\mathbf{u}$ by a Gaussian vector e' and then runs $\mathcal{D}$, we obtain the desired distinguisher.

- Revocation is only required to succeed with probability $1/\text{poly}(\lambda)$: in this case, we do not know how to formally prove that the extractor and Revoke simultaneously succeed with probability $1/\text{poly}(\lambda)$. Thus, we state this as a conjecture (see full version of this paper) and leave the investigation of this conjecture to future works.

1.3 Key-Revocable Dual-Regev Encryption with Classical Revocation

Recall that our key-revocable Dual-Regev public-key encryption scheme requires that a quantum state is *returned* as part of revocation. In the full version, we give a Dual-Regev encryption scheme with *classical key revocation*. The idea behind our scheme is the following: We use the same Gaussian decryption key from before, except that we also plant an appropriate phase into the state

$$|\psi_{\mathbf{y}}^{\mathbf{v}}\rangle = \mathbf{Z}_q^{\lfloor \frac{q}{\nu} \rfloor \cdot \mathbf{v}} |\psi_{\mathbf{y}}\rangle = \sum_{\substack{\mathbf{x} \in \mathbb{Z}_q^m \\ \mathbf{Ax}=\mathbf{y}}} \rho_\sigma(\mathbf{x}) \, \omega_q^{\langle \mathbf{x}, \lfloor \frac{q}{\nu} \rfloor \cdot \mathbf{v}\rangle} \, |\mathbf{x}\rangle \,,$$

where $\mathbf{Z}_q$ is the generalized q-ary Pauli-Z operator, $\mathbf{v} \xleftarrow{\$} \{0,1\}^m$ is a random string and ν is a sufficiently large integer with $\nu \ll q$ (to be determined later). The reason the complex phase is useful is the following: To revoke, we simply ask the recipient of the state to apply the Fourier transform and to measure in the computational basis. This results in a shifted LWE sample

$$\mathbf{w} = \hat{\mathbf{s}}^\mathsf{T}\mathbf{A} + \lfloor \frac{q}{\nu} \rfloor \cdot \mathbf{v}^\mathsf{T} + \hat{\mathbf{e}}^\mathsf{T} \in \mathbb{Z}_q^m \,,$$

where $\hat{\mathbf{s}}$ is random and $\hat{\mathbf{e}}$ is Gaussian. Note that $\mathbf{w}$ can easily be decrypted with access to a short trapdoor basis for $\mathbf{A} \in \mathbb{Z}_q^{n \times m}$. In particular, we will accept the *classical* revocation certificate $\mathbf{w}$ if and only if it yields the string $\mathbf{v}$ once we decrypt it. This way there is no need to return a quantum state as part of revocation, and we can essentially "force" the adversary to forget the decryption key. Here, we crucially rely on the fact that Dual-Regev decryption keys are encoded in the *computational basis*, whereas the revocation certificate can only be obtained via a measurement in the incompatible *Fourier basis*. Intuitively, it seems impossible for any computationally bounded adversary to recover both pieces of information *at the same time*.

To prove security, we follow a similar proof as in our previous construction from Sect. 3. First, we observe that any successful distinguisher that can distinguish Dual-Regev from uniform with quantum auxiliary input AUX (once revocation has taken place) can be converted into an extractor that obtains a valid pre-image of $\mathbf{y}$. Here, we use our Goldreich-Levin search-to-decision reduction with quantum auxiliary input. However, because the information returned to the challenger is not in fact a superposition of pre-images anymore, we cannot hope to break SIS as we did before. Instead, we make the following observation: if the adversary simultaneously succeeds at passing revocation as well as distinguishing Dual-Regev ciphertexts from uniform, this means the adversary

- knows an LWE encryption $\mathbf{w} \in \mathbb{Z}_q^m$ that yields $\mathbf{v} \in \{0,1\}^m$ when decrypted using a short trapdoor basis for $\mathbf{A} \in \mathbb{Z}_q^{n \times m}$, and
- can extract a short pre-image of $\mathbf{y}$ from its auxiliary input Aux.

In other words, the adversary simultaneously knows information about the computational basis as well as the Fourier domain of the Gaussian superposition state. We show that this violates a generic collapsing-type property of the Ajtai hash function recently proven by Bartusek, Khurana and Poremba [15, Theorem 5.5], which relies on the hardness of subexponential LWE and SIS.

1.4   Applications

We leverage our result of key-revocable Dual-Regev encryption to get key-revocable fully homomorphic encryption and revocable pseudorandom functions. While our constructions can easily be adapted to enable *classical revocation* (via our Dual-Regev scheme with classical key revocation), we choose to focus on the quantum revocation setting for simplicity.

Key-Revocable Dual-Regev Fully Homomorphic Encryption. Our first application of our key-revocable public-key encryption concerns fully homomorphic encryption schemes. In the full version, we extend our key-revocable Dual-Regev scheme towards a (leveled) FHE scheme by using the DualGSW variant of the FHE scheme by Gentry, Sahai and Waters [35,47].

To encrypt a bit $\mu \in \{0,1\}$ with respect to the public-key $(\mathbf{A}, \mathbf{y})$, sample a matrix $\mathbf{S} \xleftarrow{\$} \mathbb{Z}_q^{n \times N}$ together with a Gaussian error matrix $\mathbf{E} \in \mathbb{Z}^{m \times N}$ and row vector $\mathbf{e} \in \mathbb{Z}^N$, and output the ciphertext

$$\mathsf{CT} = \begin{bmatrix} \mathbf{A}^\mathsf{T}\mathbf{S}+\mathbf{E} \\ \mathbf{y}^\mathsf{T}\mathbf{S}+\mathbf{e} \end{bmatrix} + \mu \cdot \mathbf{G} \ (\mathrm{mod}\ q) \in \mathbb{Z}_q^{(m+1) \times N}.$$

Here, $\mathbf{G}$ is the *gadget matrix* which converts a binary vector in into its field representation over $\mathbb{Z}_q$. As before, the decryption key consists of a Gaussian superposition $|\psi_\mathbf{y}\rangle$ of pre-images of $\mathbf{y}$.

Note that the DualGSW ciphertext can be thought of as a column-wise concatenation of N-many independent Dual-Regev ciphertexts. In the full version, we prove the security of our construction by invoking the security of our key-revocable Dual-Regev scheme.

Revocable Pseudorandom Functions. Our next focus is on leveraging the techniques behind key-revocable public-key encryption to obtain revocable pseudorandom functions. Recall that the revocation security of pseudorandom functions stipulates the following: any efficient adversary (after successfully revoking the state that enables it to evaluate pseudorandom functions) cannot distinguish whether it receives pseudorandom outputs on many challenge inputs versus strings picked uniformly at random with advantage better than $\mathsf{negl}(\lambda)$. An astute reader might notice that revocation security does not even imply the traditional pseudorandomness guarantee! Hence, we need to additionally impose the requirement that a revocable pseudorandom function should also satisfy the traditional pseudorandomness guarantee.

Towards realizing a construction satisfying our definitions, we consider the following template:

1. First show that there exists a μ-revocable pseudorandom function for $\mu = 1$. Here, μ-revocation security means the adversary receives μ-many random inputs after revocation.
2. Next, we show that any 1-revocable pseudorandom function also satisfies the stronger notion of revocation security where there is no a priori bound on the number of challenge inputs received by the adversary.
3. Finally, we show that we can generically upgrade any revocable PRF in such a way that it also satisfies the traditional pseudorandomness property.

The second bullet is proven using a hybrid argument. The third bullet is realized by combining a revocable PRF with a post-quantum secure PRF (not necessarily satisfying revocation security).

Hence, we focus the rest of our attention on proving the first bullet.

1-Revocation Security. We start with the following warmup construction. The secret key k comprises of matrices $\mathbf{A}, \{\mathbf{S}c_{i,0}, \mathbf{S}c_{i,1}\}_{i \in [\ell], b \in \{0,1\}}$, where $\mathbf{A} \xleftarrow{\$} \mathbb{Z}_q^{n \times m}$, $\mathbf{S}c_{i,b} \in \mathbb{Z}_q^{n \times n}$ such that all $\mathbf{S}c_{i,b}$ are sampled from some error distribution and the output of the pseudorandom function on x is denoted to be $\lfloor \sum_{i \in [\ell]} \mathbf{S}c_{i,x_i} \mathbf{A} \rceil_p$, where $q \gg p$ and $\lfloor \cdot \rceil_p$ refers to a particular rounding operation modulo p.

In addition to handing out a regular PRF key k, we also need to generate a quantum key ρ_k such that, given ρ_k and any input x, we can efficiently compute $\mathsf{PRF}(k, x)$. Moreover, ρ_k can be revoked such that any efficient adversary after revocation loses the ability to evaluate the pseudorandom function. To enable the generation of ρ_k, we first modify the above construction. We generate $\mathbf{y} \in \mathbb{Z}_q^n$ and include this as part of the key. The modified pseudorandom function, on input x, outputs $\lfloor \sum_{i \in [\ell]} \mathbf{S}c_{i,x_i} \mathbf{y} \rceil_p$. We denote $\sum_{i \in [\ell]} \mathbf{S}c_{i,x_i}$ by $\mathbf{S}c_x$ and, with this new notation, the output of the pseudorandom function can be written as $\lfloor \mathbf{S}_x \mathbf{y} \rceil_p$.

With this modified construction, we now describe the elements as part of the quantum key ρ_k:

- For every $i \in [\ell]$, include $\mathbf{S}_{i,b}\mathbf{A} + \mathbf{E}_{i,b}$ in ρ_k, where $i \in [\ell]$ and $b \in \{0,1\}$. We sample $\mathbf{S}_{i,b}$ and $\mathbf{E}_{i,b}$ from a discrete Gaussian distribution with appropriate standard deviation $\sigma > 0$.
- Include $|\psi_{\mathbf{y}}\rangle$ which, as defined in the key-revocable Dual-Regev construction, is a Gaussian superposition of short solutions mapping $\mathbf{A}$ to $\mathbf{y}$.

To evaluate on an input x using ρ_k, compute $\sum_i \mathbf{S}_{i,x_i}\mathbf{A} + \mathbf{E}_{i,x_i}$ and then using the state $|\psi_{\mathbf{y}}\rangle$, map this to $\sum_i \mathbf{S}_{i,x_i}\mathbf{y} + \mathbf{E}_{i,x_i}$. Finally, perform the rounding operation to get the desired result.

Our goal is to show that after the adversary revokes $|\psi_{\mathbf{y}}\rangle$, on input a challenge input x^* picked uniformly at random, it cannot predict whether it has received $\lfloor \sum_{i \in [N]} \mathbf{S}c_{i,x_i^*} \mathbf{y} \rceil_p$ or a uniformly random vector in $\mathbb{Z}_p^n$.

Challenges in Proving Security: We would like to argue that when the state $|\psi_{\mathbf{y}}\rangle$ is revoked, the adversary loses its ability to evaluate the pseudorandom function. Unfortunately, this is not completely true. For all we know, the adversary could have computed the pseudorandom function on many inputs of its choice before the revocation phase and it could leverage this to break the security after revocation. For instance, suppose say the input is of length $O(\log \lambda)$ then in this case, the adversary could evaluate the pseudorandom function on all possible inputs before revocation. After revocation, on any challenge input x^*, the adversary can then successfully predict whether it receives a pseudorandom output or a uniformly chosen random output. Indeed, a pseudorandom function with $O(\log \lambda)$-length input is learnable and hence, there should be no hope of proving it to be key-revocable. This suggests that, at the very least, we need to explicitly incorporate the fact that x^* is of length $\omega(\log \lambda)$, and more importantly, should have enough entropy, in order to prove security.

Our Insight: Our insight is to reduce the security of revocable pseudorandom function to the security of key-revocable Dual-Regev public-key encryption. At a high level, our goal is to set up the parameters in such a way that the following holds:

- $(\mathbf{A}, \mathbf{y})$, defined above, is set to be the public key corresponding to the Dual-Regev public-key encryption scheme,
- $|\psi_{\mathbf{y}}\rangle$, which is part of the pseudorandom function key, is set to be the decryption key of the Dual Regev scheme,
- Suppose that the challenge ciphertext, denoted by CT^*, comprises of two parts: $\mathsf{CT}_1^* \in \mathbb{Z}_q^{n \times m}$ and $\mathsf{CT}_2^* \in \mathbb{Z}_q^n$. Note that if $\mathsf{CT}_1^* \approx \mathbf{S}^\mathsf{T} \mathbf{A}$ and $\mathsf{CT}_2^* \approx \mathbf{S}^\mathsf{T} \mathbf{y}$, for some LWE secret vector $\mathbf{S}$, then CT_1^* can be mapped onto CT_2^* using the state $|\psi_{\mathbf{y}}\rangle$. We use CT_1^* to set the challenge input x^* in such a way that CT_2^* is the output of the pseudorandom function on x^*. This implicitly resolves the entropy issue we discussed above; by the semantic security of Dual-Regev, there should be enough entropy in CT_1^* which translates to the entropy of x^*.

It turns out that our goal is quite ambitious: in particular, it is unclear how to set up the parameters such that the output of the pseudorandom function on x is exactly CT_2^*. Fortunately, this will not be a deterrant, we can set up the parameters such that the output is $\approx \mathsf{CT}_2^* + \mathbf{u}$, where $\mathbf{u}$ is a vector that is known to reduction.

Once we set up the parameters, we can then reduce the security of revocable pseudorandom functions to revocable Dual Regev.

Implementation Details: So far we established the proof template should work but the implementation details of the proof need to be fleshed out. Firstly, we set up the parameters in such a way that $\ell = nm\lceil \log q \rceil$. This means that there is a bijective function mapping $[n] \times [m] \times [\lceil \log q \rceil]$ to $[\ell]$. As a result, the quantum key ρ_k can be alternately viewed as follows:

– For every $i \in [n], j \in [m], \tau \in [\lceil \log q \rceil], b \in \{0,1\}$, include $\mathbf{S}_b^{(i,j,\tau)}\mathbf{A} + \mathbf{E}_b^{(i,j,\tau)}$ in ρ_k. We sample $\mathbf{S}_b^{(i,j,\tau)}$ and $\mathbf{E}_b^{(i,j,\tau)}$ from a discrete Gaussian with appropriate standard deviation $\sigma > 0$.

The output of the pseudorandom function on input x can now be interpreted as

$$\mathsf{PRF}(k,x) = \left\lfloor \sum_{\substack{i \in [n], j \in [m] \\ \tau \in [\lceil \log q \rceil]}} \mathbf{S}_{x_i}^{(i,j,\tau)}\mathbf{y} \right\rceil_p$$

Next, we modify ρ_k as follows: instead of generating, $\mathbf{S}_b^{(i,j,\tau)}\mathbf{A} + \mathbf{E}_b^{(i,j,\tau)}$, we instead generate $\mathbf{S}_b^{(i,j,\tau)}\mathbf{A} + \mathbf{E}_b^{(i,j,\tau)} + \mathsf{M}_b^{(i,j,k)}$, for any set of matrices $\{\mathsf{M}_b^{(i,j,\tau)}\}$. The change should be undetectable to a computationally bounded adversary, thanks to the quantum hardness of learning with errors. In the security proof, we set up the challenge input x^* in such a way that summing up the matrices $\mathsf{M}_{x_i^*}^{(i,j,\tau)}$ corresponds to CT_1^*, where CT_1^* is part of the key-revocable Dual-Regev challenge ciphertext as discussed above. With this modification, when ρ_k is evaluated on x^*, we get an output that is close to $\mathsf{CT}_2^* + \mathbf{u}$, where $\mathbf{u} \approx \sum_{i \in [n], j \in [m], \tau \in [\lceil \log(q) \rceil]} \mathbf{S}_{x_i}^{(i,j,\tau)}\mathbf{y}$ is known to the reduction (as discussed above) – thereby violating the security of key-revocable Dual-Regev scheme.

1.5   Related Work

Copy-Protection. Of particular relevance to our work is the notion of copy-protection introduced by Aaronson [1]. Informally speaking, a copy-protection scheme is a compiler that transforms programs into quantum states in such a way that using the resulting states, one can run the original program. Yet, the security guarantee stipulates that any adversary given one copy of the state cannot produce a bipartite state wherein both parts compute the original program.

While copy-protection is known to be impossible for arbitrary unlearnable functions [8,11], identifying interesting functionalities for which copy-protection is feasible has been an active research direction [9,10,28]. Of particular significance is the problem of copy-protecting cryptographic functionalities, such as decryption and signing functionalities. Coladangelo et al. [27] took the first step in this direction and showed that it is feasible to copy-protect decryption functionalities and pseudorandom functions assuming the existence of post-quantum indistinguishability obfuscation. While a very significant first step, the assumption of post-quantum iO is unsatisfactory: there have been numerous post-quantum iO candidate proposals [12,19,25,29,32,55], but not one of them have been based on well-studied assumptions[10].

Our work can be viewed as copy-protecting cryptographic functionalities based on the post-quantum hardness of the learning with errors problem under a weaker yet meaningful security guarantee.

---

[10] We remark that, there do exist post-quantum-insecure iO schemes based on well-founded assumptions [42].

Secure Software Leasing. Another primitive relevant to revocable cryptography is secure software leasing [11]. The notion of secure software leasing states that any program can be compiled into a functionally equivalent program, represented as a quantum state, in such a way that once the compiled program is returned[11], the honest evaluation algorithm on the residual state cannot compute the original functionality. Key-revocable encryption can be viewed as secure software leasing for decryption algorithms. However, unlike secure software leasing, key-revocable encryption satisfies a much stronger security guarantee, where there is no restriction on the adversary to run honestly after returning back the software. Secure leasing for different functionalities, namely, point functions [22,28], evasive functions [11,45] and pseudorandom functions [3] have been studied by recent works.

Encryption Schemes with Revocable Ciphertexts. Unruh [54] proposed a (private-key) quantum timed-release encryption scheme that is *revocable*, i.e. it allows a user to *return* the ciphertext of a quantum timed-release encryption scheme, thereby losing all access to the data. Unruh's scheme uses conjugate coding [16,56] and relies on the *monogamy of entanglement* in order to guarantee that revocation necessarily erases information about the plaintext. Broadbent and Islam [21] introduced the notion of *certified deletion*[12] and constructed a private-key quantum encryption scheme with the aforementioned feature which is inspired by the quantum key distribution protocol [16,53]. In contrast with Unruh's [54] notion of revocable quantum ciphertexts which are eventually returned and verified, Broadbent and Islam [21] consider certificates which are entirely classical. Moreover, the security definition requires that, once the certificate is successfully verified, the plaintext remains hidden even if the secret key is later revealed.

Using a hybrid encryption scheme, Hiroka, Morimae, Nishimaki and Yamakawa [40] extended the scheme in [21] to both public-key and attribute-based encryption with certified deletion via *receiver non-committing* encryption [24,43]. As a complementary result, the authors also gave a public-key encryption scheme with certified deletion which is *publicly verifiable* assuming the existence of one-shot signatures and extractable witness encryption. Using *Gaussian superpositions*, Poremba [48] proposed *Dual-Regev*-based public-key and fully homomorphic encryption schemes with certified deletion which are publicly verifiable and proven secure assuming a *strong Gaussian-collapsing conjecture* — a strengthening of the collapsing property of the Ajtai hash. Bartusek and Khurana [14] revisited the notion of certified deletion and presented a unified approach for how to generically convert any public-key, attribute-based, fully-homomorphic, timed-release or witness encryption scheme into an equivalent quantum encryption scheme with certified deletion. In particular, they

---

[11] Acording to the terminology of [11], this refers to finite term secure software leasing.

[12] This notion is incomparable with another related notion called unclonable encryption [7,9,23], which informally guarantees that it should be infeasible to clone quantum ciphertexts without losing information about the encrypted message.

considered a stronger notion called *certified everlasting security* which allows the adversary to be computationally unbounded once a valid deletion certificate is submitted.

2   Definition: Key-Revocable Public-Key Encryption

Let us now give a formal definition of key-revocable public-key encryption schemes.

Definition 1 (Key-Revocable Public-Key Encryption). *A key-revocable public-key encryption scheme* (KeyGen, Enc, Dec, Revoke) *consists of efficient algorithms, where* Enc *is a* PPT *algorithm and* KeyGen, Dec *and* Revoke *are* QPT *algorithms defined as follows:*

- KeyGen(1^λ): *given as input a security parameter* λ, *output a public key* PK, *a master secret key* MSK *and a quantum decryption key* ρ_{SK}.
- Enc(PK, x): *given* PK *and plaintext* $x \in \{0,1\}^\ell$, *output a ciphertext* CT.
- Dec(ρ_{SK}, CT): *given a key* ρ_{SK} *and ciphertext* CT, *output a message* y.
- Revoke (PK, MSK, σ): *given as input a master secret key* MSK, *a public key* PK *and quantum state* σ, *output* Valid *or* Invalid.

Correctness of Decryption. For every $x \in \{0,1\}^\ell$, the following holds:

$$\Pr\left[x \leftarrow \mathsf{Dec}(\rho_{\mathsf{SK}}, \mathsf{CT}) \;:\; \begin{matrix} \mathsf{(PK,MSK,\rho_{SK})} \leftarrow \mathsf{KeyGen}(1^\lambda) \\ \mathsf{CT} \leftarrow \mathsf{Enc(PK,}x) \end{matrix} \right] \geq 1 - \mathsf{negl}(\lambda).$$

Correctness of Revocation. The following holds:

$$\Pr\left[\mathsf{Valid} \leftarrow \mathsf{Revoke}\,(\mathsf{PK, MSK}, \rho_{\mathsf{SK}}) \;:\; (\mathsf{PK, MSK}, \rho_{\mathsf{SK}}) \leftarrow \mathsf{KeyGen}(1^\lambda) \right] \geq 1 - \mathsf{negl}(\lambda).$$

Remark 1. Using the well-known "Almost As Good As New Lemma", the procedure Dec can be purified to obtain another quantum circuit $\widetilde{\mathsf{Dec}}$ such that $\widetilde{\mathsf{Dec}}(\rho_{\mathsf{SK}}, \mathsf{CT})$ yields (x, ρ'_{SK}) with probability at least $1 - \mathsf{negl}(\lambda)$ and moreover, $\mathsf{CT} \leftarrow \mathsf{Enc}(\mathsf{PK}, x)$ and $\mathrm{TD}(\rho'_{\mathsf{SK}}, \rho_{\mathsf{SK}}) \leq \mathsf{negl}(\lambda)$.

2.1   Security Definition

Our security definition for key-revocable public-key encryption is as follows.

Definition 2. *A key-revocable public-key encryption scheme* $\Sigma = $ (KeyGen, Enc, Dec, Revoke) *is* (ϵ, δ)-*secure if, for every* QPT *adversary* $\mathcal{A}$ *with*

$$\Pr[\mathsf{Invalid} \leftarrow \mathsf{Expt}_{\Sigma,\mathcal{A}}(1^\lambda, b)] \leq \delta(\lambda)$$

for $b \in \{0,1\}$, *it holds that*

$$\left| \Pr\left[1 \leftarrow \mathsf{Expt}_{\Sigma,\mathcal{A}}(1^\lambda, 0) \right] - \Pr\left[1 \leftarrow \mathsf{Expt}_{\Sigma,\mathcal{A}}(1^\lambda, 1) \right] \right| \leq \varepsilon(\lambda),$$

where $\mathsf{Expt}_{\Sigma,\mathcal{A}}(1^\lambda, b)$ *is as defined in Fig. 1. If* $\delta(\lambda) = 1 - 1/\mathsf{poly}(\lambda)$ *and* $\varepsilon(\lambda) = \mathsf{negl}(\lambda)$, *we simply say the scheme is secure.*

$$\mathsf{Expt}_{\Sigma,\mathcal{A}}\left(1^\lambda, b\right):$$

Initialization Phase:

- The challenger runs $(\mathsf{PK}, \mathsf{MSK}, \rho_{\mathsf{SK}}) \leftarrow \mathsf{KeyGen}(1^\lambda)$ and sends $(\mathsf{PK}, \rho_{\mathsf{SK}})$ to $\mathcal{A}$.

Revocation Phase:

- The challenger sends the message REVOKE to $\mathcal{A}$.
- The adversary $\mathcal{A}$ returns a state σ.
- The challenger aborts if $\mathsf{Revoke}(\mathsf{PK}, \mathsf{MSK}, \sigma)$ outputs Invalid.

Guessing Phase:

- $\mathcal{A}$ submits a plaintext $x \in \{0,1\}^\ell$ to the challenger.
- If $b = 0$: The challenger sends $\mathsf{CT} \leftarrow \mathsf{Enc}(\mathsf{PK}, x)$ to $\mathcal{A}$. Else, if $b = 1$, the challenger sends $\mathsf{CT} \xleftarrow{\$} \mathcal{C}$, where $\mathcal{C}$ is the ciphertext space of ℓ bit messages.
- Output $b_\mathcal{A}$ if the output of $\mathcal{A}$ is $b_\mathcal{A}$.

Fig. 1. Security Experiment

Remark 2. Our security definition is similar to the one proposed by Agrawal et al. [5] in the context of public-key encryption with secure leasing.

3 Key-Revocable Dual-Regev Encryption

In this section, we present a construction of key-revocable public-key encryption. Our construction essentially involves making the Dual Regev public-key encryption of Gentry, Peikert and Vaikuntanathan [34] key revocable.

3.1 Construction

We define our Dual-Regev construction below.

Construction 1 (Key-Revocable Dual-Regev Encryption) *Let $n \in \mathbb{N}$ be the security parameter and $m \in \mathbb{N}$. Let $q \geq 2$ be a prime and let $\alpha, \beta, \sigma > 0$ be parameters. The key-revocable public-key scheme* $\mathsf{RevDual} = (\mathsf{KeyGen}, \mathsf{Enc}, \mathsf{Dec}, \mathsf{Revoke})$ *consists of the following* QPT *algorithms:*

- $\mathsf{KeyGen}(1^\lambda) \rightarrow (\mathsf{PK}, \rho_{\mathsf{SK}}, \mathsf{MSK})$: *sample* $(\mathbf{A} \in \mathbb{Z}_q^{n \times m}, \mathsf{td}_\mathbf{A}) \leftarrow \mathsf{GenTrap}(1^n, 1^m, q)$ *and generate a Gaussian superposition* $(|\psi_\mathbf{y}\rangle, \mathbf{y}) \leftarrow \mathsf{GenGauss}(\mathbf{A}, \sigma)$ *with*

$$|\psi_\mathbf{y}\rangle = \sum_{\substack{\mathbf{x} \in \mathbb{Z}_q^m \\ \mathbf{A}\mathbf{x}=\mathbf{y}}} \rho_\sigma(\mathbf{x}) |\mathbf{x}\rangle,$$

for some $\mathbf{y} \in \mathbb{Z}_q^n$. *Output* $\mathsf{PK} = (\mathbf{A}, \mathbf{y})$, $\rho_{\mathsf{SK}} = |\psi_{\mathbf{y}}\rangle$ *and* $\mathsf{MSK} = \mathsf{td}_{\mathbf{A}}$.

- $\mathsf{Enc}(\mathsf{PK}, \mu) \to \mathsf{CT}$: *to encrypt a bit* $\mu \in \{0,1\}$, *sample a random vector* $\mathbf{s} \xleftarrow{\$} \mathbb{Z}_q^n$ *and errors* $\mathbf{e} \sim D_{\mathbb{Z}^m, \alpha q}$ *and* $e' \sim D_{\mathbb{Z}, \beta q}$, *and output the ciphertext pair*

$$\mathsf{CT} = \left(\mathbf{s}^{\mathsf{T}} \mathbf{A} + \mathbf{e}^{\mathsf{T}} \ (\mathrm{mod}\ q), \mathbf{s}^{\mathsf{T}} \mathbf{y} + e' + \mu \cdot \lfloor \tfrac{q}{2} \rfloor \ (\mathrm{mod}\ q) \right) \in \mathbb{Z}_q^m \times \mathbb{Z}_q.$$

- $\mathsf{Dec}(\rho_{\mathsf{SK}}, \mathsf{CT}) \to \{0,1\}$: *to decrypt* CT, *apply the unitary* U : $|\mathbf{x}\rangle |0\rangle \to$ $|\mathbf{x}\rangle |\mathsf{CT} \cdot (-\mathbf{x}, 1)^{\mathsf{T}}\rangle$ *on input* $|\psi_{\mathbf{y}}\rangle |0\rangle$, *where* $\rho_{\mathsf{SK}} = |\psi_{\mathbf{y}}\rangle$, *and measure the second register in the computational basis. Output* 0, *if the measurement outcome is closer to* 0 *than to* $\lfloor \tfrac{q}{2} \rfloor$, *and output* 1, *otherwise.*

- $\mathsf{Revoke}(\mathsf{MSK}, \mathsf{PK}, \rho) \to \{\top, \bot\}$: *on input* $\mathsf{td}_{\mathbf{A}} \leftarrow \mathsf{MSK}$ *and* $(\mathbf{A}, \mathbf{y}) \leftarrow \mathsf{PK}$, *apply the measurement* $\{|\psi_{\mathbf{y}}\rangle\langle\psi_{\mathbf{y}}|, I - |\psi_{\mathbf{y}}\rangle\langle\psi_{\mathbf{y}}|\}$ *onto the state* ρ *using the procedure* $\mathsf{QSampGauss}(\mathbf{A}, \mathsf{td}_{\mathbf{A}}, \mathbf{y}, \sigma)$. *Output* $\top$, *if the measurement is successful, and output* $\bot$ *otherwise.*

Correctness of Decryption. Follows from the correctness of Dual-Regev public-key encryption.

Correctness of Revocation. This follows from the correctness of our discrete Gaussian sampler $\mathsf{QSampGauss}$ (formally defined in the full version).

Let us now prove the security of our key-revocable Dual-Regev scheme in Construction 1. Our first result concerns $(\mathsf{negl}(\lambda), \mathsf{negl}(\lambda))$-security, i.e., we assume that revocation succeeds with overwhelming probability.

Theorem 5. *Let* $n \in \mathbb{N}$ *and* q *be a prime modulus with* $q = 2^{o(n)}$ *and* $m \geq 2n \log q$, *each parameterized by the security parameter* $\lambda \in \mathbb{N}$. *Let* $\sqrt{8m} < \sigma < q/\sqrt{8m}$ *and let* $\alpha, \beta \in (0,1)$ *be noise ratios chosen such that* $\beta/\alpha = 2^{o(n)}$ *and* $1/\alpha = 2^{o(n)} \cdot \sigma$. *Then, assuming the subexponential hardness of the* $\mathsf{LWE}_{n,q,\alpha q}^m$ *and* $\mathsf{SIS}_{n,q,\sigma\sqrt{2m}}^m$ *problems, the scheme* $\mathsf{RevDual} = (\mathsf{KeyGen}, \mathsf{Enc}, \mathsf{Dec}, \mathsf{Revoke})$ *in Construction 1 is a* $(\mathsf{negl}(\lambda), \mathsf{negl}(\lambda))$-*secure key-revocable public-key encryption scheme according to Definition 2.*

As a first step towards the proof of Theorem 5, we first prove a technical result which concerns distinguishers with quantum auxiliary input that can distinguish between Dual-Regev samples and uniformly random samples with high probability. In Theorem 6, we give a search-to-decision reduction: we show that such distinguishers can be converted into a quantum extractor that can obtain a Dual-Regev secret key with overwhelming probability.

Theorem 6 (Search-to-Decision Reduction with Quantum Auxiliary Input). *Let* $n \in \mathbb{N}$ *and* q *be a prime modulus with* $q = 2^{o(n)}$ *and let* $m \geq 2n \log q$, *each parameterized by the security parameter* $\lambda \in \mathbb{N}$. *Let* $\sqrt{8m} < \sigma < q/\sqrt{8m}$ *and let* $\alpha, \beta \in (0,1)$ *be noise ratios with* $\beta/\alpha = 2^{o(n)}$ *and* $1/\alpha = 2^{o(n)} \cdot \sigma$. *Let* $\mathcal{A} = \{(\mathcal{A}_{\lambda, \mathbf{A}, \mathbf{y}}, \nu_\lambda)\}_{\lambda \in \mathbb{N}}$ *be any non-uniform quantum algorithm consisting of a family of polynomial-sized quantum circuits*

$$\left\{ \mathcal{A}_{\lambda, \mathbf{A}, \mathbf{y}} : \mathcal{L}(\mathcal{H}_q^m \otimes \mathcal{H}_{B_\lambda}) \to \mathcal{L}(\mathcal{H}_{R_\lambda} \otimes \mathcal{H}_{\mathrm{AUX}_\lambda}) \right\}_{\mathbf{A} \in \mathbb{Z}_q^{n \times m}, \mathbf{y} \in \mathbb{Z}_q^n}$$

and polynomial-sized advice states $\nu_\lambda \in \mathcal{D}(\mathcal{H}_{B_\lambda})$ *which are independent of* $\mathbf{A}$. *Then, assuming the quantum hardness of the* $\mathsf{LWE}^m_{n,q,\alpha q}$ *assumption, the following holds for every* QPT *distinguisher* $\mathcal{D}$. *Suppose that there exists a function* $\varepsilon(\lambda) = 1/\mathrm{poly}(\lambda)$ *such that*

$$\Pr\left[1 \leftarrow \mathsf{SearchToDecisionExpt}^{\mathcal{A},\mathcal{D}}(1^\lambda, 0)\right]$$

$$-\Pr\left[1 \leftarrow \mathsf{SearchToDecisionExpt}^{\mathcal{A},\mathcal{D}}(1^\lambda, 1)\right]\Big| = \varepsilon(\lambda).$$

$\mathsf{SearchToDecisionExpt}^{\mathcal{A},\mathcal{D}}\left(1^\lambda, b\right)$:

- If $b = 0$: output $\mathsf{lwe.Dist}^{\mathcal{A},\mathcal{D}}\left(1^\lambda\right)$ defined in Figure 3.
- If $b = 1$: output $\mathsf{unif.Dist}^{\mathcal{A},\mathcal{D}}\left(1^\lambda\right)$ defined in Figure 4.

Fig. 2. The experiment $\mathsf{SearchToDecisionExpt}^{\mathcal{A},\mathcal{D}}\left(1^\lambda, b\right)$.

Then, there exists a quantum extractor $\mathcal{E}$ *that takes as input* $\mathbf{A}$, $\mathbf{y}$ *and system* Aux *of the state* $\rho_{\mathrm{R,Aux}}$ *and outputs a short vector in the coset* $\Lambda^{\mathbf{y}}_q(\mathbf{A})$ *in time* $\mathrm{poly}(\lambda, m, \sigma, q, 1/\varepsilon)$ *such that*

$$\Pr\left[\begin{array}{c} \mathcal{E}(\mathbf{A},\mathbf{y},\rho_{\mathrm{Aux}})=\mathbf{x} \\ \wedge \\ \mathbf{x} \in \Lambda^{\mathbf{y}}_q(\mathbf{A}) \cap \mathcal{B}^m\left(0,\sigma\sqrt{\frac{m}{2}}\right) \end{array} : \begin{array}{c} \mathbf{A} \xleftarrow{\$} \mathbb{Z}^{n \times m}_q \\ (|\psi_\mathbf{y}\rangle,\mathbf{y}) \leftarrow \mathsf{GenGauss}(\mathbf{A},\sigma) \\ \rho_{\mathrm{R,Aux}} \leftarrow \mathcal{A}_{\lambda,\mathbf{A},\mathbf{y}}(|\psi_\mathbf{y}\rangle\langle\psi_\mathbf{y}|\otimes\nu_\lambda) \end{array}\right] \geq \mathrm{poly}(\varepsilon, 1/q).$$

Proof. Let $\lambda \in \mathbb{N}$ be the security parameter and let $\mathcal{A} = \{(\mathcal{A}_{\lambda,\mathbf{A},\mathbf{y}}, \nu_\lambda)\}_{\mathbf{A}\in\mathbb{Z}^{n\times m}_q}$ be a non-uniform quantum algorithm. Suppose that $\mathcal{D}$ is a QPT distinguisher with advantage $\varepsilon = 1/\mathrm{poly}(\lambda)$.

To prove the claim, we consider the following sequence of hybrid distributions.

H_0: This is the distribution $\mathsf{lwe.Dist}^{\mathcal{A},\mathcal{D}}\left(1^\lambda\right)$ in Fig. 3.

$$\mathsf{lwe.Dist}^{\mathcal{A},\mathcal{D}}\left(1^{\lambda}\right):$$

1. Sample $\mathbf{A} \xleftarrow{\$} \mathbb{Z}_q^{n \times m}$.
2. Generate $(|\psi_\mathbf{y}\rangle, \mathbf{y}) \leftarrow \mathsf{GenGauss}(\mathbf{A}, \sigma)$.
3. Generate $\rho_{R, \text{AUX}} \leftarrow \mathcal{A}_{\lambda, \mathbf{A}, \mathbf{y}}(|\psi_\mathbf{y}\rangle\langle\psi_\mathbf{y}| \otimes \nu_\lambda)$.
4. Sample $\mathbf{s} \xleftarrow{\$} \mathbb{Z}_q^n$, $\mathbf{e} \sim D_{\mathbb{Z}^m, \alpha q}$ and $e' \sim D_{\mathbb{Z}, \beta q}$.
5. Generate $\rho_{R,\text{AUX}} \leftarrow \mathcal{A}_{\lambda, \mathbf{A}, \mathbf{y}}(|\psi_\mathbf{y}\rangle\langle\psi_\mathbf{y}| \otimes \nu_\lambda)$.
6. Run $b' \leftarrow \mathcal{D}(\mathbf{A}, \mathbf{y}, \mathbf{s}^\mathsf{T}\mathbf{A} + \mathbf{e}^\mathsf{T}, \mathbf{s}^\mathsf{T}\mathbf{y} + e', \rho_{\text{AUX}})$ on the reduced state. Output b'.

Fig. 3. The distribution $\mathsf{lwe.Dist}^{\mathcal{A},\mathcal{D}}\left(1^{\lambda}\right)$.

H_1: This is the following distribution:
1. Sample a random matrix $\mathbf{A} \xleftarrow{\$} \mathbb{Z}_q^{n \times m}$.
2. Sample $\mathbf{s} \xleftarrow{\$} \mathbb{Z}_q^n$, $\mathbf{e} \sim D_{\mathbb{Z}^m, \alpha q}$ and $e' \sim D_{\mathbb{Z}, \beta q}$.
3. Sample a Gaussian vector $\mathbf{x}_0 \sim D_{\mathbb{Z}_q^m, \frac{\sigma}{\sqrt{2}}}$ and let $\mathbf{y} = \mathbf{A} \cdot \mathbf{x}_0 \pmod q$.
4. Run $\mathcal{A}_{\lambda, \mathbf{A}, \mathbf{y}}(|\mathbf{x}_0\rangle\langle\mathbf{x}_0| \otimes \nu_\lambda)$ to generate a state $\rho_{R,\text{AUX}}$ in systems R and AUX.
5. Run the distinguisher $\mathcal{D}(\mathbf{A}, \mathbf{y}, \mathbf{s}^\mathsf{T}\mathbf{A} + \mathbf{e}^\mathsf{T}, \mathbf{s}^\mathsf{T}\mathbf{y} + e', \rho_{\text{AUX}})$ on the reduced state ρ_{AUX}.

H_2 : This is the following distribution:
1. Sample a uniformly random matrix $\mathbf{A} \xleftarrow{\$} \mathbb{Z}_q^{n \times m}$.
2. Sample $\mathbf{s} \xleftarrow{\$} \mathbb{Z}_q^n$, $\mathbf{e} \sim D_{\mathbb{Z}^m, \alpha q}$ and $e' \sim D_{\mathbb{Z}, \beta q}$. Let $\mathbf{u} = \mathbf{A}^\mathsf{T}\mathbf{s} + \mathbf{e}$.
3. Sample a Gaussian vector $\mathbf{x}_0 \sim D_{\mathbb{Z}_q^m, \frac{\sigma}{\sqrt{2}}}$ and let $\mathbf{y} = \mathbf{A} \cdot \mathbf{x}_0 \pmod q$.
4. Run $\mathcal{A}_{\lambda, \mathbf{A}, \mathbf{y}}(|\mathbf{x}_0\rangle\langle\mathbf{x}_0| \otimes \nu_\lambda)$ to generate a state $\rho_{R,\text{AUX}}$ in systems R and AUX.
5. Run the distinguisher $\mathcal{D}(\mathbf{A}, \mathbf{y}, \mathbf{u}, \mathbf{u}^\mathsf{T}\mathbf{x}_0 + e', \rho_{\text{AUX}})$ on the reduced state ρ_{AUX}.

H_3 : This is the following distribution:
1. Sample a uniformly random matrix $\mathbf{A} \xleftarrow{\$} \mathbb{Z}_q^{n \times m}$.
2. Sample $\mathbf{u} \xleftarrow{\$} \mathbb{Z}_q^m$ and $e' \sim D_{\mathbb{Z}, \beta q}$.
3. Sample a Gaussian vector $\mathbf{x}_0 \sim D_{\mathbb{Z}_q^m, \frac{\sigma}{\sqrt{2}}}$ and let $\mathbf{y} = \mathbf{A} \cdot \mathbf{x}_0 \pmod q$.
4. Run $\mathcal{A}_{\lambda, \mathbf{A}, \mathbf{y}}(|\mathbf{x}_0\rangle\langle\mathbf{x}_0| \otimes \nu_\lambda)$ to generate a state $\rho_{R,\text{AUX}}$ in systems R and AUX.
5. Run the distinguisher $\mathcal{D}(\mathbf{A}, \mathbf{y}, \mathbf{u}, \mathbf{u}^\mathsf{T}\mathbf{x}_0 + e', \rho_{\text{AUX}})$ on the reduced state ρ_{AUX}.

H_4: This is the following distribution:
1. Sample a uniformly random matrix $\mathbf{A} \xleftarrow{\$} \mathbb{Z}_q^{n \times m}$.
2. Sample $\mathbf{u} \xleftarrow{\$} \mathbb{Z}_q^m$ and $r \xleftarrow{\$} \mathbb{Z}_q$.
3. Sample a Gaussian vector $\mathbf{x}_0 \sim D_{\mathbb{Z}_q^m, \frac{\sigma}{\sqrt{2}}}$ and let $\mathbf{y} = \mathbf{A} \cdot \mathbf{x}_0 \pmod q$.

4. Run $\mathcal{A}_{\lambda,\mathbf{A},\mathbf{y}}(|\mathbf{x}_0\rangle\langle\mathbf{x}_0| \otimes \nu_\lambda)$ to generate a state $\rho_{R,\text{AUX}}$ in systems R and AUX.
5. Run the distinguisher $\mathcal{D}(\mathbf{A}, \mathbf{y}, \mathbf{u}, r, \rho_{\text{AUX}})$ on the reduced state ρ_{AUX}.

H_5: This is the distribution $\mathsf{unif.Dist}^{\mathcal{A},\mathcal{D}}(1^\lambda)$ in Fig. 4.

$\underline{\mathsf{unif.Dist}^{\mathcal{A},\mathcal{D}}(1^\lambda)}:$

1. Sample $\mathbf{A} \xleftarrow{\$} \mathbb{Z}_q^{n\times m}$.
2. Sample $\mathbf{u} \xleftarrow{\$} \mathbb{Z}_q^m$ and $r \xleftarrow{\$} \mathbb{Z}_q$.
3. Run $(|\psi_{\mathbf{y}}\rangle, \mathbf{y}) \leftarrow \mathsf{GenGauss}(\mathbf{A}, \sigma)$.
4. Generate $\rho_{R,\text{AUX}} \leftarrow \mathcal{A}_{\lambda,\mathbf{A},\mathbf{y}}(|\psi_{\mathbf{y}}\rangle\langle\psi_{\mathbf{y}}| \otimes \nu_\lambda)$.
5. Run $b' \leftarrow \mathcal{D}(\mathbf{A}, \mathbf{y}, \mathbf{u}, r, \rho_{\text{AUX}})$ on the reduced state. Output b'.

Fig. 4. The distribution $\mathsf{unif.Dist}^{\mathcal{A},\mathcal{D}}(1^\lambda)$.

We now show the following:

Claim. Assuming $\mathsf{LWE}_{n,q,\alpha q}^m$, the hybrids H_0 and H_1 are computationally indistinguishable,

$$\mathsf{H}_0 \approx_c \mathsf{H}_1.$$

Proof. Here, we invoke the *Gaussian-collapsing property* which states that the following samples are indistinguishable under $\mathsf{LWE}_{n,q,\alpha q}^m$,

$$\left(\mathbf{A} \xleftarrow{\$} \mathbb{Z}_q^{n\times m},\ |\psi_{\mathbf{y}}\rangle = \sum_{\substack{\mathbf{x}\in\mathbb{Z}_q^m \\ \mathbf{A}\mathbf{x}=\mathbf{y}}} \rho_\sigma(\mathbf{x})\,|\mathbf{x}\rangle,\ \mathbf{y} \in \mathbb{Z}_q^n\right) \approx_c \left(\mathbf{A} \xleftarrow{\$} \mathbb{Z}_q^{n\times m},\ |\mathbf{x}_0\rangle,\ \mathbf{A}\cdot\mathbf{x}_0 \in \mathbb{Z}_q^n\right)$$

where $(|\psi_{\mathbf{y}}\rangle, \mathbf{y}) \leftarrow \mathsf{GenGauss}(\mathbf{A}, \sigma)$ and where $\mathbf{x}_0 \sim D_{\mathbb{Z}_q^m, \frac{\sigma}{\sqrt{2}}}$ is a sample from the discrete Gaussian distribution. Because $\mathcal{A}_{\lambda,\mathbf{A},\mathbf{y}}$ is a family efficient quantum algorithms, this implies that

$$\mathcal{A}_{\lambda,\mathbf{A},\mathbf{y}}(|\psi_{\mathbf{y}}\rangle\langle\psi_{\mathbf{y}}| \otimes \nu_\lambda) \quad\approx_c\quad \mathcal{A}_{\lambda,\mathbf{A},\mathbf{y}}(|\mathbf{x}_0\rangle\langle\mathbf{x}_0| \otimes \nu_\lambda),$$

for any polynomial-sized advice state $\nu_\lambda \in \mathcal{D}(\mathcal{H}_{B_\lambda})$ which is independent of $\mathbf{A}$.

Claim. Hybrids H_1 and H_2 are statistically indistinguishable. In other words,

$$\mathsf{H}_1 \approx_s \mathsf{H}_2.$$

Proof. Here, we invoke the *noise flooding* property to argue that $\mathbf{e}^\mathsf{T}\mathbf{x}_0 \ll e'$ holds with overwhelming probability for our choice of parameters. Therefore, the distributions in H_1 and H_2 are computationally indistinguishable.

Claim. Assuming $\mathsf{LWE}^m_{n,q,\alpha q}$, the hybrids H_2 and H_3 are computationally indistinguishable,

$$\mathsf{H}_2 \approx_c \mathsf{H}_3.$$

Proof. This follows from the $\mathsf{LWE}^m_{n,q,\alpha q}$ assumption since the reduction can sample $\mathbf{x}_0 \sim D_{\mathbb{Z}^m, \frac{\sigma}{\sqrt{2}}}$ itself and generate $\rho_{R,\mathrm{AUX}} \leftarrow \mathcal{A}_{\lambda,\mathbf{A},\mathbf{y}}(|\mathbf{x}_0\rangle\langle\mathbf{x}_0| \otimes \nu_\lambda)$ on input $\mathbf{A} \in \mathbb{Z}_q^{n \times m}$ and ν_λ.

Finally, we show the following:

Claim. Assuming $\mathsf{LWE}^m_{n,q,\alpha q}$, the hybrids H_4 and H_5 are computationally indistinguishable,

$$\mathsf{H}_4 \approx_c \mathsf{H}_5.$$

Proof. Here, we invoke the *Gaussian-collapsing property* again.

Recall that H_0 and H_5 can be distinguished with probability $\varepsilon = 1/\mathrm{poly}(\lambda)$. We proved that the hybrids H_0 and H_3 are computationally indistinguishable and moreover, hybrids H_4 and H_5 are computationally indistinguishable. As a consequence, it holds that hybrids H_3 and H_4 can be distinguished with probability at least $\varepsilon - \mathsf{negl}(\lambda)$. We leverage this to obtain a Goldreich-Levin reduction. Applying the quantum Goldreich-Levin theorem for finite fields to the previous distinguisher $\mathcal{D}$ (which additional shifts the fourth argument by $e' \sim D_{\mathbb{Z},\beta q}$), it follows that there exists an extractor $\mathcal{E}$ running in time $T(\mathcal{E}) = \mathrm{poly}(\lambda, n, m, \sigma, q, 1/\varepsilon)$ that outputs a short vector in $\Lambda_q^{\mathbf{y}}(\mathbf{A})$ with probability at least

$$\Pr\left[\begin{array}{c} \mathcal{E}(\mathbf{A},\mathbf{y},\rho_{\mathrm{AUX}})=\mathbf{x} \\ \wedge \\ \mathbf{x} \in \Lambda_q^{\mathbf{y}}(\mathbf{A}) \cap \mathcal{B}^m(0,\sigma\sqrt{\frac{m}{2}}) \end{array} : \begin{array}{c} \mathbf{A} \xleftarrow{\$} \mathbb{Z}_q^{n\times m}, \mathbf{x}_0 \sim D_{\mathbb{Z}_q^m, \frac{\sigma}{\sqrt{2}}} \\ \mathbf{y} \leftarrow \mathbf{A}\cdot\mathbf{x}_0 \pmod{q} \\ \rho_{R,\mathrm{AUX}} \leftarrow \mathcal{A}_{\lambda,\mathbf{A},\mathbf{y}}(|\mathbf{x}_0\rangle\langle\mathbf{x}_0|\otimes\nu_\lambda) \end{array}\right] \geq \mathrm{poly}(\varepsilon, 1/q).$$

Assuming the $\mathsf{LWE}^m_{n,q,\alpha q}$ assumption, we can invoke the Gaussian-collapsing property once again which implies that the quantum extractor $\mathcal{E}$ satisfies

$$\Pr\left[\begin{array}{c} \mathcal{E}(\mathbf{A},\mathbf{y},\rho_{\mathrm{AUX}})=\mathbf{x} \\ \wedge \\ \mathbf{x} \in \Lambda_q^{\mathbf{y}}(\mathbf{A}) \cap \mathcal{B}^m(0,\sigma\sqrt{\frac{m}{2}}) \end{array} : \begin{array}{c} \mathbf{A} \xleftarrow{\$} \mathbb{Z}_q^{n\times m} \\ (|\psi_\mathbf{y}\rangle, \mathbf{y}) \leftarrow \mathsf{GenGauss}(\mathbf{A},\sigma) \\ \rho_{R,\mathrm{AUX}} \leftarrow \mathcal{A}_{\lambda,\mathbf{A},\mathbf{y}}(|\psi_\mathbf{y}\rangle\langle\psi_\mathbf{y}|\otimes\nu_\lambda) \end{array}\right] \geq \mathrm{poly}(\varepsilon, 1/q).$$

This proves the claim.

3.2   Proof of Theorem 5

Proof. Let $\mathcal{A}$ be a QPT adversary and suppose that

$$\left|\Pr\left[1 \leftarrow \mathsf{Expt}_\mathcal{A}(1^\lambda, 0)\right] - \Pr\left[1 \leftarrow \mathsf{Expt}_\mathcal{A}(1^\lambda, 1)\right]\right| = \varepsilon(\lambda),$$

for some $\varepsilon(\lambda)$. We show that $\varepsilon(\lambda)$ is negligible.

Suppose for the sake of contradiction that $\epsilon(\lambda)$ is non-negligible. We show that we can use $\mathcal{A}$ to break the $\mathsf{SIS}^m_{n,q,\sigma\sqrt{2m}}$ problem. Without loss of generality, we assume that $\mathcal{A}$ submits the plaintext $x = 0$. By the assumption that revocation succeeds with overwhelming probability and since $\epsilon(\lambda) \geq 1/\mathrm{poly}(\lambda)$, we can use Theorem 6 to argue that there exists a an extractor $\mathcal{E}$ that takes as input $\mathbf{A}$, $\mathbf{y}$ and system AUX of the state $\rho_{R,\mathrm{AUX}}$ and outputs a short vector in the coset $\Lambda_q^{\mathbf{y}}(\mathbf{A})$ in time $\mathrm{poly}(\lambda, m, \sigma, q, 1/\varepsilon)$ such that

$$\Pr\left[\begin{array}{c} \mathsf{IneffRevoke}(\mathbf{A},\mathbf{y},\sigma,R)=\top \\ \wedge \\ \mathcal{E}(\mathbf{A},\mathbf{y},\mathrm{AUX}) \in \Lambda_q^{\mathbf{y}}(\mathbf{A}) \cap \mathcal{B}^m(0,\sigma\sqrt{\tfrac{m}{2}}) \end{array} : \begin{array}{c} \mathbf{A} \xleftarrow{\$} \mathbb{Z}_q^{n \times m} \\ (|\psi_{\mathbf{y}}\rangle,\mathbf{y}) \leftarrow \mathsf{GenGauss}(\mathbf{A},\sigma) \\ \rho_{R,\mathrm{AUX}} \leftarrow \mathcal{A}_{\lambda,\mathbf{A},\mathbf{y}}(|\psi_{\mathbf{y}}\rangle\langle\psi_{\mathbf{y}}|) \end{array}\right] \geq \mathrm{poly}(\varepsilon, 1/q).$$

Here, we rely on the correctness of $\mathsf{GenTrap}$ in and $\mathsf{QSampGauss}$ which are explicitly defined in the full version of this paper.

Consider the following procedure in Algorithm 1.

Algorithm 1: $\mathsf{SIS\_Solver}(\mathbf{A})$

Input: Matrix $\mathbf{A} \in \mathbb{Z}_q^{n \times m}$.
Output: Vector $\mathbf{x} \in \mathbb{Z}^m$.

1 Generate a Gaussian state $(|\psi_{\mathbf{y}}\rangle, \mathbf{y}) \leftarrow \mathsf{GenGauss}(\mathbf{A}, \sigma)$ with

$$|\psi_{\mathbf{y}}\rangle = \sum_{\substack{\mathbf{x} \in \mathbb{Z}_q^m \\ \mathbf{A}\mathbf{x} = \mathbf{y} \pmod{q}}} \rho_\sigma(\mathbf{x}) |\mathbf{x}\rangle$$

   for some vector $\mathbf{y} \in \mathbb{Z}_q^n$.
2 Run $\mathcal{A}$ to prepare $\rho_{R\,\mathrm{AUX}}$ in systems $\mathcal{H}_R \otimes \mathcal{H}_{\mathrm{AUX}}$ with $\mathcal{H}_R = \mathcal{H}_q^m$.
3 Measure system R in the computational basis, with outcome $\mathbf{x}_0 \in \mathbb{Z}_q^n$.
4 Run the quantum Goldreich-Levin extractor $\mathcal{E}(\mathbf{A}, \mathbf{y}, \rho_{\mathrm{AUX}})$ from Theorem 6, where ρ_{AUX} is the reduced state in system $\mathcal{H}_{\mathrm{AUX}}$, and let $\mathbf{x}_1 \in \mathbb{Z}_q^n$ denote the outcome.
5 Output the vector $\mathbf{x} = \mathbf{x}_1 - \mathbf{x}_0$.

To conclude the proof, we show that $\mathsf{SIS\_Solver}(\mathbf{A})$ in Algorithm 1 breaks the $\mathsf{SIS}_{n,q,\sigma\sqrt{2m}}^m$ problem whenever $\varepsilon(\lambda) = 1/\mathrm{poly}(\lambda)$. In order to guarantee that $\mathsf{SIS\_Solver}(\mathbf{A})$ is successful, we use the distinct pair extraction result (proven in the full version). This allows us to analyze the probability of simultaneously extracting two distinct short pre-images $\mathbf{x}_0 \neq \mathbf{x}_1$ such that $\mathbf{A}\mathbf{x}_0 = \mathbf{y} = \mathbf{A}\mathbf{x}_1 \pmod{q}$ – both in terms of the success probability of revocation and the success probability of extracting a pre-image from the adversary's state ρ_{AUX} in system $\mathcal{H}_{\mathrm{AUX}}$. Assuming that $\mathbf{x}_0, \mathbf{x}_1$ are distinct short pre-images such that $\|\mathbf{x}_0\| \leq \sigma\sqrt{\tfrac{m}{2}}$ and $\|\mathbf{x}_1\| \leq \sigma\sqrt{\tfrac{m}{2}}$, it then follows that the vector $\mathbf{x} = \mathbf{x}_1 - \mathbf{x}_0$ output by $\mathsf{SIS\_Solver}(\mathbf{A})$ has norm at most $\sigma\sqrt{2m}$, and thus yields a solution to $\mathsf{SIS}_{n,q,\sigma\sqrt{2m}}^m$.

Before we analyze Algorithm 1, we first make two technical remarks. First, since $\sigma \geq \omega(\sqrt{\log m})$, it follows that, for any full-rank $\mathbf{A} \in \mathbb{Z}_q^{n \times m}$ and for any $\mathbf{y} \in \mathbb{Z}_q^n$, we have

$$\max_{\substack{\mathbf{x}\in\mathbb{Z}_q^m,\,\|\mathbf{x}\|\leq\sigma\sqrt{\frac{m}{2}}\\ \mathbf{A}\mathbf{x}=\mathbf{y}\ (\mathrm{mod}\ q)}}\left\{\frac{\rho_{\frac{\sigma}{\sqrt{2}}}(\mathbf{x})}{\displaystyle\sum_{\substack{\mathbf{z}\in\mathbb{Z}_q^m,\,\|\mathbf{z}\|\leq\sigma\sqrt{\frac{m}{2}}\\ \mathbf{A}\mathbf{z}=\mathbf{y}\ (\mathrm{mod}\ q)}}\rho_{\frac{\sigma}{\sqrt{2}}}(\mathbf{z})}\right\}\leq 2^{-\Omega(m)}.$$

Second, Second, we can replace the procedure $\mathsf{Revoke}(\mathbf{A},\mathsf{td}_\mathbf{A},\mathbf{y},\rho_R)$ by an (inefficient) projective measurement $\{|\psi_\mathbf{y}\rangle\langle\psi_\mathbf{y}|,\,I-|\psi_\mathbf{y}\rangle\langle\psi_\mathbf{y}|\}$, since they produce statistically close outcomes. This follows from the fact that $\mathsf{Revoke}(\mathbf{A},\mathsf{td}_\mathbf{A},\mathbf{y},\rho_R)$ applies the procedure $\mathsf{QSampGauss}$ as a subroutine, which is correct with overwhelming probability according. Let us now analyze the success probability of Algorithm 1. Putting everything together, we get

$$\Pr\left[\begin{array}{c}\mathbf{x}\leftarrow\mathsf{SIS\_Solver}(\mathbf{A})\\ \wedge\\ \mathbf{x}\neq\mathbf{0}\ \text{s.t.}\ \|\mathbf{x}\|\leq\sigma\sqrt{2m}\end{array}:\ \mathbf{A}\xleftarrow{\$}\mathbb{Z}_q^{n\times m}\right]$$

$$\geq\left(1-\max_{\substack{\mathbf{x}\in\mathbb{Z}_q^m,\,\|\mathbf{x}\|\leq\sigma\sqrt{\frac{m}{2}}\\ \mathbf{A}\mathbf{x}=\mathbf{y}\ (\mathrm{mod}\ q)}}\left\{\frac{\rho_{\frac{\sigma}{\sqrt{2}}}(\mathbf{x})}{\displaystyle\sum_{\substack{\mathbf{z}\in\mathbb{Z}_q^m,\,\|\mathbf{z}\|\leq\sigma\sqrt{\frac{m}{2}}\\ \mathbf{A}\mathbf{z}=\mathbf{y}\ (\mathrm{mod}\ q)}}\rho_{\frac{\sigma}{\sqrt{2}}}(\mathbf{z})}\right\}\right)$$

$$\cdot\Pr\left[\mathsf{IneffRevoke}(\mathbf{A},\mathbf{y},\rho_R)=\top\ :\ \begin{array}{c}\mathbf{A}\xleftarrow{\$}\mathbb{Z}_q^{n\times m}\ \text{s.t.}\ \mathbf{A}\ \text{is full-rank}\\ (|\psi_\mathbf{y}\rangle,\mathbf{y})\leftarrow\mathsf{GenGauss}(\mathbf{A},\sigma)\\ \rho_{R,\mathrm{AUX}}\leftarrow\mathcal{A}_{\lambda,\mathbf{A},\mathbf{y}}(|\psi_\mathbf{y}\rangle\langle\psi_\mathbf{y}|)\end{array}\right]$$

$$\cdot\Pr\left[\mathcal{E}(\mathbf{A},\mathbf{y},\rho_{\mathrm{AUX}})\in\Lambda_q^\mathbf{y}(\mathbf{A})\cap\mathcal{B}^m(\mathbf{0},\sigma\sqrt{m/2})\ :\ \begin{array}{c}\mathbf{A}\xleftarrow{\$}\mathbb{Z}_q^{n\times m}\ \text{s.t.}\ \mathbf{A}\ \text{is full-rank}\\ (|\psi_\mathbf{y}\rangle,\mathbf{y})\leftarrow\mathsf{GenGauss}(\mathbf{A},\sigma)\\ \rho_{R,\mathrm{AUX}}\leftarrow\mathcal{A}_{\lambda,\mathbf{A},\mathbf{y}}(|\psi_\mathbf{y}\rangle\langle\psi_\mathbf{y}|)\\ \top\leftarrow\mathsf{IneffRevoke}(\mathbf{A},\mathbf{y},\rho_R)\end{array}\right]$$

$$\geq\left(1-2^{-\Omega(m)}\right)\cdot\Pr\left[\begin{array}{c}\mathsf{IneffRevoke}(\mathbf{A},\mathbf{y},\sigma,R)=\top\\ \wedge\\ \mathcal{E}(\mathbf{A},\mathbf{y},\mathrm{AUX})\in\Lambda_q^\mathbf{y}(\mathbf{A})\cap\mathcal{B}^m(\mathbf{0},\sigma\sqrt{\frac{m}{2}})\end{array}:\ \begin{array}{c}\mathbf{A}\xleftarrow{\$}\mathbb{Z}_q^{n\times m}\ \text{s.t.}\ \mathbf{A}\ \text{is full-rank}\\ (|\psi_\mathbf{y}\rangle,\mathbf{y})\leftarrow\mathsf{GenGauss}(\mathbf{A},\sigma)\\ \rho_{R,\mathrm{AUX}}\leftarrow\mathcal{A}_{\lambda,\mathbf{A},\mathbf{y}}(|\psi_\mathbf{y}\rangle\langle\psi_\mathbf{y}|)\end{array}\right]$$

$$\geq\left(1-2^{-\Omega(m)}\right)\cdot\left(\mathrm{poly}(\varepsilon,1/q)-q^{-n}\right)\ \geq\ \mathrm{poly}(\varepsilon,1/q).$$

Therefore, $\mathsf{SIS\_Solver}(\mathbf{A})$ in Algorithm 1 runs in time $\mathrm{poly}(q,1/\varepsilon)$ and solves $\mathsf{SIS}_{n,q,\sigma\sqrt{2m}}^m$ whenever $\varepsilon=1/\mathrm{poly}(\lambda)$, and hence $\varepsilon(\lambda)$ must be negligible.

Acknowledgements. We thank Fatih Kaleoglu and Ryo Nishimaki for several insightful discussions.

This work was done (in part) while the authors were visiting the Simons Institute for the Theory of Computing. P.A. is supported by a research gift from Cisco. A.P. is partially supported by AFOSR YIP (award number FA9550-16-1-0495), the Institute for Quantum Information and Matter (an NSF Physics Frontiers Center; NSF Grant PHY-1733907) and by a grant from the Simons Foundation (828076, TV). V.V. is supported by DARPA under Agreement No. HR00112020023, NSF CNS-2154149 and a Thornton Family Faculty Research Innovation Fellowship.

References

1. Aaronson, S.: Quantum copy-protection and quantum money. In: 2009 24th Annual IEEE Conference on Computational Complexity, pp. 229–242. IEEE (2009)
2. Aaronson, S.: The complexity of quantum states and transformations: from quantum money to black holes (2016)
3. Aaronson, S., Liu, J., Liu, Q., Zhandry, M., Zhang, R.: New approaches for quantum copy-protection. In: Malkin, T., Peikert, C. (eds.) CRYPTO 2021. LNCS, vol. 12825, pp. 526–555. Springer, Cham (2021). https://doi.org/10.1007/978-3-030-84242-0_19
4. Adcock, M., Cleve, R.: A quantum Goldreich-Levin theorem with cryptographic applications. In: Alt, H., Ferreira, A. (eds.) STACS 2002. LNCS, vol. 2285, pp. 323–334. Springer, Heidelberg (2002). https://doi.org/10.1007/3-540-45841-7_26
5. Agrawal, S., Kitagawa, F., Nishimaki, R., Yamada, S., Yamakawa, T.: Public key encryption with secure key leasing. arXiv preprint arXiv:2302.11663 (2023)
6. Ajtai, M.: Generating hard instances of lattice problems (extended abstract). In: Miller, G.L. (ed.) Proceedings of the Twenty-Eighth Annual ACM Symposium on the Theory of Computing, Philadelphia, 22–24 May 1996, pp. 99–108. ACM (1996)
7. Ananth, P., Kaleoglu, F.: Unclonable encryption, revisited. In: Nissim, K., Waters, B. (eds.) TCC 2021. LNCS, vol. 13042, pp. 299–329. Springer, Cham (2021). https://doi.org/10.1007/978-3-030-90459-3_11
8. Ananth, P., Kaleoglu, F.: A note on copy-protection from random oracles. arXiv preprint arXiv:2208.12884 (2022)
9. Ananth, P., Kaleoglu, F., Li, X., Liu, Q., Zhandry, M.: On the feasibility of unclonable encryption, and more. In: Dodis, Y., Shrimpton, T. (eds.) Advances in Cryptology – CRYPTO 2022, Part II. LNCS, pp. 212–241. Springer, Cham (2022). https://doi.org/10.1007/978-3-031-15979-4_8
10. Ananth, P., Kaleoglu, F., Liu, Q.: Cloning games: a general framework for unclonable primitives. arXiv preprint arXiv:2302.01874 (2023)
11. Ananth, P., La Placa, R.L.: Secure software leasing. In: Canteaut, A., Standaert, F.-X. (eds.) EUROCRYPT 2021. LNCS, vol. 12697, pp. 501–530. Springer, Cham (2021). https://doi.org/10.1007/978-3-030-77886-6_17
12. Badrinarayanan, S., Miles, E., Sahai, A., Zhandry, M.: Post-zeroizing obfuscation: new mathematical tools, and the case of evasive circuits. In: Fischlin, M., Coron, J.-S. (eds.) EUROCRYPT 2016. LNCS, vol. 9666, pp. 764–791. Springer, Heidelberg (2016). https://doi.org/10.1007/978-3-662-49896-5_27
13. Banerjee, A., Peikert, C., Rosen, A.: Pseudorandom functions and lattices. In: Pointcheval, D., Johansson, T. (eds.) EUROCRYPT 2012. LNCS, vol. 7237, pp. 719–737. Springer, Heidelberg (2012). https://doi.org/10.1007/978-3-642-29011-4_42
14. Bartusek, J., Khurana, D.: Cryptography with certified deletion. In: Handschuh, H., Lysyanskaya, A. (eds.) Advances in Cryptology – CRYPTO 2023, Part V. LNCS, vol. 14085, pp. 192–223. Springer, Cham (2023). https://doi.org/10.1007/978-3-031-38554-4_7
15. Bartusek, J., Khurana, D., Poremba, A.: Publicly-verifiable deletion via target-collapsing functions. In: Handschuh, H., Lysyanskaya, A. (eds.) Advances in Cryptology – CRYPTO 2023, Part V, LNCS, vol. 14085, pp. 99–128. Springer, Cham (2023). https://doi.org/10.1007/978-3-031-38554-4_4
16. Bennett, C.H., Brassard, G.: Quantum cryptography: public key distribution and coin tossing. In: Proceedings of IEEE International Conference on Computers, Systems, and Signal Processing, p. 175 (1984)

17. Bitansky, N., Brakerski, Z., Kalai, Y.T.: Constructive post-quantum reductions (2022)
18. Boneh, D., et al.: Fully key-homomorphic encryption, arithmetic circuit ABE, and compact garbled circuits. Cryptology ePrint Archive, Paper 2014/356 (2014). https://eprint.iacr.org/2014/356
19. Brakerski, Z., Döttling, N., Garg, S., Malavolta, G.: Circular-secure IWE suffices. Cryptology ePrint Archive, Factoring and pairings are not necessary for IO (2020)
20. Brakerski, Z., Vaikuntanathan, V.: Efficient fully homomorphic encryption from (standard) IWE. SIAM J. Comput. **43**(2), 831–871 (2014)
21. Broadbent, A., Islam, R.: Quantum encryption with certified deletion. In: Pass, R., Pietrzak, K. (eds.) TCC 2020. LNCS, vol. 12552, pp. 92–122. Springer, Cham (2020). https://doi.org/10.1007/978-3-030-64381-2_4
22. Broadbent, A., Jeffery, S., Lord, S., Podder, S., Sundaram, A.: Secure software leasing without assumptions. In: Nissim, K., Waters, B. (eds.) TCC 2021. LNCS, vol. 13042, pp. 90–120. Springer, Cham (2021). https://doi.org/10.1007/978-3-030-90459-3_4
23. Broadbent, A., Lord, S.: Uncloneable quantum encryption via oracles. In: Flammia, S.T. (ed.) 15th Conference on the Theory of Quantum Computation, Communication and Cryptography (TQC 2020), volume 158 of Leibniz International Proceedings in Informatics (LIPIcs), pp. 4:1–4:22. Schloss Dagstuhl-Leibniz-Zentrum für Informatik, Dagstuhl (2020)
24. Canetti, R., Feige, U., Goldreich, O., Naor, M.: Adaptively secure multi-party computation. In: Proceedings of the Twenty-Eighth Annual ACM Symposium on Theory of Computing (STOC 1996), pp. 639–648. Association for Computing Machinery, New York (1996)
25. Chen, Y., Vaikuntanathan, V., Wee, H.: GGH15 beyond permutation branching programs: proofs, attacks, and candidates. In: Shacham, H., Boldyreva, A. (eds.) CRYPTO 2018. LNCS, vol. 10992, pp. 577–607. Springer, Cham (2018). https://doi.org/10.1007/978-3-319-96881-0_20
26. Choudhuri, A.R., Jain, A., Jin, Z.: SNARGS for p from IWE. In: 2021 IEEE 62nd Annual Symposium on Foundations of Computer Science (FOCS), pp. 68–79. IEEE (2022)
27. Coladangelo, A., Liu, J., Liu, Q., Zhandry, M.: Hidden cosets and applications to unclonable cryptography. In: Malkin, T., Peikert, C. (eds.) CRYPTO 2021. LNCS, vol. 12825, pp. 556–584. Springer, Cham (2021). https://doi.org/10.1007/978-3-030-84242-0_20
28. Coladangelo, A., Majenz, C., Poremba, A.: Quantum copy-protection of compute-and-compare programs in the quantum random oracle model (2020)
29. Devadas, L., Quach, W., Vaikuntanathan, V., Wee, H., Wichs, D.: Succinct LWE sampling, random polynomials, and obfuscation. In: Nissim, K., Waters, B. (eds.) TCC 2021. LNCS, vol. 13043, pp. 256–287. Springer, Cham (2021). https://doi.org/10.1007/978-3-030-90453-1_9
30. Dieks, D.G.B.J.: Communication by EPR devices. Phys. Lett. A **92**(6), 271–272 (1982)
31. Dodis, Y., Goldwasser, S., Tauman Kalai, Y., Peikert, C., Vaikuntanathan, V.: Public-key encryption schemes with auxiliary inputs. In: Micciancio, D. (ed.) TCC 2010. LNCS, vol. 5978, pp. 361–381. Springer, Heidelberg (2010). https://doi.org/10.1007/978-3-642-11799-2_22
32. Gay, R., Pass, R.: Indistinguishability obfuscation from circular security. In: Proceedings of the 53rd Annual ACM SIGACT Symposium on Theory of Computing, pp. 736–749 (2021)

33. Gentry, C.: Fully homomorphic encryption using ideal lattices. In: Proceedings of the Forty-First Annual ACM Symposium on Theory of Computing, pp. 169–178 (2009)
34. Gentry, C., Peikert, C., Vaikuntanathan, V.: Trapdoors for hard lattices and new cryptographic constructions. Cryptology ePrint Archive, Report 2007/432 (2007). https://eprint.iacr.org/2007/432
35. Gentry, C., Sahai, A., Waters, B.: Homomorphic encryption from learning with errors: conceptually-simpler, asymptotically-faster, attribute-based. Cryptology ePrint Archive, Report 2013/340 (2013). https://ia.cr/2013/340
36. Georgiou, M., Zhandry, M.: Unclonable decryption keys. Cryptology ePrint Archive (2020)
37. Goldreich, O., Levin, L.A.: A hard-core predicate for all one-way functions. In: Proceedings of the Twenty-First Annual ACM Symposium on Theory of Computing (STOC 1989), pp. 25–32. Association for Computing Machinery, New York (1989)
38. Gottesman, D.: Uncloneable encryption. arXiv preprint quant-ph/0210062 (2002)
39. Hiroka, T., Morimae, T., Nishimaki, R., Yamakawa, T.: Certified everlasting zero-knowledge proof for QMA (2021)
40. Hiroka, T., Morimae, T., Nishimaki, R., Yamakawa, T.: Quantum encryption with certified deletion, revisited: public key, attribute-based, and classical communication. In: Tibouchi, M., Wang, H. (eds.) ASIACRYPT 2021. LNCS, vol. 13090, pp. 606–636. Springer, Cham (2021). https://doi.org/10.1007/978-3-030-92062-3_21
41. Intercept. How spies stole the keys to the encryption castle (2015). https://theintercept.com/2015/02/19/great-sim-heist/
42. Jain, A., Lin, H., Sahai, A.: Indistinguishability obfuscation from well-founded assumptions. In: Proceedings of the 53rd Annual ACM SIGACT Symposium on Theory of Computing, pp. 60–73 (2021)
43. Jarecki, S., Lysyanskaya, A.: Adaptively secure threshold cryptography: introducing concurrency, removing erasures. In: Preneel, B. (ed.) EUROCRYPT 2000. LNCS, vol. 1807, pp. 221–242. Springer, Heidelberg (2000). https://doi.org/10.1007/3-540-45539-6_16
44. Kitagawa, F., Nishimaki, R.: Functional encryption with secure key leasing. In: Agrawal, S., Lin, D. (eds.) ASIACRYPT 2022. LNCS, vol. 13794. Springer, Cham (2022). https://doi.org/10.1007/978-3-031-22972-5_20
45. Kitagawa, F., Nishimaki, R., Yamakawa, T.: Secure software leasing from standard assumptions. In: Nissim, K., Waters, B. (eds.) TCC 2021. LNCS, vol. 13042, pp. 31–61. Springer, Cham (2021). https://doi.org/10.1007/978-3-030-90459-3_2
46. Liu, J., Liu, Q., Qian, L., Zhandry, M.: Collusion resistant copy-protection for watermarkable functionalities. Cryptology ePrint Archive, Paper 2022/1429 (2022). https://eprint.iacr.org/2022/1429
47. Mahadev, U.: Classical verification of quantum computations (2018)
48. Poremba, A.: Quantum proofs of deletion for learning with errors (2022)
49. Regev, O.: On lattices, learning with errors, random linear codes, and cryptography. J. ACM 56(6), 34:1–34:40 (2005)
50. Rivest, R.L.: Can we eliminate certificate revocation lists? In: Hirchfeld, R. (ed.) FC 1998. LNCS, vol. 1465, pp. 178–183. Springer, Heidelberg (1998). https://doi.org/10.1007/BFb0055482
51. Stehlé, D., Steinfeld, R., Tanaka, K., Xagawa, K.: Efficient public key encryption based on ideal lattices. Cryptology ePrint Archive, Paper 2009/285 (2009). https://eprint.iacr.org/2009/285

52. Stubblebine, S.: Recent-secure authentication: enforcing revocation in distributed systems. In: 2012 IEEE Symposium on Security and Privacy, p. 0224. IEEE Computer Society, Los Alamitos (1995)
53. Tomamichel, M., Leverrier, A.: A largely self-contained and complete security proof for quantum key distribution. Quantum **1**, 14 (2017)
54. Unruh, D.: Revocable quantum timed-release encryption. Cryptology ePrint Archive, Report 2013/606 (2013). https://ia.cr/2013/606
55. Wee, H., Wichs, D.: Candidate obfuscation via oblivious LWE sampling. In: Canteaut, A., Standaert, F.-X. (eds.) EUROCRYPT 2021. LNCS, vol. 12698, pp. 127–156. Springer, Cham (2021). https://doi.org/10.1007/978-3-030-77883-5_5
56. Wiesner, S.: Conjugate coding. SIGACT News **15**(1), 78–88 (1983)
57. Wootters, W.K., Zurek, W.H.: A single quantum cannot be cloned. Nature **299**(5886), 802–803 (1982)
58. Zhandry, M.: Quantum lightning never strikes the same state twice or: quantum money from cryptographic assumptions. J. Cryptol. **34**(1) (2021)

Quantum Cryptography

Pseudorandomness with Proof of Destruction and Applications

Amit Behera[1]([envelope]) [iD], Zvika Brakerski[2] [iD], Or Sattath[1] [iD], and Omri Shmueli[3] [iD]

[1] Department of Computer Science, Ben Gurion University of the Negev, Beersheba, Israel
behera@post.bgu.ac.il, sattath@bgu.ac.il
[2] Weizmann Institute of Science, Rehovot, Israel
zvika.brakerski@weizmann.ac.il
[3] Tel-Aviv University, Tel Aviv, Israel
omrishmueli@mail.tau.ac.il

Abstract. Two fundamental properties of quantum states that quantum information theory explores are *pseudorandomness* and *provability of destruction*. We introduce the notion of *quantum pseudorandom states with proofs of destruction* (PRSPD) that combines both these properties. Like standard pseudorandom states (PRS), these are efficiently generated quantum states that are indistinguishable from random, but they can also be measured to create a classical string. This string is verifiable (given the secret key) and certifies that the state has been destructed. We show that, similarly to PRS, PRSPD can be constructed from any post-quantum one-way function. As far as the authors are aware, this is the first construction of a family of states that satisfies both *pseudorandomness* and *provability of destruction*.

We show that many cryptographic applications that were shown based on PRS variants using *quantum* communication can be based on (variants of) PRSPD using only *classical* communication. This includes symmetric encryption, message authentication, one-time signatures, commitments, and classically verifiable private quantum coins.

Keywords: Quantum Cryptography · Pseudorandomness · Pseudorandom States

1 Introduction

A *Pseudorandom States* family (PRS), introduced in [16]) is an efficiently samplable family of pure states such that for any polynomial t, t-copies of a (pure) quantum state $|\phi\rangle$ sampled uniformly at random from the family is computationally indistinguishable from t-copies of a truly random state sampled from the Haar measure. On the other hand, a *provably destructible* family of quantum states is accompanied by two efficient quantum algorithms, $\mathcal{D}estruct$, and $\mathcal{V}er$, such that running $\mathcal{D}estruct$ on a state $|\phi\rangle$ sampled from the family, produces a

© International Association for Cryptologic Research 2023
G. Rothblum and H. Wee (Eds.): TCC 2023, LNCS 14372, pp. 125–154, 2023.
https://doi.org/10.1007/978-3-031-48624-1_5

A. Behera et al.

classical proof $s_\phi \leftarrow \mathcal{D}estruct(|\phi\rangle)$ that can be verified using $\mathcal{V}er$, such that given a copy of a sampled state $|\phi\rangle$ one cannot output both, the state $|\phi\rangle$ and a valid proof of destruction s_ϕ. Proofs of destructions as defined above (or variants of it) have served as a crucial property for many unclonable primitives, such as tokenized digital signatures [7,12,23], classically verifiable quantum money [18,24], quantum lightning and its applications [13,21,27], one-shot signatures [1], etc.

As far as the authors are aware, there is no construction of a family of states that satisfies both pseudorandomness and provability of destruction. Previous constructions of provably destructible distributions were provably *not* pseudorandom. This stems from the fact that such techniques involved sampling a state that maintains its security only when a single copy is given. In fact, in most of these constructions (such as in [7,12]), given $O(n)$ copies of the sampled state, it is possible to not only tell the state from a Haar-random state but to completely characterize and efficiently generate the sampled state. On the side of pseudorandomness, previous techniques focused on sampled states that are uniform (or close to uniform) superpositions, with randomly sampled phases of the amplitudes. Since all known proof generation mechanisms $\mathcal{D}estruct$ in the literature are essentially, measurements in the computational basis, these constructions with uniform superposition can not be provably destructible. In this work, we study how to combine both these notions in a single primitive.

> Is it possible to construct a provably destructible family of quantum states that is also pseudorandom?

In classical cryptography, one-way functions (OWF) are considered a minimal assumption for computational-cryptography, and they are also sufficient for many applications. In the quantum setting, in contrast, (post-quantum) one-way functions are sufficient but do *not* appear to be necessary for a variety of cryptographic tasks such as symmetric encryption, digital signatures, message authentication codes, and commitments. Specifically, Ref. [16] showed that one-way functions are sufficient to build PRS, but Kretschmer [17] showed a black-box separation in the other direction, thus implying that OWFs are not necessary for PRS. Several recent works showed that PRS suffices to imply the aforementioned cryptographic applications (or variants thereof), without using OWF. For example, statistically-binding bit-commitment protocols have been shown based on PRS [4,19] (see Sect. 1.4 for other related works). However, these constructions used a different syntax than their classical counterparts—in particular in requiring *quantum* communication.

One of the aims of this work is to investigate whether this change is necessary:

> Is it possible to achieve cryptographic applications without quantum communication based on a pseudorandom states variant?

Indeed, this question has also been recently addressed by Ananth, Gulati, Qian and Yuen [2], who have shown statistically binding bit commitment and pseudo-encryption with classical communication. Their constructions were based on variants of PRS (namely, short output PRS and short output PRFS).

1.1 Our Results

Our first contribution, in Sect. 3, is defining the notion of proofs of destruction in the context of pseudorandom states, which addresses the first question raised above, see Page 2. In a PRS with proof of destruction (PRSPD), we augment a *Destruct* algorithm, which takes the pseudorandom state, and generates a classical proof; and a *Ver* algorithm, which takes a proposed proof and a key, and either accepts or rejects. We require that valid proofs should be accepted with certainty. In terms of security, we add the Unforgeability-of-proofs requirement, which guarantees that given t copies of the pseudorandom state, it should be hard to produce $t + 1$ distinct proofs of destruction. We extend the notion of proofs of destruction to a variant of PRS, called pseudorandom function-like states (PRFS), that was introduced in [4] (see Sect. 1.4 for further discussion). In a PRFS, the seed k should allow to efficiently generate a state for any input x, such that the states generated for different x's should jointly be indistinguishable from a random state. Namely, an adversary can choose $x_1, \ldots, x_m$, and should not be able to distinguish between $\bigotimes_{i \in [m]} |\psi_{k,x_i}\rangle$, where $|\psi_{k,x_i}\rangle$ are generated from the PRFS family, and $\bigotimes_{i \in [m]} |\varphi_{x_i}\rangle$ where $|\varphi_{x_i}\rangle$ is sampled from the Haar measure. We import the notion of Unforgeability-of-proofs to PRFS and define the notion of PRFSPD. We then proceed, in Sect. 4, to show how to construct PRSPD and PRFSPD from any post-quantum one-way function, which requires extending existing proof techniques for the construction of these primitives. Currently, we do not have a candidate construction of PRSPD or PRFSPD that does not use one-way functions directly.

Finally, in Sect. 5, we show how pseudorandom states (and function-like states) with proof of destruction can be used to achieve almost all of the existing known applications of pseudorandom states (and function-like states, respectively), without the need for quantum communication, thereby addressing the second question mentioned above, see Page 2. Specifically, we construct:

1. Length-restricted one-time secure digital signatures, and classically-verifiable private quantum coins[1] from any PRSPD.
2. A computational-hiding and statistically-binding bit commitment from PRSPD in which the proofs satisfy some *nice* properties, which we denote by PRSNPD—see the full version for details. While we do not know how to construct such PRSNPD from PRSPD or PRFSPD, our construction satisfies this niceness property.
3. CPA symmetric encryption (Sect. 5.2) and strong-CMA MAC (Sect. 5.1) from any PRFSPD. Note that this form of encryption is known to imply garbled circuits (see the full version for more details).

---

[1] In this primitive, the verification is quantum, but sending the proof of possession to the verifier only requires classical communication.

1.2   Our Techniques

Our construction of PRSPD is based on the following observation. Prior constructions starting with [16] showed that a uniform superposition over all computational basis elements, with a random phase, constitutes a PRS. Formally, the family $|\psi_k\rangle = \frac{1}{\sqrt{N}} \sum_{y \in \{0,1\}^n} \omega_N^{\mathsf{PRF}_k(y)} |y\rangle$ is a PRS family whenever PRF_k is a post-quantum PRF from n bits to n bits, where $N = 2^n$ and ω_N is the N-th root of unity. We show that a state which is supported on a pseudorandom subset of computational basis elements is still a PRS. More precisely, for a pseudorandom permutation PRP on $4n$ bits, let $A_{k'} = \{\mathsf{PRP}_{k'}(z || 0^{3n}) : z \in \{0,1\}^n\}$. We prove that the following states form a pseudorandom family:

$$|\psi_{k,k'}\rangle = \frac{1}{\sqrt{N}} \sum_{y \in A_{k'}} \omega_N^{\mathsf{PRF}_k(y)} |y\rangle. \tag{1}$$

This modification allows us to generate a proof of destruction as follows. The state $|\psi_{k,k'}\rangle$ is measured in the computational basis, resulting in a (uniformly random) element of $A_{k'}$, which we denote by p. The verification procedure for p is to apply $\mathsf{PRP}_{k'}^{-1}(p)$ and checking that the result is of the form $z || 0^{3n}$ for some string z. We show that this construction satisfies the Unforgeability-of-proofs property.

We observe a property of our construction from which it is easy to deduce both—the pseudorandomness property and the unforgeability of proofs property. We recall a property of the Haar-random distribution over quantum states. The following distributions (over quantum states) are equivalent: (i) Sample an n-qubit Haar-random state and output t copies of this state. (ii) Sample t elements from $\{0,1\}^n$, according to some distribution, and output a superposition over all $t!$ permutations of this t-tuple. In fact, the distribution can be $i.i.d$ uniform over the domain, with only a negligible effect on the outcome.

Now, if we sample the t elements not from the entire domain, but rather from a large enough random sub-domain, the distribution over tuples will remain statistically indistinguishable. We can apply this logic twice: First, to derive pseudorandomness, since a random state over a random subdomain is indistinguishable from a random state over the entire domain. Second, to derive the unforgeability of proofs, since providing t samples of the PRSPD state is statistically indistinguishable from a process that only uses t classical values from the sub-domain. Thus, coming up with an additional element in this random sub-domain can be done with at most negligible probability for classical information-theoretic reasons. We further show that experiment (ii) above is statistically close to experiment (iii): Sampling an exponential size subdomain A and a random function f and preparing t copies of the state $|\psi_{A,f}\rangle \propto \sum_{x \in A} \omega_N^{f(x)} |x\rangle$. Experiment (iii) and experiment (iv) in which t copies of the PRSPD states in Eq. (1) can now be seen to be computationally indistinguishable, by the pseudorandomness properties of the PRF and PRP functions. Transitions (ii)-(iv) are formalized in our main technical lemma, Lemma 6.

Extending this idea to PRFSPD is done in a straightforward manner, starting from the PRFS construction of [2]. Our PRFSPD family can be thought of as

$|\psi_{(k,k'),x}\rangle = \frac{1}{\sqrt{N}} \sum_{y \in A_{k',x}} \omega_N^{\mathsf{PRF}_k(x,y)} |y\rangle$, where $A_{k',x} = \{\mathsf{PRP}_{k'}(y||x||0^{3n}) : y \in \{0,1\}^n\}$ for $x \in \{0,1\}^n$. The destruction is done as before, and verification checks that p has the form $y||x||0^{3n}$.

How to Use Pseudorandom States with Proof of Destruction. In many cases, a template can be used to remove the quantum communication from a protocol involving pseudorandom states. Several protocols use PRS in the following manner. In the first part of the protocol, a pseudorandom state $|\psi_k\rangle$ is generated and sent via quantum communication. In a later step of the protocol, a testing procedure is applied to check if the state is indeed $|\psi_k\rangle$. In order to remove the quantum communication, we send the (classical) proof of destruction of it (instead of the state itself). Furthermore, we replace the testing whether the state is the "correct" state, with verifying that the proof of destruction is valid. This approach can also be applied with PRFS, where the state is $|\psi_{k,x}\rangle$ used.

Next, we demonstrate the use of the template above with a concrete example. Ref. [4] constructs a MAC scheme using PRFS, in which the secret key is a random k, $Sign_k(m)$ generate a *quantum* signature $|\psi_{k,m}\rangle$, and $Verify_k(m,|\varphi\rangle)$ is done by testing procedure discussed above, which tests whether $|\varphi\rangle$ is the expected state $|\psi_{k,m}\rangle$. In our scheme (see Sect. 5.1), $Sign_k(m)$ is done by preparing $|\psi_{k,m}\rangle$, and the *classical* signature is the proof of destruction, denoted p, of this state. Clearly, the signature can now be sent via a classical channel. The testing procedure above is replaced with checking that p is a valid proof of destruction for (k,m).

The template above is indeed useful as a conceptual framework, but applying it sometimes requires consideration of the specifics of the primitives. Some specific challenges that need to be addressed are as follows.

1. Pseudorandom states are pseudorandom as quantum states, but the proofs of destruction are not required to be pseudorandom strings. For example, one can easily transform a PRSPD scheme to one in which the first bit of the proof of destruction is always 0.
   This issue comes up in the context of bit-commitment. Reference [19] shows a construction that can be viewed as a quantum analog of Naor's commitments from PRG. There, we need to make the additional assumptions that the proofs *are* pseudorandom in order to prove the hiding property—see the full version for details.
   Recall that Naor's construction also requires a length-tripling PRG to prove the statistical binding. For analogous reasons, in our setting, we need a PRFSPD in which every key k accepts only a small fraction of the potential proofs.
   We define a PRSPD in which the proofs of destruction satisfy these *nice* properties as PRSNPD.

2. Pseudorandom states are known to be uncloneable [16, Theorem 2], but the proofs of destruction are classical and, therefore, can trivially be copied. We are only guaranteed that generating *new* proofs of destruction is hard. This difference means that for our quantum coins scheme to be secure, the bank

needs to keep a copy of the proofs that were already accepted, so these would be rejected in further attempts. In other words, unlike the quantum coin scheme proposed by [16], our quantum coin protocol is *stateful*—see the full version for details.

3. It can be shown that PRS are non-invertible in the following sense: Given $|\psi_k\rangle$, one cannot find k' such that $|\psi_{k'}\rangle$ has a non-negligible overlap with $|\psi_k\rangle$ [19, Lemma 4.1]. An analogous property does not necessarily hold for proofs of destruction: Given a proof p for $|\psi_k\rangle$, one might be able to find k' such that p is a valid proof of this destruction for k'. For example, given a PRSPD scheme, one can modify it so $k' = 00\ldots0$ accepts all proofs of destruction. Since that particular k' has a negligible probability of getting sampled as the key, it has no effect on the security of the scheme. But now, given a proof of destruction p, it is trivial to find a k' such that the proof of destruction is accepted. This issue arises in the context of one-time digital signatures, which we expand upon next.

To illustrate an example of such a challenge, let us describe our construction of one-time signatures from PRSPD. We recall Lamport's one-time signature scheme and assume that we only wish to sign one-bit messages (the extension to multiple bits is by repetition, as in the classical case). The idea in Lamport's OWF-based scheme is to sample uniformly random x_0, x_1 as the signing key, set $y_0 = f(x_0), y_1 = f(x_1)$ as a verification key, and set the signature on message $m \in \{0, 1\}$ to be x_m. This was adapted to PRS by [19], by replacing f with the PRS generator algorithm.

We wish to convert our quantum verification key to being classical using PRSPD. We achieve this by replacing the PRS states with their respective proofs of destruction p_0, p_1. The signature will be the key associated with the proof of destruction. However, contrary to the classical and PRS settings, we must take a different approach here. A forgery here consists of a PRSPD key k'_m which verifies p_m; indeed, if we were guaranteed that $k'_m = k_m$ then we would have been done since unforgeability of proofs would have been used in order to complete the security proof. However, this is not the case, and the unforgeability of proofs alone is insufficient: see Item 3 above.

To rule out "junk keys"—keys which accept too many proofs of destruction— we apply two modifications: the public key consists of a large number of proofs $\boldsymbol{p}_m$ for every value of m (where all proofs of destruction are generated using the same key), instead of just one. We know that all of these proofs of destruction will get accepted by the PRSPD verification by the key that generated these states. We also modify the signature verification algorithm so that given a signature k'_m, it first samples a large polynomial number of proofs of destruction with freshly random keys, and makes sure that k'_m is not verifying garbage (honestly generated keys will pass this test with overwhelming probability). Only after passing this test will the forgery be tested against $\boldsymbol{p}_m$. One can easily see that this method rules out simple "junk keys" that accept all proofs, as in the example described above. The full security proof uses a hybrid argument where the public key is not generated using a key k_m of the PRSPD, but instead, it is generated by applying the destruction algorithm to a *Haar random quantum state*.[2] This can only have a negligible change on the forgery probability by the pseudorandomness of the PRSPD. Interestingly, the construction by [19] *did not* use the pseudorandomness property and relied on a weaker notion called one-way state generators. We then show that an adversary which receives such "garbage" proofs p_m (i.e. proofs which are generated by the proof of destruction procedure on Haar random states) cannot provide forgery.

1.3 Open Problems

- A primary motivation to study pseudorandom states is that it seems as a weaker assumption than one-way functions, on which quantum cryptography could be based upon. Unfortunately, this separation result only holds for some of the PRS-variants. No such separation result is known for short-output PRS and short-output PRFS. Note that some of the applications prior to ours rely upon those. Similarly, we did not prove a similar separation for PRSPD and PRFSPD, and these challenges are left as an open problem.
- Does PRSPD imply short-input PRFSPD, i.e., PRFSPD with logarithmic input length? Ref. [4] constructs short-input PRFS from PRS generically by measuring the first $\log(\lambda)$ qubits and post-selecting the outcome being the input. The same approach may not work in the case of PRFSPD and PRSPD because the post-selection procedure as proposed in [4] may not commute with the *Destruct* algorithm for general PRSPD. An alternate yet related approach would be to run the *Destruct* algorithm on the input state without measurement, then measure only the first $\log(\lambda)$ qubits, post-select on the outcome being the input, and output the state on the unmeasured registers as the PRFSPD state.

  The hope is that if the starting state was *Haar* random, then the state on the unmeasured bits will be Haar random. However, the destruct algorithms may use ancillae qubits, and therefore the overall process becomes *non-unitary*, even before the measurement. Since non-unitary processes do not preserve *Haar*-random property, if we measure the first $\log(\lambda)$ registers, the state on the rest of the registers might not be statistically close to *Haar* random.

1.4 Related Works

Quantum forms of pseudorandomness have seen rapid development, which we summarize in this section. All the results mentioned (except the concurrent result of [3]), along with our main results are depicted in Fig. 1.

The study of pseudorandom state generators (PRS) was initiated by Ji, Liu, and Song [16]. They proved a construction based on the existence of post-quantum one-way functions. Ji, Liu, and Song's PRS construction were simplified in Ref. [10].

---

[2] One may be concerned that true random states are infeasible to generate, however for our purposes here we can use so-called "state-designs" instead of true random states.

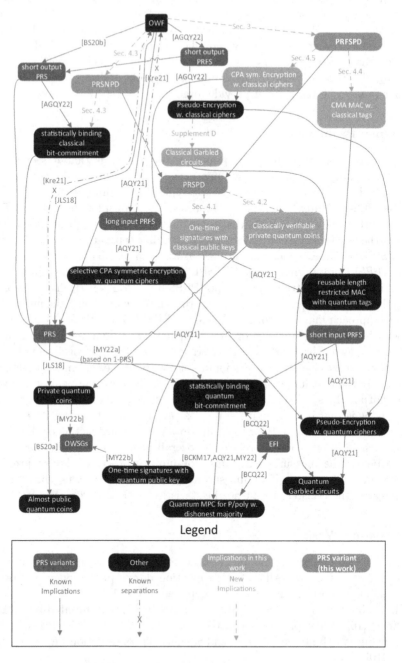

Fig. 1. Various applications of PRS and its variants. Best viewed in color. Unless stated otherwise, all applications are protocols that require *quantum communication*.

Kretschmer [17] proved a separation between one-way functions and PRSs: there exists a quantum oracle relative to which PRSs exist, but one-way functions do not exist. In other words, there is no black-box reduction from PRS to one-way functions (while a black-box reduction in the other direction is implied by [16]).

Several variants of PRS have been introduced, all of which are implied by post-quantum one-way functions. These different variants will play an important role when we discuss the applications. In Ref. [11], the authors show how to construct a *scalable* PRS based on OWFs; in this context, scalability means that for any function $n(\lambda) \leq \lambda$, one can construct a PRS with $n(\lambda)$ qubits. Perhaps counter-intuitively, and unlike pseudorandom generators, constructing pseudorandom states with a smaller number of qubits n seems harder (and definitely does not follow from the definition).

In [4], Ananth, Qian, and Yuen define pseudorandom function-like states (PRFS). An (d,n)-PRFS generator receives a key $k \in \{0,1\}^\lambda$ and an input $x \in \{0,1\}^d$ and outputs an n-qubit state[3]. In the security game, the adversary can choose (in advance) a set of inputs $x_1, \ldots, x_m$; the challenger either picks a random k and returns the PRFS states associated with $(k, x_1), (k, x_2), \ldots, (k, x_m)$, or samples a Haar random state for each distinct x_i, and send the states to the adversary. The adversary needs to distinguish between these two cases. They show how to construct a (n, d)-PRFS for $d = O(\log \lambda)$ from any $(n + d\lambda)$-PRS. We refer to PRFS in that regime (namely, $d = O(\log \lambda)$) as *short input* PRFS. They show how to construct a PRFS with $\omega(\log(\lambda))$ input length, which we refer to as long input PRFS, from any OWF. They also show that long input PRFS is separated from OWFs. It is not known how to construct long input PRFS from a short input PRFS. It is known that, similarly to vanilla PRS, *short* and *long* input PRFS are separated from post-quantum one-way functions [4].

Several applications of PRSs have been shown. In [16], it was shown that PRS implies a private quantum coin scheme—i.e., a private quantum money scheme in which all the quantum money states are exact copies. In [6], an almost public quantum coin scheme was shown based on the existence of any private coin scheme. In this context, *public* means that users can verify a quantum coin without out the bank. The scheme was *almost* public because it has several limitations. For example, it only achieves rational unforgeability; and the users must have coins in order to verify other coins. Note that there are no other *public* quantum money schemes based on one-way functions. Morimae and Yamakawa [19] construct a length-restricted one-time signature (also known as Lamport signature) with a quantum public key.

PRFS has several applications, which depend on the parameters of the PRFS. We start with those which are implied by the weakest form, namely, short input PRFS. Reference [4] construct a symmetric pseudo-encryption with quantum ciphers, which achieves one-time security. Pseudo-encryption means that the key is *shorter* than the length of the encrypted message—which is impossible to achieve unconditionally. This result requires a $\omega(\log \lambda)$-PRS or alternatively,

---

[3] For technical reasons which are outside the scope of this work, the algorithm can output abort.

an (n, d)-PRFS with $d > \log \lambda$ and $n = \omega(\log \lambda)$. As observed by [4], garbled circuits can be constructed from the symmetric pseudo-encryption mentioned above. Note that in this construction, the original circuit is classical, and the resulting garbled circuit is quantum. They also construct a statistically binding quantum bit-commitment from a $(2 \log \lambda) + \omega(\log \log \lambda))$-PRS (or, alternatively, an (n, d)-PRFS satisfying $2^d \cdot n \geq 7\lambda$); and by adapting the result in [5], they construct multi-party computation in the dishonest majority setting based on the same assumption.

Reference [4] also shows three other constructions based on *long input* PRFS: Symmetric encryption scheme secure against selective CPA with quantum ciphers based on $(\omega(\lambda), \omega(\lambda))$-PRFS; a reusable MAC with quantum tags, which is length restricted to $\ell(\lambda)$ bits, based on a (d, n)-PRFS with $d(\lambda) \geq \ell(\lambda)$ and $d = \omega(\log \lambda)$;

Recently, in [2], the authors report on statistically binding commitments and pseudo-encryption with *classical* communication. Their construction is based on *short output* PRFS, namely, $\log(\lambda)$ output and input sizes. In a concurrent and independent work [3], the authors showed a construction of non-adaptive CPA-secure symmetric encryption with classical ciphertexts from short output PRFS (this result is yet to be added in Fig. 1).

The notion of a PRS was used outside the context of cryptography in the study of the wormhole growth paradox [8] and quantum machine learning.

From the results mentioned so far, there is no indication that PRS (or any of its variants) are *minimal* assumptions for the cryptographic task that they can be used to achieve. Two recent works address this aspect: (a) Ref. [9] shows that EFI pairs—efficiently samplable, statistically far but computationally indistinguishable pairs of mixed quantum states—are equivalent to statistically binding quantum commitments, oblivious transfer, and several other functionalities. (b) Ref. [19,20] proved that a one-way state generator (OWSG) is equivalent to one-time signatures with quantum public keys.

We mention that OWSGs are known to be implied from private quantum coins and that a variant called secretly-verifiable and statistically invertible one-way state generator (SV-SI-OWSG) is equivalent to EFI [20].

2   Notations, Standard Cryptographic Definitions and Facts

For any finite set S, we use $s \xleftarrow{u} S$ to denote uniformly random sampling from the set S. Next, we recall the following result for quantum-secure Pseudorandom functions (PRF) and pseudorandom permutations (PRP), i.e., Pseudorandom functions and permutations that are secure against efficient quantum adversaries making quantum queries to the oracles, see the full version for the rigorous definitions.

Theorem 1 ([25, 26]). *PRFs and PRPs exist if quantum-secure one-way functions exist.*

Quantum Information: For any $n \in \mathbb{N}$, we use $\mathcal{H}_n$ to denote the Hilbert space on n-qubit registers, i.e., $\mathcal{H}_n = \mathbb{C}^{2^{\otimes n}}$, and N to denote N, the dimension of $\mathbb{C}^{2^{\otimes n}}$. Note that the optimal distinguishing probability between two n-qubit quantum (possibly mixed) states ρ_0 and ρ_1 is given by their trace distance $D(\rho_0, \rho_1)$, defined as

$$D(\rho_0, \rho_1) \overset{\text{def}}{=} \frac{1}{2} \|\rho_0 - \rho_1\|_1. \tag{2}$$

We now turn to discuss standard properties of symmetric subspaces; for an in-depth discussion, see [15]. For Hilbert space $\mathcal{H}_n$ of dimension N, i.e., it represents an n-qubit system, and integer t, we use $\vee^t \mathcal{H}_n$ to denote the symmetric subspace of $\mathcal{H}_n^{\otimes t}$, the subspace of states that are invariant under permutations of the subsystems. Let $\mathcal{X}$ be the set $\{0, 1, \ldots, N-1\}$ such that $\mathcal{H}_n$ is the span of $\{|x\rangle\}_{x \in \mathcal{X}}$.

For any subset $A \subset \mathcal{X}$, we use $\mathcal{H}_A$ to denote the subspace $\mathsf{Span}(A)$, and $\vee^t \mathcal{H}_A$ to denote the symmetric subspace of $\mathcal{H}_A^{\otimes t}$.

For any $t \in \mathbb{N}$, let $\mathbb{N}_t^A$ be the set of all vectors z in $\mathbb{N}^A$ such that $\sum_{j \in A} z_j = t$. We will abbreviate $\mathbb{N}_t^A$ as $\mathbb{N}_t$ for the special case $A = \mathcal{X}$. For any $\mathbf{x} = (x_1, x_2, \ldots, x_t) \in A^t$, denote $k(\mathbf{x})$ to be the associated vector in $\mathbb{N}_t^A$, i.e., the yth coordinate of z is the number of $\mathbf{x}_j$ that are y. For any $z \in \mathbb{N}_t$, define the state

$$|\mathrm{Sym}_t^z\rangle = \sqrt{\frac{1}{\binom{t}{z}}} \sum_{x \in \mathcal{X}^t : k(x) = z} |x\rangle. \tag{3}$$

For $z \in \mathbb{N}_t^A$, $|\mathrm{Sym}_t^z\rangle$ can be written as $\sqrt{\frac{1}{\binom{t}{z}}} \sum_{x \in A^t : k(x) = z} |x\rangle$.

The set of states

$$\left\{|\mathrm{Sym}_t^z\rangle\right\}_{z \in \mathbb{N}_t^A}, \left\{|\mathrm{Sym}_t^z\rangle\right\}_{z \in \mathbb{N}_t} \tag{4}$$

forms an orthonormal basis of the symmetric subspace $\vee^t \mathcal{H}_A$ and $\vee^t \mathcal{H}_n$, respectively. This implies that the dimension of the symmetric subspace $\vee^t \mathcal{H}_A$ is $|\mathbb{N}_t^A| = \binom{|A|+t-1}{t}$. In particular,

$$\dim\left(\vee^t \mathcal{H}_n\right) = |\mathbb{N}_t^{\mathcal{X}}| = \binom{N+t-1}{t}. \tag{5}$$

Let Π_t^{Sym} be the projection onto the symmetric subspace $\vee^t \mathcal{H}_n$, and for any $A \subset \mathcal{X}$, let $\Pi_t^{\mathrm{Sym}, A}$ be the orthogonal projection onto $\vee^t \mathcal{H}_A$.

Let $\mu_{\mathcal{H}_n}$ be the Haar measure on $\mathcal{H}_n$, and $\mu_{\mathcal{H}_A}$ be the induced measure on $\mathcal{H}_A$, we have

$$\int (|\psi\rangle\langle\psi|)^{\otimes t} d\mu_{\mathcal{H}_n}(\psi) = \binom{N+t-1}{t}^{-1} \Pi_t^{\mathrm{Sym}} = \rho_t^{\mathrm{Sym}} = \binom{N+t-1}{t}^{-1} \sum_z |\mathrm{Sym}_t^z\rangle\langle\mathrm{Sym}_t^z|. \tag{6}$$

$$\int (|\psi\rangle\langle\psi|)^{\otimes t} d\mu_{\mathcal{H}_A}(\psi) = \binom{|A|+t-1}{t}^{-1} \Pi_t^{\mathrm{Sym}, A} = \rho_t^{\mathrm{Sym}, A} \binom{N+t-1}{t}^{-1} \sum_{z \in \mathbb{N}_t^A} |\mathrm{Sym}_t^z\rangle\langle\mathrm{Sym}_t^z|. \tag{7}$$

3   Pseudorandom States and Function-Like States with Proofs of Destruction

In this section, we define pseudorandom states and function-like states with proofs of destruction and study some important properties and distributions related to them.

3.1   Core Definitions

Definition 1 (Pseudorandom state generator with proofs of destruction). *A PRSPD scheme with key-length $w(\lambda)$, output length $n(\lambda)$ and proof length $c(\lambda)$ is a tuple of QPT algorithms $(\mathcal{Gen}, \mathcal{Destruct}, \mathcal{Ver})$ with the following syntax:*

1. *$|\psi_k\rangle \leftarrow \mathcal{Gen}(k)$: takes a key $k \in \{0,1\}^{w(\lambda)}$, and outputs an $n(\lambda)$-qubit pure state[4] $|\psi_k\rangle$.*
2. *$p \leftarrow \mathcal{Destruct}(|\phi\rangle)$: takes an $n(\lambda)$-qubit quantum state $|\phi\rangle$, and outputs a $c(\lambda)$-bit classical string, p.*
3. *$b \leftarrow \mathcal{Ver}(k,p)$: takes a key $k \in \{0,1\}^{w(\lambda)}$, a $c(\lambda)$-bit classical string p and outputs a boolean output b.*

Correctness. A PRSPD scheme is said to be correct if

$$\Pr_{k \xleftarrow{u} \{0,1\}^{w(\lambda)}} [1 \leftarrow \mathcal{Ver}(k,p) \mid p \leftarrow \mathcal{Destruct}(|\psi_k\rangle); |\psi_k\rangle \leftarrow \mathcal{Gen}(k)] = 1$$

Security.

1. *Pseudorandomness: A PRSPD scheme is said to be pseudorandom if for any QPT adversary $\mathcal{A}$, and any polynomial $m(\lambda)$, there exists a negligible function $\mathsf{negl}(\lambda)$, such that*

$$\left| \Pr_{|\psi_k\rangle \leftarrow \mathcal{Gen}(k); k \leftarrow \{0,1\}^w}[\mathcal{A}(|\psi_k\rangle^{\otimes m}) = 1] - \Pr_{|\phi\rangle \leftarrow \mu_{(\mathbb{C}^2)^{\otimes n}}}[\mathcal{A}(|\phi\rangle^{\otimes m}) = 1] \right| = \mathsf{negl}(\lambda).$$

2. *Unforgeability-of-proofs: A PRSPD scheme satisfies Unforgeability-of-proofs if for any QPT adversary $\mathcal{A}$ in forging game (Game 1), there exists a negligible function $\mathsf{negl}(\lambda)$ such that*

$$\Pr[\text{Forging-Exp}_{\lambda}^{\mathcal{A},PRSPD} = 1] = \mathsf{negl}(\lambda).$$

Definition 2 (Pseudorandom function-like state generator with proofs of destruction). *A PRFSPD scheme with key-length $w(\lambda)$, input-length $d(\lambda)$, output length $n(\lambda)$ and proof length $c(\lambda)$ is a tuple of QPT algorithms $(\mathcal{Gen}, \mathcal{Destruct}, \mathcal{Ver})$ with the following syntax:*

---

[4] The pseudorandom security guarantee implies that with overwhelming probability over the chosen key, the state should be negligibly close to a pure state in trace distance; otherwise, pseudorandomness of the state can be violated via Swap-test.

Game 1 Forging-Exp$_\lambda^{\mathcal{A},PRSPD}$

1: Challenger samples $k \in \{0,1\}^{w(\lambda)}$ uniformly at random.
2: $\mathcal{A}^{Gen(k),Ver(k,\cdot)}(1^\lambda)$ outputs $p_1, p_2, \ldots, p_{t+1}$ to the challenger.
3: Adversary wins if: i) all p_i's are distinct, ii) the number of queries made to the $Gen(k)$ oracle was t, and iii) $Ver(k,p_i) = 1$ for $1 \leq i \leq t+1$.

1. $|\psi_k^x\rangle \leftarrow Gen(k,x)$: takes a key $k \in \{0,1\}^w$, an input string $x \in \{0,1\}^{d(\lambda)}$, and outputs an n-qubit pure state $|\psi_k^x\rangle$.
2. $p \leftarrow Destruct(|\phi\rangle)$: takes an n-qubit quantum state $|\phi\rangle$ as input, and outputs a c-bit classical string, p.
3. $b \leftarrow Ver(k,x,p)$: takes a key $k \in \{0,1\}^w$, a d-bit input string x, a c-bit classical string p and outputs a Boolean output b.

Correctness. A PRFSPD scheme is said to be correct if for every $x \in \{0,1\}^d$,

$$\Pr_{k \xleftarrow{u} \{0,1\}^w} [1 \leftarrow Ver(k,x,p) \mid p \leftarrow Destruct(|\psi_k^x\rangle)); |\psi_k^x\rangle \leftarrow Gen(k,x)] = 1$$

Security.

1. Pseudorandomness: A PRFSPD scheme is said to be quantum adaptively pseudorandom if for any QPT adversary $\mathcal{A}$ there exists a negligible function $negl(\lambda)$, such that the following absolute value is bounded by $negl(\lambda)$,

$$\left| \Pr_{k \leftarrow \{0,1\}^w} [\mathcal{A}^{Gen(k,\cdot)}(1^\lambda) = 1] - \Pr_{\forall x \in \{0,1\}^d, |\phi^x\rangle \leftarrow \mu_{(\mathbb{C}^2)^{\otimes n}}} [\mathcal{A}^{|Haar^{\{|\phi^x\rangle\}}x \in \{0,1\}^d}\rangle(\cdot)}(1^\lambda) = 1] \right|,$$
$$(8)$$

where $\forall x \in \{0,1\}^d$, $Haar^{\{|\phi^x\rangle\}}x \in \{0,1\}^d(x)$ outputs $|\phi^x\rangle$. Here $\mathcal{A}^{Gen(k,\cdot)}$ represents that $\mathcal{A}$ gets classical oracle access to $Gen(k,\cdot)$.

2. Unforgeability-of-proofs: A PRFSPD scheme satisfies Unforgeability-of-proofs if for any QPT adversary $\mathcal{A}$ in forging game (Game 2), there exists a negligible function $negl(\lambda)$ such that

$$\Pr[\text{Forging-Exp}_\lambda^{\mathcal{A},PRFSPD} = 1] = negl(\lambda).$$

Remark 1. A pseudorandom state generator or PRS(respectively, pseudorandom function-like state generator or PRFS) is the same as PRSPD (respectively, PRFSPD), but without the Destruct and Ver algorithms, and the correctness and Unforgeability-of-proofs requirements.

Remark 2 (PRFSPD Input Shortening and PRSPD). PRFSPD with input length d immediately implies PRFSPD with input length $d' \in \{0, 1, \cdots, d\}$ and in particular PRSPD. To see this, if $(Gen, Destruct, Ver)$ is a PRFSPD with input length d, then for any $d' \in \{0, 1, \cdots, d\}$, consider the d'-input-length scheme PRFSPD$_{d'} = (Gen', Destruct, Ver')$ where for $x' \in \{0,1\}^{d'}$:

Game 2 Forging-Exp$_\lambda^{\mathcal{A},\text{PRFSPD}}$

1: Given input 1^λ, Challenger samples $k \leftarrow \{0,1\}^{w(\lambda)}$ uniformly at random.
2: Initialize an empty set of variables, S.
3: $\mathcal{A}$ gets oracle access to $\mathcal{G}en(k, \cdot)$, $\mathcal{V}er(k, \cdot, \cdot)$ as oracle.
4: **for** $\mathcal{G}en$ query x made by $\mathcal{A}$ **do**
5:     **if** $\exists$ variable $t_x \in S$ **then** $t_x = t_x + 1$.
6:     **else** Create a variable t_x in S, initialized to 1.
7:     **end if**
8: **end for**
9: $\mathcal{A}$ outputs $x, p_1, p_2, \ldots, p_{t_x+1}$ to the challenger.
10: Challenger rejects if p_i's are not distinct.
11: **for** $i \in [t_x + 1]$ **do** $b_i \leftarrow \mathcal{V}er(k, x, p_i)$
12: **end for**
13: Return $\wedge_{i=1}^{t_x+1} b_i$.

- $\mathcal{G}en'(\cdot, x') = \mathcal{G}en(\cdot, (x'||0^{d-d'}))$.
- $\mathcal{V}er'(\cdot, x', \cdot) = \mathcal{V}er(\cdot, (x'||0^{d-d'}), \cdot)$.

This is similar to how pseudorandom function-like states imply pseudorandom states: A reduction that takes an adversary against the new scheme and attaches $d - d'$ zeros to its queries shows that we can use it in order to break the original scheme. Finally, PRFSPD with input length 0 exactly implies the definition of a PRSPD.

Remark 3 (Computational assumptions are necessary for PRSPD and PRFSPD). Clearly, PRSPD with $\omega(\log(1^\lambda))$ output-length implies PRS with $\omega(\log(1^\lambda))$ output-length which cannot exist unconditionally [2,17], hence PRSPD and PRFSPD with $\omega(\log(1^\lambda))$ output-length cannot exist unconditionally. It should be noted that PRSPD (and therefore PRFSPD) with $O(\log(1^\lambda))$ cannot exist since an adversary can learn an approximate description of the PRSPD state efficiently using tomography and use this description to win the forging game, see Game 1.

3.2 Distributions Related to the $\mathcal{D}estruct$ Algorithm of PRSPD, PRFSPD, and Haar Random States

Definition 3 (Correlated and independent destructions for Haar random states). *For any algorithm $\mathcal{D}estruct$, that take a n-qubit state as input and outputs a c-bit classical string as output, and for every $t \in$ poly(λ), Correlated-Destruction$_t^{\mathcal{H}aar,\mathcal{D}estruct}$ is the distribution on $\{0,1\}^{ct}$ given by, $(f_1, \ldots, f_t) \sim$ Correlated-Destruction$_t^{\mathcal{H}aar,\mathcal{D}estruct}$ where*

$$(f_1, \ldots, f_t) \leftarrow \mathcal{D}estruct^{\otimes t}(|\phi\rangle^{\otimes t}); |\phi\rangle \sim \mu_{\mathcal{H}_n}.$$

For every $t \in$ poly(λ), let Product-Destruction$_t^{\mathcal{H}aar,\mathcal{D}estruct}$ be the t-fold product of Product-Destruction$^{\mathcal{H}aar,\mathcal{D}estruct}$ which is given by

$$f \sim \text{Product-Destruction}^{\mathcal{H}aar,\mathcal{D}estruct} \equiv f \leftarrow \mathcal{D}estruct(|\phi\rangle); |\phi\rangle \sim \mu_{\mathcal{H}_n}.$$

Definition 4 (Correlated and independent destructions of PRSPD and PRFSPD). *For any PRSPD family* $\mathcal{PRSPD} = (\mathcal{Gen}, \mathcal{Destruct}, \mathcal{Ver})$ *and for every* $t \in \mathsf{poly}(\lambda)$, $\mathsf{Correlated\text{-}Destruction}_t^{\mathcal{PRSPD}}$ *is the distribution on* $\{0,1\}^{ct}$ *given by,* $(f_1, \ldots, f_t) \sim \mathsf{Correlated\text{-}Destruction}_t^{\mathcal{PRSPD}}$ *where*

$$(f_1, \ldots, f_t) \leftarrow \mathcal{Destruct}^{\otimes t}(|\psi_k\rangle^{\otimes t}); |\psi_k\rangle \leftarrow \mathcal{Gen}(k), \text{ where } k \xleftarrow{u} \{0,1\}^w.$$

For every $t \in \mathsf{poly}(\lambda)$, *let* $\mathsf{Product\text{-}Destruction}_t^{\mathcal{PRSPD}}$ *be the t-fold product of* $\mathsf{Product\text{-}Destruction}^{\mathcal{PRSPD}}$ *which is given by*

$$f \sim \mathsf{Product\text{-}Destruction}^{\mathcal{PRSPD}} \equiv f \leftarrow \mathcal{Destruct}(|\phi_k\rangle); |\phi_k\rangle \leftarrow \mathcal{Gen}(k), \text{ where } k \xleftarrow{u} \{0,1\}^w.$$

For any PRFSPD family $\mathcal{PRFSPD} = (\mathcal{Gen}, \mathcal{Destruct}, \mathcal{Ver})$, *for any* $x \in \{0,1\}^d$ *and for every* $t \in \mathsf{poly}(\lambda)$, *let* $\mathsf{Correlated\text{-}Destruction}_t^{\mathcal{PRFSPD},x} = \mathsf{Correlated\text{-}Destruction}_t^{\mathcal{PRFSPD}_x}$ *and* $\mathsf{Product\text{-}Destruction}^{\mathcal{PRFSPD},x} = \mathsf{Product\text{-}Destruction}^{\mathcal{PRFSPD}_x}$, *where* $\mathcal{PRFSPD}_x$ *is the PRSPD scheme obtained out of* $\mathcal{PRFSPD}$ *by fixing the input to* x, *see Definition 2 and Remark 2.*

3.3 Properties of Pseudorandom States and Function-Like States with Proofs of Destruction

In this section, we state a few properties of PRSPD and PRFSPD, that would be important for the applications in Sect. 5. These properties (Lemmas 1–5) are true for arbitrary PRSPD and PRFSPD, but due to space constraints, we only sketch the proofs in this version. For simplicity, some of the proofs are sketched only for a special case, where the $\mathcal{Destruct}$ algorithm of the respective PRSPD or PRFSPD family measures the state in the computational basis, and outputs the measurement outcome. Note that the $\mathcal{Destruct}$ algorithm, in general, could be more complicated and involve ancillae registers. The proof for the general case is given in full version.

Lemma 1 (PRSPD have well-distributed proofs). *For every PRSPD scheme* $(\mathcal{Gen}, \mathcal{Destruct}, \mathcal{Ver})$ *with key length* $w(\lambda)$ *proof length* $c(\lambda)$, *for every* $a \in \{0,1\}^c$, *there exists a negligible function* $\mathsf{negl}(\lambda)_a$,

$$\Pr[K \xleftarrow{u} \{0,1\}^w : \mathcal{Destruct}(\mathcal{Gen}(K)) = a] = \mathsf{negl}(\lambda)_a.$$

Furthermore, there exists a negligible function $\widetilde{\mathsf{negl}}(\lambda)_a$, *such that*

$$\Pr[|\phi\rangle \sim \mu_{\mathcal{H}_n} : \mathcal{Destruct}(|\phi\rangle) = a] = \widetilde{\mathsf{negl}}(\lambda)_a.$$

Proof sketch for the special case. The proof follows by combining pseudorandomness of the PRSPD with the observation that the $\mathcal{Destruct}$ algorithm on a *Haar* random state produces a uniformly random outcome.   □

The proof for the general case is given in the full version.

Lemma 2 (PRSPD proofs are distributed close to product distribution). *Let $\mathcal{PRSPD} = (\mathcal{Gen}, \mathcal{Destruct}, \mathcal{Ver})$ be a PRSPD scheme with key length $w(\lambda)$ proof length $c(\lambda)$. For every $t \in \mathsf{poly}(\lambda)$, and $a_1, \ldots, a_t \in \{0,1\}^c$,*[5]

$$\Pr_{\text{Correlated-Destruction}_t^{\mathcal{Haar}, \mathcal{Destruct}}} [(f_1, \ldots, f_t) = (a_1, \ldots, a_t)]$$

$$\leq \frac{N^t}{\binom{N+t-1}{t}} \Pr_{\text{Product-Destruction}_t^{\mathcal{Haar}, \mathcal{Destruct}}} [(f_1, \ldots, f_t) = (a_1, \ldots, a_t)],$$

where the subscript in the probability denotes the distribution of $(f_1, \ldots, f_t)$, and the distributions are as defined in Definition 3.

Proof sketch for the special case. Observe that for any $a_1, \ldots, a_t \in \{0,1\}^{c(\lambda)}$, there exists a unique z such that $\langle a_1, \ldots, a_t | \mathrm{Sym}_t^z \rangle$ is non-zero, see Sect. 2 for the definition of Sym_t^z. Combining this observation with Eq. (6) and the fact that $\mathcal{Destruct}$ is just a measurement in the computational basis, we conclude that $\Pr_{\text{Correlated-Destruction}_t^{\mathcal{Haar}, \mathcal{Destruct}}} [(f_1, \ldots, f_t) = (a_1, \ldots, a_t)]$, i.e.,

$$\Pr[|\phi\rangle \sim \mu_{\mathcal{H}_n} : \mathcal{Destruct}^{\otimes t}(|\phi\rangle^{\otimes t}) = (a_1, \ldots, a_t)] \leq \frac{1}{\binom{N+t-1}{t}},$$

where equality holds when $a_1 = \cdots = a_t$. Moreover, $\Pr_{\text{Product-Destruction}_t^{\mathcal{Haar}, \mathcal{Destruct}}} [(f_1, \ldots, f_t) = (a_1, \ldots, a_t)] = \frac{1}{N^t}$ for every $a_1, \ldots, a_t \in \{0,1\}^{c(\lambda)}$. Hence,

$$\Pr_{\text{Correlated-Destruction}_t^{\mathcal{Haar}, \mathcal{Destruct}}} [(f_1, \ldots, f_t) = (a_1, \ldots, a_t)]$$

$$\leq \frac{N^t}{\binom{N+t-1}{t}} \Pr_{\text{Product-Destruction}_t^{\mathcal{Haar}, \mathcal{Destruct}}} [(f_1, \ldots, f_t) = (a_1, \ldots, a_t)].$$

$\square$

The proof for the general case is given in the full version.

Remark 4. For every $t \in \mathsf{poly}(\lambda)$, Correlated-Destruction$_t^{\mathcal{Haar}, \mathcal{Destruct}}$ and Product-Destruction$_t^{\mathcal{Haar}, \mathcal{Destruct}}$ are efficiently samplable using a state t-design and a state 1-design for n-qubit quantum states, respectively.

Lemma 3 (PRSPD proofs are collision-free). *For every PRSPD scheme $\mathcal{PRSPD} = (\mathcal{Gen}, \mathcal{Destruct}, \mathcal{Ver})$ with key length $w(\lambda)$, proof length $c(\lambda)$, and $t \in \mathsf{poly}(\lambda)$, there exists a negligible function $\mathsf{negl}(\lambda)$,*

$$\Pr_{\text{Correlated-Destruction}_t^{\mathcal{PRSPD}}} [\text{Collision}] \equiv \Pr_{\text{Correlated-Destruction}_t^{\mathcal{PRSPD}}} [\exists i \neq j \mid f_i = f_j] = \mathsf{negl}(\lambda),$$

---

[5] We believe that the distributions are in fact, statistically close due to the strong concentration of the Haar measure, but we have not been able to prove it. The lemma is a weaker version of this statement, but it suffices for our purposes.

where the subscript under the probability is the distribution on $f_1, \ldots, f_t$ and Correlated-Destruction$_t^{\mathcal{PRSPD}}$ *is as defined in Definition 4.*

Moreover, by the pseudorandomness of PRSPD *(see Definition 1) there exists a negligible function* $\widetilde{\mathsf{negl}(\lambda)}$ *such that*

$$\Pr_{\mathsf{Correlated\text{-}Destruction}_t^{\mathcal{Haar},\mathcal{Destruct}}}[\text{Collision}] \equiv \Pr_{\mathsf{Correlated\text{-}Destruction}_t^{\mathcal{Haar},\mathcal{Destruct}}}[\exists i \neq j \mid f_i = f_j] = \widetilde{\mathsf{negl}(\lambda)},$$

where Correlated-Destruction$_t^{\mathcal{Haar},\mathcal{Destruct}}$ *is as defined in Definition 3.*

Proof sketch for the special case. The moreover part follows by observing that for any $t \in \mathsf{poly}(n)$, measuring t-copies of a n-qubit $\mathcal{Haar}$ random state, is statistically close up to negligible distance (in n) to the t-fold product of the uniform distribution on $\{0,1\}^n$. Hence, the probability of observing indistinct t-outcomes is negligible. The rest of the proof follows due to the pseudorandomness of the PRSPD. □

The proof for the general case is given in the full version.

Lemma 4 (PRFSPD proofs are collision-free). *For every PRFSPD scheme* $\mathcal{PRFSPD} = (\mathcal{Gen}, \mathcal{Destruct}, \mathcal{Ver})$ *with key length* $w(\lambda)$, *input length* $d(\lambda)$, *proof length* $c(\lambda)$, *and* $t \in \mathsf{poly}(\lambda)$, *and* $x \in \{0,1\}^d$ *there exists a negligible function* $\widetilde{\mathsf{negl}(\lambda)}$,

$$\Pr_{\mathsf{Correlated\text{-}Destruction}_t^{\mathcal{PRFSPD},x}}[\text{Collision}_x] \equiv \Pr_{\mathsf{Correlated\text{-}Destruction}_t^{\mathcal{PRFSPD},x}}[\exists i \neq j \mid f_i^x = f_j^x] = \widetilde{\mathsf{negl}(\lambda)},$$

where Correlated-Destruction$_t^{\mathcal{PRFSPD},x}$ *is as defined in Definition 4.*

Proof. Given a PRFSPD scheme $\mathcal{PRFSPD}$ with input length $d(\lambda)$, and any fixed input $x \in \{0,1\}^d$, we can construct a PRSPD scheme $\mathcal{PRSPD}_x$ as per Remark 2. Applying Lemma 3 on $\mathcal{PRSPD}_x$, we get the desired result. □

Lemma 5 (Classical unforgeability of PRFSPD). *Let PRFSPD = ($\mathcal{Gen}$, $\mathcal{Destruct}$, $\mathcal{Ver}$) be a Pseudorandom function-like state generator with proofs of destruction family. Then, for every QPT adversary $\mathcal{A}$, there exists a negligible function* $\mathsf{negl}(\lambda)$ *such that*

$$\Pr[\mathsf{Classical\text{-}Forging\text{-}Exp}_\lambda^{\mathcal{A},PRFSPD} = 1] = \mathsf{negl}(\lambda),$$

where Classical-Forging-Exp$_\lambda^{\mathcal{A},PRFSPD}$ *is defined in Game 3.*

Proof sketch. The proof follows by combining Lemma 4 with the Unforgeability-of-proofs property of PRFSPD. □

The proof for the general case is given in the full version.

Game 3 Classical-Forging-Exp$_\lambda^{\mathcal{A},\mathsf{PRFSPD}}$

Game 3 Classical-Forging-Exp$_\lambda^{\mathcal{A},\mathsf{PRFSPD}}$

1: Given input 1^λ, Challenger samples $k \leftarrow \{0,1\}^{w(\lambda)}$ uniformly at random. Challenger also initializes an empty set S.
2: Initialize an empty set of variables, S.
3: $\mathcal{A}$ gets oracle access to $\mathcal{D}estruct(\mathcal{G}en(k,\cdot))$, $\mathcal{V}er(k,\cdot,\cdot)$ as oracle.
4: **for** $\mathcal{D}estruct(\mathcal{G}en(k,\cdot))$ query x made by $\mathcal{A}$ **do** Add (x,σ_x) to S, where σ_x is the response of $\mathcal{D}estruct(\mathcal{G}en(k,\cdot))$ oracle on input x.
5: **end for**
6: $\mathcal{A}$ outputs x', σ_x' to the challenger.
7: Return 1 if $(x', \sigma_x') \notin S$ and $\mathcal{V}er(k, x', \sigma_x') = 1$.

4   Construction of PRFSPD from any Post-quantum One-Way Function

In this section, we construct PRFSPD (Definition 2) from post-quantum one-way functions. To be more precise, we build a PRFSPD from post-quantum pseudorandom permutations (PRP), and since post-quantum OWFs imply post-quantum PRPs [26], our statement follows. Finally, recall Remark 2 which explains why a PRFSPD with input length $d(\lambda) = \lambda$ implies a PRFSPD with input length $0 \le d'(\lambda) \le d(\lambda)$, which also means that it implies a PRSPD.

Theorem 2 (Main Theorem). *Assume there exist post-quantum one-way functions. Then, a PRFSPD scheme (Definition 2) with key length $w(\lambda) = \lambda$, input length $d(\lambda) = \lambda$, output length $n(\lambda) = 5 \cdot \lambda$ and proof length $c(\lambda) = 5 \cdot \lambda$, exists.*

The construction is given in Fig. 2 and Fig. 3. In the construction, as in the main theorem, we define the following lengths as a function of the security parameter: key length $w(\lambda) = \lambda$, input length $d(\lambda) = \lambda$, output length $n(\lambda) = 5 \cdot \lambda$ and proof length $c(\lambda) = 5 \cdot \lambda$. Our only cryptographic ingredient is a post-quantum pseudorandom permutation PRP on 5λ bits.

We next prove the security of the PRFSPD construction. This means two things: That the generated states are pseudorandom and that the classical proofs generated are unforgeable. To this end, we prove our main technical lemma that will easily imply both security aspects. Roughly, the lemma below implies that (1) classical access to the $\mathcal{G}en$ oracle, is computationally indistinguishable from an oracle that outputs truly random quantum states, and (2) for every input $x \in \{0,1\}^d$, generating more proofs of destruction than the number of queries that were made to the $\mathcal{G}en$ oracle for x is *information theoretically impossible*.

Lemma 6 (Main Technical Lemma). *Let T a polynomial and let $\mathcal{A}$ a quantum polynomial-time algorithm that outputs a bit $b \in \{0,1\}$ and has classical oracle access to some arbitrary oracle with inputs in $\{0,1\}^d$, such that for every possible input $x \in \{0,1\}^d$, $\mathcal{A}$ makes either 0 or exactly T queries to the oracle on that input x. Then the following two distributions on b are computationally indistinguishable:*

$Gen(k, x)$: For security parameter $\lambda \in \mathbb{N}$, input $k \in \{0,1\}^{w(\lambda)}, x \in \{0,1\}^{d(\lambda)}$, execute the following.

1. Generate the uniform superposition $2^{-\frac{\lambda}{2}} \cdot \sum_{y\in\{0,1\}^\lambda} |y\rangle$ over λ qubits.
2. Apply the classical PRP circuit in superposition, with the superposition as input concatenated with $(x, 0^{3\lambda}) \in \{0,1\}^{4\lambda}$:

$$2^{-\frac{\lambda}{2}} \cdot \sum_{y\in\{0,1\}^\lambda} |y\rangle |x, 0^{3\lambda}\rangle |\mathsf{PRP}_k\left(y, x, 0^{3\lambda}\right)\rangle .$$

3. Apply the inverse of the classical PRP circuit in superposition to un-compute the left 5λ qubits and get:

$$2^{-\frac{\lambda}{2}} \cdot \sum_{y\in\{0,1\}^\lambda} |0^{5\lambda}\rangle |\mathsf{PRP}_k\left(y, x, 0^{3\lambda}\right)\rangle .$$

4. Apply the following circuit $C : \{0,1\}^{5\lambda} \to \{0,1\}^{5\lambda}$ in superposition: Given input, the circuit C computes $\mathsf{PRP}_k^{-1}(\cdot)$, then flips the rightmost 3λ bits, then applies the permutation $\mathsf{PRP}_k(\cdot)$. One can verify that the state we get is

$$2^{-\frac{\lambda}{2}} \cdot \sum_{y\in\{0,1\}^\lambda} |\mathsf{PRP}_k\left(y, x, 1^{3\lambda}\right)\rangle |\mathsf{PRP}_k\left(y, x, 0^{3\lambda}\right)\rangle .$$

5. Apply on the left 5λ qubits the unitary that for every $z \in \{0,1\}^{5\lambda}$ maps $U :$ $|z\rangle \to \omega_{2^{5\lambda}}^z \cdot |z\rangle$ (this can be efficiently done with a phase kick-back algorithm, as explained in the proof of Theorem 1 in [16]),

$$2^{-\frac{\lambda}{2}} \cdot \sum_{y\in\{0,1\}^\lambda} \omega_{2^{5\lambda}}^{\mathsf{PRP}_k(y,x,1^{3\lambda})}. \tag{9}$$

$$|\mathsf{PRP}_k\left(y, x, 1^{3\lambda}\right)\rangle |\mathsf{PRP}_k\left(y, x, 0^{3\lambda}\right)\rangle . \tag{10}$$

6. Apply the circuit C again in order to un-compute the left register and trace the remaining 5λ qubits to obtain the output state:

$$|\psi_k^x\rangle := 2^{-\frac{\lambda}{2}} \cdot \sum_{y\in\{0,1\}^\lambda} \omega_{2^{5\lambda}}^{\mathsf{PRP}_k(y,x,1^{3\lambda})} \cdot |\mathsf{PRP}_k\left(y, x, 0^{3\lambda}\right)\rangle .$$

Fig. 2. The state generation procedure of our Pseudorandom Function-Like States with Proof of Destruction.

– D_0 : *Sample $k \leftarrow \{0,1\}^\lambda$ uniformly at random. $\mathcal{A}$ has classical access to $Gen(k, \cdot)$, $Ver(k, \cdot, \cdot)$ (from Fig. 2 and Fig. 3, respectively), and makes either 0 or exactly T queries to each of the possible inputs $x \in \{0,1\}^d$ to $Gen(k, \cdot)$, and outputs a bit b.*

$Destruct(|\phi\rangle)$

1. Measure the state $|\phi\rangle$ in the computational basis, and output the measurement outcome.

$Ver(k, x, q)$

1. Compute $z := \mathsf{PRP}_k^{-1}(q) \in \{0,1\}^{5\lambda}$.
2. Denote the bits of z as $(z_1, z_2, \cdots, z_{5\lambda})$. Output 1 iff $(z_{\lambda+1}, \cdots, z_{5\lambda}) = (x||0^{3\lambda})$.

Fig. 3. The state destruction and classical proof verification procedures of our Pseudorandom Function-Like States with Proof of Destruction.

- D_1 : For every $x \in \{0,1\}^d$, sample a T-sized multi-set of $\{0,1\}^{5\lambda}$: $(a_{x,1}, \cdots, a_{x,T})$, and generate the $T \cdot 5\lambda$-qubit state,

$$|\pi_x\rangle := \sum_{\sigma \in S_T} |a_{x,\sigma(1)}, \cdots, a_{x,\sigma(T)}\rangle \ ,$$

and for each $x \in \{0,1\}^d$, partition the $T \cdot 5\lambda$-qubit state $|\pi_x\rangle$ into T subregisters, each of size 5λ. The oracles are defined as follows: The generation oracle $Gen^*(\cdot)$, given $x \in \{0,1\}^d$ for the c-th query (for $c \in [T]$), outputs the c-th sub-register of the state $|\pi_x\rangle$. The proof verification oracle $Ver^*(\cdot, \cdot)$, given query $(x, q) \in (\{0,1\}^d \times \{0,1\}^{5\lambda})$, outputs 1 iff $q \in \{a_{x,1}, \cdots, a_{x,T}\}$. $\mathcal{A}$ has classical access to $Gen^*(\cdot)$, $Ver^*(\cdot, \cdot)$, makes either 0 or exactly T queries to $Gen^*(\cdot)$ for every $x \in \{0,1\}^d$, and outputs a bit b.

The proof of the lemma is deferred to the full version.

Proposition 1 (Security - Pseudorandomness). *The PRFSPD scheme in Fig. 2, Fig. 3 maintains the pseudorandomness property (as in Definition 2).*

Proof. Let $\mathcal{A}$ be a quantum polynomial-time adversary and let T be a polynomial bound on the running time of $\mathcal{A}$. We claim that one can assume without the loss of generality that for every possible input $x \in \{0,1\}^d$, $\mathcal{A}$ makes either 0 or exactly T queries to the generation oracle $Gen(\cdot)$ oracle. The reason is as follows: We can think of a new adversary $\mathcal{A}'$ that, at the end of the execution of $\mathcal{A}$, takes the inputs in $\{0,1\}^d$ that $\mathcal{A}$ queried during its execution $x_1, \cdots, x_t \in \{0,1\}^d$ (for $t \in [T]$) without considering multiplicity (i.e., some of the inputs were possibly queried more than others) and for each of these inputs, complementing the number of times that it was queried (which, as we know is bounded by T by the fact that T is an upper bound on the total running time of $\mathcal{A}$) to be T - such adversary still breaks the pseudorandomness security guarantee and also satisfies the property that for every possible input in $\{0,1\}^d$, the input was queried either 0 or T times. Now, Lemma 6 *in particular* says that the output of $\mathcal{A}$ on the classical access to the generation function $Gen(k, \cdot)$ (which is part of D_0 in the lemma's statement) is computationally indistinguishable from the output of $\mathcal{A}$ when the access is to the generation function $Gen^*(\cdot)$ defined in the distribution D_1, in the statement of the Lemma 6.

One of the standard facts in quantum information theory is that the distribution generated by T copies of a truly random, 5λ-qubit Haar state is statistically equivalent (i.e. has trace distance 0) to the projection onto the $(5\lambda, T)$-symmetric subspace ([15, Prop. 6]). In turn, an orthonormal basis for the $(5\lambda, T)$-symmetric subspace is given by the set of states defined by all T-sized multi-sets of $\{0,1\}^{5\lambda}$: For each T-sized multi-set M of $\{0,1\}^{5\lambda}$, the corresponding state $|\psi_M\rangle$ is a $5\lambda \cdot T$-qubit state which is the uniform superposition over all of the possible permutations of the T elements of M (e.g. in case M is not only a multi-set but an actual T-sized set, and all of its elements are distinct, the number of such permutations is $T!$, and if M is T times the same element, the number of such permutations is 1).

It follows that the projection onto the $(5\lambda, T)$-symmetric subspace is exactly the mixed state that corresponds to the distribution induced by sampling a T-sized multi-set M of $\{0,1\}^{5\lambda}$ and outputting the quantum state $|\psi_M\rangle$. To conclude, for T queries, the oracle access $Gen^*(\cdot)$ is equivalent to the oracle that outputs T copies of a 5λ-qubit Haar random state, and since the output bit of $\mathcal{A}$ is indistinguishable between $Gen_k(\cdot)$ and $Gen^*(\cdot)$, then the output bit of $\mathcal{A}$ is also indistinguishable between $Gen_k(\cdot)$ and an oracle that outputs Haar random states, in contradiction to the assumption that $\mathcal{A}$ breaks the pseudorandomness guarantee. $\square$

Proposition 2 (Security - Unforgeability of Proofs). *The PRFSPD scheme in Fig. 2 and Fig. 3 maintains the Unforgeability-of-proofs property (as in Definition 2).*

Proof. Assume toward contradiction there exists a quantum polynomial-time adversary $\mathcal{A}$ that breaks the proof-unforgeability property of the scheme, let ε the probability that the adversary obtains in winning the forging game (i.e. ε is non-negligible). If T is a polynomial bound on the running time of $\mathcal{A}$, note that we can assume without the loss of generality that for every possible input $x \in \{0,1\}^d$, $\mathcal{A}$ makes either 0 or exactly T queries to the generation oracle $Gen_k(\cdot)$ and arbitrarily many queries to the verification oracle $Ver_k(\cdot, \cdot)$ (in the boundaries of its running time). The reason this can be assumed w.l.o.g. is because we can consider a new adversary $\mathcal{A}'$ that uses $\mathcal{A}$ and (similarly to how we defined $\mathcal{A}'$ as a function of $\mathcal{A}$ in the proof of Proposition 1) complements the number of queries for each of its $t \in [T]$ previously-queried x's to being queried T times. However, this argument is a bit more delicate when it comes to showing how the new adversary $\mathcal{A}'$ breaks the proof-unforgeability property: At the end of the execution of the inner adversary $\mathcal{A}$, it outputs $x, p_1, \cdots, p_{t_x+1}$ (where t_x is the number of times that the input $x \in \{0,1\}^d$ was queried to $Gen_k(\cdot)$ by the inner adversary $\mathcal{A}$) such that $\forall i \in [t_x + 1] : Ver(k, x, p_i) = 1$. The outer adversary $\mathcal{A}'$ then takes the extra $\ell := T - t_x$ queries that it made (these are the queries it made in order to complement the number of queries for x from t_x to T, as part of the transformation of the inner adversary $\mathcal{A}$ to the outer adversary $\mathcal{A}'$) for the input string x and measures the ℓ copies it got in the computational basis, to obtain ℓ valid classical proofs of destruction for x.

Note that each of the ℓ copies is a uniform superposition over a set of size 2^λ, which means that the probability that any of the ℓ (which is a polynomial because T is a polynomial) proofs collides with the $t_x + 1$ proofs generated by the cheating inner adversary $\mathcal{A}$, is negligible. Thus, the new outer adversary $\mathcal{A}'$ makes a total of T queries on the input $x \in \{0,1\}^d$ but manages to generate $T+1$ distinct classical proofs of destruction, which means it breaks the security with a non-negligible probability ε'. Finally, one can think of an even outer process $\mathcal{A}^*$, that uses $\mathcal{A}'$ to generate the $T+1$ proofs, then checks by itself their validity using the verification algorithm $Ver(\cdot, \cdot)$, and outputs a bit whether or not the adversary $\mathcal{A}'$ won the forging game. Note that because $\mathcal{A}'$ wins the forging game with the non-negligible probability ε', then with the same probability, the output bit of $\mathcal{A}^*$ is 1.

Finally, by Lemma 6, it follows that the output bit of $\mathcal{A}^*$ in the above process is computationally indistinguishable from its output bit in the setting D_1 defined in Lemma 6, where $\mathcal{A}^*$ gets access only to $Gen^*(\cdot)$ and $Ver^*(\cdot, \cdot)$ (rather than $Gen_k(\cdot)$ and $Ver_k(\cdot, \cdot)$). Now, given the access to the two oracles $Gen^*(\cdot)$ and $Ver^*(\cdot, \cdot)$ (i.e., in the setting of D_1), for any algorithm, even unbounded, the probability to output $T+1$ distinct strings that are all verified by the algorithm $Ver^*(x, \cdot)$ for some $x \in \{0,1\}^d$ is zero, as by its definition, accepts at most T different elements. Our contradiction follows from the fact that ε' (the probability for $\mathcal{A}^*$ to output 1 in the setting D_0) is non-negligible, but has to be negligibly close to 0 (the probability for $\mathcal{A}^*$ to output 1 in the setting D_1, where it has access only to the oracles $Gen^*(\cdot)$ and $Ver^*(\cdot, \cdot)$). $\qquad\square$

5   Applications: Cryptography with Classical Communication

In this section, all the constructions of the cryptographic primitives are fully black-box constructions with uniform security reductions [22] from either PRSPD or PRFSPD, except for the construction of the statistically binding and computationally hiding bit-commitment scheme given in the full version, which is a fully black-box (with uniform reduction) construction from the particular class of PRSPD that satisfies some special properties, see the full version for more details. Therefore, the security guarantees of all these primitives hold even against non-uniform adversaries with quantum advice, assuming the same notion of security for the underlying PRSPD (or a special form of it) and PRFSPD. For simplicity, we only consider uniform adversaries from here onwards. Moreover, the outputs of all the algorithms in these constructions should be considered classical unless explicitly specified otherwise. Due to space constraints, some of the results and proofs have been moved to the full version.

None of the cryptographic primitives considered in the applications can exist unconditionally; see the full version for more details.

5.1   CMA-Secure MAC

Definition 5 (Length-restricted strong CMA-secure MAC (Adapted from [14, Definition 6.2.1])). *A length-restricted CMA secure MAC scheme*

(M) with message length $d(\lambda)^6$, key-length $w(\lambda)$, and tag-length $c(\lambda)$ is a tuple of QPT algorithms (Sign, Verify) with the following syntax:

- sig ← *Sign(k, m): takes a key $k \in \{0,1\}^{w(\lambda)}$, a message $m \in \{0,1\}^{d(\lambda)}$, and outputs a tag* sig $\in \{0,1\}^c$.
- b ← *Verify(k, m, sig): takes a key k, a message m, a tag* sig*, and outputs a boolean value, either accept ($b = 1$) or reject ($b = 0$).*

Correctness. For every message $m \in \{0,1\}^{d(\lambda)}$,

$$\Pr[k \xleftarrow{u} \{0,1\}^{w(\lambda)}; \text{sig} \leftarrow Sign(k, m) : Verify(k, \text{sig}) = 1] = 1.$$

Strong CMA Unforgeability. For every QPT adversary $\mathcal{A}$ in the forging game (see Game 4), there exists a negligible function $\mathsf{negl}(\lambda)$ such that

$$\Pr[\text{Strong-CMA-Forging-Exp}_\lambda^{\mathcal{A}, \mathcal{M}} = 1] = \mathsf{negl}(\lambda).$$

Game 4 Strong-CMA-Forging-Exp$_\lambda^{\mathcal{A}, \mathcal{M}}$

1: Given input 1^λ, the challenger samples $k \xleftarrow{u} \{0,1\}^{w(\lambda)}$. The challenger also initializes an empty set S.
2: $\mathcal{A}$ gets classical oracle access to $Verify(k, \cdot)$ and $Sign(k, \cdot)$.
3: **for** $Sign(k, \cdot)$ query x made by $\mathcal{A}$ **do**
4:     Add (x, σ_x) to S, where σ_x is the response of $Sign(k, \cdot)$ oracle on input x.
5: **end for**
6: $\mathcal{A}$ outputs x', σ'_x to the challenger.
7: Return 1 if $(x', \sigma'_x) \notin S$ and $Verify(k, x', \sigma'_x) = 1$.

Remark 5 (Strong vs. vanilla CMA security). Vanilla CMA security considers a similar forging game in which the adversary wins if she produces (m, σ) that passes verification and that m was never queried to the *Sign* oracle. In comparison, Definition 5 is a stronger notion because the adversary wins the forging game even if she produces a valid (m, σ) such that m was queried to the *Sign* oracle as long as σ was not received as a response in any of the m-queries she did to the *Sign* oracle. Hence, we call this notion the strong CMA security, also referred to as super-secure MACs[7] in [14, Sect. 6.5.2]. These notions are not known to be equivalent in general. However, the prominent classical MAC constructions have deterministic signing procedures, i.e., every message has a unique signature string that passes verification, and all other strings are rejected. For such MAC schemes, strong and vanilla CMA security are equivalent. This is not the case for our construction. Hence we consider the strongest possible definition.

---

[6] This is referred to as d-restricted MAC in [14].

[7] We use the term *strong* in place of *super* because *strong* is the more colloquially accepted term.

Remark 6 (Access to the verification oracle). In the classical CMA security definitions, the adversary is not given access to the verification because the classical MAC schemes usually have deterministic signing procedures; hence the verification oracle can be simulated using the signing oracle, see [14, Proposition 6.1.3]. However, MAC schemes with quantum algorithms do not have a deterministic signing in general; hence, we provide the adversary in Strong-CMA-Forging-Exp$_\lambda^{A,\mathcal{M}}$ explicit access to the verification oracle.

Construction from PRFSPD. Next we construct a length-restricted CMA secure MAC scheme with input-length $d(\lambda)$, key-length $w(\lambda)$ and tag-length $c(\lambda)$ from a PRFSPD scheme $(\mathcal{Gen}, \mathcal{Destruct}, \mathcal{Ver})$ with key-length $w(\lambda)$, input-length $d(\lambda)$ and proof-length $c(\lambda)$. The construction given in Fig. 4, combines the quantum MAC construction in [4] with the proof of destruction property of PRFSPD, to get an improved construction in the following two aspects. Firstly, the tags in our construction are classical, whereas [4] requires quantum tags. Additionally, our construction satisfies strong-CMA security while [4] considers vanilla CMA security. We also briefly mention that our construction supports any poly-size message, whereas the one in [4] is length-restricted. We note that we remove this length restriction using a standard technique, which is applicable to their construction as well.

Assumes: PRFSPD scheme, $(\mathcal{Gen}, \mathcal{Destruct}, \mathcal{Ver})$
$\mathcal{Sign}(k, m)$
Output $\mathsf{sig} = \mathcal{Destruct}(\mathcal{Gen}(k, m))$.
$\mathcal{Verify}(k, m, \mathsf{sig})$
Output $\mathcal{Ver}(k, m, \mathsf{sig})$).

Fig. 4. MAC scheme $\mathcal{M}$.

Theorem 3 (Correctness of $\mathcal{M}$). *The length-restricted MAC scheme $\mathcal{M}$ is correct (see Definition 5) if $(\mathcal{Gen}, \mathcal{Destruct}, \mathcal{Ver})$ satisfies correctness (see Definition 2).*

The proof is immediate from the correctness of the proof of destruction of the underlying PRFSPD, and hence we omit the proof.

Theorem 4 (CMA Security of $\mathcal{M}$). *The length-restricted MAC scheme $\mathcal{M}$ is CMA-secure if $(\mathcal{Gen}, \mathcal{Destruct}, \mathcal{Ver})$ is a PRFSPD (see Definition 1).*

Proof. The proof directly follows from the classical-unforgeability of proofs for PRFSPD given in Lemma 5. □

Remark 7 (Unrestricted MAC). Note that the input-length of the MAC, $d(\lambda) \in \omega(\log(\lambda))$. Hence, we can extend the MAC scheme to sign messages of arbitrary polynomial length by dividing the message into blocks and signing them individually; see [14, Theorem 6.2.2] for more details. Therefore, we conclude that PRFSPD implies CMA MAC, in a black-box manner.

5.2   CPA-Secure Symmetric Encryption

In this section, we will construct CPA-secure symmetric bit-encryption from PRFSPD, which can be easily extended to a CPA-secure and even CCA-2 encryption for arbitrary message-length, see Remarks 8 and 9.

Definition 6 (CPA-secure symmetric bit-encryption(Adapted from [14, Definition 5.4.9])). *A CPA secure symmetric bit-encryption $\mathcal{E}$ with key space $\{0,1\}^{w(\lambda)}$, and cipher space $\{0,1\}^{c(\lambda)}$ is a tuple of QPT algorithms ($\mathcal{Enc}, \mathcal{Dec}$) with the following syntax:*

- *ct $\leftarrow \mathcal{Enc}(k,m)$: takes a key k and a message bit m, and outputs a classical cipher text ct.*
- *$m \leftarrow \mathcal{Dec}(k,\text{ct})$: takes a key k, a cipher text ct, and outputs a message bit m.*

Correctness: For every message $m \in \{0,1\}$, there exists a negligible function $\text{negl}(\lambda)$, such that

$$\Pr[k \leftarrow \{0,1\}^{w(\lambda)}; \text{ct} \leftarrow \mathcal{Enc}(k,m); m' \leftarrow \mathcal{Dec}(k,\text{ct}) : m = m'] \geq 1 - \text{negl}(\lambda).$$

CPA security For every QPT adversary $\mathcal{A}$ in the distinguishability game (see Game 5, there exists a negligible function $\text{negl}(\lambda)$ such that

$$\Pr[\text{Distinguish-Exp}_{\lambda}^{\mathcal{A},\mathcal{E}} = 1] \leq \frac{1}{2} + \text{negl}(\lambda).$$

Game 5 Distinguish-Exp$_{\lambda}^{\mathcal{A},\mathcal{E}}$

1: Given input 1^λ, the challenger samples $k \xleftarrow{u} \{0,1\}^{w(\lambda)}$.
2: $\mathcal{A}$ gets classical oracle access to $\mathcal{Enc}(k,\cdot)$.
3: Challenger samples a bit b and computes $\text{ct}_b \leftarrow \mathcal{Enc}(k,b)$ and sends ct_b to $\mathcal{A}$.
4: $\mathcal{A}$ outputs b' to the challenger.
5: The output of the experiment is 1 if $b = b'$.

Construction from PRFSPD. Let ($\mathcal{Gen}, \mathcal{Destruct}, \mathcal{Ver}$) be a PRFSPD with input length $d(\lambda) \in \omega(\log(\lambda))$, and key-length $w(\lambda)$. We will give a construction of CPA secure symmetric bit-encryption from such a PRFSPD with key-length $w(\lambda)$.

In a nutshell, our construction combines the ideas in [4], with the proof of destruction property of PRFSPD state, to make the ciphers classical. The construction is given in Fig. 5.

Assumes: PRFSPD scheme, $(\mathit{Gen}, \mathit{Destruct}, \mathit{Ver})$

$\mathit{Enc}(k, b)$
1. Sample $r \leftarrow \{0,1\}^{d(\lambda)-1}$.
2. Output $\mathsf{ct} = (r, \mathit{Destruct}(\mathit{Gen}(k, r\|b)))$.

$\mathit{Dec}(k, \mathsf{ct})$
1. Interpret ct as r', c', where $r' \in \{0,1\}^{d(\lambda)-1}$.
2. Run $\mathit{Ver}(k, r'\|1, c)$. If accepted output 1 else 0.

Fig. 5. Symmetric bit-encryption $\mathcal{E}$.

Proposition 3 (Correctness of $\mathcal{E}$). *The symmetric bit-encryption scheme $\mathcal{E}$ is correct (see Definition 6) if $(\mathit{Gen}, \mathit{Destruct}, \mathit{Ver})$ satisfies correctness (see Definition 2).*

Proof. By the correctness of the underlying PRFSPD, the correctness holds for encryptions of 1, i.e.,

$$\Pr[k \leftarrow \{0,1\}^{w(\lambda)}; \mathsf{ct} \leftarrow \mathit{Enc}(k,1); m' \leftarrow \mathit{Dec}(k, \mathsf{ct}) : 1 = m'] = 1.$$

Next for encryptions of 0, it suffices to show that there exists a negligible function $\mathsf{negl}(\lambda)$ such that,

$$\mathsf{prob}_0 \equiv \Pr[k \leftarrow \{0,1\}^{w(\lambda)}; \mathsf{ct} \leftarrow \mathit{Enc}(k,0); m' \leftarrow \mathit{Dec}(k, \mathsf{ct}) : 1 = m'] = \mathsf{negl}(\lambda). \tag{11}$$

The last equation can be proven using the Unforgeability-of-proofs property of the underlying PRFSPD as follows. We construct an adversary $\mathcal{A}$ in the cloning game $\mathsf{Forging\text{-}Exp}_\lambda^{\mathcal{A},\mathsf{PRFSPD}}$ (see Game 2) that samples $r_0 \xleftarrow{u} \{0,1\}^{d-1}$ and queries the Gen oracle at $r_0\|1$ and gets a state $|\psi^{r_0\|0}\rangle$. $\mathcal{A}$ runs $\mathit{Destruct}$ on $|\psi^{r_0\|0}\rangle$ to get a proof $p \leftarrow \mathit{Destruct}(|\psi^{r_0\|0}\rangle)$, and finally submits $r\|0, p$. Note that $\mathcal{A}$ never queried $r\|0$ to Gen before, so she wins the cloning game if $r\|0, p$ passes the PRFSPD verification which by design, happens with probability exactly prob_0. Hence by the Unforgeability-of-proofs property of PRFSPD, prob_0 must be negligible. $\square$

Theorem 5 (CPA Security of $\mathcal{E}$). *The symmetric bit-encryption scheme $\mathcal{E}$ is CPA-secure (see Definition 6) if $(\mathit{Gen}, \mathit{Destruct}, \mathit{Verify})$ is a PRFSPD (see Definition 1).*

Proof. The proof follows essentially from the pseudorandomness of $(\mathit{Gen}, \mathit{Destruct}, \mathit{Verify})$ (see Definition 2). We will consider the following sequence of hybrids:

$\mathcal{H}_0$ This is the real security game $\mathsf{Distinguish\text{-}Exp}_\lambda^{\mathcal{A},\mathcal{E}}$. Since we are considering bit encryption, the challenger simply samples a bit b and feeds $\mathcal{A}$ the encryption of b, i.e., $(r, \mathit{Destruct}(\mathit{Gen}(k, r_{ch}\|b)))$ at the challenge phase. The adversary $\mathcal{A}$ is given classical access to the CPA oracle $\mathit{Enc}(k, \cdot)$ which she can query both before and after the challenge phase. Let $b_1, \ldots, b_q$ be the queries $\mathcal{A}$ makes to the CPA oracle where $q \in \mathsf{poly}(\lambda)$ (since $\mathcal{A}$ is polynomially bounded), and

$$\{\mathit{Enc}(k, b_1), \ldots \mathit{Enc}(k, b_q)\} = \{(r_1, \mathit{Destruct}(\mathit{Gen}(k, r_1\|b_1))), \ldots (r_q, \mathit{Destruct}(\mathit{Gen}(k, r_q\|b_q)))\},$$

be the respective responses from the oracle, where $r_1, \ldots, r_q$ are chosen uniformly. $\mathcal{A}$ succeeds if she submits a bit b' at the end, such that $b = b'$.

$\mathcal{H}_1$ In this hybrid, we only change the distribution on $r, r_1, \ldots, r_q$. The challenger samples r independently, and then for every $i \in [q]$, r_i is chosen uniformly from $\{0,1\}^{d(\lambda)-1} \setminus \{r, r_1, \ldots, r_{i-1}\}$, where $\{r, r_1, \ldots, r_{i-1}\}$ should be interpreted as $\{r\}$ for $i = 1$. Note that the distributions on $(r, r_1, \ldots, r_q)$ in the hybrid have negligible statistical distance from the uniformly random distribution that we had in $\mathcal{H}_0$ because $q \in \mathsf{poly}(\lambda)$ and the length of r is $d(\lambda) - 1 \in \omega(\log \lambda)$. Hence, the success probability of $\mathcal{A}$ in $\mathcal{H}_0$ and $\mathcal{H}_1$ are negligibly close.

$\mathcal{H}_2$ In this hybrid, we replace

$\{(r_1, \mathit{Destruct}(\mathit{Gen}(k, r_1\|b_1))), \ldots (r_q, \mathit{Destruct}(\mathit{Gen}(k, r_q\|b_q))), (r, \mathit{Destruct}(\mathit{Gen}(k, r\|b)))\}$ with

$\{(r_1, \mathit{Destruct}(|\phi_1\rangle)), \ldots (r_q, \mathit{Destruct}(|\phi_q\rangle)), (r, \mathit{Destruct}(|\phi_{q+1}\rangle)\}$ where $|\phi\rangle \sim \mu_{\mathcal{H}_n}$ and for each $i \in [q]$, $|\phi_i\rangle \sim \mu_{\mathcal{H}_n}$ independently.

Let the difference in the success probabilities of the $\mathcal{A}$ in $\mathcal{H}_1$ and $\mathcal{H}_2$ be p. We can construct an adversary $\mathcal{B}$ who can violate the pseudorandomness (see Definition 2) of $(\mathit{Gen}, \mathit{Destruct}, \mathit{Ver})$ with distinguishing advantage p. $\mathcal{B}$ simulates $\mathcal{A}$ and when she queries b_i in the ith query, $\mathcal{B}$ generates r_i uniformly from $\{0,1\}^{d(\lambda)-1} \setminus r_1, \ldots, r_{i-1}$, and queries the oracle (which she needs to distinguish) on $r_i\|b_i$ and performs $\mathit{Destruct}$ on the output she receives and feeds the obtained string to $\mathcal{A}$. Moreover, $\mathcal{B}$ plays the role of the challenger and samples a uniformly random bit b, and feeds the encryption of b using the challenge oracle that she has access to. $\mathcal{B}$ outputs 1 if the output of the $\mathcal{A}$ is the same as b. Clearly, the distinguishing probability is p. Hence, p must be negligible.

Now note that in $\mathcal{H}_2$, the challenge bit b is information-theoretically hidden from $\mathcal{A}$. Therefore, her success probability in $\mathcal{H}_2$ must be at most $\frac{1}{2}$.

Hence, there exists a negligible function $\mathsf{negl}(\lambda)$ such that

$$\Pr[\mathcal{A} \text{ wins } \mathcal{H}_0] \leq \frac{1}{2} + \mathsf{negl}(\lambda).$$

$\square$

Remark 8 (Encryption of arbitrarily long messages). Any CPA-secure bit encryption scheme can be extended to a CPA-secure encryption to arbitrarily long messages via bit-by-bit encryption, see [14, Sect. 5.3.2.2]. Hence, we conclude that there is a black-box construction of CPA-secure encryption for arbitrary message lengths, from PRFSPD.

Remark 9 (CCA-2 security of $\mathcal{E}$). By combining the strong MAC scheme from PRFSPD (see Theorems 3 and 4) with the CPA-secure encryption scheme mentioned in the previous remark using the Encrypt-then-MAC, we conclude that there is a black-box construction of CCA-2 secure encryption for arbitrarily long messages from PRFSPD.

Acknowledgments. Amit Behera and Or Sattath were supported by the Israeli Science Foundation (ISF) grant No. 682/18 and 2137/19, and by the Cyber Security Research Center at Ben-Gurion University. Zvika Brakerski is supported by the Israel Science Foundation (Grant No. 3426/21), and by the European Union Horizon 2020 Research and Innovation Program via ERC Project REACT (Grant 756482). Omri Shmueli is supported by the European Research Council (ERC) under the European Union's Horizon Europe research and innovation programme (grant agreements No. 101042417, acronym SPP, and No. 756482, acronym REACT), by Israeli Science Foundation (ISF) grants 18/484 and 19/2137, by Len Blavatnik and the Blavatnik Family Foundation, and by the Clore Israel Foundation. The authors would like to thank the anonymous reviewers for their valuable and insightful comments.

This work has received funding from the European Research Council (ERC) under the European Union's Horizon 2020 research and innovation programme (grant agreement No 756482).

References

1. Amos, R., Georgiou, M., Kiayias, A., Zhandry, M.: One-shot signatures and applications to hybrid quantum/classical authentication. In: Makarychev, K., Makarychev, Y., Tulsiani, M., Kamath, G., Chuzhoy, J. (eds.) Proceedings of the Annual ACM SIGACT Symposium on Theory of Computing, pp. 255–268. ACM (2020). https://doi.org/10.1145/3357713.3384304
2. Ananth, P., Gulati, A., Qian, L., Yuen, H.: Pseudorandom (function-like) quantum state generators: new definitions and applications. In: Kiltz, E., Vaikuntanathan, V. (eds.) Theory of Cryptography, TCC 2022. LNCS, vol. 13747, pp. 237–265. Springer, Cham (2022). https://doi.org/10.1007/978-3-031-22318-1_9
3. Ananth, P., Lin, Y., Yuen, H.: Pseudorandom strings from pseudorandom quantum states (2023)
4. Ananth, P., Qian, L., Yuen, H.: Cryptography from pseudorandom quantum states (2021)
5. Bartusek, J., Coladangelo, A., Khurana, D., Ma, F.: One-way functions imply secure computation in a quantum world. In: Malkin, T., Peikert, C. (eds.) Advances in Cryptology - CRYPTO 2021–41st Annual International Cryptology Conference, CRYPTO 2021, Virtual Event, 16–20 August 2021, Proceedings, Part I. LNCS, vol. 12825, pp. 467–496. Springer, Cham (2021). https://doi.org/10.1007/978-3-030-84242-0_17
6. Behera, A., Sattath, O.: Almost public coins. In: QIP 2021 (2020)
7. Ben-David, S., Sattath, O.: Quantum tokens for digital signatures. QCrypt 2017 (2016). https://doi.org/10.48550/ARXIV.1609.09047
8. Bouland, A., Fefferman, B., Vazirani, U.V.: Computational pseudorandomness, the wormhole growth paradox, and constraints on the ADS/CFT duality (abstract). In: Vidick, T. (ed.) 11th Innovations in Theoretical Computer Science Conference, ITCS 2020, 12–14 January 2020, Seattle, Washington, USA. LIPIcs, vol. 151, pp. 63:1–63:2. Schloss Dagstuhl - Leibniz-Zentrum für Informatik (2020). https://doi.org/10.4230/LIPIcs.ITCS.2020.63
9. Brakerski, Z., Canetti, R., Qian, L.: On the computational hardness needed for quantum cryptography (2022)

10. Brakerski, Z., Shmueli, O.: (Pseudo) random quantum states with binary phase. In: Hofheinz, D., Rosen, A. (eds.) TCC 2019. LNCS, vol. 11891, pp. 229–250. Springer, Cham (2019). https://doi.org/10.1007/978-3-030-36030-6_10

11. Brakerski, Z., Shmueli, O.: Scalable pseudorandom quantum states. In: Micciancio, D., Ristenpart, T. (eds.) Advances in Cryptology - CRYPTO 2020–40th Annual International Cryptology Conference, CRYPTO 2020, Santa Barbara, CA, USA, 17–21 August 2020, Proceedings, Part II. LNCS, vol. 12171, pp. 417–440. Springer, Cham (2020). https://doi.org/10.1007/978-3-030-56880-1_15

12. Coladangelo, A., Liu, J., Liu, Q., Zhandry, M.: Hidden cosets and applications to unclonable cryptography. In: Malkin, T., Peikert, C. (eds.) Advances in Cryptology - CRYPTO 2021–41st Annual International Cryptology Conference, CRYPTO 2021, Virtual Event, 16–20 August 2021, Proceedings, Part I. LNCS, vol. 12825, pp. 556–584. Springer, Cham (2021). https://doi.org/10.1007/978-3-030-84242-0_20

13. Coladangelo, A., Sattath, O.: A quantum money solution to the blockchain scalability problem. Quantum **4**, 297 (2020). https://doi.org/10.22331/q-2020-07-16-297

14. Goldreich, O.: The Foundations of Cryptography - Volume 2: Basic Applications. Cambridge University Press, Cambridge (2004). https://doi.org/10.1017/CBO9780511721656, http://www.wisdom.weizmann.ac.il/%7Eoded/foc-vol2.html

15. Harrow, A.W.: The church of the symmetric subspace (2013)

16. Ji, Z., Liu, Y., Song, F.: Pseudorandom quantum states. In: Shacham, H., Boldyreva, A. (eds.) Advances in Cryptology - CRYPTO 2018–38th Annual International Cryptology Conference, Santa Barbara, CA, USA, 19–23 August 2018, Proceedings, Part III. LNCS, vol. 10993, pp. 126–152. Springer, Cham (2018). https://doi.org/10.1007/978-3-319-96878-0_5

17. Kretschmer, W.: Quantum pseudorandomness and classical complexity. In: Hsieh, M. (ed.) 16th Conference on the Theory of Quantum Computation, Communication and Cryptography, TQC 2021, 5–8 July 2021, Virtual Conference. LIPIcs, vol. 197, pp. 2:1–2:20. Schloss Dagstuhl - Leibniz-Zentrum für Informatik (2021). https://doi.org/10.4230/LIPIcs.TQC.2021.2

18. Molina, A., Vidick, T., Watrous, J.: Optimal counterfeiting attacks and generalizations for Wiesner's quantum money. In: Iwama, K., Kawano, Y., Murao, M. (eds.) Theory of Quantum Computation, Communication, and Cryptography, TQC. LNCS, vol. 7582, pp. 45–64. Springer, Cham (2012). https://doi.org/10.1007/978-3-642-35656-8_4

19. Morimae, T., Yamakawa, T.: Quantum commitments and signatures without one-way functions. In: Dodis, Y., Shrimpton, T. (eds.) Advances in Cryptology - CRYPTO 2022–42nd Annual International Cryptology Conference, CRYPTO 2022, Santa Barbara, CA, USA, 15–18 August 2022, Proceedings, Part I. LNCS, vol. 13507, pp. 269–295. Springer, Cham (2022). https://doi.org/10.1007/978-3-031-15802-5_10

20. Morimae, T., Yamakawa, Y.: One-wayness in quantum cryptography, October 2022

21. Radian, R., Sattath, O.: Semi-quantum money. In: Proceedings of the 1st ACM Conference on Advances in Financial Technologies, AFT 2019, Zurich, Switzerland, 21–23 October 2019, pp. 132–146. ACM (2019). https://doi.org/10.1145/3318041.3355462

22. Reingold, O., Trevisan, L., Vadhan, S.P.: Notions of reducibility between cryptographic primitives. In: Naor, M. (ed.) TCC 2004, Cambridge, MA, USA Proceedings. LNCS, vol. 2951, pp. 1–20. Springer, Cham (2004). https://doi.org/10.1007/978-3-540-24638-1_1

23. Shmueli, O.: Public-key quantum money with a classical bank. In: Leonardi, S., Gupta, A. (eds.) STOC 2022: 54th Annual ACM SIGACT Symposium on Theory of Computing, Rome, Italy, 20–24 June 2022, pp. 790–803. ACM (2022). https://doi.org/10.1145/3519935.3519952
24. Shmueli, O.: Semi-quantum tokenized signatures. Cryptology ePrint Archive, Report 2022/228 (2022). https://ia.cr/2022/228
25. Zhandry, M.: How to construct quantum random functions. In: 53rd Annual IEEE Symposium on Foundations of Computer Science, FOCS 2012, New Brunswick, NJ, USA, 20–23 October 2012, pp. 679–687. IEEE Computer Society (2012). https://doi.org/10.1109/FOCS.2012.37
26. Zhandry, M.: A note on quantum-secure PRPs (2016)
27. Zhandry, M.: Quantum lightning never strikes the same state twice. Or: quantum money from cryptographic assumptions. J. Cryptol. **34**(1), 6 (2021)

Semi-quantum Copy-Protection and More

Céline Chevalier[1,2(✉)] ⓘ, Paul Hermouet[1,2,3] ⓘ, and Quoc-Huy Vu[3] ⓘ

[1] DIENS, École normale supérieure, PSL University, CNRS, INRIA, Paris, France
{celine.chevalier,paul.hermouet}@ens.fr
[2] CRED, Université Panthéon-Assas Paris II, Paris, France
[3] LIP6, Sorbonne Université, Paris, France
quoc.huy.vu@ens.fr

Abstract. Properties of quantum mechanics have enabled the emergence of quantum cryptographic protocols achieving important goals which are proven to be impossible classically. Unfortunately, this usually comes at the cost of needing quantum power from every party in the protocol, while arguably a more realistic scenario would be a network of classical clients, classically interacting with a quantum server.

In this paper, we focus on copy-protection, which is a quantum primitive that allows a program to be evaluated, but not copied, and has shown interest especially due to its links to other unclonable cryptographic primitives. Our main contribution is to show how to dequantize quantum copy-protection schemes constructed from hidden coset states, by giving a construction for classically-instructed remote state preparation for coset states, which *preserves hardness properties of hidden coset states*. We then apply this dequantizer to obtain semi-quantum cryptographic protocols for copy-protection and tokenized signatures with strong unforgeability. In the process, we present the first secure copy-protection scheme for point functions in the plain model and a new direct product hardness property of coset states which immediately implies a strongly unforgeable tokenized signature scheme.

1 Introduction

Quantum mechanical effects have enabled the construction of cryptographic primitives that are impossible classically. In particular, the no-cloning principle of quantum mechanics, which means that an unknown quantum state cannot be copied in general, has given rise to many wonderful primitives such as quantum money [2,32], quantum lightning [33], quantum copy-protection [1], one-shot signatures [3,8], secure software leasing [7], unclonable encryption [12] and many more. By standard definition, these quantum primitives can be seen as cryptographic protocols requiring quantum communication to transfer the quantumly encoded program between parties, and of course, local quantum computation from the parties. These notions thus have been mostly considered in the context of users having quantum machines with quantum communication.

Work done while at CRED and DIENS.

ⓒ International Association for Cryptologic Research 2023
G. Rothblum and H. Wee (Eds.): TCC 2023, LNCS 14372, pp. 155–182, 2023.
https://doi.org/10.1007/978-3-031-48624-1_6

Semi-quantum cryptography.[1] Besides the fact that there is a fundamental difference between classical and quantum communication, a more realistic and practical scenario would be a *classical* communication network with classical clients interacting with a single powerful quantum server. Therefore, ideally, for both theoretical and practical reasons, we might want to minimize the required model and use local quantum computation and only classical communication. In this research direction, an emerging field of "dequantizing" quantum cryptographic protocols has shown that it is possible to use local quantum computation and classical communication to obtain cryptographic constructions which are otherwise classically impossible [3,10,18,20,21,23,26,29,30]. In the following, we call these dequantized protocols *semi-quantum* protocols, i.e., cryptographic protocols between classical clients interacting with a quantum server via classical communication.

Perhaps the most striking example of quantum cryptography is the notion of *quantum copy-protection*, introduced by Aaronson [1]. Informally, quantum copy-protection allows a program to be encoded in a quantum state in such a way that the program can be evaluated, but not copied. It is also interesting to highlight the relation between copy-protection and other unclonable cryptography functionalities. Indeed, Ananth and Kaleoglu [4] show that the existence of an unclonable encryption scheme with a strong security property implies the existence of copy-protection of point-functions. Sattath and Wyborski [28] show that copy-protection of a certain family of functions allows for the construction of unclonable decryptors. We thus explore the possibility of constructing semi-quantum copy-protection in this work.

Semi-quantum copy-protection. Until now, semi-quantum copy-protection has essentially been wide open. The first and the only known semi-quantum copy-protection scheme is given in the recent work of [18]. Building on techniques introduced in [10,19,23], the authors of [18] show how to construct a *classically-instructed parallel remote state preparation of BB84 states*, which are the four following states: $\{|0\rangle, |1\rangle, |+\rangle, |-\rangle\}$ where $|\pm\rangle := \frac{1}{\sqrt{2}}(|0\rangle \pm |1\rangle)$, and whose unclonability property is based on the idea of conjugate coding. By applying this remote state preparation protocol to the construction of copy-protection of point functions in [16], they also give a construction for semi-quantum copy-protection (of point functions). However, while [18]'s framework is generic and applicable to many other quantum cryptography constructions, [18] remote state preparation protocol for BB84 states and its applicability (including their semi-quantum copy-protection of point functions) suffer from several limitations. Firstly, [18] remote state preparation protocol for BB84 states only achieve inverse polynomial security, and inherently, their dequantized protocols also only have inverse polynomial security. Secondly, we do not know how to construct copy-protection with standard malicious security from BB84 states in the plain model. We therefore ask the following question:

Can we construct semi-quantum copy-protection with standard security?

---

[1] This is called *hybrid quantum cryptography* in [3].

Semi-quantum unclonable cryptography from coset states. Given a subspace $A \subseteq \mathbb{F}_2^n$, the corresponding *subspace state* is defined as a uniform superposition over all vectors in the subspace A, i.e., $|A\rangle := \frac{1}{\sqrt{|A|}} \sum_{v \in A} |v\rangle$. The idea of using hidden subspace state to construct quantum cryptographic primitives was first proposed by Aaronson and Christiano in [2] in the oracle model where the parties have access to some membership checking oracles. This idea was realized subsequently in the plain model using indistinguishability obfuscation by Zhandry [33]. The subspace state idea was later generalized to *coset states* in [15,31], which can be seen as quantum one-time pad encrypted subspace states. Formally, for a subspace $A \subseteq \mathbb{F}_2^n$ and two vectors $s, s' \in \mathbb{F}_2^n$, the corresponding coset state is defined as $|A_{s,s'}\rangle := \frac{1}{\sqrt{|A|}} \sum_{x \in A} (-1)^{\langle x, s' \rangle} |x + s\rangle$.

Coset states possess strong unclonability properties, the so-called *direct product hardness* and *monogamy-of-entanglement* [15]. The former states that any query-bounded adversary with quantum access to oracles of membership in $A + s$ and $A^\perp + s'$ cannot produce, except with negligible probability, a pair $(v, w) \in (A + s) \times (A^\perp + s')$. On the other hand, the latter can be described as a cooperative game between three adversaries Alice, Bob and Charlie with a challenger, in which the adversaries have negligible winning probability. The game is as follows: Alice is given a random coset state $|A_{s,s'}\rangle$, outputs two (possibly entangled) quantum states and sends them to Bob and Charlie respectively. Finally, Bob and Charlie both get the description of the subspace A, and we say that the game is won if Bob outputs a vector in $A + s$ and Charlie outputs a vector in $A^\perp + s'$. Due to these unclonability properties, the coset state idea has shown a broad range of applications to signature tokens, unclonable decryptors, copy-protection [15], classical proof of quantum knowledge [31], and unclonable encryption [5].

The main distinction between random BB84 states and hidden coset states is the (un)learnability with verification oracles. Given access to membership oracles that check whether an input vector is in the primal coset or in the dual coset, a hidden coset state still maintains its unclonability properties. On the other hand, giving access to similar oracles to an adversary in the context of BB84 states would allow this adversary to break the unclonability property of BB84 states, thus making the resulting protocols insecure. This explains why coset states have more applications, mostly in the public-key setting. Indeed, to the best of our knowledge, all known provably secure copy-protection schemes with standard malicious security are based on hidden coset states [5,15].[2]

Using application-specific approaches, Shmueli further gives several semi-quantum protocols from coset states for public-key quantum money in [29] and tokenized signatures in [30]. Even though both are based on hidden coset states, his constructions are tailor-made for these applications. For example, in the case of semi-quantum tokenized signature, the signature generation process in

---

[2] The only known exception is the construction of copy-protection of single-bit point functions in the quantum random oracle model based on BB84 states [6]. In this work, we focus only on constructions in the plain model.

Shmueli's protocol ([30]) is defined specifically for the application, and it is quite different from the quantum construction given in [15]. On the other hand, modularity and generic approaches are highly desirable in cryptography, and thus our second question in this work is:

> *Can we construct classically-instructed remote state preparation for coset states which preserves hidden coset states unclonable properties, which can be used to generically dequantize quantum protocols based on coset states?*

1.1   Our Results

We answer these two open questions affirmatively. We first give an answer to the second question, by constructing a *classically-instructed remote state preparation for coset states*, based on the existence of indistinguishability obfuscation for classical circuits, and on that the Learning With Errors [27] problem. The main feature of our protocol is that it preserves unclonability properties of ideal random coset states, including the direct product hardness and monogamy-of-entanglement property, which are the core ingredients of unclonable cryptography.

Theorem 1 (Informal). *Assume that LWE is sub-exponentially hard for quantum computers and that indistinguishability obfuscation for classical circuits exists with sub-exponential security against quantum polynomial-time adversaries. Then, there is a classically-instructed remote state preparation protocol for coset states with negligible soundness (as defined in Sect. 4.1).*

Our protocol is a multi-round protocol between classical Alice and quantum polynomial-time Bob that allows Alice to delegate the construction of hidden coset states to Bob. Furthermore, Alice knows the description of the constructed coset states (which reside on Bob's device), while Bob himself does not, and no-cloning also applies to these states.[3] Hence, the situation at the end of this protocol is equivalent to one where Alice sent hidden coset states to Bob, allowing us to dequantize existing unclonable cryptography protocols from coset states in a generic and modular way, without requiring new security properties or changing the constructions (apart from making them semi-quantum).

In particular, to demonstrate the modularity of our dequantizer protocol, we construct a quantum copy-protection of point functions in the plain model whose security is also based on the idea of hidden coset states to which we can apply our dequantizer. We note that before our work, no copy-protection scheme for point functions in the plain model with negligible security was known. In fact, our copy-protection scheme is almost identical to that for pseudorandom functions given in [15]. We observe that by making few modifications to their proof, we obtain a copy-protection of point functions with a non-trivial challenge distribution (first defined in [16]) in the security definition.[4]

---

[3] These coset states actually satisfy a strong monogamy-of-entanglement property, which we elaborate later in Sect. 2.

[4] We emphasize that we use the same challenge distribution as in [16]. While being non-trivial, this is not the natural challenge distribution for point functions. Please see the full version [13] for the details.

Theorem 2 (Informal). *Assume the existence of post-quantum indistinguishability obfuscation, one-way functions, and compute-and-compare obfuscation for the class of unpredictable distributions. Then, there is a secure copy-protection scheme for point-functions in the plain model.*

By applying our dequantizer protocol to this construction, we also obtain a semi-quantum copy-protection of point functions in the plain model, with standard security. Indeed, our dequantizer is readily applicable to existing constructions of single decryptor, copy-protection of pseudorandom functions [15], and copy-protection of digital signatures [22], allowing us to obtain semi-quantum counterpart of these protocols, thus answering our first question.

Corollary 1 (Informal). *Assume that LWE is sub-exponentially hard for quantum computers and that indistinguishability obfuscation for classical circuits exists with sub-exponential security against quantum polynomial-time adversaries. Then, there is a semi-quantum copy-protection from coset states for certain class of functions, including: (decrypting) public-key encryption, (signing) signatures, (evaluating) pseudorandom functions, and (evaluating) point functions.*

To broaden the applicability of our semi-quantum protocol, we also present in this work a semi-quantum tokenized signature scheme with strong unforgeability (i.e., no efficient adversary can output two different signatures even for the same message). Previous constructions of [15] and [30] do not consider strong unforgeability and are only proven to be weakly unforgeable. Our quantum protocol of strongly unforgeable tokenized signature scheme is indeed the same as the one for weak unforgeability given in [15]. Applying our remote coset state preparation protocol immediately yields a semi-quantum tokenized signatures. Our technical contribution is a new direct product hardness of hidden coset states, which is a generalization of the direct product hardness given in [15]. Informally, we show that any query-bounded adversary given a random coset state $|A_{s,s'}\rangle$ cannot produce a pair of different vectors (v, w) in either $(A + s) \times (A + s)$ or $(A^\perp + s') \times (A^\perp + s')$. This allows us to achieve strong unforgeability.

Theorem 3 (Informal). *Assume that LWE is sub-exponentially hard for quantum computers and that indistinguishability obfuscation for classical circuits exists with sub-exponential security against quantum polynomial-time adversaries. Then, there is a semi-quantum tokenized signature scheme with strong unforgeability.*

1.2 Related Work

One can see our remote coset preparation protocol as an interactive protocol between a classical verifier and an (untrusted) prover, in which the verifier classically instructs the prover to prepare some hidden quantum states, which *satisfy certain properties*. This is highly relevant to a series of works starting with [10,23] that have developed techniques to allow the verifier to force the prover to *behave in a certain way*. We note that the former kind of protocols is implied by the latter, while the other direction is not true. For example, in our protocol, it is still possible that the prover does not behave in an expected way, but its output at the end of the protocol still satisfies the defined property.

The first semi-quantum protocol that provably forces a quantum prover to prepare a certain quantum state is the single-qubit remote state preparation protocol of [19] (see also [14] for a related result). [25] gives a protocol that allows a classical verifier to certify that a quantum prover must have prepared and measured a Bell state, i.e., an entangled 2-qubit quantum state. Finally, [18], by developing new techniques to show a n-fold parallel rigidity proof, gives the first parallel remote BB84 state preparation protocol. At the heart of the security proof of these protocols lies a *rigidity* argument. The idea of rigidity, first formally introduced by Mayers and Yao [24], is that certain games can be used to "self-test" quantum states: if such a game is won with high enough probability, then the self-test property tells us that the players must hold some quantum state, up to local isometry. Their proof technique is also the backbone of our soundness proof presented later. The most interesting point of the [18] protocol is that it allows to dequantize a number of BB84 states-based quantum cryptographic primitives, yielding a generic and modular way of translating these protocols to a setting where only classical communication is used. The downside of the [18] protocol is that it only achieves *inverse polynomial* soundness, which means that their dequantized protocols can only achieve *inverse polynomial* security at most, even if the original quantum protocols have negligible security. We note that all known self-testing protocols are developed for BB84 states and its variants, and before our work, there is no self-testing protocol for coset states (even with inverse polynomial security).

In addition to this line of work focused on rigidity statements, application-specific semi-quantum protocols were considered for quantum money [26,29], certified deletion [20], secure software leasing [21], and tokenized signature [30]. The common points of these protocols are that: (i) their approaches are less generic and modular than the [18] protocol and the protocol we present in this work; (ii) new analysis are required for each application. However, we note that all these application-specific semi-quantum protocols achieve *negligible* security, as they do not prove that the prover in their protocol behave in a certain way, but only that the output of the prover at the end satisfies certain properties. This is also the approach that we take in this work, which we describe in more details in Sect. 2.

Readers who are familiar with the context might think that our dequantization of coset state generation protocol with monogamy-of-entanglement property can be achieved readily from previous works by Shmueli ([29,30]). However, this is not quite true, due to the fact that Shmueli's works only show coset state delegation protocols with *direct product hardness* properties, and not *monogamy-of-entanglement* properties. These two kinds of unclonability properties are very different in their nature: while *direct product hardness* can be used in the constructions of quantum money and tokenized signatures (where there is only a single adversary playing the unclonability game), we do not know how to use it in the context of quantum copy-protection (where there are two or more adversaries simultaneously playing the unclonability game). In fact, *direct product hardness* does not imply *monogamy-of-entanglement*, and the former will be trivially broken if one casts it under the monogamy-of-entanglement game. We refer the readers to [15] for detailed definitions and applications of these two unclonability properties. For the application of tokenized signatures, our dequantizer protocol preserves the same direct product hardness property of ideal hidden coset states, which allows us to dequantize quantum protocols in a generic way. [30]'s protocol for semi-quantum tokenized signatures requires a new direct product hardness and a different signing procedure (compared to the quantum version of [15]), but it is unlikely that the same protocol can be shown to achieve strong unforgeability.

Copy-Protection of Point Functions. The first construction for copy protection of point functions was presented in [16], is based on BB84 states and its security is proven in the quantum random oracle model. However, [16]'s construction only achieves *constant* security. If we consider a weaker security notion, so-called *secure software leasing* [7,11] shows that we can even construct secure software leasing of point functions unconditionally in the plain model with negligible security.

On the other hand, copy-protection with negligible security against malicious adversaries are only known for pseudorandom functions, single-decryptor, point functions and digital signatures [5,15,22]. While the copy-protection schemes for pseudorandom functions, digital signatures and single-decryptor are secure in the plain model [15,22], the security of the construction for point functions is proven in the quantum random oracle model [5]. These latter constructions are all based on the idea of hidden coset states. In a recent work, [6] gives another construction for copy-protection of single-bit point functions in the quantum random oracle model based on BB84 states. In this work, we build upon the copy-protection construction of pseudorandom functions [15] to construct copy-protection of point functions in the plain model with negligible security.

Tokenized Signatures. The notion of tokenized signatures was introduced in the work of Ben-David and Sattath [8], and the first instantiation was given in [15] based on quantum-secure indistinguishability obfuscation and injective one-way functions. A dequantized construction of tokenized signatures was given in [30], assuming subexponentially quantum-secure indistinguishability obfuscation and quantum hardness of the LWE problem. However, the constructions given in [15,30] have only been proven weakly unforgeable.

2   Technical Overview

2.1   Our Remote Coset State Preparation Protocol and Its Application to Copy-Protection

In this section, we give an overview of our remote coset state preparation protocol and its proof of soundness. To give the reader a glimpse of the functionality of our protocol and how it can be used as a generic compiler to obtain semi-quantum copy-protection, we first start by analyzing security requirements for several existing quantum copy-protection schemes based on coset states.

Security Requirements. For our discussion, we focus on the copy-protection of pseudorandom functions scheme in the plain model and the single-decryptor scheme in the plain model presented in [15]. The common point is that security of these constructions all reduce to a *monogamy-of-entanglement* property of coset states [15,17]. Informally, this property states that a triple of quantum algorithms Alice, Bob and Charlie cannot cooperatively win the following monogamy game with a challenger, except with negligible probability. The challenger first prepares a uniformly random coset state $|A_{s,s'}\rangle$ and gives the state to Alice. Alice outputs two (possibly entangled) quantum states and sends them to Bob and Charlie respectively. No communication is allowed between Bob and Charlie. Finally, Bob and Charlie both get the description of the subspace A. The game is won if Bob outputs a vector in $A + s$ and Charlie outputs a vector in $A^{\perp} + s'$, where $A^{\perp}$ denote the dual subspace of A.

If our goal is to design a semi-quantum protocol for preparing coset states such that it can be used in a plug-and-play manner for the aforementioned protocols, our protocol needs to have the following properties:

- *Correctness.* If the prover is honest, at the end of the protocol execution, the prover must have a hidden coset state $|A_{s,s'}\rangle$ in its registers.
- *Soundness.* No (computationally bounded) prover after interacting with the classical verifier in the protocol, can win the monogamy-of-entanglement game described above (with a single modification in the first step of the game: instead of sending the coset state to the prover, we run the protocol). For a formal definition of the soundness, see Definition 3. We note that the soundness property also implies the blindness property: an untrusted prover cannot know the description of A and s, s' through the interaction.

The first attempt. Having described all requirements needed, we now turn into our protocol construction. Our starting point is the recent coset state delegation protocol introduced by Shmueli in [29], which uses hybrid quantum homomorphic encryption (QFHE)[5] and indistinguishability obfuscation ($i\mathcal{O}$) as the building blocks. The idea is indeed very simple: the verifier can simply send an (encrypted) classical description of a random subspace to the prover, and ask the prover to homomorphically generate the subspace state using the quantum homomorphic encryption. By the property of the hybrid QFHE, the subspace state is one-time pad encrypted with random Pauli keys, which is exactly equivalent to a random coset state. More formally, the scheme is as follows.

---

[5] A hybrid QFHE scheme is one where every encryption of a quantum state $|\psi\rangle$ consists of a quantum one-time pad encryption of $|\psi\rangle$ with Pauli keys $(x, z) \in \{0,1\}^*$, and $\mathrm{ct}_{x,z}$ which is a classical FHE encryption of the Pauli keys.

1. The classical verifier $\mathcal{V}$ samples a random $\frac{\lambda}{2}$-dimensional subspace $A \subseteq \mathbb{F}_2^\lambda$ (represented by a matrix $\mathbf{M}_A \in \{0,1\}^{\frac{\lambda}{2} \times \lambda}$), and sends $(\mathbf{M}_A^{p_x}, \mathrm{ct}_{p_x})$ to the prover $\mathcal{P}$, an encryption of the matrix $\mathbf{M}_A$ under QFHE.

2. $\mathcal{P}$ homomorphically evaluates the circuit C, which is a quantum circuit that gets as input the classical description of a subspace $A \subseteq \mathbb{F}_2^\lambda$ and generates a uniform superposition over A. $\mathcal{P}$ obtains a homomorphically evaluated ciphertext

$$(|A_{x,z}\rangle, \mathrm{ct}_{x,z}) \leftarrow \mathsf{QFHE.Eval}(\mathsf{pk}, (\mathbf{M}_A^{p_x}, \mathrm{ct}_{p_x}), C),$$

and sends the classical part $\mathrm{ct}_{x,z}$ to $\mathcal{V}$.

3. $\mathcal{V}$ decrypts $(x,z) \leftarrow \mathsf{QFHE.Decrypt}(\mathsf{sk}, \mathrm{ct}_{x,z})$ and sends obfuscated membership check programs $i\mathcal{O}(A + x), i\mathcal{O}(A^\perp + z)$ to $\mathcal{P}$.

Unfortunately, there is an efficient "splitting" attack that breaks the monogamy game described above (even if the adversary does not receive the description of A in the question phase): a malicious prover can adversarially homomorphically compute two vectors, one in $A + x$, the other in $A^\perp + z$, thus trivially breaking the monogamy of entanglement. Intuitively, the attack is possible due to the fact that there is no mechanism to verify the quantum homomorphic evaluation. (Here, we need to have a classical verification procedure for a quantum statement, which is not an NP or QMA statement.) However, as we will see later in the proof of soundness, we do not need a notion of quantum homomorphic evaluation verification for our protocol. Instead, we will show that a weak notion of verification, in which the malicious prover is forced to homomorphically compute a state that is close to ideal coset states (and it can freely evaluate to obtain other things), is enough to obtain the monogamy-of-entanglement property. The weak notion of verification we are seeking is stated in the form of a self-testing argument, which leads us to the second attempt.

The second attempt: running self-testing protocol under QFHE. Our second attempt is be based on the recent [18,19] self-testing protocols for BB84 states. At first sight, it is not clear how one can directly obtain a self-testing protocol for coset states from these protocols. One of our technical contributions is the following observation: in the self-testing protocol for BB84 states of [18], instead of asking the prover $\mathcal{P}$ to prepare its own states (which are polynomially many $|+\rangle$ states if $\mathcal{P}$ is honest), the verifier $\mathcal{V}$ can send the input to $\mathcal{P}$ using QFHE. In particular, $\mathcal{V}$ sends encryption of $\mathbf{M}_0$, which is the all-zero matrix. $\mathcal{P}$ homomorphic evaluates a quantum circuit C on the received ciphertext such that if the input matrix is all-zero, C evaluates to a uniform superposition over $\mathbb{F}_2^\lambda$, which is product of $|+\rangle$ states. Under QFHE encryption, the quantum part of the evaluated ciphertext is product of random $|\pm\rangle$ states. $\mathcal{P}$ then uses this in the [18] self-testing protocol. We will show that an honest prover $\mathcal{P}$ using product of $|+\rangle$ states as in the [18] protocol or $\mathcal{P}$ using product of $|\pm\rangle$ states does not change the correctness of the protocol, while its soundness is maintained (since the soundness does not depend on which input the prover has used in the protocol execution).

We now briefly give a description of the [18] self-testing protocol, which is an n-fold parallel of the single-qubit self-testing protocol from [19], and explain later how to go from self-testing for BB84 states to self-testing for coset states using QFHE. The main cryptographic primitive underlying the [18] protocol (as well as other self-testing protocols [19,25]) is the so-called extended noisy trapdoor claw-free function (ENTCF) family[6], which can be constructed assuming the quantum hardness of LWE [23]. An ENTCF family is a family of functions indexed by a set of keys $\mathcal{K}_0 \cup \mathcal{K}_1$. $\mathcal{K}_0$ and $\mathcal{K}_1$ are disjoint sets of keys with the property that the two sets are computationally indistinguishable.

1. For a given *basis choice* $\theta \in \{0,1\}$ (where "0" corresponds to the computational and "1" to the Hadamard basis), the verifier $\mathcal{V}$ samples a key $k \in \mathcal{K}_\theta$, alongside some trapdoor information t. $\mathcal{V}$ sends k to the prover $\mathcal{P}$ and keeps t private.
2. The verifier and prover then interact classically.
3. For us, the most relevant part is the last round of the protocol, i.e., the last message from the verifier to the prover and back. Before the last round, the remaining quantum state of an *honest* prover is the single-qubit state $|v\rangle_\theta$ for $v \in \{0,1\}$, where $|v\rangle_\theta$ is a conjugate encoding of v in the basis θ: if $\theta = 0$, $|v\rangle_\theta = |v\rangle$, otherwise $|v\rangle_\theta = \frac{1}{\sqrt{2}}(|0\rangle + (-1)^v |1\rangle)$. From the transcript and the trapdoor information, the verifier can compute v; in contrast, the prover, which does not know the trapdoor, cannot efficiently compute θ or v. In the last round, the verifier sends θ to the prover, who returns $v' \in \{0,1\}$; the verifier then checks whether $v' = v$. The honest prover would generate v' by measuring its remaining qubit $|v\rangle_\theta$ in the basis θ and therefore always pass the verifier's check.

In the [18] test protocol, $\mathcal{V}$ runs n independent copies of [19] in parallel, except that the basis choice θ_i is the same for each copy. Next, from the [18] protocol, we describe a self-testing protocol for coset states.

Assume that now the verifier has private input which is a description of a coset state (A, x, z). We modify the verification procedure of the [18] test protocol in the last round as follows. Let v be the last message sent by $\mathcal{P}$ to $\mathcal{V}$ in the protocol above. If $\theta = 0$ (note that the basis choice is the same for n copies), $\mathcal{V}$ checks if $v \in A + x$, otherwise, it decodes[7] v to get a vector w and checks if $w \in A^\perp + z$. An honest prover would use the coset state $|A_{x,z}\rangle$, which it obtains after running the [29] protocol described above, as the input to this self-testing protocol. The honest prover would have measured its state in the computational basis when $\theta = 0$, and in the Hadamard basis when $\theta = 1$. Thus, any honest prover would pass this self-testing protocol for coset states with probability 1.

The crucial point is that, since the prover's input in both the [18] self-testing protocol and the self-testing protocol for coset states described above

---

[6] We refer the reader to [23, Section 4] for further details on ENTCF families.

[7] We omit the details of this decoding procedure, and refer the reader to Sect. 4.2. We note that with the trapdoor t, this procedure can be implemented efficiently by the verifier.

is encrypted under QFHE, and the fact that the two protocols are identical from the prover point's of view (except the last verification procedure, which is hidden from the prover), the two protocols are computationally indistinguishable. In other words, any computationally bounded prover cannot distinguish if it is playing in the [18] self-testing protocol or the coset-state self-testing protocol. This allows us to "embed" a self-testing for coset states into self-testing for BB84 states and to carry the rigidity argument of the [18] protocol to our setting. Note that in our protocol, we need to run both kind of tests, as self-testing for coset states alone is not enough to establish a rigidity argument. We elaborate more on this later in Sect. 2.2. For time being, let's say we have showed that if the prover $\mathcal{P}$ passes the verification, it must have "used" a coset state in the self-testing protocol (with inverse polynomial soundness).

Our final protocol. However, our ultimate goal is to perform a remote state preparation protocol (and not just self-testing, as the states used for the self-testing protocol will be destroyed due to the measurements). Our final step would be to run this coset-state self-testing protocol in the n-over-$2n$ cut-and-choose fashion: the verifier first sends $2n$ encrypted coset states and $|+\rangle$ to the prover, and it picks n instances uniformly at random for the self-testing protocol. The remaining n instances are used as the output of the final protocol. Building on the simple but powerful "quantum cut-and-choose" formalism of Bouman and Fehr [9], we can show that if the prover passes all the test instances, it must have at least 1 coset state in its registers at the end of the protocol (with inverse polynomial soundness). Notably, we will show that even if we only obtain inverse polynomial soundness at this step, our final protocol still achieves negligible security for a monogamy-of-entanglement game, which is the main property used in many copy-protection schemes. (An overview of the soundness proof is given below in Sect. 2.2.)

Our final protocol (Protocol 5) works as follows:

(1) The verifier first sends homomorphic encryption that allows the prover to either construct coset states or BB84 states.

(2) The prover is asked to homomorphically evaluate the instructed circuits and return classical encryption of the one-time pads of the homomorphic encryption, and keep the quantum parts.

(3) Next, the prover and the verifier run a number of self-testing rounds (Protocol 3), in which each test round consists of testing either BB84 states (Protocol 1) or coset states (Protocol 2), forming several test blocks. (In particular, a test block consists of a number of BB84 states testing rounds, and one coset states testing round.) All the BB84 states are consumed after this step, while only half of the coset states are consumed.

(4) Once the verifier is convinced, the verifier runs the coset states generation round on the remaining half of the coset states, in which the verifier sends back to the prover obfuscation of the membership checking programs. The final state of the prover can then be used in coset states based constructions. To be more precise, the output state of a single run of our protocol would satisfy the monogamy-of-entanglement property that we described above. If a quantum copy-protection scheme requires n random coset states, we can simply run our protocol n times (with independent randomness for each instance).

2.2   Soundness Proof

In this overview, we only give a brief intuition for the monogamy-of-entanglement soundness of our protocol. However, we note that the same proof technique can be used to show a direct product soundness.

Rigidity argument for the [18] **self-testing protocol.** Since the soundness proof uses the rigidity argument of the [18] protocol as the backbone, we briefly recall it here. Consider the last round of the [18] self-testing protocol: at the start, the prover has a state $\sigma^{(\theta,v)}$, which it produced as a result of the previous rounds of the protocol. Upon receiving $\theta \in \{0,1\}$ the prover measures a binary observable Z_i (if $\theta = 0$) or X_i (if $\theta = 1$) and returns the outcome v_i', one for each copy. Let $Z(a) := Z_1^{a_1} \cdots Z_n^{a_n}$, similarly for $X(b)$. The main goal of the [18] soundness proof is to show that when acting on the prover's (unknown) state $\sigma^{(\theta)}$ (where $\sigma^{(\theta)}$ is like $\sigma^{(\theta,v)}$, but averaged over all v), the operators $\{Z(a)X(b)\}$ behave essentially like Pauli operators. Formally, this means showing that on average over $a, b \in \{0,1\}^n$,

$$\mathrm{Tr}\Big[Z(a)X(b)Z(a)X(b)\sigma^{(\theta)}\Big] \approx (-1)^{a \cdot b}. \tag{1}$$

Rigidity argument for our coset-state self-testing protocol. Using the [18] rigidity argument, we now turn into our coset-state self-testing protocol. Crucially, since the two protocols are identical from the prover's point of view, and the fact that the input of the prover is encrypted, Equation (1) also carries to the coset-state self-testing. Specifically, it means that under the isometry V, the prover's observables in the coset-state self-testing protocol also behave like Pauli observables. Roughly speaking, the isometry "teleport" the prover's state into a "concrete" state by means of EPR pairs. In our case, the concrete state would be (close to) a mixed state of vectors $v \in A + x$ if $\theta = 0$, or $v' \in A^{\perp} + z$ if $\theta = 1$ (up to some classical post-processing), for a coset state instance (A, x, z).

This means that we can fix a prover $\mathcal{P}$ and consider a "hypothetical" quantum verifier, which runs the *purified version* of the protocol with $\mathcal{P}$, that is, we do not measure to get the prover's classical message as in the original protocol, but only do a projective measurement at the end for the verification. Then under the isometry V, if $\theta = 0$, we should obtain a state that is close to $|A + x\rangle$, and if $\theta = 1$, a state that is close to $|A^{\perp} + z\rangle$. In other words, consider that we run $\mathcal{P}$ with $\theta = 0$ in superposition, check the obtained state is $|A + x\rangle$, then undo the prover computation (described by a unitary), then run $\mathcal{P}$ with $\theta = 1$ in superposition, check the obtained state is $|A^{\perp} + z\rangle$. If both checks pass, it is easy to see that the prover must have a coset state $|A_{x,z}\rangle$ in its registers.

Note that this does not constitute a classical verification of QFHE. What it says is that after the evaluation and if $\mathcal{P}$ passes verification with overwhelming probability it is necessary that it must have a coset state in its register up to an isometry.

We stress that the above rigidity statement has $1/\text{poly}(n)$ closeness, due to the $1/\text{poly}(n)$ closeness in the rigidity argument of the [18] protocol.

Going from self-testing to remote state preparation. We then simply run the self-testing protocol sequentially in the cut-and-choose style. Say we have $2N$ coset state instances, and we run the self-testing protocol over N instances, chosen uniformly at random. The remaining N instances are the output of the protocol. By a particular "quantum sample-and-estimate" strategy defined in [9], it means that after running the self-testing rounds, the prover has at least one coset state $|A_{x,z}\rangle$ among N remaining coset state instances in its registers, with inverse polynomial closeness. We can write the prover's state at this step as (inverse polynomially δ-close to) $|A_{x,z}\rangle \otimes \rho$, where ρ can depend on the protocol's transcript and the encryption of (A, x, z).

Establishing a monogamy-of-entanglement property. In this final step, we want to show that now if the prover involves in a monogamy-of-entanglement game, it would have negligible probability of winning. The security game is defined as follows.

1. The prover and the verifier jointly execute our semi-quantum protocol to obtain (supposedly) N coset states, which are hidden but kept by the prover.
2. The prover and the verifier play the monogamy game using the output of the semi-quantum protocol:
   (a) The prover splits its state into a bipartite state and sends each part to Bob and Charlie, respectively. No communication is allowed between Bob and Charlie.
   (b) The verifier sends the description of the *subspace* to both Bob and Charlie.
   (c) Bob and Charlie are asked to output N vectors belonging to N cosets (for Bob), and N dual cosets (for Charlie).

However, our current situation is different from the standard monogamy game setting in which the prover only has the coset state, while here the prover also has an auxiliary state that depends on the coset state description. (Even worse, it might be possible that the prover can have two copies of the coset state after the interactive protocol.) The proof of the standard monogamy game does not carry over directly. Hence, for our monogamy-of-entanglement proof, new ideas are needed.

Injecting quantumness into the reduction. Our idea is to consider an intermediate game as follows.

1. The prover and the verifier jointly execute our semi-quantum protocol.
2. After finishing the protocol execution, the verifier asks the prover to send it a coset state among the remaining coset state instances uniformly at random.
3. Upon receiving a quantum state from the prover, the verifier verifies whether the received state is indeed the expected coset state, then it sends it back unmodified to the prover.

4. The prover and the verifier play the monogamy game.

Here we make few notes. First, with probability $\frac{1}{N}$ the coset state instance that the verifier asked is (A, x, z). It is easy to see that with probability $\frac{(1-\delta)}{N}$, which is non-negligible, any adversary for the original security experiment can be turned into an adversary for this experiment with identical winning probability. Secondly, defining this intermediate game is possible because of our rigidity argument above. Indeed, only in this step we inject quantumness into the reduction and make it a quantum verifier.

The proof continues with the following steps.

- We make another important observation that when considering only the coset instance (A, x, z), it is exactly the same as the public-key semi-quantum protocol introduced by Shmueli in [29]. We then follow proof strategies in previous works and carefully modify the experiment to remove the QFHE secret key (corresponding to this coset instance (A, x, z)) from the reduction. This is essentially done by changing the obfuscated membership checking programs sent to the prover in the last step of the protocol, using the following two techniques: subspace-hiding obfuscation [33], and complexity leveraging to blindly sample the obfuscations [29]. To use Shmueli's complexity leveraging technique, we will need sub-exponential security of the building blocks (which include the QFHE and the indistinguishability obfuscation).

- Then we make a final change in the reduction: upon receiving the coset state from the prover and if the check passes, the verifier keeps the received coset state in its internal memory, and send back to the prover another random coset state $|A'_{x',z'}\rangle$. In the monogamy game, instead of sending a description of A (as a basis matrix), the verifier sends a description of A'. Note that now the winning condition is also changed subject to this change in the challenge coset. We can think of $|A'_{x',z'}\rangle$ as the challenge of the original monogamy-of-entanglement game (with quantum communication).

- In this final experiment, if the prover managed to win the monogamy game, it means that Bob has successfully output a vector $v \in A' + x'$, and Charlie has successfully output a vector $w \in A'^{\perp} + z'$. The verifier then outputs v, w and wins the monogamy game with quantum communication. We conclude that no efficient prover can win this experiment except with negligible probability.

- The last part of the proof is to show that this final experiment is computationally indistinguishable from the previous experiment (in which the QFHE secret key was removed). We do this by invoking the security of the QFHE. However, there is a subtlety that needs to be taken care of. That is, even if we do not use the QFHE secret key in the reduction at this step, the adversary still receives predicate programs on the ciphertext, which are the obfuscated membership checking programs. Thus, we cannot simply send a uniformly random coset state $|A'_{x',z'}\rangle$ to the prover. In the protocol, we change the obfuscation programs so that both $|A_{x,z}\rangle$ and $|A'_{x',z'}\rangle$ make the programs accept. We refer to the formal construction and proof for the description of how these obfuscation programs are generated. Once this is shown, we can complete the proof.

2.3   Copy-Protection of Point Functions

Next, we give some intuition and obstacles behind our construction of copy-protection of point functions in this section. Informally, a copy-protection scheme of point functions is composed of a protection algorithm that takes as input a point function and returns a quantum encoding of this function; and an evaluation algorithm that takes as input the encoding and an input point and evaluates the function on this point. The (anti-piracy) security of such a scheme is defined through a game played by three adversaries Alice, non-communicating Bob and Charlie, where Alice is asked to "split" the quantum encoding into a two-register quantum state and to send one register to Bob and the other one to Charlie. In order to win the game, Bob and Charlie then must correctly evaluate the point function on two challenge inputs sampled from a certain distribution. The most natural distribution to take is the one that yields two inputs (x_B, x_C) such that (x_B, x_C) equals to either (y, y), (x_1, y), (y, x_2), or (x_1, x_2), each with probability $\frac{1}{4}$, where y is the protected point and x_1, x_2 are uniformly sampled.

A natural idea to construct copy-protection of point functions would be as follows. In order to protect a point y, sample a pseudorandom function (PRF) secret key k, protect it using the PRF copy-protection scheme to get ρ_k, and let the copy-protection of y be $(\rho_k, \mathsf{PRF}(k, y))$. The evaluation of an input x then consists, given a copy-protection of a point (ρ, z), on using the PRF copy-protection's evaluation procedure to compute $\mathsf{PRF}(k, x)$ and returning whether the outcome is z or not. At first glance, it may look like this idea has good chances to result in a secure scheme, since copy-protection of PRFs with a strong security property was shown in [15]. This so-called *indistinguishable anti-piracy security* of copy-protection of PRFs is defined as a game between a challenger and three adversaries Alice, Bob and Charlie. Bob and Charlie are not given a challenge only, but a pair (x, z) such that z is either $\mathsf{PRF}(k, x)$, or a uniformly random string, depending on the challenger's random coins. Then they are asked to return the value of the coins.

Unfortunately, we do not know how to reduce the security of our protocol directly to the indistinguishable anti-piracy security of copy-protection of PRFs, and thus we need to make few modifications to the indistinguishable anti-piracy game described above in order to carry out the reduction: (i) first, we change the definition by allowing Alice to have access to the z part of each challenge pair before she sends the bipartite state to Bob and Charlie; (ii) secondly, it is no longer the z part of the challenge that is either real or random, but the x part. More precisely, the challenge pairs (x, z) become such that z is an image of the PRF and x is either its pre-image or a uniformly random string. Furthermore, the image value z is sent to Alice and thus it is the same for both Bob and Charlie, only the x values are sampled independently based on the challenger's random coins. Even though we conjecture that our construction is secure if the underlying copy-protection of PRF scheme has security with respect to these modifications, it turns out that we have incompatible distributions when we do the reduction. The reason is essentially that, in order to prove the security, we do a reduction to the monogamy-of-entanglement of coset states. In this game,

Bob and Charlie must each return a vector from different spaces, which - in the reduction - they extract from the challenge they are given. Because of our last change, they receive the same challenge with probability 1/4, and then they return the same vector with probability 1/4. Unfortunately, this does not lead to any contradiction. Indeed, the same problem occurs as long as Bob and Charlie are given the same challenge with non-negligible probability.

Instead, in this work, we use another challenge distribution first defined in [16] - namely the distribution that yields either (y, x_2), (x_1, y), or (x_1, x_2), each with probability $\frac{1}{3}$. In this challenge distribution, Bob and Charlie never receive the same challenge, and thus it allows us to apply the extracting technique described above to finish the security proof. We refer the reader to Sect. 5 for a formal description of the construction, and we note that even though the challenge distribution that we use is less ideal, it is still a non-trivial challenge distribution in the context of copy-protection of point functions.

3   Preliminaries

Notation. Throughout this paper, λ denotes the security parameter. The notation $\mathsf{negl}(n)$ denotes any function f such that $f(\lambda) = \lambda^{-\omega(1)}$, and $\mathsf{poly}(n)$ denotes any function f such that $f(\lambda) = \mathcal{O}(\lambda^c)$ for some $c > 0$. For $a, b \in \mathbb{R}$, $[a, b] := \{x \in \mathbb{R} \mid a \leq x \leq b\}$ and $[\![a, b]\!] := \{x \in \mathbb{Z} \mid a \leq x \leq b\}$ will denote the closed real and integer interval with endpoints a and b. With an abuse of notation, we will write $[\![n]\!]$ as shorthand for $[\![0, n-1]\!]$. For a set $I = \{i_1, \ldots, i_\ell\} \subseteq [\![n]\!]$ and a n-bit string $x \in \{0,1\}^n$, we write $x|_I := x_{i_1} \cdots x_{i_\ell}$. When sampling uniformly at random a value a from a set $\mathcal{U}$, we employ the notation $a \xleftarrow{\$} \mathcal{U}$. When sampling a value a from a probabilistic algorithm $\mathcal{A}$, we employ the notation $a \leftarrow \mathcal{A}$. Let $|\cdot|$ denote either the length of a string, or the cardinal of a finite set, or the absolute value. By PPT we mean a polynomial-time non-uniform family of probabilistic circuits, and by QPT we mean a polynomial-time family of quantum circuits. For a probabilistic algorithm f, we write $f(x; r)$ to denote the computation of f on input x with randomness r drawn uniformly at random. We sometimes omit the randomness and just write $f(x)$. We refer the reader to the full version [13] for a complete presentation.

3.1   Cryptographic Primitives

We will use several cryptographic primitives in this paper: (i) indistinguishability obfuscation $i\mathcal{O}$, (ii) pseudorandom functions PRF, (iii) leveled hybrid quantum fully homomorphic encryption $\mathsf{QFHE} := \langle \mathsf{KeyGen}, \mathsf{Encrypt}, \mathsf{QOTP}, \mathsf{Eval}, \mathsf{Decrypt} \rangle$. We refer the reader to the full version for formal definitions of these primitives.

3.2   Extended Trapdoor Claw-Free Functions

Our remote state preparation protocol is based on a cryptographic primitive called extended noisy trapdoor claw free function families (ENTCF families), which are defined in [23, Section 4] and can be constructed from the Learning with Errors assumption [10, 27]. We use the same notation as in [23, Section 4], with the exception that we write $\mathcal{K}_0$ instead of $\mathcal{K}_{\mathcal{G}}$ and $\mathcal{K}_1$ instead of $\mathcal{K}_{\mathcal{F}}$. In addition, we also define the following functions for convenience:

Definition 1. (Decoding maps, [25, Definition 2.1]).

1. *For a key* $k \in \mathcal{K}_0 \cup \mathcal{K}_1$, *an image* $y \in \mathcal{Y}$, *a bit* $b \in \{0,1\}$, *and a pre-image* $x \in \mathcal{X}$, *we define* $\mathsf{Chk}(k, y, b, x)$ *to return 1 if* $y \in \mathsf{Supp}(f_{k,b}(x))$, *and 0 otherwise. (This definition is as in [23, Definition 4.1 and 4.2].)*
2. *For a key* $k \in \mathcal{K}_0$ *and a* $y \in \mathcal{Y}$, *we define* $\hat{b}(k,y)$ *by the condition* $y \in \cup_x \mathsf{Supp}\left(f_{k,\hat{b}(k,y)}(x)\right)$. *(This is well-defined because* $f_{k,0}$ *and* $f_{k,1}$ *form an injective pair.)*
3. *For a key* $k \in \mathcal{K}_0 \cup \mathcal{K}_1$ *and a* $y \in \mathcal{Y}$, *we define* $\hat{x}_b(k,y)$ *by the condition* $y \in \mathsf{Supp}(f_{k,b}(\hat{x}_b(k,y)))$, *and* $\hat{x}_b(k,y) = \bot$ *if* $y \notin \cup_x \mathsf{Supp}(f_{k,b}(x))$. *For* $k \in \mathcal{K}_0$, *we also use the shorthand* $\hat{x}(k,y) := \hat{x}_{\hat{b}(k,y)}(k,y)$.
4. *For a key* $k \in \mathcal{K}_1$, *a* $y \in \mathcal{Y}$, *and a* $d \in \{0,1\}^w$, *we define* $\hat{u}(k,y,d)$ *by the condition* $d \cdot (\hat{x}_0(k,y) \oplus \hat{x}_1(k,y)) = \hat{u}(k,y,d)$.

The above decoding maps applied to vector inputs are understood to act in an element-wise fashion. For example, for $\boldsymbol{k} \in \mathcal{K}_1^{\times n}, \boldsymbol{y} \in \mathcal{Y}^{\times n}$, *and* $\boldsymbol{d} \in \{0,1\}^{w \times n}$, *we denote by* $\hat{u}(\boldsymbol{k}, \boldsymbol{y}, \boldsymbol{d}) \in \{0,1\}^n$ *the string defined by* $(\hat{u}(\boldsymbol{k}, \boldsymbol{y}, \boldsymbol{d}))_i := \hat{u}(k_i, y_i, d_i)$.

4   Remote Coset State Preparation Protocol

In this section, we introduce our protocol for remote hidden coset state preparation. We first give a definition of completeness and soundness in Sect. 4.1. Our construction is given in Sect. 4.2, and its formal proofs are given in the full version [13].

4.1   Definitions

Definition 2 (Remote Coset State Preparation Protocol). *A remote coset state preparation protocol is an interactive classical communication protocol between a* PPT *verifier (or sender, denoted as* $\mathcal{V}$*) and a* QPT *prover (or receiver, denoted as* $\mathcal{P}$*) such that at the end of the protocol, the verifier obtains a list* $T \subset \mathbb{N}$ *of classical description of cosets* $\{S_i, \alpha_i, \beta_i\}_{i \in T}$ *and the prover outputs a quantum state* ψ. *The two parties also obtain a common output which is obfuscated membership checking programs of* $S_i + \alpha_i$ *and* $S_i^\perp + \beta_i$ *for all* $i \in T$.

We denote an execution of the protocol as $(\{S_i, \alpha_i, \beta_i\}_{i \in T}, \psi, \{P_{0,i}, P_{1,i}\}_{i \in T})$ $\leftarrow \langle \mathcal{P}(1^\lambda), \mathcal{V}(1^\lambda) \rangle$, *where* $P_{0,i}$ *is an obfuscated membership checking program of* $S_i + \alpha_i$ *and* $P_{1,i}$ *is an obfuscated membership checking program of* $S_i^\perp + \beta_i$. *Note that* $\{P_{0,i}, P_{1,i}\}_{i \in T}$ *is the common output of both parties. When it is clear from the context, we omit the common output and just write* $(\{S_i, \alpha_i, \beta_i\}_{i \in T}, \psi) \leftarrow \langle \mathcal{P}(1^\lambda), \mathcal{V}(1^\lambda) \rangle$.

The protocol is correct *if the protocol does not abort and at the end of the execution, there exists a negligible function $\varepsilon(\lambda)$ such that*

$$\Pr\left[\psi \approx_\varepsilon \bigotimes_{i \in T} |S_{i,\alpha_i,\beta_i}\rangle\right] \geq 1 - \mathsf{negl}(n),$$

where the probability is taken over randomness of the verifier $\mathcal{V}$.

We now formally define the notions of soundness of remote coset state preparation protocol. We will give two different definitions: one for the monogamy-of-entanglement property (Definition 3), and another for the direct product hardness property (see the full version for the details).

Definition 3. *Let $(\{S_i, \alpha_i, \beta_i\}_{i \in T}, \psi) \leftarrow \langle \mathcal{P}_\lambda(\rho_\lambda), \mathcal{V}(1^\lambda)\rangle$ be an execution of a remote coset state preparation protocol between a* QPT *prover $\mathcal{P} = \{\mathcal{P}_\lambda, \rho_\lambda\}_{\lambda \in \mathbb{N}}$ and a* PPT *verifier $\mathcal{V}$, after which $\mathcal{V}$ outputs $\{S_i, \alpha_i, \beta_i\}_{i \in T}$ and $\mathcal{P}$ outputs a state ψ. The prover (now modeled as a triple algorithm $(\mathcal{P}, \mathcal{B}, \mathcal{C})$) then interacts with the verifier in the following monogamy game.*

1. *The prover applies a CPTP map to split ψ into a bipartite state ψ_{BC}; it sends the register B to $\mathcal{B}$ and the register C to $\mathcal{C}$. No communication is allowed between $\mathcal{B}$ and $\mathcal{C}$ after this phase.*
2. *Question. The verifier sends the description of $\{S_i\}_{i \in T}$, to both $\mathcal{B}$ and $\mathcal{C}$.*
3. *Answer. $\mathcal{B}$ returns $s_1^{(i)} \in \mathbb{F}_2^n$ and $\mathcal{C}$ returns $s_2^{(i)} \in \mathbb{F}_2^n$ for all $i \in T$.*

The prover $(\mathcal{P}, \mathcal{B}, \mathcal{C})$ wins if and only if $s_1^{(i)} \in S_i + \alpha_i$ and $s_2^{(i)} \in S_i^\perp + \beta_i$ for all $i \in T$. Let $\mathsf{SMCosetMonogamy}(\mathcal{P}, \lambda)$ *be a random variable which takes the value 1 if the game above is won by the prover $(\mathcal{P}, \mathcal{B}, \mathcal{C})$, and takes the value 0 otherwise.*

The protocol is secure if the winning probability of any QPT *adversary is negligible. Formally, for any* QPT *malicious prover, the protocol is computationally sound with the monogamy-of-entanglement property if*

$$\Pr[\mathsf{SMCosetMonogamy}(\mathcal{P}, \lambda) = 1] \leq \mathsf{negl}(n).$$

4.2   Construction

Notation. Our Protocol 1 and Protocol 2 will be (almost) a parallel repetition of a sub-protocol. We make use of vector notation to denote tuples of items corresponding to the different copies of the sub-protocol. For example, if each of the n parallel sub-protocols requires a key k_i, we denote $\boldsymbol{k} = (k_1, \ldots, k_n)$. A function that takes as input a single value can be extended to input vectors in the obvious way: for example, if f takes as input a single key k, then we write $f(\boldsymbol{k})$ for the vector $(f(k_1), \ldots, f(k_n))$. We will also use $\boldsymbol{0}$ and $\boldsymbol{1}$ for the bit strings consisting only of 0 and 1, respectively (and whose length will be clear from the context), and $\boldsymbol{1}^i \in \{0, 1\}^n$ for the bit string whose i-th bit is 1 and whose remaining bits are 0. Let n the length of a vector in a coset state (i.e., if $v \in A$ then $|v| = n$). In our constructions below, we set $n := 2\lambda$.

Ingredients. Our constructions use the following building blocks:

- A quantum hybrid fully homomorphic encryption scheme $\mathsf{QFHE} := \langle \mathsf{KeyGen}, \mathsf{QOTP}, \mathsf{Encrypt}, \mathsf{Eval}, \mathsf{Decrypt} \rangle$, with sub-exponential advantage security.
- A post-quantum secure indistinguishability obfuscation scheme $i\mathcal{O}$.
- A post-quantum secure extended noisy trapdoor claw-free function (ENTCF) family $(\mathcal{F}, \mathcal{G})$.

Our main protocol's construction is given in Protocol 5. The protocol involves two parties: a QPT prover (or receiver, denoted as $\mathcal{P}$), and a PPT verifier (or sender, denoted as $\mathcal{V}$).

Protocol 1: Semi-quantum Protocol: BB84 Test Round

Input. The verifier initially receives Pauli keys (α, β) with $\alpha, \beta \in \{0,1\}^n$ as private inputs.

1. The verifier selects a uniformly random basis $\theta \xleftarrow{\$} \{0,1\}$, where 0 corresponds to the computational and 1 to the Hadamard basis.
2. The verifier samples keys and trapdoors $\{(k_i, t_i)\}_{i=1}^n$ by computing $(k_i, t_i) \leftarrow \mathsf{Gen}_{\mathcal{K}_\theta}(1^\lambda)$. The verifier then sends $\{k_i\}_{i=1}^n$ to the prover (but keeps the trapdoors $\{t_i\}_{i=1}^n$ private).
3. The verifier receives $\{y_i\}_{i=1}^n$ where $y_i \in \mathcal{Y}$ from the prover.
4. The verifier selects a round type $\in \{\text{pre-image round}, \text{Hadamard round}\}$ uniformly at random and sends the round type to the prover.
   (a) For a *pre-image round*: the verifier receives $\{(b_i, x_i)\}_{i=1}^n$ from the prover, with $b_i \in \{0,1\}$, and $x_i \in \mathcal{X}$. The verifier sets $\mathtt{flag}_{\mathsf{bb84}} \leftarrow \mathtt{flag}_{\mathsf{Pre}}$ and aborts if $\mathsf{Chk}(k_i, t_i, b_i, x_i) = 0$ for any $i \in [\![1, n]\!]$.
   (b) For a *Hadamard round*: the verifier receives $\{d_i\}_{i=1}^n$ from the prover with $d_i \in \{0,1\}^w$ (for some w depends on the security parameter λ). The verifier sends $q = \theta$ to the prover, and receives answers $\{v_i\}_{i=1}^n$ with $v_i \in \{0,1\}$. The verifier performs the following:
      - If $q = \theta = 0$, set $\mathtt{flag}_{\mathsf{bb84}} \leftarrow \mathtt{flag}_{\mathsf{Had}}$ and abort if $\hat{b}(k_i, y_i) \neq v_i$ for some $i \in [\![1, n]\!]$.
      - If $q = \theta = 1$, set $\mathtt{flag}_{\mathsf{bb84}} \leftarrow \mathtt{flag}_{\mathsf{Had}}$ and abort if $\hat{u}(k_i, y_i, d_i) \neq v_i \oplus \beta_i$ for some $i \in [\![1, n]\!]$.

Protocol 2: Semi-quantum Protocol: Coset-state Test Round

Input. The verifier initially receives a subspace $A \subseteq \mathbb{F}_2^n$ and Pauli keys (α, β) with $\alpha, \beta \in \{0,1\}^n$ as private inputs.

1. The verifier selects a uniformly random basis $\theta \xleftarrow{\$} \{0,1\}$, where 0 corresponds to the computational and 1 to the Hadamard basis.
2. The verifier samples keys and trapdoors $\{(k_i, t_i)\}_{i=1}^n$ by computing $(k_i, t_i) \leftarrow \mathsf{Gen}_{\mathcal{K}_\theta}(1^\lambda)$. The verifier then sends $\{k_i\}_{i=1}^n$ to the prover (but keeps the trapdoors $\{t_i\}_{i=1}^n$ private).
3. The verifier receives $\{y_i\}_{i=1}^n$ where $y_i \in \mathcal{Y}$ from the prover.

4. The verifier sends "Hadamard round" as the round type to the prover.
5. The verifier receives $\{d_i\}_{i=1}^n$ from the prover with $d_i \in \{0,1\}^w$ (for some w depends on the security parameter λ). The verifier sends $q = \theta$ to the prover, and receives answers $\{v_i\}_{i=1}^n$ with $v_i \in \{0,1\}$.
   The verifier performs the following:
   - If $q = \theta = 0$, let $v := v_1 \ldots v_n$. Set $\texttt{flag}_{\text{coset}} \leftarrow \texttt{flag}_{\text{Had}}$ and abort if $v \notin A + \alpha$.
   - If $q = \theta = 1$, let $s_i \leftarrow v_i \oplus \hat{u}(k_i, y_i, d_i)$ and let $s := s_1 \ldots s_n$. Set $\texttt{flag}_{\text{coset}} \leftarrow \texttt{flag}_{\text{Had}}$ and abort if $s \notin A^{\perp} + \beta$.

Protocol 3: Semi-quantum Protocol: Self-Testing

Let M^2 the maximum number of test rounds (for $M \in \mathbb{N}$).
Input. The verifier initially receives a subspace $A \subseteq \mathbb{F}_2^n$ and Pauli keys (α', β') and $\{(\alpha_i, \beta_i)\}_{i=1}^{M^2}$ with $\alpha', \beta', \alpha_i, \beta_i \in \{0,1\}^n$ as private inputs. Note that (A, α', β') corresponds to one coset-state instance, and $\{(\alpha_i, \beta_i)\}_{i=1}^{M^2}$ corresponds to M^2 BB84 instances.

1. The verifier privately samples $B \xleftarrow{\$} [\![1, M-1]\!]$ (this determines the number of BB84 test rounds that will be performed).
2. The verifier performs BM executions of Protocol 1 (with corresponding private inputs $\{(\alpha_i, \beta_i)\}$) with the prover. The verifier aborts if Protocol 1 aborts for some execution.
3. The verifier privately samples $R \xleftarrow{\$} [\![1, M]\!]$ and executes Protocol 1 with the prover $R - 1$ times (with corresponding private inputs $\{(\alpha_i, \beta_i)\}$). Then the verifier executes Protocol 2 with the prover (with private inputs (A, α', β')) and aborts if Protocol 2 aborts.

Protocol 4: Semi-quantum Protocol: Self-Testing (with Soundness Amplification)

Let $N := \lambda$ the number of iterations.
Input. The verifier initially receives $\{(A_i, \alpha'_i, \beta'_i)\}_{i=1}^N$ and $\{(\alpha_i, \beta_i)\}_{i=1}^{NM^2}$ as private inputs. Each tuple in the first set corresponds to a coset-state instance, and each tuple in the second set corresponds to a BB84 instance.
The verifier and the prover sequentially run Protocol 3 N times as follows.

1. For each run, the verifier and the prover interactively run Protocol 3 with one coset state instance $(A_i, \alpha'_i, \beta'_i)$ and M^2 BB84 instances $\{(\alpha_i, \beta_i)\}_{i=1}^{M^2}$, each is picked uniformly at random from the input sets. (If some instance has been picked before, it will be excluded).
2. The verifier aborts unless Protocol 3 does not abort in all N iterations.

Protocol 5: Semi-quantum Protocol: Main Protocol

Verifier's preparation.

1. **Coset-state instances.** For each $i \in [\![1, 2N]\!]$, the verifier samples a random $\frac{n}{2}$-dimensional subspace $S_i \subseteq \mathbb{F}_2^n$, described by a matrix $\mathbf{M}_{S_i} \in \{0,1\}^{\frac{n}{2} \times n}$. Samples Pauli keys $p_{\alpha_i} \xleftarrow{\$} \{0,1\}^{\frac{n^2}{2}}$ to encrypt $\mathbf{M}_{S_i}^{p_{\alpha_i}} \leftarrow \mathsf{QFHE.QOTP}(p_{\alpha_i}, \mathbf{M}_{S_i})$,

and then $(\mathsf{pk}_i, \mathsf{sk}_i) \leftarrow \mathsf{QFHE.KeyGen}(1^\lambda, 1^{\ell(\lambda)})$ for some polynomial $\ell(\cdot)$, $\mathsf{ct}_i \leftarrow$ $\mathsf{QFHE.Encrypt}(\mathsf{pk}_i, p_{\alpha_i})$.

2. n-**qubit BB84 instances.** For each $i \in [\![1, NM^2]\!]$, the verifier samples Pauli keys $p_{\alpha_i} \overset{\$}{\leftarrow} \{0,1\}^{\frac{n^2}{2}}$ to encrypt $\mathbf{M}_0^{p_{\alpha_i}} \leftarrow \mathsf{QFHE.QOTP}(p_{\alpha_i}, \mathbf{M}_0)$ (here, $\mathbf{M}_0$ is the all-zero vector of length $\frac{n^2}{2}$), and then $(\mathsf{pk}_i, \mathsf{sk}_i) \leftarrow \mathsf{QFHE.KeyGen}(1^\lambda, 1^{\ell(\lambda)})$, $\mathsf{ct}_i \leftarrow \mathsf{QFHE.Encrypt}(\mathsf{pk}_i, p_{\alpha_i})$.

3. For each index $i \in [\![1, 2N + NM^2]\!]$, the verifier picks uniformly at random one instance from either the set of (encrypted) coset states or the set of (encrypted) n-qubit BB84 states prepared above. For each index i, denote the i-th instance as $(\mathsf{pk}_i, \mathbf{M}^{p_{\alpha_i}}, \mathsf{ct}_i)$ with secrets (sk_i, S_i). (If this instance is from the set of n-qubit BB84 states, we understand that $S_i = \mathbf{M}_0$.)

4. The verifier sends $\{\mathsf{pk}_i, \mathbf{M}^{p_{\alpha_i}}, \mathsf{ct}_i\}_{i=1}^{2N+NM^2}$ to the prover.

Prover's homomorphic evaluation

5. Let C the quantum circuit that for an input matrix $\mathbf{M} \in \{0,1\}^{\frac{n}{2} \times n}$, outputs a uniform superposition of its row span, except that if $\mathbf{M} = \mathbf{M}_0$, it outputs a uniform superposition of all vectors in the space $\mathbb{F}_2^n$. The prover homomorphically evaluates C for each $i \in [\![1, 2N + NM^2]\!]$: $(|S_{i,\alpha_i,\beta_i}\rangle, \mathsf{ct}_{i,\alpha_i,\beta_i}) \leftarrow$ $\mathsf{QFHE.Eval}\big(\mathsf{pk}_i, (\mathbf{M}^{p_{\alpha_i}}, \mathsf{ct}_i), C\big)$, saves the quantum part $|S_{i,\alpha_i,\beta_i}\rangle$ and sends the classical part $\mathsf{ct}_{i,\alpha_i,\beta_i}$ to the verifier.

Self-testing for the prover.

6. For each $i \in [\![1, 2N + NM^2]\!]$, the verifier decrypts $(\alpha_i, \beta_i) \leftarrow$ $\mathsf{QFHE.Decrypt}(\mathsf{sk}_i, \mathsf{ct}_{i,\alpha_i,\beta_i})$. For all coset-state instances, if $\alpha_i \in S_i$, the protocol is terminated.

7. The verifier then runs Protocol 4 with these NM^2 prepared BB84 instances and N coset-state instances, where each coset-state instance is picked uniformly at random among $2N$ prepared instances. (If some instance has been picked before, it will be excluded). It aborts if Protocol 4 aborts.

Coset-state generation.

8. The verifier samples a random $\frac{n}{2}$-dimensional coset $(\hat{S}, \hat{\alpha}, \hat{\beta}) \subseteq \mathbb{F}_2^n$ independently.[a] Let $\mathbf{M}_{\hat{S}}, \mathbf{M}_{\hat{S}^\perp} \in \{0,1\}^{\frac{n}{2} \times n}$ bases for $\hat{S}$ and $\hat{S}^\perp$, respectively.

9. Let T the set of indexes of the remaining N instances of the coset-states which have not been used in the self-testing protocol above. For each $i \in T$, the verifier does the following:
   (a) Let $\mathbf{M}_{S_i^\perp} \in \{0,1\}^{\frac{n}{2} \times n}$ a basis for $S_i^\perp$ (as a matrix). Compute indistinguishability obfuscations $P_{0,i} \leftarrow i\mathcal{O}\big(i\mathcal{O}(\mathbf{M}_{S_i} + \alpha_i) \vee i\mathcal{O}(\mathbf{M}_{\hat{S}} + \hat{\alpha})\big)$ and $P_{1,i} \leftarrow$ $i\mathcal{O}\big(i\mathcal{O}(\mathbf{M}_{S_i^\perp} + \beta_i) \vee i\mathcal{O}(\mathbf{M}_{\hat{S}^\perp} + \hat{\beta})\big)$, all with appropriate padding.[b]
   (b) Record $\{(\alpha_i, \beta_i, S_i)\}_{i \in T}$.
   (c) Send T and $\{P_{0,i}, P_{1,i}\}_{i \in T}$ to the prover.

The output of the prover is $\{P_{0,i}, P_{1,i}, |S_{i,\alpha_i,\beta_i}\rangle\}_{i \in T}$ where $|T| = N$.

---

[a] This step is merely an artifact that we will need later for the security proof.

[b] Here, we understand that for any two programs C, C' with binary output, $i\mathcal{O}(C \vee C')(x)$ outputs $C(x) \vee C'(x)$.

Notation. For each execution of Protocol 5, we abuse the notation and denote $(|A_{s,s'}\rangle, \mathsf{R}^0, \mathsf{R}^1)$ the state obtained by the receiver, where R^b the obfuscated membership checking programs, computed by concatenating all the obfuscated programs $P_{b,i}$ in Protocol 5, and (A, s, s') the "coset" (which in fact consists of polynomial many different real cosets) obtained by the sender. That is, we consider the whole output state of the protocol as a single unclonable state (which we also call "coset state"). This notation will only be used later when we describe the applications of our protocol in the context of semi-quantum copy-protection and semi-quantum tokenized signatures.

We refer the reader to the full version [13] for the proofs of correctness and security.

5   (Semi-quantum) Copy-Protection of Point Functions

In this section, we give a construction of quantum copy-protection of point functions and we also show how to instantiate a semi-quantum copy-protection scheme by applying our remote state preparation protocol Protocol 5 to this quantum copy-protection scheme. We note that our semi-quantum copy-protection scheme is interactive, while its quantum version is non-interactive.

We first recall security definition of (semi-)quantum copy-protection of point functions in Sect. 5.1, and present our constructions in Sect. 5.2, followed by a sketch of security proofs. (The formal proofs are given in the full version [13].)

5.1   Definition

Recall that a point functions family $\{\mathsf{PF}_y\}_{y \in \mathcal{X}}$ is indexed by points $y \in \mathcal{X}$ and a point function PF_y returns 1 on input y and 0 on any other input.

We give a security definition for copy-protection of point functions by instantiating the general definition of copy-protection with the following family: $\mathcal{F} := \{\mathsf{PF}_y\}_{y \in \{0,1\}^n}$, where each function $f = \mathsf{PF}_y$ in the family is described by $d_f := y$. For the anti-piracy security, we will consider the function distribution $\mathcal{D}_f := \mathcal{U}(\{0,1\}^n)$: the uniform distribution over $\{0,1\}^n$; and the family of distributions $\mathcal{X} := \{\mathcal{X}_y\}_{y \in \{0,1\}^n}$ such that for any $y \in \{0,1\}^n$, $\mathcal{X}_y$:

- samples $x \xleftarrow{\$} \{0,1\}^n$ and yields (y, x) with probability $1/3$;
- samples $x \xleftarrow{\$} \{0,1\}^n$ and yields (x, y) with probability $1/3$;
- samples $x, x' \xleftarrow{\$} \{0,1\}^n$ and yields (x, x') with probability $1/3$.

5.2   Constructions

Let $\{\mathsf{PF}_y\}_{y \in \{0,1\}^n}$ be the family to be copy-protected, where $n := n(\lambda)$ is a polynomial in λ. We define ℓ_0, ℓ_1, ℓ_2 such that $n = \ell_0 + \ell_1 + \ell_2$ and $\ell_2 - \ell_0$ is large enough. For this construction, we need three pseudorandom functions (PRFs):

- A puncturable extracting PRF $\mathsf{PRF}_1 : \mathcal{K}_1 \times \{0,1\}^n \to \{0,1\}^m$ with error $2^{-\lambda-1}$, where m is a polynomial in λ and $n \geq m + 2\lambda + 4$.

- A puncturable injective PRF $\mathsf{PRF}_2 : \mathcal{K}_2 \times \{0,1\}^{\ell_2} \to \{0,1\}^{\ell_1}$ with failure probability $2^{-\lambda}$, with $\ell_1 \geq 2\ell_2 + \lambda$.
- A puncturable PRF $\mathsf{PRF}_3 : \mathcal{K}_3 \times \{0,1\}^{\ell_1} \to \{0,1\}^{\ell_2}$.

Construction 1: Quantum Copy-Protection of Point Functions

$\mathsf{PF.Protect}(y)$:

- Sample ℓ_0 random coset states $\{|A_{i,s_i,s'_i}\rangle\}_{i \in [\![1,\ell_0]\!]}$, where each subspace $A_i \subseteq \mathbb{F}_2^n$ if of dimension $\frac{n}{2}$.
- For each coset state $|A_{i,s_i,s'_i}\rangle$, prepare the obfuscated membership programs $\mathsf{R}_i^0 = i\mathcal{O}(A_i + s_i)$ and $\mathsf{R}_i^1 = i\mathcal{O}(A_i^\perp + s'_i)$.
- Sample $k_i \leftarrow \mathsf{PRF}_i.\mathsf{KeyGen}(1^\lambda)$ for $i \in \{1,2,3\}$.
- Prepare the program $\hat{\mathsf{P}} \leftarrow i\mathcal{O}(\mathsf{P})$, where P is described in Figure 1.
- Compute $z := \mathsf{PRF}_1(k_1, y)$.
- Return $\rho_y := \left(\{|A_{i,s_i,s'_i}\rangle\}_{i \in [\![1,\ell_0]\!]}, \hat{\mathsf{P}}, z \right)$.

$\mathsf{PF.Eval}(\rho_y, x)$:

- Parse $\rho_y = \left(\{|A_{i,s_i,s'_i}\rangle\}_{i \in [\![1,\ell_0]\!]}, \hat{\mathsf{P}}, z \right)$.
- Parse x as $x := x_0 \| x_1 \| x_2$.
- For each $i \in [\![1,\ell_0]\!]$, if $x_{0,i} = 1$, apply $\mathsf{H}^{\otimes n}$ to $|A_{i,s_i,s'_i}\rangle$; if $x_{0,i} = 0$, leave the state unchanged.
- Let σ be the resulting state (which can be interpreted as a superposition over tuples of ℓ_0 vectors). Run $\hat{\mathsf{P}}$ coherently on input x and σ, and measure the final output register to obtain z'.
- Return 1 if $z' = z$, otherwise return 0.

Hardcoded: Keys $(k_1, k_2, k_3) \in \mathcal{K}_1 \times \mathcal{K}_2 \times \mathcal{K}_3$, programs $\mathsf{R}_i^0, \mathsf{R}_i^1$ for all $i \in [\![1,\ell_0]\!]$.

On input $x = x_0 \| x_1 \| x_2$ and vectors $v_0, v_1, \cdots, v_{\ell_0}$ where each $v_i \in \mathbb{F}_2^n$, do the following:

1. **(Hidden Trigger Mode)** If $\mathsf{PRF}_3(k_3, x_1) \oplus x_2 = x_0 \| Q'$ and $x_1 = \mathsf{PRF}_2(k_2, x_0 \| Q')$: treat Q' as a classical circuit and output $Q'(v_1, \cdots, v_{\ell_0})$.

2. **(Normal Mode)** If for all $i \in [\![1,\ell_0]\!]$, $\mathsf{R}_i^{x_i}(v_i) = 1$, then output $\mathsf{PRF}_1(k_1, x)$. Otherwise, output $\perp$.

Fig. 1. Program P.

The semi-quantum copy-protection scheme for point functions is presented in Construction 2, which is essentially obtained by applying our compiler in Sect. 4 to Construction 1.

Construction 2: Semi-Quantum Copy-Protection of Point Functions

PF.Protect(y): This is now an interactive protocol between a sender and a receiver.
The sender does the following:

- Run Protocol 5 independently ℓ_0 times with the receiver to obtain

$$\left(\{A_i, s_i, s_i'\}_{i \in [\![1,\ell_0]\!]}, \{(\mathsf{R}_i^0, \mathsf{R}_i^1)\}_{i \in [\![1,\ell_0]\!]}\right).$$

The receiver obtains the corresponding $\{|A_{i,s_i,s_i'}\rangle\}_{i \in [\![1,\ell_0]\!]}$.

- Sample PRF keys k_i for PRF_i with $i \in \{1,2,3\}$.
- Prepare the program $\hat{\mathsf{P}} \leftarrow i\mathcal{O}(\mathsf{P})$, where P is described in Figure 1.
- Compute $z := \mathsf{PRF}_1(\mathsf{k}_1, y)$.
- Send $\left(\hat{\mathsf{P}}, z\right)$ to the receiver.

PF.Eval(ρ_y, x):

- Parse $\rho_y = \left(\{|A_{i,s_i,s_i'}\rangle\}_{i \in [\![1,\ell_0]\!]}, \hat{\mathsf{P}}, z\right).$
- Parse x as $x := x_0 \| x_1 \| x_2$.
- For each $i \in [\![1,\ell_0]\!]$, if $x_{0,i} = 1$, apply $H^{\otimes n}$ to $|A_{i,s_i,s_i'}\rangle$; if $x_{0,i} = 0$, leave the state unchanged.
- Let σ be the resulting state (which can be interpreted as a superposition over tuples of ℓ_0 vectors). Run $\hat{\mathsf{P}}$ coherently on input x and σ, and measure the final output register to obtain z'.
- Return 1 if $z' = z$, otherwise return 0.

Theorem 4. *Assuming the existence of post-quantum indistinguishability obfuscation, one-way functions, and compute-and-compare obfuscation for the class of unpredictable distributions, Construction 1 and Construction 2 have correctness and anti-piracy security.*

The correctness of our protocols follows directly from the correctness of the copy-protection of PRFs construction of [15, Lemma 7.13].

The security of our protocols relies on a new security notion for (semi-quantum) single-decryptors. We recall its definitions and introduce this new security notion – which we call anti-piracy security (real-or-random style). We show that the [15]'s single-decryptor scheme also achieves this new security definition. The security proof of our constructions then follows the same strategy as that of copy-protection of PRFs given in [15], except that we reduce security to our new single-decryptors definitions. We refer the reader to the full version [13] for a detailed proof.

6   Semi-quantum Tokenized Digital Signatures

In this section, we present a semi-quantum construction of tokenized digital signatures with strong unforgeability security, using our compiler presented in Sect. 4.

6.1   Definitions

A definition for a strongly unforgeable semi-quantum tokenized signature is given below. We note that our definition is similar to the one for weak unforgeability given in [30].

Definition 4 (Semi-quantum Tokenized Digital Signature). *A semi-quantum tokenized signature scheme consists of five* QPT *algorithms* sqTDS = ⟨Send, Rec, Sign, TokenVerif, Verif⟩ *with the following properties:*

- (vk, *sig*) ← ⟨Send, Rec⟩(1^λ). *On input the security parameter* λ, *a classical-communication protocol between* Send *and* Rec *outputs a classical verification key* pk *and a signing token* sig. *We emphasize that* Send *is a* PPT *algorithm.*
- σ ← Sign(m, *sig*). *On input a message* m ∈ {0, 1} *and a signing token* sig, *the signing algorithm* Sign *outputs a classical signature* σ ∈ {0, 1}^{p(λ)}.
- (b, *sig'*) ← TokenVerif(vk, *sig*). *On input the verification key* vk, *and a signing token* sig, *the token verification* TokenVerif *outputs a single bit* b ∈ {0, 1}, *and a post-verified token* sig'.
- b ← Verif(vk, m, σ). *On input the verification key* vk, *a message* m *and a classical signature* σ, *the verification algorithm outputs a bit* b ∈ {0, 1}.

A semi-quantum tokenized digital signature scheme sqTDS *must satisfy the following requirements for all* λ ∈ ℕ.

- ***Correctness.*** *For every message* m ∈ {0, 1}, *we have that*

$$\Pr_{(vk,sig)\leftarrow\langle\text{Send},\text{Rec}\rangle(1^\lambda)}\left[\text{Verif}(vk, \text{Sign}(m, sig)) = 1\right] \geq 1 - \text{negl}(n).$$

- ***(Strong) Unforgeability.*** sqTDS *is strongly unforgeable if for every* QPT *adversary* $\mathcal{A} = \{\mathcal{A}_\lambda, \rho_\lambda\}_{\lambda\in\mathbb{N}}$,

$$\text{Adv}^{\text{sqTDS}}(\lambda, \mathcal{A}) :=$$

$$\Pr\left[\begin{array}{c}\forall b \in \{0, 1\} : \text{Verif}(pk, m_b, \sigma_b) = 1 \wedge \\ (m_0, \sigma_0) \neq (m_1, \sigma_1)\end{array}\middle|\begin{array}{c}(vk, sig) \leftarrow \langle\text{Send}, \mathcal{A}\rangle(1^\lambda) \\ \{(m_b, \sigma_b)\}_{b\in\{0,1\}} \leftarrow \mathcal{A}(\rho_\lambda)\end{array}\right]$$
$$\leq \text{negl}(n).$$

- ***Testability.*** *The token testing algorithm* TokenVerif, *unlike the signing algorithm, does not consume the signing token. If a signing token passes this test, the post-verified token also passes the test, and it can be used to sign a document. That is, for any* QPT *adversary* $\mathcal{A}$,

$$\Pr\left[\text{TokenVerif}(sig') = (1, sig')\middle|\begin{array}{c}(vk, sig) \leftarrow \langle\text{Send}, \mathcal{A}\rangle(1^\lambda) \\ (1, sig') \leftarrow \text{TokenVerif}(vk, sig)\end{array}\right] \geq 1 - \text{negl}(n).$$

Furthermore, for every m ∈ {0, 1}, *we have that:*

$$\Pr\left[\text{Verif}(vk, m, \text{Sign}(m, sig')) = 1\middle|\begin{array}{c}(vk, sig) \leftarrow \langle\text{Send}, \mathcal{A}\rangle(1^\lambda) \\ (1, sig') \leftarrow \text{TokenVerif}(vk, sig)\end{array}\right]$$
$$\geq 1 - \text{negl}(n).$$

6.2 Semi-quantum Strongly Unforgeable Tokenized Digital Signatures

Our remote coset state preparation protocol (Protocol 5) directly gives a semi-quantum tokenized signature scheme in the plain model. The formal description of the scheme is given in Construction 3, whose security proof is discussed in the full version [13].

Construction 3: Our semi-quantum tokenized signature scheme

Token Generation Protocol. The input of the protocol is the security parameter $\lambda \in \mathbb{N}$.
- Run Protocol 5 between a classical sender and a quantum receiver. Send is the sender's procedure in the protocol and Rec is the receiver's procedure in the protocol.
- The output of the protocol is $\mathsf{vk} := (\mathsf{R}^0, \mathsf{R}^1)$ and $\mathit{sig} := |A_{s,s'}\rangle$ using the notation in Section 4.

$\mathsf{Sign}(m, \mathit{sig})$: Take as input $m \in \{0, 1\}$, and a state sig on n qubits.
- Compute $\mathsf{H}^{\otimes n} \mathit{sig}$ if $m = 1$, otherwise do nothing to the quantum state.
- Measure the state in the computational basis. Let σ be the outcome.
- Output (m, σ).

$\mathsf{Verif}(\mathsf{vk}, (m, \sigma))$: Parse vk as $(\mathsf{R}^0, \mathsf{R}^1)$ where R^0 and R^1 are circuits.
- Output $\mathsf{R}^m(\sigma)$.

$\mathsf{TokenVerif}(\mathsf{vk}, \mathit{sig})$: Parse vk as $(\mathsf{R}^0, \mathsf{R}^1)$ where R^0 and R^1 are circuits.
- Let V_i be the unitary implementing the following operation:

$$V_i |v, z\rangle \mapsto |v, z \oplus \mathsf{R}^i(v)\rangle .$$

Compute $\mathit{sig}' := (\mathsf{H}^{\otimes n} \otimes \mathcal{I}) V_1 (\mathsf{H}^{\otimes n} \otimes \mathcal{I}) V_0 \mathit{sig} \otimes |0\rangle$.
- Measure the last register in the computational basis.
- If the outcome is 1, return $(0, \mathit{sig}')$. Otherwise, return $(1, \mathit{sig}')$.

Acknowledgements. This work was supported in part by the French ANR projects CryptiQ (ANR-18-CE39-0015) and SecNISQ (ANR-21-CE47-0014). QHV was supported in part by the French ANR project TCS-NISQ (ANR-22-CE47-0004), and by the PEPR integrated project EPiQ ANR-22-PETQ-0007 part of Plan France 2030. The authors would like to thank Thomas Vidick, Christian Majenz, Alexandru Gheorghiu, as well as the anonymous reviewers for their helpful discussion and feedback.

References

1. Aaronson, S.: Quantum copy-protection and quantum money. In: 2009 24th Annual IEEE Conference on Computational Complexity, pp. 229–242. IEEE (2009)
2. Aaronson, S., Christiano, P.: Quantum money from hidden subspaces. In: Karloff, H.J., Pitassi, T. (eds.) 44th ACM STOC, pp. 41–60. ACM Press (2012). https://doi.org/10.1145/2213977.2213983

3. Amos, R., Georgiou, M., Kiayias, A., Zhandry, M.: One-shot signatures and applications to hybrid quantum/classical authentication. In: Makarychev, K., Makarychev, Y., Tulsiani, M., Kamath, G., Chuzhoy, J. (eds.) 52nd ACM STOC, pp. 255–268. ACM Press (2020). https://doi.org/10.1145/3357713.3384304

4. Ananth, P., Kaleoglu, F.: Unclonable encryption, revisited. In: Nissim, K., Waters, B. (eds.) TCC 2021. LNCS, vol. 13042, pp. 299–329. Springer, Cham (2021). https://doi.org/10.1007/978-3-030-90459-3_11

5. Ananth, P., Kaleoglu, F., Li, X., Liu, Q., Zhandry, M.: On the feasibility of unclonable encryption, and more. In: Dodis, Y., Shrimpton, T. (eds.) CRYPTO 2022, Part II. LNCS, vol. 13508, pp. 212–241. Springer, Heidelberg (2022). https://doi.org/10.1007/978-3-031-15979-4_8

6. Ananth, P., Kaleoglu, F., Liu, Q.: Cloning games: a general framework for unclonable primitives. In: Handschuh, H., Lysyanskaya, A. (eds.) Advances in Cryptology - CRYPTO 2023, pp. 66–98. Springer Nature Switzerland, Cham (2023). https://doi.org/10.1007/978-3-031-38554-4_3

7. Ananth, P., La Placa, R.L.: Secure software leasing. In: Canteaut, A., Standaert, F.-X. (eds.) EUROCRYPT 2021. LNCS, vol. 12697, pp. 501–530. Springer, Cham (2021). https://doi.org/10.1007/978-3-030-77886-6_17

8. Ben-David, S., Sattath, O.: Quantum tokens for digital signatures. Cryptology ePrint Archive, Report 2017/094 (2017). https://eprint.iacr.org/2017/094

9. Bouman, N.J., Fehr, S.: Sampling in a quantum population, and applications. In: Rabin, T. (ed.) CRYPTO 2010. LNCS, vol. 6223, pp. 724–741. Springer, Heidelberg (2010). https://doi.org/10.1007/978-3-642-14623-7_39

10. Brakerski, Z., Christiano, P., Mahadev, U., Vazirani, U.V., Vidick, T.: A cryptographic test of quantumness and certifiable randomness from a single quantum device. In: Thorup, M. (ed.) 59th FOCS, pp. 320–331. IEEE Computer Society Press (2018). https://doi.org/10.1109/FOCS.2018.00038

11. Broadbent, A., Jeffery, S., Lord, S., Podder, S., Sundaram, A.: Secure software leasing without assumptions. In: Nissim, K., Waters, B. (eds.) TCC 2021. LNCS, vol. 13042, pp. 90–120. Springer, Cham (2021). https://doi.org/10.1007/978-3-030-90459-3_4

12. Broadbent, A., Lord, S.: Uncloneable quantum encryption via oracles **158**, 4:1–4:22 (2020)

13. Chevalier, C., Hermouet, P., Vu, Q.H.: Semi-quantum copy-protection and more. Cryptology ePrint Archive, Report 2023/244 (2023). https://eprint.iacr.org/2023/244

14. Cojocaru, A., Colisson, L., Kashefi, E., Wallden, P.: QFactory: classically-instructed remote secret qubits preparation. In: Galbraith, S.D., Moriai, S. (eds.) ASIACRYPT 2019. LNCS, vol. 11921, pp. 615–645. Springer, Cham (2019). https://doi.org/10.1007/978-3-030-34578-5_22

15. Coladangelo, A., Liu, J., Liu, Q., Zhandry, M.: Hidden cosets and applications to unclonable cryptography. In: Malkin, T., Peikert, C. (eds.) CRYPTO 2021. LNCS, vol. 12825, pp. 556–584. Springer, Cham (2021). https://doi.org/10.1007/978-3-030-84242-0_20

16. Coladangelo, A., Majenz, C., Poremba, A.: Quantum copy-protection of compute-and-compare programs in the quantum random oracle model. Cryptology ePrint Archive, Report 2020/1194 (2020). https://eprint.iacr.org/2020/1194

17. Culf, E., Vidick, T.: A monogamy-of-entanglement game for subspace coset states. Quantum **6**, 791 (2022)

18. Gheorghiu, A., Metger, T., Poremba, A.: Quantum cryptography with classical communication: Parallel remote state preparation for copy-protection, verification, and more. In: Etessami, K., Feige, U., Puppis, G. (eds.) 50th International Colloquium on Automata, Languages, and Programming, ICALP 2023, July 10–14, 2023, Paderborn, Germany. LIPIcs, vol. 261, pp. 67:1–67:17. Schloss Dagstuhl - Leibniz-Zentrum für Informatik (2023). https://doi.org/10.4230/LIPIcs.ICALP.2023.67

19. Gheorghiu, A., Vidick, T.: Computationally-secure and composable remote state preparation. In: Zuckerman, D. (ed.) 60th FOCS, pp. 1024–1033. IEEE Computer Society Press (2019). https://doi.org/10.1109/FOCS.2019.00066

20. Hiroka, T., Morimae, T., Nishimaki, R., Yamakawa, T.: Quantum encryption with certified deletion, revisited: public key, attribute-based, and classical communication. In: Tibouchi, M., Wang, H. (eds.) ASIACRYPT 2021. LNCS, vol. 13090, pp. 606–636. Springer, Cham (2021). https://doi.org/10.1007/978-3-030-92062-3_21

21. Kitagawa, F., Nishimaki, R., Yamakawa, T.: Secure software leasing from standard assumptions. In: Nissim, K., Waters, B. (eds.) TCC 2021. LNCS, vol. 13042, pp. 31–61. Springer, Cham (2021). https://doi.org/10.1007/978-3-030-90459-3_2

22. Liu, J., Liu, Q., Qian, L., Zhandry, M.: Collusion resistant copy-protection for watermarkable functionalities. In: Kiltz, E., Vaikuntanathan, V. (eds.) TCC 2022, Part I. LNCS, vol. 13747, pp. 294–323. Springer, Heidelberg (2022). https://doi.org/10.1007/978-3-031-22318-1_11

23. Mahadev, U.: Classical verification of quantum computations. In: Thorup, M. (ed.) 59th FOCS, pp. 259–267. IEEE Computer Society Press (2018). https://doi.org/10.1109/FOCS.2018.00033

24. Mayers, D., Yao, A.: Self testing quantum apparatus. Quantum Info. Comput. 4(4), 273–286 (2004)

25. Metger, T., Vidick, T.: Self-testing of a single quantum device under computational assumptions. In: Lee, J.R. (ed.) ITCS 2021, vol. 185, pp. 19:1–19:12. LIPIcs (2021). https://doi.org/10.4230/LIPIcs.ITCS.2021.19

26. Radian, R., Sattath, O.: Semi-quantum money. Cryptology ePrint Archive, Report 2020/414 (2020). https://eprint.iacr.org/2020/414

27. Regev, O.: On lattices, learning with errors, random linear codes, and cryptography. In: Gabow, H.N., Fagin, R. (eds.) 37th ACM STOC, pp. 84–93. ACM Press (2005). https://doi.org/10.1145/1060590.1060603

28. Sattath, O., Wyborski, S.: Uncloneable decryptors from quantum copy-protection (2022). https://arxiv.org/abs/2203.05866

29. Shmueli, O.: Public-key quantum money with a classical bank. In: Proceedings of the 54th Annual ACM SIGACT Symposium on Theory of Computing, pp. 790–803 (2022)

30. Shmueli, O.: Semi-quantum tokenized signatures. In: Dodis, Y., Shrimpton, T. (eds.) CRYPTO 2022, Part I. LNCS, vol. 13507, pp. 296–319. Springer, Heidelberg (2022). https://doi.org/10.1007/978-3-031-15802-5_11

31. Vidick, T., Zhang, T.: Classical proofs of quantum knowledge. In: Canteaut, A., Standaert, F.-X. (eds.) EUROCRYPT 2021. LNCS, vol. 12697, pp. 630–660. Springer, Cham (2021). https://doi.org/10.1007/978-3-030-77886-6_22

32. Wiesner, S.: Conjugate coding. ACM SIGACT News 15(1), 78–88 (1983)

33. Zhandry, M.: Quantum lightning never strikes the same state twice. In: Ishai, Y., Rijmen, V. (eds.) EUROCRYPT 2019. LNCS, vol. 11478, pp. 408–438. Springer, Cham (2019). https://doi.org/10.1007/978-3-030-17659-4_14

Weakening Assumptions
for Publicly-Verifiable Deletion

James Bartusek[1]($\boxtimes$), Dakshita Khurana[2], Giulio Malavolta[3],
Alexander Poremba[4], and Michael Walter[5]

[1] UC Berkeley, Berkeley, USA
bartusek.james@gmail.com
[2] UIUC, Champaign, USA
dakshita@illinois.edu
[3] Bocconi University and Max Planck Institute for Security and Privacy,
Bochum, Germany
giulio.malavolta@hotmail.it
[4] Caltech, Pasadena, USA
aporemba@caltech.edu
[5] Ruhr-Universität Bochum, Bochum, Germany
michael.walter@rub.de

Abstract. We develop a simple compiler that generically adds publicly-verifiable deletion to a variety of cryptosystems. Our compiler only makes use of one-way functions (or one-way state generators, if we allow the public verification key to be quantum). Previously, similar compilers either relied on indistinguishability obfuscation along with any one-way function (Bartusek et al., ePrint:2023/265), or on almost-regular one-way functions (Bartusek, Khurana and Poremba, CRYPTO 2023).

1 Introduction

Is it possible to *provably* delete information by leveraging the laws of quantum mechanics? An exciting series of recent works [1–6,9–11,18,19] have built a variety of quantum cryptosystems that support certifiable deletion of plaintext data and/or certifiable revocation of ciphertexts or keys.

The notion of certified deletion was formally introduced by Broadbent and Islam [6] for the one-time pad, where once the certificate is successfully verified, the plaintext remains hidden even if the secret (one-time pad) key is later revealed. This work has inspired a large body of research, aimed at understanding what kind of cryptographic primitives can be certifiably deleted. Recently, [4] built a compiler that generically adds the certified deletion property described above to any computationally secure commitment, encryption, attribute-based encryption, fully-homomorphic encryption, witness encryption or timed-release encryption scheme, *without making any additional assumptions*. Furthermore, it provides a strong *information-theoretic* deletion guarantee: Once an adversary generates a valid (classical) certificate of deletion, they cannot recover the

© International Association for Cryptologic Research 2023
G. Rothblum and H. Wee (Eds.): TCC 2023, LNCS 14372, pp. 183–197, 2023.
https://doi.org/10.1007/978-3-031-48624-1_7

plaintext that was previously computationally determined by their view even given *unbounded time*. However, the compiled schemes satisfy privately verifiable deletion – namely, the encryptor generates a ciphertext together with secret parameters which are necessary for verification and must be kept hidden from the adversary.

Publicly Verifiable Deletion. The above limitation was recently overcome in [3], which obtained *publicly-verifiable* deletion (PVD) for all of the above primitives as well as new ones, such as CCA encryption, obfuscation, maliciously-secure blind delegation and functional encryption[1]. However, the compilation process proposed in [3] required the strong notion of indistinguishability obfuscation, regardless of what primitive one starts from. This was later improved in [5], which built commitments with PVD from injective (or almost-regular) one-way functions, and X encryption with PVD for $X \in \{$attribute-based, fully-homomorphic, witness, timed-release$\}$, assuming X encryption and trapdoored variants of injective (or almost-regular) one-way functions.

Weakening Assumptions for PVD. Given this state of affairs, it is natural to ask whether one can further relax the assumptions underlying publicly verifiable deletion, essentially matching what is known in the private verification setting. In this work, we show that the injectivity/regularity constraints on the one-way functions from prior work [5] are not necessary to achieve publicly-verifiable deletion; *any* one-way function suffices, or even a quantum weakening called a one-way state generator (OWSG) [17] if we allow the verification key to be quantum. Kretschmer [14] showed that, relative to an oracle, pseudorandom state generators (PRSGs) [12,17] exist even if $\mathsf{BQP} = \mathsf{QMA}$ (and thus $\mathsf{NP} \subseteq \mathsf{BQP}$). Because PRSGs are known to imply OWSGs [17], this allows us to base our generic compiler for PVD on something potentially even weaker than the existence of one-way functions.w

In summary, we improve [5] to obtain X with PVD for $X \in \{$statistically-binding commitment, public-key encryption, attribute-based encryption, fully-homomorphic encryption, witness encryption, timed-release encryption$\}$, assuming only X and any one-way function. We also obtain X with PVD for all the X above, assuming only X and any one-way state generator [17], but with a *quantum* verification key. Our primary contribution is conceptual: Our construction is inspired by a recent work on quantum-key distribution [16], which we combine with a proof strategy that closely mimics [3,5] (which in turn build on the proof technique of [4]).

1.1 Technical Outline

Prior Approach. We begin be recalling that prior work [5] observed that, given an appropriate *two-to-one* one-way function f, a commitment (with certified deletion) to a bit b can be

---

[1] A concurrent updated version of [10] also obtained functional encryption with certified deletion, although in the private-verification settings.

$$\mathsf{ComCD}(b) \propto \left(y, |x_0\rangle + (-1)^b |x_1\rangle \right)$$

where $(0, x_0), (1, x_1)$ are the two pre-images of (a randomly sampled) image y. Given an image y and a quantum state $|\psi\rangle$, they showed that any pre-image of y constitutes a valid certificate of deletion of the bit b. This certificate can be obtained by measuring the state $|\psi\rangle$ in the computational basis.

Furthermore, it was shown in [5] that in fact two-to-one functions are not needed to instantiate this template, it is possible to use more general types of one-way functions to obtain a commitment of the form

$$\mathsf{ComCD}(b) \propto \left(y, \sum_{x:f(x)=y, M(x)=0} |x\rangle + (-1)^b \sum_{x:f(x)=y, M(x)=1} |x\rangle \right).$$

where M denotes some binary predicate applied to the preimages of y. The work of [5] developed techniques to show that this satisfies certified deletion, as well as binding as long as the sets

$$\sum_{x:f(x)=y, M(x)=0} |x\rangle \quad \text{and} \quad \sum_{x:f(x)=y, M(x)=1} |x\rangle$$

are somewhat "balanced", i.e. for a random image y and the sets $S_0 = \{x : f(x) = y, M(x) = 0\}$ and $S_1 = \{x : f(x) = y, M(x) = 1\}$, it holds that $\frac{|S_0|}{|S_1|}$ is a fixed constant. Such "balanced" functions can be obtained from injective (or almost-regular) one-way functions by a previous result of [8].

Using Any One-Way Function. Our first observation is that it is not necessary to require x_0, x_1 to be preimages of the same image y. Instead, we can modify the above template to use randomly sampled $x_0 \neq x_1$ and compute $y_0 = F(x_0), y_1 = F(x_1)$ to obtain

$$\mathsf{ComCD}(b) \propto \left((y_0, y_1), |x_0\rangle + (-1)^b |x_1\rangle \right)$$

Unfortunately, as described so far, the phase b may not be statistically fixed by the commitment when F is a general one-way function, since if F is not injective, the y_0, y_1 do not determine the choice of x_0, x_1 that were used to encrypt the phase. To restore binding, we can simply append a commitment to $(x_0 \oplus x_1)$ to the state above, resulting in

$$\mathsf{ComCD}(b) \propto \left((y_0, y_1), \mathsf{Com}(x_0 \oplus x_1), |x_0\rangle + (-1)^b |x_1\rangle \right)$$

Assuming that Com is statistically binding, the bit b is (statistically) determined by the commitment state above, and in fact, can even be efficiently determined given $x_0 \oplus x_1$. This is because a measurement of $|x_0\rangle + (-1)^b |x_1\rangle$ in the Hadamard basis yields a string z such that $b = (x_0 \oplus x_1) \cdot z$.

Relation to [3]. In fact, one can now view this scheme as a particular instantiation of the subspace coset state based compiler from [3]. To commit to a bit b using the compiler of [3], we would sample (i) a random subspace S of $\mathbb{F}_2^n$, (ii) a random coset of S represented by a vector v, and (iii) a random coset of $S^\perp$ represented by a vector w. Then, the commitment would be

$$\mathsf{ComCD}(b) = \mathsf{Com}(S), |S_{v,w}\rangle, b \oplus \bigoplus_i v_i,$$

where $|S_{v,w}\rangle \propto \sum_{s\in S}(-1)^{s\cdot w}|s+v\rangle$ is the subspace coset state defined by S, v, w. A valid deletion certificate would be any vector in $S^\perp + w$, obtained by measuring $|S_{v,w}\rangle$ in the Hadamard basis.

However, in order to obtain publicly-verifiable deletion, [3] publish an obfuscated membership check program for $S^\perp + w$, which is general requires post-quantum indistinguishability obfuscation. Our main observation here is that we can sample S as an $(n-1)$-dimensional subspace, which means that $S^\perp + w$ will only consist of two vectors. Then, to obfuscate a membership check program for $S^\perp + w$, it suffices to publish a one-way function evaluated at each of the two vectors in $S^\perp + w$, which in our notation are x_0 and x_1.

To complete the derivation of our commitment scheme, note that to describe S, it suffices to specify the hyperplane that defines S, which in our notation is $x_0 \oplus x_1$. Finally, we can directly encode the bit b into the subspace coset state rather than masking it with the description of a random coset (in our case, there are only two cosets of S), and if we look at the resulting state in the Hadamard basis, we obtain $\propto |x_0\rangle + (-1)^b |x_1\rangle$.

Proving Security. Naturally, certified deletion security follows by adapting the proof technique from [3], as we discuss now. Recall that we will consider an experiment where the adversary is given an encryption of b and outputs a deletion certificate. If the certificate is valid, the output of the experiment is defined to be the adversary's left-over state (which we will show to be independent of b), otherwise the output of the experiment is set to $\perp$.

We will consider a sequence of hybrid experiments to help us prove that the adversary's view is statistically independent of b when their certificate verifies. The first step is to defer the dependence of the experiment on the bit b. In more detail, we will instead imagine sampling the distribution by guessing a uniformly random $c \leftarrow \{0,1\}$, and initializing the adversary with the following: $((y_0, y_1), \mathsf{Com}(x_0 \oplus x_1), |x_0\rangle + (-1)^c |x_1\rangle)$. The challenger later obtains input b and aborts the experiment (outputs $\perp$) if $c \neq b$. Since c was a uniformly random guess, the trace distance between the $b = 0$ and $b = 1$ outputs of this modified experiment is at least half the trace distance between the outputs of the original experiment. Moreover, we can actually consider a *purification* of this experiment where a register C is initialized in a superposition $|0\rangle + |1\rangle$ of two choices for c, and is later measured to determine the bit c.

Now, we observe that the joint quantum state of the challenger and adversary can be written as

$$\frac{1}{2} \sum_{c\in\{0,1\}} |c\rangle_\mathsf{C} \otimes (|x_0\rangle + (-1)^c |x_1\rangle)_\mathsf{A} = \frac{1}{\sqrt{2}}(|+\rangle_\mathsf{C} |x_0\rangle_\mathsf{A} + |-\rangle_\mathsf{C} |x_1\rangle_\mathsf{A}),$$

where the adversary is initialized with the register A. Intuitively, if the adversary returns a successful deletion certificate x such that $F(x) = y_{c'}$ for bit c', then they must have done this by measuring in the standard basis and collapsing the joint state to $Z^{c'} |+\rangle_C |x_{c'}\rangle_A$. We can formalize this intuition by introducing an extra abort condition into the experiment. That is, if the adversary returns some x such that $F(x) = y_{c'}$, the challenger will then measure their register in the Hadamard basis and abort if the result $c'' \neq c'$. By the one-wayness of F, we will be able to show that no adversary can cause the challenger to abort with greater than $\mathrm{negl}(\lambda)$ probability as a result of this measurement. This essentially completes the proof of our claim, because at this point the bit c is always obtained by measuring a Hadamard basis state in the standard basis, resulting in a uniformly random bit outcome that completely masks the dependence of the experiment on b.

Applications. Finally, we note that encryption with PVD can be obtained similarly by committing to each bit of the plaintext as

$$\mathsf{EncCD}(b) \propto \big((y_0, y_1), \mathsf{Enc}(x_0 \oplus x_1), |x_0\rangle + (-1)^b |x_1\rangle\big)$$

We also note that, following prior work [4], a variety of encryption schemes (e.g., ABE, FHE, witness encryption) can be plugged into the template above, replacing Enc with the encryption algorithm of ABE/FHE/witness encryption, yielding the respective schemes with publicly-verifiable deletion.

1.2   Concurrent and Independent Work

A concurrent work of Kitagawa, Nishimaki, and Yamakawa [13] obtains similar results on publicly-verifiable deletion from one-way functions. Similarly to our work, they propose a generic compiler to obtain X with publicly-verifiable deletion only assuming X plus one-way functions, for a variety of primitives, such as commitments, quantum fully-homomorphic encryption, attribute-based encryption, or witness encryption. One subtle difference, is that they need to assume the existence of *quantum* fully-homomorphic encryption (QFHE), even for building *classical* FHE with PVD, due to the evaluation algorithm computing over a quantum state. On the other hand, we obtain FHE with PVD using only plain FHE. At a technical level, their approach is based on one-time signatures for BB84 states, whereas our approach can (in retrospect) be thought of as using one-time signatures on the $|+\rangle$ state.

Differently from our work, [13] shows that their compiler can be instantiated from *hard quantum planted problems for NP*, whose existence is *implied* by most cryptographic primitives with PVD. In this sense, their assumptions can be considered minimal. Although we do not explore this direction in our work, we believe that a similar implication holds for our compiler as well. On the other hand, we propose an additional compiler, whose security relies solely on one-way state generators (OWSG), which is an assumption conjectured to be even *weaker* than one-way function.

2 Preliminaries

Let λ denote the security parameter. We write negl($\cdot$) to denote any *negligible* function, which is a function f such that for every constant $c \in \mathbb{N}$ there exists $N \in \mathbb{N}$ such that for all $n > N$, $f(n) < n^{-c}$.

A finite-dimensional complex Hilbert space is denoted by $\mathcal{H}$, and we use subscripts to distinguish between different systems (or registers); for example, we let $\mathcal{H}_A$ be the Hilbert space corresponding to a system A. The tensor product of two Hilbert spaces $\mathcal{H}_A$ and $\mathcal{H}_B$ is another Hilbert space denoted by $\mathcal{H}_{AB} = \mathcal{H}_A \otimes \mathcal{H}_B$. We let $\mathcal{L}(\mathcal{H})$ denote the set of linear operators over $\mathcal{H}$. A quantum system over the 2-dimensional Hilbert space $\mathcal{H} = \mathbb{C}^2$ is called a *qubit*. For $n \in \mathbb{N}$, we refer to quantum registers over the Hilbert space $\mathcal{H} = (\mathbb{C}^2)^{\otimes n}$ as n-qubit states. We use the word *quantum state* to refer to both pure states (unit vectors $|\psi\rangle \in \mathcal{H}$) and density matrices $\rho \in \mathcal{D}(\mathcal{H})$, where we use the notation $\mathcal{D}(\mathcal{H})$ to refer to the space of positive semidefinite linear operators of unit trace acting on $\mathcal{H}$. The *trace distance* of two density matrices $\rho, \sigma \in \mathcal{D}(\mathcal{H})$ is given by

$$\mathsf{TD}(\rho, \sigma) = \frac{1}{2}\mathsf{Tr}\left[\sqrt{(\rho - \sigma)^{\dagger}(\rho - \sigma)}\right].$$

A quantum channel $\Phi : \mathcal{L}(\mathcal{H}_A) \to \mathcal{L}(\mathcal{H}_B)$ is a linear map between linear operators over the Hilbert spaces $\mathcal{H}_A$ and $\mathcal{H}_B$. We say that a channel Φ is *completely positive* if, for a reference system R of arbitrary size, the induced map $I_R \otimes \Phi$ is positive, and we call it *trace-preserving* if $\mathsf{Tr}[\Phi(X)] = \mathsf{Tr}[X]$, for all $X \in \mathcal{L}(\mathcal{H})$. A quantum channel that is both completely positive and trace-preserving is called a quantum CPTP channel.

A *unitary* $U : \mathcal{L}(\mathcal{H}_A) \to \mathcal{L}(\mathcal{H}_A)$ is a special case of a quantum channel that satisfies $U^{\dagger}U = UU^{\dagger} = I_A$. A *projector* Π is a Hermitian operator such that $\Pi^2 = \Pi$, and a *projective measurement* is a collection of projectors $\{\Pi_i\}_i$ such that $\sum_i \Pi_i = I$.

A quantum polynomial-time (QPT) machine is a polynomial-time family of quantum circuits given by $\{\mathcal{A}_\lambda\}_{\lambda \in \mathbb{N}}$, where each circuit $\mathcal{A}_\lambda$ is described by a sequence of unitary gates and measurements; moreover, for each $\lambda \in \mathbb{N}$, there exists a deterministic polynomial-time Turing machine that, on input 1^λ, outputs a circuit description of $\mathcal{A}_\lambda$.

Imported Theorem 1 (Gentle Measurement [20]). *Let ρ^X be a quantum state and let $(\Pi, \mathbb{I} - \Pi)$ be a projective measurement on X such that $\mathsf{Tr}(\Pi\rho) \geq 1 - \delta$. Let*

$$\rho' = \frac{\Pi\rho\Pi}{\mathsf{Tr}(\Pi\rho)}$$

be the state after applying $(\Pi, \mathbb{I} - \Pi)$ to ρ and post-selecting on obtaining the first outcome. Then, $\mathsf{TD}(\rho, \rho') \leq 2\sqrt{\delta}$.

Imported Theorem 2 (Distinguishing implies Mapping [7]). *Let D be a projector, Π_0, Π_1 be orthogonal projectors, and $|\psi\rangle \in \mathsf{Im}\,(\Pi_0 + \Pi_1)$. Then,*

$$\|\Pi_1 D\Pi_0 |\psi\rangle\|^2 + \|\Pi_0 D\Pi_1 |\psi\rangle\|^2 \geq \frac{1}{2}\left(\|D|\psi\rangle\|^2 - \left(\|D\Pi_0 |\psi\rangle\|^2 + \|D\Pi_1 |\psi\rangle\|^2\right)\right)^2.$$

3 Main Theorem

Theorem 3. *Let $F : \{0,1\}^{n(\lambda)} \rightarrow \{0,1\}^{m(\lambda)}$ be a one-way function secure against QPT adversaries. Let $\{\mathcal{Z}_\lambda(\cdot,\cdot,\cdot,\cdot)\}_{\lambda \in \mathbb{N}}$ be a quantum operation with four arguments: an $n(\lambda)$-bit string z, two $m(\lambda)$-bit strings y_0, y_1, and an $n(\lambda)$-qubit quantum state $|\psi\rangle$. Suppose that for any QPT adversary $\{\mathcal{A}_\lambda\}_{\lambda \in \mathbb{N}}$, $z \in \{0,1\}^{n(\lambda)}, y_0, y_1 \in \{0,1\}^{m(\lambda)}$, and $n(\lambda)$-qubit state $|\psi\rangle$,*

$$\left| \Pr\left[\mathcal{A}_\lambda(\mathcal{Z}_\lambda(z, y_0, y_1, |\psi\rangle)) = 1 \right] - \Pr\left[\mathcal{A}_\lambda(\mathcal{Z}_\lambda(0^\lambda, y_0, y_1, |\psi\rangle)) = 1 \right] \right| = \mathrm{negl}(\lambda).$$

That is, $\mathcal{Z}_\lambda$ is semantically-secure with respect to its first input.[2] Now, for any QPT adversary $\{\mathcal{A}_\lambda\}_{\lambda \in \mathbb{N}}$, consider the following distribution $\left\{ \widetilde{\mathcal{Z}}_\lambda^{\mathcal{A}_\lambda}(b) \right\}_{\lambda \in \mathbb{N}, b \in \{0,1\}}$ over quantum states, obtained by running $\mathcal{A}_\lambda$ as follows.

- *Sample $x_0, x_1 \leftarrow \{0,1\}^{n(\lambda)}$ conditioned on $x_0 \neq x_1$, define $y_0 = F(x_0), y_1 = F(x_1)$ and initialize $\mathcal{A}_\lambda$ with*

$$\mathcal{Z}_\lambda \left(x_0 \oplus x_1, y_0, y_1, \frac{1}{\sqrt{2}} \left(|x_0\rangle + (-1)^b |x_1\rangle \right) \right).$$

- *$\mathcal{A}_\lambda$'s output is parsed as a string $x' \in \{0,1\}^{n(\lambda)}$ and a residual state on register A'.*
- *If $F(x') \in \{y_0, y_1\}$, then output A', and otherwise output $\bot$.*

Then,

$$\mathsf{TD} \left(\widetilde{\mathcal{Z}}_\lambda^{\mathcal{A}_\lambda}(0), \widetilde{\mathcal{Z}}_\lambda^{\mathcal{A}_\lambda}(1) \right) = \mathrm{negl}(\lambda).$$

Proof. We define a sequence of hybrids.

- $\mathsf{Hyb}_0(b)$: This is the distribution $\left\{ \widetilde{\mathcal{Z}}_\lambda^{\mathcal{A}_\lambda}(b) \right\}_{\lambda \in \mathbb{N}, b \in \{0,1\}}$ described above.
- $\mathsf{Hyb}_1(b)$: This distribution is sampled as follows.
  - Sample $x_0, x_1, y_0 = F(x_0), y_1 = F(x_1)$, prepare the state

$$\frac{1}{2} \sum_{c \in \{0,1\}} |c\rangle_{\mathsf{C}} \otimes (|x_0\rangle + (-1)^c |x_1\rangle)_{\mathsf{A}},$$

  and initialize $\mathcal{A}_\lambda$ with

$$\mathcal{Z}_\lambda \left(x_0 \oplus x_1, y_0, y_1, \mathsf{A} \right).$$

---

[2] One can usually think of $\mathcal{Z}_\lambda$ as just encrypting its first input and leaving the remaining in the clear. However, we need to formulate the more general definition of $\mathcal{Z}_\lambda$ that operates on all inputs to handle certain applications, such as attribute-based encryption. See [4] for details.

- $\mathcal{A}_\lambda$'s output is parsed as a string $x' \in \{0,1\}^{n(\lambda)}$ and a residual state on register A'.
- If $F(x') \notin \{y_0, y_1\}$, then output $\perp$. Next, measure register C in the computational basis and output $\perp$ if the result is $1 - b$. Otherwise, output A'.

- $\mathsf{Hyb}_2(b)$: This distribution is sampled as follows.
  - Sample $x_0, x_1, y_0 = F(x_0), y_1 = F(x_1)$, prepare the state

  $$\frac{1}{2} \sum_{c \in \{0,1\}} |c\rangle_\mathsf{C} \otimes (|x_0\rangle + (-1)^c |x_1\rangle)_\mathsf{A},$$

  and initialize $\mathcal{A}_\lambda$ with

  $$\mathcal{Z}_\lambda (x_0 \oplus x_1, y_0, y_1, \mathsf{A}).$$

  - $\mathcal{A}_\lambda$'s output is parsed as a string $x' \in \{0,1\}^{n(\lambda)}$ and a residual state on register A'.
  - If $F(x') \notin \{y_0, y_1\}$, then output $\perp$. Next, let $c' \in \{0,1\}$ be such that $F(x') = y_{c'}$, measure register C in the Hadamard basis, and output $\perp$ if the result is $1 - c'$. Next, measure register C in the computational basis and output $\perp$ if the result is $1 - b$. Otherwise, output A'.

We define $\mathsf{Advt}(\mathsf{Hyb}_i) := \mathsf{TD}(\mathsf{Hyb}_i(0), \mathsf{Hyb}_i(1))$. To complete the proof, we show the following sequence of claims.

Claim. $\mathsf{Advt}(\mathsf{Hyb}_2) = 0$.

Proof. This follows by definition. Observe that Hyb_2 only depends on the bit b when it decides whether to abort after measuring register C in the computational basis. But at this point, it is guaranteed that register C is in a Hadamard basis state, so this will result in an abort with probability $1/2$ regardless of the value of b.

Claim. $\mathsf{Advt}(\mathsf{Hyb}_1) = \mathsf{negl}(\lambda)$.

Proof. Given Sect. 3, it suffices to show that for each $b \in \{0,1\}$, $\mathsf{TD}(\mathsf{Hyb}_1(b), \mathsf{Hyb}_2(b)) = \mathsf{negl}(\lambda)$. The only difference between these hybrids is the introduction of a measurement of C in the Hadamard basis. By Gentle Measurement (Theorem 1), it suffices to show that this measurement results in an abort with probability $\mathsf{negl}(\lambda)$.

So suppose otherwise. That is, the following experiment outputs 1 with probability non-$\mathsf{negl}(\lambda)$.

- Sample $x_0, x_1, y_0 = F(x_0), y_1 = F(x_1)$, prepare the state

$$\frac{1}{2} \sum_{c \in \{0,1\}} |c\rangle_\mathsf{C} \otimes (|x_0\rangle + (-1)^c |x_1\rangle)_\mathsf{A},$$

and initialize $\mathcal{A}_\lambda$ with

$$\mathcal{Z}_\lambda (x_0 \oplus x_1, y_0, y_1, \mathsf{A}).$$

- $\mathcal{A}_\lambda$'s output is parsed as a string $x' \in \{0,1\}^{n(\lambda)}$ and a residual state on register A'.
- If $F(x') \notin \{y_0, y_1\}$, then output $\perp$. Next, let $c' \in \{0,1\}$ be such that $F(x') = y_{c'}$, measure register C in the Hadamard basis, and output 1 if the result is $1 - c'$.

Next, observe that we can commute the measurement of C in the Hadamard basis to before the adversary is initialized, without affecting the outcome of the experiment:

- Sample $x_0, x_1, y_0 = F(x_0), y_1 = F(x_1)$, prepare the state

$$\frac{1}{2} \sum_{c \in \{0,1\}} |c\rangle_C \otimes (|x_0\rangle + (-1)^c |x_1\rangle)_A = \frac{1}{\sqrt{2}} (|+\rangle_C |x_0\rangle_A + |-\rangle_C |x_1\rangle_A),$$

measure C in the Hadamard basis to obtain $c'' \in \{0,1\}$ and initialize $\mathcal{A}_\lambda$ with the resulting information

$$\mathcal{Z}_\lambda (x_0 \oplus x_1, y_0, y_1, |x_{c''}\rangle_A).$$

- $\mathcal{A}_\lambda$'s output is parsed as a string $x' \in \{0,1\}^{n(\lambda)}$ and a residual state on register A'.
- If $F(x') \notin \{y_0, y_1\}$, then output $\perp$. Next, let $c' \in \{0,1\}$ be such that $F(x') = y_{c'}$, and output 1 if $c'' = 1 - c'$.

Finally, note that any such $\mathcal{A}_\lambda$ can be used to break the one-wayness of F. To see this, we can first appeal to the semantic security of $\mathcal{Z}_\lambda$ and replace $x_0 \oplus x_1$ with $0^{n(\lambda)}$. Then, note that the only information $\mathcal{A}_\lambda$ receives is two images and one preimage F, and $\mathcal{A}_\lambda$ is tasked with finding the *other* preimage of F. Succeeding at this task with probability non-negl(λ) clearly violates the one-wayness of F.

Claim. $\mathsf{Advt}(\mathsf{Hyb}_0) = \mathsf{negl}(\lambda)$.

Proof. This follows because $\mathsf{Hyb}_1(b)$ is identically distributed to the distribution that outputs $\perp$ with probability $1/2$ and otherwise outputs $\mathsf{Hyb}_0(b)$, so the advantage of Hyb_0 is at most double the advantage of Hyb_1.

4   Cryptography with Publicly-Verifiable Deletion

Let us now introduce some formal definitions. A public-key encryption (PKE) scheme with publicly-verifiable deletion (PVD) has the following syntax.

- $\mathsf{PVGen}(1^\lambda) \to (\mathsf{pk}, \mathsf{sk})$: the key generation algorithm takes as input the security parameter λ and outputs a public key pk and secret key sk.
- $\mathsf{PVEnc}(\mathsf{pk}, b) \to (\mathsf{vk}, |\mathsf{ct}\rangle)$: the encryption algorithm takes as input the public key pk and a plaintext b, and outputs a (public) verification key vk and a ciphertext $|\mathsf{ct}\rangle$.

- PVDec(sk, $|ct\rangle$) → b: the decryption algorithm takes as input the secret key sk and a ciphertext $|ct\rangle$ and outputs a plaintext b.
- PVDel($|ct\rangle$) → π: the deletion algorithm takes as input a ciphertext $|ct\rangle$ and outputs a deletion certificate π.
- PVVrfy(vk, π) → $\{\top, \bot\}$: the verify algorithm takes as input a (public) verification key vk and a proof π, and outputs $\top$ or $\bot$.

Definition 1 (Correctness of deletion). *A PKE scheme with PVD satisfies correctness of deletion if for any b, it holds with $1 - \mathrm{negl}(\lambda)$ probability over $(\mathsf{pk}, \mathsf{sk}) \leftarrow \mathsf{PVGen}(1^\lambda), (\mathsf{vk}, |ct\rangle) \leftarrow \mathsf{PVEnc}(\mathsf{pk}, b), \pi \leftarrow \mathsf{PVDel}(|ct\rangle), \mu \leftarrow \mathsf{PVVrfy}(\mathsf{vk}, \pi)$ that $\mu = \top$.*

Definition 2 (Certified deletion security). *A PKE scheme with PVD satisfies certified deletion security if it satisfies standard semantic security, and moreover, for any QPT adversary $\{\mathcal{A}_\lambda\}_{\lambda \in \mathbb{N}}$, it holds that*

$$\mathsf{TD}\left(\mathsf{EvPKE}_{\mathcal{A},\lambda}(0), \mathsf{EvPKE}_{\mathcal{A},\lambda}(1)\right) = \mathrm{negl}(\lambda),$$

where the experiment $\mathsf{EvPKE}_{\mathcal{A},\lambda}(b)$ is defined as follows.

- *Sample $(\mathsf{pk}, \mathsf{sk}) \leftarrow \mathsf{PVGen}(1^\lambda)$ and $(\mathsf{vk}, |ct\rangle) \leftarrow \mathsf{PVEnc}(\mathsf{pk}, b)$.*
- *Run $\mathcal{A}_\lambda(\mathsf{pk}, \mathsf{vk}, |ct\rangle)$, and parse their output as a deletion certificate π and a state on register A'.*
- *If $\mathsf{PVVrfy}(\mathsf{vk}, \pi) = \top$, output A', and otherwise output $\bot$.*

Construction via OWF. We now present our generic compiler that augments any (post-quantum secure) PKE scheme with the PVD property, assuming the existence of one-way functions.

Construction 4. *[PKE with PVD from OWF] Let $\lambda \in \mathbb{N}$, let*

$$F : \{0,1\}^{n(\lambda)} \rightarrow \{0,1\}^{m(\lambda)}$$

be a one-way function, and let $(\mathsf{Gen}, \mathsf{Enc}, \mathsf{Dec})$ be a standard (post-quantum) public-key encryption scheme. Consider the PKE scheme with PVD consisting of the following efficient algorithms:

- *$\mathsf{PVGen}(1^\lambda)$: Same as $\mathsf{Gen}(1^\lambda)$.*
- *$\mathsf{PVEnc}(\mathsf{pk}, b)$: Sample $x_0, x_1 \leftarrow \{0,1\}^{n(\lambda)}$, define $y_0 = F(x_0), y_1 = F(x_1)$, and output*

$$\mathsf{vk} := (y_0, y_1), \quad |ct\rangle := \left(\mathsf{Enc}(\mathsf{pk}, x_0 \oplus x_1), \frac{1}{\sqrt{2}}\left(|x_0\rangle + (-1)^b |x_1\rangle\right)\right).$$

- *$\mathsf{PVDec}(\mathsf{sk}, |ct\rangle)$: Parse $|ct\rangle$ as a classical ciphertext ct' and a quantum state $|\psi\rangle$. Compute $z \leftarrow \mathsf{Dec}(\mathsf{sk}, \mathsf{ct}')$, measure $|\psi\rangle$ in the Hadamard basis to obtain $w \in \{0,1\}^{n(\lambda)}$, and output the bit $b = z \cdot w$.*

- PVDel($|ct\rangle$): *Parse* $|ct\rangle$ *as a classical ciphertext* ct′ *and a quantum state* $|\psi\rangle$. *Measure* $|\psi\rangle$ *in the computational basis to obtain* $x' \in \{0,1\}^{n(\lambda)}$, *and output* $\pi := x'$.
- PVVrfy(vk, π): *Parse* vk *as* (y_0, y_1) *and output* $\top$ *if and only if* $F(\pi) \in \{y_0, y_1\}$.

Theorem 5. *If one-way functions exist, then Theorem 4 instantiated with any (post-quantum) public-key encryption scheme satisfies correctness of deletion (according to Definition 1) as well as (everlasting) certified deletion security according to Definition 2.*

Proof. Let (Gen, Enc, Dec) be a standard (post-quantum) public-key encryption scheme. Then, correctness of deletion follows from the fact that measuring $\frac{1}{\sqrt{2}}(|x_0\rangle + |x_1\rangle)$ in the Hadamard basis produces a vector orthogonal to $x_0 \oplus x_1$, whereas measuring the state $\frac{1}{\sqrt{2}}(|x_0\rangle - |x_1\rangle)$ in the Hadamard basis produces a vector that is not orthogonal to $x_0 \oplus x_1$.

Next, we note that semantic security follows from a sequence of hybrids. First, we appeal to the semantic security of the public-key encryption scheme (Gen, Enc, Dec) to replace Enc(pk, $x_0 \oplus x_1$) with Enc(pk, $0^{n(\lambda)}$). Next, we introduce a measurement of $\frac{1}{\sqrt{2}}(|x_0\rangle + (-1)^b |x_1\rangle)$ in the standard basis before initializing the adversary. By a straightforward application of Theorem 2, a QPT adversary that can distinguish whether or not this measurement was applied can be used to break the one-wayness of F. Finally, note that the ciphertext now contains no information about b, completing the proof.

Finally, the remaining part of certified deletion security follows from Theorem 3, by setting $\mathcal{Z}_\lambda(x_0 \oplus x_1, y_0, y_1, |\psi\rangle) = $ Enc(pk, $x_0 \oplus x_1$), $y_0, y_1, |\psi\rangle$ and invoking the semantic security of the public-key encryption scheme (Gen, Enc, Dec).

Remark 1. Following [4], we can plug various primitives into the above compiler to obtain X with PVD for $X \in \{$commitment, attribute-based encryption, fully-homomormphic encryption, witness encryption, timed-release encryption$\}$.

5 Publicly-Verifiable Deletion from One-Way State Generators

In this section, we show how to relax the assumptions behind our generic compiler for PVD to something potentially even weaker than one-way functions, namely the existence of so-called one-way state generators (if we allow for quantum verification keys). Morimae and Yamakawa [17] introduced one-way state generator (OWSG) as a quantum analogue of a one-way function.

Definition 3 (One-Way State Generator). *Let* $n \in \mathbb{N}$ *be the security parameter. A one-way state generator* (OWSG) *is a tuple* (KeyGen, StateGen, Ver) *consisting of QPT algorithms:*

KeyGen(1^n) $\rightarrow k$: *given as input* 1^n, *it outputs a uniformly random key* $k \leftarrow \{0,1\}^n$.

StateGen(k) $\rightarrow$ ϕ_k: *given as input a key* $k \in \{0,1\}^n$, *it outputs an* m-*qubit quantum state* ϕ_k.

Ver(k', ϕ_k) $\rightarrow$ $\top/\bot$: *given as input a supposed key* k' *and state* ϕ_k, *it outputs* $\top$ *or* $\bot$.

We require that the following property holds:

Correctness: For any $n \in \mathbb{N}$, *the scheme* (KeyGen, StateGen, Ver) *satisfies*

$$\Pr[\top \leftarrow \text{Ver}(k, \phi_k) : k \leftarrow \text{KeyGen}(1^n), \phi_k \leftarrow \text{StateGen}(k)] \geq 1 - \text{negl}(n).$$

Security: For any computationally bounded quantum algorithm $\mathcal{A}$ *and any* $t = \text{poly}(\lambda)$:

$$\Pr[\top \leftarrow \text{Ver}(k', \phi_k) : k \leftarrow \text{KeyGen}(1^n), \phi_k \leftarrow \text{StateGen}(k), k' \leftarrow \mathcal{A}(\phi_k^{\otimes t})] \leq \text{negl}(n).$$

Morimae and Yamakawa [17] showed that if pseudorandom quantum state generators with $m \geq c \cdot n$ for some constant $c > 1$ exist, then so do one-way state generators. Informally, a pseudorandom state generator [12] is a QPT algorithm that, on input $k \in \{0,1\}^n$, outputs an m-qubit state $|\phi_k\rangle$ such that $|\phi_k\rangle^{\otimes t}$ over uniformly random k is computationally indistinguishable from a Haar random states of the same number of copies, for any polynomial $t(n)$. Recent works [14,15] have shown oracle separations between pseudorandom state generators and one-way functions, indicating that these quantum primitives are potentially weaker than one-way functions.

Publicly Verifiable Deletion from OWSG. To prove that our generic compiler yields PVD even when instantiated with a OWSG, it suffices to extend Theorem 3 as follows.

Theorem 6. *Let* (KeyGen, StateGen, Ver) *be a OSWG from* $n(\lambda)$ *bits to* $m(\lambda)$ *qubits. Let* $\{\mathcal{Z}_\lambda(\cdot, \cdot, \cdot, \cdot)\}_{\lambda \in \mathbb{N}}$ *be a quantum operation with four arguments: an* $n(\lambda)$-*bit string* z, *two* $m(\lambda)$-*qubit quantum states* ϕ_0, ϕ_1, *and an* $n(\lambda)$-*qubit quantum state* $|\psi\rangle$. *Suppose that for any QPT adversary* $\{\mathcal{A}_\lambda\}_{\lambda \in \mathbb{N}}$, $z \in \{0,1\}^{n(\lambda)}$, $m(\lambda)$-*qubit states* ϕ_0, ϕ_1, *and* $n(\lambda)$-*qubit state* $|\psi\rangle$,

$$\left| \Pr[\mathcal{A}_\lambda (\mathcal{Z}_\lambda (z, \phi_0, \phi_1, |\psi\rangle)) = 1] - \Pr[\mathcal{A}_\lambda (\mathcal{Z}_\lambda (0^{n(\lambda)}, \phi_0, \phi_1, |\psi\rangle)) = 1] \right| = \text{negl}(\lambda).$$

That is, $\mathcal{Z}_\lambda$ *is semantically-secure with respect to its first input. Now, for any QPT adversary* $\{\mathcal{A}_\lambda\}_{\lambda \in \mathbb{N}}$, *consider the following distribution* $\left\{ \widetilde{\mathcal{Z}}_\lambda^{\mathcal{A}_\lambda}(b) \right\}_{\lambda \in \mathbb{N}, b \in \{0,1\}}$ *over quantum states, obtained by running* $\mathcal{A}_\lambda$ *as follows.*

- *Sample* $x_0, x_1 \leftarrow \{0,1\}^{n(\lambda)}$, *generate quantum states* ϕ_{x_0} *and* ϕ_{x_1} *by running the procedure* StateGen *on input* x_0 *and* x_1, *respectfully, and initialize* $\mathcal{A}_\lambda$ *with*

$$\mathcal{Z}_\lambda \left(x_0 \oplus x_1, \phi_{x_0}, \phi_{x_1}, \frac{1}{\sqrt{2}} \left(|x_0\rangle + (-1)^b |x_1\rangle \right) \right).$$

- A_λ's output is parsed as a string $x' \in \{0,1\}^{n(\lambda)}$ and a residual state on register A'.
- If $\mathsf{Ver}(x', \psi_{x_i})$ outputs $\top$ for some $i \in \{0,1\}$, then output A', and otherwise output $\bot$.

Then,

$$\mathsf{TD}\left(\widetilde{\mathcal{Z}}_\lambda^{A_\lambda}(0), \widetilde{\mathcal{Z}}_\lambda^{A_\lambda}(1)\right) = \mathrm{negl}(\lambda).$$

Proof. The proof is analogus to Theorem 3, except that we invoke the security of the OWSG, rather than the one-wayness of the underlying one-way function.

Construction from OWSG. We now consider the following PKE scheme with PVD. The construction is virtually identical to Theorem 4, except that we replace one-way functions with one-way state generators. This means that the verification key is now quantum.

Construction 7 (PKE with PVD from OWSG). *Let $\lambda \in \mathbb{N}$ and let* $(\mathsf{KeyGen}, \mathsf{StateGen}, \mathsf{Ver})$ *be a OSWG, and let* $(\mathsf{Gen}, \mathsf{Enc}, \mathsf{Dec})$ *be a standard (post-quantum) public-key encryption scheme. Consider the following PKE scheme with PVD:*

- $\mathsf{PVGen}(1^\lambda)$*: Same as* $\mathsf{Gen}(1^\lambda)$*.*
- $\mathsf{PVEnc}(\mathsf{pk}, b)$*: Sample* $x_0, x_1 \leftarrow \{0,1\}^{n(\lambda)}$ *and generate quantum states* ϕ_{x_0} *and* ϕ_{x_1} *by running the procedure* $\mathsf{StateGen}$ *on input* x_0 *and* x_1*, respectfully. Then, output*

$$\mathsf{vk} := (\phi_{x_0}, \phi_{x_1}), \quad |\mathsf{ct}\rangle := \left(\mathsf{Enc}(\mathsf{pk}, x_0 \oplus x_1), \frac{1}{\sqrt{2}}\left(|x_0\rangle + (-1)^b |x_1\rangle\right)\right).$$

- $\mathsf{PVDec}(\mathsf{sk}, |\mathsf{ct}\rangle)$*: Parse* $|\mathsf{ct}\rangle$ *as a classical ciphertext* ct' *and a quantum state* $|\psi\rangle$*. Compute* $z \leftarrow \mathsf{Dec}(\mathsf{sk}, \mathsf{ct})$*, measure* $|\psi\rangle$ *in the Hadamard basis to obtain* $w \in \{0,1\}^{n(\lambda)}$*, and output the bit* $b = z \cdot w$*.*
- $\mathsf{PVDel}(|\mathsf{ct}\rangle)$*: Parse* $|\mathsf{ct}\rangle$ *as a classical ciphertext* ct' *and a quantum state* $|\psi\rangle$*. Measure* $|\psi\rangle$ *in the computational basis to obtain* $x' \in \{0,1\}^{n(\lambda)}$*, and output* $\pi := x'$*.*
- $\mathsf{PVVrfy}(\mathsf{vk}, \pi)$*: Parse* vk *as* (ϕ_{x_0}, ϕ_{x_1}) *and output* $\top$ *if and only if* $\mathsf{Ver}(\pi, \phi_{x_i})$ *outputs* $\top$*, for some* $i \in \{0,1\}$*. Otherwise, output* $\bot$*.*

Remark 2. Unlike in Theorem 4, the verification key vk in Theorem 7 is quantum. Hence, the procedure $\mathsf{PVVrfy}(\mathsf{vk}, \pi)$ in Theorem 7 may potentially consume the public verification key (ϕ_{x_0}, ϕ_{x_1}) when verifying a dishonest deletion certificate π. However, by the security of the OWSG scheme, we can simply hand out $(\phi_{x_0}^{\otimes t}, \phi_{x_1}^{\otimes t})$ for any number of $t = \mathrm{poly}(\lambda)$ many copies without compromising security. This would allow multiple users to verify whether a (potentially dishonest) deletion certificate is valid. We focus on the case $t = 1$ for simplicity.

Theorem 8. *If one-way state generators exist, then Theroem 7 instantiated with any (post-quantum) public-key encryption scheme satisfies correctness of deletion (according to Definition 1) as well as (everlasting) certified deletion security according to Definition 2.*

Proof. The proof is analogous to Theroem 5, except that we again invoke security of the OWSG, rather than the one-wayness of the underlying one-way function.

Following [4], we also immediately obtain:

Theorem 9. *If one-way state generators exist, then there exists a generic compiler that adds PVD to any (post-quantum) public-key encryption scheme. Moreover, plugging X into the compiler yields X with PVD for*

$$X \in \left\{ \begin{array}{c} commitment,\ attribute\text{-}based\ encryption,\ fully\text{-}homomormphic \\ encryption,\ witness\ encryption,\ timed\text{-}release\ encryption \end{array} \right\}.$$

Acknowledgements. DK was supported in part by NSF 2112890, NSF CNS-2247727, and DARPA SIEVE. This material is based upon work supported by the Defense Advanced Research Projects Agency through Award HR00112020024. GM was partially funded by the Deutsche Forschungsgemeinschaft (DFG, German Research Foundation) under Germany's Excellence Strategy - EXC 2092 CASA - 390781972.

References

1. Agrawal, S., Kitagawa, F., Nishimaki, R., Yamada, S., Yamakawa, T.: Public key encryption with secure key leasing. In: Hazay, C., Stam, M. (eds.) EUROCRYPT 2023, vol. 14004, pp. 581–610. Springer, Cham (2023). https://doi.org/10.1007/978-3-031-30545-0_20
2. Ananth, P., Poremba, A., Vaikuntanathan, V.: Revocable cryptography from learning with errors. Cryptology ePrint Archive, Paper 2023/325 (2023). https://eprint.iacr.org/2023/325
3. Bartusek, J., et al.: Obfuscation and outsourced computation with certified deletion. Cryptology ePrint Archive, Paper 2023/265 (2023). https://eprint.iacr.org/2023/265
4. Bartusek, J., Khurana, D.: Cryptography with certified deletion. In: Crypto 2023 (2023, to appear)
5. Bartusek, J., Khurana, D., Poremba, A.: Publicly-verifiable deletion via target-collapsing functions. In: Crypto 2023 (2023, to appear)
6. Broadbent, A., Islam, R.: Quantum encryption with certified deletion. In: Pass, R., Pietrzak, K. (eds.) TCC 2020. LNCS, vol. 12552, pp. 92–122. Springer, Cham (2020). https://doi.org/10.1007/978-3-030-64381-2_4
7. Dall'Agnol, M., Spooner, N.: On the necessity of collapsing. Cryptology ePrint Archive, Paper 2022/786 (2022). https://eprint.iacr.org/2022/786
8. Haitner, I., Horvitz, O., Katz, J., Koo, C.-Y., Morselli, R., Shaltiel, R.: Reducing complexity assumptions for statistically-hiding commitment. J. Cryptol. **22**(3), 283–310 (2007). https://doi.org/10.1007/s00145-007-9012-8

9. Hiroka, T., Morimae, T., Nishimaki, R., Yamakawa, T.: Quantum encryption with certified deletion, revisited: public key, attribute-based, and classical communication. In: Tibouchi, M., Wang, H. (eds.) ASIACRYPT 2021. LNCS, vol. 13090, pp. 606–636. Springer, Cham (2021). https://doi.org/10.1007/978-3-030-92062-3_21

10. Hiroka, T., Morimae, T., Nishimaki, R., Yamakawa, T.: Certified everlasting functional encryption. Cryptology ePrint Archive, Paper 2022/969 (2022). https://eprint.iacr.org/2022/969, https://eprint.iacr.org/2022/969

11. Hiroka, T., Morimae, T., Nishimaki, R., Yamakawa, T.: Certified everlasting zero-knowledge proof for QMA. In: Dodis, Y., Shrimpton, T. (eds.) CRYPTO 2022, Part I. LNCS, vol. 13507, pp. 239–268. Springer, Cham (2022)

12. Ji, Z., Liu, Y.-K., Song, F.: Pseudorandom quantum states. In: Shacham, H., Boldyreva, A. (eds.) CRYPTO 2018. LNCS, vol. 10993, pp. 126–152. Springer, Cham (2018). https://doi.org/10.1007/978-3-319-96878-0_5

13. Kitagawa, F., Nishimaki, R., Yamakawa, T.: Publicly verifiable deletion from minimal assumptions. Cryptology ePrint Archive, Paper 2023/538 (2023). https://eprint.iacr.org/2023/538

14. Kretschmer, W.: Quantum pseudorandomness and classical complexity. Schloss Dagstuhl - Leibniz-Zentrum für Informatik (2021). https://doi.org/10.4230/LIPICS.TQC.2021.2, https://drops.dagstuhl.de/opus/volltexte/2021/13997/

15. Kretschmer, W., Qian, L., Sinha, M., Tal, A.: Quantum cryptography in algorithmica. In: Saha, B., Servedio, R.A. (eds.) Proceedings of the 55th Annual ACM Symposium on Theory of Computing, STOC 2023, Orlando, FL, USA, June 20–23, 2023, pp. 1589–1602. ACM (2023). https://doi.org/10.1145/3564246.3585225

16. Malavolta, G., Walter, M.: Non-interactive quantum key distribution. Cryptology ePrint Archive, Paper 2023/500 (2023). https://eprint.iacr.org/2023/500

17. Morimae, T., Yamakawa, T.: Quantum commitments and signatures without one-way functions. In: Dodis, Y., Shrimpton, T. (eds.) CRYPTO 2022. LNCS, vol. 13507, pp. 269–295. Springer, Heidelberg (2022). https://doi.org/10.1007/978-3-031-15802-5_10

18. Poremba, A.: Quantum proofs of deletion for learning with errors. In: Kalai, Y.T. (ed.) 14th Innovations in Theoretical Computer Science Conference, ITCS 2023, January 10–13, 2023, MIT, Cambridge, Massachusetts, USA. LIPIcs, vol. 251, pp. 90:1–90:14. Schloss Dagstuhl - Leibniz-Zentrum für Informatik (2023). https://doi.org/10.4230/LIPIcs.ITCS.2023.9

19. Unruh, D.: Revocable quantum timed-release encryption. J. ACM **62**(6) (2015). https://doi.org/10.1145/2817206

20. Winter, A.J.: Coding theorem and strong converse for quantum channels. IEEE Trans. Inf. Theory **45**(7), 2481–2485 (1999). https://doi.org/10.1109/18.796385

Public-Key Encryption with Quantum Keys

Khashayar Barooti[1], Alex B. Grilo[2], Loïs Huguenin-Dumittan[1],
Giulio Malavolta[3,4]iD, Or Sattath[5]iD, Quoc-Huy Vu[2(✉)]iD,
and Michael Walter[6]

[1] EPFL, Lausanne, Switzerland
[2] Sorbonne Université, CNRS, LIP6, Paris, France
quoc.huy.vu@ens.fr
[3] Bocconi University, Milan, Italy
[4] Max-Planck Institute in Security and Privacy, Bochum, Germany
[5] Computer Science Department, Ben-Gurion University of the Negev,
Beersheba, Israel
[6] Faculty of Computer Science, Ruhr University Bochum, Bochum, Germany

Abstract. In the framework of Impagliazzo's five worlds, a distinction
is often made between two worlds, one where public-key encryption
exists (Cryptomania), and one in which only one-way functions exist
(MiniCrypt). However, the boundaries between these worlds can change
when quantum information is taken into account. Recent work has shown
that quantum variants of oblivious transfer and multi-party computation,
both primitives that are classically in Cryptomania, can be constructed
from one-way functions, placing them in the realm of quantum MiniCrypt
(the so-called MiniQCrypt). This naturally raises the following question:
*Is it possible to construct a quantum variant of public-key encryption,
which is at the heart of Cryptomania, from one-way functions or potentially weaker assumptions?*

In this work, we initiate the formal study of the notion of quantum
public-key encryption (qPKE), i.e., public-key encryption where keys
are allowed to be quantum states. We propose new definitions of security and several constructions of qPKE based on the existence of one-
way functions (OWF), or even weaker assumptions, such as pseudorandom function-like states (PRFS) and pseudorandom function-like states
with proof of destruction (PRFSPD). Finally, to give a tight characterization of this primitive, we show that computational assumptions are
necessary to build quantum public-key encryption. That is, we give a
self-contained proof that no quantum public-key encryption scheme can
provide information-theoretic security.

1 Introduction

The use of quantum resources to enable cryptographic tasks under weaker
assumptions than classically needed (or even *unconditionally*) were actually the
first concrete proposals of quantum computing, with the seminal quantum money

© International Association for Cryptologic Research 2023
G. Rothblum and H. Wee (Eds.): TCC 2023, LNCS 14372, pp. 198–227, 2023.
https://doi.org/10.1007/978-3-031-48624-1_8

protocol of Wiesner [34] and the key-exchange protocol of Bennett and Brassard [11]. Ever since, the field of quantum cryptography has seen a surge of primitives that leverage quantum information to perform tasks that classically require stronger assumptions, or are downright impossible. Recent works [9,19] have shown that there exist quantum protocols for oblivious transfer, and therefore arbitrary multi-party computation (MPC), based solely on the existence of one-way functions (OWF) [9,19], or pseudorandom states (PRS) [23], which potentially entail even weaker computational assumptions [26,27]. It is well-known that, classically, oblivious transfer and MPC are "Cryptomania" objects, i.e., they can only be constructed from more structured assumptions that imply public-key encryption (PKE). Thus, the above results seem to challenge the boundary between Cryptomania and MiniCrypt, in the presence of quantum information. Motivated by this state of affairs, in this work we investigate the notion of *PKE itself*, the heart of Cryptomania, through the lenses of quantum computing. That is, we ask the following question:

Does public-key encryption (PKE) belong to MiniQCrypt?

Known results around this question are mostly negative: It is known that PKE cannot be constructed in a black-box manner from OWFs [22], and this result has been recently re-proven in the more challenging setting where the encryption or decryption algorithms are quantum [5]. However, a tantalizing possibility left open by these works is to realize PKE schemes from OWFs (or weaker assumptions), where public-key or ciphertexts are quantum states.

1.1 Our Results

In this work we initiate the systematic study of quantum public-key encryption (qPKE), i.e., public-key encryption where public-keys and ciphertexts are allowed to be quantum states. We break down our contributions as follows.

1. Definitions. We provide a general definitional framwork for qPKE, where both the public-key and ciphertext might be general quantum states. In the classical setting, there is no need to provide oracle access to the encryption, since the public-key can be used to implement that. In contrast, if the public-key is a quantum state, it might be measured during the encryption procedure, and the ciphertexts might depend on the measurement outcome. In fact, this is the approach taken in some of our constructions. This motivates a stronger security definition, similar to the classical counterpart, in which the adversary gets additional access to an encryption oracle that uses the same quantum public-key that is used during the challenge phase. We define IND-CPA-EO (respectively, IND-CCA-EO) security by adding the encryption oracle (EO) to the standard IND-CPA (respectively, IND-CCA) security game.

2. Constructions. With our new security definition at hand, we propose three protocols for implementing qPKE from OWF and potentially weaker assumptions, each with its own different advantages and disadvantages. More concretely, we show the existence of:

1. A qPKE scheme with quantum public-keys and classical ciphertexts that is IND-CCA-EO[1] secure, based on post-quantum OWF, in Sect. 4.1.
2. A qPKE scheme with quantum public-key and quantum ciphertext that is IND-CCA1 secure, based on pseudo-random function-like states (PRFS) with super-logarithmic input-size[2], in Sect. 4.2. Since this scheme is not EO secure, each quantum public-key enables the encryption of a single message.
3. A qPKE scheme with quantum public-key and classical ciphertext that is IND-CPA-EO secure based on pseudo-random function-like states with proof of destruction (PRFSPDs), in Sect. 5.

We wish to remark that it has been recently shown that OWF imply PRFS with super-logarithmic input-size [4] and PRFSPDs [10]. Therefore, the security of the second and third protocols is based on a potentially weaker cryptographic assumption than the first one. Furthermore, PRFS with super-logarithmic input-size are *oracle separated* from one-way functions [26]; therefore, our second result shows a black-box separation between a certain form of quantum public-key encryption and one-way functions. On the other hand, for the other two constructions, even if the public-key is a quantum state, the ciphertexts are classical and, furthermore, one quantum public-key can be used to encrypt multiple messages. The first protocol is much simpler to describe and understand since it only uses standard (classical) cryptographic objects. Moreover, we show that this scheme guarantees the notion of adaptive CCA2 security and is the only scheme that achieves perfect correctness.

3. Lower Bounds. To complete the picture, we demonstrate that *information-theoretically secure* qPKE does not exist. Due to the public-keys being quantum states, this implication is much less obvious than for the classical case. In fact, some of the existing constructions of qPKE [18] have been conjectured to be unconditionally secure, a conjecture that we invalidate in this work. While this general statement follows by known implications in the literature (see Sect. 6 for more details), in this work we present a self-contained proof of this fact, borrowing techniques from shadow tomography, which we consider to be of independent interest.

1.2   Technical Overview

In this section, we provide a technical overview of our results. In Sect. 1.2.1, we explain the challenges and choices to define qPKE and its security definition. In Sect. 1.2.2, we present 3 instantiations of qPKE, each based on a different assumption and with different security guarantees. Ultimately, Sect. 1.2.3 is dedicated to the impossibility of information-theoretically secure qPKE and a high-level overview of the proof technique.

---

[1] Throughout this paper, unless explicitly specified, by IND-CCA we refer to the notion of adaptive IND-CCA2 security.

[2] Note that PRS implies PRFS with logarithmic size inputs, but no such implication is known for super-logarithmic inputs.

1.2.1 Definitions of qPKE

In order to consider public-key encryption schemes with quantum public-keys, we need to revisit the traditional security definitions. In the case of quantum public-keys, there are several immediate issues that require revision.

The first issue is related to the access the adversary is given to the public-key. In the classical-key case (even with quantum ciphertexts), the adversary is given the classical public-key pk. Given a single quantum public-key, one cannot create arbitrary number of copies of the quantum public-key, due to no-cloning. Hence, to naturally extend notions such as IND-CPA security, we provide multiple copies of the quantum public-key to the adversary (via the mean of oracle access to the quantum public-key generation algorithm).

The second issue concerns the quantum public-key's *reusability*. Classically, one can use the public-key to encrypt multiple messages. With quantum public-keys, this might not be the case: the quantum public-key might be consumed during the encryption. In a non-reusable scheme, the user needs a fresh quantum public-key for every plaintext they wish to encrypt. This is not only a theoretical concern: in the PRFS-based construction (see Sect. 4.2), part of the quantum public-key is sent as the (quantum) ciphertext, so clearly, this construction is *not* reusable.

Thirdly, it could be the case that in a reusable scheme, each encryption call changes the public-key state ρ_{qpk} in an irreversible way. Hence, we make a syntactic change: $\mathsf{Enc}(\rho_{qpk}, m)$ outputs (ρ'_{qpk}, c), where c is used as the ciphertext and ρ'_{qpk} is used as the key to encrypt the next message. Note that in this scenario the updated public-key is not publicly available anymore and is only held by the party who performed the encryption.

Lastly, the syntactic change mentioned above also has security effects. Recall that classically, there is no need to give the adversary access to an encryption oracle, since the adversary can generate encryption on their own. Alas, with quantum public-keys, the distribution of ciphers might depend on the changes that were made to the quantum public-key by the challenger whenever the key is used to encrypt several messages. Therefore, for reusable schemes, we define two new security notions, denoted CPA-EO and CCA-EO, that are similar to CPA and CCA but where the adversary is given access to an encryption oracle (EO). We note there are several works considering the notions of chosen-ciphertext security in the quantum setting, because it is not clear how to prevent the adversary from querying the challenge ciphertext, if it contains a quantum states. However, we only consider CCA-security for schemes with classical ciphertexts, and therefore this issue does not appear in this work.

Pure vs Mixed States. We mention explicitly that we require our public-keys to be *pure states*. This is motivated by the following concern: there is no general method to authenticate quantum states. One proposal to ensure that the certificate authority (CA) is sending the correct state is to distribute various copies of the keys to different CAs and test whether they are all sending the same state [18]. This ensures that, as long as at least one CA is honest, the user will reject a malformed key with some constant probability. However, this argument crucially relies on the public-key being a pure state (in which case comparison can be implemented with a SWAP-test). On the other hand, if the public-key was a mixed state, there would be no way to run the above test without false positives.

We also mention that, if mixed states are allowed, then there is a trivial construction of qPKE from any given symmetric encryption scheme (SKE.key-gen, SKE.Enc, SKE.Dec), as also observed in [29, Theorem C.6].

1.2.2   Constructions for qPKE

As previously mentioned, we propose in this work three schemes for qPKE, based on three different assumptions, each providing a different security guarantee.

qPKE from OWF. Our first instantiation of qPKE is based on the existence of post-quantum OWFs. For this construction, we aim for the strong security notion of indistinguishability against adaptive chosen ciphertext attacks with encryption oracle referred to as IND-CCA-EO. We start with a simple bit-encryption construction that provides IND-CCA security and we discuss how one can modify the scheme to encrypt multi-bit messages and also provide EO security.

Our first scheme assumes the existence of a *quantum-secure pseudorandom function* (PRF), which can be built from quantum-secure one-way functions [35]. Given a PRF ensemble $\{f_k\}_k$, the public key consists of a pair of pure quantum states $qpk = (|qpk_0\rangle, |qpk_1\rangle)$ and the secret key consists of a pair of bit-strings $dk = (dk_0, dk_1)$ such that, for all $b \in \{0, 1\}$,

$$|qpk_b\rangle = \frac{1}{\sqrt{2^n}} \sum_{x \in \{0,1\}^n} |x, f_{dk_b}(x)\rangle,$$

where f_k denotes the quantum-secure PRF keyed by k. To encrypt a bit b, one simply measures all qubits of $|qpk_b\rangle$ in the computational basis. The result takes the form $(x, f_{dk_b}(x))$ for some uniformly random $x \in \{0, 1\}^n$ and this is returned as the ciphertext, i.e., $(qc_0, qc_1) = (x, f_{dk_b}(x))$.

To decrypt a ciphertext (qc_0, qc_1), we apply both f_{dk_0} and f_{dk_1} to qc_0 and return the value of $b \in \{0, 1\}$ such that $f_{dk_b}(qc_0) = qc_1$. In case this does happen for neither or both of the keys, the decryption aborts.

The IND-CCA security of the simple bit-encryption scheme can be proven with a hybrid argument. However, there are a few caveats to the scheme that can be pointed out. First, the scheme is not reusable. It can be easily noticed that after using a public-key for an encryption, the public-key state collapses, meaning that all the subsequent encryption calls are derandomized. This would mean if the same public-key is reused, it can not even guarantee IND-CPA security as the encryption is deterministic.

The second issue is lifting this CCA-secure bit-encryption scheme to a many-bit CCA-secure encryption scheme. Note that although not trivial, as proven by Myers and Shelat [31], classically it is possible to construct CCA-secure many-bit encryption from CCA-secure bit-encryption. However, the argument cannot be extended to qPKE in a generic way. The main issue is that the construction from [31], similar to the Fujisaki-Okamoto transform, derandomizes the encryption procedure for some fixed random coins. Later these fixed random coins are encrypted and attached to the ciphertext, so that the decryptor can re-encrypt the plaintext to make sure they were handed the correct randomness. Looking at our construction, it is quite clear that it is not possible to derandomize the encryption procedure as the randomness is a consequence of the measurement.

Let us show how the same approach can be modified to circumvent the issues mentioned. Our main observation is that we can use public-keys of the form mentioned before for a key agreement stage and then use the agreed key to encrypt many-bit messages with a symmetric-key encryption scheme (SKE). Let us elaborate. Let $\{f_k\}_k$ be a PRF family and (SE.Enc, SE.Dec) be a symmetric-key encryption scheme. Note that quantum-secure one-way functions imply a quantum-secure PRF [35], and post-quantum IND-CCA symmetric encryption [12]. Consider the following scheme: the secret key dk is a uniformly random key for the PRF, and for a fixed dk, the quantum public-key state is

$$|qpk_{dk}\rangle = \frac{1}{\sqrt{2^\lambda}} \sum_{x \in \{0,1\}^\lambda} |x\rangle |f_{dk}(x)\rangle. \tag{1}$$

The encryption algorithm will then measure $|qpk_{dk}\rangle$ in the computational basis leading to the outcome $(x^*, y^* = f_{dk}(x^*))$. The ciphertext of a message m is given by $(x^*, \text{SE.Enc}(y^*, m))$. To decrypt a ciphertext $(\hat{x}, \hat{c})$, we first compute $\hat{y} = f_{dk}(x)$ and return $\hat{m} = \text{SE.Dec}(f_{dk}(\hat{x}), \hat{c})$.

We emphasize that this scheme is reusable since it allows the encryption of many messages using the same measurement outcome $(x^*, f_{dk}(x^*))$. Using a hybrid argument, it can be shown that if the underlying SKE guarantees IND-CCA security, this construction fulfills our strongest security notion, i.e. IND-CCA-EO security. A formal description of the scheme, along with a security proof can be found in Sect. 4.1.

QPKE from PRFS. The second construction we present in this paper is an IND-CCA1 secure public-key scheme based on the existence of pseudorandom function-like state generators. Our approach is based on first showing bit encryption, and the discussion regarding how to lift that restriction is discussed in Sect. 4.2. The ciphertexts generated by our scheme are quantum states, and as the public-keys of this construction are not reusable, we do not consider the notion of EO security. A family of states $\{|\psi_{k,x}\rangle\}_{k,x}$ is pseudo-random function-like [4] if

1. There is a quantum polynomial-time algorithm Gen such that

$$\text{Gen}(k, \sum_x \alpha_x |x\rangle) = \sum_x \alpha_x |x\rangle |\psi_{k,x}\rangle, \text{ and}$$

2. No QPT adversary can distinguish $(|\psi_1\rangle, ..., |\psi_\ell\rangle)$ from $(|\phi_1\rangle, ..., |\phi_\ell\rangle)$, where $|\psi_i\rangle = \sum_x \alpha_x^i |x\rangle |\psi_{k,x}\rangle$, $|\phi_i\rangle = \sum_x \alpha_x^i |x\rangle |\phi_x\rangle$, and $\{|\phi_x\rangle\}_x$ are Haar random states and the states $|\sigma_i\rangle = \sum_x \alpha_x^i |x\rangle$ are chosen by the adversary.

We continue by providing a high-level description of the scheme. The key generation algorithm picks a uniform PRFS key dk and generates the corresponding public-keys as stated below:

$$\frac{1}{\sqrt{2^\lambda}} \sum_{x \in \{0,1\}^\lambda} |x\rangle |\psi_{\mathsf{dk},x}\rangle^{\otimes n}, \tag{2}$$

where $\{|\psi_{k,x}\rangle\}_{k,x}$ is a PRFS family, the size of the input x is super-logarithmic in the security parameter and n is a polynomial in the security parameter.

To encrypt a bit m, the encryptor will then measure the first register of $|qpk\rangle$ to obtain x^* and the residual state after this measurement will be of form $|x^*\rangle |\psi_{\mathsf{dk},x^*}\rangle^{\otimes n}$. They also sample a uniform key dk_1 and compute the state $|\psi_{\mathsf{dk}_1,x^*}\rangle$ then compute the ciphertext $c = (x^*, \rho)$ where

$$\rho = \begin{cases} |\psi_{\mathsf{dk},x^*}\rangle^{\otimes n}, & \text{if } m = 0 \\ |\psi_{\mathsf{dk}_1,x^*}\rangle^{\otimes n}, & \text{if } m = 1 \end{cases}. \tag{3}$$

To decrypt a ciphertext $(\hat{x}, \hat{\rho})$, we first compute n copies of the state $|\psi_{\mathsf{dk},\hat{x}}\rangle$ and performs a SWAP tests between each copy and the subsystems of $\hat{\rho}$ with the same size as $|\psi_{\mathsf{dk},\hat{x}}\rangle$. If all the SWAP tests return 0 the decryption algorithm returns $\hat{m} = 0$ and otherwise it returns $\hat{m} = 1$. For a large enough n, our scheme achieves statistical correctness.

We prove that this construction guarantees IND-CCA1 security by a hybrid argument in Sect. 4.2. We emphasize that as the ciphertexts of the scheme are quantum states it is challenging to define adaptive CCA2 security.

QPKE from PRFSPDs. Our third scheme is based on pseudo-random function-like states with proof of destruction (PRFSPDs), which was recently defined in [10]. The authors extended the notion of PRFS to pseudo-random function-like states with proof of destruction, where we have two algorithms $\mathcal{Destruct}$ and $\mathcal{Ver}$, which allows us to verify if a copy of the PRFS was destructed.

We will discuss now how to provide non-reusable CPA security security[3] of the encryption of a one-bit message and we discuss later how to use it to achieve reusable security, i.e., CPA-EO security. The quantum public-key in this simplified case is

$$\frac{1}{\sqrt{2^\lambda}} \sum_{x \in \{0,1\}^\lambda} |x\rangle |\psi_{\mathsf{dk},x}\rangle. \tag{4}$$

The encryptor will then measure the first register of $|qpk\rangle$ and the post measurement state is $|x^*\rangle |\psi_{\mathsf{dk},x^*}\rangle$. The encryptor will then generate a (classical) proof of destruction $\pi = \mathcal{Destruct}(|\psi_{\mathsf{dk},x^*}\rangle)$. The encryption procedure also picks dk_1 uniformly at random, generated $|\psi_{\mathsf{dk}_1,x^*}\rangle$ and generates the proof of destruction

---

[3] Meaning that one can only encrypt once using a $|qpk\rangle$.

$\pi' = \mathcal{D}estruct(|\psi_{\mathsf{dk}_1,x^*}\rangle)$. The corresponding ciphertext for a bit b is given by $c = (x^*, y)$, where

$$y = \begin{cases} \pi', & \text{if } b = 0 \\ \pi, & \text{if } b = 1 \end{cases}.$$

The decryptor will receive some value $(\hat{x}, \hat{y})$ and decrypt the message $\hat{b} = \mathcal{V}er(\mathsf{dk}, \hat{x}, \hat{y})$. The proof of the security of the aforementioned construction follows from a hybrid argument reminiscent of the security proof of the previous schemes (see Sect. 5). Notice that repeating such a process in parallel trivially gives a one-shot security of the encryption of a string m and moreover, such an encryption is classical. Therefore, in order to achieve IND-CPA-EO secure qPKE scheme, we can actually encrypt a secret key sk that is chosen by the encryptor, and send the message encrypted under sk. We leave the details of such a construction and its proof of security to Sect. 5.

1.2.3   Impossibility of Information-Theoretically Secure qPKE

So far, we have established that qPKE can be built from assumptions weaker than the ones required for the classical counterpart, and potentially even weaker than those needed to build secret-key encryption classically. This naturally leads to the question of whether it is possible to build an information-theoretically secure qPKE. In the following, we present a self-contained proof of this fact, using techniques from the literature on shadow tomography. Although proving the impossibility for classical PKE is immediate, there are a few challenges when trying to prove a result of a similar flavor for qPKE. Even when considering security against a computationally unbounded adversary, there is a limitation that such adversary has, namely, they are only provided with polynomially many copies of the public-key.

The first step of the proof is reducing winning the IND-CPA game to finding a secret-key/public-key pair $(\mathsf{dk}, |qpk_{\mathsf{dk}}\rangle)$ such that

$$\langle qpk^* | qpk_{\mathsf{dk}} \rangle \approx 1.$$

In other words, we show that if $|qpk_{\mathsf{dk}}\rangle$ is relatively close to $|qpk^*\rangle$, there is a good chance that dk can decrypt ciphertexts encrypted by $|qpk^*\rangle$ correctly. A formal statement and the proof of this argument can be found in Lemma 1.

Given this lemma, the second part of the proof consists in constructing an adversary that takes polynomially many copies of $|qpk^*\rangle$ as input and outputs $(\mathsf{dk}, |qpk_{\mathsf{dk}}\rangle)$ such that $|qpk_{\mathsf{dk}}\rangle$ is relatively close to $|qpk^*\rangle$. The technique to realize this adversary is *shadow tomography*, which shows procedures to estimate the values $\langle qpk_{\mathsf{dk}} | qpk^*\rangle$ for all $(|qpk_{\mathsf{dk}}\rangle, \mathsf{dk})$ pairs. Note that doing this naively, i.e. by SWAP-testing multiple copies of $|qpk^*\rangle$ with each $|qpk_{\mathsf{dk}}\rangle$, would require exponentially many copies of the public-key $|qpk^*\rangle$. The way we circumvent this problem is by using the a recent result by Huang, Kueng, and Preskill [21]. Informally, this theorem states that for M rank 1 projective measurements $O_1, \ldots, O_M$ and an unknown n-qubit state ρ, it is possible to estimate $\text{Tr}(O_i \rho)$ for all i, up to precision ϵ, by only performing $T = O(\log(M)/\epsilon^2)$ single-copy random Clifford measurements on ρ.

Employing this theorem, we show that a computationally unbounded adversary can estimate all the values $\langle qpk_{dk}|qpk^*\rangle$ from random Clifford measurements on polynomially many copies of $|qpk^*\rangle$. Having the estimated values of $\langle qpk_{dk}|qpk^*\rangle$ the adversary picks a dk such that the estimated value is relatively large and uses this key to decrypt the challenge ciphertext. Now invoking Lemma 1 we conclude that the probability of this adversary winning the IND-CPA game is significantly more than $1/2$.

1.3   Related Works

The notion of qPKE was already considered in the literature, although without introducing formal security definitions. For instance, Gottesman [18] proposed a candidate construction in an oral presentation, without a formal security analysis. The scheme has quantum public-keys and quantum ciphers, which consumes the public-key for encryption. Kawachi et al. [24] proposed a construction of qPKE (with quantum keys and ciphertexts) from a newly introduced hardness assumption, related to the graph automorphism problem. [33] defines and constructs a public-key encryption where the keys, plaintexts and ciphers are classical, but the algorithms are quantum the (key-generation uses Shor's algorithm). One of the contributions of this work, is to provide a unifying framework for these results, as well as improve in terms of computational assumptions and security guarantees.

In [32], the authors define and provide impossibility results regarding encryption with quantum public-keys. Classically, it is easy to show that a (public) encryption scheme cannot have deterministic ciphers; in other words, encryption must use randomness. They show that this is also true for a quantum encryption scheme with quantum public-keys. In [17], a secure encryption scheme with quantum public keys based on the LWE assumption is introduced. That work shows (passive) indistinguishable security, and is not IND-CPA secure.

In [29,30], the authors study digital signatures with quantum signatures, and more importantly in the context of this work, quantum public-keys.

The study of quantum pseudorandomness and its applications has recently experienced rapid advancements. One of the most astonishing aspects is that PRS (Pseudorandom states) and some of its variations are considered weaker than one-way functions. In other words, they are implied by one-way functions, and there exists a black-box separation between them. However, it has been demonstrated that these primitives are sufficient for many applications in Minicrypt and even extend beyond it. A graph presenting the various notions of quantum pseudorandomness and its application is available at https://sattath.github.io/qcrypto-graph/.

1.4   Concurrent and Subsequent Work

This work is a merge of two concurrent and independent works [8,20], with a unified presentation and more results.

In a concurrent and independent work, Coladangelo [16] proposes a qPKE scheme with a construction that is very different from ours, and uses a quantum trapdoor function, which is a new notion first introduced in their work. Their construction is based on the existence of quantum-secure OWF. However, in their construction, each quantum public-key can be used to encrypt a single message (compared to our construction from OWF, where the public-key can be used to encrypt multiple messages), and the ciphertexts are quantum (whereas our construction from OWF has classical ciphertexts). They do not consider the stronger notion of IND-CCA security.

Our paper has already generated interest in the community: Two follow-up works [25,28] consider a *stronger* notion of qPKE where the public-key consists of a classical and a quantum part, and the adversary is allowed to tamper arbitrarily with the quantum part (but not with the classical component).[4] The authors provide constructions assuming quantum-secure OWF. While their security definition is stronger, we remark that our approach is more general, as exemplified by the fact that we propose constructions from potentially weaker computational assumptions. In [6], the authors give another solution for the quantum public-key distribution problem using time-dependent signatures, which can be constructed from quantum-secure OWF, but the (classical) verification key needs to be continually updated.

2   Preliminaries

We refer the reader to the full version [7] for a complete presentation of this section.

2.1   Notation

Throughout this paper, λ denotes the security parameter. The notation $\mathsf{negl}(\lambda)$ denotes any function f such that $f(\lambda) = \lambda^{-\omega(1)}$, and $\mathsf{poly}(\lambda)$ denotes any function f such that $f(\lambda) = \lambda^{\mathcal{O}(1)}$. When sampling uniformly at random a value a from a set $\mathcal{U}$, we employ the notation $a \leftarrow_\$ \mathcal{U}$. When sampling a value a from a probabilistic algorithm $\mathcal{A}$, we employ the notation $a \leftarrow \mathcal{A}$. Let $|\cdot|$ denote either the length of a string, or the cardinal of a finite set, or the absolute value. By PPT we mean a polynomial-time non-uniform family of probabilistic circuits, and by QPT we mean a polynomial-time family of quantum circuits.

---

[4] Because of this stronger security definition, here the notion of public-keys with mixed states is meaningful since there is an alternative procedure to ensure that the key is well-formed (e.g., signing the classical component).

2.2   Pseudorandom Function-Like State (PRFS) Generators

The notion of pseudorandom function like states was first introduced by Ananth, Qian and Yuen in [4]. A stronger definition where the adversary is allowed to make superposition queries to the challenge oracles was introduced in the follow-up work [3]. We reproduce their definition here:

Definition 1 (Quantum-accessible PRFS generator). *We say that a QPT algorithm G is a quantum-accessible secure pseudorandom function-like state generator if for all QPT (non-uniform) distinguishers A if there exists a negligible function ϵ, such that for all λ, the following holds:*

$$\left| \Pr_{k \leftarrow \{0,1\}^{1^\lambda}} \left[A_\lambda^{|\mathcal{O}_{\mathsf{PRFS}}(k,\cdot)\rangle}(\rho_\lambda) = 1 \right] - \Pr_{\mathcal{O}_{\mathsf{Haar}}} \left[A_\lambda^{|\mathcal{O}_{\mathsf{Haar}}(\cdot)\rangle}(\rho_\lambda) = 1 \right] \right| \leq \epsilon(\lambda),$$

where:

- *$\mathcal{O}_{\mathsf{PRFS}}(k,\cdot)$, on input a d-qubit register $\mathbf{X}$, does the following: it applies an isometry channel that is controlled on the register $\mathbf{X}$ containing x, it creates and stores $G_{1^\lambda}(k,x)$ in a new register $\mathbf{Y}$. It outputs the state on the registers $\mathbf{X}$ and $\mathbf{Y}$.*
- *$\mathcal{O}_{\mathsf{Haar}}(\cdot)$, modeled as a channel, on input a d-qubit register $\mathbf{X}$, does the following: it applies a channel that controlled on the register $\mathbf{X}$ containing x, stores $|\vartheta_x\rangle\langle\vartheta_x|$ in a new register $\mathbf{Y}$, where $|\vartheta_x\rangle$ is sampled from the Haar distribution. It outputs the state on the registers $\mathbf{X}$ and $\mathbf{Y}$.*

Moreover, A_{1^λ} has superposition access to $\mathcal{O}_{\mathsf{PRFS}}(k,\cdot)$ and $\mathcal{O}_{\mathsf{Haar}}(\cdot)$ (denoted using the ket notation).

We say that G is a $(d(\lambda), n(\lambda))$-QAPRFS generator to succinctly indicate that its input length is $d(\lambda)$ and its output length is $n(\lambda)$.

2.3   Quantum Pseudorandomness with Proofs of Destruction

We import the definition of pseudorandom function-like states with proofs of destruction (PRFSPD) from [10].

Definition 2 (PRFS generator with proof of destruction). *A PRFSPD scheme with key-length $w(\lambda)$, input-length $d(\lambda)$, output length $n(\lambda)$ and proof length $c(\lambda)$ is a tuple of QPT algorithms* Gen, Destruct, Ver *with the following syntax:*

1. *$|\psi_k^x\rangle \leftarrow$ Gen(k,x): takes a key $k \in \{0,1\}^w$, an input string $x \in \{0,1\}^{d(\lambda)}$, and outputs an n-qubit pure state $|\psi_k^x\rangle$.*
2. *$p \leftarrow$ Destruct$(|\phi\rangle)$: takes an n-qubit quantum state $|\phi\rangle$ as input, and outputs a c-bit classical string, p.*
3. *$b \leftarrow$ Ver(k,x,q): takes a key $k \in \{0,1\}^w$, a d-bit input string x, a c-bit classical string p and outputs a boolean output b.*

Correctness. *A PRFSPD scheme is said to be correct if for every* $x \in \{0,1\}^d$,

$$\Pr_{k \xleftarrow{u} \{0,1\}^w} [1 \leftarrow \mathcal{V}er(k,x,p) \mid p \leftarrow \mathcal{D}estruct(|\psi_k^x\rangle); |\psi_k^x\rangle \leftarrow \mathsf{Gen}(k,x)] = 1$$

Security.

1. **Pseudorandomness:** *A PRFSPD scheme is said to be (adaptively) pseudo-random if for any QPT adversary $\mathcal{A}$, and any polynomial $m(\lambda)$, there exists a negligible function $\mathsf{negl}(\lambda)$, such that*

$$\Big| \Pr_{k \leftarrow \{0,1\}^w} [\mathcal{A}^{|\mathsf{Gen}(k,\cdot)\rangle}(1^\lambda) = 1]$$

$$- \Pr_{\forall x \in \{0,1\}^d, |\phi^x\rangle \leftarrow \mu_{(\mathbb{C}^2)^{\otimes n}}} [\mathcal{A}^{|\mathcal{H}aar^{\{|\phi^x\rangle\}}x \in \{0,1\}^d}(\cdot)\rangle}(1^\lambda) = 1]\Big| = \mathsf{negl}(\lambda)$$

   where $\forall x \in \{0,1\}^d$, $\mathcal{H}aar^{\{|\phi^x\rangle\}}x \in \{0,1\}^d}(x)$ outputs $|\phi^x\rangle$. Here we note that $\mathcal{A}$ gets quantum access to the oracles.
2. **Unclonability-of-proofs:** *A PRFSPD scheme satisfies* unclonability of proofs *if for any QPT adversary $\mathcal{A}$ in cloning game (see Game 1), there exists a negligible function $\mathsf{negl}(\lambda)$ such that*

$$\Pr[\mathsf{Cloning\text{-}Exp}_\lambda^{\mathcal{A},PRFSPD} = 1] = \mathsf{negl}(\lambda).$$

Game 1 Cloning-Exp$_\lambda^{\mathcal{A},PRFSPD}$

1: Given input 1^λ, Challenger samples $k \leftarrow \{0,1\}^{w(\lambda)}$ uniformly at random.
2: Initialize an empty set of variables, S.
3: $\mathcal{A}$ gets oracle access to $\mathsf{Gen}(k,\cdot)$, $\mathcal{V}er(k,\cdot,\cdot)$ as oracle.
4: **for** Gen query x made by $\mathcal{A}$ **do**
5:     **if** $\exists$ variable $t_x \in S$ **then** $t_x = t_x + 1$.
6:     **else** Create a variable t_x in S, initialized to 1.
7:     **end if**
8: **end for**
9: $\mathcal{A}$ outputs $x, c_1, c_2, \ldots, c_{t_x+1}$ to the challenger.
10: Challenger rejects if c_i's are not distinct.
11: **for** $i \in [m+1]$ **do** $b_i \leftarrow \mathcal{V}er(k,x,c_i)$
12: **end for**
13: Return $\wedge_{i=1}^{m+1} b_i$.

---

3 Definitions of qPKE

In this section, we introduce the new notion of encryption with quantum public keys (Definition 3). The indistinguishability security notions are defined in Sect. 3.1 and Sect. 3.2.

Definition 3 (Encryption with quantum public keys). *Encryption with quantum public keys (qPKE) consists of 4 algorithms with the following syntax:*

1. dk ← *Gen*(1^λ): *a QPT algorithm, which receives the security parameter and outputs a classical decryption key.*
2. $|qpk\rangle$ ← *QPKGen*(dk): *a QPT algorithm, which receives a classical decryption key* dk, *and outputs a quantum public key* $|qpk\rangle$. *In this work, we require that the output is a pure state, and that t calls to QPKGen*(dk) *should yield the same state, that is,* $|qpk\rangle^{\otimes t}$.
3. (qpk', qc) ← *Enc*(qpk, m): *a QPT algorithm, which receives a quantum public key* qpk *and a plaintext* m, *and outputs a (possibly classical) ciphertext* qc *and a recycled public key* qpk'.
4. m ← *Dec*(dk, qc): *a QPT algorithm, which uses a decryption key* dk *and a ciphertext* qc, *and outputs a classical plaintext* m.

We say that a qPKE scheme is *correct* if for every message $m \in \{0,1\}^*$ and any security parameter $\lambda \in \mathbb{N}$, the following holds:

$$\Pr\left[Dec(\text{dk}, qc) = m \;\middle|\; \begin{array}{c} \text{dk} \leftarrow Gen(1^\lambda) \\ |qpk\rangle \leftarrow QPKGen(\text{dk}) \\ (qpk', qc) \leftarrow Enc(|qpk\rangle, m) \end{array} \right] \geq 1 - \mathsf{negl}(\lambda),$$

where the probability is taken over the randomness of *Gen*, *QPKGen*, *Enc* and *Dec*. We say that the scheme is reusable if completeness holds to polynomially many messages using a single quantum public key. More precisely, we say that a qPKE scheme is *reusable* if for every security parameter $\lambda \in \mathbb{N}$, polynomial number of messages $m_1, \ldots, m_{n(\lambda)} \in \{0,1\}^*$, the following holds:

$$\Pr\left[\forall i \in [n(\lambda)], Dec(\text{dk}, qc_i) = m_i \;\middle|\; \begin{array}{c} \text{dk} \leftarrow Gen(1^\lambda) \\ |qpk_1\rangle \leftarrow QPKGen(\text{dk}) \\ (qpk_2, qc_2) \leftarrow Enc(|qpk_1\rangle, m_1) \\ \vdots \\ (qpk_{n+1}, qc_n) \leftarrow Enc(|qpk_i\rangle, m_{n(\lambda)}) \end{array} \right]$$
$$\geq 1 - \mathsf{negl}(\lambda).$$

3.1 Security Definitions for qPKE with Classical Ciphertexts

In this section, we present a quantum analogue of classical indistinguishability security for qPKE with classical ciphertexts. We note that there are few differences. Firstly, since in general the public keys are quantum states and unclonable, in the security games, we allow the adversary to receive polynomially many copies of $|qpk\rangle$, by making several calls to the *QPKGen*(dk) oracle. Secondly, in the classical setting, there is no need to provide access to an encryption oracle since the adversary can use the public key to apply the encryption themself. In the quantum setting, this is not the case: as we will see, the quantum public key might be measured, and the ciphertexts might depend on the measurement outcome. Furthermore, the quantum public key can be reused to encrypt multiple different messages. This motivates a stronger definition of indistinguishability with encryption oracle, in which the adversary gets oracle access to the encryption, denoted as IND-ATK-EO security, where ATK can be either chosen-plaintext attacks (CPA), (adaptive or non-adaptive) chosen-ciphertext attacks (CCA1 and CCA2).

Game 2 Indistinguishability security with an encryption oracle (IND-ATK-EO) for encryption with quantum public key and classical ciphertext schemes.

1: The challenger generates $\mathsf{dk} \leftarrow \mathcal{G}en(1^\lambda)$.
2: The adversary gets 1^λ as an input, and oracle access to $\mathcal{QPKGen}(\mathsf{dk})$.
3: The challenger generates $|qpk\rangle \leftarrow \mathcal{QPKGen}(\mathsf{dk})$. Let $qpk_1 := |qpk\rangle$.
4: For $i = 1, \ldots, \ell$, the adversary creates a classical message m_i and send it to the challenger.
5: The challenger computes $(qc_i, qpk_{i+1}) \leftarrow \mathcal{E}nc(qpk_i, m_i)$ and send qc_i to the adversary.
6: During step (2) to step (5), the adversary also gets classical oracle access to an oracle $\mathcal{O}_1$.
7: The adversary sends two messages m'_0, m'_1 of the same length to the challenger.
8: The challenger samples $b \in_R \{0,1\}$, computes $(qc^*, qpk_{l+2}) \leftarrow \mathcal{E}nc(qpk_{\ell+1}, m'_b)$ and sends qc^* to the adversary.
9: For $i = \ell + 2, \ldots, \ell'$, the adversary creates a classical message m_i and send it to the challenger.
10: The challenger computes $(qc_i, qpk_{i+1}) \leftarrow \mathcal{E}nc(qpk_i, m_i)$ and send qc_i to the adversary.
11: During step (9) to step (10), the adversary also gets classical oracle access to an oracle $\mathcal{O}_2$. Note that after step (7), the adversary no longer gets access to oracle $\mathcal{O}_1$.
12: The adversary outputs a bit b'.

We say that the adversary wins the game (or alternatively, that the outcome of the game is 1) iff $b = b'$.

We define the oracles $\mathcal{O}_1, \mathcal{O}_2$ depending on the level of security as follows.

ATK	Oracle $\mathcal{O}_1$	Oracle $\mathcal{O}_2$
CPA	$\varnothing$	$\varnothing$
CCA1	$\mathcal{D}ec(\mathsf{dk}, \cdot)$	$\varnothing$
CCA2	$\mathcal{D}ec(\mathsf{dk}, \cdot)$	$\mathcal{D}ec^*(\mathsf{dk}, \cdot)$

Here $\mathcal{D}ec^*(\mathsf{dk}, \cdot)$ is defined as $\mathcal{D}ec(\mathsf{dk}, \cdot)$, except that it return $\perp$ on input the challenge ciphertext qc^*.

Definition 4. *A qPKE scheme is IND-ATK-EO secure if for every QPT adversary, there exists a negligible function ϵ such that the probability of winning the IND-ATK-EO security game (Game 2) is at most $\frac{1}{2} + \epsilon(\lambda)$.*

Remark 1. The definition presented in Definition 4 is stated for the single challenge query setting. m, id argument, it is straightforward to show that single-challenge definitions also imply many-challenge definitions where the adversary can make many challenge queries.

Remark 2. Note that the IND-CCA2-EO definition is only defined for schemes with classical ciphertexts. The other two notions are well-defined even for quantum ciphertexts, though we do not use those.

3.2   Security Definitions for qPKE with Quantum Ciphertexts

We now give a definition for qPKE with quantum ciphertexts. In the case of adaptive chosen ciphertext security, the definition is non-trivial due to the no-cloning and the destructiveness of quantum measurements. We note there are indeed several works considering the notions of chosen-ciphertext security in the quantum setting: [2] defines chosen-ciphertext security for quantum symmetric-key encryption (when the message is a quantum state), and [13,14] defines chosen-ciphertext security for classical encryption under superposition attacks. However, extending the technique from [2] to the public-key setting is non-trivial, and we leave this open problem for future work. In this section, we only consider security notions under chosen-plaintext attacks and non-adaptive chosen-ciphertext attacks.

Even though one can similarly define security notions with encryption oracle for schemes with quantum ciphertexts as in Sect. 3.1, we note that in all constructions of qPKE with quantum ciphertexts present in this work are not reusable, and thus we do not present the definition in which the adversary has oracle access to the encryption oracle (with reusable public keys) for the sake of simplicity. However, we note that the adversary still gets access to the encryption oracle in which a new fresh copy of the public key is used for each invocation. We denote these notions as IND-ATK, where ATK is either chosen-plaintext attacks (CPA) or non-adaptive chosen-ciphertext attacks (CCA1).

Game 3 IND-ATK security game for encryption with quantum public key and quantum ciphertexts schemes.

1: The challenger generates $\mathsf{dk} \leftarrow \mathcal{G}en(1^\lambda)$.
2: The adversary $\mathcal{A}_1$ gets 1^λ as an input, and oracle access to $\mathcal{QPKGen}(\mathsf{dk})$, $\mathcal{E}nc(qpk, \cdot)$ and $\mathcal{O}_1$, and sends m_0, m_1 of the same length to the challenger. $\mathcal{A}_1$ also output a state $|\mathsf{st}\rangle$ and sends it to $\mathcal{A}_2$.
3: The challenger samples $b \in_R \{0,1\}$, generates $|qpk\rangle \leftarrow \mathcal{QPKGen}(\mathsf{dk})$ and sends $c^* \leftarrow \mathcal{E}nc(|qpk\rangle, m_b)$ to the adversary $\mathcal{A}_2$.
4: $\mathcal{A}_2$ gets oracle access to $\mathcal{QPKGen}(\mathsf{dk})$, $\mathcal{E}nc(qpk, \cdot)$.
5: The adversary $\mathcal{A}_2$ outputs a bit b'.

We say that the adversary wins the game (or alternatively, that the outcome of the game is 1) iff $b = b'$.

The oracles $\mathcal{O}_1$ is defined depending on the level of security as follows.

ATK	Oracle $\mathcal{O}_1$
CPA	$\varnothing$
CCA1	$\mathcal{D}ec(\mathsf{dk}, \cdot)$

Definition 5. *A qPKE scheme with quantum ciphertexts is IND-ATK secure if for every QPT adversary $\mathcal{A} := (\mathcal{A}_1, \mathcal{A}_2)$, there exists a negligible function ϵ such that the probability of winning the IND-ATK security game (Game 3) is at most $\frac{1}{2} + \epsilon(\lambda)$.*

4   Constructions of CCA-Secure qPKE

In this section, we present our qPKE constructions from OWF and PRFS and prove that their CCA security. The former (given in Sect. 4.1) has classical ciphertexts, and allows to encrypt arbitrary long messages. The latter (given in Sect. 4.2) has quantum ciphertexts, and only allows to encrypt a single-bit message. However, we note that the latter is based on a weaker assumption than the former. Finally, in Sect. 4.3, we give a remark on the black-box construction of non-malleable qPKE from CPA-secure qPKE using the same classical approach.

4.1   CCA-Secure Many-Bit Encryption from OWF

We start by presenting a simple qPKE construction from OWF which prove that it provides our strongest notion of security, i.e. IND-CCA-EO security. The scheme is formally presented in Construction 1. The ciphertexts produced by the scheme are classical, and the public-keys are reusable. The cryptographic components of our construction are a quantum secure PRF family $\{f_k\}$ and a post-quantum IND-CCA secure symmetric-key encryption scheme $(\mathsf{SE.Enc}, \mathsf{SE.Dec})$ which can both be built from a quantum-secure OWF [12,35].

Construction 1 (IND-CCA-EO secure qPKE from OWF).

- **Assumptions:** *A family of quantum-secure pseudorandom functions $\{f_k\}_k$, and post-quantum IND-CCA SKE $(\mathsf{SE.Enc}, \mathsf{SE.Dec})$.*
- $\mathcal{G}en(1^\lambda)$
    1. $\mathsf{dk} \xleftarrow{\$} \{0,1\}^\lambda$
    2. $|qpk\rangle \leftarrow \sum_{x \in \{0,1\}^\lambda} |x, f_{\mathsf{dk}}(x)\rangle$
- $\mathcal{E}nc(|qpk\rangle, m)$
    1. *Measure $|qpk\rangle$ to obtain classical strings x, y.*
    2. *Let $c_0 \leftarrow x$ and $c_1 \leftarrow \mathsf{SE.Enc}(y, m)$.*
    3. *Output (c_0, c_1)*

- $\mathcal{D}ec(\mathsf{dk}, (c_0, c_1))$
  1. *Compute* $y \leftarrow f_{\mathsf{dk}}(c_0)$.
  2. *Compute* $m \leftarrow \mathsf{SE.Dec}(y, c_1)$ *and return* m.

It can be trivially shown that the scheme achieves perfect correctness if the underlying SKE provides the perfect correctness property.

Theorem 1. *Let* $\{f_k\}_k$ *be a quantum secure PRF and* $(\mathsf{SE.Enc}, \mathsf{SE.Dec})$ *be a post-quantum IND-CCA secure SKE. Then, the quantum qPKE given in Construction 1 is IND-CCA-EO secure.*

Proof. We proceed with a sequence of hybrid games detailed in

- **Hybrid H_0:** This is the IND-CCA game with Π with the challenge ciphertext fixed to $(x^*, c^*) = \mathcal{E}nc(|\mathsf{pk}\rangle, m_0')$.
- **Hybrid H_1:** This is identical to H_0 except instead of measuring $|qpk\rangle$ when the adversary queries the encryption oracle, the challenger measures a copy of $|qpk\rangle$ in advance to obtain $(x^*, y^* = f_{\mathsf{dk}}(x^*))$ and answers queries to the encryption oracle using (x^*, y^*) instead. The decryption oracle still returns $\bot$ when queried (x^*, c^*). This change is only syntactical so the two hybrids are the same from the adversary's view.

The hybrids H_2 to H_5 have 2 main goals: (i) to decorrelate the encryption, decryption oracles $\mathcal{D}ec^*$, $\mathcal{E}nc$ from the public-keys handed to the adversary and (ii) to remove the oracles' dependency on dk.

- **Hybrid H_2:** This is identical to H_1, except (x^*, y^*) is removed from the copies of $|qpk\rangle$ handed to the adversary. More precisely, the adversary is handed $|qpk'\rangle$ of the following form:

$$|qpk'\rangle = \frac{1}{\sqrt{2^{|x^*|} - 1}} \sum_{x : x \neq x'} |x\rangle |f_{\mathsf{dk}}(x)\rangle \tag{5}$$

The decryption oracle still returns $\bot$ when queried on the challenge ciphertext. Note that $|qpk\rangle$ and $|qpk'\rangle$ have $\mathsf{negl}(\lambda)$ trace distance so the advantage of distinguishing H_1 and H_2 is $\mathsf{negl}(\lambda)$.

- **Hybrid H_3:** This (inefficient) hybrid is identical to H_2 other than f_{dk} being replaced with a truly random function f, i.e. the public-keys are change to:

$$|qpk'\rangle = \frac{1}{\sqrt{2^{|x^*|} - 1}} \sum_{x : x \neq x'} |x\rangle |f(x)\rangle \tag{6}$$

The encryption and decryption oracle can be simulated by oracle access to f. The decryption oracle returns $\bot$ when queried (x^*, c^*). The indistinugishability of H_3 and H_2 follows directly from pseudorandomness property of $\{f_k\}_k$.

- **Hybrid H_4:** This hybrid is identical to H_3 other than y^* being sampled uniformly at random. Upon quering (c_0, c_1) to the decryption oracle if $c_0 \neq x^*$, the oracle computes $y = f(c_0)$ and returns $m = \mathsf{SE.Dec}(y, c_1)$. In case $c_0 = x^*$ and $c_1 \neq c^*$, the decryption oracle returns $m = \mathsf{SE.Dec}(y^*, c_1)$. On (x^*, c^*) the oracle returns $\perp$. The encryption oracle returns $(x^*, \mathsf{SE.Enc}(y^*, m))$ when queried on m. As x^* does not appear in any of the public-keys this change is only syntactical.

- **Hybrid H_5:** This hybrid reverts the changes of H_3, i.e. dk' is sampled uniformly at random and the public-keys are changed as follows:

$$|qpk'\rangle = \frac{1}{\sqrt{2^{|x^*|} - 1}} \sum_{x : x \neq x'} |x\rangle |f_{\mathsf{dk}'}(x)\rangle \qquad (7)$$

  With this change, on query (c_0, c_1) if $c_0 \neq x^*$, the decryption oracle computes $y = f_{\mathsf{dk}'}(c_0)$ and returns $m = \mathsf{SE.Dec}(y, c_1)$. In case $c_0 = x^*$, the decryption oracle simply returns $m = \mathsf{SE.Dec}(y^*, c_1)$ when $c_1 \neq c^*$ and $\perp$ otherwise. The encryption oracle is unchanged from H_4. The indistinguishability of H_4 and H_5 follows from the pseudorandomness of f and the fact that $|qpk'\rangle$ and (x^*, y^*) are decorrelated. The hybrid is efficient again.

The next step is to remove the dependency of the encryption and decryption oracles on y^*. This is done by querying the encryption and decryption oracles of the SKE.

- **Hybrid H_6:** Let $\mathsf{SE.OEnc}$ and $\mathsf{SE.ODec}^*$ be two oracles implementing the encryption and decryption procedures of SE with the key y^*. $\mathsf{SE.ODec}^*$ returns $\perp$ when queried y^*. In this hybrid, we syntactically change the encryption and decryption oracle using these two oracles. To implement the encryption oracle, on query m we simply query $\mathsf{SE.OEnc}$ on message m and return $(x^*, \mathsf{SE.OEnc}(m))$. To simulate the decryption oracle, on query (c_0, c_1) we act the same as in H_5 when $c_0 \neq x^*$, but on queries of form (x^*, c) we query $\mathsf{SE.ODec}^*$ on c and return $\mathsf{SE.ODec}^*(c)$. Due to the definition of OEnc and ODec^* these changes are also just syntactical. Note that although $\mathsf{SE.ODec}^*$ always returns $\perp$ on y^*, it is only queried when $c_0 = x^*$, i.e. to cause this event the decryption oracle should be queried on the challenge ciphertext (x^*, c^*).

- **Hybrid H_7:** We provide the adversary with $x^*, \mathsf{SE.OEnc}, \mathsf{SE.ODec}^*$, instead of access to the encryption and decryption oracle. Note that the adversary can implement the encryption and decryption oracles themselves by having access to $x^*, \mathsf{SE.OEnc}, \mathsf{SE.ODec}^*$ and sampling a uniform dk' themselves and vice versa ($\mathsf{SE.ODec}^*$ can be queried on c by querying the decryption oracle (x^*, c) and $\mathsf{SE.OEnc}$ can be queried on m by querying the encryption oracle on m). This demonstrates that the hybrids are only syntactically different and hence are indistinguishable.

- **Hybrid H_8:** This hybrid is identical to H_7 with the only difference that the challenge ciphertext is swapped with $(x^*, \mathsf{SE.OEnc}(0))$. Now notice that any adversary that can distinguish H_8 from H_7 can effectively break the IND-CCA security of SE. Hence, the indistinguishability of the two hybrids follows directly from the IND-CCA security of SE.

Following the same exact hybrids for challenge ciphertext $\mathcal{E}nc(|qpk\rangle, m_1')$ we can deduce that the scheme is IND-CCA-EO secure.   □

4.2   CCA1-Secure Many-Bit Encryption from PRFS

We continue by presenting a CCA1-secure bit-encryption from PRFS. Extending this scheme to polynomially many bits is discussed at the end of this section, see Remark 3. The description of the scheme is given below in Construction 2.

Construction 2 (IND-CCA1 secure qPKE from PRFS).

- **Assumptions:** *A PRFS family* $\{|\psi_{\mathsf{dk},x}\rangle\}_{\mathsf{dk},x}$ *with super-logarithmic input-size. Let* $n := n(\lambda)$.
- $\mathcal{G}en(1^\lambda)$
    1. *Output* $\mathsf{dk} \leftarrow_R \{0,1\}^\lambda$.
- $Q\mathcal{P}\mathcal{K}\mathcal{G}en(\mathsf{dk})$
    1. *Output* $|qpk\rangle \leftarrow \sum_x |x\rangle_R |\psi_{\mathsf{dk},x}\rangle_S^{\otimes n}$, *where* $x \in \{0,1\}^{\omega(\log \lambda)}$.
- $\mathcal{E}nc(|qpk\rangle, m)$ *for* $m \in \{0,1\}$
    1. *Measure the R registers of* $|qpk\rangle$ *to obtain a classical string* x. *Let* $|\phi\rangle := |\psi_{\mathsf{dk},x}\rangle^{\otimes n}$ *denote the residual state.*
    2. *If* $m = 0$, *output the ciphertext as* $(x, |\phi\rangle)$.
    3. *Else, sample a uniformly random key* dk_1, *and output the ciphertext as* $(x, |\psi_{\mathsf{dk}_1,x}\rangle^{\otimes n})$.
- $\mathcal{D}ec(\mathsf{dk}, (x, \Psi))$
    1. *Compute* $|\psi_{\mathsf{dk},x}\rangle^{\otimes n}$ *and perform* n *SWAP tests for each subsystem of* Ψ *of the same size as* $|\psi_{\mathsf{dk},x}\rangle$ *with* $|\psi_{\mathsf{dk},x}\rangle$.
    2. *If the outcome of the SWAP tests is* 0 *all the time, output* 0, *otherwise output* 1.

Our scheme described in Construction 2 has correctness, which follows from the correctness of the (parallel amplification) of SWAP test.

Theorem 2. *Construction 2 has correctness.*

Proof. The correctness of the scheme follows from the fact that the states $|\psi_{\mathsf{dk}_1,x}\rangle$ are relatively well spread out for a random choice of dk. This is due to the pseudorandomness of the state generator. Note that if in step 3. instead of picking dk_1 randomly and computing $|\psi_{\mathsf{dk}_1,x}\rangle$, the encryption algorithm could sample $|\vartheta\rangle^{\otimes n}$, from the Haar measure, the expected probability of n SWAP tests between $|\psi_{x,\mathsf{dk}}\rangle$ and $|\vartheta\rangle$ all returning 0 would be 2^{-n}. Hence, if the probability is more than negligibly apart for n SWAP tests between $|\psi_{x,\mathsf{dk}_1}\rangle$ and $|\psi_{x,\mathsf{dk}}\rangle$ for a random choice of dk_1, with a Chernoff bound argument one can show that this would lead to a distinguisher for the PRFS. Hence, for n polynomial in λ the scheme has negligible correctness error. $\square$

Theorem 3. *The construction in Construction 2 is IND-CCA1 secure (see Definition 5), assuming* $\{|\psi_{\mathsf{dk},x}\rangle\}_{\mathsf{dk},x}$ *is a PRFS with super-logarithmic input-size.*

Proof. We prove the theorem via a series of hybrids.

- **Hybrid H_0.** The original security game as defined in Definition 5.
- **Hybrid H_1.** This is identical to hybrid H_0, except that the challenger, instead of measuring $|qpk\rangle$ when the adversary queries the encryption oracle for the first time, the challenger measures (the R registers of) this state before providing the copies of $|qpk\rangle$ to the adversary. Note that by measuring $|qpk\rangle$ in the computational basis, the challenger would obtain a classical uniformly random string x^*, let the residual state be $|\phi^*\rangle := |\psi_{\mathsf{dk},x^*}\rangle^{\otimes n}$.

  Note that the two operations corresponding to the challenger's measurement of $|qpk\rangle$ and the creation of the copies of $|qpk\rangle$ given to the adversary commute. Thus, the distribution of the two hybrids are identical and no adversary can distinguish H_0 from H_1 with non-zero advantage.
- **Hybrid H_2.** This is identical to hybrid H_1, except that the challenger samples x^* as in the previous hybrid, and instead of providing $|qpk\rangle$ to the adversary, it provides

$$|qpk'\rangle := \frac{1}{\sqrt{2^{|x^*|} - 1}} \sum_{x:x\neq x^*} |x\rangle |\psi_{\mathsf{dk},x}\rangle^{\otimes n}.$$

  Moreover, in the challenge query, the challenger uses $(x^*, |\phi^*\rangle)$ for the encryption of the chosen message m, without measuring a fresh copy of $|qpk\rangle$ (that is, it skips the first step of the encryption algorithm). We note that this state $|qpk'\rangle$ can be efficiently prepared.

  The distinguishing probability of the two hybrids H_1 and H_2 implies that we can distinguish the following quantum states $|qpk\rangle^{\otimes p} \otimes |x^*\rangle$ and $|qpk'\rangle^{\otimes p} \otimes |x^*\rangle$ with the same probability, but these two quantum states have $\mathsf{negl}(\lambda)$ trace-distance for any polynomial p. Therefore, any adversary can only distinguish H_1 and H_2 with success probability at most $\mathsf{negl}(\lambda)$.
- **Hybrid H_3.** This (inefficient) hybrid is identical to H_2, except that the challenger uses a Haar oracle $\mathcal{O}_{\mathsf{Haar}}$ to generate $|qpk'\rangle$ in place of $|\psi_{\mathsf{dk},\cdot}\rangle$. In particular, the quantum public key in the hybrid H_3 is computed as:

$$|qpk'\rangle \leftarrow \sum_{x:x\neq x^*} |x\rangle \otimes |\vartheta_x\rangle^{\otimes n},$$

  where each $|\vartheta_x\rangle$ is an output of $\mathcal{O}_{\mathsf{Haar}}$ on input x. The decryption oracle is the same as the decryption algorithm with the difference that $\mathcal{O}_{\mathsf{PRFS}}$ (the algorithm generating the PRFS) is swapped with $\mathcal{O}_{\mathsf{Haar}}$. The crucial point here is that the decryption oracle only uses the PRFS in a black-box way (in particular, it only uses $\mathcal{O}_{\mathsf{PRFS}}$ and does not use $\mathcal{O}_{\mathsf{PRFS}}^\dagger$).

  Note that the decryption oracle can return $\perp$ on query $(x^*, \cdot)$. This can not be used to distinguish the two hybrids as the adversary has a negligible chance of querying x^* as x^* is picked uniformly at random. The adversary is only provided with the value of x^* when given the challenge ciphertext, at which point they do not have access to the decryption oracle anymore.

  We note that the adversary does not have direct access to this $\mathcal{O}_{\mathsf{Haar}}$, but only via the decryption oracle. By pseudorandomness property of $|\psi_{\mathsf{dk},\cdot}\rangle$, we have that H_2 and H_3 are computationally indistinguishable.

- **Hybrid H_4.** In this hybrid, we revert the changes in H_3, except that the challenger samples a uniformly random key dk' to compute all states in $|qp\mathsf{k}'\rangle$, except for the one used to encrypt the challenge query. In particular, the public key $|qp\mathsf{k}'\rangle$ is now generated using the PRFS generator with the key dk', and the secret key dk and its public counterpart $(x^*, |\psi_{\mathsf{dk},x^*}\rangle^{\otimes n})$ are used for the challenge encryption. We note that the hybrid is now efficient again. Similar to the previous argument, H_3 and H_4 are also computationally indistinguishable due to pseudorandomness property of $|\psi_{\mathsf{dk}',.}\rangle$.
- **Hybrid H_5.** This hybrid is identical to H_4, except that in the challenge query, instead of encrypting 0 as $(x^*, |\psi_{\mathsf{dk},x^*}\rangle^{\otimes n})$, the challenger encrypts 0 as $(x^*, |\vartheta_{x^*}\rangle^{\otimes n})$, where each $|\vartheta_x\rangle$ is an output of $\mathcal{O}_{\mathsf{Haar}}$ on input x.

  Notice that in this hybrid, the secret key dk and its public counterpart $(x^*, |\psi_{\mathsf{dk},x^*}\rangle)^{\otimes n})$ are not correlated with any of other variables in the hybrid. Furthermore, after receiving the challenge ciphertext, the adversary no longer gets access to the decryption oracle. By the pseudorandomness property of $|\psi_{\mathsf{dk},x^*}\rangle$, we have that H_4 and H_5 are computationally indistinguishable.

  Furthermore, in this final hybrid, the adversary needs to distinguish the output of PRFS with a uniformly random key dk_1 (for encryption of 1) and the output of a Haar random oracle (for encryption of 0). By the same argument as above, the winning advantage of the adversary is also negligible.

Overall, since all hybrids are negligibly close and the winning advantage of the adversary in the last hybrid in negligible, we conclude the proof. $\qquad\square$

Remark 3. We sketch here how to achieve many-bit encryption from our scheme present above. We do this through several steps.

- The scheme stated in Construction 2 can easily be extended to a length-restricted scheme, by applying bit-by-bit encryption.
- Given a qPKE length-restricted CCA1 encryption, and a (non-restricted length) symmetric key encryption, we can define a hybrid encryption scheme, where the qPKE scheme is used first to encrypt a random (fixed length) secret key, which is later used to encrypt an arbitrarily long message. The entire scheme is CPA- (respectively, CCA1-) secure if the symmetric key encryption has CPA- (respectively, CCA1-) security.
- Finally, we note that the following many-bit symmetric key encryption scheme can be proven to be CCA1 secure, using the same proof strategy as in Theorem 3, based on the existence of PRFS alone. Given a secret key dk, to encrypt a message $m \in \{0,1\}^\ell$, we sample ℓ distinct uniformly random strings x_i, and compute $|\psi_{\mathsf{dk},x_i}\rangle^{\otimes n}$. Then each bit m_i will be encrypted using as $(x_i, |\psi_{\mathsf{dk},x_i}\rangle^{\otimes n})$ if $m_i = 0$, or $(x_i, |\psi_{\mathsf{dk}',x_i}\rangle^{\otimes n})$ if $m_i = 1$ for a fresh key dk'.

4.3   Generic Construction of Non-Malleable qPKE

We remark that known implications from the literature can be used to show that IND-CPA secure qPKE *with classical ciphertexts* implies non-malleable qPKE:

The work of [15] shows a black-box compiler from IND-CPA encryption to non-malleable encryption, which also applies to the settings of quantum public-keys. The only subtlety is that the compiler assumes the existence of a one-time signature scheme to sign the ciphertext. In [29,30] it is shown that one-time signatures (with quantum verification keys) exist assuming one-way state generators, which in turn are implied by qPKE. Combining the implications of these two works, we obtain a generic construction of non-malleable qPKE from any IND-CPA secure one.

5   IND-CPA-EO Secure qPKE from PRFSPD

In this section, we propose a construction for qPKE from pseudorandom function-like states with proof of destruction. The construction is reusable, has classical ciphers, and is CPA-EO secure.

We first import the following result that builds *symmetric*-key encryption from PRFSPD.

Proposition 1 ([10]). *If quantum-secure PRFSPD exists, then there exists a quantum CPA symmetric encryption with classical ciphertexts.*

We give the formal construction for many-bit reusable encryption scheme from PRFSPD in Construction 3.

Construction 3 (IND-CPA-EO secure qPKE from PRFSPD).

- **Assumptions:** *A PRFSPD family* $\{|\psi_{\mathsf{dk},x}\rangle\}_{\mathsf{dk},x}$ *and a quantum symmetric encryption scheme with classical ciphers* $\{\mathsf{Enc}, \mathsf{Dec}\}$.
- $\underline{\mathcal{Gen}(1^\lambda)}$
  1. *Let* $\mathsf{dk}_{0,i} \leftarrow_R \{0,1\}^\lambda$ *for all* $i \in [1,\lambda]$.
  2. *Output* $\mathsf{dk} \leftarrow \{\mathsf{dk}_{0,i}\}_{i\in[1,\lambda]}$.
- $\underline{\mathcal{QPKGen}(\mathsf{dk})}$
  1. *Output* $|qpk\rangle = \bigotimes_{i\in[\lambda]} \frac{1}{\sqrt{2^\lambda}} \sum_{x_i\in\{0,1\}^\lambda} |x_i\rangle|\psi_{\mathsf{dk}_{0,i},x_i}\rangle$.
- $\underline{\mathcal{Enc}(|qpk\rangle, m)}$ *for* $m \in \{0,1\}^*$
  1. *Let* $|qpk_i\rangle := \frac{1}{\sqrt{2^\lambda}} \sum_{x_i\in\{0,1\}^\lambda} |x_i\rangle|\psi_{\mathsf{dk}_{0,i},x_i}\rangle$, *and write* $|qpk\rangle$ *as* $|qpk\rangle = \bigotimes_{i\in[\lambda]} |qpk_i\rangle$.
  2. *Measure the left registers of* $|qpk_i\rangle$ *to obtain classical strings* x_i. *Denote the post-measurement states as* $|\psi_i'\rangle$.
  3. *Set* $y_i \leftarrow \mathcal{Destruct}(|\psi_i'\rangle)$.
  4. *For* $i \in [1,\lambda]$, *pick* $\mathsf{dk}_{1,i} \leftarrow \{0,1\}^\lambda$ *and compute* $|\psi_{\mathsf{dk}_{1,i},x_i}\rangle$.
  5. *Set* $y_i' \leftarrow \mathcal{Destruct}(|\psi_{\mathsf{dk}_{1,i},x_i}\rangle)$ *for all* $i \in [\lambda]$.
  6. *Pick a uniformly random key* $k \leftarrow \{0,1\}^\lambda$.
  7. *Set* $\tilde{y}_i = \begin{cases} y_i' & , if\ k_i = 0 \\ y_i & , if\ k_i = 1 \end{cases}$.
  8. *Output* $(\mathsf{Enc}(k,m), ((x_i, \tilde{y}_i))_i)$ *as ciphertext and* $(k, ((x_i, \tilde{y}_i))_i)$ *as the recycled public-key.*

- $\underline{\mathcal{Dec}(\mathsf{dk}, c)}$
    1. *Interpret c as $(c', ((x_i, \tilde{y}_i))_i)$.*
    2. *Let $k'_i = \mathcal{Ver}(\mathsf{dk}_{0,i}, x_i, \tilde{y}_i)$ and let $k' = k'_0 \ldots k'_\lambda$.*
    3. *Output $\mathsf{Dec}(k', c')$.*

The correctness of our scheme relies on the existence of PRFSPD with pseudorandomness and unclonability of proofs properties. The proof of correctness can be shown similarly to that of Construction 2. Next, we show that this construction achieves IND-CPA-EO security in Lemma 4.

Theorem 4. *If quantum-secure PRFSPD with super-logarithmic input size exists, then there exists a public-key encryption with classical ciphertexts which is IND-CPA-EO secure.*

Proof. Our construction is given in Construction 3. It uses a PRFSPD family $\{|\psi_{\mathsf{dk},x}\rangle\}_{\mathsf{dk},x}$ and a quantum symmetric encryption scheme with classical ciphers $\{\mathsf{Enc}, \mathsf{Dec}\}$. We prove the security of our scheme through a series of hybrids.

- **Hybrid H_0.** The original security game as defined in Definition 4.
- **Hybrid H_1.** This is identical to hybrid H_0, except that the challenger, instead of measuring $|qpk_i\rangle$ (for all $i \in [\lambda]$) when the adversary queries the encryption oracle for the first time, the challenger measures the left register of each $|qpk_i\rangle$ before providing the copies of $|qpk\rangle$ to the adversary. Note that by measuring $|qpk_i\rangle$ in the computational basis, the challenger would obtain a classical uniformly random string x_i^*.
  Note that the two operations corresponding to the challenger's measurement of $|qpk\rangle$ and the creation of the copies of $|qpk\rangle$ given to the adversary commute. Thus, the distribution of the two hybrids are identical and no adversary can distinguish H_0 from H_1 with non-zero advantage.
- **Hybrid H_2.** This is identical to hybrid H_1, except that the challenger samples x_i^* as in the previous hybrid, and instead of providing $|qpk\rangle$ to the adversary, it provides

$$|qpk'\rangle := \bigotimes_{i \in [\lambda]} \frac{1}{\sqrt{2^{|x_i^*|} - 1}} \sum_{x_i : x_i \neq x_i^*} |x_i\rangle |\psi_{\mathsf{dk}_{0,i}, x_i}\rangle.$$

  Moreover, in the challenge query, the challenger uses $(x_i^*, |\psi_{\mathsf{dk}_{0,i}, x_i^*}\rangle)$ for all $i \in [\lambda]$ for the encryption of the chosen message m, without measuring a fresh copy of $|qpk\rangle$ (that is, it skips the first step of the encryption algorithm). We note that this state $|qpk'\rangle$ can be efficiently prepared.
  The distinguishing probability of the two hybrids H_1 and H_2 implies that we can distinguish the following quantum states $|qpk\rangle^{\otimes p} \otimes \bigotimes_{i \in [\lambda]} |x_i^*\rangle$ and $|qpk'\rangle^{\otimes p} \otimes \bigotimes_{i \in [\lambda]} |x_i^*\rangle$ with the same probability, but these two quantum states have $\mathsf{negl}(\lambda)$ trace-distance for any polynomial p. Therefore, any adversary can only distinguish H_1 and H_2 with success probability at most $\mathsf{negl}(\lambda)$.

- **Hybrid $H_{2,i}$ for $i \in [0, \lambda]$.** We define a series of hybrids $H_{2,i}$, in which $H_{2,0} := H_2$, and we denote $H_{2,\lambda} := H_3$. Each $H_{2,i+1}$ is identical as $H_{2,i}$, except that the challenger uses a Haar oracle $\mathcal{O}_{\mathsf{Haar}_i}$ in place of $|\psi_{\mathsf{dk}_{0,i},\cdot}\rangle$. In particular, the quantum public key in the hybrid $H_{2,i}$ is computed as:

$$|qpk'\rangle \leftarrow \bigotimes_{j=1}^{i} \sum_{x_j : x_j \neq x_j^*} |x_j\rangle \otimes |\vartheta_{x_j}\rangle \otimes \bigotimes_{j=i+1}^{\lambda} \sum_{x_j : x_j \neq x_j^*} |x_j\rangle |\psi_{\mathsf{dk}_{0,j}, x_j}\rangle,$$

where each $|\vartheta_{x_j}\rangle$ is an output of $\mathcal{O}_{\mathsf{Haar}_j}$ on input x_j. For the challenge encryption query, the challenger uses $(x_j^*, |\vartheta_{x_j^*}\rangle)$ for all $j \in [1, i]$, and $(x_j^*, |\psi_{\mathsf{dk}_{0,j}, x_j^*}\rangle)$ for all $j \in [i+1, \lambda]$.

  By pseudorandomness property of $|\psi_{\mathsf{dk}_{0,i},\cdot}\rangle$, we have that $H_{2,i}$ and $H_{2,i+1}$ are computationally indistinguishable.

- **Hybrid $H_{3,i}$ for $i \in [0, \lambda]$.** We define a series of (inefficient) hybrids $H_{3,i}$, in which $H_{3,0} := H_3$, and we denote $H_{3,\lambda} := H_4$. In each $H_{3,i+1}$, we revert the changes in $H_{3,i}$, except that the challenger samples uniformly random keys dk_i' to compute the i-the component in $|qpk'\rangle$, except for the one used to encrypt the challenge query.

  Similar to the previous argument, $H_{3,i+1}$ and $H_{3,i}$ are also computationally indistinguishable due to pseudorandomness property of $|\psi_{\mathsf{dk}_i',\cdot}\rangle$.

- **Hybrid $H_{4,i}$ for $i \in [0, \lambda]$.** We define a series of (inefficient) hybrids $H_{4,i}$, in which $H_{4,0} := H_4$, and we denote $H_{4,\lambda} := H_5$.

  Each hybrid $H_{4,i}$ is identical to $H_{4,i+1}$, except that for the challenge encryption, the challenger does not sample $\mathsf{dk}_{1,i}$ and compute $|\psi_{\mathsf{dk}_{1,i}, x_i^*}\rangle$. Instead, the challenger generates $|\vartheta_{x_i^*}\rangle$ using a Haar random oracle $\mathcal{O}_{\mathsf{Haar}_i}$ and uses this state to compute y_i' (by applying $\mathcal{D}estruct$ to $|\vartheta_{x_i^*}\rangle$).

  By the pseudorandomness of $|\psi_{\mathsf{dk}_{1,i},\cdot}\rangle$, $H_{4,i}$ and $H_{4,i+1}$ are computationally indistinguishable.

- **Hybrid H_6.** This hybrid is identical to H_5, except that now the challenger sets $\tilde{y}_i = y_i$ for all i for the challenge encryption query.

  Note that in this hybrid, both y_i and y_i' are computed by applying $\mathcal{D}estruct$ to a Haar random state, thus they are output of the same distribution. Therefore, H_5 and H_6 are identical.

- **Hybrid $H_{6,i}$ for $i \in [0, \lambda]$.** We define a series of hybrids $H_{6,i}$, in which $H_{6,0} := H_6$, and we denote $H_{6,\lambda} := H_7$.

  Each hybrid $H_{6,i+1}$ is identical to $H_{6,i}$, except now instead of using a Haar random oracle in encryption of the challenge query, the challenger samples a fresh key dk_i and uses this key to compute $\tilde{y}_i$ which is a proof of destruction of the state $|\psi_{\mathsf{dk}_i, x_i^*}\rangle$.

  By pseudorandomness of $|\psi_{\mathsf{dk}_i,\cdot}\rangle$, $H_{6,i+1}$ and $H_{6,i}$ are computationally indistinguishable.

  We also note that the hybrid H_7 is now efficient again. In this final hybrid, we note that the secret key k of the symmetric key encryption scheme is uniformly random and independent from all the other variables in the hybrid. Thus, we can easily reduce the winning probability of the adversary in this hybrid to the security of the symmetric key encryption scheme, which is negligible.

Overall, we obtain the winning probability of the adversary in the first hybrid H_0 is negligible, and conclude the proof.   □

6   Impossibility of Unconditionally Secure qPKE

In the following, we investigate the question on whether qPKE is possible to construct with information-theoretic security, and we give strong bounds against this. First, let us mention that a recent work by Morimae et al. [29] shows that an object called quantum pseudo-one-time pad (QPOTP) implies the existence of efficiently samplable, statistically far but computationally indistinguishable pairs of (mixed) quantum states (EFI pairs). QPOTP is a one-time symmetric encryption with quantum ciphertexts and classical keys, whose key length is shorter than the message length. qPKE immediately implies the existence of QPOTP, by increasing the message length, using bit-by-bit encryption. Since EFI pairs cannot exist information-theoretically, this chain of implications rules out the existence of unconditionally secure qPKE.[5]

For the sake of completeness, we provide a new and direct proof of the impossibility statement using a shadow tomography argument.

A Proof from Shadow Tomography. In order to prove our impossibility result, we first show that if two public-keys $|qpk\rangle$ and $|qpk^*\rangle$ are close, if we encrypt a random bit using $|qpk^*\rangle$, the probability of decrypting correctly with dk is high, where dk is the corresponding secret-key of $|qpk\rangle$.

Lemma 1. *Let λ be the security parameter and $\Gamma = (Gen, QPKGen, Enc, Dec)$ be a qPKE. Let $dk^*, |qpk\rangle^*$ be a fixed pair of honestly generated keys and for all decryption keys dk define p_{dk} to be:*

$$p_{dk} = \Pr\left[Dec(dk, qc) = pt \;\middle|\; \begin{array}{c} pt \xleftarrow{\$} \{0,1\} \\ (qc, \cdot) \leftarrow Enc(qpk^*, pt) \end{array}\right]$$

and let $|qpk_{dk}\rangle \leftarrow QPKGen(dk)$. For all dk, if $|\langle qpk^*|qpk_{dk}\rangle| \geq 1 - \epsilon$, then $p_{dk} \geq 1 - \sqrt{3\epsilon}$.

We defer the proof of this lemma to the full version [7].

Given Lemma 1 one can reduce the adversary's task in the IND-CPA game to finding a decryption key dk such that the state $|qpk_{dk}\rangle \leftarrow QPKGen(dk)$ is close to $|qpk^*\rangle$ in inner product distance. The main technique we use to realize this subroutine of the adversary is shadow tomography introduced by Aaronson et al. [1]. At the core of our proof is the following theorem by Huang, Kueng, and Preskill [21].

Theorem 5 (Theorem 1 and S16 [21]). *Let $O_1, \ldots, O_M$ be M fixed observables and let ρ be an unknown n-qubit state. Given $T = O(\log(M/\delta)/\epsilon^2 \times$*

---

[5] This observation was pointed out to us by Takashi Yamakawa.

$\max_i \text{Tr}(O_i^2))$ *copies of ρ, there exists a quantum algorithm that performs measurements in random Clifford basis on each copy and outputs $\tilde{p}_1, \ldots, \tilde{p}_M$ such that, with probability at least $1 - \delta$, we have that $\forall i, |\tilde{p}_i - \text{Tr}(O_i \rho)| \le \epsilon$.*

At a high level, the theorem states that outcomes of polynomially many random Clifford measurements on a state, i.e. a polynomial number of classical shadows, are enough to reconstruct an estimate of the statistics obtained by measuring an exponential number of observables. Note that, the post-processing required to reconstruct $\tilde{p}_i$ values is often inefficient, however for our purpose, i.e. proving the impossibility of an information-theoretically secure quantum PKE the efficiency of the procedure is not of concern. Using Theorem 5 we are able to prove the impossibility statement.

Theorem 6. *For any security parameter λ and qPKE $\Gamma = (Gen, QPKGen, Enc, Dec)$ there exists a polynomial m and a computationally unbounded adversary $\mathcal{A}$ who can win the IND-CPA game with significant advantage only given $m(\lambda)$ copies of the public-key.*

Remark 4. Actually our attack allows us to recover the secret key with high probability, and thus the attack also breaks the one-wayness security of qPKE (which is a weaker security notion than IND-CPA). Thus, our theorem indeed shows a generic impossibility of unconditionally secure qPKE.

Proof. Let us describe the adversary given m copies of the public-key $|qpk^*\rangle$ alongside a challenge ciphertext qc. We set the value of m later in the proof. For a value N, we define the following rank 1 projection ensemble $\{\Pi_{dk}^1 = |qpk_{dk}\rangle\langle qpk_{dk}|^{\otimes N}\}_{dk \leftarrow Gen(1^\lambda)}$. The adversary tries to find a decryption key dk such that $\text{Tr}(\Pi_{dk}^1 |qpk^*\rangle\langle qpk^*|^{\otimes N})$ is relatively large. In order to do so the adversary computes $\text{Tr}(\Pi_{dk}^1 |qpk^*\rangle\langle qpk^*|^{\otimes N})$ for all decryption keys dk. By following the procedure from Theorem 5 on $\rho = |qpk^*\rangle\langle qpk^*|^{\otimes N}$, the adversary performs random Clifford measurements on

$$T = O\left(\log\left(\frac{\#\{dk | dk \leftarrow Gen(1^\lambda)\}}{\delta} \right) \frac{1}{\epsilon^2} \text{Tr}(\Pi_{dk}^{1\ 2}) \right)$$

copies of ρ to compute values $\tilde{p}_{dk}$ such that with probability $1 - \delta$, for all dk

$$\left| \tilde{p}_{dk} - \text{Tr}(\Pi_{dk}^1 |qpk^*\rangle\langle qpk^*|^{\otimes N}) \right| \le \epsilon.$$

Let us set $\epsilon < 1/6$ and δ to be a small constant, e.g. $1/100$. Immediately it can be noticed that as ϵ and δ are constants and $\text{Tr}(\Pi_{dk}^{1\ 2}) = 1$[6], T is $O(\log(\#\{dk | dk \leftarrow Gen(1^\lambda)\}))$ which is $poly(\lambda)$ as the key-lengths should be polynomial in the security parameter.

We claim that if the adversary picks any key such that $\tilde{p}_{dk} > 1/2$, they have found a key that has a high chance of decrypting the challenge ciphertext correctly. Let us elaborate. First of all, note that the adversary finds at least

---

[6] This is due to Π_{dk}^1 operators being rank-1 projections.

one such dk with probability at least $1 - \frac{1}{100}$, as for the correct decryption key dk*, $\mathrm{Tr}(\Pi^1_{\mathsf{dk}^*}|qpk^*\rangle\langle qpk^*|^{\otimes N}) = 1$ hence $\tilde{p}_{\mathsf{dk}^*} > 1 - 1/6$ with probability at least $1 - \frac{1}{100}$.

The next thing to show is that any dk such that $\tilde{p}_{\mathsf{dk}} > 1/2$ is a *good* decryption key. Note that due to Lemma 1 we have,

$$\mathrm{Tr}(\Pi^1_{\mathsf{dk}}|qpk^*\rangle\langle qpk^*|^{\otimes N}) = \left|\langle qpk_{\mathsf{dk}}|qpk^*\rangle\right|^{2N} \tag{8}$$

We note that for all dk such that $p_{\mathsf{dk}} \leq 1 - \sqrt{\frac{3}{\log(N)}}$ we have:

$$p_{\mathsf{dk}} \leq 1 - \sqrt{\frac{3}{\log(N)}} \Rightarrow \langle qpk_{\mathsf{dk}}|qpk^*\rangle \leq 1 - \frac{1}{\log(N)} \tag{9}$$

$$\Rightarrow \mathrm{Tr}(\Pi^1_{\mathsf{dk}}|qpk^*\rangle\langle qpk^*|^{\otimes N}) \leq (1 - \frac{1}{\log(N)})^{2N} \tag{10}$$

$$\leq e^{-2N/\log(N)} \ll 1/3, \text{ for a large enough } N \tag{11}$$

Given our choice of δ, ϵ, this ensures that if the adversary picks any dk such that $\tilde{p}_{\mathsf{dk}} > 1/2$, with probability at least $1 - \frac{1}{100}$ we have that,

$$\left|\tilde{p}_{\mathsf{dk}} - \mathrm{Tr}(\Pi^1_{\mathsf{dk}}|qpk^*\rangle\langle qpk^*|^{\otimes N})\right| \leq 1/6, \text{ and } \mathrm{Tr}(\Pi^1_{\mathsf{dk}}|qpk^*\rangle\langle qpk^*|^{\otimes N}) > 1/3.$$

Hence, $p_{\mathsf{dk}} > 1 - \sqrt{\frac{3}{\log(N)}}$.

As the last step, the adversary uses the dk they obtain from the previous procedure to decrypt the challenge ciphertext qc^*. By union bound and following the discussion above the adversary's advantage to decrypt the challenge ciphertext correctly is greater than $1 - \frac{1}{100} - \sqrt{\frac{3}{\log(N)}}$ which by setting N to be a large constant is significantly larger than $1/2$. Finally note that this adversary uses $m = NT$ copies of the public-key, where $T = \mathsf{poly}(\lambda)$ and N is a constant, so the total number of public-key copies used are polynomial in λ. $\square$

Acknowledgments. The authors wish to thank Prabhanjan Ananth and Umesh Vazirani for related discussions, and Takashi Yamakawa for pointing out a simple argument to rule out the existence of information-theoretically secure qPKE. The argument is replicated here with his permission.

ABG and QHV are supported by ANR JCJC TCS-NISQ ANR-22-CE47-0004, and by the PEPR integrated project EPiQ ANR-22-PETQ-0007 part of Plan France 2030. GM was partially funded by the German Federal Ministry of Education and Research (BMBF) in the course of the 6GEM research hub under grant number 16KISK038 and by the Deutsche Forschungsgemeinschaft (DFG, German Research Foundation) under Germany's Excellence Strategy - EXC 2092 CASA - 390781972. OS was supported by the Israeli Science Foundation (ISF) grant No. 682/18 and 2137/19, and by the Cyber Security Research Center at Ben-Gurion University. KB and LH were supported by the Swiss National Science Foundation (SNSF) through the project grant 192364 on Post Quantum Cryptography. OS has received funding from the European Research Council (ERC) under the European Union's Horizon 2020 research and innovation programme (grant agreement No 756482). MW acknowledges support by the the European Union (ERC, SYMOPTIC, 101040907), by the Deutsche Forschungsgemeinschaft (DFG, German Research Foundation) under Germany's Excellence Strategy - EXC 2092 CASA - 390781972, by the BMBF through project QuBRA, and by the Dutch Research Council (NWO grant OCENW.KLEIN.267). Views and opinions expressed are those of the author(s) only and do not necessarily reflect those of the European Union or the European Research Council Executive Agency. Neither the European Union nor the granting authority can be held responsible for them.

References

1. Aaronson, S.: Shadow tomography of quantum states. In: Diakonikolas, I., Kempe, D., Henzinger, M. (eds.) 50th ACM STOC, pp. 325–338. ACM Press (2018). https://doi.org/10.1145/3188745.3188802
2. Alagic, G., Gagliardoni, T., Majenz, C.: Unforgeable quantum encryption. In: Nielsen, J.B., Rijmen, V. (eds.) EUROCRYPT 2018. LNCS, vol. 10822, pp. 489–519. Springer, Cham (2018). https://doi.org/10.1007/978-3-319-78372-7_16
3. Ananth, P., Gulati, A., Qian, L., Yuen, H.: Pseudorandom (function-like) quantum state generators: New definitions and applications. In: Kiltz, E., Vaikuntanathan, V. (eds.) TCC 2022, Part I. LNCS, vol. 13747, pp. 237–265. Springer, Heidelberg (2022). https://doi.org/10.1007/978-3-031-22318-1_9
4. Ananth, P., Qian, L., Yuen, H.: Cryptography from pseudorandom quantum states. In: Dodis, Y., Shrimpton, T. (eds.) CRYPTO 2022, Part I. LNCS, vol. 13507, pp. 208–236. Springer, Heidelberg (2022). https://doi.org/10.1007/978-3-031-15802-5_8
5. Austrin, P., Chung, H., Chung, K.M., Fu, S., Lin, Y.T., Mahmoody, M.: On the impossibility of key agreements from quantum random oracles. In: Dodis, Y., Shrimpton, T. (eds.) CRYPTO 2022, Part II. LNCS, vol. 13508, pp. 165–194. Springer, Heidelberg (2022). https://doi.org/10.1007/978-3-031-15979-4_6
6. Barhoush, M., Salvail, L.: How to sign quantum messages. arXiv preprint arXiv:2304.06325 (2023)
7. Barooti, K., et al.: Public-key encryption with quantum keys. Cryptology ePrint Archive, Paper 2023/877 (2023). https://eprint.iacr.org/2023/877
8. Barooti, K., Malavolta, G., Walter, M.: A simple construction of quantum public-key encryption from quantum-secure one-way functions. Cryptology ePrint Archive, Paper 2023/306 (2023). https://eprint.iacr.org/2023/306
9. Bartusek, J., Coladangelo, A., Khurana, D., Ma, F.: One-way functions imply secure computation in a quantum world. In: Malkin, T., Peikert, C. (eds.) CRYPTO 2021. LNCS, vol. 12825, pp. 467–496. Springer, Cham (2021). https://doi.org/10.1007/978-3-030-84242-0_17
10. Behera, A., Brakerski, Z., Sattath, O., Shmueli, O.: Pseudorandomness with proof of destruction and applications. Cryptology ePrint Archive, Paper 2023/543 (2023). https://eprint.iacr.org/2023/543
11. Bennett, C.H., Brassard, G.: An update on quantum cryptography (impromptu talk). In: Blakley, G.R., Chaum, D. (eds.) CRYPTO'84. LNCS, vol. 196, pp. 475–480. Springer, Heidelberg (1984)
12. Boneh, D., Zhandry, M.: Quantum-secure message authentication codes. In: Johansson, T., Nguyen, P.Q. (eds.) EUROCRYPT 2013. LNCS, vol. 7881, pp. 592–608. Springer, Heidelberg (2013). https://doi.org/10.1007/978-3-642-38348-9_35

13. Boneh, D., Zhandry, M.: Secure signatures and chosen ciphertext security in a quantum computing world. In: Canetti, R., Garay, J.A. (eds.) CRYPTO 2013. LNCS, vol. 8043, pp. 361–379. Springer, Heidelberg (2013). https://doi.org/10.1007/978-3-642-40084-1_21

14. Chevalier, C., Ebrahimi, E., Vu, Q.H.: On security notions for encryption in a quantum world. In: Isobe, T., Sarkar, S. (eds.) Progress in Cryptology - INDOCRYPT 2022–23rd International Conference on Cryptology in India, Kolkata, India, 11–14 December 2022, Proceedings. Lecture Notes in Computer Science, vol. 13774, pp. 592–613. Springer, Heidelberg (2022). https://doi.org/10.1007/978-3-031-22912-1_26

15. Choi, S.G., Dachman-Soled, D., Malkin, T., Wee, H.: A black-box construction of non-malleable encryption from semantically secure encryption. J. Cryptol. **31**(1), 172–201 (2018). https://doi.org/10.1007/s00145-017-9254-z

16. Coladangelo, A.: Quantum trapdoor functions from classical one-way functions. Cryptology ePrint Archive, Paper 2023/282 (2023). https://eprint.iacr.org/2023/282

17. Doliskani, J.: Efficient quantum public-key encryption from learning with errors. Cryptology ePrint Archive, Paper 2020/1557 (2020). https://eprint.iacr.org/2020/1557

18. Gottesman, D.: Quantum public key cryptography with information-theoretic security (2005). https://www2.perimeterinstitute.ca/personal/dgottesman/Public-key.ppt

19. Grilo, A.B., Lin, H., Song, F., Vaikuntanathan, V.: Oblivious transfer is in MiniQCrypt. In: Canteaut, A., Standaert, F.-X. (eds.) EUROCRYPT 2021. LNCS, vol. 12697, pp. 531–561. Springer, Cham (2021). https://doi.org/10.1007/978-3-030-77886-6_18

20. Grilo, A.B., Sattath, O., Vu, Q.H.: Encryption with quantum public keys. Cryptology ePrint Archive, Paper 2023/345 (2023). https://eprint.iacr.org/2023/345

21. Huang, H.Y., Kueng, R., Preskill, J.: Predicting many properties of a quantum system from very few measurements. Nat. Phys. **16**(10), 1050–1057 (2020)

22. Impagliazzo, R., Rudich, S.: Limits on the provable consequences of one-way permutations. In: Goldwasser, S. (ed.) CRYPTO 1988. LNCS, vol. 403, pp. 8–26. Springer, New York (1990). https://doi.org/10.1007/0-387-34799-2_2

23. Ji, Z., Liu, Y.-K., Song, F.: Pseudorandom quantum states. In: Shacham, H., Boldyreva, A. (eds.) CRYPTO 2018. LNCS, vol. 10993, pp. 126–152. Springer, Cham (2018). https://doi.org/10.1007/978-3-319-96878-0_5

24. Kawachi, A., Koshiba, T., Nishimura, H., Yamakami, T.: Computational indistinguishability between quantum states and its cryptographic application. In: Cramer, R. (ed.) EUROCRYPT 2005. LNCS, vol. 3494, pp. 268–284. Springer, Heidelberg (2005). https://doi.org/10.1007/11426639_16

25. Kitagawa, F., Morimae, T., Nishimaki, R., Yamakawa, T.: Quantum public-key encryption with tamper-resilient public keys from one-way functions. Cryptology ePrint Archive, Paper 2023/490 (2023). https://eprint.iacr.org/2023/490

26. Kretschmer, W.: Quantum pseudorandomness and classical complexity. In: Hsieh, M. (ed.) 16th Conference on the Theory of Quantum Computation, Communication and Cryptography, TQC 2021, 5–8 July 2021, Virtual Conference. LIPIcs, vol. 197, pp. 2:1–2:20. Schloss Dagstuhl - Leibniz-Zentrum für Informatik (2021). https://doi.org/10.4230/LIPIcs.TQC.2021.2

27. Kretschmer, W., Qian, L., Sinha, M., Tal, A.: Quantum cryptography in algorithmica. arXiv preprint arXiv:2212.00879 (2022)

28. Malavolta, G., Walter, M.: Non-interactive quantum key distribution. Cryptology ePrint Archive, Paper 2023/500 (2023). https://eprint.iacr.org/2023/500

29. Morimae, T., Yamakawa, T.: One-wayness in quantum cryptography. Cryptology ePrint Archive, Paper 2022/1336 (2022). https://eprint.iacr.org/2022/1336

30. Morimae, T., Yamakawa, T.: Quantum commitments and signatures without one-way functions. In: Dodis, Y., Shrimpton, T. (eds.) CRYPTO 2022, Part I. LNCS, vol. 13507, pp. 269–295. Springer, Heidelberg (2022). https://doi.org/10.1007/978-3-031-15802-5_10

31. Myers, S., Shelat, A.: Bit encryption is complete. In: 50th FOCS, pp. 607–616. IEEE Computer Society Press (2009). https://doi.org/10.1109/FOCS.2009.65

32. Nikolopoulos, G.M., Ioannou, L.M.: Deterministic quantum-public-key encryption: forward search attack and randomization. Phys. Rev. A **79**, 042327 (2009). https://doi.org/10.1103/PhysRevA.79.042327

33. Okamoto, T., Tanaka, K., Uchiyama, S.: Quantum public-key cryptosystems. In: Bellare, M. (ed.) CRYPTO 2000. LNCS, vol. 1880, pp. 147–165. Springer, Heidelberg (2000). https://doi.org/10.1007/3-540-44598-6_9

34. Wiesner, S.: Conjugate coding. SIGACT News **15**(1), 78–88 (1983). https://doi.org/10.1145/1008908.1008920

35. Zhandry, M.: How to construct quantum random functions. In: 53rd FOCS, pp. 679–687. IEEE Computer Society Press (2012). https://doi.org/10.1109/FOCS.2012.37

Publicly Verifiable Deletion from Minimal Assumptions

Fuyuki Kitagawa, Ryo Nishimaki, and Takashi Yamakawa[✉]

NTT Social Informatics Laboratories, Tokyo, Japan
{fuyuki.kitagawa,ryo.nishimaki,takashi.yamakawa}@ntt.com

Abstract. We present a general compiler to add the publicly verifiable deletion property for various cryptographic primitives including public key encryption, attribute-based encryption, and quantum fully homomorphic encryption. Our compiler only uses one-way functions, or more generally hard quantum planted problems for NP, which are implied by one-way functions. It relies on minimal assumptions and enables us to add the publicly verifiable deletion property with no additional assumption for the above primitives. Previously, such a compiler needs additional assumptions such as injective trapdoor one-way functions or pseudorandom group actions [Bartusek-Khurana-Poremba, CRYPTO 2023]. Technically, we upgrade an existing compiler for privately verifiable deletion [Bartusek-Khurana, CRYPTO 2023] to achieve publicly verifiable deletion by using digital signatures.

1 Introduction

1.1 Background

Quantum mechanics yields new cryptographic primitives that classical cryptography cannot achieve. In particular, the uncertainty principle enables us to certify deletion of information. Broadbent and Islam [10] introduced the notion of quantum encryption with certified deletion, where we can generate a classical certificate for the deletion of quantum ciphertext. We need a verification key generated along with a quantum ciphertext to check the validity of a certificate. The root of this concept is revocable quantum time-release encryption by Unruh [24], where a sender can revoke quantum ciphertext if a receiver returns it before a predetermined time. Encryption with certified deletion is useful because encryption security holds *even if adversaries obtain a secret decryption key after they generate a valid certificate for deletion*. After the work by Broadbent and Islam [10], many works presented extended definitions and new constructions of quantum (advanced) encryption with certified deletion [7–9,16,17,23]. In particular, Bartusek and Khurana [8], and Hiroka, Kitagawa, Morimae, Nishimaki, Pal, and Yamakawa [16] considered certified everlasting security, which guarantees that computationally *unbounded* adversaries cannot obtain information about plaintext *after a valid certificate was generated*. Several works [7,9,17,23] considered

G. Rothblum and H. Wee (Eds.): TCC 2023, LNCS 14372, pp. 228–245, 2023.
https://doi.org/10.1007/978-3-031-48624-1_9

public verifiability, where we can reveal verification keys without harming certified deletion security. These properties are desirable for encryption with certified deletion in real-world applications.

In this work, we focus on cryptographic primitives with publicly verifiable deletion (PVD) [9], which satisfy certified everlasting security and public verifiability. Known schemes based on BB84 states are privately verifiable [8,10,16,17], where we need to keep verification keys secret to ensure encryption security. Some schemes are publicly verifiable [7,9,17,23]. Public verifiability is preferable to private verifiability since we need to keep many verification keys secret when we generate many ciphertexts of encryption with privately verifiable deletion. More secret keys lead to more risks. In addition, anyone can verify deletion in cryptography with PVD.

Hiroka, Morimae, Nishimaki, and Yamakawa [17] achieved interactive public key encryption with non-everlasting PVD from extractable witness encryption [14], which is a strong knowledge-type assumption, and one-shot signatures which require classical oracles [3]. Poremba [23] achieved public key encryption (PKE) and fully homomorphic encryption (FHE) with non-everlasting PVD based on lattices. He conjectured Ajtai hash function satisfies a strong Gaussian collapsing property and proved the security of his constructions under the conjecture. Later, Bartusek, Khurana, and Poremba [9] proved the conjecture is true under the LWE assumption.

Bartusek, Garg, Goyal, Khurana, Malavolta, Raizes, and Roberts [7] achieved primitive X with PVD from X and post-quantum secure indistinguishability obfuscation (IO) [6] where $X \in$ {SKE, COM, PKE, ABE, FHE, TRE, WE}.[1] They also achieved functional encryption with PVD and obfuscation with PVD, which rely on post-quantum IO. All their constructions use subspace coset states [12]. Bartusek et al. [9] achieved PKE (resp. COM) with PVD from injective trapdoor one-way functions (or superposition-invertible regular trapdoor functions) or pseudorandom group actions [15] (resp. almost-regular one-way functions). They also achieved primitive Y with PVD from injective trapdoor one-way functions (or superposition-invertible regular trapdoor functions) or pseudorandom group actions, and primitive Y where $Y \in$ {ABE, QFHE, TRE, WE}. They obtained these results by considering certified everlasting target-collapsing functions as an intermediate primitive.

As we explained above, known encryption with PVD constructions need strong and non-standard assumptions [7,17], algebraic assumptions [9,23], or additional assumptions [9]. This status is unsatisfactory because Bartusek and Khurana [8] prove that we can achieve X with *privately* verifiable deletion[2]

---

[1] SKE, COM, ABE, TRE, and WE stand for secret key encryption, commitment, attribute-based encryption, time-release encryption, and witness encryption, respectively. Although Bartusek et al. [7] did not mention, we can apply their transformation to SKE and COM as the results by Bartusek and Khurana [8].

[2] We do not abbreviate when we refer to this type to avoid confusion.

from X where $X \in \{$SKE, COM, PKE, ABE, FHE, TRE, WE$\}^3$ *without any additional assumptions*. Thus, our main question in this work is the following.

Can we achieve encryption with PVD from minimal assumptions?

1.2 Our Results

We affirmatively answer the main question described in the previous section. We present a general transformation from primitive Z into Z with PVD where $Z \in \{$SKE, COM, PKE, ABE, QFHE, TRE, WE$\}$. In the transformation, we only use one-way functions, or more generally, hard quantum planted problems for NP, which we introduce in this work and are implied by one-way functions.

More specifically, we extend the certified everlasting lemma by Bartusek and Khurana [8], which enables us to achieve encryption with privately verifiable deletion, to a publicly verifiable certified everlasting lemma. We develop an authentication technique based on (a variant of) the Lamport signature [21] to reduce our publicly verifiable certified everlasting lemma to Bartusek and Khurana's certified everlasting lemma.

Our new lemma is almost as versatile as Bartusek and Khurana's lemma. It is easy to apply it to all-or-nothing type encryption[4], where a secret key (or witness) holder can recover the entire plaintext. One subtle issue is that we need to use QFHE for (Q)FHE with PVD. The reason is that we need to apply an evaluation algorithm to quantum ciphertext. Note that we can use FHE and Bartusek and Khurana's lemma to achieve FHE with privately verifiable deletion.

The advantages of our techniques are as follows:

- For $Z' \in \{$SKE, COM, PKE, ABE, QFHE, TRE$\}$, we can convert plain Z' into Z' with PVD with no additional assumption. For WE, we can convert it into WE with PVD additionally assuming one-way functions (or hard quantum planted problems for NP).[5] Bartusek et al. [9] require injective (or almost-regular) trapdoor one-way functions, pseudorandom group actions, or almost-regular one-way functions for their constructions.
- Our transformation is applicable even if the base scheme has quantum encryption and decryption (or committing) algorithms.[6] This means that our assumptions are minimal since Z with PVD implies both plain Z with quantum encryption and decryption (or committing) algorithms and hard quantum planted problems for NP for $Z \in \{$SKE, COM, PKE, ABE, QFHE, TRE, WE$\}$.

---

[3] Although Bartusek and Khurana [8] did not mention, we can apply their transformation to SKE.

[4] SKE, PKE, ABE, (Q)FHE, TRE, and WE fall into this category.

[5] WE does not seem to imply one-way functions.

[6] The compilers of [8,9] are also applicable to schemes that have quantum encryption and decryption (or committing) algorithms though they do not explicitly mention it.

– Our approach is simple. Bartusek et al. [9] introduced an elegant intermediate notion, certified everlasting target-collapsing, to achieve cryptography with PVD. However, they use a few more intermediate notions (such as balanced binary-measurement target-collision-resistance) for their approach.

1.3 Technical Overview

As explained in Sect. 1.1, Bartusek and Khurana [8] gave a generic compiler to add the *privately verifiable* deletion property for various types of encryption. Our finding is that there is a surprisingly simple way to upgrade their compiler to achieve *publicly verifiable* deletion by additionally using digital signatures.

Notations. For a bit string x, we write x_j to mean j-th bit of x. For bit strings $x, \theta \in \{0,1\}^\ell$, we write $|x\rangle_\theta$ to mean the BB84 state $\bigotimes_{j \in [\ell]} H^{\theta_j} |x_j\rangle$ where H is the Hadamard operator.

Certified Everlasting Lemma of [8]. The compiler of [8] is based on the *certified everlasting lemma* described below.[7] We describe it in the dual version, where the roles of computational and Hadamard bases are swapped for convenience. We stress that the dual version is equivalent to the original one because they coincide under an appropriate basis change.

Consider a family of distributions $\{\mathcal{Z}(m)\}_{m \in \{0,1\}^{\lambda+1}}$ over classical strings, such that for any $m \in \{0,1\}^{\lambda+1}$, the distribution $\mathcal{Z}(m)$ is computationally indistinguishable from the distribution $\mathcal{Z}(0^{\lambda+1})$. In other words, each distribution $\mathcal{Z}(m)$ can be thought of as an "encryption" of the input m. Let $\widetilde{\mathcal{Z}}(b)$ be an experiment between an adversary and challenger defined as follows for $b \in \{0,1\}$:

– The challenger samples $x, \theta \leftarrow \{0,1\}^\lambda$ and sends $|x\rangle_\theta$ and $\mathcal{Z}(\theta, b \oplus \bigoplus_{j:\theta_j=1} x_j)$ to the adversary.
– The adversary sends a classical string $x' \in \{0,1\}^\lambda$ and a quantum state ρ to the challenger.
– The challenger outputs ρ if $x'_j = x_j$ for all j such that $\theta_j = 0$, and otherwise outputs a special symbol $\perp$ as the output of the experiment.

The certified everlasting lemma states that for any QPT adversary, the trace distance between $\widetilde{\mathcal{Z}}(0)$ and $\widetilde{\mathcal{Z}}(1)$ is negligible in λ.

The above lemma immediately gives a generic compiler to add the privately verifiable deletion property. To encrypt a message $b \in \{0,1\}$, we set the ciphertext to be $(|x\rangle_\theta, \mathsf{Enc}(\theta, b \oplus \bigoplus_{j:\theta_j=1} x_j))$, where x and θ are randomly chosen from $\{0,1\}^\lambda$, and Enc is the encryption algorithm of the underlying scheme.[8]

---

[7] For simplicity, we state a simplified version of the lemma that is sufficient for the conversion for PKE, FHE, TRE, and WE, but not for ABE. See Lemma 4.1 for the general version.

[8] We write $\mathsf{Enc}(\theta, b \oplus \bigoplus_{j:\theta_j=1} x_j)$ to mean an encryption of the message $(\theta, b \oplus \bigoplus_{j:\theta_j=1} x_j)$ where we omit the encryption key.

The decryptor first decrypts the second component to get $(\theta, b \oplus \bigoplus_{j:\theta_j=1} x_j)$, recovers $\bigoplus_{j:\theta_j=1} x_j$ from $|x\rangle_\theta$ and θ, and then XORs it with $b \oplus \bigoplus_{j:\theta_j=1} x_j$ to recover b. To delete the ciphertext and obtain a certificate x', we measure $|x\rangle_\theta$ in the standard basis. To verify the certificate, we check if $x'_j = x_j$ for all j such that $\theta_j = 0$. By utilizing the above lemma, we can see that an adversary's internal state will not contain any information about b given the verification algorithm's acceptance. Therefore, the scheme offers certified everlasting security. However, this scheme has only privately verifiable deletion because the verification algorithm needs to know x and θ, which are part of the encryption randomness that has to be hidden from the adversary.

Making Verification Public via Digital Signatures. We show a publicly verifiable variant of the certified everlasting lemma by using digital signatures. Roughly speaking, our idea is to generate a signature for the BB84 state $|x\rangle_\theta$ by coherently running the signing algorithm so that the verification of deletion can be done by the verification of the signature, which can be done publicly. Note that the signature does *not* certify $|x\rangle_\theta$ as a quantum state. It rather certifies its computational basis part (i.e., x_j for j such that $\theta_j = 0$). This is sufficient for our purpose because the verification of deletion just checks the computational basis part.

With the above idea in mind, we modify the experiment $\widetilde{\mathcal{Z}}(b)$ as follows:

- The challenger generates a key pair $(\mathsf{vk}, \mathsf{sigk})$ of a digital signature scheme and samples $x, \theta \leftarrow \{0,1\}^\lambda$. Let U_{sign} be a unitary that works as follows:

$$|m\rangle |0\ldots 0\rangle \mapsto |m\rangle |\mathsf{Sign}(\mathsf{sigk}, m)\rangle.$$

where $\mathsf{Sign}(\mathsf{sigk}, \cdot)$ is a deterministic signing algorithm with a signing key sigk. The challenger sends vk, $U_{\mathsf{sign}} |x\rangle_\theta |0\ldots 0\rangle$, and $\mathcal{Z}(\mathsf{sigk}, \theta, b \oplus \bigoplus_{j:\theta_j=1} x_j)$ to the adversary.
- The adversary sends a classical string $x' \in \{0,1\}^\lambda$, a signature σ, and a quantum state ρ to the challenger.
- The challenger outputs ρ if σ is a valid signature for x', and otherwise outputs a special symbol $\perp$ as the output of the experiment.

We show that for any QPT adversary, the trace distance between $\widetilde{\mathcal{Z}}(0)$ and $\widetilde{\mathcal{Z}}(1)$ is negligible in λ if we instantiate the digital signatures with an appropriate scheme as explained later. The crucial difference from the original lemma is that the challenger does not need to check if $x'_j = x_j$ for all j such that $\theta_j = 0$ and only needs to run the verification algorithm of the digital signature scheme.

By using the above variant similarly to the original privately verifiable construction, we obtain a generic compiler that adds publicly verifiable deletion property. For clarity, we describe the construction below. To encrypt a message $b \in \{0,1\}$, the encryption algorithm generates a key pair $(\mathsf{vk}, \mathsf{sigk})$ of the digital signature scheme, chooses $x, \theta \leftarrow \{0,1\}^\lambda$, and outputs a ciphertext $(U_{\mathsf{sign}} |x\rangle_\theta, \mathsf{Enc}(\mathsf{sigk}, \theta, b \oplus \bigoplus_{j:\theta_j=1} x_j))$ and a public verification key vk. The decryptor first decrypts the second component to get $(\mathsf{sigk}, \theta, b \oplus \bigoplus_{j:\theta_j=1} x_j)$, uncompute the signature register of the first component by using sigk to get $|x\rangle_\theta$, recovers $\bigoplus_{j:\theta_j=1} x_j$ from $|x\rangle_\theta$ and θ, and then XORs it with $b \oplus \bigoplus_{j:\theta_j=1} x_j$ to recover b. To delete the ciphertext and obtain a certificate (x', σ), we measure $U_{\mathsf{sign}}|x\rangle_\theta$ in the standard basis to get (x', σ). To verify the certificate, we check if σ is a valid signature for x'. By utilizing the above lemma, we can see that the above scheme achieves certified everlasting security with public verification.

Proof Idea and Instantiation of Digital Signatures. We prove the above publicly verifiable version by reducing it to the original one in [8]. Noting that $\mathcal{Z}(\mathsf{sigk}, \theta, b \oplus \bigoplus_{j:\theta_j=1} x_j)$ computationally hides sigk by the assumption, a straightforward reduction works if the digital signature scheme satisfies the following security notion which we call one-time unforgeability for BB84 states.

Definition 1.1 (One-time unforgeability for BB84 states (informal)).
Given vk *and* $U_{\mathsf{sign}}|x\rangle_\theta|0\ldots0\rangle$ *for uniformly random* $x, \theta \leftarrow \{0,1\}^\lambda$, *no QPT adversary can output* $x' \in \{0,1\}^\lambda$ *and a signature* σ *such that* σ *is a valid signature for* x' *and* $x'_j \neq x_j$ *for some* j *such that* $\theta_j = 0$ *with a non-negligible probability.*

It is easy to show that the Lamport signature satisfies the above property. This can be seen as follows. Recall that a verification key of the Lamport signature consists of $(v_{j,b})_{j\in[\lambda], b\in\{0,1\}}$ where $v_{j,b} := f(u_{j,b})$ for a one-way function f and uniformly random inputs $(u_{j,b})_{j\in[\lambda], b\in\{0,1\}}$, and a signature for a message $m \in \{0,1\}^\lambda$ is $\sigma := (u_{j,m_j})_{j\in[\lambda]}$. Suppose that there is an adversary that breaks the above property. Then, there must exist $j \in [\lambda]$ such that $x'_j \neq x_j$ and $\theta_j = 0$, in which case the input state $U_{\mathsf{sign}}|x\rangle_\theta|0\ldots0\rangle$ does not have any information of $u_{j,1-x_j}$. On the other hand, to generate a valid signature for x', the adversary has to find a preimage of $v_{j,x'_j} = v_{j,1-x_j}$. This is impossible by the one-wayness of f. Thus, a digital signature scheme that satisfies one-time unforgeability for BB84 states exists assuming the existence of one-way functions.

Achieving Minimal Assumptions. In the above, we explain that one-way functions are sufficient for instantiating the digital signature scheme needed for our compiler. On the other hand, encryption schemes with publicly verifiable deletion does not seem to imply the existence of one-way functions because ciphertexts can be quantum. Thus, one-way functions may not be a necessary assumption for them. To weaken the assumption, we observe that we can use hard quantum planted problems for NP instead of one-way functions in the Lamport signature. Here, hard quantum planted problems for a NP language L is specified by a quantum polynomial-time sampler that samples an instance-witness pair (x, w) for the language L in such a way that no QPT adversary can find a witness for x with non-negligible probability. Given such a sampler, it is easy to see that we can instantiate the digital signature scheme similar to the above except that $(v_{j,b}, u_{j,b})$ is now replaced with an instance-witness pair sampled by the sampler.

We observe that Z with PVD implies the existence of hard quantum planted problems for NP where $Z \in \{\text{SKE, COM, PKE, ABE, QFHE, TRE, WE}\}$.[9] This can be seen by considering the verification key as an instance and certificate as a witness for an NP language. Our construction relies on hard quantum planted problems for NP and plain Z with quantum encryption and decryption (or committing) algorithms, both of which are implied by Z with PVD, and thus it is based on the minimal assumptions.

1.4 More on Related Works

Certified Deletion for Ciphertext with private verifiability. Broadbent and Islam [10] achieved one-time SKE with privately verifiable deletion without any cryptographic assumptions. Hiroka et al. [17] achieved PKE and ABE with non-everlasting privately verifiable deletion. They also achieve interactive PKE with non-everlasting privately verifiable deletion and classical communication in the quantum random oracle model (QROM) from the LWE assumption. However, none of their constructions satisfy certified everlasting security. Hiroka, Morimae, Nishimaki, and Yamakawa [18] defined certified everlasting commitment and zero-knowledge (for QMA) by extending everlasting security [22]. They achieved these notions by using plain commitment and QROM. Bartusek and Khurana [8] defined certified everlasting security for various all-or-nothing type encryption primitives and presented a general framework to achieve certified everlasting secure all-or-nothing type encryption and commitment with privately verifiable deletion using BB84 states. They also studied secure computation with everlasting security transfer. Hiroka et al. [16] also defined and achieved certified everlasting security for various cryptographic primitives. In particular, they defined and achieved certified everlasting (collusion-resistant) functional encryption, garbled circuits, and compute-and-compare obfuscation, which are outside of all-or-nothing type encryption. Their constructions are also based on BB84 states and are privately verifiable. They also use a signature-based authentication technique for BB84 states. However, its role is not achieving public verifiability but functional encryption security. See the paper by Hiroka et al. [16] for the differences between their results and Bartusek and Khurana's results [8].

Certified Deletion for Keys or Secure Key Leasing. Kitagawa and Nishimaki [19] defined secret key functional encryption with secure key leasing, where we can generate a classical certificate for the deletion of functional keys. They achieved such a primitive with bounded collusion-resistance from one-way functions. Agrawal, Kitagawa, Nishimaki, Yamada, and Yamakawa [2] defined PKE with secure key leasing, where we lose decryption capability after we return a quantum decryption key. They achieved it from standard PKE. They also extended

---

[9] We assume that the verification algorithm of Z with PVD is a classical deterministic algorithm. If we allow it to be a quantum algorithm, we have to consider hard quantum planted problems for QCMA, which are also sufficient to instantiate our compiler.

the notion to ABE with secure key leasing and public key functional encryption with secure key leasing. They achieved them from standard ABE and public key functional encryption, respectively. Garg et al. [7] presented a public key functional encryption with secure key leasing scheme based on IO and injective one-way functions. Ananth, Poremba, and Vaikuntanathan [5] also defined the same notion as PKE with secure key leasing (they call key-revocable PKE). However, their definition differs slightly from that of Agrawal et al. [2]. They also studied key-revocable FHE and PRF. They achieved them from the LWE assumption.

Secure Software Leasing. Ananth and La Placa [4] defined secure software leasing, where we lose software functionality after we return a quantum software. They achieved secure software leasing for a subclass of evasive functions from public key quantum money and the LWE assumptions. After that, several works proposed extensions, variants, and improved constructions of secure software leasing [1,11,13,20].

2 Preliminaries

2.1 Notations

Here we introduce basic notations we will use in this paper.

In this paper, standard math or sans serif font stands for classical algorithms (e.g., C or Gen) and classical variables (e.g., x or pk). Calligraphic font stands for quantum algorithms (e.g., $\mathcal{Gen}$) and calligraphic font and/or the bracket notation for (mixed) quantum states (e.g., q or $|\psi\rangle$).

Let $x \leftarrow X$ denote selecting an element x from a finite set X uniformly at random, and $y \leftarrow A(x)$ denote assigning to y the output of a quantum or probabilistic or deterministic algorithm A on an input x. When D is a distribution, $x \leftarrow D$ denotes sampling an element x from D. $y := z$ denotes that y is set, defined, or substituted by z. Let $[n] := \{1, \ldots, n\}$. Let λ be a security parameter. For a bit string $s \in \{0, 1\}^n$, s_i denotes the i-th bit of s. QPT stands for quantum polynomial time. PPT stands for (classical) probabilistic polynomial time. We say that a quantum (resp. probabilistic classical) algorithm is efficient if it runs in QPT (resp. PPT). A function $f : \mathbb{N} \to \mathbb{R}$ is a negligible function if for any constant c, there exists $\lambda_0 \in \mathbb{N}$ such that for any $\lambda > \lambda_0$, $f(\lambda) < \lambda^{-c}$. We write $f(\lambda) \leq \mathsf{negl}(\lambda)$ to denote $f(\lambda)$ being a negligible function. The trace distance between two quantum states ρ and σ denoted as $\mathsf{TD}(\rho, \sigma)$ is given by $\frac{1}{2} \|\rho - \sigma\|_{\mathrm{tr}}$, where $\|A\|_{\mathrm{tr}} := \mathrm{tr}\sqrt{A^\dagger A}$ is the trace norm.

2.2 Cryptographic Tools

In this section, we review the cryptographic tools used in this paper.

Definition 2.1 (Signature). *Let $\mathcal{M}$ be a message space. A signature scheme for $\mathcal{M}$ is a tuple of efficient algorithms* (Gen, Sign, Vrfy) *where:*

$\mathsf{Gen}(1^\lambda) \to (\mathsf{vk}, \mathsf{sigk})$: *The key generation algorithm takes as input the security parameter 1^λ and outputs a verification key vk and a signing key sigk.*

$\mathsf{Sign}(\mathsf{sigk}, m) \to \sigma$: *The signing algorithm takes as input a signing key sigk and a message $m \in \mathcal{M}$ and outputs a signature σ.*

$\mathsf{Vrfy}(\mathsf{vk}, m, \sigma) \to \top$ **or** $\bot$: *The verification algorithm is a deterministic algorithm that takes as input a verification key vk, a message m and a signature σ and outputs $\top$ to indicate acceptance of the signature and $\bot$ otherwise.*

Correctness: *For all $m \in \mathcal{M}$, $(\mathsf{vk}, \mathsf{sigk})$ in the range of $\mathsf{Gen}(1^\lambda)$, and $\sigma \in \mathsf{Sign}(\mathsf{sigk}, m)$, we have $\mathsf{Vrfy}(\mathsf{vk}, m, \sigma) = \top$.*

Definition 2.2 (Deterministic Signature). *We say that a signature scheme $\mathsf{SIG} = (\mathsf{Gen}, \mathsf{Sign}, \mathsf{Vrfy})$ is a deterministic signature if $\mathsf{Sign}(\mathsf{sigk}, \cdot)$ is a deterministic function.*

Definition 2.3 (Public Key Encryption). *A PKE scheme is a tuple of efficient algorithms $\mathsf{PKE} = (\mathsf{Gen}, \mathsf{Enc}, \mathsf{Dec})$.*

$\mathsf{Gen}(1^\lambda) \to (\mathsf{pk}, \mathsf{sk})$: *The key generation algorithm takes the security parameter 1^λ as input and outputs a public key pk and a secret key sk.*

$\mathsf{Enc}(\mathsf{pk}, m) \to \mathsf{ct}$: *The encryption algorithm takes pk and a plaintext $m \in \{0, 1\}$ as input, and outputs a ciphertext ct.*

$\mathsf{Dec}(\mathsf{sk}, \mathsf{ct}) \to m'$: *The decryption algorithm takes sk and ct as input, and outputs a plaintext $m' \in \mathcal{M}$ or $\bot$.*

Correctness: *For any $m \in \mathcal{M}$, we have*

$$\Pr\left[m' \neq m \;\middle|\; \begin{array}{l} (\mathsf{pk}, \mathsf{sk}) \leftarrow \mathsf{Gen}(1^\lambda) \\ \mathsf{ct} \leftarrow \mathsf{Enc}(\mathsf{pk}, m) \\ m' \leftarrow \mathsf{Dec}(\mathsf{sk}, \mathsf{ct}) \end{array} \right] \leq \mathsf{negl}(\lambda).$$

Semantic Security: *For any QPT $\mathcal{A}$, we have*

$$\left| \Pr\left[\mathcal{A}(\mathsf{pk}, \mathsf{ct}) = 1 \;\middle|\; \begin{array}{l} (\mathsf{pk}, \mathsf{sk}) \leftarrow \mathsf{Gen}(1^\lambda) \\ \mathsf{ct} \leftarrow \mathsf{Enc}(\mathsf{pk}, 0) \end{array} \right] \right.$$
$$\left. - \Pr\left[\mathcal{A}(\mathsf{pk}, \mathsf{ct}) = 1 \;\middle|\; \begin{array}{l} (\mathsf{pk}, \mathsf{sk}) \leftarrow \mathsf{Gen}(1^\lambda) \\ \mathsf{ct} \leftarrow \mathsf{Enc}(\mathsf{pk}, 1) \end{array} \right] \right| = \mathsf{negl}(\lambda).$$

3   Signature with One-Time Unforgeability for BB84 States

Definition. We first provide the definition of one-time unforgeability for BB84 states.

Definition 3.1 (One-Time Unforgeability for BB84 states). *Let $\mathsf{SIG} = (\mathsf{Gen}, \mathsf{Sign}, \mathsf{Vrfy})$ be a signature scheme. We define the experiment $\mathsf{Exp}_{\mathsf{SIG}, \mathcal{A}}^{\mathsf{otu\text{-}bb84}}(1^\lambda)$ between an adversary $\mathcal{A}$ and challenger as follows.*

1. *The challenger runs* $(\mathsf{vk}, \mathsf{sigk}) \leftarrow \mathsf{Gen}(1^\lambda)$ *and generates* $x, \theta \leftarrow \{0,1\}^\lambda$. *The challenger generates a quantum state* $|\psi\rangle$ *by applying the map* $|m\rangle |0 \dots 0\rangle \rightarrow |m\rangle |\mathsf{Sign}(\mathsf{sigk}, m)\rangle$ *to* $|x\rangle_\theta \otimes |0 \dots 0\rangle$. *The challenger gives* vk *and* $|\psi\rangle$ *to* $\mathcal{A}$.
2. $\mathcal{A}$ *outputs a pair of message and signature* (x', σ') *as the challenge message-signature pair to the challenger.*
3. *The experiment outputs 1 if the followings are satisfied.*
   - $x_i \neq x'_i$ *holds for some* i *such that* $\theta_i = 0$.
   - $\mathsf{Vrfy}(\mathsf{vk}, x', \sigma') = 1$ *holds.*

We say SIG *is one-time unforgeable for BB84 states if, for any QPT adversary* $\mathcal{A}$, *it holds that*

$$\mathsf{Adv}_{\mathsf{SIG},\mathcal{A}}^{\mathsf{otu\text{-}bb84}}(\lambda) := \Pr[\mathsf{Exp}_{\mathsf{SIG},\mathcal{A}}^{\mathsf{otu\text{-}bb84}}(1^\lambda) = 1] = \mathsf{negl}(\lambda).$$

Construction. We construct a classical deterministic signature scheme $\mathsf{SIG} = (\mathsf{Gen}, \mathsf{Sign}, \mathsf{Vrfy})$ satisfying one-time unforgeability for BB84 states using OWF f. The message space of SIG is $\{0,1\}^\ell$.

$\mathsf{Gen}(1^\lambda)$:
   - Generate $u_{i,b} \leftarrow \{0,1\}^\lambda$ for every $i \in [\ell]$ and $b \in \{0,1\}$.
   - Compute $v_{i,b} \leftarrow f(u_{i,b})$ for every $i \in [\ell]$ and $b \in \{0,1\}$.
   - Output $\mathsf{vk} := (v_{i,b})_{i \in [\ell], b \in \{0,1\}}$ and $\mathsf{sigk} := (u_{i,b})_{i \in [\ell], b \in \{0,1\}}$.
$\mathsf{Sign}(\mathsf{sigk}, m)$:
   - Parse $(u_{i,b})_{i \in [\ell], b \in \{0,1\}} \leftarrow \mathsf{sigk}$.
   - Output $(u_{i,m_i})_{i \in [\ell]}$.
$\mathsf{Vrfy}(\mathsf{vk}, m, \sigma)$:
   - Parse $(v_{i,b})_{i \in [\ell], b \in \{0,1\}} \leftarrow \mathsf{vk}$ and $(w_i)_{i \in [\ell]} \leftarrow \sigma$.
   - Output $\top$ if $u_{i,m_i} = f(w_i)$ holds for every $i \in [\ell]$ and otherwise output $\bot$.

It is clear that SIG is a correct classical deterministic signature. Also, we have the following theorem.

Theorem 3.1. *Assume* f *is OWF. Then,* SIG *satisfies one-time unforgeability for BB84 states.*

Proof. For a computational basis position $i \in [\lambda]$ (that is, i such that $\theta_i = 0$), when we generate $|\psi\rangle$ by applying the map $|m\rangle |0 \dots 0\rangle \rightarrow |m\rangle |\mathsf{Sign}(\mathsf{sigk}, m)\rangle$ to $|x\rangle_\theta \otimes |0 \dots 0\rangle$, $|\psi\rangle$ contains only $u_{i,b}$ and not $u_{i,1-b}$ if $x_i = b$. From this fact, the one-time unforgeability of SIG directly follows from the security of f. $\square$

4   Certified Everlasting Lemmas

In this section, we first review the certified everlasting lemma by Bartusek and Khurana [8], which provides cryptography with privately verifiable deletion. Next, we present our new certified everlasting lemma, which provides cryptography with PVD.

Lemma 4.1 (Certified Everlasting Lemma [8]). *Let* $\{\mathcal{Z}_\lambda(\cdot,\cdot,\cdot)\}_{\lambda\in\mathbb{N}}$ *be an efficient quantum operation with three arguments: a λ-bit string θ, a bit β, and a quantum register* A. *For any QPT* $\mathcal{B}$, *consider the following experiment* $\widetilde{\mathcal{Z}}_\lambda^{\mathcal{B}}(b)$ *over quantum states, obtained by running* $\mathcal{B}$ *as follows.*

- *Sample* $x, \theta \leftarrow \{0,1\}^\lambda$ *and initialize* $\mathcal{B}$ *with* $\mathcal{Z}_\lambda(\theta, b \oplus \bigoplus_{i:\theta_i=1} x_i, |x\rangle_\theta)$.
- $\mathcal{B}$'s *output is parsed as a string* $x' \in \{0,1\}^\lambda$ *and a residual state on register* B.
- *If* $x_i = x'_i$ *for all i such that* $\theta_i = 0$, *output* B, *and otherwise output a special symbol* $\bot$.
  Assume that for any QPT $\mathcal{A}$, $\theta \in \{0,1\}^\lambda$, $\beta \in \{0,1\}$, *and an efficiently samplable state* $|\psi\rangle^{\mathsf{A,C}}$ *on registers* A *and* C, *we have*

$$\left| \Pr[\mathcal{A}(\mathcal{Z}_\lambda(\theta,\beta,\mathsf{A}),\mathsf{C}) = 1] - \Pr[\mathcal{A}(\mathcal{Z}_\lambda(0^\lambda,\beta,\mathsf{A}),\mathsf{C}) = 1] \right| \le \mathsf{negl}(\lambda).$$

Then, for any QPT $\mathcal{B}$, *we have*

$$\mathsf{TD}(\widetilde{\mathcal{Z}}_\lambda^{\mathcal{B}}(0), \widetilde{\mathcal{Z}}_\lambda^{\mathcal{B}}(1)) \le \mathsf{negl}(\lambda).$$

Remark 4.1. Besides notational differences, the above lemma has the following differences from the original lemma by [8].

- We focus on QPT adversaries $\mathcal{A}$ and $\mathcal{B}$, though the original lemma by [8] captures more general classes of adversaries.
- The roles of computational basis position and Hadamard basis position in $\widetilde{\mathcal{Z}}_\lambda^{\mathcal{A}'}(b)$ are switched.

We can upgrade Lemma 4.1 to a publicly verifiable one by using signatures with one-time unforgeability for BB84 state introduced in Sect. 3.

Lemma 4.2 (Publicly Verifiable Certified Everlasting Lemma). *Let* $\mathsf{SIG} = (\mathsf{Gen}, \mathsf{Sign}, \mathsf{Vrfy})$ *be a signature scheme satisfying one-time unforgeability for BB84 states. Let* $\{\mathcal{Z}_\lambda(\cdot,\cdot,\cdot,\cdot,\cdot)\}_{\lambda\in\mathbb{N}}$ *be an efficient quantum operation with five arguments: a verification key* vk *and a signing key* sigk *of* SIG, *a λ-bit string θ, a bit β, and a quantum register* A. *For any QPT* $\mathcal{B}$, *consider the following experiment* $\widetilde{\mathcal{Z}}_\lambda^{\mathcal{B}}(b)$ *over quantum states, obtained by running* $\mathcal{B}$ *as follows.*

- *Sample* $x, \theta \leftarrow \{0,1\}^\lambda$ *and generate* $(\mathsf{vk}, \mathsf{sigk}) \leftarrow \mathsf{Gen}(1^\lambda)$. *Generate a quantum state* $|\psi\rangle$ *by applying the map* $|m\rangle |0\ldots0\rangle \rightarrow |m\rangle |\mathsf{Sign}(\mathsf{sigk}, m)\rangle$ *to* $|x\rangle_\theta \otimes |0\ldots0\rangle$. *Initialize* $\mathcal{B}$ *with* $\mathcal{Z}_\lambda(\mathsf{vk}, \mathsf{sigk}, \theta, b \oplus \bigoplus_{i:\theta_i=1} x_i, |\psi\rangle)$.
- $\mathcal{B}$'s *output is parsed as a pair of strings* (x', σ') *and a residual state on register* B.
- *If* $\mathsf{Vrfy}(\mathsf{vk}, x', \sigma') = \top$, *output* B, *and otherwise output a special symbol* $\bot$.
  Assume that for any QPT $\mathcal{A}$, *key pair* $(\mathsf{vk}, \mathsf{sigk})$ *of* SIG, $\theta \in \{0,1\}^\lambda$, $\beta \in \{0,1\}$, *and an efficiently samplable state* $|\psi\rangle^{\mathsf{A,C}}$ *on registers* A *and* C, *we have*

$$\left| \Pr[\mathcal{A}(\mathcal{Z}_\lambda(\mathsf{vk}, \mathsf{sigk}, \theta, \beta, \mathsf{A}), \mathsf{C}) = 1] - \Pr[\mathcal{A}(\mathcal{Z}_\lambda(\mathsf{vk}, 0^{\ell_{\mathsf{sigk}}}, \theta, \beta, \mathsf{A}), \mathsf{C}) = 1] \right|$$
$$\le \mathsf{negl}(\lambda), \tag{1}$$

and

$$\left| \Pr[\mathcal{A}(\mathcal{Z}_\lambda(\mathsf{vk}, \mathsf{sigk}, \theta, \beta, \mathsf{A}), \mathsf{C}) = 1] - \Pr[\mathcal{A}(\mathcal{Z}_\lambda(\mathsf{vk}, \mathsf{sigk}, 0^\lambda, \beta, \mathsf{A}), \mathsf{C}) = 1] \right|$$
$$\leq \mathsf{negl}(\lambda). \tag{2}$$

Then, for any QPT $\mathcal{B}$, we have

$$\mathsf{TD}(\widetilde{\mathcal{Z}}_\lambda^{\mathcal{B}}(0), \widetilde{\mathcal{Z}}_\lambda^{\mathcal{B}}(1)) \leq \mathsf{negl}(\lambda).$$

Proof. We first define the following event Forge.

Forge: For (x', σ') output by $\mathcal{B}$ in $\widetilde{\mathcal{Z}}_\lambda^{\mathcal{B}}(b)$, the followings are satisfied.
- $x_i \neq x_i'$ holds for some i such that $\theta_i = 0$.
- $\mathsf{Vrfy}(\mathsf{vk}, x', \sigma') = \top$ holds.

We also define the event Forge* in the same way as Forge except that $\mathcal{B}$ is initialized with $\mathcal{Z}_\lambda(\mathsf{vk}, 0^{\ell_{\mathsf{sigk}}}, \theta, b \oplus \bigoplus_{i:\theta_i=1} x_i, |\psi\rangle)$. From Eq. (1), we have $\Pr[\mathsf{Forge}] = \Pr[\mathsf{Forge}^*] + \mathsf{negl}(\lambda)$. Also, from the one-time unforgeability for BB84 states, we have $\Pr[\mathsf{Forge}^*] = \mathsf{negl}(\lambda)$. Thus, we obtain $\Pr[\mathsf{Forge}] = \mathsf{negl}(\lambda)$.

We define $\widehat{\mathcal{Z}}_\lambda^{\mathcal{B}}(b)$ as the experiment defined in the same way as $\widetilde{\mathcal{Z}}_\lambda^{\mathcal{B}}(b)$ except that the experiment outputs the register B if and only if $x_i = x_i'$ holds for all i such that $\theta_i = 0$. Since $\Pr[\mathsf{Forge}] = \mathsf{negl}(\lambda)$, if $\mathsf{Vrfy}(\mathsf{vk}, x', \sigma') = \top$ holds, then $x_i = x_i'$ holds for all i such that $\theta_i = 0$, except negligible probability. Thus, we have

$$\mathsf{TD}(\widetilde{\mathcal{Z}}_\lambda^{\mathcal{B}}(0), \widetilde{\mathcal{Z}}_\lambda^{\mathcal{B}}(1)) \leq \mathsf{TD}(\widehat{\mathcal{Z}}_\lambda^{\mathcal{B}}(0), \widehat{\mathcal{Z}}_\lambda^{\mathcal{B}}(1)) + \mathsf{negl}(\lambda).$$

From Eq. (2) and Lemma 4.1, we have $\mathsf{TD}(\widehat{\mathcal{Z}}_\lambda^{\mathcal{B}}(0), \widehat{\mathcal{Z}}_\lambda^{\mathcal{B}}(1)) = \mathsf{negl}(\lambda)$. This completes the proof.   □

5   Instantiations

We can apply Lemma 4.2 to various cryptographic primitives.

5.1   Public-Key Encryption

First, we show how to apply Lemma 4.2 to PKE and obtain PKE with PVD.

Definition. We define PKE with publicly verifiable deletion (PKE-PVD).

Definition 5.1 (PKE with Publicly Verifiable Deletion). *A PKE scheme with publicly verifiable deletion is a tuple of efficient algorithms* $\mathsf{PKE\text{-}PVD} = (\mathsf{Gen}, \mathcal{E}nc, \mathcal{D}ec, \mathcal{D}el, \mathsf{Vrfy})$.

$\mathsf{Gen}(1^\lambda) \to (\mathsf{pk}, \mathsf{sk})$**:** *The key generation algorithm takes the security parameter* 1^λ *as input and outputs a public key* pk *and a secret key* sk.
$\mathcal{E}nc(\mathsf{pk}, m) \to (\mathsf{vk}, \mathsf{ct})$**:** *The encryption algorithm takes* pk *and a plaintext* $m \in \{0, 1\}$ *as input, and outputs a verification key* vk *and a ciphertext* ct.

$\mathcal{Dec}(\mathsf{sk}, ct) \rightarrow m'$: *The decryption algorithm takes* sk *and* ct *as input, and outputs a plaintext* $m' \in \mathcal{M}$ *or* $\perp$.

$\mathcal{Del}(ct) \rightarrow$ cert: *The deletion algorithm takes* ct *as input and outputs a certification* cert.

$\mathsf{Vrfy}(\mathsf{vk}, \mathsf{cert}) \rightarrow \top$ *or* $\perp$: *The verification algorithm is a deterministic algorithm that takes* vk *and* cert *as input, and outputs* $\top$ *or* $\perp$.

Decryption Correctness: *For any* $m \in \mathcal{M}$, *we have*

$$\Pr\left[m' \neq m \; \middle| \; \begin{array}{l} (\mathsf{pk}, \mathsf{sk}) \leftarrow \mathsf{Gen}(1^\lambda) \\ (\mathsf{vk}, ct) \leftarrow \mathcal{Enc}(\mathsf{pk}, m) \\ m' \leftarrow \mathcal{Dec}(\mathsf{sk}, ct) \end{array} \right] \leq \mathsf{negl}(\lambda).$$

Verification Correctness: *For any* $m \in \mathcal{M}$, *we have*

$$\Pr\left[\mathsf{Vrfy}(\mathsf{vk}, \mathsf{cert}) = \perp \; \middle| \; \begin{array}{l} (\mathsf{pk}, \mathsf{sk}) \leftarrow \mathsf{Gen}(1^\lambda) \\ (\mathsf{vk}, ct) \leftarrow \mathcal{Enc}(\mathsf{pk}, m) \\ \mathsf{cert} \leftarrow \mathcal{Del}(ct) \end{array} \right] \leq \mathsf{negl}(\lambda).$$

Semantic Security: *For any QPT* $\mathcal{A}$, *we have*

$$\left| \Pr\left[\mathcal{A}(\mathsf{pk}, \mathsf{vk}, ct) = 1 \; \middle| \; \begin{array}{l} (\mathsf{pk}, \mathsf{sk}) \leftarrow \mathsf{Gen}(1^\lambda) \\ (\mathsf{vk}, ct) \leftarrow \mathcal{Enc}(\mathsf{pk}, 0) \end{array} \right] \right.$$

$$\left. - \Pr\left[\mathcal{A}(\mathsf{pk}, \mathsf{vk}, ct_1) = 1 \; \middle| \; \begin{array}{l} (\mathsf{pk}, \mathsf{sk}) \leftarrow \mathsf{Gen}(1^\lambda) \\ (\mathsf{vk}, ct) \leftarrow \mathcal{Enc}(\mathsf{pk}, 1) \end{array} \right] \right| = \mathsf{negl}(\lambda).$$

Definition 5.2 (Certified Deletion Security for PKE-PVD). *Let* $\mathsf{PKE} - PVD = (\mathsf{Gen}, \mathcal{Enc}, \mathcal{Dec}, \mathcal{Del}, \mathsf{Vrfy})$ *be a PKE-PVD scheme. We consider the following security experiment* $\mathsf{Exp}^{\mathsf{cert\text{-}del}}_{\mathsf{PKE\text{-}PVD}, \mathcal{A}}(\lambda, b)$ *against a QPT adversary* $\mathcal{A}$.

1. *The challenger computes* $(\mathsf{pk}, \mathsf{sk}) \leftarrow \mathsf{Gen}(1^\lambda)$, *and sends* pk *to* $\mathcal{A}$.
2. *The challenger computes* $(\mathsf{vk}, ct) \leftarrow \mathcal{Enc}(\mathsf{pk}, b)$, *and sends* vk *and* ct *to* $\mathcal{A}$.
3. *At some point,* $\mathcal{A}$ *sends* cert *and its internal state* ρ *to the challenger.*
4. *The challenger computes* $\mathsf{Vrfy}(\mathsf{vk}, \mathsf{cert})$. *If the outcome is* $\top$, *the challenger outputs* ρ *and otherwise outputs* $\perp$.

We say that PKE-PVD *satisfies certified deletion security if for any QPT* $\mathcal{A}$, *it holds that*

$$\mathsf{TD}(\mathsf{Exp}^{\mathsf{cert\text{-}del}}_{\mathsf{PKE\text{-}PVD}, \mathcal{A}}(\lambda, 0), \mathsf{Exp}^{\mathsf{cert\text{-}del}}_{\mathsf{PKE\text{-}PVD}, \mathcal{A}}(\lambda, 1)) \leq \mathsf{negl}(\lambda).$$

Remark 5.1. We define PKE-PVD and the certified deletion security for it as the plaintext space of PKE-PVD is $\{0, 1\}$ by default. We can generalize them into one for the plaintext space $\{0, 1\}^\ell$ for any polynomial ℓ. Also, such a multi-bit plaintext PKE-PVD can be constructed from a single-bit plaintext PKE-PVD by the standard hybrid argument.

Construction. We construct a PKE-PVD scheme PKE-PVD = (Gen, $\mathcal{E}nc$, $\mathcal{D}ec$, $\mathcal{D}el$, Vrfy) for the plaintext space $\{0,1\}$. The building blocks are as follows.

- A public-key encryption scheme PKE = PKE.(Gen, Enc, Dec).
- A deterministic signature SIG = SIG.(Gen, Sign, Vrfy).

Gen(1^λ):
- Output (pk, sk) $\leftarrow$ PKE.Gen(1^λ).

$\mathcal{E}nc$(pk, $m \in \{0,1\}$):
- Generate $x, \theta \leftarrow \{0,1\}^\lambda$ and generate (vk, sigk) $\leftarrow$ SIG.Gen(1^λ). Generate a quantum state $|\psi\rangle$ by applying the map $|\mu\rangle |0\ldots0\rangle \rightarrow |\mu\rangle |\text{SIG.Sign}(\text{sigk}, \mu)\rangle$ to $|x\rangle_\theta \otimes |0\ldots0\rangle$.
- Generate pke.ct $\leftarrow$ PKE.Enc(pk, (sigk, θ, $m \oplus \bigoplus_{i:\theta_i=1} x_i$)).
- Output vk and $ct := (|\psi\rangle, \text{pke.ct})$.

$\mathcal{D}ec$(sk, ct):
- Parse ct into a quantum states ρ and classical bit string pke.ct.
- Compute (sigk, θ, β) $\leftarrow$ PKE.Dec(sk, pke.ct).
- Apply the map $|\mu\rangle |0\ldots0\rangle \rightarrow |\mu\rangle |\text{SIG.Sign}(\text{sigk}, \mu)\rangle$ to ρ, measure the first λ qubits of the resulting state in Hadamard basis, and obtain $\bar{x}$.
- Output $m \leftarrow \beta \oplus \bigoplus_{i:\theta_i=1} \bar{x}_i$.

$\mathcal{D}el$(ct):
- Parse ct into a quantum state ρ and a classical string pke.ct.
- Measure ρ in the computational basis and obtain x' and σ'.
- Output (x', σ').

Vrfy(vk, cert):
- Parse $(z', \sigma') \leftarrow$ cert.
- Output the result of SIG.Vrfy(vk, z', σ').

We see that PKE-PVD satisfies decryption correctness and verification correctness if SIG and PKE satisfy their correctness notions. Also, the semantic security of PKE-PVD immediately follows from that of PKE. Also, we have the following theorem.

Theorem 5.1. *Assume* SIG *satisfies one-time unforgeability for BB84 states and* PKE *satisfies semantic security. Then,* PKE-PVD *satisfies certified deletion security.*

Proof. We define $\mathcal{Z}_\lambda$(vk, sigk, θ, β, A) be an efficient quantum process such that it generates (pk, sk) $\leftarrow$ Gen(1^λ) and outputs (pk, vk, Enc(pk, (sigk, θ, β))). Then, from the semantic security of PKE, for any QPT $\mathcal{A}$, key pair (vk, sk) of SIG, $\theta \in \{0,1\}^\lambda$, $\beta \in \{0,1\}$, and an efficiently samplable state $|\psi\rangle^{A,C}$ on registers A and C, we have

$$\left| \Pr[\mathcal{A}(\mathcal{Z}_\lambda(\text{vk}, \text{sigk}, \theta, \beta, A), C) = 1] - \Pr[\mathcal{A}(\mathcal{Z}_\lambda(\text{vk}, 0^{\ell_{\text{sigk}}}, \theta, \beta, A), C) = 1] \right| \leq \text{negl}(\lambda),$$

and

$$\left| \Pr[\mathcal{A}(\mathcal{Z}_\lambda(\text{vk}, \text{sigk}, \theta, \beta, A), C) = 1] - \Pr[\mathcal{A}(\mathcal{Z}_\lambda(\text{vk}, \text{sigk}, 0^\lambda, \beta, A), C) = 1] \right| \leq \text{negl}(\lambda).$$

Then, the certified deletion security of PKE-PVD follows from Lemma 4.2. $\square$

In Sect. 3, we show that a deterministic signature scheme with one-time unforgeability for BB84 states is implied by OWF that is implied by a PKE scheme. Thus, we obtain the following theorem.

Theorem 5.2. *Assume that there exists PKE. Then, there exists PKE-PVD.*

5.2   Other Primitives

By combining Lemma 4.2 with other types of primitives instead of PKE, we immediately obtain them with publicly verifiable deletion. That is, we instantiate $\mathcal{Z}_\lambda$ in Lemma 4.2 with these primitives. Formally, we have the following theorem.

Theorem 5.3. *If there exists*

$$Z' \in \{SKE,\ COM,\ PKE,\ ABE,\ QFHE,\ TRE\},$$

then, there exists Z' with publicly verifiable deletion. If there exist WE and one-way functions, then there exists WE with publicly verifiable deletion.

Remark 5.2. We additionally assume one-way functions for the case of WE since WE is unlikely to imply one-way functions while every one of SKE, COM, PKE, ABE, QFHE, and TRE implies them.

We omit the definitions of these primitives (with publicly verifiable deletion) and refer the reader to [8,9] for them.[10]

6   Making Assumptions Minimal

In Sect. 5, we show that $Z \in \{SKE, COM, PKE, ABE, QFHE, TRE, WE\}$ (and one-way functions in the case of $Z = WE$) imply Z with publicly verifiable deletion. However, Z with publicly verifiable deletion does not seem to imply either of plain (classical) Z or one-way functions in general. In this section, we explain how to weaken the assumptions to minimal ones implied by Z with publicly verifiable deletion.

First, we observe that our compiler works even if we start with primitive $Z \in \{SKE, COM, PKE, ABE, QFHE, TRE, WE\}$ that has quantum encryption and decryption (or committing) algorithms. Second, we observe our compiler works even if the underlying digital signature scheme has a quantum key generation algorithm since the quantum encryption algorithm runs it. Moreover, such a digital signature scheme with a quantum key generation algorithm that satisfies one-time security for BB84 states can be constructed from hard quantum planted problems for NP defined below.

---

[10] The definitions in [8] only consider privately verifiable deletion, but it is straightforward to extend them to ones with publicly verifiable deletion.

Definition 6.1 (Hard Quantum Planted Problem for NP). *A quantum polynomial-time algorithm $\mathcal{G}$ is a sampler for an NP relation $\mathcal{R} \subseteq \{0,1\}^* \times \{0,1\}^*$ if, for every n, $\mathcal{G}(1^n)$ outputs a pair (x,w) such that $(x,w) \in \mathcal{R}$ with probability 1. We say that the quantum planted problem corresponding to $(\mathcal{G}, \mathcal{R})$ is hard if, for every QPT $\mathcal{A}$, it holds that*

$$\Pr[(x, \mathcal{A}(x)) \in \mathcal{R} \mid (x,w) \leftarrow \mathcal{G}(1^n)] \leq \mathsf{negl}(n).$$

It is clear that the construction in Sect. 3 works using hard quantum planted problems for NP instead of one-way functions where input-output pairs of the one-way function are replaced with witness-instance pairs of the NP problem if we allow the key generation algorithm of the signature scheme to be quantum. Combining the above observations, we obtain the following theorem.

Theorem 6.1. *Assume that there exists*

$$Z \in \{SKE,\ COM,\ PKE,\ ABE,\ QFHE,\ TRE,\ WE\}$$

with quantum encryption and decryption (or committing) algorithms and hard quantum planted problems for NP. Then, there exists Z with publicly verifiable deletion.

The assumption in the above theorem is minimal since

1. Z with quantum encryption and decryption (or committing) algorithms is immediately implied by Z with publicly verifiable deletion by simply ignoring the deletion and verification algorithms, and
2. Hard quantum planted problems for NP are implied by Z with publicly verifiable deletion by regarding the verification key and certificate as instance and certificate, respectively.

Remark 6.1. In the second item above, we assume that the verification algorithm of Z with publicly verifiable deletion is a classical deterministic algorithm. If it is allowed to be a quantum algorithm, we need to consider hard quantum planted problems for QCMA instead of NP. The construction in Sect. 3 works with such problems if we allow the verification algorithm to be quantum. Thus, the minimality of the assumption holds in this setting as well.

References

1. Aaronson, S., Liu, J., Liu, Q., Zhandry, M., Zhang, R.: New approaches for quantum copy-protection. In: Malkin, T., Peikert, C. (eds.) CRYPTO 2021, Part I. LNCS, vol. 12825, pp. 526–555. Springer, Cham (2021). https://doi.org/10.1007/978-3-030-84242-0_19
2. Agrawal, S., Kitagawa, F., Nishimaki, R., Yamada, S., Yamakawa, T.: Public key encryption with secure key leasing. IACR Cryptol. ePrint Arch., p. 264 (2023). https://eprint.iacr.org/2023/264, eurocrypt 2023 (to appear)

3. Amos, R., Georgiou, M., Kiayias, A., Zhandry, M.: One-shot signatures and applications to hybrid quantum/classical authentication. In: Makarychev, K., Makarychev, Y., Tulsiani, M., Kamath, G., Chuzhoy, J. (eds.) 52nd ACM STOC, pp. 255–268. ACM Press, June 2020. https://doi.org/10.1145/3357713.3384304

4. Ananth, P., La Placa, R.L.: Secure software leasing. In: Canteaut, A., Standaert, F.-X. (eds.) EUROCRYPT 2021, Part II. LNCS, vol. 12697, pp. 501–530. Springer, Cham (2021). https://doi.org/10.1007/978-3-030-77886-6_17

5. Ananth, P., Poremba, A., Vaikuntanathan, V.: Revocable cryptography from learning with errors. Cryptology ePrint Archive, Report 2023/325 (2023). https://eprint.iacr.org/2023/325

6. Barak, B., et al.: On the (im)possibility of obfuscating programs. J. ACM **59**(2), 6:1–6:48 (2012)

7. Bartusek, J., et al.: Obfuscation and outsourced computation with certified deletion. Cryptology ePrint Archive, Report 2023/265 (2023). https://eprint.iacr.org/2023/265

8. Bartusek, J., Khurana, D.: Cryptography with certified deletion. Cryptology ePrint Archive, Report 2022/1178 (2022). https://eprint.iacr.org/2022/1178

9. Bartusek, J., Khurana, D., Poremba, A.: Publicly-verifiable deletion via target-collapsing functions. IACR Cryptol. ePrint Arch. p. 370 (2023). https://eprint.iacr.org/2023/370

10. Broadbent, A., Islam, R.: Quantum encryption with certified deletion. In: Pass, R., Pietrzak, K. (eds.) TCC 2020, Part III. LNCS, vol. 12552, pp. 92–122. Springer, Cham (2020). https://doi.org/10.1007/978-3-030-64381-2_4

11. Broadbent, A., Jeffery, S., Lord, S., Podder, S., Sundaram, A.: Secure software leasing without assumptions. In: Nissim, K., Waters, B. (eds.) TCC 2021, Part I. LNCS, vol. 13042, pp. 90–120. Springer, Cham (2021). https://doi.org/10.1007/978-3-030-90459-3_4

12. Coladangelo, A., Liu, J., Liu, Q., Zhandry, M.: Hidden Cosets and applications to unclonable cryptography. In: Malkin, T., Peikert, C. (eds.) CRYPTO 2021, Part I. LNCS, vol. 12825, pp. 556–584. Springer, Cham (2021). https://doi.org/10.1007/978-3-030-84242-0_20

13. Coladangelo, A., Majenz, C., Poremba, A.: Quantum copy-protection of compute-and-compare programs in the quantum random oracle model. Cryptology ePrint Archive, Report 2020/1194 (2020). https://eprint.iacr.org/2020/1194

14. Goldwasser, S., Kalai, Y.T., Popa, R.A., Vaikuntanathan, V., Zeldovich, N.: How to run turing machines on encrypted data. In: Canetti, R., Garay, J.A. (eds.) CRYPTO 2013, Part II. LNCS, vol. 8043, pp. 536–553. Springer, Heidelberg (2013). https://doi.org/10.1007/978-3-642-40084-1_30

15. Hhan, M., Morimae, T., Yamakawa, T.: From the hardness of detecting superpositions to cryptography: quantum public key encryption and commitments. Cryptology ePrint Archive, Report 2022/1375 (2022). https://eprint.iacr.org/2022/1375

16. Hiroka, T., Kitagawa, F., Morimae, T., Nishimaki, R., Pal, T., Yamakawa, T.: Certified everlasting secure collusion-resistant functional encryption, and more. Cryptology ePrint Archive, Report 2023/236 (2023). https://eprint.iacr.org/2023/236

17. Hiroka, T., Morimae, T., Nishimaki, R., Yamakawa, T.: Quantum encryption with certified deletion, revisited: public key, attribute-based, and classical communication. In: Tibouchi, M., Wang, H. (eds.) ASIACRYPT 2021, Part I. LNCS, vol. 13090, pp. 606–636. Springer, Cham (2021). https://doi.org/10.1007/978-3-030-92062-3_21

18. Hiroka, T., Morimae, T., Nishimaki, R., Yamakawa, T.: Certified everlasting zero-knowledge proof for QMA. In: Dodis, Y., Shrimpton, T. (eds.) CRYPTO 2022, Part I. LNCS, vol. 13507, pp. 239–268. Springer, Heidelberg (2022). https://doi.org/10.1007/978-3-031-15802-5_9
19. Kitagawa, F., Nishimaki, R.: Functional encryption with secure key leasing. In: Agrawal, S., Lin, D. (eds.) ASIACRYPT 2022, Part IV. LNCS, vol. 13794, pp. 569–598. Springer, Heidelberg (2022). https://doi.org/10.1007/978-3-031-22972-5_20
20. Kitagawa, F., Nishimaki, R., Yamakawa, T.: Secure software leasing from standard assumptions. In: Nissim, K., Waters, B. (eds.) TCC 2021, Part I. LNCS, vol. 13042, pp. 31–61. Springer, Cham (2021). https://doi.org/10.1007/978-3-030-90459-3_2
21. Lamport, L.: Constructing digital signatures from a one-way function. Technical report SRI-CSL-98, SRI International Computer Science Laboratory, October 1979
22. Müller-Quade, J., Unruh, D.: Long-term security and universal composability. J. Cryptol. 23(4), 594–671 (2010). https://doi.org/10.1007/s00145-010-9068-8
23. Poremba, A.: Quantum proofs of deletion for learning with errors. In: Kalai, Y.T. (ed.) 14th Innovations in Theoretical Computer Science Conference, ITCS 2023, 10–13 January 2023. LIPIcs, vol. 251, pp. 90:1–90:14, MIT. Cambridge. Schloss Dagstuhl - Leibniz-Zentrum für Informatik (2023). https://doi.org/10.4230/LIPIcs.ITCS.2023.90
24. Unruh, D.: Revocable quantum timed-release encryption. J. ACM 62(6), 49:1–49:76 (2015)

One-Out-of-Many Unclonable Cryptography: Definitions, Constructions, and More

Fuyuki Kitagawa$^{(\boxtimes)}$ and Ryo Nishimaki

NTT Social Informatics Laboratories, Tokyo, Japan
{fuyuki.kitagawa,ryo.nishimaki}@ntt.com

Abstract. The no-cloning principle of quantum mechanics enables us to achieve amazing unclonable cryptographic primitives, which is impossible in classical cryptography. However, the security definitions for unclonable cryptography are tricky. Achieving desirable security notions for unclonability is a challenging task. In particular, there is no indistinguishable-secure unclonable encryption and quantum copy-protection for single-bit output point functions in the standard model. To tackle this problem, we introduce and study relaxed but meaningful security notions for unclonable cryptography in this work. We call the new security notion *one-out-of-many* unclonable security.

We obtain the following results.
- We show that one-time strong anti-piracy secure secret key single-decryptor encryption (SDE) implies one-out-of-many indistinguishable-secure unclonable encryption.
- We construct a one-time strong anti-piracy secure secret key SDE scheme in the standard model from the LWE assumption. This scheme can encrypt multi-bit messages.
- We construct one-out-of-many copy-protection for single-bit output point functions from one-out-of-many indistinguishable-secure unclonable encryption and the LWE assumption.
- We construct one-out-of-many unclonable predicate encryption (PE) from one-out-of-many indistinguishable-secure unclonable encryption and the LWE assumption.

Thus, we obtain one-out-of-many indistinguishable-secure unclonable encryption, one-out-of-many copy-protection for single-bit output point functions, and one-out-of-many unclonable PE in the standard model from the LWE assumption. In addition, our one-time SDE scheme is the first multi-bit SDE scheme that does not rely on any oracle heuristics and strong assumptions such as indistinguishability obfuscation and witness encryption.

1 Introduction

1.1 Background

Unclonable Encryption and Quantum Copy-Protection. Quantum information enables us to achieve new cryptographic primitives beyond classical cryptography. Especially the no-cloning principle of quantum information has given

© International Association for Cryptologic Research 2023
G. Rothblum and H. Wee (Eds.): TCC 2023, LNCS 14372, pp. 246–275, 2023.
https://doi.org/10.1007/978-3-031-48624-1_10

rise to amazing unclonable cryptographic primitives. This includes quantum money [28], quantum copy-protection [1], unclonable encryption [12], one-shot signatures [3], single-decryptor encryption [13,17], and many more. In this work, we mainly focus on unclonable encryption and quantum copy-protection.

Broadbent and Lord [12] introduced unclonable encryption. Unclonable encryption is a one-time secure secret key encryption where a plaintext is encoded into a quantum ciphertext that is impossible to clone. More specifically, an unclonable encryption scheme encrypts a plaintext m into a quantum ciphertext ct. The user who has the secret key can recover m from ct. The security notion of unclonable encryption ensures that it is impossible to convert ct into possibly entangled bipartite states ct_1 and ct_2, both of which can be used to recover m when the secret key is given. Ananth and Kaleoglu [4] later introduced unclonable public key encryption. Unclonable encryption has interesting applications, such as preventing cloud storage attacks where an adversary steals ciphertexts from cloud storage with the hope that they can be decrypted if the secret key is leaked later.

Quantum copy-protection [1] is a cryptographic primitive that prevents users from creating pirated copies of a program. More specifically, a quantum copy-protection scheme transforms a classical program C into a quantum program ρ that is impossible to copy. We can compute $C(x)$ for any input x using ρ. The security notion of copy-protection ensures that it is impossible to convert ρ into possibly entangled bipartite states ρ_1 and ρ_2, both of which can be used to compute C. As shown by Ananth and La Placa [8], it is impossible to have quantum copy-protection for general unlearnable functions. For this reason, recent works have been studying quantum copy-protection for a simple class of functions such as point functions [4-6,14].[1] Moreover, Coladangelo, Majenz, and Poremba [14] show that quantum copy-protection for point functions can be transformed into quantum copy-protection for a more general class of compute-and-compare programs (C&C programs) that includes conjunctions with wildcards, affine testers, plaintext testers, and so on. We focus on quantum copy-protection for point functions in this work.

Definition of Unclonability: One-Wayness and Indistinguishability. To describe our research questions and contributions, we first explain a general template for unclonable security games played by a tuple of three adversaries $(\mathcal{A}_0, \mathcal{A}_1, \mathcal{A}_2)$. The template is common to unclonable encryption and quantum copy-protection. In the first stage, the challenger sends a challenge copy-protected object (such as a quantum ciphertext in unclonable encryption and copy-protected program in quantum copy-protection) to an adversary $\mathcal{A}_0$. Then, $\mathcal{A}_0$ generates possibly

---

[1]   Some lines of works [13,22] studied quantum copy-protection for cryptographic functionalities that are not captured by C&C programs. Quantum copy-protections for cryptographic functionalities have different names, such as unclonable decryption or single decryptor encryption. In this work, unless stated otherwise, we use the term quantum copy-protection to indicate quantum copy-protection for point functions. For the previous works on quantum copy-protection for cryptographic functionalities, see Sect. 1.5.

entangled bipartite states ρ_1 and ρ_2 and sends ρ_α to $\mathcal{A}_\alpha$ for $\alpha \in \{1,2\}$. In the second phase, the challenger sends extra information (such as secret keys in unclonable encryption and some inputs for the program in quantum copy-protection) to $\mathcal{A}_1$ and $\mathcal{A}_2$, and they try to compute target information about the copy-protected object (such as plaintexts in unclonable encryption and computation results on the given inputs in quantum copy-protection). Here, $\mathcal{A}_1$ and $\mathcal{A}_2$ are not allowed to communicate. If both $\mathcal{A}_1$ and $\mathcal{A}_2$ succeed in computing target information, the adversaries win. Note that if $\mathcal{A}_\alpha$ has the original objects, computing target information is easy.

Using the above game, we can define both one-wayness-based notion and indistinguishability-based notion depending on which one the task of $\mathcal{A}_1$ and $\mathcal{A}_2$ is, recovering entire bits of high min-entropy information or detecting 1-bit information. Similarly to standard security notions, indistinguishability-based one is more general and enables us to have a wide range of applications. Also, indistinguishability-based unclonability usually implies standard cryptographic security notions, but one-wayness-based unclonability does not necessarily imply them.[2] In this work, we focus on indistinguishability-based unclonability notions.

Toward Indistinguishability-Based Unclonability in the Standard Model. Unclonable encryption and quantum copy-protection have been studied actively and there are many constructions. Although we have constructions with one-wayness-based unclonability from standard assumptions in the standard model [4,12], we have constructions with indistinguishability-based unclonability *only in the oracle model*, in both unclonable encryption and quantum copy-protection [6]. Ananth, Kaleoglu, Li, Liu, and Zhandry [6] proposed the only indistinguishability-based secure unclonable encryption and quantum copy-protection schemes. Their proof technique is highly specific to the oracle model. Thus, it still remains elusive to achieve unclonable encryption and quantum copy-protection with indistinguishability-based unclonability in the standard model.

Given the above situation, it is natural and reasonable to explore relaxed but meaningful indistinguishability-based unclonability and ask whether the notion can be achieved in the standard model. Such a standard model construction with a relaxed notion would provide new insights toward achieving full-fledged indistinguishability-based unclonability in the standard model.

1.2   Our Result

Our contributions are proposing new definitions for unclonability and constructions satisfying them under the LWE assumption in the standard model.

New Definitions: One-Out-of-Many Unclonability Notions. We introduce a relaxed indistinguishability-based unclonability for unclonable encryption and

---

[2] For example, indistinguishability-based unclonability for unclonable encryption implies (one-time) IND-CPA security, but one-wayness-based unclonability does not.

copy-protection, called *one-out-of-many* unclonable security. This notion captures a meaningful unclonability, as we argue below. It guarantees that no adversary can generate n copies with probability significantly better than $\frac{1}{n}$ for any n. Thus, roughly speaking, it guarantees that the expected number of successful target objects generated by any copying adversary is not noticeably more than 1. We define one-out-of-many unclonability by extending the unclonable game played by a tuple of three adversaries into a game played by $n + 1$ adversaries, where $n \geq 2$ is arbitrary.

Although one-out-of-many unclonable security looks weaker than existing unclonable security, it is useful in some applications. For example, suppose we publish many quantum objects, say ℓ objects. Then, one-out-of-many security guarantees that no matter what copying attacks are applied to those objects, there are expected to be only ℓ objects on average in this world. Another nice property of one-out-of-many security is that it implies standard cryptographic security notions. For example, one-out-of-many unclonability for unclonable encryption implies (one-time) IND-CPA security. This result contrasts one-wayness-based unclonability notions that do not necessarily imply standard indistinguishability notions.

Unclonable Encryption in the Standard Model via Single Decryptor Encryption. We provide unclonable encryption satisfying one-out-of-many unclonability under the LWE assumption in the standard model. We obtain this result as follows.

We first define one-out-of-many unclonability for (one-time) single decryptor encryption (SDE) [13,17]. One-time SDE is a dual of unclonable encryption in the sense that one-time SDE is a one-time secret key encryption scheme where a secret key is encoded into a quantum state, and its security notion guarantees that any adversary cannot copy the quantum secret key. Under appropriate definitions, it is possible to go back and forth between unclonable encryption and one-time SDE, as shown by Georgiou and Zhandry [17]. We show that we can transform any one-time SDE with one-out-of-many unclonability to unclonable encryption with one-out-of-many unclonability.

We then show that we can obtain one-time SDE with one-out-of-many unclonability from the LWE assumption. More specifically, assuming the LWE assumption, we construct one-time SDE satisfying strong anti-piracy introduced by Coladangelo, Liu, Liu, and Zhandry [13], and show that strong anti-piracy implies one-out-of-many unclonability. Combining this result with the above transformation, we obtain unclonable encryption with one-out-of-many security under the LWE assumption.

Theorem 1 (informal). *Assuming the LWE assumption holds, there exists strong anti-piracy secure one-time SDE for multi-bit messages.*

Theorem 2 (informal). *Assuming the LWE assumption holds, there exists one-out-of-many indistinguishable-secure unclonable encryption.*

To achieve one-time SDE satisfying strong anti-piracy, we develop a technique enabling us to use a BB84 [10] state as a copy-protected secret key. Our crucial tool is single-key ciphertext-policy functional encryption (CPFE) with a succinct key, which we introduce in this work. We instantiate it with hash encryption (HE) [16] implied by the LWE assumption. The technique of the post-quantum watermarking by Kitagawa and Nishimaki [21] inspired our proof technique. We emphasize that *our one-time SDE scheme is the first SDE scheme that does not require either oracle heuristic or strong assumptions such as indistinguishability obfuscation and witness encryption.*

Quantum Copy-Protection in the Standard Model via Unclonable Encryption. We propose quantum copy protection for single-bit output point functions based on unclonable encryption and the LWE assumption. Known constructions from unclonable encryption [4,14] support only multi-bit output point functions.[3] Although we formally prove this result with our new one-out-of-many security notion, our construction also works under standard indistinguishability-based unclonability definitions defined using three adversaries $(\mathcal{A}_0, \mathcal{A}_1, \mathcal{A}_2)$.

Theorem 3 (informal). *Assuming (resp. one-out-of-many) indistinguishable-secure unclonable encryption and the LWE assumption holds, there exits (resp. one-out-of-many) copy-protection for single-bit output point functions.*

Unclonable Predicate Encryption. Using the technique proposed by Ananth and Kaleoglu [4], we can convert our one-out-of-many secure unclonable encryption into one-out-of-many secure unclonable public-key encryption. We construct a one-out-of-many unclonable predicate encryption (PE) scheme from one-out-of-many unclonable encryption and the LWE assumption. PE is a stronger variant of attribute-based encryption (ABE). ABE is an advanced public-key encryption system where we can generate a user secret key for an attribute x and a ciphertext of a message m under a policy P.[4] We can decrypt a ciphertext and obtain m if $P(x) = 1$. In PE, ciphertexts hide not only plaintexts but also policies.

Theorem 4 (informal). *Assuming (resp. one-out-of-many) indistinguishable-secure unclonable encryption and the LWE assumption, there exists (resp. one-out-of-many) unclonable PE.*

1.3 Concurrent and Independent Work

Ananth, Kaleoglu, and Liu [7] introduce a new framework called cloning games to study unclonable cryptography. They obtain many implications to unclonable

---

[3] One might think that copy protection for multi-bit output point functions implies that for single-bit output point functions. However, this is not the case. This is because the security of copy protection for multi-bit output point functions usually relies on the high min-entropy of the multi-bit output string, and it is broken if the output string does not have enough entropy as in the case of single-bit output. Realizing copy protection for single-bit output point function is challenging in the sense that we have to achieve the security without relying on the entropy of the output string.

[4] We focus on ciphertext-policy ABE in this work.

cryptography thanks to the framework. In particular, they obtain information-theoretically secure one-time SDE in the standard model. The scheme is *single-bit* encryption while our computationally secure scheme is multi-bit encryption. *Note that we do not know how to obtain multi-bit encryption from single-bit one via parallel repetition and the standard hybrid argument in unclonable cryptography.* Thus, their results on SDE is incomparable with ours. We also note that it is not clear whether we can obtain one-out-of-many indistinguishable-secure unclonable encryption from their SDE, since it seems that we need strong anti-piracy secure one-time SDE to obtain one-out-of-many secure one, but their scheme is only proved to satisfy (non-strong) indistinguishability-based security. For the detailed reason on the need of strong anti-piracy for the implication, see the "SDE from LWE" paragraph in Sect. 1.4.

1.4 Technical Overview

We provide a high-level overview of our techniques in this subsection. In this paper, standard math or sans serif font stands for classical algorithms and classical variables. The calligraphic font stands for quantum algorithms and the calligraphic font and/or the bracket notation for (mixed) quantum states.

Relaxed definition of Unclonable Cryptography. We introduce relaxed security notions for unclonable cryptography called *one-out-of-many* unclonable security that roughly guarantees that no adversary can generate n copies with a probability significantly better than $\frac{1}{n}$ for any n. The one-out-of-many unclonability is defined by extending the unclonable game played by $(\mathcal{A}_0, \mathcal{A}_1, \mathcal{A}_2)$ explained in Sect. 1.1. The one-out-of-many unclonability game is played by a tuple of $n + 1$ adversaries $(\mathcal{A}_0, \mathcal{A}_1, \cdots, \mathcal{A}_n)$, where n is arbitrary. At the first stage of the game, $\mathcal{A}_0$ is given a single quantum object, generates possibly entangled n-partite states $\rho_1, \ldots, \rho_n$, and sends ρ_k to $\mathcal{A}_k$ for $k \in \{1, \ldots, n\}$. At the second stage, the challenger selects one of $(\mathcal{A}_1, \ldots, \mathcal{A}_n)$ by a random $\alpha \leftarrow \{1, \ldots, n\}$ and sends additional information *only to* $\mathcal{A}_\alpha$, and only $\mathcal{A}_\alpha$ tries to detect the target 1-bit information. Recall that we focus on indistinguishability-based setting. The one-out-of-many unclonability guarantees that the adversary cannot win this game with probability significantly better than the trivial winning probability $\frac{1}{n} \cdot 1 + \frac{n-1}{n} \cdot \frac{1}{2} = \frac{1}{2} + \frac{1}{2n}$. The definition captures the above intuition because if $\mathcal{A}_0$ could make n copies with probability $\frac{1}{n} + \delta$ for some noticeable δ, the adversary would win the game with probability at least $(\frac{1}{n} + \delta) \cdot 1 + (1 - \frac{1}{n} - \delta) \cdot \frac{1}{2} = \frac{1}{2} + \frac{1}{2n} + \frac{\delta}{2}$. See Remark 3 for more discussion.

We consider one-out-of-many unclonable security for the following security notions in this work: (1) (one-time) unclonable-indistinguishable security for unclonable encryption, (2) copy-protection security for single-bit output point functions, (3) (one-time) indistinguishability-based security for one-time SDE, (4) unclonable-simulation security for PE, which is introduced in this work.

The nice property of one-out-of-many security are as follows. One-out-of-many security implies standard cryptographic security notions. For example, one-out-of-many unclonability for unclonable encryption implies (one-time) IND-CPA security, and one for copy-protection implies distributional indistinguishability as virtual black-box obfuscation. Moreover, we can use one-out-of-many secure unclonable cryptographic primitives as a drop-in-replacement of standard indistinguishability-based unclonable cryptographic primitives if our goal is constructing a one-out-of-many secure unclonable cryptographic primitive (and vice versa). For example, the transformation from unclonable encryption to unclonable public-key encryption proposed by Ananth and Kaleoglu [4] works also in the one-out-of-many setting. Moreover, all of the generic constructions from an unclonable primitive to another unclonable primitive that we propose work in both the standard (three adversary style) setting and the one-out-of-many setting.

In addition to the above nice properties, we can prove that *one-out-of-many indistinguishability-based secure one-time SDE is equivalent to one-out-of-many unclonable-indistinguishable secure unclonable encryption*. In this work, we first obtain one-out-of-many indistinguishability-based secure one-time SDE from the LWE assumption, and using this equivalence, we obtain one-out-of-many secure unclonable encryption, copy protection for single-bit output point functions, and unclonable PE.

Before our work, Georgiou and Zhandry [17] showed a transformation from one-time SDE to unclonable encryption under the standard three adversary style setting. Informed readers may think that by combining their result with the result by Coladangelo et al. [13] (and the result by Culf and Vidick [15]), we can obtain indistinguishability-based unclonable encryption in the standard model based on indistinguishability obfuscation. However, this is not the case due to the fact that those two works used different definitions of the indistinguishability-based security for SDE, and we do not know any relation between them. For more details, see Remark 2.

SDE from LWE. We next explain how to obtain one-out-of-many indistinguishability-based secure one-time SDE. In fact, we obtain one-time SDE satisfying much stronger security notion called strong anti-piracy [13] from the LWE assumption, and prove that *strong anti-piracy implies one-out-of-many indistinguishability-based security*. Below, we first introduce the definition of strong anti-piracy for one-time SDE, briefly explain the intuition of the implication, and finally present the high level ideas on how to realize strong anti-piracy secure one-time SDE from the LWE assumption.

Recall the general template of the security game for unclonability played by three adversaries $(\mathcal{A}_0, \mathcal{A}_1, \mathcal{A}_2)$ explained in Sect. 1.1. This template also captures the security game of strong anti-piracy for SDE. In strong anti-piracy security for SDE, $\mathcal{A}_0$ receives a copy-protected decryption key $\tilde{dk}$ in the first stage. In the second stage, $\mathcal{A}_1$ and $\mathcal{A}_2$ outputs quantum decryptors $\mathcal{D}_1$ and $\mathcal{D}_2$, respectively, and the challenger tests whether both $\mathcal{D}_1$ and $\mathcal{D}_2$ are "good" (or "live") quantum decryptors [13,30]. Intuitively, good quantum decryptors can distinguish encryption of m_0 from that of m_1 with probability $\frac{1}{2} + \frac{1}{\text{poly}(\lambda)}$, and do not lose the decryption capability even after its goodness was tested. Strong anti-piracy guarantees that the probability that both $\mathcal{D}_1$ and $\mathcal{D}_2$ are tested as good is negligible. See Definition 4 for the precise definition.

The intuition behind the implication from strong anti-piracy to one-out-of-many security is as follows. The one-out-of-many security game for a one-time SDE scheme played by a tuple of $n + 1$ adversaries $(\mathcal{A}_0, \cdots, \mathcal{A}_n)$ is defined as follows. In the first stage, $\mathcal{A}_0$ is given a quantum decryption key dk, generates possibly entangled n-partite states $\rho_1, \cdots \rho_n$, and sends ρ_k to the second stage adversary $\mathcal{A}_k$ for every $k \in \{1, \cdots, n\}$. In the second stage, only randomly chosen single second stage adversary $\mathcal{A}_\alpha$ is given the challenge ciphertext and required to guess the challenge bit. The n-partite state $(\rho_1, \cdots, \rho_n)$ generated by $\mathcal{A}_0$ can be regarded as a tuple of n quantum decryptors. If the one-time SDE scheme is strong anti-piracy secure, all n quantum decryptors *except one* must have success probabilities at most $1/2 + \mathsf{negl}(\lambda)$. Hence, the success probability of $(\mathcal{A}_0, \cdots, \mathcal{A}_{n+1})$ in the one-out-of-many security game is at most $1/n \cdot 1 + (n-1)/n \cdot (1/2 + \mathsf{negl}(\lambda)) = 1/2 + 1/2n + \mathsf{negl}(\lambda)$, which proves the one-out-of-many security. It seems that "strong" anti piracy is required for this argument and it is difficult to prove a similar implication from (non-strong) indistinguishability-based security defined by Coladangelo et al. [13]. To formally prove the implication, we have to construct a reduction algorithm that finds two "good" decryptors from n decryptors output by $\mathcal{A}$. If the reduction attacks strong anti-piracy, it is sufficient to randomly pick two decryptors out of n since the reduction's goal is to output two "good" decryptors with inverse polynomial probability. However, if the reduction attacks (non-strong) indistinguishability-based security, the reduction cannot use such random guessing and needs to detect whether each decryptor is "good" since the reduction's goal is to make a distinguishing gap. We are considering the one-time setting where the adversaries are not given the encryption key. Thus, it seems difficult to perform such detection of "good" decryptors.

We next explain how to achieve strong anti-piracy secure one-time SDE based on the LWE assumption in the standard model. We use the monogamy of entanglement property of BB84 states [26] differently from the previous work on SDE [13] that used the monogamy of entanglement property of coset states.

We combine BB84 states and ciphertext-policy FE with succinct key to achieve strong anti-piracy. We first explain the definition of single-key CPFE. A single-key CPFE scheme CPFE consists of three algorithms $(\mathsf{FE.Setup}, \mathsf{FE.Enc}, \mathsf{FE.Dec})$. $\mathsf{FE.Setup}$ takes as input a string x and outputs a public key pk and a decryption key sk_x.[5] Here, we assume that x itself works as a decryption key sk_x for x, thus $\mathsf{FE.Setup}$ outputs only pk. We can achieve such a CPFE (we will explain later). $\mathsf{FE.Enc}$ takes as input pk and a circuit C, and outputs a ciphertext ct. We can decrypt ct with sk_x using $\mathsf{FE.Dec}$, and obtain $C(x)$. The single-key security of CPFE guarantees that $\mathsf{FE.Enc}(\mathsf{pk}, C_0)$ and $\mathsf{FE.Enc}(\mathsf{pk}, C_1)$ are computationally indistinguishable for an adversary who has a decryption key sk_x for x of its choice as long as $C_0(x) = C_1(x)$ holds.

---

[5] We omit the security parameter for simplicity in this overview. The same is applied to other cryptographic primitives.

Let $s[i]$ is the i-th bit of a string $s \in \{0,1\}^n$. Our one-time SDE scheme is as follows. The key generation algorithm generate a BB84 state $|x^\theta\rangle :=$ $H^{\theta[1]}|x[1]\rangle \otimes \cdots \otimes H^{\theta[n]}|x[n]\rangle$, where H is the Hadamard gate, and a public key pk $\leftarrow$ FE.Setup(x) of CPFE. It outputs an encryption key ek $:= (\theta, \text{pk})$ and decryption key $dk := |x^\theta\rangle$. Note that although our one-time SDE scheme is secret key encryption, an encryption key and a decryption key are different. The encryption algorithm takes as input the encryption key and a plaintext m, and generates a ciphertext fe.ct $\leftarrow$ FE.Enc$(\text{pk}, C[\text{m}])$, where $C[\text{m}]$ is a constant circuit that outputs m for all inputs. It outputs a ciphertext $(\theta, \text{fe.ct})$. We can decrypt fe.ct and obtain m by recovering x from $|x^\theta\rangle$ and θ since x works as a decryption key of CPFE as we assumed. Intuitively, it is hard to copy $dk = |x^\theta\rangle$ by the monogamy of entanglement property. The monogamy of entanglement property can be explained by the template of unclonable cryptography. In the first stage, $\mathcal{A}_0$ is given $|x^\theta\rangle$. In the second stage, $\mathcal{A}_1$ and $\mathcal{A}_2$ receive θ and try to output x. It is proved that the winning probability of the adversaries is exponentially small without any assumptions [26].

To prove the strong anti-piracy security, we need to extract x both from good decryptors $\mathcal{D}_1$ and $\mathcal{D}_2$ respectively output by $\mathcal{A}_1$ and $\mathcal{A}_2$ to reduce the SDE security to the monogamy of entanglement property. The idea for the extraction is as follows. Let $\widetilde{C}[b, \text{m}_0, \text{m}_1, i]$ be a circuit that takes as input x and outputs $\text{m}_{b \oplus x[i]}$. We estimate the probability that a good decryptor outputs the correct b when we feed FE.Enc$(\text{pk}, \widetilde{C}[b, \text{m}_0, \text{m}_1, i])$ to it. The security of CPFE guarantees that FE.Enc$(\text{pk}, \widetilde{C}[b, \text{m}_0, \text{m}_1, i])$ is indistinguishable from FE.Enc$(\text{pk}, C[\text{m}_{b \oplus x[i]}])$ since $\widetilde{C}[b, \text{m}_0, \text{m}_1, i](x) = \text{m}_{b \oplus x[i]} = C[\text{m}_{b \oplus x[i]}](x)$. Hence, we can analyze the probability as follows.

- If $x[i] = 0$, the distinguishing probability should be greater than $\frac{1}{2}$ since a good decryptor receives FE.Enc$(\text{pk}, C[\text{m}_b])$ in its view and correctly guesses b with probability $\frac{1}{2} + \frac{1}{\text{poly}(\lambda)}$.
- If $x[i] = 1$, the distinguishing probability should be smaller than $\frac{1}{2}$ since a good decryptor receives FE.Enc$(\text{pk}, C[\text{m}_{1 \oplus b}])$ in its view and outputs the flipped bit $1 \oplus b$ with probability $\frac{1}{2} + \frac{1}{\text{poly}(\lambda)}$.

This means that we can decide $x[i] = 0$ or $x[i] = 1$ by estimating the success probability of a good decryptor that receives FE.Enc$(\text{pk}, \widetilde{C}[b, \text{m}_0, \text{m}_1, i])$. Thus, we can extract x from good decryptors. This extraction technique is based on the post-quantum watermarking extraction technique by Kitagawa and Nishimaki [21]. Hence, the extraction succeeds without collapsing good quantum decryptors $\mathcal{D}_1$ and $\mathcal{D}_2$. See Sect. 4 for the detail.

There is one subtle issue in the argument above. Since pk depends on x, we need leakage information about x to simulate pk in the reduction. More specifically, let Leak$(\cdot)$ be a leakage function and the reduction needs Leak(x) to simulate pk of CPFE. We can consider such a leakage variant of the monogamy of entanglement game, where $\mathcal{A}_0$ receives $|x^\theta\rangle$ and Leak(x) in the first stage. The variant holds if $|\text{Leak}(x)| = \lambda$ that is short enough compared to $n = |x|$ since we can simply guess Leak(x) with probability $\frac{1}{2^\lambda}$. Although the bound is degraded to $\frac{2^\lambda}{\exp(n)}$, it is still negligible by setting n appropriately. Hence, we use single-key CPFE with *succinct key* to ensure that $\mathsf{Leak}(x)$ does not have much information about x.

A single-key CPFE scheme has a succinct key if it satisfies the following properties. FE.Setup consists of two algorithms $(\mathsf{HKG}, \mathsf{Hash})$, computes a hash key $\mathsf{hk} \leftarrow \mathsf{HKG}(1^{|x|})$ and a hash value $h \leftarrow \mathsf{Hash}(\mathsf{hk}, x)$ from x, and outputs a public key $\mathsf{pk} := (\mathsf{hk}, h)$ and a decryption key $\mathsf{sk}_x := x$. The length of h should be the same as the security parameter (no matter how large x is). These properties are crucial for our construction since we consider $\mathsf{Leak}(x) := \mathsf{Hash}(\mathsf{hk}, \cdot)$ and a hash value h does not have much information about x.

We can achieve single-key CPFE with succinct key from hash encryption (HE) [16], which can be achieved from the LWE. We use HE instead of plain PKE in the well-known single-key FE scheme based on PKE [24]. Thanks to the compression property of hash encryption, we can achieve the succinct key property. A decryption key of HE is a pre-image of a hash. Hence, we can use x as a decryption key sk_x.

One-Out-of-Many Unclonable Encryption. Georgiou and Zhandry [17] showed that under appropriate definitions, it is possible to transform one-time SDE to unclonable encryption. We show that by using the same transformation, we can transform any one-out-of-many secure SDE to one-out-of-many secure unclonable encryption. By combining this transformation with the above one-out-of-many SDE, we can obtain one-out-of-many secure unclonable encryption based on the LWE assumption.

Copy Protection for Single-Bit Output Point Functions. A point function $f_{y,\mathsf{m}}$ is a function that outputs m on input y and outputs $0^{|\mathsf{m}|}$ otherwise. When we say single-bit output, we set $\mathsf{m} = 1$. When we say multi-bit output, we set m as a multi-bit string sampled from some high min-entropy distribution. We denote the family of single-bit output point functions and multi-bit output point functions as $\mathcal{PF}^1$ and $\mathcal{PF}^{\mathsf{mlt}}$, respectively.

We introduce a simplified security game for copy protection for point functions. It follows the template given in Sect. 1.1. The first stage adversary is given a copy protected program ρ of a randomly generated point function $f_{y,\mathsf{m}}$. In the second stage, $\mathcal{A}_1$ and $\mathcal{A}_2$ are given a challenge input x sampled from some distribution and try to output $f_{y,\mathsf{m}}(x)$ simultaneously. The copy protection security guarantees that the success probability of the adversary is bounded by the trivial winning probability.

Coladangelo et al. [14] proposed a generic construction of copy protection for $\mathcal{PF}^{\mathsf{mlt}}$ using unclonable encryption.[6] The construction is as follows. To copy protect a multi-bit output point function $f_{y,\mathsf{m}}$, it generates a quantum ciphertext of m of an unclonable encryption scheme UE under the key y, that is $ct \leftarrow \mathsf{UE}.\mathcal{E}nc(y, \mathsf{m})$. For simplicity, we assume that given a key y' and a ciphertext ct' of UE, we can efficiently check whether ct' is generated under the key y' or not.

---

[6] Ananth and Kaleoglu [4] also proposed a similar construction.

Then, to evaluate this copy protected program with input x, it first checks if x and ct match or not, and if so, just output the decryption result of ct under the key x. We see that the construction satisfies the correctness. Coladangelo et al. also show that if UE satisfies one-wayness-based unclonability, the construction satisfies copy protection security.

In this work, we propose a generic construction of copy protection for $\mathcal{PF}^1$ using unclonable-indistinguishable secure unclonable encryption. The above simple construction by Coladangelo et al. does not work if our goal is copy protection for $\mathcal{PF}^1$, even if the underlying unclonable encryption is unclonable-indistinguishable secure. The above construction crucially relies on the fact that m is sampled from high min-entropy distribution in $\mathcal{PF}^{\mathsf{mlt}}$. In fact, if m is fixed as the case of $\mathcal{PF}^1$, the construction is completely insecure under the above condition that we can efficiently check the correspondence between a key and a ciphertext of UE, which is required to achieve correctness.

To fix this issue, our construction uses quantum FHE [23] and obfuscation for C&C programs [20,27], both of which can be realized from the LWE assumption. Roughly speaking, in our construction, the above UE-based copy protected program is encrypted by QFHE. The evaluation of the new copy protected program is done by the homomorphic evaluation of QFHE, and we obtain the evaluation result from the QFHE ciphertext by using decryption circuit of QFHE obfuscated by obfuscation for C&C programs. Our construction works in both standard three adversary style setting explained above and one-out-of-many setting.

Unclonable PE. We also define and construct unclonable PE. Our security definition of unclonable PE is simulation-based. It also can be seen as an extension of simulation-based security notion for (not unclonable) PE defined by Gorbunov et al. [18].

Our construction of unclonable PE is an extension of ABE-to-PE transformation based on obfuscation for C&C programs proposed in classical cryptography [20,27]. The above construction of copy protection for $\mathcal{PF}^1$ can be extended to copy protection for C&C programs by encrypting a C&C program together with the ciphertext of unclonable encryption into the QFHE ciphertext. At a high level, we show that by replacing obfuscation for C&C programs with this copy protection for C&C programs in the ABE-to-PE transformation, we can obtain unclonable PE. To achieve hiding of policies in PE, the construction crucially uses the security notions of the underlying QFHE and obfuscation for C&C programs. Thus, we do not use the abstraction of copy protection for C&C programs, and present our construction directly using ABE and the building blocks of our copy protection construction. Our construction works in both standard three adversary style setting and one-out-of-many setting.

In the above transformation, we use a simulation-based secure ABE instead of an indistinguishability-based one. As far as we know, simulation-based secure ABE was not studied before and there is no existing construction. Thus, we construct simulation-based secure ABE by ourselves. The construction is based on indistinguishability-based secure ABE and obfuscation for C&C programs, both of which can be based on the LWE assumption. Interestingly, we can also use our simulation-based secure ABE to convert unclonable encryption into the first unclonable ABE via the standard KEM-DEM framework.

1.5   More on Related Work

Copy-Protection for C&C Programs. Aaronson proposed candidate constructions of copy-protection for point functions [1]. However, he did not provide reduction-based proofs. Coladangelo, Majenz, and Poremba proposed copy-protection for C&C programs in the quantum random oracle model (QROM) and copy-protection for multi-bit output point functions based on one-way-secure unclonable encryption [14]. They also show that we can convert copy-protection for point functions into copy-protection for C&C programs. Ananth and Kaleoglu proposed copy-protected point functions based on indistinguishable-secure unclonable encryption [4]. Ananth et al. [6] proposed indistinguishable-secure unclonable encryption and copy-protection for single-bit output point functions in the QROM. Ananth and La Placa [8] show that there exists a class of functions that we cannot achieve copy-protection in the plain model. Ananth and Kaleoglu [5] extend the impossibility result by Ananth and La Placa [8] and show that there exists a class of functions that we cannot achieve copy-protection in the classical-accessible random oracle model (CAROM). CAROM is a model where both constructions and adversaries can only classically access the random oracle.

Unclonable Encryption. Broadbent and Lord [12] proposed the notion of unclonable encryption based on the idea by Gottesman [19].[7] They considered two security definitions for unclonable encryption. One is one-wayness against cloning attacks (one-way-secure unclonable encryption) and they achieve information-theoretic one-wayness by using BB84 states. The other is indistinguishability against cloning attacks (indistinguishable-secure unclonable encryption). However, they did not achieve it. They constructed indistinguishable-secure unclonable encryption only in a very restricted model by using PRFs. Ananth and Kaleoglu [4] proposed a transformation from unclonable encryption to public key unclonable encryption. Ananth et al. [6] proposed the first indistinguishable-secure unclonable encryption in the QROM.

Unclonable Decryption. Georgiou and Zhandry [17] proposed the notion of SDE and show the equivalence between indistinguishable-secure unclonable encryption and their SDE.[8], Coladangelo et al. [13] proposed new definitions of SDE and constructed a *public key* SDE scheme that satisfies their definitions from IO and the LWE assumption. Although they needed the strong monogamy of entanglement property conjecture for their constructions, the conjecture was proved without any assumptions by Culf and Vidick [15]. It is unclear whether SDE under

---

[7] The notion of unclonable encryption by Gottesman is slightly different from the one in this paper. His definition focuses on tamper detection.

[8] Selectively secure secret key SDE in the setting of honestly generated keys. See [17] for the detail.

the definitions by Coladangelo et al. [13] is equivalent to unclonable encryption. Liu, Liu, Qian, and Zhandry [22] achieved bounded collusion-resistant public key SDE, where adversaries can receive many copy-protected decryption keys, from IO and the LWE assumption. They also consider bounded collusion-resistant copy-protection for PRFs and signatures. Sattath and Wyborski [25] also extend SDE to unclonable decryptors, where we can generate multiple copy-protected decryption keys from a classical decryption key. They constructed a secret key unclonable decryptors scheme from copy-protection for balanced binary functions. However, they need IO or a quantum oracle to instantiate copy-protection for balanced binary functions.

Rational Security for Quantum Money. Behera and Sattath [9] studied a notion of unclonability for quantum money that has a similar flavor to our one-out-of-many unclonability. Their notion also guarantees that the expected number of successful quantum money output by an adversary is less than the number of money that the adversary originally had. They call this notion rational security since counterfeiting is possible only if adversaries risk their original object and rational adversaries would not try to do it. We can apply the same argument to our one-out-of-many unclonability.[9] We believe that one-out-of-many security and rational security are meaningful and useful notions. It is an important future direction to tackle whether, by considering our relaxed notions, we can remove strong assumptions or oracle heuristics from unclonable primitives.

1.6   Organization

Due to the space limitation, we provide the result on unclonable PE only in the full version. Also, please refer the full version for background on quantum information and definitions of standard cryptographic primitives.

In Sect. 3, we introduce the notion of one-out-of-many unclonable security and prove some implications. In Sect. 4, we show how to construct secret key one-time SDE based on the LWE assumption. In Sect. 5, we show how to realize one-out-of-many copy protection for single-bit output point functions.

2   Preliminaries

Notations and Conventions. In this paper, standard math or sans serif font stands for classical algorithms (e.g., C or Gen) and classical variables (e.g., x or pk). Calligraphic font stands for quantum algorithms (e.g., $\mathcal{G}en$) and calligraphic font and/or the bracket notation for (mixed) quantum states (e.g., q or $|\psi\rangle$). For strings x and y, $x\|y$ denotes the concatenation of x and y. Let $[\ell]$ denote the set of integers $\{1,\cdots,\ell\}$, λ denote a security parameter, and $y := z$ denote that y is set, defined, or substituted by z.

---

[9] For the detail on the rational security flavor of one-out-of-many unclonability, see Remark 3.

In this paper, for a finite set X and a distribution D, $x \leftarrow X$ denotes selecting an element from X uniformly at random, $x \leftarrow D$ denotes sampling an element x according to D. Let $y \leftarrow \mathsf{A}(x)$ and $y \leftarrow \mathcal{A}(\chi)$ denote assigning to y the output of a probabilistic or deterministic algorithm A and a quantum algorithm $\mathcal{A}$ on an input x and χ, respectively. When we explicitly show that A uses randomness r, we write $y \leftarrow \mathsf{A}(x; r)$. PPT and QPT algorithms stand for probabilistic polynomial-time algorithms and polynomial-time quantum algorithms, respectively. Let negl denote a negligible function. Let $\overset{c}{\approx}$ denote computational indistinguishability.

2.1 Quantum Cryptographic Tools

Unclonable Encryption. We introduce the definition of secret key unclonable encryption (SKUE) [12] and one-time indistinguishability for it.

Definition 1 (SKUE (Syntax)). *A SKUE scheme with the message space $\mathcal{M}$ is a tuple of quantum algorithms* $(\mathsf{KG}, \mathcal{E}nc, \mathcal{D}ec)$.

$\mathsf{KG}(1^\lambda) \to \mathsf{uk}$: *The key generation algorithm takes as input the security parameter 1^λ and outputs a key* uk.
$\mathcal{E}nc(\mathsf{uk}, \mathsf{m}) \to \mathsf{ct}$: *The encryption algorithm takes as input uk and a plaintext $\mathsf{m} \in \mathcal{M}$ and outputs a ciphertext* ct.
$\mathcal{D}ec(\mathsf{uk}, \mathsf{ct}) \to \mathsf{m}'$: *The decryption algorithm takes as input uk and ct and outputs a plaintext $\mathsf{m}' \in \mathcal{M}$ or* $\bot$.
Decryption Correctness: *For any $\mathsf{m} \in \mathcal{M}$, it holds that*

$$\Pr\left[\mathcal{D}ec(\mathsf{uk}, \mathsf{ct}) = \mathsf{m} \,\middle|\, \begin{array}{l} \mathsf{uk} \leftarrow \mathsf{KG}(1^\lambda) \\ \mathsf{ct} \leftarrow \mathcal{E}nc(\mathsf{uk}, \mathsf{m}) \end{array}\right] = 1 - \mathsf{negl}(\lambda).$$

Definition 2 (One-Time Unclonable-Indistinguishable Security for SKUE). *Let $\mathsf{UE} = (\mathcal{E}nc, \mathcal{D}ec)$ be an SKUE scheme with the key space $\mathcal{K}$ and the message space $\mathcal{M}$. We consider the following security experiment* $\mathsf{Exp}_{\mathsf{UE},\mathcal{A}}^{\mathsf{ot\text{-}ind\text{-}clone}}(\lambda)$, *where* $\mathcal{A} = (\mathcal{A}_0, \mathcal{A}_1, \mathcal{A}_2)$.

1. $\mathcal{A}_0$ *sends (m_0, m_1) to the challenger.*
2. *The challenger generates* $\mathsf{coin} \leftarrow \{0, 1\}$, $\mathsf{uk} \leftarrow \mathsf{KG}(1^\lambda)$, *and* $\mathsf{ct} \leftarrow \mathcal{E}nc(\mathsf{uk}, m_{\mathsf{coin}})$, *and sends ct to $\mathcal{A}_0$.*
3. $\mathcal{A}_0$ *creates a bipartite state q over registers R_1 and R_2. $\mathcal{A}$ sends $q[\mathsf{R}_1]$ and $q[\mathsf{R}_2]$ to $\mathcal{A}_1$ and $\mathcal{A}_2$, respectively.*
4. *The challenger sends uk to $\mathcal{A}_1$ and $\mathcal{A}_2$. $\mathcal{A}_1$ and $\mathcal{A}_2$ respectively output coin'_1 and coin'_2. If $\mathsf{coin}'_i = \mathsf{coin}$ for $i \in \{1, 2\}$, the challenger outputs 1, otherwise outputs 0.*

We say that UE is one-time unclonable-indistinguishable secure SKUE scheme if for any QPT $\mathcal{A}$, it holds that

$$\mathsf{Adv}_{\mathsf{UE},\mathcal{A}}^{\mathsf{ot\text{-}ind\text{-}clone}}(\lambda) := \Pr[\mathsf{Exp}_{\mathsf{UE},\mathcal{A}}^{\mathsf{ot\text{-}ind\text{-}clone}}(\lambda) = 1] \leq \frac{1}{2} + \mathsf{negl}(\lambda).$$

Single-Decryptor Encryption. We review the definition of single-decryptor encryption (SDE). We consider a one-time secret key variant of SDE by Coladangelo et al. [13] in this work.

Definition 3 (Secret Key SDE (Syntax)). *A secret key SDE scheme* SDE *is a tuple of quantum algorithms* $(\mathcal{KG}, \mathsf{Enc}, \mathcal{Dec})$ *with plaintext space* $\mathcal{M}$.

$\mathcal{KG}(1^\lambda) \to (\mathsf{ek}, \mathit{dk})$: *The key generation algorithm takes as input the security parameter* 1^λ *and outputs an encryption key* ek *and a quantum decryption key* dk.

$\mathsf{Enc}(\mathsf{ek}, m) \to \mathsf{ct}$: *The encryption algorithm takes as input* ek *and a plaintext* $m \in \mathcal{M}$ *and outputs a ciphertext* ct.

$\mathcal{Dec}(\mathit{dk}, \mathsf{ct}) \to m'$: *The decryption algorithm takes as input* dk *and* ct *and outputs a plaintext* $m' \in \mathcal{M}$ *or* $\perp$.

Decryption Correctness: *There exists a negligible function* negl *such that for any* $m \in \mathcal{M}$,

$$\Pr\left[\mathcal{Dec}(\mathit{dk}, \mathsf{ct}) = m \;\middle|\; \begin{array}{l}(\mathsf{ek}, \mathit{dk}) \leftarrow \mathcal{KG}(1^\lambda) \\ \mathsf{ct} \leftarrow \mathsf{Enc}(\mathsf{ek}, m)\end{array}\right] = 1 - \mathsf{negl}(\lambda).$$

Definition 4 (One-Time Strong Anti-Piracy Security for Secret Key SDE]). *Let* $\gamma \in [0, 1]$. *Let* SDE $= (\mathcal{KG}, \mathsf{Enc}, \mathcal{Dec})$ *be a secret key SDE scheme. We consider the one-time strong anti-piracy game* $\mathsf{Exp}^{\text{ot-santi-piracy}}_{\mathsf{SDE}, \mathcal{A}}(\lambda, \gamma)$ *between the challenger and an adversary* $\mathcal{A} = (\mathcal{A}_0, \mathcal{A}_1, \mathcal{A}_2)$ *below.*

1. *The challenger generates* $(\mathsf{ek}, \mathit{dk}) \leftarrow \mathcal{KG}(1^\lambda)$ *and sends* dk *to* $\mathcal{A}_0$.
2. *$\mathcal{A}_0$ creates a bipartite state* q *over registers* R_1 *and* R_2. *$\mathcal{A}$ sends* (m_0, m_1), *$q[\mathsf{R}_1]$, and* $q[\mathsf{R}_2]$ *to the challenger,* $\mathcal{A}_1$, *and* $\mathcal{A}_2$, *respectively.*
3. *$\mathcal{A}_1$ and* $\mathcal{A}_2$ *respectively output* $\mathcal{D}_1 = (\rho[\mathsf{R}_1], U_1)$ *and* $\mathcal{D}_2 = (\rho[\mathsf{R}_2], U_2)$.
4. *For* $\alpha \in [2]$, *let* $\boldsymbol{P}_\alpha = (\boldsymbol{P}_{\alpha, b, \mathsf{ct}}, \boldsymbol{I} - \boldsymbol{P}_{\alpha, b, \mathsf{ct}})_{b, \mathsf{ct}}$ *be a collection of binary projective measurements, where*

$$\boldsymbol{P}_{\alpha, b, \mathsf{ct}} = \boldsymbol{U}^\dagger_{\alpha, \mathsf{ct}} |b\rangle\langle b| \boldsymbol{U}_{\alpha, \mathsf{ct}}.$$

We also define D as the distribution that generates $b \leftarrow \{0, 1\}$ *and* $\mathsf{ct} \leftarrow \mathsf{Enc}(\mathsf{ek}, m_b)$ *and outputs* (b, ct). *Also, for* $\alpha \in [2]$, *we denote the mixture of* $\boldsymbol{P}_\alpha$ *with respect to D as* $\boldsymbol{P}_{\alpha, D}$. *Then, for every* $\alpha \in [2]$, *the challenger applies* $\mathsf{ProjImp}(\boldsymbol{P}_{\alpha, D})$ *to* $\rho[\mathsf{R}_\alpha]$ *and obtains* p_α. *If* $p_\alpha > \frac{1}{2} + \gamma$ *for every* $\alpha \in [2]$, *the challenger outputs 1. Otherwise, the challenger outputs 0.*

We say that SDE *is one-time strong anti-piracy secure if for any* $\gamma \in [0, 1]$ *and QPT adversary* $\mathcal{A}$, *it satisfies that*

$$\mathsf{Adv}^{\text{ot-santi-piracy}}_{\mathsf{SDE}, \mathcal{A}}(\lambda, \gamma) := \Pr[\mathsf{Exp}^{\text{ot-santi-piracy}}_{\mathsf{SDE}, \mathcal{A}}(\lambda, \gamma) = 1] = \mathsf{negl}(\lambda).$$

Remark 1. Readers might think the meaning of "one-time" is unclear in Definition 4. Here, "one-time" means that $\mathcal{A}_0$ cannot access an encryption oracle that returns a ciphertext for a query m. This naming might sound strange since $\mathcal{A}_0$ does not receive any ciphertext. However, we stick to this naming for correspondence with one-time unclonable-indistinguishable security of unclonable encryption in Definition 2.

Remark 2 (On the issue in indistinguishability-based definitions). There are two indistinguishability-based security notions for SDE. The first one is defined by Georgiou and Zhandry (denoted by GZ) [17] and the second one is defined by Coladangelo et al. (denoted by CLLZ)[10] [13]. Both of them are defined using a security game similar to that in Definition 4, except that $\mathcal{A}_1$ and $\mathcal{A}_2$ are given the challenge ciphertexts and required to guess the challenge bits. In the GZ definition, $\mathcal{A}_1$ and $\mathcal{A}_2$ receive the same ciphertext $\mathsf{Enc}(\mathsf{sk}, m_{\mathsf{coin}})$ for the single challenge bit. However, in the CLLZ definition, $\mathcal{A}_1$ and $\mathcal{A}_2$ receive different ciphertexts $\mathsf{Enc}(\mathsf{sk}, m_{\mathsf{coin}_1})$ and $\mathsf{Enc}(\mathsf{sk}, m_{\mathsf{coin}_2})$, respectively, where coin_1 and coin_2 are independent challenge bits. Currently, the relationship between these two security notions for SDE remains elusive.[11] The GZ definition is known to imply unclonable-indistinguishable secure unclonable encryption, but the CLLZ definition is not. Also, strong anti-piracy security defined in Definition 4 implies the CLLZ definition but not the GZ definition.

Quantum Fully Homomorphic Encryption. We introduce quantum fully homomorphic encryption (QFHE) with classical ciphertexts.

Definition 5 (QFHE with Classical Ciphertexts [11,23]). *A QFHE scheme with classical ciphertext is a tuple of algorithms* $(\mathsf{KG}, \mathsf{Enc}, \mathcal{E}val, \mathsf{Dec})$.

$\mathsf{KG}(1^\lambda) \rightarrow (\mathsf{pk}, \mathsf{sk})$: *The key generation algorithm takes as input the security parameter* 1^λ *and outputs a key pair* $(\mathsf{pk}, \mathsf{sk})$.

$\mathsf{Enc}(\mathsf{pk}, m) \rightarrow \mathsf{ct}$: *The encryption algorithm takes as input a public key* pk *and a plaintext* m, *and outputs a ciphertext* ct. *Without loss of generality, we can assume that a ciphertext includes the public key* pk.

$\mathcal{E}val(C, \rho, \mathsf{ct}_1, \cdots, \mathsf{ct}_n) \rightarrow \mathsf{evct}$: *The evaluation algorithm takes as input a quantum circuit* C *with classical outputs, quantum state* ρ, *and ciphertexts* $\mathsf{ct}_1, \cdots, \mathsf{ct}_n$, *and outputs a classical ciphertext* evct.

$\mathsf{Dec}(\mathsf{sk}, \mathsf{ct}) \rightarrow m'$: *The decryption algorithm takes as input a secret key* sk *and a ciphertext* ct, *and outputs a plaintext* m.

Decryption Correctness: *Let* $(\mathsf{pk}, \mathsf{sk}) \leftarrow \mathsf{KG}(1^\lambda)$. *Let* $(m_1, \cdots, m_n)$ *be any* n *messages. For any* $i \in [n]$, *let* $\mathsf{ct}_i \leftarrow \mathsf{Enc}(\mathsf{pk}, m_i)$ *for every* $i \in [n]$. *Let* C *be a quantum circuit that takes a quantum state and* n *classical input,* ρ *a quantum state, and* $\mathsf{evct} \leftarrow \mathcal{E}val(C, \rho, \mathsf{ct}_1, \cdots, \mathsf{ct}_n)$. *Then, we have* $\mathsf{Dec}(\mathsf{sk}, \mathsf{evct}) = C(\rho, m_1, \cdots, m_n)$.

Semantic Security: *For any two messages of equal length* m_0, m_1, *we have*

$$(\mathsf{pk}, \mathsf{Enc}(\mathsf{pk}, m_0)) \stackrel{c}{\approx} (\mathsf{pk}, \mathsf{Enc}(\mathsf{pk}, m_1)),$$

where $(\mathsf{pk}, \mathsf{sk}) \leftarrow \mathsf{KG}(1^\lambda)$.

The existing QFHE schemes [11,23] can be seen as QFHE with classical ciphertexts, since they have a property that if the encrypted plaintext is classical, we can make the ciphertext classical. Thus, the following theorem holds.

---

[10] They call "CPA-style anti-piracy security".

[11] Ananth et al. [7] show the relationship between *one-wayness-based* security with the same ciphertext and one with the different ciphertexts.

Theorem 5 ([11,23]). *If the LWE assumption holds, there exists QFHE with classical ciphertexts.*

QFHE with classical ciphertexts was previously used in the context of impossibility on copy protection [8] and quantum obfuscation [2]. For the detailed explanation for how to use the existing QFHE schemes as QFHE with classical ciphertexts, please refer to [2].

3 One-Out-of-Many Unclonable Security

This section introduces new unclonable security notions that we call one-out-of-many unclonable security. The definition is roughly as follows. The one-out-of-many unclonable security game is an indistinguishability-style game played by a tuple of $n+1$ adversaries $(\mathcal{A}_0, \mathcal{A}_1, \cdots, \mathcal{A}_n)$, where $2 \le n$ is arbitrary. At the first stage of the game, $\mathcal{A}_0$ is given a single quantum object (such as ciphertext in unclonable encryption), generates possibly entangled n-partite states $\rho_1, \ldots, \rho_n$, and sends ρ_k to $\mathcal{A}_k$ for $k \in \{1, \ldots, n\}$. At the second stage, the challenger selects one of $(\mathcal{A}_1, \ldots, \mathcal{A}_n)$ by a random $\alpha \leftarrow \{1, \ldots, n\}$ and sends additional information (such as a secret key in unclonable encryption) *only to* $\mathcal{A}_\alpha$, and only $\mathcal{A}_\alpha$ tries to guess the challenge bit $\mathsf{coin} \in \{0, 1\}$. The one-out-of-many unclonable security guarantees that the adversary cannot win this game with a probability significantly better than the trivial winning probability $\frac{1}{2} + \frac{1}{2n}$.[12]

The one-out-of-many unclonable security notion guarantees that no adversary can generate n copies with a probability significantly better than $\frac{1}{n}$ for any n. This is because an adversary who can generate n copies with probability $\frac{1}{n} + \delta$ can win the one-out-of-many game with probability at least $(\frac{1}{n} + \delta) \cdot 1 + (1 - \frac{1}{n} - \delta) \cdot \frac{1}{2} = \frac{1}{2} + \frac{1}{2n} + \frac{\delta}{2}$, which violates to the one-out-of-many unclonable security. The one-out-of-many unclonable security notion does not rule out a copying process that can generate n copies with probability $\frac{1}{n}$. However, it guarantees that such a process must completely destroy the original object with probability $1 - \frac{1}{n}$. In fact, it guarantees that the expected number of successful copies generated by any copying adversary is at most 1.

Although one-out-of-many unclonable security looks weaker than existing unclonable security, it still seems useful in some applications. For example, suppose we publish many quantum objects, say ℓ objects. Then, the one-out-of-many security guarantees that no matter what copying attacks are applied to those objects, there are expected to be only ℓ objects on average in this world.

Below, we define one-out-of-many one-time unclonable-indistinguishable security for SKUE and one-out-of-many one-time anti-piracy for secret key SDE.

---

[12] Suppose $\mathcal{A}_0$ forwards the given quantum state to $\mathcal{A}_1$ and nothing to $(\mathcal{A}_2, \ldots, \mathcal{A}_n)$. If $\alpha = 1$ is chosen, the adversaries win with probability 1 because the additional information, together with the original quantum object, can be used to compute the challenge bit coin correctly. If one of $(\mathcal{A}_2, \ldots, \mathcal{A}_n)$ is chosen, the adversaries win with probability $\frac{1}{2}$ by random guess. Hence, the advantage is $\frac{1}{n} \cdot 1 + \frac{n-1}{n} \cdot \frac{1}{2} = \frac{1}{2} + \frac{1}{2n}$, which we consider as the trivial advantage.

We prove that one-out-of-many one-time unclonable-indistinguishable security for SKUE implies one-time IND-CPA security. We also prove that one-time strong anti-piracy for secret key SDE implies one-out-of-many one-time anti-piracy for secret key SDE. Then, we show that we can transform secret key SDE with one-out-of-many one-time anti-piracy into one-out-of-many one-time unclonable-indistinguishable secure SKUE.

In Sect. 5, we define one-out-of-many copy protection security for single-bit output point functions. In the full version, we also define simulation-based security for unclonable PE and introduce its one-out-of-many variant.

3.1   One-Out-of-Many Security Notions for SKUE and Secret Key SDE

Definition 6 (One-out-of-Many One-Time Unclonable-Indistinguishability for SKUE). *Let* $\mathsf{UE} = (\mathsf{KG}, \mathcal{E}nc, \mathcal{D}ec)$ *be an SKUE scheme with the message space* $\mathcal{M}$. *We consider one-out-of-many one-time unclonable-indistinguishability game* $\mathsf{Exp}^{\mathsf{om\text{-}ot\text{-}clone\text{-}ind}}_{\mathsf{UE},\mathcal{A}}(\lambda, n)$ *between the challenger and an adversary* $\mathcal{A} = (\mathcal{A}_0, \mathcal{A}_1, \cdots, \mathcal{A}_n)$ *below.*

1. $\mathcal{A}_0$ *sends* $(\mathsf{m}_0, \mathsf{m}_1)$ *to the challenger.*
2. *The challenger generates* $\mathsf{coin} \leftarrow \{0,1\}$, $\mathsf{uk} \leftarrow \mathsf{KG}(1^\lambda)$, *and* $\mathsf{ct} \leftarrow \mathcal{E}nc(\mathsf{uk}, \mathsf{m}_{\mathsf{coin}})$, *and sends* ct *to* $\mathcal{A}_0$.
3. $\mathcal{A}_0$ *creates a quantum state* q *over* n *registers* $\mathsf{R}_1, \cdots, \mathsf{R}_n$. $\mathcal{A}_0$ *sends* $q[\mathsf{R}_i]$ *to* $\mathcal{A}_i$ *for every* $i \in [n]$.
4. *The challenger generates* $\alpha \leftarrow [n]$, *and gives* uk *to* $\mathcal{A}_\alpha$. $\mathcal{A}_\alpha$ *outputs* coin'. *The challenger outputs* 1 *if* $\mathsf{coin}' = \mathsf{coin}$ *and outputs* 0 *otherwise.*

We say that UE *is one-out-of-many one-time unclonable-indistinguishable if for any polynomial* $n = n(\lambda)$ *and QPT adversary* $\mathcal{A} = (\mathcal{A}_0, \mathcal{A}_1, \cdots, \mathcal{A}_n)$, *it satisfies that*

$$\mathsf{Adv}^{\mathsf{om\text{-}ot\text{-}clone\text{-}ind}}_{\mathsf{UE},\mathcal{A}}(\lambda, n) := \Pr[\mathsf{Exp}^{\mathsf{om\text{-}ot\text{-}unclone\text{-}ind}}_{\mathsf{UE},\mathcal{A}}(\lambda, n) = 1] \leq \frac{1}{2} + \frac{1}{2n} + \mathsf{negl}(\lambda).$$

Theorem 6. *Let* $\mathsf{UE} = (\mathsf{KG}, \mathcal{E}nc, \mathcal{D}ec)$ *be a one-out-of-many one-time unclonable-indistinguishable secure SKUE scheme with the message space* $\mathcal{M}$. *Then,* UE *satisfies one-time IND-CPA security, that is,*

$$\mathcal{E}nc(\mathsf{uk}, \mathsf{m}_0) \overset{c}{\approx} \mathcal{E}nc(\mathsf{uk}, \mathsf{m}_1)$$

for any $(\mathsf{m}_0, \mathsf{m}_1) \in \mathcal{M}$, *where* $\mathsf{uk} \leftarrow \mathsf{KG}(1^\lambda)$.

Proof. Suppose there exists $\mathcal{B}$ who can distinguish $\mathcal{E}nc(\mathsf{uk}, \mathsf{m}_0)$ from $\mathcal{E}nc(\mathsf{uk}, \mathsf{m}_1)$ with probability $\frac{1}{2} + p$ for some $(\mathsf{m}_0, \mathsf{m}_1) \in \mathcal{M}$ and inverse polynomial p, where $\mathsf{uk} \leftarrow \mathsf{KG}(1^\lambda)$. Consider the following $n = \frac{1}{p}$ tuple of adversaries $\mathcal{A} = (\mathcal{A}_0, \mathcal{A}_1, \cdots, \mathcal{A}_n)$ for the one-out-of-many one-time unclonable-indistinguishable security. On input ct, $\mathcal{A}_0$ gives them to $\mathcal{B}$ and obtains $\mathcal{B}$'s guess coin', and sends it to $\mathcal{A}_i$ for every $i \in [n]$. $\mathcal{A}_i$ just outputs coin' if $\alpha = i$ is chosen by the challenger. We have $\mathsf{Adv}^{\mathsf{om\text{-}ot\text{-}unclone\text{-}ind}}_{\mathsf{UE},\mathcal{A}}(\lambda, n) = \frac{1}{2} + p$, which contradicts to the one-out-of-many unclonable-indistinguishable security since $p > \frac{1}{2n} = \frac{p}{2}$. $\qquad \square$

Definition 7 (One-out-of-Many One-Time Anti-Piracy Security for Secret Key SDE). *Let* SDE $= (\mathcal{KG}, \mathsf{Enc}, \mathcal{Dec})$ *be a secret key SDE scheme. We consider one-out-of-many one-time anti-piracy game* $\mathsf{Exp}_{\mathsf{SDE},\mathcal{A}}^{\mathsf{om-otanti-piracy}}(\lambda, n)$ *between the challenger and an adversary* $\mathcal{A} = (\mathcal{A}_0, \mathcal{A}_1, \cdots, \mathcal{A}_n)$ *below.*

1. *The challenger generates* $(\mathsf{ek}, d\!k) \leftarrow \mathcal{KG}(1^\lambda)$ *and sends* $d\!k$ *to* $\mathcal{A}_0$.
2. $\mathcal{A}_0$ *creates a quantum state* q *over* n *registers* $\mathsf{R}_1, \cdots, \mathsf{R}_n$. $\mathcal{A}_0$ *sends* $(\mathsf{m}_0, \mathsf{m}_1)$ *to the challenger.* $\mathcal{A}_0$ *also sends* $q[\mathsf{R}_i]$ *to* $\mathcal{A}_i$ *for every* $i \in [n]$.
3. $\mathcal{A}_i$ *outputs* $\mathcal{D}_i = (\rho[\mathsf{R}_i], U_i)$ *for every* $i \in [n]$.
4. *The challenger generates* $\alpha \leftarrow [n]$ *and* coin $\leftarrow \{0, 1\}$, *and generates* ct $\leftarrow$ $\mathsf{Enc}(\mathsf{ek}, \mathsf{m}_{\mathsf{coin}})$. *The challenge runs* $\mathcal{D}_\alpha$ *on input* ct *and obtains* coin$'$. *The challenger outputs* 1 *if* coin$'$ = coin *and outputs* 0 *otherwise.*

We say that SDE *is one-out-of-many one-time anti-piracy secure if for any polynomial* $n = n(\lambda)$ *and QPT adversary* $\mathcal{A} = (\mathcal{A}_0, \mathcal{A}_1, \cdots, \mathcal{A}_n)$, *it satisfies that*

$$\mathsf{Adv}_{\mathsf{SDE},\mathcal{A}}^{\mathsf{om-otanti-piracy}}(\lambda, n) := \Pr[\mathsf{Exp}_{\mathsf{SDE},\mathcal{A}}^{\mathsf{om-otanti-piracy}}(\lambda, n) = 1] \leq \frac{1}{2} + \frac{1}{2n} + \mathsf{negl}(\lambda).$$

We show that one-time strong anti-piracy security for secret key SDE implies one-ouf-of-many one-time anti-piracy for secret key SDE.

Theorem 7. *Let* SDE *be a secret key SDE scheme. If* SDE *is one-time strong anti-piracy secure, then* SDE *is also one-out-of-many one-time anti-piracy secure.*

Proof. $\mathsf{Exp}_{\mathsf{SDE},\mathcal{A}}^{\mathsf{om-anti-piracy}}(\lambda, n)$ is equivalent to the security game where item 4 is replaced with the following.

- The challenger generates $\alpha \leftarrow [n]$. For every $\alpha' \in [n]$, the challenger applies $\mathsf{ProjImp}(P_{\alpha',D})$ to $\rho[\mathsf{R}_{\alpha'}]$ and obtains $p_{\alpha'}$. The challenger outputs 1 with probability p_α.

This equivalence follows from the definition of $\mathsf{ProjImp}$. Using this version of $\mathsf{Exp}_{\mathsf{SDE},\mathcal{A}}^{\mathsf{om-anti-piracy}}(\lambda, n)$, we prove that $\mathsf{Adv}_{\mathsf{SDE},\mathcal{A}}^{\mathsf{om-anti-piracy}}(\lambda, n) \leq \frac{1}{2} + \frac{1}{2n} + \gamma$ for any inverse polynomial γ. Since SDE is strong anti-piracy secure, except for some single index i^*, p_i computed by the challenger is smaller than $\frac{1}{2} + \gamma$, with overwhelming probability. Thus, we have

$$\mathsf{Adv}_{\mathsf{SDE},\mathcal{A}}^{\mathsf{om-anti-piracy}}(\lambda, n) \leq \frac{1}{n} \cdot 1 + \frac{n-1}{n} \cdot (\frac{1}{2} + \gamma) + \mathsf{negl}(\lambda)$$

$$\leq \frac{1}{2} + \frac{1}{2n} + \gamma.$$

This completes the proof. □

Remark 3 (On the rational security flavor). One-out-of-many security guarantees that the expected number of successful quantum objects generated by any copying adversary is at most 1. This means that cloning is possible only if adversaries risk their original objects. Unclonability with such a flavor was previously studied by Behera and Sattath [9] for quantum money. They call the unclonability rational security since rational adversaries would not try to copy if it risks the original objects. We explain in detail why one-out-of-many security has the rational security flavor.

We first make our claim more precise. We simply focus on the $n = 2$ case as the standard unclonability game. The definition of one-out-of-many unclonability is equivalent to the variant where both second-stage adversaries $\mathcal{A}_1$ and $\mathcal{A}_2$ are given extra information (e.g., secret keys in unclonable encryption) and asked to compute the target information (e.g., the challenge bit), but the challenger checks only the answer output by $\mathcal{A}_\alpha$ for randomly chosen $\alpha \in \{1, 2\}$. Then, with this equivalent definition, one-out-of-many unclonability guarantees that the expected number of correct answers among outputs of $\mathcal{A}_1$ and $\mathcal{A}_2$ is roughly at most $1 + \frac{1}{2}$. This matches the adversary's trivial strategy where $\mathcal{A}_1$ always uses the original quantum object obtained from $\mathcal{A}_0$ to compute the target information and $\mathcal{A}_2$ always does random guessing. We can see this fact as follows.

We define the following four probabilities for some fixed state at the end of the first stage (the copying stage played by $\mathcal{A}_0$).

p_{CC} (resp. p_{II}): The probability that both $\mathcal{A}_1$ and $\mathcal{A}_2$ output the correct (resp. incorrect) answers.

p_{CI} (resp. p_{IC}): The probability that $\mathcal{A}_1$ outputs the correct (resp. incorrect) answer but $\mathcal{A}_2$ outputs the incorrect (resp. correct) one.

Then, one-out-of-many unclonability guarantees that $E[\frac{1}{2} \cdot (p_{\text{CC}} + p_{\text{CI}}) + \frac{1}{2} \cdot (p_{\text{CC}} + p_{\text{IC}})] \leq \frac{1}{2} + \frac{1}{4} + \mathsf{negl}(\lambda)$, where the expectation is taken over the states at the end of the first stage. This inequality is equal to $E[2 \cdot p_{\text{CC}} + 1 \cdot p_{\text{CI}} + 1 \cdot p_{\text{IC}}] \leq 1 + \frac{1}{2} + \mathsf{negl}(\lambda)$. The left-hand side is the expected number of correct answers. Thus, this is what we want.

One-out-of-many unclonability is weaker than the standard unclonable-indistinguishability requiring that $E[p_{\text{CC}}] \leq \frac{1}{2} + \mathsf{negl}(\lambda)$ with the above notions. However, the guarantee on the expected number of correct answers is the same between the standard unclonable-indistinguishability and one-out-of-many unclonability. Thus, one-out-of-many unclonability is meaningful and useful when we are interested in only the number of successful objects on average.

We remark that unclonability focusing on the expected number of successful copies was previously studied by Aaronson [1] for quantum copy protection. His definition is more general than ours in the sense that it captures situations where an adversary is given multiple copy protected programs of a single function. We emphasize that our security definition considers the situation where an adversary is given a single copy protected object, but, from the linearity of the expectation, it still provides the security guarantee on the expectation explained above if an adversary is given independently generated copy protected objects.

3.2 From Secret-Key SDE to SKUE: One-out-of-Many Setting

We present a transformation from a secret key SDE scheme that satisfies Definition 7 into a SKUE scheme that satisfies Definition 6. Georgiou and Zhandry developed this transformation [17]. Note that they do not consider one-out-of-many security for secret key SDE and SKUE. We show that their transformation works even in the one-out-of-many setting.

Let SDE = (SDE.$\mathcal{KG}$, SDE.Enc, SDE.$\mathcal{Dec}$) be a secret key SDE scheme. We also let ℓ be the length of ciphertexts of SDE. We construct a SKUE scheme UE = (UE.KG, UE.$\mathcal{Enc}$, UE.$\mathcal{Dec}$) as follows.

UE.KG(1^λ):
- Output uk $\leftarrow \{0,1\}^\ell$.

UE.$\mathcal{Enc}$(uk, m):
- Generate (sde.ek, sde.$d\mathcal{k}$) $\leftarrow$ SDE.$\mathcal{KG}(1^\lambda)$.
- Compute sde.ct $\leftarrow$ SDE.Enc(sde.ek, m).
- Output ue.ct := (sde.ct $\oplus$ uk, sde.$d\mathcal{k}$).

UE.$\mathcal{Dec}$(uk, ue.ct):
- Parse (ct$_1'$, sde.$d\mathcal{k}$) = ue.ct.
- Compute sde.ct' := ct$_1' \oplus$ uk.
- Output m' $\leftarrow$ SDE.$\mathcal{Dec}$(sde.$d\mathcal{k}$, sde.ct').

Theorem 8. *If* SDE *is one-out-of-many one-time anti-piracy secure,* UE *is one-out-of-many one-time unclonable-indistinguishable secure.*

Proof. Let n be any polynomial of λ. We construct an adversary $\mathcal{B} = (\mathcal{B}_0, \mathcal{B}_1, \cdots, \mathcal{B}_n)$ for SDE by using the adversary $\mathcal{A} = (\mathcal{A}_0, \mathcal{A}_1, \cdots, \mathcal{A}_n)$ for UE.

1. $\mathcal{B}_0$ is given sde.$d\mathcal{k}$ from its challenger.
2. $\mathcal{B}_0$ runs $\mathcal{A}_0$ and receives (m$_0$, m$_1$), and passes (m$_0$, m$_1$) to its challenger.
3. $\mathcal{B}_0$ generates uk $\leftarrow \{0,1\}^\ell$, sets ue.ct := (uk, sde.$d\mathcal{k}$), and passes ue.ct to $\mathcal{A}_0$. Then, $\mathcal{A}_0$ create a quantum state $q_{\mathcal{A}}$ over n registers C$_1, \cdots,$ C$_n$. $\mathcal{B}_0$ receives them.
4. $\mathcal{B}_0$ creates a quantum state $q_{\mathcal{B}}$ over n registers R$_1, \cdots,$ R$_n$ such that $q_{\mathcal{B}}[$R$_i]$:= (uk, $q_{\mathcal{A}}[$C$_i]$) for every $i \in [n]$, then $\mathcal{B}_0$ sends $q_{\mathcal{B}}[$R$_i]$ to $\mathcal{B}_i$ for every $i \in [n]$.
5. For every $i \in [n]$, $\mathcal{B}_i$ outputs $\mathcal{D}_i = (q_{\mathcal{B}}[R_1], \boldsymbol{U}_i)$, where $\boldsymbol{U}_i$ is a unitary that takes sde.ct and $q_{\mathcal{B}}[$R$_1]$ as inputs, and outputs coin' $\leftarrow \mathcal{A}_i(q_{\mathcal{A}}[C_i],$ uk $\oplus$ sde.ct).

If the challenger of one-out-of-many security of SDE chooses $\alpha \leftarrow [n]$ and coin $\leftarrow \{0,1\}$, and generates sde.ct $\leftarrow$ SDE.Enc(sde.ek, m$_{\text{coin}}$), then the challenger runs $\mathcal{D}_\alpha$ on input sde.ct and obtains the output coin' $\leftarrow \mathcal{A}_\alpha(q_{\mathcal{A}}[C_\alpha],$ uk $\oplus$ sde.ct). If sde.ct = SDE.Enc(sde.ek, m$_{\text{coin}}$), then ue.ct = (uk, sde.$d\mathcal{k}$) = UE.$\mathcal{Enc}$(sde.ct $\oplus$ uk, m$_{\text{coin}}$). $\mathcal{B}$ correctly simulates the one-out-of-many security game of SKUE for $\mathcal{A}$ since uk is a uniformly random string. Therefore, the probability that $\mathcal{A}$ succeeds in breaking UE is bounded by the probability that $\mathcal{B}$ succeeds in breaking SDE. This completes the proof. $\square$

4 One-Time Secret Key SDE from LWE

We construct secret key SDE satisfying one-time strong anti-piracy based on the LWE assumption in this section.

4.1 Tools

Ciphertext-Policy Functional Encryption. We introduce ciphertext-policy functional encryption (CPFE). Since we consider single-key setting by default, we use a simplified syntax where the setup algorithm takes as input x and outputs a master public key and a functional decryption key for x. There is no key generation algorithm.

Definition 8 (Single-Key Ciphertext-Policy Functional Encryption). *A single-key CPFE scheme for the circuit space $\mathcal{C}$ and the input space $\mathcal{X}$ is a tuple of algorithms* (Setup, Enc, Dec).

- *The setup algorithm* Setup *takes as input a security parameter 1^λ and an input $x \in \mathcal{X}$, and outputs a master public key* MPK *and functional decryption key* sk_x.
- *The encryption algorithm* Enc *takes as input the master public key* MPK *and $C \in \mathcal{C}$, and outputs a ciphertext* ct.
- *The decryption algorithm* Dec *takes as input a functional decryption key* sk_x *and a ciphertext* ct, *and outputs y.*

Decryption Correctness: *We require* $\mathsf{Dec}(\mathsf{sk}_x, \mathsf{Enc}(\mathsf{MPK}, C)) = C(x)$ *for every $C \in \mathcal{C}$, $x \in \mathcal{X}$, and* $(\mathsf{MPK}, \mathsf{sk}_x) \leftarrow \mathsf{Setup}(1^\lambda, x)$.

Definition 9 (1-Bounded Security). *Let* CPFE *be a single-key CPFE scheme. We define the game* $\mathsf{Expt}_{\mathsf{CPFE},\mathcal{A}}^{\mathsf{1\text{-}bounded}}(\lambda, \mathsf{coin})$ *as follows.*

1. $\mathcal{A}$ *sends $x \in \mathcal{X}$ to the challenger.*
2. *The challenger generates* $(\mathsf{MPK}, \mathsf{sk}_x) \leftarrow \mathsf{Setup}(1^\lambda, x)$ *and sends* $(\mathsf{MPK}, \mathsf{sk}_x)$ *to $\mathcal{A}$.*
3. $\mathcal{A}$ *outputs (C_0, C_1) such that $C_0(x) = C_1(x)$. The challenger generates* ct $\leftarrow$ $\mathsf{Enc}(\mathsf{MPK}, C_{\mathsf{coin}})$, *and sends* ct *to $\mathcal{A}$.*
4. $\mathcal{A}$ *outputs* coin$' \in \{0,1\}$.

We say that CPFE *is 1-bounded secure if for every QPT $\mathcal{A}$, we have*

$$\mathsf{Adv}_{\mathsf{CPFE},\mathcal{A}}^{\mathsf{1\text{-}bounded}}(\lambda) = |\Pr[\mathsf{Expt}_{\mathsf{CPFE},\mathcal{A}}^{\mathsf{1\text{-}bounded}}(\lambda, 0) = 1] - \Pr[\mathsf{Expt}_{\mathsf{CPFE},\mathcal{A}}^{\mathsf{1\text{-}bounded}}(\lambda, 1) = 1]| = \mathsf{negl}(\lambda).$$

Definition 10 (Succinct Key). *We say that a single-key CPFE scheme satisfies succinct key property if there exist two algorithms* HKG *and* Hash *satisfying the following conditions.*

- Setup$(1^\lambda, x)$ *runs* hk $\leftarrow$ HKG$(1^\lambda, 1^{|x|})$, *compute $h \leftarrow$* Hash(hk, x), *and outputs* MPK $:= (hk, h)$ *and* $\mathsf{sk}_x := x$. *For the setup of a CPFE scheme with succinct key property, we omit to write* $\mathsf{sk}_x := x$ *from the output of* Setup *and we simply write* MPK $\leftarrow$ Setup$(1^\lambda, x)$.
- *The length of h output by* Hash *is λ regardless of the length of the input x.*

Theorem 9. *If the LWE or exponentially-hard LPN assumption holds, there exists single-key CPFE with succinct key for P/poly.*

See the full version for the proof of Theorem 9.

Monogamy of Entanglement. We review the monogamy of entanglement property of of BB84 states [26] and its variant.

Theorem 10 (Monogamy Property of BB84 States [26]). *Consider the following game between a challenger and an adversary* $\mathcal{A} = (\mathcal{A}_0, \mathcal{A}_1, \mathcal{A}_2)$.

1. *The challenger picks a uniformly random strings* $x \in \{0,1\}^n$ *and* $\theta \in \{0,1\}^n$. *It sends* $|x^{\theta}\rangle := H^{\theta[1]}|x[1]\rangle \otimes \cdots \otimes H^{\theta[n]}|x[n]\rangle$ *to* $\mathcal{A}_0$.
2. $\mathcal{A}_0$ *creates a bipartite state* q *over registers* R_1 *and* R_2. *Then,* $\mathcal{A}_0$ *sends register* R_1 *to* $\mathcal{A}_1$ *and register* R_2 *to* $\mathcal{A}_2$.
3. θ *is then sent to both* $\mathcal{A}_1$ *and* $\mathcal{A}_2$. $\mathcal{A}_1$ *and* $\mathcal{A}_2$ *return respectively* x'_1 *and* x'_2.

Let $\mathsf{MoEBB84}(\mathcal{A}, \lambda)$ *be a random variable which takes the value* 1 *if* $x'_1 = x'_2 = x$, *and takes the value* 0 *otherwise. Then, there exists an exponential function* $\exp$ *such that for any adversary* $\mathcal{A} = (\mathcal{A}_0, \mathcal{A}_1, \mathcal{A}_2)$, *it holds that*

$$\Pr[\mathsf{MoEBB84}(\mathcal{A}, \lambda) = 1] \leq 1/\exp(n).$$

We introduce a variant of the monogamy property above where the adversary can select a leakage function Leak and obtain $\mathsf{Leak}(x)$.

Theorem 11 (Monogamy Property of BB84 States with Leakage). *Consider the following game between a challenger and an adversary* $\mathcal{A} = (\mathcal{A}_0, \mathcal{A}_1, \mathcal{A}_2)$.

1. $\mathcal{A}$ *sends a function* Leak *whose output length is* ℓ *to the challenger.*
2. *The challenger picks a uniformly random strings* $x \in \{0,1\}^n$ *and* $\theta \in \{0,1\}^n$. *It sends* $|x^{\theta}\rangle := H^{\theta[1]}|x[1]\rangle \otimes \cdots \otimes H^{\theta[n]}|x[n]\rangle$ *and* $\mathsf{Leak}(x)$ *to* $\mathcal{A}_0$.
3. $\mathcal{A}_0$ *creates a bipartite state* q *over registers* R_1 *and* R_2. *Then,* $\mathcal{A}_0$ *sends register* R_1 *to* $\mathcal{A}_1$ *and register* R_2 *to* $\mathcal{A}_2$.
4. θ *is then sent to both* $\mathcal{A}_1$ *and* $\mathcal{A}_2$. $\mathcal{A}_1$ *and* $\mathcal{A}_2$ *return respectively* x'_1 *and* x'_2.

Let $\mathsf{MoEBB84Leak}(\mathcal{A}, \lambda)$ *be a random variable which takes the value* 1 *if* $x'_1 = x'_2 = x$, *and takes the value* 0 *otherwise. Then, there exists an exponential function* $\exp$ *such that for any adversary* $\mathcal{A} = (\mathcal{A}_0, \mathcal{A}_1, \mathcal{A}_2)$, *it holds that*

$$\Pr[\mathsf{MoEBB84Leak}(\mathcal{A}, \lambda) = 1] \leq 2^{\ell}/\exp(n).$$

Especially, if ℓ *is independent of* n, *the right hand side is negligible in* λ *by setting* n *appropriately.*

We can reduce Theorem 11 to Theorem 10 by guessing $\mathsf{Leak}(x)$ with probability $1/2^{\ell}$.

4.2   Construction

We use a CPFE scheme with succinct key property $\mathsf{CPFE} = (\mathsf{Setup}, \mathsf{Enc}, \mathsf{Dec})$ to construct a secret key SDE scheme $\mathsf{SDE} = (\mathsf{SDE}.\mathcal{KG}, \mathsf{SDE}.\mathsf{Enc}, \mathsf{SDE}.\mathcal{Dec})$. The description of SDE is as follows. The plaintext space of SDE is $\{0,1\}^{\ell}$.

SDE.$\mathcal{KG}(1^\lambda)$:
- Generate $x, \theta \leftarrow \{0,1\}^n$.
- Generate $|x^\theta\rangle = H^{\theta[1]}|x[1]\rangle \otimes \ldots H^{\theta[n]}|x[n]\rangle$.
- Generate MPK $\leftarrow$ Setup($1^\lambda, x$).
- Output ek $:= (\theta, \mathsf{MPK})$ and $\mathcal{dk} := |x^\theta\rangle$.

SDE.Enc(ek, m):
- Parse ek $= (\theta, \mathsf{MPK})$.
- Let $C[m]$ be a constant circuit that outputs m on any input. C is padded so that it has the same size as C^* appeared in the security proof.
- Compute ct $\leftarrow$ CPFE.Enc(MPK, $C[m]$).
- Output sdct $:= (\theta, \mathsf{ct})$.

SDE.$\mathcal{Dec}(\mathcal{dk}, \mathsf{sdct})$:
- Parse $\mathcal{dk} = |x^\theta\rangle$ and sdct $= (\theta, \mathsf{ct})$.
- Compute x from $|x^\theta\rangle$ and θ.
- Output $m \leftarrow$ Dec(x, ct).

Theorem 12. *If* CPFE *is a CPFE scheme that satisfies succinct key property and 1-bounded security,* SDE *is a one-time strong anti-piracy secure single-decryptor SKE.*

From Theorems 7 to 9 and 12, we immediately obtain the following corollary.

Corollary 1. *If the LWE assumption holds, there exists one-out-of-many unclonable-indistinguishable secure unclonable encryption.*

We prove Theorem 12 in the full version.

5 Quantum Copy-Protection from Unclonable Encryption

We introduce one-out-of-many copy protection security for single-bit output point functions and present how to achieve it using one-out-of-many secure unclonable encryption in this section.

5.1 Definition

Definition 11 (Copy-Protection (Syntax)). *A copy-protection scheme* CP *for a family of circuits* $\mathcal{C}$ *consists of two algorithms* (*CopyProtect, Eval*).

CopyProtect$(1^\lambda, C) \rightarrow \rho$: *The copy-protection algorithm takes as input the security parameter* 1^λ, *a circuit* $C \in \mathcal{C}$, *and outputs a quantum state* ρ.

Eval(ρ, x): *The evaluation algorithm takes as input a quantum state* ρ *and an input* x, *and outputs* y.

Evaluation Correctness: *For every circuit* C *and input* x, *we have*

$$\Pr[\mathit{Eval}(\rho, x) = C(x) \mid \rho \leftarrow \mathit{CopyProtect}(1^\lambda, C)] = 1 - \mathsf{negl}(\lambda).$$

Remark 4. We can assume without loss of generality that a copy protected program ρ output by *CopyProtect* is reusable, that is, it can be reused polynomially many times. This is because the output of *Eval* on input ρ and any input x is almost deterministic by correctness, and thus such an operation can be done without almost disturbing ρ by the gentle measurement lemma [29].

We focus on copy protection scheme for a family of single-bit output point functions that we denote $\mathcal{PF}^1$. We also define a family of single-bit output point functions $\mathcal{PF}^1_{\ell_{\mathrm{inp}}}$ as $\mathcal{PF}^1_{\ell_{\mathrm{inp}}} = \{f_y\}_{y \in \{0,1\}^{\ell_{\mathrm{inp}}}}$, where f_y outputs 1 if the input is $y \in \{0,1\}^{\ell_{\mathrm{inp}}}$ and 0 otherwise.

We review the widely used copy-protection security for $\mathcal{PF}^1$ originally introduced by Coladangelo et al. [14].

Definition 12 (Copy-Protection Security for $\mathcal{PF}^1$). *Let* CP *be a copy protection scheme for* $\mathcal{PF}^1_{\ell_{\mathrm{inp}}}$. *Let* D_Y *be a distribution over* $\{0,1\}^{\ell_{\mathrm{inp}}}$. *Let* $D_X(\cdot)$ *be a distribution over* $\{0,1\}^{\ell_{\mathrm{inp}}} \times \{0,1\}^{\ell_{\mathrm{inp}}}$, *where* $D_X(\cdot)$ *takes as input* $y' \in \{0,1\}^{\ell_{\mathrm{inp}}}$. *We consider the following security experiment* $\mathsf{Exp}^{\mathrm{cp\text{-}pf1}}_{\mathsf{CP},D_Y,D_X,\mathcal{A}}(\lambda)$ *for* $\mathcal{A} = (\mathcal{A}_0, \mathcal{A}_1, \mathcal{A}_2)$.

1. *The challenger generates* $y \leftarrow D_Y$. *The challenger generates* $\rho \leftarrow$ *CopyProtect*$(1^\lambda, f_y)$ *and sends* ρ *to* $\mathcal{A}_0$.
2. *$\mathcal{A}_0$ creates a bipartite state* q *over registers* R_1 *and* R_2. *$\mathcal{A}_0$ sends* $q[\mathsf{R}_1]$ *and* $q[\mathsf{R}_2]$ *to* $\mathcal{A}_1$ *and* $\mathcal{A}_2$, *respectively.*
3. *The challenger generates* $(x_1, x_2) \leftarrow D_X(y)$, *and sends* x_1 *and* x_2 *to* $\mathcal{A}_1$ *and* $\mathcal{A}_2$, *respectively.*
4. *$\mathcal{A}_1$ and $\mathcal{A}_2$ respectively output* b_1 *and* b_2. *If* $b_i = f_y(x_i)$ *for* $i \in \{1,2\}$, *the challenger outputs* 1, *otherwise outputs* 0.

We define $p^{\mathrm{triv}} = \max_{i \in \{1,2\}, S} p_{i,S}$, *where*

$$
p_{i,S} = \Pr\left[b_i = f_y(x_i) \;\middle|\; \begin{matrix} y \leftarrow D_Y, (x_1, x_2) \leftarrow D_X(y) \\ b_i \leftarrow S(x_i) \end{matrix}\right]
$$

and the maximization is done by all possibly computationally unbounded algorithm S.

We say that CP *satisfies copy-protection security for* $\mathcal{PF}^1$ *with respect to* D_Y *and* D_X *if for any QPT* $\mathcal{A}$, *it holds that*

$$
\mathsf{Adv}^{\mathrm{cp\text{-}pf1}}_{\mathsf{CP},D_Y,D_X,\mathcal{A}}(\lambda) := \Pr[\mathsf{Exp}^{\mathrm{cp\text{-}pf1}}_{\mathsf{CP},D_Y,D_X,\mathcal{A}}(\lambda) = 1] \le p^{\mathrm{triv}} + \mathsf{negl}(\lambda).
$$

The following definition is a natural adaptation of Definition 12 into one-out-of-many setting.

Definition 13 (One-out-of-Many Copy-Protection Security for $\mathcal{PF}^1$). *Let* CP *be a copy protection scheme for* $\mathcal{PF}^1_{\ell_{\mathrm{inp}}}$. *Let* D_Y *and* $D_X(\cdot)$ *be distributions over* $\{0,1\}^{\ell_{\mathrm{inp}}}$, *where* $D_X(\cdot)$ *takes as input* $y' \in \{0,1\}^{\ell_{\mathrm{inp}}}$. *We consider the following security experiment* $\mathsf{Exp}^{\mathrm{cp\text{-}pf1\text{-}om}}_{\mathsf{CP},D_Y,D_X,\mathcal{A}}(\lambda, n)$ *for* $\mathcal{A} = (\mathcal{A}_0, \mathcal{A}_1, \cdots, \mathcal{A}_n)$.

1. *The challenger generates* $y \leftarrow D_Y$. *The challenger generates* $\rho \leftarrow$ *CopyProtect*$(1^\lambda, f_y)$ *and sends* ρ *to* $\mathcal{A}_0$.
2. $\mathcal{A}_0$ *creates a quantum state* q *over* n *registers* $\mathsf{R}_1, \cdots, \mathsf{R}_n$. $\mathcal{A}_0$ *sends* $q[\mathsf{R}_i]$ *to* $\mathcal{A}_i$ *for every* $i \in [n]$.
3. *The challenger generates* $\alpha \leftarrow [n]$. *The challenger generates* $x \leftarrow D_X(y)$ *and sends* x *to* $\mathcal{A}_\alpha$. $\mathcal{A}_\alpha$ *outputs* b_α. *If* $b_\alpha = f_y(x)$, *the challenger outputs* 1, *otherwise outputs* 0.

We define $p^{\mathtt{triv}} = \max_S p_S$, *where*

$$p_S = \Pr\left[b = f_y(x) \,\middle|\, \begin{matrix} y \leftarrow D_Y, x \leftarrow D_X(y) \\ b \leftarrow S(x) \end{matrix} \right]$$

and the maximization is done by all possibly computationally unbounded algorithm S.

We say that CP *satisfies one-out-of-many copy-protection security for* $\mathcal{PF}^1$ *with respect to* D_Y *and* D_X *if for any polynomial* $n = n(\lambda)$ *and QPT* $\mathcal{A}$, *it holds that*

$$\mathsf{Adv}_{\mathsf{CP},D_Y,D_X,\mathcal{A}}^{\mathrm{cp\text{-}pf1\text{-}om}}(\lambda, n) := \Pr[\mathsf{Exp}_{\mathsf{CP},D_Y,D_X,\mathcal{A}}^{\mathrm{cp\text{-}pf1\text{-}om}}(\lambda, n) = 1] \leq \frac{1}{n} \cdot 1 + \frac{n-1}{n} \cdot p^{\mathtt{triv}} + \mathsf{negl}(\lambda).$$

5.2   Construction

We construct a copy-protection scheme for single-bit output point functions $\mathcal{PF}^1_{\ell_{\mathsf{inp}}}$, where ℓ_{inp} is specified later. We use the following tools:

- SKUE UE = (UE.KG, UE.$\mathcal{E}nc$, UE.$\mathcal{D}ec$). Suppose the plaintext space of UE is $\{0,1\}^\lambda$ and the key length is ℓ_{uk}.
- Injective commitment scheme with equivocal mode Com = (Setup, Commit, EqSetup, Open). Suppose the message space of Com is $\{0,1\}^{\ell_{\mathsf{uk}}}$ and the random coin space is $\{0,1\}^{\ell_{\mathsf{comr}}}$.
- Compute-and-compare obfuscation CC.Obf with the simulator CC.Sim. In this section, the message feed to CC.Obf is fixed to 1. Thus, we omit to write it from the input.
- QFHE with classical ciphertexts QFHE = (QFHE.KG, QFHE.Enc, QFHE.$\mathcal{E}val$, QFHE.Dec).

We set $\ell_{\mathsf{inp}} = \ell_{\mathsf{uk}} + \ell_{\mathsf{comr}}$. The description of CP is as follows.

CopyProtect$(1^\lambda, f_y)$:
- Generate $(\mathsf{pk}, \mathsf{sk}) \leftarrow$ QFHE.KG(1^λ), $\mathsf{uk} \leftarrow$ UE.KG(1^λ), and $\mathsf{ck} \leftarrow$ Setup(1^λ).
- Generate $\mathsf{lock} \leftarrow \{0,1\}^\lambda$.
- Parse $y_{\mathsf{mask}} \| y_{\mathsf{comr}} \leftarrow y$ and generate , $\leftarrow$ Commit$(\mathsf{ck}, y_{\mathsf{mask}}; y_{\mathsf{comr}})$.
- Generate $\mathsf{ct}_{\mathsf{uk}} \leftarrow y_{\mathsf{mask}} \oplus \mathsf{uk}$.
- Generate $\mathsf{qfhe.ct} \leftarrow$ QFHE.Enc$(\mathsf{pk}, (\mathsf{ck}, , , \mathsf{ct}_{\mathsf{uk}}))$.
- Generate $\mathsf{ue}.ct \leftarrow$ UE.$\mathcal{E}nc(\mathsf{uk}, \mathsf{lock})$.
- Generate $\widetilde{D} \leftarrow$ CC.Obf$(1^\lambda, \mathsf{QFHE.Dec}(\mathsf{sk}, \cdot), \mathsf{lock})$.

  - Output $\rho = (\text{qfhe.ct}, \text{ue.}ct, \widetilde{D})$.
$\mathcal{Eval}\,(\rho, x)$:
  - Parse $\rho = (\text{qfhe.ct}, \text{ue.}ct, \widetilde{D})$.
  - Compute evct $\leftarrow$ QFHE.$\mathcal{Eval}\,(C[x], \text{ue.}ct, \text{qfhe.ct})$, where the circuit $C[x]$ is described in Fig. 1.
  - Output $y \leftarrow \widetilde{D}(\text{evct})$.

Quantum circuit $C[x]$

Constant: A string x.
Input: A quantum state ue.ct and strings ck, com, and ct_{uk}.

1. Parse $x_{\text{mask}} \| x_{\text{comr}} \leftarrow x$.
2. If com $\neq$ Commit(ck, $x_{\text{mask}}; x_{\text{comr}}$), output 0^λ. Otherwise, go to the next step.
3. Compute uk$' \leftarrow x_{\text{mask}} \oplus \text{ct}_{\text{uk}}$.
4. Output lock$' \leftarrow$ UE.$\mathcal{Dec}(\text{uk}', \text{ue.}ct)$.

Fig. 1. The description of $C[x]$

Evaluation Correctness. It is easy to see that CP satisfies evaluation correctness from the correctness of CC.Obf, QFHE, and UE, and injectivity of Com.

Security. For security, we have the following theorems.

Theorem 13. *Let $0 \leq w \leq 1$. We define the distributions $U_{\ell_{\text{inp}}}$ and $D_{w\text{-resamp}}(\cdot)$ as follows.*

  - *$U_{\ell_{\text{inp}}}$ is the uniform distribution over $\{0,1\}^{\ell_{\text{inp}}}$.*
  - *$D_{w\text{-resamp}}(\cdot)$ is a distribution such that $D_{w\text{-resamp}}(y)$ outputs y with probability $1 - w$ and outputs a resampled value $z \leftarrow U_{\ell_{\text{inp}}}$ with probability w.*

Let $D = \{D_\lambda\}$ be a family of distributions where each D_λ outputs $(\text{QFHE.Dec}(\text{sk}, \cdot), \text{lock}, aux := \text{pk})$ generated as those in CopyProtect. If CC.Obf is secure with respect to D, QFHE satisfies semantic security, UE satisfies one-out-of-many one-time unclonable-indistinguishable security, and Com satisfies trapdoor equivocality, then CP satisfies one-out-of-many copy protection security for $\mathcal{PF}^1$ with respect to the distributions $D_Y = U_{\ell_{\text{inp}}}$ and $D_X(\cdot) = D_{w\text{-resamp}}(\cdot)$.

Theorem 14. *We define $D^2_{w\text{-resamp}}(\cdot)$ as follows.*

  - *$D^2_{w\text{-resamp}}(\cdot)$ is a distribution such that $D^2_{w\text{-resamp}}(y)$ outputs (y, y) with probability $1 - w$ and outputs (z, z) for a resampled value $z \leftarrow U_{\ell_{\text{inp}}}$ with probability w.*

In Theorem 13, if we use one-time unclonable-indistinguishable secure UE, CP satisfies copy protection security for $\mathcal{PF}^1$ with respect to the distributions $D_Y = U_{\ell_{\text{inp}}}$ and $D_X(\cdot) = D^2_{w\text{-resamp}}(\cdot)$.

Remark 5 (On instantiations). When we instantiate CP based on Theorem 14, we need to be careful about the fact that the existing one-time unclonable-indistinguishable secure SKUE scheme uses QROM. The construction of CP evaluates the decryption circuit of UE by QFHE. Thus, to use the QROM based SKUE scheme as the building block of CP, we have to assume that it is secure when we replace QRO with real hash functions so that the decryption algorithm has a concrete description that QFHE can evaluate. Note that we always need this assumption to use QROM-based SKUE schemes in the real world.

When we instantiate CP based on Theorem 13, there is no such issue and we can obtain a construction secure in the standard model, since we have one-out-of-many one-time unclonable-indistinguishable secure SKUE based on the LWE assumption in the standard model.

We provide the proof of Theorem 13 in the full version, and omit the proof of Theorem 14.

References

1. Aaronson, S.: Quantum copy-protection and quantum money. In: Proceedings of the 24th Annual IEEE Conference on Computational Complexity, CCC 2009, Paris, France, 15–18 July 2009, pp. 229–242. IEEE Computer Society (2009). https://doi.org/10.1109/CCC.2009.42
2. Alagic, G., Brakerski, Z., Dulek, Y., Schaffner, C.: Impossibility of quantum virtual black-box obfuscation of classical circuits. In: Malkin, T., Peikert, C. (eds.) CRYPTO 2021, Part I. LNCS, vol. 12825, pp. 497–525. Springer, Cham (2021). https://doi.org/10.1007/978-3-030-84242-0_18
3. Amos, R., Georgiou, M., Kiayias, A., Zhandry, M.: One-shot signatures and applications to hybrid quantum/classical authentication. In: Makarychev, K., Makarychev, Y., Tulsiani, M., Kamath, G., Chuzhoy, J. (eds.) 52nd ACM STOC, pp. 255–268. ACM Press, June 2020. https://doi.org/10.1145/3357713.3384304
4. Ananth, P., Kaleoglu, F.: Unclonable encryption, revisited. In: Nissim, K., Waters, B. (eds.) TCC 2021, Part I. LNCS, vol. 13042, pp. 299–329. Springer, Cham (2021). https://doi.org/10.1007/978-3-030-90459-3_11
5. Ananth, P., Kaleoglu, F.: A note on copy-protection from random oracles. Cryptology ePrint Archive, Report 2022/1109 (2022). https://eprint.iacr.org/2022/1109
6. Ananth, P., Kaleoglu, F., Li, X., Liu, Q., Zhandry, M.: On the feasibility of unclonable encryption, and more. In: Dodis, Y., Shrimpton, T. (eds.) CRYPTO 2022, Part II. LNCS, vol. 13508, pp. 212–241. Springer, Heidelberg (2022). https://doi.org/10.1007/978-3-031-15979-4_8
7. Ananth, P., Kaleoglu, F., Liu, Q.: Cloning games: a general framework for unclonable primitives. arXiv (CoRR) abs/2302.01874 (2023). https://doi.org/10.48550/arXiv.2302.01874, https://arxiv.org/pdf/2302.01874.pdf
8. Ananth, P., La Placa, R.L.: Secure software leasing. In: Canteaut, A., Standaert, F.-X. (eds.) EUROCRYPT 2021, Part II. LNCS, vol. 12697, pp. 501–530. Springer, Cham (2021). https://doi.org/10.1007/978-3-030-77886-6_17
9. Behera, A., Sattath, O.: Almost public quantum coins. CoRR abs/2002.12438 (2020). https://arxiv.org/abs/2002.12438

10. Bennett, C.H., Brassard, G.: Quantum cryptography: public key distribution and coin tossing. Theor. Comput. Sci. **560**, 7–11 (2014). https://doi.org/10.1016/j.tcs. 2014.05.025

11. Brakerski, Z.: Quantum FHE (almost) as secure as classical. In: Shacham, H., Boldyreva, A. (eds.) CRYPTO 2018, Part III. LNCS, vol. 10993, pp. 67–95. Springer, Cham (2018). https://doi.org/10.1007/978-3-319-96878-0_3

12. Broadbent, A., Lord, S.: Uncloneable quantum encryption via oracles. In: Flammia, S.T. (ed.) 15th Conference on the Theory of Quantum Computation, Communication and Cryptography, TQC 2020, Riga, Latvia, 9–12 June 2020. LIPIcs, vol. 158, pp. 4:1–4:22. Schloss Dagstuhl - Leibniz-Zentrum für Informatik (2020)

13. Coladangelo, A., Liu, J., Liu, Q., Zhandry, M.: Hidden Cosets and applications to unclonable cryptography. In: Malkin, T., Peikert, C. (eds.) CRYPTO 2021, Part I. LNCS, vol. 12825, pp. 556–584. Springer, Cham (2021). https://doi.org/10.1007/978-3-030-84242-0_20

14. Coladangelo, A., Majenz, C., Poremba, A.: Quantum copy-protection of compute-and-compare programs in the quantum random oracle model. arXiv (CoRR) abs/2009.13865 (2020). https://arxiv.org/abs/2009.13865

15. Culf, E., Vidick, T.: A monogamy-of-entanglement game for subspace coset states. Quantum **6**, 791 (2022)

16. Döttling, N., Garg, S., Hajiabadi, M., Masny, D.: New constructions of identity-based and key-dependent message secure encryption schemes. In: Abdalla, M., Dahab, R. (eds.) PKC 2018, Part I. LNCS, vol. 10769, pp. 3–31. Springer, Cham (2018). https://doi.org/10.1007/978-3-319-76578-5_1

17. Georgiou, M., Zhandry, M.: Unclonable decryption keys. Cryptology ePrint Archive, Report 2020/877 (2020). https://eprint.iacr.org/2020/877

18. Gorbunov, S., Vaikuntanathan, V., Wee, H.: Predicate encryption for circuits from LWE. In: Gennaro, R., Robshaw, M. (eds.) CRYPTO 2015, Part II. LNCS, vol. 9216, pp. 503–523. Springer, Heidelberg (2015). https://doi.org/10.1007/978-3-662-48000-7_25

19. Gottesman, D.: Uncloneable encryption. Quantum Inf. Comput. **3**(6), 581–602 (2003). https://doi.org/10.26421/QIC3.6-2

20. Goyal, R., Koppula, V., Waters, B.: Lockable obfuscation. In: Umans, C. (ed.) 58th FOCS, pp. 612–621. IEEE Computer Society Press, October 2017. https://doi.org/10.1109/FOCS.2017.62

21. Kitagawa, F., Nishimaki, R.: Watermarking PRFs against quantum adversaries. In: Dunkelman, O., Dziembowski, S. (eds.) EUROCRYPT 2022, Part III. LNCS, vol. 13277, pp. 488–518. Springer, Heidelberg (2022). https://doi.org/10.1007/978-3-031-07082-2_18

22. Liu, J., Liu, Q., Qian, L., Zhandry, M.: Collusion-resistant copy-protection for watermarkable functionalities. In: Kiltz, E., Vaikuntanathan, V. (eds.) TCC 2022. LNCS, vol. 13747, pp. 294–323. Springer, Cham (2022). https://doi.org/10.1007/978-3-031-22318-1_11

23. Mahadev, U.: Classical homomorphic encryption for quantum circuits. In: Thorup, M. (ed.) 59th FOCS, pp. 332–338. IEEE Computer Society Press, October 2018. https://doi.org/10.1109/FOCS.2018.00039

24. Sahai, A., Seyalioglu, H.: Worry-free encryption: functional encryption with public keys. In: Al-Shaer, E., Keromytis, A.D., Shmatikov, V. (eds.) ACM CCS 2010, pp. 463–472. ACM Press, October 2010. https://doi.org/10.1145/1866307.1866359

25. Sattath, O., Wyborski, S.: Uncloneable decryptors from quantum copy-protection. arXiv (CoRR) abs/2203.05866 (2022). https://doi.org/10.48550/arXiv.2203.05866

26. Tomamichel, M., Fehr, S., Kaniewski, J., Wehner, S.: A monogamy-of-entanglement game with applications to device-independent quantum cryptography. New J. Phys. **15**(10), 103002 (2013). https://doi.org/10.1088/1367-2630/15/10/103002

27. Wichs, D., Zirdelis, G.: Obfuscating compute-and-compare programs under LWE. In: Umans, C. (ed.) 58th FOCS, pp. 600–611. IEEE Computer Society Press, October 2017. https://doi.org/10.1109/FOCS.2017.61

28. Wiesner, S.: Conjugate coding. SIGACT News **15**(1), 78–88 (1983). https://doi.org/10.1145/1008908.1008920

29. Winter, A.: Coding theorem and strong converse for quantum channels. IEEE Trans. Inf. Theory **45**(7), 2481–2485 (1999). https://doi.org/10.1109/18.796385

30. Zhandry, M.: Schrödinger's Pirate: how to trace a quantum decoder. In: Pass, R., Pietrzak, K. (eds.) TCC 2020, Part III. LNCS, vol. 12552, pp. 61–91. Springer, Cham (2020). https://doi.org/10.1007/978-3-030-64381-2_3

Group-Based Cryptography

Limits in the Provable Security
of ECDSA Signatures

Dominik Hartmann$^{(\boxtimes)}$ and Eike Kiltz

Ruhr University Bochum, Bochum, Germany
{dominik.hartmann,eike.kiltz}@rub.de

Abstract. Digital Signatures are ubiquitous in modern computing. One of the most widely used digital signature schemes is ECDSA due to its use in TLS, various Blockchains such as Bitcoin and Etherum, and many other applications. Yet the formal analysis of ECDSA is comparatively sparse. In particular, all known security results for ECDSA rely on some idealized model such as the generic group model or the programmable (bijective) random oracle model.

In this work, we study the question whether these strong idealized models are necessary for proving the security of ECDSA. Specifically, we focus on the programmability of ECDSA's "conversion function" which maps an elliptic curve point into its x-coordinate modulo the group order. Unfortunately, our main results are negative. We establish, by means of a meta reductions, that an algebraic security reduction for ECDSA can only exist if the security reduction is allowed to program the conversion function. As a consequence, a meaningful security proof for ECDSA is unlikely to exist without strong idealization.

Keywords: ECDSA · random oracle model · programmability · meta reductions

1 Introduction

The digital signature algorithm (DSA) [35][1] and its elliptic curve variant ECDSA [29] are two of the most prevalent digital signatures to date, used in TLS [4] and various cryptocurrencies such as Bitcoin and Ethereum. Furthermore, there has been a lot of recent interest in designing threshold signing protocols for ECDSA such as [12,14–19,25,31–33].

Despite its practical importance, only a few research papers so far have studied the provable security of (EC)DSA. Further, all security proofs require some form of strong idealization, e.g. the random oracle model [5,21], the bijective random oracle model [20], the (elliptic curve) generic group model (GGM) [8,27], or the algebraic bijective random oracle model [38].

Generic DSA signatures (GenDSA) are defined over a group $\mathbb{G}$ of prime order p with generator g, a hash function H, and a so-called "conversion function"

---

[1] FIPS 186-5 from February 2023 does no longer approve DSA signatures for digital signature generation. However, DSA may still be used for signature verification.

© International Association for Cryptologic Research 2023
G. Rothblum and H. Wee (Eds.): TCC 2023, LNCS 14372, pp. 279–309, 2023.
https://doi.org/10.1007/978-3-031-48624-1_11

$f : \mathbb{G}^* \to \mathbb{Z}_p$ mapping group elements to exponents. A public key consists of a single group element $X = g^x$ with its discrete logarithm x being the secret key. To sign a message m, the signer samples a random exponent r, computes g^r and then applies the conversion function to compute $t = f(g^r)$. Next, it hashes the message m and computes $s = \frac{H(m)+tx}{r} \bmod p$. The signature is the tuple $(s,t) \in \mathbb{Z}_p^* \times \mathbb{Z}_p^*$. DSA and ECDSA can be seen as special cases of GenDSA, instantiated over specific groups and with specific conversion functions. For ECDSA, $\mathbb{G}$ is an elliptic curve group and the conversion function f maps an element on the elliptic curve to its x-coordinate modulo p; for DSA, $\mathbb{G}$ is a subgroup of order p of a prime order field, and f reduces a group element modulo p.

Whereas in most previous security proofs of GenDSA, the hash function H was modeled as a perfect random function (i.e., a random oracle [3]), properly modeling the conversion function $f : \mathbb{G}^* \to \mathbb{Z}_p$ turned out to be problematic. In both DSA and ECDSA, the conversion functions in essence reduce (part of) the group element modulo the order of the group generator, but they completely disrupt the algebraic meaning of their input. Specifically, for ECDSA, f is "almost invertible", i.e., inverting f only loses the sign of the elliptic curve point. However, all known security proofs (of full UF-CMA security) have the following drawback:

Observation: *All existing security proofs of (EC)DSA model (parts of) the conversion function f as some programmable, idealized function.*

Specifically, they either model f *explicitly* using a random function/bijection [5, 20, 38] or they hide the group elements via the random encoding of the GGM and hence model f *implicitly* as a random function [8, 27]. While this approach does mimic how f breaks the algebraic meaning of its inputs, it actually does even more. By using a random oracle/bijection, a reduction is allowed to *program* the random function, as long as the adversary cannot detect the changes. Similarly, the GGM allows for programming of the representations of the group elements, which makes any non-algebraic function f mapping from $\mathbb{G}$ implicitly programmable. Programmability is already somewhat debatable when modeling hash functions [22], but it is especially unsatisfying when modeling the conversion function f, as the function is conceptually very simple and not random at all, which makes programmability especially unrealistic. Yet, all known proofs for (EC)DSA crucially rely (explicitly or implicitly) on programming the conversion function f. So in this work, we ask the following natural question:

Question: *Is (EC)DSA provably secure without relying on the programmability of the conversion function f?[2]*

---

[2] We stress that we do not question the modeling of GenDSA's hash function H as a programmable random oracle. Even though the programmable random oracle model has received valid criticism (e.g., [13]), it is generally viewed as a valid heuristic for a modern hash function which was designed to behave randomly.

1.1 Main Contributions

Unfortunately, our results are negative: We show that without modeling (part of) the conversion function f as a programmable idealized object, there is little hope for proving (EC)DSA secure. Together with the known positive results on (EC)DSA by Fersch, Kiltz, and Poettering [20,21], we obtain the following complete picture on the provable security of (EC)DSA:

> **Main result (informal):** *(EC)DSA is provably secure if and only if the conversion function f is modeled using a programmable idealized function.*

To be a bit more precise, we follow the framework of [20] and decompose the conversion function f into three functions φ, ψ, Π, with $f = \psi \circ \Pi \circ \varphi$, where only $\Pi : \{0,1\}^L \rightarrow \{0, \dots, 2^L - 1\}$ is an idealized random bijection and φ and ψ are standard model functions. (More details on the modeling of f will be given in Sect. 3.2.) To simplify the presentation of our results, in the remainder of this introduction we call conversion function f programmable iff the random bijection Π is programmable.

Our main results are summarized in Fig. 1, where the considered security notions are Unforgeability against Chosen-Message Attack (UF-CMA), Unforgeability against No-Message Attack (UF-NMA – no signing queries allowed), and Multi-User UF-CMA (n-UF-CMA).

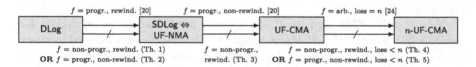

Fig. 1. Relations between hardness assumptions DLog and SDLog (relative to conversion function f) and security notions for GenDSA (relative to hash function H and conversion function f). A crossed arrow refers to an impossibility result, together with the condition under which it holds. "f = progr." means that the conversion function f is modeled as programmable, "f = non-progr." means that f is modeled as non-programmable, and "f = arb." means that f can be arbitrary; "rewind." and "non-rewind." means that the security reduction is rewinding and non-rewinding, respectively. In all negative relations, GenDSA's hash function H (if available) is modeled as a programmable random oracle.

RELATION BETWEEN DLog AND UF-NMA SECURITY OF GenDSA. We first study the question whether the standard Discrete Logarithm assumption (DLog) can provably imply UF-NMA security of GenDSA (i.e., no signing queries allowed). Since for arbitrary conversion functions f, UF-NMA security is known to be equivalent to the SDLog assumption when modeling the hash function H as a programmable random oracle [6,21], we equivalently study the (simpler) relation between the DLog and the SDLog assumption. Here SDLog refers to the *Semi*

Discrete Logarithm assumption relative to conversion function f [6].[3] On the positive side, [20] use a rewinding reduction to show that DLog is equivalent to SDLog if f is programmable. We contrast their positive result with two negative results.

Firstly, we present a meta reduction showing that if the conversion function f is *non-programmable*, then there exists no *algebraic* reduction that reduces the SDLog to the DLog assumption, as long as the *Free-Base One-More Discrete Logarithm assumption* (FBOMDL) holds in the group. FBOMDL, introduced by Paillier and Vergnaud [37], is a stronger variant of the regular One-More Discrete Logarithm assumption (OMDL) [2]. (See below for a general discussion on assumptions in the context of meta reductions.) Secondly, we show that even if the conversion function f is *programmable*, SDLog cannot be reduced to the DLog assumption by an algebraic, *non-rewinding* reduction, as long as FBOMDL holds.

By the equivalence of SDLog and the UF-NMA security of GenDSA, the relation between DLog and UF-NMA security of GenDSA can be summarized as follows: DLog provably implies UF-NMA security of GenDSA if and only if f is programmable *and* the reduction is allowed to rewind the adversary.

RELATION BETWEEN UF-NMA AND UF-CMA SECURITY. On the positive side, [20] use a non-rewinding reduction to show that UF-NMA implies UF-CMA security of GenDSA if f is programmable. Contrasting their positive result, we prove that there cannot exist an algebraic reduction from the UF-CMA security of GenDSA to its UF-NMA security, if the DLog assumption holds and f is *non-programmable*.

Note that UF-NMA and UF-1CMA security are known to be equivalent for GenDSA [21], where in UF-1CMA security the adversary is only allowed to query *one* signature for each message. By transitivity, our negative result also shows that UF-1CMA does not imply full UF-CMA security, unless f is programmable. This gives a negative answer to an open question of [21].

RELATION BETWEEN SINGLE-USER AND MULTI-USER SECURITY. We also consider the multi-user security of GenDSA. While single-user and multi-user security are tightly equivalent for other schemes such as Schnorr signatures [30], we prove that the generic security loss linear in the number of users proven in [24] is indeed optimal for GenDSA, if the reduction is algebraic and f is non-programmable. We also show optimality of the linear loss for the case if the conversion function f is *programmable* but the reduction is restricted to be *non-rewinding*. Our interpretation is that GenDSA's multi-user security inherently loses a linear factor compared to single-user security, unless the reduction can program f and is allowed to rewind the adversary. But rewinding reductions usually require the forking lemma and therefore result in an even worse (quadratic) security loss.

INTERPRETATION OF OUR RESULTS. Our results show that there can be no *algebraic* reductions under the conditions mentioned above. More specifically,

---

[3] The SDLog assumption essentially says that it is hard to forge a GenDSA signature relative to a message m with $H(m) = 1$, see Definition 3.

we have to restrict the class of reductions even further (see Sect. 3.2). So how relevant are our results then? First, note that almost all security reductions are *generic*, i.e. they do not use anything other than the group structure of a cryptographic group. All generic algorithms are also algebraic [23] and have to fulfill the additional requirements we make on our reductions, so most reductions commonly used are covered by our impossibility results. Another formulation of our results would be that in order to prove GenDSA secure without programming f, one would either have to break FBOMDL, find some new, non-algebraic proof technique or apply additional idealized model such as the AGM or GGM.

GENERIC HARDNESS OF THE FBOMDLASSUMPTION. As we are dealing with meta-reductions, all our negative results are naturally conditioned on certain computational assumptions. Some of them are non-standard and quite strong assumptions, such as the FBOMDL assumption. We would like to stress that we only prove "unprovability" based on such strong assumptions. That is, if the strong assumption gets broken, we only lose the impossibility result and (EC)DSA signatures are most likely still secure. The natural interpretation of our results is that a formal security proof is impossible unless one finds a way to break the assumptions. In that sense for impossibility results from meta-reductions there is only a small risk in using strong assumptions. Other examples following a similar approach include the impossibility result of [10], which is conditioned on the existence of indistinguishability obfuscation (iO). This is in stark contrast to an actual security proofs from strong assumptions where the security of the whole system would be jeopardized in case the assumption is broken.

The OMDL assumption was recently proven secure in the GGM [1]. Their proof mainly uses that each query to the discrete logarithm oracle reveals a linear relation. While the free-base variant allows queries to a different basis point, answers still only reveal linear relations, so their proof applies to the FBOMDL assumption as well. For completeness, we provide a formal proof of the FBOMDL assumption in the GGM in the full version [28].

1.2   Related Work

The first formal security results on *unmodified* (EC)DSA are due to Brown [7–9] and prove security of ECDSA in the generic group model. However, the proof is somewhat problematic in that it not only idealizes the underlying group $\mathbb{G}$ but also implicitly the conversion function f. This allows Brown to prove that ECDSA is *strongly* unforgeable (as observed by Stern et al. [40]), which it obviously is not. Additionally, Brown shows different necessary and sufficient conditions for the security of ECDSA, however the sufficient conditions are significantly stronger than the discrete logarithm problem.

As already mentioned, [20,21] take a different approach in that they do not idealize the underlying group but conversion function f and hash function H. Modeling f as a programmable idealized object, [20] show that DLog implies UF-NMA security, which in turn implies full UF-CMA security. Furthermore, [21] model only H as a random oracle, and show that, for any function f, the Semi Discrete Logarithm assumption (SDLog) implies the UF-NMA security of GenDSA, which in turn implies UF-1CMA security, i.e. an adversary is only allowed a single signature on each message.

Recently, Groth and Shoup [27] revisited the security of ECDSA in the generic group model. They avoid the shortcomings of Brown's proof by considering ECDSA in the so-called Elliptic Curve GGM (EC-GGM). This variant of the GGM keeps some relationships in the elliptic curve intact, such as the fact which points share the same x-coordinate. Their proof still implicitly idealizes the conversion function f, but only requires standard properties for the hash function H. They also consider the security of ECDSA with additive key derivation and when using presignatures (i.e. an adversary gets a number of random group elements and can choose which the challenger has to use to answer signature queries).

In terms of impossibility results, Pailler and Vergnaud [37] show that a large class of signatures including DSA and ECDSA cannot be proven secure in the standard model via a meta reduction to a variant of the One-More Discrete Logarithm problem. We prove a stronger impossibility result, since we model f as in [20] with a (non-programmable) ideal bijection and make no restrictions on the modeling of H (i.e., even allow it to be a *programmable* RO).

Further research either considered variants of GenDSA (or DSA and ECDSA) [34] or analyzed their behavior in the presence of specific faults such as (partial) randomness reuse [36] or collisions [41,42]. Blind signatures and threshold signatures based on ECDSA were proposed in [11,38] and [15,26] respectively.

2 Preliminaries

For integers $m, n \in \mathbb{Z}$, let $[m : n] = \{m, m + 1, \ldots, n\}$. If $m = 1$, we write $[n]$ instead. Let S be a (finite) set, then we write $s \xleftarrow{\$} S$ for sampling an element s uniformly at random from S.

2.1 Algebraic Algorithms

We model all algorithms (i.e. adversaries, reductions and meta reductions) as stateful and probabilistic (the specific computational model is not relevant, but one can think of interactive Turing machines). For a probabilistic algorithm $\mathcal{A}$, we write $y \xleftarrow{\$} \mathcal{A}(x_1, \ldots, x_n)$ when $\mathcal{A}$ outputs y on input $(x_1, \ldots, x_n)$ using fresh random coins. For deterministic algorithms, we use $y \leftarrow \mathcal{A}(x_1, \ldots, x_n)$. We write $\mathcal{A}^{O(\cdot)}$ to indicate that $\mathcal{A}$ gets black-box access to algorithm O which is also called an oracle. That is, $\mathcal{A}$ can make arbitrary many queries x_i to O and obtains $O(x_i)$ as answers.

Throughout this paper, we fix a cryptographic group $\mathcal{G} = (\mathbb{G}, p, g)$, where $\mathbb{G}$ is a finite multiplicative group $\mathbb{G}$ of prime order p, generated by g. An algorithm $\mathcal{A}$ is called *algebraic* [23,37], if it outputs every group element together with a representation relative to its inputs. We also consider oracle-aided algorithms, where an oracle can output (random) group elements. If this is the case, an algebraic algorithm treats these group elements as additional inputs. On the other hand, if an oracle takes group elements as input, an algebraic algorithm is also required to output a representation for these inputs.

Definition 1 (Algebraic Algorithm). *An algorithm $\mathcal{A}$ is called* algebraic *relative to a group $\mathcal{G} = (\mathbb{G}, p, g)$, if whenever it outputs a group element $X \in \mathbb{G}$ it additionally outputs a representation vector $z \in \mathbb{Z}_p^n$ s.t. $X = \prod_{i=1}^{n} Y_i^{z_i}$, where $Y_1, \ldots, Y_n$ denote the group elements previously known to $\mathcal{A}$.*

Our meta reductions will require that the assumed reduction is algebraic, yet the meta reductions themselves (and therefore also the adversaries simulated by them) will not be algebraic. This is analogue to security reductions in the AGM, where an adversary is assumed to be algebraic, but the reduction and the oracles it provides are not algebraic.

As noted by in [43,44], it is somewhat imprecise to talk about the group elements "known" to an algorithm, because additional group elements might be encoded in its inputs. However, all adversaries that we consider only receive group elements as inputs (most only a single group element), so we assume that those are the only group elements known.

2.2 Idealized Functions

In our security reductions we will model the conversion function f and the hash function H of GenDSA as publicly accessible, idealized functions. The most prominent idealized function is a random oracle [3], where a hash function $H : \mathcal{X} \to \mathcal{Y}$ is modeled as a perfect random function $\mathbf{H} \xleftarrow{\$} \{H : \mathcal{X} \to \mathcal{Y}\}$ that can only be accessed through oracle queries. Note that oracle $\mathbf{H}$ can be efficiently implemented using lazy sampling.

Let $\mathrm{Func}(\mathcal{X}, \mathcal{Y})$ be the set of all functions from $\mathcal{X}$ to $\mathcal{Y}$ and let $\mathrm{Bij}(\mathcal{X}, \mathcal{Y})$ be the set of all bijections from $\mathcal{X}$ to $\mathcal{Y}$. The idealized functions that we will use in this work, together with their oracle interfaces, are listed in the following table.

Idealized object	Function type	Oracle	Distribution
Random Oracle (RO)	Function $H : \mathcal{X} \to \mathcal{Y}$	$\mathbf{H}$	$\mathbf{H} \xleftarrow{\$} \mathrm{Func}(\mathcal{X}, \mathcal{Y})$
Bijective Random Oracle (bRO)	Bijection $\Pi : \mathcal{X} \to \mathcal{Y}$	$(\mathbf{\Pi}, \mathbf{\Pi}^{-1})$	$\mathbf{\Pi} \xleftarrow{\$} \mathrm{Bij}(\mathcal{X}, \mathcal{Y})$

2.3 Security Reductions and Programmability

Proving that a hard problem P (e.g., DLog) implies the security of some cryptographic protocol S (e.g., the ECDSA signature scheme) is commonly done via a security reduction. In a security reduction, an adversary $\mathcal{A}$ against S is executed by a reduction $\mathcal{R}$, denoted as $\mathcal{R}^{\mathcal{A}}$, which uses $\mathcal{A}$ to solve its own hard problem P. If further $\mathcal{R}$'s success is meaningfully related to that of $\mathcal{A}$, then one can deduce P $\Rightarrow$ S. In this work, we always consider *Fully Black Box* reductions [39], i.e. the reduction can not depend on any internal properties of the adversary like its code. However, we assume that upper bounds on the number of oracle queries of all algorithms are known.

PROGRAMMABLE IDEALIZED FUNCTIONS. If $\mathcal{A}$ is an adversary with oracle access to an idealized function $\mathbf{O}$ (see Sect. 2.2), then reduction $\mathcal{R}$ executes $\mathcal{A}$ by providing its inputs, randomness, and answering all queries made to the expected oracle $\mathbf{O}$. Using our notation, we write $\mathcal{R}^{\mathcal{A}^{\mathbf{O}}}$ to denote the reduction executing $\mathcal{A}^{\mathbf{O}}$. Consequently, $\mathcal{R}$ has complete control over $\mathcal{A}$'s input and output channel and therefore in particular over oracle $\mathbf{O}$. In the most general case, $\mathcal{R}$ can even rewind the adversary $\mathcal{A}$ in a black-box manner by running it again with the same initial inputs (including randomness) and altering the oracle answers at some point of the execution. Hence in the context of a security reduction, such idealized functions are also called programmable. Most prominently, if $\mathbf{O}$ is modeled as a random function $\mathbf{H}$, then $\mathbf{H}$ is the well known programmable random oracle or simply random oracle [3].

NON-PROGRAMMABLE IDEALIZED FUNCTIONS. One can also model $\mathcal{A}$'s oracle as an idealized function that reduction $\mathcal{R}$ does *not* control but is only able to observe. We call such an oracle a non-programmable idealized function $\bar{\mathbf{O}}$. We use the notion $\bar{\mathbf{O}}$ ("overline") to make the non-programmability of the function explicit. Here, observing means that whenever $\mathcal{A}$ makes a query X to $\bar{\mathbf{O}}$, it obtains the response $\bar{\mathbf{O}}(X)$ directly from $\bar{\mathbf{O}}$, but $\mathcal{R}$ also gets the pair $(X, \bar{\mathbf{O}}(X))$.[4] Furthermore, we also provide the reduction $\mathcal{R}$ black-box access to $\bar{\mathbf{O}}$. (In the programmable case this is not necessary since $\mathcal{R}$ has already full control over the oracle $\mathbf{O}$.) In the context of a security reduction, we use the notation $\mathcal{R}^{\bar{\mathbf{O}}, \mathcal{A}^{\bar{\mathbf{O}}}}$ to indicate that $\bar{\mathbf{O}}$ is non-programmable by $\mathcal{R}$.

The special case where $\bar{\mathbf{O}}$ is a perfectly random function $\bar{\mathbf{H}}$ yields the well-known non-programmable random oracle [22].

The differences between a programmable and a non-programmable idealized function in the context of a security reduction are visualized in Fig. 2.

2.4 Meta Reductions

Meta reductions are a useful tool for proving the (conditional) impossibility of security reductions. On a technical level, a meta reduction $\mathcal{M}$ assumes the existence of a reduction $\mathcal{R} = \mathcal{R}^{\mathcal{A}}$ proving $\mathsf{P} \Rightarrow \mathsf{S}$, i.e., $\mathcal{R}$ solves problem P with black-box access to an adversary $\mathcal{A}$. Meta reduction $\mathcal{M}$ then uses said assumed reduction to break some (potentially different) hard problem P'. As a consequence, such a security reduction $\mathcal{R}$ proving $\mathsf{P} \Rightarrow \mathsf{S}$ cannot exist unless problem P' turns out to be easy. The above requires simulating an adversary $\mathcal{A}$ for $\mathcal{R}$ to work, which is often the main challenge of constructing a meta reduction.

The meta reduction has to provide $\mathcal{R}$ with all oracles it expects in its game as well as (programmable or non-programmable) idealized functions, while $\mathcal{R}$ in

---

[4] [22] consider a more general modeling where $\mathcal{R}$ gets X before the query and can make its own oracle queries which could influence the response $\bar{\mathbf{O}}(X)$. However, since such queries would never alter the behavior in all of our reductions, we only consider this simplified definition.

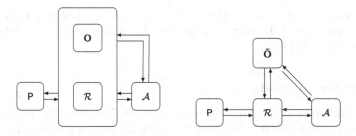

Fig. 2. Left: Security reduction $\mathcal{R}$ running adversary $\mathcal{A}$ with access to a programmable idealized function **O**. Reduction $\mathcal{R}$ has full control over $\mathcal{A}$'s queries to **O**. Right: Security reduction $\mathcal{R}$ running $\mathcal{A}$ with access to a non-programmable idealized function $\bar{\mathbf{O}}$. Reduction $\mathcal{R}$ can only observe $\mathcal{A}$'s queries to $\bar{\mathbf{O}}$. (Color figure online)

turn provides all *programmable* oracles **O** to the (simulated) adversary $\mathcal{A}$. This is depicted in Fig. 3. For the case of a non-programmable ideal function, there are some intricacies to the modeling. Specifically, if $\mathcal{R}$ expects a non-programmable idealized function, $\mathcal{M}$ can itself simulate a *programmable* idealized function (via standard lazy sampling), which is indistinguishable from a non-programmable idealized function for $\mathcal{R}$.

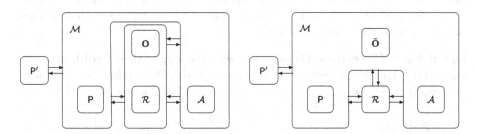

Fig. 3. Depiction of a meta reduction $\mathcal{M}$ interacting with a game P$'$ with a *programmable* oracle **O** (left) and *non-programmable* oracle $\bar{\mathbf{O}}$ (right), and a reduction $\mathcal{R}$. In the programmable case, the oracle is "internal" to the reduction, i.e., **O** can be controlled arbitrarily by $\mathcal{R}$. In the non-programmable case, the oracle is external to $\mathcal{R}$ and hence meta-reduction $\mathcal{M}$ is able to control $\bar{\mathbf{O}}$.

Fischlin et al. [22] argue that one should allow the reduction the same programming and observability capabilities as the meta reduction, as it keeps the modeling of the function replaced by the random oracle consistent. Intuitively, if the goal is to model realistic functions, it is unreasonable to assume that one (efficient) algorithm has more control over some function than another (efficient) algorithm without any trapdoors. However in our proofs, we have to allow the meta-reduction to program while the reduction sees the random oracle as non-programmable. Indeed, programmability for the meta-reduction seems necessary in order to extract solutions in the end of the meta reduction. Looking ahead, the meta-reduction will use the solution of the reduction together with the observed random oracle queries to extract a discrete logarithm from the solution and previously simulated signatures.

2.5 Hardness Assumptions

We now recall three hard problems over a group $\mathcal{G} = (\mathbb{G}, p, g)$: The standard Discrete Logarithm problem, the Semi Discrete Logarithm problem [6], and the Free-Base One-More Discrete Logarithm problem [37].

Definition 2 (Discrete Logarithm Problem).] *The discrete logarithm (DLog) problem is (t, ϵ)-hard in group $\mathcal{G} = (\mathbb{G}, p, g)$, if for all adversaries $\mathcal{A}$ running in time at most t, $\Pr[x' = x \mid x \xleftarrow{\$} \mathbb{Z}_p; X := g^x; x' \xleftarrow{\$} \mathcal{A}(X)] \leq \epsilon$.*

Definition 3 (Semi-Discrete Logarithm Problem). *The* Semi-Discrete Logarithm (SDLog) *problem is (t, ϵ)-hard relative to group $\mathcal{G} = (\mathbb{G}, p, g)$ and conversion function $f : \mathbb{G} \rightarrow \mathbb{Z}_p$, if for any adversary $\mathcal{A}$ running in time at most t, $\Pr[t^* \neq 0 \wedge s^* \neq 0 \wedge t^* = f((g \cdot X^{t^*})^{s^{*-1}}) \mid x \xleftarrow{\$} \mathbb{Z}_p; X = g^x; (s^*, t^*) \xleftarrow{\$} \mathcal{A}(X)] \leq \epsilon$.*

We remark that the SDLog problem can equivalently be seen as "forging a GenDSA signature (see Definition 8) on a message m with $H(m) = 1$". While SDLog is defined relative to a specific conversion function f, it can be replaced by an idealized function in a reduction similar to how explicit hash functions can be replaced with random oracles.

Definition 4 (Free-Base One-More Discrete Logarithm Problem). *The q-Free-Base One-More Discrete Logarithm (q-FBOMDL) problem is (t, ϵ)-hard in group $\mathcal{G} = (\mathbb{G}, p, g)$, if for all adversaries $\mathcal{A}$ running in time at most t,*

$$\Pr\left[\forall 0 \leq i \leq q : X_i = g^{x_i} \,\middle|\, \begin{array}{c} X_0 \xleftarrow{\$} \mathbb{G} \\ (x_0, \dots, x_q) \xleftarrow{\$} \mathcal{A}^{\mathbf{DL}(\cdot, \cdot), \mathbf{Chal}}(X_0) \end{array}\right] \leq \epsilon,$$

where the oracles are defined as follows. The challenge oracle **Chal***, on its i-th query, outputs a group element $X_i \xleftarrow{\$} \mathbb{G}^*$. It can be queried at most q times. The free-base discrete logarithm oracle* **DL**$(\cdot, \cdot)$*, on input $(X, R) \in \mathbb{G} \times \mathbb{G}^*$, outputs $z \in \mathbb{Z}_p$ s.t. $R^z = X$. It can be queried as many times as the* **Chal** *oracle was queried.*

q-FBOMDL is a stronger variant of the regular One-More Discrete Logarithm assumption [2], where the discrete logarithm oracle is restricted to base g. To increase the confidence in q-FBOMDL, we will prove its unconditional hardness in the GGM in the full version [28].

2.6 Digital Signatures

We recall the definition of digital signatures and their standard notions of security.

Definition 5 (Digital Signatures). *A digital signature scheme* $SIG = ($Gen, Sign, Ver$)$ *is a tuple of three algorithms with the following properties:*

Gen $\xrightarrow{\$}$ (sk, vk)*: The key generation algorithm outputs a public key/secret key pair. The public key implicitly defines the message space* $\mathcal{M}$*.*

Sign(sk, m) $\xrightarrow{\$}$ σ*: The signing algorithm takes a secret key* sk *and a message* m *as input and returns a signature* σ*.*

Ver(vk, m, σ)*: The (deterministic) verification algorithm gets a public key* vk*, a message* m *and a signature* σ *and outputs 1 for accept and 0 for reject.*

A digital signature scheme is ϵ-correct*, if for all* (sk, vk) $\in$ Gen *and all messages* $m \in \mathcal{M}$

$$Pr[\text{Ver}(\text{vk}, m, \text{Sign}(\text{sk}, m)) = 0] \leq \epsilon$$

Definition 6 (Signature Security). *Let* $n \in \mathbb{N}$ *and* $SIG = ($Gen, Sign, Ver$)$ *be a digital signature scheme.* SIG *is said to be* (t, ϵ, q_S)-n-UF-ATK *secure (*Multi-User Unforgeability against ATK attacks*), if for every adversary* $\mathcal{A}$ *running in time at most* t *and making at most* q_S *queries to the oracle* SIGN,

$$Pr\left[\begin{array}{c} (i^*, m^*) \notin \mathcal{Q} \wedge \\ \text{Ver}(\text{vk}_{i^*}, m^*, \sigma^*) = 1 \end{array} \middle| \begin{array}{c} \text{For } i \in [n] : (\text{vk}_i, \text{sk}_i) \xleftarrow{\$} \text{Gen} \\ (i^*, m^*, \sigma^*) \xleftarrow{\$} \mathcal{A}^{\text{SIGN}(\cdot, \cdot)}((\text{vk}_i)_{i \in [n]}) \end{array} \right] \leq \epsilon,$$

where depending on ATK*, the oracle* SIGN *is defined as follows:*

- ATK = NMA*: The oracle* SIGN *always returns* $\perp$*.*
- ATK = CMA*: On input of a message* m *and an index* $i \in [n]$*,* SIGN *returns a signature* σ *for* m *under secret key* sk_i *and adds* (i, m) *to* $\mathcal{Q}$*.*

If the adversary has additionally access to an idealized function via oracle $\mathbf{O}(\cdot)$*, we denote this as* (t, ϵ, q_S, q_O)-n-UF-ATK *security, where* q_O *denotes the number of queries to* $\mathbf{O}$*. For* NMA *security, we omit the parameter* q *from the description and simply write* (t, ϵ)-n-UF-NMA*. If* $n = 1$*, i.e. we are in a single-user setting, we instead write* (t, ϵ, q_S)-UF-ATK = (t, ϵ, q_S)-1-UF-ATK*.*

3 Generic DSA and the Conversion Function

In this section, we recall the definition of GenDSA from [20] and discuss the modeling of the conversion function f in our meta reductions. We also recall some basic definitions beforehand.

Definition 7 (Semi-Injective Function). *Let* $\mathbb{G}$ *be a prime order group and* $\mathcal{Y}$ *a set. A function* $\varphi : \mathbb{G}^* \to \mathcal{Y}$ *is called semi-injective if*

1. *its range* $\varphi(\mathbb{G}^*) \subseteq \mathcal{Y}$ *is efficiently decidable and*
2. *it is either injective or a 2-to-1 function with* $\varphi(x) = \varphi(y) \implies x \in \{y, y^{-1}\}$

3.1   Generic DSA Signatures

In this work, we will study Generic DSA (GenDSA) [20], an abstract signature framework which subsumes both DSA and ECDSA. It models the conversion function as $f = \psi \circ \Pi \circ \varphi$ for efficient functions ψ, φ and a bijection Π. According to [20], the idea is to reflect in φ the structure of f that involves only its domain and to reflect in ψ the structure that involves only its range; the component that is responsible for disrupting any algebraic link between the domain and the range is modeled by Π. In security proofs we, Π will be replaced by a bijective random oracle. DSA and ECDSA can naturally be obtained, together with the specific peculiarities of their conversion functions, by correspondingly instantiating φ and ψ. For a more in-depth discussion of GenDSA, we refer the reader to [20].

Definition 8 (GenDSA). *Let $L \in \mathbb{N}$. The signature scheme GenDSA = (Gen, Sign, Ver) relative to a group $\mathcal{G} = (\mathbb{G}, p, g)$, a hash function $H : \{0,1\}^* \to \mathbb{Z}_p$ and a conversion function $f : \mathbb{G}^* \to \mathbb{Z}_p$ with $f = \psi \circ \Pi \circ \varphi$ for efficient functions ψ, φ and bijection Π with*

$$\mathbb{G}^* \xrightarrow{\varphi} \{0,1\}^L \xrightarrow{\Pi} [0 : 2^L - 1] \xrightarrow{\psi} \mathbb{Z}_p$$

is defined as follows.

Gen:

$x \xleftarrow{\$} \mathbb{Z}_p; X := g^x$
$\mathsf{vk} := X; \mathsf{sk} := x$
return $(\mathsf{vk}, \mathsf{sk})$

Sign(sk = x, m):

$r \xleftarrow{\$} \mathbb{Z}_p^*; R := g^r$
$t := f(R); h := H(m)$
$s := \frac{h + x \cdot t}{r}$
if $(t = 0) \vee (s = 0)$ **then**
    return $\bot$
return (s, t)

Ver(vk = $X, m, \sigma = (s,t)$):

if $(t = 0) \vee (s = 0)$ **then**
    return $\bot$
$h := H(m)$
$t' := f\left(\left(g^h X^t\right)^{\frac{1}{s}}\right)$
return $t = t'$

To the function ψ from Definition 8, we associate the quantity

$$\epsilon_\psi = \max_{t \in \mathbb{Z}_p} \Pr_{y \in [0:2^L-1]} [\psi(y) = t], \tag{1}$$

ECDSA AND DSA. For ECDSA [29], $\mathcal{G}$ is instantiated with a prime-order subgroup $\mathbb{G}$ of an elliptic curve group over $\mathbb{F}_q$. For $L = \lceil \log_2(q) \rceil$, $\varphi : \mathbb{G}^* \to \{0,1\}^L$ maps an elliptic curve point $R = (R_x, R_y) \in \mathbb{F}_q \times \mathbb{F}_q$ to the binary representation of its x-coordinate R_x, which makes it a semi-injective 2-to-1 function. Note that $\varphi(\mathbb{G})$ is efficiently decidable. Function $\psi : [0 : 2^L - 1] \to \mathbb{Z}_p$ is the modular reduction modulo p. By Hasse's theorem, we get $p \leq 2q$ for all $q \geq 13$ (see [27]). If $q \geq p$, then the probability that ψ maps an element from $[0 : 2^L - 1]$ with $L = \lceil \log_2(q) \rceil$ to a specific $y \in \mathbb{Z}_p$ is at most $2/p$, since there are at most $\lceil 2^L/p \rceil$ preimages per y. On the other hand, if $q \leq p$, we get that the same probability is bounded by $1/q \leq 1/(p/2) = 2/p$, where the inequality follows from the Hasse bound. So in both cases $\epsilon_\psi \leq 2/p$.

For DSA, $\mathcal{G}$ is instantiated with a multiplicative prime order subgroup of the a prime order field $\mathbb{F}_q$, i.e. $\mathbb{G} \subset \mathbb{F}_q^*$. For $L = \lceil \log_2(q) \rceil$ $\varphi : \mathbb{G}^* \to \{0,1\}^L$ is the mapping of a group element to its binary representation, hence it is injective (so also semi-injective). $\varphi(\mathbb{G})$ is efficiently decidable since the group order is known. $\psi : [0 : 2^L - 1] \to \mathbb{Z}_p$ is the reduction modulo p. Since we always have $p \leq 2q + 1$, it is straight forward to see $\epsilon_\psi \leq 2/p$.

3.2 Modeling the Conversion Function in Proofs

As observed by Brown [9], the non-algebraic conversion function $f : \mathbb{G}^* \to \mathbb{Z}_p$ is an integral part of a security analysis of GenDSA. However, modeling the abstract properties of f in formal proofs turns out to be a non-trivial task.

We use Definition 8 and decompose f as $f = \psi \circ \Pi \circ \varphi$. In our meta reductions, permutation $\Pi : \{0,1\}^L \to [0 : 2^L - 1]$ is modeled as a *bijective Random Oracle* (bRO) (Π, Π^{-1}) and the two functions $\varphi : \mathbb{G}^* \to \{0,1\}^L$, $\psi : [0 : 2^L - 1] \to \mathbb{Z}_p$ are standard model functions. This allows to accurately model the biases introduced by the real conversion functions while having a clear interface to work with in (meta-)reductions.

THE CONVERSION FUNCTION IN THE AGM. In our results we will provide an *algebraic* algorithm $\mathcal{A}$ (i.e., a reduction) access to a bijective Random Oracle (Π, Π^{-1}). Since algorithm $\mathcal{A}$ is algebraic, we make the following constraints:

1. Whenever an algebraic algorithm $\mathcal{A}$ queries $\Pi^{-1}(y)$ for some $y \in [0 : 2^L - 1]$, it receives the output $x = \Pi^{-1}(y) \in \{0,1\}^L$ of the bRO. If $x \in \varphi(\mathbb{G}^*)$ (which can be efficiently decided by Definition 7), then we add $\varphi^{-1}(x)$ to the list of known group elements relative to which the algebraic algorithm can output representations. Note that, by using lazy sampling, queries to $\Pi^{-1}(y)$ can be efficiently simulated even if φ is *not* efficiently invertible: We first sample a fresh random element $x \in \{0,1\}^L$. If $x \notin \varphi(\mathbb{G}^*)$, we define $\Pi^{-1}(y) := x$. If $x \in \varphi(\mathbb{G})$, we discard x and define $\Pi^{-1}(y) := \varphi(g^r)$ for $r \xleftarrow{\$} \mathbb{Z}_p$.
2. Whenever an algebraic algorithm $\mathcal{A}$ queries $\Pi(x)$ for some $x \in \varphi(\mathbb{G}^*)$, it also has to provide a group element $R \in \varphi^{-1}(x)$, together with an algebraic representation of R. (Note that φ is semi-injective, and hence the exact choice of $R \in \varphi^{-1}(x)$ is irrelevant).

The latter constraint above was previously introduced in [38] as the *Algebraic Bijective Random Oracle model*. However they only consider algebraic use of the bRO interface Π used in f in contrast to the fully algebraic reductions in our meta reductions. Therefore, we make the need for a representation relative to φ part of the algebraic adversary instead of (Π, Π^{-1}) and add the potentially new group elements computable from (Π, Π^{-1}) to $\mathcal{A}$'s inputs. Specifically, this is *not* an additional idealization of φ for (Π, Π^{-1}) but a restriction on the class of algorithms we consider.

Why is this a reasonable modeling of the conversion function in the algebraic group model? First, as argued in [20], the composition of the three functions allows to accurately model the biases and intricacies of the conversion function in many different settings such as DSA and ECDSA. However, since the bijective random oracle $(\mathbf{\Pi}, \mathbf{\Pi}^{-1})$ does not receive group elements as inputs, it is generally incompatible with the AGM. The second constraint bridges this gap somewhat artificially by demanding a representation of a preimage under φ whenever $\mathbf{\Pi}$ is queried, which implicitly assumes that an algorithm will always use $\mathbf{\Pi}$ in composition with φ (it can still use φ without querying $\mathbf{\Pi}$). This assumption can be seen as a simply another convenient constraint on algorithms similar to the ones already made by the AGM. From this point of view, we simply consider an even more limited class of algorithms.

Note that all *generic* algorithms are still covered by this limited class. Specifically, in the GGM, a representation of a preimage under φ is always known for every $z \in \{0,1\}^L$ as long as $\varphi^{-1}(z)$ is a valid label. This is due to the fact that the GGM can simply track all calls to the group oracle and therefore knows a representation for all defined labels relative to the inputs. If φ^{-1} produces a new, valid label, the GGM can internally simply assign it a random group element for which it knows a representation, keeping this invariant intact. For invalid labels, nothing has to be done.

However, this restriction is indeed also a reasonable assumption if we look at the concrete instantiations of the conversion function. For ECDSA, φ is essentially the projection of an elliptic curve point (R_x, R_y) to is x-coordinate. While it is easy for many curves to sample x-coordinates uniformly at random, doing so samples the curve point obliviously, i.e. without knowledge of the discrete logarithm or a representation relative to other points. If an algorithm were to use such a group element in its solution, it would have to produce a non-trivial equation in the secret key or challenge *and* this unknown discrete logarithm. Worse still, this choice of an x-coordinate also does not give any more control over the output of $\mathbf{\Pi}$ or $\psi \circ \mathbf{\Pi}$, since $\mathbf{\Pi}$ is a random function, so using $\mathbf{\Pi}$ without φ only loses information.

4   Impossibility Results

4.1   DLog $\not\Rightarrow$ SDLog

Our first result is to show that DLog does not imply SDLog if we consider only non-programming, algebraic reductions. Specifically, the following theorem states that there cannot exist an algebraic reduction from SDLog to DLog that does not program the random bijection $(\bar{\mathbf{\Pi}}, \bar{\mathbf{\Pi}}^{-1})$, unless the FBOMDL assumption is false.

Theorem 1 (DLog $\overset{\Pi \text{ non-progr.}}{\not\Rightarrow}$ SDLog). *Let $f = \psi \circ \Pi \circ \varphi$ be a conversion function with semi-injective $\varphi : \mathbb{G}^* \to \{0,1\}^L$, $\psi : [0 : 2^L - 1] \to \mathbb{Z}_p$ and $\Pi : \{0,1\}^L \to [0 : 2^L - 1]$ modeled by a non-programmable bijective random oracle $(\bar{\mathbf{\Pi}}, \bar{\mathbf{\Pi}}^{-1})$. If there exists an algebraic reduction $\mathcal{R}$ that $(t_\mathcal{R}, \epsilon_\mathcal{R}, q'_{\bar{\mathbf{\Pi}}}, q'_{\bar{\mathbf{\Pi}}^{-1}})$-breaks the DLog assumption given q_P-times access to an adversary $\mathcal{A}$ that $(t_\mathcal{A}, \epsilon_\mathcal{A}, q_{\bar{\mathbf{\Pi}}}, q_{\bar{\mathbf{\Pi}}^{-1}})$-breaks the SDLog assumption, then there* *exists a meta-reduction $\mathcal{M}$ which $(t_\mathcal{M}, \epsilon_\mathcal{M})$-breaks the q_P-FBOMDL assumption with*

$$\epsilon_\mathcal{M} \geq \epsilon_\mathcal{R} - 2q_P\epsilon_\psi - \frac{q^2}{2^L}, \quad t_\mathcal{M} \approx t_\mathcal{R} + q_P t_\mathcal{A},$$

where $q = q_P(q_{\bar{\Pi}} + q_{\bar{\Pi}^{-1}}) + q'_{\bar{\Pi}} + q'_{\bar{\Pi}^{-1}}$ is the total amount of queries to $(\bar{\Pi}, \bar{\Pi}^{-1})$ made by $\mathcal{A}$ and $\mathcal{R}$.

We state an orthogonal impossibility result for non-rewinding reductions which have access to a *programmable* bRO (Π, Π^{-1}). Specifically, the following theorem states that there cannot exist an algebraic reduction $\mathcal{R}$ that reduces SDLog to DLog without rewinding the adversary, unless the FBOMDL assumption is false.

Theorem 2 (DLog $\overset{\text{non-rew.}}{\not\Rightarrow}$ SDLog). *Let $f = \psi \circ \Pi \circ \varphi$ be a conversion function with semi-injective $\varphi : \mathbb{G}^* \to \{0,1\}^L$, $\psi : [0 : 2^L - 1] \to \mathbb{Z}_p$ and $\Pi : \{0,1\}^L \to [0 : 2^L - 1]$ modeled by a programmable bijective random oracle (Π, Π^{-1}). If there exists an algebraic reduction $\mathcal{R}$ that $(t_\mathcal{R}, \epsilon_\mathcal{R})$-breaks the DLog assumption given one-times access to an adversary $\mathcal{A}$ that $(t_\mathcal{A}, \epsilon_\mathcal{A}, q_\Pi, q_{\Pi^{-1}})$-breaks the SDLog assumption, then there exists a meta-reduction $\mathcal{M}$ which $(t_\mathcal{M}, \epsilon_\mathcal{M})$-breaks the 1-FBOMDL assumption with*

$$\epsilon_\mathcal{M} \geq \epsilon_\mathcal{R}, \quad t_\mathcal{M} \approx t_\mathcal{R} + t_\mathcal{A}.$$

We now prove Theorem 1. The proof of Theorem 2 is similar and can be found in the full version [28].

Proof (of Theorem 1). Let $\mathcal{A}$ be an adversary that $(t_\mathcal{A}, \epsilon_\mathcal{A}, q_{\bar{\Pi}}, q_{\bar{\Pi}^{-1}})$-breaks the SDLog assumption, and let $\mathcal{R}$ be the security reduction that $(t_\mathcal{R}, \epsilon_\mathcal{R}, q'_{\bar{\Pi}}, q'_{\bar{\Pi}^{-1}})$-breaks the DLog assumption. $\mathcal{R} = \mathcal{R}^{(\bar{\Pi}(\cdot), \bar{\Pi}^{-1}(\cdot))}$ has access to the non-programmable bRO $(\bar{\Pi}, \bar{\Pi}^{-1})$ and executes up to q_P-times adversary $\mathcal{A}$. (Recall that the bars of $(\bar{\Pi}, \bar{\Pi}^{-1})$ indicate non-programmability.) We denote the i-th execution of $\mathcal{A}$ as $\mathcal{A}_i$. $\mathcal{A}_i = \mathcal{A}_i^{(\bar{\Pi}(\cdot), \bar{\Pi}^{-1}(\cdot))}$ has access to the non-programmable bRO $(\bar{\Pi}, \bar{\Pi}^{-1})$ of the SDLog game and $\mathcal{R}$ can observer all queries made by $\mathcal{A}$ to $(\bar{\Pi}, \bar{\Pi}^{-1})$. We will construct a meta-reduction $\mathcal{M}$ trying to solve the q_P-FBOMDL game by running the reduction $\mathcal{R}$, simulating the DLog experiment, the non-programmable bRO $(\bar{\Pi}, \bar{\Pi}^{-1})$ via lazy sampling, and the q_P executions $\mathcal{A}_i$ of adversary $\mathcal{A}$.

$\mathcal{M}^{\mathbf{Chal}, \mathbf{DL}(\cdot, \cdot)}(X)$ receives X as its q_P-FBOMDL input, has access to FBOMDL's challenge oracle **Chal** and discrete logarithm oracle **DL** and executes the reduction $\mathcal{R}^{\bar{\Pi}, \bar{\Pi}^{-1}}(X)$ with X as its DLog challenge. Reduction $\mathcal{R}$ in turn executes up to q_P adversaries $\mathcal{A}_i(\hat{X}_i)$ (simulated by $\mathcal{M}$) on an arbitrary group element $\hat{X}_i$ as its SDLog challenge. Meta reduction $\mathcal{M}$ and $\mathcal{A}_i(\hat{X}_i)$ simulated by $\mathcal{M}$ are shown in Fig. 4. Since $\mathcal{R}$ is algebraic, it provides $\mathcal{A}_i$ (and hence also $\mathcal{M}$) with the representations $(a_i, b_i, c_{i,1}, \ldots, c_{i,i-1})_{i \in [q_P]}$ of $\hat{X}_i$. That is, $\hat{X}_i = g^{a_i} X^{b_i} \prod_{j<i} X_j^{c_{i,j}}$ for $a_i, b_i, c_{i,j} \in \mathbb{Z}_p$, where X_j is the j-th challenge

Meta Reduction $\mathcal{M}^{\mathbf{Chal},\mathbf{DL}(\cdot,\cdot)}(X)$	Adversary $\mathcal{A}_i^{\bar{\Pi}(\cdot),\bar{\Pi}^{-1}(\cdot)}(\hat{X}_i)$ $/\!/\hat{X}_i = g^{a_i}X^{b_i}\prod_{j<i}X_j^{c_{i,j}}$
1: Run $\mathcal{R}(X)$	8: $X_i \leftarrow \mathbf{Chal}$
2: for $i \in [q_P]$ do	9: $t_i^* \leftarrow \psi(\bar{\Pi}(\varphi(X_i)))$ $/\!/$via oracle query to $\bar{\Pi}$
3: Receive $\hat{X}_i$ from $\mathcal{R}$	10: Make remaining $q_{\bar{\Pi}} - 1$ dummy queries to $\bar{\Pi}$
4: Simulate $\mathcal{A}_i^{\bar{\Pi}(\cdot),\bar{\Pi}^{-1}(\cdot)}(\hat{X}_i)$ for $\mathcal{R}$	11: Make $q_{\bar{\Pi}^{-1}}$ dummy queries to $\bar{\Pi}^{-1}$
5: Receive solution x from $\mathcal{R}$	12: if $t_i^* = 0 \vee g \cdot \hat{X}_i^{t_i^*} = 1$ then $/\!/\Leftrightarrow s_i^* = 0$
6: Solve equations for $x_1,\dots x_{q_P}$	13: abort
7: return $(x, x_1,\dots,x_{q_P})$	14: $s_i^* \leftarrow \mathbf{DL}(g \cdot \hat{X}_i^{t_i^*}, X_i)$ $/\!/$from FBOMDL game
	15: return $\begin{cases}(s_i^*, t_i^*) & \text{with prob. } \epsilon_{\mathcal{A}} \\ \perp & \text{else}\end{cases}$

Fig. 4. Meta reduction $\mathcal{M}$ and simulated adversaries $\mathcal{A}_i$ against the SDLog assumption. DL and **Chal** are $\mathcal{M}$'s oracles from the FBOMDL assumption. If the $\mathcal{A}_i$ is run with the same randomness and public key as $\mathcal{A}_j$, then $\mathcal{M}$ simply replays the queries made by $\mathcal{A}_j$ and does not query the **Chal** or **DL** oracle.

returned by the **Chal** oracle. $\mathcal{R}$ will learn exactly one new X_j for each execution of $\mathcal{A}$ through its queries to Π, so $\hat{X}_i$ can only depend on g, X, and $X_1,\dots,X_{i-1}$.

$\mathcal{A}_i$ embeds one of the FBOMDL challenges X_i into its first query to $\bar{\Pi}$.[5] Next, it makes $q_{\bar{\Pi}} - 1$ dummy queries to $\bar{\Pi}$ and $q_{\bar{\Pi}^{-1}}$ queries to $\bar{\Pi}^{-1}$. Here, all queries are chosen such that the group elements corresponding to them via φ are independent of the X_i, so the representation of all public keys for future executions of $\mathcal{A}$ still collapses as described above. After making all of its queries, $\mathcal{A}_i$ checks if the challenge X_i results in an invalid solution (line 12) and ends its execution if so. Otherwise, it uses one query to the **DL** oracle to obtain $s_i^* = \mathbf{DL}(g \cdot \hat{X}_i^{t_i^*}, X_i) = \frac{1+\hat{x}_i t_i^*}{x_i} \neq 0$, where $\hat{X}_j = g^{\hat{x}_j}$ and $X_j = g^{x_j} \in \mathbb{G}^*$. Next, it returns a valid SDLog solution $(s_i^*, t_i^*) \in \mathbb{Z}_p^* \times \mathbb{Z}_p^*$ relative to public key $\hat{X}_i$. Note that every $\mathcal{A}_i$ makes one **Chal** query and at most one **DL** query.

We can assume w.l.o.g. that all executions of $\mathcal{A}_i$ are distinct. (If $\mathcal{A}_i$ is run with the same randomness and public key as $\mathcal{A}_j$ for $j < i$, then $\mathcal{M}$ simply replays the same queries as made in $\mathcal{A}_j$. Specifically, it does not query the **Chal** oracle and sets $X_i = X_j$. This results in a correct simulation, since $(\bar{\Pi}, \bar{\Pi}^{-1})$ is a non-programmable bRO, so $\mathcal{R}$ can only control the randomness and input of $\mathcal{A}_i$ and nothing else.)

The simulation of $\mathcal{A}_i$ is perfect, as it wins with exactly probability $\epsilon_{\mathcal{A}}$, unless $t_i^* = 0$ or $t_i^* \cdot \hat{x}_i + 1 = 0$ with $\hat{X}_i = g^{\hat{x}_i}$ (line 12). We call the overall abort BAD and the two sub-events BAD$_1$ and BAD$_2$ respectively. In order to analyze $\Pr[\text{BAD}]$, we assume that $(\bar{\Pi}, \bar{\Pi}^{-1})$ is a random *function* instead of a random permutation. This allows us to assume that all output values are always chosen uniformly at random, but might incur an error if a collision occurs. The latter can be bounded by the birthday bound as $q^2/2^L$, where q is the total number of queries to $(\bar{\Pi}, \bar{\Pi}^{-1})$ observed by $\mathcal{R}$.

We now analyze BAD$_1$ and BAD$_2$ for each individual execution of $\mathcal{A}_i$. Event BAD$_1$ occurs iff $t_i^* = f(X_i) = \psi(\bar{\Pi}(\varphi(X_i))) = 0$. The random variable $y_i := \bar{\Pi}(\varphi(X_i))$ is distributed uniformly random since $\bar{\Pi}$ is a random function. Therefore, $\Pr[\text{BAD}_1] = \Pr[f(X_i) = 0] = \Pr[\psi(\bar{\Pi}(\varphi(X_i))) = 0] =$

---

[5] This fixed embedding is not exploitable by $\mathcal{R}$ since $(\bar{\Pi}, \bar{\Pi}^{-1})$ is non-programmable.

$\Pr_{y_i \xleftarrow{\$} [0:2^L-1]}[\psi(y_i) = 0] \leq \epsilon_\psi$. Similarly, for each execution of $\mathcal{A}_i$, event BAD_2 occurs iff $\hat{x}_i t_i^* + 1 = 0$ with $t_i^* \neq 0$ and $\hat{x}_i \neq 0$. $\hat{x}_i$ is (implicitly) chosen by $\mathcal{R}$ *before* t_i^* is computed by $\mathcal{A}_i$ with its first query to $\bar{\Pi}$, so it is independent of t_i^*. So in order for BAD_2 to occur, we have to bound the probability that $t_i^* = -\hat{x}_i^{-1}$. With the same argument as for BAD_1, we get $\Pr[\text{BAD}_2] = \Pr[t_i^* = -\hat{x}_i] \leq \epsilon_\psi$. So overall, $\Pr[\text{BAD}] \leq \Pr[\text{BAD}_1] + \Pr[\text{BAD}_2] \leq 2\epsilon_\psi$ for each execution of $\mathcal{A}_i$. A union bound over all executions of $\mathcal{A}$ and the birthday bound yields that the probability that BAD occurs in *any* execution is

$$\Pr[\text{BAD}] \leq 2q_P\epsilon_\psi + q^2/2^L.$$

Now assume that none of the $\mathcal{A}_i$ aborts, i.e., BAD does not happen. Then all $\mathcal{A}_i$ are simulated perfectly, so $\mathcal{R}$ will be successful with probability $\epsilon_\mathcal{R}$ and output x s.t. $g^x = X$. Let x_i ($i \in [q_P]$) be the unknown discrete logarithms of the FBOMDL challenges $X_i = g^{x_i}$ from line 8. Using the representations $a_i, b_i, (c_{i,j})_{j \in [q_P]}$ of $\hat{X}_i = g^{a_i} X^{b_i} \prod_{j<i} X_j^{c_{i,j}}$, $\mathcal{M}$ gets the equations

$$s_i^* x_i = 1 + t_i^* a_i + t_i^* b_i x + t_i^* \sum_{1 \leq j < i} c_{i,j} x_j,$$

for $i \in [q_P]$ in the variables $x_1, \ldots, x_{q_P}$.

There are q_P equations in q_P variables, so there exists a unique solution unless its determinant is zero. Looking at these equations as a matrix, we see that it is a triangle matrix with the s_i^* on the diagonal. Its determinant is $\prod_{i \in [q_P]} s_i^* \neq 0$ since $s_i^* \neq 0$. $\mathcal{M}$ computes the x_i using standard linear algebra and returns all $q_P + 1$ discrete logarithms $(x, x_1, \ldots, x_{q_P})$ as its solution. Hence, $\mathcal{M}$ wins the q_P-FBOMDL game if $\mathcal{R}$ is successful and BAD occurs in no execution of $\mathcal{A}$, so

$$\epsilon_\mathcal{M} \geq \epsilon_\mathcal{R} - \Pr[\text{BAD}] \geq \epsilon_\mathcal{R} - 2q_P\epsilon_\psi - \frac{q^2}{2^L},$$

which concludes the proof. □

4.2 NMA $\not\Rightarrow$ CMA

Next, we prove that with non-programmable bijective random oracles, GenDSA's UF-NMA security does not imply UF-CMA security. By transitivity, this also implies that UF-1CMA security does not imply UF-CMA security without programmability of (Π, Π^{-1}).

Specifically, the following theorem states that there cannot exist an algebraic reduction $\mathcal{R}$ that reduces the UF-CMA security of GenDSA to its UF-NMA security that does not program the random bijection $(\bar{\Pi}, \bar{\Pi}^{-1})$, unless the DLog assumption does not hold in the group.

Theorem 3 (UF-NMA $\overset{\Pi \text{ non-progr.}}{\not\Rightarrow}$ UF-CMA). *Let $\mathbf{H}, \mathbf{H}' : \{0,1\}^* \to \mathbb{Z}_p$ be hash functions modeled as a programmable random oracle and $f = \psi \circ \Pi \circ \varphi$ be* a conversion function with semi-injective $\varphi : \mathbb{G}^* \to \{0,1\}^L$, $\psi : [0 : 2^L - 1] \to \mathbb{Z}_p$ and $\bar{\Pi} : \{0,1\}^L \to [0 : 2^L - 1]$ a non-programmable bijective random oracle $(\bar{\Pi}, \bar{\Pi}^{-1})$. If there exists an algebraic reduction $\mathcal{R}$ that $(t_\mathcal{R}, \epsilon_\mathcal{R}, q'_{\bar{\Pi}}, q'_{\bar{\Pi}^{-1}}, q'_\mathbf{H})$-breaks the UF-NMA security of GenDSA (instantiated with $\mathbf{H}$) with q_P-time access to an adversary $\mathcal{A}$ that $(t_\mathcal{A}, \epsilon_\mathcal{A}, q_s, q_{\bar{\Pi}}, q_{\bar{\Pi}^{-1}}, q_{\mathbf{H}'})$-breaks the UF-CMA security of GenDSA (instantiated with $\mathbf{H}'$), then there exists an algorithm $\mathcal{M}$ that $(t_\mathcal{M}, \epsilon_\mathcal{M})$-breaks the DLog assumption where

$$\epsilon_\mathcal{M} \geq \epsilon_\mathcal{R} - (2(q'_{\bar{\Pi}} + q'_{\bar{\Pi}^{-1}})q'_\mathbf{H} + 1)\epsilon_\psi - q'_\mathbf{H}/p - q^2/2^L, \quad t_\mathcal{M} \approx t_\mathcal{R},$$

where $q = q'_{\bar{\Pi}} + q'_{\bar{\Pi}^{-1}} + q_P(q_{\bar{\Pi}} + q_{\bar{\Pi}^{-1}})$ is total number of queries made to $(\bar{\Pi}, \bar{\Pi}^{-1})$ by $\mathcal{R}$ and $\mathcal{A}$.

Since the goals of $\mathcal{R}$ and $\mathcal{A}$ are identical, i.e. producing a valid signature for a given key, we cannot generally use the output of $\mathcal{R}$ to make $\mathcal{M}$ work, since if $\mathcal{R}$ just forwards its own challenge key, the solution of $\mathcal{A}$ is also a solution for $\mathcal{R}$. So in this case, the idea of the meta-reduction is to ask for two signatures on the same message and then extract a DLog solution from the oracle queries and the signatures that $\mathcal{R}$ produces. Disallowing the reduction from programming the bRO $(\bar{\Pi}, \bar{\Pi}^{-1})$ is necessary, as otherwise the proof from [20] applies. For the same reason, an analogue of Theorem 2 is impossible here, as the reduction of [20] is non-rewinding.

Proof. Let $\mathcal{A}$ be an adversary that $(t_\mathcal{A}, \epsilon_\mathcal{A}, q_s, q_{\bar{\Pi}}, q_{\bar{\Pi}^{-1}}, q_{\mathbf{H}'})$-breaks the UF-CMA security of GenDSA and let $\mathcal{R}$ be the security reduction that $(t_\mathcal{R}, \epsilon_\mathcal{R}, q'_{\bar{\Pi}}, q'_{\bar{\Pi}^{-1}}, q'_\mathbf{H})$-breaks the UF-NMA security of GenDSA. $\mathcal{A} = \mathcal{A}^{\mathbf{H}', \bar{\Pi}, \bar{\Pi}^{-1}}(\mathsf{vk}')$ has access to the non-programmable bRO $(\bar{\Pi}, \bar{\Pi}^{-1})$ and the programmable random oracle $\mathbf{H}'$ of the UF-CMA game. $\mathcal{R} = \mathcal{R}^{\mathbf{H}, \bar{\Pi}, \bar{\Pi}^{-1}}$ has access to the non-programmable bRO $(\bar{\Pi}, \bar{\Pi}^{-1})$ and the random oracle $\mathbf{H}$ of the UF-NMA game, internally simulates the programmable random oracle $\mathbf{H}'$ of the UF-CMA game (accessed by $\mathcal{A}$) and observes all queries made by $\mathcal{A}$ to $(\bar{\Pi}, \bar{\Pi}^{-1})$. Meta-reduction $\mathcal{M}$ tries to solve the DLog game by running the reduction $\mathcal{R}$, simulating the UF-NMA experiment together with its RO $\mathbf{H}$ and the non-programmable bRO $(\bar{\Pi}, \bar{\Pi}^{-1})$, and simulating adversary $\mathcal{A}$.

$\mathcal{M}(X)$ receives a DLog challenge $X = g^x$ as input and sets $\mathsf{vk} = X$. It runs $\mathcal{R}^{\mathbf{H}, \bar{\Pi}, \bar{\Pi}^{-1}}(\mathsf{vk})$ with the signature key vk as input and simulates the random oracle $\mathbf{H}$ and the bRO $(\bar{\Pi}, \bar{\Pi}^{-1})$ via lazy sampling. It keeps a list L where it stores previous queries and assorted information on the queries. When $\mathcal{R}$ queries $\bar{\Pi}(z)$ for a fresh $z \in \{0,1\}^L$, $\mathcal{M}$ samples a fresh random $y \in [0 : 2^L - 1]$. If $z \notin \varphi(\mathbb{G}^*)$, it stores $(\bot, z, \bot, y)$ in L and returns y. If $z \in \varphi(\mathbb{G}^*)$, $\mathcal{R}$ has to provide a representation a, b s.t. $\varphi(g^a \cdot X^b) = z$ and $\mathcal{M}$ stores $(g^a X^b, z, (a,b), y)$ (and $(g^{-a} X^{-b}, z, (-a, -b), y)$ if φ is 2-to-1) in L. When $\mathcal{R}$ queries $\bar{\Pi}^{-1}(z')$ on a fresh $z' \in [0 : 2^L - 1]$, $\mathcal{M}$ samples a random $x \in \{0,1\}^L$. If $x \notin \varphi(\mathbb{G}^*)$, $\mathcal{M}$ sets $\bar{\Pi}^{-1}(z') = x$ (i.e. stores $(\bot, x, \bot, z')$ in L) and returns x. Otherwise, it samples $(a,b) \xleftarrow{\$} \mathbb{Z}_p^2$ s.t. $a + xb \neq 0$, computes $R := g^a \cdot X^b$ and sets $\bar{\Pi}^{-1}(z') := \varphi(R)$. In the latter case, it additionally stores $(R, \varphi(R), (a,b), z')$

(and $(R^{-1}, \varphi(R), (-a, -b), \psi(z'))$ if φ is 2-to-1) in L and returns $\varphi(R)$ to $\mathcal{R}$. Note that this simulation of $(\bar{\Pi}, \bar{\Pi}^{-1})$ implements a random *function* instead of a random bijection. By the birthday bound, this incurs a statistical loss $q^2/2^L$, where $q = q'_{\bar{\Pi}} + q'_{\bar{\Pi}^{-1}} + q_P(q_{\bar{\Pi}} + q_{\bar{\Pi}^{-1}})$ is the total number of queries made to $(\bar{\Pi}, \bar{\Pi}^{-1})$ by $\mathcal{R}$ and $\mathcal{A}$ due to it possibly introducing collisions.

When $\mathcal{R}$ invokes the UF-NMA adversary $\mathcal{A} = \mathcal{A}^{\mathbf{H}', \bar{\Pi}, \bar{\Pi}^{-1}}$, $\mathcal{M}$ simulates it for $\mathcal{R}$. Note that $\mathcal{A}$ has access to the same oracles $\bar{\Pi}$ and $\bar{\Pi}^{-1}$ as $\mathcal{R}$, since we model $(\bar{\Pi}, \bar{\Pi}^{-1})$ as a non-programmable bRO, but $\mathbf{H}'$ is fully controlled by $\mathcal{R}$. $\mathcal{R}$ starts $\mathcal{A}$ by sending a public key vk'. Since $\mathcal{R}$ is algebraic, it also outputs a representation of vk' relative to all its inputs, including group elements calculated from answers to $\bar{\Pi}^{-1}$ queries. Since $\mathcal{M}$ knows all discrete logarithms except for X from the simulation described above, this representation implicitly collapses to one relative to g and X:

$$\mathsf{vk}' = g^\alpha X^\beta \in \mathbb{G} . \tag{2}$$

At this point, $\mathcal{M}$ reacts differently depending on whether $\beta = 0$ or not.

CASE 1: $\beta = 0$. In this case, $\mathcal{R}$ effectively does not need the adversary $\mathcal{A}$ as it can compute any signature produced by $\mathcal{A}$ on its own. (Note that the simulation of adversary $\mathcal{A}$ is trivial in this case as $\mathcal{R}$ is algebraic and therefore $\mathcal{M}$ knows $\mathsf{sk}' = \alpha$, which also makes rewinding/multiple executions trivial.) Meta-reduction $\mathcal{M}$ continues the execution of $\mathcal{R}$ until it terminates and produces a forgery $(m^*, \sigma^* = (s^*, t^*))$. Assume the forgery is valid, i.e., it satisfies

$$t^* = f(R^*), \text{ where } R^* = \left(g^{\mathbf{H}(m^*)} X^{t^*}\right)^{\frac{1}{s^*}} . \tag{3}$$

We we will now use another case distinction to show that $\mathcal{M}$ can solve its DLog challenge in Case 1 except with probability $2\epsilon_\psi q'_{\mathbf{H}}(q'_{\bar{\Pi}} + q'_{\bar{\Pi}^{-1}})$.

CASE 1.A: $\beta = 0$ AND $\nexists (R^*, *, (a^*, b^*), y^*) \in L$ WITH $\psi(y^*) = t^*$. In this case, t^* does not correspond to a query made by $\mathcal{R}$ to $\bar{\Pi}$ or $\bar{\Pi}^{-1}$ and $\mathcal{M}$ *can not* compute a discrete logarithm solution in this case and aborts. We call this case BAD$_1$. We will show that $\Pr[\text{BAD}_1] \leq \epsilon_\psi$. First, note that since $\bar{\Pi}$ is random, the random variable $y^* = \bar{\Pi}(\varphi(R^*))$ is distributed uniformly over $[0 : 2^L - 1]$. Therefore, we have

$$\Pr[\text{BAD}_1] = \Pr[\psi(\bar{\Pi}(\varphi(R^*))) = t^*] = \Pr[\psi(y^*) = t^*] \leq \epsilon_\psi .$$

CASE 1.B: $\beta = 0$ AND $\exists (R^*, *, (a^*, b^*), y^*) \in L$ WITH $\psi(y^*) = t^*$. Since $R^* = g^{a^*} X^{b^*}$, (3) simplifies to

$$s^*(a^* + b^* x) = \mathbf{H}(m^*) + t^* x . \tag{4}$$

Consequently, unless $s^* b^* = t^*$ (which we denote as event BAD$_2$), $\mathcal{M}$ can extract $x = \frac{s^* a^* - \mathbf{H}(m^*)}{t^* - s^* b^*}$ and solve its DLog challenge. To finish the analysis of Case 1.B, it remains to show

$$\Pr[\text{BAD}_2] = \Pr[t^* = s^* b^*] \leq 2\epsilon_\psi q'_{\mathbf{H}}(q'_{\bar{\Pi}} + q'_{\bar{\Pi}^{-1}}) + q'_{\mathbf{H}}/p . \tag{5}$$

Assuming $t^* = s^*b^*$, the verification Eq. (4) can be rearranged as

$$t^*a^* = \mathbf{H}(m^*)b^*. \tag{6}$$

For every fixed m^*, a^*, b^*, the value t^* satisfying (6) is unique unless $a^* = 0$. However in that case, (6) implies that either $b^* = 0$ or $\mathbf{H}(m^*) = 0$. The first case already reveals $x = \mathbf{H}(m^*)/t^*$ from (4). The second case only occurs with probability $q'_{\mathbf{H}}/p$, since $\mathbf{H}$ is a random oracle that $\mathcal{R}$ can not program and we also abort in this case. Hence, conditioned on $\mathbf{H}(m^*) \neq 0$, $\Pr[\psi(\bar{\mathbf{\Pi}}(\varphi(g^{a^*}X^{b^*}))) = t^*] \leq \epsilon_\psi$, where the probability is over the random function $(\bar{\mathbf{\Pi}}, \bar{\mathbf{\Pi}}^{-1})$. $\mathcal{R}$ can chose from $q'_{\mathbf{H}}$ many tuples $(m^*, \mathbf{H}(m^*))$ ($\mathbf{H}$ is the oracle provided by the UF-NMA game to $\mathcal{R}$ so it is not programmable) and from $2(q'_{\bar{\mathbf{\Pi}}} + q'_{\bar{\mathbf{\Pi}}^{-1}})$ many tuples (a^*, b^*) (φ is semi-injective, i.e., there are potentially 2 preimages for every t^*). So a union bound over the number of tuples yields that the probability that $\mathcal{R}$ finds a tuple (a^*, b^*, t^*, m^*) satisfying (6) is at most $2\epsilon_\psi q'_{\mathbf{H}}(q'_{\bar{\mathbf{\Pi}}} + q'_{\bar{\mathbf{\Pi}}^{-1}}) + q'_{\mathbf{H}}/p$.

Overall, $\mathcal{M}$ is successful in Case 1 iff BAD_1 and BAD_2 do not happen.

CASE 2: $\beta \neq 0$. In this case, $\mathcal{R}$ effectively uses the adversary $\mathcal{A}$. $\mathcal{M}$ continues simulating $\mathcal{A}$ by picking an arbitrary message m satisfying $\mathbf{H}'(m) \neq 0$ and asks for two signatures $\sigma_1 = (s_1, t_1)$ and $\sigma_2 = (s_2, t_2)$ on the same m. Without loss of generality, we assume that $\sigma_1 \neq \sigma_2$. Next, $\mathcal{M}$ aborts the execution of $\mathcal{A}$ and $\mathcal{R}$. Note that $\mathcal{M}$ has simulated the UF-NMA game and an UF-CMA adversary perfectly up to this point. Again, rewinding/multiple executions are handled trivially, as every instance of $\mathcal{A}$ only queries two signatures on a random message m with $\mathbf{H}'(m) \neq 0$.

Let $r_1, r_2 \in \mathbb{Z}_p$ s.t. $R_i := g^{r_i}$ and $f(R_i) = t_i$ for $i \in \{1, 2\}$. Note that there might be multiple such r_1, r_2 as f is generally not injective. We assume that the two values chosen here are the ones used by the reduction in its answer and its queries to f (if they were made, see case distinction below). Assuming the signatures σ_1 and σ_2 are valid, we have

$$\forall i \in \{1, 2\}: \quad s_i r_i - \mathbf{H}'(m) = t_i \alpha + t_i \beta x, \tag{7}$$

with $s_i \neq 0$, $t_i \neq 0$ and α, β are from (2). Note that $\mathcal{M}$ only knows $R_i = g^{r_i}$ and not r_i. We now distinguish two cases depending on whether R_1 and R_2 have been recorded as a query to $(\bar{\mathbf{\Pi}}, \bar{\mathbf{\Pi}}^{-1})$ or not.

- Case 2.A: $\nexists (R_i, z_i, (a_i, b_i), z'_i) \in L$ s.t. $g^{r_i} = R_i$ for at least one $i \in \{1, 2\}$
- Case 2.B: $\exists (R_i, z_i, (a_i, b_i), z'_i) \in L$ s.t. $g^{r_i} = R_i$, i.e. $r_i = a_i + xb_i$ for $i \in \{1, 2\}$

CASE 2.A: This case is almost identical to Case 1.A, as $\mathcal{M}$ can again not extract a DLog solution and aborts. We call this event BAD_3. As in Case 1.A, we have that the probability of $\mathcal{R}$ succeeding in this case is upper bounded by ϵ_ψ, because $\mathcal{R}$ has to simulate a proper signing oracle, so the signatures σ_1, σ_2 need to verify and with the same argument as in the other case, we get

$$\Pr[\text{BAD}_3] \leq \epsilon_\psi.$$

CASE 2.B: In this case, $\mathcal{R}$ made queries to $(\bar{\Pi}, \bar{\Pi}^{-1})$ to compute $f(R_i)$ for both signatures (or $f^{-1}(t_i)$ respectively). Therefore due to the way $(\bar{\Pi}, \bar{\Pi}^{-1})$ is programmed and the fact that the reduction is algebraic, $\mathcal{M}$ knows a representation of $R_i = g^{a_i} X^{b_i}$, which it can use to solve for x. Plugging $r_i = a_i + x b_i$ for $i \in \{1, 2\}$ into (7) we obtain

$$\forall i \in \{1, 2\} : \quad -\mathbf{H}'(m) - t_i \alpha + s_i a_i = (t_i \beta - s_i b_i) x . \tag{8}$$

$\mathcal{M}$ can solve any of these two equations for x (and hence solve its own challenge), unless

$$\forall i \in \{1, 2\} : \quad : t_i \beta = s_i b_i . \tag{9}$$

We call this event BAD$_4$. Assuming (9) is the case, (8) simplifies to $-\mathbf{H}'(m) - t_i \alpha + s_i a_i = 0$ which implies

$$\mathbf{H}'(m) b_i = t_i \Delta_i \tag{10}$$
$$t_2 b_1 \Delta_2 = t_1 b_2 \Delta_1, \tag{11}$$

where $\Delta_i := a_i \beta - b_i \alpha$.

Assume $b_1 \neq 0$ and $\Delta_2 \neq 0$. By (11), t_2 directly depends on t_1 and the exponents a_2, b_2, which are used in the bRO query that outputs t_2 (or chosen at random by $\mathcal{M}$ when a $\psi^{-1}(t_2)$ is queried to $\bar{\Pi}^{-1}$). Most importantly, $\mathcal{R}$ has to fix w.l.o.g. t_1 before it can choose t_2. So similar to Case 1.B, the probability that $\mathcal{R}$ computes a t_2 which satisfies Eq. (11) is upper bounded by $2\epsilon_\psi(q'_{\bar{\Pi}} + q'_{\bar{\Pi}^{-1}})$ since it can only evaluate $(\bar{\Pi}, \bar{\Pi}^{-1})$ up to $q'_{\bar{\Pi}} + q'_{\bar{\Pi}^{-1}}$ many times. Therefore

$$\Pr[\text{BAD}_4] \leq 2\epsilon_\psi(q'_{\bar{\Pi}} + q'_{\bar{\Pi}^{-1}})$$

and $\mathcal{M}$ extracts a DLog solution unless BAD$_4$ occurs. Note that the bound does not depend on $q_{\mathbf{H}}$, because both signatures are for the same message and $\mathbf{H}(m^*)$ cancels in (11).

It remains to argue why we could assume $b_1 \neq 0$ and $\Delta_2 \neq 0$. If $b_1 = 0$, then (9) and $t_1 \neq 0$ implies $\beta = 0$ contradicting (2). If $\Delta_2 = 0$, then (10) implies $b_2 = 0$ (and hence $\beta = 0$ as in the case above) or $\mathbf{H}'(m) = 0$ (contradicting $\mathbf{H}'(m) \neq 0$).

As in Case 1, $\mathcal{M}$ is successful in Case 2, if BAD$_3$ and BAD$_4$ do not occur.

Combining the probabilities for the two cases and the collision bound, the theorem follows:

$$\epsilon_{\mathcal{M}} \geq \epsilon_{\mathcal{R}} - \max_{i \in \{1,3\}} (\text{BAD}_i + \text{BAD}_{i+1}) - q^2/2^L$$
$$\geq \epsilon_{\mathcal{R}} - \epsilon_\psi(2q'_{\mathbf{H}}(q'_{\bar{\Pi}} + q'_{\bar{\Pi}^{-1}}) + 1) - q'_{\mathbf{H}}/p - q^2/2^L$$

$\square$

Remark 1. Note that it is necessary for the meta reduction to program the responses to $\bar{\Pi}^{-1}$ queries in order to know the discrete logarithms of the R corresponding to the responses. Suppose that this was not allowed. Then if the reduction makes a query $\bar{\mathbf{\Pi}}^{-1}(z)$ for some t, $\mathcal{M}$ does not know a representation for the resulting group element R with $\varphi(R) = \bar{\mathbf{\Pi}}^{-1}(z)$. So if a signature provided by the reduction includes this R, the meta-reduction will not be able extract a solution. Yet, it seems intuitive that an adversary that uses such a random group element already needs to know its discrete logarithm, because a valid solution fulfills a non-trivial equation with this group element. So such an adversary would break the DLog problem in $\mathbb{G}$. However, in order to "use" this (implicit) DLog adversary, we need to embed a DLog challenge in the random oracle. But without programming, the challenge will only occur with negligible probability, leaving us with the same problem.

We avoid this seemingly technical problem by allowing the meta-reduction to program the random oracle. Note that we only use it for exactly this purpose, namely so that the meta-reduction knows the discrete logarithms of all results of $\bar{\mathbf{\Pi}}^{-1}$ queries.

4.3 Single-User Security Does Not Tightly Imply Multi-user Security

Lastly, we show that for GenDSA, single user security does not tightly imply multi-user security with algebraic, non-programming reductions.

The following theorem states that there cannot exist an algebraic reduction from the multi-user UF-NMA-security of GenDSA to its single-user security that does not program the random bijection $(\bar{\mathbf{\Pi}}, \bar{\mathbf{\Pi}}^{-1})$ and loses less then a factor linear in the number of users, unless the FBOMDL assumption does not hold.

Theorem 4 (UF-NMA $\overset{\text{loss} < n}{\not\Rightarrow}$ n-UF-NMA). *Let $H : \{0,1\}^* \to \mathbb{Z}_p$ be a hash function modeled as a programmable random oracle $\mathbf{H}$ and $f = \psi \circ \mathbf{\Pi} \circ \varphi$ be a conversion function with semi-injective $\varphi : \mathbb{G}^* \to \{0,1\}^L$, $\psi : [0 : 2^L - 1] \to \mathbb{Z}_p$ and $\mathbf{\Pi} : \{0,1\}^L \to [0 : 2^L - 1]$ modeled by a non-programmable bijective random oracle $(\bar{\mathbf{\Pi}}, \bar{\mathbf{\Pi}}^{-1})$. If there exists an algebraic reduction $\mathcal{R}$ that $(t_\mathcal{R}, \epsilon_\mathcal{R}, q'_{\bar{\mathbf{\Pi}}}, q'_{\bar{\mathbf{\Pi}}^{-1}}, q'_{\mathbf{H}})$-breaks the UF-NMA security of GenDSA with q_P-time black-box access to an adversary $\mathcal{A}$ that $(n, t_\mathcal{A}, \epsilon_\mathcal{A}, q_{\bar{\mathbf{\Pi}}}, q_{\bar{\mathbf{\Pi}}^{-1}}, q_{\mathbf{H}'})$-breaks the n-UF-NMA security of GenDSA, then there exists an algorithm $\mathcal{M}$ that $(t_\mathcal{M}, \epsilon_\mathcal{M})$-breaks the q_P-FBOMDL assumption where*

$$\epsilon_\mathcal{M} \geq \epsilon_\mathcal{R} - \frac{q_P}{n}\epsilon_\mathcal{A} - \left(2(q'_{\bar{\mathbf{\Pi}}} + q'_{\bar{\mathbf{\Pi}}^{-1}})q'_{\mathbf{H}} + q_P + 2\right)\epsilon_\psi - q^2/2^L, t_\mathcal{M} \approx t_\mathcal{R} + q_P t_\mathcal{A}$$

where $q = (q'_{\bar{\mathbf{\Pi}}} + q'_{\bar{\mathbf{\Pi}}^{-1}} + q_P(q_{\bar{\mathbf{\Pi}}} + q_{\bar{\mathbf{\Pi}}^{-1}}))$ is the total amount of queries to $(\bar{\mathbf{\Pi}}, \bar{\mathbf{\Pi}}^{-1})$ made by $\mathcal{A}$ and $\mathcal{R}$.

As an orthogonal impossibility result we prove that single user security does not tightly imply multi-user security with algebraic, non-rewinding reductions. Specifically, the following theorem states that there cannot exist an algebraic reduction from the multi-user UF-NMA-security of GenDSA to its single-user security that does not rewind the multi-user adversary $\mathcal{A}$ and loses less than a factor linear in the number of users, unless the FBOMDL assumption does not hold.

Theorem 5. *Let $H : \{0,1\}^* \to \mathbb{Z}_p$ be a hash function modeled as a programmable random oracle $\mathbf{H}$ and $f = \psi \circ \mathbf{\Pi} \circ \varphi$ be a conversion function with semi-injective $\varphi : \mathbb{G}^* \to \{0,1\}^L$, $\psi : [0 : 2^L - 1] \to \mathbb{Z}_p$ and $\mathbf{\Pi} : \{0,1\}^L \to [0 : 2^L - 1]$ modeled by a programmable bijective random oracle $(\mathbf{\Pi}, \mathbf{\Pi}^{-1})$. If there exists an algebraic reduction $\mathcal{R}$ that $(t_{\mathcal{R}}, \epsilon_{\mathcal{R}}, q_{\mathbf{\Pi}}, q_{\mathbf{\Pi}^{-1}}, q_{\mathbf{H}})$-breaks the* UF-NMA *security of* GenDSA *with one-time black-box access to an adversary $\mathcal{A}$ that $(n, t_{\mathcal{A}}, \epsilon_{\mathcal{A}}, q_{\mathbf{\Pi}'}, q_{\mathbf{\Pi}'^{-1}}, q_{\mathbf{H}'})$-breaks the n-*UF-NMA* security of* GenDSA, *then there exists an algorithm $\mathcal{M}$ that $(t_{\mathcal{M}}, \epsilon_{\mathcal{M}})$-breaks the* 1-FBOMDL *assumption where*

$$\epsilon_{\mathcal{M}} \geq \epsilon_{\mathcal{R}} - \frac{1}{n}\epsilon_{\mathcal{A}} - (2(q_{\mathbf{\Pi}} + q_{\mathbf{\Pi}^{-1}})q_{\mathbf{H}} + 1)\epsilon_{\psi} - q^2/2^L, \quad t_{\mathcal{M}} \approx t_{\mathcal{R}} + t_{\mathcal{A}}$$

where $q = q_{\mathbf{\Pi}} + q_{\mathbf{\Pi}^{-1}}$ is the total number of queries to $(\mathbf{\Pi}, \mathbf{\Pi}^{-1})$ made by $\mathcal{R}$. We now prove Theorem 4. The proof of Theorem 5 is similar and can be found in the full version [28].

Remark 2. The results of Theorem 4 and Theorem 5 also hold for UF-CMA and n-UF-CMA security with small adjustments. The main difference is that the meta reduction now uses the $q_S + q_P$-FBOMDL (resp. $q_S + 1$-FBOMDL) assumption, as we need the additional oracle queries to answer signature queries. The additional challenges used in the signatures do not pose a problem when eventually extracting the discrete logarithm solutions. Similar to the proof of Theorem 1, they form a random upper triangular matrix, so unless the forgery lies in the span of the new signatures (which can only happen with negligible probability) a solution can be extracted in the same way as in Theorem 4 (resp. Theorem 5).

Proof (of Theorem 4). Let $\mathcal{A}$ be an adversary that $(t_{\mathcal{A}}, \epsilon_{\mathcal{A}}, q_{\bar{\mathbf{\Pi}}}, q_{\bar{\mathbf{\Pi}}^{-1}}, q_{\mathbf{H}})$-breaks the n-UF-NMA security of GenDSA, and let $\mathcal{R}$ be the algebraic security reduction that $(t_{\mathcal{R}}, \epsilon_{\mathcal{R}}, q'_{\bar{\mathbf{\Pi}}}, q'_{\bar{\mathbf{\Pi}}^{-1}}, q'_{\mathbf{H}})$-breaks the UF-NMA security of GenDSA. $\mathcal{A} = \mathcal{A}^{\mathbf{H}'(\cdot), \bar{\mathbf{\Pi}}(\cdot), \bar{\mathbf{\Pi}}^{-1}(\cdot)}$ has access to the non-programmable bRO $(\bar{\mathbf{\Pi}}, \bar{\mathbf{\Pi}}^{-1})$ and the random oracle $\mathbf{H}'$ of the n-UF-NMA game. $\mathcal{R} = \mathcal{R}^{\mathbf{H}(\cdot), \bar{\mathbf{\Pi}}(\cdot), \bar{\mathbf{\Pi}}^{-1}(\cdot)}$ has access to the same non-programmable bRO $(\bar{\mathbf{\Pi}}, \bar{\mathbf{\Pi}}^{-1})$ and the programmable random oracle $\mathbf{H}$ of the UF-NMA game and internally simulates the programmable RO $\mathbf{H}'$, which is accessed by $\mathcal{A}$. Meta reduction $\mathcal{M}$ tries to solve the q_P-FBOMDL assumption by running the reduction $\mathcal{R}$, simulating the UF-NMA game, the adversary $\mathcal{A}$ up to q_P times and the oracles $\mathbf{H}$ and $(\bar{\mathbf{\Pi}}, \bar{\mathbf{\Pi}}^{-1})$.

Meta-reduction $\mathcal{M}$ and simulated $\mathcal{A}$ are described in Fig. 5. Note that since $\mathcal{A}$ is simulated by $\mathcal{M}$, it has access to the **DL** and **Chal** oracles. The meta reduction $\mathcal{M}$ gets a FBOMDL challenge X as input and has to output $x, x_1, \ldots, x_{q_P}$ s.t. $X = g^x$ and $X_i = g^{x_i}$, where the X_i are returned by its **Chal** oracle. It simulates the UF-NMA game for $\mathcal{R}$ by setting $\mathsf{vk} = X$ and runs $\mathcal{R}^{\mathbf{H}, \bar{\mathbf{\Pi}}, \bar{\mathbf{\Pi}}^{-1}}(\mathsf{vk})$. $\mathcal{M}$ simulates the bRO $(\bar{\mathbf{\Pi}}, \bar{\mathbf{\Pi}}^{-1})$ and the regular random oracle $\mathbf{H}$ via lazy sampling. When $\mathcal{R}$ queries $\bar{\mathbf{\Pi}}$ on a fresh bitstring z with preimage group element R under φ, it has to provide a representation $a, b, c_1, \ldots, c_{q_P}$ s.t. $R = g^a \cdot X^b \cdot \prod_{j<i} X_j^{c_j}$, which $\mathcal{M}$ stores together with the random answer z'. If no such representation exists, $\mathcal{M}$

Meta Reduction $\mathcal{M}^{\mathbf{DL}(\cdot,\cdot),\mathbf{Chal}}(X)$

1: $L = \emptyset$
2: Run $\mathcal{R}^{\mathbf{H}(\cdot),\bar{\mathbf{\Pi}}(\cdot),\bar{\mathbf{\Pi}}^{-1}(\cdot)}(X)$
3: **for** $i \in [q_P]$ **do**
4:      Simulate $\mathcal{A}_i^{\mathbf{H}'(\cdot),\bar{\mathbf{\Pi}}(\cdot),\bar{\mathbf{\Pi}}^{-1}(\cdot)}((\mathsf{vk}_{i,j})_{j\in[n]})$
5:      **if** $\mathcal{A}_i$ aborts **then**
6:          **abort**
7: Receive forgery $(m^*, \sigma^*) = (s^*, t^*)$ from $\mathcal{R}$
8: **if** $\exists i \in [q_P]$ s.t. $\sigma^* = (s_i, t_i)$ **then** // $\mathcal{R}$ guessed n_i^*
9:      **abort**
10: **if** $\nexists (R^*, \varphi(R^*), (*, \ldots, *), \psi^{-1}(t^*)) \in L$ **then**
11:      **abort**
12: Solve verification equations for $x, x_1, \ldots, x_{q_P}$
13: **return** $(x, x_1, \ldots, x_{q_P})$

Oracle $\bar{\mathbf{\Pi}}(z)$

14: **if** $\nexists (*, z, *, z') \in L$ **then**
15:      $z' \xleftarrow{\$} [0 : 2^L - 1]$
16:      **if** $z \in \varphi(\mathbb{G}^*)$ **then** // $\mathcal{R}$ provides representation
17:          Let $z = \varphi(Y) = \varphi(g^a X^b \prod_{j \in [q_P]} X_j^{c_j})$
18:          $L \mathrel{+}\!\leftarrow (Y, z, (a, b, (c_j)_{j \in [q_P]}), z')$
19:          $L \mathrel{+}\!\leftarrow (Y^{-1}, z, (-a, -b, (-c_j)_{j \in [q_P]}), z')$
20:      **else**
21:          $L \mathrel{+}\!\leftarrow (\perp, z, \perp, z')$
22: Let $(*, z, *, z') \in L$
23: **return** z'

Adv. $\mathcal{A}_i^{\mathbf{H}'(\cdot),\bar{\mathbf{\Pi}}(\cdot),\bar{\mathbf{\Pi}}^{-1}(\cdot)}((\mathsf{vk}_{i,j})_{j\in[n]})$
     // $\mathsf{vk}_{i,j} = g^{a_{i,j}} X^{b_{i,j}} \prod_{k<i} X_k^{c_{i,j,k}}$

24: **for** $j \in [q_H]$ **do**
25:      $m_j \xleftarrow{\$} \mathcal{M}$, $h_j \leftarrow \mathbf{H}'(m_j)$
26: $n_i^* \xleftarrow{\$} [n]$; $k_i^* \xleftarrow{\$} [q_{\bar{\Pi}}]$; $j_i^* \xleftarrow{\$} [q_H]$
27: **for** $j \in [q_{\bar{\Pi}}] \setminus k_i^*$ **do**
28:      $r_j \xleftarrow{\$} \mathbb{Z}_p$, $R_j \leftarrow g^{r_j}$
29:      $t_j \leftarrow \psi(\bar{\mathbf{\Pi}}(\varphi(R_j)))$ // via oracle query to $\bar{\mathbf{\Pi}}$
30: $X_i \leftarrow \mathbf{Chal}$
31: $R_{k_i^*} \leftarrow X_i$, $t_{k_i^*} \leftarrow \psi(\bar{\mathbf{\Pi}}(\varphi(X_i)))$ // Embed challenge
32: **if** $t_{k_i^*} = 0$ **then**
33:      **abort**
34: Make $q_{\bar{\Pi}^{-1}}$ dummy queries to $\bar{\mathbf{\Pi}}^{-1}$
35: $t_i \leftarrow t_{k_i^*}$
36: $h_i \leftarrow h_{j_i^*}$; $m_i \leftarrow m_{j_i^*}$
37: **if** $g^{h_i} \cdot \mathsf{vk}_{i,n_i^*}^{t_i} = 1$ **then**
38:      **abort**
39: $s_i \leftarrow \mathbf{DL}(g^{h_i} \cdot \mathsf{vk}_{i,n_i^*}^{t}, X_i)$ // From FBOMDL game
40: $\sigma_i \leftarrow (s_i, t_i)$
41: **return** $\begin{cases} (n_i^*, m_i, \sigma_i) & \text{with prob. } \epsilon_{\mathcal{A}} \\ \perp & \text{else} \end{cases}$

Oracle $\bar{\mathbf{\Pi}}^{-1}(z')$

42: **if** $\nexists (*, z, *, z') \in L$ **then**
43:      $x \xleftarrow{\$} \{0,1\}^L$
44:      **if** $x \notin \varphi(\mathbb{G}^*)$ **then**
45:          $L \mathrel{+}\!\leftarrow (\perp, x, \perp, z')$
46:      **else**
47:          $(a, b) \xleftarrow{\$} \mathbb{Z}_p^2$ s.t. $g^a \cdot X^b \neq 1$
48:          $z \leftarrow \varphi(g^a X^b)$
49:          $L \mathrel{+}\!\leftarrow (g^a X^b, z, (a, b, 0, \ldots, 0), z')$
50:          $L \mathrel{+}\!\leftarrow (g^{-a} X^{-b}, z, (-a, -b, 0, \ldots, 0), z')$
51: Let $(*, z, *, z') \in L$
52: **return** z

Fig. 5. Meta reduction $\mathcal{M}$ and simulated n-UF-NMA adversary for Theorem 4. For ease of notation, we group queries to $\bar{\mathbf{\Pi}}, \bar{\mathbf{\Pi}}^{-1}$ and $\mathbf{H}$ and write the challenge queries separately, but assume that $\mathcal{A}$ interweaves them at position k_i^* and j_i^* respectively. If two executions of $\mathcal{A}$ receive the same randomness, public keys and answers to all $\mathbf{H}$ queries, then $\mathcal{M}$ replays the previous execution of $\mathcal{A}$ and makes no additional **Chal** query.

only samples z' and returns it. Similarly, when $\mathcal{R}$ queries $\bar{\mathbf{\Pi}}^{-1}$ on some z', $\mathcal{M}$ first samples a random $z \in \{0,1\}^L \setminus L$ (i.e. a random z that it hasn't returned yet) and if $z \in \varphi(\mathbb{G}^*)$ $\mathcal{M}$ chooses random $(a, b) \in \mathbb{Z}_p^2$ s.t. $R' = g^a X^b \neq 1$ and returns $\varphi(R')$. Otherwise, it simply returns z. In both cases, $\mathcal{M}$ stores the input/output pairs together with the potential representation in a list L in order to keep the random oracles consistent. Note that it is necessary to first sample a uniformly random $x \in \{0,1\}^L$ and check if it lies in $\varphi(\mathbb{G}^*)$ to keep the distribution of $(\bar{\mathbf{\Pi}}, \bar{\mathbf{\Pi}}^{-1})$ consistent. Furthermore, $(\bar{\mathbf{\Pi}}, \bar{\mathbf{\Pi}}^{-1})$ is simulated as a random *function*, instead of a random permutation. By the birthday bound, this incurs a statistical error of $q^2/2^L$, where $q = q'_{\bar{\Pi}} + q'_{\bar{\Pi}^{-1}} + q_P(q_{\bar{\Pi}} + q_{\bar{\Pi}^{-1}})$ is the total number of queries made to $(\bar{\mathbf{\Pi}}, \bar{\mathbf{\Pi}}^{-1})$ by $\mathcal{A}$ and $\mathcal{R}$ due to the possibility of collisions. The random oracle $\mathbf{H}$ is simulated honestly, i.e. via lazy sampling without programming any values.

Eventually, $\mathcal{R}$ invokes up to q_P copies $\mathcal{A}_i^{\mathbf{H}',\bar{\mathbf{\Pi}},\bar{\mathbf{\Pi}}^{-1}}((\mathsf{vk}_{i,j})_{j\in[n]})$ of the adversary $\mathcal{A}$ with n verification keys of its choosing. Note that all adversaries get access to the same $\bar{\mathbf{\Pi}}$ and $\bar{\mathbf{\Pi}}^{-1}$ because it is non-programmable for $\mathcal{R}$, but $\mathbf{H}'$ is fully controlled by $\mathcal{R}$. Since $\mathcal{R}$ is algebraic, it also outputs representations of all keys, so let $\mathsf{vk}_{i,j} = g^{a_{i,j}} \cdot X^{b_{i,j}} \cdot \prod_{k\in[q_P]} X_k^{c_{i,j,k}}$ for $i \in [q_P], j \in [n]$. To be precise, $\mathcal{R}$ provides a representation relative to $g, X, X_1, \dots, X_{q_P}$ and all elements it can compute from outputs of $\bar{\mathbf{\Pi}}^{-1}$. Due to the programming described above, $\mathcal{M}$ knows a representation of all these group elements relative to X and $X_1, \dots, X_{q_P}$, so we can assume that $\mathcal{M}$ gets a representation only relative to them. Note however that at the start of the first execution of $\mathcal{A}$, $\mathcal{R}$ did not receive any of the X_i yet, so the first verification keys only depend on g and X. In the second, it has only seen X_1 and so on (w.l.o.g. we order the adversary executions such that the i-th adversary is the adversary that queried its challenge after $i - 1$ other adversaries queried theirs). So for the i-th adversary, $c_{i,j,k} = 0$ for $k \geq i$.

Note that $\mathcal{R}$ can only program $\mathbf{H}'$. So if $\mathcal{R}$ executes an adversary $\mathcal{A}_i$ with the same randomness and inputs as $\mathcal{A}_j$, $\mathcal{A}_i$ makes the same queries to $\mathbf{H}'$ as $\mathcal{A}_j$ and if they are answered identically, then $\mathcal{A}_i$ uses the same challenge as $\mathcal{A}_j$ and does not query **Chal** or **DL**. However if the answers to $\mathbf{H}'$ differ in at least one place, then $\mathcal{A}_i$ behaves as depicted in Fig. 5 (i.e. queries a fresh challenge, etc.). To detect which is the case, $\mathcal{A}$ has to make all queries to $\mathbf{H}'$ *before* querying a new challenge. Otherwise, $\mathcal{M}$ would have to use two queries to **DL** with the same challenge if $\mathcal{R}$ reprograms $\mathbf{H}'$ on the message $\mathcal{A}_i$ intends to forge on *after* all queries to $\bar{\mathbf{\Pi}}$ have already been made, making $\mathcal{M}$ unable to win the FBOMDL game. So w.l.o.g., we assume that all adversaries $\mathcal{A}_i$ for $i \in [q_P]$ are distinct.

Each $\mathcal{A}_i$ clearly $(t_{\mathcal{A}}, \epsilon_{\mathcal{A}}, q_{\bar{\mathbf{\Pi}}}, q_{\bar{\mathbf{\Pi}}^{-1}}, q_{\mathbf{H}})$-breaks the n-UF-NMA security of GenDSA, unless the aborts in line 33 or 38 occur and $\mathcal{M}$ makes exactly one **Chal** query and at most one **DL** query per simulation of $\mathcal{A}$. The abort in line 33 occurs if $t_{k^*} = \psi(\bar{\mathbf{\Pi}}(\varphi(X_i))) = 0$ for any $i \in [q_P$ and we call this event BAD_1. Since $(\bar{\mathbf{\Pi}}, \bar{\mathbf{\Pi}}^{-1})$ is a random function, it follows that the random variable $y^* = \bar{\mathbf{\Pi}}(\varphi(X_i))$ is uniformly random over $[0 : 2^L - 1]$. Therefore, we have $\Pr[\psi(\bar{\mathbf{\Pi}}(\varphi(X_i)) = 0] = \Pr[\psi(y^*) = 0] \leq \max_{t\in\mathbb{Z}_p} \Pr_{y\xleftarrow{\$}[0:2^L-1]}[\psi(y) = t] \leq \epsilon_\psi$, so $\Pr[\mathrm{BAD}_1] \leq \epsilon_\psi$ for any single execution of $\mathcal{A}_i$. A union bound over the q_P executions of $\mathcal{A}$ allows us to bound the probability of BAD_1 occurring in *any* execution of $\mathcal{A}_i$ by

$$\Pr[\mathrm{BAD}_1] \leq q_P \epsilon_\psi.$$

Now consider the abort in line 38, i.e. $g^{h_i} \cdot \mathsf{vk}_{i,n_i^*}^{t_i} = 1$, which we call BAD_2. If BAD_2 occurs, it implies that

$$\mathbf{H}'(m_i^*) = t_i\Big(a_{i,n_i^*} + b_{i,n_i^*}x + \sum_{j\in[i-1]} c_{i,n_i^*,j}x_j\Big).$$

Note that $\mathcal{R}$ can program $\mathbf{H}'$, so it can trigger BAD_2 if it programs $\mathbf{H}'(m_i^*)$ correctly. However, $\mathcal{A}_i$ makes all of its queries to $\mathbf{H}'$ *before* it makes any queries to $(\bar{\mathbf{\Pi}}, \bar{\mathbf{\Pi}}^{-1})$. Therefore, in order to correctly program $\mathbf{H}'(m_i^*)$, $\mathcal{R}$ has to guess the correct indices n_i^*, j_i^* and a group element R' s.t. $f(R') = t_i$, since they are all information-theoretically hidden from $\mathcal{R}$. With the same argument as for BAD_1, the probability of finding a R' that maps to t_i can be bounded by ϵ_ψ, so together with guessing the indices, we get that

$$\Pr[\mathrm{BAD}_2] \leq \frac{\epsilon_\psi}{n q_{\mathbf{H}}}$$

If $\mathcal{R}$ aborts at any point or does not return a valid signature, $\mathcal{M}$ aborts as well. So assume $\mathcal{R}$ eventually outputs a valid forgery $(m^*, \sigma^* = (s^*, t^*))$ for key vk^*. Since $\mathcal{R}$ can choose all verification keys $\mathsf{vk}_{i,j}$, it can set one to its own challenge key for each execution of $\mathcal{A}$ (It can only do this at one point since the challenge keys need to be distinct). So with probability at most $1/n$, an $\mathcal{A}_i$ produced a forgery for the public key that $\mathcal{M}$ gave to $\mathcal{R}$, in which case $\mathcal{R}$ can just forwards the signature it got from $\mathcal{A}_i$ and $\mathcal{M}$ aborts (line 9). We call the event that this happens for any execution of $\mathcal{A}$ BAD_3. This abort occurs with probability $\frac{1}{n}\epsilon_\mathcal{A}$ for each execution of $\mathcal{A}$, so via a union bound, the probability of BAD_3 occurring in *any* execution of $\mathcal{A}$ is

$$\Pr[\mathrm{BAD}_3] \leq \frac{q_P}{n}\epsilon_\mathcal{A}.$$

Otherwise, $\mathcal{R}$ produces a fresh forgery and together with the signatures from the simulated adversaries $\mathcal{A}_i$ and the verification equation of GenDSA, we get that

$$s_1 \cdot x_1 - b_{n_1^*} t_1 x = h_1 + a_{n_1^*} t_1 \qquad (12)$$

$$\vdots$$

$$s_{q_P} \cdot x_{q_P} - t_{q_P} \sum_{j \in [q_P-1]} c_{q_P, n_{q_P}^*, j} x_j - b_{n_{q_P}^*} t_{q_P} x = h_{q_P} + a_{n_{q_P}^*} t_{q_P} \qquad (13)$$

$$s^* \cdot r^* - t^* x = \mathbf{H}(m^*) \qquad (14)$$

with $f(g^{r^*}) = t^*$.

Now $\mathcal{M}$ checks L for an entry $(g^{r^*}, z, (\alpha, \beta, (\gamma_i)_{i \in [q_P]}), z')$ with $\psi(z') = t^*$. If such an entry exists, we have $r^* = \alpha + \beta x + \sum_{i \in [q_P]} \gamma_i x_i$, yielding the equation system

$$s_1 \cdot x_1 - b_{n_1^*} t_1 x = h_1 + a_{n_1^*} t_1$$

$$\vdots$$

$$s_{q_P} \cdot x_{q_P} - t_{q_P} \sum_{j \in [q_P-1]} c_{q_P, n_{q_P}^*, j} x_j - b_{n_{q_P}^*} t_{q_P} x = h_{q_P} + a_{n_{q_P}^*} t_{q_P}$$

$$s^* \sum_{j \in [q_P]} \gamma_j x_j + (\beta s^* - t^*) x = \mathbf{H}(m^*) - \alpha s^*$$

If no such r^* exists, then $\mathcal{R}$ never queried the bRO on a preimage of t^* or received a preimage of t^* from the bRO. We call this case BAD_4 and $\mathcal{M}$ aborts (line 11) as it can not solve its FBOMDL challenge in this case. By the same argument as for BAD_1, we get

$$\Pr[\text{BAD}_4] \leq \epsilon_\psi.$$

Otherwise, the signatures form a system of $q_P + 1$ equations with $q_P + 1$ variables, where each variable represents a solution to one of the discrete logarithm challenges. So unless the determinant of the system is 0, $\mathcal{M}$ can extract a solution for its FBOMDL instance. So all that is left is to analyze the probability of this bad case.

In matrix notation, we can write this condition as

$$\Delta := \det \begin{bmatrix} b_{n_1^*} t_1 & s_1 & 0 & \cdots & 0 \\ \vdots & t_2 c_{2,n_2^*,1} & s_2 & 0 & \vdots \\ \vdots & \vdots & \ddots & & \vdots \\ b_{n_{q_P-1}^*} t_{q_P-1} & t_{q_P-1} c_{q_P-1,n_{q_P-1}^*,1} & & s_{q_P-1} & 0 \\ b_{n_{q_P}^*} t_{q_P} & t_{q_P} c_{q_P,n_{q_P}^*,1} & \cdots & t_{q_P} c_{q_P,n_{q_P}^*,q_P-1} & s_{q_P} \\ \beta s^* - t^* & s^* \gamma_1 & \cdots & \cdots & s^* \gamma_{q_P} \end{bmatrix} \neq 0$$

Using the Leibnitz formula on the last row, we see that Δ is of the form $\Delta = (s^* \beta - t^*) \prod_{i \in [q_P]} s_i + s^* d$, where d is the sum of the determinants of the q_P submatrices resulting from eliminating the last row and the i-th column for all i except for the first column. Note that d is independent of s^* and t^*, but depends on β and the γ_i. Collecting all terms containing s^*, we get

$$s^*\left(\beta \prod_{i \in [q_P]} s_i + d\right) = t^* \prod_{i \in [q_P]} s_i \tag{15}$$

By definition, we have $s_i \neq 0$ for all $i \in [q_P]$ as well as $s^* \neq 0$ and $t^* \neq 0$. Therefore, if $\beta \prod_{i \in [q_P]} s_i + d = 0$, we get $\Delta \neq 0$. So assume $\beta \prod_{i \in [n]} s_i + d \neq 0$. Then $s^* = t^* \frac{\prod_{i \in [q_P]} s_i}{\beta \prod_{i \in [q_P]} s_i + d}$ and substitution in Eq. (14) yields the equation

$$t^* \frac{\prod_{i \in [q_P]} s_i}{\beta \prod_{i \in [q_P]} s_i + d}\left(\alpha + (\beta - 1)x + \sum_{j \in [q_P]} \gamma_j x_j\right) = \mathbf{H}(m^*). \tag{16}$$

Here, $\mathbf{H}$ is the random oracle provided to $\mathcal{R}$, so it can *not* be programmed. For every fixed $m^*, \alpha, \beta, (\gamma_i)_{i \in [q_P]}$, there is a unique t^* that satisfies Eq. (16) and since $(\bar{\mathbf{\Pi}}, \bar{\mathbf{\Pi}}^{-1})$ is a random function, we have $\Pr[\psi(\bar{\mathbf{\Pi}}(\varphi(R) = t^*] \leq \epsilon_\psi$ for every $R \in \mathbb{G}$. $\mathcal{R}$ can choose from $q_\mathbf{H}$ tuples $(m^*, \mathbf{H}(m^*)$ and from $2(q'_{\bar{\mathbf{\Pi}}} + q'_{\bar{\mathbf{\Pi}}^{-1}})$ tuples $(\alpha, \beta, (\gamma_i)_{i \in [q_P]})$ (φ is semi-injective, so there are 2 tuples for every query). So a union bound over the number of tuples yields that the probability of $\mathcal{R}$ finding a tuple $(\mathbf{H}(m^*), \alpha, \beta, (\gamma_i)_{i \in [q_P]}, t^*)$ that satisfies Eq. (16) is at most $2\epsilon_\psi q_\mathbf{H}(q_{\bar{\mathbf{\Pi}}} + q_{\bar{\mathbf{\Pi}}^{-1}})$ and

$$\Pr[\text{BAD}_5] \leq 2\epsilon_\psi q_\mathbf{H}(q_{\bar{\mathbf{\Pi}}} + q_{\bar{\mathbf{\Pi}}^{-1}}).$$

Combining all probabilities, we get

$$\epsilon_{\mathcal{M}} \geq \epsilon_{\mathcal{R}} - \sum_{i=1}^{5} \Pr[\text{BAD}_i] - q^2/2^L$$

$$\geq \epsilon_{\mathcal{R}} - \frac{2q_P}{n}\epsilon_{\mathcal{A}} - \epsilon_{\psi}\left(2(q'_{\hat{\Pi}} + q'_{\hat{\Pi}-1})q'_{\mathbf{H}} + q_P + 2\right) - q^2/2^L$$

which concludes the proof. □

Acknowledgments. Dominik Hartmann was supported by the European Union (ERC AdG REWORC - 101054911). Eike Kiltz was supported by the Deutsche Forschungsgemeinschaft (DFG, German Research Foundation) under Germany's Excellence Strategy - EXC 2092 CASA - 390781972, and by the European Union (ERC AdG REWORC - 101054911).

References

1. Bauer, B., Fuchsbauer, G., Plouviez, A.: The one-more discrete logarithm assumption in the generic group model. In: Tibouchi, M., Wang, H. (eds.) ASIACRYPT 2021. LNCS, vol. 13093, pp. 587–617. Springer, Cham (2021). https://doi.org/10.1007/978-3-030-92068-5_20

2. Bellare, M., Namprempre, C., Pointcheval, D., Semanko, M.: The one-more-RSA-inversion problems and the security of Chaum's blind signature scheme. J. Cryptol. **16**(3), 185–215 (2003)

3. Bellare, M., Rogaway, P.: Random oracles are practical: A paradigm for designing efficient protocols. In: Denning, D.E., Pyle, R., Ganesan, R., Sandhu, R.S., Ashby, V. (eds.) ACM CCS 93: 1st Conference on Computer and Communications Security, pp. 62–73. ACM Press, Fairfax (1993)

4. Blake-Wilson, S., Bolyard, N., Gupta, V., Hawk, C., Moeller, B.: Elliptic curve cryptography (ECC) cipher suites for transport layer security (TLS). RFC 4492, RFC Editor (2016)

5. Brickell, E., Pointcheval, D., Vaudenay, S., Yung, M.: Design validations for discrete logarithm based signature schemes. In: Imai, H., Zheng, Y. (eds.) PKC 2000. LNCS, vol. 1751, pp. 276–292. Springer, Heidelberg (2000). https://doi.org/10.1007/978-3-540-46588-1_19

6. Brown, D.: On the Provable Security of ECDSA. London Mathematical Society Lecture Note Series, pp. 21–40. Cambridge University Press (2005)

7. Brown, D.R.L.: The exact security of ECDSA. Contributions to IEEE P1363a (2001). http://grouper.ieee.org/groups/1363/

8. Brown, D.R.L.: Generic groups, collision resistance, and ECDSA. Cryptology ePrint Archive, Report 2002/026 (2002). https://eprint.iacr.org/2002/026

9. Brown, D.R.L.: Generic groups, collision resistance, and ECDSA. Contributions to IEEE P1363a (2002). Updated version for "The Exact Security of ECDSA". http://grouper.ieee.org/groups/1363/

10. Brzuska, C., Farshim, P., Mittelbach, A.: Random-oracle uninstantiability from indistinguishability obfuscation. In: Dodis, Y., Nielsen, J.B. (eds.) TCC 2015, Part II. LNCS, vol. 9015, pp. 428–455. Springer, Heidelberg (2015). https://doi.org/10.1007/978-3-662-46497-7_17

11. Camenisch, J., Piveteau, J.M., Stadler, M.: Blind signatures based on the discrete logarithm problem (rump session). In: Santis, A.D. (ed.) EUROCRYPT 1994. LNCS, vol. 950, pp. 428–432. Springer, Heidelberg (1995). https://doi.org/10.1007/bfb0053458

12. Canetti, R., Gennaro, R., Goldfeder, S., Makriyannis, N., Peled, U.: UC noninteractive, proactive, threshold ECDSA with identifiable aborts. In: Ligatti, J., Ou, X., Katz, J., Vigna, G. (eds.) ACM CCS 2020: 27th Conference on Computer and Communications Security, pp. 1769–1787. ACM Press, Virtual Event (2020)

13. Canetti, R., Goldreich, O., Halevi, S.: The random oracle methodology, revisited (preliminary version). In: 30th Annual ACM Symposium on Theory of Computing, pp. 209–218. ACM Press, Dallas (1998)

14. Castagnos, G., Catalano, D., Laguillaumie, F., Savasta, F., Tucker, I.: Two-party ECDSA from hash proof systems and efficient instantiations. In: Boldyreva, A., Micciancio, D. (eds.) CRYPTO 2019, Part III. LNCS, vol. 11694, pp. 191–221. Springer, Cham (2019). https://doi.org/10.1007/978-3-030-26954-8_7

15. Castagnos, G., Catalano, D., Laguillaumie, F., Savasta, F., Tucker, I.: Bandwidth-efficient threshold EC-DSA. In: Kiayias, A., Kohlweiss, M., Wallden, P., Zikas, V. (eds.) PKC 2020, Part II. LNCS, vol. 12111, pp. 266–296. Springer, Cham (2020). https://doi.org/10.1007/978-3-030-45388-6_10

16. Dalskov, A., Orlandi, C., Keller, M., Shrishak, K., Shulman, H.: Securing DNSSEC keys via threshold ECDSA from generic MPC. In: Chen, L., Li, N., Liang, K., Schneider, S. (eds.) ESORICS 2020, Part II. LNCS, vol. 12309, pp. 654–673. Springer, Cham (2020). https://doi.org/10.1007/978-3-030-59013-0_32

17. Damgård, I., Jakobsen, T.P., Nielsen, J.B., Pagter, J.I., Østergaard, M.B.: Fast threshold ECDSA with honest majority. In: Galdi, C., Kolesnikov, V. (eds.) SCN 2020. LNCS, vol. 12238, pp. 382–400. Springer, Cham (2020). https://doi.org/10.1007/978-3-030-57990-6_19

18. Doerner, J., Kondi, Y., Lee, E., shelat, a.: Secure two-party threshold ECDSA from ECDSA assumptions. In: 2018 IEEE Symposium on Security and Privacy, pp. 980–997. IEEE Computer Society Press, San Francisco (2018)

19. Doerner, J., Kondi, Y., Lee, E., Shelat, A.: Threshold ECDSA from ECDSA assumptions: the multiparty case. In: 2019 IEEE Symposium on Security and Privacy, pp. 1051–1066. IEEE Computer Society Press, San Francisco (2019)

20. Fersch, M., Kiltz, E., Poettering, B.: On the provable security of (EC)DSA signatures. In: Weippl, E.R., Katzenbeisser, S., Kruegel, C., Myers, A.C., Halevi, S. (eds.) ACM CCS 2016: 23rd Conference on Computer and Communications Security, pp. 1651–1662. ACM Press, Vienna (2016)

21. Fersch, M., Kiltz, E., Poettering, B.: On the one-per-message unforgeability of (EC)DSA and its variants. In: Kalai, Y., Reyzin, L. (eds.) TCC 2017, Part II. LNCS, vol. 10678, pp. 519–534. Springer, Cham (2017). https://doi.org/10.1007/978-3-319-70503-3_17

22. Fischlin, M., Lehmann, A., Ristenpart, T., Shrimpton, T., Stam, M., Tessaro, S.: Random oracles with(out) programmability. In: Abe, M. (ed.) ASIACRYPT 2010. LNCS, vol. 6477, pp. 303–320. Springer, Heidelberg (2010). https://doi.org/10.1007/978-3-642-17373-8_18

23. Fuchsbauer, G., Kiltz, E., Loss, J.: The Algebraic Group Model and its Applications. In: Shacham, H., Boldyreva, A. (eds.) CRYPTO 2018, Part II. LNCS, vol. 10992, pp. 33–62. Springer, Cham (2018). https://doi.org/10.1007/978-3-319-96881-0_2

24. Galbraith, S., Malone-Lee, J., Smart, N.: Public key signatures in the multi-user setting. Inf. Process. Lett. **83**(5), 263–266 (2002). https://www.sciencedirect.com/science/article/pii/S0020019001003386
25. Gennaro, R., Goldfeder, S.: Fast multiparty threshold ECDSA with fast trustless setup. In: Lie, D., Mannan, M., Backes, M., Wang, X. (eds.) ACM CCS 2018: 25th Conference on Computer and Communications Security, pp. 1179–1194. ACM Press, Toronto (2018)
26. Gennaro, R., Goldfeder, S., Narayanan, A.: Threshold-optimal DSA/ECDSA signatures and an application to bitcoin wallet security. In: Manulis, M., Sadeghi, A.-R., Schneider, S. (eds.) ACNS 2016. LNCS, vol. 9696, pp. 156–174. Springer, Cham (2016). https://doi.org/10.1007/978-3-319-39555-5_9
27. Groth, J., Shoup, V.: On the security of ECDSA with additive key derivation and presignatures. In: Dunkelman, O., Dziembowski, S. (eds.) EUROCRYPT 2022. LNCS, vol. 13275, pp. 365–396. Springer, Cham (2022). https://doi.org/10.1007/978-3-031-06944-4_13
28. Hartmann, D., Kiltz, E.: Limits in the provable security of ECDSA signatures. Cryptology ePrint Archive, Paper 2023/914 (2023). https://eprint.iacr.org/2023/914, https://eprint.iacr.org/2023/914
29. Johnson, D., Menezes, A., Vanstone, S.: The elliptic curve digital signature algorithm (ECDSA). Int. J. Inf. Secur. **1**(1), 36–63 (2001)
30. Kiltz, E., Masny, D., Pan, J.: Optimal security proofs for signatures from identification schemes. In: Robshaw, M., Katz, J. (eds.) CRYPTO 2016, Part II. LNCS, vol. 9815, pp. 33–61. Springer, Heidelberg (2016). https://doi.org/10.1007/978-3-662-53008-5_2
31. Kondi, Y., Magri, B., Orlandi, C., Shlomovits, O.: Refresh when you wake up: proactive threshold wallets with offline devices. In: 2021 IEEE Symposium on Security and Privacy, pp. 608–625. IEEE Computer Society Press, San Francisco (2021)
32. Lindell, Y.: Fast secure two-party ECDSA signing. In: Katz, J., Shacham, H. (eds.) CRYPTO 2017, Part II. LNCS, vol. 10402, pp. 613–644. Springer, Cham (2017). https://doi.org/10.1007/978-3-319-63715-0_21
33. Lindell, Y., Nof, A.: Fast secure multiparty ECDSA with practical distributed key generation and applications to cryptocurrency custody. In: Lie, D., Mannan, M., Backes, M., Wang, X. (eds.) ACM CCS 2018: 25th Conference on Computer and Communications Security, pp. 1837–1854. ACM Press, Toronto (2018)
34. Malone-Lee, J., Smart, N.P.: Modifications of ECDSA. In: Nyberg, K., Heys, H. (eds.) SAC 2002. LNCS, vol. 2595, pp. 1–12. Springer, Heidelberg (2003). https://doi.org/10.1007/3-540-36492-7_1
35. National Institute of Standards and Technology: Digital signature standard (DSS) - FIPS 186-4. Technical report, U.S. Department of Commerce (2013)
36. Nguyen, P.Q., Shparlinski, I.: The insecurity of the digital signature algorithm with partially known nonces. J. Cryptol. **15**(3), 151–176 (2002)
37. Paillier, P., Vergnaud, D.: Discrete-log-based signatures may not be equivalent to discrete log. In: Roy, B. (ed.) ASIACRYPT 2005. LNCS, vol. 3788, pp. 1–20. Springer, Heidelberg (2005). https://doi.org/10.1007/11593447_1
38. Qin, X., Cai, C., Yuen, T.H.: One-more unforgeability of blind ECDSA. Cryptology ePrint Archive, Report 2021/1449 (2021). https://ia.cr/2021/1449
39. Reingold, O., Trevisan, L., Vadhan, S.: Notions of reducibility between cryptographic primitives. In: Naor, M. (ed.) TCC 2004. LNCS, vol. 2951, pp. 1–20. Springer, Heidelberg (2004). https://doi.org/10.1007/978-3-540-24638-1_1

40. Stern, J., Pointcheval, D., Malone-Lee, J., Smart, N.P.: Flaws in applying proof methodologies to signature schemes. In: Yung, M. (ed.) CRYPTO 2002. LNCS, vol. 2442, pp. 93–110. Springer, Heidelberg (2002). https://doi.org/10.1007/3-540-45708-9_7

41. Vaudenay, S.: Hidden collisions on DSS. In: Koblitz, N. (ed.) CRYPTO 1996. LNCS, vol. 1109, pp. 83–88. Springer, Heidelberg (1996). https://doi.org/10.1007/3-540-68697-5_7

42. Vaudenay, S.: The security of DSA and ECDSA. In: Desmedt, Y.G. (ed.) PKC 2003. LNCS, vol. 2567, pp. 309–323. Springer, Heidelberg (2003). https://doi.org/10.1007/3-540-36288-6_23

43. Zhandry, M.: To label, or not to label (in generic groups). In: Dodis, Y., Shrimpton, T. (eds.) CRYPTO 2022, Part IV. LNCS, vol. 13509, pp. 66–96. Springer, Cham (2022). https://doi.org/10.1007/978-3-031-15982-4_3

44. Zhang, C., Zhou, H.S., Katz, J.: An analysis of the algebraic group model. In: Agrawal, S., Lin, D. (eds.) ASIACRYPT 2022. LNCS, vol. 3794, pp. 310–322. Springer, Cham (2022). https://doi.org/10.1007/978-3-031-22972-5_11

Round-Robin is Optimal: Lower Bounds for Group Action Based Protocols

Daniele Cozzo[1]([✉]) [ID] and Emanuele Giunta[1,2] [ID]

[1] IMDEA Software Institute, Madrid, Spain
{daniele.cozzo,emanuele.giunta}@imdea.org
[2] Universidad Politecnica de Madrid, Madrid, Spain

Abstract. An hard homogeneous space (HHS) is a finite group acting on a set with the group action being hard to invert and the set lacking any algebraic structure. As such HHS could potentially replace finite groups where the discrete logarithm is hard for building cryptographic primitives and protocols in a post-quantum world.

Threshold HHS-based primitives typically require parties to compute the group action of a secret-shared input on a public set element. On one hand this could be done through generic MPC techniques, although they incur in prohibitive costs due to the high complexity of circuits evaluating group actions known to date. On the other hand round-robin protocols only require black box usage of the HHS. However these are highly sequential procedures, taking as many rounds as parties involved. The high round complexity appears to be inherent due the lack of homomorphic properties in HHS, yet no lower bounds were known so far.

In this work we formally show that round-robin protocols are optimal. In other words, any *at least passively secure* distributed computation of a group action making black-box use of an HHS must take a number of rounds greater or equal to the threshold parameter. We furthermore study *fair* protocols in which all users receive the output in the same round (unlike plain round-robin), and prove communication and computation lower bounds of $\Omega(n \log_2 n)$ for n parties. Our results are proven in Shoup's Generic Action Model (GAM), and hold regardless of the underlying computational assumptions.

1 Introduction

It is known from the '80s that Shor's algorithms [31] on a powerful enough quantum computer solves in polynomial time the hidden subgroup problem for abelian groups of which Factoring and Discrete Logarithm (DL) are particular instances. This poses a menace to existing public-key cryptography and has motivated the exploration and study of post-quantum cryptographic problems.

One potential candidate are hard homogeneous spaces (HHS), where a finite group $\mathbb{G}$ acts on a set $\mathcal{E}$ through an action $\star : \mathbb{G} \times \mathcal{E} \to \mathcal{E}$ which is hard to invert. These resemble prime order groups where the group action corresponds to the exponentiation. However, unlike groups, in HHS the set $\mathcal{E}$ lacks a group

© International Association for Cryptologic Research 2023
G. Rothblum and H. Wee (Eds.): TCC 2023, LNCS 14372, pp. 310–335, 2023.
https://doi.org/10.1007/978-3-031-48624-1_12

structure, making it immune to Schor's algorithms. So far the only known practical instantiations come from the Commutative Supersingular Diffie-Hellman (CSIDH) key-exchange, based on isogenies between supersingular elliptic curves. Remarkably, recent attacks [11,23,27] directed at SIDH, a different family of isogeny-based key exchange, did not affect the security of CSIDH.

Over the last years CSIDH has been used to build a variety of primitives. Examples include cryptosystems [20,25,33], signatures [1,8,15,19] and identification schemes [4] as well as more advanced primitives such as ID-based signatures [30], adaptor signatures [34], oblivious transfer [22], linkable ring signatures [7], group signatures [6] and importantly threshold schemes [1–3,5,10,14,16].

HHS-based threshold schemes in particular have gained a lot of attention as post-quantum alternatives to replace currently deployed solutions. Typically protocols based on group action involve the evaluation of $s \star E$ for a secret shared $s \in \mathbb{G}$ and a public set element E. However, as opposed to the DL group setting, parties with shares s_i cannot simply compute $s_i \star E$ locally and aggregate them to get $s \star E$ in a single round due to the lack of group structure in $\mathcal{E}$. Because of such a limitation, only two orthogonal approaches are know to date.

One is through generic multi-party computation (MPC) techniques. These require to express the group action as an explicit arithmetic circuit and then compute it gate-by-gate, theoretically achieving constant round complexity in the number of parties. The downside though is that either round or communication complexity highly depends on the multiplicative depth of the circuit, for instance when using protocol based respectively on linear secret sharing schemes or garbled circuits. Unfortunately, currently known circuits for CSIDH (Algorithm 2 in [12]) are not MPC-friendly, as they involve extensive looping over secret shared values. Hence the MPC approach does not appear to be practical yet.

On the other hand there are *round-robin* protocols. These require users to sequentially apply (a function of) their secret share on a given set element. An example to compute $s = s_1 + \ldots + s_4$ acting on E_0 among 4 parties is given in Fig. 1. The main advantage of such procedures is that they only make black-box usage of the HHS, avoiding the overheads of generic MPC. However, they require as many rounds as users involved in the computation, which in a t out of n secret sharing would amount to t rounds. This solution then appears hard to scale.

$$E_0 \xrightarrow[P_1]{s_1} E_1 \xrightarrow[P_2]{s_2} E_{21} \xrightarrow[P_3]{s_3} E_{321} \xrightarrow[P_4]{s_4} E_{4321} = s \star E_0$$

Fig. 1. Round-robin protocol for four parties. Here $E_{i_1 i_2 \ldots i_t} = (s_{i_1} + s_{i_2} + \cdots + s_{i_t}) \star E_0$

Given the current unsatisfactory state of the art, we ask whether best of both worlds constructions exist. In other words:

Is it possible to securely compute the group action of a t out of n secret shared group element through black-box usage of the HHS with less than t rounds of communication?

1.1 Our Contributions

We answer the above question in the negative proving the following lower bounds:

Round Lower Bound. We show that *any* protocol which, given a t out of n secret shared s, attempts to compute $f(s) \star E_0$ making only black-box usage of the group action either:

- Requires t or more rounds of communication[1]
- Is insecure against $t - 1$ passively corrupted users, which can recover $f(s)$.

The notion of black-box group action is formalized through Shoup's Generic Action Model (GAM) recently proposed in [18]. Here set elements are represented by random labels, and actions are computed through oracle calls to $\mathcal{O}_{act}$. We prove this by describing for any k round protocol an explicit PPT adversary which, provided a transcript and the secret inputs of k users, recovers $f(s)$. Our result cannot therefore be circumvented by

- *Using external hardness assumptions.* Our adversary is PPT, not only polynomially bounded in the number of queries to $\mathcal{O}_{act}$, and it could be used by any reduction to efficiently break the underlying assumption.
- *Using element's representation*, because this is already allowed in the GAM.

The only way we see to avoid our lower bound is through explicit usage of a circuit for the group action. In this case generic MPC techniques can be applied to improve asymptotic round complexity, however incurring in the overheads discussed previously.

Round-Optimal Fair Protocols Lower Bounds. Although we prove round-robin protocols to be optimal in the GAM, in concrete applications they present some vulnerabilities. The most notable one is that only the last user receives the result. That party may then refuse to share it with the others or an adversary could cause him to crash, forcing the protocol to restart[2]. For this reason variants have been proposed [16] in which all parties get the output in the same round (we call such protocols *fair*).

A trivial solution would be to run n parallel round robin protocols (see Fig. 2 for an example with $n = 4$), but this would require $O(n^2)$ communication and computation.

A better one, the *binary splitting strategy* [16], allows computing only $n(1 + \log_2 n)$ group actions and communicating $n(1 + \log_2 n) - 2$ set elements, at least when the number of parties is a power of two. An example for $n = 4$ is shown in Fig. 3.

---

[1] Including one round to broadcast the result to other users.

[2] Or, in honest majority, to publicly reconstruct this user's secret share.

$$E_0 \xrightarrow{s_1} E_1 \xrightarrow{s_2} E_{21} \xrightarrow{s_3} E_{321} \xrightarrow{s_4} E_{4321} = s \star E_0$$
$$E_0 \xrightarrow{s_2} E_2 \xrightarrow{s_3} E_{32} \xrightarrow{s_4} E_{432} \xrightarrow{s_1} E_{1432} = s \star E_0$$
$$E_0 \xrightarrow{s_3} E_3 \xrightarrow{s_4} E_{43} \xrightarrow{s_1} E_{143} \xrightarrow{s_2} E_{2143} = s \star E_0$$
$$E_0 \xrightarrow{s_4} E_4 \xrightarrow{s_1} E_{14} \xrightarrow{s_2} E_{214} \xrightarrow{s_3} E_{3214} = s \star E_0$$

Fig. 2. Fair Round-robin protocol for four parties. Naive approach.

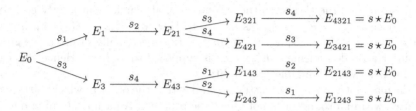

Fig. 3. Fair round-robin protocol for four parties. Optimal strategy.

We show that in the GAM this strategy is optimal for n a power of two, assuming the protocol does not allow $n-1$ honest-but-curious parties to recover $f(s)$. More precisely, we prove that any n rounds protocol[3] in the GAM computing $s \star E_0$ among n parties, with s being a function of user's private input, satisfying

- No set of $n-1$ can recover s
- All users obtain the output in the last round

involves at least $n(1 + \log_2 n)$ action evaluations and the communication of at least $n(1 + \log_2 n) - 2$ set elements. As for the previous result, this lower bound holds in spite of the computational assumptions and the usage of element's representation.

1.2 Our Techniques

Our results are both based on the fact that in the GAM every computed set element is either randomly sampled or returned by the oracle call $\mathcal{O}_{act}(a, D)$ with $a \in \mathbb{G}$ and a previously computed $D \in \mathcal{E}$. This allows us to construct a graph among set elements[4] where there is an edge from D to E if D was computed before E and $E = \mathcal{O}_{act}(a, D)$. In particular if there exists a path from D to E then, knowing the group elements used in all queries associated to the edges of this path, one can compute $a \in \mathbb{G}$ such that $a \star D = E$ by taking their sum.

---

[3] Due to our first result, this is also the best round complexity in this case.
[4] More precisely we later introduce a relation "$\rightarrow$" among *query indices*.

Round-Robin Lower Bound. Our proof consists of two steps. First, we show that a path from E_0 to $f(s) \star E_0$ exists with high probability. Second, we prove that among all paths from E_0 to $f(s) \star E_0$ there exists w.h.p. one involving for each round queries performed by at most one user. Because the protocol has k rounds, this path can involve queries of at most k users. Our result then follows because these k users can then jointly compute $f(s)$ as described above.

The first step, which we call *Sequentiality Lemma*[5], is proved observing that the output is either connected to E_0 or to a randomly sampled element E'. In the first case, we get the thesis. In the second case, all parties can jointly compute $a \in \mathbb{G}$ such that $a \star E' = E_{\text{out}}$ as observed. However $E_{\text{out}} = f(s) \star E_0$ implies that $E' = (-a + f(s)) \star E_0$, meaning that parties successfully inverted the group action for a random element E', which is supposed to be hard. Hence this case only happens with negligible probability.

The main idea in the second step instead is that the order in which parties are executed within a round does not affect the protocol. A path containing queries of at most one user for each round can then be constructed by induction. Given F a set element computed by P_i at round r, we can assume P_i was executed before any other user (so its queries occurs *before* any other user's ones in the same round). In this way, given a path from E_0 to F, all the queries in the path at round r can only come from P_i. The remaining queries at previous rounds can then be handled through the inductive hypothesis.

Optimality of Fair Round-Robin. Regarding fair protocols, we exploit the fact that all parties eventually return the output E_{out_i}. A first approach to bound computation would be to find a path from E_0 to each E_{out_i}, and count the total number of queries involved. If we only had one path this would work: Since we assume the protocol to have n rounds and that no subset of $n - 1$ users can recover $f(s)$, all users must contribute to this path by performing at least a query as discussed above. As a consequence each path contains $\Omega(n)$ queries. The issue however is that when many paths are considered, they may potentially share a large fraction of associated queries.

We address through the following critical abstraction: To each path connecting E_0 with E_{out_i} we associate the sequence $\pi_i(1), \ldots, \pi_i(n)$ of users performing queries in this path. Up to carefully choosing the paths, $\pi_i(r)$ is then the index of the only user performing queries at round r which contributes to the chosen path from E_0 to E_{out_i}. Our key observation is then that[6] two paths can share the same queries at round r only if π_i and π_j share the same prefix of length r. In other words, shared queries only occurs if for the first r rounds the two paths involve the same users in the same order.

With this crucial result we can then link the total number of queries to properties of the *prefix tree* of $\pi_1, \ldots, \pi_n$. We then shift our focus to the study of this graph. Because $\pi_1, \ldots, \pi_n$ can be proved to be permutations, their prefix tree

---

[5] Because it implies that computing $a \star E_0$ can only be done through sequential applications of the group action starting from E_0.

[6] Up to choosing paths satisfying a rather technical minimality condition.

must satisfy what we call the *tall sub-tree* (TS) property. Namely a tree is *tall* if all leaves have the same distance from the root and its height is greater than the number of leaves. A tree where all its sub-trees are tall is TS. We eventually translate our communication and computation lower bounds into bounds for TS trees and prove them with elementary graph-theoretic techniques.

Interestingly, the connection between TS trees and optimal fair protocols turned out to be more than a mere proof artifact: in the full version, we informally show how from any optimal TS tree one can derive optimal fair protocols to reconstruct an additive secret sharing over commutative group actions (such as CSIDH).

1.3 Related Work

The study of idealized models of computation dates back to the formalization of Shoup's [32] and Maurer's [24] Generic Group Models, where in the former group elements are labeled with random strings while in the latter no label is ever provided. In these frameworks many primitives were shown to be impossible including VDFs [28], efficient accumulators [29], signature schemes [13,17], vector commitments [13] and NIZKs [21]. All these results are limited to Maurer's GGM either because the primitive is known to exists in Shoup's GGM, or because negative results in Shoup's GGM are typically harder, such as the IBE impossibility [26,35]. Moreover all these negative results are proved providing an *unbounded* adversary restricted to perform at most polynomially many GGM queries. This means that using non group theoretic assumptions could be enough to bypass them. We remark that our results instead do not suffer from such a limitation.

Regarding group actions, a Shoup-like model was proposed in [18] capturing the concrete case of CSIDH, in which quadratic twists are efficiently computable, through an external oracle. Our result is based on their model, but we will not use for simplicity their twisting oracle. Instead we capture twists by allowing non-commutative and non-free actions as proposed in [9]. We discuss this further in the full version's Appendix.

Conversely a Maurer-like model for group actions was proposed in [9] and used to prove lower bounds on identification schemes. These apply to signature and zero-knowledge proofs obtained via the Fiat-Shamir transform. We stress that like any negative result in Maurer-like models, their bounds on interactive identification schemes only hold if set elements representation is never used. We again remark that this is not the case in our results.

2 Preliminaries

2.1 Notation

λ is the security parameter and a function of λ is *negligible* if it approaches zero faster than the inverse of any polynomial. For a Turing machine $\mathcal{A}$, $y \leftarrow \mathcal{A}(x)$

means y was *deterministically* computed on input x, whereas $y \leftarrow^\$ \mathcal{A}(x)$ means y was computed *probabilistically*. These must not be confused with "$\rightarrow$" and "$\dashrightarrow$", two relations we define in Sects. 3.1 and 3.3. $x \sim \mathcal{X}$ is a random variable with support $\mathcal{X}$. $H(x)$ is the Shannon's entropy of x and $I(x; y)$ is the mutual information between x and y, defined as $H(x) - H(x|y)$. $x \leftarrow^\$ \mathcal{X}$ means x is uniformly sampled from $\mathcal{X}$. For a finite group, denoted by $(\mathbb{G}, +)$, we always use additive notation and denote by 0 the identity element. We will not implicitly assume groups to be commutative or prime order.

2.2   Hard Homogeneous Space

Here we recall the notion of possibly non-commutative group actions.

Definition 1. *An action of a finite group $(\mathbb{G}, +)$ on a set $\mathcal{E}$ is given by a map $\star : \mathbb{G} \times \mathcal{E} \rightarrow \mathcal{E}$ satisfying the following properties:*

1. *Identity: $0 \star E = E$ for all $E \in \mathcal{E}$.*
2. *Associativity: $(h + g) \star E = h \star (g \star E)$ for every $h, g \in \mathbb{G}$ and $E \in \mathcal{E}$.*

The action is transitive if for all $E_1, E_2 \in \mathcal{E}$ there exists $g \in \mathbb{G}$ such that $E_2 = g \star E_1$. If g is unique the action is called free.

For a group action to be *effectively computable* we further assume that deciding membership in $\mathbb{G}$, $\mathcal{E}$ and equality between elements in $\mathbb{G}$ and $\mathcal{E}$ is efficient. Moreover sampling uniformly from both sets, computing the operations and inverses in $\mathbb{G}$, and the group action $\star$ is also efficient.

Typically, the set $\mathcal{E}$ equipped with an effective group action $\star$ is called *Homogeneous Space* if $\star$ is transitive and free. However we will extend this notion to actions that are not necessarily free. This, in line with the approach of [9], allows for instance encoding quadratic twists for CSIDH as the action of specific group elements.

For a PPT $\mathcal{A}$ adversary we define the advantage for the *vectorization* and *parallelization* problems as

$$\mathsf{Adv}^{\mathsf{Vec}}(\mathcal{A}) = \Pr\left[g = g' \;\middle|\; \begin{array}{l} g \leftarrow^\$ \mathbb{G},\ E \leftarrow^\$ \mathcal{E},\ E' = g \star E \\ g' \leftarrow \mathcal{A}(E, E') \end{array} \right],$$

$$\mathsf{Adv}^{\mathsf{Par}}(\mathcal{A}) = \Pr\left[E_t = (g + h) \star E \;\middle|\; \begin{array}{l} g, h \leftarrow^\$ \mathbb{G},\ E \leftarrow^\$ \mathcal{E} \\ E_g \leftarrow g \star E,\ E_h \leftarrow h \star E \\ E_t \leftarrow \mathcal{A}(E, E_g, E_h) \end{array} \right].$$

Definition 2. *An homogeneous space is called hard if the vectorization and parallelization problems are hard. That is, if for any PPT adversary $\mathcal{A}$ there exists negligible functions $\varepsilon_{\mathsf{vec}}, \varepsilon_{\mathsf{par}}$ such that*

$$\mathsf{Adv}^{\mathsf{Vec}}(\mathcal{A}) \leq \varepsilon_{\mathsf{vec}}(\lambda), \qquad \mathsf{Adv}^{\mathsf{Par}}(\mathcal{A}) \leq \varepsilon_{\mathsf{par}}(\lambda).$$

2.3 Shoup's Generic Action Model

In order to capture generic usage of the group action, we use an adaptation of Shoup's Generic Group Model [32]. In this setting the group action $\star : \mathbb{G} \times \mathcal{E} \to \mathcal{E}$ is modeled through an oracle $\mathcal{O}_{\mathrm{act}}$. Initially a random injective labeling function $\sigma : \mathcal{E} \to \{0,1\}^{\mu}$ is sampled and users receive $E_0 = \sigma(E_0')$ the encoding of an element in $\mathcal{E}$. Action queries are then replied to with

$$\mathcal{O}_{\mathrm{act}}(a, E) = \begin{cases} \sigma(a \star E') & \text{If } E = \sigma(E') \\ \bot & \text{If } E \notin \mathrm{Im}\,\sigma \end{cases}$$

We do not provide an oracle to test membership in $\sigma(\mathcal{E})$ as this can be checked querying $\mathcal{O}_{\mathrm{act}}(0, E)$, which returns E if $E \in \sigma(\mathcal{E})$ and $\bot$ if $E \notin \sigma(\mathcal{E})$. We further remark that if $\mu = \log_2 |\mathcal{E}| + O(\log \lambda)$ the model allows sampling random elements of unknown "discrete logarithm" in base E_0. Conversely if $\mu = \log_2 |\mathcal{E}| + \Omega(\lambda)$ sampling random elements is computationally hard.

In relation to previously proposed models [9,18] for generic group actions, ours allows parties to have an explicit representation for set elements as done in [18] and as opposed to [9]. However, as in [9] we allow non-free and non-commutative group actions in order to encode external operations such as quadratic twists as particular action evaluations. In this sense we do not need a separate oracle to capture twists as done in [18].

3 Technical Lemmas

3.1 Sequentiality Lemma

In this section we present our starting point, the *Sequentiality Lemma*, stating that any procedure computing $s \star E_0$ can obtain the right result only through sequential applications of the group action to E_0. A full proof of this Lemma can be found in the extended version's appendix.

First let us introduce some notation. Given $\mathcal{A}$ a PPT algorithm with oracle access to $\mathcal{O}_{\mathrm{act}}$ initially receiving E_0 and performing q queries, we denote these with $E_k \leftarrow \mathcal{O}_{\mathrm{act}}(a_k, D_k)$ for $k \in \{1, \dots, q\}$. Next we introduce a relation $\to$ among indices $\{0, \dots, q\}$.

$$k_1 \to k_2 \quad \Leftrightarrow \quad k_1 < k_2, \quad E_{k_1} = D_{k_2}.$$

Intuitively this means that the k_1-th set element was used to compute the k_2-th. Note this relation is not yet a (strict) partial order as it is not transitive, but its transitive closure is. This is explicitly defined as

$$i \to^{+} j \quad \Leftrightarrow \quad \exists k_1, \dots, k_m : \quad k_1 \to k_2 \to \dots \to k_m, \quad k_1 = i, \quad k_m = j$$

The lemma then ensures that if an algorithm computes $s \star E_0$ for a known s in the GAM, with high probability $s \star E_0$ is the output of some query, say the k-th (meaning $s \star E_0 = E_k$), and $0 \to^{+} k$.

Lemma 1. *For any $\mathcal{A}$ PPT algorithm with oracle access to $\mathcal{O}_{act}$ making at most q queries and any $s \in \mathbb{G}$, such that $(s, E_{out}) \leftarrow \mathcal{A}(E_0)$ then*

$$\Pr\left[E_{out} = s \star E_0, \; \nexists k \left(E_{out} = E_k, \; 0 \rightarrow^+ k\right)\right] \leq \varepsilon_{vec}(2q) + \frac{1}{|\mathcal{E}| - (q+1)} := \varepsilon_{seq}(q)$$

where $\varepsilon_{vec}(q)$ is the advantage of breaking the vectorization problem in q queries, see Definition 2.

3.2 Interactive Protocols

The main limitation of the Sequentiality Lemma is that it only applies to a single machine. Here we introduce notation for interactive protocols in the GAM in order to extend in the next section this result to the interactive case.

An interactive protocol is defined by n PPT machines $P_1, \ldots, P_n$ with access to point-to-point (i.e. non-broadcast[7]) communication channels. We assume them to be synchronous and simultaneous i.e. such that messages from all parties are atomically sent at the beginning of each round and delivered at the end. To formally describe this model we initially call $trs_0 = \bot$ and inductively define for initial inputs $x_1, \ldots, x_n$ the messages sent and transcript at round r as

$$M_{r,i} \leftarrow^\$ P_i(x_i, trs_{r-1}), \quad trs_r = (trs_{r-1}, M_{r,1}, \ldots, M_{r,n})$$

where $M_{r,i} = (M_{r,i}^{(1)}, \ldots, M_{r,i}^{(n)})$ is the tuple of messages sent by P_i, and in particular $M_{r,i}^{(j)}$ is the message P_i sends to P_j. To ensure parties only use message delivered to them, we assume P_j can only read entries of the form $M_{r,i}^{(j)}$ in trs for any r and i.

Regarding the interaction with the GAM we denote $E_{r,i,j} \leftarrow \mathcal{O}_{act}(a_{r,i,j}, D_{r,i,j})$ the j-th query made by P_i to $\mathcal{O}_{act}$ during the r-th round. As done in Sect. 3.1 we then define a relation $\rightarrow$ among the indices (r, i, j) and (r', i', j') which indicates that the result from the former was used as input in the latter. Formally

$$(r, i, j) \rightarrow (r', i', j') \quad \Leftrightarrow \quad \left(r < r' \vee (r = r', \; i = i', \; j < j')\right) \wedge E_{r,i,j} = D_{r',i',j'}.$$

This condition on the indices says that one query precedes another one only if it was performed on a previous round, or if both were asked in the same round *by the same party P_i* one before the other. Like $\rightarrow$, the relation $\rightarrow$ is not yet a (strict) partial order. However its transitive closure $\rightarrow^+$ is. This is explicitly defined as $(r, i, j) \rightarrow^+ (r', i', j') \quad \Leftrightarrow$

$$\Leftrightarrow \exists (r_1, i_1, j_1), \ldots, (r_t, i_t, j_t):$$
$$(r_1, i_1, j_1) \rightarrow \ldots \rightarrow (r_t, i_t, j_t), \quad (r_1, i_1, j_1) = (r, i, j), \quad (r_t, i_t, j_t) = (r', i', j').$$

---

[7] Even though broadcast could be achieved simply sending the same message to all parties, as we only focus on semi-honest adversaries.

Finally, to further include E_0 in this relation, which might be technically never queried, we could either assume that parties initially query $E_0 \leftarrow \mathcal{O}_{\mathsf{act}}(0, E_0)$, or more simply say that

$$0 \dashrightarrow (r, i, j) \quad \Leftrightarrow \quad D_{r,i,j} = E_0.$$

We conclude this section with two elementary properties of $\dashrightarrow$. The proofs appears in the full version.

Lemma 2. *Let* $(r_1, i_1, j_1) \dashrightarrow \ldots \dashrightarrow (r_t, i_t, j_t)$. *Then*

$$E_{r_t, i_t, j_t} = (a_{r_t, i_t, j_t} + \ldots + a_{r_1, i_1, j_1}) \star D_{r_1, i_1, j_1}.$$

Lemma 3. *Let* $0 \dashrightarrow (r_1, i_1, j_1) \dashrightarrow \ldots \dashrightarrow (r_t, i_t, j_t)$. *Then*

$$|\{i_1, \ldots, i_t\}| \le |\{r_1, \ldots, r_t\}|.$$

3.3 Interactive Sequentiality Lemma

In this section we state the Interactive Sequentiality Lemma, which extends Lemma 1. This applies to a set of parties $P_1, \ldots, P_n$ each holding an input $s_i \in \{0, 1\}^{\mathsf{poly}(\lambda)}$ and wishing to compute $f(s_1, \ldots, s_n) \star E_0$ for a given function f. Informally it states that the result must, up to negligible probability, come from the sequential application of $\mathcal{O}_{\mathsf{act}}$ to E_0 *and* that such sequence of queries involves at most one player for each round.

Lemma 4. *Let* $P_1, \ldots, P_n$ *be a* k *round protocol in the GAM and* f *a function such that given inputs* $s_1, \ldots, s_n \sim \{0, 1\}^{\mathsf{poly}(\lambda)}$ *there exists* P_i *which at round* k *returns* $E_{\mathsf{out}} = f(s_1, \ldots, s_n) \star E_0$. *Then*

$$\Pr\left[\exists (r', i', j') \; : \; E_{\mathsf{out}} = E_{r', i', j'}, \quad 0 \dashrightarrow^+ (r', i', j')\right] \ge 1 - (k+1) \cdot \varepsilon_{\mathsf{seq}}(q)$$

where q *is an upper bound on the total number of queries performed.*

A full proof of this lemma appears in the full version.

4 Round Lower Bound

We now present our first result for distributed computation over black box HHS. We assume that parties $P_1, \ldots, P_n$ initially receive a secret input $s_i \in \{0, 1\}^{\mathsf{poly}(\lambda)}$ and a public function f and execute a protocol compute $f(s_1, \ldots, s_n) \star E_0$ in Shoup's GAM. In this setting then we will prove that if such computation only requires k rounds, then a subset of k users can passively collude, and recover $f(s_1, \ldots, s_n)$.

Evaluating the group action of a t out of n secret shared group element $s \in \mathbb{G}$ is then a specific case of interest, as it affects threshold signatures and cryptosystems. This is captured by our result setting f as the reconstruction function. More concretely, for n out of n additive secret sharing, $f(s_1, \ldots, s_n)$ is simply the sum of all shares. Similarly, for t out of n Shamir secret sharing f is

$$f(s_1, \ldots, s_n) = \sum_{i \in R} \lambda_{i,R} s_i$$

with R being a reconstruction set of size t and $\lambda_{i,R} \in \mathbb{Z}$ the Lagrange coefficients[8]. In all these cases, since any set with less than t users is not entitled to recover s, our result implies that passive security cannot be achieved with less than t rounds. Finally, this will further imply the optimality of round-robin protocols in such cases.

Theorem 1. *Let $P_1, \ldots, P_n$ be a k-round protocol in the GAM and f a function such that on input $s_1, \ldots, s_n \sim \{0,1\}^{\mathsf{poly}(\lambda)}$ there exists P_i returning at round k the element $E_{\mathsf{out}} = f(s_1, \ldots, s_n) \star E_0$.*

Then up to probability $(k+1)\varepsilon_{\mathsf{seq}}$ there exists $S \subseteq \{1, \ldots, n\}$ and a PPT machine $\mathcal{A}$ such that, calling ρ_i the random coins of P_i

1. *$|S| \leq k$*
2. *$s' \leftarrow \mathcal{A}(\mathsf{trs}, \{s_i, \rho_i\}_{i \in S})$ with $s' \star E_0 = E_{\mathsf{out}}$.*

Proof. We begin by applying the *Interactive Sequentiality Lemma* 4, stating that up to probability $(k+1)\varepsilon_{\mathsf{seq}}$ there exists (r, i, j) such that $E_{\mathsf{out}} = E_{r,i,j}$ and $0 \twoheadrightarrow^+ (r, i, j)$. Next let $(r_1, i_1, j_1), \ldots (r_t, i_t, j_t) = (r, i, j)$ be a chain for the above relation, i.e.

$$0 \twoheadrightarrow (r_1, i_1, j_1) \twoheadrightarrow \ldots \twoheadrightarrow (r_t, i_t, j_t).$$

We define $S = \{i_1, \ldots, i_t\}$ the set of users involved in the chain[9]. To upper bound the size of S we use Lemma 3: because the protocol has k round, $|S| \leq |\{r_1, \ldots, r_t\}| \leq k$. Next we provide an explicit description of $\mathcal{A}$ computing s' from $\{s_i, \rho_i\}_{i \in S}$ and trs. Initially $\mathcal{A}$ executes P_i with $i \in S$ for all rounds. In this way it performs all queries $(r_1, i_1, j_1), \ldots, (r_t, i_t, j_t)$ and in particular knows the group elements used in those queries. The sum s' of all these group elements then is such that $s' \star E_0 = E_{\mathsf{out}}$. A formal description is provided in Fig. 4.

Since the query $(r_\alpha, i_\alpha, j_\alpha)$ for $\alpha \in \{1, \ldots, t\}$ is performed by P_{i_α} at round r_α, then $\mathcal{A}$ also performs this query as by construction $i_\alpha \in S$ and $\mathcal{A}$ runs $P_{i_\alpha}^{\mathcal{O}_{\mathsf{act}}}(s_{i_\alpha}, \mathsf{trs}_{r_\alpha - 1}; \rho_{i_\alpha})$ in line 4. Finally, by Lemma 2

$$s' \star E_0 = (a_{r_t, i_t, j_t} + \ldots + a_{r_1, i_1, j_1}) \star E_0 = E_{r_t, i_t, j_t} = E_{\mathsf{out}}.$$

This completes the proof.

---

[8] These can be defined for $\mathbb{G}$ if $\mathbb{Z}_N$ has an *exceptional set* of size at least n, with N being the order of $\mathbb{G}$.

[9] Note $|S|$ may be smaller than t if there are repetitions among $i_1, \ldots, i_t$.

$\mathcal{A}^{\mathcal{O}_{\mathsf{act}}}(\mathsf{trs}, \{s_i, \rho_i\}_{i \in S})$

---

1 :   Compute $\mathsf{trs}_0, \mathsf{trs}_1 \ldots, \mathsf{trs}_r$ from trs

2 :   // Execute all users in S. Note that at round r' users get $\mathsf{trs}_{r'-1}$

3 :   **For all** $i' \in S$ and $r \in \{1, \ldots, k\}$:

4 :   Run $P_{i'}^{\mathcal{O}_{\mathsf{act}}}(s_{i'}, \mathsf{trs}_{r'-1}; \rho_{i'})$

5 :   // Compute s' from the users' queries

6 :   Find $(r_1, i_1, j_1), \ldots (r_t, i_t, j_t)$ such that $0 \dashrightarrow (r_1, i_1, j_1) \dashrightarrow \ldots \dashrightarrow (r_t, i_t, j_t)$

7 :   Retrieve queried group elements $a_{r_1, i_1, j_1}, \ldots, a_{r_t, i_t, j_t}$

8 :   **Return** $s' \leftarrow a_{r_t, i_t, j_t} + \ldots + a_{r_1, i_1, j_1}$

Fig. 4. Adversary $\mathcal{A}$ computing s' such that $s' \star E_0 = E_{\mathsf{out}}$

5   Fair Protocols Lower Bounds

5.1   Fair Protocols

As proven in the previous section, round-robin protocols achieve the best round complexity in the GAM. These however do not achieve *fairness* even against weak adversaries. Indeed, since only the last user gets the result, it can simply halt instead of communicating it to others. Remarkably, in order to carry out this attack, an adversary only needs to be able to

- corrupt only 1 user.
- deviate from the protocol only through crashes.

Moreover, it does not even have to be *rushing*, i.e. able to receive for each round honest users' messages before computing and sending its own.

In this section we will study protocols that address this issue, and eventually provide communication and computation lower bounds for them in the GAM. More specifically we focus on protocols among n users to compute a function of all parties' private inputs acting on a given set elements such that:

1. it prevents $n - 1$ honest-but-curious users from reconstructing the secret,
2. in honest executions, all parties obtain their output in the last round,
3. it requires exactly n rounds of communication (i.e. it is round optimal according to Theorem 1).

We immediately observe that these simple restrictions, the second one being necessary for fairness in general, imply fairness against the weak class of attacks described above. The idea is that if an adversary obtains the output before the n-th round, and then crashes the corrupted party, then using Theorem 1, one could find a subset of $n - 1$ or less users who are able to recover the secret group element. Conversely, if it crashes at round n, as we assumed it not to be rushing, it can only halt after sending its own messages. Hence all parties eventually get their output as well.

Noticeably, the above argument does not imply that fair protocols have to be round-optimal. Even more so, as our lower bounds will only apply to round-optimal protocols, this leaves open the possibility that fair solutions with sub-optimal round complexity but better communication and computational costs exist. Since our techniques do not seem to easily generalize in such case, we leave this as an interesting open question.

Finally, it may appear as uninteresting in practice to only study security against such a weak class of attacks. We remark that, as we will prove lower bounds for these protocols, our results applies to stronger models of corruption as well.

5.2   Refined Interactive Sequentiality Lemma

In order to provide our second lower bound we will need an improved version of the Interactive Sequentiality Lemma, Sect. 3.3. First let us recall its statement. Given n parties with inputs $s_1, \ldots, s_n$ jointly computing $E_{\text{out}} = f(s_1, \ldots, s_n) \star E_0$, Lemma 4 states that up to negligible probability, $E_{\text{out}} = E_{r,i,j}$ and $0 \dashrightarrow^+ (r, i, j)$. Let $(r_1, i_1, j_1), \ldots, (r_t, i_t, j_t)$ be a chain of queries for $0 \dashrightarrow^+ (r, i, j)$, i.e. such that

$$0 \dashrightarrow (r_1, i_1, j_1) \dashrightarrow (r_2, i_2, j_2) \dashrightarrow \ldots \dashrightarrow (r_t, i_t, j_t) = (r, i, j).$$

In our improved lemma we will show that this chain can be chosen so that the first query occurring at round r_α is *minimal* among all queries performed in the same round r_α with respect to the relation $\dashrightarrow^+$. This means that the set elements used to perform this minimal query was not computed in the same round by P_{i_α}. This property will prove useful when studying communication lower bounds, as it roughly implies that the set element used in minimal queries highly depends on messages previously received. More formally we give the following definition:

Definition 3. *Given* $P_1, \ldots, P_n$ *PPT defining a* k *rounds protocol, and a sequence of queries* $(r_1, i_1, j_1), \ldots, (r_t, i_t, j_t)$ *such that*

$$0 \dashrightarrow (r_1, i_1, j_1) \dashrightarrow \ldots \dashrightarrow (r_t, i_t, j_t)$$

we call this a refined chain if for all $r \in \{r_1, \ldots, r_t\}$ *there exists an index* α *such that* $(r_\alpha, i_\alpha, j_\alpha)$ *is minimal among all queries of the form* $(r_\alpha, \cdot, \cdot)$ *with respect to* $\dashrightarrow^+$.

Lemma 5. *Let* $P_1, \ldots, P_n$ *be a* k *round protocol in the GAM and* f *a function such that on inputs* $s_1, \ldots, s_n \sim \{0, 1\}^{\text{poly}(\lambda)}$, *there exists* P_i *which at round* k *returns* $E_{\text{out}} = f(s_1, \ldots, s_n) \star E_0$. *Up to probability* $(k+1)\varepsilon_{\text{seq}}$ *then* $E_{\text{out}} = E_{r,i,j}$ *and there exists a refined chain such that* $0 \dashrightarrow^+ (r, i, j)$.

The proof appears in the full version.

5.3   Tall Sub-tree Property

Our technique to study fair protocols will be to associate a tree with special properties to the protocol, and translate bounds for the tree size to communication and computation lower bounds. In this section we therefore introduce the *tall sub-tree* (TS for short) property for tree graphs, and lower bound their size.

Informally a tree is *tall* if all leaves have the same distance from the root, and its height is higher than the number of leaves. A tree then satisfies the TS property if all its (non-trivial) sub-trees are tall. To be more formal we introduce some notation. Given $T = (V, E)$ a tree, height(T) is its height (the longest path's length) and leaves(T) its number of leaves. T_v for $v \in V$ is the sub-tree rooted in v (Fig. 5).

Definition 4. *A tree $T = (V, E)$ is tall if all leaves have the same distance from the root and either $|V| = 1$ or* height(T) $\geq$ leaves(T). *T satisfies the tall sub-tree (TS) property if T_v is tall for all $v \in V$.*

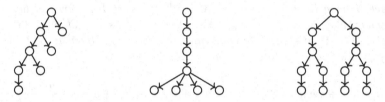

Fig. 5. Examples of non-TS (left), tall but non-TS (center) and TS (right) trees.

Proposition 1. *Let $T = (V, E)$ be a TS tree with* height(T) $= m$ *and* leaves(T) $= n$. *Then*

$$|E| \geq m + n \log_2 n.$$

We quickly observe that because in any tree $|V| = |E| + 1$, the Proposition above could be restated as $|V| \geq m + 1 + n \log_2 n$. Next we prove a bound for the number of nodes of distance at least two from the root.

Proposition 2. *Let $T = (E, V)$ a TS tree with* height(T) $= m$ *and* leaves(T) $= n$. *Furthermore let $V_{\geq 2}$ the set of nodes with distance at least two from the root. Then*

$$|V_{\geq 2}| \geq m + n \log_2 n - 2.$$

Proofs for Proposition 1 and 2 appears in the full version.

5.4   Main Result

We are finally ready to state and prove our second lower bound for fair protocols with optimal round complexity. Regarding our notation, we remind that μ denotes the GAM label size, i.e. the number of bits used to represent set elements, and that trs denotes the tuple of messages exchanged throughout the protocol's execution. In order to give meaningful lower bound on the communication complexity we define for the tuple of messages $M_r^{(i)}$ received by P_i at round r

$$\ell(M_r^{(i)}) \ := \ \mathsf{H}(M_r^{(i)} \,|\, \mathsf{trs}_{r-1}) \qquad \ell_{\mathsf{tot}} \ = \ \sum_{r=1}^{k} \sum_{i=1}^{n} \ell_{\mathsf{tot}}(M_r^{(i)}).$$

Roughly $\ell(\,\cdot\,)$ represent the amount of information contained in $M_r^{(i)}$ given all previous messages, and lower bound the information P_i receives conditioned only to messages it previously saw. Hence ℓ_{tot} lower bounds the total information sent throughout the protocol.

Theorem 2. *Let $P_1, \ldots, P_n$ be an n-round protocol in the GAM and f a function such that on input $s_1, \ldots, s_n \sim \{0,1\}^{\mathsf{poly}(\lambda)}$, every P_i returns at last round the element $E_{\mathsf{out}_i} = f(s_1, \ldots, s_n) \star E_0$. If there exists no set $S \subseteq \{1, \ldots, n\}$ and adversary $\mathcal{A}$ satisfying the conditions of Theorem 1 then up to probability $(n+1)\varepsilon_{\mathsf{seq}}$, calling q the total number of $\mathcal{O}_{\mathsf{act}}$ queries*

$$q \geq n(1 + \log n), \qquad \ell_{\mathsf{tot}} \geq (n(1 + \log n) - 2) \cdot \left(\mu - \frac{q}{2^{\mu-1} - q} \right).$$

As for Theorem 1, this result readily generalizes to protocol reconstructing the action of a t out of n secret shared value, which requires exactly t rounds and at least a subset of t users get the output. In such case the protocol must involve at least $t(1 + \log_2 t)$ queries and no less than $\approx t(1 + \log_2)\mu$ bits of communication.

Proof. The proof consists of four steps:

1. Observing that any chain for $0 \rightarrowtail^+ \mathsf{out}_i$ contains at least a query from each user. In particular we can associate to each chain a permutation π_i assigning to round r the (only) user whose round r queries appears in the chain.
2. Given $\pi_1, \ldots, \pi_n$ permutations we build their *prefix tree* and show it is a TS tree, see Sect. 5.3. In particular it contains at least $n(1 + \log_1 n)$ nodes, excluding the root.
3. Using Lemma 5, we find refined chains for $0 \rightarrowtail^+ \mathsf{out}_i$ so that the prefix tree of the associated permutations $\pi_1, \ldots, \pi_n$ satisfies a certain minimality condition. Then we build an injective function f from the nodes (root excluded) to the set of query indexes. By Proposition 1 this yields $q \geq n(1 + \log n)$.
4. Proving each $M_r^{(i)}$ must have enough information about set element which figures as input in queries in $\mathrm{Im}\, f$ performed by P_i at round $r+1$. The bound on ℓ_{tot} is then a consequence of Proposition 2.

Regarding the first step, we begin with the following claim, stating that each chain for $0 \dashrightarrow^+ \mathsf{out}_i$ must contain queries from all users and cannot skip any round.

Claim 1. *For all* $(r_1, i_1, j_1), \ldots, (r_t, i_t, j_t)$ *such that*

$$0 \dashrightarrow (r_1, i_1, j_1) \dashrightarrow \ldots \dashrightarrow (r_t, i_t, j_t) = \mathsf{out}_i$$

then $\{i_1, \ldots, i_t\} = \{1, \ldots, n\} = \{r_1, \ldots, r_t\}$.

Using this, for all chains $(r_1, i_1, j_1), \ldots, (r_t, i_t, j_t)$ for $0 \dashrightarrow^+ \mathsf{out}_i$ we define a function π_i associating to each round r_α the user i_α who performed at least one query in the chain at that round

$$\pi_i : \{1, \ldots, n\} \to \{1, \ldots, n\} \quad : \quad \pi_i(r_\alpha) = i_\alpha \quad \forall \alpha \in \{1, \ldots, t\}.$$

This is a function because $\dashrightarrow$ implies there is at most one user performing queries for each round and, by Claim 1, π_i is defined for all r. In fact this is a permutation as stated in the next claim, which completes the first step.

Claim 2. *For all* $(r_1, i_1, j_1), \ldots, (r_t, i_t, j_t)$ *chain for* $0 \dashrightarrow^+ \mathsf{out}_i$, π_i *is a bijection and* $\pi_i(n) = i$.

Regarding the second step, assuming $0 \dashrightarrow^+ \mathsf{out}_i$ for all i, we can define $\pi_1, \ldots, \pi_n$ for any choice of chains realizing these relations. We then construct their prefix tree. This is done by defining for each $r \in \{0, \ldots, n\}$ an equivalence relation where π_i is equivalent to π_j if the two functions agree on the first r evaluations. Note that for $r = 0$ all permutations are equivalent and, due to Claim 2, for $r = n$ no two distinct permutations are. Then the equivalence classes are

$$[\pi_i]_r = \{\pi_j : \pi_j(1) = \pi_i(1), \ldots, \pi_i(r) = \pi_j(r)\}.$$

For the sake of clarity we notice that $[\pi_i]_0 = \{\pi_1, \ldots, \pi_n\}$ and, by Claim 2, $[\pi_i]_n = \{\pi_i\}$. With this notation their prefix tree $T = (V, E)$ is defined as

$$v_{i,r} := ([\pi_i]_r, r)$$
$$V = \{v_{i,r} : i \in \{1, \ldots, n\}, r \in \{0, \ldots, n\}\}$$
$$E = \{(v_{i,r}, v_{i,r+1}) : i \in \{1, \ldots, n\}, r \in \{1, \ldots, n-1\}\}.$$

i.e. the class $[\pi_i]_{r+1}$ is connected to the class $[\pi_i]_r$ it refines. We conclude the second step with the next claim.

Claim 3. *If* $0 \dashrightarrow^+ \mathsf{out}_i$ *for all* $i \in \{1, \ldots, n\}$, *then for all chains realizing them and associated permutations* $\pi_1, \ldots, \pi_n$, *their prefix tree* T *is a TS tree with* $\mathsf{height}(T) = n$ *and* $\mathsf{leaves}(T) = n$.

For the third step we use Lemma 5. Since each P_i returns $E_{\mathsf{out}_i} = f(s_1, \ldots, s_n) \star E_0$, up to probability $(n+1)\varepsilon_{\mathsf{seq}}$, for all i there exists a refined chain for $0 \dashrightarrow^+ \mathsf{out}_i$, see Definition 3. Conditioning on this event, we can chose n refined chains with associated permutations $\pi_1, \ldots, \pi_n$ so that, calling $V_t = \{v_{i,r} : i \in \{1, \ldots, t\}, r \in \{0, \ldots, n\}\}$, the tuple

$$(|V_1|, |V_2|, \ldots, |V_n|)$$

is minimal w.r.t. the lexicographic order. This means that for any other choice of refined chains, the associated permutations $\pi'_1, \ldots, \pi'_n$ defines a prefix tree $T' = (V', E')$ so that either $|V_t| = |V'_t|$ for all t or there exists a t such that

$$|V_1| = |V'_1| \wedge \ldots \wedge |V_t| = |V'_t| \wedge |V_{t+1}| < |V'_{t+1}|.$$

Using this we will construct an injective function f from the tree nodes (excluding the root) to the set of query indices. Each node $v = ([\pi_i]_r, r)$ for some π_i will be mapped to a query that is:

- in the chain for $0 \rightarrowtail^+ \text{out}_i$ used to construct π,
- minimal among round r queries, with respect to $\rightarrowtail^+$.

Claim 4. *There exists refined chains for $0 \rightarrowtail^+ \text{out}_i$ so that, calling $T = (V, E)$ the resulting prefix tree and V^* the set of nodes excluding the root, there exists $f : V^* \rightarrow \mathbb{N}^3$ such that*

1. *For each $v \in V$ there exist r, i, j so that $v = v_{i,r}$ and $f(v) = (r, \pi_i(r), j)$ is a query in the chain used to construct π_i. Moreover $f(v)$ is minimal w.r.t. $\rightarrowtail^+$ among all queries of the form $(r, \cdot, \cdot)$.*
2. *f is injective.*
3. *Calling $a_{r,i,j}, D_{r,i,j}$ the input of $\mathcal{O}_{\text{act}}$ in the (r, i, j)-th query, then*

$$D_{f(u)} = D_{f(v)} \quad \Rightarrow \quad \exists w : (w, u), (w, v) \in E.$$

The first two properties combined implies that the set of queries contains at least $|V^*| = |E| \geq n(1 + \log_2 n)$ elements, where the last bound follows from Claim 3 and Proposition 1.

Finally we go through the last step. In order to bound communication we first bound the number of minimal queries using different set elements as input performed by P_i at round r. Next we will prove $M_{r-1}^{(i)}$ has to contain enough information about these elements. Toward this goal we define $U_{r,i}$ as the set of nodes to which f associate a query performed by P_i at round r, and $\Delta_{r,i}$ the collection of set elements used in those queries.

$$U_{r,i} := \{v \in V : \exists j : f(v) = (r, i, j)\} \qquad \Delta_{r,i} := \{D_{f(v)} : v \in U_{r,i}\}$$

First we give a bound on the size of $\Delta_{r,i}$.

Claim 5. $\sum_{r=1}^{n-1} \sum_{i=1}^{n} |\Delta_{r+1,i}| \geq n(1 + \log_2 n) - 2.$

Then, we relate the size of $\Delta_{r+1,i}$ with the entropy in $M_r^{(i)}$

Claim 6. *With the previous notation,*

$$H\left(M_r^{(i)}\,\Big|\,\mathsf{trs}_{r-1}\right) \geq |\Delta_{r+1,i}| \cdot \left(\mu - \frac{q}{2^{\mu-1} - q}\right).$$

This eventually concludes the proof of Theorem 2 because

$$\ell_{\text{tot}} = \sum_{r=1}^{n-1} \sum_{i=1}^{n} \ell(M_r^{(i)})$$

$$\geq \sum_{r=1}^{n-1} \sum_{i=1}^{n} |\Delta_{r+1,i}| \cdot \left(\mu - \frac{q}{2^{\mu-1} - q}\right)$$

$$\geq (n(1 + n\log_2 n) - 2) \cdot \left(\mu - \frac{q}{2^{\mu-1} - q}\right).$$

Proof of Claim 1. Assume by contradiction that there exists a chain for $0 \dashrightarrow^+$ out_i such that $S := \{i_1, \ldots, i_t\} \subsetneq \{1, \ldots, n\}$. Then, as shown in the proof of Theorem 1, the adversary $\mathcal{A}$ described in Fig. 4 on input trs and $(s_i, \rho_i)_{i \in S}$, with ρ_i being the random coins of P_i, recovers s' such that $s' \star E_0 = E_{\mathsf{out}_i}$. This contradicts the assumption that such a pair $(S, \mathcal{A})$ does not exist.

Next, using Lemma 3 and the fact that the protocol has n rounds,

$$n = |\{i_1, \ldots, i_t\}| \leq |\{r_1, \ldots, r_t\}| = n \quad \Rightarrow \quad \{r_1, \ldots, r_t\} = \{1, \ldots, n\}.$$

Proof of Claim 2. We begin showing that π_i is a total function from $\{1, \ldots, n\}$. Let $\alpha < \beta$ be two indexes such that $r_\alpha = r_\beta$. Because $(r_\alpha, i_\alpha, j_\alpha) \dashrightarrow^+ (r_\beta, i_\beta, j_\beta)$, by the definition of $\dashrightarrow^+$, $r_\alpha = r_\beta$ implies $i_\alpha = i_\beta$. Hence π_i associate the same value to r_α and r_β. Moreover, by Claim 1, for each $r \in \{1, \ldots, n\}$ there exists an α such that $r = r_\alpha$. As a consequence π_i is well defined function with domain $\{1, \ldots, n\}$.

Next we observe that $\mathrm{Im}\,\pi_i = \{i_1, \ldots, i_t\} = \{1, \ldots, n\}$ where we used again Claim 1, implying that $\pi_i : \{1, \ldots, n\} \rightarrow \{1, \ldots, n\}$ is a surjective function between finite sets of the same size, and therefore also a bijection.

Finally, since the query out_i is performed by P_i, it has the form (r_t, i, j_t). If $r_t < n$ then we would find a chain with $\{r_1, \ldots, r_t\}$ of size strictly smaller than n, contradicting Claim 1. Therefore $r_t = n$ and $\pi_i(n) = \pi_i(r_t) = i$.

Proof of Claim 3. T is a tree because each node $v_{i,r}$ is connected to the root by the path

$$\big((v_{i,0}, v_{i,1}), \ldots, (v_{i,r-1}, v_{i,r})\big),$$

with $v_{i,0} = (\{\pi_1, \ldots, \pi_n\}, 0)$ being equal for all i, and each node has in-degree 1 because

$$(v_{j,r-1}, v_{i,r}), (v_{k,r-1}, v_{i,r}) \in E \quad : \quad \begin{cases} v_{i,r} = ([\pi_i]_r, r) \\ v_{j,r-1} = ([\pi_j]_{r-1}, r-1) \\ v_{k,r-1} = ([\pi_k]_{r-1}, r-1) \end{cases}$$

$$\Rightarrow \quad \pi_j(x) = \pi_i(x) = \pi_k(x) \quad \forall x \in \{1, \ldots, r-1\}$$

$$\Rightarrow \quad [\pi_j]_{r-1} = [\pi_k]_{r-1} \quad \Rightarrow \quad v_{j,r-1} = v_{k,r-1}.$$

By construction the leaves of T are $v_{i,n}$ with i ranging from 1 to n, and these are all distinct. Indeed for $i \neq j$ we have $\pi_i(n) = i \neq j = \pi_j(n)$ implying $v_{i,n} \neq v_{j,n}$. Thus $\mathsf{leaves}(T) = n$. Moreover each leaf has distance n from the root, so $\mathsf{height}(T) = n$.

Next we show that the sub-tree of $v_{i,r} = ([\pi_i]_r, r)$ is a tall tree. By previous observations its height is $n - r$. If $r = n$ the node is a leaf and it is trivially tall. Conversely let $v_{j_1}, \ldots, v_{j_n}$ be all the leaves of this sub-tree, so that $v_{j_\alpha} = ([\pi_{j_\alpha}]_n, n)$. Then for all α we have that $v_{i,r} = v_{j_\alpha, r}$ because from both nodes there exists a path to $v_{j_\alpha, n}$, and there exists no path connecting the two nodes. As a consequence

$$[\pi_i]_r = [\pi_{j_1}]_r = \ldots = [\pi_{j_m}]_r.$$

Hence $\pi_{j_1}, \ldots, \pi_{j_m}$ have the same values when evaluated on the indexes from 1 to r. Moreover, since these are all permutations, their value on n (as we assumed $n > r$) must differ from their value on previous points. Thus

$$\{\pi_{j_1}(n), \ldots, \pi_{j_m}(n)\} \cap \{\pi_i(1), \ldots, \pi_i(r)\} = \varnothing$$
$$\Rightarrow \quad \{j_1, \ldots, j_m\} \cap \{\pi_i(1), \ldots, \pi_i(r)\} = \varnothing$$

where the implication uses Claim 2. Since $j_1, \ldots, j_m$ are all distinct by construction, $\pi_i(1), \ldots, \pi_i(r)$ are all distinct as π_i is a bijection, and all these indexes lies in the range $\{1, \ldots, n\}$ we conclude

$$|\{j_1, \ldots, j_m\}| + |\{\pi_i(1), \ldots, \pi_i(r)\}| \leq n \quad \Rightarrow \quad m + r \leq n \quad \Rightarrow \quad m \leq n - r.$$

The sub-tree of $v_{i,r}$ is therefore tall, concluding the claim's proof.

Proof of Claim 4. We recall $V_t = \{v_{i,r} : i \in \{1, \ldots, t\}, r \in \{0, \ldots, n\}\}$ and further define $V_t^* = V_t \setminus \{v_{1,0}\}$, i.e. the set of vertices in V_t without the root. To prove the claim we proceed by induction on t showing the existence of a function $f : V_t^* \to \mathbb{N}^3$ satisfying the required properties.

If $t = 1$, we set $f(v_{1,r}) = (r, \pi_1(r), j)$ to be the query in the refined chain, see Definition 3, minimal w.r.t. $\twoheadrightarrow^+$ among queries performed at round r. Then f is injective over V_1^* and satisfies the first condition by construction. Regarding the third property if $D_{f(v_{1,r})} = D_{f(v_{1,r'})}$ with $r < r'$ then we could create a shorter chain skipping round r, thus violating Claim 1. Hence $r = r'$, and in particular $v_{1,r}, v_{1,r'}$ are the same, meaning that $v \mapsto D_{f(v)}$ is injective over V_1^* and thus satisfies the third property.

Assuming the statement to be true for $t - 1$, i.e. that we have $f : V_{t-1}^* \to \mathbb{N}^3$ satisfying the three properties, we show f can be extended to V_t^*. To so, let j_r be such that $(r, \pi_t(r), j_r)$ is the minimal query at round r of the chain for $0 \twoheadrightarrow^+ \mathsf{out}_t$. We then define for all $v_{i,r} \in V_t^* \setminus V_{t-1}^*$ the function to be $f(v_{i,r}) = (r, \pi_t(r), j_r)$. The first property is thus satisfied by construction.

Next we show f is injective. If $f(v_{i,r}) = f(v_{i',r'})$ then $r = r'$ from the first property[10]. By inductive hypothesis f is injective over V_{t-1}^*. Without loss of generality we can then assume $v_{i',r'} \in V_t^* \setminus V_{t-1}^*$, in which case $t = i'$. In order

---

[10] r and r' are the first component of respectively the LHS and the RHS.

to prove $v_{i,r} = v_{t,r}$ we proceed by contradiction assuming the two nodes to be different.

This implies that $v_{i,r} \in V_{t-1}^*$. With loss of generality we can further assume because of the first property that $f(v_{i,r}) = (r, \pi_i(r), j^*)$ is a minimal query at round r for $0 \dashrightarrow^+ \text{out}_i$. This implies that there exist refined chains for the relations

$$0 \dashrightarrow^+ (r, \pi_t(r), j_r) \dashrightarrow^+ \text{out}_t \qquad 0 \dashrightarrow^+ (r, \pi_i(r), j^*) \dashrightarrow^+ \text{out}_i.$$

Since $(r, \pi_t(r), j_r) = (r, \pi_i(r), j^*)$ we can combine the first half of the second chain with the second half of the first one to obtain a new refined chain for $0 \dashrightarrow^+ \text{out}_t$. Let $\widehat{\pi}_t$ be the associated permutations. By construction $\widehat{\pi}_t(x) = \pi_i(x)$ for all $x \in \{1, \dots, t\}$, and in particular $[\widehat{\pi}_t]_r = [\pi_i]_r$. Hence, calling $\widehat{T} = (\widehat{V}, \widehat{E})$ the prefix tree for $\pi_1, \dots, \widehat{\pi}_t, \dots, \pi_n$, we will show it violates our minimality condition on T. Indeed

- $|V_{t-1}^*| = |\widehat{V}_{t-1}^*|$, because the first $t-1$ permutations used to build $T, \widehat{T}$ are the same.
- $|V_t^*| \geq |V_{t-1}^*| + (n - r + 1)$, because $v_{t,r} \in V_{t-1}^* \setminus V_t^*$ and in particular, $v_{t,r'} \notin V_{t-1}^*$ for $r' > r$, or else $v_{t,r'} = v_{i,r'}$ for some $i < t$ which implies $v_{t,r} = v_{i,r} \in V_{t-1}^*$. Hence

$$\{v_{i,r}, \dots, v_{i,n}\} \subseteq V_t^* \setminus V_{t-1}^* \quad \Rightarrow \quad |V_t^* \setminus V_{t-1}^*| \geq (n - r + 1)$$

- $|\widehat{V}_t^*| \leq |\widehat{V}_{t-1}^*| + (n - r)$, because $[\widehat{\pi}_t]_r = [\pi_i]_r$ implies $[\widehat{\pi}_t]_{r'} = [\pi_i]_{r'}$ for all $r' \leq r$. Hence, again for all $r' \leq r$, $\widehat{v}_{t,r'} = \widehat{v}_{i,r'} \in \widehat{V}_{t-1}^*$ and in particular

$$\widehat{V}_t^* \setminus \widehat{V}_{t-1}^* \subseteq \{\widehat{v}_{t,r+1}, \dots, \widehat{v}_{t,n}\} \quad \Rightarrow \quad |\widehat{V}_t^* \setminus \widehat{V}_{t-1}^*| \leq n - t.$$

Combining the three relations we conclude that our minimality assumption on T is violated because

$$|\widehat{V}_t^*| \leq |\widehat{V}_{t-1}^*| + (n - r) < |V_{t-1}^*| + (n - r + 1) \leq |V_t^*|.$$

This means that the assumption $v_{i,r} \neq v_{t,r}$ leads to a contradiction, implying that $v_{i,r} = v_{t,r}$ and that f is injective.

To conclude we need to prove the third property holds for f. Let $D_{f(v_{i,r})} = D_{f(v_{i',r'})}$. We study two cases:

1. $r \neq r'$. Then without loss of generality $r < r'$ and by the first property $v_{i,r}$, $v_{i',r'}$ are such that $f(v_{i,r}) = (r, \pi_i(r), j)$ and $f(v_{i',r'}) = (r', \pi_{i'}(r'), j')$ are minimal queries in their respective rounds with respect to $\dashrightarrow^+$. Among the queries appearing in the chain for $0 \dashrightarrow^+ \text{out}_i$ let (r'', i'', j'') be the predecessor of $(r, \pi_i(r), j)$, i.e. such that

$$0 \dashrightarrow^+ (r'', i'', j'') \dashrightarrow (r, \pi_i(r), j) \dashrightarrow^+ \text{out}_i.$$

Note that since $(r, \pi_i(r), j)$ is minimal among the queries at round r, we must have $r'' < r$. Then if we call $E_{r'', i'', j''}$ the output of $\mathcal{O}_{\text{act}}$ for query (r'', i'', j''), by the definition of $\twoheadrightarrow$ we have $E_{r'',i'',j''} = D_{(r,\pi_r(i),j)}$. Therefore, again by the definition of $\twoheadrightarrow^+$

$$E_{r'',i'',j''} = D_{(r',\pi_{r'}(i'),j')}, \wedge r'' < r' \quad \Rightarrow$$
$$\Rightarrow \quad 0 \twoheadrightarrow^+ (r'',i'',j'') \twoheadrightarrow (r',i',j') \twoheadrightarrow^+ \mathsf{out}_{i'}.$$

Since $r'' < r < r'$ the resulting chain would not include any query from round r, contradicting Claim 1. Therefore $r \neq r'$ is impossible.

2. $r = r'$. By the inductive hypothesis if both vertices lie in V_{t-1}^* the property holds, so without loss of generality assume $v_{i',r} \in V_t^* \setminus V_{t-1}^*$ and $f(v_{i,r}) = (r, \pi_i(r), j_r)$, i.e. that the image of $v_{i,r}$ is a query on the chain for $0 \twoheadrightarrow^+ \mathsf{out}_i$. We will denote p_i the predecessor of $f(v_{i,r})$ on the refined chains for $0 \twoheadrightarrow^+ \mathsf{out}_i$. This means we have

$$0 \twoheadrightarrow^+ p_i \to f(v_{i,r}) \twoheadrightarrow^+ \mathsf{out}_i$$

Then by how $\twoheadrightarrow$ was defined $E_{p_i} = D_{f(v_{i,r})} = D_{f(v_{t,r})}$ and by minimality of $f(v_{i,r})$ among the queries occurring at round r, p_i occurs at a round strictly smaller than r. Thus $p_i \twoheadrightarrow f(v_{t,r})$ and in particular we can find a chain for

$$0 \twoheadrightarrow^+ p_i \to f(v_{t,r}) \twoheadrightarrow^+ \mathsf{out}_t$$

that is equal to the chain for $0 \twoheadrightarrow^+ \mathsf{out}_i$ until query p_i. Calling $\widehat{\pi}_t$ the associated permutation we would then have $[\widehat{\pi}_t]_{r-1} = [\pi_i]_{r-1}$ since the chains are equal until round $r-1$ (we use Claim 1 to observe p_i occurs at round $r-1$).

Finally assume that for the current chain chosen for $0 \twoheadrightarrow^+ \mathsf{out}_t$ the nodes $v_{i,r}$ and $v_{t,r}$ are no siblings (otherwise the claim is proven), i.e. $v_{i,r-1} \neq v_{t,r-1}$, we distinguish two cases:

- $v_{t,r-1} \notin V_{t-1}^*$. Then as done previously we can use $\widehat{\pi}_t$ to build a prefix tree $\widehat{T} = (\widehat{V}, \widehat{E})$ with $|\widehat{V}_t| < |V_t|$, which contradicts our minimality assumption.
- $v_{t,r-1} \in V_{t-1}^*$. Again using the new path we can build a prefix tree such that for all $t' < t$

$$|V_{t'}^*| = |\widehat{V}_{t'}^*| \qquad |V_t^*| = |V_{t-1}^*| + (n-r+1) \qquad |\widehat{V}_t^*| \leq |\widehat{V}_{t-1}^*| + (n-r+1).$$

with the first equality holding as we are only replacing π_t with $\widehat{\pi}_t$ and using the same $\pi_1, \ldots, \pi_{t-1}$ in both prefix trees, the second one because $v_{t,r-1} \in V_t^* \setminus V_{t-1}^*$ while $v_{t,r-1} \in V_{t-1}^*$, and the third because $\widehat{v}_{t,r-1} = \widehat{v}_{i,r-1} \in \widehat{V}_{t-1}^*$. We thus conclude $|\widehat{V}_t| \leq |V_t|$ while preserving the size of smaller sub-trees.

Replacing the chain for $0 \twoheadrightarrow^+ \mathsf{out}_t$, we finally have that for the new tree $\widehat{v}_{i,r-1} = \widehat{v}_{i,r-1}$. Notice that this change occurs only once since there can only be one node $v_{i,r} \in V_t \setminus V_{t-1}$ with $v_{i,r-1} \in V_{t-1}$. Furthermore after the change we still have $\widehat{v}_{i,r} \in \widehat{V}_t \setminus \widehat{V}_{t-1}$ with $\widehat{v}_{i,r-1} \in \widehat{V}_{t-1}$ because

$$\widehat{v}_{t,r} \in \widehat{V}_{t-1}^* \quad \Rightarrow \quad |\widehat{V}_t^*| \leq |\widehat{V}_{t-1}^*| + (n-r) < |V_{t-1}^*| + (n-r+1) = |V_t^*|$$
$$\Rightarrow \quad |\widehat{V}_t| < |V_t|$$

contradicting our minimality assumption. Therefore, all remaining nodes in $\widehat{V}_t \setminus \widehat{V}_{t-1}$ falls into the previous case.

This concludes the proof of the Claim.

Proof of Claim 5. Calling $V_{\geq 2}$ as in Sect. 5.3 the set of nodes of distance at least 2 from the root we observe that

$$V_{\geq 2} = \bigcup_{r=2}^{n} \bigcup_{i=1}^{n} U_{r,i}$$

Indeed given $v \in V_{\geq 2} \subseteq V^*$, by Claim 4 there exists r, i, j such that $v = v_{i,r}$ and $f(v) = (r, i, j)$, implying $r \geq 2$ and $v \in U_{r,i}$. Next we show $|U_{r,i}| = |\Delta_{r,i}|$. To do so it suffices to show that the map $v \mapsto D_{f(v)}$ is injective over $U_{r,i}$. Let $u, v \in U_{r,i}$ such that $D_{f(u)} = D_{f(v)}$. By Claim 4 they must have the same parent. In particular if $u = ([\pi_\ell]_r, r)$ and $v = ([\pi_{\ell'}]_r, r)$ then having the same parent implies

$$[\pi_\ell]_{r-1} = [\pi_{\ell'}]_{r-1}, \quad \pi_\ell(r) = i = \pi_{\ell'}(r) \quad \Rightarrow \quad [\pi_\ell]_r = [\pi_{\ell'}]_r \quad \Rightarrow \quad u = v$$

where the second and third equality follows since $u, v \in U_{r,i}$. Finally, using Proposition 2 and Claim 3 stating that T is a TS tree we conclude

$$\sum_{r=1}^{n-1} \sum_{i=1}^{n} |\Delta_{r+1,i}| = \sum_{r=2}^{n} \sum_{i=1}^{n} |\Delta_{r,i}| \geq |V_{\geq 2}| \geq (n-2) + n \log_2 n.$$

Proof of Claim 6. In the following we denote input $= (s_1, \ldots, s_n, \rho_1, \ldots, \rho_n, E_0)$ where s_i, ρ_i are the private input and random coins of P_i. Furthermore, we will denote

$$\Gamma_{r+1,i,j} = \{E_{r+1,i,j'} : j' < j\} \cup \{D_{r+1,i,j'} : j' < j\}$$

We furthermore index $\Delta_{r+1,i} = \{D_{r+1,i,j_1}, \ldots, D_{r+1,i,j_m}\}$. Then

$$\mathrm{H}\left(M_r^{(i)} \,\middle|\, \mathsf{trs}_{r-1}\right) \geq \mathrm{H}\left(M_r^{(i)} \,\middle|\, \mathsf{trs}_{r-1}, \mathsf{input}\right)$$

$$\geq \sum_{\alpha=1}^{m} \mathrm{I}\left(M_r^{(i)}; D_{r+1,i,j_\alpha} \,\middle|\, \mathsf{trs}_{r-1}, \mathsf{input}, \{D_{r+1,i,j_\beta}\}_{\beta=1}^{\alpha-1}\right)$$

$$\geq \sum_{\alpha=1}^{m} \mathrm{I}\left(M_r^{(i)}; D_{r+1,i,j_\alpha} \,\middle|\, \mathsf{trs}_{r-1}, \mathsf{input}, \Gamma_{r+1,i,j_\alpha}\right).$$

We will then lower bound each of these terms. The key observation is that, given $M_j^{(i)}$, trs_{r-1}, input and $\Gamma_{r+1,i,j}$, the execution of P_i becomes deterministic until the next query to $\mathcal{O}_{\mathsf{act}}$ is performed, meaning that $D_{r+1,i,j}$ is univocally determined. Therefore, if $\Delta_{r,i} = \{D_{r+1,i,j_1}, \ldots, D_{r+1,i,j_m}\}$, we have that

$$\mathrm{H}\left(D_{r+1,i,j_\alpha} \,\middle|\, M_r^{(i)}, \mathsf{trs}_{r-1}, \mathsf{input}, \Gamma_{r+1,i,j_\alpha}\right) = 0.$$

Conversely we observe that before round r, D_{r+1,i,j_α} was not returned as an output by $\mathcal{O}_{\mathsf{act}}$, or else we could build a chain for D_{r+1,i,j_α} skipping round r, which violates Claim 1. Moreover by the minimality of D_{r+1,i,j_α} (see Claim 4), this set elements was not computed previously on the same round by P_i, meaning that is does not belong in Γ_{r+1,i,j_α}. Moreover D_{r+1,i,j_α} is independent from the random coins and inputs of parties (which are sampled before any query is ever made to $\mathcal{O}_{\mathsf{act}}$). Hence we conclude that D_{r+1,i,j_α} conditioned to trs_{r-1}, input, Γ_{r+1,i,j_α} is uniform in the set of not-yet queried labels, which has size $2^\mu - 2q$. Thus

$$H\left(D_{r+1,i,j_\alpha} \mid \mathsf{trs}_{r-1}, \text{input}, \Gamma_{r+1,i,j_\alpha}\right) \geq \log_2(2^\mu - 2q)$$

$$\geq \mu - \frac{2q}{2^\mu - 2q} = \mu - \frac{q}{2^{\mu-1} - q}.$$

Where second in equality follows since $\log(x)$ is concave and for all $x > y > 0$

$$\frac{1}{x} \leq \frac{\log(x) - \log(y)}{x - y} \leq \frac{1}{y}$$

replacing $x = 2^\mu$ and $y = 2^\mu - 2q$. As the mutual information is the difference of the above quantities, we have that $\mu - \frac{q}{2^{\mu-1}-q}$ lower bounds each term in the summation above. We can therefore conclude

$$H\left(M_r^{(i)} \mid \mathsf{trs}_{r-1}\right) \geq m \cdot \frac{q}{2^{\mu-1} - q} \geq |\Delta_{r+1,i}| \cdot \frac{q}{2^{\mu-1} - q}.$$

6 Conclusions

In conclusion we proved two lower bounds for multi-party computation in the GAM, i.e. through black box usage of a group action. First, protocols that are at least passively secure cannot perform better than Round-Robin in terms of round complexity. Second, *fair* computation, in the sense of Sect. 5.1, requires $\Omega(n \log_2 n)$ computation and communication complexity. Remarkably, both results still hold under *any* computational assumptions, and even if parties make explicit use of the bit representation of elements in $\mathcal{E}$.

In the context of threshold protocols, including those for digital signatures and public-key encryptions schemes, these bounds hinder the scalability to large sets of parties. In these cases, if lower round complexity or communication is required, our result could be bypassed only through explicit usage of a circuit implementing the group action. General purpose MPC techniques for instance would apply in such case. Therefore future research in this direction should either focus on reducing the complexity for computing group actions (e.g. lowering the multiplicative depth), or on designing specialized *non-black box* protocols.

Finally, we leave two open questions related to fair protocols: First, as mentioned in Sect. 5.1, our lower communication and computation lower bounds only affect round-optimal constructions. We thus ask whether increasing the round complexity allows violating our bounds. Secondly, our result is tight only for n users with n being a power of 2. More generally we conjecture optimal solutions to require

$$n(1 + \log_2 n) \leq q \leq n(1 + \log_2 n) + c \cdot n$$

many queries, for a tight constant c. We numerically estimate $c \approx 0.087$ for $n \leq 2^{24}$ and leave the question of whether such condition holds in general to future studies.

Acknowledgment. This work received funding from projects from the European Research Council (ERC) under the European Union's Horizon 2020 research and innovation program under project PICOCRYPT (grant agreement No. 101001283), from SECURING Project (ref. PID2019-110873RJ-I00), from the Spanish Government under projects PRODIGY (TED2021-132464B-I00) and ESPADA (PID2022-142290OB-I00). The last two projects are co-funded by European Union EIE, and NextGenerationEU/PRTR fund.

References

1. Atapoor, S., Baghery, K., Cozzo, D., Pedersen, R.: CSI-SharK: CSI-FiSh with sharing-friendly keys. In: Simpson, L., Rezazadeh Baee, M.A. (eds.) ACISP 2023. LNCS, vol. 13915, pp. 471–502. Springer, Cham (2023). https://doi.org/10.1007/978-3-031-35486-1_21
2. Atapoor, S., Baghery, K., Cozzo, D., Pedersen, R.: Practical robust DKG protocols for CSIDH. In: Tibouchi, M., Wang, X. (eds.) ACNS 2023. LNCS, pp. 219–247. Springer, Cham (2023). https://doi.org/10.1007/978-3-031-33491-7_9
3. Atapoor, S., Baghery, K., Cozzo, D., Pedersen, R.: VSS from distributed ZK proofs and applications. IACR Cryptology ePrint Archive, p. 992 (2023). https://eprint.iacr.org/2023/992
4. Baghery, K., Cozzo, D., Pedersen, R.: An isogeny-based ID protocol using structured public keys. In: Paterson, M.B. (ed.) IMACC 2021. LNCS, vol. 13129, pp. 179–197. Springer, Cham (2021). https://doi.org/10.1007/978-3-030-92641-0_9
5. Beullens, W., Disson, L., Pedersen, R., Vercauteren, F.: CSI-RAShi: distributed key generation for CSIDH. In: Cheon, J.H., Tillich, J.-P. (eds.) PQCrypto 2021 2021. LNCS, vol. 12841, pp. 257–276. Springer, Cham (2021). https://doi.org/10.1007/978-3-030-81293-5_14
6. Beullens, W., Dobson, S., Katsumata, S., Lai, Y.F., Pintore, F.: Group signatures and more from isogenies and lattices: generic, simple, and efficient. In: Dunkelman, O., Dziembowski, S. (eds.) EUROCRYPT 2022, Part II. LNCS, vol. 13276, pp. 95–126. Springer, Cham (2022). https://doi.org/10.1007/978-3-031-07085-3_4
7. Beullens, W., Katsumata, S., Pintore, F.: Calamari and Falafl: logarithmic (linkable) ring signatures from isogenies and lattices. In: Moriai, S., Wang, H. (eds.) ASIACRYPT 2020, Part II. LNCS, vol. 12492, pp. 464–492. Springer, Cham (2020). https://doi.org/10.1007/978-3-030-64834-3_16
8. Beullens, W., Kleinjung, T., Vercauteren, F.: CSI-FiSh: efficient isogeny based signatures through class group computations. In: Galbraith, S.D., Moriai, S. (eds.) ASIACRYPT 2019, Part I. LNCS, vol. 11921, pp. 227–247. Springer, Cham (2019). https://doi.org/10.1007/978-3-030-34578-5_9
9. Boneh, D., Guan, J., Zhandry, M.: A lower bound on the length of signatures based on group actions and generic isogenies. In: Hazay, C., Stam, M. (eds.) EUROCRYPT 2023, Part V. LNCS, vol. 14008, pp. 507–531. Springer, Cham (2023). https://doi.org/10.1007/978-3-031-30589-4_18

10. Campos, F., Muth, P.: On actively secure fine-grained access structures from isogeny assumptions. In: Cheon, J.H., Johansson, T. (eds.) PQCrypto 2022. LNCS, vol. 13512, pp. 375–398. Springer, Cham (2022). https://doi.org/10.1007/978-3-031-17234-2_18

11. Castryck, W., Decru, T.: An efficient key recovery attack on SIDH. In: Hazay, C., Stam, M. (eds.) EUROCRYPT 2023, Part V. LNCS, vol. 14008, pp. 423–447. Springer, Cham (2023). https://doi.org/10.1007/978-3-031-30589-4_15

12. Castryck, W., Lange, T., Martindale, C., Panny, L., Renes, J.: CSIDH: an efficient post-quantum commutative group action. In: Peyrin, T., Galbraith, S. (eds.) ASIACRYPT 2018, Part III. LNCS, vol. 11274, pp. 395–427. Springer, Cham (2018). https://doi.org/10.1007/978-3-030-03332-3_15

13. Catalano, D., Fiore, D., Gennaro, R., Giunta, E.: On the impossibility of algebraic vector commitments in pairing-free groups. In: Kiltz, E., Vaikuntanathan, V. (eds.) TCC 2022, Part II. LNCS, vol. 13748, pp. 274–299. Springer, Heidelberg (2022). https://doi.org/10.1007/978-3-031-22365-5_10

14. Cozzo, D., Smart, N.P.: Sashimi: cutting up CSI-FiSh secret keys to produce an actively secure distributed signing protocol. In: Ding, J., Tillich, J.-P. (eds.) PQCrypto 2020. LNCS, vol. 12100, pp. 169–186. Springer, Cham (2020). https://doi.org/10.1007/978-3-030-44223-1_10

15. De Feo, L., Galbraith, S.D.: SeaSign: compact isogeny signatures from class group actions. In: Ishai, Y., Rijmen, V. (eds.) EUROCRYPT 2019, Part III. LNCS, vol. 11478, pp. 759–789. Springer, Cham (2019). https://doi.org/10.1007/978-3-030-17659-4_26

16. De Feo, L., Meyer, M.: Threshold schemes from isogeny assumptions. In: Kiayias, A., Kohlweiss, M., Wallden, P., Zikas, V. (eds.) PKC 2020, Part II. LNCS, vol. 12111, pp. 187–212. Springer, Cham (2020). https://doi.org/10.1007/978-3-030-45388-6_7

17. Döttling, N., Hartmann, D., Hofheinz, D., Kiltz, E., Schäge, S., Ursu, B.: On the impossibility of purely algebraic signatures. In: Nissim, K., Waters, B. (eds.) TCC 2021, Part III. LNCS, vol. 13044, pp. 317–349. Springer, Cham (2021). https://doi.org/10.1007/978-3-030-90456-2_11

18. Duman, J., Hartmann, D., Kiltz, E., Kunzweiler, S., Lehmann, J., Riepel, D.: Generic models for group actions. In: Boldyreva, A., Kolesnikov, V. (eds.) PKC 2023, Part I. LNCS, vol. 13940, pp. 406–435. Springer, Heidelberg (2023). https://doi.org/10.1007/978-3-031-31368-4_15

19. El Kaafarani, A., Katsumata, S., Pintore, F.: Lossy CSI-FiSh: efficient signature scheme with tight reduction to decisional CSIDH-512. In: Kiayias, A., Kohlweiss, M., Wallden, P., Zikas, V. (eds.) PKC 2020, Part II. LNCS, vol. 12111, pp. 157–186. Springer, Cham (2020). https://doi.org/10.1007/978-3-030-45388-6_6

20. Fouotsa, T.B., Petit, C.: SHealS and HealS: isogeny-based PKEs from a key validation method for SIDH. In: Tibouchi, M., Wang, H. (eds.) ASIACRYPT 2021, Part IV. LNCS, vol. 13093, pp. 279–307. Springer, Cham (2021). https://doi.org/10.1007/978-3-030-92068-5_10

21. Giunta, E.: On the impossibility of algebraic NIZK in pairing-free groups. In: Handschuh, H., Lysyanskaya, A. (eds.) CRYPTO 2023. LNCS, vol. 14084, pp. 702–730. Springer, Cham (2023). https://doi.org/10.1007/978-3-031-38551-3_22

22. Lai, Y.-F., Galbraith, S.D., Delpech de Saint Guilhem, C.: Compact, efficient and UC-secure isogeny-based oblivious transfer. In: Canteaut, A., Standaert, F.-X. (eds.) EUROCRYPT 2021, Part I. LNCS, vol. 12696, pp. 213–241. Springer, Cham (2021). https://doi.org/10.1007/978-3-030-77870-5_8

23. Maino, L., Martindale, C., Panny, L., Pope, G., Wesolowski, B.: A direct key recovery attack on SIDH. In: Hazay, C., Stam, M. (eds.) EUROCRYPT 2023. LNCS, vol. 14008, pp. 448–471. Springer, Cham (2023). https://doi.org/10.1007/978-3-031-30589-4_16

24. Maurer, U.: Abstract models of computation in cryptography (invited paper). In: Smart, N.P. (ed.) Cryptography and Coding. LNCS, vol. 3796, pp. 1–12. Springer, Heidelberg (2005). https://doi.org/10.1007/11586821_1

25. Moriya, T., Onuki, H., Takagi, T.: SiGamal: a supersingular isogeny-based PKE and its application to a PRF. In: Moriai, S., Wang, H. (eds.) ASIACRYPT 2020, Part II. LNCS, vol. 12492, pp. 551–580. Springer, Cham (2020). https://doi.org/10.1007/978-3-030-64834-3_19

26. Papakonstantinou, P.A., Rackoff, C., Vahlis, Y.: How powerful are the DDH hard groups? Electron. Colloquium Comput. Complex. 167 (2012). https://eccc.weizmann.ac.il/report/2012/167

27. Robert, D.: Breaking SIDH in polynomial time. In: Hazay, C., Stam, M. (eds.) EUROCRYPT 2023, Part V. LNCS, vol. 14008, pp. 472–503. Springer, Cham (2023). https://doi.org/10.1007/978-3-031-30589-4_17

28. Rotem, L., Segev, G., Shahaf, I.: Generic-group delay functions require hidden-order groups. In: Canteaut, A., Ishai, Y. (eds.) EUROCRYPT 2020, Part III. LNCS, vol. 12107, pp. 155–180. Springer, Cham (2020). https://doi.org/10.1007/978-3-030-45727-3_6

29. Schul-Ganz, G., Segev, G.: Accumulators in (and beyond) generic groups: non-trivial batch verification requires interaction. In: Pass, R., Pietrzak, K. (eds.) TCC 2020, Part II. LNCS, vol. 12551, pp. 77–107. Springer, Cham (2020). https://doi.org/10.1007/978-3-030-64378-2_4

30. Shaw, S., Dutta, R.: Identification scheme and forward-secure signature in identity-based setting from isogenies. In: Huang, Q., Yu, Yu. (eds.) ProvSec 2021. LNCS, vol. 13059, pp. 309–326. Springer, Cham (2021). https://doi.org/10.1007/978-3-030-90402-9_17

31. Shor, P.W.: Algorithms for quantum computation: discrete logarithms and factoring. In: Proceedings of the 35th Annual Symposium on Foundations of Computer Science, pp. 124–134 (1994)

32. Shoup, V.: Lower bounds for discrete logarithms and related problems. In: Fumy, W. (ed.) EUROCRYPT 1997. LNCS, vol. 1233, pp. 256–266. Springer, Heidelberg (1997). https://doi.org/10.1007/3-540-69053-0_18

33. Stolbunov, A.: Cryptographic schemes based on isogenies (2012)

34. Tairi, E., Moreno-Sanchez, P., Maffei, M.: Post-quantum adaptor signature for privacy-preserving off-chain payments. In: Borisov, N., Diaz, C. (eds.) FC 2021, Part II. LNCS, vol. 12675, pp. 131–150. Springer, Heidelberg (2021). https://doi.org/10.1007/978-3-662-64331-0_7

35. Zhandry, M.: To label, or not to label (in generic groups). In: Dodis, Y., Shrimpton, T. (eds.) CRYPTO 2022, Part III. LNCS, vol. 13509, pp. 66–96. Springer, Cham (2022). https://doi.org/10.1007/978-3-031-15982-4_3

(Verifiable) Delay Functions from Lucas Sequences

Charlotte Hoffmann[1]([envelope]) [iD], Pavel Hubáček[2,3] [iD], Chethan Kamath[4], and Tomáš Krňák[3] [iD]

[1] Institute of Science and Technology Austria, Klosterneuburg, Austria
charlotte.hoffmann@ist.ac.at
[2] Institute of Mathematics, Czech Academy of Sciences, Prague, Czech Republic
[3] Faculty of Mathematics and Physics, Charles University, Prague,
Czech Republic
hubacek@iuuk.mff.cuni.cz, tomas@krnak.cz
[4] Tel Aviv University, Tel Aviv, Israel
ckamath@protonmail.com

Abstract. Lucas sequences are constant-recursive integer sequences with a long history of applications in cryptography, both in the design of cryptographic schemes and cryptanalysis. In this work, we study the sequential hardness of computing Lucas sequences over an RSA modulus.

First, we show that modular Lucas sequences are at least as sequentially hard as the classical delay function given by iterated modular squaring proposed by Rivest, Shamir, and Wagner (MIT Tech. Rep. 1996) in the context of time-lock puzzles. Moreover, there is no obvious reduction in the other direction, which suggests that the assumption of sequential hardness of modular Lucas sequences is strictly weaker than that of iterated modular squaring. In other words, the sequential hardness of modular Lucas sequences might hold even in the case of an algorithmic improvement violating the sequential hardness of iterated modular squaring.

Second, we demonstrate the feasibility of constructing practically-efficient *verifiable* delay functions based on the sequential hardness of modular Lucas sequences. Our construction builds on the work of Pietrzak (ITCS 2019) by leveraging the intrinsic connection between the problem of computing modular Lucas sequences and exponentiation in an appropriate extension field.

Keywords: Delay functions · Verifiable delay functions · Lucas sequences

1 Introduction

A verifiable delay function (VDF) $f : \mathcal{X} \to \mathcal{Y}$ is a function that satisfies two properties. First, it is a delay function, which means it must take a prescribed (wall) time T to compute f, irrespective of the amount of parallelism available.

© International Association for Cryptologic Research 2023
G. Rothblum and H. Wee (Eds.): TCC 2023, LNCS 14372, pp. 336–362, 2023.
https://doi.org/10.1007/978-3-031-48624-1_13

Second, it should be possible for anyone to quickly verify – say, given a short proof π – the value of the function (even without resorting to parallelism), where by quickly we mean that the verification time should be independent of or significantly smaller than T (e.g., logarithmic in T). If we drop either of the two requirements, then the primitive turns out trivial to construct. For instance, for an appropriately chosen hash function h, the delay function $f(x) = h^T(x)$ defined by T-times iterated hashing of the input is a natural heuristic for an inherently sequential task which, however, seems hard to verify more efficiently than by recomputing. On the other hand, the identity function $f(x) = x$ is trivial to verify but also easily computable. Designing a simple function satisfying the two properties simultaneously proved to be a nontrivial task.

The notion of VDFs was introduced in [31] and later formalised in [9]. In principle, since the task of constructing a VDF reduces to the task of incrementally-verifiable computation [9,53], constructions of VDFs could leverage succinct non-interactive arguments of knowledge (SNARKs): take any sequentially-hard function f (for instance, iterated hashing) as the delay function and then use the SNARK on top of it as the mechanism for verifying the computation of the delay function. However, as discussed in [9], the resulting construction is not quite practical since we would rely on a general-purpose machinery of SNARKs with significant overhead.

Efficient VDFs via Algebraic Delay Functions. VDFs have recently found interesting applications in design of blockchains [17], randomness beacons [43,51], proofs of data replication [9], or short-lived zero-knowledge proofs and signatures [3]. Since efficiency is an important factor there, this has resulted in a flurry of constructions of VDFs that are tailored with application and practicality in mind. They rely on more algebraic, structured delay functions that often involve iterating an *atomic operation* so that one can resort to custom proof systems to achieve verifiability. These constructions involve a range of algebraic settings like the RSA or class groups [5,8,25,42,55], permutation polynomials over finite fields [9], isogenies of elliptic curves [21,52] and, very recently, lattices [15,28]. The constructions in [42,55] are arguably the most practical and the mechanism that underlies their delay function is the same: carry out iterated *squaring* in groups of unknown order, like RSA groups [47] or class groups [12]. What distinguishes these two proposals is the way verification is carried out, i.e., how the underlying "proof of exponentiation" works: while Pietrzak [42] resorts to an LFKN-style recursive proof system [35], Wesolowski [55] uses a clever linear decomposition of the exponent.

Iterated Modular Squaring and Sequentiality. The delay function that underlies the VDFs in [5,25,42,55] is the same, and its security relies on the conjectured *sequential* hardness of iterated squaring in a group of unknown order (suggested in the context of time-lock puzzles by Rivest, Shamir, and Wagner [48]). Given that the practically efficient VDFs all rely on the above single delay function, an immediate open problem is to identify additional sources of sequential hardness that are structured enough to support practically efficient verifiability.

1.1   Our Approach to (Verifiable) Delay Functions

In this work, we study an alternative source of sequential hardness in the algebraic setting and use it to construct efficient verifiable delay functions. The sequentiality of our delay function relies on an atomic operation that is related to the computation of so-called Lucas sequences [29,34,57], explained next.

Lucas Sequences. A Lucas sequence is a constant-recursive integer sequence that satisfies the recurrence relation

$$x_i = Px_{i-1} - Qx_{i-2}$$

for integers P and Q.[1] Specifically, the Lucas sequences of integers $(U_i(P,Q))_{i\in\mathbb{N}}$ and $(V_i(P,Q))_{i\in\mathbb{N}}$ of the first and second type (respectively) are defined recursively as

$$U_i(P,Q) = PU_{i-1}(P,Q) - QU_{i-2}(P,Q)$$

with $U_1(P,Q) = 1, U_0(P,Q) = 0$, and

$$V_i(P,Q) = PV_{i-1}(P,Q) - QV_{i-2}(P,Q)$$

with $V_1(P,Q) = P, V_0(P,Q) = 2$.

These sequences can be alternatively defined by the characteristic polynomial $x^2 - Px + Q$. Specifically, given the discriminant $D = P^2 - 4Q$ of the characteristic polynomial, one can alternatively compute the above sequences by performing operations in the extension field

$$\mathbb{Z}[\sqrt{D}] \simeq \mathbb{Z}[x]/(x^2 - D)$$

using the identities

$$U_i = \frac{\omega^i - \overline{\omega}^i}{\omega - \overline{\omega}} \quad \text{and} \quad V_i = \omega^i + \overline{\omega}^i,$$

where $\omega = (P + \sqrt{D})/2$ and its conjugate $\overline{\omega} = (P - \sqrt{D})/2$ are roots of the characteristic polynomial. Since conjugation and exponentiation commute in the extension field (i.e., $\overline{\omega^i} = \overline{\omega}^i$), computing the i-th terms of the two Lucas sequences over integers reduces to computing ω^i in the extension field, and vice versa.

The intrinsic connection between computing the terms in the Lucas sequences and that of exponentiation in the extension has been leveraged to provide alternative instantiations of public-key encryption schemes like RSA and ElGamal in terms of Lucas sequences [7,30]. However, as we explain later, the corresponding underlying computational hardness assumptions are not necessarily equivalent.

---

[1] Note that integer sequences like Fibonacci numbers and Mersenne numbers are special cases of Lucas sequences.

Overview of Our Delay Function. The delay function in [5,25,42,55] is defined as the iterated squaring base x in a (safe) RSA group[2] modulo N:

$$f_N(x, T) := x^{2^T} \bmod N.$$

Our delay function is its analogue in the setting of Lucas sequences:

$$f_N(P, Q, T) := (U_{2^T}(P, Q) \bmod N, V_{2^T}(P, Q) \bmod N).$$

As mentioned above, computing $f_N(P, Q, T)$ can be carried out equivalently in the extension field $\mathbb{Z}_N[\sqrt{D}]$ using the known relationship to roots of the characteristic polynomial of the Lucas sequence. Thus, the delay function can be alternatively defined as

$$f_N(P, Q, T) := \omega^{2^T} \quad \text{in} \quad \mathbb{Z}_N[\sqrt{D}].$$

Note that the atomic operation of our delay function is "doubling" the index of an element of the Lucas sequence modulo N (i.e., $V_i \mapsto V_{2i}$) or, equivalently, squaring in the extension field $\mathbb{Z}_N[\sqrt{D}]$ (as opposed to squaring in $\mathbb{Z}_N$). Using the representation of $\mathbb{Z}_N[\sqrt{D}]$ as $\{a + b\sqrt{D} \mid a, b \in \mathbb{Z}_N\}$, squaring in $\mathbb{Z}_N[\sqrt{D}]$ can be expressed as a combination of squaring, multiplication and addition modulo N, since

$$(a + b\sqrt{D})^2 = (a^2 + b^2 D) + 2ab\sqrt{D}. \tag{1}$$

Since $\mathbb{Z}_N[\sqrt{D}]$ is a group of unknown order (provided the factorization of N is kept secret), iterated squaring remains hard here. In fact, we show in Sect. 3.2 that iterated squaring in $\mathbb{Z}_N[\sqrt{D}]$ is *at least as hard as* iterated squaring for RSA moduli N. Moreover, we conjecture in Conjecture 1 that it is, in fact, strictly harder (also see discussion below on advantages of our approach).

Verifying Modular Lucas Sequence. To obtain a VDF, we need to show how to efficiently verify our delay function. To this end, we show how to adapt the interactive proof of exponentiation from [42] to our setting, which then – via the Fiat-Shamir Transform [22] – yields the non-interactive verification algorithm.[3] Thus, our main result is stated informally below.

Theorem 1 (Informally stated, see Theorem 2). *Assuming sequential hardness of modular Lucas sequence, there exists statistically-sound VDF in the random-oracle model.*

However, the modification of Pietrzak's protocol is not trivial and we have to overcome several hurdles that we face in this task, which we elaborate on in Sect. 1.2. We conclude this section with discussions about our results.

---

[2] The choice of modulus N is said to be safe if $N = pq$ for safe primes $p = 2p' + 1$ and $q = 2q' + 1$, where p' and q' are also prime.

[3] Further, using the ideas from [14,20], it is possible to construct so-called *continuous* VDFs from Lucas sequences.

Advantage of Our Approach. Our main advantage is the reliance on a potentially weaker (sequential) hardness assumption while maintaining efficiency: we show in Sect. 3.2 that modular Lucas sequences are *at least* as sequentially-hard as the classical delay function given by iterated modular squaring [48]. Despite the linear recursive structure of Lucas sequences, there is no obvious reduction in the other direction, which suggests that the assumption of sequential hardness of modular Lucas sequences is strictly weaker than that of iterated modular squaring (Conjecture 1). In other words, the sequential hardness of modular Lucas sequences might hold even in the case of an algorithmic improvement violating the sequential hardness of iterated modular squaring. Even though both assumptions need the group order to be hidden, we believe that there is need for a nuanced analysis of sequential hardness assumptions in hidden order groups, especially because all current delay functions that provide sufficient structure for applications are based on iterated modular squaring. If the iterated modular squaring assumption is broken, our delay function is currently the only practical alternative in the RSA group.

Delay Functions in Idealised Models. Recent works studied the relationship of group-theoretic (verifiable) delay functions to the hardness of factoring in idealised models such as the algebraic group model and the generic ring model [27,50]. In the generic ring model, Rotem and Segev [50] showed the equivalence of straight-line delay functions in the RSA setting and factoring. Our construction gives rise to a straight-line delay function and, by their result, its sequentiality is equivalent to factoring *for generic algorithms*. However, their result holds only in the generic ring model and leaves the relationship between the two assumptions unresolved in the standard model.

Compare this with the status of the RSA assumption and factoring. On one hand, we know that *in the generic ring model*, RSA and factoring are equivalent [2]. Yet, it is possible to rule out certain classes of reductions from factoring to RSA in the standard model [11]. Most importantly, despite the equivalence in the generic ring model, there is currently no reduction from factoring to RSA in the standard model and it remains one of the major open problems in number theory related to cryptography since the introduction of the RSA assumption.

In summary, speeding up iterated squaring by a non-generic algorithm could be possible (necessarily exploiting the representations of ring elements modulo N), while such an algorithm may not lead to a speed-up in the computation of modular Lucas sequences despite the result of Rotem and Segev [50].

1.2   Technical Overview

Pietrzak's VDF. Let $N = pq$ be an RSA modulus where p and q are safe primes and let x be a random element from $\mathbb{Z}_N^*$. At its core, Pietrzak's VDF relies on the interactive protocol for the statement

"(N, x, y, T) satisfies $y = x^{2^T} \bmod N$".

The protocol is recursive and, in a round-by-round fashion, reduces the claim to a smaller statement by halving the time parameter. To be precise, in each round, the (honest) prover sends the "midpoint" $\mu = x^{2^{T/2}}$ of the current statement to the verifier and they together reduce the statement to

"$(N, x', y', T/2)$ satisfies $y' = (x')^{2^{T/2}} \bmod N$",

where $x' = x^r \mu$ and $y' = \mu^r y$ for a random challenge r. This is continued till $(N, x, y, T = 1)$ is obtained at which point the verifier simply checks whether $y = x^2 \bmod N$ using a single modular squaring.

Since the challenges r are public, the protocol can be compiled into a non-interactive one using the Fiat-Shamir transform [22] and this yields a means to verify the delay function

$$f_N(x, T) = x^{2^T} \bmod N.$$

It is worth pointing out that the choice of safe primes is crucial for proving soundness: in case the group has easy-to-find elements of small order then it becomes easy to break soundness (see, e.g., [10]).

Adapting Pietrzak's Protocol to Lucas Sequences. For a modulus $N = pq$ and integers $P, Q, T \in \mathbb{N}$, recall that our delay function is defined as

$$f_N(T, P, Q) = (U_{2^T}(P, Q) \bmod N, V_{2^T}(P, Q) \bmod N),$$

or equivalently
$$f_N(T, P, Q) = \omega^{2^T} \quad \text{in} \quad \mathbb{Z}_N[\sqrt{D}],$$

for the discriminant $D = P^2 - 4Q$ of the characteristic polynomial $x^2 - Px + Q$. Towards building a verification algorithm for this delay function, the natural first step is to design an interactive protocol for the statement

"(N, P, Q, y, T) satisfies $y = \omega^{2^T}$ in $\mathbb{Z}_N[\sqrt{D}]$."

It turns out that the interactive protocol from [42] can be adapted for this purpose. However, we encounter two technicalities in this process.

Dealing with elements of small order. The main problem that we face while designing our protocol is avoiding elements of small order. In the case of [42], this was accomplished by moving to the setting of signed quadratic residues [26] in which the sub-groups are all of large order. It is not clear whether a corresponding object exists for our algebraic setting. However, in an earlier draft of Pietrzak's protocol [41], this problem was dealt with in a different manner: the prover sends a square root of μ, from which the original μ can be recovered easily (by squaring it) with a guarantee that the result lies in a group of quadratic residues QR_N. Notice that the prover knows the square root of μ, because it is just a previous term in the sequence he computed.

In our setting, we cannot simply ask for the square root of the midpoint as the subgroup of $\mathbb{Z}_N[\sqrt{D}]$ we effectively work in has a different structure. Nevertheless, we can use a similar approach: for an appropriately chosen small a, we provide an a-th root of ω (instead of ω itself) to the prover in the beginning of the protocol. The prover then computes the whole sequence for $\omega^{\frac{1}{a}}$. In the end, he has the a-th root of every term of the original sequence and he can recover any element of the original sequence by raising to the a-th power.

Sampling strong modulus. The second technicality is related to the first one. In order to ensure that we can use the above trick, we require a modulus where the small subgroups are reasonably small not only in the group $\mathbb{Z}_N$ but also in the extension $\mathbb{Z}_N[\sqrt{D}]$. Thus the traditional sampling algorithms that are used to sample strong primes (e.g., [46]) are not sufficient for our purposes. However, sampling strong primes that suit our criteria can still be carried out efficiently as we show in the full version.

Comparing Our Technique with [8,25]. The VDFs in [8,25] are also inspired by [42] and, hence, faced the same problem of low-order elements. In [8], this is dealt with by amplifying the soundness at the cost of parallel repetition and hence larger proofs and extra computation. In [25], the number of repetitions of [8] is reduced significantly by introducing the following technique: The exponent of the initial instance is reduced by some parameter q^C and at the end of an interactive phase, the verifier performs final exponentiation with q^C, thereby weeding out potential false low-order elements in the claim. This technique differs from the approach taken in our work in the following ways: The technique from [25] works in arbitrary groups but it requires the parameter q^C to be large and of a specific form. In particular, the VDF becomes more efficient when q^C is larger than 2^λ. In our protocol, we work in RSA groups whose modulus is the product of primes that satisfy certain conditions depending on a. This enables us to choose a parameter a that is smaller than a statistical security parameter and thereby makes the final exponentiation performed by the verifier much more efficient. Further, a can be any natural number, while q^C must be set as powers of all small prime numbers up a certain bound in [25].

1.3 More Related Work

Timed Primitives. The notion of VDFs was introduced in [31] and later formalised in [9]. VDFs are closely related to the notions of time-lock puzzles [48] and proofs of sequential work [36]. Roughly speaking, a time-lock puzzle is a delay function that additionally allows efficient sampling of the output via a trapdoor. A proof of sequential work, on the other hand, is a delay "multi-function", in the sense that the output is not necessarily unique. Constructions of time-lock puzzles are rare [6,38,48], and there are known limitations: e.g., that it cannot exist in the random-oracle model [36]. However, we know how to construct proofs of sequential work in the random-oracle model [1,16,19,36].

Since VDFs have found several applications, e.g., in the design of resource-efficient blockchains [17], randomness beacons [43,51] and proof of data replication [9], there have been several constructions. Among them, the most notable are the iterated-squaring based construction from [8,25,42,55], the permutation-polynomial based construction from [9], the isogenies-based construction from [13,21,52] and the construction from lattice problems [15,28]. The constructions in [42,55] are quite practical (see the survey [10]) and the VDF deployed in the cryptocurrency Chia is basically their construction adapted to the algebraic setting of class groups [17]. This is arguably the closest work to ours. On the other hand, the constructions from [21,52], which work in the algebraic setting of isogenies of elliptic curves where no analogue of square and multiply is known, simply rely on "exponentiation". Although, these constructions provide a certain form of quantum resistance, they are presently far from efficient. Freitag et al. [23] constructed VDFs from any sequentially hard function and polynomial hardness of learning with errors, the first from standard assumptions. The works of Cini, Lai, and Malavolta [15,28] constructed the first VDF from lattice-based assumptions and conjectured it to be post-quantum secure.

Several variants of VDFs have also been proposed. A VDF is said to be unique if the proof that is used for verification is unique [42]. Recently, Choudhuri et al. [5] constructed unique VDFs from the sequential hardness of iterated squaring in *any* RSA group and polynomial hardness of LWE. A VDF is tight [18] if the gap between simply computing the function and computing it *with* a proof is small. Yet another extension is a continuous VDF [20]. The feasibility of time-lock puzzles and proofs of sequential works were recently extended to VDFs. It was shown [50] that the latter requirement, i.e., working in a group of unknown order, is inherent in a black-box sense. It was shown in [18,37] that there are barriers to constructing tight VDFs in the random-oracle model.

VDFs also have surprising connection to complexity theory [14,20,33].

Work Related to Lucas Sequences. Lucas sequences have long been studied in the context of number theory: see for example [45] or [44] for a survey of its applications to number theory. Its earliest application to cryptography can be traced to the $(p+1)$ factoring algorithm [56]. Constructive applications were found later thanks to the parallels with exponentiation. Several encryption and signature schemes were proposed, most notably the LUC family of encryption and signatures [30,39]. It was later shown that some of these schemes can be broken or that the advantages it claimed were not present [7]. Other applications can be found in [32].

2   Preliminaries

2.1   Interactive Proof Systems

Interactive Protocols. An interactive protocol consists of a pair (P, V) of interactive Turing machines that are run on a common input x. The first machine P

is the prover and is computationally unbounded. The second machine V is the verifier and is probabilistic polynomial-time.

In an ℓ-round (i.e., $(2\ell - 1)$-message) interactive protocol, in each round $i \in [1, \ell]$, first P sends a message $\alpha_i \in \Sigma^a$ to V and then V sends a message $\beta_i \in \Sigma^b$ to P, where Σ is a finite alphabet. At the end of the interaction, V runs a (deterministic) Turing machine on input $\{x, (\beta_1, \ldots, \beta_\ell), (\alpha_1, \ldots, \alpha_\ell)\}$. The interactive protocol is *public-coin* if β_i is a uniformly distributed random string in Σ^b.

Interactive Proof Systems. The notion of an interactive proof for a language L is due to Goldwasser, Micali and Rackoff [24].

Definition 1. *For a function $\epsilon : \mathbb{N} \to [0, 1]$, an interactive protocol* (P, V) *is an ϵ-statistically-sound* interactive proof system for L *if:*

- **Completeness:** *For every $x \in L$, if V interacts with P on common input x, then V accepts with probability 1.*
- **Soundness:** *For every $x \notin L$ and every (computationally-unbounded) cheating prover strategy $\widetilde{P}$, the verifier V accepts when interacting with $\widetilde{P}$ with probability less than $\epsilon(|x|)$, where ϵ is called the* soundness error.

2.2 Verifiable Delay Functions

We adapt the definition of verifiable delay functions from [9] but we decouple the verifiability and sequentiality properties for clarity of exposition of our results. First, we present the definition of a delay function.

Definition 2. *A delay function* DF = (DFSetup, DFGen, DFEval) *consists of a triple of algorithms with the following syntax:*

pp $\leftarrow$ DFSetup(1^n):
    On input a security parameter 1^n, the algorithm DFSetup *outputs public parameters* pp.
$x \leftarrow$ DFGen(pp, T):
    On input public parameters pp *and a time parameter $T \in \mathbb{N}$, the algorithm* DFGen *outputs a challenge x.*
$y \leftarrow$ DFEval(pp, (x, T)):
    On input a challenge pair (x, T), the (deterministic) algorithm DFEval *outputs the value y of the delay function in time T.*

The security property required of a delay function is sequential hardness as defined below.

Definition 3 (Sequentiality). *We say that a delay function* DF *satisfies the sequentiality property, if there exists an $\epsilon \in (0, 1)$ such that for all $T(\lambda) \in$ poly(λ) and for every adversary $A = (A_0, A_1)$, where A_1 uses poly(λ) processors and runs in time $O(T^\epsilon(\lambda))$, there exists a negligible function μ such that*

$$\Pr\left[\begin{array}{c} A_1(\text{pp}, \text{state}, (x, T(\lambda))) = y \\ where \\ \text{pp} \leftarrow \text{DFSetup}(1^n) \\ \text{state} \leftarrow A_0(\text{pp}) \\ x \leftarrow \text{DFGen}(\text{pp}, T(\lambda)) \\ y \leftarrow \text{DFEval}(\text{pp}, (x, T(\lambda))) \end{array}\right] \leq \mu(\lambda).$$

A few remarks about our definition of sequentiality are in order:

1. We require computing $\text{DFEval}(\text{pp}, (x, T))$ to be hard in less than T sequential steps even using any polynomially-bounded amount of parallelism and pre-computation. Note that it is necessary to bound the amount of parallelism, as an adversary could otherwise break the underlying hardness assumption (e.g. hardness of factorization). Analogously, T should be polynomial in λ as, otherwise, breaking the underlying hardness assumptions becomes easier than computing $\text{DF}(x, T)$ itself for large values of T.

2. Another issue is what bound on the number of sequential steps of the adversary should one impose. For example, the delay function based on T repeated modular squarings can be computed in sequential time $O(T/\log\log T)$ using polynomial parallelism [4]. Thus, one cannot simply bound the sequential time of the adversary by $o(T)$. Similarly to [38], we adapt the $O(T^\epsilon)$ bound for $\epsilon \in (0, 1)$ which, in particular, is asymptotically smaller than $O(T/\log\log T)$.

3. Without loss of generality, we assume that the size of pp is at least linear in n and the adversary A does not have to get the unary representation of the security parameter 1^n as its input.

The definition of *verifiable* delay function extends a delay function with the possibility to compute publicly-verifiable proofs of correctness of the output value.

Definition 4. *A delay function* $\text{VDF} = (\text{VDFSetup}, \text{VDFGen}, \text{VDFEval})$ *is a verifiable delay function if it is equipped with two additional algorithms* VDFProve *and* VDFVerify *with the following syntax:*

$(y, \pi) \leftarrow \text{VDFProve}(\text{pp}, (x, T))$:
   On input public parameters and a challenge pair (x, T), *the* VDFProve *algorithm outputs* (y, π), *where* π *is a proof that the output* y *is the output of* $\text{VDFEval}(\text{pp}, (x, T))$.
$\{\text{accept}/\text{reject}\} \leftarrow \text{VDFVerify}(\text{pp}, (x, T), (y, \pi))$:
   On input public parameters, a challenge pair (x, T), *and an output/proof pair* (y, π), *the (deterministic) algorithm* VDFVerify *outputs either* accept *or* reject.

In addition to sequentiality (inherited from the underlying delay function), the VDFProve and VDFVerify algorithms must together satisfy correctness and (statistical) soundness as defined below.

Definition 5. (Correctness). *A verifiable delay function* VDF *is* correct *if for all* $T \in \mathbb{N}$

$$\Pr \begin{bmatrix} \texttt{VDF.Verify}(\texttt{pp}, (x, T), (y, \pi)) = \texttt{accept} \\ \textit{where} \\ \texttt{pp} \leftarrow \texttt{VDFSetup}(1^n) \\ x \leftarrow \texttt{VDFGen}(\texttt{pp}, T) \\ (y, \pi) \leftarrow \texttt{VDFProve}(\texttt{pp}, (x, T)) \end{bmatrix} = 1.$$

Definition 6. (Statistical soundness). *A verifiable delay function* VDF *is statistically sound if for every (computationally unbounded) malicious prover* P^* *there exists a negligible function* $\mu(\lambda)$ *such that for all* $\lambda \in \mathbb{N}$

$$\Pr \begin{bmatrix} \texttt{VDF.Verify}(\texttt{pp}, (x, T), (\tilde{y}, \tilde{\pi})) = \texttt{accept} \\ \textit{and} \quad y \neq \tilde{y} \\ \textit{where} \\ \texttt{pp} \leftarrow \texttt{VDFSetup}(1^n) \\ x \leftarrow \texttt{VDFGen}(\texttt{pp}, T) \\ y \leftarrow \texttt{VDFEval}(\texttt{pp}, (x, T)) \\ (\tilde{y}, \tilde{\pi}) \leftarrow P^*(\texttt{pp}, (x, T)) \end{bmatrix} \leq \mu(\lambda).$$

3   Delay Functions from Lucas Sequences

In this section, we propose a delay function based on Lucas sequences and prove its sequentiality assuming that iterated squaring in a group of unknown order is sequential (Sect. 3.1). Further, we conjecture (Sect. 3.2) that our delay function candidate is even more robust than its predecessor proposed by Rivest, Shamir, and Wagner [48]. Finally, we turn our delay function candidate into a *verifiable* delay function (Sect. 4).

3.1   The Atomic Operation

Our delay function is based on subsequences of Lucas sequences, whose indexes are powers of two. Below, we use $\mathbb{N}$ to denote the set of non-negative integers.

Definition 7. *For integers* $P, Q \in \mathbb{Z}$, *the* Lucas sequences $(U_i)_{i \in \mathbb{N}}$ *and* $(V_i)_{i \in \mathbb{N}}$ *are defined for all* $i > 1$ *as*

$$U_i(P, Q) = PU_{i-1}(P, Q) - QU_{i-2}(P, Q)$$

with $U_1(P, Q) = 1$ *and* $U_0(P, Q) = 0$, *and*

$$V_i(P, Q) = PV_{i-1}(P, Q) - QV_{i-2}(P, Q)$$

with $V_1(P, Q) = P$ *and* $V_0(P, Q) = 2$.

We define subsequences $(u_t)_{t \in \mathbb{N}}$, respectively $(v_t)_{t \in \mathbb{N}}$, of $(U_i)_{i \in \mathbb{N}}$, respectively $(V_i)_{i \in \mathbb{N}}$ for all $t \in \mathbb{N}$ as

$$u_t := U_{2^t}(P, Q) \quad \textit{and} \quad v_t := V_{2^t}(P, Q). \tag{2}$$

Although the value of (u_t, v_t) depends on parameters (P, Q), we omit (P, Q) from the notation because these parameters will be always obvious from the context.

The underlying atomic operation for our delay function is

$$f_N(T, P, Q) = (u_T \bmod N, v_T \bmod N).$$

There are several ways to compute (u_t, v_t) in T sequential steps, and we describe two of them below.

An Approach Based on Squaring in a Suitable Extension Ring. To compute the value $f_N(T, P, Q)$, we can use the extension ring $\mathbb{Z}_N[\sqrt{D}]$, where $D := P^2 - 4Q$ is the discriminant of the characteristic polynomial $f(z) = z^2 - Pz + Q$ of the Lucas sequence. The characteristic polynomial $f(z)$ has a root $\omega := (P + \sqrt{D})/2 \in \mathbb{Z}_N[\sqrt{D}]$, and it is known that, for all $i \in \mathbb{N}$, it holds that

$$\omega^i = \frac{V_i + U_i\sqrt{D}}{2} \quad \left(\text{i.e.,} \quad \omega^{2^t} = \frac{v_t + u_t\sqrt{D}}{2} \right).$$

Thus, by iterated squaring of ω, we can compute terms of our target subsequences. To get a better understanding of squaring in the extension ring, consider the representation of the root $\omega = a + b\sqrt{D}$ for some $a, b \in \mathbb{Z}_N$. Then,

$$(a + b\sqrt{D})^2 = (a^2 + b^2D) + 2ab\sqrt{D}.$$

Then, the atomic operation of our delay function can be interpreted as $g \colon \mathbb{Z}_N \times \mathbb{Z}_N \to \mathbb{Z}_N \times \mathbb{Z}_N$, defined for all $a, b \in \mathbb{Z}_N$ as

$$g \colon (a, b) \mapsto (a^2 + b^2D, 2ab) \quad g^t\left(\frac{P}{2}, \frac{1}{2}\right) = \left(\frac{v_t}{2}, \frac{u_t}{2}\right). \tag{3}$$

An Approach Based on Known Identities. Many useful identities for members of modular Lucas sequences are known, such as

$$U_{j+i} = U_jV_i - Q^iU_{j-i}, \quad \text{and} \quad V_{j+i} = V_jV_i - Q^iV_{j-i}. \tag{4}$$

Setting $j = i$ we get

$$U_{2i} = U_iV_i, \quad \text{and} \quad V_{2i} = V_i^2 - 2Q^i. \tag{5}$$

The above identities are not hard to derive (see, e.g., Lemma 12.5 in [40]). Indexes are doubled on each of application of the identities in Eq. (5), and, thus, for $t \in \mathbb{N} \cup \{0\}$, we define an auxiliary sequence (q_t) by $q_t := Q^{2^t}$. Using the identities in Eq. (5), we get recursive equations

$$u_{t+1} = u_tv_t, \quad v_{t+1} = v_t^2 - 2q_t \quad \text{and} \quad q_{t+1} = q_t^2. \tag{6}$$

Then, the atomic operation of our delay function can be interpreted as $g \colon \mathbb{Z}_N \times \mathbb{Z}_N \times \mathbb{Z}_N \to \mathbb{Z}_N \times \mathbb{Z}_N \times \mathbb{Z}_N$, defined for all $u, v, q \in \mathbb{Z}_N$ as

$$g \colon (u, v, q) \mapsto (uv, v^2 - 2q, q^2), \quad g^t(1, P, Q) = (u_t, v_t, Q^{2^t}). \tag{7}$$

LCS.Setup(1^n): Samples two n-bit primes p and q and outputs $N := p \cdot q$.
LCS.Gen(N, T): Samples P and Q independently from the uniform distribution on
$\quad$ $\mathbb{Z}_N$, sets $D := P^2 - 4Q$ and outputs (P, D, T).
LCS.Eval($N, (P, D, T)$): Sets

$$g\colon \mathbb{Z}_N \times \mathbb{Z}_N \to \mathbb{Z}_N \times \mathbb{Z}_N$$
$$(a, b) \mapsto (a^2 + b^2 D, 2ab),$$

$\quad$ computes

$$\left(\frac{v_T}{2}, \frac{u_T}{2}\right) := g^T\left(\frac{P}{2}, \frac{1}{2}\right)$$

$\quad$ and outputs (u_T, v_T).

Fig. 1. Our delay function candidate LCS based on a modular Lucas sequence.

After a closer inspection, the reader may have an intuition that an auxiliary sequence q_t, which introduces a third state variable, is redundant. This intuition is indeed right. In fact, there is another easily derivable identity

$$q_t = \frac{v_t^2 - u_t^2 D}{4}, \tag{8}$$

which can be found, e.g., as Lemma 12.2 in [40]. On the other hand, Eq. (8) is quite interesting because it allows us to compute large powers of an element $Q \in \mathbb{Z}_N$ using two Lucas sequences. We use this fact in the security reduction in Sect. 3.2. Our construction of a delay function, denoted LCS, is given in Fig. 1.

On the Discriminant D. Notice that whenever D is a quadratic residue modulo N, the value $\sqrt{D}$ is an element of $\mathbb{Z}_N$ and hence $\mathbb{Z}_N[\sqrt{D}] = \mathbb{Z}_N$. By definition, LCS.Gen generates a parameter D that is a quadratic residue with probability $1/4$, so it might seem that in one fourth of the cases there is another approach to compute (u_t, v_t): find the element $\sqrt{D}$ and then perform n sequential squarings in the group $\mathbb{Z}_N$. However, it is well known that finding square roots of uniform elements in $\mathbb{Z}_N$ is equivalent to factoring the modulus N, so this approach is not feasible. We can therefore omit any restrictions on the discriminant D in the definition of our delay function LCS.

3.2   Reduction from RSW Delay Function

In order to prove the sequentiality property (Definition 3) of our candidate LCS, we rely on the standard conjecture of the sequentiality of the RSW time-lock puzzles, implicitly stated in [48] as the underlying hardness assumption.

Definition 8 (RSW delay function). *The* RSW *delay function is defined as follows:*

RSWSetup(1^n): *Samples two n-bit primes p and q and outputs* $N := p \cdot q$.
RSWGen(N, T): *Outputs an x sampled from the uniform distribution on* $\mathbb{Z}_N^*$.
RSWEval($N, (x, T)$): *Outputs* $y := x^{2^T} \bmod N$.

Theorem 2. *If the* RSW *delay function has the sequentiality property, then the* LCS *delay function has the sequentiality property.*

Proof. Suppose there exists an adversary (A_0, A_1) who contradicts the sequentiality of LCS, where A_0 is a precomputation algorithm and A_1 is an online algorithm. We construct an adversary (B_0, B_1) who contradicts the sequentiality of RSW as follows:

– The algorithm B_0 is defined identically to the algorithm A_0.
– On input $(N, \text{state}, (x \in \mathbb{Z}_N^*, T))$, B_1 picks a P from the uniform distribution on $\mathbb{Z}_N$, sets

$$Q := x, \quad D := P^2 - 4Q$$

and it runs $A_1(N, \text{state}, (P, D, T))$ to compute (u_T, v_T). The algorithm B_1 computes $y = x^{2^T} = Q^{2^T} = q_T$ using the identity in Eq. (8).

Note that the input distribution for the algorithm A_1 produced by B_1 differs from the one produced by LCS.Gen, because the LCS generator samples Q from the uniform distribution on $\mathbb{Z}_N$ (instead of $\mathbb{Z}_N^*$). However, this is not a problem since the size of $\mathbb{Z}_N \setminus \mathbb{Z}_N^*$ is negligible compared to the size of $\mathbb{Z}_N$, so the statistical distance between the distribution of D produced by B_1 and the distribution of D sampled by LCS.Gen is negligible in the security parameter. Thus, except for a negligible multiplicative loss, the adversary (B_0, B_1) attains the same success probability of breaking the sequentiality of RSW as the probability of (A_0, A_1) breaking the sequentiality of LCS – a contradiction to the assumption of the theorem.   □

We believe that the converse implication to Theorem 2 is not true, i.e., that breaking the sequentiality of RSW does not necessarily imply breaking the sequentiality of LCS. Below, we state it as a conjecture.

Conjecture 1. Sequentiality of LCS cannot be reduced to sequentiality of RSW.

One reason why the above conjecture might be true is that, while the RSW delay function is based solely only on multiplication in the group $\mathbb{Z}_N^*(\cdot)$, our LCS delay function uses the full arithmetic (addition and multiplication) of the commutative ring $\mathbb{Z}_N$.

One way to support the conjecture would be to construct an algorithm that speeds up iterated squaring but is not immediately applicable to Lucas sequences. By [49] we know that this cannot be achieved by a generic algorithm. A non-generic algorithm that solves iterated squaring in time $O(T/\text{loglog}(T))$ is presented in [4]. The main tool of their construction is the Explicit Chinese Remainder Theorem modulo N. However, a similiar theorem exists also for univariate polynomial rings, which suggests that a similar speed-up can be obtained for our delay function by adapting the techniques in [4] to our setting.

4   VDF from Lucas Sequences

In Sect. 3.1 we saw different ways of computing the atomic operation of the delay function. Computing (u_t, v_t) in the extension field seems to be the more natural and time and space effective approach. Furthermore, writing the atomic operation $g(a, b) = (a^2 + b^2 D, 2ab)$ as $\omega \mapsto \omega^2$ is very clear, and, thus, we follow this approach throughout the rest of the paper.

4.1   Structure of $\mathbb{Z}_N[x]/(x^2 - Px + Q)$

To construct a VDF based on Lucas sequences, we use an algebraic extension

$$\mathbb{Z}_N[x]/(x^2 - Px + Q), \tag{9}$$

where N is an RSA modulus and $P, Q \in \mathbb{Z}_N$. In this section, we describe the structure of the algebraic extension given in Expression (9). Based on our understanding of the structure of the above algebraic extension, we can conclude that using modulus N composed of safe primes (i.e., for all prime factors p of N, $p-1$ has a large prime divisor) is necessary but not sufficient condition for security of our construction. We specify some sufficient conditions on factors of N in the subsequent Sect. 4.2.

First, we introduce some simplifying notation for quotient rings.

Definition 9. *For* $m \in \mathbb{N}$ *and* $f(x) \in \mathbb{Z}_m[x]$, *we denote by* $\mathbb{Z}_{m,f}$ *the quotient ring* $\mathbb{Z}[x]/(m, f(x))$, *where* $(m, f(x))$ *denotes the ideal of the ring* $\mathbb{Z}[x]$ *generated by* m *and* $f(x)$.

Observation 1, below, allows us to restrict our analysis only to the structure of $\mathbb{Z}_{p,f}$ for prime $p \in \mathbb{P}$.

Observation 1. *Let* $p, q \in \mathbb{P}$ *be distinct primes,* $N := p \cdot q$ *and* $f(x) \in \mathbb{Z}_N[x]$. *Then*

$$\mathbb{Z}_{N,f} \simeq \mathbb{Z}_{p,f} \times \mathbb{Z}_{q,f} .$$

Proof. Using the Chinese reminder theorem, we get

$$\mathbb{Z}_{N,f} \simeq \frac{\mathbb{Z}[x]/(f(x))}{(N)} \simeq \frac{\mathbb{Z}[x]/(f(x))}{(p)} \times \frac{\mathbb{Z}[x]/(f(x))}{(q)} \simeq \mathbb{Z}_{p,f} \times \mathbb{Z}_{q,f}$$

as claimed.   □

The following lemma characterizes the structure of $\mathbb{Z}_{p,f}$ with respect to the discriminant of f. We use $\left(\frac{a}{p}\right)$ to denote the standard Legendre symbol.

Lemma 1. *Let* $p \in \mathbb{P} \setminus \{2\}$ *and* $f(x) \in \mathbb{Z}_p[x]$ *be a polynomial of degree 2 with the discriminant* D. *Then*

$$\mathbb{Z}_{p,f}^*(\cdot) \simeq \begin{cases} \mathbb{Z}_{p^2-1}(+) & \left(\frac{D}{p}\right) = -1 \\ \mathbb{Z}_{p-1}(+) \times \mathbb{Z}_p(+) & \left(\frac{D}{p}\right) = 0 \\ \mathbb{Z}_{p-1}(+) \times \mathbb{Z}_{p-1}(+) & \left(\frac{D}{p}\right) = 1 \end{cases} .$$

Proof. We consider each case separately:

- If $\left(\frac{D}{p}\right) = -1$, then $f(x)$ is irreducible over $\mathbb{Z}_p$ and $\mathbb{Z}_{p,f}$ is a field with p^2 elements. Since $\mathbb{Z}_{p,f}$ is a finite field, $\mathbb{Z}_{p,f}^*$ is cyclic and contains $p^2 - 1$ elements.
- If $\left(\frac{D}{p}\right) = 0$, then $D = 0$ and f has some double root α and it can be written as $\beta(x - \alpha)^2$ for some $\beta \in \mathbb{Z}_p^*$. Since the ring $\mathbb{Z}_{p,\beta(x-\alpha)^2}$ is isomorphic to the ring $\mathbb{Z}_{p,x^2}$ (consider the isomorphism $g(x) \mapsto g(x + \alpha)$), we can restrict ourselves to describing the structure of $\mathbb{Z}_{p,x^2}$.

We will prove that the function ψ,

$$\psi : \mathbb{Z}_p^*(\cdot) \times \mathbb{Z}_p(+) \to \mathbb{Z}_{p,x^2}^*(\cdot),$$
$$\psi : (a, b) \mapsto a \cdot (1 + x)^b,$$

is an isomorphism. First, the polynomial $a + cx \in \mathbb{Z}_{p,x^2}$ is invertible if and only if $a \neq 0$ (inverse is $a^{-1} - a^{-2}cx$). For the choice $b = a^{-1}c$, we have

$$\psi(a, b) = a(1 + x)^b \equiv a(1 + bx) \equiv a(1 + a^{-1}cx) \equiv a + cx \quad \mathrm{mod}\ (p, x^2).$$

Thus ψ is onto. Second, ψ is, in fact, a bijection, because

$$|\mathbb{Z}_{p,x^2}^*(\cdot)| = p^2 - p = (p - 1) \cdot p = |\mathbb{Z}_p^*(\cdot) \times \mathbb{Z}_p(+)|. \tag{10}$$

Finally, ψ is a homomorphism, because

$$\psi(a_1, b_1) \cdot \psi(a_2, b_2) = a_1 a_2 (1 + x)^{b_1 + b_2} = \psi(a_1 a_2, b_1 + b_2).$$

If $\left(\frac{D}{p}\right) = 1$, then $f(x)$ has two roots $\beta_1, \beta_2 \in \mathbb{Z}_p$. We have an isomorphism

$$\psi : \mathbb{Z}_p[x]/(f(x)) \to \mathbb{Z}_p \times \mathbb{Z}_p$$
$$\psi : g(x) + (f(x)) \mapsto (g(\beta_1), g(\beta_2))$$

and $(\mathbb{Z}_p \times \mathbb{Z}_p)^* \simeq \mathbb{Z}_p^* \times \mathbb{Z}_p^* \simeq \mathbb{Z}_{p-1}(+) \times \mathbb{Z}_{p-1}(+)$. $\qquad\square$

4.2   Strong Groups and Strong Primes

To achieve the verifiability property of our construction, we need $\mathbb{Z}_{p,f}^*$ to contain a strong subgroup (defined next) of order asymptotically linear in p. We remark that our definition of strong primes is stronger than the one by Rivest and Silverman [46].

Definition 10 (Strong groups). *For $\lambda \in \mathbb{N}$, we say that a non-trivial group $\mathbb{G}$ is λ-strong, if the order of each non-trivial subgroup of $\mathbb{H}$ is greater than 2^λ.*

Observation 2. *If $\mathbb{G}_1$ and $\mathbb{G}_2$ are λ-strong groups, then $\mathbb{G}_1 \times \mathbb{G}_2$ is a λ-strong group.*

It can be seen from Lemma 1 that $\mathbb{Z}^*_{p,f}$ always contains groups of small order (e.g. $Z_2(+)$). To avoid these, we descend into the subgroup of a-th powers of elements of $\mathbb{Z}^*_{p,f}$. Below, we introduce the corresponding notation.

Definition 11. *For an Abelian group* $\mathbb{G}$ *and* $a \in \mathbb{N}$, *we define the subgroup* $\mathbb{G}^{(a)} := \{x^a \mid x \in \mathbb{G}\}$ *of* $\mathbb{G}$ *in the multiplicative notation and* $a\mathbb{G} := \{ax \mid x \in \mathbb{G}\}$ *in the additive notation.*

Further, we show in Lemma 2 below that (λ, a)-strong primality (defined next) is a sufficient condition for $(\mathbb{Z}^*_{p,f})^{(a)}$ to be a λ-strong group.

Definition 12 (Strong primes). *Let* $p \in \mathbb{P}$ *and* $\lambda, a \in \mathbb{N}$. *We say that* p *is a* (λ, a)-*strong prime, if* $\lambda > a$ *and there exists* $W \in \mathbb{N}$, $W > 1$, *such that* $p^2 - 1 = aW$ *and every prime factor of* W *is greater than* 2^λ.

Since a is a public parameter in our setup, super-polynomial a could reveal partial information about the factorization of N. However, we could allow a to be polynomial in λ while maintaining hardness of factoring N.[4] For the sake of simplicity of Definition 12, we rather use stronger condition $a < \lambda$. The following simple observation will be useful for proving Lemma 2.

Observation 3 *For* $\forall m, n \in \mathbb{N} : n\mathbb{Z}_m \simeq \mathbb{Z}_{m/\gcd(m,n)}$.

Lemma 2. *Let* p *be a* (λ, a)-*strong prime and* $f(x) \in \mathbb{Z}_p[x]$ *be a quadratic polynomial. Then,* $(\mathbb{Z}^*_{p,f})^{(a)}$ *is a* λ-*strong group.*

Proof. From definition of the strong primes, there exists $W \in \mathbb{N}$, whose factors are bigger than 2^λ and $p^2 - 1 = aW$. We denote $W^- := \gcd(p-1, W)$ a factor of W. Applying Observation 3 to Lemma 1, we get

$$
(\mathbb{Z}^*_{p,f})^{(a)} \simeq
\begin{cases}
a\mathbb{Z}_{p^2-1}(+) \simeq a\mathbb{Z}_{aW}(+) \simeq \mathbb{Z}_W(+) & \left(\frac{D}{p}\right) = -1 \\
a\mathbb{Z}_p(+) \times a\mathbb{Z}_{p-1}(+) \simeq \mathbb{Z}_p(+) \times \mathbb{Z}_{W^-}(+) & \left(\frac{D}{p}\right) = 0 \\
a\mathbb{Z}_{p-1}(+) \times a\mathbb{Z}_{p-1}(+) \simeq \mathbb{Z}_{W^-}(+) \times \mathbb{Z}_{W^-}(+) & \left(\frac{D}{p}\right) = 1.
\end{cases}
$$

In particular, we used above the fact that Observation 2 implies that $a\mathbb{Z}_{p-1}(+) \simeq \mathbb{Z}_{W^-}$ as explained next. Since $(p-1)(p+1) = aW$, all divisors of $p-1$ are divisors of aW. By definition of a and W in Definition 12, we also have that $\gcd(a, W) = 1$, which implies that any factor of $p-1$ divides either a or W, but *not both*. When we divide $p - 1$ by all the common divisors with a, only the common divisors with W are left, which implies $(p-1)/\gcd(a, p-1) = \gcd(W, p-1) = W^-$. The proof of the lemma is now completed by Observation 2.

Corollary 1. *Let* p *be a* (λ, a_p)-*strong prime,* q *be a* (λ, a_q)-*strong prime,* $N = p \cdot q$, $a = \text{lcm}(a_p, a_q)$, $P, Q \in \mathbb{Z}_N$ *and* $f(x) = x^2 - Px + Q$. *Then* $(Z^*_{N,f})^{(a)}$ *is* λ-*strong.*

---

[4] Since we set a to be at most polynomial in λ, its is possible to go over all possible candidate values for a in time polynomial in λ. Thus, any algorithm that could factor N using the knowledge of a can be efficiently simulated even without the knowledge of a.

4.3 Our Interactive Protocol

Our interactive protocol is formally described in Fig. 3. To understand this protocol, we first recall the outline of Pietrzak's interactive protocol from Sect. 1.2 and then highlight the hurdles. Let $N = p \cdot q$ be an RSA modulus where p and q are strong primes and let x be a random element from $\mathbb{Z}_N^*$. The interactive protocol in [42] allows a prover to convince the verifier of the statement

"(N, x, y, T) satisfies $y = x^{2^T} \bmod N$".

The protocol is recursive and in a round-by-round fashion reduces the claim to a smaller statement by halving the time parameter. To be precise, in each round the (honest) prover sends the "midpoint" $\mu = x^{2^{T/2}}$ of the current statement to the verifier and they together reduce the statement to

"$(N, x', y', T/2)$ satisfies $y' = (x')^{2^{T/2}} \bmod N$",

where $x' = x^r \mu$ and $y' = \mu^r y$ for a random challenge r. This is continued until $(N, x, y, T = 1)$ is obtained at which point the verifier simply checks whether $y = x^2 \bmod N$.

The main problem, we face while designing our protocol is ensuring that the verifier can check whether μ sent by prover lies in an appropriate subgroup of $\mathbb{Z}_N[\sqrt{D}]$. In the first draft of Pietrzak's protocol [41], prover sends a square root of μ, from which the original μ can be recovered easily (by simply squaring it) with a guarantee, that the result lies in a group of quadratic residues QR_N. Notice that the prover knows the square root of μ, because it is just a previous term in the sequence he computed.

Using Pietrzak's protocol directly for our delay function would require computing a-th roots in RSA group for some arbitrary a. Since this is a computationally hard problem, we cannot use the same trick. In fact, the VDF construction of Wesolowski [54] is based on similar hardness assumption.

While Pietrzak shifted from QR_N to the group of signed quadratic residues QR_N^+ in his following paper [42] to get unique proofs, we resort to his old idea of 'squaring a square root' and generalise it.

The high level idea is simple. First, on input ω, prover computes the sequence $(\omega, \omega^2, \ldots, \omega^{2^T})$. Next, during the protocol, verifier maps all elements sent by the prover by homomorphism

$$\psi : \mathbb{Z}_{N,f}^* \to (\mathbb{Z}_{N,f}^*)^{(a)}, \quad \psi(x) = x^a \tag{11}$$

into the target strong group $(\mathbb{Z}_{N,f}^*)^{(a)}$. This process is illustrated in Fig. 2. Notice that the equality $y = \omega^{2^T}$ for the original sequence implies the equality $y^a = (\omega^a)^{2^T}$ for the mapped sequence $(\omega^a, \omega^{2a}, \ldots, \omega^{a2^T})$.

Restriction to Elements of $(\mathbb{Z}_{N,f}^*)^{(a)}$. Mapping Eq. (11) introduces a new technical difficulty. Since ψ is not injective, we narrow the domain inputs, for which the output of our VDF is verifiable, from $\mathbb{Z}_{N,f}^*$ to $(\mathbb{Z}_{N,f}^*)^{(a)}$. Furthermore,

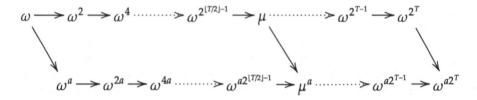

Fig. 2. Illustration of our computation of the iterated squaring using the a-th root of ω. Horizontal arrows are $x \mapsto x^2$ and diagonal arrows are $x \mapsto x^a$.

the only way to verify that a certain x is an element of $(\mathbb{Z}_{N,f}^*)^{(a)}$ is to get an a-th root of x and raise it to the ath power. So we have to represent elements of $(\mathbb{Z}_{N,f}^*)^{(a)}$ by elements of $\mathbb{Z}_{N,f}^*$ anyway. To resolve these two issues, we introduce a non-unique representation of elements of $(\mathbb{Z}_{N,f}^*)^{(a)}$.

Definition 13. *For $a \in \mathbb{N}$ and $x \in \mathbb{Z}_{N,f}^*$, we denote x^a (an element of $(\mathbb{Z}_{N,f}^*)^{(a)}$) by $[x]$. Since this representation of x^a is not unique, we define an equality relation by*

$$[x] = [y] \overset{def}{\leftrightarrow} x^a = y^a$$

We will denote by tilde ($\tilde{x}$) the elements that were already powered to the a by a verifier (i.e. $\tilde{x} = x^a$). Thus tilded variables verifiably belong to the target group $(\mathbb{Z}_{N,f}^*)^{(a)}$.

In the following text, the goal of the brackets notation in Definition 13 is to distinguish places where the equality means the equality of elements of $Z_{N,f}^*$ from those places, where the equality holds up to $\mathrm{Ker}(\psi)$. A reader can also see the notation in Definition 13 as a concrete representation of elements of a factor group $\mathbb{Z}_{N,f}/\mathrm{Ker}(\psi)$.

Our security reduction 2 required the delay function to operate everywhere on $\mathbb{Z}_N$. This is not a problem if the LCS.Setup algorithm is modified to output the set $\mathrm{Ker}(\psi)$.

4.4   Security

Recall here that $(\mathbb{Z}_{N,f}^*)^{(a)}$ is λ-strong group, so there exist $p_1, \ldots, p_m \in \mathbb{P} \cap (2^\lambda, \infty)$ and $k_1, \ldots, k_m \in \mathbb{N}$ such that

$$(\mathbb{Z}_{N,f}^*)^{(a)} \simeq \mathbb{Z}_{p_1^{k_1}}(+) \times \cdots \times \mathbb{Z}_{p_m^{k_m}}(+) \tag{12}$$

Definition 14. *For $z \in (\mathbb{Z}_{N,f}^*)^{(a)}$ and $i \in [m]$, we define z_i as i-th coordinate of $\psi(z)$, where ψ is the isomorphism given by Eq. (12).*

Setting

$n \in \mathbb{N}$ computational security parameter
$\lambda \in \mathbb{N}$ statistical security parameter
$a \in \mathbb{N}$ exponentiation parameter
$N \in \mathbb{N}$ a product of n-bit (λ, a_p)-safe prime p and
(λ, a_q)-safe prime q such that $a = \mathrm{lcm}(a_p, a_q)$
$f(x) = x^2 - Px + Q$ for some $P, Q \in \mathbb{Z}_N$
$((N, a), [\omega], T)$ a challenge tuple
$((N, a), [\omega], T, [y])$ a solution tuple

The Interactive Protocol
1. Prover and verifier get a challenge tuple $((N, a), [\omega], T)$ as a common input.
2. Prover computes the sequence

$$\omega \to \omega^2 \to \omega^4 \to \ldots \to \omega^{2^T}$$

and sends its last element $[y] := [\omega^{2^T}]$ to the verifier.
3. Prover and verifier repeat the halving protocol, initiated with solution tuple $((N, a), [\omega], T, [y])$, until verifier either **accept** or **reject**.

The Halving Protocol
1. Prover and verifier get solution tuple $((N, a), [\omega], T, [y])$ as common input.
2. If $T = 1$, then the verifier computes $(\tilde{\omega}, \tilde{y}) = (\omega^a, y^a)$ and it outputs **accept** provided that $\tilde{y} = \tilde{\omega}^2$ or **reject** otherwise.
3. Prover sends $[\mu] := [\omega^{2^{\lfloor T/2 \rfloor}}]$ to verifier.
4. If $\mu \notin \mathbb{Z}^*_{N,f}$, then verifier output **reject**.
5. Verifier picks a random r from uniform distribution on $\mathbb{Z}_{2^\lambda}$ and he sends r to the prover.
6. Finally prover and verifier merge solution tuples

$$((N, a), [\omega], \lfloor T/2 \rfloor, [\mu]) \qquad \text{and}$$

$$\begin{cases} ((N, a), [\mu], T/2, [y]) & \text{for even } T \\ ((N, a), [\mu], \lceil T/2 \rceil, [y^2]) & \text{for odd } T \end{cases}$$

into the new solution tuple

$$\begin{cases} ((N, a), [\omega^r \mu], T/2, [\mu^r y]) & \text{for even } T \\ ((N, a), [\omega^r \mu], \lceil T/2 \rceil, [(\mu^r y)^2]) & \text{for odd } T. \end{cases}$$

Fig. 3. Our Interactive Protocol for LCS.

Lemma 3. *Let $T \in \mathbb{N}$ and $\omega, \mu, y \in (\mathbb{Z}^*_{N,f})^{(a)}$. If $y \neq \omega^{2^T}$, then*

$$\Pr \begin{bmatrix} y' = (\omega')^{2^{T/2}} \\ \text{where} \\ r \leftarrow \mathbb{Z}_{2^\lambda} \\ \omega' := \omega^r \mu \\ y' := \mu^r y \end{bmatrix} < \frac{1}{2^\lambda}. \tag{13}$$

Proof. Fix ω, μ and y. Let some $r \in \mathbb{Z}_{2^\lambda}$ satisfy

$$\mu^r y = (\omega^r \mu)^{2^{T/2}}. \tag{14}$$

Using notation from Definition 14, we rewrite Eq. (14) as a set of equations

$$r\mu_1 + y_1 \equiv 2^{T/2}(r\omega_1 + \mu_1) \mod p_1^{k_1},$$

$$\vdots$$

$$r\mu_m + y_m \equiv 2^{T/2}(r\omega_m + \mu_m) \mod p_m^{k_m}.$$

For every $j \in [m]$, by reordering the terms, the j-th equation becomes

$$r(2^{T/2}\omega_j - \mu_j) + (2^{T/2}\mu_j - y_j) \equiv 0 \mod p_j^{k_j} \tag{15}$$

If $\forall j \in [m] : 2^{T/2}\omega_j - \mu_j \equiv 0 \mod p_j^{k_j}$, then $\mu = \omega^{2^{T/2}}$. Further for every $j \in [m] : 2^{T/2}\mu_j - y_j \equiv 0 \mod p_j^{k_j}$. It follows that $y = \mu^{2^{T/2}}$. Putting these two equations together gives us $y = \omega^{2^T}$, which contradicts our assumption $y \neq \omega^{2^T}$.

It follows that there exists $j \in [m]$ such that

$$2^{T/2}\omega_j - \mu_j \not\equiv 0 \mod p_j^{k_j}. \tag{16}$$

Thereafter there exists $k < k_j$ such that p_j^k divides $(2^{T/2}\omega_j - \mu_j)$ and

$$(2^{T/2}\omega_j - \mu_j)/p_j^k \not\equiv 0 \mod p_j. \tag{17}$$

Furthermore, from Eq. (15), p_j^k divides $(2^{T/2}\mu_j - y_j)$. Finally, dividing eq. Eq. (15) by p_j^k, we get that r is determined uniquely (mod p_j),

$$r \equiv -\frac{(2^{T/2}\mu_j - y_j)/p_j^k}{(2^{T/2}\omega_j - \mu_j)/p_j^k} \mod p_j.$$

Using the fact that $2^\lambda < p_j$, this uniqueness of r upper bounds number of $r \in \mathbb{Z}_{2^\lambda}$, such that Eq. (14) holds, to one. It follows that the probability that Eq. (14) holds for r chosen randomly from the uniform distribution over $\mathbb{Z}_{2^\lambda}$ is less than $1/2^\lambda$. $\qquad\square$

Corollary 2. *The halving protocol will turn an invalid input tuple (i.e. $[y] \neq [\omega^{2^T}]$) into a valid output tuple (i.e. $[y'] = [(\omega')^{2^{T/2}}]$) with probability less than $1/2^\lambda$.*

Theorem 3. *For any computationally unbounded prover who submits anything other than $[y]$ such that $[y] = [\omega^{2^T}]$ in phase 2 of the protocol, the soundness error is upper-bounded by $\log(T)/2^\lambda$*

Proof. In each round of the protocol, T decreases to $\lceil T/2 \rceil$. It follows that the number of rounds of the halving protocol before reaching $T = 1$ is upper bounded by $\log T$.

If the verifier accepts the solution tuple $((N, a), [\omega''], 1, [y''])$ in the last round, then the equality $[y''] = [(\omega'')^2]$ must hold. It follows that the initial inequality must have turned into equality in some round of the halving protocol. By Lemma 3, the probability of this event is bounded by $1/2^\lambda$. Finally, using the union bound for all rounds, we obtain the upper bound $(\log T)/2^\lambda$.   □

4.5   Our VDF

Analogously to the VDF of Pietrzak [42], we compile our public-coin interactive proof given in Fig. 3 into a VDF using the Fiat-Shamir heuristic. The complete construction is given in Fig. 4. For ease of exposition, we assume that the time parameter T is always a power of two.

As discussed in Sect. 4.3, it is crucial for the security of the protocol that the prover computes a sequence of powers of the a-th root of the challenge and the resulting value (as well as the intermediate values) received from the prover is lifted to the appropriate group by raising it to the a-th power. We use the tilde notation in Fig. 4 in order to denote elements on the sequence relative to the a-th root.

Note that, by the construction, the output of our VDF is the $a \cdot 2^T$-th power of the root of the characteristic polynomial for Lucas sequence with parameters P and Q. Therefore, the value of the delay function implicitly corresponds to the $a \cdot 2^T$-th term of the Lucas sequence.

Theorem 4. *Let λ be the statistical security parameter. The* LCS *VDF defined in Fig. 4 is correct and statistically-sound with a negligible soundness error if* hash *is modelled as a random oracle, against any adversary that makes $2^{o(\lambda)}$ oracle queries.*

Proof. The correctness follows directly by construction.

To prove its statistical soundness, we proceed in a similar way to [42]. We cannot apply Fiat-Shamir transformation directly, because our protocol does not have constant number of rounds, thus we use Fiat-Shamir heuristic to each round separately.

First, we use a random oracle as the hash function. Second, if a malicious prover computed a proof accepted by verifier for some tuple $((N, a), ([\omega], T), [y])$ such that

$$[y] \neq [\omega^{2^T}], \tag{19}$$

then he must have succeeded in turning inequality from Eq. (19) into equality in some round. By Lemma 3, probability of such a flipping is bounded by $1/2^\lambda$. Every such an attempt requires one query to random oracle. Using a union bound, it follows that the probability that a malicious prover who made q queries to random oracle succeeds in flipping initial inequality into equality in some round is upper-bounded by $q/2^\lambda$.

LCS.Setup$(1^n, 1^\lambda)$: Runs a strong primes generator on input $1^n, 1^\lambda$ to get an n-bit (λ, a_p)-strong prime p and an n-bit (λ, a_q)-strong prime q, such that $N = p \cdot q$ is a Blum integer. Then it chooses a hash function

$$\text{hash} : \mathbb{Z} \times \mathbb{Z}_N^3 \to \mathbb{Z}_{2^\lambda}.$$

and it outputs the public parameters

$$(N := p \cdot q, a := \text{lcm}(a_p, a_q), \text{hash}).$$

LCS.Gen(N, T): Samples P and Q independently from the uniform distribution on $\mathbb{Z}_N$, sets

$$D := P^2 - 4Q \quad \text{and} \quad \omega := \frac{P + z}{2},$$

where z is a formal variable satisfying $z^2 = D$, and outputs (ω, T).

LCS.Eval$(N, (\omega, T))$: Computes the sequence

$$\omega \to \omega^2 \to \omega^4 \to \omega^8 \to \ldots \to \omega^{2^{T-1}} \to \omega^{2^T}$$

and outputs its last term ω^{2^T}.

LCS.Prove$((N, a, \text{hash}), ([\omega], T))$: Computes

$$y := [\omega^{2^T}]$$

and sets $(\omega_1, y_1) = (\omega, y)$. For $i = 1, \ldots, t$ computes

$$\mu_i := \omega_i^{2^{T/2^i}},$$
$$r_i := \text{hash}(T/2^{i-1}, \omega_i^a, y_i^a, \mu_i^a),$$
$$\omega_{i+1} := \omega_i^{r_i} \mu_i,$$
$$y_{i+1} := \mu_i^{r_i} y_i.$$

It outputs $([y], \pi = ([\mu_1], \ldots, [\mu_t]))$.

LCS.Verify$((N, a, \text{hash}), ([\omega], T), ([y], \pi))$: Sets $\tilde{\omega}_1 = \omega^a$, $\tilde{y}_1 = y^a$ and for each $i = 1, \ldots, t$, computes

$$\tilde{\mu}_i := \mu_i^a,$$
$$r_i := \text{hash}(T/2^{i-1}, \tilde{\omega}_i, \tilde{y}_i, \tilde{\mu}_i),$$
$$\tilde{\omega}_{i+1} := \tilde{\omega}_i^{r_i} \tilde{\mu}_i,$$
$$\tilde{y}_{i+1} := \tilde{\mu}_i^{r_i} \tilde{y}_i.$$

It outputs accept if

$$\tilde{y}_{t+1} = \tilde{\omega}_{t+1}^2, \tag{18}$$

otherwise it outputs reject.

Fig. 4. VDF based on Lucas sequences

Since q is $o(2^\lambda)$, $q/2^\lambda$ is a negligible function and thus the soundness error is negligible.   □

Acknowledgements. We thank Krzysztof Pietrzak and Alon Rosen for several fruitful discussions about this work and the anonymous reviewers of SCN 2022 and TCC 2023 for valuable suggestions.

Pavel Hubáček is supported by the Czech Academy of Sciences (RVO 67985840), by the Grant Agency of the Czech Republic under the grant agreement no. 19-27871X, and by the Charles University project UNCE/SCI/004. Chethan Kamath is supported by Azrieli International Postdoctoral Fellowship, by the European Research Council (ERC) under the European Union's Horizon Europe research and innovation programme (grant agreement No. 101042417, acronym SPP), and by ISF grant 1789/19.

References

1. Abusalah, H., Kamath, C., Klein, K., Pietrzak, K., Walter, M.: Reversible proofs of sequential work. In: Ishai, Y., Rijmen, V. (eds.) EUROCRYPT 2019. LNCS, vol. 11477, pp. 277–291. Springer, Cham (2019). https://doi.org/10.1007/978-3-030-17656-3_10
2. Aggarwal, D., Maurer, U.: Breaking RSA generically is equivalent to factoring. IEEE Trans. Inf. Theory **62**(11), 6251–6259 (2016). https://doi.org/10.1109/TIT.2016.2594197
3. Arun, A., Bonneau, J., Clark, J.: Short-lived zero-knowledge proofs and signatures. In: Agrawal, S., Lin, D. (eds.) Advances in Cryptology – ASIACRYPT 2022. Lecture Notes in Computer Science, vol. 13793, pp. 487–516. Springer, Cham (2022). https://doi.org/10.1007/978-3-031-22969-5_17
4. Bernstein, D., Sorenson, J.: Modular exponentiation via the explicit Chinese remainder theorem. Math. Comput. **76**, 443–454 (2007). https://doi.org/10.1090/S0025-5718-06-01849-7
5. Bitansky, N., et al.: PPAD is as hard as LWE and iterated squaring. IACR Cryptol. ePrint Arch., p. 1072 (2022)
6. Bitansky, N., Goldwasser, S., Jain, A., Paneth, O., Vaikuntanathan, V., Waters, B.: Time-lock puzzles from randomized encodings. In: ITCS, pp. 345–356. ACM (2016)
7. Bleichenbacher, D., Bosma, W., Lenstra, A.K.: Some remarks on Lucas-based cryptosystems. In: Coppersmith, D. (ed.) CRYPTO 1995. LNCS, vol. 963, pp. 386–396. Springer, Heidelberg (1995). https://doi.org/10.1007/3-540-44750-4_31
8. Block, A.R., Holmgren, J., Rosen, A., Rothblum, R.D., Soni, P.: Time- and space-efficient arguments from groups of unknown order. In: Malkin, T., Peikert, C. (eds.) CRYPTO 2021. LNCS, vol. 12828, pp. 123–152. Springer, Cham (2021). https://doi.org/10.1007/978-3-030-84259-8_5
9. Boneh, D., Bonneau, J., Bünz, B., Fisch, B.: Verifiable delay functions. In: Shacham, H., Boldyreva, A. (eds.) CRYPTO 2018. LNCS, vol. 10991, pp. 757–788. Springer, Cham (2018). https://doi.org/10.1007/978-3-319-96884-1_25
10. Boneh, D., Bünz, B., Fisch, B.: A survey of two verifiable delay functions. IACR Cryptol. ePrint Arch. **2018**, 712 (2018)
11. Boneh, D., Venkatesan, R.: Breaking RSA may not be equivalent to factoring. In: Nyberg, K. (ed.) Advances in Cryptology - EUROCRYPT '98. Lecture Notes in Computer Science, vol. 1403, pp. 59–71. Springer, Cham (1998). https://doi.org/10.1007/BFb0054117

12. Buchmann, J., Williams, H.C.: A key-exchange system based on imaginary quadratic fields. J. Cryptol. **1**(2), 107–118 (1988). https://doi.org/10.1007/BF02351719

13. Chavez-Saab, J., Rodríguez-Henríquez, F., Tibouchi, M.: Verifiable Isogeny walks: towards an isogeny-based postquantum VDF. In: AlTawy, R., Hülsing, A. (eds.) SAC 2021. LNCS, vol. 13203, pp. 441–460. Springer, Cham (2022). https://doi.org/10.1007/978-3-030-99277-4_21

14. Choudhuri, A.R., Hubáček, P., Kamath, C., Pietrzak, K., Rosen, A., Rothblum, G.N.: PPAD-hardness via iterated squaring modulo a composite. IACR Cryptol. ePrint Arch. **2019**, 667 (2019)

15. Cini, V., Lai, R.W.F., Malavolta, G.: Lattice-based succinct arguments from vanishing polynomials. In: Handschuh, H., Lysyanskaya, A. (eds.) Advances in Cryptology - CRYPTO 2023. Lecture Notes in Computer Science, pp. 72–105. Springer Nature Switzerland, Cham (2023). https://doi.org/10.1007/978-3-031-38545-2_3

16. Cohen, B., Pietrzak, K.: Simple proofs of sequential work. In: Nielsen, J.B., Rijmen, V. (eds.) EUROCRYPT 2018. LNCS, vol. 10821, pp. 451–467. Springer, Cham (2018). https://doi.org/10.1007/978-3-319-78375-8_15

17. Cohen, B., Pietrzak, K.: The Chia network blockchain. Technical report, Chia Network (2019). https://www.chia.net/assets/ChiaGreenPaper.pdf. Accessed 29 July 2022

18. Döttling, N., Garg, S., Malavolta, G., Vasudevan, P.N.: Tight verifiable delay functions. In: Galdi, C., Kolesnikov, V. (eds.) SCN 2020. LNCS, vol. 12238, pp. 65–84. Springer, Cham (2020). https://doi.org/10.1007/978-3-030-57990-6_4

19. Döttling, N., Lai, R.W.F., Malavolta, G.: Incremental proofs of sequential work. In: Ishai, Y., Rijmen, V. (eds.) EUROCRYPT 2019. LNCS, vol. 11477, pp. 292–323. Springer, Cham (2019). https://doi.org/10.1007/978-3-030-17656-3_11

20. Ephraim, N., Freitag, C., Komargodski, I., Pass, R.: Continuous verifiable delay functions. In: Canteaut, A., Ishai, Y. (eds.) EUROCRYPT 2020. LNCS, vol. 12107, pp. 125–154. Springer, Cham (2020). https://doi.org/10.1007/978-3-030-45727-3_5

21. De Feo, L., Masson, S., Petit, C., Sanso, A.: Verifiable delay functions from supersingular isogenies and pairings. In: Galbraith, S.D., Moriai, S. (eds.) ASIACRYPT 2019. LNCS, vol. 11921, pp. 248–277. Springer, Cham (2019). https://doi.org/10.1007/978-3-030-34578-5_10

22. Fiat, A., Shamir, A.: How to prove yourself: practical solutions to identification and signature problems. In: Odlyzko, A.M. (ed.) CRYPTO 1986. LNCS, vol. 263, pp. 186–194. Springer, Heidelberg (1987). https://doi.org/10.1007/3-540-47721-7_12

23. Freitag, C., Pass, R., Sirkin, N.: Parallelizable delegation from LWE. IACR Cryptol. ePrint Arch., p. 1025 (2022)

24. Goldwasser, S., Micali, S., Rackoff, C.: The knowledge complexity of interactive proof systems. SIAM J. Comput. **18**(1), 186–208 (1989)

25. Hoffmann, C., Hubáček, P., Kamath, C., Klein, K., Pietrzak, K.: Practical statistically sound proofs of exponentiation in any group. In: Dodis, Y., Shrimpton, T. (eds.) Advances in Cryptology – CRYPTO 2022. Lecture Notes in Computer Science, vol. 13508, pp. 1–30. Springer, Cham (2022). https://doi.org/10.1007/978-3-031-15979-4_13

26. Hofheinz, D., Kiltz, E.: The group of signed quadratic residues and applications. In: Halevi, S. (ed.) CRYPTO 2009. LNCS, vol. 5677, pp. 637–653. Springer, Heidelberg (2009). https://doi.org/10.1007/978-3-642-03356-8_37

27. Katz, J., Loss, J., Xu, J.: On the security of time-lock puzzles and timed commitments. In: Pass, R., Pietrzak, K. (eds.) TCC 2020, Part III. LNCS, vol. 12552, pp. 390–413. Springer, Cham (2020). https://doi.org/10.1007/978-3-030-64381-2_14

28. Lai, R.W.F., Malavolta, G.: Lattice-based timed cryptography. In: Handschuh, H., Lysyanskaya, A. (eds.) Advances in Cryptology - CRYPTO 2023. Lecture Notes in Computer Science, pp. 782–804. Springer Nature Switzerland, Cham (2023). https://doi.org/10.1007/978-3-031-38554-4_25

29. Lehmer, D.H.: An extended theory of Lucas' functions. Ann. Math. **31**(3), 419–448 (1930). https://www.jstor.org/stable/1968235

30. Lennon, M.J.J., Smith, P.J.: LUC: A new public key system. In: Douglas, E.G. (ed.) Ninth IFIP Symposium on Computer Security, pp. 103–117. Elsevier Science Publishers (1993)

31. Lenstra, A.K., Wesolowski, B.: Trustworthy public randomness with sloth, unicorn, and trx. IJACT **3**(4), 330–343 (2017)

32. Lipmaa, H.: On Diophantine complexity and statistical zero-knowledge arguments. In: Laih, C.-S. (ed.) ASIACRYPT 2003. LNCS, vol. 2894, pp. 398–415. Springer, Heidelberg (2003). https://doi.org/10.1007/978-3-540-40061-5_26

33. Lombardi, A., Vaikuntanathan, V.: Fiat-Shamir for repeated squaring with applications to PPAD-hardness and VDFs. In: Micciancio, D., Ristenpart, T. (eds.) CRYPTO 2020. LNCS, vol. 12172, pp. 632–651. Springer, Cham (2020). https://doi.org/10.1007/978-3-030-56877-1_22

34. Lucas, E.: Théorie des fonctions numériques simplement périodiques. Am. J. Math. **1**(4), 289–321 (1878). https://www.jstor.org/stable/2369373

35. Lund, C., Fortnow, L., Karloff, H.J., Nisan, N.: Algebraic methods for interactive proof systems. J. ACM **39**(4), 859–868 (1992)

36. Mahmoody, M., Moran, T., Vadhan, S.P.: Publicly verifiable proofs of sequential work. In: ITCS, pp. 373–388. ACM (2013)

37. Mahmoody, M., Smith, C., Wu, D.J.: A note on the (Im)possibility of verifiable delay functions in the random oracle model. IACR Cryptol. ePrint Arch. **2019**, 663 (2019)

38. Malavolta, G., Thyagarajan, S.A.K.: Homomorphic time-lock puzzles and applications. In: Boldyreva, A., Micciancio, D. (eds.) CRYPTO 2019. LNCS, vol. 11692, pp. 620–649. Springer, Cham (2019). https://doi.org/10.1007/978-3-030-26948-7_22

39. Müller, W.B., Nöbauer, W.: Some remarks on public-key cryptosystems. Studia Sci. Math. Hungar. **16**, 71–76 (1981)

40. Bressoud, D.M.: Factorization and primality testing. Math. Comput. **56**(193), 400 (1991)

41. Pietrzak, K.: Simple verifiable delay functions. IACR Cryptol. ePrint Arch. **2018**, 627 (2018). https://eprint.iacr.org/2018/627/20180720:081000

42. Pietrzak, K.: Simple verifiable delay functions. In: ITCS. LIPIcs, vol. 124, pp. 1–15. Schloss Dagstuhl - Leibniz-Zentrum für Informatik (2019)

43. Rabin, M.O.: Transaction protection by beacons. J. Comput. Syst. Sci. **27**(2), 256–267 (1983)

44. Ribenboim, P.: My Numbers, My Friends: Popular Lectures on Number Theory. Springer-Verlag, New York (2000)

45. Riesel, H.: Prime Numbers and Computer Methods for Factorization, Progress in Mathematics, vol. 57. Birkhäuser, Basel (1985)

46. Rivest, R., Silverman, R.: Are 'strong' primes needed for RSA. Cryptology ePrint Archive, Report 2001/007 (2001). https://eprint.iacr.org/2001/007

47. Rivest, R.L., Shamir, A., Adleman, L.M.: A method for obtaining digital signatures and public-key cryptosystems (reprint). Commun. ACM **26**(1), 96–99 (1983)

48. Rivest, R.L., Shamir, A., Wagner, D.A.: Time-lock puzzles and timed-release crypto. Technical report, Massachusetts Institute of Technology (1996)

49. Rotem, L., Segev, G.: Generically speeding-up repeated squaring is equivalent to factoring: sharp thresholds for all generic-ring delay functions. In: Micciancio, D., Ristenpart, T. (eds.) CRYPTO 2020. LNCS, vol. 12172, pp. 481–509. Springer, Cham (2020). https://doi.org/10.1007/978-3-030-56877-1_17

50. Rotem, L., Segev, G., Shahaf, I.: Generic-group delay functions require hidden-order groups. In: Canteaut, A., Ishai, Y. (eds.) EUROCRYPT 2020. LNCS, vol. 12107, pp. 155–180. Springer, Cham (2020). https://doi.org/10.1007/978-3-030-45727-3_6

51. Schindler, P., Judmayer, A., Hittmeir, M., Stifter, N., Weippl, E.R.: RandRunner: distributed randomness from trapdoor VDFs with strong uniqueness. In: 28th Annual Network and Distributed System Security Symposium, NDSS 2021, virtually, 21–25 February 2021. The Internet Society (2021)

52. Shani, B.: A note on isogeny-based hybrid verifiable delay functions. IACR Cryptol. ePrint Arch. **2019**, 205 (2019)

53. Valiant, P.: Incrementally verifiable computation or proofs of knowledge imply time/space efficiency. In: Canetti, R. (ed.) TCC 2008. LNCS, vol. 4948, pp. 1–18. Springer, Heidelberg (2008). https://doi.org/10.1007/978-3-540-78524-8_1

54. Wesolowski, B.: Efficient verifiable delay functions. In: Ishai, Y., Rijmen, V. (eds.) EUROCRYPT 2019. LNCS, vol. 11478, pp. 379–407. Springer, Cham (2019). https://doi.org/10.1007/978-3-030-17659-4_13

55. Wesolowski, B.: Efficient verifiable delay functions. J. Cryptol. **33**(4), 2113–2147 (2020). https://doi.org/10.1007/s00145-020-09364-x

56. Williams, H.C.: A $p+1$ method of factoring. Math. Comput. **39**(159), 225–234 (1982)

57. Williams, H.C.: Édouard lucas and primality testing. Math. Gaz. **83**, 173 (1999)

Algebraic Group Model with Oblivious Sampling

Helger Lipmaa[1]($\boxtimes$)(iD), Roberto Parisella[2](iD), and Janno Siim[2](iD)

[1] University of Tartu, Tartu, Estonia
helger.lipmaa@gmail.com
[2] Simula UiB, Bergen, Norway

Abstract. In the algebraic group model (AGM), an adversary has to return with each group element a linear representation with respect to input group elements. In many groups, it is easy to sample group elements obliviously without knowing such linear representations. Since the AGM does not model this, it can be used to prove the security of spurious knowledge assumptions. We show several well-known zk-SNARKs use such assumptions. We propose AGM with oblivious sampling (AGMOS), an AGM variant where the adversary can access an oracle that allows sampling group elements obliviously from some distribution. We show that AGM and AGMOS are different by studying the family of "total knowledge-of-exponent" assumptions, showing that they are all secure in the AGM, but most are not secure in the AGMOS if the DL holds. We show an important separation in the case of the KZG commitment scheme. We show that many known AGM reductions go through also in the AGMOS, assuming a novel falsifiable assumption TOFR.

Keywords: Admissible encoding · algebraic group model ·
elliptic-curve hashing · FindRep · KZG extractability · oblivious
sampling

1 Introduction

GGM. One of the most influential idealized models of computation in cryptography is the generic group model (GGM, [30,35]). GGM models the situation where an adversary $\mathcal{A}$ operates in a (usually abelian, possibly bilinear) group. In the GGM, $\mathcal{A}$'s operations on group elements are "generic" (typically addition, equality test, pairing operation), i.e., they do not depend on the concrete group. One models this either by giving the adversary access to random encodings [35] or abstract handles of group elements [30], together with oracles that perform group operations and equality tests on given encodings (resp., handles). $\mathcal{A}$ cannot access any other information about the group elements, including their bit representations. $\mathcal{A}$ does not even have access to the group description, except (usually) its order. Most elliptic-curve cryptanalysis algorithms are generic. That is, the algorithms do not exploit any particular structure of the group.

© International Association for Cryptologic Research 2023
G. Rothblum and H. Wee (Eds.): TCC 2023, LNCS 14372, pp. 363–392, 2023.
https://doi.org/10.1007/978-3-031-48624-1_14

While the GGM is used widely to argue about security in group-based settings, the GGM has several well-known weaknesses [14,15] that have motivated researchers to propose more realistic idealized models. In particular, GGM makes the questionable assumption that the adversary cannot conduct more efficient attacks by accessing the bit-presentation of group elements.

AGM. Fuchsbauer et al. [18] proposed the more realistic algebraic group model (AGM) with *algebraic* adversaries. The AGM does not assume the adversary's ignorance about the group description or bit-representation of the group elements. Instead, the AGM is a generalized knowledge assumption [12], stating that an algebraic adversary $\mathcal{A}$ must know a linear representation of an output group element with respect to input group elements. Notably, a group element's creation can depend on the group description and already known group elements' bit-presentation. The knowledge of the linear representation is modeled by requiring the adversary, together with each group element, to output a linear dependence from the group elements seen thus far. More formally, given (for example) input group elements $[x_1, \ldots, x_n]_1{}^1$, if the adversary outputs $[y]_1$, it has to also output integers $v_1, \ldots, v_n$ such that $[y]_1 = \sum_{i=1}^n v_i[x_i]_1$.

Oblivious Sampling. Since a real-life adversary is not restricted to group operations and equality tests, AGM does not always capture all (known) possible attacks. In particular, it was realized early [9] in the context of GGM that one must additionally model the adversary's ability to sample group elements obliviously without knowing the linear representations.

We point out (we seem to be the first to make this connection) that in the case of elliptic curve groups, oblivious sampling is not just a theoretical possibility but concrete and *provable* (see Sect. 2.1 for a proof) attack due to admissible encodings [5,8,17,22,37]. Admissible encodings are efficiently computable functions E from $\mathbb{F} = \mathbb{Z}_p$ to elliptic curve groups that are regular (small preimage sizes) and preimage sampleable (given $[y]_1 \in \text{Im}(E)$, one can efficiently recover its whole preimage). Admissible encodings allow an adversary $\mathcal{A}$ to sample group elements obliviously without knowing their discrete logarithms [22] and even linear representations: $\mathcal{A}$ can do it by sampling $s \leftarrow_\$ \mathbb{F}$ and outputting $E(s)$. Since admissible encodings exist for all curves and are often constant-time computable, *we argue that elliptic curve group adversaries are not algebraic.* We emphasize that admissible encodings are just one approach to oblivious sampling. Many others may exist, and it is crucial to guarantee security against all of them.

Without modeling oblivious sampling, one can prove in the GGM and the AGM the security of spurious knowledge assumptions [3,9,36]. Consider the following *SpurKE* (*spurious knowledge of exponent*) assumption: if the adversary on input $[1]_1$ outputs $[x]_1$ then it must know x. First, we only consider groups where the DL (discrete logarithm) assumption holds since otherwise, SpurKE

---

[1] Let $\hat{e} : \mathbb{G}_1 \times \mathbb{G}_2 \to \mathbb{G}_T$ be a bilinear pairing. Let the order of the groups be a prime p and denote $\mathbb{F} = \mathbb{Z}_p$. We use the standard additive bracket notation, denoting a group element as $z \cdot [1]_\kappa = [z]_\kappa \in \mathbb{G}_\kappa$, where $[1]_\kappa$ is a generator of an additive abelian group $\mathbb{G}_\kappa$, by $[z]_\kappa$. We denote the pairing by $\bullet : \mathbb{G}_1 \times \mathbb{G}_2 \to \mathbb{G}_T$.

and many other knowledge assumptions hold trivially. As already argued in [9], if the adversary samples $[x]_1$ obliviously (and DL holds), then SpurKE does not hold. However, SpurKE holds in the standard GGM and AGM (even when DL holds); in AGM, the linear representation is just x. It is a severe shortcoming of standard GGM and AGM that assumptions like SpurKE can be proven secure. SpurKE is not the only bad apple: the AGM allows one to prove the security of many similar spurious knowledge assumptions.

This shortcoming of AGM has misled researchers to use SpurKE. In the KZG polynomial commitment scheme [24], the committer gets as an input a public key $\mathsf{pk} = ([1, x, \ldots, x^d]_1, [1, x]_2)$. To commit to a polynomial $f(X) = \sum_{i=0}^{d} f_i X^i$, the committer computes $[c]_1 \leftarrow \sum_{i=1}^{d} f_i [x^i]_1$. (See Sect. 5.3 for the full construction.) Campanelli et al. [10] (the full version of [11]), Sect. 7.3, suggest a trivial proof of knowledge for KZG commitment, where the proof is empty. They motivate this by AGM since, in AGM, the polynomial coefficients can be extracted from $[c]_1$ alone. However, extracting the polynomial directly from a commitment corresponds to the SpurKE assumption and is thus intractable.

Similarly, in the knowledge-soundness proof of Plonk [20], Gabizon et al. write the following (Remark 3.2, [20]): *"the algebraic group model is crucial for allowing us to model both binding and knowledge soundness in one clean game - without it, we typically cannot require E to return the polynomial immediately after A's commitment."*. Again, the authors rely on immediate extraction from the commitment, hence relying on SpurKE. This does not necessarily imply a vulnerability in Plonk. (We show later that the polynomial can be extracted if a KZG commitment is opened at some evaluation point.) However, it shows that SpurKE has been used (albeit sneakily) in well-known, widely deployed SNARKs like Plonk. We will leave it to future work to establish whether such SNARKs (including other KZG-based SNARKs in the literature) can be proven secure in AGMOS. Even if they are secure, they will need a different security proof. More generally, this shows that relying on SpurKE and equivalent assumptions is more common than expected.

Modelling Oblivious Sampling. An augmented GGM that models oblivious sampling is often called *GGM with hashing* (GGMH, [2,3,9]). In GGMH, the adversary is given access to an oracle that obliviously samples from the uniform distribution over the group.

[18] briefly discusses the oblivious sampling issue under the heading of "Integrating AGM with random oracles," stating that algebraic adversaries cannot do oblivious sampling. They extend AGM to the setting of protocols that explicitly use a random oracle (RO) that outputs group elements (in particular, to prove the security of the BLS signature scheme). In such cases, they consider RO answers semantically equivalent to input elements. Thus, they require that an algebraic adversary knows a representation of its output group elements as a linear combination of inputs and RO answers. We will call this extension *RO-AGM*. [18] does not analyze the security of protocols where the honest participants do not use RO, but the adversary uses RO to obliviously sample group elements.

[28] added oblivious sampling to the AGM. However, for this, [28] uses the *fully-programmable random oracle* (FPRO, [16,31]) model. FPRO is even less realistic than the *non-programmable random oracle* (NPRO) model, where the reduction is only allowed to query and forward the answers of the RO. Moreover, this does *not* model admissible encodings that are real-world, well-defined, non-programmable, deterministic functions.

Let us try to understand the issues we face, including how the FPRO comes in. First, by the definition of the AGM, an algebraic adversary $\mathcal{A}$ always returns a linear representation of its output, which is typically used in a reduction proof. For instance, we can prove in AGM that Computational Diffie-Hellman (CDH) is not easier to break than DL. An algebraic CDH adversary $\mathcal{A}$, on input $[1, a, b]_\kappa$, computes $[ab]_\kappa$, and must also output integers v_1, v_2, v_3 such that $[ab]_\kappa = v_1[1]_\kappa + v_2[a]_\kappa + v_3[b]_\kappa$. A DL reduction $\mathcal{B}$ can set the DL challenge as $[a]_\kappa$, sample a random integer b, and invoke $\mathcal{A}$. Observe that if $\mathcal{A}$ succeeds in attacking CDH, the polynomial $V(X) = v_1 + v_2 X + v_3 y - X b$ has a as a root. Thus, $\mathcal{B}$ can compute and return a. The discrete logarithm a will be correctly computed if V is a non-zero polynomial in X.[2] However, when proving SpurKE and similar assumptions, we should not assume that $\mathcal{A}$ returns the linear representation.

The (more challenging) second issue concerns how one constructs reductions $\mathcal{B}$ in the AGM, like the one above. In a typical AGM proof, one analyzes an assumption with a verification polynomial $V(\boldsymbol{X})$ that depends on the discrete logarithms of the input and output group elements. $\mathcal{B}$ uses the extracted linear representation to extract all V's coefficients. The verification equation stipulates that $V(\boldsymbol{x}) = 0$. After that, one analyzes two cases. "Case A" (*algebraic*), where V is a zero polynomial: typically, either $V(\boldsymbol{X}) = 0$ is impossible (computational assumptions) or the extraction succeeds (knowledge assumptions).

Alternatively, one is in "Case X" (*$\boldsymbol{X}$-related case*) where $V(\boldsymbol{X}) \neq 0$ as a polynomial but $V(\boldsymbol{x}) = 0$. In this case, one constructs a reduction to a standard computational assumption like (d_1, d_2)-PDL (Power Discrete Logarithm, given $[1, y, \ldots, y^{d_1}]_1$ and $[1, y, \ldots, y^{d_2}]_2$ for random y, it is intractable to recover y).

A typical reduction $\mathcal{B}$ to PDL implicitly embeds random affine functions of $\mathcal{B}$'s input trapdoor y to all the coordinates of $\boldsymbol{x}$. (This step is only needed when V is multivariate.) This results in a *univariate* polynomial V^*, such that $V^*(Y) \neq 0$ but $V^*(y) = 0$. Using univariate polynomial factorization, $\mathcal{B}$ recovers y. Consider the case of oblivious sampling with RO. Then, $[\boldsymbol{x}]_1$ also includes RO answers, which means that a PDL reduction must implicitly embed y to the RO answers. Since now the RO must be programmed, this results in using the FPRO model in [28]. See [28] for a discussion on the differences between this approach and the approach of [18].

Since SpurKE-like assumptions do not hold (assuming DL holds) in [28]'s version of AGM, this answers one of our concerns. Unfortunately, it still relies on using FPRO. Pitfalls of FPRO are well understood; see [16,31] for extended discussions. Modeling admissible encodings (existing, efficient functions) via a RO would remove one of the advantages of the AGM over the GGM, the ability to argue about concrete bit representations of existing real-life objects.

---

[2] The actual reduction is slightly more complicated since we need to guarantee that V is a non-zero polynomial.

Moreover, the outputs of most admissible encodings are not distributed uniformly, while the GGMH, the RO-AGM of [18], and [28] only consider the uniform distribution. Since both GGMH and RO-AGM only consider uniformly distributed outputs, they do not model properly admissible encodings also in this aspect. For example, Icart's admissible encoding [22] has domain size $\approx 5/8$ of the group size, and thus it can be easily distinguished from an RO that outputs uniformly random group elements. In addition, one can choose a non-uniform input distribution for the admissible encoding or combine several known admissible encodings. Even if one is willing to use the FPRO model, one has the problem of embedding the input of the PDL adversary to the RO answers that come from non-uniform distributions. It is not clear how to do it generically.

Main Questions of this Work. The previous discussion leads us to the following question: *how to extend the AGM to model oblivious sampling without needing the FPRO (or even the NPRO)?* This modeling should take into account that admissible encodings can be used to sample from non-uniform distributions.

Our Contributions. Firstly, we formally establish that oblivious sampling is possible in elliptic curve groups using admissible encodings. Thus, an oblivious sampling extension to AGM is indeed needed.

Our modeling focuses on the bilinear setting; the non-bilinear setting follows directly by restricting the adversary. We consider $(\mathcal{EF}, \mathcal{DF})$-*AGMOS adversaries (AGM with oblivious sampling)* $\mathcal{A}$ that obtain group elements as inputs and output field or group elements. Here, $\mathcal{EF}$ is a family of encoding functions, and $\mathcal{DF}$ is a family of distributions. We allow $\mathcal{A}$ to use an oracle $\mathcal{O}$ to obliviously sample elements from $\mathbb{G}_1$ or $\mathbb{G}_2$. $\mathcal{A}$ inputs to $\mathcal{O}$ adversarially chosen $E \in \mathcal{EF}$ and $D \in \mathcal{DF}$. $\mathcal{O}$ samples a random $s \leftarrow_s D$ and then outputs $E(s)$ and s. The model executes $\mathcal{O}$ correctly and honestly (it is non-programmable) without leaking any side information. With any group element $[z]_\kappa$, $\mathcal{A}$ must output a linear representation with respect to all previously seen group elements, including oracle answers from the same group. Reasonable choices for $\mathcal{EF}$ may be admissible encodings or some other oblivious sampling functions. We also describe a simpler version of AGMOS where oracles respond with uniformly random group elements and discuss the implications of that.

To tackle the issue of reductions to PDL, we define a new family of falsifiable assumptions, $(\mathcal{EF}, \mathcal{DF})$-TOFR (Tensor Oracle FindRep). In the full version [29], we prove that $(\mathcal{EF}, \mathcal{DF})$-TOFR holds in a version of GGM augmented by a distribution oracle $\mathcal{O}$ (all previous GGMH variants consider uniform distributions), under the assumption that $\mathcal{DF}$ contains well-spread distributions (i.e., distributions with min-entropy $\omega(\log \lambda)$, where λ is the security parameter).

We prove that (a version of) the Flexible Uber assumption [4,6], the Power Knowledge of Exponent (PKE) assumption [13], EUF-CMA of Schnorr's signature [34], and the extractability of the KZG polynomial commitment scheme [24] hold in the AGMOS. Crucially, in the last case, extractability is only possible when the committer additionally opens the polynomial at some point. Immediate extraction from the commitment is intractable, as we discussed earlier. In typical

AGMOS proofs, we construct two reductions: one to the new TOFR assumption and the second one to the PDL assumption. To simplify PDL reductions, we define an intermediate assumption FPR (*Find Polynomial Representation*) and reduce it to PDL. The FPR assumption hides many of the complexities of typical PDL reductions and can also be used in standard AGM proofs.

Let TotalKE be the assumption family stating that an adversary, whose input is $([1]_1, [1]_2)$, knows the discrete logarithms of all output group elements. Most of such assumptions are insecure in the standard model due to oblivious sampling (if DL holds), while they hold in the AGM. We show that such spurious assumptions do not hold in AGMOS, under the hardness of DL, obtaining a (conditional) separation with AGM.

1.1   Technical Overview

Feasibility of Oblivious Sampling. We give a more detailed proof of a claim from [22] that computing the DL of a group element $G = E(s)$, given G and s, where E is an admissible encoding and s is a random input, is roughly as hard as computing the discrete logarithm of a random group element. This implies that adversaries in the elliptic curve setting can indeed sample group elements obliviously (i.e., without knowing their DLs).

Definition of AGMOS. Suppose $\mathsf{p} = (p, \mathbb{G}_1, \mathbb{G}_2, \mathbb{G}_T, \hat{e})$ is a concrete bilinear group, $\kappa \in \{1, 2\}$, and $\mathbb{F} = \mathbb{Z}_p$. Let $\mathcal{EF} = \{\mathcal{EF}_{\mathsf{p},\kappa}\}_{\mathsf{p},\kappa}$ be a set of encodings (e.g., admissible encodings), with $\mathcal{EF}_{\mathsf{p},\kappa}$ containing encodings from $\mathbb{F}$ to $\mathbb{G}_\kappa$. Let $\mathcal{DF} = \{\mathcal{DF}_{\mathsf{p}}\}_{\mathsf{p}}$ be a family of distributions over $\mathbb{F}$.

We allow $(\mathcal{EF}, \mathcal{DF})$-*AGMOS adversaries* to query (p-dependent) *non-programmable* oracles $\mathcal{O}_1$ and $\mathcal{O}_2$. Given adversarially chosen E and D as inputs, $\mathcal{O}_\kappa(E, D)$ is defined as follows: if $E \notin \mathcal{EF}_{\mathsf{p},\kappa}$ or $D \notin \mathcal{DF}_{\mathsf{p}}$, it aborts. Otherwise, it samples $s \leftarrow_{\$} D$, computes $[\mathsf{q}]_\kappa \leftarrow E(s)$, and returns $[\mathsf{q}]_\kappa$ and s.

We require that for every non-uniform probabilistic polynomial time (PPT) $\mathcal{A}$, there exists a non-uniform PPT extractor $\mathsf{Ext}_{\mathcal{A}}$, such that: if the adversary returns a group element $[\mathsf{y}]_\kappa$, $\mathsf{Ext}_{\mathcal{A}}$ returns with an overwhelming probability a linear representation $(\gamma_\kappa, \delta_\kappa)$ of $[\mathsf{y}]_\kappa$ with respect to the already seen group elements (including oracle answers) from $\mathbb{G}_\kappa$. More precisely, for $\kappa \in \{1, 2\}$, $\mathsf{Ext}_{\mathcal{A}}$ extracts vectors γ_κ and δ_κ and a vector of oracle answers $[\mathsf{q}_\kappa]_\kappa$, such that $\mathsf{y}_\kappa = \gamma_\kappa^{\mathsf{T}} \mathsf{x}_\kappa + \delta_\kappa^{\mathsf{T}} \mathsf{q}_\kappa$.

Security Proofs in AGMOS. Security proofs in the AGMOS follow the general strategy of security proofs in the AGM but with some crucial differences. Since the adversary's output $\mathsf{y} = \gamma^{\mathsf{T}} \mathsf{x}_\kappa + \delta^{\mathsf{T}} \mathsf{q}_\kappa$ depends on the oracle answers, the usual PDL reduction strategy is not sufficient. In the AGM, the polynomial $V(\boldsymbol{X})$ corresponding to the assumption's verification (a pairing-product equation) depends only on the challenger's trapdoors (e.g., a and b in the CDH assumption). In the case of several trapdoors, the PDL reduction embeds its input $[x]_\kappa$ to all trapdoors. Since we want to avoid FPRO, in the AGMOS, the reduction cannot embed $[x]_\kappa$ to the oracle answers.

Due to that, the AGMOS proof strategy looks as follows. We work with a verification polynomial $V(\boldsymbol{X}, \mathbb{Q})$, where $\mathbb{Q}_{\kappa i}$ is an indeterminate corresponding to $[q_{\kappa i}]_\kappa$ (the ith answer of $\mathcal{O}_\kappa$). This polynomial is such that $V(\boldsymbol{x}, q)$ is equal to 0 iff the challenger accepts the adversary's output. Note that the actual verification equation, used in the definition of the assumption, is a function of the adversary's inputs and outputs. However, since the outputs have all the form $\boldsymbol{y} = \boldsymbol{\gamma}^\mathsf{T} \mathbf{x}_\kappa + \boldsymbol{\delta}^\mathsf{T} q_\kappa$, V can be written as a polynomial in $(\boldsymbol{X}, \mathbb{Q})$. Importantly, V's coefficients can be computed from the internal variables of the challenger and the elements extracted by the AGMOS extractor.

In the AGM proof of a computational assumption, one considers two cases. In Case A of an AGM proof, $V(\boldsymbol{X}) = 0$ as a polynomial. One typically shows that this case never materializes.

In Case X of an AGM proof, $V(\boldsymbol{X}) \neq 0$ as a polynomial but $V(\boldsymbol{x}) = 0$. One then constructs a PDL reduction that embeds the challenge (given as a tuple of group elements) to $\boldsymbol{x}$ (given as group elements), obtaining a univariate polynomial $V^*(X)$. The reduction uses polynomial factorization to find $V^*(X)$'s roots. One of these roots is necessarily the discrete logarithm of the reduction's input.

An AGMOS proof strategy of computational assumptions is more complicated. In Case A of an AGMOS proof, $V(\boldsymbol{X}, \mathbb{Q}) = 0$ as a polynomial. However, V is generally more complicated than in an AGM proof, and thus one has to be more careful when showing that $V(\boldsymbol{X}, \mathbb{Q}) = 0$ is impossible. Later, we use this difference to separate AGM and AGMOS.

Assuming $V(\boldsymbol{X}, \mathbb{Q}) \neq 0$, an AGMOS proof has more cases. Case X of an AGMOS proof corresponds to the case where we can construct a PDL adversary. Due to how the sampling oracle's answers are created, one can write $V(\boldsymbol{X}, \mathbb{Q}) = V^h(\boldsymbol{X}) + V^t(\boldsymbol{X}, \mathbb{Q})$, where V^h does not depend on $\mathbb{Q}$ while each term of V^t depends on some indeterminate $\mathbb{Q}_{\kappa i}$. In Case X, $V(\boldsymbol{X}, \mathbb{Q}) \neq 0$ as a polynomial but $V^t(\boldsymbol{x}, \mathbb{Q}) = 0$ as a polynomial. We divide Case X into two subcases. In Subcase X.1, the adversary does not use oracle answers, which means that $V^t(\boldsymbol{X}, \mathbb{Q}) = 0$ as a polynomial ($\boldsymbol{\delta} = \boldsymbol{0}$ for all group elements output by the adversary). Thus, the non-zero polynomial $V(\boldsymbol{X}, \mathbb{Q})$ does not depend on $\mathbb{Q}$. As in the AGM, we reduce the security of the proved assumption to the PDL.

In Subcase X.2, $V^t(\boldsymbol{X}, \mathbb{Q}) \neq 0$ but $V^t(\boldsymbol{x}, \mathbb{Q}) = 0$. In this case, the coefficient of some $\mathbb{Q}_{\kappa i}$ or $\mathbb{Q}_{1i}\mathbb{Q}_{2j}$ is a non-zero polynomial in $\boldsymbol{X}$ that evaluates to zero at $\boldsymbol{X} = \boldsymbol{x}$. As in Subcase X.1, we can reduce the security to the PDL by using polynomial factorization to return PDL's input, but the reduction is different.

Case Q of an AGMOS proof is the remaining case when Cases A and X do not hold. That is, $V^t(\boldsymbol{x}, \mathbb{Q}) \neq 0$ (but the verifier accepts, $V(\boldsymbol{x}, q) = 0$). Now we are in a situation where $V^t \neq 0$ as a polynomial (thus, V depends nontrivially on at least one $\mathbb{Q}_{\kappa i}$) but $V(\boldsymbol{x}, q) = V^h(\boldsymbol{x}) + V^t(\boldsymbol{x}, q) = 0$ for $[q_{\kappa i}]_\kappa$ chosen from some distribution from $\mathcal{DF}_p$.

For a concrete V, the probability that $V(x, q) = 0$ is negligible over the choice of q. However, V (whose coefficients depend on the linear representations) is fixed after the adversary $\mathcal{A}$ sees the oracle's answers. Since, for any q, one can choose a bad V so that $V(\boldsymbol{x}, q) = 0$, this probabilistic argument does not work. Fortunately, $\mathcal{A}$ only knows $[q_{\kappa i}]_\kappa$ as group elements. It seems reasonable to *assume* that for any adversarial input (chosen by the reduction) and for $[q]_\kappa$ coming from a well-spread distribution (in particular, q is non-zero with an overwhelming probability), it is difficult to construct a low-degree polynomial in $\mathbb{Q}$ that evaluates to zero at the oracle answers. In a few paragraphs, we formulate this as a new assumption, TOFR. In Case Q, we construct a reduction to TOFR.

To summarize, an AGMOS proof of a computational assumption has the following structure:

- Case A: $V(\boldsymbol{X}, \mathbb{Q}) = 0$. This case is typically impossible.
- Case X: $V(\boldsymbol{X}, \mathbb{Q}) \neq 0$ and $V^t(\boldsymbol{x}, \mathbb{Q}) = 0$.
  - Case X.1: $V^t(\boldsymbol{X}, \mathbb{Q}) = 0$. Reduces to PDL.
  - Case X.2: $V^t(\boldsymbol{X}, \mathbb{Q}) \neq 0$. Reduces (differently) to PDL.
- Case Q: $V(\boldsymbol{X}, \mathbb{Q}) \neq 0$ and $V^t(\boldsymbol{x}, \mathbb{Q}) \neq 0$. Reduces to TOFR.

FPR Assumption. To automatize PDL reductions in AGMOS proofs, we define a new intermediate assumption Find Polynomial Representation (FPR). FPR is a tautological assumption of Case X (both subcases). FPR states that it is hard to find a non-zero multivariate polynomial f that evaluates to zero at the given input trapdoor. We first reduce FPR to PDL (without using idealized models). We define two variants of FPR that have incomparable reductions to PDL; the best choice depends on the context. The actual security reductions of Case X to FPR are straightforward. The definition of FPR is an independent contribution applicable to both AGM and AGMOS proofs.

Handling Knowledge Assumptions. The AGMOS proofs of knowledge assumptions follows the above blueprint for AGMOS proofs of computational assumptions. In particular, there will be Case A, Case X, and Case Q. Case X and Case Q are similar to the case of computational assumptions. (Although, as we will see, case X may not be needed in some knowledge assumption reductions.) Depending on the case, we construct a reduction to either FPR or TOFR. Recall that Case A did not materialize in the case of computational assumptions. In the case of knowledge assumptions, in an AGMOS proof, we construct a knowledge assumption extractor Ext that uses the AGMOS extractor $\overline{\mathsf{Ext}}$ as a subroutine. We show that if $\overline{\mathsf{Ext}}$ succeeds, so does Ext.

The New Assumption TOFR. The new $(\mathcal{EF}, \mathcal{DF})$-TOFR (*Tensor Oracle Find-Rep*, see Definition 2) assumption states the following. Given oracle access to the sampling oracles $\mathcal{O}_1$ and $\mathcal{O}_2$ (that are defined w.r.t. some $(\mathcal{EF}, \mathcal{DF})$ as before), it is intractable to output a vector $\boldsymbol{v} \neq \boldsymbol{0}$ such that $(1 \| q_1^{\mathsf{T}} \| q_2^{\mathsf{T}} \| (q_1 \otimes q_2)^{\mathsf{T}}) \cdot \boldsymbol{v} = 0$. Here, $[q_\kappa]_\kappa$ is the vector of $\mathcal{O}_\kappa$ answers.

TOFR generalizes the classical FindRep [7] and KerMDH assumptions. Recall that FindRep assumes that given a uniformly random vector of group elements $[x]_\kappa$, it is difficult to find a non-zero vector $\boldsymbol{v}$, such that $\boldsymbol{v}^{\mathsf{T}} x = 0$. FindRep is tightly secure under the discrete logarithm assumption.

Our AGMOS reductions work for any family $(\mathcal{EF}, \mathcal{DF})$ for which $(\mathcal{EF}, \mathcal{DF})$-TOFR is secure, but clearly, TOFR itself is not secure for any $(\mathcal{EF}, \mathcal{DF})$. For example, it is trivial to break TOFR if the encoding function is a constant function that maps any input to $[1]_\kappa$. The adversary can easily output $v = (1, \ldots, 1, -(\ell - 1))$, where ℓ is the length of the vector $(1 \| \mathsf{q}_1^\mathsf{T} \| \mathsf{q}_2^\mathsf{T} \| (\mathsf{q}_1 \otimes \mathsf{q}_2)^\mathsf{T})$.

However, when $(\mathcal{EF}, \mathcal{DF})$ implements oblivious sampling (adversary does not know DL of $E(s)$ for $s \leftarrow_\$ D$), we expect $(\mathcal{EF}, \mathcal{DF})$-TOFR to hold since it is similar to the FindRep assumption. Such is the case with admissible encodings.

We provide further confidence to this claim in the full version [29]. We first define GGM with oblivious sampling (GGMOS), a novel version of GGM where the generic adversary has (in addition to the regular operations) access to an oblivious sampling oracle. The oracle takes as an input a distribution $D \in \mathcal{OF}_\mathsf{p}$ over $\mathbb{F}$ and returns a GGM label of x sampled from D. Here D can be seen as distribution over $\mathbb{F}$, induced by $E(D')$ where $E \in \mathcal{EF}_{\mathsf{p},\kappa}$ and $D' \in \mathcal{DF}_\mathsf{p}$. Note that modeling $\mathcal{EF}_{\mathsf{p},\kappa}$ itself is not possible in GGMOS since it may depend on the concrete structure of the group.

We prove that $(\mathcal{EF}, \mathcal{DF})$-TOFR is secure in GGMOS, assuming that all distributions from $\mathcal{DF}_\mathsf{p}$ have min-entropy $\omega(\log \lambda)$, i.e., are well-spread. Thus, the strength of TOFR depends crucially on $\mathcal{DF}$. However, this proof should only be taken as implying a necessary requirement for $\mathcal{DF}$ since $\mathcal{EF}$ cannot be entirely accurately modeled in GGMOS, as mentioned above.

Example AGMOS Proofs. In Sect. 5, we present a few example AGMOS security proofs. We picked our examples such that they showcase a variety of different aspects of AGMOS. We prove that a variant of the Flexible Uber assumption [4,6] is secure under FPR and TOFR (see Sect. 5.1 for why we chose a variant). This proof follows closely the general proof strategy mentioned above. We also prove that the (bilinear) Power Knowledge of Exponent (PKE) assumption [13] is secure under TOFR. As with many knowledge assumptions, this AGMOS proof does not need to rely on FPR or PDL. Intuitively this is because knowledge assumptions (typically) do not require that computing something is hard. We prove that the KZG polynomial commitment scheme [24] is extractable under FPR and TOFR. Crucially, extractability is only possible when the committer opens the polynomial at some point. Extractability based only on the commitment corresponds to SpurKE, as discussed earlier. Here, we see a combination of an extractability property and a computational hardness property (binding), which is why both assumptions are needed. In the full version, we show that Schnorr's signature [34] is tightly EUF-CMA secure under DL and TOFR. This one is mainly interesting because it shows another advantage of AGM/AGMOS, the ability to prove tight reductions for protocols, which are not known to be tightly secure in the standard or RO model.

Separating AGM and AGMOS. As demonstrated with SpurKE, unconditional security of knowledge assumptions in the AGM does not imply the same in the AGMOS (or in the standard model). In Sect. 6, we consider the TotalKE assumption that states that an adversary $\mathcal{A}$ on input $([1]_1, [1]_2)$ must know the discrete logarithm of each of its output group elements. We prove that if $\mathcal{A}$ outputs more than R elements either in $\mathbb{G}_1$ or $\mathbb{G}_2$, where R is the number of distinct (pairing-product) verification equations that define the assumption, then $\mathcal{A}$'s some output element must depend non-trivially on some $\mathsf{q}_{\kappa i}$. Thus, under the DL assumption, $\mathcal{A}$ does not know its discrete logarithm.

Interestingly, this result uses the Chevalley-Warning theorem on the number of roots a low-degree multivariate polynomial can have over finite fields. To our knowledge, this is the first use of the Chevalley-Warning theorem to prove impossibility results in the pairing-based setting. We hope our result inspires further use of this theorem in (pairing-based) cryptography.

When $R = 1$, we give a characterization of all TotalKE assumptions that can be proven secure in groups where the DL assumption holds. Since all TotalKE assumptions hold in the AGM, this separates the AGM and the AGMOS in all but a small number of TotalKE cases. Here, separation means the following: in the AGM, most of the TotalKE assumptions hold independently of the DL, while in the AGMOS, these assumptions do not hold if the DL holds.

In the GGMH and GGMOS, one is only concerned about Case A (Case X and Case Q cannot appear). However, Case A is handled similarly in GGMOS and AGMOS. Hence, we also obtain a separation between GGMH and GGMOS.

AGMOS with Uniform Oracle. We also present a more simplified version of AGMOS where the oracle responds with uniformly random group elements. This model is more restrictive (for example, admissible encodings do not produce uniform outputs) but has other benefits. In particular, it relies on a weaker version of TOFR. We prove that if we did allow programming, then that version of TOFR would be implied by the PDL assumption.

More Related Work. Rotem and Segev [33] formalized algebraic adversaries for decisional problems. We only focus on computational and knowledge problems in this work. Recently, Zhandry and Zhang et al. [38,39] have shown uninstantiability results for AGM. Although significant issues, we are not trying to solve these problems in the current work.

Many more works combine RO and AGM [19,21,25] to model idealized hash functions. However, the point of those works is not to strengthen AGM with oblivious sampling.

[27] was an early eprint that was never published. It contained a few mistakes. In particular, it considered an initial variant of AGMOS, but without the "TOFR" case. As such, it was incomplete and has been since withdrawn. [28] covers some of the results of [27] (like a new variant of Groth16 SNARK and its proof in [28] AGM model), but importantly it did not consider arbitrary oblivious sampling distributions and encodings. [28] got over the missing TOFR case by using the FPRO. The current paper corrects and improves on another set of techniques from [27]. It also does not use FPRO.

2   Preliminaries

Let $\mathbb{F} = \mathbb{Z}_p$. Vectors are, by default, column vectors. We write $(\boldsymbol{a}//\boldsymbol{b})$ to show concatenation of vectors $\boldsymbol{a}$ and $\boldsymbol{b}$. For a matrix $\boldsymbol{A}$, $\boldsymbol{A}_i$ denotes its ith row and $\boldsymbol{A}^{(j)}$

denotes its jth column. Let $\mathbf{0}_n$ be a zero vector of length n. $\mathbb{F}^{(\leq d)}[X_1, \ldots, X_k]$ denotes the set of k-variate polynomials of total degree $\leq d$ over $\mathbb{F}$. For $f \in \mathbb{F}[X_1, \ldots, X_m]$, $\deg(f)$ denotes the total degree of f and $\deg_{X_i}(f)$ denotes the individual degree of X_i in f. PPT denotes probabilistic polynomial-time; $\lambda \in \mathbb{N}$ is the security parameter. Let $\mathsf{negl}(\lambda)$ be an arbitrary negligible function and $\mathsf{poly}(\lambda)$ be an arbitrary polynomial function. A probability is overwhelming if it is greater $1 - \mathsf{negl}(\lambda)$ for some negligible function $\mathsf{negl}(\lambda)$. A random variable X has min-entropy k, denoted $\mathbf{H}_\infty(X) = k$, if $\max_x \Pr[X = x] = 2^{-k}$. A distribution is *well-spread* if it has super-logarithmic min-entropy, $\mathbf{H}_\infty(X) = \omega(\log \lambda)$; that is, $\max_x \Pr[X = x] = 2^{-\omega(\log \lambda)} = \lambda^{-\omega(1)} = \mathsf{negl}(\lambda)$. For an algorithm $\mathcal{A}$, $\mathrm{Im}(\mathcal{A})$ is the image of $\mathcal{A}$, i.e., the set of valid outputs of $\mathcal{A}$. $\mathsf{RND}_\lambda(\mathcal{A})$ denotes the random tape of $\mathcal{A}$ (for given λ), and $r \leftarrow_\$ \mathsf{RND}_\lambda(\mathcal{A})$ denotes the uniformly random choice of r from $\mathsf{RND}_\lambda(\mathcal{A})$. By $y \leftarrow \mathcal{A}(\mathrm{x}; r)$ we denote the fact that $\mathcal{A}$, given an input x and a randomizer r, outputs y. Let $[1, n]$ denote $\{1, 2, \ldots, n\}$.

Bilinear Groups. A bilinear group generator $\mathsf{Pgen}(1^\lambda)$ returns $(p, \mathbb{G}_1, \mathbb{G}_2, \mathbb{G}_T, \hat{e})$, where $\mathbb{G}_1$, $\mathbb{G}_2$, and $\mathbb{G}_T$ are three additive cyclic (thus, abelian) groups of prime order p, and $\hat{e} : \mathbb{G}_1 \times \mathbb{G}_2 \to \mathbb{G}_T$ is a non-degenerate efficiently computable bilinear pairing. Recall $\mathbb{F} = \mathbb{Z}_p$. The bilinear pairing is Type-3 (there is no efficient isomorphism between $\mathbb{G}_1$ and $\mathbb{G}_2$). We use the standard additive bracket notation, writing $[a]_\kappa$ to denote $a g_\kappa$ where $g_\kappa = [1]_\kappa$ is a fixed generator of $\mathbb{G}_\kappa$, $\kappa \in \{1, 2, T\}$. We denote $\hat{e}([a]_1, [b]_2)$ by $[a]_1 \bullet [b]_2$. We use the bracket notation together with matrix notation, e.g., $\boldsymbol{AB} = \boldsymbol{C}$ iff $[\boldsymbol{A}]_1 \bullet [\boldsymbol{B}]_2 = [\boldsymbol{C}]_T$.

Let $d_1(\lambda), d_2(\lambda) \in \mathsf{poly}(\lambda)$. Pgen is $(d_1(\lambda), d_2(\lambda))$-PDL *(Power Discrete Logarithm [26]) secure* if for any λ and non-uniform PPT $\mathcal{A}$, $\mathsf{Adv}^{\mathrm{pdl}}_{d_1, d_2, \mathsf{Pgen}, \mathcal{A}}(\lambda) :=$

$$\Pr\left[\mathcal{A}(\mathsf{p}, [(x^i)_{i=0}^{d_1}]_1, [(x^i)_{i=0}^{d_2}]_2) = x \mid \mathsf{p} \leftarrow \mathsf{Pgen}(1^\lambda), x \leftarrow_\$ \mathbb{F}\right] = \mathsf{negl}(\lambda) .$$

Algebraic Group Model. AGM [18] is a recent idealized model of computation. Essentially, in the AGM, one assumes that each non-uniform PPT algorithm $\mathcal{A}$ is algebraic in the following sense. Assume $\mathcal{A}$'s input includes $\mathrm{x}_\kappa = [\boldsymbol{x}_\kappa]_\kappa$ and no other elements from the group $\mathbb{G}_\kappa$. We assume that if $\mathcal{A}$ outputs a vector $[\mathrm{y}_\kappa]_\kappa$ of group elements, then $\mathcal{A}$ knows a matrix $\boldsymbol{\gamma}_\kappa$, such that $\mathrm{y}_\kappa = \boldsymbol{\gamma}_\kappa^\mathsf{T} \mathrm{x}_\kappa$. Note that the underlying protocol can be interactive. In such a case, the outputs of earlier rounds cannot depend on the inputs of the later rounds. One can formalize this by requiring specific entries of $\boldsymbol{\gamma}_\kappa$ are zero.

Fix Pgen. More precisely, a non-uniform PPT algorithm $\mathcal{A}$ is *algebraic* if there exists a non-uniform PPT extractor $\mathsf{Ext}_\mathcal{A}$, such that for any vector of group elements $\mathrm{x} = ([\mathrm{x}_1]_1, [\mathrm{x}_2]_2)$, $\mathsf{Adv}^{\mathrm{agm}}_{\mathsf{Pgen}, \mathcal{A}, \mathsf{Ext}_\mathcal{A}}(\lambda) :=$

$$\Pr\left[\begin{matrix} \mathrm{y}_1 \neq \boldsymbol{\gamma}_1^\mathsf{T} \mathrm{x}_1 \vee \\ \mathrm{y}_2 \neq \boldsymbol{\gamma}_2^\mathsf{T} \mathrm{x}_2 \end{matrix} \middle| \begin{matrix} \mathsf{p} \leftarrow_\$ \mathsf{Pgen}(1^\lambda); r \leftarrow_\$ \mathsf{RND}_\lambda(\mathcal{A}); \\ ([\mathrm{y}_1]_1, [\mathrm{y}_2]_2) \leftarrow \mathcal{A}(\mathsf{p}, \mathrm{x}; r); (\boldsymbol{\gamma}_1, \boldsymbol{\gamma}_2) \leftarrow \mathsf{Ext}_\mathcal{A}(\mathrm{x}; r) \end{matrix}\right] = \mathsf{negl}(\lambda) .$$

2.1 Admissible Encodings

A map $E : \mathcal{S} \to \mathcal{R}$ between finite sets is an *admissible encoding* [8] iff

Computable: E is PPT computable,

ϱ-regular: for any $y \in \mathcal{R}$, the preimage size $|E^{-1}(y)|$ of y under E is $\leq \varrho$ for a small constant ϱ ($\varrho = 4$ in [22]),

Sampleable: given y in the image of E, one can efficiently compute its full preimage $E^{-1}(y)$.

Boneh and Franklin [5] defined admissibility slightly differently; we follow the definition of [8]. Many admissible encodings are known. We discuss some of them in the full version of the paper.

Next, we present a claim of Icart [22] that computing the discrete logarithm of $E(s)$ is roughly as hard as computing the discrete logarithm of a uniformly random element of $\mathbb{G}$. (Icart [22] only gave a proof sketch.) We give a detailed proof of it in the full version. This result is significant since it shows that efficient oblivious sampling is possible in elliptic curve groups.

Another corollary of the sampleability is that one can efficiently recognize whether some $P \in \mathbb{G}_\kappa$ belongs to $\mathrm{Im}(E)$. Within the proof (the claim does not depend on it), we use the quantity $\psi_E := |\mathrm{Im}(E)|/|\mathbb{F}|$. As proven in [17], while Icart's admissible encoding has $\varrho = 4$, it has $\psi_E \approx 5/8 > 1/\varrho$.

Let D be a distribution over $\mathbb{G}_\kappa$ for some $\kappa \in \{1, 2\}$. We say that the discrete logarithm assumption over D holds in Pgen if, for any non-uniform PPT $\mathcal{A}$,

$$\mathsf{Adv}^{\mathrm{dl}}_{\mathsf{Pgen}, D, \mathcal{A}}(\lambda) := \Pr\left[\mathcal{A}(\mathsf{p}, [x]_\kappa) = x \mid \mathsf{p} \leftarrow \mathsf{Pgen}(1^\lambda), [x]_\kappa \leftarrow_{\!\$} D\right] = \mathsf{negl}(\lambda) \ .$$

In the following, $E(\mathbb{F})$ refers to the distribution $E(s)$ for $s \leftarrow_{\!\$} \mathbb{F}$ and $\mathbb{G}_\kappa$ is the uniform distribution over $\mathbb{G}_\kappa$.

Theorem 1. *Let $E : \mathbb{F} \to \mathbb{G}_\kappa$ be a ϱ-regular admissible encoding. For any non-uniform PPT $\mathcal{A}$, there exists a non-uniform PPT $\mathcal{C}$ such that $\mathsf{Adv}^{\mathrm{dl}}_{\mathsf{Pgen}, E(\mathbb{F}), \mathcal{A}}(\lambda) \leq \frac{\varrho|\mathbb{G}_\kappa|}{|\mathbb{F}|} \cdot \mathsf{Adv}^{\mathrm{dl}}_{\mathsf{Pgen}, \mathbb{G}_\kappa, \mathcal{C}}(\lambda).$*

3   AGM with Oblivious Sampling

Next, we define AGMOS, a more realistic variant of AGMOS that gives the adversary oblivious sampling oracles that return group elements without revealing their discrete logarithm. We define AGMOS in the pairing-based setting. However, it can be restricted to a group-based setting or generalized to a multilinear-map-based setting.

Sampling Oracles. Fix $\mathsf{p} \leftarrow \mathsf{Pgen}(1^\lambda)$. Let $\mathcal{EF}_{\mathsf{p}, \kappa}$ be a set of (polynomially many) functions $\mathbb{F} \to \mathbb{G}_\kappa$. Let $\mathcal{DF}_\mathsf{p}$ be a family of distributions over $\mathbb{F}$. We introduce two oracles $\mathcal{O}_1$ and $\mathcal{O}_2$, one for each group $\mathbb{G}_1$ and $\mathbb{G}_2$. To simplify notation, we denote $\mathcal{O} = (\mathcal{O}_1, \mathcal{O}_2)$. The ith query (E, D) to $\mathcal{O}_\kappa$ consists of a function $E \in \mathcal{EF}_{\mathsf{p}, \kappa}$ and a distribution $D \in \mathcal{DF}_\mathsf{p}$. The oracle samples a random field element $s_i \leftarrow_{\!\$} D$ and returns $[\mathsf{q}_{\kappa_i}]_\kappa \leftarrow E(s_i)$ and s_i.

We will denote the adversary's initial input (e.g., input from the challenger) in $\mathbb{G}_\kappa$ by $[\mathbf{x}_\kappa]_\kappa$. We assume $[\mathbf{x}_\kappa]_\kappa$ always includes $[1]_\kappa$. Let $\mathbf{x} = ([\mathbf{x}_1]_1, [\mathbf{x}_2]_2)$. In interactive protocols, $\mathbf{x}$ is updated sequentially (we will not formalize it). The adversary's view consists of all group elements that the adversary has seen up to the given moment. This includes the adversary's initial input, elements sent by other parties during the interaction, and oracle answers.

$$
\begin{array}{|l|}
\hline
\mathcal{O}_\kappa(E, D) \\
\hline
\text{if } E \notin \mathcal{EF}_{\mathsf{p},\kappa} \vee D \notin \mathcal{DF}_\mathsf{p} \text{ then return } \bot; \text{fi} \\
s \twoheadleftarrow D; [\mathsf{q}]_\kappa \leftarrow E(s); \text{return } ([\mathsf{q}]_\kappa, s); \\
\hline
\end{array}
$$

Fig. 1. The description of the oblivious sampling oracle $\mathcal{O}_\kappa$, where $\kappa \in \{1, 2\}$.

Definition. Let $\mathcal{O}$ be as above. We require that for any non-uniform PPT oracle adversary $\mathcal{A}^\mathcal{O}$, there exists a non-uniform PPT extractor $\mathsf{Ext}_\mathcal{A}^\mathcal{O}$, such that: if $\mathcal{A}^\mathcal{O}(\mathbf{x})$ outputs a vector of group elements $[\mathbf{y}]_\kappa$, on input $\mathbf{x} = ([\mathbf{x}_1]_1, [\mathbf{x}_2]_2)$, then with an overwhelming probability, $\mathsf{Ext}_\mathcal{A}^\mathcal{O}$ outputs field-element matrices $\boldsymbol{\gamma}$, $\boldsymbol{\delta}$, and $[\mathsf{q}_\kappa]_\kappa$ ($\mathcal{O}_\kappa$'s answer vector), such that

$$
\mathbf{y} = \boldsymbol{\gamma}^\mathsf{T} \mathbf{x}_\kappa + \boldsymbol{\delta}^\mathsf{T} \mathsf{q}_\kappa . \tag{1}
$$

Here, $\boldsymbol{\gamma}$ and $\boldsymbol{\delta}$ have the natural restriction that outputted group elements should only depend on the current state (group elements, including oracle answers, seen thus far) and not on the future information.

Definition 1 (AGMOS). *Let $\mathcal{EF} = \{\mathcal{EF}_{\mathsf{p},\kappa}\}$ be a collection of functions. Let $\mathcal{DF} = \{\mathcal{DF}_\mathsf{p}\}$ be a family of distributions. A non-uniform PPT algorithm $\mathcal{A}$ is an $(\mathcal{EF}, \mathcal{DF})$-AGMOS adversary for Pgen if there exists a non-uniform PPT extractor $\mathsf{Ext}_\mathcal{A}$, such that for any $\mathbf{x} = (\mathbf{x}_1, \mathbf{x}_2)$, $\mathsf{Adv}_{\mathsf{Pgen}, \mathcal{EF}, \mathcal{DF}, \mathcal{A}, \mathsf{Ext}_\mathcal{A}}^{\mathrm{agmos}}(\lambda) :=$*

$$
\Pr\left[
\begin{array}{l}
\mathbf{y}_1 \neq \boldsymbol{\gamma}_1^\mathsf{T} \mathbf{x}_1 + \boldsymbol{\delta}_1^\mathsf{T} \mathsf{q}_1 \vee \\
\mathbf{y}_2 \neq \boldsymbol{\gamma}_2^\mathsf{T} \mathbf{x}_2 + \boldsymbol{\delta}_2^\mathsf{T} \mathsf{q}_2
\end{array}
\middle|
\begin{array}{l}
\mathsf{p} \leftarrow \mathsf{Pgen}(1^\lambda); r \leftarrow \mathsf{RND}_\lambda(\mathcal{A}); \\
([\mathbf{y}_1]_1, [\mathbf{y}_2]_2) \twoheadleftarrow \mathcal{A}^\mathcal{O}(\mathsf{p}, \mathbf{x}; r); \\
(\boldsymbol{\gamma}_\kappa, \boldsymbol{\delta}_\kappa, [\mathsf{q}_\kappa]_\kappa)_{\kappa=1}^2 \leftarrow \mathsf{Ext}_\mathcal{A}^\mathcal{O}(\mathsf{p}, \mathbf{x}; r) :
\end{array}
\right] = \mathsf{negl}(\lambda) .
$$

$\mathcal{O}$ is the non-programmable oracle depicted in Fig. 1. Here, $[\mathsf{q}_\kappa]_\kappa$ is required to be the tuple of elements output by $\mathcal{O}_\kappa$. We denote by ql_κ the number of $\mathcal{O}_\kappa$ calls.

In Sect. 7, we present a simplified version of the model, where $\mathcal{O}_\kappa$ returns only uniformly random group elements.

Discussion. In modeling, we will stay agnostic to the concrete choice of the families $\mathcal{EF}$ and $\mathcal{DF}$, but as we will see, the security of the TOFR assumption will significantly depend on this choice. Functions that can be reasonably included in $\mathcal{EF}$ should satisfy two properties:

1. They should induce well-spread distributions from well-spread distributions. Thus, for each well-spread distribution D, the distribution defined by $E(s)$, where $s \leftarrow_\$ D$, should be well-spread.
2. It should be hard to compute the discrete logarithm of $E(s)$, knowing s, when s is sampled from a well-spread distribution.

For example, if $\mathcal{EF}$ includes scalar multiplication map $[\cdot]_1 : s \mapsto [s]_1$, which does not satisfy 2, the intuition that any party cannot know the discrete logarithm of $E(s)$ does not work anymore. Thus, including $[\cdot]_1$ to $\mathcal{EF}$ will not result in a meaningful model.

3.1   Further Formalization

Next, we will introduce more notation. We assume that the adversary's input is $\mathrm{x}(\boldsymbol{x}) = (\mathrm{x}_1(\boldsymbol{x}), \mathrm{x}_2(\boldsymbol{x}))$, where $\boldsymbol{x}$ is a vector of trapdoors not known to the adversary. For simplicity, the input always includes group generators $([1]_1, [1]_2)$. Here, $\boldsymbol{x}$ includes both CRS trapdoors and the trapdoors generated by other parties (e.g., the challenger) during the protocol. Let $\boldsymbol{X}$ be a vector of indeterminates corresponding to trapdoors $\boldsymbol{x}$ and thus $\mathrm{x}(\boldsymbol{X})$ is a vector of polynomials (or possibly rational functions, though we will not analyze this case) in $\boldsymbol{X}$.

Let $\mathbb{Q} = (\mathbb{Q}_1, \mathbb{Q}_2)$ be the vector of indeterminates corresponding to the concatenation of vectors of oracle outputs $[q_1]_1$ and $[q_2]_2$. As in Sect. 3, $[q_{\kappa i}]_\kappa = E_{\kappa i}(s_{\kappa i})$ for $s_{\kappa i} \leftarrow_\$ D_{\kappa i}$, where $E_{\kappa i} \in \mathcal{EF}_{\mathsf{p},\kappa}$ and $D_{\kappa i} \in \mathcal{DF}_{\mathsf{p}}$. We denote the adversary's outputs in $\mathbb{G}_\kappa$ as a vector $\mathrm{y}_\kappa(\boldsymbol{x}, q_\kappa)$ corresponding to a vector of polynomials $\mathrm{y}_\kappa(\boldsymbol{X}, \mathbb{Q}_\kappa)$.

In an AGMOS security proof, the proved assumption[3] is accompanied by one or more "verification polynomials" V_i. For example, on input $[1, x_1, x_2]_1$, the CDH-in-$\mathbb{G}_1$ adversary outputs $[\mathrm{y}]_1 = [\mathrm{y}(x_1, x_2, q_1)]_1$, where (due to the definition of the AGMOS) y is an adversarially chosen polynomial. The adversary is successful if $V(x_1, x_2, \mathrm{y}) = 0$, where $V(X_1, X_2, \mathrm{y}) := X_1 X_2 - \mathrm{y}(X_1, X_2, \mathbb{Q}_1)$. In the general case, the adversary is successful if each verification polynomial evaluates to 0 at the concrete point $(\boldsymbol{x}, \mathrm{y})$, where y depends on $(\boldsymbol{x}, q)$.

Formalizing Verification Equations. In the pairing-based setting, assumptions are defined by one (or more) verification polynomial equation in the challenger input and the adversary's output. Let us call this explicit verification polynomial V^{expl}.

In AGMOS (as it was in AGM) the challenger, upon queried the knowledge extractor, checks the polynomial equation, defined by replacing adversary's outputs in V^{expl} with their linear representation. Since the adversary's outputs y_κ are affine functions in $\mathbb{Q}_\kappa$, each addend in the linear representation of $[\mathrm{y}_{\kappa i}]_\kappa$ in

---

[3] One can prove the security of a concrete assumption or a concrete primitive/protocol. We will call all things we prove in the AGMOS assumptions instead of each time saying "an assumption or the security of a protocol".

$\mathbb{G}_\kappa$ must depend on at most one oracle answer. Therefore, we can define the *implicit verification polynomial* as

$$V(\boldsymbol{X}, \mathbb{Q}) := V^h(\boldsymbol{X}) + V^t(\boldsymbol{X}, \mathbb{Q}) \text{ for } V^h(\boldsymbol{X}) := \boldsymbol{\gamma}^\mathsf{T} \mathrm{p}^h, \ V^t(\boldsymbol{X}, \mathbb{Q}) := \boldsymbol{\delta}^\mathsf{T} \mathrm{p}^t \quad (2)$$

for vectors $\boldsymbol{\gamma}$ and $\boldsymbol{\delta}$ that can be computed from the outputs of the AGMOS extractor, and vectors p^h and p^t that depend on $\boldsymbol{X}$. The latter two equalities follow from Eq. (1).

Example 1 (CDH in $\mathbb{G}_1$). Recall that on input $[1, x_1, x_2]_1$, the CDH adversary outputs $[\mathrm{y}]_1 = [\mathrm{y}(x_1, x_2, \mathbb{q}_1)]_1$. The challenger checks if $[x_1]_1 \bullet x_2[1]_2 = [\mathrm{y}]_1 \bullet [1]_2$. Thus, the *explicit verification polynomial* is $V^{\mathsf{expl}}(\boldsymbol{X}, \mathrm{y}) = X_1 X_2 - \mathrm{y}$. Taking into account that $\mathrm{y} = \boldsymbol{\gamma}^\mathsf{T} \mathrm{x}_1(\boldsymbol{X}) + \boldsymbol{\delta}^\mathsf{T} \mathbb{Q}_1$ (and changing signs), we get that

$$V(\boldsymbol{X}, \mathbb{Q}) = \gamma_1 + \gamma_2 X_1 + \gamma_3 X_2 - X_1 X_2 + \sum \delta_i \mathbb{Q}_{1i} \ .$$

Thus, $\mathrm{p}^h = (1, X_1, X_2, X_1 X_2)^\mathsf{T}$, $\mathrm{p}^t = \mathbb{Q}_1$, $\boldsymbol{\gamma} = (\gamma_1, \gamma_2, \gamma_3, -1)^\mathsf{T}$, and $\boldsymbol{\delta} = (\delta_1, \dots)$.

Observe that $V^h(\boldsymbol{X})$ does not depend on $\mathbb{Q}$ while each term of $V^t(\boldsymbol{X}, \mathbb{Q})$ depends on either some indeterminate $\mathbb{Q}_{\kappa i}$ or some product $\mathbb{Q}_{1i} \mathbb{Q}_{2j}$. Since $\mathbb{Q}_{\kappa i}$ are indeterminates, it follows from $\boldsymbol{\delta} \neq \boldsymbol{0}$ that $V^t(\boldsymbol{X}, \mathbb{Q}) \neq 0$ and hence $V(\boldsymbol{X}, \mathbb{Q}) \neq 0$. If $\boldsymbol{\delta} = \boldsymbol{0}$, then the verification success does not depend on the answers of the oracles. In this case, one essentially has an AGM proof where one does not have to consider the additional details of AGMOS. On the other hand, if $\boldsymbol{\delta} \neq \boldsymbol{0}$ is non-zero, then the verification polynomial has at least one term, say $v\mathbb{Q}_{\kappa k}$ or $vX\mathbb{Q}_{\kappa k}$, with a non-zero coefficient v. This case is new to AGMOS and has to be analyzed separately.

4 New Assumptions

4.1 TOFR

According to Sect. 1.1, in Case Q of AGMOS proofs, we have to handle the case when $V^t(\boldsymbol{x}, \mathbb{Q}) \neq 0$ but (since the verifier accepts) $V(\boldsymbol{x}, \mathbb{q}) = 0$. As outlined in Sect. 1.1, there are several differences between the AGM and the AGMOS proofs. However, only Case Q requires us to rely on a new assumption.

Intuitively, TOFR is a simplified version of the tautological assumption in Case Q of AGMOS proofs. The latter states that it is difficult to output the coefficients of a polynomial V (see Eq. (2)), such that $V^t(\boldsymbol{x}, \mathbb{Q}) \neq 0$ but $V(\boldsymbol{x}, \mathbb{q}) = 0$. Recall that $V(\boldsymbol{X}, \mathbb{Q}) = \boldsymbol{\gamma}^\mathsf{T} \mathrm{x}^h + \boldsymbol{\delta}^\mathsf{T} \mathrm{x}^t$. In our AGMOS proofs, we let the TOFR reduction generate the input trapdoors $\boldsymbol{x}$. Thus, the input of a TOFR assumption is just $([1]_1, [1]_2)$; moreover, $\mathrm{x}^h = 1$, and γ is a single field element. Writing $\boldsymbol{v} := \binom{\gamma}{\delta}$, by Eq. (2), $V^t(\boldsymbol{X}, \mathbb{Q}) = \boldsymbol{\delta}^\mathsf{T} \mathrm{x}^t \neq 0$ iff $\boldsymbol{\delta} \neq \boldsymbol{0}$ and $V(\mathrm{x}, \mathbb{q}) = 0$ iff $\boldsymbol{v}^\mathsf{T} \mathrm{x} = 0$. Here, $\mathrm{x}^t = \begin{pmatrix} \mathbb{q}_1 \\ \mathbb{q}_2 \\ \mathbb{q}_1 \otimes \mathbb{q}_2 \end{pmatrix}$, and $\mathrm{x} = \binom{\mathrm{x}^h}{\mathrm{x}^t} = \binom{1}{\mathrm{x}^t}$. Clearly, $\boldsymbol{v}^\mathsf{T} \mathrm{x} = 0$ cannot hold if $\boldsymbol{\delta} = \boldsymbol{0}$ but $\gamma \neq 0$. Hence $\boldsymbol{\delta} \neq \boldsymbol{0}$ and $\boldsymbol{v}^\mathsf{T} \mathrm{x} = 0$ is equivalent to $\boldsymbol{v} \neq \boldsymbol{0}$ and $\boldsymbol{v}^\mathsf{T} \mathrm{x} = 0$. We get the following assumption.

Definition 2 (TOFR). *Let $\mathcal{EF}$ be some family of function and $\mathcal{DF}$ a family of distributions. We say that* Pgen *is* $(\mathcal{EF}, \mathcal{DF})$-*TOFR (Tensor Oracle FindRep) secure if for any non-uniform PPT $\mathcal{A}$, $\mathsf{Adv}^{\mathrm{tofr}}_{\mathsf{Pgen},\mathcal{EF},\mathcal{DF},\mathcal{A}}(\lambda) :=$*

$$\Pr\left[\boldsymbol{v} \neq \boldsymbol{0} \wedge \boldsymbol{v}^{\mathsf{T}} \cdot \begin{pmatrix} 1 \\ \mathsf{q}_1 \\ \mathsf{q}_2 \\ \mathsf{q}_1 \otimes \mathsf{q}_2 \end{pmatrix} = 0 \,\middle|\, \mathsf{p} \leftarrow \mathsf{Pgen}(1^\lambda); \boldsymbol{v} \leftarrow \mathcal{A}^{\mathcal{O}}(\mathsf{p}) \right] = \mathsf{negl}(\lambda) \ .$$

Here, $\mathcal{O}$, q_1, and q_2 are as in Definition 1.

Discussion. In the full version, we prove that TOFR is secure in a variant of GGM where the adversary can call an oracle that samples group elements from well-spread distributions, i.e., has more power compared to the GGM.

TOFR is related to the following well-known assumption. Let $d(\lambda) \in \mathsf{poly}(\lambda)$. Pgen is d-*FindRep (Find Representation, [7])* secure in $\mathbb{G}_\kappa$ if for any non-uniform PPT $\mathcal{A}$, $\mathsf{Adv}^{\mathrm{findrep}}_{d,\mathsf{Pgen},\kappa,\mathcal{A}}(\lambda) := \Pr\left[\boldsymbol{v} \neq \boldsymbol{0} \wedge \boldsymbol{v}^{\mathsf{T}}\boldsymbol{x} = 0 \mid \mathsf{p} \leftarrow \mathsf{Pgen}(1^\lambda); \boldsymbol{x} \leftarrow_\$ \mathbb{F}^d; \boldsymbol{v} \leftarrow \mathcal{A}(\mathsf{p},[\boldsymbol{x}]_\kappa) \right] = \mathsf{negl}(\lambda)$.

FindRep can be tightly reduced to the discrete logarithm assumption. For the sake of completeness, we reprove this well-known result.

Lemma 1 (*[7]*). *Let $d \geq 1$. For any non-uniform PPT $\mathcal{A}$, there exist a non-uniform PPT $\mathcal{B}$ such that $\mathsf{Adv}^{\mathrm{findrep}}_{d,\mathsf{Pgen},\kappa,\mathcal{A}}(\lambda) \leq \mathsf{Adv}^{\mathrm{dl}}_{\mathsf{Pgen},\kappa,\mathcal{B}}(\lambda) + 1/|\mathbb{F}|$.*

Proof. The discrete logarithm adversary $\mathcal{B}$ embeds its challenge $[y]_\kappa$ to a Find-Rep challenge $[\boldsymbol{x}]_\kappa$ by sampling $\boldsymbol{r}, \boldsymbol{s} \leftarrow_\$ \mathbb{F}^d$ and then setting $[\boldsymbol{x}]_\kappa \leftarrow \boldsymbol{r}[1]_\kappa + \boldsymbol{s}[y]_\kappa$. If $\mathcal{A}$ succeeds, i.e., returns a non-zero representation $\boldsymbol{v}$, such that $\boldsymbol{v}^{\mathsf{T}}\boldsymbol{x} \neq 0$, then $\mathcal{B}$ returns $y' \leftarrow -\boldsymbol{v}^{\mathsf{T}}\boldsymbol{r}/\boldsymbol{v}^{\mathsf{T}}\boldsymbol{s}$. Note that $[\boldsymbol{x}]_\kappa$ is uniformly random over $\mathbb{G}^d_\kappa$ and $\boldsymbol{s}$ is independent of $\boldsymbol{x}$ and thus of $\boldsymbol{v}$. Thus, if $\boldsymbol{v}$ is non-zero, $\Pr[\boldsymbol{v}^{\mathsf{T}}\boldsymbol{s} = 0] = 1/|\mathbb{F}|$. Then, $0 = \boldsymbol{v}^{\mathsf{T}}\boldsymbol{x} = \boldsymbol{v}^{\mathsf{T}}(\boldsymbol{r} + \boldsymbol{s}y)$. Solving for y, we get $y = -\boldsymbol{v}^{\mathsf{T}}\boldsymbol{r}/\boldsymbol{v}^{\mathsf{T}}\boldsymbol{s}$. Thus, if $\mathcal{A}$ succeeds, then $\mathcal{B}$ works correctly, except with the probability $1/|\mathbb{F}|$. $\square$

There are two essential differences between FindRep and TOFR. Firstly, instead of getting $[\mathsf{q}_{\kappa i}]_\kappa$ as inputs, a TOFR adversary $\mathcal{A}$ can query the oracle to obtain $[\mathsf{q}_{\kappa i}]_\kappa$ adaptively. Secondly, TOFR oracle is non-programmable. However, even if we ignore the second issue, the reduction to DL is non-obvious. We could modify the described reduction so that r_i and s_i are sampled on the fly. However, before each query, the adversary can adaptively choose a new distribution for the oracle answer. It is unclear how to choose r_i and s_i to make each $[\mathsf{q}_{\kappa i}]_\kappa$ to be from the correct distribution. We propose a more restrictive model in Sect. 7, where the oracle returns only uniformly random group elements. In that case, relying on a weaker version of TOFR is possible. We prove that if we allow programming, this weaker version of TOFR is equivalent to $(1,1)$-PDL.

4.2 FPR

Recall a typical step in an AGM/AGMOS security proof. According to Eq. (2), the verification polynomial has form $V(\boldsymbol{X}, \mathbb{Q}) = V^h(\boldsymbol{X}) + V^t(\boldsymbol{X}, \mathbb{Q})$. We know that $V(\boldsymbol{x}, \mathsf{q}) = 0$ for (uniformly random) $\boldsymbol{x}$ and oracle answers q. In one of the proof branches (that we call Case X), we have $V^t(\boldsymbol{x}, \mathbb{Q}) = 0$ but $V(\boldsymbol{X}, \mathbb{Q}) \neq 0$. One then constructs a reduction to PDL. We automate this step by defining a tautological assumption for a typical Case X and then relate it to PDL.

Definition 3 (FPR). *Let* $m \geq 1$, $d_1, d_2, d_T, d_g \geq 0$ *and* $\boldsymbol{d} = (d_1, d_2, d_T, d_g)$. *Let* $\boldsymbol{X} = (X_1, \ldots, X_m)$. *We say that* Pgen *is* $(\boldsymbol{d}, m)$-FPR *(Find Polynomial Representation) secure if for any non-uniform PPT adversary* $\mathcal{A}$, $\mathsf{Adv}^{\mathrm{fpr}}_{\mathsf{Pgen}, \boldsymbol{d}, m, \mathcal{A}}(\lambda) :=$

$$
\Pr \left[
\begin{array}{l}
g(\boldsymbol{X}) \in \mathbb{F}^{(\leq d_g)}[X_1, \ldots, X_m] \wedge \\
g(\boldsymbol{X}) \neq 0 \wedge g(\boldsymbol{x}) = 0
\end{array}
\middle|
\begin{array}{l}
\mathsf{p} \leftarrow \mathsf{Pgen}(1^\lambda); \boldsymbol{x} \leftarrow_\$ \mathbb{F}^m; \\
g(\boldsymbol{X}) \leftarrow \mathcal{A}^{\mathcal{O}^{\mathrm{fpr}}_{\boldsymbol{d}, m}(\boldsymbol{x}, \cdot)}(\mathsf{p})
\end{array}
\right] = \mathsf{negl}(\lambda) \ ,
$$

$\mathcal{B}(\mathsf{p}, [(x^i)^{d_1}_{i=0}]_1, [(x^i)^{d_2}_{i=0}]_2)$

$i^* \leftarrow_\$ [1, m]; \alpha_1, \ldots, \alpha_{i^*-1}, \alpha_{i^*+1}, \ldots, \alpha_m \leftarrow_\$ \mathbb{F}^{m-1}$;
Define implicitly $\alpha_{i^*} = x$;
$g(\boldsymbol{X}) \leftarrow \mathcal{A}^{\mathcal{O}^{\mathrm{fpr}}(\boldsymbol{x}, \cdot)}(\mathsf{p})$;
Define $\mathsf{seq}(g) = \{h_1, \ldots, h_m\}$;
$v(X) := h_{i^*}(X, \alpha_{i^*+1}, \ldots, \alpha_m)$; if $v(X) = 0$ then return $\bot$; fi
Find the set of roots S of $v(X)$;
return $s \in S$ such that either $s \cdot [1]_1 = [x]_1$ or $s \cdot [1]_2 = [x]_2$;

Fig. 2. The FPR reduction $\mathcal{B}$ to PDL assumption in Theorem 2.

where the oracle $\mathcal{O}^{\mathrm{fpr}}_{\boldsymbol{d}, m}(\boldsymbol{x}, \cdot)$ *takes an input* (κ, f). *If* $\kappa \in \{1, 2, T\}$ *and* $f \in \mathbb{F}[\boldsymbol{X}]$ *such that* $\deg_{X_i}(f) \leq d_\kappa$ *for all* i, *it returns* $[f(\boldsymbol{x})]_\kappa$. *Otherwise, it returns* $\bot$. *We will omit the subscript for simplicity and write* $\mathcal{O}^{\mathrm{fpr}}(\boldsymbol{x}, \cdot)$.

We use techniques from [32,33] to show that FPR reduces to PDL. Let us borrow some notation from [32]. For a non-zero polynomial $f \in \mathbb{F}[X_1, \ldots, X_m]$, define $h_i \in \mathbb{F}[X_i, \ldots, X_m]$ as follows: (1) $h_1 = f$, (2) for $i \in [2, m]$: If $h_{i-1} = 0$, then $h_i := 0$. Otherwise, write $h_{i-1} = \sum_{j=0}^d g_j(X_i, \ldots X_m) X_{i-1}^j$ as a polynomial in $(\mathbb{F}[X_i, \ldots, X_m])[X_{i-1}]$; here, $d = \deg_{X_{i-1}} h_{i-1}$. Let j^* be the minimal index, such that g_{j^*} is a non-zero polynomial over $\mathbb{F}$. Define $h_i := g_{j^*}$. If no such index j^* exists, set $h_i = 0$. Define $\mathsf{seq}(f) := \{h_1, \ldots, h_m\}$.

Proposition 1 (Lemma 5.5 of *[32]*). *Let* $f \in \mathbb{F}[X_1, \ldots, X_m]$ *be non-zero. Let* $\mathsf{seq}(f) = \{h_1, \ldots, h_m\}$ *be as above. Then: (1) For each* $i \in [1, m]$, $h_i \neq 0$. *(2) For each root* $\boldsymbol{\alpha} = (\alpha_1, \ldots, \alpha_m) \in \mathbb{F}^m$ *of* $f(\boldsymbol{X})$, *there exists* $i_0 \in [1, m]$ *such that* $v(X_{i_0}) := h_{i_0}(X_{i_0}, \alpha_{i_0+1}, \ldots, \alpha_m)$ *is a non-zero polynomial and* $v(\alpha_{i_0}) = 0$.

We reduce FPR to PDL in the standard model (not in the AGMOS).

Theorem 2. *Let* $m \geq 1$ *and* $d_1, d_2, d_g \geq 0$ *with* $d_g = \mathsf{poly}(\lambda)$. *Let* $\boldsymbol{d} = (d_1, d_2, d_1 + d_2, d_g)$. *If the* (d_1, d_2)-PDL *assumption holds, then the* $(\boldsymbol{d}, m)$-FPR *assumption holds.*

Proof. Let $\mathcal{A}$ be a non-uniform PPT $(\boldsymbol{d}, m)$-FPR adversary. In Fig. 1, we depict a (d_1, d_2)-PDL adversary $\mathcal{B}$. $\mathcal{B}$ gets $(\mathsf{p}, [(x^i)_{i=0}^{d_1}]_1, [(x^i)_{i=0}^{d_2}]_2)$ as an input. $\mathcal{B}$ samples $\boldsymbol{\alpha} \leftarrow_\$ \mathbb{F}^m$, except that for a randomly chosen position i^*, it implicitly sets $\alpha_{i^*} \leftarrow x$. If $\mathcal{A}$ queries (κ, f) for some κ and f, $\mathcal{B}$ answers with $[f(\boldsymbol{x})]_\kappa \leftarrow \sum_{i=0}^{d_i} f_i(\alpha_1, \ldots, \alpha_{i^*-1}, \alpha_{i^*+1}, \ldots, \alpha_m)[x^i]_\kappa$, where f_i is defined by $f(\boldsymbol{X}) = \sum_{i=0}^{d_i} f_i(X_1, \ldots, X_{i^*-1}, X_{i^*+1}, \ldots, X_m) X_{i^*}^i$ and $d_i = \deg_{X_i} f$. In case of $\mathbb{G}_T$ queries, $\mathcal{B}$ can compute $[1, \ldots, x^{d_1+d_2}]_T$ by pairing input elements.

If $\mathcal{A}$ succeeds, then g is a non-zero multivariate polynomial satisfying $g(\boldsymbol{x}) = 0$. By Proposition 1, there exists $i_0 \in [1, m]$ such that $v(X_{i_0}) := h_{i_0}(X_{i_0}, \alpha_{i_0+1}, \ldots, \alpha_m)$ is a non-zero *univariate* polynomial. Suppose that $i_0 = i^*$, which happens with probability $1/m$. Using Proposition 1 again, $v(X)$ is a non-zero polynomial satisfying $v(x) = 0$. Thus, $\mathcal{B}$ succeeds in computing x. Here, $d_g = \mathsf{poly}(\lambda)$ since it might otherwise take superpolynomial time to find the roots. Thus, $\mathsf{Adv}^{\mathsf{fpr}}_{\mathsf{Pgen}, \boldsymbol{d}, m, \mathcal{A}}(\lambda) \leq m \cdot \mathsf{Adv}^{\mathsf{pdl}}_{d_1, d_2, \mathsf{Pgen}, \mathcal{B}}(\lambda)$.   □

Note that $(\boldsymbol{d}, m)$-FPR is secure even when $d_T > d_1 + d_2$. Let us denote $d_\Delta := d_T - (d_1 + d_2)$. Then $(\boldsymbol{d}, m)$-FPR reduces trivially to $(\boldsymbol{d}', m)$-FPR, where $\boldsymbol{d}' = (d_1 + d_\Delta, d_2, d_T, d_g)$. By Theorem 2, $(\boldsymbol{d}', m)$-FPR (and thus also $(\boldsymbol{d}, m)$-FPR) reduces to $(d_1 + d_\Delta, d_2)$-PDL.

In the full version, we construct another reduction to PDL, which sometimes gives a tighter reduction to PDL.

5   Example AGMOS Security Proofs

We give an explicit security proof for the Uber assumption and state the results for the PKE assumption and the KZG commitment. Complete proofs of the latter two are available in the full version (in addition to the security proof for Schnorr's signature).

In the rest of this section, we assume that $\mathcal{EF}$ is some family of encoding and $\mathcal{DF}$ is some family of distributions for which the $(\mathcal{EF}, \mathcal{DF})$-TOFR holds.

5.1   The Split Flexible Uber Assumption

The Flexible Uber assumption [4,6] is a family that covers many commonly used computational assumptions. Instead of proving that each such assumption is secure, proving the Flexible Uber assumption makes sense. However, a Flexible Uber adversary outputs a $\mathbb{G}_T$ element. Since $\mathbb{G}_T$ (a subgroup of the multiplicative group of a finite field) is not a generic group [23], we prefer not to handle adversaries who output $\mathbb{G}_T$ elements.[4] Instead, we prove the AGM security of a slightly weaker assumption, Split Flexible Uber.

For a vector of m-variate polynomials $\mathcal{R} = (f_1, \ldots, f_r)$ over $\mathbb{F}$ and $\boldsymbol{x} \in \mathbb{F}^m$, we denote $\mathcal{R}(\boldsymbol{x}) := (f_1(\boldsymbol{x}), \ldots, f_r(\boldsymbol{x}))$.

---

[4] One can extend AGMOS to allow arguing about adversarial outputs from $\mathbb{G}_T$, but it is just our preference not to do so. See [23] for a discussion.

Definition 4 (Split Flexible Uber Assumption). *Let* $m \geq 1$ *be an integer and* $\boldsymbol{X} = (X_1, \ldots, X_m)$. *Let* $\mathsf{p} \leftarrow \mathsf{Pgen}(1^\lambda)$. *Let* $\mathcal{R}_1 = (f_1, \ldots, f_{r_1})$, $\mathcal{R}_2 = (g_1, \ldots, g_{r_2})$, *and* $\mathcal{R}_T = (h_1, \ldots, h_{r_T})$ *be three tuples of* m-*variate polynomials from* $\mathbb{F}[\boldsymbol{X}]$, *where* $f_1 = g_1 = h_1 = 1$. *The* $(\mathcal{R}_1, \mathcal{R}_2, \mathcal{R}_T, d_t)$-*computational Split Uber assumption for* Pgen, *states that for any non-uniform PPT adversary* $\mathcal{A}$, $\mathsf{Adv}^{\mathrm{sfuber}}_{\mathsf{Pgen}, \mathcal{R}_1, \mathcal{R}_2, \mathcal{R}_T, \mathcal{A}}(\lambda) :=$

$$
\Pr \left[\begin{array}{l} t \in \mathbb{F}[\boldsymbol{X}] \wedge \deg t \leq d_t \wedge \\ t(\boldsymbol{X}) \notin \mathrm{span}\{f_i g_j\} \cup \{h_k\} \wedge \\ [y_1]_1 \bullet [y_2]_2 = [t(\boldsymbol{x})]_T \end{array} \middle| \begin{array}{l} \mathsf{p} \leftarrow \mathsf{Pgen}(1^\lambda); \boldsymbol{x} \leftarrow_\$ \mathbb{F}^m; \\ \mathsf{ck} \leftarrow ([\mathcal{R}_1(\boldsymbol{x})]_1, [\mathcal{R}_2(\boldsymbol{x})]_2, [\mathcal{R}_T(\boldsymbol{x})]_T); \\ (t, [y_1]_1, [y_2]_2) \leftarrow \mathcal{A}(\mathsf{ck}) \end{array} \right] = \mathsf{negl}(\lambda) \ .
$$

We say t is *non-trivial* if $t \in \mathbb{F}[\boldsymbol{X}]$, $\deg t \leq d_t$, and $t(\boldsymbol{X}) \notin \mathrm{span}\{f_i g_j\} \cup \{h_k\}$.

In the Flexible Uber assumption, the adversary outputs $(t, [z]_T)$ and the requirement is that $[z]_T = [t(\boldsymbol{x})]_T$. Given $(t, [y_1]_1, [y_2]_2)$ output by a Split Flexible Uber adversary, one can construct a Flexible Uber adversary that outputs t together with $[z]_T \leftarrow [y_1]_1 \bullet [y_2]_2$. Thus, if one can break the Split Flexible Uber assumption, one can break the Flexible Uber assumption.

It is easy to see that the Split Flexible Uber assumption implies (among many other assumptions) the CDH assumption in $\mathbb{G}_1$. One sets $\mathcal{R}_1 = \{f_1, f_2\}$ where $f_1(X_1) = X_1$ and $f_2(X_2) = X_2$ (and $\mathcal{R}_2 = \mathcal{R}_T = \emptyset$). This means the adversary gets an input $[x_1, x_2]_1$ for $x_1, x_2 \leftarrow_\$ \mathbb{F}$. To break the CDH assumption, the adversary should output $[y]_1 = [x_1 x_2]_1$, which is computationally hard since otherwise, the uber adversary could output $[y]_1, [1]_2$ and $t(X_1, X_2) = X_1 \cdot X_2$.

Let us introduce some additional notation for Theorem 3. For $\kappa \in \{1, 2, T\}$, let d_κ be such that for any $f \in \mathcal{R}_\kappa$ and any $i \in [1, m]$, $\deg_{X_i}(f) \leq d_\kappa$. Let $\boldsymbol{d} = (d_1, d_2, d_T, d_g)$, where $d_g = \max(d_t, m \cdot (d_1 + d_2))$.

Theorem 3. *If the* $(\boldsymbol{d}, m)$-*FPR and* $(\mathcal{EF}, \mathcal{DF})$-*TOFR assumptions hold, then the* $(\mathcal{R}_1, \mathcal{R}_2, \mathcal{R}_T, d_t)$-*computational Split Flexible Uber assumption holds in the AGMOS.*

Proof. Let $\mathcal{A}$ be a non-uniform PPT Split Flexible Uber assumption AGMOS adversary that with some non-negligible probability outputs t, $[y_1]_1$, and $[y_2]_2$, such that t is non-trivial and $y_1 y_2 = t(\boldsymbol{x})$. Since $\mathcal{A}$ is an AGMOS adversary, there exists an extractor $\overline{\mathsf{Ext}}_\mathcal{A}$ that extracts $\boldsymbol{\gamma}, \boldsymbol{\delta}$, such that $[y_1]_1 = \boldsymbol{\gamma}_1^\mathsf{T}[\boldsymbol{f}(\boldsymbol{x})]_1 + \boldsymbol{\delta}_1^\mathsf{T}[\mathsf{q}_1]_1$ and $[y_2]_2 = \boldsymbol{\gamma}_2^\mathsf{T}[\boldsymbol{g}(\boldsymbol{x})]_2 + \boldsymbol{\delta}_2^\mathsf{T}[\mathsf{q}_2]_2$, where $[\mathsf{q}_\kappa]_\kappa$ is the tuple of sampling oracle answers in $\mathbb{G}_\kappa$. Let ql_κ be the number of oracle queries in $\mathbb{G}_\kappa$ for $\kappa \in \{1, 2\}$. Define

$$
Y_1(\boldsymbol{X}, \mathbb{Q}_1) = \sum_{f_i \in \mathcal{R}_1} \gamma_{1i} f_i(\boldsymbol{X}) + \sum \delta_{1i} \mathbb{Q}_{1i} \ ,
$$

$$
Y_2(\boldsymbol{X}, \mathbb{Q}_2) = \sum_{g_i \in \mathcal{R}_2} \gamma_{2i} g_i(\boldsymbol{X}) + \sum \delta_{2i} \mathbb{Q}_{2i} \ .
$$

Thus, $[y_1]_1 = [Y_1(\boldsymbol{x}, \mathsf{q}_1)]_1$ and $[y_2]_2 = [Y_2(\boldsymbol{x}, \mathsf{q}_2)]_2$. Next, assume that both $\mathcal{A}$ and $\overline{\mathsf{Ext}}_\mathcal{A}$ succeeded. The verifier checks that $[V(\boldsymbol{x}, \mathsf{q})]_T = [0]_T$, where for $s_1(\boldsymbol{X}) := \sum_{i=1}^{r_1} \gamma_{1i} f_i(\boldsymbol{X})$ and $s_2(\boldsymbol{X}) := \sum_{i=1}^{r_2} \gamma_{2i} g_i(\boldsymbol{X})$,

$$
\begin{aligned}
V(\boldsymbol{X}, \mathbb{Q}) &:= Y_1(\boldsymbol{X}, \mathbb{Q}_1) Y_2(\boldsymbol{X}, \mathbb{Q}_2) - t(\boldsymbol{X}) \\
&= (s_1(\boldsymbol{X}) + \sum \delta_{1i} \mathbb{Q}_{1i})(s_2(\boldsymbol{X}) + \sum \delta_{2i} \mathbb{Q}_{2i}) - t(\boldsymbol{X}) \quad (3) \\
&= V^h(\boldsymbol{X}) + V^t(\boldsymbol{X}, \mathbb{Q}) \ ,
\end{aligned}
$$

where $V^h(\boldsymbol{X}) = s_1(\boldsymbol{X})s_2(\boldsymbol{X}) - t(\boldsymbol{X})$ and $V^t(\boldsymbol{X}, \mathbb{Q}) = s_1(\boldsymbol{X})\sum_i \delta_{2i}\mathbb{Q}_{2i} + s_2(\boldsymbol{X})\sum_i \delta_{1i}\mathbb{Q}_{1i} + \sum_{i,j} \delta_{1i}\delta_{2j}\mathbb{Q}_{1i}\mathbb{Q}_{2j}$. Observe that $\deg s_\kappa \leq m \cdot d_\kappa$ for $\kappa \in \{1, 2\}$. Note that $V^t = 0$ in an AGM proof.

Let us now consider the three AGMOS cases.

$\mathcal{B}_{\mathsf{fpr}}^{\mathcal{O}^{\mathsf{fpr}}(\boldsymbol{x}, \cdot),\, \mathcal{A}^{\mathcal{O}}}(\mathsf{p})$ $\mathcal{B}_{\mathsf{tofr}}^{\mathcal{A}^{\mathcal{O}}}(\mathsf{p})$

For $\kappa \in \{1, 2, T\}$, $q \in \mathcal{R}_\kappa$: $[q(\boldsymbol{x})]_\kappa \leftarrow \mathcal{O}^{\mathsf{fpr}}(\boldsymbol{x}, (\iota, q));$ $\boldsymbol{x} \leftarrow_{\$} \mathbb{F}^m;$
$\mathsf{ck} \leftarrow ([\mathcal{R}_1(\boldsymbol{x})]_1, [\mathcal{R}_2(\boldsymbol{x})]_2, [\mathcal{R}_T(\boldsymbol{x})]_T)$;
$r \leftarrow \mathsf{RND}_\lambda(\mathcal{A}); (t, [y_1]_1, [y_2]_2) \leftarrow \mathcal{A}^{\mathcal{O}}(\mathsf{p}, \mathsf{ck}; r)$;
$(\boldsymbol{\gamma}_\kappa, \boldsymbol{\delta}_\kappa, [\mathsf{q}_\kappa]_\kappa)_{\kappa=1}^2 \leftarrow \overline{\mathsf{Ext}}_{\mathcal{A}}^{\mathcal{O}}(\mathsf{p}, \mathsf{ck}; r);$ // e.g., $[y_1]_1 = \boldsymbol{\gamma}_1^{\mathsf{T}}[\boldsymbol{f}(\boldsymbol{x})]_1 + \boldsymbol{\delta}_1^{\mathsf{T}}[\mathsf{q}_1]_1;$
if $\overline{\mathsf{Ext}}_{\mathcal{A}}$ failed then return $\perp;$ fi
Define V, V^h, V^t as in Eq. (3);
if $V(\boldsymbol{X}, \mathbb{Q}) \neq 0 \wedge V^t(\boldsymbol{X}, \mathbb{Q}) = 0$ then return $V^h(\boldsymbol{X});$ fi
if $V^t(\boldsymbol{X}, \mathbb{Q}) \neq 0 \wedge V^t(\boldsymbol{x}, \mathbb{Q}) = 0$ then
    $s_1(\boldsymbol{X}) \leftarrow \sum \gamma_{1i}f_i(\boldsymbol{X}); s_2(\boldsymbol{X}) \leftarrow \sum \gamma_{2i}g_i(\boldsymbol{X});$
    find $s_\kappa(\boldsymbol{X})\delta_{\kappa i^*} \neq 0;$ return $s_\kappa(\boldsymbol{X})\delta_{\kappa i^*};$ fi
if $V^t(\boldsymbol{x},\ ) \neq 0$ then return $v = (V^h(\boldsymbol{x}) // s_2(\boldsymbol{X})\delta_1 // s_1(\boldsymbol{X})\delta_2 // \delta_1 \otimes \delta_2);$
return $\perp;$

Fig. 3. Flexible Uber assumption: the FPR adversary $\mathcal{B}_{\mathsf{fpr}}$ and the TOFR adversary $\mathcal{B}_{\mathsf{tofr}}$ in Theorem 3. The differences are dashed boxed ($\mathcal{B}_{\mathsf{fpr}}$) or dotted boxed ($\mathcal{B}_{\mathsf{tofr}}$).

Case A: $V(\boldsymbol{X}, \mathbb{Q}) = 0$. Then also $V^h(\boldsymbol{X}) = s_1(\boldsymbol{X})s_2(\boldsymbol{X}) - t(\boldsymbol{X}) = 0$. However, $s_1(\boldsymbol{X})$ is in the span of f_i and $s_2(\boldsymbol{X})$ is in the span of g_i. Contradiction to the assumption $t \notin \mathrm{span}\{f_i g_j\}$. Thus, this case never materializes.

Case X: $V(\boldsymbol{X}, \mathbb{Q}) \neq 0$ and $V^t(\boldsymbol{x}, \mathbb{Q}) = 0$. In Fig. 3, we define a $(\boldsymbol{d}, m)$-FPR adversary $\mathcal{B}_{\mathsf{fpr}}$. Recall that $\mathcal{B}_{\mathsf{fpr}}$ has access to an oracle $\mathcal{O}^{\mathsf{fpr}}(\boldsymbol{x}, \cdot)$, where $\boldsymbol{x} \leftarrow_{\$} \mathbb{F}^m$ is a trapdoor vector sampled by the challenger. $\mathcal{B}_{\mathsf{fpr}}$ queries $[r(\boldsymbol{x})]_\kappa \leftarrow \mathcal{O}^{\mathsf{fpr}}(\boldsymbol{x}, (\kappa, r))$ for various $\kappa \in \{1, 2, T\}$ and $r(\boldsymbol{X}) \in \mathcal{R}_\kappa$ to construct $\mathsf{ck} \leftarrow ([\mathcal{R}_1(\boldsymbol{x})]_1, [\mathcal{R}_2(\boldsymbol{x})]_2, [\mathcal{R}_T(\boldsymbol{x})]_T)$. Note that $\mathcal{O}^{\mathsf{fpr}}(\boldsymbol{x}, \cdot)$ will accept those queries since $\deg_{X_i}(r) \leq d_\kappa$ for all $i \in [1, m]$. Then, $\mathcal{B}_{\mathsf{fpr}}$ will run $\mathcal{A}$ and $\overline{\mathsf{Ext}}_{\mathcal{A}}$ on input ck. $\mathcal{B}_{\mathsf{fpr}}$ aborts if $\overline{\mathsf{Ext}}_{\mathcal{A}}$ fails. Otherwise, $\mathcal{B}_{\mathsf{fpr}}$ learns polynomials defined Eq. (3).

Next, $\mathcal{B}_{\mathsf{fpr}}$ follows one of the two strategies. Case X.1: if $V^t(\boldsymbol{X}, \mathbb{Q}) = 0$, then $V(\boldsymbol{X}, \mathbb{Q}) = V^h(\boldsymbol{X}) \neq 0$, but $0 = V(\boldsymbol{x}, \mathsf{q}) = V^h(\boldsymbol{x})$. Since $\deg V^h \leq \max(m \cdot (d_1 + d_2), d_t) = d_g$, then $\mathcal{B}_{\mathsf{fpr}}$ can output V^h to break $(\boldsymbol{d}, m)$-FPR.

Case X.2: if $V^t(\boldsymbol{X}, \mathbb{Q}) \neq 0 \wedge V^t(\boldsymbol{x}, \mathbb{Q}) = 0$ (this subcase does not occur in AGM proofs), at least one of the coefficients of some $\mathbb{Q}_{\kappa i}$ or $\mathbb{Q}_{1i}\mathbb{Q}_{2j}$ is a non-zero polynomial that evaluates to 0 at $\boldsymbol{X} = \boldsymbol{x}$. Since the coefficient of each $\mathbb{Q}_{1i}\mathbb{Q}_{2j}$ does not depend on $\boldsymbol{X}$, it must be that for some κ and i^*, $p(\boldsymbol{X}) := s_\kappa(\boldsymbol{X})\delta_{\kappa i^*}$ is a non-zero polynomial that has $\boldsymbol{x}$ as a root. Observe that $\deg p(\boldsymbol{X}) \leq \max(m \cdot d_1, m \cdot d_2) \leq d_g$. Thus, $\mathcal{B}_{\mathsf{fpr}}$ can output $p(\boldsymbol{X})$ to break (d, m)-FPR.   Case Q: $V^t(x, \mathbb{Q}) \neq 0$. (This case does not occur in AGM.) In Fig. 3, we depict a TOFR adversary $\mathcal{B}_{\text{tofr}}$. $\mathcal{B}_{\text{tofr}}$ samples x to construct $\mathsf{ck} \leftarrow ([\mathcal{R}_1(x)]_1, [\mathcal{R}_2(x)]_2, [\mathcal{R}_T(x)]_T)$. It runs $\mathcal{A}$ to obtain $(t, [y_1]_1, [y_2]_2)$, such that t is a non-trivial polynomial and $[y_1]_1 \bullet [y_2]_2 = [t(x)]_T$ and then uses $\overline{\mathsf{Ext}}_{\mathcal{A}}$ to extract field elements γ, δ such that $[y_1]_1 = \gamma_1^{\mathsf{T}}[f(x)]_1 + \delta_1^{\mathsf{T}}[\mathsf{q}_1]_1$ and $[y_2]_2 = \gamma_2^{\mathsf{T}}[f(x)]_2 + \delta_2^{\mathsf{T}}[\mathsf{q}_2]_2$. If the verifier accepts, $0 = V(x, \mathsf{q}) = V^h(x) + s_2(x) \sum \delta_{1i}\mathsf{q}_{1i} + s_1(x) \sum \delta_{2i}\mathsf{q}_{2i} + \sum \delta_{1i}\delta_{2j}\mathsf{q}_{1i}\mathsf{q}_{2j}$ (see Eq. (3)). Thus, $\mathcal{B}$ outputs $v = (V^h(x) // s_2(x)\delta_1 // s_1(x)\delta_2 // \delta_1 \otimes \delta_2)$. Since $V^t(x, \mathbb{Q}) \neq 0$, then $v \neq 0$ and $\mathcal{B}$ breaks the TOFR assumption.

Thus, either the algebraic extractor fails, or, if it succeeds, we get one of the above cases. Hence, $\mathsf{Adv}^{\text{sfuber}}_{\mathsf{Pgen}, \mathcal{R}_1, \mathcal{R}_2, \mathcal{R}_T, d_t, \mathcal{A}}(\lambda) \leq \mathsf{Adv}^{\text{agmos}}_{\mathsf{Pgen}, \mathcal{EF}, \mathcal{DF}, \mathcal{A}, \mathsf{Ext}_{\mathcal{A}}}(\lambda) + \mathsf{Adv}^{\text{fpr}}_{\mathsf{Pgen}, d, m, \mathcal{B}_{\text{fpr}}}(\lambda) + \mathsf{Adv}^{\text{tofr}}_{\mathsf{Pgen}, \mathcal{EF}, \mathcal{DF}, \mathcal{B}_{\text{tofr}}}(\lambda)$. This concludes the proof.   □

5.2   The PKE Assumption

Let us recall the Power Knowledge of Exponent (PKE) assumption [13].

Definition 5. *The (asymmetric) $d(\lambda)$-PKE assumption holds for* Pgen, *if for every non-uniform PPT adversary $\mathcal{A}$, there exists a non-uniform PPT extractor* $\mathsf{Ext}_{\mathcal{A}}$, *such that* $\mathsf{Adv}^{\text{pke}}_{d, \mathsf{Pgen}, \mathcal{A}, \mathsf{Ext}_{\mathcal{A}}}(\lambda) :=$

$$\Pr \left[\begin{array}{l} y_1 = y_2 \wedge \\ y_1 \neq \sum_{i=0}^{d} \gamma_i x^i \end{array} \middle| \begin{array}{l} \mathsf{p} \leftarrow \mathsf{Pgen}(1^\lambda); x \leftarrow_{\$} \mathbb{F}; r \leftarrow \mathsf{RND}_\lambda(\mathcal{A}); \\ ([y_1]_1, [y_2]_2) \leftarrow \mathcal{A}(\mathsf{p}, ([x^i]_1, [x^i]_2)_{i=0}^{d}; r); \\ (\gamma_i)_{i=0}^{d} \leftarrow \mathsf{Ext}_{\mathcal{A}}(\mathsf{p}, ([x^i]_1, [x^i]_2)_{i=0}^{d}; r) \end{array} \right] = \mathsf{negl}(\lambda) \ .$$

Our AGMOS analysis shows that the PKE stays secure even if the adversary can sample new group elements from non-uniform distributions. We are not aware of any prior result of this type. See the full version for the proof.

Theorem 4 (*d-PKE*). *If the $(\mathcal{EF}, \mathcal{DF})$-TOFR assumption holds, then $d(\lambda)$-PKE holds in the AGMOS.*

5.3   Extractability of the KZG Polynomial Commitment Scheme

In a polynomial commitment scheme (PCS, [24]), the committer first commits to a polynomial $f(X)$ and then opens it to an evaluation $f(\alpha)$ at some point α chosen by the verifier. In the current paper, we focus on the non-randomized PCSs (like the first PCS construction in [24]) since such PCSs are used to construct many efficient SNARKs.

More formally, a polynomial commitment scheme over a field $\mathbb{F}$ is a tuple of PPT algorithms $\mathsf{PC} = (\mathsf{KC}, , , \mathsf{open}, \mathsf{V})$, such that:

(1) $\mathsf{KC} : (1^\lambda, d) \mapsto (\mathsf{ck}, \mathsf{td})$ is a randomized commitment key generation algorithm, where d is the maximum degree of committed polynomials, ck is a commitment key and td is a trapdoor.
(2) $\mathsf{com} : (\mathsf{ck}, f(X)) \mapsto (\mathsf{c}, \mathsf{d})$ is a deterministic commitment algorithm that, given a polynomial $f(X) \in \mathbb{F}[X]$ of degree $\leq d$, outputs commitment information c and decommitment information d.

(3) open : $(\mathsf{ck}, \mathbb{c}, \alpha, \mathbb{d}) \mapsto (f(\alpha), \pi)$ is a deterministic opening algorithm that, given an evaluation point α, outputs $f(\alpha)$ together with opening proof π.

(4) V : $(\mathsf{ck}, \mathbb{c}, \alpha, \eta, \pi) \mapsto 0/1$ is a deterministic verification algorithm that, given candidate value η for $f(\alpha)$, outputs 1 if $\eta = f(\alpha)$ and 0, otherwise.

Definition 6. *A polynomial commitment scheme* PC *is extractable for* Pgen, *if for any* $d = \mathsf{poly}(\lambda)$ *and every non-uniform PPT adversary* $\mathcal{A}$, *there exists a non-uniform PPT extractor* $\mathsf{Ext}_{\mathcal{A}}$, *such that* $\mathsf{Adv}^{\mathsf{ext}}_{\mathsf{Pgen}, \mathsf{PC}, d, \mathcal{A}, \mathsf{Ext}_{\mathcal{A}}}(\lambda) :=$

$$\Pr \left[\begin{array}{l} \mathsf{V}(\mathsf{ck}, \mathbb{c}, \alpha, \eta, \pi) = 1 \wedge \\ (\mathbb{c} \neq, (f(X)) \vee \\ \deg f > d \vee f(\alpha) \neq \eta) \end{array} \middle| \begin{array}{l} \mathsf{p} \leftarrow \mathsf{Pgen}(1^\lambda); (\mathsf{ck}, \mathsf{td}) \leftarrow \mathsf{KC}(\mathsf{p}, d); \\ r \leftarrow \mathsf{RND}_\lambda(\mathcal{A}); (\mathbb{c}, \alpha, \eta, \pi) \leftarrow \mathcal{A}(\mathsf{p}, \mathsf{ck}; r); \\ f(X) \leftarrow \mathsf{Ext}_{\mathcal{A}}(\mathsf{p}, \mathsf{ck}; r) \end{array} \right] = \mathsf{negl}(\lambda) \ .$$

$\mathsf{KC}(1^\lambda, d)$: output $\mathsf{p} \leftarrow \mathsf{Pgen}(1^\lambda)$, $x \leftarrow_\$ \mathbb{Z}_p^*$, $\mathsf{ck} = ([(x^i)_{i=0}^d]_1, [1, x]_2)$.
$\mathsf{com}(\mathsf{ck}, f(X))$: $[\mathbb{c}]_1 \leftarrow [f(x)]_1 = \sum_{j=0}^d f_j [x^j]_1$; return $([\mathbb{c}]_1, \mathbb{d} = f(X))$.
$\mathsf{open}(\mathsf{ck}, [\mathbb{c}]_1, \alpha, \mathbb{d} = f(X))$: $\pi(X) \leftarrow (f(X) - f(\alpha))/(X - \alpha)$; $[\pi(x)]_1 \leftarrow$
$\sum_{j=0}^{n-1} \pi_j [x^j]_1$; return $(\eta = f(\alpha), [\pi(x)]_1)$;
$\mathsf{V}(\mathsf{ck}, [\mathbb{c}]_1, \alpha, \eta, [\pi(x)]_1)$: check $[\mathbb{c} - \eta]_1 \bullet [1]_2 = [\pi(x)]_1 \bullet [x - \alpha]_2$.

Fig. 4. The KZG polynomial commitment scheme.

The KZG PCS. Let $f(X)$ be a polynomial of degree $\leq d$. In Fig. 4, we depict the famous Kate-Zaverucha-Goldberg (KZG, [24]) polynomial commitment scheme. Its security is based on the fact that $(X - \alpha) \mid (f(X) - \eta) \Leftrightarrow f(\alpha) = \eta$. Next, we prove in AGMOS that KZG is extractable. Since KZG extractability is a knowledge assumption, one could expect that it is sufficient to assume TOFR just as in the proof of PKE. However, if the adversary can efficiently compute x (i.e., PDL does not hold), then one can compute an accepting opening $[\pi]_1 = [\mathbb{c} - \eta]_1/(x - \alpha)$ for any values η and α. Thus, similarly to the AGM proofs of KZG extractability, one has to assume FPR (or PDL). The extractability of a PCS combines both an extractability property (extracting $f(X)$) and a computational hardness property (it is hard to find (α, η) such that $f(\alpha) \neq \eta$).

Remark 1. In the case of KZG, the stronger extractability notion, where the adversary who only produces $\mathbb{c}$ must know f is not secure in the AGMOS (assuming DL is secure); essentially, this notion is equivalent to SpurKE. This is the flaw in say [11,20], mentioned in the introduction. While we leave the study of the security of such SNARKs for future work (it might be that they are secure but need a different security proof), we emphasize that one should not use the stronger extractability notion.

Below, we consider $\boldsymbol{d} = (d, 1, d + 1, d_g)$. See the full version for the proof.

Theorem 5 (Extractability of KZG). *If the* $(\boldsymbol{d}, m)$-FPR *and* $(\mathcal{EF}, \mathcal{DF})$-TOFR *assumptions hold, then KZG is extractable in the AGMOS.*

6   AGM-AGMOS Separation

Next, we will explain why some knowledge assumptions that are secure in the AGM, by definition, are not secure in the AGMOS (assuming DL is hard) while others might be secure. We will study general (publicly-verifiable) knowledge assumptions with some fixed verification equations. For the sake of simplicity, we will somewhat restrict the latter class. In particular, we only study the strongest possible knowledge assumption (the "TotalKE"). Later results of this section also only hold when the adversary's input is $([1]_1, [1]_2)$ (i.e., it does not depend on any trapdoors; this means that outputting a linear representation is the same as outputting discrete logarithms), but we will start with the general case.

We will extensively rely on the notation introduced in Sect. 3.1. We will also introduce matrix-vector notation to clarify the exposition; while this notation is only used in the current section, we find the tensor notation to be more cumbersome in this concrete case. Let $\mathsf{il}_\kappa / \mathsf{ol}_\kappa$ be the length of the input/output in $\mathbb{G}_\kappa$ and ql_κ be the number of oracle queries in $\mathbb{G}_\kappa$. A publicly-verifiable pairing-product verification polynomial can be written as $V^{\mathsf{expl}}(\mathbf{x}, \mathbf{y}) = \left(\begin{smallmatrix} \mathbf{x}_1 \\ \mathbf{y}_1 \end{smallmatrix}\right)^{\mathsf{T}} M \left(\begin{smallmatrix} \mathbf{x}_2 \\ \mathbf{y}_2 \end{smallmatrix}\right)$ for some public matrix M. Let $M = \left(\begin{smallmatrix} M_{11} & M_{12} \\ M_{21} & M_{22} \end{smallmatrix}\right)$ for submatrices M_{ij}. Here, say, $M_{11} \in \mathbb{F}^{\mathsf{il}_1 \times \mathsf{il}_2}$ and $M_{22} \in \mathbb{F}^{\mathsf{ol}_1 \times \mathsf{ol}_2}$. The AGMOS extractor extracts the matrices $\gamma_\kappa \in \mathbb{F}^{\mathsf{ol}_\kappa \times \mathsf{il}_\kappa}$ and $\delta_\kappa \in \mathbb{F}^{\mathsf{ol}_\kappa \times \mathsf{ql}_\kappa}$ from $[\mathbf{y}_1]_1$ and $[\mathbf{y}_2]_2$.

Let Γ and Δ be indeterminates corresponding to γ and δ. Similarly to γ_κ and δ_κ, we think of Γ_κ and Δ_κ as $(\mathsf{ol}_\kappa \times \mathsf{il}_\kappa$ and $\mathsf{ol}_\kappa \times \mathsf{ql}_\kappa)$ matrices. Let $P_\kappa(\Gamma, \Delta) := \left(\begin{smallmatrix} I_{\mathsf{il}_\kappa} & 0_{\mathsf{il}_\kappa \times \mathsf{ql}_\kappa} \\ \Gamma_\kappa & \Delta_\kappa \end{smallmatrix}\right)$ be the matrix so that $\left(\begin{smallmatrix} \mathbf{x}_\kappa \\ \mathbf{y}_\kappa \end{smallmatrix}\right) = P_\kappa(\gamma, \delta) \left(\begin{smallmatrix} \mathbf{x}_\kappa \\ \mathbf{q}_\kappa \end{smallmatrix}\right)$. Define

$$N(\Gamma, \Delta) := P_1^{\mathsf{T}}(\Gamma, \Delta) M P_2(\Gamma, \Delta)$$

$$= \left(\begin{matrix} I_{\mathsf{il}_1} & 0_{\mathsf{il}_1 \times \mathsf{ql}_1} \\ \Gamma_1 \in \mathbb{F}^{\mathsf{ol}_1 \times \mathsf{il}_1} & \Delta_1 \end{matrix}\right)^{\mathsf{T}} \cdot \left(\begin{matrix} M_{11} & M_{12} \\ M_{21} & M_{22} \end{matrix}\right) \cdot \left(\begin{matrix} I_{\mathsf{il}_2} & 0_{\mathsf{il}_2 \times \mathsf{ql}_2} \\ \Gamma_2 & \Delta_2 \end{matrix}\right)$$

$$= \left(\begin{matrix} M_{11} + \Gamma_1^{\mathsf{T}} M_{21} + (M_{12} + \Gamma_1^{\mathsf{T}} M_{22})\Gamma_2 & (M_{12} + \Gamma_1^{\mathsf{T}} M_{22})\Delta_2 \\ \Delta_1^{\mathsf{T}}(M_{21} + M_{22}\Gamma_2) & \Delta_1^{\mathsf{T}} M_{22}\Delta_2 \end{matrix}\right) .$$

Note that while M corresponds to V^{expl}, N corresponds to V. Let

$$f_M(\Gamma, \Delta) = \left(\begin{matrix} 0_{\mathsf{il}_1 \times \mathsf{il}_2} & (M_{12} + \Gamma_1^{\mathsf{T}} M_{22})\Delta_2 \\ \Delta_1^{\mathsf{T}}(M_{21} + M_{22}\Gamma_2) & \Delta_1^{\mathsf{T}} M_{22}\Delta_2 \end{matrix}\right)$$

be equal to $N(\Gamma, \Delta)$, except that its top left submatrix is $\mathbf{0}$. We rewrite $f_M = \mathbf{0}$ as the following equivalent system of polynomial equations in $(\Gamma_1, \Gamma_2, \Delta_1, \Delta_2)$:

$$(M_{12} + \Gamma_1^{\mathsf{T}} M_{22})\Delta_2 = 0_{\mathsf{il}_1 \times \mathsf{ql}_2}, \quad \Delta_1^{\mathsf{T}}(M_{21} + M_{22}\Gamma_2) = 0_{\mathsf{ql}_1 \times \mathsf{il}_2},$$
$$\Delta_1^{\mathsf{T}} M_{22}\Delta_2 = 0_{\mathsf{ql}_1 \times \mathsf{ql}_2}. \tag{4}$$

Clearly, for a fixed $\Gamma = \gamma$, Eq. (4) is a system of $\mathsf{il}_1\mathsf{ql}_2 + \mathsf{il}_2\mathsf{ql}_1 + \mathsf{ql}_1\mathsf{ql}_2$ polynomial equations, where the sum of the total degrees of all polynomials is at most $\mathsf{il}_1\mathsf{ql}_2 + \mathsf{il}_2\mathsf{ql}_1 + 2\mathsf{ql}_1\mathsf{ql}_2$. Moreover, the system Eq. (4) has $\mathsf{ol}_1\mathsf{ql}_1 + \mathsf{ol}_2\mathsf{ql}_2$ indeterminates. Note also that $V^t(\boldsymbol{X}, \mathbb{Q}) = \left(\begin{smallmatrix} \mathbf{x}_1(\boldsymbol{X}) \\ \mathbb{Q}_1 \end{smallmatrix}\right)^{\mathsf{T}} f_M(\gamma, \delta) \left(\begin{smallmatrix} \mathbf{x}_2(\boldsymbol{X}) \\ \mathbb{Q}_2 \end{smallmatrix}\right)$.

Analysis of the TotalKE assumption. Let us assume $il_1 = il_2 = 1$, in particular, there are no input indeterminates $\boldsymbol{X}$. We will leave the general case for future work. Let TotalKE be the parameterized assumption that states the following: if the adversary, on input $([1]_1, [1]_2)$, outputs the specified number of group elements in $\mathbb{G}_1$ and $\mathbb{G}_2$ and the specified verification equation holds, then one can extract a linear representation of any output element with respect to the adversary's input elements. Since $il_1 = il_2 = 1$, the nontrivial linear relation is just the discrete logarithm of the output element.

Definition 7. *Let* $il_1 = il_2 = 1$, $ol_1, ol_2 \geq 1$, *and* $R \geq 1$. *Let* $\boldsymbol{M}[i] \in \mathbb{F}^{(ol_1 + il_1) \times (ol_2 + il_2)}$ *for* $i \in [1, R]$. *Let* $V_i(\boldsymbol{y}) = \left(\begin{smallmatrix} 1 \\ y_1 \end{smallmatrix}\right)^{\mathsf{T}} \boldsymbol{M}[i] \left(\begin{smallmatrix} 1 \\ y_2 \end{smallmatrix}\right)$. *The* $(ol_1, ol_2, \{V_i\}_{i=1}^R)$-*TotalKE assumption holds for* Pgen, *if for every non-uniform PPT adversary* $\mathcal{A}$, *there exists a non-uniform PPT extractor* $\mathsf{Ext}_{\mathcal{A}}$, *such that* $\mathsf{Adv}^{\mathrm{totalke}}_{\mathsf{Pgen}, ol_1, ol_2, \{V_i\}_{i=1}^R, \mathcal{A}, \mathsf{Ext}_{\mathcal{A}}}(\lambda) :=$

$$
\Pr \left[
\begin{array}{l}
\boldsymbol{y} \in \mathbb{F}^{ol_1} \wedge \boldsymbol{z} \in \mathbb{F}^{ol_2} \wedge \\
\forall i \in [1, R]. V_i(\boldsymbol{y}, \boldsymbol{z}) = 0 \wedge \\
(\boldsymbol{y}, \boldsymbol{z}) \neq (\boldsymbol{y}^*, \boldsymbol{z}^*)
\end{array}
\middle|
\begin{array}{l}
\mathsf{p} \leftarrow \mathsf{Pgen}(1^\lambda); r \leftarrow \mathsf{RND}_\lambda(\mathcal{A}); \\
([\boldsymbol{y}]_1, [\boldsymbol{z}]_2) \leftarrow \mathcal{A}(\mathsf{p}, [1]_1, [1]_2; r); \\
(\boldsymbol{y}^*, \boldsymbol{z}^*) \leftarrow \mathsf{Ext}_{\mathcal{A}}(\mathsf{p}, [1]_1, [1]_2; r)
\end{array}
\right] = \mathsf{negl}(\lambda) .
$$

We emphasize that for any choice of il_κ and ol_κ, TotalKE is secure in the AGM. The simplest TotalKE-type assumption is the SpurKE assumption, mentioned in the introduction: if $\mathcal{A}(\mathsf{p}, [1]_1)$ outputs $[x]_1$, then one can extract x. SpurKE holds in the AGM, but it is clearly false when one can sample obliviously. Thus, it is also false in the AGMOS, and in the standard model due to the existence of admissible encodings Sect. 2.1.

We are interested in for which choices of $(ol_1, ol_2, \{V_i\})$, the TotalKE assumption is secure in AGMOS, assuming both TOFR and DL holds.

Theorem 6. *Fix* $(p, \mathbb{G}_1, \mathbb{G}_2, \mathbb{G}_T, \hat{e})$ *such that DL is hard in each group. Fix* $il_1 = il_2 = 1$ *and* $ql_1, ql_2, ol_1, ol_2 \geq 1$. *If* $\boldsymbol{f}_{M[1]}(\boldsymbol{\Gamma}, \boldsymbol{\Delta}) = \ldots = \boldsymbol{f}_{M[R]}(\boldsymbol{\Gamma}, \boldsymbol{\Delta}) = \boldsymbol{0}$ *has a common solution* $(\boldsymbol{\gamma}, \boldsymbol{\delta})$ *such that* $\boldsymbol{\delta} \neq \boldsymbol{0}$, *then the* $(ol_1, ol_2, \{V_i\})$-*TotalKE assumption is* not *secure in the AGMOS. If this holds, we say* $\boldsymbol{M}$ *is TotalKE-incompatible. Otherwise, it is TotalKE-compatible.*

As a first step, we show that it is sufficient to consider one oracle query in both groups.

Lemma 2. *Let* $\boldsymbol{M} \in \mathbb{F}^{n \times m}$, *where* $n = il_1 + ol_1$ *and* $m = il_2 + ol_2$. *If the system in Eq. (4) has a solution* $(\boldsymbol{\gamma}_\kappa, \boldsymbol{\delta}_\kappa \in \mathbb{F}^{ol_\kappa \times ql_\kappa})_{\kappa=1}^2$ *for some* $ql_1, ql_2 > 1$ *with nonzero* $\boldsymbol{\delta}_1 \neq \boldsymbol{0}$, *then it has a non-zero solution* $(\boldsymbol{\gamma}_\kappa, \boldsymbol{\delta}'_\kappa \in \mathbb{F}^{ol_\kappa})_{\kappa=1}^2$ *with* $\boldsymbol{\delta}'_2 = \boldsymbol{0}_{ol_2}$. *A dual claim holds for* $\boldsymbol{\delta}_2 \neq \boldsymbol{0}$.

Proof. For any $\boldsymbol{M} \in \mathbb{F}^{n \times m}$, let Eq. (4) hold for some $\boldsymbol{\gamma}_1, \boldsymbol{\gamma}_2$, and $\boldsymbol{\delta}_1 \in \mathbb{F}^{ol_1 \times ql_1}$, $\boldsymbol{\delta}_2 \in \mathbb{F}^{ol_2 \times ql_2}$, such that $\boldsymbol{\delta}_\kappa \neq \boldsymbol{0}$ for some $\kappa \in \{1, 2\}$. W.l.o.g., assume $\kappa = 1$. Then, $\boldsymbol{\delta}_1^{(k)} \neq \boldsymbol{0}$ for some k. Then, clearly, Eq. (4) has a non-zero solution when setting $ql_1 = ql_2 = 1$: the solution is $(\boldsymbol{\gamma}_\kappa, \boldsymbol{\delta}'_\kappa)_{\kappa=1}^2$ with $\boldsymbol{\delta}'_1 = \boldsymbol{\delta}_1^{(k)}$, $\boldsymbol{\delta}'_2 = \boldsymbol{0}_{ol_2}$. □

Thus, in the rest of this subsection, we assume $\mathsf{ql}_\kappa = 1$; in particular, $\boldsymbol{\delta}_\kappa \in \mathbb{F}^{\mathsf{ol}_\kappa}$. For the same reason, Theorem 6 can be equivalently stated for $\mathsf{ql}_1 = \mathsf{ql}_2 = 1$.

Assume the system $\boldsymbol{f}_M(\boldsymbol{\Gamma}, \boldsymbol{\Delta}) = \mathbf{0}$ has a common solution $(\boldsymbol{\gamma}, \boldsymbol{\delta})$ where $\boldsymbol{\delta}$ is non-zero. We emphasize that $\boldsymbol{\delta}$ has different semantics than $\boldsymbol{\gamma}$, and, under TOFR and DL, recovering the discrete logarithm of $\boldsymbol{\delta}$ is hard for any party. Thus, the TotalKE extractor can only recover the discrete logarithms in the case $\boldsymbol{\delta} = \mathbf{0}$.

If such a non-zero solution exists, then from the fact that the verifier accepts, it does not follow that one can extract the discrete logarithms of all adversary's outputs. Thus, on our hypothesis, the TotalKE assumption is secure iff for any $\boldsymbol{\Gamma} = \boldsymbol{\gamma}$, $\boldsymbol{f}_M(\boldsymbol{\Gamma}, \boldsymbol{\Delta}) = \mathbf{0}$ has only a zero solution in $\boldsymbol{\Delta}$.

6.1   Classification of TotalKE-Compatible Matrices

We will use the following classic result.

Proposition 2 (Chevalley-Warning theorem). *Let $\mathbb{F}_q$ be a finite field of size q and characteristic p. If r polynomials $f_j \in \mathbb{F}[t_1, \dots, t_n]$ satisfy $\sum \deg f_j < n$, then the number of common roots of f_j is divisible by p.*

TotalKE-Incompatible Cases. Let $\deg \boldsymbol{f}_{M[i]}$ be the sum of the degrees of all $\mathsf{il}_1\mathsf{ql}_2 + \mathsf{il}_2\mathsf{ql}_1 + 2\mathsf{ql}_1\mathsf{ql}_2$ polynomials involved in the system $\boldsymbol{f}_{M[i]} = \mathbf{0}$, where we consider only $\boldsymbol{\Delta}$ as the indeterminates. For a fixed R, let $\deg \boldsymbol{f} := \sum_{i \le R} \deg \boldsymbol{f}_{M[i]}$. Lemma 3 separates AGM and AGMOS. We leave the proof for the full version.

Lemma 3. *Let $\mathsf{il}_1, \mathsf{il}_2 = 1$ and $\mathsf{ql}_1 = \mathsf{ql}_2 = 1$. For $i \in [1, R]$, fix any $M[i]$ and the corresponding verification equation V_i. If either $\mathsf{ol}_1 > R$ or $\mathsf{ol}_2 > R$, then there exists a non-zero common solution with $\boldsymbol{\delta} \ne \mathbf{0}$. Thus, if DL holds, $(\mathsf{ol}_1, \mathsf{ol}_2, \{V_i\}_{i=1}^R)$-TotalKE is not secure in the AGMOS for any $M[i]$.*

TotalKE-Compatible Cases. Let $R = 1$. It follows from Lemma 3 that (if DL holds) TotalKE does not hold unless $\mathsf{ol}_1 \le 1$ and $\mathsf{ol}_2 = 0$, or $\mathsf{ol}_1 + \mathsf{ol}_2 \le 2$ and $\mathsf{ol}_2 \ge 1$. That is, either $\mathsf{ol}_1 = 1$ and $\mathsf{ol}_2 = 0$ (the case $\mathsf{ol}_1 = \mathsf{ol}_2 = 0$ is vacuous) or $\mathsf{ol}_1 = 1$ and $\mathsf{ol}_2 = 1$. (The case $\mathsf{ol}_1 = 0$ and $\mathsf{ol}_2 = 1$ is dual.)

In the rest of this section, we will give a list of all TotalKE-compatible matrices in the case of a single verification equation. We will leave the case of $\mathsf{il}_1 > 1$ or $\mathsf{il}_2 > 1$ or $R > 1$ for future work.

Lemma 4. *Let $\mathsf{il}_\kappa = \mathsf{ql}_\kappa = 1$ and $R = 1$ (thus there is a single matrix M). Assume that DL holds.*

1. *Let $\mathsf{ol}_1 = 1$ and $\mathsf{ol}_2 = 0$. Then M is TotalKE-compatible iff $M_{21} \ne 0$. Thus, the only possibly secure TotalKE assumption involves verification equation $[y]_1 \bullet [1]_2 = M_{11}[1]_1 \bullet [1]_2$ for M_{11} chosen by the verifier.*
2. *Let $\mathsf{ol}_1 = 1$ and $\mathsf{ol}_2 = 1$. Then M is TotalKE-compatible iff $M_{22} = 0$ and either $M_{21} \ne 0$ or $M_{12} \ne 0$. Thus, the only possibly secure TotalKE assumption involves verification equation $M_{12}[y]_1 \bullet [1]_2 + [1]_1 \bullet M_{21}[z]_2 = -M_{11}[1]_1 \bullet [1]_2$ for non-zero M_{12} or M_{21}, where the verifier chooses M_{12}, M_{21}, and M_{11}.*

Proof. We recall from Theorem 6 that M is TotalKE-incompatible iff $f(\boldsymbol{\Gamma}, \boldsymbol{\Delta}) = 0$ has a solution $(\boldsymbol{\gamma}, \boldsymbol{\delta})$ such that $\boldsymbol{\delta}$ is non-zero.

(Item 1). Since $\mathsf{il}_1 = \mathsf{ol}_1 = \mathsf{ql}_1 = 1$, $\boldsymbol{\gamma}_1 = \gamma_1 \in \mathbb{F}^{\mathsf{ol}_1 \times \mathsf{il}_1} = \mathbb{F}$ and $\boldsymbol{\delta}_1 = \delta_1 \in \mathbb{F}^{\mathsf{ol}_1 \times \mathsf{ql}_1} = \mathbb{F}$. Since $\mathsf{ol}_2 = 0$, there is no $\boldsymbol{\delta}_2$ and thus the system Eq. (4) consists of only one polynomial, $f(\boldsymbol{\Gamma}, \boldsymbol{\Delta}) = \Delta_1 M_{21}$. Thus, $f(\boldsymbol{\gamma}, \boldsymbol{\delta}) = 0$ iff $\delta_1 M_{21} = 0$. This has a non-zero solution $\delta_1 \neq 0$ iff $M_{21} = 0$. Then, $M = \left(\begin{smallmatrix} M_{11} \\ 0 \end{smallmatrix}\right)$ for some $M_{11} \in \mathbb{F}$. The claim follows.

(Item 2). Then $\boldsymbol{\gamma}_1$, $\boldsymbol{\gamma}_2$, $\boldsymbol{\delta}_1$, and $\boldsymbol{\delta}_2$ have dimension one. In this case, the equation $f(\boldsymbol{\gamma}, \boldsymbol{\delta}) = 0$ in Eq. (4) simplifies to

$$\delta_2(\gamma_1 M_{22} + M_{12}) = 0 \ , \qquad \delta_1(\gamma_2 M_{22} + M_{21}) = 0 \ , \qquad \delta_1 \delta_2 M_{22} = 0 \ .$$

For this to have a non-zero solution in (δ_1, δ_2), we need that, say, $\delta_1 \neq 0$. From the second equation, we then get $M_{21} = -\gamma_2 M_{22}$. Hence, there are only zero solutions iff $M_{22} = 0$ and $M_{21} \neq 0$ (that is, $M = \left(\begin{smallmatrix} M_{11} & M_{12} \\ M_{21} & 0 \end{smallmatrix}\right)$ for $M_{21} \neq 0$); in every other case, one can choose γ_2 that makes the equation hold. Choosing $\delta_2 = 0$ means no other restrictions exist.

The case $\delta_2 \neq 0$ is dual. The claim follows since $\left(\begin{smallmatrix} 1 \\ z \end{smallmatrix}\right)^{\mathsf{T}} \left(\begin{smallmatrix} M_{11} & M_{12} \\ M_{21} & 0 \end{smallmatrix}\right) \left(\begin{smallmatrix} 1 \\ y \end{smallmatrix}\right) = M_{11} + M_{12} y + M_{21} z$ and we either need $M_{21} \neq 0$ or $M_{12} \neq 0$. □

Clearly, the result makes intuitive sense. For example, the verification equation in Item 2 includes one unknown group element in both groups and some constants. Since $\mathbb{Q}_{\kappa i}$ is only available in $\mathbb{G}_\kappa$, they cancel out, and thus $\boldsymbol{\delta} = \mathbf{0}$.

We will give some concrete examples in the full version of the paper.

7   AGMOS with Uniform Oracle

We propose a simplification of the general AGMOS, where the oracle produces uniformly random group elements. We call this AGM with Uniform Oblivious Sampling (AGMUOS). GGM with uniform sampling is known [1,3], and Lipmaa's variant of AGMOS [28] also focused on uniform sampling.

Note that AGMUOS with uniform sampling does not accurately model, for example, admissible encodings. Since a noticeable fraction of the group is not in the image of an admissible encoding, outputs of standard admissible encodings are easily distinguishable from uniformly random group elements. Nevertheless, the uniform model is easier to state, will rely on a weaker assumption, and is still helpful as a predictor for the security of assumptions. In fact, we are unaware of any assumption that can be proven secure in the uniform model but is insecure in $(\mathcal{EF}, \mathcal{DF})$-AGMOS when $(\mathcal{EF}, \mathcal{DF})$-TOFR holds. Moreover, the standard security proof approach for AGMOS (such as in Sect. 5) carries over to AGMUOS, with the only difference being the underlying assumption.

We define AGMOS with uniform sampling in the pairing-based setting, just as the general model. Let $\mathsf{p} \leftarrow \mathsf{Pgen}(1^\lambda)$ be the description of the pairing. We define a uniform sampling oracle $\mathcal{U}$ that takes as an input $\kappa \in \{1, 2\}$ and returns a uniformly random group element $[\mathsf{q}]_\kappa \leftarrow_\$ \mathbb{G}_\kappa$. Importantly, we assume that $\mathcal{U}$ is non-programmable. That is, security reductions cannot modify outputs of $\mathcal{U}$.

Besides that, the model is almost identical. For the sake of completeness, we state the complete definition below.

Definition 8 (AGMUOS). *A non-uniform PPT algorithm $\mathcal{A}$ is an AGMUOS adversary for* Pgen *if there exists a non-uniform PPT extractor* $\mathsf{Ext}_{\mathcal{A}}$, *such that for any* $\mathbf{x} = (\mathbf{x}_1, \mathbf{x}_2)$, $\mathsf{Adv}_{\mathsf{Pgen}, \mathcal{A}, \mathsf{Ext}_{\mathcal{A}}}^{\mathrm{agmuos}}(\lambda) :=$

$$\Pr \left[\begin{array}{l} y_1 \neq \gamma_1^{\mathsf{T}} \mathbf{x}_1 + \delta_1^{\mathsf{T}} \mathbf{q}_1 \vee \\ y_2 \neq \gamma_2^{\mathsf{T}} \mathbf{x}_2 + \delta_2^{\mathsf{T}} \mathbf{q}_2 \end{array} \middle| \begin{array}{l} \mathsf{p} \leftarrow \mathsf{Pgen}(1^{\lambda}); r \leftarrow \mathsf{RND}_{\lambda}(\mathcal{A}); \\ ([y_1]_1, [y_2]_2) \leftarrow_{\$} \mathcal{A}^{\mathcal{U}}(\mathsf{p}, \mathbf{x}; r); \\ (\gamma_{\kappa}, \delta_{\kappa}, [\mathbf{q}_{\kappa}]_{\kappa})_{\kappa=1}^{2} \leftarrow \mathsf{Ext}_{\mathcal{A}}^{\mathcal{U}}(\mathsf{p}, \mathbf{x}; r) : \end{array} \right] = \mathsf{negl}(\lambda) \ .$$

Here, $[\mathbf{q}_{\kappa}]_{\kappa}$ is the tuple of elements output by $\mathcal{U}$ on input $\kappa \in \{1, 2\}$. We denote by ql_{κ} the number of $\mathcal{U}$ calls on input κ.

As mentioned before, proofs are essentially identical in AGMUOS, except we can rely on a weaker version of TOFR. We define a uniform oracle version of the TOFR assumption that we call Uniform Tensor Oracle FindRep (UTOFR).

Definition 9 (UTOFR). *We say that* Pgen *is* UTOFR *(Uniform Tensor Oracle FindRep) secure if for any non-uniform PPT $\mathcal{A}$, $\mathsf{Adv}_{\mathsf{Pgen}, \mathcal{A}}^{\mathrm{utofr}}(\lambda) :=$*

$$\Pr \left[\boldsymbol{v} \neq \mathbf{0} \wedge \boldsymbol{v}^{\mathsf{T}} \cdot \begin{pmatrix} 1 \\ \mathbf{q}_1 \\ \mathbf{q}_2 \\ \mathbf{q}_1 \otimes \mathbf{q}_2 \end{pmatrix} = 0 \middle| \mathsf{p} \leftarrow \mathsf{Pgen}(1^{\lambda}); \boldsymbol{v} \leftarrow \mathcal{A}^{\mathcal{U}}(\mathsf{p}) \right] = \mathsf{negl}(\lambda) \ .$$

Here, $\mathcal{U}$, $\mathbf{q}_1$, and $\mathbf{q}_2$ are as in Definition 8.

In fact, if we did allow programming $\mathcal{U}$, then this assumption could be reduced to the $(1, 1)$- PDL assumption. Although we do not allow programming in general, it does indicate that UTOFR is a relatively weak assumption.

Lemma 5. *Suppose $\mathcal{U}$ is programmable. Then, $(1,1)$-PDL implies UTOFR. More formally, for any non-uniform PPT $\mathcal{A}$, there exist a non-uniform PPT $\mathcal{B}$ such that $\mathsf{Adv}_{\mathsf{Pgen}, \mathcal{A}}^{\mathrm{utofr}}(\lambda) \leq \mathsf{Adv}_{1,1,\mathsf{Pgen}, \mathcal{B}}^{\mathrm{pdl}}(\lambda) + \mathsf{negl}(\lambda)$.*

Proof. The discrete logarithm adversary $\mathcal{B}$ runs $\mathcal{A}$ while embedding its challenge $([y]_1, [y]_2)$ to the queries of the oracle $\mathcal{U}$. On a query κ to $\mathcal{U}$, $\mathcal{B}$ samples $r_{\kappa,i}, s_{\kappa,i} \leftarrow_{\$} \mathbb{F}$ and returns $[\mathbf{q}_{\kappa i}]_{\kappa} \leftarrow r_{\kappa,i}[1]_{\kappa} + s_{\kappa i}[y]_{\kappa}$. If $\mathcal{A}$ succeeds, it returns a non-zero representation $\boldsymbol{v}$, such that $\boldsymbol{v}^{\mathsf{T}} \mathbf{q} \neq 0$. Let us denote $\boldsymbol{v} = (v_0 // \boldsymbol{v}_1 // \boldsymbol{v}_2 // \boldsymbol{v}_3)$, where subvectors correspond to 1, $\mathbf{q}_1$, $\mathbf{q}_2$ and $\mathbf{q}_1 \otimes \mathbf{q}_2$ respectively. Then,

$$\begin{aligned} 0 =& v_0 + \boldsymbol{v}_1^{\mathsf{T}} \mathbf{q}_1 + \boldsymbol{v}_2^{\mathsf{T}} \mathbf{q}_2 + \boldsymbol{v}_3^{\mathsf{T}} (\mathbf{q}_1 \otimes \mathbf{q}_2) \\ =& v_0 + \boldsymbol{v}_1^{\mathsf{T}} (\boldsymbol{r}_1 + \boldsymbol{s}_1 y) + \boldsymbol{v}_2^{\mathsf{T}} (\boldsymbol{r}_2 + \boldsymbol{s}_2 y) + \boldsymbol{v}_3^{\mathsf{T}} ((\boldsymbol{r}_1 + \boldsymbol{s}_1 y) \otimes (\boldsymbol{r}_2 + \boldsymbol{s}_2 y)) \\ =& v_0 + \boldsymbol{v}_1^{\mathsf{T}} \boldsymbol{r}_1 + \boldsymbol{v}_2^{\mathsf{T}} \boldsymbol{r}_2 + \boldsymbol{v}_3^{\mathsf{T}} (\boldsymbol{r}_1 \otimes \boldsymbol{r}_2) \\ & + (\boldsymbol{v}_1^{\mathsf{T}} \boldsymbol{s}_1 + \boldsymbol{v}_2^{\mathsf{T}} \boldsymbol{s}_2 + \boldsymbol{v}_3^{\mathsf{T}} (\boldsymbol{r}_1 \otimes \boldsymbol{s}_2 + \boldsymbol{s}_1 \otimes \boldsymbol{r}_2)) \cdot y + \boldsymbol{v}_3^{\mathsf{T}} (\boldsymbol{s}_1 \otimes \boldsymbol{s}_2) \cdot y^2 \ . \end{aligned}$$

We can view this as a quadratic equation in y. If the coefficient of y or y^2 is non-zero, then $\mathcal{B}$ can solve the equation for y and break the PDL assumption.

Let us analyze the probability of that happening. Note that v_1, v_2, v_3 cannot be zero vectors at the same time since then also $v_0 = 0$, which implies that the whole vector v is a zero-vector.

The vectors s_1 and s_2 are information-theoretically hidden from the adversary (they are blinded by r_1 and r_2 respectively). The probability that s_1 or s_2 contain a zero element is bounded by $(q l_1 + q l_2)/\mathbb{F}$. Additionally, if s_1 and s_2 do not contain a zero, then neither does $s_1 \otimes s_2$. Let us suppose that this is the case. Now, we look at two cases.

1) Suppose $v_3 \neq \mathbf{0}$. Then, according to Schwartz-Zippel lemma, the probability that $v_3^\mathsf{T}(s_1 \otimes s_2) = 0$ is bounded by $2/\mathbb{F}^{q l_1 + q l_2}$.

2) Suppose $v_3 = \mathbf{0}$, but v_1 or v_2 are non-zero. Then the coefficient of y is $v_1^\mathsf{T} s_1 + v_2^\mathsf{T} s_2$. The probability that this coefficient is 0 is bounded by $1/\mathbb{F}^{q l_1 + q l_2}$.

Thus, except for negligible probability, $\mathcal{B}$ breaks $(1,1)$-PDL.   □

Acknowledgment. We thank Markulf Kohlweiss and anonymous reviewers for helpful comments.

References

1. Abdolmaleki, B., Baghery, K., Lipmaa, H., Zajac, M.: A subversion-resistant SNARK. In: Takagi, T., Peyrin, T. (eds.) ASIACRYPT 2017, Part III. LNCS, vol. 10626, pp. 3–33. Springer, Cham (2017). https://doi.org/10.1007/978-3-319-70700-6_1

2. Abdolmaleki, B., Lipmaa, H., Siim, J., Zajac, M.: On subversion-resistant SNARKs. J. Cryptol. **34**(3), 17 (2021). https://doi.org/10.1007/s00145-021-09379-y

3. Bellare, M., Fuchsbauer, G., Scafuro, A.: NIZKs with an untrusted CRS: security in the face of parameter subversion. In: Cheon, J.H., Takagi, T. (eds.) ASIACRYPT 2016, Part II. LNCS, vol. 10032, pp. 777–804. Springer, Heidelberg (2016). https://doi.org/10.1007/978-3-662-53890-6_26

4. Boneh, D., Boyen, X., Goh, E.-J.: Hierarchical identity based encryption with constant size ciphertext. In: Cramer, R. (ed.) EUROCRYPT 2005. LNCS, vol. 3494, pp. 440–456. Springer, Heidelberg (2005). https://doi.org/10.1007/11426639_26

5. Boneh, D., Franklin, M.: Identity-based encryption from the weil pairing. In: Kilian, J. (ed.) CRYPTO 2001. LNCS, vol. 2139, pp. 213–229. Springer, Heidelberg (2001). https://doi.org/10.1007/3-540-44647-8_13

6. Boyen, X.: The uber-assumption family. In: Galbraith, S.D., Paterson, K.G. (eds.) Pairing 2008. LNCS, vol. 5209, pp. 39–56. Springer, Heidelberg (2008). https://doi.org/10.1007/978-3-540-85538-5_3

7. Brands, S.: Untraceable off-line cash in wallet with observers (extended abstract). In: Stinson, D.R. (ed.) CRYPTO 1993. LNCS, vol. 773, pp. 302–318. Springer, Heidelberg (1994). https://doi.org/10.1007/3-540-48329-2_26

8. Brier, E., Coron, J.-S., Icart, T., Madore, D., Randriam, H., Tibouchi, M.: Efficient indifferentiable hashing into ordinary elliptic curves. In: Rabin, T. (ed.) CRYPTO 2010. LNCS, vol. 6223, pp. 237–254. Springer, Heidelberg (2010). https://doi.org/10.1007/978-3-642-14623-7_13

9. Brown, D.R.L.: The exact security of ECDSA. Contributions to IEEE P1363a, January 2001. https://grouper.ieee.org/groups/1363/

10. Campanelli, M., Faonio, A., Fiore, D., Querol, A., Rodríguez, H.: Lunar: a tool-box for more efficient universal and updatable zkSNARKs and commit-and-prove extensions. Cryptology ePrint Archive, Report 2020/1069 (2020). https://eprint.iacr.org/2020/1069

11. Campanelli, M., Faonio, A., Fiore, D., Querol, A., Rodríguez, H.: Lunar: a tool-box for more efficient universal and updatable zkSNARKs and commit-and-prove extensions. In: Tibouchi, M., Wang, H. (eds.) ASIACRYPT 2021, Part III. LNCS, vol. 13092, pp. 3–33. Springer, Cham (2021). https://doi.org/10.1007/978-3-030-92078-4_1

12. Damgård, I.: Towards practical public key systems secure against chosen ciphertext attacks. In: Feigenbaum, J. (ed.) CRYPTO 1991. LNCS, vol. 576, pp. 445–456. Springer, Heidelberg (1992). https://doi.org/10.1007/3-540-46766-1_36

13. Danezis, G., Fournet, C., Groth, J., Kohlweiss, M.: Square span programs with applications to succinct NIZK arguments. In: Sarkar, P., Iwata, T. (eds.) ASIACRYPT 2014, Part I. LNCS, vol. 8873, pp. 532–550. Springer, Heidelberg (2014). https://doi.org/10.1007/978-3-662-45611-8_28

14. Dent, A.W.: Adapting the weaknesses of the random oracle model to the generic group model. In: Zheng, Y. (ed.) ASIACRYPT 2002. LNCS, vol. 2501, pp. 100–109. Springer, Heidelberg (2002). https://doi.org/10.1007/3-540-36178-2_6

15. Fischlin, M.: A note on security proofs in the generic model. In: Okamoto, T. (ed.) ASIACRYPT 2000. LNCS, vol. 1976, pp. 458–469. Springer, Heidelberg (2000). https://doi.org/10.1007/3-540-44448-3_35

16. Fischlin, M., Lehmann, A., Ristenpart, T., Shrimpton, T., Stam, M., Tessaro, S.: Random oracles with(out) programmability. In: Abe, M. (ed.) ASIACRYPT 2010. LNCS, vol. 6477, pp. 303–320. Springer, Heidelberg (2010). https://doi.org/10.1007/978-3-642-17373-8_18

17. Fouque, P.-A., Tibouchi, M.: Estimating the size of the image of deterministic hash functions to elliptic curves. In: Abdalla, M., Barreto, P.S.L.M. (eds.) LATIN-CRYPT 2010. LNCS, vol. 6212, pp. 81–91. Springer, Heidelberg (2010). https://doi.org/10.1007/978-3-642-14712-8_5

18. Fuchsbauer, G., Kiltz, E., Loss, J.: The algebraic group model and its applications. In: Shacham, H., Boldyreva, A. (eds.) CRYPTO 2018, Part II. LNCS, vol. 10992, pp. 33–62. Springer, Cham (2018). https://doi.org/10.1007/978-3-319-96881-0_2

19. Fuchsbauer, G., Plouviez, A., Seurin, Y.: Blind Schnorr signatures and signed ElGamal encryption in the algebraic group model. In: Canteaut, A., Ishai, Y. (eds.) EUROCRYPT 2020, Part II. LNCS, vol. 12106, pp. 63–95. Springer, Cham (2020). https://doi.org/10.1007/978-3-030-45724-2_3

20. Gabizon, A., Williamson, Z.J., Ciobotaru, O.: PLONK: permutations over lagrange-bases for oecumenical noninteractive arguments of knowledge. Cryptology ePrint Archive, Report 2019/953 (2019). https://eprint.iacr.org/2019/953

21. Ghoshal, A., Tessaro, S.: Tight state-restoration soundness in the algebraic group model. In: Malkin, T., Peikert, C. (eds.) CRYPTO 2021, Part III. LNCS, vol. 12827, pp. 64–93. Springer, Cham (2021). https://doi.org/10.1007/978-3-030-84252-9_3

22. Icart, T.: How to hash into elliptic curves. In: Halevi, S. (ed.) CRYPTO 2009. LNCS, vol. 5677, pp. 303–316. Springer, Heidelberg (2009). https://doi.org/10.1007/978-3-642-03356-8_18

23. Jager, T., Rupp, A.: The semi-generic group model and applications to pairing-based cryptography. In: Abe, M. (ed.) ASIACRYPT 2010. LNCS, vol. 6477, pp. 539–556. Springer, Heidelberg (2010). https://doi.org/10.1007/978-3-642-17373-8_31

24. Kate, A., Zaverucha, G.M., Goldberg, I.: Constant-size commitments to polynomials and their applications. In: Abe, M. (ed.) ASIACRYPT 2010. LNCS, vol. 6477, pp. 177–194. Springer, Heidelberg (2010). https://doi.org/10.1007/978-3-642-17373-8_11

25. Kohlweiss, M., Maller, M., Siim, J., Volkhov, M.: Snarky ceremonies. In: Tibouchi, M., Wang, H. (eds.) ASIACRYPT 2021, Part III. LNCS, vol. 13092, pp. 98–127. Springer, Cham (2021). https://doi.org/10.1007/978-3-030-92078-4_4

26. Lipmaa, H.: Progression-free sets and sublinear pairing-based non-interactive zero-knowledge arguments. In: Cramer, R. (ed.) TCC 2012. LNCS, vol. 7194, pp. 169–189. Springer, Heidelberg (2012). https://doi.org/10.1007/978-3-642-28914-9_10

27. Lipmaa, H.: Simulation-extractable ZK-SNARKs revisited. Technical report 2019/612, IACR, 31 May 2019. https://ia.cr/2019/612. Accessed 8 Feb 2020

28. Lipmaa, H.: A unified framework for non-universal SNARKs. In: Hanaoka, G., Shikata, J., Watanabe, Y. (eds.) PKC 2022, Part I. LNCS, vol. 13177, pp. 553–583. Springer, Heidelberg (2022). https://doi.org/10.1007/978-3-030-97121-2_20

29. Lipmaa, H., Siim, J., Parisella, R.: Algebraic group model with oblivious sampling. Technical report 2023/?, IACR, September 2023. https://eprint.iacr.org/2023/?

30. Maurer, U.M.: Abstract models of computation in cryptography (invited paper). In: Smart, N.P. (ed.) Cryptography and Coding 2005. LNCS, vol. 3796, pp. 1–12. Springer, Heidelberg (Dec (2005). https://doi.org/10.1007/11586821_1

31. Nielsen, J.B.: Separating random oracle proofs from complexity theoretic proofs: the non-committing encryption case. In: Yung, M. (ed.) CRYPTO 2002. LNCS, vol. 2442, pp. 111–126. Springer, Heidelberg (2002). https://doi.org/10.1007/3-540-45708-9_8

32. Rotem, L.: Revisiting the uber assumption in the algebraic group model: fine-grained bounds in hidden-order groups and improved reductions in bilinear groups. In: Dachman-Soled, D. (ed.) ITC 2022. LIPIcs, vol. 230, pp. 13:1–13:13. Cambridge, MA, USA, 5–7 July 2022. https://doi.org/10.4230/LIPIcs.ITC.2022.13

33. Rotem, L., Segev, G.: Algebraic distinguishers: from discrete logarithms to decisional uber assumptions. In: Pass, R., Pietrzak, K. (eds.) TCC 2020, Part III. LNCS, vol. 12552, pp. 366–389. Springer, Cham (2020). https://doi.org/10.1007/978-3-030-64381-2_13

34. Schnorr, C.P.: Efficient signature generation by smart cards. J. Cryptol. 4(3), 161–174 (1991). https://doi.org/10.1007/BF00196725

35. Shoup, V.: Lower bounds for discrete logarithms and related problems. In: Fumy, W. (ed.) EUROCRYPT 1997. LNCS, vol. 1233, pp. 256–266. Springer, Heidelberg (1997). https://doi.org/10.1007/3-540-69053-0_18

36. Stern, J., Pointcheval, D., Malone-Lee, J., Smart, N.P.: Flaws in applying proof methodologies to signature schemes. In: Yung, M. (ed.) CRYPTO 2002. LNCS, vol. 2442, pp. 93–110. Springer, Heidelberg (2002). https://doi.org/10.1007/3-540-45708-9_7

37. Wahby, R.S., Boneh, D.: Fast and simple constant-time hashing to the BLS12-381 elliptic curve. IACR TCHES 2019(4), 154–179 (2019). https://doi.org/10.13154/tches.v2019.i4.154-179, https://tches.iacr.org/index.php/TCHES/article/view/8348

38. Zhandry, M.: To label, or not to label (in generic groups). In: Dodis, Y., Shrimpton, T. (eds.) CRYPTO 2022. LNCS, vol. 13509, pp. 66–96. Springer, Heidelberg (2022). https://doi.org/10.1007/978-3-031-15982-4_3

39. Zhang, C., Zhou, H.S., Katz, J.: An Analysis of the Algebraic Group Model, pp. 310–322 (2022)

Byzantine Agreement, Consensus and Composability

Zombies and Ghosts: Optimal Byzantine Agreement in the Presence of Omission Faults

Julian Loss[1] and Gilad Stern[2(✉)]

[1] CISPA Helmholtz Center for Information Security, Saarbrücken, Germany
[2] The Hebrew University of Jerusalem, Jerusalem, Israel
gilad.stern@mail.huji.ac.il

Abstract. Studying the feasibility of Byzantine Agreement (BA) in realistic fault models is an important question in the area of distributed computing and cryptography. In this work, we revisit the mixed fault model with Byzantine (malicious) faults and omission faults put forth by Hauser, Maurer, and Zikas (TCC 2009), who showed that BA (and MPC) is possible with t Byzantine faults, s send faults (whose outgoing messages may be dropped) and r receive faults (whose incoming messages may be lost) if $n > 3t + r + s$. We generalize their techniques and results by showing that BA is possible if $n > 2t + r + s$, given the availability of a cryptographic setup. Our protocol is the first to match the recent lower bound of Eldefrawy, Loss, and Terner (ACNS 2022) for this setting.

Keywords: Consensus · Synchrony · Mixed-Faults

1 Introduction

Byzantine agreement (BA) is a fundamental problem in distributed computing where n parties $1, \ldots, n$ each hold an input v_i and want to agree on a common output v by running some distributed protocol Π. However, their task is complicated by some $t < n$ out of the parties deviating from the protocol description, e.g., by crashing or sending incorrect messages. BA forms the backbone of many distributed protocols and has wide-ranging applications such as multi-party computation, verifiable secret sharing, and replicated state machines. For this reason, an extensive body of literature has studied the feasibility of BA under various conditions, e.g., different types of network behaviors and/or faults. If no setup is assumed, the celebrated work of Lamport, Shostak and Pease [16] demonstrates that BA is possible if and only if the number of *malicious faults* t satisfies $t < \frac{n}{3}$. On the other hand, a protocol can tolerate any number of *crash faults* (i.e., where a party crashes). As a middle ground between these two types of faults, many previous works have also considered so-called *omission faults*. An omission fault is a party that remains honest and online, but for which some of its incoming and outgoing messages may not be delivered. This makes omission faults a very realistic, but also particularly difficult type of fault to deal with.

© International Association for Cryptologic Research 2023
G. Rothblum and H. Wee (Eds.): TCC 2023, LNCS 14372, pp. 395–421, 2023.
https://doi.org/10.1007/978-3-031-48624-1_15

Toward a more general understanding of fault tolerance with omission faults, Hauser, Maurer, and Zikas [28], studied BA (and multi-party computation) in a mixed model with malicious faults and omission faults. Their work considers two types of omission faults, *receive omission faults* (a party does not receive some incoming messages) and *send omission faults* (some messages of a party are not delivered). Their result shows that BA and MPC are possible if $n > 3t + r + s$, where t is the number of malicious faults, r is the number of receive omission faults, and s is the number of send omission faults.[1] Much more recently, Eldefrawy, Loss, and Terner [11] make a first attempt at translating this result to a setting where cryptographic setup (i.e., a PKI) is available to the parties. In this setting, they show that BA is possible only if $n > 2t + r + s$. On the converse, they show a protocol that matches this bound when considering a special type of send omission fault called a *spotty fault*. Spotty faults must drop either *all or none* of their messages in any given protocol round; a feature which their protocols crucially exploit. Their work explicitly leaves open the question of finding a protocol matching the lower bound even for general send omission faults. In this work, we answer this question in the affirmative. More concretely, we show the following results:

- We begin by revisiting the protocol framework of Hauser et al. used by parties to detect and silence themselves upon becoming receive omission faulty. To overcome additional obstacles that we are presented with as a result of our more general fault regime, we extend their framework to the much more challenging case of send omission faults.
- Using our new framework, we then give the first protocol matching the $2t + r + s < n$ lower bound of Eldefrawy et al. in the mixed model with malicious faults and general send/receive omission faults. Our definitions and protocol designs are modular and lend themselves ideally as building blocks to future works in this area.

1.1   Our Techniques

We now give a technical overview of our results. We begin with a recap of the model and necessary definitions.

The Mixed Fault Model. Let us first revisit the standard security properties of BA (i.e., without omission faults): (1) *validity*: if all honest parties input v, all honest parties output v. (2) *consistency*: if an honest party i outputs v, then all honest parties output v. From the onset, it is clear that we cannot hope to achieve this definition for omission faulty parties. For example, a receive faulty party may not receive all of the necessary messages to output in protocol Π at all. Similarly, a send omission faulty party may not be able to share its input, so any validity property that is sensitive to its input cannot be achieved. On the other hand, we *can hope* to achieve a validity property that takes into account

---

[1] Parties who are both send and receive omission faulty are counted twice in this bound.

receive faulty parties' inputs as well as to guarantee output for parties that are only send faulty. Indeed, the protocols of Hauser et al. and Eldefrawy et al. satisfy these properties.

Zombies. Central to the protocol design of existing works is a means for receive omission faulty parties to detect that they are not receiving messages as they should. A self-detected party can then react by ceasing to propagate potentially incorrect information in the future. To this end, parties overlay communication with a protocol that constantly checks whether they receive messages from sufficiently many parties, i.e., $n - t - s$ many of them. If not, a party i can be certain that it is not receiving messages from at least one party who is neither malicious nor send omission faulty. Hence, i concludes that it is receive faulty and shuts itself off in the protocol so as to not cause further harm to the remaining honest parties. In line with existing works, we will refer to such parties as *zombies*. To deal with $t < \frac{n}{3}$ malicious faults, Hauser et al. now obtain a weak consensus protocol as follows.[2] Suppose that from party i's view, there is a value $b \in \{0, 1\}$ that is supported by at least $n - s - r > 2t$ parties, whereas $1 - b$ is supported by fewer than $t + 1$ many parties. Then i can decide b, as it is sure that among the (at least) $2t + 1$ supporters of b, there were $t + 1$ honest parties. Those parties would have also communicated their support to all other parties, who, by the same rule, would not decide $1 - b$, unless they are receive faulty. Moreover, if all honest parties input b to the protocol, b will always be the decided value for all honest parties and send omission faulty parties. Since zombie parties can detect themselves and cease to send messages, Hauser et al. now manage to transform the above weak consensus, into strong consensus via standard techniques.

Additional Challenges When $\frac{n}{3} \leq t < \frac{n}{2}$. Even when signatures are available, it is unclear how the above approach would be made to work. Note that the standard strategy in this setting (i.e., when there are no omission faults) is for parties to gather *certificates* of at least $t + 1$ signatures on either b or $1 - b$, which they then pass on to all other parties. Upon obtaining $t + 1$ certificates on a value b and no certificate on a conflicting value $1 - b$, a party i deems that it is safe to output b. Much as above, P would usually infer that at least one certificate on b was sent to it by another honest party, j, who also sent it to all other parties. Hence, no other party decides $1 - b$.

This strategy is not applicable when there are send omission faults, as i's $t + 1$ certificates could have been sent by t malicious parties and one send faulty party j. Contrary to an honest, party, j might not be able to pass on the certificate to all other honest parties, and so they may yet decide on $1 - b$. It may seem tempting for i to just wait for more certificates. But, since zombies are still needed to make the remaining steps of the construction work, this is also not possible, since i, in the worst case, will receive messages from at most $t + 1$ honest parties. Hence i may not decide on a value b, even if all honest parties

---

[2] Weak consensus is a precursor to full consensus in which any honest party outputs either some $y \in \{0, 1\}$ or a special symbol $\perp$ (but no honest party outputs $1 - y$). Moreover, if all honest parties input y, they all output y.

input b to weak consensus. The issue with send faulty parties described above is sidestepped by Eldefrawy et al. who consider spotty omissions that drop all or none of the messages in a single protocol round.

Ghosts. We now introduce our new tool that allows us to deal with fully fledged send omission faults. As with zombies, our main idea is for parties to self-detect whether or not they are send faulty and take measures to prevent themselves from causing further harm in the protocol. Looking ahead, we will again let parties who self-detect as send omission faulty silence themselves in all subsequent protocol steps. Different from zombies, however, self-detected send omission faulty parties will remain as silent observers in the protocol and output along with the honest parties. Therefore, we refer to such parties as *ghosts*.

Putting ghost parties to good use turns out to be subtle. To see the issue, consider the following scenario. In some round, a party i becomes aware that at least $n - t - s > t + r$ parties (and thus at least one honest party) haven't heard from it in the previous round and haven't become zombies. This can easily be achieved by running our protocol via an overlay in which parties confirm each others messages in each round. Party i promptly concludes that it must be send omission faulty and stops speaking in all further rounds. However, the problem is that i might already have caused a problematic situation. For example, i might have sent a certificate for some value b to a party j. Party j would like to conclude that b is a safe value to decide on. However, even if j sees $t + 1$ certificates (including i's) for b in a given round, and no conflicting certificate for $1 - b$, it still cannot do so, as i's message may not have arrived in that round at all other honest parties. As a result some of those parties might still deem $1 - b$ a value that is safe to decide on.

To prevent this scenario, we introduce some extra rounds after every round of sending messages. During these rounds, parties confirm to each other that they didn't turn themselves into ghosts in any of the previous rounds. At the same time, parties are instructed to echo all of the messages they receive to all other parties and to keep confirming receipts of messages to each other in all rounds. In order to guarantee the delivery of a message, i sends the message once, and then sends it again if it hasn't become a ghost. Every party that receives the message during the first round also forwards that message in the second round. Party i knows that if it didn't become a ghost, at least one non-faulty party received its message in the first round and will forward that message to all parties. In addition, a party that receives messages from i in both rounds knows that every party will hear about the message for similar reasons (i.e., because i has not turned itself ghost). Using this technique, in addition to detecting its own failures, every party can also grade received messages according to how confident it is that every other party will receive them as well. Then, if some party receives a certificate with high confidence that every other party will do so as well, it can count it towards its tally of $t + 1$ supporting certificates for a given value.

Putting Things Together: Undead Consensus. Using the above template, we use a modular approach to build protocols of increasingly strong consistency guarantees. Here, we follow a more or less standard structure of going from weak consensus to full consensus. We adapt all of our definitions to explicitly take into account *undead parties* (i.e., zombies or ghosts). This is important, because zombie parties cannot be expected to have the same consistency guarantees as the live (i.e., honest) ones, whereas ghost parties cannot be expected to have their inputs taken into account for protocols they participate in. Our definitions are tailored to modular protocol design and depart from prior works, in which these guarantees were left implicit. In particular, our definitions account for parties to be undead even before the protocol starts, which may occur as the result of running a previous subprotocol in the overall protocol stack. We believe that our modular notions will serve as important definitional pillars for future work in this area.

2 Model and Definitions

2.1 Network Model

We assume a network of n parties with point-to-point authenticated communication channels. In addition, we assume a PKI setup used for signing messages, meaning that each party i has a well-known public key pk_i associated with it and a signing key sk_i known only to it. Parties can sign a message using the Sign algorithm and verify signatures using the Verify algorithm. As is standard in this line of literature, we model the signatures as perfectly unforgeable. It is, however, straight-forward to instantiate signatures in any of our protocols with any existentially unforgeable signature scheme, in which case our properties hold against computationally bounded adversaries.

The network is assumed to be synchronous, meaning that there is a well-known upper bound Δ on message delay. Any message sent by an honest party at time t is delivered by time $t + \Delta$. In such systems, it is possible to define discrete communication rounds. All parties start each protocol at time 0, and then actions taken between time $(r-1)\Delta$ and $r\Delta$ are said to take place in round r. In particular, if a party sends a message at time $(r-1)\Delta$ in the beginning of round r, it is guaranteed to be delivered by time $r\Delta$, at the beginning of the next round. In the below protocols, each bullet-point defines the actions to be taken in the beginning of a specific round, unless specifically stated otherwise. When a bullet-point contains a call to a subprotocol that requires k rounds to complete, parties continue to the next bullet-point only after k rounds.

2.2 Adversary Model

The aim of this work is to deal with mixed-fault networks. The n parties can experience one of three types of faults/corruptions:

- **Send Omission Faults.** Send faulty parties follow the protocol description. For any message that a send faulty party sends, the adversary can choose not to deliver that message. We assume that there are at most s send faulty parties.

- **Receive Omission Faults.** Receive faulty parties follow the protocol description. For any message sent to a receive faulty party, the adversary can choose not to deliver that message. We assume that there are at most r receive faulty parties.
- **Byzantine/Malicious Faults.** A Byzantine/Malicious party can deviate from a protocol description arbitrarily. We assume that there are at most t Byzantine parties.

Throughout this work, we will assume that $n > 2t+s+r$. As shown by Eldefrawy, Loss, and Terner, this is the best-possible tolerance that can be achieved. The adversary is assumed to be *rushing* and *strongly adaptive*. This means that it can corrupt parties at any time throughout a protocol execution with one of the three types of corruptions explained above. In any round of a protocol execution, the adversary can observe the messages of all honest parties and then choose the messages of corrupt parties as well as what new parties to corrupt adaptively for that round. For send faulty parties, the adversary chooses which of their messages to deliver for that round, whereas for receive faulty parties, it chooses which of the (honest) messages to deliver to those parties. If a party newly becomes Byzantine and/or send faulty in a round, the adversary can erase (or replace, in case of a Byzantine corruption) any of the messages that party sent while it was honest, as long as those messages have not been delivered yet. Similarly, for a newly receive faulty party, the adversary may erase any of the messages that were sent to that party while it was still honest, as long as those messages have not been delivered. We assume the adversary to have full control over the network, subject to the constraint of delivering messages of honest and receive faulty parties within Δ time.

2.3 Zombies and Ghosts

Our overarching goal is constructing a mixed-fault tolerant consensus protocol, allowing all parties to agree on a value. As has been done in previous works, our protocols are designed in a way that an omission-faulty party should either behave correctly (or correctly enough), or find out that it is faulty and stop communicating in order not to cause harm.

Using the terminology of [28], if a party finds out that it is receive faulty, it becomes a "zombie". This means that it sets a flag Z to the value true, stops sending messages, and eventually outputs the flag from the protocol in addition to any other value. Similarly, if a party sees that it is send faulty it becomes a "ghost" by setting a flag G to true, stops sending messages, and eventually outputs this flag as well. Parties also receive such flags as inputs, denoting whether they were zombies or ghosts in the beginning of the protocol, and output those flags in addition to any regular output in order to relay this information to any calling protocol. For simplicity, whenever a party sends a message via a protocol with a designated sender, we assume all parties participate in the protocol. In addition, whenever parties call an internal protocol, they also input their current Z, G flags to the called protocol.

We say that a party has become a zombie or a ghost during a protocol if it set its corresponding flag to the value true while executing the protocol. Similarly, we say that a party is a zombie or a ghost in the beginning of a protocol if its corresponding input flags are set to the value true. A party that has become a zombie or a ghost is said to be "undead", and a non-Byzantine party that isn't undead at a given moment is said to be alive.

2.4 Protocol Definitions

We now give basic protocol definitions used throughout this paper. Our definitions extend classical definitions in the literature with properties for undead parties. The original definitions without the notion of undead parties are provided in Appendix B.

No Living Undead Protocol. In all of the following definitions, we consider undead versions of classic protocols. That is, if parties output a value x in some protocol, in the undead version parties output x, z, g, with x being analogous to the original output, z being a flag indicating whether the party became a zombie while running the protocol, and g being a flag indicating whether it became a ghost. A general property we would like in any such protocol is that parties only become zombies or ghosts if they are indeed receive or send faulty, respectively. We formalize this notion in the following definition, indicating that the protocol does not produce any undead parties that are actually alive.

Definition 1. *Let Π be a protocol executed by parties $1, \ldots, n$, where every party outputs a triplet (x, z, g) such that z and g are boolean values. We say that Π is (t, s, r)-no living undead (NLU) if the following holds whenever at most t parties are Byzantine, s parties are send faulty and r parties are receive faulty: if a non-Byzantine party is alive in the beginning of the protocol and it outputs (x, z, g) such that $z = $ true (resp. $g = $ true), then it is receive faulty (resp. send faulty).*

Undead Weak Multicast. An undead weak multicast protocol is a basic building block, replacing the simple multicast implementation. In the protocol, a known sender has a message to send to all parties. The sender then attempts to send the message to all parties, checking whether it should become a ghost and allowing parties to check whether they should become zombies. This primitive is weak in the sense that if a party does not become a ghost, it only knows that at least one nonfaulty party heard its message.

Definition 2. *Let Π be a protocol executed by parties $1, \ldots, n$, with a designated sender i^* starting with an input $m \neq \bot$. In addition, every party i has two values $z_i, g_i \in \{$true, false$\}$ as input. Every party outputs a triplet (x, z, g) such that x is either a possible message or $\bot$, and z, g are boolean values.*

- **Validity.** *Π is (t, s, r)-valid if the following holds whenever at most t parties are Byzantine, s parties are send faulty and r parties are receive faulty: if i^* is nonfaulty or receive faulty and is alive in the beginning of the protocol, every* *non-Byzantine party either outputs (x, z, g) such that $x = m$, or becomes a zombie by the end of the protocol. In addition, if i^* is send faulty, no non-Byzantine party outputs (x, z, g) such that $x \notin \{m, \bot\}$.*

- **Detection.** *Π is (t, s, r)-detecting if the following holds whenever at most t parties are Byzantine, s parties are send faulty and r parties are receive faulty: if i^* is send faulty and it is alive at the end of the protocol, at least one nonfaulty party output (x, z, g) such that $x = m$.*

- **Termination.** *Π is (t, s, r)-terminating if the following holds whenever at most t parties are Byzantine, s parties are send faulty and r parties are receive faulty: all parties complete the protocol and output a value.*

If Π is (t, s, r)-valid, (t, s, r)-detecting, (t, s, r)-terminating, and (t, s, r)-no living undead we say that it is a (t, s, r)-secure multicast protocol with undead parties.

Undead Graded Multicast. Using the undead weak multicast primitive, it is possible to construct a slightly stronger multicast primitive. An undead graded multicast protocol also has a designated sender that attempts to send its message to all parties in such a way that parties can detect their own faults. In addition to outputting a message m, parties also output a grade y, intuitively indicating how confident they are that the protocol succeeded. In such a protocol, if some party is very confident that the protocol succeeded for some non-Byzantine sender, all parties will receive a message from the sender, even if it is send faulty. This protocol is also "stronger" than the previous protocol in the sense that if a sender does not become a ghost, it knows that every party received its message.

Definition 3. *Let Π be a protocol executed by parties $1, \ldots, n$, with a designated sender i^* starting with an input $m \neq \bot$. In addition, every party i has two values $z_i, g_i \in \{\text{true}, \text{false}\}$ as input. Every party outputs a tuple (x, y, z, g) such that x is either a possible message or $\bot$, $y \in \{0, 1, 2\}$ and z, g are boolean values.*

- **Validity.** *Π is (t, s, r)-valid if the following holds whenever at most t parties are Byzantine, s parties are send faulty and r parties are receive faulty: if i^* is nonfaulty or receive faulty and is alive in the beginning of the protocol, every non-Byzantine party either outputs (x, y, z, g) such that $x = m, y = 2$, or becomes a zombie by the end of the protocol. In addition, if i^* is send faulty, no non-Byzantine party outputs (x, y, z, g) such that $x \notin \{m, \bot\}$.*

- **Detection.** *Π is (t, s, r)-detecting if the following holds whenever at most t parties are Byzantine, s parties are send faulty and r parties are receive faulty: if i^* is send faulty and it is alive at the end of the protocol, every nonfaulty party output (x, y, z, g) such that $x = m$ and $y \geq 1$.*

- **Consistency.** *Π is (t, s, r)-consistent if the following holds whenever at most t parties are Byzantine, s parties are send faulty and r parties are receive faulty: if i^* is non-Byzantine, for every two non-Byzantine parties j, k that output (x_j, y_j, z_j, g_j) and (x_k, y_k, z_k, g_k) respectively, either $|y_j - y_k| \leq 1$, or at least one of the parties becomes a zombie by the end of the protocol. In addition, either $x_j = \bot$ and $y_j = 0$ or $x_j = m$.*

– **Termination.** Π is (t, s, r)-terminating *if the following holds whenever at most t parties are Byzantine, s parties are send faulty and r parties are receive faulty: all parties complete the protocol and output a value.*

If Π is (t, s, r)-valid, (t, s, r)-detecting, (t, s, r)-consistent, (t, s, r)-terminating, and (t, s, r)-no living undead we say that it is a (t, s, r)-(secure) graded multicast with undead parties protocol.

Note that in the above, the output of a party is x, y, z, g with z, g being boolean flags. For the no living undead property, we consider x, y as the first element of the output and omit the parentheses for convenience, and z, g as the two flags.

Undead Weak Consensus. An undead weak consensus protocol is a mixed-fault version of a weak consensus protocol. In such a protocol, every party has a binary input, 0 or 1. The goal of the protocol is for there to be some value y such that every party either outputs y or $\bot$.

Definition 4. *Let Π be a protocol executed by parties $1, \ldots, n$, in which every party i starts with an input $v_i \neq \bot$. In addition, every party i has two values $z_i, g_i \in \{\mathsf{true}, \mathsf{false}\}$ as input. Every party outputs a triplet (x, z, g) such that x is either a possible input message or $\bot$, and z, g are boolean values.*

– **Validity.** Π is (t, s, r)-valid *if the following holds whenever at most t parties are Byzantine, s parties are send faulty and r parties are receive faulty: if all parties that are alive in the beginning of the protocol have the same input v, every non-Byzantine party either outputs (x, z, g) such that $x = v$, or becomes a zombie by the end of the protocol.*
– **Consistency.** Π is (t, s, r)-consistent *if the following holds whenever at most t parties are Byzantine, s parties are send faulty and r parties are receive faulty: if two parties are either alive or ghosts at the end of the protocol and they output (x, z, g) and (x', z', g'), then either $x = x'$, $x = \bot$ or $x' = \bot$.*
– **Termination.** Π is (t, s, r)-terminating *if the following holds whenever at most t parties are Byzantine, s parties are send faulty and r parties are receive faulty: all parties complete the protocol and output a value.*

If Π is (t, s, r)-valid, (t, s, r)-consistent, (t, s, r)-terminating, and (t, s, r)-no living undead we say that it is a (t, s, r)-secure undead weak consensus protocol.

Undead Consensus. Similarly, an undead consensus protocol is a mixed-fault version of a consensus protocol, in which all parties output the same value.

Definition 5. *Let Π be a protocol executed by parties $1, \ldots, n$, in which every party i starts with an input $v_i \neq \bot$. Every party outputs a triplet (x, z, g) such that x is a possible input value or $\bot$, and z, g are boolean values.*

- **Validity.** Π is (t, s, r)-valid *if the following holds whenever at most t parties are Byzantine, s parties are send faulty and r parties are receive faulty: if all parties that are alive in the beginning of the protocol have the same input v, every non-Byzantine party either outputs (x, z, g) such that $x = v$, or becomes a zombie by the end of the protocol.*
- **Consistency.** Π is (t, s, r)-consistent *if the following holds whenever at most t parties are Byzantine, s parties are send faulty and r parties are receive faulty: if two parties are either alive or ghosts at the end of the protocol and they output (x, z, g) and (x', z', g'), then $x = x'$.*
- **Termination.** Π is (t, s, r)-terminating *if the following holds whenever at most t parties are Byzantine, s parties are send faulty and r parties are receive faulty: all parties complete the protocol and output a value.*

If Π is (t, s, r)-valid, (t, s, r)-consistent, (t, s, r)-terminating, and (t, s, r)-no living undead *we say that it is a (t, s, r)-secure undead consensus protocol.*

Undead Common Coin. As done in previous works, in order to construct a consensus protocol with a constant expected number of rounds, we use an unbiasable common-coin protocol in each iteration of the protocol. Using the same construction as the ones in [4,11], we assume a common coin protocol, CoinFlip. This protocol can be constructed using a threshold signature scheme with unique signatures and a multicast protocol which allows parties to detect their own failures and turn into zombies or ghosts. Using this construction, the protocol informally achieves the following properties:

- Until at least one non-Byzantine party calls the common coin protocol for a given iteration, the output is distributed uniformly from the point of view of the adversary.
- All parties that are not zombies at the end of the protocol output the same value.

As done in other protocols, parties output a bit b, as well as two flags Z, G indicating whether they became zombies or ghosts throughout the protocol.

As described in [4], this protocol can be viewed as an ideal functionality. Parties can input a round number k into the functionality. Upon receiving the input k from $t + 1$ parties, the functionality uniformly samples a bit $b \in \{0, 1\}$ and sends k, b to all parties signifying that the coin's value for round k is b. Note that as described above, the value b is unpredictable from the point of view of Byzantine parties before $t + 1$ parties call the functionality for round k, which must include at least one non-Byzantine party. Considering also receive-faulty parties, the adversary can have the functionality send the message $\perp$ to receive-faulty parties instead of k, b, after which they can become zombies.

One common way to instantiate such a coin is by the use of threshold signatures with unique signatures. Using such a threshold signature scheme with a threshold of $t + 1$, a simple protocol for a Byzantine coin can be constructed by having all parties sign the round number and send the signature to all parties. Parties can then generate a unique threshold signature from any set of $t + 1$

such signature, and use a randomness extractor such as a random oracle to get a coin from the signature. In our setting, parties multicast these messages using the undead weak multicast protocol. Every party that doesn't become a zombie receives the multicasts sent by the $t + 1$ nonfaulty parties (in addition to other possible signatures), and thus can compute the coin correctly. Note that the unique signatures of the scheme allow taking any set of $t + 1$ correct signatures and computing the same threshold signature from them, meaning that parties will have a consistent coin even when $n > 2t + s + r$.

3   Protocols

In this section we construct protocols solving the tasks defined in Sect. 2.4. We generally follow many of the ideas and structure of Eldefrawy et al. [11]. Importantly, we both adjust the protocols to deal with ghosts and slightly change their protocol design. We use an undead graded multicast protocol instead of a weak broadcast protocol, which does not allow Byzantine parties to equivocate, but does not output grades as well as messages. In addition, we reduce our weak consensus protocol directly to a consensus protocol while they construct a graded consensus protocol as a step in between the two protocols.

In all of the following protocols, when we say that a party calls a protocol, we assume that it also inputs its current flags Z and G to the protocols without explicitly stating that it does so. In addition parties always participate in multicast and broadcast protocols with other parties as senders without explicitly stating so.

The proofs of all theorems in this section are provided in Appendix A

3.1   Undead Weak Multicast

The simplest primitive constructed in this work is an undead weak multicast protocol. This protocol is an adaptation of the FixReceive protocol of [28] and the all-to-all FixReceive protocol of [11]. In the protocol, the sender i^* attempts to send its message m to all parties, while allowing parties to detect their own faults. This is done by i^* sending the message m along with a signature σ to all parties, which then forward any message they received, or $\perp$ if they received no message. Parties then output m' if they receive this message along with a verifying signature from any party. Every party that isn't receive faulty knows that it should receive some message (either m or $\perp$) from all of the nonfaulty and receive faulty parties, totalling in $n - t - s$ parties. Therefore, if some party receives fewer than $n - t - s$ messages, it knows that it should become a zombie. In order for i^* to be able to detect its own faults, non-zombie parties inform it if they received no message and resorted to outputting $\perp$. If i^* receives $t + 1$ such messages, it knows that at least one non-Byzantine party output $\perp$, and can conclude that it should become a ghost. The full description of the protocol is provided in Fig. 1 and the proof of Theorem 1 is provided in Appendix A.1.

Theorem 1. *The protocol described in Fig. 1 is a (t, s, r)-secure undead weak multicast protocol if $n > 2t + s + r$.*

Undead Weak Multicast, sender i^* with input m, every party j with inputs z_j, g_j

1. Every party j sets $Z_j = z_j, G_j = g_j$. Party i^* sends $m, \mathsf{Sign}(\mathsf{sk}_{i^*}, m)$ to every party if it is alive.
2. If a party receives m, σ from i^* such that $\mathsf{Verify}(\mathsf{pk}_{i^*}, m, \sigma) = 1$, forward m, σ to every j. Otherwise, send $\perp$ to every j.
3. Every $j \neq i^*$ that received fewer than $n - t - s$ messages becomes a zombie by setting $Z_j = \mathsf{true}$ and outputs $(\perp, Z_j, G_j)$. If j hasn't become a zombie and it received at least one pair m, σ such that $\mathsf{Verify}(\mathsf{pk}_{i^*}, m, \sigma) = 1$, it outputs (m, Z_j, G_j) (choose arbitrarily). If j hasn't become a zombie or output a tuple, it sends "no output" to i^* and outputs $(\perp, Z_j, G_j)$ (note that zombies don't send this message). In all cases, parties wait an additional round before terminating.
4. If i^* receives at least $t + 1$ "no output" messages, it becomes a ghost by setting $G_{i^*} = \mathsf{true}$. Regardless of whether it has become a ghost, if $Z_{i^*} = \mathsf{false}$, i^* outputs (m, Z_{i^*}, G_{i^*}) and otherwise it outputs $(\perp, Z_{i^*}, G_{i^*})$.

Fig. 1. An undead weak multicast protocol

3.2 Undead Graded Multicast

We turn to construct a slightly stronger version of an undead weak multicast protocol. In the previous protocol, if the sender party did not become a ghost, it only knows that one nonfaulty party received its message. The undead graded multicast protocol described in Fig. 2 allows a non-ghost sender to know that all parties received its message. In addition, parties output a message x as well as a grade $y \in \{0, 1, 2\}$. Informally, the grades represent parties' confidence that all parties heard the message sent by the sender. A grade of 2 guarantees that all parties hear the message sent by a non-Byzantine sender, and a grade of 0 is only given in the case that some party heard no value and had to output $\perp$.

The protocol consists of two rounds. In the first round, i^* signs its message m and sends m, σ to all parties with the undead weak multicast protocol described above. In the second round, parties forward the received message and signature if they received such values, and $\perp, \perp$ otherwise. Parties then output $m, 2$ if they heard (m, σ) from i^* in both rounds; $m, 1$ if they heard (m, σ) from some party in the second round; and $\perp, 0$ if they heard no message with a verifying signature. Intuitively, if some party outputs $m, 2$, it knows that i^* did not become a ghost in the first round because it sent a message in the second round. This means that some nonfaulty party heard that message and forwarded it to all parties, which either receive it and output m with a grade of at least 1, or become zombies. It is important to note that we require that if some party is receive faulty, but is alive in the beginning of the protocol, all parties receive its message and output $m, 2$. In order to make sure this happens, if i^* finds out that it is a zombie after the first round, it sends its message again in the second round and only then becomes a zombie. The proof of Theorem 2 is provided in Appendix A.2.

Undead Graded Multicast, sender i^* with input m, every j with inputs z_j, g_j

1. Every party j sets $Z_j = z_j$, $G_j = g_j$. Party i^* sends $m, \mathsf{Sign}(\mathsf{sk}_{i^*}, m)$ using an undead weak multicast protocol if it is alive.

2. Every party j checks whether it became a zombie in the previous round, and if not forwards whichever message it received. As an exception, i^* sends its message again even if it became a zombie (but not if it became a ghost). More precisely, let x_j, Z'_j, G'_j be j's output in the previous round. If $Z'_j = \mathsf{true}$ for some $j \neq i^*$, j sets $Z_j = \mathsf{true}$ and if $G'_j = \mathsf{true}$ (for any j), j sets $G_j = \mathsf{true}$. Then, if $Z'_{i^*} = \mathsf{true}$, i^* first sends (m, σ) again using an undead weak multicast protocol and then sets $Z_{i^*} = \mathsf{true}$. Every $j \neq i^*$ checks if $x_j = (m', \sigma')$ such that $\mathsf{Verify}(\mathsf{pk}_{i^*}, m', \sigma') = 1$. If this is the case, j sets $(m_j, \sigma_j) = (m', \sigma')$, and otherwise $(m_j, \sigma_j) = (\bot, \bot)$. Every $j \neq i^*$ that is alive sends (m_j, σ_j) using an undead weak multicast protocol.

3. For every pair of parties j, k, define $x_{j,k}, Z_{j,k}, G_{j,k}$ to be the value j received from k in the previous round. If j has become a ghost or a zombie in any of the calls to the undead weak multicast protocol, it becomes one in the undead graded multicast protocol as well. That is, it sets $G_j = \mathsf{true}$ if $G_{j,j} = \mathsf{true}$ and sets $Z_j = \mathsf{true}$ if there exists a k such that $Z_{j,k} = \mathsf{true}$. Then, if j has $Z_j = \mathsf{true}$, it outputs $\bot, 0, Z_j, G_j$. If $Z_j \neq \mathsf{true}$, $(m_j, \sigma_j) \neq (\bot, \bot)$ and j received $x_{j,i^*} = (m_j, \sigma_j)$ from i^* in the previous round as well, it outputs $m_j, 2, Z_j, G_j$. If j did not output a value yet and there exists some k such that $x_{j,k} = (m', \sigma')$ and $\mathsf{Verify}(\mathsf{pk}_{i^*}, m', \sigma') = 1$, j outputs $m', 1, Z_j, G_j$ and if no such k exists it outputs $\bot, 0, Z_j, G_j$.

Fig. 2. An undead graded multicast protocol

Theorem 2. *The protocol described in Fig. 2 is a (t, s, r)-secure undead graded multicast protocol if $n > 2t + s + r$.*

3.3 Undead Weak Consensus

Using the undead graded multicast protocol, we construct an undead weak consensus protocol with binary inputs. In this protocol, parties send each other their signed inputs. Each party i then collect all of the signed inputs it heard in a set S_i and forwards the set to all parties using the undead graded multicast protocol. These sets are used as certificates, proving that a large enough number of parties reported having a certain input. Generally, we say that S_i is a certificate for the value x if it contains signatures from $t + 1$ parties on the value x. Parties then output a value x if it is possible that all nonfaulty parties had the input x. They check whether this is possible by seeing if at least $t + 1$ parties signed a value x and at most t parties signed the opposite value $1 - x$ (this can be generalized to $t + 1$ signatures for x and at most t signatures on any other value).

The protocol, described in Fig. 3, consists of two rounds. Each party starts by signing its input and sending it to all parties. Every party then defines S_i to be the set of signed messages it receives and forwards it using an undead graded multicast protocol. If a party receives a certificate S_j for a value v with a grade of 2 from $t + 1$ parties j, and it does not receive a conflicting certificate S_k for the value $1 - v$ from any party k, it outputs v. Intuitively, a party that outputs v knows that at least one of the certificates that was received with grade 2 was sent by a non-Byzantine party. All parties receive that certificate with grade 1 or greater, or become zombies. Therefore, a party that chooses to output v knows that all other parties will either become zombies or hear about at least one certificate for v and thus won't output $1 - v$. The proof of Theorem 3 is provided in Appendix A.3.

Undead Weak Consensus, each party i has input $x_i \in \{0, 1\}$ and two inputs z_i, g_i

1. Each party i sets $Z_i = z_i, G_i = g_i$. Each party i that is alive at this time sends $x_i, \mathsf{Sign}(\mathsf{sk}_i, x_i)$ to all other parties.

2. Each party i defines the set S_i to contain tuples of the form (j, x, σ) such that i received the message x, σ from j and $\mathsf{Verify}(\mathsf{pk}_j, x, \sigma) = 1$ and calls the undead graded multicast protocol with input S_i.

3. For every party i, j, define $S_{j,i}, y_{j,i}, Z_{j,i}, G_{j,i}$ to be i's output from the undead graded multicast call with j as sender. If there exists some j such that $Z_{j,i} = \mathsf{true}$, i sets $Z_i = \mathsf{true}$, and if there exists some j such that $G_{j,i} = \mathsf{true}$, i sets $G_i = \mathsf{true}$. A set S with enough signatures on the value v is called a certificate for v. That is, S is said to be a certificate for v if $|\{k | \exists \sigma \ s.t. (k, v, \sigma) \in S \land \mathsf{Verify}(\mathsf{pk}_k, v, \sigma) = 1\}| \geq t + 1$. Each party i checks if there is a value v_i such that there are at least $t + 1$ parties j from which it received a certificate $S_{j,i}$ with grade 2, and checks that none of the $S_{j,i}$ sets it received contained a certificate for the value $1 - v_i$, before outputting v_i. More precisely if there exists some value v such that for $t + 1$ parties j, $S_{j,i}$ is a certificate for v and $y_{j,i} = 2$; and for every k, $S_{k,i}$ is not a certification for $1 - v$ (with any grade $y_{k,i}$); then i sets $v_i = v$. Otherwise, it sets $v_i = \bot$. Finally, i outputs v_i, Z_i, G_i.

Fig. 3. An undead weak consensus protocol

Theorem 3. *The protocol described in Fig. 3 is a (t, s, r)-secure undead weak consensus protocol if $n > 2t + s + r$.*

3.4   Undead Consensus

Finally, we use the undead weak consensus protocol above to construct an undead consensus protocol with expected constant round complexity, similarly to the construction of [11]. Parties start by setting a local variable v_i to be their input, and then perform several actions in a loop until terminating. In the beginning of each iteration, parties call an undead weak consensus protocol with v_i as input, and after completing that protocol also call a common coin protocol. If some party outputs $u \neq \bot$ from the protocol, it adopts it as its value by updating $v_i = u$. On the other hand, if $u = \bot$, i defaults to using the output from the common coin protocol as its input to the next round. If some party outputs the same value u from both the weak consensus protocol and from the common coin protocol, it signs the value and send the signature to all parties. At this point, it already knows that v is going to be the output from the protocol and could output v if desired. Parties store all signatures received throughout the protocol in a set D_v. Once parties receive $t+1$ such signatures on v, they forward D_v to all parties and output v. They then continue for one more iteration of the protocol in order to help parties complete the protocol without becoming zombies or ghosts.

The protocol works by having parties check whether they already agree on a value v using the weak consensus protocol. If all parties have the same input to the protocol, they will output it from the weak consensus protocol and always have their v_i variables equal v. Unfortunately, parties don't know that the weak consensus protocol succeeded, so they also need to choose when to complete the protocol. This is done by also flipping a common coin, and checking whether its result b equals the output from the weak consensus protocol u. Every party that sees that $b = u$ knows that every party j either sets its v_j variable to u because it output u from the weak consensus protocol, or because it output $b = u$ from the common coin protocol. From this point on, all parties have the same input u in each iteration and will output u from any subsequent call to the weak consensus protocol. Note that this event also takes place if all parties output $\bot$ from the weak consensus protocol and then adopted the value of the common coin as their inputs to the next iteration. Parties now simply need to wait for b to equal u, at which point all parties will send signatures and complete the protocol. A formal description of the protocol is provided in Fig. 4 and a proof of Theorem 4 is provided in Appendix A.4.

Theorem 4. *The protocol described in Fig. 4 is a (t, s, r)-secure undead consensus protocol if $n > 2t + s + r$.*

4   Related Work and Future Directions

Byzantine Agreement, originally defined as the Byzantine Generals problem, has been researched as a foundational task in the field of distributed computing. Early results showed that the task is only solveable in synchronous systems with t Byzantine parties and without a PKI setup if $n > 3t$ and with a PKI setup if $n > 2t$ [16]. The highly related task of authenticated broadcast has been shown to be possible as long as $n > t$ [10]. Following that, research into the task of consensus in synchronous systems with omission faults yielded protocols that are resilient to any number of omission faults if the faulty parties aren't required to output correct values [20], and in the presence of k omission faults (of either type) if $n > 2k$ when they are required to output correct values [19, 21].

Undead Consensus, each party i has input $x_i \in \{0, 1\}$ and two inputs z_i, g_i

– Set $v_i = x_i$, $Z_i = z_i$, $G_i = g_i$, $k = 0$ and $D_0 = D_1 = \emptyset$, then loop until terminating:

1. Call the undead weak consensus protocol with input v_i. Define u_i, Z_i', G_i' to be the output from the undead weak consensus call. If $Z_i' = $ true, set $Z_i = $ true and if $G_i' = $ true, set $G_i = $ true.

2. Update $k = k + 1$ and invoke $\mathsf{CoinFlip}(k)$. Define b, Z_i', G_i' to be the output of the protocol. If $Z_i' = $ true, set $Z_i = $ true and if $G_i' = $ true set $G_i = $ true. If $u_i \neq \perp$, update $v_i = u_i$. If also $u_i = b$, send the message $v_i, \mathsf{Sign}(\mathsf{sk}_i, v_i)$ to all parties. On the other hand, if $u_i = \perp$, update $v_i = b$.

3. If for some $v \in \{0, 1\}$, $|D_v| \geq t + 1$, send v, D_v to all parties and continue for one more iteration of the loop but stop updating the flags Z_i, G_i. Output v, Z_i, G_i and terminate at the end of the next iteration of the loop.

– If at any point in the protocol, $Z_i = $ true, send "Zombie" to all parties, output $\perp, Z_i, G_i$ and terminate. If at any point in the protocol a "Zombie" message is received from some party j, act as if it forwards $\perp$ messages in every undead weak multicast protocol from this point on, or messages corresponding to receiving no values in other protocols. If at any point $G_i = $ true, stop sending any message in the protocol, but continue processing messages.

– If at any point in the protocol, a v, σ message is received from some party j such that $\mathsf{Verify}(\mathsf{pk}_j, v, \sigma) = 1$ and there is no tuple of the form $(j, \sigma') \in D_v$, add (j, σ) to D_v.

– If at any point in the protocol, a message v, D_v' is received such that D_v' is a set of tuples of the form (j, σ), for every $(j, \sigma) \in D_v'$, $\mathsf{Verify}(\mathsf{pk}_j, \sigma, v) = 1$ and $|\{j | \exists \sigma \ s.t. \ (j, \sigma) \in D_v'\}| \geq t + 1$, set $D_v = D_v'$.

Fig. 4. An undead consensus protocol

A long line of research has been done on consensus in systems with mixed faults. The earliest works dealing with mixed faults considered a mix of t Byzantine faults and k non-malicious faults, consisting of both crash and omission faults. Crash faults are relatively mild, allowing the adversary to crash parties and stop them from sending or receiving any messages in the protocol. In the below discussion, t is always considered as the number of Byznatine faults, and k is the number of non-malicious faults when the works do not specify any further or allow for a mix of non-malicious faults. When works specify the exact number of crash, receive-omission and send-omission faults we specify these numbers as c, r and s respectively.

Early works such as that of Siu, Chin and Yang [24] a synchronous consensus protocol when $n > 3f + k$. A similar work by Garay and Perry [13] constructed a similar protocol with $n > 3f + c$. Additional works such as that of Thambidurai and Park [25] and of Lincoln and Rushby [18] constructed broadcast protocols for $n > 3t + 2f + k$, when k parties may have non-malicious faults and f parties may deviate from the protocol, but must send the same message to all parties in each round. The work of Hauser, Maurer and Zikas [28] presents several protocols, including a consensus, a broadcast and a secure function evaluation protocol under the assumption that $n > 3t + r + s$, also using the notion of zombies. More recently, the works of Eldefrawy, Loss and Terner [11] and of Abraham, Dolev, Kagan and Stern [1] construct mixed-fault consensus and state machine replication (SMR) protocols in an authenticated setting. Abraham *et al.* construct authenticated consensus and SMR protocols when $n > 2t + c$, only allowing crash faults. On the other hand, Elderfrawy *et al.* construct an authenticated consensus protocol for $n > 2t + 2s + r$. They also improve their resilience to $n > 2t + s + r$ when dealing only with *spotty* omission faults in which either all messages sent by a party are delivered in a given round, or none of them are. Our work adapts many of the ideas of the work of Elderfrawy *et al.*, achieving a resilience of $n > 2t + s + r$ while removing the additional assumptions on fault structure.

More research has been done into mixed faults in partially synchronous systems, in which the network starts off as an unstable network with asynchronous message delivery, but after some point in time (unknown to the participating parties), all messages are delivered within a well known time bound. The Scrooge [22], Upright [7] and SBFT [14] protocols are authenticated mixed-fault protocols for partially synchronous systems which are secure as long as $n > 4t + 2c$, $n > 3t + 2k$ and $n > 3f + 2c$ respectively. Some protocols achieve increased resilience by disallowing some actions by the adversary. Some of the works [6,8,9,17,26] make use of specialized hardware to make sure that the adversary does not act in a Byzantine manner in important code sections and de-facto make it an omission or crash party that can only choose not to send incorrect messages. Additional approaches include protocols which assume that specific parties with special roles are not Byzantine [23] and protocols which can deal with either Byzantine or crash faults, but not with both at the same time [3].

Future Directions. This work intends to simply show that authenticated consensus is possible in synchronous systems when $n > 2t + s + r$, matching the known lower bound. Seeing as this is simply a possibility result, this work adapted techniques and structures while making small adjustments for clarity and simplicity. Some of these adjustments included removing unnecessary layers in the protocol stack (mentioned in Sect. 3), which had the nice side effect of making the protocol slightly more efficient. A natural future line of work deals with improving the efficiency of such protocols. For example, it could be possible to improve the round complexity of the protocol by breaking down the modular structure of the protocols and bundling several protocol messages together. On the other hand, it is very likely that improvements can be made in the number of messages or bits sent by parties by using stronger cryptographic primitives such as threshold signatures, as seen in modern Byzantine consensus protocols such as HotStuff [27] and VABA [2].

Another avenue of research is forgoing the use of threshold cryptography in the common coin protocol. This can be done either by having a $t + r + s + 1$-iteration consensus protocol with a rotating leader, as done in [28], or by generating randomness in a different way. For example, classic Byzantine agreement protocols such as those of Feldman and Micali [12] and Katz and Koo [15] use verifiable secret sharing in order to generate randomness, and constructing such protocols for the authenticated mixed-fault setting can be of independent interest.

Finally, using this protocol, it could be possible to construct more complex primitives such as state machine replication and secure multiparty computation protocols in mixed-fault settings with $n > 2t + s + r$. In a state machine replication protocol, parties agree on a (possibly infinite) log of values, with a numbered slot for each value. Well-known constructions, such as the PBFT protocol of Catsro and Liskov [5] use many instances of byzantine agreement protocols, and the recent work of Abraham et al. [1] constructed such protocols to settings where parties may either be Byzantine or crash. In addition, MPC protocols have been constructed using consensus protocols, allowing parties to securely compute arbitrary functions (or interactive functionalities). Hauser et al. construct such a protocol in an unauthenticated mixed-fault setting with $n > 3t + s + r$ [28] using their consensus protocol, and it could be possible to adapt synchronous cryptographic MPC protocols to mixed-fault protocols using a consensus protocol as an important building block.

Acknowledgements. Julian Loss was supported by the European Union, ERC-2023-STG, Project ID: 101116713. Views and opinions expressed are however those of the author(s) only and do not necessarily reflect those of the European Union. Neither the European Union nor the granting authority can be held responsible for them. Gilad Stern was supported by the HUJI Federmann Cyber Security Research Center in conjunction with the Israel National Cyber Directorate (INCD) in the Prime Minister's Office.

A   Security Proofs

This section includes security proofs not included in the body of the paper.

A.1   Undead Weak Multicast

Theorem 1. *The protocol described in Fig. 1 is a (t, s, r)-secure undead weak multicast protocol if $n > 2t + s + r$.*

Proof. **Validity.** If i^* is nonfaulty or is receive faulty and alive in the beginning of the protocol, it sends m, σ to every party and all nonfaulty parties receive it and forward it. Every party that isn't receive faulty receives those messages. Since i^* is non-Byzantine, it only sends one verifying signature and thus this is the only received value, which will then be output. In addition, if a receive faulty party j receives fewer than $n - t - s$ messages, it becomes a zombie. Otherwise, it receives at least $n - t - s \geq 2t + s + r + 1 - t - s = t + r + 1$ messages, and at least one of those messages was sent by a party that is neither Byzantine nor receive faulty. Those parties receive the message m, σ from i^* and forward it, and thus every $j \neq i^*$ outputs m. In addition, if i^* isn't a zombie by the end of the protocol, it outputs (m, Z_{i^*}, G_{i^*}) as well. Finally, if i^* is send faulty, it only signs the message m. This means that no nonfaulty party receives any other signed message from i^*, and thus output either m or $\bot$.

Detection. If i^* did not become a ghost, then it received "no output" from fewer than $t + 1$ parties. It receives all messages from all $t + 1$ nonfaulty parties, so at least one of those parties did not send "no output", and has thus output m, Z, G.

Termination. All parties terminate after exactly 3 rounds.

No Living Undead. Any party that isn't receive faulty receives messages from at least $n - t - s$ parties in round 2. Therefore, only receive faulty parties become zombies. If i^* is nonfaulty or receive faulty, then all nonfaulty parties receive m, σ in round 1 and forward it. Every non-Byzantine party that hasn't become a zombie received $n - t - s$ messages, i.e. at least $t + r + 1$. Therefore, at least one of those messages was from a nonfaulty or send faulty party. As stated above, it received m, σ and thus did not send "no output". This means that i^* receives at most t messages of the form "no output" from Byzantine parties and does not become a ghost.

A.2 Undead Graded Multicast

Theorem 2. *The protocol described in Fig. 2 is a (t, s, r)-secure undead graded multicast protocol if $n > 2t + s + r$.*

Proof. **Validity.** If i^* is nonfaulty or is receive faulty and alive in the beginning of the protocol, it sends m, σ using an undead weak multicast protocol. The protocol has no living undead, and thus i^* does not become a ghost, and sends the same message again in the second round. From the Validity property of that protocol, every non-Byzantine party either outputs $(m, \sigma), Z, G$ in both rounds, or becomes a zombie. Therefore, every party that didn't become a zombie received both messages and output $m, 2, Z, G$. In addition, if i^* is send faulty, it only signs m and thus no party receives a message $m' \neq m$ with a verifying signature. Therefore, every party outputs x, y, Z, G such that $x = m$ or $x = \bot$.

Detection. If i^* is send faulty and alive at the end of the protocol, it did not become a ghost after sending (m, σ) for the first time. From the Detection property of the undead weak multicast protocol, at least one nonfaulty party j received that message and forwarded it using the undead weak multicast protocol in the second round. From the Validity property of the protocol, every party that doesn't become a zombie in the protocol receives (m, σ) from j and outputs $m, 1, Z, G$ if it hasn't received (m, σ) from i^* and output $m, 2, Z, G$ instead.

Consistency. Assume i^* is not Byzantine and that some party j output $m, 2, Z, G$ with $Z = $ false. This means that j received the same message (m, σ) from i^* in both calls to the undead weak multicast protocol. From the Validity property, i^* must have sent those messages, and a non-Byzantine party only sends the second message if it does not become a ghost during the first call to the protocol. As argued above, at least one nonfaulty party receives that message and forwards it to all parties, either because of the Validity property if i^* is nonfaulty or receive faulty, or from the Detection property if it is send faulty. Every party either becomes a zombie or receives the message, and thus outputs $m, 1, Z, G$ if it hasn't also received (m, σ) from i^* in the second round, causing it to output $m, 2, Z, G$ instead. This means that for every nonfaulty j, k that don't become zombies, $y_j, y_k \in \{1, 2\}$ and thus $|y_j - y_k| \leq 1$. Note that if no nonfaulty party outputs the grade $y = 2$, then for every j, k the grades y_j, y_k are either 0 or 1 and thus $|y_j - y_k| \leq 1$ also holds. Finally, note that if $y_j \neq 0$, then j output m', y_j, Z, G after receiving a pair m', σ' such that $\mathsf{Verify}(\mathsf{pk}_{i^*}, m', \sigma') = 1$. As stated above, i^* only signs m, so $m' = m$.

Termination. All parties terminate after exactly 2 rounds.

No Living Undead. Parties only become ghosts or zombies after doing so in the undead weak multicast protocol, and thus are either send or receive omission respectively since that protocol has no living undead as well.

A.3   Undead Weak Consensus

Theorem 3. *The protocol described in Fig. 3 is a (t, s, r)-secure undead weak consensus protocol if $n > 2t + s + r$.*

Proof. **Validity.** Assume all parties that are alive in the beginning of the protocol have the same input x. Each alive i sends x, σ_i to all other parties. Each nonfaulty party receives at least $t + 1$ such messages from all nonfaulty parties, and no non-Byzantine party receives more than t messages x', σ' such that $x' \neq x$. Every nonfaulty party then calls the undead graded multicast protocol with the set of values it received. From the Validity property of the protocol every non-Byzantine party that isn't a zombie at this time receives the S_j set sent by every nonfaulty party. Therefore, every party i that isn't a zombie by that time received at least $t + 1$ certificates S_j for the input x sent by the nonfaulty parties, and no set contains more than t signatures on $1 - v$. Therefore every party i that isn't a zombie at that time outputs x, Z_i, G_i.

Consistency. Assume some non-Byzantine party outputs v, Z, G such that $v \neq \perp$. By construction, this means that this party is not a zombie at that time. Since it output $v \neq \perp$, there are $t + 1$ parties j from which it received a certificate $S_{j,i}$ for v with $y_{j,i} = 2$. At least one of these parties is non-Byzantine, and let that party be j. From the Validity and Consistency properties of the undead graded multicast protocol, all parties that aren't zombies received the same set $S_{j,i}$ with either grade 1 or 2. This set is a certificate for v and thus every party that isn't a zombie won't output $1 - v$. In addition, parties that do become zombies output $\perp$. Therefore, no non-Byzantine party outputs $1 - v$ from the protocol.

Termination. All parties complete the protocol after exactly 2 rounds.

No Living Undead. Parties only become zombies or ghosts in the protocol after seeing they do so in the undead graded multicast protocol. The protocol has no living undead, so parties only do so if they are indeed send or receive faulty respectively.

A.4   Undead Consensus

Theorem 4. *The protocol described in Fig. 4 is a (t, s, r)-secure undead consensus protocol if $n > 2t + s + r$.*

Proof. **Validity.** Assume all parties that are alive in the beginning of the protocol have the same input v. All parties set $v_i = v$ and start the first iteration of the protocol. We will now prove inductively that every party i that hasn't terminated has $v_i = u_i = v$ in all iterations of the protocol. From the Validity property of the undead weak consensus protocol, every party that isn't a zombie by the end of the protocol outputs $u_i = v$ and sets $v_i = v$. Any party that is a zombie by the end of the protocol outputs $\perp, \mathsf{Z}, \mathsf{G}$. Following that, all parties that are not zombies start the next iteration with $v_i = v$. Note that parties only send messages of the form x, σ with $x = v_i$ and thus at most t parties sign any value other than v in the protocol. This means that at all times, there are signatures from at most t different parties in D_{1-v} and thus no nonfaulty party outputs $1 - v$. In order to complete the proof, it is required to show that all parties eventually terminate, which will be shown in the Termination property of the protocol.

Consistency. Assume some nonfaulty party output some value. It does so after seeing that there are signatures from at least $t + 1$ parties in either D_0 or D_1. Let i be the first non-Byzantine party to send a v, σ message for any value v. If it does so, it is alive at that time, and both output $u_i = v$ from the undead weak consensus protocol and saw that $b = v$ in the same iteration. In that case, every party j that is alive at that point in the protocol outputs either $u_j = v$ or $u_j = \perp$ because of the Consistency property of the undead weak consensus protocol and outputs $b = v$ from CoinFlip in that iteration. Then, every alive j either updates v_j to u_j if $u_j \neq \perp$ (and thus $u_j = v_j = v$), or updates v_j to $b = v$. Following the same arguments as the ones in the Validity property, no non-Byzantine party ever sends a signature on $1 - v$, and thus every party that completes the protocol and isn't a zombie outputs v.

Termination. First note that if some nonfaulty party completes the protocol after outputting v, it sends v, D_v to all parties. Every party that isn't receive faulty receives that message and terminates in a finite number of rounds, and every party that is receive faulty will become a zombie after all other parties stop participating and don't send it messages, causing it to become a zombie if it hasn't terminated earlier. This means that it is enough to show that some nonfaulty party completes the protocol in a finite amount of time. We will show that this even takes place with probability 1 and that the expected number of rounds until this happens is constant.

Observe a single iteration of the protocol in which no nonfaulty party terminated, and assume without loss of generality that all parties that are alive at the end of the call to the undead weak consensus protocol either output v or $\perp$ for some $v \in \{0, 1\}$. With probability $\frac{1}{2}$, all parties output $b = v$ from the CoinFlip protocol as well in that iteration. Therefore, every party i that is alive in the next iteration has $v_i = v$. As shown in the proof of the Validity property, from this point on, all parties have $v_i = u_i = v$ in all subsequent iterations of the protocol. From the consistency property of the undead weak consensus protocol, all nonfaulty parties output v from the protocol in each iteration from this point on. In each one of those iterations, with probability $\frac{1}{2}$, every nonfaulty party also outputs $b = v$ from the CoinFlip protocol. At that point, each nonfaulty party sends a v, σ message to all other parties. Every nonfaulty party receives those messages, adds the a tuple (j, σ) to D_v for every nonfaulty j and outputs v in the end of the iteration. From the above discussion, all parties complete the protocol in a constant number of rounds after that.

Note that the number of iterations required for each of the above events is a geometric random variable with probability $\frac{1}{2}$ of succeeding in each iteration, and thus the expected number of rounds is bounded by 4. In addition, for any ℓ, the probability that it takes more than ℓ iterations for each of the events to take place is no greater than $\frac{1}{2^\ell}$, and thus the probability that some party does not terminate in at most 2ℓ iterations is no greater than $\frac{2}{2^\ell} = \frac{1}{2^{\ell-1}}$, which decreases exponentially as ℓ grows with a 0 probability of an infinite run.

No Living Undead. Parties only become zombies or ghosts in the protocol if they do so in the undead weak consensus and CoinFlip protocols. Both of these protocols have no living undead, so parties do so if they are receive or send faulty respectively. Note that if a party is alive and it completes the protocol after outputting v, it sends its D_v set to all parties and continues participating in another iteration of the loop. This means that any party that is alive at the time the first nonfaulty party completes the protocol either receives the message or is receive faulty. It then outputs v, Z, G in the next iteration of the loop. Since all parties are still participating in the protocol, the undead weak consensus protocol has no living undead at that point in time. Any receive-omission party that hasn't terminated by that point in time will either become a zombie because it receives no messages or eventually output v. In addition, note that if parties become zombies, all parties are informed and act as if the zombies sent messages consistent with receiving no messages in all protocols, which is a possible behaviour of theirs in a regular run of the protocols, and thus the protocols still have no living undead.

B Original Protocol Definitions

As stated in Sect. 2.4, the definitions used in this paper are variations on well-known protocols, which also add the notion of undead parties. Below are the original definitions, which do not use undead parties. Note that in the undead versions of the protocols, parties also output the flags Z and G, which are not part of the output in the original setting. This means that the undead versions technically do not solve the original tasks, but can be easily adjusted to solve them by simply omitting these flags from the output. Note that in the below protocols we actually consider uniform versions of the protocols. In these versions, even omission faulty parties are required to output the correct values or ⊥ if they can't (specifically, if they are receive faulty). This reflects the above constructions of the undead versions of the protocols, which also have these guarantees for faulty outputs. Weaker versions of such protocols also exist in which no restrictions are made on the output of faulty parties, but we do not define such protocols below.

Multicast. This notion is usually not defined separately, and is often just used as a simple instruction to send a message to all parties. One could define a multicast task in which a known sender has a message to send to all parties, and all parties output a message or ⊥.

Definition 6. *Let Π be a protocol executed by parties $1, \ldots, n$, with a designated sender i^* starting with an input $m \neq \bot$. Every party outputs a value x such that x is either a possible message or $\bot$.*

- **Validity.** *Π is (t, s, r)-valid if the following holds whenever at most t parties are Byzantine, s parties are send faulty and r parties are receive faulty: if i^* is nonfaulty or receive faulty, every party that is neither Byzantine nor receive faulty outputs m. In addition, if i^* is send faulty, no non-Byzantine party outputs x such that $x \notin \{m, \bot\}$.*
- **Termination.** *Π is (t, s, r)-terminating if the following holds whenever at most t parties are Byzantine, s parties are send faulty and r parties are receive faulty: all parties complete the protocol and output a value.*

If Π is (t, s, r)-valid and (t, s, r)-terminating we say that it is a (t, s, r)-secure multicast protocol.

Graded Multicast. A graded multicast protocol also has a designated sender that attempts to send its message to all parties. In addition to outputting a message x, parties also output a grade y, indicating how confident they are that the protocol succeeded.

Definition 7. *Let Π be a protocol executed by parties $1, \ldots, n$, with a designated sender i^* starting with an input $m \neq \bot$. Every party outputs a pair of values (x, y) such that x is either a possible message or $\bot$ and $y \in \{0, 1, 2\}$.*

- **Validity.** Π is (t, s, r)-valid *if the following holds whenever at most t parties are Byzantine, s parties are send faulty and r parties are receive faulty: if i^* is nonfaulty or receive faulty, every party that is neither Byzantine nor receive faulty outputs x, y such that $x = m, y = 2$. In addition, if i^* is send faulty, no non-Byzantine party outputs x, y such that $x \notin \{m, \bot\}$.*
- **Consistency.** Π is (t, s, r)-consistent *if the following holds whenever at most t parties are Byzantine, s parties are send faulty and r parties are receive faulty: if i^* is non-Byzantine and j, k are neither Byzantine nor receive faulty, and j, k output x_j, y_j and x_k, y_k respectively, then $|y_j - y_k| \leq 1$. In addition, if j is non-Byzantine (but is possibly receive faulty) then either $x_j = \bot$ and $y_j = 0$ or $x_j = m$.*
- **Termination.** Π is (t, s, r)-terminating *if the following holds whenever at most t parties are Byzantine, s parties are send faulty and r parties are receive faulty: all parties complete the protocol and output a value.*

If Π is (t, s, r)-valid, (t, s, r)-consistent and (t, s, r)-terminating we say that it is a (t, s, r)-(secure) *graded multicast protocol.*

Weak Consensus. In a weak consensus protocol, every party has a binary input, 0 or 1. The goal of the protocol is for there to be some value y such that every party either outputs y or $\bot$.

Definition 8. *Let Π be a protocol executed by parties $1, \ldots, n$, in which every party i starts with an input $v_i \neq \bot$. Every party outputs a value x such that x is either a possible input message or $\bot$.*

- **Validity.** Π is (t, s, r)-valid *if the following holds whenever at most t parties are Byzantine, s parties are send faulty and r parties are receive faulty: if all nonfaulty parties have the same input v, every party that is neither Byzantine nor receive faulty outputs v.*
- **Consistency.** Π is (t, s, r)-consistent *if the following holds whenever at most t parties are Byzantine, s parties are send faulty and r parties are receive faulty: if two non-Byzantine parties output x and x' respectively, then either $x = x'$, $x = \bot$ or $x' = \bot$.*
- **Termination.** Π is (t, s, r)-terminating *if the following holds whenever at most t parties are Byzantine, s parties are send faulty and r parties are receive faulty: all parties complete the protocol and output a value.*

If Π is (t, s, r)-valid, (t, s, r)-consistent and (t, s, r)-terminating we say that it is a (t, s, r)-secure *weak consensus protocol.*

Consensus. In a consensus protocol, all parties output the same value. In addition, if all parties have the same input, they must output that value.

Definition 9. *Let Π be a protocol executed by parties $1, \ldots, n$, in which every party i starts with an input $v_i \neq \bot$. Every party outputs a possible output value x or possibly $\bot$ if it is faulty.*

- **Validity.** Π is (t, s, r)-valid *if the following holds whenever at most t parties are Byzantine, s parties are send faulty and r parties are receive faulty: if all nonfaulty parties have the same input v, every party that is neither Byzantine nor receive faulty outputs v. In addition, receive faulty parties either output v or $\perp$.*
- **Consistency.** Π is (t, s, r)-consistent *if the following holds whenever at most t parties are Byzantine, s parties are send faulty and r parties are receive faulty: if two parties non-Byzantine and they output x, x', then either $x = x'$ or one of them is receive faulty and it outputs $\perp$.*
- **Termination.** Π is (t, s, r)-terminating *if the following holds whenever at most t parties are Byzantine, s parties are send faulty and r parties are receive faulty: all parties complete the protocol and output a value.*

If Π is (t, s, r)-valid, (t, s, r)-consistent and (t, s, r)-terminating we say that it is a (t, s, r)-secure consensus protocol.

References

1. Abraham, I., Dolev, D., Kagan, A., Stern, G.: Brief announcement: authenticated consensus in synchronous systems with mixed faults. In: Scheideler, C. (ed.) 36th International Symposium on Distributed Computing, DISC 2022, 25–27 October 2022, Augusta, Georgia, USA. LIPIcs, vol. 246, pp. 38:1–38:3. Schloss Dagstuhl - Leibniz-Zentrum für Informatik (2022). https://doi.org/10.4230/LIPIcs.DISC.2022.38

2. Abraham, I., Malkhi, D., Spiegelman, A.: Validated asynchronous Byzantine agreement with optimal resilience and asymptotically optimal time and word communication. CoRR abs/1811.01332 (2018). arXiv arXiv:1811.01332

3. Bessani, A.N., Sousa, J., Alchieri, E.A.P.: State machine replication for the masses with BFT-SMART. In: 44th Annual IEEE/IFIP International Conference on Dependable Systems and Networks, DSN 2014, Atlanta, GA, USA, 23–26 June 2014, pp. 355–362. IEEE Computer Society (2014). https://doi.org/10.1109/DSN.2014.43

4. Blum, E., Katz, J., Loss, J.: Synchronous consensus with optimal asynchronous fallback guarantees. In: Hofheinz, D., Rosen, A. (eds.) TCC 2019. LNCS, vol. 11891, pp. 131–150. Springer, Cham (2019). https://doi.org/10.1007/978-3-030-36030-6_6

5. Castro, M., Liskov, B.: Practical Byzantine fault tolerance. In: Seltzer, M.I., Leach, P.J. (eds.) Proceedings of the Third USENIX Symposium on Operating Systems Design and Implementation (OSDI), New Orleans, Louisiana, USA, 22–25 February 1999, pp. 173–186. USENIX Association (1999). https://dl.acm.org/citation.cfm?id=296824

6. Chun, B., Maniatis, P., Shenker, S., Kubiatowicz, J.: Attested append-only memory: making adversaries stick to their word. In: Bressoud, T.C., Kaashoek, M.F. (eds.) 2007 Proceedings of the 21st ACM Symposium on Operating Systems Principles, SOSP 2007, Stevenson, Washington, USA, 14–17 October 2007, pp. 189–204. ACM (2007). https://doi.org/10.1145/1294261.1294280

7. Clement, A., et al.: Upright cluster services. In: Matthews, J.N., Anderson, T.E. (eds.) 2009 Proceedings of the 22nd ACM Symposium on Operating Systems Principles, SOSP 2009, Big Sky, Montana, USA, 11–14 October 2009, pp. 277–290. ACM (2009). https://doi.org/10.1145/1629575.1629602

8. Correia, M., Lung, L.C., Neves, N.F., Veríssimo, P.: Efficient Byzantine-resilient reliable multicast on a hybrid failure model. In: 21st Symposium on Reliable Distributed Systems, SRDS 2002, 13–16 October 2002, Osaka, Japan, pp. 2–11. IEEE Computer Society (2002). https://doi.org/10.1109/RELDIS.2002.1180168

9. Correia, M., Neves, N.F., Veríssimo, P.: How to tolerate half less one Byzantine nodes in practical distributed systems. In: 23rd International Symposium on Reliable Distributed Systems, SRDS 2004, 18–20 October 2004, Florianpolis, Brazil, pp. 174–183. IEEE Computer Society (2004). https://doi.org/10.1109/RELDIS.2004.1353018

10. Dolev, D., Strong, H.R.: Authenticated algorithms for Byzantine agreement. SIAM J. Comput. 12(4), 656–666 (1983). https://doi.org/10.1137/0212045

11. Eldefrawy, K., Loss, J., Terner, B.: How Byzantine is a send corruption? In: Ateniese, G., Venturi, D. (eds.) Proceedings of the 20th International Conference on Applied Cryptography and Network Security, ACNS 2022, Rome, Italy, 20–23 June 2022, pp. 684–704. Springer, Heidelberg (2022). https://doi.org/10.1007/978-3-031-09234-3_34

12. Feldman, P., Micali, S.: Optimal algorithms for Byzantine agreement. In: Simon, J. (ed.) Proceedings of the 20th Annual ACM Symposium on Theory of Computing, Chicago, Illinois, USA, 2–4 May 1988, pp. 148–161. ACM (1988). https://doi.org/10.1145/62212.62225

13. Garay, J.A., Perry, K.J.: A continuum of failure models for distributed computing. In: Segall, A., Zaks, S. (eds.) WDAG 1992. LNCS, vol. 647, pp. 153–165. Springer, Heidelberg (1992). https://doi.org/10.1007/3-540-56188-9_11

14. Golan-Gueta, G., et al.: SBFT: a scalable and decentralized trust infrastructure. In: 49th Annual IEEE/IFIP International Conference on Dependable Systems and Networks, DSN 2019, Portland, OR, USA, 24–27 June 2019, pp. 568–580. IEEE (2019). https://doi.org/10.1109/DSN.2019.00063

15. Katz, J., Koo, C.-Y.: On expected constant-round protocols for Byzantine agreement. In: Dwork, C. (ed.) CRYPTO 2006. LNCS, vol. 4117, pp. 445–462. Springer, Heidelberg (2006). https://doi.org/10.1007/11818175_27

16. Lamport, L., Shostak, R.E., Pease, M.C.: The Byzantine generals problem. ACM Trans. Program. Lang. Syst. 4(3), 382–401 (1982). https://doi.org/10.1145/357172.357176

17. Levin, D., Douceur, J.R., Lorch, J.R., Moscibroda, T.: Trinc: small trusted hardware for large distributed systems. In: Rexford, J., Sirer, E.G. (eds.) Proceedings of the 6th USENIX Symposium on Networked Systems Design and Implementation, NSDI 2009, 22–24 April 2009, Boston, MA, USA, pp. 1–14. USENIX Association (2009). http://www.usenix.org/events/nsdi09/tech/full_papers/levin/levin.pdf

18. Lincoln, P., Rushby, J.M.: A formally verified algorithm for interactive consistency under a hybrid fault model. In: Digest of Papers: FTCS-23, The Twenty-Third Annual International Symposium on Fault-Tolerant Computing, Toulouse, France, 22–24 June 1993, pp. 402–411. IEEE Computer Society (1993). https://doi.org/10.1109/FTCS.1993.627343

19. Parvédy, P.R., Raynal, M.: Uniform agreement despite process omission failures. In: 17th International Parallel and Distributed Processing Symposium, IPDPS 2003, 22–26 April 2003, Nice, France, CD-ROM/Abstracts Proceedings, p. 212. IEEE Computer Society (2003). https://doi.org/10.1109/IPDPS.2003.1213388

20. Perry, K.J., Toueg, S.: Distributed agreement in the presence of processor and communication faults. IEEE Trans. Softw. Eng. **12**(3), 477–482 (1986). https://doi.org/10.1109/TSE.1986.6312888

21. Raynal, M.: Consensus in synchronous systems: a concise guided tour. In: 9th Pacific Rim International Symposium on Dependable Computing, PRDC 2002, 16–18 December 2002, Tsukuba-City, Ibarski, Japan, pp. 221–228. IEEE Computer Society (2002). https://doi.org/10.1109/PRDC.2002.1185641

22. Serafini, M., Bokor, P., Dobre, D., Majuntke, M., Suri, N.: Scrooge: reducing the costs of fast Byzantine replication in presence of unresponsive replicas. In: Proceedings of the 2010 IEEE/IFIP International Conference on Dependable Systems and Networks, DSN 2010, Chicago, IL, USA, 28 June–1 July 2010, pp. 353–362. IEEE Computer Society (2010). https://doi.org/10.1109/DSN.2010.5544295

23. Serafini, M., Suri, N.: The fail-heterogeneous architectural model. In: 26th IEEE Symposium on Reliable Distributed Systems, SRDS 2007, Beijing, China, 10–12 October 2007, pp. 103–113. IEEE Computer Society (2007). https://doi.org/10.1109/SRDS.2007.33

24. Siu, H.S., Chin, Y.H., Yang, W.P.: Byzantine agreement in the presence of mixed faults on processors and links. IEEE Trans. Parallel Distrib. Syst. **9**(4), 335–345 (1998). https://doi.org/10.1109/71.667895

25. Thambidurai, P.M., Park, Y.: Interactive consistency with multiple failure modes. In: Proceedings of the Seventh Symposium on Reliable Distributed Systems, SRDS 1988, Columbus, Ohio, USA, 10–12 October 1988, pp. 93–100. IEEE Computer Society (1988). https://doi.org/10.1109/RELDIS.1988.25784

26. Veronese, G.S., Correia, M., Bessani, A.N., Lung, L.C., Veríssimo, P.: Efficient Byzantine fault-tolerance. IEEE Trans. Comput. **62**(1), 16–30 (2013). https://doi.org/10.1109/TC.2011.221

27. Yin, M., Malkhi, D., Reiter, M.K., Golan-Gueta, G., Abraham, I.: HotStuff: BFT consensus with linearity and responsiveness. In: Robinson, P., Ellen, F. (eds.) Proceedings of the 2019 ACM Symposium on Principles of Distributed Computing, PODC 2019, Toronto, ON, Canada, 29 July–2 August 2019, pp. 347–356. ACM (2019). https://doi.org/10.1145/3293611.3331591

28. Zikas, V., Hauser, S., Maurer, U.: Realistic failures in secure multi-party computation. In: Reingold, O. (ed.) TCC 2009. LNCS, vol. 5444, pp. 274–293. Springer, Heidelberg (2009). https://doi.org/10.1007/978-3-642-00457-5_17

Concurrent Asynchronous Byzantine Agreement in Expected-Constant Rounds, Revisited

Ran Cohen[1]([⊠]), Pouyan Forghani[2], Juan Garay[2], Rutvik Patel[2], and Vassilis Zikas[3]

[1] Reichman University, Herzliya, Israel
cohenran@runi.ac.il
[2] Texas A&M University, College Station, USA
{pouyan.forghani,garay,rsp7}@tamu.edu
[3] Purdue University, West Lafayette, USA
vzikas@cs.purdue.edu

Abstract. It is well known that without randomization, Byzantine agreement (BA) requires a linear number of rounds in the synchronous setting, while it is flat out impossible in the asynchronous setting. The primitive which allows to bypass the above limitation is known as *oblivious common coin* (OCC). It allows parties to agree with constant probability on a random coin, where agreement is oblivious, i.e., players are not aware whether or not agreement has been achieved.

The starting point of our work is the observation that no known protocol exists for information-theoretic multi-valued OCC with optimal resiliency in the asynchronous setting (with eventual message delivery).

This apparent hole in the literature is particularly problematic, as multi-valued OCC is implicitly or explicitly used in several constructions.

In this paper, we present the first information-theoretic multi-valued OCC protocol in the asynchronous setting with optimal resiliency, i.e., tolerating $t < n/3$ corruptions, thereby filling this important gap. Further, our protocol efficiently implements OCC with an exponential-size domain, a property which is not even achieved by known constructions in the simpler, synchronous setting.

We then turn to the problem of round-preserving parallel composition of asynchronous BA. A protocol for this task was proposed by Ben-Or and El-Yaniv [Distributed Computing '03]. Their construction, however, is flawed in several ways. Thus, as a second contribution, we provide a simpler, more modular protocol for the above task. Finally, and as a contribution of independent interest, we provide proofs in Canetti's Universal Composability framework; this makes our work the first one offering composability guarantees, which are important as BA is a core building block of secure multi-party computation protocols.

The full version of this paper can be found at the *IACR Cryptology ePrint Archive*, report 2023/1003.

G. Rothblum and H. Wee (Eds.): TCC 2023, LNCS 14372, pp. 422–451, 2023.
https://doi.org/10.1007/978-3-031-48624-1_16

1   Introduction

Byzantine agreement (BA) [63,74] enables n parties to reach agreement on one of their inputs in an adversarial setting, facing up to t colluding and cheating parties. The core properties require all honest parties to eventually terminate with the same output (*agreement*), which equals their input value in case they all begin with the same common input (*validity*). BA and its closely related single-sender variant, *broadcast*, are fundamental building blocks in the construction of cryptographic protocols, in particular for *secure multi-party computation* (MPC) [13,28,56,82], in which parties wish to privately compute a joint function over their inputs.

We consider a complete network of authenticated and private point-to-point (P2P) channels, which enables every pair of parties to communicate directly. The central settings in which BA has been studied are:

The *synchronous* setting. Here the protocol proceeds in a round-by-round fashion, and messages sent in a given round are guaranteed to be delivered by the start of the next round. The round structure can be achieved given synchronized clocks and a known bound on message delivery, and enables the use of *timeouts*. This clean abstraction allows for simpler analyses of protocols, but comes at the cost that parties must wait for the worst-case delay in each round before they can proceed.

The *asynchronous* setting. Here no assumptions are made on the clocks or on the bound of message delivery (other than that each message will be eventually delivered), and messages may be adversarially delayed by an arbitrary (yet finite) amount of time. The main challenge is that timeouts cannot be used, implying the inability to distinguish a slow honest party from a silent, noncooperative corrupted party. On the positive side, asynchronous protocols can advance as fast as the network allows, irrespectively of the worst-case delay, and each party can proceed to the next step as soon as it gets sufficiently many messages.

The *feasibility* of BA is inherently related to the synchrony assumptions of the system. Synchronous BA with *perfect* security is achievable with deterministic protocols for $t < n/3$ [15,54,74]; this bound is tight in the plain model[1] even when considering weaker, computational security [17,47,74], but can be overcome with setup assumptions, yielding computationally secure BA [37], and even information-theoretically secure BA [75], for $t < n/2$.[2] On the other hand, deterministic asynchronous BA (A-BA) is impossible even facing a single crash failure [48], and randomized solutions are a necessity. Following Ben-Or [9] and Rabin [76], information-theoretic randomized A-BA has been achieved with $t < n/3$ corruptions [2,18,24], which, as opposed to the synchronous case, is a tight bound even given setup and cryptographic assumptions [19,39].

---

[1] That is, without setup assumptions and without imposing resource restrictions on the adversary.

[2] The bound $t < n/2$ is tight for BA [49]; however, under the same setup assumptions, broadcast can be solved for any number of corruptions.

Round Complexity of BA. In the synchronous setting, it is known that *deterministic* BA requires $t + 1$ rounds [37,46], a bound that is matched by early feasibility results [37,54,74]. It is also known that t-secure randomized BA for $t \in \Theta(n)$ cannot terminate in a *strict* constant number of rounds [26,29,60]; yet, *expected* constant-round protocols have been constructed both for $t < n/3$ in the plain model [45] and for $t < n/2$ in the PKI model [50,61].[3] The latter protocols follow the approach of Rabin [76] and rely on an *oblivious common coin* (OCC), that is, a distributed coin-tossing protocol over a domain V such that the output of every honest party is a common random value $v \in V$ with constant probability p, but with probability $1 - p$ is independently and adversarially chosen; the coin toss is "oblivious" since the parties cannot distinguish between a successful coin toss and an adversarial one.[4]

Loosely speaking, round complexity in the asynchronous setting can be defined based on the expected number of times an honest party has to alternate between sending and receiving messages that are "causally related" [36]. In an unpublished manuscript, Feldman [41] generalized the expected-constant-round synchronous protocol of [42] to asynchronous networks with $t < n/4$; at the core of the construction lies a **binary** (asynchronous) OCC protocol which actually has resiliency $\min(t', \lceil n/3 \rceil - 1)$, where t' is the corruption threshold of an *asynchronous verifiable secret sharing* (A-VSS) scheme.[5] Canetti and Rabin [24] constructed A-VSS for $t < n/3$, thereby obtaining A-BA in expected-constant rounds for the optimal threshold $t < n/3$.

Concurrent BA. All of the above constructions are for solving a *single* instance of BA. However, most applications, particularly MPC protocols, require composing multiple instances of BA: sequentially, in parallel, or concurrently. While the composition of synchronous, deterministic protocols is relatively simple (although care must be taken in the cryptographic setting [65]), composing expected-constant-round protocols with probabilistic termination is a much more challenging task.

Indeed, Ben-Or and El-Yaniv [11,12] observed that running m instances of a probabilistic-termination protocol in parallel may incur a blow-up in the expected number of rounds until they all terminate. The technical reason is that the expectation of the maximum of m independent, identically distributed random variables does not necessarily equal the maximum of their expectations. In particular, for expected-constant-round BA with a geometric termination probability (which is the case in all known protocols), the parallel composition of m instances terminates after expected $\Theta(\log m)$ rounds [31]. Further, even when all

---

[3] Fitzi and Garay [50] devised expected-constant-round BA for $t < n/2$ in the PKI model under number-theoretic assumptions. Katz and Koo [61] established a similar result from the minimal assumption of digital signatures, which yields an information-theoretic variant using pseudo-signatures [75].

[4] This primitive is sometimes known as a "weak" common coin in the literature.

[5] Feldman's A-VSS suffers from a negligible error probability. An *errorless* A-VSS scheme for $t < n/4$ is given in [10] and used to construct a *perfectly* secure asynchronous MPC protocol with resiliency $t < n/4$.

parties start the protocol together, simultaneous termination is not guaranteed as the adversary can force some honest parties to terminate after the others; although this gap can be reduced to a single round, inaccurate sequential re-synchronization of ℓ instances of BA may lead to an exponential blow up in ℓ if not done with care [64]. Following [12,61,64,65], recent works have shown how to compose synchronous BA in a round-preserving way with simulation-based security in Canetti's framework for universal composability (UC) [23], with optimal resiliency and *perfect* security in the plain model for $t < n/3$ [31], and with cryptographic security in the PKI model for $t < n/2$ [32].

In the asynchronous setting, the parties are not assumed to begin the proto-col at the same time, so intuitively, sequential composition is not problematic. However, running m instances of expected-constant-round A-BA concurrently would yield a $\Theta(\log m)$ blowup as in the synchronous case. Ben-Or and El-Yaniv [12] further showed how to execute m instances of A-BA in expected-constant rounds and with optimal resiliency $t < n/3$; however, their solution is more com-plicated than the synchronous one. In addition, they only prove a property-based security definition of A-BA that does not necessarily address modern security requirements such as security under composition, or facing adaptive adversaries.

1.1 Concurrent A-BA in Expected-Constant Rounds: Cracks in the Concrete

The underlying idea behind the synchronous protocol of Ben-Or and El-Yaniv [12] for parallel BA is to execute each BA instance multiple times over the same inputs, but only for a constant number of rounds. For a suitable choice of parameters, this ensures that with high probability each party will have obtained at least one output value in each such batch. To coordinate these outputs, the parties then run an *oblivious leader election* (OLE) protocol, which guarantees that with constant probability, a random leader is elected. In the event that the leader is honest and the parties obtained an output in each batch (which, again, occurs with constant probability) the parties will terminate; otherwise they repeat the process.

The same general technique underlies Ben-Or and El-Yaniv's asynchronous protocol, but great care is needed to deal with the low message dispersion inher-ent in asynchronous networks while maintaining optimal resiliency $t < n/3$. A closer look at their security proof indeed raises a number of subtle issues. First, they point to Canetti and Rabin [24] for instantiating the (asynchronous) OLE primitive used in their construction (called *A-Election()*). (Recall that Canetti and Rabin construct an OCC to obtain A-BA in expected-constant rounds; an n-valued OCC would indeed imply OLE.) As it turns out, the OCC construc-tion in [24, Sec. 8] (as well as the more detailed versions [22, Sec. 5.7] and [25, Sec. 8]) is only *binary* (i.e., it only works for $V = \{0, 1\}$), and it does not seem straightforward to generalize to larger (non-constant-sized) domains.

Further, running $\log n$ executions of a binary OCC in parallel to make it multi-valued yields only $1/\text{poly}(n)$ probability of agreement, and as long as the coin is not *perfectly* fair (i.e., non-oblivious and unbiased, which is impossible in the asynchronous setting [77]), that would not imply OLE with constant success probability. We note that Patra *et al.* [73] claim to construct a $(t + 1)$-bit asynchronous OCC, but their main focus is on communication complexity, and the agreement probability of their protocol is no better than would be obtained by running $t + 1$ executions of a binary OCC protocol (i.e., exponentially small). Techniques used to get OLE in the synchronous setting [42,61] do not seem to extend in asynchrony for $t < n/3$ (we elaborate on this in Sect. 1.2). Thus, to the best of our knowledge, no existing OCC construction is *simultaneously* optimally resilient, multi-valued, and asynchronous, without relying on computational assumptions (in Sect. 1.3 we discuss solutions in the cryptographic setting).

Second, there is a subtle issue in the logic of one of the proofs in [12]. This issue raises concerns about the validity of the proof claiming an expected-constant round complexity of one of the main subroutines—namely, the Π_{select} subroutine, which handles the shortcomings of their message-distribution mechanism. Specifically, in the analysis of Π_{select} it is claimed that if the leader is chosen from a certain set, the protocol will terminate. However, further examination reveals that there are scenarios in which the protocol may not terminate for certain leaders from that set. As a result, this issue casts doubt on the promised expected-constant round complexity of their concurrent A-BA protocol.

Finally, the concurrent asynchronous (resp., synchronous) BA protocol in [12] relies on *multi-valued* asynchronous (resp., synchronous) BA in expected-constant rounds.[6] Recall that running the binary protocols in [45] or [24] $\omega(1)$ times in parallel would terminate in expected $\omega(1)$ rounds, so they cannot be naïvely used for this task. In the synchronous setting, Turpin and Coan [79] extended binary BA to multi-valued BA for $t < n/3$ with an overhead of just two rounds. Ben-Or and El-Yaniv claim that this technique can be adapted for asynchronous networks by using Bracha's "A-Cast" primitive [18] for message distribution. However, a closer look reveals that although the Turpin-Coan extension works (with appropriate modifications) in the asynchronous setting for $t < n/5$, it **provably does not work** when $t \geq n/5$, regardless of the specific choice of the underlying binary A-BA protocol and even when the adversary is limited to static corruptions (see further discussion in the full version of this paper [33]).

More recently, an optimally resilient multi-valued A-BA protocol with expected-constant round complexity was proposed by Patra [72], but it relies on the *Agreement on a Common Subset* (ACS) protocol in [14]; however, as we explain below, this ACS protocol does not achieve expected-constant round complexity without some modifications, which require either expected-constant-round concurrent A-BA (this would be circular), or information-theoretic asynchronous OLE with optimal resiliency. Fortunately, Mostéfaoui and Raynal [70] recently gave a black-box, constant-round reduction from multi-valued to binary

---

[6] This is true even if one is interested only in *binary* concurrent BA (i.e., when the input vectors consist of bits). Multi-valued BA is needed to agree on the leader's output vector.

A-BA for $t < n/3$,[7] using just one invocation of the underlying binary protocol as in [79].

We emphasize that the asynchronous protocol of Ben-Or and El-Yaniv [11,12] lies, either explicitly or implicitly, at the core of virtually every round-efficient asynchronous MPC construction [8,10,14,16,30,36,57,58,66]. The concerns raised above regarding the result of [12] render this extensive follow-up work unsound. In this paper, we revisit this seminal result and rectify these issues.

1.2   Overview of Our Results

We now present an overview of our results, which are three-fold, including a detailed exposition of our techniques.

Multi-valued and Asynchronous Oblivious Common Coin. As a starting point, we look at the *binary* asynchronous OCC protocol of Canetti and Rabin [24]. The idea (following the approach of [45] in the synchronous setting and [41] in the asynchronous setting) is that each party secret-shares a random vote for each party, using an optimally resilient A-VSS scheme. Each party accepts $t + 1$ of the votes cast for him (at least one of which must have come from an honest party), and once it is determined that enough secrets have been fixed (based on several rounds of message exchange, using Bracha's A-Cast primitive [18] for message distribution), the parties begin reconstructing the accepted votes. The sum or "tally" of these votes becomes the value associated with the corresponding party. After computing the values associated with an appropriate set of at least $n - t$ parties, an honest party outputs 0 if at least one of those tallies is 0, and outputs 1 otherwise. Note that each tally must be uniformly random, and the properties of A-Cast guarantee that no two honest parties can disagree on the value of any given tally (although up to t tallies may be "missing" in an honest party's local view); moreover, Canetti and Rabin show using a counting argument that at least $n/3$ of the tallies are known to all honest parties (i.e., common to their local views). This can be used to show that with probability at least $1/4$ all honest parties output 0, and similarly for 1.

In the conference version of Feldman and Micali's paper [42], there is a brief remark suggesting that the synchronous version of the above protocol can be modified to obtain (oblivious) leader election.[8] Rather than outputting a bit, parties output the index of the party whose tally is minimum; when the domain of secrets is large enough, with constant probability the same *honest* party is chosen. This approach was fully materialized by Katz and Koo [61] for $t < n/3$ in the information-theoretic setting and $t < n/2$ in the computational setting.

---

[7] They are also concerned with obtaining $O(n^2)$ message complexity. The novelty of their result, even without this more stringent requirement, does not seem to be acknowledged in the paper.

[8] This claim no longer appears in the ICALP [43] or journal [45] versions of the paper, or in Feldman's thesis [44].

We note that what is obtained is not exactly OLE as we have defined it, as the adversary can of course bias the index of the elected party, but nevertheless, this is sufficient for the concurrent BA protocols of Ben-Or and El-Yaniv [12].

Unfortunately, the approach effective in the synchronous setting cannot be directly applied to the asynchronous setting while maintaining optimal resiliency. The challenge arises from the fact that the adversary can selectively remove t coordinates from the honest parties' local views of the tallies, ensuring that the leader is not chosen from the parties corresponding to those missing coordinates. This poses a significant obstacle as the original concurrent A-BA protocol by Ben-Or and El-Yaniv [12] terminates successfully when the leader is honest and selected from an adversarially chosen subset of $n - 2t$ parties. Consequently, when $t < n/3$, the size of this subset is only $t + 1$, allowing the adversary to reduce the probability of choosing an appropriate leader to as low as $\frac{1}{n-t}$. The same issue arises in our simplified concurrent A-BA protocol, where we also require the leader to be selected from an adversarially chosen subset of parties, but with size greater than $n/3$. Again, when $t < n/3$, this subset can be of size $t + 1$, leading to the same challenge. However, when $t < n/4$, the set of potential appropriate leaders becomes larger in both concurrent A-BA protocols, enabling us to circumvent this issue. Therefore, in addition to the inherent value in obtaining a true OCC (where a successful coin toss produces a uniform value), we specifically need such a primitive to obtain optimal resiliency for concurrent A-BA.

In conclusion, no OLE construction—and therefore no concurrent A-BA protocol in expected-constant rounds—exists with optimal resiliency $t < n/3$ in asynchronous networks. We now describe our solution to this problem, which is based on the following simple combinatorial observation. If we work over a field of size $N \in \Theta(n^2)$, then with *constant* probability, at least one value will be repeated in the global view of tallies, and, moreover, all repeats will occur within the subset of indices known to all honest parties. The intuition for this fact is that when $N \in O(n^2)$ there is, due to the birthday paradox, at least one repeat in any constant fraction of the indices with constant probability, and when $N \in \Omega(n^2)$, there are no repeats at all with constant probability. There is a "sweet spot" between these extremes that can be leveraged to extract shared randomness: Honest parties output the value that is repeated in their local views of the tallies and has the minimum index in the vector of tallies. With this modification of Canetti and Rabin's protocol [24], we obtain the first n^2-valued asynchronous OCC for $t < n/3$ in the information-theoretic setting. We remark that the above combinatorial observation at the heart of our construction may be of independent interest.

It is straightforward to extend our OCC protocol to accommodate arbitrary domains V. One approach is to work over a prime field of size at least $\text{lcm}(n^2, |V|)$. In this setting, we can still identify "repeats" by considering the tallies modulo n^2. Once the repeat with minimum index is determined, we can generate a common random output by reducing the corresponding (original) field element modulo $|V|$. In particular, when $|V| = n$, we get asynchronous OLE with optimal resiliency.

Proving the security of our multi-valued OCC protocol in a *simulation-based* manner is not without its own challenges. The issue is that the simulator must expose a view of the vector of tallies that both adheres to the distribution in the real world and is consistent with the random value chosen by the OCC functionality (in the case of a successful coin toss) in the ideal world. While the simulator can easily determine the exact set of indices known to all honest parties from its internal execution with the real-world adversary, properly sampling the "repeat pattern" according to these constraints is a delicate task; furthermore, since the functionality is only parameterized by a (constant) lower bound on the probability of a successful coin toss, the simulator must handle the complementary case carefully in order to avoid skewing the distribution. It is not immediately clear how to perform this inverse sampling efficiently.

A heavy-handed solution is to simply have the functionality sample the tallies itself, and then determine the output based on the location of repeats relative to the subset of indices (supplied by the simulator) that are known to all honest parties. This protocol-like functionality would certainly allow for simulation— and would in fact be sufficient for our purposes—but its guarantees are more difficult to reason about and, more importantly, it cannot be realized by other protocols! Instead, we construct a simulator that, given the exact probabilities of certain events in the protocol, can also efficiently sample from those events, potentially conditioned on the output of a successful coin toss. By selecting the appropriate sampling procedure, the simulator can derive a vector of tallies that preserves the (perfect) indistinguishability of the real and ideal worlds. Equipped with the means to carry out the inverse sampling, we can now realize a more abstract (and natural) OCC functionality, which is ready to be plugged into higher-level protocols.

Simplified Concurrent A-BA. Ben-Or and El-Yaniv [12] devised an expected-constant-round concurrent A-BA protocol. However, in addition to relying on unspecified building blocks, as mentioned above, it suffers from logical issues in its proof. Although our new OCC protocol can instantiate the missing primitive, doubts remain about the expected-constant round complexity due to a lingering issue in the proof. This issue stems from the steps taken to address low message dispersion, and the possibility of resolving it without changing the protocol is unclear. To tackle this, we redesign the message-distribution phase, avoiding the problem in the proof and obtaining stronger guarantees. These guarantees simplify the protocol structure, achieving a level of simplicity comparable to the synchronous solution.

In more detail, we build on Ben-Or and El-Yaniv's work, where parties initiate multiple executions for each A-BA instance that are "truncated" after a fixed number of iterations. However, we adopt a different approach to message distribution, allowing us to establish the rest of the protocol based on the simpler structure of their synchronous solution. Similarly to [12], we set parameters to ensure that each party receives at least one output from each batch of truncated A-BA executions (for each instance) with constant probability. Based on their local results from those truncated A-BAs, parties create suggestions for the final output. Subsequently, the message-distribution phase begins with parties running a binary A-BA to verify a precondition, ensuring the ability to validate each other's suggestions. If they choose to proceed, they A-Cast their suggestions and only accept those they can validate using their local results from the truncated A-BAs. This validation relies on the property that honest parties terminate within two consecutive iterations in each A-BA execution, ensuring the validity of suggestions even when provided by corrupted parties. Once parties receive $n - t$ suggestions, they proceed by A-Casting the set of the first $n - t$ suggestions they receive, along with the identity of their providers. The checked precondition guarantees that everyone can move on to the next step.

Parties then wait until they receive enough suggestions and enough sets, ensuring that at least $n - t$ sets are completely contained within the set of suggestions they received. By employing a counting argument similar to [24, 41], we can ensure the delivery of suggestions from at least $n/3$ parties to all honest participants. Moreover, the validation process applied to the suggestions guarantees that each honest party only accepts valid suggestions, even if they originate from corrupted sources. These robust guarantees in the distribution of suggested outputs establish that the $n/3$ suggestions commonly received by honest parties are legitimate outputs. This enables us to directly utilize the synchronous protocol in the asynchronous setting.

We employ our new asynchronous OCC protocol to elect a leader for party coordination. Every party adopts the leader's suggestion and runs a multi-valued A-BA to handle the obliviousness of the leader-election mechanism. If the leader is chosen from those $n/3$ commonly received suggestions, all honest parties initiate the A-BA protocol with the leader's suggestion and output the same value. If the leader is not among those $n/3$ parties, precautions are taken to ensure no malicious value is output. For this purpose, we utilize an "intrusion-tolerant" A-BA protocol that guarantees the output to be either a default value or one of the honest parties' inputs.[9] Finally, parties run a binary A-BA to determine if they have reached consensus on a non-default value and terminate.

By following the above approach, we overcome the issues in the proof and achieve a significantly simpler protocol structure for the asynchronous setting compared to the one presented in [12]. Somewhat surprisingly, the resulting protocol is conceptually as simple as its synchronous counterpart.

Applications to Asynchronous MPC. Asynchronous MPC crucially relies on ACS for determining the set of input providers [10]; this task commonly boils down to concurrently executing n instances of A-BA. Our expected-constant-round concurrent A-BA protocol can be directly plugged into the asynchronous MPC protocols in [8,10,30,57,58,66], preserving their (expected) round complexity.

---

[9] Ben-Or and El-Yaniv [12] introduced and used a strengthened property for (A-)BA without naming it, which was later called "non-intrusion" validity in [70]. Non-intrusion validity lies between standard validity and "strong" validity [50], as it requires that a value decided by an honest party is either an honest party's input or a special symbol $\perp$ (i.e., the adversary cannot intrude malicious values into the output).

However, despite folklore belief, concurrent A-BA cannot be used in a black-box way in the BKR protocol [14] to achieve asynchronous MPC with round complexity linear in the depth of the circuit. The issue (as pointed out in [1,83]) is that the ACS protocol outlined in [14] assigns input values for certain A-BA instances based on the outputs of other instances. This problem also affects other works like [16,36] that rely on [14].

Fortunately, this issue can be readily addressed by modifying the ACS protocol from BCG [10] (which is secure for $t < n/3$). Recall that this protocol involves a preprocessing step for distributing input shares before initiating concurrent A-BA, which necessitates $O(\log n)$ rounds. Replacing the $O(\log n)$-round preprocessing step with the constant-round "gather" protocol described in [4]-an enhanced version of Canetti and Rabin's counting argument [24]-results in an ACS protocol with constant round complexity. This modified ACS protocol can be seamlessly integrated into both [10] and [14], effectively rendering their round complexity independent of the number of parties. Alternatively, one can leverage the expected-constant-round ACS protocol recently proposed by Abraham *et al.* [1], or the one by Duan *et al.* [38] (instantiating all building blocks with information-theoretic realizations; in particular, the assumption of a "Rabin dealer" [76], used for leader election, can be replaced by our multi-valued OCC).

Composable Treatment of Expected-Constant-Round Concurrent A-BA. We choose to work in Canetti's Universal Composability (UC) framework [23], and as such, we prove the security of our protocols in a *simulation-based* manner. The UC framework provides strong composability guarantees when secure protocols are run as a subroutine in higher-level protocols (this is absolutely critical in our context given that expected-constant-round concurrent A-BA is a key building block in many round-efficient cryptographic protocols, as mentioned above), and even in *a priori* unknown or highly adversarial environments (such as asynchronous networks). Moreover, it enables us to provide a modular, bottom-up security analysis. However, obtaining a composable and round-preserving treatment of "probabilistic-termination" BA is non-trivial, as pointed out by Cohen *et al.* [31,32] in the synchronous setting. In the following, we discuss some unique issues in asynchrony and how we address them.

To model eventual message delivery, we follow [30,36,62] and require parties to repeatedly attempt fetching messages from the network. The first D such requests are ignored by the functionality, where D is a value provided by the adversary in unary so that it remains bounded by the adversary's running time (i.e., so that messages cannot be delayed *indefinitely*). It is straightforward then to derive a formal notion of asynchronous rounds in UC, based on this mechanism. We remark that unlike in the synchronous setting [62], (asynchronous) rounds cannot be used by the environment to distinguish the real and ideal worlds in the asynchronous setting. Thus, as opposed to [31,32], our functionalities are round-unaware. Similarly, we do not need to deal with standard issues in sequential composition, namely, non-simultaneous start/termination ("slack"), since asynchronous protocols are already robust to slack. Indeed, it is entirely possible that some parties receive output from a (secure) asynchronous protocol before other parties have even started the protocol!

On the other hand, the issue of *input incompleteness* is trickier to address. This refers to the problem that in the asynchronous setting, the inputs of up to t honest parties may not be considered in the result of the computation; the remaining $n - t$ parties form a "core set" of input providers. Note that in the worst case, the core set is adversarially chosen and includes all corrupted parties. Prior work [30,36] allowed the adversary to send an explicit core set to the functionality; however, this approach does not always accurately model what happens in the real world, and can cause difficulties in the simulation. Instead, our solution is to allow the adversary to define the core set *implicitly*, by delaying the submission of inputs to the functionality in the same way that it delays the release of outputs from the functionality. Using this novel modeling approach, we obtain updated functionalities for some standard asynchronous primitives that more accurately capture realizable security guarantees.

1.3   Additional Related Work

As mentioned earlier, the $t + 1$ lower bounds for deterministic BA [37,46] were extended to rule out *strict*-constant-round t-secure randomized BA for $t = \Theta(n)$ [26,29,60]; these bounds show that any such r-round BA must fail with probability at least $(c \cdot r)^{-r}$ for a constant c, a result that is matched by the protocol of [55]. Cohen *et al.* [35] showed that for $t > n/3$, two-round BA are unlikely to reach agreement with constant probability, implying that the *expected* round complexity must be larger; this essentially matches Micali's BA [68] that terminates in three rounds with probability $1/3$. Attiya and Censor-Hillel [6] extended the results on worst-case round complexity for $t = \Theta(n)$ from [29,60] to the asynchronous setting, showing that any r-round A-BA must fail with probability $1/c^r$ for some constant c.

In the dishonest-majority setting, expected-constant-round broadcast protocols were initially studied by Garay *et al.* [53], who established feasibility for $t = n/2 + O(1)$ as well as a negative result. A line of work [27,51,78,80,81] established expected-constant-round broadcast for any constant fraction of corruptions under cryptographic assumptions.

Synchronous and (binary) asynchronous OCC protocols in the information-theoretic setting were discussed earlier. Using the synchronous protocol in [12], Micali and Rabin [69] showed how to realize a *perfectly unbiased* common coin in expected-constant rounds for $t < n/3$ over secure channels (recall that this task is impossible in asynchronous networks [77]). In the cryptographic setting, both synchronous and asynchronous OCC protocols with optimal resiliency are known, relying on various computational assumptions; we mention a few here. Beaver and So [7] gave two protocols tolerating $t < n/2$ corruptions in synchronous networks, which are secure under the quadratic residuosity assumption and the hardness of factoring, respectively. Cachin *et al.* [21] presented two protocols for $t < n/3$ and asynchronous networks, which are secure in the random oracle model based on the RSA and Diffie-Hellman assumptions, respectively.

Nielsen [71] showed how to eliminate the random oracle and construct an asynchronous OCC protocol relying on standard assumptions alone (RSA and DDH). Although these constructions are for asynchronous networks, they can be readily extended to work in synchronous networks for $t < n/2$ (e.g., so that they can be used in the computationally secure BA protocol from [50]). We also note that while the resiliency bounds for asynchronous OCC protocols coincide in the information-theoretic and computational settings, working in the latter typically yields expected-constant-round A-BA protocols that are much more efficient in terms of communication complexity (i.e., *interaction*) than the unconditionally secure protocol of Canetti and Rabin [24].

Lastly, we discuss solutions to multi-valued A-BA in the computational setting. Cachin *et al.* [20] studied a more general version of this problem, in which the validity property is replaced with "external" validity, where the output domain can be arbitrarily large but the agreed-upon value must only satisfy an application-specific predicate. They gave a construction for multi-valued "validated" A-BA that runs in expected-constant rounds for $t < n/3$, assuming a PKI and a number of threshold cryptographic primitives (including an asynchronous OCC), and used it to obtain an efficient protocol for asynchronous *atomic* broadcast. Recently, Abraham *et al.* [5] (and follow-ups, e.g., [4,52,67]) have improved the communication complexity. The work of Fitzi and Garay [50] also considered *strong* (A-)BA. Here we require "strong" validity: the common output must have been one of the honest parties' inputs (note that this is equivalent to standard validity in the binary case). When the size of the input domain is $m > 2$, neither a Turpin-Coan-style reduction [79] nor the obvious approach of running $\log m$ parallel executions of a binary protocol would suffice to realize this stronger notion of agreement; indeed, Fitzi and Garay showed that strong A-BA is possible if and only if $t < n/(m + 1)$. This bound holds in both the information-theoretic and computational settings. Their unconditionally secure asynchronous protocol actually involves oblivious coin flipping on the domain, but $m > 2$ forces $t < n/4$ and the binary asynchronous OCC protocols in [24,41] can be extended to multi-valued in this regime, as discussed in Sect. 1.2.

In the next section, we start with some preliminaries. Due to space constraints, we refer the reader to the full version [33] for proofs and other details.

2   Model and Preliminaries

For $m \in \mathbb{N}$, we use $[m]$ to denote the set $\{1, \ldots, m\}$.

We prove our constructions secure in the UC framework [23], with which we assume the reader has some familiarity. However, the base communication model in UC is completely unprotected. To capture asynchronous networks with eventual message delivery, we work in a hybrid model with access to the multi-use *asynchronous secure message transmission* functionality $\mathcal{F}_{\text{a-smt}}$, which was introduced in [36] and is itself based on the (single-use) *eventual-delivery secure channel* functionality $\mathcal{F}_{\text{ed-sec}}$ from [62]. In the full version [33], we include a formal specification of $\mathcal{F}_{\text{a-smt}}$.

The functionality $\mathcal{F}_{\text{a-smt}}$ models a *secure* eventual-delivery channel between a sender P_s and receiver P_r.[10] To reflect the adversary's ability to delay the message by an arbitrary finite duration (even when P_s and P_r are not corrupted), the functionality operates in a "pull" mode, managing a message buffer M and a counter D that represents the current message delay. This counter is decremented every time P_r tries to fetch a message, which is ultimately sent once the counter hits 0. The adversary can at any time provide an additional integer delay T, and if it wishes to immediately release the messages, it needs only to submit a large negative value. It is important to note that T must be encoded in unary; this ensures that the delay, while arbitrary, remains bounded by the adversary's computational resources or running time. Also, note that $\mathcal{F}_{\text{a-smt}}$ guarantees eventual message delivery assuming that the environment gives sufficient resources to the protocol, i.e., activates P_r sufficiently many times.

Finally, we note that while the UC framework has no notion of time, and we are in the asynchronous setting (with eventual message delivery) where parties may proceed at different rates, one can still formally define a notion of asynchronous rounds along the lines of [36], which will be referred to in our statements. We defer an in-depth discussion to the full version [33], as there are some subtleties that need to be addressed.

3   Ideal Functionalities for a Few Standard Primitives

In this section, we present ideal functionalities for asynchronous primitives used in our constructions. This seemingly simple task requires careful consideration of certain aspects, as the adversary's ability to delay messages in the network has an upstream impact on the achievable security guarantees of distributed tasks. In particular, the adversary can obstruct the output release procedure and impede honest parties' participation. To model *delayed output release*, we extend the mechanism discussed in Sect. 2 (using per-party delay counters). However, to model *delayed participation*, we introduce a novel and more natural approach that addresses limitations of prior work and more closely captures the effects of asynchrony.

3.1   Modeling Delayed Participation

In the asynchronous setting, honest parties cannot distinguish whether uncooperative parties are corrupted and intentionally withholding messages, or if they are honest parties whose messages have been delayed. Consequently, when the number of corruptions is upper-bounded by t, waiting for the participation of the last t parties can result in an indefinite wait. In ideal functionalities, this translates to expecting participation and/or input only from a subset of adversarially chosen parties, known as the "core set," with a size of $n - t$. Observe

---

[10] Recall that while (concurrent) A-BA is not a private task, secure channels are needed to construct an OCC.

that the value of t is closely related to the behavior of the functionality. In this work, we specifically consider optimal resiliency, where $t = \lceil \frac{n}{3} \rceil - 1$. However, our functionalities can be easily adapted to accommodate other resiliency bounds.

In our modeling approach, the adversary implicitly determines the core set by strategically delaying participation (or input submission) to the functionality. If we instruct the ideal functionality to proceed once $n - t$ parties have participated, the adversary can precisely determine the core set by manipulating the order of participation (or input submissions). To accommodate arbitrary but finite delays for input submissions, we employ a technique similar to the one we use for the output-release mechanism. That is, in addition to a per-party *output delay counter*, there is an *input delay counter* (updatable by the adversary) which is decremented every time the party pings the functionality; once the counter reaches zero, the party is allowed to participate.

This approach contrasts with the work of Cohen [30] and Coretti *et al.* [36], wherein the adversary (simulator) **explicitly** sends a core set to the functionality. Obtaining the core set from the adversary all at once does not accurately mimic real-world executions and requires careful consideration to ensure the implementation works in all scenarios. For instance, a challenging case to model is when the simulator sets the core set, but the environment never activates some parties in that core set. If not handled properly, this situation can lead to either the ideal functionality stalling indefinitely while the real-world execution proceeds, or allowing for core sets of smaller sizes, neither of which is acceptable.

There are other aspects of modeling the core set that can potentially cause issues. If the simulator is required to set the core set early on, it may encounter issues during the simulation because in some real-world protocols, such as the asynchronous MPC protocol of Ben-Or *et al.* [14], the core set is not fixed in the early stages of the execution. Similarly, if the functionality allows late submission of the core set, then when using the functionality as a hybrid, the adversary can potentially stall the functionality unless appropriate preventive mechanisms are in place. In contrast, implicitly defining the core set by delaying parties' participation aligns more closely with real-world executions, reducing the probability of errors. Additionally, it can potentially simplify the simulation process, as the simulator can gradually define the core set as the protocol progresses.

3.2   Ideal Functionalities for a Few Standard Primitives

We now cast a few standard asynchronous primitives as UC functionalities, following our novel modeling approach. We also present security statements showing how classical protocols can be used to realize these primitives.

Asynchronous Broadcast (A-Cast). The first essential primitive used in both our OCC and concurrent A-BA protocols, which also finds numerous applications in other asynchronous protocols, is *Bracha's Asynchronous Broadcast* (A-Cast) [18]. A-Cast enables a distinguished sender to distribute its input, such that if an honest party outputs a value, then all honest parties must (eventually) output the same value. Moreover, if the sender is honest, then all honest parties must (eventually) output the sender's input. While these are essentially the agreement and validity properties required from regular (synchronous) broadcast, we stress that honest parties may not terminate when the sender is corrupted. We formulate A-Cast as the ideal functionality $\mathcal{F}_{\text{a-cast}}$, presented in the full version [33].

Note that although A-Cast is a single-sender primitive, assuming it can proceed to the output generation phase without sufficient participation from other parties is too idealized. A realizable functionality should only proceed to the output generation phase when $n - t$ parties (which may include the sender) have participated. Parties demonstrate their participation by sending (dummy) input messages, followed by issuing fetch requests to the functionality. An important technicality here is that the participation of parties before the sender initiates the session should not contribute to the count. Therefore, $\mathcal{F}_{\text{a-cast}}$ starts a session only once the input from the sender is received. Consequently, any efforts for participation before that point will not be taken into account. An implication of this design choice when using $\mathcal{F}_{\text{a-cast}}$ as a hybrid is that parties other than the sender will not know when the session has started. As a result, they should constantly switch between sending input messages and fetch requests until they receive the output.

Bracha's asynchronous broadcast protocol [18] can be used to UC-realize $\mathcal{F}_{\text{a-cast}}$ with perfect security:

Proposition 1. $\mathcal{F}_{\text{a-cast}}$ *can be UC-realized with perfect security in the $\mathcal{F}_{\text{a-smt}}$-hybrid model, in constant rounds and against an adaptive and malicious t-adversary, provided $t < \frac{n}{3}$.*

Asynchronous Verifiable Secret Sharing (A-VSS). Another crucial primitive we require, mainly for our OCC protocol, is *Asynchronous Verifiable Secret Sharing* (A-VSS). A-VSS allows a dealer to secret-share a value among all parties, ensuring that no unauthorized subset of colluding parties can learn any information about the secret. However, any authorized subset of parties should be able to efficiently reconstruct the secret using their shares. The term "verifiable" reflects that the dealer cannot cheat, for example by causing the reconstruction to fail or by inducing inconsistent output values from honest parties. In particular, whenever the sharing phase succeeds, any authorized subset of parties should be able to efficiently complete the reconstruction phase, and all honest parties doing so must recover the same secret. Moreover, if the dealer is honest, the sharing phase must always succeed, and everyone should recover the value originally shared by the dealer. In our context, we consider only the threshold access structure, where a subset of parties can recover the secret if and only if it contains at least $1/3$ of the parties. The formulation of A-VSS as an ideal functionality, $\mathcal{F}_{\text{a-vss}}$, can be found in the full version [33].

A-VSS, being a single-sender primitive, also requires the participation of at least $n - t$ parties to be realizable. We adopt a similar approach to $\mathcal{F}_{\text{a-cast}}$ in modeling this requirement. Parties other than the dealer demonstrate their participation by sending (dummy) input messages and issuing fetch requests, ensuring that the minimum participation threshold is met for the A-VSS protocol to proceed. Also, it is important to note that $\mathcal{F}_{\text{a-vss}}$ only initiates a session once it receives the first input from the dealer. Any participation efforts made before that point are not taken into account.

The A-VSS protocol given by Canetti and Rabin in [24] can be used to UC-realize $\mathcal{F}_{\text{a-vss}}$ with statistical security for $t < n/3$. This result is formally stated in the following proposition. It is worth noting that perfectly secure A-VSS is impossible for $t \geq n/4$ [3,14].

Proposition 2. *For any finite field $\mathbb{F}$ (with $|\mathbb{F}| > n$), $\mathcal{F}_{\text{a-vss}}^{\mathbb{F}}$ can be UC-realized with statistical security, in constant rounds and in the $\mathcal{F}_{\text{a-smt}}$-hybrid model against an adaptive and malicious t-adversary, provided $t < \frac{n}{3}$.*

Asynchronous Byzantine Agreement (A-BA). We use A-BA for both binary and multi-valued domains V in our revised concurrent A-BA protocol. In this primitive, each party P_i has an input $v_i \in V$. The goal is for all parties to output the same value, such that if $n - 2t$ input values are the same, that value is chosen as the output; otherwise, the adversary determines the output. We initially consider *corruption-unfair* A-BA, where the adversary learns the input of each party the moment it is provided. Corruption fairness, as introduced in [59] and later coined in [34], essentially ensures that the (adaptive) adversary cannot corrupt a party and subsequently influence the input value of that party based on the original input value. It is worth noting that corruption-fair A-BA can easily be defined by avoiding leaking honest parties' inputs before the output is generated. We formulate A-BA as the ideal functionality $\mathcal{F}_{\text{a-ba}}$, presented in the full version [33].

The functionality $\mathcal{F}_{\text{a-ba}}$ encompasses an additional property known as "non-intrusion" validity (see Sect. 1.2). In a nutshell, this property guarantees that no malicious value can be present in the output. In other words, the output must be either an honest party's input or a default value $\bot$. This stronger notion of A-BA is vital for the security of our concurrent A-BA protocol.

The expected-constant-round binary A-BA protocol of Canetti and Rabin [24] can be used to UC-realize $\mathcal{F}_{\text{a-ba}}^{V}$ with statistical security for binary domains ($|V| = 2$) and $t < n/3$. However, our concurrent A-BA protocol (and the one in [12]) require **multi-valued** A-BA, where $|V|$ is not constant (in fact, exponential), in expected-constant rounds. Ben-Or and El-Yaniv [12] claim that the constant-round reduction of multi-valued to binary BA proposed by Turpin and Coan [79], which works in the synchronous setting for $t < n/3$, can be extended to work in the asynchronous setting by using A-Cast for message distribution. However, in the full version of the paper [33], we demonstrate that the asynchronous version of this reduction works if and only if $t < n/6$, even when using A-Cast and considering a static adversary. Some additional modifications can improve this bound to $t < n/5$, but achieving optimal resiliency is not straightforward.

More recently, Mostéfaoui and Raynal [70] presented a constant-round transformation from binary to multi-valued A-BA that works for $t < n/3$. Furthermore, the resulting protocol satisfies the non-intrusion validity property mentioned above. By applying this transformation to the binary A-BA protocol of Canetti and Rabin [24], we can UC-realize $\mathcal{F}_{\text{a-ba}}^{V}$ for arbitrary V with statistical security:

Proposition 3. *For any domain V, $\mathcal{F}_{\text{a-ba}}^{V}$ can be UC-realized with statistical security in the $\mathcal{F}_{\text{a-smt}}$-hybrid model, in expected-constant rounds and against an adaptive and malicious t-adversary, provided $t < \frac{n}{3}$.*

4   Asynchronous Oblivious Common Coin

As highlighted in the Introduction, none of the existing OCC proposals is simultaneously information-theoretic, asynchronous, multi-valued, and optimally resilient. Furthermore, no straightforward adaptation of the existing schemes yields an OCC with all of these properties. In this section, we propose our own OCC protocol that aims to satisfy all of these properties. Recall that we are primarily interested in the case where the output domain has size equal to the number of parties; this can be used for asynchronous OLE (defined in Sect. 5), which sets the stage for concurrent A-BA in expected-constant rounds.

At a high level, our protocol is based on the binary OCC of Feldman [41] and Canetti and Rabin [24], and incorporates a novel combinatorial technique derived from our observation stated in Lemma 1 below. By leveraging this lemma, we unveil interesting and powerful properties of the local views formed during the protocol's execution, leading to enhanced extraction capabilities. In fact, instead of extracting a single bit, by choosing appropriate parameters we can extract random values from any arbitrary domain still with a constant probability.

A-OCC Ideal Functionality. An oblivious common coin is parameterized by a set V and some constant probability p. Each party starts with an empty input λ, and every party P_i outputs a value from V where with probability at least $p > 0$ every party outputs the same uniformly random value $x \in V$ and with probability $1 - p$ the adversary chooses each party's output.[11]

The above goal can be translated to a UC functionality as follows: Initially, the ideal functionality samples a "fairness bit" $b \leftarrow \text{Bernoulli}(p)$ and a random value $y \xleftarrow{\text{R}} V$. Then, if $b = 1$ or no meaningful input is received from the adversary, it outputs y to every party. However, if $b = 0$ and meaningful input is received from the adversary, it assigns each party the value provided by the adversary. The functionality also informs the adversary about the fairness bit and the random value once they have been sampled. Asynchronous aspects, including delayed output release and participation, are handled as in Sect. 3. The resulting functionality is shown in Fig. 1.

---

[11] It is important to note that the term "oblivious" in this context refers to the fact that parties do not learn whether an agreement on a random coin value has been achieved or not, while the adversary does.

Functionality $\mathcal{F}_{\text{a-occ}}^{V,p}$

The functionality is parameterized by a set V of possible outcomes and a fairness probability p, and it proceeds as follows. At the first activation, verify that $\mathsf{sid} = (\mathcal{P}, \mathsf{sid}')$, where $\mathcal{P}$ is a player set of size n. For each $P_i \in \mathcal{P}$, initialize y_i to a default value $\bot$, $\mathsf{participated}_i := 0$, and delay values $D_i^{\text{input}} = D_i^{\text{output}} := 1$. Also initialize a, y, and b to $\bot$, and $t := \lceil \frac{n}{3} \rceil - 1$.

- Upon receiving $(\mathsf{delay}, \mathsf{sid}, P_i, \mathsf{type}, D)$ from the adversary for $P_i \in \mathcal{P}$, $\mathsf{type} \in \{\mathsf{input}, \mathsf{output}\}$, and $D \in \mathbb{Z}$ represented in unary notation, update $D_i^{\mathsf{type}} := \max(1, D_i^{\mathsf{type}} + D)$ and send $(\mathsf{delay\text{-}set}, \mathsf{sid})$ to the adversary.
- Upon receiving $(\mathsf{input}, \mathsf{sid})$ from $P_i \in \mathcal{P}$ (or the adversary on behalf of corrupted P_i), run the Input Submission Procedure and send $(\mathsf{leakage}, \mathsf{sid}, P_i)$ and any other messages set by the Input Release Procedure to the adversary.
- Upon receiving $(\mathsf{replace}, \mathsf{sid}, v)$ from the adversary, record $a := v$.
- Upon receiving $(\mathsf{fetch}, \mathsf{sid})$ from $P_i \in \mathcal{P}$ (or the adversary on behalf of corrupted P_i) run the Input Submission and Output Release Procedures, and send $(\mathsf{fetched}, \mathsf{sid}, P_i)$ to the adversary and any messages set by the Output Release Procedure to P_i.

Input Submission Procedure: If $\mathsf{participated}_i = 0$ and $(\mathsf{input}, \mathsf{sid})$ was already received from P_i, then do:

1. Update $D_i^{\text{input}} := D_i^{\text{input}} - 1$.
2. If $D_i^{\text{input}} = 0$ then set $\mathsf{participated}_i := 1$.
3. If $b = \bot$ then sample a "fairness bit" $b \leftarrow \text{Bernoulli}(p)$ and a random value $y \xleftarrow{\text{R}} V$, and set $(\mathsf{reveal}, \mathsf{sid}, b, y)$ to be sent to the adversary.

Output Release Procedure: If $\sum_{j=1}^{n} \mathsf{participated}_j \geq n - t$ then do:

1. Update $D_i^{\text{output}} := D_i^{\text{output}} - 1$.
2. If $D_i^{\text{output}} = 0$, then do the following. If $y_i = \bot$:
   - If $b = 1$ or a cannot be parsed as $(a_1, \ldots, a_n) \in V^n$, set $y_k := y$ for each $P_k \in \mathcal{P}$.
   - If $b = 0$ and a can be parsed as $(a_1, \ldots, a_n) \in V^n$, set $y_k := a_k$ for each $P_k \in \mathcal{P}$.
   Additionally, set $(\mathsf{output}, \mathsf{sid}, y_i)$ to be sent to P_i.

Fig. 1. The asynchronous OCC functionality.

The A-OCC Protocol. We proceed to present our asynchronous and multi-valued OCC protocol. We begin by discussing all the essential building blocks employed in our protocol. Subsequently, we provide a high-level overview of the protocol, highlighting its key ideas. A detailed description appears in the full version [33].

The basic building blocks of our A-OCC protocol are A-VSS and A-Cast. A-VSS enables parties to contribute by privately providing their local randomness and only revealing this randomness when the contributions to the output are determined. Thus, A-VSS ensures the secrecy and verifiability of the shared secrets in an asynchronous setting. The A-VSS primitive is formally modeled as the ideal functionality $\mathcal{F}_{\text{a-vss}}$, described in Sect. 3.2. On the other hand, A-Cast facilitates communication among parties by providing stronger guarantees than simple message distribution. This is especially crucial in asynchronous settings where challenges such as low message dispersion can occur. A-Cast helps in overcoming these challenges and ensures reliable message dissemination among the parties. We use the ideal functionality $\mathcal{F}_{\text{a-cast}}$, described in Sect. 3.2, to model this primitive.

As previously mentioned, our multi-valued protocol is built upon existing binary A-OCC constructions [24,41] and introduces a novel combinatorial technique for extracting values from arbitrary domains. In both the binary protocol and our proposed protocol, each party secret-shares n random elements from a field. It can be observed that at some point during the protocol execution, a vector of length n consisting of random elements from the same field is established (with up to t missing values due to asynchrony). For each coordinate of this vector, random elements shared by $t+1$ parties are utilized to prevent the adversary, controlling up to t parties, from biasing any specific coordinate. Subsequently, each party starts reconstructing secrets shared by other parties to form the same vector locally. In the asynchronous setting, due to the low dispersion of messages, not all coordinates can be reconstructed by honest parties. This can result in different parties reconstructing different subsets of coordinates. However, by using mechanisms to improve message dispersion, as originally demonstrated by Feldman [41], it has been proven that when $t \le n/3$, while the local vectors of honest parties may have up to t missing coordinates, they have an overlap of size at least $n/3$.[12] This is significant because without such mechanisms, and allowing for t missing components when $n = 3t + 1$, the overlap in the local vectors of just four parties could be empty.

Traditionally, existing protocols extract a single bit from the local views of the random vector by instructing parties to take all existing coordinates modulo n and output 0 if any coordinate is 0 or output 1 otherwise. In contrast, our protocol represents a significant improvement by going beyond the extraction of a single bit from the local views of the random vector. This enhanced randomness extraction is through a combinatorial observation regarding vectors of random values, as formulated in Lemma 1. This observation, allows the parties to agree non-interactively on certain coordinates of the random vector with a constant probability, while also ensuring that these agreed-upon coordinates lie within their overlap section. The minimum such coordinate is then used to select a common output value from the vector.

Another important observation regarding existing binary A-OCC protocols is the lack of a proper termination mechanism. This poses significant challenges as network delays can cause parties to operate out of sync. In such cases, some

---

[12] Feldman calculated the size of the overlap, denoted as x, based on the number of participants n and the maximum number of corruptions t. The general relation is $x \ge n - t - \frac{t^2}{n-2t}$, which yields $x \ge n/3$ and $x \ge 5n/8$ when $t \le n/3$ and $t \le n/4$, respectively. This argument was later used in [24] to achieve optimal resiliency.

parties may receive the output before completing their role in the execution, and if they stop, others may not be able to generate the output at all. This directly affects the simulator's ability to accurately simulate the protocol, especially in managing input and output delays in the ideal functionality. This is mainly because, unlike the protocol, the ideal functionality ensures that once a party receives the output, sufficient participation has occurred, and any other party, regardless of others' participation, can fetch the output if sufficiently activated. One potential solution could be invoking A-BA on the output at the end; however, this would create a circular dependency since A-OCC itself is used in A-BA. Instead, we choose to adopt a simpler approach inspired by Bracha's termination mechanism. This approach resolves the participation issue without causing deadlocks and ensures agreement once all parties initiate the procedure with the same value. The formal description of our asynchronous OCC protocol $\Pi_{\text{a-occ}}$ appears in the full version [33].

Having described our A-OCC protocol, we proceed to present the formal security statement that demonstrates how the protocol UC-realizes $\mathcal{F}_{\text{a-occ}}$. However, we first state a combinatorial observation regarding vectors of random values that facilitates the security proof. We formulate this observation separately in the following lemma, as it may be of independent interest.

Lemma 1. *Let V be a vector of n values chosen independently and uniformly at random from a set S of size $N \in \Theta(n^2)$, and let α be a constant satisfying $0 < \alpha \leq 1$. Then for any subset of indices $I \subseteq [n]$ such that $|I| \geq \alpha n$, with constant probability p there is at least one repeated value in V; moreover, all of the repeated values are constrained to the indices in I.*

With the groundwork laid out, we now state the security of protocol $\Pi_{\text{a-occ}}$:

Theorem 1. *There exists a probability $p \in \Theta(1)$ such that for any integer domain V, protocol $\Pi_{\text{a-occ}}^V$ UC-realizes $\mathcal{F}_{\text{a-occ}}^{V,p}$ with perfect security in the $(\mathcal{F}_{\text{a-cast}}, \mathcal{F}_{\text{a-vss}}^{\mathbb{F}})$-hybrid model where $\mathbb{F}$ is the smallest prime field of size at least $\text{lcm}(|V|, n^2)$, in constant rounds and in the presence of an adaptive and malicious t-adversary, provided $t < \frac{n}{3}$.*

5   Concurrent A-BA in Expected-Constant Rounds

In this section, we dive into the important problem of achieving concurrent A-BA in an expected-constant number of rounds. As discussed in the Introduction, Ben-Or and El-Yaniv [12] highlighted the potential issue of running multiple executions of a probabilistic-termination protocol in parallel, which could lead to an increase in the expected number of rounds required for *all* executions to terminate. The concurrent A-BA protocol proposed in [12] relies on A-OLE and multi-valued A-BA, which can be instantiated using our A-OCC protocol from Sect. 4 and the extended A-BA protocol from [24,70], respectively. However, during our analysis, we discovered certain issues in their analysis that cast doubt on the expected-constant round complexity of one of their main building blocks and, consequently, their concurrent A-BA protocol. For a more comprehensive presentation of these issues, see the full version of the paper [33]. It is unclear how to address these issues without modifying the protocol itself.

To rectify these concerns, we modify the underlying message distribution mechanism and incorporate an additional layer of message validation. These changes not only resolve the identified issues, but also significantly simplify the protocol. It is worth emphasizing that our revised concurrent A-BA protocol achieves a level of simplicity that is comparable to the synchronous version proposed in [12]. This accomplishment is significant because when designing an asynchronous counterpart to a synchronous protocol, achieving a level of simplicity on par with the synchronous version is often considered the ideal outcome. In the following, we describe an ideal functionality for concurrent A-BA, our protocol, and its required building blocks, and provide a security statement.

Concurrent A-BA Ideal Functionality. Concurrent A-BA, as the name suggests, refers to a primitive that enables parties to solve N instances of A-BA concurrently. We are primarily interested in the case $N = n$, corresponding to the emulation of n ideal A-BA primitives, commonly used in asynchronous MPC protocols to form the core set and overcome low message dispersion. However, in our study, we consider a more general version that allows for a broader range of values for N. In this setting, each party P_i initiates the concurrent A-BA by providing N values, namely $v_{i,1}, \ldots, v_{i,N}$. Subsequently, all parties receive the same set of N output values, denoted as $y_1, \ldots, y_N$. Each individual output value y_j is computed based on the input values $v_{1,j}, \ldots, v_{n,j}$, following the prescribed procedure outlined in the standard A-BA primitive. Specifically, if $n - 2t$ input values are identical, that common value is selected as the output; otherwise, the output is determined by the adversary. We capture the task of concurrent A-BA using the ideal functionality $\mathcal{F}_{\text{conc-a-ba}}$, defined in the full version [33]. Since we are able to achieve non-intrusion validity (i.e., for each instance, the corresponding output must be either $\bot$ or the corresponding input of an honest party), we consider an *intrusion-tolerant* concurrent A-BA functionality.

Building Blocks. Our concurrent A-BA protocol relies on A-Cast as the fundamental communication primitive due to its enhanced guarantees compared to basic message distribution mechanisms. The ideal functionality $\mathcal{F}_{\text{a-cast}}$, which models the A-Cast primitive, was described in Sect. 3.2.

As another crucial building block, our protocol incorporates asynchronous oblivious leader election (A-OLE) as a coordination mechanism among the parties. A-OLE enables parties to randomly elect a leader from among themselves. The term "oblivious" indicates that parties are unaware of whether or not agreement on a random leader has been achieved. In our concurrent A-BA protocol, similar to the approach described in [12], there comes a point where all parties suggest outputs, and A-OLE assists them in reaching agreement on the output by adopting the suggestion of the elected leader. To capture the task of A-OLE, we parameterize the A-OCC functionality $\mathcal{F}_{\text{a-occ}}$, given in Sect. 4, by a domain with size equal to the number of parties. This yields an ideal functionality for

A-OLE, denoted as $\mathcal{F}_{\text{a-ole}}$, which is defined as $\mathcal{F}_{\text{a-occ}}^{[n],p}$ for appropriate $p \in \Theta(1)$. Recall from Theorem 1 that $\mathcal{F}_{\text{a-ole}}$ can be realized using protocol $\Pi_{\text{a-occ}}^{[n]}$.

Our concurrent A-BA protocol leverages both binary and multi-valued A-BA. Binary A-BA is employed to achieve agreement on critical decisions within the protocol, such as whether to continue a particular iteration, or whether to terminate the protocol. On the other hand, the use of multi-valued A-BA addresses the inherent obliviousness of the A-OLE primitive by providing a means for parties to reach an agreement on the output. The ideal functionality for A-BA was described in Sect. 3.2.

As in [12], another essential component in our concurrent A-BA protocol is *truncated* executions of an A-BA protocol limited to a predefined number of iterations, consequently implying a fixed number of rounds. In the spirit of [31], we model those executions with the ideal functionality $\mathcal{F}_{\text{trunc-a-ba}}$, defined in the full version [33]. $\mathcal{F}_{\text{trunc-a-ba}}$ is parameterized with V, p, and itr, where V denotes the domain, p represents the termination probability in each iteration, and itr indicates the maximum number of iterations in the execution.

This ideal functionality also encapsulates a "1-shift" property for termination, meaning that all honest parties produce the output within two consecutive iterations. We note that the adversary has the discretion to determine which parties discover the output first. Unlike a traditional A-BA functionality that outputs a single value, $\mathcal{F}_{\text{trunc-a-ba}}$ produces a vector of values that includes the output after each iteration of the execution. Modeling the 1-shift property and providing outputs for all iterations is crucial since our concurrent A-BA protocol relies on those properties of truncated executions of A-BA.

It is worth mentioning that $\mathcal{F}_{\text{trunc-a-ba}}^{V,p,\text{itr}}$ can be implemented by executing any intrusion-tolerant A-BA protocol with the 1-shift property and a termination probability of p in each iteration, precisely for itr iterations, and concatenating the output of all iterations to get the final output (with λ representing iterations without output). Canetti and Rabin's binary A-BA protocol [24] possesses the desired properties of intrusion tolerance and terminating with a constant probability in each iteration. However, using Bracha's technique for termination [18] in Canetti and Rabin's binary A-BA protocol does not admit the 1-shift property. The main reason is that parties may take the shortcut and use Bracha termination messages to generate the output in their very early iterations. Fortunately, Bracha's termination procedure is unnecessary in the truncated execution of Canetti and Rabin's binary A-BA protocol. This is primarily due to the fact that all parties will naturally terminate after a fixed number of iterations. With this adjustment, Canetti and Rabin's binary A-BA protocol also successfully attains the 1-shift property. Moreover, Mostéfaoui and Raynal's multi-valued A-BA protocol [70] offers intrusion tolerance, the 1-shift property, and terminating with a constant probability in each iteration if the underlying binary A-BA used in their construction also exhibits these characteristics. Thus, we can formulate the following proposition about realizing $\mathcal{F}_{\text{trunc-a-ba}}^{V,p,\text{itr}}$.

Proposition 4. *For some constant probability p, any domain V, and any integer* itr, $\mathcal{F}_{\text{trunc-a-ba}}^{V,p,\text{itr}}$ *can be UC-realized with statistical security in the $\mathcal{F}_{\text{a-smt}}$-hybrid* *model, in constant rounds and in the presence of an adaptive and malicious t-adversary, provided $t < n/3$.*

The above statement guarantees statistical security since the A-BA protocols we consider rely on the A-VSS primitive, which can only be realized with statistical security when $t < n/3$. In fact, by working in the $\mathcal{F}_{\text{a-vss}}$-hybrid model, we can achieve perfectly secure $\mathcal{F}_{\text{trunc-a-ba}}$. We remark that the intrusion tolerance of $\mathcal{F}_{\text{trunc-a-ba}}$ is not a requirement in our concurrent A-BA protocol; however, employing a non-intrusion-tolerant version of truncated A-BA will naturally lead to a non-intrusion-tolerant concurrent A-BA protocol.

The New Concurrent A-BA Protocol. Our protocol builds on the core ideas presented in [12]. In addition to instantiating the missing OLE building block using our OCC protocol from Sect. 4, we address the issue in the analysis by redesigning the message distribution phase. Our revised message distribution mechanism not only resolves the issue in the proof but also provides stronger guarantees, which in turn simplifies the final protocol design. In fact, apart from the message distribution phase, the overall structure of our protocol closely resembles the synchronous version of the protocol described in [12].

Before diving into the high-level description of our protocol, we highlight the choices we made in the message distribution mechanism and discuss some alternative approaches that fail to meet our requirements. In the eventual-delivery model, at least $n - t$ parties will receive each other's messages if they wait for a sufficient duration, as messages from honest parties will eventually be delivered to one another, but determining the exact waiting time required is not straightforward. One possible approach is to instruct parties to A-Cast the identities of the parties from which they have received messages. After constructing a graph with parties as vertices and adding edges between parties that have reported message receipts from each other, we can look for a clique of size $n - t$; however, finding a maximum clique is known to be NP-complete and also difficult to approximate [40].

To overcome this challenge, one possible approach is to investigate alternative structures that offer weaker guarantees regarding message dispersion but can be efficiently identified [10,14,22,72]. However, it is important to note that this approach does not guarantee the precise message dispersion required for our specific application. In our analysis, it is crucial that *all* honest parties receive messages from a linear fraction of other parties. Even finding a clique of size $n - t$ does not guarantee this level of message dispersion, rendering this approach unsuitable for our protocol. Thus, we adopt another approach that has been used in prior works [24,41], and extend it by incorporating a precondition check before the process and introducing a validation layer during the execution. These additions enhance the guarantees, making them more suitable and effective for our specific purpose. We proceed to explain our protocol.

Similar to the (synchronous) protocol described in [12], in our concurrent A-BA protocol, each party initiates for every A-BA instance a batch of m executions of the A-BA protocol (over the same inputs) for a fixed number of iterations, denoted as itr. If the A-BA protocol has a termination probability of at least a constant value p in each iteration, which is the case for most existing A-BA protocols, suitable values of m and itr can be determined so that each party obtains at least one output value for each batch. Each party then selects an output for each instance and forms a suggestion for the final output. The next paragraph, which explains the mechanism for distributing suggestions among parties, is our main modification to the protocol. Then, for the remaining part, we can use a similar structure as the synchronous version of the protocol.

Firstly, parties initiate a binary A-BA protocol to determine a specific condition that allows for choosing and validating suggested outputs later in the execution. Based on the outcome of this binary A-BA, parties decide whether to continue or start over. In the case of continuation, parties perform A-Cast operations to distribute their suggestions and wait to receive suggestions from other parties. Each party only accepts an A-Cast message containing a suggested output if the value is consistent with the outputs obtained from their own truncated A-BA executions. This validation step is crucial as it ensures that even corrupted parties provide acceptable (correct) suggestions. The validation is based on the 1-shift property of A-BA that ensures all honest parties terminate within two consecutive iterations. Parties wait to accept A-Casts of suggested outputs from at least $n - t$ parties and then A-Cast the set of all these $n - t$ suggestions along with the identities of the corresponding senders. They continue accepting A-Casts of suggestions and sets until they receive at least $n - t$ sets that are fully contained within their accepted suggestions. At this point, a sufficient number of messages have been exchanged, and using a counting argument similar to the one in [24,41], it can be deduced that at least $n/3$ parties have their suggested outputs received by all honest parties.

After the message distribution phase described above, our protocol proceeds similarly to the synchronous protocol presented in [12]. Specifically, parties execute OLE to elect a random leader to adopt its suggested output. Subsequently, a multi-valued A-BA is performed on the adopted output to address the oblivious nature of OLE. Finally, a binary A-BA is executed to determine whether an agreement on the output has been reached, resulting in the termination or restarting of the protocol. The intrusion-tolerance property of multi-valued A-BA is crucial to make sure that the result of the agreement on the output is not provided by a corrupted party. It is worth noting that the favorable scenario occurs when the leader is among the $n/3$ parties whose suggested outputs have been accepted by all honest parties. If the leader is elected randomly, this event happens with a probability of $1/3$. In this case, all parties adopt the same output, leading to termination in the subsequent A-BA calls.

It is worth noting that the set of $n/3$ parties whose suggested outputs have been accepted by all honest parties may only contain a single honest party. This single honest party can only be elected with a probability of $O(1/n)$ by the OLE. However, due to the validation step in the message-distribution phase, there is no longer a need to ensure that an honest leader is elected, as the suggested values from corrupted parties are considered valid outputs. Refer to the full version [33] for a formal description of protocol $\Pi_{\text{conc-a-ba}}$.

We now consider the security of our concurrent A-BA protocol. Before stating the theorem, it is worth noting that the specific parameters of the hybrid model, which combine the different ideal functionalities, are not explicitly specified in the theorem statement. However, they can be determined from the protocol's parameters and are integral to the overall security guarantees of the protocol. Now, let us state the theorem formally:

Theorem 2. *For any domain V, integer N, constant $0 < p < 1$, and constant integer* itr > 1, *setting* $m := \log_{\frac{1}{1-p}} N$, *the protocol* $\Pi_{\text{conc-a-ba}}^{V,N,m,p,\text{itr}}$ *UC-realizes* $\mathcal{F}_{\text{conc-a-ba}}^{V,N}$ *with statistical security in the* $(\mathcal{F}_{\text{a-cast}}, \mathcal{F}_{\text{a-ba}}, \mathcal{F}_{\text{trunc-a-ba}}, \mathcal{F}_{\text{a-ole}})$-*hybrid model, in expected-constant rounds and in the presence of an adaptive and malicious t-adversary, provided $t < n/3$.*

Acknowledgements. Our original motivation for this project was to provide a simulation-based treatment of concurrent A-BA protocols, such as Ben-Or and El-Yaniv's [12], but the search for building blocks, in particular of an optimally resilient asynchronous OCC protocol became a bit of a "detective story," as many references pointed to an unpublished manuscript by Feldman [41], which was nowhere to be found. We thank Michael Ben-Or for providing it to us, which corroborated its in-existence.

Ran Cohen's research is supported in part by NSF grant no. 2055568. Juan Garay's research is supported in part by NSF grants no. 2001082 and 2055694. Vassilis Zikas's research is supported in part by NSF grant no. 2055599 and by Sunday Group. The authors were also supported by the Algorand Centres of Excellence programme managed by Algorand Foundation. Any opinions, findings, and conclusions or recommendations expressed in this material are those of the author(s) and do not necessarily reflect the views of Algorand Foundation.

References

1. Abraham, I., Asharov, G., Patra, A., Stern, G.: Perfectly secure asynchronous agreement on a core set in constant expected time. IACR Cryptology ePrint Archive, Report 2023/1130 (2023). https://eprint.iacr.org/2023/1130
2. Abraham, I., Dolev, D., Halpern, J.Y.: An almost-surely terminating polynomial protocol for asynchronous byzantine agreement with optimal resilience. In: 27th ACM PODC, pp. 405–414. ACM (2008)
3. Abraham, I., Dolev, D., Stern, G.: Revisiting asynchronous fault tolerant computation with optimal resilience. Distributed Comput. **35**(4), 333–355 (2022)
4. Abraham, I., Jovanovic, P., Maller, M., Meiklejohn, S., Stern, G., Tomescu, A.: Reaching consensus for asynchronous distributed key generation. In: 40th ACM PODC, pp. 363–373. ACM (2021)

5. Abraham, I., Malkhi, D., Spiegelman, A.: Asymptotically optimal validated asynchronous byzantine agreement. In: 38th ACM PODC, pp. 337–346. ACM (2019)
6. Attiya, H., Censor-Hillel, K.: Lower bounds for randomized consensus under a weak adversary. SIAM J. Comput. **39**(8), 3885–3904 (2010)
7. Beaver, D., So, N.: Global, unpredictable bit generation without broadcast. In: Helleseth, T. (ed.) EUROCRYPT 1993. LNCS, vol. 765, pp. 424–434. Springer, Heidelberg (1994). https://doi.org/10.1007/3-540-48285-7_36
8. Beerliová-Trubíniová, Z., Hirt, M.: Simple and efficient perfectly-secure asynchronous MPC. In: Kurosawa, K. (ed.) ASIACRYPT 2007. LNCS, vol. 4833, pp. 376–392. Springer, Heidelberg (2007). https://doi.org/10.1007/978-3-540-76900-2_23
9. Ben-Or, M.: Another advantage of free choice: completely asynchronous agreement protocols (extended abstract). In: 2nd ACM PODC, pp. 27–30. ACM (1983)
10. Ben-Or, M., Canetti, R., Goldreich, O.: Asynchronous secure computation. In: 25th ACM STOC, pp. 52–61. ACM Press (1993)
11. Ben-Or, M., El-Yaniv, R.: Interactive consistency in constant expected time. Technical report, Inst. of Math. and Comp. Sci., Hebrew University, Jerusalem (1988)
12. Ben-Or, M., El-Yaniv, R.: Resilient-optimal interactive consistency in constant time. Distrib. Comput. **16**(4), 249–262 (2003)
13. Ben-Or, M., Goldwasser, S., Wigderson, A.: Completeness theorems for non-cryptographic fault-tolerant distributed computation (extended abstract). In: 20th ACM STOC, pp. 1–10. ACM Press (1988)
14. Ben-Or, M., Kelmer, B., Rabin, T.: Asynchronous secure computations with optimal resilience (extended abstract). In: 13th ACM PODC, pp. 183–192. ACM (1994)
15. Berman, P., Garay, J.A., Perry, K.J.: Towards optimal distributed consensus (extended abstract). In: 30th FOCS, pp. 410–415. IEEE Computer Society Press (1989)
16. Blum, E., Liu-Zhang, C.-D., Loss, J.: Always have a backup plan: fully secure synchronous MPC with asynchronous fallback. In: Micciancio, D., Ristenpart, T. (eds.) CRYPTO 2020, Part II. LNCS, vol. 12171, pp. 707–731. Springer, Cham (2020). https://doi.org/10.1007/978-3-030-56880-1_25
17. Borcherding, M.: Levels of authentication in distributed agreement. In: Babaoğlu, Ö., Marzullo, K. (eds.) WDAG 1996. LNCS, vol. 1151, pp. 40–55. Springer, Heidelberg (1996). https://doi.org/10.1007/3-540-61769-8_4
18. Bracha, G.: Asynchronous byzantine agreement protocols. Inf. Comput. **75**(2), 130–143 (1987)
19. Bracha, G., Toueg, S.: Asynchronous consensus and broadcast protocols. J. ACM **32**(4), 824–840 (1985)
20. Cachin, C., Kursawe, K., Petzold, F., Shoup, V.: Secure and efficient asynchronous broadcast protocols. In: Kilian, J. (ed.) CRYPTO 2001. LNCS, vol. 2139, pp. 524–541. Springer, Heidelberg (2001). https://doi.org/10.1007/3-540-44647-8_31
21. Cachin, C., Kursawe, K., Shoup, V.: Random oracles in constantinople: practical asynchronous byzantine agreement using cryptography. J. Cryptol. **18**(3), 219–246 (2005)
22. Canetti, R.: Studies in secure multiparty computation and applications. Ph.D. thesis, Weizmann Institute of Science (1996)
23. Canetti, R.: Universally composable security. J. ACM **67**(5), 1–94 (2020)
24. Canetti, R., Rabin, T.: Fast asynchronous byzantine agreement with optimal resilience. In: 25th ACM STOC, pp. 42–51. ACM Press (1993)

25. Canetti, R., Rabin, T.: Fast asynchronous byzantine agreement with optimal resilience. Full version of [24] (1998). https://www.cs.tau.ac.il/~canetti/materials/cr93.ps
26. Chan, T.H., Pass, R., Shi, E.: Round complexity of Byzantine agreement, revisited. IACR Cryptology ePrint Archive, Report 2019/886 (2019). https://eprint.iacr.org/2019/886
27. Chan, T.-H.H., Pass, R., Shi, E.: Sublinear-round byzantine agreement under corrupt majority. In: Kiayias, A., Kohlweiss, M., Wallden, P., Zikas, V. (eds.) PKC 2020, Part II. LNCS, vol. 12111, pp. 246–265. Springer, Cham (2020). https://doi.org/10.1007/978-3-030-45388-6_9
28. Chaum, D., Crépeau, C., Damgård, I.: Multiparty unconditionally secure protocols (extended abstract). In: 20th ACM STOC, pp. 11–19. ACM Press (1988)
29. Chor, B., Merritt, M., Shmoys, D.B.: Simple constant-time consensus protocols in realistic failure models. J. ACM 36(3), 591–614 (1989)
30. Cohen, R.: Asynchronous secure multiparty computation in constant time. In: Cheng, C.-M., Chung, K.-M., Persiano, G., Yang, B.-Y. (eds.) PKC 2016, Part II. LNCS, vol. 9615, pp. 183–207. Springer, Heidelberg (2016). https://doi.org/10.1007/978-3-662-49387-8_8
31. Cohen, R., Coretti, S., Garay, J., Zikas, V.: Probabilistic termination and composability of cryptographic protocols. J. Cryptol. 32(3), 690–741 (2019)
32. Cohen, R., Coretti, S., Garay, J.A., Zikas, V.: Round-preserving parallel composition of probabilistic-termination cryptographic protocols. J. Cryptol. 34(2), 12 (2021)
33. Cohen, R., Forghani, P., Garay, J.A., Patel, R., Zikas, V.: Concurrent asynchronous byzantine agreement in expected-constant rounds, revisited. IACR Cryptology ePrint Archive, Report 2023/1003 (2023). https://eprint.iacr.org/2023/1003
34. Cohen, R., Garay, J., Zikas, V.: Completeness theorems for adaptively secure broadcast (2023), cRYPTO '23 (2023, to appear)
35. Cohen, R., Haitner, I., Makriyannis, N., Orland, M., Samorodnitsky, A.: On the round complexity of randomized byzantine agreement. J. Cryptol. 35(2), 10 (2022)
36. Coretti, S., Garay, J., Hirt, M., Zikas, V.: Constant-round asynchronous multiparty computation based on one-way functions. In: Cheon, J.H., Takagi, T. (eds.) ASIACRYPT 2016, Part II. LNCS, vol. 10032, pp. 998–1021. Springer, Heidelberg (2016). https://doi.org/10.1007/978-3-662-53890-6_33
37. Dolev, D., Strong, H.R.: Authenticated algorithms for byzantine agreement. SIAM J. Comput. 12(4), 656–666 (1983)
38. Duan, S., Wang, X., Zhang, H.: Practical signature-free asynchronous common subset in constant time. Cryptology ePrint Archive (2023), cCS '23 (2023, to appear)
39. Dwork, C., Lynch, N.A., Stockmeyer, L.J.: Consensus in the presence of partial synchrony. J. ACM 35(2), 288–323 (1988)
40. Feige, U., Goldwasser, S., Lovász, L., Safra, S., Szegedy, M.: Approximating clique is almost NP-complete (preliminary version). In: 32nd FOCS, pp. 2–12. IEEE Computer Society Press (1991)
41. Feldman, P.: Asynchronous byzantine agreement in constant expected time (1989), unpublished manuscript
42. Feldman, P., Micali, S.: Optimal algorithms for byzantine agreement. In: 20th ACM STOC, pp. 148–161. ACM Press (1988)
43. Feldman, P., Micali, S.: An optimal probabilistic algorithm for synchronous Byzantine agreement. In: Ausiello, G., Dezani-Ciancaglini, M., Della Rocca, S.R. (eds.) ICALP 1989. LNCS, vol. 372, pp. 341–378. Springer, Heidelberg (1989). https://doi.org/10.1007/BFb0035770

44. Feldman, P.N.: Optimal Algorithms for Byzantine Agreement. Ph.D. thesis, Massachusetts Institute of Technology (1988)
45. Feldman, P., Micali, S.: An optimal probabilistic protocol for synchronous byzantine agreement. SIAM J. Comput. **26**(4), 873–933 (1997)
46. Fischer, M.J., Lynch, N.A.: A lower bound for the time to assure interactive consistency. Inf. Process. Lett. **14**(4), 183–186 (1982)
47. Fischer, M.J., Lynch, N.A., Merritt, M.: Easy impossibility proofs for distributed consensus problems. Distrib. Comput. **1**(1), 26–39 (1986)
48. Fischer, M.J., Lynch, N.A., Paterson, M.: Impossibility of distributed consensus with one faulty process. J. ACM **32**(2), 374–382 (1985)
49. Fitzi, M.: Generalized communication and security models in Byzantine agreement. Ph.D. thesis, ETH Zurich, Zürich, Switzerland (2003)
50. Fitzi, M., Garay, J.A.: Efficient player-optimal protocols for strong and differential consensus. In: 22nd ACM PODC, pp. 211–220. ACM (2003)
51. Fitzi, M., Nielsen, J.B.: On the number of synchronous rounds sufficient for authenticated byzantine agreement. In: Keidar, I. (ed.) DISC 2009. LNCS, vol. 5805, pp. 449–463. Springer, Heidelberg (2009). https://doi.org/10.1007/978-3-642-04355-0_46
52. Gao, Y., Lu, Y., Lu, Z., Tang, Q., Xu, J., Zhang, Z.: Efficient asynchronous byzantine agreement without private setups. In: 42nd ICDCS, pp. 246–257. IEEE (2022)
53. Garay, J.A., Katz, J., Koo, C., Ostrovsky, R.: Round complexity of authenticated broadcast with a dishonest majority. In: 48th FOCS, pp. 658–668. IEEE Computer Society Press (2007)
54. Garay, J.A., Moses, Y.: Fully polynomial byzantine agreement for n > 3t processors in t + 1 rounds. SIAM J. Comput. **27**(1), 247–290 (1998)
55. Ghinea, D., Goyal, V., Liu-Zhang, C.: Round-optimal byzantine agreement. In: Dunkelman, O., Dziembowski, S. (eds.) EUROCRYPT 2022, Part I. LNCS, vol. 13275, pp. 96–119. Springer, Heidelberg (2022). https://doi.org/10.1007/978-3-031-06944-4_4
56. Goldreich, O., Micali, S., Wigderson, A.: How to play any mental game or A completeness theorem for protocols with honest majority. In: 19th ACM STOC, pp. 218–229. ACM Press (1987)
57. Hirt, M., Nielsen, J.B., Przydatek, B.: Cryptographic asynchronous multi-party computation with optimal resilience. In: Cramer, R. (ed.) EUROCRYPT 2005. LNCS, vol. 3494, pp. 322–340. Springer, Heidelberg (2005). https://doi.org/10.1007/11426639_19
58. Hirt, M., Nielsen, J.B., Przydatek, B.: Asynchronous multi-party computation with quadratic communication. In: Aceto, L., Damgård, I., Goldberg, L.A., Halldórsson, M.M., Ingólfsdóttir, A., Walukiewicz, I. (eds.) ICALP 2008, Part II. LNCS, vol. 5126, pp. 473–485. Springer, Heidelberg (2008). https://doi.org/10.1007/978-3-540-70583-3_39
59. Hirt, M., Zikas, V.: Adaptively secure broadcast. In: Gilbert, H. (ed.) EUROCRYPT 2010. LNCS, vol. 6110, pp. 466–485. Springer, Heidelberg (2010). https://doi.org/10.1007/978-3-642-13190-5_24
60. Karlin, A.R., Yao, A.C.: Probabilistic lower bounds for Byzantine agreement and clock synchronization (1986). unpublished manuscript
61. Katz, J., Koo, C.: On expected constant-round protocols for byzantine agreement. J. Comput. Syst. Sci. **75**(2), 91–112 (2009)
62. Katz, J., Maurer, U., Tackmann, B., Zikas, V.: Universally composable synchronous computation. In: Sahai, A. (ed.) TCC 2013. LNCS, vol. 7785, pp. 477–498. Springer, Heidelberg (2013). https://doi.org/10.1007/978-3-642-36594-2_27

63. Lamport, L., Shostak, R.E., Pease, M.C.: The byzantine generals problem. ACM Trans. Program. Lang. Syst. **4**(3), 382–401 (1982)

64. Lindell, Y., Lysyanskaya, A., Rabin, T.: Sequential composition of protocols without simultaneous termination. In: 21st ACM PODC, pp. 203–212. ACM (2002)

65. Lindell, Y., Lysyanskaya, A., Rabin, T.: On the composition of authenticated byzantine agreement. J. ACM **53**(6), 881–917 (2006)

66. Liu-Zhang, C.-D., Loss, J., Maurer, U., Moran, T., Tschudi, D.: MPC with synchronous security and asynchronous responsiveness. In: Moriai, S., Wang, H. (eds.) ASIACRYPT 2020, Part III. LNCS, vol. 12493, pp. 92–119. Springer, Cham (2020). https://doi.org/10.1007/978-3-030-64840-4_4

67. Lu, Y., Lu, Z., Tang, Q., Wang, G.: Dumbo-MVBA: optimal multi-valued validated asynchronous byzantine agreement, revisited. In: 39th ACM PODC, pp. 129–138. ACM (2020)

68. Micali, S.: Very simple and efficient byzantine agreement. In: ITCS 2017. LIPIcs, vol. 4266, pp. 6:1–6:1. Schloss Dagstuhl (2017)

69. Micali, S.: Very simple and efficient byzantine agreement. In: ITCS 2017. LIPIcs, vol. 4266, pp. 6:1–6:1. Schloss Dagstuhl (2017)

70. Mostéfaoui, A., Raynal, M.: Signature-free asynchronous byzantine systems: from multivalued to binary consensus with $t < n/3$, $O(n^2)$ messages, and constant time. Acta Informatica **54**(5), 501–520 (2017)

71. Nielsen, J.B.: A threshold pseudorandom function construction and its applications. In: Yung, M. (ed.) CRYPTO 2002. LNCS, vol. 2442, pp. 401–416. Springer, Heidelberg (2002). https://doi.org/10.1007/3-540-45708-9_26

72. Patra, A.: Error-free multi-valued broadcast and byzantine agreement with optimal communication complexity. In: Fernàndez Anta, A., Lipari, G., Roy, M. (eds.) OPODIS 2011. LNCS, vol. 7109, pp. 34–49. Springer, Heidelberg (2011). https://doi.org/10.1007/978-3-642-25873-2_4

73. Patra, A., Choudhury, A., Rangan, C.P.: Asynchronous byzantine agreement with optimal resilience. Distrib. Comput. **27**(2), 111–146 (2014)

74. Pease, M.C., Shostak, R.E., Lamport, L.: Reaching agreement in the presence of faults. J. ACM **27**(2), 228–234 (1980)

75. Pfitzmann, B., Waidner, M.: Unconditional Byzantine agreement for any number of faulty processors. In: Finkel, A., Jantzen, M. (eds.) STACS 1992. LNCS, vol. 577, pp. 337–350. Springer, Heidelberg (1992). https://doi.org/10.1007/3-540-55210-3_195

76. Rabin, M.O.: Randomized byzantine generals. In: 24th FOCS. pp. 403–409. IEEE Computer Society Press (1983)

77. de Souza, L.F., Kuznetsov, P., Tonkikh, A.: Distributed randomness from approximate agreement. In: 36th DISC. LIPIcs, vol. 246, pp. 24:1–24:21. Schloss Dagstuhl - Leibniz-Zentrum für Informatik (2022)

78. Srinivasan, S., Loss, J., Malavolta, G., Nayak, K., Papamanthou, C., Thyagarajan, S.A.K.: Transparent batchable time-lock puzzles and applications to byzantine consensus. In: PKC 2023, Part I. LNCS, pp. 554–584. Springer, Heidelberg (2023). https://doi.org/10.1007/978-3-031-31368-4_20

79. Turpin, R., Coan, B.A.: Extending binary byzantine agreement to multivalued byzantine agreement. Inf. Process. Lett. **18**(2), 73–76 (1984)

80. Wan, J., Xiao, H., Devadas, S., Shi, E.: Round-efficient byzantine broadcast under strongly adaptive and majority corruptions. In: Pass, R., Pietrzak, K. (eds.) TCC 2020, Part I. LNCS, vol. 12550, pp. 412–456. Springer, Cham (2020). https://doi.org/10.1007/978-3-030-64375-1_15

81. Wan, J., Xiao, H., Shi, E., Devadas, S.: Expected constant round byzantine broadcast under dishonest majority. In: Pass, R., Pietrzak, K. (eds.) TCC 2020, Part I. LNCS, vol. 12550, pp. 381–411. Springer, Cham (2020). https://doi.org/10.1007/978-3-030-64375-1_14

82. Yao, A.C.: Protocols for secure computations (extended abstract). In: 23rd FOCS, pp. 160–164. IEEE Computer Society Press (1982)

83. Zhang, H., Duan, S.: PACE: fully parallelizable BFT from reproposable byzantine agreement. In: ACM CCS 2022, pp. 3151–3164. ACM (2022)

Simplex Consensus: A Simple and Fast Consensus Protocol

Benjamin Y. Chan[1]([⊠])[iD] and Rafael Pass[2]

[1] Cornell Tech, New York, USA
byc@cs.cornell.edu
[2] Tel-Aviv University & Cornell Tech, Tel Aviv, Israel
rafaelp@tau.ac.il

Abstract. We present a theoretical framework for analyzing the efficiency of consensus protocols, and apply it to analyze the optimistic and pessimistic confirmation times of state-of-the-art partially-synchronous protocols in the so-called "rotating leader/random leader" model of consensus (recently popularized in the blockchain setting).

We next present a new and simple consensus protocol in the partially synchronous setting, tolerating $f < n/3$ byzantine faults; in our eyes, this protocol is essentially as simple to describe as the simplest known protocols, but it also enjoys an even simpler security proof, while matching and, even improving, the efficiency of the state-of-the-art (according to our theoretical framework).

As with the state-of-the-art protocols, our protocol assumes a (bare) PKI, a digital signature scheme, collision-resistant hash functions, and a random leader election oracle, which may be instantiated with a random oracle (or a CRS).

1 Introduction

Distributed consensus algorithms [48] allow large numbers of machines to agree on a single ground truth, even when some machines malfunction. Born out of research towards fault-tolerant aircraft control [60] in the 1970s, consensus algorithms have since then touched every corner of the Internet, and are used by the Internet's most important services to replicate data at scale (e.g. Google's Chubby lock service [15], Apache Zookeeper [8], and many more). Today, new varieties of consensus algorithms power blockchains such as Bitcoin [51] and Ethereum [17], where users propose transactions which are then batched into agreed-upon blocks, and where—unlike in classical consensus algorithms—the set of servers is not known ahead of time, and instead miners can join the system at any time (in other words, the system is "permissionless"). Subsequently,

B. Y. Chan—Supported in part by NSF CNS-2128519, NSF Award RI-1703846 and AFOSR Award FA9550-18-1-0267.

R. Pass—Supported in part by NSF Award RI-1703846, AFOSR Award FA9550-18-1-0267, a JP Morgan Faculty Award and an award from the Algorand Foundation.

G. Rothblum and H. Wee (Eds.): TCC 2023, LNCS 14372, pp. 452–479, 2023.
https://doi.org/10.1007/978-3-031-48624-1_17

blockchains have found new applications in cryptocurrency and also in bringing liquidity to otherwise illiquid markets (such as the market for art [7]).

At their core, consensus algorithms allow people to work together and collaborate without needing to trust each other. In some sense, they (and their evolution as multi-party computation algorithms [61]) are the epitome of enabling collaboration without needing trust. In a society that heavily depends on trust-mitigation protocols (such as markets, democracy, a justice system, etc.) to keep people safe, boost productivity, and to provide a high standard of living, continued innovation on trustless algorithms is of fundamental importance.

Relevance of the Permissioned Setting. In this paper, we return our focus to *classical permissioned consensus protocols*, where the set of participants is known ahead of time. This setting has by now been studied for four decades [48], but importantly, many modern techniques for realizing scalable, energy efficient *permissionless* blockchains (see e.g. Ethereum [16], Algorand [28]) rely on classical permissioned consensus as a building block. In particular, blockchain applications bring forth new desiderata for such consensus protocols, and require them to be faster and more robust than ever before, which we will soon make more precise.

Our focus here is on the *partially-synchronous* model of computation [31], which is specified by a worst-case bound on message delivery Δ, but where the actual message delivery time may be much smaller $\delta < \Delta$. The protocol is aware of Δ, but is not aware of δ; additionally, even the worst-case bound may not always hold, but is only required to hold after GST (the global stabilization time); liveness is only required to hold after GST, and consistency holds always[1]. As we are in the partially-synchronous model, we assume the byzantine attacker can control at most 1/3 of the players (which is optimal [31]). The partial-synchronous model is well-suited for settings that require security even if the network is partitioned (e.g. due to a Denial-of-Service attack), or if message delivery is unreliable (e.g. on today's Internet). Note that the partially-synchronous approach underlies many of the most successful consensus protocols deployed today, including Paxos [46] and PBFT [23].

The Multicast Model. We adopt the *multicast model* of communication. In the multicast model, players communicate by multicasting a message to the entire network, as opposed in the point-to-point model, where players send each message to a single recipient (whose identity must usually be known). The multicast model is the model of choice for protocols built for the large-scale peer-to-peer setting (see Bitcoin, Ethereum, and Algorand as examples). Protocols often have different communication complexities depending on whether they are analyzed in a point-to-point model, or a multicast setting. We note that when analyzing protocols implemented on top of peer-to-peer gossip networks, the communication complexity in the multi-cast model is most realistic, especially if point-to-point communication is implemented by what is essentially a multicast.

---

[1] As usual, the model can also be extended a more general model where liveness hold during "periods of synchrony"; for simplicity, we ignore this distinction.

Consensus with Rotating/Random Leaders. In a blockchain protocol or a state-machine replication system, clients send the system a series of transactions (txs) over time and the protocol participants must collectively decide the order in which the transactions are executed, outputting a LOG of transactions. Suppose that there are two conflicting pending transactions txs and txs' (for instance, comprising a double spend), and that the protocol must decide which of them to include in the final log of transactions. Typically, protocols (in the partially synchronous setting) decide which of the transactions to include by either flipping an imperfect global coin [18,22] to directly choose one of the transactions, or by *electing a leader process* to decide on behalf of all of the participants. Nearly all modern protocols deployed in practice fall into the second category, including blockchains, where the leader is equivalent to the block proposer (see Paxos [47], PBFT [23], Bitcoin [51], Ethereum [17], Algorand [34]). The reason is one of *scalability*: a block proposer can sequence many transactions in a row (as in PBFT), and more importantly also aggregate transactions together into blocks to improve throughput (as in blockchains). In contrast, flipping a global coin for each pair of transactions is expensive and is largely restricted to solving binary consensus, unless the coin is itself used to elect a leader.

Consequently, block proposers (or leaders) have disproportionate power when deciding the order of transactions within blocks, or across blocks if it is propos-ing many blocks in a sequence. In a system such as Ethereum, where block proposers can profit from ordering transactions at will, such a disproportionate balance of power affects the security and fairness of the underlying protocol (e.g. via "miner extractable value" [30]). Mitigating the power of block proposers to reorder transactions within a block is an active area of research (e.g. see [38,43]). Over multiple blocks, it is prudent to ensure that each new block is proposed by a different, "fresh" block proposer[2], if only to ensure that no process is 'in power' for too long.

A slow leader can additionally cause blocks to be confirmed slowly and dras-tically reduce throughput. In a 'stable leader' protocol such as PBFT, where the leader is never changed unless it detectably misbehaves, this can be problematic. Even if there is only a *single* slow process, if that process is the leader, then every block proposal may take much longer than the true network speed δ. Thus one more reason to rotate leaders frequently is to ensure that a single slow leader cannot slow down the entire operation for too long (e.g. see [6]).

In this paper, we focus on leader-based consensus protocols in the permis-sioned setting, specifically those protocols that rotate its leaders, or randomly choose their leaders for each block. This seems essential for both fairness and performance in the common case where proposers can be corrupt.

Efficiency Measures for Consensus with Rotating Leaders. There has been a recent explosion in new leader-based consensus protocols. To compare these var-

---

[2] See the related notion of chain quality [32], which (informally) requires that any sufficiently long chain contain a large fraction of blocks that are mined by honest parties.

ious approaches, and to understand whether they are "optimal" in some well-defined way, we need to specify some *efficiency measures*. In this paper, we consider the following notions of efficiency:

– *Optimistic confirmation time:* Suppose that all block proposers are honest. When a transaction is provided to the protocol (after GST), how long does it take for the transaction to be finalized? The optimistic confirmation time is (informally) the sum of the "proposal confirmation time" and the "optimistic block time" (both rather imprecise, but popular, notions):

  • *Proposal confirmation time:* Suppose an honest proposer is elected and proposes a block; how long does it take for that block to be finalized?
  • *Optimistic block time:* Suppose all block proposers are honest. How long does a pending transaction need to wait to be included in the next honest block proposal?

  If the optimistic confirmation time depends only on the true message delivery time δ and not on the known upper bound Δ, we say that the protocol is *optimistically responsive* [54]. In practice, Δ is usually set conservatively s.t. δ is much smaller than Δ, in which case a protocol that runs at the speed of δ (instead of the parameter Δ) is much preferable.

– *Pessimistic confirmation time:* Suppose that some number f of eligible proposers are corrupt. When a transaction is provided to the protocol (after GST), how long does it take for the transaction to be finalized? This is an important metric in practice, where there are almost certainly leaders who are offline, or even downright malicious. Uncooperative leaders may choose to exclude a transaction from its block proposals, whereas slow leaders may not propose it at all. There are two notions here:

  • *Worst-case confirmation time.* In the very worst-case, how long must we wait for a transaction to be finalized? The bound must hold for any transaction arrival time t.
  • *(Expected) pessimistic confirmation time.* In expectation, how long does it take for a transaction to be finalized?

  Essentially all protocols in the literature consider a "view-based liveness" notion that is tailored for rotating leader based protocols.[3] Following the literature, we will also consider this notion of expected "view-based" liveness: Suppose that the protocol proceeds in incrementing "views" or "iterations" $v := 1, 2, \ldots$ where each view v is assigned a single leader L_v. Fix some view number v ahead of time, and suppose that a transaction is provided to every honest player at the time they enter view v. How long (in expectation) does it take for the transaction to be finalized, once every honest process has entered view v?

---

[3] We may also consider an *expected worst-case confirmation time*, where, for any transaction arrival time t after GST, both fixed ahead of time, a transaction must be finalized soon after t in expectation over the coins of the execution. Such a bound may be useful to capture real-world liveness, but is typically difficult to analyze in a setting where the adversary can control the scheduling of messages.

We focus mainly on the expected pessimistic confirmation time. For our protocol, as well as many other protocols in the literature, we can turn an expected liveness bound into a worst-case liveness bound by losing an additive term of $\omega(\log \lambda) \cdot \Theta(\Delta)$, where λ is the security parameter. Note that, if a protocol requires multiple honest leaders in a row to confirm transactions, the worst-case bound will be worse.

The State of the Art. Before describing our contributions, we summarize the current start of the art; we focus only on leader-based protocols that rotate their leaders or elect random leaders. (The interested reader will find further comparisons of related works in Sect. 4, building on the survey below.) Throughout, denote n the number of participants, and f the number of faults; we consider static corruptions only.

Roughly speaking, the literature has focused on optimizing the *optimistic confirmation times*, but this has come at the expense of sacrificing the *pessimistic confirmation time*. In more details, let's first examine optimistic confirmation time:

- *Proposal confirmation-time favoring.* The seminal paper of PBFT [23] achieves a proposal confirmation time of 3δ for honest block proposals, but has stable leaders. Instead, consider an optimistically responsive "base version" of the Algorand agreement protocol [28], denote Algorand*[4], which is similar to PBFT but allows a different leader for each block. Algorand* achieves a proposal confirmation time of 3δ, and an optimistic block time of 3δ. [5] later showed that a 3δ proposal confirmation time is optimal when $f \geq (n+2)/5$.[5]
- *Block-time favoring.* Following Hotstuff [62], a new class of pipe-lined protocols were subsequently designed to improve the optimistic block time of rotating-leader protocols from 3δ to 2δ. These protocols pipe-line proposals, similar to Nakamoto style consensus [51], and achieve an optimistic block time of 2δ. However, these protocols require a worse proposal confirmation time: proposals take 4δ time (Pala [26]), or 5δ time (Jolteon [33]/Pipelined Fast-Hotstuff [39]) or 7δ time (Hotstuff [62]) to be confirmed, and additionally require 2, 3, and 4 honest leaders in a row respectively to confirm each block. In essence, these protocols improve the blocktime to just 2δ, but they sacrifice the proposal confirmation time. Moreover, the pessimistic confirmation time blows up significantly. Note that Hotstuff and its variants are generally

---

[4] While the version of Algorand agreement in [28] is not optimistically responsive, it can be easily made so if every period has a unique leader known ahead of time (provided by a leader election oracle in lieu of using a VRF). Then, players can simply 'soft-vote' immediately on seeing a proposal from the leader, and 'cert-vote' immediately on seeing $2n/3$ soft-votes, much like in PBFT.

[5] We do not consider optimizations of the variety made in Parametrized FaB Paxos [49] and SBFT [36], where if $f < (n + 2)/5$, a proposal confirmation time of 2δ is possible without affecting worst-case fault tolerance. We are particularly interested in the case when leaders are honest, but $1/3$ of voters are not.

Table 1. Latency of Popular Consensus Protocols (Random Leaders)

	ProposalConf. Time	OptimisticBlock Time	Pessimistic Liveness ($f = \lceil n/3 \rceil - 1$)
Simplex	**3δ**	**2δ**	**3.5δ + 1.5Δ**
Algorand* [28]	3δ	3δ	4δ + 2Δ
ICC [19]	3δ	2δ	5.5δ + 1.5Δ
PaLa [26]	4δ	2δ	6.25δ + 9.25Δ
Pipeline Fast-Hotstuff [39] Jolteon [33]	5δ	2δ	10.87δ + 9.5Δ
Chained Hotstuff (v6) [62]	7δ	2δ	19.31δ + 12.18Δ
P-Sync Bullshark [59]	6δ	3δ	6δ + 9Δ
Streamlet [24]	6Δ	2Δ	35.56Δ

*Base protocol without sortition.

designed for the point-to-point messaging model, where, to reduce communication, players often send their votes to a single recipient who aggregates them; if players instead multicast their votes, the confirmation time improves slightly (but only shaves off δ, or one less honest leader in a row).

- *Simultaneously proposal confirmation-time and block-time friendly:* The recent ICC protocol [19] simultaneously achieves the state-of-the-art 3δ proposal confirmation time and 2δ optimistic block time. However, this protocol again requires (essentially) 2 honest leaders in a row to confirm a block if a faulty leader was previously elected. Requiring multiple honest leaders in a row to finalize a block severely impacts the pessimistic confirmation time, which we will explore next.

Pessimistic Liveness. Few protocols explicitly analyze their expected or worst-case confirmation time under pessimistic conditions, despite it being an important performance desiderata in practice—after all, it is natural to assume that a fraction of the participants will be offline if not outright malicious. To explicitly compare the different approaches, we focus on the setting where each "iteration" of the protocol is associated with a randomly selected leader (essentially all the protocols in the literature, for this setting, assume or instantiate such a sequence of leaders). Throughout, assume that $f = \lfloor n/3 \rfloor$.

The current state-of-the-art is achieved by Algorand* (as defined above), which achieves $4δ + 2Δ$ expected view-based liveness. Protocols that require multiple honest leaders in a row to confirm transactions generally achieve degraded expected liveness: ICC [19], PaLa [26], Pipelined Fast-Hotstuff/Jolteon [33,39], and Chained Hotstuff (v6) [62] have expected liveness of $5.5\delta + 1.5\Delta$, $6.25\delta + 9.25\Delta$, $10.87\delta + 9.5\Delta$, and $19.31\delta + 12.18\Delta$ respectively.[6] Generally speaking, the more honest leaders required in a row to finalize a block, the worse the expected pessimistic liveness.

These protocols also get an even worse *worst-case confirmation time*: a protocol that requires k honest leaders in a row would need a longer sequence of random leaders to guarantee that k honest leaders in a row are elected, compared to if it only required 1 honest leader for confirmation.[7] Protocols with random leaders generally require just a sequence of at least $\omega(\log \lambda)$ leaders to guarantee one honest leader.

So, summarizing the state of the art, there is a trade-off between achieving good optimistic liveness bounds, and achieving pessimistic liveness bounds.

Our Contributions. In this paper, we present a simple consensus protocol, named Simplex, that matches the best optimistic liveness bounds, while at the same time matching and even improving the best known pessimistic liveness bounds (both in expectation and in the worst-case). Most importantly, our protocol is simple to describe and has an, in our eyes, a very simple proof of correctness—including an easy liveness proof. In contrast, most protocols in the literature have somewhat informal or difficult liveness arguments or do not analyze their own theoretical latency at all. (In terms of simplicity, while the protocol itself is arguably more complicated to describe than Streamlet [24], the proof of correctness is significantly easier, which may make it more understandable.)

In more details, assuming a "bare" PKI, collision-resistant hash functions, and a random leader election oracle (which can be instantiated using a Random Oracle), Simplex implements partially-synchronous consensus (tolerating the standard $f < n/3$ static byzantine faults), while achieving

- an optimal proposal confirmation time of 3δ,
- an optimistic block time of 2δ,
- an expected pessimistic confirmation time of $3.5\delta + 1.5\Delta$,
- a worst-case pessimistic confirmation time of $4\delta + \omega(\log \lambda) \cdot (3\Delta + \delta)$,
- and using $O(n)$ multicast complexity.

As observed by [53], the Random Oracle can be replaced with a PRF (which follows from collision-resistant hash functions [37]) and a CRS chosen after the public keys.

---

[6] Here, Chained Hotstuff is analyzed using a timeout-based pacemaker from LibraBFT [11] and a timeout of 3Δ, since they don't instantiate their own pacemaker. PaLa is analyzed with a less conservative timeout of $1\text{min}=5\Delta$, and $1\text{sec}=2\Delta$ than the ones presented in their paper.

[7] An alternative is to have a single leader be in power for k iterations in a row, before switching to the next leader; this sacrifices fairness, since we would like to rotate leaders more frequently, and the latency is still not ideal, since a faulty leader can delay the execution for k iterations.

We also note that using now standard techniques, we can bring down the communication complexity to $\mathsf{polylog}(\lambda)$ (in the multi-cast model) and linear (in the point-to-point model) through subsampling the committee of voters [26, 29]. This gives a scalable protocol that may be suitable for deployment in practice on large-scale peer-to-peer networks. We do not innovate on this subsampling and therefore just focus on the "base protocol" (which determines the concrete efficiency also of the protocol with subsampling).

Comparison of Techniques. Our contributions build on the techniques of many prior works. In contrast with the pipelined protocols of [24, 26, 33, 39, 62], which generally fall into a streamlined "propose/vote" paradigm where processes only send one vote type, our protocol follows [23] and requires processes to multicast a second "finalize" message to finalize blocks (in parallel with the next block proposal). We posit that the resulting protocol is actually simpler despite the second voting step.[8] Moreover, having a second voting step makes for a faster protocol in the optimistic case, matching the proposal confirmation time of PBFT. Another technique that we use is that of a "dummy block": if, during some iteration, a process detects no progress (i.e. due to a faulty leader or network), it will timeout and vote for the dummy block. On seeing $2n/3$ votes for the dummy block, a player may move to the next iteration and try again with a new leader. It is similar to the notion of a timeout certificate in [26, 33, 62]; the difference is that, in our protocol, a process must either vote for the dummy block of height h, or vote "finalize" for a block of height h (whereas no such stipulation was made in prior work). Then, if we see $2n/3$ finalize messages, we can be sure that no process saw $2n/3$ votes for the dummy block at that height, and it is safe to finalize the block. The result is a simpler consistency and liveness proof; moreover, a block proposer never needs to wait extra time before proposing (unlike in [14, 26]) even after seeing a timeout block.

Comparison with Asynchronous Protocols. Consensus protocols have also been designed for the *asynchronous setting* [4, 18, 22, 50, 55, etc], where protocols should make progress even before GST, as long as messages are eventually delivered. Asynchronous protocols generally have worse latency than their partial-synchronous counterparts after GST. Here, we only mention the elegant DAGRider protocol [42], which requires 4 rounds of reliable broadcast ($\approx 12\delta$ time) in the optimistic case, and Bullshark [58], which adds a synchronous fast-path but still requires 2 rounds of reliable broadcast (or 6δ time) optimistically, as opposed to the optimal 3δ. Moreover, essentially every asynchronous protocol requires a common coin, which is most practically implemented using threshold signatures, following [18]. Threshold signatures require a private setup or

---

[8] To recover a streamlined protocol, it is possible to "piggyback" the finalize message onto the first vote message of the next block; this would only make liveness a little slower, and consistency would still hold.

trusted dealer, which aside from being hard to implement, makes it difficult to subsample the protocol for scalability.

Note on Adaptive Security. Following the approach of Algorand [28], our protocol can also be adapted to support adaptive adversaries. Since these techniques are by now well-known, we just briefly review them here: a description of the concrete approach can be found e.g., in Section A.1 of [26]. It requires preforming leader election using a VRF and either a RO (as in [28]) or a CRS (as in [26]), that is chosen after the PKI. Using a VRF leads to a minor complication that multiple leaders may be chosen in an epoch. The key point to note is that (exactly as in [26]): consistency of our protocol holds irregardless (think of an epoch with multiple elected leader as simply a single corrupted leader), and liveness requires just a *single* epoch with a single (honest) leader, which still happens with some reasonable probability. Since there can be epochs with multiple leaders, the liveness parameters worsen, in the same way as it would with other protocols.

2   The Protocol

We describe the Simplex consensus protocol in the framework of blockchains, which provides an elegant framework for reasoning about consensus on a sequence of values.

To start, the protocol assumes a (bare) public-key infrastructure (PKI), and a digital signature scheme. Additionally, let $H : \{0,1\}^* \rightarrow \{0,1\}^*$ be a publicly known collision-resistant hash function.

- **Bare PKI setup.** Before the protocol execution, a trusted party generates a $(\mathsf{pk}_i, \mathsf{sk}_i)$ keypair for each process $i \in [n]$ using the key generation algorithm for the digital signature scheme, and for each $i \in [n]$ sends $(\mathsf{pk}_i, \mathsf{sk}_i)$ to process i. Each process replies with a pk_i', where honest processes reply with the same $\mathsf{pk}_i' = \mathsf{pk}_i$. The trusted party then sends $\{\mathsf{pk}_i'\}_{i \in [n]}$ to all parties.[9]
- **Notation for digital signatures.** For any message $m \in \{0,1\}^*$ and a process $p \in [n]$, we denote by $\langle m \rangle_p$ a tuple of the form (m, σ), where σ is a valid signature for m under process p's public key.

The protocol uses the following data structures.

- **Blocks, block heights, and the genesis block.** A *block* b is a tuple $(h, \mathsf{parent}, \mathsf{txs})$, where $h \in \mathbb{N}$ is referred to as the *height* of the block, parent is a string that (typically) is meant to be the hash of a "parent" blockchain, and txs is an arbitrary sequence of strings, corresponding to transactions contained in the block.
  Define the *genesis block* to be the special tuple $b_0 := (0, \emptyset, \emptyset)$.

---

[9] Note that this is referred to as a Bare PKI [10] since malicious parties may pick their own, potentially malformed, public keys.

- **Dummy blocks.** The special *dummy block* of height h is the tuple $\perp_h :=$ $(h, \perp, \perp)$. This is an empty block that will be inserted into the blockchain at heights where no agreement is reached. A dummy block does not point to a specific parent.
- **Blockchains.** A *blockchain* of *height* h is a sequence of blocks $(b_0, b_1, \ldots, b_h)$ such that b_0 is the genesis block, and for each $i \in [h]$, either $b_i = \perp_i$ or $b_i = (i, H(b_0, \ldots, b_{i-1}), \text{txs})$ for some txs.
- **Notarized blocks and blockchains.** A *notarization* for a block b —which may be the dummy block— is a set of signed messages of the form $\langle \text{vote}, h, b \rangle_p$ from $\geq 2n/3$ unique processes $p \in [n]$, where h is the height of the block b. A *notarized block* is a block augmented with a notarization for that block. A *notarized blockchain* is a tuple $(b_0, \ldots, b_h, S)$, where $b_0, \ldots, b_h$ is a blockchain, and S is a set of notarizations, one for each block $b_1, \ldots, b_h$. We stress that a notarized blockchain may contain notarized dummy blocks.
- **Finalized blocks and blockchains.** A *finalization* for a height h is a set of signed messages of the form $\langle \text{finalize}, h \rangle_p$ from $\geq 2n/3$ unique processes $p \in [n]$. We say that a block of height h is *finalized* if it is notarized and accompanied by a finalization for h. A *finalized blockchain* is either just the genesis block b_0, or a notarized blockchain accompanied by a finalization for the last block.
- **Linearizing a blockchain.** Given a blockchain $b_0, b_1, \ldots, b_h$, denote

$$\text{linearize}(b_0, b_1, \ldots, b_h)$$

to be the (most natural) operation that takes the sequences of transactions from each individual block, in order, and outputs the concatenation, to form a total ordering of all transactions in the blockchain.

2.1 The Protocol Description and Main Theorem

We are now ready to describe the protocol. The protocol runs in sequential iterations $h = 1, 2, 3, \ldots$ where each process starts in iteration $h = 1$. Note that each process may advance through iterations at a different speed, and at any given time, two processes may be in two different iterations, due to network delay (since we are in the partially synchronous setting). As local state, each process $p \in [n]$ keeps track of which iteration h it is currently in, and also stores all of the notarized blocks and messages that it has seen thus far.

Additionally, we assume that each iteration h has a pre-determined block proposer or leader $L_h \in [n]$ that is randomly chosen ahead of time; this is referred to as a *random leader election oracle* and can be implemented using a random oracle: namely, $L_h := H^*(h) \mod n$, where $H^*(\cdot)$ is some public hash function modeled as a random oracle.

Player p on entering iteration h does the following:

1. **Leader proposal:** If $p = L_h$, p multicasts a single proposal of the form

$$\langle \text{propose}, h, b_0, \ldots, b_{h-1}, b_h, S \rangle_p.$$

Here, $b_0, \ldots, b_h$ is p's choice of a blockchain of height h, where $(b_0, \ldots, b_{h-1}, S)$ is a notarized parent blockchain, and $b_h \neq \perp_h$. The new block b_h should contain every pending transaction that p has seen that is not already in the parent chain.

2. **Dummy blocks:** Each process p starts a new timer T_h, set to fire locally after 3Δ time.[10] If T_h fires, vote for the dummy block by multicasting $\langle \text{vote}, h, \perp_h \rangle_p$.

3. **Notarizing block proposals:** On seeing the *first* proposal of the form

$$\langle \text{propose}, h, b_0, \ldots, b_h, S \rangle_{\mathsf{L}_h}$$

check that $b_h \neq \perp_h$, that $b_0, \ldots, b_h$ is a valid blockchain, and that $(b_0, \ldots, b_{h-1}, S)$ is a notarized blockchain. If all checks pass, multicast

$$\langle \text{vote}, h, b_h \rangle_p.$$

4. **Next iteration and finalize votes:** On seeing a notarized blockchain of height h, enter iteration $h + 1$. At the same time, p multicasts its view of the notarized blockchain to everyone else.

    At this point in time, if the timer T_h did not fire yet: cancel T_h (so it never fires) and multicast $\langle \text{finalize}, h \rangle_p$.

5. **Finalized Outputs:** Whenever p sees a finalized blockchain $b_0, \ldots, b_{h'}$, output the contents $\mathsf{LOG} \leftarrow \text{linearize}(b_0, \ldots, b_{h'})$.

Let us informally describe the intuition behind the protocol. In each iteration, the processes collectively try to get the leader's block (proposal) notarized; if this fails due to a faulty leader or a faulty network, then the timer will fire. The timer thus upper bounds the amount of time each leader has to get its block notarized; when it fires, processes now have the option of voting for the dummy block and (on seeing a notarization for this dummy block) moving to next height to try again with the next leader. Eventually, we will hit a good leader and have good network conditions and an iteration h will complete without the timer T_h firing for any honest process. Consistency, on the other hand, will follow from a straight-forward use of the standard "quorum intersection lemma".

Summarizing, we get the following theorem.

Theorem 1 (Partially-synchronous Consensus). *Assuming collision-resistant hash functions, digital signatures, a PRF, a bare PKI, and a CRS, there is a partially-synchronous blockchain protocol for $f < n/3$ static corruptions that has $O(n)$ multicast complexity, optimistic confirmation time of 5δ, worst-case confirmation time of $4\delta + \omega(\log \lambda) \cdot (3\Delta + \delta)$, and expected view-based liveness of $3.5\delta + 1.5\Delta$.*

Note that the existence of digital signatures and PRFs follows from the existence of collison-resistant hash functions (see [37,57] respectively), but we include it here to emphasize what cryptographic building blocks we rely on. Also, as noted

---

[10] In addition, we could optimistically fire the timer when the leader "equivocates"; we omit the rule for brevity.

in [53], we can replace the random oracle with a common reference string (CRS) that is chosen after the adversary has registered its public keys, and instead use $L_h = \text{PRF}_{\text{crs}}(h) \mod n$ (and note that existence of PRFs follow from the existence of collision-resistant hash functions [37]).

2.2   Proof Outline

Let us provide a proof outline which conveys the essence of the whole proof:

Consistency. The consistency proof is straightforward. Let Alice and Bob be two honest players. We want to show that if Alice finalizes a chain $b_0, \ldots, b_h$, and Bob finalizes a longer chain $b_0, \ldots, b'_h, \ldots, b'_{h'}$, then Alice's chain is a prefix of Bob's, namely that $b_0 \ldots, b_h = b_0, \ldots, b'_h$. It suffices to show that Bob's block at height h is identical to Alice's, namely that $b'_h = b_h$; by the collision resistant hash function, the parent chains must be the same.

First, since Alice saw a finalization for height h, then the dummy block $\perp_h$ cannot be notarized in Bob's view, by the standard "quorum intersection" lemma. This is because an honest player only votes for either $\langle \text{finalize}, h \rangle$, or $\langle \text{vote}, h, \perp_h \rangle$, and never both. Likewise, since Alice saw that b_h is notarized, then a competing non-dummy block $b'_h \neq b_h$ also cannot be notarized in Bob's view, again by the standard "quorum intersection" lemma. This follows because an honest player only votes for a single (non-dummy) block proposal per iteration. Immediately it must be that $b'_h = b_h$, as required.

Liveness. Perhaps more interestingly, the liveness proof is also simple—this is in contrast to all previous protocols in the partially-synchronous setting that we are aware of, each of which require a subtle/complex analysis. We first claim that any honest leader can drive the protocol forward after GST. To see this, let us first observe that honest players need to be "synchronized" after GST:

> *"Synchronization after GST" (Sync): If an honest player enters an iteration h by time $t > \text{GST}$, then every honest player enters iteration h by time $t + \delta$.*

This follows because when an honest player enters iteration h, it forwards a notarized blockchain of height $h - 1$ to everyone else (and thus they will enter iteration h once they receive it, unless they had already entered iteration h before).

Now, assume the honest leader for height h proposes a block at time $t > \text{GST}$. We shall argue that the block it proposes will be finalized by time $t + 3\delta$. This follows from the following observations.

1. *Every honest player must enter iteration $h + 1$ by time $t + 2\delta$.* This is because either (a) *every* honest player votes for the leader's block by time $t + \delta$ (thus they all see a notarized blockchain for h by time $t + 2\delta$), or (b) *some* honest player i did *not* vote for the leader's block. In the latter case, player i must

have already been in iteration $h+1$ (or higher) when it saw the block proposal by time $t + \delta$ (since otherwise it would have voted as by Sync, it must be in iteration at least h by time $t + \delta$) and thus would have forwarded a notarized blockchain of height h by $t + \delta$. So again, every honest player will enter iteration $h + 1$ by time $t + 2\delta$.

2. *No timer of an honest player can fire until after time $t + 2\delta$.* This is because no honest player could have entered iteration h before time $t - \delta$ by Sync. Consequently, the earliest any (honest) timer can fire is after time $t - \delta + 3\Delta > t + 2\delta$.

Combining Observation 1 and 2, we have that every honest player must vote $\langle \mathsf{finalize}, h \rangle$ when it enters iteration $h + 1$ (because none of their timers have fired by the time they enter iteration $h + 1$). Consequently, by time $t + 3\delta$, every honest player sees that h is finalized. Since no honest player voted for the dummy block (since by Observation 2, their timers did not fire), it must be the leader's block that is finalized, which concludes the proof for the case that the leader is honest.

Let us next consider the case that the leader for iteration h is malicious. We shall argue that in this case, the iteration will be "skipped" (and all honest processes move on to iteration $h + 1$) after at most $3\Delta + \delta$ time: Suppose that every honest player is in iteration h by time $t > \mathsf{GST}$. Either every honest player fires its timer (by time $t + 3\Delta$), or some honest player does not fire its timer. In the first case, they all vote for the dummy block and see a notarized dummy block by time $t + 3\Delta + \delta$, thus entering iteration $h + 1$. In the second case, that player must have entered iteration $h + 1$ before its timer could fire, i.e. before $t + 3\Delta$; but as before, then every honest player will follow it into iteration $h + 1$ by time $t + 3\Delta + \delta$.

3   Formal Analysis

3.1   Preliminaries

We analyze the Simplex protocol in the framework of blockchains. Throughout, when we say that a message is "in honest view", we mean that it is in the view of some honest process (but perhaps not all honest processes).

The Permissioned Setting. We consider static byzantine corruptions. Denote n the number of players, $f < n/3$ of which are set to be "corrupted". The corrupted players are chosen ahead of time, before the setup phase. The remaining players are "honest".

Protocol Execution. In our setting the adversary has power over the network and can choose when to deliver messages sent by honest players. However, in good network conditions, message delivery should occur "quickly". This requires that we formalize a notion of time, in addition to specifying the execution of a distributed protocol.[11] In the spirit of the UC framework [20], consider n player machines, an adversary machine $\mathcal{A}$, and an environment $\mathcal{Z}$, where each is modeled as an instance of a non-uniform probabilistic polynomial time (nuPPT) interactive Turing Machine (ITM) that takes as input the security parameter 1^λ. The adversary $\mathcal{A}$ controls the f (statically corrupted) faulty players. Each player additionally has access to an authenticated multicast channel $\mathcal{F}_{\mathsf{mult}}$ over which $\mathcal{A}$ has scheduling power. We use the notation $\mathsf{EXEC}_\Pi(1^\lambda, \mathcal{Z}, \mathcal{A})$ to denote a random execution of the protocol Π with $\mathcal{A}$ and $\mathcal{Z}$, over the coins of the setup, the players, $\mathcal{A}$, and $\mathcal{Z}$.

To model time, we consider environments $\mathcal{Z}$ that send special "tick" messages to the n player machines. Fix any execution of a protocol with $\mathcal{Z}$ and $\mathcal{A}$ on some 1^λ. Recall that an execution is a sequence of activations of instances of machines. Given an execution, we say that it proceeds in timesteps $t = 0, 1, 2, \ldots$ where timestep t starts at the first point (in the execution) where the environment $\mathcal{Z}$ has sent any player machine exactly t "tick" messages. An event happens before/at/after time t if it occurs before/during/after timestep t in the execution. The execution ends when $\mathcal{Z}$ halts.

Network Model and Clocks. We consider adversaries that are partially synchronous [31]. An environment/attacker tuple $(\mathcal{Z}, \mathcal{A})$ is "δ-bounded partially synchronous" if, for every protocol Π, for every security parameter λ, there exists a time $\mathsf{GST} \in \mathbb{N}$ s.t. in every execution of Π with $\mathcal{Z}$ and $\mathcal{A}$ on 1^λ:

- *Synchronized clocks.* Denote t^* the time at which $\mathcal{Z}$ halts. It must be that $\mathcal{Z}$ sends every honest player exactly one "tick" message at each time $t \in [t^*]$.
- *Message delivery guarantee after GST.* For every time $t \in \mathbb{N}$, if some honest player sends a message by time t, the message is delivered by time $\max(\mathsf{GST}, t + \delta)$. Note that GST is not publicly known.

Definition of a Blockchain Protocol. Let $T : \mathbb{N} \times \mathbb{N} \to \mathbb{N}$, and $t \in \mathbb{N}$. A protocol Π, parametrized by Δ, is said to compute a blockchain with (expected) $T(\delta, \Delta)$-*liveness* if for every environment $\mathcal{Z}$ and attacker $\mathcal{A}$, in executions of Π in $\mathcal{Z}$ with $\mathcal{A}$ on 1^λ, the following properties hold with all but negligible probability in λ:

- *Consistency.* If two honest players ever output sequences of transactions LOG and LOG' respectively, either $\mathsf{LOG} \preceq \mathsf{LOG}'$ or $\mathsf{LOG}' \preceq \mathsf{LOG}$, where "$\preceq$" means "is a prefix of or is equal to".
- $T(\delta, \Delta)$-*Liveness.* Fix any time $t \in \mathbb{N}$. Suppose that $(\mathcal{A}, \mathcal{Z})$ is additionally δ-bounded partially synchronous for some $\delta < \Delta$ and $\mathsf{GST} < t$. Suppose that $\mathcal{Z}$ never halts early and that it always delivers some input txs to every honest player by time t. Then txs is in the output of every honest player by time $t + T(\delta, \Delta)$.

---

[11] Doing this composably has been visited in-depth in works such as [9,12,21,40,41,44]. However, here we ignore the question of composability and use an simple stand-alone model for convenience.

We say that a protocol has $T(\delta, \Delta)$ *optimistic confirmation time* if it is $T(\delta, \Delta)$-live when $f = 0$. Similarly, a protocol has $T(\delta, \Delta)$ *worst-case confirmation time* if it is $T(\delta, \Delta)$-live for any $f < n/3$. Now, suppose that a protocol proceeds in incrementing views (or iterations) $v = 1, 2, \ldots$, implemented by a local counter on each process. We say that a protocol has *expected $T(\delta, \Delta)$ view-based liveness* (w.r.t. the counter v) if:

- *Expected $T(\delta, \Delta)$ View-Based Liveness.* Fix any view $v \in \mathbb{N}$. Suppose that $(\mathcal{A}, \mathcal{Z})$ is additionally δ-bounded partially synchronous for some $\delta < \Delta$ and some GST. Suppose that $\mathcal{Z}$ never halts early and that it always delivers some input txs to every honest player before they enter view v. Suppose that every honest player enters view v by time t. If $t >$ GST, then txs is in the output of every honest player by time $t + T(\delta, \Delta)$, in expectation (over the coins of the execution).

Optimistic Responsiveness. (Variant of definition from [54].) We say that a blockchain protocol is *optimistically responsive* if it is has $T(\delta)$-time liveness for some function $T(\cdot)$ that is not a function of Δ, conditioned on all processes being honest. In other words, when all processes are honest, the liveness depends only on δ, not Δ.

3.2   Consistency of Simplex

In this section, we present a consistency proof for the protocol. We start with a simple fact about digital signatures:

Lemma 1. *With overwhelming probability in λ, for any honest process i, no honest process will see a valid signature of the form $\langle m \rangle_i$ in honest view unless process i previously signed m.*

Proof. This is by a direct reduction to the unforgeability of the signature scheme. $\qquad\square$

We next state the standard *quorum-intersection lemma*, and for completeness provide its proof. (This is a very standard technique.)

Lemma 2. *Let $h \in \mathbb{N}$. Let b_h and b_h' be two distinct blocks s.t. neither are equal to the dummy block $\perp_h$. It cannot be that both b_h and b_h' are both notarized in honest view (except with negligible probability in λ).*

Proof. Consider a random execution and let b_h and b_h' be any two blocks of height h in the execution transcript, s.t. $b_h \neq b_h'$ and moreover $b_h \neq \perp_h$ and $b_h' \neq \perp_h$. We call a tuple (i, m) "good" if $m \in \{(\text{vote}, h, b_h), (\text{vote}, h, b_h')\}$ and there exists a valid signature $\langle m \rangle_i$ in the view of some honest player. By the construction of the protocol, each honest process signs at most one of (vote, h, b_h) and (vote, h, b_h'). On the other hand, each corrupted player can sign both messages. Applying Lemma 1, then there are at most $(n - f) + f \cdot 2 = n + f < 4n/3$ good tuples with all but negligible probability in the security parameter. Now assume for the sake of contradiction that there are both notarizations for b_h and b'_h in honest view. Then there are $\geq 2n/3$ signatures for $\langle \mathsf{vote}, h, b_h \rangle$ and likewise $\geq 2n/3$ signatures for $\langle \mathsf{vote}, h, b'_h \rangle$ in honest view; thus there are $\geq 4n/3$ good tuples in honest view, which is a contradiction. □

We can also apply the exact same quorum-intersection technique to finalize and $\perp$ messages; for completeness, we write out the proof (again).

Lemma 3. *If there is a finalization for height h in honest view, $\perp_h$ cannot be notarized in honest view (except with negligible probability in λ).*

Proof. We call a tuple (i, m) "good" if $m \in \{(\mathsf{finalize}, h), (\mathsf{vote}, h, \perp_h)\}$ and there exists a valid signature $\langle m \rangle_i$ in the view of some honest player. By the construction of the protocol, each honest process signs at most one of $\langle \mathsf{finalize}, h \rangle$ or $\langle \mathsf{vote}, h, \perp_h \rangle$, whereas each corrupted player can sign either message. Applying Lemma 1, there are thus at most $(n - f) + f \cdot 2 = n + f < 4n/3$ good tuples (with all but negligible probability in λ). But now assume for the sake of contradiction that b_h is finalized and $\perp_h$ is also notarized. Since b_h is finalized, there are $\geq 2n/3$ signatures for $\langle \mathsf{finalize}, h \rangle$ in honest view, and likewise since $\perp_h$ is notarized, there are $\geq 2n/3$ signatures for $\langle \mathsf{vote}, h, \perp_h \rangle$ in honest view; thus there are $\geq 4n/3$ good tuples, which is a contradiction. □

The main theorem immediately follows:

Theorem 2 (Consistency). *Suppose that two sequences of transactions, denote* LOG *and* LOG$'$, *are both output in honest view. Then either* LOG $\preceq$ LOG$'$ *or* LOG$'$ $\preceq$ LOG *(with overwhelming probability in λ).*

Proof. Immediately, there must be two blockchains denoted $b_0, b_1, \ldots, b_h$ and $b_0, b'_1, \ldots, b'_{h'}$, such that both are finalized in honest view, where LOG $\leftarrow$ linearize$(b_0, b_1, \ldots, b_h)$ and LOG$'$ $\leftarrow$ linearize$(b_0, b'_1, \ldots, b'_{h'})$. Without loss of generality, we assume that $h \leq h'$.

It suffices to show that $b_h = b'_h$ and moreover that $b_h \neq \perp_h$. In plainer English, the two chains should contain the same block at height h, and moreover this block is not the dummy block. Then by collision-resistant property of the hash function $H(\cdot)$, the parent chains are the same $b_0, b_1, \ldots, b_{h-1} = b_0, b'_1, \ldots, b'_{h-1}$, and thus LOG $\preceq$ LOG$'$.

To prove that $b_h = b'_h$, first observe that both $b'_{h'}$ and b_h are finalized in honest view, and thus both $b'_{h'}$ and b_h are notarized in honest view. Because $b'_{h'}$ is notarized in honest view, then some honest process must have voted for it in iteration h' which implies that b'_h is also notarized in honest view. By Lemma 3, observing that b_h is finalized in honest view, it must be that $b_h \neq \perp_h$, and likewise $b'_h \neq \perp_h$ (except with negligible probability in λ). Finally, we apply Lemma 2, which says that since b_h and b'_h are both notarized and not the dummy block, it must be that $b_h = b'_h$ (except with negligible probability), concluding the proof. □

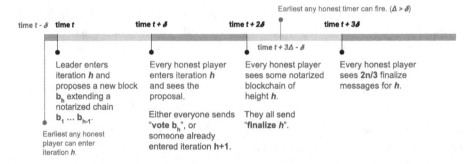

Fig. 1. Timeline of events when the leader of iteration h is honest ($t >$ GST).

3.3   Liveness of Simplex

In this section, we analyze the liveness of the protocol. Throughout, suppose that $(\mathcal{A}, \mathcal{Z})$ is additionally δ-bounded partially synchronous, for some $\delta < \Delta$. Recall that the protocol is parametrized by Δ and not δ. When we say that "an honest process has entered iteration h by time t", we mean that the process previously entered iteration h at some time $t' \leq t$; when time t comes around, the process may well be in a larger iteration $h' > h$.

Lemma 4 (Synchronized Iterations). *If some honest process has entered iteration h by time t, then every honest process has entered iteration h by time* $\max(GST, t + \delta)$.

Proof. By the assumption that some honest process p has entered iteration h by time t, we know that process p must have seen a notarized blockchain of height $h - 1$ at or before time t. By the protocol design, p will multicast their view of this notarized blockchain immediately before entering iteration h. Subsequently, every honest process will have seen a notarized blockchain of height $h - 1$, and thus also a notarized blockchain for every height $h' \leq h - 1$, by time $\max(\mathsf{GST}, t+\delta)$. Thus, by time $\max(\mathsf{GST}, t+\delta)$, every honest process that is not yet in an iteration $\geq h$ will have incremented its iteration number until it is in iteration h.   □

We show that the proposal confirmation time is 3δ, and that the optimistic block time is 2δ (Fig. 1).

Lemma 5 (The Effect of Honest Leaders). *Let h be any iteration with an honest leader L_h. Suppose that L_h entered iteration h by some time $t >$ GST. Then, with all but negligible probability, every honest process will have entered iteration $h + 1$ by time $t + 2\delta$. Moreover, every honest process will see a finalized block at height h, proposed by L_h, by time $t + 3\delta$.*

We break the proof down into two subclaims.

Subclaim 1. Every honest player will see a notarized blockchain of height h, and thus enter iteration $h + 1$, by time $t + 2\delta$ (except with negligible probability).

Proof. Recall that L_h enters iteration h by time t. Thus, L_h must multicast a proposal for a new non-dummy block b_h by time t. Thus, by time $t+\delta$ (observing that $t > \mathsf{GST}$), every honest process must have seen a valid proposal from the leader for b_h. There are now two cases:

- *Case 1.* Every honest process p casts a vote $\langle\mathsf{vote}, h, b_h\rangle_p$ by time $t+\delta$. Subsequently every honest process will see a notarization for b_h and thus a notarized blockchain of height h by time $t + 2\delta$, if not earlier, and enter iteration $h + 1$, as required.
- *Case 2.* There is some honest process p that did not multicast a vote $\langle\mathsf{vote}, h, b_h\rangle_p$ by time $t+\delta$. However, by Lemma 4, every honest process should have entered iteration h by time $t+\delta$, so the only way this could happen is if p entered iteration $h+1$ before time $t + \delta$. Then, every honest process will have entered iteration $h + 1$ (and thus seen a notarized blockchain of height h) by time $t + 2\delta$, again by Lemma 4. (This case may have occured if, for instance, p saw a notarization for L_h's proposed block without seeing the proposal itself.) $\square$

Subclaim 2. Every honest player p will multicast $\langle\mathsf{finalize}, h\rangle_p$ by time $t + 2\delta$, and thus see a finalized block of height h by time $t + 3\delta$ (except with negligible probability).

Proof. By Subclaim 1, every honest player sees a notarized blockchain of height h (thus finishing iteration h) by time $t + 2\delta$. We will show below that no honest player's timer for iteration h can fire before time $\leq t + 2\delta$. Then, when each honest player p finishes iteration h, they must multicast a $\langle\mathsf{finalize}, h\rangle_p$ message, as their timer cannot have fired yet, showing the claim.

Let $t' \leq t$ be the time at which the first honest process enters iteration h. By Lemma 4, all honest processes—including the leader L_h—will have entered iteration h by $\max(\mathsf{GST}, t'+\delta)$, implying that $t \leq t'+\delta$ (since t is strictly greater than GST). The earliest an honest timer can fire is at or after $t'+3\Delta > t'+3\delta \geq t + 2\delta$ time (noting that $\Delta > \delta$), as desired. $\square$

Finishing the Proof of Lemma 5. It remains to show that this finalized block is proposed by the leader. Recall that by Subclaim 2, every honest player p will have seen a finalized block b_h of height h by time $t + 3\delta$. Applying Lemma 3, we know that $b_h \neq \perp_h$. Thus, b_h must be proposed by L_h, because for it to be notarized, some honest player must have voted for it. The lemma follows. $\square$

Theorem 3 (Optimistic Confirmation Time). *Simplex has an optimistic confirmation time of 5δ.*

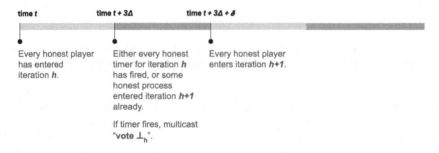

Fig. 2. Timeline of events when the leader of iteration h is faulty ($t > $ GST).

Proof. Suppose that there is a set of transactions txs in the view of every honest player by time t, where $t > $ GST, where txs is not yet in the output of any honest player. Let h be the highest iteration that any honest player is in at time t. There are two cases. If L_h has not entered iteration h yet by time t, then by Lemma 4, it will enter iteration h by time $t + \delta$, at which point it proposes a blockchain that contains txs; applying Lemma 5 then completes the proof. In the second case, by time t, L_h has already started iteration h, and by Lemma 5 every honest process will be in iteration $h + 1$ by time $t + 2\delta$, and see a finalized block from L_{h+1} by $t + 5\delta$. □

Now, we are ready to reason about worst-case confirmation time (Fig. 2).

Lemma 6 (The Effect of Faulty Leaders). *Suppose every honest process has entered iteration h by time t, for some $t > $ GST. Then every honest process will have entered iteration $h + 1$ by time $t + 3\Delta + \delta$.*

Proof. There are two cases. First, suppose that for every honest process, its timer in iteration h fires; then every honest process p will cast a vote $\langle$vote, h, $\perp_h\rangle_p$ at some time $\leq t + 3\Delta$, and subsequently this vote will be in the view of every honest process by time $\max($GST$, t+3\Delta+\delta) = t+3\Delta+\delta$. These votes comprise a notarization for $\perp_h$ and thus every honest process will see a notarized blockchain of height h by time $t + 3\Delta + \delta$ (if not earlier) and subsequently enter iteration $h + 1$ as required. The second case is if an iteration h timer does not fire for some honest process p. Then it must be that p entered iteration $h + 1$ at a time before its timer could fire, i.e. before time $t + 3\Delta$, and applying Lemma 4 yields the claim. □

Theorem 4 (Worst-Case Confirmation Time). *Simplex has worst-case confirmation time of $(4\delta + \omega(\log \lambda) \cdot (3\Delta + \delta))$.*

Proof. Suppose that there is a set of transactions txs in the view of every honest player by time t, where $t > $ GST, where txs is not yet in the output of any honest player. Let h be the highest iteration that any honest player is in at time t. By Lemma 4 every honest process must have entered iteration h by time $t+\delta$. Now, suppose that at least one iteration $i \in \{h+1, \ldots, h+k\}$ has an honest leader L_i, for some choice of $k \in \mathbb{N}$. Then, applying Lemmas 5 and 6, every honest process will see a finalized block containing txs by time $t + 4\delta + k(3\Delta + \delta)$.

It remains to analyze the probability that, in a random execution, there is a sequence of k iterations in a row $h, h+1, \ldots, h+k-1$ s.t. for every $i \in [k]$, L_{h+i-1} is corrupt. First, observe that the attacker (and the environment) is PPT, and so there is a polynomial function $m(\cdot)$ s.t. any execution of the protocol on a security parameter 1^λ must contain at most $m(\lambda)$ number of iterations. Fix any $\lambda \in \mathbb{N}$. Recall that, for all $i \in [m(\lambda)]$, L_i is selected using a random oracle, and is thus corrupt with independent probability $f/n \leq 1/3$. (Recall that we instantiated the leader election oracle to be either $\mathsf{L}_i := H^*(i) \mod n$ or $\mathsf{L}_i := H^*(\sigma_i) \mod n$, where H^* is a random oracle and σ_i is a unique threshold signature on i.)

To help, we analyze the probability that in a sequence of $m(\lambda)$ unbiased coin flips, there is a consecutive sequence of at least k tails. There are at most $(m(\lambda) - k + 1) \cdot 2^{m(\lambda)-k}$ possible sequences with at least k consecutive tails, out of $2^{m(\lambda)}$ total; thus the probability is less than $\frac{(m(\lambda)-k+1)}{2^k}$. Immediately, the probability there are k corrupt leaders in a row is $< \frac{(m(\lambda)-k+1)}{2^k}$, since the probability a leader is corrupt is less than the probability an unbiased coin is tails. Observing that $\frac{(m(\lambda)-k+1)}{2^k}$ is a negligible function in λ when $k = \omega(\log \lambda)$, the theorem follows. $\qquad\square$

For the sake of comparison, we also compute the expected view-based liveness. Recall that it says that, if every honest process sees some transaction txs before they enter iteration h, once every honest process enters iteration h, then txs will soon be confirmed:

Theorem 5 (Expected View-Based Liveness). *Simplex has expected* $3.5\delta + 1.5\Delta$ *view-based liveness.*

Proof. Fix any iteration $h \in \mathbb{N}$. Suppose that there is a set of transactions txs in the view of every honest player before they enter iteration h, and moreover suppose that every honest player entered iteration h by some time $t > \mathsf{GST}$. Recall that for each iteration i, we defined the leader to be $\mathsf{L}_i := H^*(i) \mod n$, where H^* is a random oracle (chosen independently of GST and h). Immediately, for each $i \in \mathbb{N}$, L_i must be an honest player with independent probability $(n - f)/n \geq 2/3$. Denote X the number s.t. L_{h+X} is honest but, when $X > 0$, L_i is faulty $\forall i$ where $h \leq i < h + X$. Here X is a random variable, and immediately $\mathbb{E}[X] \leq 3/2 - 1 = 1/2$. Observe that, importantly, L_{h+X} will propose a blockchain that contains txs.

It remains to upper bound the time at which some honest process enters iteration $h + X$. By Lemma 6, every honest process will have entered iteration $h + X$ by time $t + X \cdot (3\Delta + \delta)$. Applying Lemma 5, we conclude that every honest process will see a finalized block proposed by L_{h+X} by time $t + 3\delta + (X) \cdot (3\Delta + \delta)$. Moreover, this block contains txs if not already in a previous block. Taking the expectation of the time elapsed since t, the theorem statement follows. $\qquad\square$

3.4   Communication Complexity

Each iteration of the Simplex protocol (without subsampling) requires $O(n)$ multicasts. Note that we do not make any additional "relay rule assumptions", unlike other protocols in the multicast model (e.g. Streamlet [24], Algorand Agreement [28], PaLa [26]).

Lemma 7. *In each iteration h, each honest process will multicast at most 4 messages.*

Proof. For each iteration $h \in \mathbb{N}$, an honest process p will multicast at most one propose message, at most one vote message for a non-$\bot$ block, at most one of $\langle \text{vote}, h, \bot_h \rangle_p$ and $\langle \text{finalize}, h \rangle_p$, and will relay their view of a notarized blockchain of height h at most once.   □

Each message is at most size $O(\lambda^\varepsilon \cdot n)$ (since a notarization contains up to n signatures of $O(\lambda^\varepsilon)$ size each, where $0 < \varepsilon \leq 1$), so in each iteration, at most $O(\lambda^\varepsilon \cdot n^2)$ bits total are multicast (in the system as a whole, summing over all players). We note that this matches the multicast bit complexity of the base Algorand Agreement protocol [28]. By using now standard techniques, we can bring down the multicast bit complexity to $O(\lambda^\varepsilon \cdot \text{polylog}(\lambda))$ through subsampling the committee of voters [29]. Assuming the sub-exponential security of OWFs, then the length of a signature can be made to be $O(\text{polylog}(\lambda))$, yielding a total multicast bit complexity of $O(\text{polylog}(\lambda))$. We do not innovate on these methods, and focus on the base protocol.

Multicast can be implemented in various different ways on an underlying communication network. In a point-to-point network, each multicast involves sending the message to every other player; thus, our protocol—without subsampling—has $O(\lambda^\varepsilon \cdot n^3)$ total bit complexity in a point-to-point setting (counting every bit that was sent in the whole system). However, in modern peer-to-peer networks or gossip networks, peers do not need to directly communicate with every other peer. In the same vein as e.g. [13,27] or the implementation of [34], it is possible to simulate all-to-all communication if each peer talks to $O(\text{polylog}(n))$ other peers (if chosen appropriately). Then, total communication can be reduced to $O(\lambda^\varepsilon \cdot n^2) \cdot \text{polylog}(n)$ bits (assuming that players do not relay the same message twice when gossiping messages). This may be reduced further by subsampling (again, following the techniques in Algorand).

We note that many nice works, starting with Hotstuff [62], propose base protocols that achieve $O(\lambda^\varepsilon \cdot n)$ bit complexity in a point-to-point setting, when all players are honest. Pessimistically, the bit complexity is $O(\lambda^\varepsilon \cdot n^2)$. Hotstuff and many follow-up works use threshold signatures to compress the size of notarizations, which requires a private setup, making it unclear how to do subsampling. Indeed, our protocol with subsampling (without gossip) matches the asymptotic communication complexity of their base protocols, achieving $O(\lambda^\varepsilon \cdot \text{polylog}(\lambda) \cdot n)$ total bit complexity, or $O(\text{polylog}(\lambda) \cdot n)$ assuming subexponentially secure OWFs. Moreover, this bound holds both pessimistically and optimistically for our protocol, as opposed to just the optimistic case in Hotstuff.

Table 2. Extended Comparison of Popular Consensus Protocols (Random Leaders)

	Proposal Conf. Time	OptimisticBlock Time	Expected View-Based Liveness ($\gamma := \frac{n}{n-f}$)
Simplex	3δ	2δ	$3\delta + (\gamma - 1) \cdot (3\Delta + \delta)$
Algorand*[†] [28]	3δ	3δ	$3\delta + (\gamma - 1) \cdot (4\Delta + 2\delta)$
ICC [19]	3δ	2δ	$3\delta + (\gamma - 1) \cdot (\gamma \cdot (2\Delta + 2\delta) + 2\delta)$
PaLa [26]	4δ	2δ	$4\delta + (\gamma^2 - 1) \cdot (5\Delta + \delta) + (\gamma - 1) \cdot 2\delta + \gamma \cdot 2\Delta$
Pipelined Fast-Hotstuff^ [39] Jolteon^ [33]	5δ	2δ	$5\delta + (\gamma^3 - 1) \cdot (4\Delta + \delta) + (\gamma^2 + \gamma - 2) \cdot 2\delta$
Chained Hotstuff (v6)^ [62]	7δ	2δ	$7\delta + (\gamma^4 - 1) \cdot (3\Delta + \delta) + (\gamma^3 + \gamma^2 + \gamma - 3) \cdot 2\delta$
Streamlet [24]	6Δ	2Δ	$6\Delta + (\gamma^5 + \gamma^4 + \gamma^3 + \gamma^2 + \gamma - 5) \cdot 2\Delta$
P-Sync Bullshark[‡] [59]	6δ	3δ	$6\delta + (\gamma - 1) \cdot 18\Delta$
Hotstuff (v1)^ [1,3] Casper FFG^ [16] Chained Tendermint^ [1,14]	5δ	2δ	$5\delta + (\gamma^3 - 1) \cdot (5\Delta + \delta) + \gamma^2 \cdot 2\Delta$

^With random leaders. *Base protocol without sortition, with optimistic responsiveness. [†]Following the techniques of Algorand [34], by using subsampling, many (if not all) of the protocols here built for the multicast model can be adapted to use only polylog(λ) multicasts per block. [‡]Assuming that it takes 3δ to generate a vertex (optimistically), and where the timeout is set to 9Δ according to Section C.2 in [58].

4 Related Work

The roots of consensus research in the permissioned and partially-synchronous setting dates back to the seminal paper of [31]. Subsequently, the classical approaches in Paxos [46] and PBFT [23] became mainstream and were further studied in [35,45,49,52]. These protocols typically adopt an expensive or complex "view-change" phase for switching out a faulty leader for a new leader, and are built mainly for the stable leader setting, where a single leader can propose many blocks in a row without ceding its leadership.

More recently, the rise of blockchain applications (in particular, Proof-of-Stake systems) motivated a new line of work towards building fairer and simpler consensus protocols, where each leader generally only gets to propose a single block. In particular, Casper FFG [16], Hotstuff (v1) [3], Tendermint [14], and PaLa [26] introduced a new "streamlined" approach where consensus is reached on many pipelined blocks at once, largely avoiding the complexity of a dedicated view-change subroutine. All four protocols proceed in incrementing epochs $e = 1, 2, \ldots$ and have a similar voting rule, where voters vote only for proposals extending the "freshest block" they've seen, that is, the one with the highest epoch number. As a consequence of the voting rule, the protocols maintain some intricacy when arguing liveness (i.e. the proposer may have to wait an extra 2Δ before proposing a new block, if the previous proposer crashed).[12] (Note that Simplex does not have this intricacy.) Somewhat separately, but also building on the streamlined paradigm, Streamlet [24] achieves a simple protocol description but has worse optimistic and pessimistic liveness. In Streamlet, players are allowed to vote for any "longest chain," even if it is not the "freshest block" that they have seen, and thus requires a different consistency and liveness argument than do Hotstuff/Tendermint/PaLa.

PBFT [23] remains the fastest protocol when leaders are honest, requiring only 3δ timesteps to confirm transactions; [5] showed that this is optimal in the partially synchronous setting for $f \leq n/3$. (We mention works such as Parametrized FaB Paxos [49] and SBFT [36], which achieve even faster optimistic confirmation when $f \leq n/5$, but this requires that the fraction of faulty voters also be small, in addition to honest leaders.) However, we are more interested in the setting with rotating/random leaders, due to issues of fairness. (Random leaders also give better worst-case confirmation time.) Consequently, many works have adapted PBFT to a setting with rotating leaders; we mention Algorand [28], Fast-Hotstuff [39], and Jolteon [33]. In particular, Pipelined Fast-Hotstuff and Jolteon propose streamlined versions of PBFT-like protocols that also seek to reduce the complexity of the view-change, again by pipelining proposals; both are slower than Algorand. Algorand and Fast-Hotstuff (without pipelining) achieve 3δ proposal confirmation time, but worse 3δ block time.

A major concern when designing modern consensus protocols is that of communication complexity. A low communication complexity is essential for a scalable protocol. In the multicast model, Algorand [29] showed an elegant way to subsample the committee of voters to achieve $\mathsf{polylog}(\lambda)$ multicasts (or $O(n)$ messages in the point-to-point model). We remark that their techniques also apply to our protocol. (If we additionally trade off optimistic responsiveness, Algorand [29] can also achieve *adaptive security*.) In the point-to-point messaging model, a nice line of works, starting with Hotstuff [62], sought to reduce communication complexity by funneling all messages through the leader (a technique from [56]) and by using threshold signatures to reduce the size of certificates (a technique from [18]). Hotstuff, Pipelined Fast-Hotstuff [39] and Jolteon [33] all achieve $O(n)$ messages per block optimistically, and $O(n^2)$ messages in the case of a faulty leader (or better when amortized over many round-robin leaders, depending on the implementation of the 'pacemaker'). It remains unclear how realistic it is to funnel communication through a single leader on a peer-to-peer network. We note that their optimizations to message size using threshold signatures or aggregate signatures also apply to other protocols; of course, threshold signatures require a much stronger private setup (e.g. see [18]) that we wish to avoid. Apart

---

[12] Sometimes, this is referred to as the 'hidden lock problem'.

from requiring additional complexity to instantiate the private setup, it is also not clear how to do subsampling for protocols that require threshold signatures, as an example.

Our protocol has a similar 'notarize/finalize' voting procedure to that of [19] (Dfinity ICC) and an old variant of Streamlet ([25], Appendix A), but uses different techniques for proposals and for switching leaders. The ICC protocol [19] is also quite nice but does not use timeout/dummy blocks, and incurs some complexity in how they rank leaders and allow multiple leaders in each round (they additionally assume threshold signatures and a trusted private setup, which we avoid). Consequently, if the first leader in a round is corrupt, they need essentially two honest leaders in a row to confirm a subsequent block. It is worth exploring whether their techniques for block dissemination can be used to improve Simplex. Independently, we also note structural similarities between Simplex and the Graded Binding Crusader Agreement protocol (using a weak common coin) in [2], albeit that protocol is for the asynchronous setting.

In a somewhat distinct line of work, [58] propose a partially synchronous version of Bullshark built on top of what they call a DAG. These protocols are well-suited for the asynchronous setting, but when adapted for partial-synchrony, much care is needed when integrating timeouts into the DAG construction, to ensure that a slow honest leader is not left behind before it can propose a block; moreover, it trades-off latency.

We summarize the comparisons in Table 2 (for the random leader setting). When computing the expected view-based liveness, we define a parameter $\gamma := n/(n - f)$ that corresponds to the inverse fraction of eligible leaders who are honest.[13] Table 1 presents concrete values for expected liveness when $f = \lceil n/3 \rceil - 1$. Importantly, we remark that the landscape of consensus protocols is rich and ever-changing; this survey may not be comprehensive. In particular, while we compare only theoretical works here, much has been done to improve the performance of consensus protocols in practice by the systems community.

References

1. Abraham, I.: Two round hotstuff. https://decentralizedthoughts.github.io/2022-11-24-two-round-HS/. Accessed: 2022-12-30
2. Abraham, I., Ben-David, N., Yandamuri, S.: Efficient and adaptively secure asynchronous binary agreement via binding crusader agreement. In: Proceedings of the 2022 ACM Symposium on Principles of Distributed Computing, pp. 381–391 (2022)
3. Abraham, I., Gueta, G., Malkhi, D.: Hot-stuff the linear, optimal-resilience, one-message bft devil. CoRR, abs/1803.05069 (2018)

---

[13] Another reason we use a different variable is to make clear that it is possible to elect leaders from an entirely different set of processes than the main set of protocol processes; indeed, our protocol supports a setting where most leaders are corrupt (i.e. $\gamma > 3/2$) even when the number of faulty voters is required to be small ($f < n/3$).

4. Abraham, I., Malkhi, D., Spiegelman, A.: Asymptotically optimal validated asynchronous byzantine agreement. In: Proceedings of the 2019 ACM Symposium on Principles of Distributed Computing, pp. 337–346 (2019)

5. Abraham, I., Nayak, K., Ren, L., Xiang, Z.: Good-case latency of byzantine broadcast: a complete categorization. In: Proceedings of the 2021 ACM Symposium on Principles of Distributed Computing, pp. 331–341 (2021)

6. Aiyer, A.S., Alvisi, L., Clement, A., Dahlin, M., Martin, J.P., Porth, C.: Bar fault tolerance for cooperative services. In: Proceedings of the Twentieth ACM Symposium on Operating Systems Principles, pp. 45–58 (2005)

7. Allen, S., Juels, A., Khaire, M., Kell, T., Shrivastava, S.: Nfts for art and collectables: Primer and outlook (2022)

8. Apache Software Foundation: ZooKeeper internals. https://zookeeper.apache.org/doc/r3.4.13/zookeeperInternals.html. Accessed 24 Feb 2023

9. Backes, M., Manoharan, P., Mohammadi, E.: Tuc: time-sensitive and modular analysis of anonymous communication. In: 2014 IEEE 27th Computer Security Foundations Symposium, pp. 383–397. IEEE (2014)

10. Barak, B., Canetti, R., Nielsen, J.B., Pass, R.: Universally composable protocols with relaxed set-up assumptions. In: 45th Annual IEEE Symposium on Foundations of Computer Science, pp. 186–195. IEEE (2004)

11. Baudet, M., et al.: State machine replication in the libra blockchain. The Libra Assn., Technical report 7 (2019)

12. Baum, C., David, B., Dowsley, R., Nielsen, J.B., Oechsner, S.: Tardis: a foundation of time-lock puzzles in UC. In: Annual International Conference on the Theory and Applications of Cryptographic Techniques, pp. 429–459. Springer (2021)

13. Boyle, E., Chung, K.M., Pass, R.: Large-scale secure computation: Multi-party computation for (parallel) ram programs. In: Advances in Cryptology-CRYPTO 2015: 35th Annual Cryptology Conference, Santa Barbara, CA, USA, August 16–20, 2015, Proceedings, Part II, pp. 742–762. Springer (2015)

14. Buchman, E., Kwon, J., Milosevic, Z.: The latest gossip on bft consensus. arXiv preprint arXiv:1807.04938 (2018)

15. Burrows, M.: The chubby lock service for loosely-coupled distributed systems. In: Proceedings of the 7th Symposium on Operating Systems Design and Implementation, pp. 335–350 (2006)

16. Buterin, V., Griffith, V.: Casper the friendly finality gadget. arXiv preprint arXiv:1710.09437 (2017)

17. Buterin, V., et al.: A next-generation smart contract and decentralized application platform. White Paper **3**(37), 2–1 (2014)

18. Cachin, C., Kursawe, K., Shoup, V.: Random oracles in constantinopole: practical asynchronous byzantine agreement using cryptography. In: Proceedings of the Nineteenth Annual ACM Symposium on Principles of Distributed Computing, pp. 123–132 (2000)

19. Camenisch, J., Drijvers, M., Hanke, T., Pignolet, Y.A., Shoup, V., Williams, D.: Internet computer consensus. In: Proceedings of the 2022 ACM Symposium on Principles of Distributed Computing, pp. 81–91 (2022)

20. Canetti, R.: Universally composable security: a new paradigm for cryptographic protocols. In: Proceedings 42nd IEEE Symposium on Foundations of Computer Science, pp. 136–145. IEEE (2001)

21. Canetti, R., Hogan, K., Malhotra, A., Varia, M.: A universally composable treatment of network time. In: 2017 IEEE 30th Computer Security Foundations Symposium (CSF), pp. 360–375. IEEE (2017)

22. Canetti, R., Rabin, T.: Fast asynchronous byzantine agreement with optimal resilience. In: Proceedings of the Twenty-Fifth Annual ACM Symposium on Theory of Computing, pp. 42–51 (1993)
23. Castro, M., Liskov, B., et al.: Practical byzantine fault tolerance. In: OsDI. 99, pp. 173–186 (1999)
24. Chan, B.Y., Shi, E.: Streamlet: Textbook streamlined blockchains. In: Proceedings of the 2nd ACM Conference on Advances in Financial Technologies, pp. 1–11 (2020)
25. Chan, B.Y., Shi, E.: Streamlet: Textbook streamlined blockchains (earlier version). Cryptology ePrint Archive, Paper 2020/088 (2020). https://eprint.iacr.org/archive/2020/088/20200204:124247
26. Chan, T.H., Pass, R., Shi, E.: Pala: A simple partially synchronous blockchain. Cryptology ePrint Archive (2018)
27. Chandran, N., Chongchitmate, W., Garay, J.A., Goldwasser, S., Ostrovsky, R., Zikas, V.: The hidden graph model: communication locality and optimal resiliency with adaptive faults. In: Proceedings of the 2015 Conference on Innovations in Theoretical Computer Science, pp. 153–162 (2015)
28. Chen, J., Gorbunov, S., Micali, S., Vlachos, G.: Algorand agreement: super fast and partition resilient byzantine agreement. Cryptology ePrint Archive (2018)
29. Chen, J., Micali, S.: Algorand: a secure and efficient distributed ledger. Theoret. Comput. Sci. **777**, 155–183 (2019)
30. Daian, P., Goldfeder, S., Kell, T., Li, Y., Zhao, X., Bentov, I., Breidenbach, L., Juels, A.: Flash boys 2.0: frontrunning in decentralized exchanges, miner extractable value, and consensus instability. In: 2020 IEEE Symposium on Security and Privacy (SP), pp. 910–927. IEEE (2020)
31. Dwork, C., Lynch, N., Stockmeyer, L.: Consensus in the presence of partial synchrony. J. ACM (JACM) **35**(2), 288–323 (1988)
32. Garay, J., Kiayias, A., Leonardos, N.: The bitcoin backbone protocol: analysis and applications. In: Oswald, E., Fischlin, M. (eds.) EUROCRYPT 2015. LNCS, vol. 9057, pp. 281–310. Springer, Heidelberg (2015). https://doi.org/10.1007/978-3-662-46803-6_10
33. Gelashvili, R., Kokoris-Kogias, L., Sonnino, A., Spiegelman, A., Xiang, Z.: Jolteon and ditto: network-adaptive efficient consensus with asynchronous fallback. In: Financial Cryptography and Data Security: 26th International Conference, FC 2022, Grenada, May 2–6, 2022, Revised Selected Papers, pp. 296–315. Springer, Cham (2022). https://doi.org/10.1007/978-3-031-18283-9_14
34. Gilad, Y., Hemo, R., Micali, S., Vlachos, G., Zeldovich, N.: Algorand: scaling byzantine agreements for cryptocurrencies. In: Proceedings of the 26th Symposium on Operating Systems Principles, pp. 51–68 (2017)
35. Guerraoui, R., Knežević, N., Quéma, V., Vukolić, M.: The next 700 bft protocols. In: Proceedings of the 5th European Conference on Computer Systems, EuroSys 2010, pp. 363–376. ACM, New York (2010)
36. Gueta, G.G., et al.: Sbft: a scalable and decentralized trust infrastructure. In: 2019 49th Annual IEEE/IFIP International Conference on Dependable Systems and Networks (DSN), pp. 568–580. IEEE (2019)
37. Håstad, J., Impagliazzo, R., Levin, L.A., Luby, M.: A pseudorandom generator from any one-way function. SIAM J. Comput. **28**(4), 1364–1396 (1999)
38. Hubert Chan, T.-H., Pass, R., Shi, E.: Consensus through herding. In: Ishai, Y., Rijmen, V. (eds.) EUROCRYPT 2019. LNCS, vol. 11476, pp. 720–749. Springer, Cham (2019). https://doi.org/10.1007/978-3-030-17653-2_24
39. Jalalzai, M.M., Niu, J., Feng, C., Gai, F.: Fast-hotstuff: a fast and resilient hotstuff protocol. arXiv preprint arXiv:2010.11454 (2020)

40. Kalai, Y.T., Lindell, Y., Prabhakaran, M.: Concurrent general composition of secure protocols in the timing model. In: Proceedings of the Thirty-Seventh Annual ACM Symposium on Theory of Computing, pp. 644–653 (2005)
41. Katz, J., Maurer, U., Tackmann, B., Zikas, V.: Universally composable synchronous computation. In: Sahai, A. (ed.) TCC 2013. LNCS, vol. 7785, pp. 477–498. Springer, Heidelberg (2013). https://doi.org/10.1007/978-3-642-36594-2_27
42. Keidar, I., Kokoris-Kogias, E., Naor, O., Spiegelman, A.: All you need is dag. In: Proceedings of the 2021 ACM Symposium on Principles of Distributed Computing, pp. 165–175 (2021)
43. Kelkar, M., Zhang, F., Goldfeder, S., Juels, A.: Order-fairness for byzantine consensus. In: Micciancio, D., Ristenpart, T. (eds.) CRYPTO 2020. LNCS, vol. 12172, pp. 451–480. Springer, Cham (2020). https://doi.org/10.1007/978-3-030-56877-1_16
44. Kiayias, A., Zhou, H.-S., Zikas, V.: Fair and robust multi-party computation using a global transaction ledger. In: Fischlin, M., Coron, J.-S. (eds.) EUROCRYPT 2016. LNCS, vol. 9666, pp. 705–734. Springer, Heidelberg (2016). https://doi.org/10.1007/978-3-662-49896-5_25
45. Kotla, R., Alvisi, L., Dahlin, M., Clement, A., Wong, E.L.: Zyzzyva: speculative byzantine fault tolerance. In: Proceedings of the 21st ACM Symposium on Operating Systems Principles 2007, SOSP 2007, Stevenson, Washington, USA, October 14–17, 2007, pp. 45–58 (2007)
46. Lamport, L.: The part-time parliament. ACM Trans. Comput. Syst. 16(2), 133–169 (1998)
47. Lamport, L.: Paxos made simple. ACM SIGACT News (Distributed Computing Column) 32, 4 (Whole Number 121, December 2001), pp. 51–58 (2001)
48. Lamport, L., Shostak, R., Pease, M.: The byzantine generals problem. ACM Trans. Program. Lang. Syst. 4(3), 382–401 (1982)
49. Martin, J.P., Alvisi, L.: Fast byzantine consensus. IEEE Trans. Dependable Secur. Comput. 3(3) (2006)
50. Miller, A., Xia, Y., Croman, K., Shi, E., Song, D.: The honey badger of BFT protocols. In: Proceedings of the 2016 ACM SIGSAC Conference on computer and communications security, pp. 31–42 (2016)
51. Nakamoto, S.: Bitcoin: A peer-to-peer electronic cash system. Decentralized business review, p. 21260 (2008)
52. Ongaro, D., Ousterhout, J.: In search of an understandable consensus algorithm. In: Proceedings of the 2014 USENIX Conference on USENIX Annual Technical Conference, USENIX ATC 2014, pp. 305–320. USENIX Association, USA (2014)
53. Pass, R., Shi, E.: The sleepy model of consensus. In: Takagi, T., Peyrin, T. (eds.) ASIACRYPT 2017. LNCS, vol. 10625, pp. 380–409. Springer, Cham (2017). https://doi.org/10.1007/978-3-319-70697-9_14
54. Pass, R., Shi, E.: Thunderella: blockchains with optimistic instant confirmation. In: Nielsen, J.B., Rijmen, V. (eds.) EUROCRYPT 2018. LNCS, vol. 10821, pp. 3–33. Springer, Cham (2018). https://doi.org/10.1007/978-3-319-78375-8_1
55. Rabin, M.O.: Randomized byzantine generals. In: 24th Annual Symposium on Foundations of Computer Science (sfcs 1983), pp. 403–409. IEEE (1983)
56. Reiter, M.K.: Secure agreement protocols: reliable and atomic group multicast in rampart. In: Proceedings of the 2nd ACM Conference on Computer and Communications Security, pp. 68–80 (1994)
57. Rompel, J.: One-way functions are necessary and sufficient for secure signatures. In: Proceedings of the Twenty-Second Annual ACM Symposium on Theory of Computing, pp. 387–394 (1990)

58. Spiegelman, A., Giridharan, N., Sonnino, A., Kokoris-Kogias, L.: Bullshark: Dag BFT protocols made practical. In: Proceedings of the 2022 ACM SIGSAC Conference on Computer and Communications Security, pp. 2705–2718 (2022)
59. Spiegelman, A., Giridharan, N., Sonnino, A., Kokoris-Kogias, L.: Bullshark: the partially synchronous version. arXiv preprint arXiv:2209.05633 (2022)
60. Wensley, J.H., et al.: Sift: design and analysis of a fault-tolerant computer for aircraft control. Proc. IEEE **66**(10), 1240–1255 (1978)
61. Yao, A.C.: Protocols for secure computations. In: 23rd Annual Symposium on Foundations of Computer Science (sfcs 1982), pp. 160–164. IEEE (1982)
62. Yin, M., Malkhi, D., Reiter, M.K., Gueta, G.G., Abraham, I.: Hotstuff: BFT consensus with linearity and responsiveness. In: Proceedings of the 2019 ACM Symposium on Principles of Distributed Computing, pp. 347–356 (2019)

Agile Cryptography: A Universally Composable Approach

Christian Badertscher[1]([✉])[ID], Michele Ciampi[2][ID], and Aggelos Kiayias[2,3]

[1] Input Output, Zurich, Switzerland
christian.badertscher@iohk.io
[2] University of Edinburgh, Edinburgh, UK
{michele.ciampi,aggelos.kiayias}@ed.ac.uk
[3] Input Output, Edinburgh, UK

Abstract. Being capable of updating cryptographic algorithms is an inevitable and essential practice in cryptographic engineering. This *cryptographic agility*, as it has been called, is a fundamental desideratum for long term cryptographic system security that still poses significant challenges from a modeling perspective. For instance, current formulations of agility fail to express the fundamental security that is expected to stem from timely implementation updates, namely the fact that the system retains some of its security properties provided that the update is performed prior to the deprecated implementation becoming exploited.

In this work we put forth a novel framework for expressing updateability in the context of cryptographic primitives within the universal composition model. Our updatable ideal functionality framework provides a general template for expressing the security we expect from cryptographic agility capturing in a fine grained manner all the properties that can be retained across implementation updates. We exemplify our framework over two basic cryptographic primitives, digital signatures and non-interactive zero-knowledge (NIZK), where we demonstrate how to achieve updateability with consistency and backwards-compatibility across updates in a composable manner. We also illustrate how our notion is a continuation of a much broader scope of the concept of agility introduced by Acar, Belenkiy, Bellare, and Cash in Eurocrypt 2010 in the context of symmetric cryptographic primitives.

1 Introduction

A lesson we all know well is that cryptographic implementations are not forever. And while in theory, switching between implementations may be as easy as wiping a whiteboard, in cryptographic engineering, transitioning between implementations of the same primitive can be very challenging. This was exemplified in the efforts of deprecating MD5 and SHA-1 that were brought about by the attacks of [27,28] which eventually culminated to a complete collapse of collision resistance for these functions, [24,25]. Despite significant communication efforts

M. Ciampi—Supported by the Sunday Group.

G. Rothblum and H. Wee (Eds.): TCC 2023, LNCS 14372, pp. 480–509, 2023.
https://doi.org/10.1007/978-3-031-48624-1_18

and the practical attacks that were developed, the functions lingered for years, see for example [23]. Developing computer systems in a way that they are capable of updating the underlying cryptographic implementations they use has been an important engineering objective for over a decade. It is the main objective behind the concept of cryptographic *agility* [26], that promotes software engineering practices that facilitate the easy swapping of cryptographic algorithms. Agility has been identified as a key requirement in standardization of cryptographic systems, see e.g., the NIST report on post-quantum security [12] and remains a much discussed topic in cryptographic engineering circles and one that is also, still, not sufficiently researched, cf. [21].

Given the above state of affairs, an important question is whether there is a way to formally study implementation updates in cryptographic systems and even realize them in a safe manner. In [1] cryptographic agility is given a formal treatment identifying it as a special case of the problem of key-reuse between cryptographic algorithms. While key re-use is important security consideration in cryptographic systems and indeed highly relevant in the context of updates, we argue that cryptographic implementation updateability and agility itself, is a much broader and not sufficiently understood topic. The reason is that "agility" as defined in [1] *"is about individually secure schemes sharing a key. It is not about what happens when a scheme is broken and replaced by another that is (hopefully) secure."* However it is clear that in a broader cryptographic engineering context, the agility desideratum is exactly about broken cryptographic algorithms and the need to update them. Indeed, it is in this context that the term is mentioned in [26] and [12], where the objective is to move from broken hash function implementations and, respectively, broken classical cryptographic algorithms, to ones that are more secure. As stated explicitly in [26], agility is about *"an administrator [who] might choose to replace an algorithm that was recently broken with one still considered secure."* At first sight, this direction might seem hopeless: a security collapse of a cryptographic algorithm seems catastrophic for security. Key material may be exposed, privacy of past transactions can be compromised and integrity of future interactions can be at risk. Furthermore, even attempting to model security in this setting seems problematic. How to model an event like an "efficient algorithm for factoring is just discovered" in the timeline of events of a cryptographic system? The cryptographic assumptions that are used to assemble the conditional statements in the security theorems we are so fond of have a truth-value that is universal and definite—it is not meant to change in the course of the system deployment based on our understanding.

Contrary to these theoretical barriers, security practitioners have no issue to envision the concept of a secure update. They know that taking advantage of the specifics of the system at hand, an update process can be followed to sanitize the parts that are deemed vulnerable and provided that such process is completed on time—prior to an algorithm compromise or other adversarial exploit—the system will retain a fair amount of its security properties. This final point is the main motivation behind our work that bridges the cryptographic theoretical design and modeling toolset with the engineering practices of software updates. We study the notion of cryptographic agility in UC which allows us to master the complexity of interactions present in computer systems where multiple cryptographic modules interact with each other. Such a composable definition of what a secure update system for a cryptographic task ideally is, allows us not only to theoretically reason about the security properties of update protocols, but also to rely on the composition theorem to construct complex systems with clear security semantics that contain updatable modules.

1.1   Contributions

We present a novel modeling of cryptographic agility within the setting of Universal Composition and illustrate it with concrete protocols for important cryptographic primitives. Our results include:

A Generic Framework for Updates. Our model framework captures the concept of securely updating a cryptographic implementation in the form of a generic update functionality we denote by $U_{SttUp,UpPred}^{\mathscr{F}}$ that is parameterized by a class of ideal functionalities $\mathscr{F}$ as well as two programs UpPred and SttUp. Each member of the class $\mathscr{F}$ is indexed by a particular implementation and provides the same interface to the users who engage with it. At any given time the session participants of the functionality are connected to a particular member of $\mathscr{F}$ which initially is a designated member $\mathcal{F}_0$ for all parties. As time passes, participants, even in different sessions, may initiate an update to another implementation, by pointing to another member of $\mathscr{F}$. While the interface of $U_{SttUp,UpPred}^{\mathscr{F}}$ contains that of the members of $\mathscr{F}$, the additional update interface of $U_{SttUp,UpPred}^{\mathscr{F}}$ enables users of the functionality to coordinate an update. The security properties of the update are captured by a *state-update* function SttUp and the *update* predicate UpPred. SttUp represents the (ideal) initialization of the state of the updated functionality (as a function of its history), and UpPred dictates the circumstances under which a party successfully completes the update:

– *Security across updates.* In the most simple parameterization, $UpPred \equiv 1$ and $SttUp \equiv \emptyset$, amounting to a "clean install", we have that the new primitive substitutes the old one without retaining any properties or guarantees from the past instantiation. There are many reasons that a "clean install" is a very limiting way of approaching the concept of updatable cryptographic primitives. One thing is that key material has to be re-generated. A more crucial downside however is that backwards compatibility is lost—something highly desirable from an engineering perspective and difficult to attain as pointed out in [19]. This can be a very serious consideration since the updated system may still need to interoperate with components using the previous algorithm. Our framework captures naturally such considerations by suitably defining via the SttUp program which portion of the past state, such as of functionality $\mathcal{F}_{i-1}$, should be retained when updating to the functionality $\mathcal{F}_i$ during the i-th update.

- *Update coordination patterns.* Updating the implementation of a particular primitive requires some action by all participants engaged in a certain execution session. This may be done by varying degrees of coordination and our framework is capable of doing this by programming the UpPred predicate to grant the update successfully at the right conditions. For instance, the update predicate could demand that all parties transition in tandem, or could ensure the update unifies a set of parties currently working with different versions.

Fine-Grain Corruption Interface. By specializing the UC corruption model to capture explicit subroutine corruptions, we are able to propose a unified modeling tool capturing the seemingly different security breaches of (1) corrupted implementations, (2) key leakage, or (3) failed security assumptions, without having to declare parties affected by such failures as *fully corrupted*. While such a fine-grain look at corruption is of independent interest, in the context of updates, such a formalization is important because it allows us to express advanced features of updates. For example, we can capture that if an update happens prior to any of the above failures, the system is uninterruptedly secure. We can also capture that as long as a party is not fully corrupted (but suffering from any of the above failures), an update regains the party's full security guarantees.

Updatable Signatures and NIZKs. We present two extensive studies applying our framework to the setting of digital signatures and non-interactive zero-knowledge schemes. In both cases, we explore the ramifications of the requirement of consistency, backwards compatibility across updates, and healing from sub-corruptions. In particular, the desideratum is that past signatures and NIZKs still verify after an update, while mitigating any side-effects by a collapsed cryptographic implementation, in the sense of regaining security after the update takes place. We achieve this via an update process that transfers information about the state onwards, while eliminating algorithmic dependencies on previous versions which may be compromised. In the signature case, we obtain a general and provably secure blueprint of how computer systems can become post-quantum ready today without sacrificing efficiency. In the NIZK case, we show that more effort is required by the prover to ensure the preservation of soundness of the proof system across updates while ensuring that no leakage occurs due to the update system itself. Due to space limitations, we have deferred the NIZK result to the full version.

Comparison with Previous Notion. Finally, for completeness, we demonstrate how our framework subsumes the concept of agility as defined in [1]. Following that work, we focus on pseudorandom functions (PRFs) and we show what exact type of an updatable PRF functionality in our framework corresponds to their agility notion. Expectedly, the result does not account for (adaptive) corruptions since agility in [1] is equated to key reuse and hence it fundamentally requires the protection of the key as algorithms are being swapped across updates.

1.2   Related Work

As mentioned above, our work recasts the issue of cryptographic agility in the universal composition setting taking a broader view of what cryptographic agility means compared to [1] who consider it a special case of key sharing across primitives. This notion is subsumed within our framework, which in a similar manner, can also accommodate protocol substitution attacks [6,15]. Our work also relates to key-insulated cryptosystems [14] and key-evolving cryptography [16] in the sense that our notion can encompass forward security with previous key compromise. The important distinction though of our cryptographic agility framework is that we do not outsource the version coordination to the users and the fact that implementations of the underlying primitive can be independent; in contrast, key-insulated and key-evolving cryptographic primitives require a single monolithic implementation that has the users themselves specify at each invocation which version of the key they engage with. The case of "updatable encryption" [8,20] is similar. Another treatment of a specific primitive in the context of software updates is given in the context of blockchain protocols in [13]. In the context of key exchange [7], agility has been casted as having a configurable selection of multiple protocol and cipher modes that can be chosen via running a negotiation protocol. In our agility framework such negotiations can take arbitrary form between parties and culminate to a particular input to the updatable functionality which will be then be responsible for facilitating the coordination steps needed for parties to implement the switch to the negotiated mode of operation. It follows that it is straightforward to express the concept of downgrade attacks as well as the concept of downgrade-resilience (cf. [7]), by suitably restricting to environments that prohibit honest parties from "shooting themselves in the foot" and agreeing to switch (downgrade) to a weak implementation. Finally, we note that our topic bears a superficial resemblance to the concept of "cryptography with updates" [2] which in fact relates to incremental cryptography [5], as well as to firewall-based constructions [11] that tame dishonest behavior by sanitizing the messages from a cryptographic protocol. Recently Poettering et al. [22] propose a forward secure signature scheme suitable to authenticate software versions by the vendors with two main features: first, assuming secure erasures, the scheme is forward secure, and second, based on a natural incentive structure, the scheme enjoys a particular self-enforcement mechanism that strongly disincentivizes coercion attacks in which vendors are forced, e.g. by nation state actors, to misuse or disclose their keys.

1.3   Notation

We denote the security parameter with $\lambda \in \mathbb{N}$. A randomized algorithm $\mathcal{A}$ is running in *probabilistic polynomial time* (PPT) if there exists a polynomial $p(\cdot)$ such that for every input x the running time of $\mathcal{A}(x)$ is bounded by $p(|x|)$. We call a function negl : $\mathbb{N} \to \mathbb{R}^+$ *negligible* if for every positive polynomial $p(\lambda)$ a $\lambda_0 \in \mathbb{N}$ exists, such that for all $\lambda > \lambda_0 : \epsilon(\lambda) < 1/p(\lambda)$. We denote by $[n]$ the set $\{1, \ldots, n\}$ for $n \in \mathbb{N}$. We use "=" to check equality of two different elements (i.e.

$a = b$ then...) and "$\leftarrow$" as the assigning operator (e.g. to assign to a the value of b we write $a \leftarrow b$). A randomized assignment is denoted with $a \xleftarrow{\$} \mathsf{alg}$, where alg is a randomized algorithm and the randomness used by alg is not explicit. If the randomness is explicit we write $a := \mathsf{alg}(x; r)$ where x is the input and r is the randomness. Let $\mathbf{v}$ be a sequence of elements (vector); by $\mathbf{v}[i]$ we mean the i-th element of $\mathbf{v}$. Analogously, for a bi-dimensional vector M, we denote with $M[i, j]$ the element identified by the i-th row and the j-th column of M.

2 UC Basics and Corruption Models

2.1 Overview

We use the UC framework [10] in this work and give here a brief overview.

Protocol and Protocol Instances. A protocol π is an algorithm for a distributed system formalized as an interactive Turing machine (ITM) with several tapes. For this paper, we are mainly referring to three tapes: (1) the input tape, holding inputs written by a calling program, (2) the subroutine-output tape, which holds return values from called programs, and (3) the backdoor tape which formalizes the interaction of an ITM with the adversary (for example to capture corruption modes). Of great formal interest are the so-called *structured protocols* that are protocols that consist of a *shell* part that takes care of model-related instructions such as corruption handling, and a *body* part that encodes the actual cryptographic protocol. The body can again consist of a protocol (consisting of shell and body) which yields a sequence of shells. Towards defining a UC execution, UC defines an ITM instance (denoted ITI), which is defined as the pair $M = (\mu, \mathsf{id})$, where μ is the description of an ITM and $\mathsf{id} = (\mathsf{sid}\|\mathsf{pid})$ is its identity, consisting of a session identifier sid and a party identifier pid. An instance is associated with a Turing machine configuration, which can be seen as this machine's state. An *instance or session of a protocol* π, with respect to a session identifier sid, is defined as a set of ITIs $(\pi, \mathsf{id}_1), (\pi, \mathsf{id}_2), \ldots$ with $\mathsf{id}_i = \mathsf{sid}\|\mathsf{pid}_i$. Each such ITI is referred to as a (main) *party*, and the *extended instance* is the transitive closure of machines spawned as a consequence of running π, in particular, it encompasses all the subroutines.

Ideal Functionalities. Special types of protocols are ideal protocols that formalize the idealization of a cryptographic task. They are represented by an ideal functionality and its specification is usually referred to by $\mathcal{F}$. An instance of this functionality can be thought of as a "trusted third party". Parties are formally represented as dummy machines that forward inputs and outputs to and from this particular ITI, respectively. $\mathcal{F}$ therefore has to specify all outputs generated for each party, and the amount of information the ideal-world adversary learns (via the backdoor tape) and what its active influence is via its interaction with $\mathcal{F}$. Functionalities directly handle the corruption requests by an adversary (and usually adjust their behavior based on this information). We denote the corruption set maintained by parties by $\mathcal{C}$ and this will play an essential role in our treatment.

Execution of a Protocol, Adversary, and Corruption Models. In a UC execution, an environment is allowed to spawn a session of a protocol μ. Often, this is either a real protocol π or an instance of some ideal functionality running with dummy parties. Additionally, the environment is allowed to invoke the adversary. The adversary can communicate with other ITIs by writing (only) on their respective backdoor tapes. This tape is used to model security properties provided by functionalities (e.g., a secure channel could leak the length of the message via the backdoor tape). The backdoor tapes are also used to model party corruption. The corruption model is formally specified by how machines react to these messages on the backdoor tape. The plain UC model does not prescribe any specific corruption model, but there is a standard corruption mode that we describe in more detail below in Sect. 2.2 as it is relevant to this work because we are going to propose an extension to it.

UC Emulation and Composition. While UC emulation is a very general notion, we are only interested in the special case that a protocol π UC-realizes an ideal functionality $\mathcal{F}$: A protocol π UC-realizes $\mathcal{F}$, if for any (efficient) real-world adversary $\mathcal{A}$ there is an (efficient) ideal-world adversary (the simulator) $\mathcal{S}$ such that no (efficient) environment can distinguish the (real) execution of protocol π from the (ideal) execution of $\mathcal{F}$. This emulation notion is composable: if a protocol π_1 UC-realizes $\mathcal{F}_1$, and another protocol π_2 uses $\mathcal{F}_1$ as a subroutine to UC-realize some other functionality $\mathcal{F}_2$, then one can replace invocations of $\mathcal{F}_1$ by invocations to π_1 and the composed protocol (consisting of π_2 calling π_1) UC-realizes $\mathcal{F}_2$.

Standard Functionalities. In this work, we will make use of the standard formalism of signatures, non-interactive zero-knowledge (NIZK), and pseudo-random functions (PRFs). We refer to the full version for the formal definitions of the tools we are using [4].

2.2   Fine-Grained Corruption Model

The standard way of modeling byzantine corruptions in UC has two important aspects: when a machine is corrupted, the adversary takes full control over the future input-output behavior(and learns all previous inputs and outputs). Second, the machine reports itself as corrupted to a *corruption aggregation ITI* that aggregates all corruption information of an extended session. In more detail, this aggregation machine records corruptions within the main session and is further made aware of all subroutines and their respective session-IDs in order to be able to (recursively) retrieve the corruption status via the corruption aggregation machines of those invoked (sub)sessions. In this way, the environment receives "genuine" information about the corruption set in an execution. The corruption aggregation is identified by a special PID $\mathscr{A}$. When invoked to report the corruption set, in the standard party-wise (pid-wise) corruption model, the machine reports the list of known party identities that are listed as corrupted.

This is however only a restricted use of the entire formalism put forth in [10]. In general, if a machine with (extended) identity $id := (\pi, \text{sid}, \text{pid})$ is registered as corrupted, the corruption-aggregation machine can store any function $f(id)$ to model a fine-grained level of corruption and not just report pid. Similarly, an ideal functionality, which models all interaction including the faithful reporting of the corruption information can report a more fine-grained set of corrupted machines.

In our model, we follow pid-wise corruption with the following simple addition. Let π be a protocol and let $\mathcal{H}$ be a dedicated hybrid functionality invoked only by a single party (imagine $\mathcal{H}$ to be a private memory functionality of party pid). Then we allow the corruption aggregation machine to report two kinds of information: $f(\rho, s, p) = p$ if ρ is any other code than $\mathcal{H}$ (as usual, the entire party is considered corrupted in this case). If ρ corresponds to the ideal protocol for $\mathcal{H}$, then the entire identity is revealed, i.e., the session, the party-id and the label of the functionality. A protocol in this model has hence two corruption modes: session sid of π run by party pid follows the standard corruption mechanism except that when its hybrid functionality $\mathcal{H}$ obtains the corruption message to corrupt party pid, the protocol reports $(\mathcal{H}, \text{pid}, s)$ where s is the session-id within which $\mathcal{H}$ was invoked. If $\mathcal{H}$ models a local memory, then this corruption mode allows to corrupt the memory of a party without corrupting the entire party.

Ideal-World Correspondence. In the ideal world, the realized functionality $\mathcal{F}$ must support more complex corruption instructions to reflect the different corruption states that are possible based on the fine-grained information contained in $\mathcal{C}$ (note that since corruption is modeled in UC as part of the protocol execution, it is the functionality that is responsible for the reporting in the ideal execution). Instead of just reacting on ordinary party corruptions, our ideal functionalities will incorporate specific instructions to reflect the more fine-grained model. For example, an ideal functionality $\mathcal{F}$ will allow backdoor messages from the adversary to specify that e.g. a memory of some party pid is corrupted, upon which the security would downgrade to the extent defined by the functionality $\mathcal{F}$, which is presumably less severe than when the functionality receives an ordinary request to corrupt the *full* party pid. Recall from [10] that standard PID-wise corruption in the ideal world refers to a minimally supported interface of a functionality when a party P is (fully) corrupted. In particular, at the point the party is corrupted via a corruption message on the functionality's backdoor tape, the functionality outputs to the adversary all the values received from P and output to P so far. External inputs to P are ignored and given to the adversary, and the adversary is free to specify any message to be output by P (that is, externally written by the dummy protocol for P without changing the state of the functionality). Moreover, the adversary can decide to formally invoke the functionality with (INPUT, P, v) upon which the functionality executes its defined instructions for input v as coming from P (based on the current state which includes the corruptions status of parties).

2.3   Further Conventions Relevant to This Work

State, behavior, and functionality classes. Without loss of generality we assume that each instance of a functionality manages a *state* data-structure which encodes all the information relevant for its input-output behavior (such as inputs that the functionality receives and the output that it provides). We describe the state of a functionality by means of a variable state. Note that the behavior of a functionality (defined as a Turing machine in UC) can equivalently be described using a state-transition model, i.e., as a sequence of conditional probability distributions (defined for output space Y, input space X and state space S) $p^{\mathcal{F}}_{(Y,S_i)|(X,S_{i-1})}((y, \mathsf{state}_i)|(x, \mathsf{state}_{i-1}))$ for $i > 0$ assuming an initial well-defined state state_0. The formal inputs correspond to the content of the respective input tapes and the outputs define the content on the outgoing message tape. We give a quick overview of this correspondence in [4] for completeness.

We introduce the notion of a *class of functionalities* $\mathscr{F}$, which in its full generality can be thought as being defined by a language $L \subseteq \{0,1\}^*$ such that a functionality $\mathcal{F}$ belongs to $\mathscr{F}$ if the state state of any instance of $\mathcal{F}$ satisfies state $\in L$ and its initial state (representing the initial configuration before any interaction) as $\perp$. Further, we assume that the corruption set (which the functionality has to export e.g. to the environment) is represented by an explicit state variable $\mathcal{C}$. That is, we write state $= (\mathsf{state}', \mathcal{C})$ (initially, the corruption set is empty). We assume that we have a fixed party universe $\mathcal{P}$ and our functionalities interact with this set (of party identifiers). However, it is easy to extend the treatment to dynamic party sets [3].

Functionalities Running Arbitrary Code. We will specify functionalities that receive code or algorithm, say alg, as part of their input from some caller which they are expected to execute on certain inputs x. In order for this to be unproblematic [10] defines how an ideal functionality evaluates $\mathsf{alg}(x)$: instead of running it internally, the functionality invokes a new subroutine (a new machine) that executes alg. Since the runtime of any new machine depends on the so-called *import* it receives (until it runs out of import), the execution of alg can therefore be made safe as follows: whenever the party receives the request to execute alg on input x, it expects the calling party to provide the import for this, which it relays to the subroutine executing alg. This way, the algorithm's runtime uses up the runtime budget of the entity instructing the execution of alg on input x. In order to keep the descriptions simple, we assume the above mechanism implicitly.

3   Our Model for Updatable Functionalities

3.1   A Fine-Grained Corruption Model for Update Systems

Intuitively, we want to be able to capture sub-routine corruption (and not consider it as a full corruption) because it is updates that will make parties recover from sub-routine corruptions. To make this idea more precise, we introduce a generic modeling tool that captures subversion of any kind building on top of Sect. 2.2. That is, we introduce a machinery by which we formally model that a certain algorithm used by a party P becomes insecure (without P being corrupted). Our machinery can be seen as a particular way to model the leakage of secret keys, subverted and broken algorithms.

Corruptions in the Real World. To model real-world attacks on specific cryptographic schemes (e.g., the adversary gets access to secret keys of the honest parties, or installs a malware into the machine of the honest users that changes the behavior of the cryptographic algorithms, or obtains access to inputs due to a broken algorithm), we introduce a new modeling technique. We present a functionality $\mathcal{F}_{\mathsf{Comp}}$ (Fig. 1) that internally runs arbitrary procedures and stores all the input-output pairs. This device is corruptible in the sense that upon corruption (with respect to a certain party P) the adversary gets full access to the memory and can also fully control it. It is a sub-routine corruption, and thus the party P does not become corrupted automatically. The functionality $\mathcal{F}_{\mathsf{Comp}}$ can be used as a modeling tool to express, in a fine-grained way, which parts of a system we do consider as potentially risky and vulnerable (it need not stand for a real-world object such as a computing module). This includes three important special cases:

- If we believe some cryptographic key material is more exposed than others (e.g., because a long-term private key is stored on a hardware device, while a short-term key is stored in memory), one can formally model key exposure by introducing $\mathcal{F}_{\mathsf{Comp}}$ for computations involving the short-term key.
- As a second use case, if we want to study the impact on security that a deployed algorithm has in case it turns out to be unsafe (such as algorithms vulnerable to quantum attacks), this potential attack surface is modeled by formally running the algorithm in question on $\mathcal{F}_{\mathsf{Comp}}$ (without the expectation that this is a special hardware of any sort).
- The abstraction further can capture security assumptions that might be broken at some point. Consider for example the DDH assumption, that is, the assumption that in some group $\mathbb{G} = \langle g \rangle$ random triples (g^a, g^b, g^c) are indistinguishable from DH triples of the form (g^a, g^b, g^{ab}) (where the exponents a, b, and c are picked at random). We can capture the case where the DDH assumption does not hold (anymore) by having the algorithm that generates the DH triple be run inside $\mathcal{F}_{\mathsf{Comp}}$, and model the case that the DDH assumption fails by leaking toward the adversary (via the sub-corrupt command) the randomness used to generate the triples, hence giving a noticeable distinguishing advantage to the adversary.

Corruptions in the Ideal World. As soon as we have a more fine-grained corruption model in the real world, we must reflect it in the ideal world, too as explained in Sect. 2.2. In particular, the corruption mode is more fine grained and the corruption set $\mathcal{C}$ does contain not only party identities but also particular "(sub-)sessions". Consequently, ideal functionalities can give more fine-grained guarantees depending on which subroutines are corrupted.

Functionality $\mathcal{F}_{\mathsf{Comp}}$

The functionality maintains a corruption set denoted by $\mathcal{C}$ (initially empty).

1. Upon receiving a command (INITIALIZE, sid, $\{\mathsf{alg}\}_{i\in[\lambda]}$) from an honest party P store ($\{\mathsf{alg}\}_{i\in[\lambda]}, P, \mathsf{sid}$) and send ($\{\mathsf{alg}\}_{i\in[\lambda]}, P$) to $\mathcal{A}$.
2. Upon receiving a command (QUERY, sid, alg, input) from an honest party P.
   - If $P \notin \mathcal{C}$ then if the tuple (alg, P) is stored then compute output $\leftarrow$ alg(input), store (input, output, P) and return output to P (note that the input also specifies the random tape for alg).
   - If $P \in \mathcal{C}$ then send (input, sid, P) to $\mathcal{A}$.
3. Upon receiving (output, P) from $\mathcal{A}$, where $P \in \mathcal{C}$ send output to P.
4. Upon receiving (SUB-CORRUPT, P) from $\mathcal{A}$ return all the entries $(\cdot, P)$ stored so far to $\mathcal{A}$ and add P to $\mathcal{C}$.

Fig. 1. Functionality $\mathcal{F}_{\mathsf{Comp}}$.

More concretely, in the case that the real-world protocol is formulated w.r.t. $\mathcal{F}_{\mathsf{Comp}}$, the ideal functionality accepts inputs (SUB-CORRUPT, id, P) for $id = (\mathcal{F}_{\mathsf{Comp}}, \mathsf{ssid})$ on its backdoor tape and add ($\mathcal{F}_{\mathsf{Comp}}, \mathsf{ssid}, P$) to $\mathcal{C}$ (and thus reports this extended identity as corrupted). The subsequent behavior of the functionality can thus be dependent on which subroutine is corrupted to give a fine-grained analysis of what happens when which subroutine is corrupted.

In the same spirit, additional modes for further subroutines can be specified. Note that a functionality with a fine-grained corruption model will typically manage subroutine identities that reflect the subroutines of its realizing protocol (e.g., an identity denoting a CRS). Of course, it will always be possible to abstract the naming conventions and impose an ordering of subroutines (to keep the definition of the ideal functionality independent of the exact resources realizing it). However, we stick to the more suggestive notation for clarity.

Update Systems: Healing from Sub-corruptions. For a given functionality $\mathcal{F}$ in the standard corruption model (i.e., maintaining a corruption set consisting of the identifiers of corrupted parties), one can formally extend its behavior to the more detailed case of sub-corruptions by making the effect of sub-corruption equivalent to full corruption: the code of the functionality considers P as corrupted as soon as P gets standard corrupted or there is some entry $(id, P) \in \mathcal{C}$ for some id (which happens if just some subroutine of P, like $\mathcal{F}_{\mathsf{Comp}}$, is corrupted). We denote this extension of a standard functionality to the more fine grain setting by $\widehat{\mathcal{F}}$. Based on the above corruption model, the goal of an update system can now be understood in a concise way: an update system should guarantee that even if a party P is sub-corrupted in some instance of, say, functionality $\widehat{\mathcal{F}}$ (and thus can still perform updates as it is not fully corrupted) then after the update to the new functionality $\widehat{\mathcal{F}}'$, P should regain its desired security guarantees (until the adversary decides to sub-corrupt again). Hence, the update is healing the party P and formally corresponds to removing the sub-corruptions entries from the corruption set of the updating protocol instance.

Example: Signatures. We show two examples for fine-grained corruptions with standard functionalities in [4] for completeness. The standard signature functionality $\mathcal{F}_{\mathtt{SIG}}^S$ for example can be modeled as being subject to sub-corruptions yielding the induced functionality $\widehat{\mathcal{F}}_{\mathtt{SIG}}^S$. As we will see later, the protocol realizing $\widehat{\mathcal{F}}_{\mathtt{SIG}}^S$ is a UC signature protocol as described in Sect. 2 where the algorithms are executed formally on $\mathcal{F}_{\mathsf{Comp}}$. On the other hand, recall that $\mathcal{F}_{\mathtt{SIG}}^S$ is realized by a signature protocol which is modeled as not being sub-corruptible e.g. to express a different security assumption or more trusted setup. In order to differentiate the two modeling assumptions, we refer to the latter as a *cold signature scheme*. An analogous treatment applies to other cryptographic primitives.

3.2   The Update Functionality

We present the update functionality $\mathsf{U}_{\mathtt{SttUp},\mathtt{UpPred}}^{\mathscr{F}}$ in Fig. 2 and describe its defining elements here. The update functionality serves as the abstract ideal goal that any real-world update mechanism (defined for a cryptographic primitive or scheme) must satisfy. The functionality is parameterized by three elements: first, by a class of functionalities (or ideal specifications) $\mathscr{F}$ between which transitions (aka updates) are performed, where we demand that there is a dedicated root functionality that we simply call $\mathcal{F}_0$. Second, a function $\mathtt{UpPred}$, which, depending on the current state of the system and inputs by parties, decides whether an update is either in progress, failed, or succeeded. And finally, a function $\mathtt{SttUp}$ which determines the initial state of the new instance of a functionality after a successful update. For any concrete update system, the above three elements fully determine the corresponding ideal update process.

Basic Mode of Operation. $\mathsf{U}_{\mathtt{SttUp},\mathtt{UpPred}}^{\mathscr{F}}$ maintains a rooted graph $\mathsf{UpGraph}$ where each node v stores an instance of an ideal functionality (see Sect. 2 for the formal definition of an instance). In particular, the values $v.\mathsf{function}$ and $v.\mathsf{ssid}$ determine the code and session of the functionality, respectively (formally, we speak of sub-sessions not to confuse it with the session of the update system as a whole). The root node contains the description of $\mathcal{F}_0$ and its initial state is the initial configuration of $\mathcal{F}_0$. The maintained graph is by construction a directed acyclic graph (DAG) for reasons outlined below. We follow the convention that for two nodes v and v' we call v' a child of v if there is a directed edge from v to v'. Likewise, we call v a parent of v' in this case. As we will see, the directed paths away from the root constitute update paths of parties.

At any point in time, every party is assigned to one instance in this DAG structure to which its inputs are relayed toward, and from which it receives the outputs. It is worth to point out that formally following the concept of structured protocols, this makes the actions described in Fig. 2 to be *shell-code* (cf. Sect. 2) as the code deals only with model-related instructions, i.e., how to re-direct inputs and outputs to the correct instances, which are executed as part of the body. The DAG structure models several natural aspects of update systems. For example, a child node v' of v typically contains in $v'.\mathsf{function}$ the description

---

Functionality $\mathsf{U}^{\mathscr{F}}_{\mathsf{SttUp,UpPred}}$

A rooted, directed acyclic graph UpGraph is maintained, which is initialized with only the root node v_0 with v_0.function $:= \mathcal{F}_0$. The functionality maintains the lists UpdateReq$_F$ which are lazily created and initially empty. The functionality manages the vector PartiesFunctions. For each $P \in \mathcal{P}$ initially set PartiesFunctions$[P] \leftarrow v_0$.

Interaction with most up-to-date functionality per party:

- If $I := (\text{INPUT}, \text{sid}, x)$ is received from a party $P \in \mathcal{P}$ (formally sent via a dummy party that has matching party and session identifiers), set $v \leftarrow$ PartiesFunctions$[P]$. Then invoke the instance of v.function on input $(v.\text{ssid}, x)$ from P.
- If $I := (\text{INPUT-ADV}, \text{sid}, x, v)$ is received from the adversary (on the backdoor tape), where v specifies a node of UpGraph then invoke the instance v.function on value $(v.\text{ssid}, x)$ on its backdoor tape. Otherwise, ignore the input.
- Upon subroutine-output generation by an instance v that specifies an output value y and destination entity D then output y to D.   ▷ See Remark 1.
- Upon any other output produced by an instance v destined for the backdoor tape of the adversary, forward the output to the adversary.

Update Process:

- If $I := (\text{UPDATE}, \text{sid}, \mathcal{F})$ for $\mathcal{F} \in \mathscr{F}$ is received from P check that UpdateStatus$_{P,\mathcal{F}} \neq$ *Done* and that for all $\mathcal{F}' \neq \mathcal{F}$: UpdateStatus$_{P,\mathcal{F}'} \neq$ *Updating*. If the check succeeds then append (sid, P) to UpdateReq$_{\mathcal{F}}$ and set UpdateStatus$_{P,\mathcal{F}} \leftarrow$ *Updating*. Ignore the input if the check fails. Send $(\text{UPDATE\_NOTIFICATION}, \text{sid}, \text{UpdateReq}_{\mathcal{F}}, P, \mathcal{F})$ to $\mathcal{A}$.
- If $I := (\text{GRANTUPDATE}, \text{sid}, P, \text{ssid}, \mathcal{F}', aux)$ for $\mathcal{F}' \in \mathscr{F}$ from the adversary $\mathcal{A}$, then evaluate the predicate $b \leftarrow$ UpPred$(P, \text{ssid}, \mathcal{F}', \text{UpdateReq}_{\mathcal{F}'}, \text{UpdateStatus}_{P,\mathcal{F}}, \text{PartiesFunctions}, \text{UpGraph}, aux)$ and do the following:
  - If $b = \perp$ then output $(P, \text{ssid}, b = \perp)$ to $\mathcal{A}$.
  - If $b = 0$ then append $(\text{Fail}, P, \text{sid}, \text{ssid})$ to UpdateReq$_{\mathcal{F}'}$ and set UpdateStatus$_{P,\mathcal{F}'} \leftarrow$ *Done*. Output $(\text{Fail}, \text{sid}, \text{ssid}, \mathcal{F}')$ to P.
  - If $b = 1$ then append $(\text{Success}, P, \text{sid}, \text{ssid})$ to UpdateReq$_{\mathcal{F}'}$, set UpdateStatus$_{P,\mathcal{F}'} \leftarrow$ *Done*, and perform the following tasks to complete the update.
    1. Let $v \leftarrow$ PartiesFunctions$[P]$.
    2. If there is no node v' in UpGraph with v'.function $= \mathcal{F}'$ and v'.ssid $=$ ssid, then create this node as a child of v: initialize v'.function $\leftarrow \mathcal{F}'$, v'.ssid $\leftarrow$ ssid, and v'.state $= (\perp, \emptyset)$. Otherwise, let v' be the already existing node and define v' to be a child of v in UpGraph.
    3. Parse v'.state as $(s, \mathcal{C})$. Assign PartiesFunctions$[P] \leftarrow v'$ and Compute state$' \leftarrow$ SttUp$(v, P, \text{UpdateReq}_{\mathcal{F}'}, \text{PartiesFunctions}, \text{UpGraph}, aux)$, and update v'.state $\leftarrow (\text{state}', \mathcal{C})$.
    4. Output $(\text{Success}, \text{sid}, \text{ssid}, \mathcal{F}')$ to P.

Corruption: Upon party corruption of party P via a direct corruption message or via a corruption message to its current instance PartiesFunctions$[P]$, party P is marked as corrupted and the standard UC corruption mode applies to $\mathsf{U}^{\mathscr{F}}_{\mathsf{SttUp,UpPred}}$. The functionality further reports upon request the aggregated corruption set consisting of all corrupted parties and all reported sub-corruptions (if any) of the instances in UpGraph.   ▷ See Section 3.1 for corruption model.

Fig. 2. The Generic UC Ideal Update Mechanism.

of an updated version of v.function. For example, if v is a leaf of UpGraph (i.e., does not have children) then v.function represents an updated functionality that some subset of parties is currently using. In fact, the update functionality will ensure that if parties which start off, say, in the same node v_i, agree on the new code, and agree on the same session id, then their inputs and outputs once the update completes are received and returned from the same new instance. On the other hand, the model supports that parties might split and fork into different versions, or to merge previously split parties again into the same, updated session. Furthermore, we demand that in principle, the corruption status of parties is cleared when the new instance starts. This is in essence what captures the basic requirements of a useful update. We note in passing that clearing the corruption status makes only a non-trivial difference when we model sub-corruptions. For full corruptions in the pid-wise corruption model, an attacker can without loss of generality continue to corrupt a party in any instance. Our abstract update therefore captures the requirement that an update system can heal from the less severe corruptions. To give an example, if some subset of parties decides to switch to a new functionality, let us call it $\mathcal{F}'$, then we would add a new node v' to UpGraph as a child of v. At a high level, we use UpGraph to take track of all the updates between instances that occur. The reason why we need to keep track of all the functionalities is that not all the parties might update at the same time. Hence, some parties might still want to use the old functionalities.[1] In the code, PartiesFunctions is used to store which party is registered to what functionality (i.e., to which node the party is assigned). Any time that a party P queries $\mathsf{U}^{\mathcal{F}}_{\mathsf{SttUp,UpPred}}$ with the command (INPUT, sid, x), $\mathsf{U}^{\mathcal{F}}_{\mathsf{SttUp,UpPred}}$ derives the actual instance of a program $\mathcal{F}$ this party P is currently talking to and executes the instance of $\mathcal{F}$.

Updating Functionalities and Security-Relevant Parameters. $\mathsf{U}^{\mathcal{F}}_{\mathsf{SttUp,UpPred}}$ can receive an update command UPDATE from any party P that is willing to *update* to a new specification $\mathcal{F}$. We demand that each party is part of at most one update process by maintaining a flag $\mathsf{UpdateStatus}_{P,\mathcal{F}}$. The command UPDATE comes with an input that specifies the new version. We choose to represent this by the label of the ideal specification for simplicity. If clear from the context, this could also be an index into the functionality class, or any unique label we desire. $\mathsf{U}^{\mathcal{F}}_{\mathsf{SttUp,UpPred}}$ keeps track of all the update requests and of the identifier of the parties that sent the update command by means of a data structure UpdateReq. Whether an update for a party P succeeds depends on a predicate called UpPred. If the adversary admits party P to update, UpPred decides whether the update can actually be performed. It is therefore the predicate that specifies the ideal conditions for an update to go through (and has to be made concrete in concrete applications).

As said above, the functionality only mandates an abstract update structure such that parties can only be updated along paths in the graph and only if they are willing to update (and, as indicated above, that they have some minimal

---

[1] We call old functionalities all the functionalities that are not in the leaves of UpGraph.

guarantee whether they are interacting with the same instance. We point out that the predicate also steers whether a party that has been inactive the entire time can *fast-forward* to a more recent version. Last but not least, core of an update mechanism is to offer a useful form of *state preservation*. For example, with signatures, we have to ensure that legitimate past signatures still verify (in case of an honest signer) whereas the signature scheme is consistent for verifiers. On an abstract level, the state preservation property of an update mechanism for the class $\mathscr{F}$ is given by the function $\mathtt{SttUp}(.)$ which defines how the state of the "new" functionality depends on the ancestor states when an update is made. In Fig. 3 we provide graphical illustration of an execution of $\mathsf{U}^{\mathscr{F}}_{\mathtt{SttUp},\mathtt{UpPred}}$: the initial configuration of $\mathsf{U}^{\mathscr{F}}_{\mathtt{SttUp},\mathtt{UpPred}}$, denoted with **A**, maintains only one node representing the functionality $\mathcal{F}_0$ and the parties $p_1, \ldots, p_5$ registered to it. From this initial configuration, p_1 and p_2 update to a new functionality $\mathcal{F}_1$, and a new node is created in the graph. Similarly, the parties (p_3, p_4) update to $\mathcal{F}_2$, thus yielding to the creation of a new node (represented in the configuration **B**). The adversary then can send any input on the adversarial interface of $\mathcal{F}_2$, in this example we assume that $\mathcal{F}_2$ allows the sub-corruption of the registered parties, and in particular assume that p_3 gets corrupted this way. This concludes the description of the configuration we denote with **B**. We have assumed that all the parties that wanted to update manage to do so, but we recall that it is the update-predicate that mandates whether an update will be successful, depending on the adversarial influence, and the current configuration of the graph. At this point, p_3 and p_4 may fear that the functionality $\mathcal{F}_2$ has been compromised, and decide to reinitiate $\mathcal{F}_2$. This can be done by letting the parties update to $\mathcal{F}_2$. We note that this creates a new node in the graph with a sub-session identifier $ssid'_2 \neq ssid_2$. The state $\mathtt{state}'_2$ depends on $\mathtt{state}_2$, hence some of the work done by the previous instantiation of $\mathcal{F}_2$ may be preserved (how much is preserved is expressed by the state-update function $\mathtt{SttUp}$). We stress that in this configuration, denoted with **C**, $\mathcal{F}_2$ now treats p_3 like an honest party, (i.e., it heals from the sub-corruption). In the final configuration (denoted with **D**) some of the nodes that were initially in $\mathcal{F}_0$ merge again in a new functionality denoted with $\mathcal{F}_3$.

At this abstract level of defining updates, we can make two natural basic observations: first, a so-called clean install is always possible and corresponds to the case where no state from the past must be preserved and hence is one of the simplest forms of an update. We formally state this in the full version [4]. Second, it is the (amount of) state preservation that steers the complexity and assumptions of any update system. Intuitively, if state preservation is required, some joint view from the past is retained once the update completes and the state-update formalism is precisely the idealization of that real-world process where parties must reach some agreement. While intuitively clear, in the full version [4] we show how one can formalize this claim.

3.3   Concluding Remarks

We conclude this section on the model with two important observations.

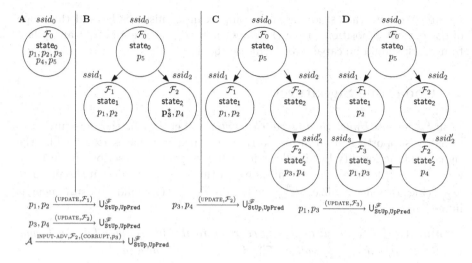

Fig. 3. Sample execution of $U^{\mathscr{F}}_{\mathtt{SttUp,UpPred}}$.

Remark 1 (On Subroutine Outputs). As specified in the ideal system in Fig. 2, subroutine outputs by functionalities towards some party P are provided to that party. This holds even if the functionality is not the most recent one. We leave it to the higher-level protocol to decide what happens with such outputs by "old" session. Note that one can always define a filter protocol that, based on the sub-session identifier of the most recent functionality, blocks all outputs not belonging to that session. This has the effect that any party only interacts locally with the most recent functionality. We do not hardcode this behavior in the generic update functionality. Observing the old session could turn out useful in settings where a party monitors participation in prior sessions or to detect whether another party is active in two protocol versions. In such cases, further useful actions could be taken thanks to more transparency, which are outside the scope of a pure update protocol.

Remark 2. Our DAG based formulation enables the modeling of arbitrary update patterns. We note that even though we do not formally allow cycles in the graph, an update pattern oscillating between functionalities is still easy to capture by assigning unique labels in each invocation of UPDATE. This, for instance, can capture different "ciphersuite" negotiation interactions that occur in the context of key-exchange protocols. Furthermore, multi-parent nodes in the graph open up the opportunity to design more complex update procedures where a set of parties initially diverges from a single functionality and subsequently converges to a single functionality. Such modeling capability can come handy if one wishes to capture complex multiparty settings such as that of a distributed ledger where parties may diverge due to an implementation difference and subsequently negotiate the merging of their states as part of a "convergence" update. We note that studying such complex mechanisms is beyond the scope of our current exposition—nevertheless we believe it is essential that an update framework should be capable to facilitate them.

4   Updatable Signatures

Ideal Signatures Under Subroutine Corruptions. Let $\widehat{\mathcal{F}}^S_{\text{SIG}}$ be the signature functionality supporting sub-routine corruptions (i.e., it behaves exactly like the signature functionality but it allows for sub-corruption as described in Sect. 3.1, we refer to [4] for the formal definition). In this section, we design the protocol $\widehat{\Pi}^S_{\mathcal{DS}}$ (Fig. 4) which realizes $\widehat{\mathcal{F}}^S_{\text{SIG}}$ relying on $\mathcal{F}_{\text{Comp}}$. The following statement is immediate:

Lemma 1. *If $\Pi^S_{\mathcal{DS}}$ realizes $\mathcal{F}_{\text{SIG}}$ (we refer to the fill version for the formal definition [4]) then $\widehat{\Pi}^S_{\mathcal{DS}}$ realizes $\widehat{\mathcal{F}}^S_{\text{SIG}}$ in the $\mathcal{F}_{\text{Comp}}$-hybrid model.*

Recall from Sect. 3.1 that a scheme is modeled using $\mathcal{F}_{\text{Comp}}$ to indicate the belief that the honest usage can turn out to be unsafe. Recall the distinction to a signature scheme that we assume to actually be safe under honest usage in that it realizes $\mathcal{F}_{\text{SIG}}$ (and thus subroutine corruptions of an honest party are not a concern), which are referred to as cold schemes.

Remark 3. In our update mechanisms, we make use of cold vs. hot signature keys as a way to recover from sub-corruptions across updates and to reflect different trust assumptions. We point out that our security goal necessitates a form of "authenticated communication" post sub-corruption and is enabled by this cold signature mechanism. We make that choice due to two reasons: first, it is a practical assumption (in particular when accessing cold keys only rarely or hardware tokens are assumed) and second, because it allows us to describe a generic approach to post-quantum readiness as described in Sect. 4.3.

4.1   Ideal Updatable Signature System

We want to provide a scheme that implements the update system for signatures. More formally, we describe a protocol to UC-realize $U^{\mathscr{F}_{\text{SIG}}}_{\text{SttUp}_{\text{SIG}}, \text{UpPred}_{\text{SIG}}}$ for $\mathscr{F}_{\text{SIG}} := \{\widehat{\mathcal{F}}^{S, \mathcal{DS}_i}_{\text{SIG}}\}_i$, where $\mathscr{F}_{\text{SIG}}$ denotes the family of signature functionalities as defined above which are formally indexed with $\mathcal{DS}_i$. Note that S (the signer identity) appears as an explicit identifier in this family.

To formalize the ideal update for signatures, we first define how $\text{SttUp}_{\text{SIG}}$ and $\text{UpPred}_{\text{SIG}}$ work. The state $\text{state}_{\text{SIG}}$ of a signature functionality (aside of the corruption set) is represented by the verification key of the sender and the set of tuples (vk, m, σ, b) stored by the functionality (we refer to the full version [4] for a more detailed discussion).

Protocol $\widehat{\Pi}^S_{DS}$

Initialization

Let $DS = (\mathsf{KGen}, \mathsf{Sign}, \mathsf{Ver})$ be the signature scheme. Each party $P \in \mathcal{P}$ sends to $\mathcal{F}_{\mathsf{Comp}}$ the input $(\text{INITIALIZE}, \text{sid}, \{\mathsf{KGen}, \mathsf{Sign}, \mathsf{Ver}\})$.

Key Generation:

Upon receiving the command $I := (\text{INPUT}, \text{sid}, \text{KEY-GEN})$ S sends $(\text{QUERY}, \text{sid}, \mathsf{KGen}, 1^\lambda)$ to $\mathcal{F}_{\mathsf{Comp}}$ and upon receiving (vk, sk) outputs $(\text{VERIFICATION-KEY}, \text{sid}, vk)$.

Signing and Verification:

- Upon receiving the command $I := (\text{SIGN}, m)$ the signer send $(\text{QUERY}, \text{sid}, \mathsf{KGen}, (sk, m))$ to $\mathcal{F}_{\mathsf{Comp}}$. Upon receiving (m, σ) from $\mathcal{F}_{\mathsf{Comp}}$ output $(\text{SIGNATURE}, \text{sid}, m, \sigma)$.
- Upon receiving the command $I = (\text{VERIFY}, vk, m, \sigma)$ send $(\text{QUERY}, \text{sid}, \mathsf{Ver}, (vk, m, \sigma))$ to $\mathcal{F}_{\mathsf{Comp}}$, and upon receiving a reply b output $(\text{VERIFIED}, \text{sid}, m, b)$.

Fig. 4. Corruptible signature

- $\mathsf{UpPred}_{\mathsf{SIG}}$: On input $(P, \text{ssid}, \mathcal{F}', \mathsf{UpdateReq}_{\mathcal{F}'}, \mathsf{UpdateStatus}_{P,\mathcal{F}'},$ $\mathsf{PartiesFunctions}, \mathsf{UpGraph}, 0^\lambda)$ do the following: if P appears in $\mathsf{UpdateReq}$ and $\mathsf{UpdateStatus}_{P,\mathcal{F}'} = \textit{Updating}$ then let $v \leftarrow \mathsf{PartiesFunctions}[P]$ and perform the following steps to compute the decision (otherwise, return $\perp$):
  - If P is the signer of instance v and $\mathsf{UpGraph}$ has no node v' with $v'.\text{function} = \mathcal{F}'$ and $v'.\text{ssid} = \text{ssid}$ then return 1.
  - Else, if P is not the signer and if there is a node v' with $v'.\text{function} = \mathcal{F}'$ and $v'.\text{ssid} = \text{ssid}$ that is a child of v and $(S, vk) \in v'.\text{state}$ then do the following:
    * If S is honest then return 1.
    * If S is corrupted then let M_P be the set of all the pairs (m, σ) s.t. $(P, vk, m, \sigma, 1) \in v.\text{state}$ and let M be the set of all the pairs (m, σ) for which a tuple $(\cdot, vk, m, \sigma, 1)$ is stored in $v'.\text{state}$, if $M_P \subseteq M$ then return 1.
  - Return 0.

The update predicate thus ensures that it only allows a party to transition, if it can be guaranteed that the party will remain consistent with respect to the set of messages it has seen and successfully verified. Furthermore, as long as the signer is honest, the update graph $\mathsf{UpGraph}$ is a chain of instances of the signature functionality. We next define the state updates:

- $\mathsf{SttUp}_{\mathsf{SIG}}$: On input $\mathsf{SttUp}(v^\star, P, \mathsf{UpdateReq}, \mathsf{PartiesFunctions}, \mathsf{UpGraph}, \text{aux})$ first obtain the instance $v \leftarrow \mathsf{PartiesFunctions}[P]$ (note that by definition, $v^\star$ is the parent node of v party P is updating from):

- If P is the signer in instance $v^\star$ and P is honest, define the new state s and insert the tuple $(P, vk) \in v^\star.\mathsf{state}$ as well as all tuples $(S, vk, m, \sigma, 1) \in v^\star.\mathsf{state}$.
- Else, if P is the signer for the instance $v^\star$ and P is corrupted then define an empty state s, and set $s \leftarrow aux$.
- If P is not the signer then set $s \leftarrow v.\mathsf{state}$.
- Return s.

The definition means that we keep all generated signatures of the honest signer, even if the signer has been sub-corrupted. If instead the signer is fully corrupted, then we let the adversary decide the state of the updated functionality.

4.2   The Protocol and Security Statement

The main underlying primitives that we use to realize our update system are a cold signature scheme $\mathcal{DS}_c$ and a message registry that we formally introduce in the full version [4]. At a very high level, $\mathcal{DS}_c$ will be used only during the update phase by the signer to authenticate the information that concerns the updates which are sent to each individual verifier. We prove that as long as the security of $\mathcal{DS}_c$ holds then our scheme realizes the updatable functionality $\mathsf{U}^{\mathcal{F}_{\mathrm{SIG}}}_{\mathsf{SttUp}_{\mathrm{SIG}}, \mathsf{UpPred}_{\mathrm{SIG}}}$. Our approach is justified by the fact that $\mathcal{DS}_c$ might be a particularly inefficient signature scheme, but at the same time difficult to attack. Given the inefficiency of $\mathcal{DS}_c$, it might not be practical to directly use it as a signature scheme, hence we use it just to support an update between one signature scheme and another (which are more efficient than $\mathcal{DS}_c$ but they might be compromised more easily). In order to provide the security guarantees we modularize our construction with a simple cryptographic primitive we call a message registry. The primitive uses three algorithms $(\mathsf{Gen}, \mathsf{Add}, \mathsf{Vmr})$ and enables to deposit messages to a "container", a process that may generate a witness, while given a message and witness one can verify reliably whether the message is in the container. A message registry can be trivially realized information theoretically, or cryptographically for more efficiency. We give more details in the full version [4].

Equipped with these tools, our update system works as follows. The signer registers his cold verification-key to a PKI[2], and starts issuing signatures using the (sub-corruptible) signature functionality $\widehat{\mathcal{F}}^{S,\mathcal{DS}_0}_{\mathrm{SIG}} \in \mathscr{F}_{\mathrm{SIG}}$ while the verifier simply uses the same functionality to verify the signatures. The signer keeps the memory of all the signatures he issues (by recording them in the message registry), and the verifiers do something similar, i.e., memorizing valid signatures.

When the signer wants to update, he hashes the message registry, together with the description of the new functionality he wants to update to (let us call it $\widehat{\mathcal{F}}^{S,\mathcal{DS}_\star}_{\mathrm{SIG}}$) and a verification key freshly generated by querying $\widehat{\mathcal{F}}^{S,\mathcal{DS}_\star}_{\mathrm{SIG}}$. Then he signs the hash with the cold signature scheme and sends the signature, the message registry, $\widehat{\mathcal{F}}^{S,\mathcal{DS}_\star}_{\mathrm{SIG}}$ and the new verification key to each verifier.

---

[2] This enables authenticated communication from the honest signer to other parties. In the protocol, we also store the initial verification key of the signer for efficiency and simplicity, as otherwise, the first update message would have to include it.

If a verifier has received an update command for the functionality $\widehat{\mathcal{F}}_{\text{SIG}}^{S,\mathcal{DS}\star}$ (which is the same functionality he receives from the signer, then), and if all the information are authenticated as described above, then the verifier does the following. He checks whether all the signatures he has ever verified are contained in the message registry received from the signer, and if this is the case then the verifier will accept the update. The reason for this check is to maintain consistency throughout the updates. That is, if a verifier has verified successfully a signature for a message m, then any verifier registered to the same functionality must correctly verify the same pair, even if the verification of m happened in a previous epoch.

To fully enable consistency, we also need to modify how the verification procedure works after an update. The verifier now, upon receiving a message and a signature, would first check if the pair is valid with respect to the new key by querying $\widehat{\mathcal{F}}_{\text{SIG}}^{S,\mathcal{DS}\star}$. If it is, then the verifier memorizes the pair as before, if instead $\widehat{\mathcal{F}}_{\text{SIG}}^{S,\mathcal{DS}\star}$ returns 0, then the verifier looks in the message registry (received during the update) for the pair. If there is a match, the verifier outputs 1, else he returns 0.

The overall idea is simple, but we need to deal with some subtle technicalities to be able to prove that the scheme does realize $\mathsf{U}_{\mathsf{SttUp}_{\text{SIG}},\mathsf{UpPred}_{\text{SIG}}}^{\mathscr{F}_{\text{SIG}}}$. The first is related to the fact that in $\mathsf{U}_{\mathsf{SttUp}_{\text{SIG}},\mathsf{UpPred}_{\text{SIG}}}^{\mathscr{F}_{\text{SIG}}}$ the sub-session identifiers play an important role since they define to which node in the graph (maintained by $\mathsf{U}_{\mathsf{SttUp}_{\text{SIG}},\mathsf{UpPred}_{\text{SIG}}}^{\mathscr{F}_{\text{SIG}}}$) each party should be registered to. In the real world protocol the ssid is computed by hashing the descriptor of $\widehat{\mathcal{F}}_{\text{SIG}}^{S,\mathcal{DS}\star}$ with the message registry the signer sends during the update. The idea is that we want verifiers with the same sub-session identifier to share the same history of signed messages (i.e., they are registered to the same functionality with the same state). The collision resistance of the hash function guarantees that if two verifiers accept an update for the same ssid, then they must have received the same message-registry and the same functionality descriptor from the adversary, creating the correct connection between ideal and real world. A final technicality is that we must keep the honest signer key the same across epochs to be compatible with standard signatures (this is an important aspect looking ahead on Sect. 4.4). The full description of the protocol is given in Figs. 5 and 6.

Remark 4. It is instructive to compare the above construction to a simple construction that works as follows: during the update, simply sign the message set with the next instance of the signature public key. There are two drawbacks of this update system compared to our proposal: first, the party has to update its record with the PKI (and hence revoke the old one as it might become compromised later). Second, while the system meets the minimal requirement that we have uninterrupted security as long as the security breach of a scheme always happens "after an update" to the next version, the simple construction falls short in enabling the honest signer to regain security after a security breach of the current implementation. In particular, our $\mathsf{SttUp}_{\text{SIG}}$ demands that an honest signer (despite being subcorrupted) regains full security in the updated session, while

---

Protocol $\Pi_{\text{SIG}}^{S,up}$ - Part I

Initialization

All the parties initially interact to the root functionality $\widehat{\mathcal{F}}_{\text{SIG}}^{S,\mathcal{DS}_0} \in \mathscr{F}_{\text{SIG}}$. Each party $P \in \mathcal{P}$ initializes $\text{Version}^P \leftarrow 0$, $\text{sid}^P \leftarrow \text{sid}$ (where sid is the session-ID of the protocol instance), $M^P \leftarrow \emptyset$, and defines Ver^P which on input $(vk, m, (\sigma, w))$ sends $(\text{VERIFY}, \text{sid}^P, vk, m, \sigma)$ to $\widehat{\mathcal{F}}_{\text{SIG}}^{S,\mathcal{DS}_0}$ and returns whatever $\widehat{\mathcal{F}}_{\text{SIG}}^{S,\mathcal{DS}_0}$ returns.

Key Generation:

Upon receiving the command $I := (\text{INPUT}, \text{sid}, \text{KEY-GEN})$ S does the following.
- Send $(\text{KEY-GEN}, \text{sid}^S)$ to $\widehat{\mathcal{F}}_{\text{SIG}}^{S,\mathcal{DS}_0}$ thus obtaining vk_0.
- Compute $(vk_c, sk_c) \leftarrow \text{KGen}_c(1^\lambda)$ and $k \xleftarrow{\$} \text{Gen}_H(1^\lambda)$
- Register (vk_0, vk_c, k) with the PKI.
- Generate $trap, A \xleftarrow{\$} \text{Gen}(1^\lambda)$ and define Sign which is a stateful algorithm that on input m does the following steps.
    - Send (SIGN, m) to $\widehat{\mathcal{F}}_{\text{SIG}}^{S,\mathcal{DS}_0}$ and upon receiving $(\text{SIGNATURE}, \text{sid}, m, \sigma)$ continue.
    - Compute $A', w \xleftarrow{\$} \text{Add}(trap, A, (m, vk_0, \sigma))$.
    - Set $A \leftarrow A'$ and return $(m, (\sigma, w))$.
Return $(\text{VERIFICATION-KEY}, \text{sid}, vk_0)$.

Signing and Verification:

- Upon receiving the command $I := (\text{INPUT}, \text{sid}, y)$,
    - if $y = (\text{SIGN}, m)$ and I is received by the signer, then run $\text{Sign}(m)$ and return whatever Sign returns.
    - if $y = (\text{VERIFY}, vk, m, (\sigma, w))$ and I is received by a party P then run Ver^P on input $(vk, m, (\sigma, w))$ to receive $(\text{VERIFIED}, \text{sid}, m, b)$; add $(m, vk, (\sigma, w))$ to M^P if $b = 1$, and finally return $(\text{VERIFIED}, \text{sid}, m, b)$.

Fig. 5. Updatable signatures: initialization and operation.

for the above simpler protocol, the update guarantees are lost when the active key is compromised (since the most recent update messages can be equivocated by an attacker). Note that an even stronger PKI with a richer interface could salvage the scheme (in spirit along the lines of our construction), but assuming such a strong PKI does not appear to be a practical assumption. In contrast, our scheme works with the basic CA-functionality of Canetti [9] and hence with the minimal root of trust (just a single key per signer must be distributed authentically in the beginning), which is easily seen to be a necessary assumption to achieve any non-trivial form of state preservation. We elaborate on this crucial aspect when we discuss the benefits of our construction in the larger context of post-quantum readiness in Sect. 4.3.

Theorem 1. *Assume* (Gen_H, H) *is a collision-resistant hash function,* $\mathcal{DS}_c$ *is a (cold) signature scheme which is only used during the update, and* $(\text{Gen}, \text{Add}, \text{Vmr})$

Protocol $\Pi_{\text{SIG}}^{S,up}$ - Part II

Update:

- If the signer S receives the command $I := (\text{UPDATE}, \text{sid}, \widehat{\mathcal{F}}_{\text{SIG}}^{S,\mathcal{DS}\star})$ (with $\widehat{\mathcal{F}}_{\text{SIG}}^{S,\mathcal{DS}\star} \in \mathscr{F}_{\text{SIG}}$ then she sets $\text{sid}^S \leftarrow H_k(A||\widehat{\mathcal{F}}_{\text{SIG}}^{S,\mathcal{DS}\star})$ does the following steps.
  1. Send $(\text{KEY-GEN}, \text{sid}^S)$ to $\widehat{\mathcal{F}}_{\text{SIG}}^{S,\mathcal{DS}\star}$ thus obtaining $vk_\star$.
  2. Redefine Sign. On input m, Sign does the following steps.
     - Send $(\text{SIGN}, \text{sid}^S, m)$ to $\widehat{\mathcal{F}}_{\text{SIG}}^{S,\mathcal{DS}\star}$ and upon receiving $(\text{SIGNATURE}, \text{sid}^S, m, \sigma)$ continue.
     - Compute $A', w \xleftarrow{\$} \text{Add}(trap, A, (m, vk_0, \sigma))$.
     - Set $A \leftarrow A'$ and return $(m, (\sigma, w))$.
  3. Set Version $\leftarrow$ Version $+ 1$.
  4. Compute $\sigma_c \leftarrow \text{Sign}_c(sk_c, \text{Version}||vk_\star||h)$, define $\tau \leftarrow \widehat{\mathcal{F}}_{\text{SIG}}^{S,\mathcal{DS}\star}||\text{Version}||vk_\star||A||h||\sigma_c$ and send τ to each verifier.
- If a party P receives the command $I := (\text{UPDATE}, \text{sid}, \widehat{\mathcal{F}}_{\text{SIG}}^{S,\mathcal{DS}\star})$, if $\widehat{\mathcal{F}}_{\text{SIG}}^{S,\mathcal{DS}\star} \in \mathscr{F}_{\text{SIG}}$ then she does the following steps.
  1. Wait to receive τ from the signer S. Once the message τ is received, first retrieve the signer's public keys and hash key (vk_0, vk_c, k) from the PKI. Then parse τ as $\mathcal{F}||\text{Version}||vk_\star||A||h||\sigma_c$, check if $\text{Ver}_c(vk_c, \text{Version}||vk_\star||h, \sigma_c) = 1$ and $h = H_k(A||\mathcal{F})$ and $\mathcal{F} = \widehat{\mathcal{F}}_{\text{SIG}}^{S,\mathcal{DS}\star}$ and Version $>$ Version^P and $\wedge_{(m, vk_0, (\sigma, w)) \in M^P} \text{Vmr}(A, w, (m, \sigma, vk_0))$. If the check fails then ignore the input, else set $A^P \leftarrow A$, $\text{sid}^P \leftarrow h$, set Version$^P \leftarrow$ Version and redefine Ver^P as follows.
     Ver$^P(vk', m, (\sigma, w))$:
     - If $vk' = vk_0$, then send $(\text{VERIFY}, \text{sid}^P, vk_\star, m, \sigma)$ to $\widehat{\mathcal{F}}_{\text{SIG}}^{S,\mathcal{DS}\star}$; upon receiving $(\text{VERIFIED}, \text{sid}^P, m, b)$, if $b = 1$ then append $(m, vk_0, (\sigma, w))$ to M^P and return 1. If $b = 0$ then return $\text{Vmr}(A, w, (m, \sigma, vk_0))$.
     - else return 0.

Fig. 6. Updatable signatures: update step

is a *Message Registry* then $\Pi_{\text{SIG}}^{S,up}$ *realizes* $\mathsf{U}_{\text{SttUp}_{\text{SIG}}, \text{UpPred}_{\text{SIG}}}^{\mathscr{F}_{\text{SIG}}}$ *for the function family defined above in the standard PKI hybrid model.*

The proof is provided in the full version [4].

4.3 Practical Impact: Preparation for Post-Quantum Readiness

Our construction in Sect. 4.2 is written in a formal language that abstracts a few key components. First, $\mathcal{F}_{\text{Comp}}$ models the belief about which parts of the system might fail by reasoning about two types of signatures: hot and cold; second, the construction is based on signature functionalities and thus fully generic, and third, our solution just requires a very simple root of trust (CA without updates). It is important to map these abstractions to real-world use cases to appreciate the value of the protocol.

Assume you had a signing service that currently cannot afford to sign with anything less efficient than (DL-based) systems like ECDSA or EdDSA. At the same time, you would like to be ready to transition to a signature scheme that is based, say, on lattices as soon as either (i) the quantum threat (against authentication schemes) becomes real or (ii) a post-quantum signature scheme has been developed with efficiency as ECDSA and widely deployed to enable a frictionless operation post-transition.

When you "flip the switch" to the new signature algorithm, your system should definitely not forget the documents it has signed in the past. Clearly, if all you do is to sign old documents issued earlier with a new secret key, then an attacker can impersonate your service unless you cryptographically connect your new key to your old key to preserve the link. This latter step requires interaction, either through a (post-quantum ready) PKI that allows you to record your key update, or via a direct method (as in our solution) secured by an additional scheme that remains secure despite the threat (the cold signature scheme).

Therefore, when used to prepare for a transition in the context of post-quantum readiness, our scheme has the following features.

- When the initial public key is distributed (before the quantum threat is practical), our construction does not rely on a quantum secure PKI since we do not have to update our key in the PKI, but we secure the update ourselves based on this initial root of trust (e.g., downloaded by parties or stored in the browser). This is an important feature for another reason: the developer of a post-quantum ready PKI for example cannot rely itself on a post-quantum secure PKI as this would end up in a circular dependency.
- The update itself is secured by a post-quantum secure signature (corresponding in the formal model to what we call cold signature scheme). Since we do not use it often, this can be a signature scheme that is not very efficient or even limited, and therefore be based on extremely conservative assumptions like one-way functions.
- The system we transition to can be some new algorithm that was not known at the time we set up the initial public key. We can transition to the most favorite signing algorithm at the point of the update. This means that the decision of which post-quantum signature to use in the daily business can be deferred to the point when the need arises (where presumably a better understanding of post-quantum signatures will facilitate more efficient schemes).

Our protocol gives a way to be post-quantum ready w.r.t. signatures without relying on external post-quantum secure services to be ready, and without committing *now* to the signature scheme used after the transition.

4.4   A Succinct Representation of the Update System

It is interesting to see how a "compiled" version of $\mathsf{U}^{\mathcal{F}_{\mathsf{SIG}}}_{\mathsf{SttU}_{\mathsf{P_{SIG}}},\mathsf{UpPred}_{\mathsf{SIG}}}$ formally compares to the standard signature functionality. While intuitively clear based on the above statements, we can make the claim more formal by introducing the following protocol π_{upd}^S that wraps the update system in the most obvious way to obtain an abstraction that then looks like a signature functionality with updates:

1. All machines keep track of a local counter ep of the number of successful updates, initially $ep \leftarrow 0$.
2. On input (KEY-GEN, sid) or (SIGN, sid, m) the signer S issues this command to $U_{SttUp_{SIG},UpPred_{SIG}}^{\mathcal{F}_{SIG}}$ and returns the result to the caller.
3. On (VERIFY, sid, m, σ, vk') relay the verification request to $U_{SttUp_{SIG},UpPred_{SIG}}^{\mathcal{F}_{SIG}}$ and return any answer to the caller.
4. On (UPDATE, sid) for signer S, issue the update request (UPDATE, sid, $\widehat{\mathcal{F}}_{SIG}^{S,\mathcal{DS}_{ep+1}}$) to $U_{SttUp_{SIG},UpPred_{SIG}}^{\mathcal{F}_{SIG}}$ and return any answer to the caller. Upon a successful update notification (Success, ssid, F) set $ep \leftarrow ep + 1$. If the update fails, abort the execution.
5. On (UPDATE, sid), issue the update request (UPDATE, sid, $\widehat{\mathcal{F}}_{SIG}^{S,\mathcal{DS}_{ep+1}}$) to $U_{SttUp_{SIG},UpPred_{SIG}}^{\mathcal{F}_{SIG}}$. Upon a successful update notification (Success, ssid', $\widehat{\mathcal{F}}_{SIG}^{S,\mathcal{DS}_{ep+1}}$) set $ep \leftarrow ep + 1$. If the update fails or the identities do not match, abort the execution.

In Fig. 7 we describe the concise signature functionality with updates that the above protocol realizes, and which has the following features: we have consistency throughout the execution of the system as long as the signer is not fully corrupted. This means that no party will see a tuple (m, σ, vk) fail to verify if it did successfully verify in the past. Next, if the signer updates before it is sub-corrupted, the set of signed messages remains exactly the set of messages formed by the messages that were input by the signer. In this case, every verifier in the same epoch as the signer enjoys the normal unforgeability guarantees—and always with respect to the one registered public key of the signer—despite the fact that forgeries are allowed for older epochs or during periods of signer sub corruptions. We can summarize this observation as a lemma.

Lemma 2. *Protocol π_{upd}^S defined above UC-realizes $\mathcal{F}_{SIG}^{\star,S}$.*

Proof. We first describe the simulator $\mathcal{S}$ for this construction that interacts with $\mathcal{F}_{SIG}^{\star,S}$. The simulator internally emulates the instance of $U_{SttUp_{SIG},UpPred_{SIG}}^{\mathcal{F}_{SIG}}$. It behaves as follows from inputs from $\mathcal{F}_{SIG}^{\star,S}$:

– On receiving (KEY-GEN, sid), (SIGN, sid, m), or (VERIFY, sid, m, σ, v') from a particular party P, hand the corresponding input to the emulated instance ep_P of the session $U_{SttUp_{SIG},UpPred_{SIG}}^{\mathcal{F}_{SIG}}$ and send to the environment the output that is produced. Return the answer from the environment (which is either (VERIFICATION-KEY, sid, v), (SIGNATURE, sid, m, σ), or (VERIFIED, sid, m, ϕ)) to any of these requests back to the very same instance and forward the reply to $\mathcal{F}_{SIG}^{\star,S}$ to produce the matching output towards P.
– On receiving (SIGNERADVANCES, sid, ep_S) the simulator $\mathcal{S}$ simulates the update request (UPDATE_NOTIFICATION, sid, UpdateReq$_F$, S, $\widehat{\mathcal{F}}_{SIG}^{S,\mathcal{DS}_{ep_S+1}}$)

(where each $\mathsf{UpdateReq}_F$ is simply filled with all parties that want to update to F) to the environment.

- On receiving $(\text{UPDATE}, \text{sid}, P)$, the simulator $\mathcal{S}$ simulates the update request analogous to above, i.e., by sending $(\text{UPDATE\_NOTIFICATION}, \text{sid}, \mathsf{UpdateReq}_F, P, \widehat{\mathcal{F}}_{\text{SIG}}^{S, \mathcal{DS}_{ep_P+1}})$ to the environment.
- On receiving $(\text{GRANTUPDATE}, \text{sid}, P, \text{ssid}, F', aux)$, the simulator internally evaluates the request on its running instance. If the update is successful, it returns $(\text{ALLOWUPDATE}, \text{sid}, 1)$ to $\mathcal{F}_{\text{SIG}}^{\star, S}$, and if the update is not successful, it returns $(\text{ALLOWUPDATE}, \text{sid}, 1)$ to $\mathcal{F}_{\text{SIG}}^{\star, S}$.

This simulation yields an execution that is indistinguishable from an execution of π_{up}. This is obvious before the first update, as both worlds simply talk to an ideal signature functionality they have an identical behavior by definition. Furthermore, if the signer ever gets sub-corrupted, both worlds weaken the ideal unforgeability guarantees and the simulator is free to decide on the outputs by S. Regarding the updates, as long as the signer is honest, the update, i.e., epoch changes can only be triggered by the signer by definition of $\mathsf{UpPred}_{\text{SIG}}$, as otherwise, no child node exists. Furthermore, the update graph is in fact a chain: the only admissible ssid for everyone is the ssid obtained by the signer S when the update succeeds and the functionality must be the one requested by the signer, because an honest signer only performs one update a time and $\mathsf{UpPred}_{\text{SIG}}$ would only let this one update go through and otherwise the update fails. Thus, as long as the signer is honest, both systems behave identically. We are thus left with analyzing the case that the signer becomes fully corrupted. To this end, let ep^* denote the epoch during which the signer becomes fully corrupted. We observe that the ideal system lifts the unforgeability and global consistency guarantees and the simulator is free to decide the output of a signature verification. The only restriction that is maintained is local consistency. However, by definition of $\mathsf{UpPred}_{\text{SIG}}$, no matter what transition a party P does, local consistency is retained also in the real world. This concludes the proof. □

Outlook: Non-interactive Zero-Knowledge Proof Systems. As a second use-case, we consider updatable NIZK systems, where we consider the NIZK functionality from [17] in our framework, which simply means that, as in the previous section, we formally equip it with the standard sub-routine corruption mode. Recall that a proof system is called a UC-NIZK scheme if, cast as a straightforward UC protocol $\Pi_{\mathcal{PS}}$, UC-realizes $\mathcal{F}_{\text{NIZK}}$. Due to space limitations, we defer the treatment to the full version [4], where we formalize several forms of CRS corruptions (as our security statements do hold w.r.t. any such form of corruption), by formally defining a CRS functionality that outlines several assumptions about the corruptibility of the CRS (where we capture leakage about the CRS generation procedure). Similar to before, subversion is captured by our formalism using the computation devices $\mathcal{F}_{\text{Comp}}$.

Functionality $\mathcal{F}_{\text{SIG}}^{\star,S}$

The functionality interacts with parties $P \in \mathcal{P}$ and initializes $ep_P \leftarrow 0$, $\mathcal{M}_P \leftarrow \emptyset$ for all $P \in \mathcal{P}$, as well as a set $\mathcal{M} \leftarrow \emptyset$. The function is parameterized by the signer identity $S \in \mathcal{P}$. The corruption set consists of identities $P \in \mathcal{P}$, (full corruption) or $(\mathcal{F}_{\text{Comp}}, s, P)$ for $P \in \mathcal{P}$ (subroutine corruption).

- Upon receiving (KEY-GEN, sid) from signer S for the first time, hand (KEY-GEN, sid) to the $\mathcal{A}$. Upon receiving (VERIFICATION-KEY, sid, vk) from $\mathcal{A}$, verify that no entry $(\cdot, m, \cdot, vk, 1)$ is recorded and ignore the reply if there is such an entry. Else, record the pair (S, vk) and output (VERIFICATION-KEY, sid, vk) to S. Otherwise, ignore the request.

- Upon receiving (SIGN, sid, m) is received from signer S, send (SIGN, sid, m) to $\mathcal{A}$. Upon receiving $I = $ (SIGNATURE, sid, m, σ) from $\mathcal{A}$, verify that no entry $(ep, m, \sigma, vk, 0)$ for any ep is stored. If it is, then ignore the reply. Else, send (SIGNATURE, sid, m, σ) to S, and store the record $(ep_S, m, \sigma, vk, 1)$ in $\mathcal{M}$. Additionally, store the record $(m, \sigma, vk, 1)$ in $\mathcal{M}_S$.

- Upon receiving (VERIFY, sid, m, σ, vk') from some party P, hand (VERIFY, sid, m, σ, vk') to the adversary. Upon receiving (VERIFIED, sid, m, ϕ) from the adversary do:
  1. If $vk' = vk$ and $S \notin \mathcal{C}$, and the entry $(ep_P, m, \sigma, vk, 1) \in \mathcal{M}$ is recorded, then set $f \leftarrow 1$. *(Completeness)*
  2. Else, if $vk' = vk$ and $S \notin \mathcal{C}$ and $(\cdot, ep_P, S) \notin \mathcal{C}$, and if no entry $(ep_P, m, \cdot, vk, 1)$ is already stored, then set $f \leftarrow 0$ and record the entry $(ep_P, m, \sigma, vk, 0)$. *(Unforgeability)*
  3. Else, if the entry $(ep_P, m, \sigma, vk', f') \in \mathcal{M}$ is recorded and $S \notin \mathcal{C}$ then let $f \leftarrow f'$. *(Consistency across all parties in epoch)*
  4. Else, if the entry $(m, \sigma, vk', f') \in \mathcal{M}_P$ is recorded, then let $f \leftarrow f'$. *(Local consistency)*
  5. Else, let $f \leftarrow \phi$. If $S \notin \mathcal{C}$, record the entry $(ep_P, m, \sigma, vk', \phi)$.
  Store the tuple (m, σ, vk', f) in $\mathcal{M}_P$ if the result is $f = 1$. Output (VERIFIED, sid, m, f) to P.

- Upon receiving (UPDATE, sid) from signer S, output (SIGNERADVANCES, sid, ep_S) to the adversary. Upon receiving (ALLOWUPDATE, sid, d) from the adversary then do the following: if $d = 0$ then abort; otherwise set $ep_S \leftarrow ep_S + 1$ and store for each record $(m, \sigma, vk, b) \in \mathcal{M}_S$ the record (ep_S, m, σ, vk, b).

- Upon receiving (UPDATE, sid) from some party $P \in \mathcal{P}$ perform the following: hand (UPDATE, sid, P) to the adversary. Upon receiving the answer (ALLOWUPDATE, sid, d), do the following: if $d = 0$, then abort. If $d = 1$ and if $ep_P < ep_S$ then set $ep_P \leftarrow ep_P + 1$ and store for each record $(m, \sigma, vk, b) \in \mathcal{M}_P$ the record (ep_P, m, σ, vk, b) in $\mathcal{M}$.

- The functionality follows the fine-grained corruption mode explained in Section 3.1.

Fig. 7. The signature functionality $\mathcal{F}_{\text{SIG}}^{\star,S}$ with explicit updates.

Game FF.PR.Gm^b

procedure **KeySetup**(prf)

   – $K \xleftarrow{\$} \text{prf.KGen}(1^\kappa)$.

   – Return K

procedure **Fn**(prf, x)

   – if $b = 1$ then $y \leftarrow \text{prf.Eval}(K, x)$ else $y \xleftarrow{\$} \mathcal{Y}_\kappa$.

   – Return y.

Fig. 8. Game FF.PR.Gm^b from [1]. We simplified the description for clarity. We omit the parameters because they are not relevant for our treatment. We formulate security as an equivalent distinguishing problem, and not as a bit-guessing problem.

5   Comparison with a Prior Notion of Agility

We start this section by recalling the notion of crypto-agility introduced in [1] for the case of pseudo-random functions (the other case treated in [1], authenticated encryption, could be represented analogously in our framework). We refer to the full version [4] for the standard definitions.

Definition 1 (Compatible PRF schemes). *We say that a set $\mathcal{S}$ of PRF schemes is compatible if all schemes prf $\in \mathcal{S}$ have the same key generator.*

Consider the games of Fig. 8. In [1] an adversary is called $\mathcal{S}$-restricted if (1) it specifies in its queries only schemes from $\mathcal{S}$, (2) it makes only one **KeySetup** query which is its first oracle query in any execution, (3) it never repeats an oracle query, and (4) any **Fn**(prf, x) query it makes satisfies $x \in \mathcal{X}_\kappa$. (All this must hold with probability 1 regardless of how queries are answered). $\mathcal{S}$ being compatible means the parameter and key generation algorithms invoked during setup will be the same regardless of the PRF scheme that is provided as input to the function evaluation oracle.)

Definition 2 (PRF agility). *Let $\mathcal{A}^{\text{Gm}^b}$ be the output of the adversary in the game* FF.PR.Gm^b *of Fig. 8. We say that a finite, compatible set $\mathcal{S}$ of PRF schemes is agile if $|\Pr[\mathcal{A}^{\text{Gm}^0} = 1] - \Pr[\mathcal{A}^{\text{Gm}^1} = 1]|$ is negligible for all efficient $\mathcal{S}$-restricted adversaries.*

5.1   Comparison with Crypto-Agility from [1]

In this section, we define a simple update system that leads to the above prior notion of agility. The instantiation is simple since in [1] the algorithms are always executed honestly and as such, no guarantees in the presence of corruptions are given. We can therefore just consider a single party under the UC static corruption model—we point out that as we have seen in prior sections, our formalism can capture a much richer corruption model (see for example [18] on how to obtain PRFs with adaptive security in the random oracle model).

Ideal Updatable (Pseudo-) Random Functions. Again, the ideal update system that we achieve is fully specified by defining the core functions and noting that we aim to realize $U_{\mathsf{SttUp}_{\mathsf{URF}},\mathsf{UpPred}_{\mathsf{URF}}}^{\mathscr{F}_{\mathsf{URF}}}$, for $\mathscr{F}_{\mathsf{URF}} := \{\mathcal{F}_{\mathsf{URF},\mathcal{X},\mathcal{Y}}^{\mathsf{P},(\mathsf{KGen},\mathsf{Eval}_i)}\}_i$, the family of URF functionalities and formally indexed with prf_i, where as explained above, all schemes share the key generation process and the single party in the system is denoted by P.

- $\mathsf{UpPred}_{\mathsf{URF}}$:   On   input $(\mathsf{P}, \mathsf{ssid}, \mathcal{F}', \mathsf{UpdateReq}_{\mathcal{F}'}, \mathsf{UpdateStatus}_{\mathsf{P},\mathcal{F}'},$
  $\mathsf{PartiesFunctions}, \mathsf{UpGraph})$ do the following: if P appears in $\mathsf{UpdateReq}$ and $\mathsf{UpdateStatus}_{\mathsf{P},\mathcal{F}'} = \textit{Updating}$ and return 1 (otherwise, return $\perp$).

- $\mathsf{SttUp}_{\mathsf{URF}}$: On input $\mathsf{SttUp}(v^*, \mathsf{P}, \mathsf{UpdateReq}, \mathsf{PartiesFunctions}, \mathsf{UpGraph}, \mathsf{aux})$, obtain the instance $v \leftarrow \mathsf{PartiesFunctions}[\mathsf{P}]$ (note that by definition, v^* is the parent node of v party P is updating from):
  - If P is honest and $\exists v' \in \mathsf{UpGraph} : v'.\mathsf{function} = v.\mathsf{function}$ then initialize a new state $s := v'.\mathsf{state}$.
  - Else, if P is honest and a table has been initialized in $v^*.\mathsf{state}$, then initialize a new state s with an empty table T and return s.
  - Else return the empty state.

We observe that if we repeat the function from a previous update, then the queries are answered consistently (the update graph is actually a chain for an honest P). Furthermore, if we switch to an entirely new function, then we check whether the initialization event has happened or not.

Protocol and Security Statement. The protocol $\Pi_{\mathsf{URF}}^{\mathsf{P},up}$ is specified as follows:

- Upon initialization, party P initializes the empty key $sk := \perp$ and the algorithm $\mathsf{Eval}^* := \mathsf{Eval}_0$.
- On input $I := (\mathsf{INPUT}, \mathsf{sid}, y)$ where $y = (\mathsf{INITIALIZE}, \mathsf{sid})$, do the following: if $sk = \perp$, execute $sk \xleftarrow{\$} \mathsf{KGen}$, otherwise ignore the input.
- On input $I := (\mathsf{INPUT}, \mathsf{sid}, y)$ where $y = (\mathsf{EVAL}, \mathsf{sid}, x)$, verify that $sk \neq \perp$ and ignore the request if this does not hold. Otherwise, return $s \xleftarrow{\$} \mathsf{Eval}^*(sk, x)$.
- On input $I := (\mathsf{UPDATE}, \mathsf{sid}, \mathcal{F}_{\mathsf{URF},\mathcal{X},\mathcal{Y}}^{\mathsf{P},\mathsf{prf}_j})$ with $\mathcal{F}_{\mathsf{URF},\mathcal{X},\mathcal{Y}}^{\mathsf{P},\mathsf{prf}_j} \in \mathscr{F}_{\mathsf{URF}}$ set $\mathsf{Eval}^* := \mathsf{Eval}_j$.

Security Statement. Let $\mathcal{S}$ be the set containing all the compatible schemes, and the corresponding functionality class $\mathscr{F}_{\mathsf{URF}}$ indexed with these schemes. We obtain the following theorem whose proof is given in the full version [4].

Theorem 2. *Let $\mathscr{F}_{\mathsf{URF}}$ and $\mathcal{S}$ be as defined above. The set $\mathcal{S}$ is agile if and only if protocol $\Pi_{\mathsf{URF}}^{\mathsf{P},up}$ as defined above realizes $U_{\mathsf{SttUp}_{\mathsf{URF}},\mathsf{UpPred}_{\mathsf{URF}}}^{\mathscr{F}_{\mathsf{URF}}}$ (with respect to static corruption of party P).*

References

1. Acar, T., Belenkiy, M., Bellare, M., Cash, D.: Cryptographic agility and its relation to circular encryption. In: Gilbert, H. (ed.) EUROCRYPT 2010. LNCS, vol. 6110, pp. 403–422. Springer, Heidelberg (2010). https://doi.org/10.1007/978-3-642-13190-5_21

2. Ananth, P., Cohen, A., Jain, A.: Cryptography with updates. In: Coron, J.-S., Nielsen, J.B. (eds.) EUROCRYPT 2017. LNCS, vol. 10211, pp. 445–472. Springer, Cham (2017). https://doi.org/10.1007/978-3-319-56614-6_15

3. Badertscher, C., Canetti, R., Hesse, J., Tackmann, B., Zikas, V.: Universal composition with global subroutines: capturing global setup within plain UC. In: Pass, R., Pietrzak, K. (eds.) TCC 2020, Part III. LNCS, vol. 12552, pp. 1–30. Springer, Cham (2020). https://doi.org/10.1007/978-3-030-64381-2_1

4. Badertscher, C., Ciampi, M., Kiayias, A.: Agile cryptography: a universally composable approach. Cryptology ePrint Archive, Paper 2022/1367 (2022). https://eprint.iacr.org/2022/1367

5. Bellare, M., Goldreich, O., Goldwasser, S.: Incremental cryptography: the case of hashing and signing. In: Desmedt, Y.G. (ed.) CRYPTO 1994. LNCS, vol. 839, pp. 216–233. Springer, Heidelberg (1994). https://doi.org/10.1007/3-540-48658-5_22

6. Bellare, M., Paterson, K.G., Rogaway, P.: Security of symmetric encryption against mass surveillance. In: Garay, J.A., Gennaro, R. (eds.) CRYPTO 2014, Part I. LNCS, vol. 8616, pp. 1–19. Springer, Heidelberg (2014). https://doi.org/10.1007/978-3-662-44371-2_1

7. Bhargavan, K., Brzuska, C., Fournet, C., Green, M., Kohlweiss, M., Zanella-Béguelin, S.: Downgrade resilience in key-exchange protocols. In: 2016 IEEE Symposium on Security and Privacy, pp. 506–525. IEEE Computer Society Press, May 2016. https://doi.org/10.1109/SP.2016.37

8. Boyd, C., Davies, G.T., Gjøsteen, K., Jiang, Y.: Fast and secure updatable encryption. In: Micciancio, D., Ristenpart, T. (eds.) CRYPTO 2020, Part I. LNCS, vol. 12170, pp. 464–493. Springer, Cham (2020). https://doi.org/10.1007/978-3-030-56784-2_16

9. Canetti, R.: Universally composable signatures, certification and authentication. Cryptology ePrint Archive, Report 2003/239 (2003). https://eprint.iacr.org/2003/239

10. Canetti, R.: Universally composable security. J. ACM **67**(5), 2020 (2020)

11. Chakraborty, S., Magri, B., Nielsen, J.B., Venturi, D.: Universally composable subversion-resilient cryptography. In: Dunkelman, O., Dziembowski, S. (eds.) EUROCRYPT 2022, Part I. LNCS, vol. 13275, pp. 272–302. Springer, Heidelberg (2022). https://doi.org/10.1007/978-3-031-06944-4_10

12. Chen, L., et al.: Report on post-quantum cryptography. NISTIR 8105, National Institute of Standards and Technology, April 2016. https://nvlpubs.nist.gov/nistpubs/ir/2016/nist.ir.8105.pdf

13. Ciampi, M., Karayannidis, N., Kiayias, A., Zindros, D.: Updatable blockchains. In: Chen, L., Li, N., Liang, K., Schneider, S. (eds.) ESORICS 2020, Part II. LNCS, vol. 12309, pp. 590–609. Springer, Cham (2020). https://doi.org/10.1007/978-3-030-59013-0_29

14. Dodis, Y., Katz, J., Xu, S., Yung, M.: Strong key-insulated signature schemes. In: Desmedt, Y.G. (ed.) PKC 2003. LNCS, vol. 2567, pp. 130–144. Springer, Heidelberg (2003). https://doi.org/10.1007/3-540-36288-6_10

15. Fischlin, M., Mazaheri, S.: Self-guarding cryptographic protocols against algorithm substitution attacks. In: Chong, S., Delaune, S. (eds.) CSF 2018 Computer Security Foundations Symposium, pp. 76–90. IEEE Computer Society Press (2018). https://doi.org/10.1109/CSF.2018.00013

16. Franklin, M.K.: A survey of key evolving cryptosystems. Int. J. Secur. Netw. **1**(1/2), 46–53 (2006). https://doi.org/10.1504/IJSN.2006.010822

17. Groth, J., Ostrovsky, R., Sahai, A.: New techniques for noninteractive zero-knowledge. J. ACM **59**(3) (2012)

18. Jaeger, J., Tyagi, N.: Handling adaptive compromise for practical encryption schemes. In: Micciancio, D., Ristenpart, T. (eds.) CRYPTO 2020, Part I. LNCS, vol. 12170, pp. 3–32. Springer, Cham (2020). https://doi.org/10.1007/978-3-030-56784-2_1

19. Jager, T., Paterson, K.G., Somorovsky, J.: One bad apple: backwards compatibility attacks on state-of-the-art cryptography. In: NDSS 2013. The Internet Society, February 2013

20. Lehmann, A., Tackmann, B.: Updatable encryption with post-compromise security. In: Nielsen, J.B., Rijmen, V. (eds.) EUROCRYPT 2018, Part III. LNCS, vol. 10822, pp. 685–716. Springer, Cham (2018). https://doi.org/10.1007/978-3-319-78372-7_22

21. Ott, D., Paterson, K., Moreau, D.: Where is the research on cryptographic transition and agility? RWC (2022). Video of the talk https://www.youtube.com/watch?v=nF2CB8VD-IA at 1:03:00

22. Poettering, B., Rastikian, S.: Sequential digital signatures for cryptographic software-update authentication. In: Atluri, V., Pietro, R.D., Jensen, C.D., Meng, W. (eds.) ESORICS 2022, Part II. LNCS, vol. 13555, pp. 255–274. Springer, Cham (2022). https://doi.org/10.1007/978-3-031-17146-8_13

23. Rashid, F.Y.: Oracle to Java DEVs: stop signing jar files with md5. https://www.infoworld.com/article/3159186/oracle-to-java-devs-stop-signing-jar-files-with-md5.html. Accessed 19 Jan 2017

24. Stevens, M., Bursztein, E., Karpman, P., Albertini, A., Markov, Y.: The first collision for full SHA-1. In: Katz, J., Shacham, H. (eds.) CRYPTO 2017, Part I. LNCS, vol. 10401, pp. 570–596. Springer, Cham (2017). https://doi.org/10.1007/978-3-319-63688-7_19

25. Stevens, M., et al.: Short chosen-prefix collisions for MD5 and the creation of a rogue CA certificate. In: Halevi, S. (ed.) CRYPTO 2009. LNCS, vol. 5677, pp. 55–69. Springer, Heidelberg (2009). https://doi.org/10.1007/978-3-642-03356-8_4

26. Sullivan, B.: Security briefs - cryptographic agility. MSDN Mag. **24**(8) (2009)

27. Wang, X., Yin, Y.L., Yu, H.: Finding collisions in the full SHA-1. In: Shoup, V. (ed.) CRYPTO 2005. LNCS, vol. 3621, pp. 17–36. Springer, Heidelberg (2005). https://doi.org/10.1007/11535218_2

28. Wang, X., Yu, H.: How to break MD5 and other hash functions. In: Cramer, R. (ed.) EUROCRYPT 2005. LNCS, vol. 3494, pp. 19–35. Springer, Heidelberg (2005). https://doi.org/10.1007/11426639_2

Composable Long-Term Security
with Rewinding

Robin Berger[1] ⓘ, Brandon Broadnax[3], Michael Klooß[2(✉)] ⓘ,
Jeremias Mechler[1] ⓘ, Jörn Müller-Quade[1], Astrid Ottenhues[1] ⓘ,
and Markus Raiber[1] ⓘ

[1] KASTEL Security Research Labs, Karlsruhe Institute of Technology, Karlsruhe,
Germany
{robin.berger,jeremias.mechler,joern.mueller-quade,astrid.ottenhues,
markus.raiber}@kit.edu
[2] Aalto University, Espoo, Finland
michael.klooss@aalto.fi
[3] Karlsruhe, Germany
broadnax@mail.informatik.kit.edu

Abstract. Long-term security, a variant of Universally Composable (UC)
security introduced by Müller-Quade and Unruh (TCC '07, JoC '10),
allows to analyze the security of protocols in a setting where all hardness assumptions no longer hold after the protocol execution has finished.
Such a strict notion is highly desirable when properties such as input
privacy need to be guaranteed for a long time, e.g. with zero-knowledge
proofs for secure electronic voting. Strong impossibility results rule out so-
called *long-term-revealing* setups, e.g. a common reference string (CRS), to
achieve long-term security, with known constructions for long-term security requiring hardware assumptions, e.g. signature cards.

We circumvent these impossibility results with new techniques,
enabling rewinding-based simulation in a way that universal composability is achieved. This allows us to construct a long-term-secure composable
commitment scheme in the CRS-hybrid model, which is provably impossible in the notion of Müller-Quade and Unruh. We base our construction on
a statistically hiding commitment scheme in the CRS-hybrid model with
CCA-like properties. To provide a CCA oracle, we cannot rely on super-
polynomial extraction techniques and instead extract the value committed to via rewinding. To this end, we incorporate rewinding-based commitment extraction into the UC framework via a *helper* in analogy to Canetti,
Lin and Pass (FOCS 2010), allowing both adversary and environment to
extract statistically hiding commitments.

Our new framework provides the *first* setting in which a commitment
scheme that is both *statistically hiding* and *universally composable* can be
constructed from standard polynomial-time hardness assumptions and a
CRS only. We also prove that our CCA oracle is *k-robust extractable*. This
asserts that extraction is possible without rewinding a concurrently executed k-round protocol. Consequently any k-round (standard) UC-secure
protocol remains secure in the presence of our helper.

M. Klooß—Research was conducted at Karlsruhe Institute of Technology.
For the full version [5], see https://eprint.iacr.org/2023/363.

G. Rothblum and H. Wee (Eds.): TCC 2023, LNCS 14372, pp. 510–541, 2023.
https://doi.org/10.1007/978-3-031-48624-1_19

Finally, we prove that building long-term-secure oblivious transfer (and thus general two-party computations) from long-term-revealing setups remains impossible in our setting. Still, our long-term-secure commitment scheme suffices for natural applications, such as long-term secure and composable (commit-and-prove) zero-knowledge arguments of knowledge.

1 Introduction

Secure multi-party computation (MPC) allows mutually distrusting parties to perform computations on their private inputs, guaranteeing properties such as correctness, privacy or independence of inputs. To this end, the parties that wish to perform an MPC jointly execute a *protocol*, i.e. exchange messages with each other over a network.

In today's highly connected world where devices are usually connected to the Internet, it is important to judge the security of cryptographic protocols not only in a *stand-alone setting* where only *one* instance of a protocol is executed at any time. Indeed, it is known that protocols which are stand-alone-secure may lose *all* security even if only two instances of *the same* protocol are executed in parallel [17].

In contrast, *composable security* considers security when multiple, possibly adversarially chosen, protocols may be executed concurrently. A very important notion for this setting is the so-called *Universally Composable (UC)* security, introduced by [6]. By default, UC security offers *computational* security only, i.e. crucially relies on hardness assumptions. If these hardness assumptions turn out to be wrong or eventually become invalid (e.g. due to the availability of universal quantum computers), all security may be lost. For data that is very sensitive and must be kept secure for a long time, e.g. genomic data or electoral choices with secure online voting, computational (UC) security may be insufficient. In contrast, *statistical* security does not rely on hardness assumptions at all—offering, in principle, adequate security guarantees even for the most sensitive data. However, statistical (UC) security is often much harder to achieve than computational (UC) security, for example because a 2/3 honest majority [4] or a very strong *trusted setup* [3,15] is needed.

Interestingly, there is a middle ground between statistical and computational security, called *long-term security*, introduced by [23,24]. With long-term security, hardness assumptions only hold *during* the execution of a protocol. However, *after* the protocol execution has finished, all hardness assumptions become invalid and security must hold against (now) unbounded adversaries. Thus, long-term security offers a very interesting trade-off, in particular when considering that many protocol executions only take a comparatively short time compared to the assumed (and believed) validity of today's used cryptographic hardness assumptions, which is often measured in years.

Impossibility Results of Long-Term Security. Unfortunately, long-term security is subject to very strong impossibility results: Many commonly used and natural setup assumptions (e.g. a common reference string (CRS) or certain public-key infrastructures (PKIs)) that suffice for UC security are too weak to construct long-term-secure composable commitment schemes. Indeed, the known constructions for long-term-secure and composable commitment schemes require very strong *hardware assumptions* such as (trusted) signature cards [24] or fully malicious physically unclonable functions (PUFs) [22]. While these hardware assumptions are weaker than the assumptions required for statistical UC security, they are very impractical, as they require a great deal of coordination between protocol parties in order to exchange the necessary hardware.

Very informally, the strong impossibility results of long-term security come from the fact that commitments created by a malicious committer must be *extractable*, i.e. the simulator must be able to determine the value committed to. In a UC-secure commitment scheme that uses a CRS, this can be achieved by embedding an extraction trapdoor into the CRS (say, a public key used for encryption for which the secret decryption key is known). Using this extraction trapdoor, the value committed to can be determined in a *straight-line* way, i.e. without rewinding the malicious committer.

If long-term security is desired, the above approach fails: If a commitment scheme is straight-line extractable via an extraction trapdoor embedded into the CRS, the commitment must *statistically* contain the value committed to. When the protocol execution has finished, this extraction trapdoor can be (inefficiently) obtained and used to extract the commitment, contradicting the very requirement that the value committed to must be statistically hidden. Conversely, choosing the CRS distribution so that the commitment is statistically hiding makes straight-line extraction impossible. The example is generalized in [24], ruling out any "long-term revealing"[1] setup, in particular *any* CRS distribution.

This problem, namely the insufficiency of widely-used and practical classes of setups such as common reference strings, raises our main research question:

Can we circumvent the impossibility results of [24] that rule out composable and long-term-secure commitment schemes from many natural setups?

Perhaps surprisingly, we can answer this question affirmatively and construct a long-term-secure composable commitment scheme in the CRS-hybrid model. In order to circumvent the prior impossibility result, we propose a new security notion based on (long-term) UC security which covers the possibility of extracting statistically hiding commitment schemes via rewinding.

Having circumvented the impossibility results of [24] for commitment schemes, we raise our second research question:

Can our techniques be used to construct protocols for composable general two-party computation with long-term security from natural setups?

---

[1] Informally, a functionality $\mathcal{F}$ is long-term revealing for party P if the communication between $\mathcal{F}$ and P can be (inefficiently) computed from the communication between $\mathcal{F}$ and all entities except P.

We answer this question negatively by giving an impossibility result for oblivious transfer (OT) with long-term security for both sender and receiver. On the positive side, we sketch how OT with long-term security for *one* party can be achieved. This construction can then be generalized to (reactive) composable general two-party computation with long-term security for one party. Given our new impossibility result, this is the best one can hope for in the setting considered in this paper.

For the special case of (commit-and-prove) zero-knowledge, we give a positive result: Using our long-term-secure composable commitment scheme, we construct composable and long-term-secure (commit-and-prove) zero-knowledge.

1.1   Outline and Contribution

In this work, we construct protocols with composable long-term security for many important tasks. Our main contributions are as follows:

1. We introduce *pseudo-oracles* in Sect. 3.1. A pseudo-oracle $\mathcal{O}$ is defined as an oracle which is given its caller's current view (and code), so that $\mathcal{O}$ can rewind the caller "in its head". With this, it is possible to extract a value from statistically hiding commitment schemes via rewinding.
2. As a building block for the long-term-secure commitment scheme, we construct a statistically hiding and equivocal CCA-secure commitment scheme in the CRS-hybrid model in Sect. 3. Here, we use pseudo-oracles to instantiate the CCA oracle.
3. We extend the notions of Universal Composability [6] and Long-Term Security [24] to a setting where commitments can be extracted by rewinding via a helper. As the helper is accessible by environment and adversary, we retain universal composability. We call the resulting security notion *Long-Term UC Security with Rewinding*.
4. We construct a composable commitment scheme which is long-term-Rewinding-UC-secure in the $\mathcal{F}_{\mathrm{CRS}}$-hybrid model, circumventing the impossibility results of [24] in Sect. 6. To the best of our knowledge, we are the *first* to achieve such a strong notion of security for commitment schemes without resorting to hardware assumptions (or assumptions that already imply statistical UC security).
5. We present several applications of our commitment scheme in Sect. 7. Using our composable and long-term-secure commitment scheme, we can realize zero-knowledge as well as commit-and-proof with long-term security. Moreover, we obtain composable oblivious transfer with long-term security for one party. As we will show in Sect. 5, this is provably the best possible security in our setting.

Unless noted otherwise, we assume ideally authenticated communication and consider static corruptions only.

1.2 Related Work

Long-Term Security. In this paper, we build upon the notion of long-term security as introduced by [24]. In [24], a composable long-term secure commitment scheme is constructed from a trusted signature card. Conversely, large classes of setup assumptions, namely *long-term revealing* setups , have been shown to not admit long-term composable commitment schemes. In contrast to standard UC security [13], long-term composable commitment schemes do not admit composable general multi-party computation with long-term security. Composable long-term commitment schemes also have previously been constructed from other hardware assumptions, namely fully malicious PUFs (together with a CRS) [22].

Statistical Security. Assuming the existence of *ideally secure communication* and an honest majority of more than 2/3, composable general MPC with even statistical security is possible [1].

When there is no honest majority, strong setups such as tamper-proof hardware tokens (e.g. [15]) also admit statistically secure composable general MPC. However, the use of such token-based protocols is often impractical, in particular when computations with many participants are desired. An alternative approach for statistical security is the use of pre-distributed correlated randomness [3]. However, if the party providing the randomness is untrusted or becomes corrupted at any point, all security is lost.

[29] have presented several composable OT protocols. By using a CRS with appropriate distribution, statistical security for either the OT sender or the OT receiver is possible. However, if a CRS admitting statistical security for one party is chosen, composability is lost. The same holds for many composable commitment schemes with statistical security for one party, e.g. [14].

Rewinding and Composable Security. With respect to concurrent self-composability, in particular for game-based security notions, several approaches using rewinding exist, e.g. for the case of commitment schemes [10,19] or zero-knowledge [21,26]. To this end, a very helpful tool is a robust extraction lemma [19], which allows rewinding-based extraction without disturbing "left sides" up to a certain round complexity. While our protocol is based on [19] and their robust rewinding lemma, we modify it so that we can prove that the resulting pseudo-oracle satisfies essential properties, such as composition-order invariance.

Allowing a UC simulator to rewind the execution has first been proposed by [25], leading to a security notion with properties reminiscent of SPS security, namely limited composability.

[10] have presented the first CCA-secure commitment scheme that can be extracted either straight-line by inefficient computations or efficiently using rewinding. Using this commitment scheme, they realize composable general MPC in the plain model, using the inefficient but straight-line extraction. Instead of allowing the simulator to perform these inefficient computations itself, they are performed by a special party called the *helper*. By also giving the environment access to the helper, the notion achieves universal composability. A drawback of

the proposed approach is that UC compatibility is limited. Intuitively, this means that there exists a protocol π that UC-emulates a protocol ϕ, but that does not emulate ϕ under the new notion. However, for any polynomial k, the notion can be adapted such that any k-round UC-secure protocol remains secure, at the expense of a higher round complexity of the CCA-secure commitment scheme. This result has subsequently been improved, e.g. by [11].

We use an approach that is reminiscent of the techniques of [10]. In particular, we also use a helper to extract commitments. As we are interested in commitment schemes with a statistical hiding property, straight-line extraction is not possible anymore. Instead, we let the helper rewind the execution, requiring changes to the execution experiment. For details, see Sect. 5.

2 Preliminaries

We use standard notation. The security parameter is denoted by κ. All inputs are assumed to be of length polynomial in κ. Often, we will provide machines (usually the adversary, the environment as well as entities helping them) with input $(1^\kappa, z)$, where 1^κ denotes the unary encoding of κ and z is some (possibly non-uniform) input depending on κ. We use the usual notation for probability ensembles and write $\overset{c}{\approx}$ for computational and $\overset{s}{\approx}$ statistical indistinguishability.

For two interactive machines $\mathcal{B}$ and $\mathcal{A}$, we write $\langle \mathcal{B}, \mathcal{A} \rangle$ to denote the system where $\mathcal{B}$ and $\mathcal{A}$ interact. We call $\mathcal{B}$ the "left side" and $\mathcal{A}$ the "right side". We write $\mathcal{B} \| \mathcal{A}$ to denote the "parallel composition" of $\mathcal{B}$ and $\mathcal{A}$. We write $\mathrm{out}_\mathcal{B} \langle \mathcal{B}(x), \mathcal{A}(y) \rangle (1^\kappa, z)$ (or similar) to denote the output of $\mathcal{B}$ after interaction with $\mathcal{A}$, where $\mathcal{A}$ and $\mathcal{B}$ receive common input $(1^\kappa, z)$, and $\mathcal{A}$ (resp. $\mathcal{B}$) receives private input x (resp. y). Similarly, we write $\mathrm{view}_\mathcal{A}$ for the view of party $\mathcal{A}$, which consists of the party's random tape, all its inputs and all messages it received. By abuse of notation, we sometimes write $\langle \mathcal{B}, \mathcal{A} \rangle$ for a protocol. A k-round protocol sends at most k messages between its parties. An oracle algorithm $\mathcal{A}$ has an "oracle interface" (i.e. expected input-output behavior), which can be filled in by an oracle $\mathcal{O}$ (but also by a pseudo-oracle, cf. Sect. 3.1), and we write $\mathcal{A}^\mathcal{O}$ for the composed machine; an oracle $\mathcal{O}$ is itself a (potentially unbounded) machine.

Two (oracle-)machines $\mathcal{A}_0$ and $\mathcal{A}_1$ are *indistinguishable w.r.t. rewinding*, if no unbounded distinguisher $\mathcal{D}$ can distinguish black-box (rewinding) access to $\mathcal{A}_0$ or $\mathcal{A}_1$ (where $\mathcal{D}$ receives (and can respond to) any oracle queries of $\mathcal{A}_0$ and $\mathcal{A}_1$).

2.1 Commitment Schemes

In our constructions, we use (stand-alone) commitment schemes as building blocks. In the following, we give a definition.

Definition 1 (Commitment Scheme). *A commitment scheme (with setup), non-interactive unveil phase and message space $\mathcal{M}$ is a tuple* (Setup, C, R), *where* Setup *is a PPT algorithm and* C *and* R *are interactive PPT algorithms, with* *the following syntax:* 1. Setup *takes* (1^κ) *as input and outputs a commitment key* ck, 2. C *and* R *have common input* $(1^\kappa, \text{ck})$. *We usually write* (c, d) *for the commitment-decommitment pair after the* commit *phase. The* decommit *phase or* unveil *phase is non-interactive and we write* OPEN(ck, c, v, d) *for the function which outputs* 1 *if a decommitment* d *of commitment* c *to value* v *is accepted w.r.t. commitment key* ck.

Definition 2 (Stateless and Public-Coin Receivers). *A commitment scheme* $\langle C, R \rangle$ *is* stateless, *or more concretely, has a* stateless receiver, *if every message and output of the receiver is computed from the current (possibly empty) transcript. If, additionally, the receiver's messages are a (fixed) portion of its random tape (independent of the transcript), we call it a* public-coin *receiver.*

Many commitment schemes, in particular all non-interactive ones, are public-coin. Binding and hiding are defined as expected and omitted for space reasons.

3 A Statistically Hiding Concurrently Extractable and Equivocal Commitment Scheme

In this section, we define pseudo-oracles which capture oracles that use rewinding. Building on this, we define CCA security of commitment schemes w.r.t. a committed-value pseudo-oracle in Definitions 7 and 8. Lastly, we construct a commitment scheme which is computationally CCA-binding and statistically CCA-equivocal (so in particular, statistically CCA-hiding). Our constructions and definitions are in the CRS-hybrid model.

3.1 Pseudo-oracles

We define pseudo-oracles, which, as noted before, can capture rewinding-based techniques. There is some freedom in the definition of pseudo-oracles and their properties. Our definition intentionally limits the power of pseudo-oracles as much as possible.

Definition 3 ((Pseudo-)oracle). *Suppose* $\mathcal{A}$ *is an (interactive) oracle algorithm. Suppose* $\mathcal{O}$ *is a (stateful) algorithm which behaves like an oracle, i.e. interfaces with* $\mathcal{A}$ *by responding to a query* x *with response* y.

- *For (stateful)* oracles, y *is computed from* $\mathcal{O}$'s *state, randomness, and query* x.
- *For (stateful)* pseudo-oracles, y *is computed from* $\mathcal{O}$'s *state, randomness, and the current* view *of* $\mathcal{A}$ *(which includes the query* x *to* $\mathcal{O}$*) as well as* $\mathcal{A}$'s *code.*

Remark 1 (Alternative Interpretation). We give pseudo-oracles access to their caller's code and view. Alternatively, we may restrict to *admissible callers*, which pass their code and current view to the oracle (turning the pseudo-oracle into an ordinary oracle). Evidently, any oracle algorithm which uses a pseudo-oracle can be turned into an *admissible* oracle algorithm which uses an *ordinary* oracle.

The familiar properties of ordinary oracles do not carry over to pseudo-oracles in general, and we must make explicit the properties which a (pseudo-)oracle should have. In our setting, all pseudo-oracles of interest are *black-box*.

Definition 4 (Black-Box Oracle). *A (possibly stateful) pseudo-oracle $\mathcal{O}$ is black-box, if its output y is computed from $\mathcal{O}$'s state, randomness, black-box (rewinding) access to $\mathcal{A}$, and the current view of $\mathcal{A}$ but with $\mathcal{A}$'s randomness removed (i.e. only all inputs and messages which $\mathcal{A}$ received).*

Like ordinary oracles, black-box pseudo-oracles are independent of implementation details of their caller. We record following trivial consequence.

Corollary 1. *Let $\mathcal{O}$ be a black-box pseudo-oracle. Let $\mathcal{A}$ and $\mathcal{B}$ be oracle algorithms which are perfectly indistinguishable w.r.t. rewinding. Then $\mathcal{A}^{\mathcal{O}}$ and $\mathcal{B}^{\mathcal{O}}$ are again perfectly indistinguishable w.r.t. rewinding.*

In this paper, we only consider pseudo-oracles that fulfill the black-box property.

Another property of ordinary oracles is *composition-order invariance*, which asserts that, in a larger system of composed machines, it does not matter when a (pseudo-)oracle is connected to its caller.

Definition 5 (k-Robust Composition-Order Invariance (COI)). *A pseudo-oracle $\mathcal{O}$ is k-robust composition-order invariant w.r.t. PPT algorithms, if for a pair of interacting PPT algorithms $\mathcal{A}, \mathcal{B}$, where $\langle \mathcal{B}, \mathcal{A} \rangle$ has at most k rounds, we have*

$$\{\mathrm{out}_{\mathcal{B},\mathcal{A}}\langle \mathcal{B}(x), \ \mathcal{A}^{\mathcal{O}}(y)\rangle(1^{\kappa}, z)\}_{\kappa \in \mathbb{N}, x, y, z \in \{0,1\}^*}$$

$$\overset{s}{\approx} \{\mathrm{out}_{\mathcal{B},\mathcal{A}}\langle \mathcal{B}(x), \ \mathcal{A}(y)\rangle^{\mathcal{O}}(1^{\kappa}, z)\}_{\kappa \in \mathbb{N}, x, y, z \in \{0,1\}^*}.$$

That is, it is statistically indistinguishable whether the system was composed as

- *$\langle \mathcal{B}, \mathcal{A}^{\mathcal{O}} \rangle$, that is, first the pseudo-oracle $\mathcal{O}$ is composed with $\mathcal{A}$, and then $\mathcal{A}^{\mathcal{O}}$ is composed with $\mathcal{B}$, or*
- *$\langle \mathcal{B}, \mathcal{A} \rangle^{\mathcal{O}}$, that is, first $\mathcal{A}$ is composed with $\mathcal{B}$, and then the pseudo-oracle $\mathcal{O}$ is composed with $\langle \mathcal{B}, \mathcal{A} \rangle$.*

We note that in the above, $\langle \mathcal{B}, \mathcal{A} \rangle$ is considered as a single *entity, i.e. it is a single machine which emulates both $\mathcal{B}$, $\mathcal{A}$ and their interaction. Consequently, for $\langle \mathcal{B}, \mathcal{A}^{\mathcal{O}} \rangle$, the pseudo-oracle has access to $\mathrm{view}_{\mathcal{A}}$ only, whereas in $\langle \mathcal{B}, \mathcal{A} \rangle^{\mathcal{O}}$ it has access to $\mathrm{view}_{\langle \mathcal{B}, \mathcal{A} \rangle}$ (where, by abuse of notation, we write $\mathrm{view}_{\langle \mathcal{B}, \mathcal{A} \rangle}$ for the view of the entity $\langle \mathcal{B}, \mathcal{A} \rangle$ as explained above).*

Definition 5 is quite abstract. It helps to consider the pseudo-oracle $\mathcal{O}_{\mathsf{CCA}}$ from Sect. 3.2. There, the core difference between $\langle \mathcal{B}, \mathcal{A}^{\mathcal{O}} \rangle$ and $\langle \mathcal{B}, \mathcal{A} \rangle^{\mathcal{O}}$ is, whether it is possible to rewind $\mathcal{B}$ alongside $\mathcal{A}$, or not (because $\mathcal{B}$ is an external entity). Composition-order invariance for $\mathcal{O}_{\mathsf{CCA}}$ intuitively ensures that, despite this difference, the values extracted by $\mathcal{O}_{\mathsf{CCA}}$ for $\mathcal{A}$ remain unchanged.

Remark 2 (Relation to Oracles). Ordinary oracles are evidently black-box and ∞-robust composition-order invariant (w.r.t. unbounded algorithms).

We stress that composition-order invariance is a non-trivial property of pseudo-oracles. Indeed, to verify that the CCA-commitment pseudo-oracle $\mathcal{O}_{\mathsf{CCA}}$ satisfies composition-order invariance, we crucially rely on computational assumptions; and we do not know whether it holds without such assumptions. For that reason, Definition 5 restricts to PPT algorithms.

Another useful property allows the elimination of a pseudo-oracle altogether. This corresponds to the k-robustness property of [10,19].

Definition 6 (k-Robust Pseudo-PPT). *A black-box pseudo-oracle is k-robust pseudo-PPT if for every (interactive) PPT oracle algorithm $\mathcal{A}$, there exists a PPT algorithm $\mathcal{S}$ such that for every interactive PPT algorithm $\mathcal{B}$ interacting with $\mathcal{A}$ in at most k rounds, we have*

$$\{\mathsf{out}_{\mathcal{B},\mathcal{A}}\langle\mathcal{B}(x),\ \mathcal{A}^{\mathcal{O}}(y)\rangle(1^{\kappa},z)\}_{\kappa\in\mathbb{N},x,y,z\in\{0,1\}^*}$$
$$\overset{s}{\approx}\{\mathsf{out}_{\mathcal{B},\mathcal{S}}\langle\mathcal{B}(x),\ \mathcal{S}(y)\rangle(1^{\kappa},z)\}_{\kappa\in\mathbb{N},x,y,z\in\{0,1\}^*}.$$

Terminology 1 (Asymptotics). *We say that a pseudo-oracle $\mathcal{O}$ is $O(k)$-robust composition-order-invariant resp. pseudo-PPT if $\mathcal{O}$ is f-robust composition-order-invariant resp. pseudo-PPT for all $f \in O(k)$.*

3.2 Properties of Commitment Schemes

We require a commitment scheme which is *concurrently extractable* and *statistically hiding* (indeed, equivocal) to achieve concurrent security. Consequently, we define security notions in the presence of a committed-value oracle $\mathcal{O}_{\mathsf{CCA}}$. The security w.r.t. a committed-value oracle will be important, as it allows to concurrently extract adversarial inputs to commitments, while at the same time simulating commitments of honest parties. The committed-value oracle $\mathcal{O}_{\mathsf{CCA}}$ for COM plays the receiver of COM in an arbitrary number of sessions. Upon completion of a commitment phase in session s, $\mathcal{O}_{\mathsf{CCA}}$ outputs $(\mathsf{End}, s, v_s, \mathsf{view}_{\mathsf{R}_s})$. (The view of the receiver is outputted for technical reasons. For public-coin COM, it contains no additional information anyway.)

We start with a variant of the binding property, which must hold even in the presence of a committed-value oracle $\mathcal{O}_{\mathsf{CCA}}$ for the committer.

Definition 7 (CCA-Binding). *Let COM be a commitment scheme with message space $\mathcal{M}$. Let $\mathcal{O}_{\mathsf{CCA}}$ be a pseudo-oracle whose interface is described below. Let $\mathrm{Exp}_{\mathcal{A},\mathcal{O}_{\mathsf{CCA}},\mathsf{COM}}^{\mathsf{CCA\text{-}bind}}(\kappa, z)$ be the output of the following experiment:*

1. *Run the adversary $\mathcal{A}$ on input $(1^{\kappa}, z)$ with access to a (committed-value) pseudo-oracle $\mathcal{O}_{\mathsf{CCA}}$ provided through the game $\mathcal{G}$. Formally, this means $\langle\mathcal{G},\mathcal{A}\rangle^{\mathcal{O}_{\mathsf{CCA}}}$ where game $\mathcal{G}$ passes messages between $\mathcal{A}$ and $\mathcal{O}_{\mathsf{CCA}}$ as follows:*
   - *$\mathcal{O}_{\mathsf{CCA}}$ is proxied through $\mathcal{G}$ and allows $\mathcal{A}$ to choose common[2] inputs $(1^{\kappa}, t)$ and interact with an honest receiver R_s in session s (for arbitrarily many concurrent sessions). For this, $\mathcal{O}_{\mathsf{CCA}}$ first generates a fresh setup $\mathsf{ck}_s \leftarrow \mathsf{Setup}(1^{\kappa}, t)$ and sends it to $\mathcal{A}$ (through $\mathcal{G}$).*

---

[2] Here, $\mathcal{A}$ must not modify the security parameter, i.e. 1^{κ} is the same as $\mathcal{A}$'s input.

- *Whenever a session s is finished, $\mathcal{O}_{\text{CCA}}$ responds with $(\text{End}, s, v_s, \text{view}_{R_s})$, where v_s is the* extracted *value of commitment (which may be $\bot$, e.g. if the receiver does not accept) or $\bot_{ext}$ if extraction failed. The game passes (End, s, v_s) to $\mathcal{A}$ (but not view_{R_s}).*

2. *In any session s whose commit phase finished, the adversary may complete the unveil phase for s. This phase is simulated by the game (which has access to view_{R_s}). Suppose receiver R_s accepts opening to $v \neq \bot$. If $v \neq v_s$ and $v \in \mathcal{M}$, then the game outputs 1, i.e. $\mathcal{A}$ wins. (For $v = \bot$, $\mathcal{A}$ does not win.)*

3. *If $\mathcal{A}$ stops, the game outputs 0, i.e. $\mathcal{A}$ loses the game.*

We say COM *is* CCA-binding *w.r.t. $\mathcal{O}_{\text{CCA}}$, if for every PPT adversary $\mathcal{A}$, there exists a negligible function* negl, *such that for all $\kappa \in \mathbb{N}$ and all $z \in \{0,1\}^*$, $\Pr[\text{Exp}_{\mathcal{A},\mathcal{O}_{\text{CCA}},\text{COM}}^{\text{CCA-bind}}(\kappa, z) = 1] \leq$ negl. We then call $\mathcal{O}_{\text{CCA}}$ a* committed-value pseudo-oracle.

Some remarks are in order: Firstly, Definition 7 is the binding analogue to *CCA-hiding* of [10]. Secondly, it is a multi-challenge variant (but as usual, multi- and single-challenge are equivalent by a standard argument). Thirdly, it would have been more straightforward to have the game or $\mathcal{O}_{\text{CCA}}$ play the honest receivers in both commit and unveil phase. However, we want a committed-value pseudo-oracle with the interface as in Definition 7, i.e. only the commitment phase. Lastly, $\mathcal{O}_{\text{CCA}}$ even rewinds the game, but this only strengthens the notion of binding. We note that, if $\mathcal{O}_{\text{CCA}}$ is $O(1)$-robust COI, then a game with a constant number of challenge sessions can be handled as a left side, so that $\mathcal{O}_{\text{CCA}}$ does not rewind the game anymore.

Terminology 2 (Value Committed to). *Let* COM *be a commitment scheme with message space $\mathcal{M}$ which is CCA-binding w.r.t. committed-value oracle $\mathcal{O}_{\text{CCA}}$. Let $v \in \mathcal{M} \cup \{\bot, \bot_{ext}\}$ be the value which is part of the output of $\mathcal{O}_{\text{CCA}}$ in an interaction with a (possibly malicious) committer. If $v \in \mathcal{M}$, we say that v is the* value committed to. *If $v \notin \mathcal{M}$, i.e. $v \in \{\bot, \bot_{ext}\}$, we do not consider the commitment to have a value.*

For the straight-line simulation of commitments, we define trapdoor commitment schemes. These allow to generate dummy commitments that can be equivocated to an arbitrary value in the opening phase.

Definition 8 (Trapdoor Commitment Scheme). *Let* $(\text{Setup}, \text{C}, \text{R})$ *be a commitment scheme with message space $\mathcal{M}$, and let $(\text{TSetup}, \text{C}_{\text{trap}})$ be algorithms which can be used in place of (Setup, C). Let $\mathcal{O}_{\text{CCA}}$ be a committed-value pseudo-oracle. Then* $\text{TRAPCOM} = (\text{Setup}, \text{C}, \text{R}, \text{TSetup}, \text{C}_{\text{trap}})$ *is called* trapdoor *w.r.t. $\mathcal{O}_{\text{CCA}}$ if*

- *$\langle \text{C}, \text{R} \rangle$ and $\langle \text{C}_{\text{trap}}, \text{R} \rangle$ are commitment schemes with message space $\mathcal{M}$, and*
- *for all PPT adversaries $\mathcal{A}$, it holds that*

$$\{\text{Exp}_{\mathcal{A},\mathcal{O}_{\text{CCA}},\text{TRAPCOM}}^{\text{TDC}}(\kappa, 0, z)\}_{\kappa \in \mathbb{N}, z \in \{0,1\}^*}$$

$$\overset{s}{\approx} \{\text{Exp}_{\mathcal{A},\mathcal{O}_{\text{CCA}},\text{TRAPCOM}}^{\text{TDC}}(\kappa, 1, z)\}_{\kappa \in \mathbb{N} z \in \{0,1\}^*}$$

that is, the ensembles are statistically indistinguishable.

The experiment $\mathrm{Exp}_{\mathcal{A},\mathcal{O}_{\mathsf{CCA}}\mathsf{TRAPCOM}}^{\mathrm{TDC}}(\kappa, b, z)$ *is defined as follows:*

1. *Run* $\mathcal{A}(1^\kappa, z)$ *where* $\mathcal{A}$ *interacts with the game* $\mathcal{G}$ *as follows.*
2. *First,* $\mathcal{A}$ *sends* (Setup). *If* $b = 0$, *set* ck $\leftarrow$ Setup(1^κ). *Otherwise, set* (ck, td) $\leftarrow$ TSetup(1^κ). *The experiment sends* ck *to* $\mathcal{A}$.
3. *By sending* (Start, v) *to* $\mathcal{G}$, $\mathcal{A}$ *starts the commit phase of* TRAPCOM, *acting as receiver. If* $b = 0$, *the experiment runs the code of the honest committer* C *on input* (1^κ, ck, v). *If* $b = 1$, *the experiment runs the code of the trapdoor committer* $\mathsf{C}_{\mathrm{trap}}$ *on input* (1^κ, ck, $|v|$, td).
4. *After the commit phase has finished, wait for a message* (Unveil) *and perform the unveil phase. If* $b = 1$, *the trapdoor committer receives* v *as additional private input.*
5. *The experiment gives* $\mathcal{A}$ *access to a committed-value pseudo-oracle* $\mathcal{O}_{\mathsf{CCA}}$ *as in Definition 7. Concretely, we consider* $\langle \mathcal{G}, \mathcal{A} \rangle^{\mathcal{O}_{\mathsf{CCA}}}$ *as the complete experiment.*
6. *The experiment outputs the view of* $\mathcal{A}$.

As for CCA-binding, in the CCA-equivocation experiment, $\mathcal{O}_{\mathsf{CCA}}$ rewinds the whole game. This only makes the adversary (and hence security notion) stronger. Unlike CCA-binding, Definition 8 is single-challenge.

3.3 Constructions

We first recall the definition of a PRS commitment for μ-bit messages from [19].

Construction 1 (PRS Commitment Scheme (Adapted from [19])). *Let* $\kappa \in \mathbb{N}$ *be a security parameter. Let* COM$'$ = (Setup$'$, C$'$, R$'$) *be a commitment scheme with message space* $\mathcal{M} = \{0,1\}^{\mu(\kappa)}$ *for polynomial* μ. *Let* $\ell = \ell(\kappa)$ *denote a round parameter. The PRS commitment scheme with* ℓ *rounds and base commitment* COM$'$ *is denoted* PRS$_\ell$ *or just* PRS. *It has message space* $\mathcal{M}$ *and is defined as follows.*

Setup. *Generate* ck$_{i,j}^b \leftarrow$ Setup$'(1^\kappa)$ *for* $b \in \{0,1\}$, $i \in [\kappa]$, $j \in [\ell]$.
Commit Phase. *On common input* (1^κ) *and private input* $v \in \mathcal{M}$ *for* C:
   1. *The committer* C *chooses* $\kappa \cdot \ell$ *pairs of random shares* $(s_{i,j}^0, s_{i,j}^1)$ *of* v, *i.e. for all* i, j *it holds that* $s_{i,j}^0 \oplus s_{i,j}^1 = v$. *Then,* C *runs* C$'$ *to commit to* $s_{i,j}^b$ *for* $b \in \{0,1\}$, $i \in [\kappa]$, $j \in [\ell]$ *under commitment key* ck$_{i,j}^b$ *(in parallel) to obtain commitments* $c_{i,j}^b$.
   2. *For* $j = 1, \dots, \ell$ *sequentially:*
      (a) *The receiver* R *sends a challenge string* $r_j = (r_{1,j}, \dots, r_{\kappa,j}) \overset{\$}{\leftarrow} \{0,1\}^\kappa$.
      (b) *The committer* C *unveils the commitments* $c_{1,j}^{r_{1,j}}, \dots, c_{\kappa,j}^{r_{\kappa,j}}$. *The receiver aborts if any unveil is invalid.*
Unveil Phase.
   1. *The committer unveils all remaining shares that have not been opened in the commit phase.*
   2. *The receiver accepts a value* v *if* $u_{1,1}^0 \oplus u_{1,1}^1 = \dots = u_{\kappa,\ell}^0 \oplus u_{\kappa,\ell}^1 = v$, *where* $u_{i,j}^b$ *is the message unveiled for commitment* $c_{i,j}^b$.

Terminology 3. *In the following, we call the commitment schemes used within the PRS commitment scheme* base commitment schemes, *to distinguish them from the PRS commitment scheme itself.*

We use the PRS commitment scheme, which is concurrently and robustly extractable [19], as a basis to build our CCA-secure commitment scheme. Our basic construction follows [19], but is simpler thanks to the use of a CRS. The protocol first commits to the committer's input using the PRS commitment scheme (built from some suitable base commitment scheme). Then, it provides a proof of knowledge for consistency, which (due to the CRS) will be simulatable. This ensures that all slots of the PRS commitment commit to the same value (even if not unveiled). We crucially rely on this to prove composition-order invariance.

Construction 2. *Let* COM′ *be a base commitment scheme (for the PRS commitment scheme). Define the commitment scheme* CCACOM *for round parameter* $\ell = \ell(\kappa)$ *as follows:*

- **Inputs:** *Common input is* (1^κ). *Private input to* C *is* v.
- **Setup:** *Setup for* PRS$_\ell$ *(i.e. for base commitment* COM′ *and* ℓ *rounds).*
- **Commit Phase:**
  1. **PRS commit:** *Run the PRS commitment phase of* PRS$_\ell$. *Let* τ_{prs} *be the PRS commitment transcript.*
  2. **Argument of knowledge (AoK):** *Run Blum's graph hamiltonicity AoK protocol* κ-*fold in parallel with base commitments* COM′ *to prove:* τ_{prs} *is a valid PRS commitment to some value* $v \in \mathcal{M}$.
- **Unveil Phase:** *Run the corresponding PRS unveil phase.*

Note that in Theorem 1, we use a parallel repetition of Blum's graph hamiltonicity protocol instead of a general AoK. This is primarily for simplicity. Next, we state and prove CCACOM secure for suitable choices of COM′ and ℓ.

Theorem 1. *Consider a base commitment scheme* COM′ *such that*

1. COM′ *has a stateless receiver and non-interactive unveil phase.*
2. *The commitment phase of* COM′ *has at most* $k = k(\kappa)$ *rounds and the first message is sent by the committer* C$_t$.
3. COM′ *is binding.*
4. COM′ *is trapdoor with trapdoor committing algorithm* C$'_{\mathsf{trap}}$.

Let CCACOM *be Construction 2 with round parameter* $\ell \in \omega(k(\kappa)\log(\kappa))$ *and* COM′. *Let* $\mathcal{O}_{\mathsf{CCA}}$ *be the following pseudo-oracle, where* $\mathcal{A}$ *denotes its caller:*

- $\mathcal{O}_{\mathsf{CCA}}$ *allows* $\mathcal{A}$ *to choose common inputs* (1^κ) *and interact with an honest receiver* R$_s$ *in session* s *in arbitrarily many concurrent sessions. For this,* $\mathcal{O}_{\mathsf{CCA}}$ *first generates the setup* ck$_s \leftarrow$ Setup(1^κ) *per session and sends it to* $\mathcal{A}$.
- $\mathcal{O}_{\mathsf{CCA}}$ *runs the rewinding-based extraction of PRS commitments, formally defined via* recurse *in Sect. 4.1 below.[3] Let* v_s *denote the extracted value (which*

---

[3] We note that $\mathcal{O}_{\mathsf{CCA}}$ needs to process the extracted values and present $\mathcal{A}$ with the expected game interface. Hence, formally, an adversary $\mathcal{A}_{\mathcal{O}_{\mathsf{CCA}}}$ is defined which handles this, and recurse is invoked for $\mathcal{A}_{\mathcal{O}_{\mathsf{CCA}}}$ (not $\mathcal{A}$).

may be ⊥) received in (main thread) session s. (If extraction failed, v_s is the special symbol $⊥_{ext}$.)

- *When the commitment phase of session s completes, $\mathcal{O}_{CCA}$ outputs (End, s, v_s, viewR_s) where v_s is replaced by ⊥ if R rejected the AoK.*

Then the following holds for CCACOM w.r.t. $\mathcal{O}_{CCA}$:

1. CCACOM *has at most $O(k + \ell)$ rounds and non-interactive unveil phase.*
2. CCACOM *is CCA-binding w.r.t. $\mathcal{O}_{CCA}$.*
3. CCACOM *is trapdoor for some trapdoor committing algorithm C_{trap}.*
4. $\mathcal{O}_{CCA}$ *is black-box and $O(k)$-robust composition-order invariant.*
5. $\mathcal{O}_{CCA}$ *is $O(k)$-robust pseudo-PPT.*

Proof (Proof Sketch). The claims in Item 1 follow immediately. Item 2, i.e. CCA-binding w.r.t. $\mathcal{O}_{CCA}$, follows immediately from the generalized robust extraction lemma of [19] (adapted to our setting). The rewinding schedule of [19] (cf. Sect. 4.1) only uses black-box rewinding access and at most squares the worst-case runtime, hence Item 5, i.e. black-boxness and pseudo-PPT, follow as well. It remains to show Item 3 and Item 4.

Claim 1 (Item 4). $\mathcal{O}_{CCA}$ *is $O(k)$-robust composition-order invariant w.r.t. PPT algorithms.*

We defer the proof of this claim to Sect. 4.2 Finally, we show the trapdoor property, Item 3. The trapdoor commitment setup is obtained by (in the PRS commitment) replacing Setup' with TSetup' and C' with C'_{trap}, i.e., simply using the trapdoor commitment algorithms of the base commitment COM', in the PRS commitments and the AoK commitments.

Claim 2 (Item 3). COM *is trapdoor w.r.t. $\mathcal{O}_{CCA}$ for trapdoor commitment algorithms (TSetup, C_{trap}) as described above.*

Proof. To prove indistinguishability we argue over following hybrids.

- Hybrid G_0: Real game, i.e. the bit b in $\mathrm{Exp}^{TDC}_{\mathcal{A},\mathcal{O}_{CCA},TRAPCOM}$ is 0.
- Hybrid G_1: Same as G_0, except that the AoK also uses TSetup' and C'_{trap} (and trapdoor unveil) instead of the real algorithms.
- Hybrid G_2: Same as G_1, except that the AoK is simulated using the (perfect) special honest-verifier zero-knowledge (SHVZK) simulation for Blum's graph hamiltonicity, by equivocating commitments after the challenge was received.
- Hybrid H_j: Same as $H_0 := G_2$, except that for PRS slots $j' \leq j$, the hybrid executes the left commit phase using trapdoor algorithms TSetup' and C'_{trap} (and trapdoor unveil) instead of the real algorithms.
- Hybrid $G_3 := H_\ell$: The simulation, i.e. the bit b in $\mathrm{Exp}^{TDC}_{\mathcal{A},\mathcal{O}_{CCA},TRAPCOM}$ is 1.

All hybrids output the view of $\mathcal{A}$, denoted by view$_\mathcal{A}$. Intuitively, indistinguishability of G_0 and G_1, as well as H_i and H_{i+1}, obviously follows from the trapdoor property (Definition 8). However, the presence of rewinding $\mathcal{O}_{CCA}$ makes the argument non-trivial and we have to rely on COI. We demonstrate the argument for the hybrids H_i; the completely analogous case of $G_0 \overset{s}{\approx} G_1$ is left to the reader.

We sketch the formal arguments for the reduction. Let $\mathcal{H}_i$ be the experiment H_i with $\mathcal{O}_{\mathsf{CCA}}$ factored out, i.e. $H_i = \mathcal{H}_i^{\mathcal{O}_{\mathsf{CCA}}}$. Let $E_b :=$ $\mathrm{Exp}_{\mathcal{H}_i, \mathcal{O}_{\mathsf{CCA}}, \mathsf{TRAPCOM}'^{2\kappa}}^{\mathrm{TDC}}(1^\kappa, b, z)$ be the TDC experiment from Definition 8. Finally, let $\mathcal{B}_i$ be defined such that $\mathcal{H}_i = \langle E_0, \mathcal{B}_i \rangle$, i.e. make session i explicit and "move" it into E_b. Also observe that $\mathcal{H}_{i+1} = \langle E_1, \mathcal{B}_i \rangle$. This gives us

$$H_i = \mathcal{H}_i^{\mathcal{O}_{\mathsf{CCA}}} = \mathrm{out}_{\mathcal{B}_i} \langle E_0, \mathcal{B}_i \rangle^{\mathcal{O}_{\mathsf{CCA}}} \overset{s}{\approx} \mathrm{out}_{\mathcal{B}_i} \langle E_0, \mathcal{B}_i^{\mathcal{O}_{\mathsf{CCA}}} \rangle,$$

where the first equality holds by definition, the next equality follows by *black-boxness* of $\mathcal{O}_{\mathsf{CCA}}$ (Corollary 1), and the statistical indistinguishability follows from $O(k)$-robust COI of $\mathcal{O}_{\mathsf{CCA}}$ (for PPT algorithms). We stress that this indistinguishability is *not* automatic for pseudo-oracles and *requires justification*, given by COI. Next, we find

$$\mathrm{out}_{\mathcal{B}_i} \langle E_0, \mathcal{B}_i^{\mathcal{O}_{\mathsf{CCA}}} \rangle \overset{s}{\approx} \mathrm{out}_{\mathcal{B}_i} \langle E_1, \mathcal{B}_i^{\mathcal{O}_{\mathsf{CCA}}} \rangle,$$

by using that COM' is a trapdoor commitment by assumption (and applying another hybrid argument over the commitment instances).[4] Now, we reverse the previous steps, with the same arguments but E_1 as left side to find

$$\mathrm{out}_{\mathcal{B}_i} \langle E_1, \mathcal{B}_i^{\mathcal{O}_{\mathsf{CCA}}} \rangle \overset{s}{\approx} \mathrm{out}_{\mathcal{B}_i} \langle E_1, \mathcal{B}_i \rangle^{\mathcal{O}_{\mathsf{CCA}}} = \mathcal{H}_{i+1}^{\mathcal{O}_{\mathsf{CCA}}} = H_{i+1}.$$

Thus, we have shown that $H_0 \overset{s}{\approx} H_\ell$, via uniform reductions $H_i \overset{s}{\approx} H_{i+1}$ (for $0 \leq i \leq \ell - 1$). As noted, $G_0 \overset{s}{\approx} G_1$ follows completely analogously.

It remains to show that $G_1 \overset{s}{\approx} G_2$, i.e., that we can simulate the AoK. To do so, instead of unveiling the real values (using the algorithm of the trapdoor committer), we instead use the special honest-verifier zero-knowledge (SHVZK) simulator for Blum's graph hamiltonicity protocol to generate the messages to unveil. Since the SHVZK simulation is perfect (given perfectly hiding commitments), for any challenge the distribution of unveiled messages is identical for real and simulated commitments. Thus, we can let $\mathsf{C}_{\mathrm{trap}}$ unveil the simulation, instead of the real messages. Again, due to the presence of the pseudo-oracle (which may rewind the interaction, breaking the perfect indistinguishability), we formally argue this by first moving $\mathsf{C}_{\mathrm{trap}}$ to the left side, doing the switch, and then moving it back to the right side. This is done completely analogous to the hybrid steps. This completes the proof of Claim 2.   □

The base commitment COM' in Theorem 1 can be instantiated using a number of assumptions. We note that COM' is a stand-alone commitment scheme, in particular, it need not be universally composable.

---

[4] It is easy to see that a 2κ-fold parallel composition of $\mathsf{TRAPCOM}'$ is still a trapdoor commitment (w.r.t. $\mathcal{O}_{\mathsf{CCA}}$). And switching E_0 to E_1 is exactly a switch from parallel real to parallel trapdoor commitments. Moreover, while the TDC experiment E_b has *more than* k moves, it is only $O(1)$ more. So, it is clear that it is still $O(k)$ rounds, and hence $O(k)$-robust COI and $O(k)$-robust pseudo-PPT are applicable.

Proposition 1 (Possible Instantiations). *Under the RSA assumption, the DLOG assumption and the SIS assumption, there exist commitment schemes* COM'_{RSA} *[20],* $\text{COM}'_{\text{DLOG}}$ *[28] and* COM'_{SIS} *[18] in the CRS-hybrid model with*

1. *a public-coin receiver and non-interactive unveil phase,*
2. *a commit phase of* $O(1)$ *rounds and the first message is sent by the committer,*
3. *a computational binding property and*
4. *a statistical trapdoor property.*

4   Analysis of the Committed-Value Oracle $\mathcal{O}_{\text{CCA}}$

In this section, we recall the PRS rewinding schedule from [19], presented in our setting. Moreover, we show that the committed-value oracle $\mathcal{O}_{\text{CCA}}$ from Theorem 1 satisfies composition-order invariance.

4.1   The Rewinding Schedule from [19]

In Fig. 1 below, we recall the rewinding schedule of [19], which itself is based on [27,30]. In [19], an adversary $\mathcal{A}$ interacting with an external party $\mathcal{B}$ and an (external) PRS receiver is considered. Thus, $\mathcal{A}$ can send messages to

– the PRS receiver, which offers rewinding slots,
– the external party $\mathcal{B}$, which is a barrier to rewinding.

As usual, we assume (for presentational simplicity) that PRS messages from (and to) $\mathcal{A}$ are of the form (Type, values). Thus, we have following message types, where m is the "actual" message. Firstly, messages which are irrelevant to the rewinding schedule:

– (Init, s): Initiate PRS session s.
– (Other, s, m): These are all other messages (to and from $\mathcal{A}$) which are not covered below (e.g. the commit phase step 1).

The messages related to the challenge-response phase/the slots, and message to the external party $\mathcal{B}$, are used in the rewinding schedule. These are the following:

– (Start, s, m): Start of challenge-response in PRS session s.[5] (Sent by $\mathcal{A}$.)
– (Chall$_i$, s, m): Challenge for i-th slot of PRS session s. (Sent by PRS oracle.)
– (Resp$_i$, s, m): Response to i-th slot of PRS session s. (Sent by $\mathcal{A}$.)
– (End, s, m): Extracted PRS session result. (Sent by PRS oracle.)
– (ExtSend$_i$, m): The i-th message from $\mathcal{A}$ to $\mathcal{B}$. (Sent by $\mathcal{A}$.)
– (ExtResp$_i$, m): The i-th response from $\mathcal{B}$ to $\mathcal{A}$. (Sent by PRS oracle.)

---

[5] Either m is the last message of the commit phase step 1. Or one lets (Other, s, m) finish that step and sets $m = \bot$ here. Either way, the message is a "start marker" initiating the first challenge. The choice does not affect the rewinding schedule.

We assume for simplicity that $\mathcal{A}$ is well-behaved, i.e. never sends unexpected or malformed messages, skips steps, etc. Moreover, we note (and will see) that the presence of a CRS does not affect the rewinding schedule of PRS extractor, which only depends on challenge slots.

We use the PRS preamble as defined in Construction 1. We ignore the messages $(\texttt{Init}, s)$ and $(\texttt{Other}, s, m)$ in the description, as they are simply handled "honestly" and do not affect the rewinding schedule in any way. Rewinds only happen to sample fresh challenges $(\texttt{Chall}_i, s, m)$ and gather (fresh) responses, while respecting external messages $(\texttt{ExtResp}_i, m)$ which cannot be rewound.

The **procedure** $\mathsf{recurse}(t, \mathsf{st}, \mathcal{T}, \mathsf{f}, \mathsf{aux}, \mathsf{id})$ is recursively defined with base case for step size $t = 1$. We assume w.l.o.g. that t is a power of 2.

Parameter Explanation. The rewinding schedule of [19], adapted to our notation, is given in Fig. 1. We first explain the arguments of $\mathsf{recurse}(t, \mathsf{st}, \mathcal{T}, \mathsf{f}, \mathsf{aux}, \mathsf{id})$: 1. t denotes the number of message (between $\mathcal{A}$ and left/right sides) which is handled by this recursive calls. Only the base case $t = 1$ actually handles messages. 2. st is the state of the adversary. 3. $\mathcal{T}$ denotes a "repository", a subset of (accepting) responses to challenges in slots which have been played in previous recursive calls. 4. f is a bit which identifies if the current recursive call contains the "main thread" of execution ($\mathsf{f} = 1$) or not ($\mathsf{f} = 0$). 5. id denotes the recursive call's identifier. The recursive calls form a 4-ary tree structure, where id pin-points the position of the recursion in that tree. This tree structure is the most relevant property of $\mathsf{recurse}$ for our analysis, see Remark 4. The initial call to $\mathsf{recurse}$ has the form $\mathsf{recurse}(t = 2^n, \mathsf{st} = state_{\mathcal{A},\text{initial}}, \mathcal{T} = \emptyset, \mathsf{f} = 1, aux = \emptyset, \mathsf{id} = \epsilon)$, where t^n is an upper bound on the number of messages $\mathcal{A}$ sends.

High-level Description. Due to space constraints, we focus on the recursive structure of the extraction, which is the most relevant part in our proofs. We refer to [27,30] for excellent introductions to this type of rewinding schedule, where [27] is very close to [19]. Following the naming of [19], we call a (recursive) call of $\mathsf{recurse}(\ldots, \mathsf{id})$ a *block* and id is the blocks identifier. A base case call is also called an *atomic block*. A *thread* is a sequence of atomic blocks which correspond to a continuous execution of $\mathcal{A}$ (i.e., the starting state of one block is the output state of the previous block). A block is called a *main block* if $\mathsf{f} = 1$.[6] The *main thread* is the thread of atomic blocks with $\mathsf{f} = 1$. All non-main blocks or threads are called *look-ahead*. Blocks and threads have a natural partial order, namely one identity being a prefix of the other, e.g., a block 11 containing 112.

A call $\mathsf{recurse}(t, \ldots)$ only continues for up to t messages which $\mathcal{A}$ sends. The structure of the rewinding schedule is to always handle $t/2$ the messages by two recursions which start at the same state. These are called *sibling calls* and the blocks are also *siblings*; they use the same $\mathcal{T}$, but aux may differ. The first call is always a look-ahead ($\mathsf{f} = 0$). The recursions have a repository $\mathcal{T}$ which contains information gathered by prior (look-ahead) recursions. These are used in $\mathsf{extract}$ to obtain the committed messages. (Recall that the committer's secret in the

---

[6] Note that f could be defined as a function of id, so this is well-defined.

Fig. 1. The rewinding schedule from [19].

Base case: **procedure** $\mathsf{recurse}(1, \mathsf{st}, \mathcal{T}, \mathsf{f}, \mathsf{aux}, \mathsf{id})$

1. If the next message is $(\mathtt{Start}, s, m)$, start a new session s:[a]
   - Send $(\mathtt{Chall}_1, s, r_1)$ for $r_1 \leftarrow \mathcal{C}$, where $\mathcal{C} = \{0,1\}^\kappa$.
   - Add $(s, 1, r_1, m)$ to $\mathcal{T}$.
2. If the next message is $(\mathtt{Resp}_i, s, m)$:
   - If the simulated PRS receiver in session s would abort (due to a failing check), abort session s and add $(s, i, \bot, \bot)$ to $\mathcal{T}$. Else continue.
   - If $i \in \{1, \ldots, \ell\}$
     • Add (s, i, r_i, m) to $\mathcal{T}$
     • If $i < \ell$: Send $(\mathtt{Chall}_i, s, r_i)$ for $r \leftarrow \mathcal{C}$.
     • If $i = \ell$: Send $(\mathtt{End}, s, \mathsf{extract}(s, \mathsf{id}, \mathcal{T}, \mathsf{aux}))$.
3. If the next message is $(\mathtt{ExtSend}_i, m)$:
   - If $\mathsf{f} = 0$, i.e. this is a *look-ahead* thread, **return** $(\mathsf{st}, \mathcal{T})$. (Early return.)
   - If $\mathsf{f} = 1$, i.e. this is the *main thread*, then:
     • For every live session $s \in \mathsf{LIVE}(\mathsf{id})$ do:[b]
       * Set $\times_{s, \mathsf{id}'} = 1$ for every block id' that contains id, including $\mathsf{id}' = \mathsf{id}$.
     • Send m to $\mathcal{B}$ and receive response m'. Forward $(\mathtt{ExtResp}_i, m')$ to $\mathcal{A}$.
4. If not early returned, update state st to current state of $\mathcal{A}$ and return $(\mathsf{st}, \mathcal{T})$.

Recursive case: **procedure** $\mathsf{recurse}(t, \mathsf{st}, \mathcal{T}, \mathsf{f}, \mathsf{aux}, \mathsf{id})$

// Rewind the first half twice:
1. $(\mathsf{st}_1, \mathcal{T}_1) \leftarrow \mathsf{recurse}(t/2, \mathsf{st}, \mathcal{T}, 0, \mathsf{aux}, \mathsf{id} \circ 1)$ (look-ahead block)
2. Let $\mathsf{aux}_2 = (\mathsf{aux}, \mathcal{T}_1 \setminus \mathcal{T})$
   $(\mathsf{st}_2, \mathcal{T}_2) \leftarrow \mathsf{recurse}(t/2, \mathsf{st}, \mathcal{T}, \mathsf{f}, \mathsf{aux}_2, \mathsf{id} \circ 2)$ (main block)
// Rewind the second half twice:
3. Let $\mathcal{T}^* = \mathcal{T}_1 \cup \mathcal{T}_2$
   $(\mathsf{st}_3, \mathcal{T}_3) \leftarrow \mathsf{recurse}(t/2, \mathsf{st}_2, \mathcal{T}^*, 0, \mathsf{aux}, \mathsf{id} \circ 3)$ (look-ahead block)
4. Let $\mathsf{aux}_4 = (\mathsf{aux}, \mathcal{T}_3 \setminus \mathcal{T}^*)$
   $(\mathsf{st}_4, \mathcal{T}_4) \leftarrow \mathsf{recurse}(t/2, \mathsf{st}_2, \mathcal{T}^*, \mathsf{f}, \mathsf{aux}_4, \mathsf{id} \circ 4)$ (main block)

Extraction: **procedure** $\mathsf{extract}(s, \mathsf{id}, \mathcal{T}, \mathsf{aux})$

1. Search in $\mathcal{T}$ for a pair of (s, i, r_i, m), (s, i, r_i', m') with $r_i' \neq r_i$. If found, extract that pair and return an extracted value.
2. If no such pair exists in $\mathcal{T}$, consider every block id_1 for which $\times_{s, \mathsf{id}_1} = 1$.
   - Let id_1' be the sibling[c] of id_1 with input/output tables $\mathcal{T}_{\mathsf{in}}, \mathcal{T}_{\mathsf{out}}$ respectively.
   - Attempt to extract (as before) from $\mathsf{aux}_{\mathsf{id}_1'} := \mathcal{T}_{\mathsf{in}} \setminus \mathcal{T}_{\mathsf{out}}$.
   - If all attempts fail, return $\mathtt{ExtFail}$, otherwise return the extracted value.

---

[a] W.l.o.g., assume that s uniquely identifies a session *among all threads*. This can be achieved by using (s, id) instead of s as the unique handle for a session. (For any id', there is a unique id, such that id and id' lie on the same thread and $((s, \mathsf{id}), 1, \cdot, \cdot) \in \mathcal{T}$; namely, id is the elementary block where session s started (on this thread). This disambiguates identifier s to (s, id) in all situations.)

[b] $\mathsf{LIVE}(\mathsf{id})$ denotes all initiated sessions s which are alive (i.e., not completed or aborted) at atomic block id.

[c] The sibling of a block/identity if the other block/identity in the paired calls, e.g. the sibling of $\mathsf{id} \circ 1$ is $\mathsf{id} \circ 2$ and vice versa.

PRS commitment is secret-shared. Once two different shares are unveiled, the committed message can be extracted.) For this overview, we ignore the influence of aux, which is required in the robustness proof of [19]. Overall, a quadratic number of base calls, and hence rewinds, is generated by this recursive procedure.

The base case recurse$(1, \ldots)$ handles a single message from $\mathcal{A}$, and effectively stores data about responses to challenges in $\mathcal{T}$ (Items 1 and 2). External messages are handled specially: If recurse is on a look-ahead thread, then execution stops— we must not query the left side during look-ahead as it cannot be rewound. On the main thread, the left side is queried and execution continues, but we remember that an external message arrived via $\times_{s,\text{id}}$, as this is needed in extract. For the sake of this overview, we ignore the details of extract, $\times_{s,\text{id}}$ and aux and refer to [19]. To establish COI, the high-level recursive structure and handling of external messages on the main thread suffices. The success analysis for recurse from [19] is used unchanged.

Lastly, the concurrent extraction algorithm $\mathcal{E}$ for PRS commitments is defined by running recurse for a given adversary $\mathcal{A}$ and left side $\mathcal{B}$. (Observe that recurse sends the extracted message to $\mathcal{A}$ when a commit phase completes, see Item 2.) We recall properties of the extraction from [19], in particular, bounds for the probability of extraction failure (ExtFail).

Remark 3 (Ambiguous Extraction). In extract$(s, \text{id}, \mathcal{T}, \text{aux})$, it can happen that multiple *distinct* values are be extracted, e.g. because the PRS preamble was inconsistent, and different values were shared in different slots or within a slot. We do not specify which value should be extracted in this case; any choice is fine.

Remark 4 ((Hierarchically) Structured Randomness). The procedure recurse is deterministic in all recursive calls, except the base calls. It will be helpful to assume that recurse interprets its randomness in a structured manner into disjoint/independent parts as follows:

- A tuple $(r_{\text{id}}^{\text{Chall}})_{\text{id}}$ which specifies challenge messages the for slot in atomic block id, i.e. base call ids (i.e. strings in $\{1, 2, 3, 4\}^{\log(t)}$).
- A tuple $(r_{\text{id}}^{\text{Other}})_{\text{id}}$ which specifies randomness for all other probabilistic computations, e.g. the receiver randomness used in base commitments in the PRS commit phase.

In particular, it is possible to *identify and fix the randomness of the main thread*, and thus all messages and challenges "sent" by recurse on the main thread. This separation of randomness into atomic blocks will be conceptually helpful later.

4.2   Composition-Order Invariance of $\mathcal{O}_{\text{CCA}}$

In this section, we prove the k-robust composition-order invariance of $\mathcal{O}_{\text{CCA}}$ from Theorem 1. For this, we consider an adversary $\mathcal{A}$ with access to $\mathcal{O}_{\text{CCA}}$ and an external protocol $\mathcal{B}$, so that the interaction $\langle \mathcal{B}, \mathcal{A} \rangle$ has at most k rounds.

Remark 5. The switch from $\mathcal{A}$ interacting with external $\mathcal{B}$ to $\langle \mathcal{B}, \mathcal{A} \rangle$ as a composed system effectively corresponds to making the previously external messages between $\mathcal{A}$ and $\mathcal{B}$ "internal", hence they are not visible to recurse anymore. For example, in a system composed of three machines and a pseudo-oracle $\mathcal{O}_{\mathsf{CCA}}$, we can compose the system in several ways:

- $\langle \mathcal{C}, \langle \mathcal{B}, \mathcal{A}^{\mathcal{O}_{\mathsf{CCA}}} \rangle \rangle$: Here, all messages from $\mathcal{A}$ and to $\mathcal{B}$ or $\mathcal{C}$ are external (for $\mathcal{O}_{\mathsf{CCA}}$), whereas $\mathcal{C}$ and $\mathcal{B}$ are the single external entity to $\mathcal{O}_{\mathsf{CCA}}$. Indeed, this is equivalent to $\langle \mathcal{C} \parallel \mathcal{B}, \mathcal{A}^{\mathcal{O}_{\mathsf{CCA}}} \rangle$.
- $\langle \mathcal{C}, \langle \mathcal{B}, \mathcal{A} \rangle^{\mathcal{O}_{\mathsf{CCA}}} \rangle$: Here, all messages from $\mathcal{A}$ or $\mathcal{B}$ (i.e., from the composed system $\langle \mathcal{B}, \mathcal{A} \rangle$) to $\mathcal{C}$ are external (for $\mathcal{O}_{\mathsf{CCA}}$).
- $\langle \mathcal{B}, \langle \mathcal{C}, \mathcal{A} \rangle^{\mathcal{O}_{\mathsf{CCA}}} \rangle$: Same as above, with roles of $\mathcal{B}$ and $\mathcal{C}$ swapped.
- $\langle \mathcal{B}, \langle \mathcal{C}, \mathcal{A} \rangle \rangle^{\mathcal{O}_{\mathsf{CCA}}}$: Here, there are no external messages. Indeed, this is equivalent to $(\mathcal{C} \parallel \mathcal{B} \parallel \mathcal{A})^{\mathcal{O}_{\mathsf{CCA}}}$.

Before analyzing $\mathcal{O}_{\mathsf{CCA}}$ from Theorem 1 further, note that it generates the setup and outputs the receiver's view $\mathsf{view}_{\mathsf{R}_s}$, unlike the PRS extractor. This does not affect security in any way. Indeed, setup generation is clearly not a problem. And, perhaps surprisingly, outputting the receiver's view also poses no problem in the security reduction.

Lemma 1. *Let $\mathcal{A}$, $\mathcal{B}$, $\mathcal{O}_{\mathsf{CCA}}$ as above and recall that $\langle \mathcal{B}, \mathcal{A} \rangle$ has at most k rounds. Suppose that COM' has a stateless receiver. Suppose $M = 2^m$ is an upper bound on the number of messages $\mathcal{A}$ sends to the PRS oracle or to $\mathcal{B}$. Let T be an upper bound of the number of sessions started by $\mathcal{A}$ on the main thread. Define the random variables*

- $\mathsf{out}_1(\kappa, x, y, z)$ *as* $\mathsf{out}_{\mathcal{B}, \mathcal{A}} \langle \mathcal{B}(x), \mathcal{A}^{\mathcal{O}_{\mathsf{CCA}}}(y) \rangle (1^\kappa, z)$, *and*
- $\mathsf{out}_2(\kappa, x, y, z)$ *as* $\mathsf{out}_{\mathcal{B}, \mathcal{A}} \langle \mathcal{B}(x), \mathcal{A}(y) \rangle^{\mathcal{O}_{\mathsf{CCA}}}(1^\kappa, z)$.

Then there exists an adversary $\mathcal{A}_{\mathsf{COM}'}$ against the binding property of COM' with expected[7] run-time bounded roughly by the (strict) runtime of extractor $\mathcal{E}^{\langle \mathcal{B}, \mathcal{A} \rangle}$. Concretely, if $\langle \mathcal{B}, \mathcal{A} \rangle$ has worst-case run-time S, then $\mathcal{E}^{\langle \mathcal{B}, \mathcal{A} \rangle}$ and $\mathcal{A}_{\mathsf{COM}'}$ has expected run-time bounded roughly by $2 \cdot M^2 S$. In particular, if $\mathcal{B}$ and $\mathcal{A}$ are PPT, then $\mathcal{A}_{\mathsf{COM}'}$ is expected polynomial time. For $\mathcal{A}_{\mathsf{COM}'}$, it holds that for all $\kappa \in \mathbb{N}$ and all $z \in \{0,1\}^*$:

$$\Delta(\mathsf{out}_1(\kappa, x, y, z), \mathsf{out}_2(\kappa, x, y, z)) \leq 2 \cdot (2^{-\ell + (k+2)\log(M)} + M^2/|\mathcal{C}|) + 2^{-\kappa}$$

$$+ \frac{1}{T \cdot \mathsf{poly}} \cdot \mathrm{Adv}^{\mathrm{bind}}_{\mathsf{COM}', \mathcal{A}_{\mathsf{COM}'}}(\kappa, z)$$

where $\mathsf{poly}(\kappa) = \mathsf{poly}_{\mathsf{AoK}}(\kappa) + \kappa \cdot \ell(\kappa)$ and $\mathsf{poly}_{\mathsf{AoK}}$ is a bound on the number of commitments made during in the AoK step and Δ denotes the statistical distance.

---

[7] Expected run-time stems from extraction of the AoK via rewinding. It can be traded for only one rewind, hence strict PPT, but with a quadratic loss in advantage.

The proof idea is straightforward: Whenever extract is called for a session which is *visible on the main thread* and thus part of the view, the extracted value must be the same for *both* $\Pi_1 = \langle \mathcal{B}, \mathcal{A}^{\mathcal{O}_{CCA}} \rangle$ and $\Pi_2 = \langle \mathcal{B}, \mathcal{A} \rangle^{\mathcal{O}_{CCA}}$. Indeed, running the extractor, i.e. recurse, with fixed randomness for $\mathcal{E}$, and $\mathcal{A}$ and $\mathcal{B}$ (and fixed inputs x, y) either the outputs of Π_1 and Π_2 are identical, or at some point, the result of an extraction, i.e. the output of $\mathcal{O}_{CCA}$, *on the main thread* must have been different. Since extraction succeeds with overwhelming probability (statistically), the only failure case is a break of the binding property of the base commitment or an inconsistent PRS commitment, which is a break of the AoK (which reduces to a binding break). Moreover, despite the different rewinding schedules, $\mathcal{O}_{CCA}$ (i.e. $\mathcal{E}$) sends the same challenges on the main thread. This is a simple consequence of the "disjoint partition of randomness" we postulated in Remark 4. The claim follows. When embedding the binding game on the main thread, one must simulate the receiver in look-ahead threads (in such a way that the PRS analysis still applies). This is where the *stateless receiver* property is used, as it ensures that anyone can continue the receiver's interactions. A more detailed proof is provided below.

Proof. Suppose w.l.o.g. that $\mathcal{A}$ resp. $\mathcal{B}$ are deterministic and fix inputs x resp. y. Draw and fix the random tape r for recurse and all other randomness of $\mathcal{O}_{CCA}$. Note that we assume (Remark 4) that the randomness r is of the form $r = (r_{id})_{id \in \{1,2,3,4\}^{\log(M)}}$ such that all atomic blocks use disjoint randomness. W.l.o.g., the rewinding sets $t = M$. Let $\Pi_1 = \langle \mathcal{B}, \mathcal{A}^{\mathcal{O}_{CCA}} \rangle$ and $\Pi_2 = \langle \mathcal{B}, \mathcal{A} \rangle^{\mathcal{O}_{CCA}}$, Since the extractor $\mathcal{E}$, i.e., recurse, is used to implement the PRS extraction in $\mathcal{O}_{CCA}$, we will talk about *threads* of Π_1 resp. Π_2 by an abuse of notation.

Now, compare the main thread on Π_1 and Π_2. Since randomness r for recurse is fixed and $\mathcal{A}$ and $\mathcal{B}$ assumed deterministic, we observe (by induction) that:

1. If all messages received by $\mathcal{A}$ or $\mathcal{B}$ in Π_1 resp. Π_2 on the main thread are identical, then the next message of $\mathcal{A}$ or $\mathcal{B}$ will again be identical.
2. Only $\mathcal{O}_{CCA}$ may send messages which are not identical in Π_1 and Π_2. We say that (the responses of $\mathcal{O}_{CCA}$ in) Π_1 and Π_2 *diverge*.

Thus, we will, in the following, view the execution of Π_1 and Π_2 in parallel and in lockstep on the main thread, until they diverge.

There are two possible cases for diverging responses on the main thread: For some session s, the AoK was accepting but

1. Extraction via recurse failed for one of Π_1 or Π_2 (but not both). Denote such an extraction failure event in Π_i by F_i for $i = 1, 2$. Clearly, the event by $F_1 \vee F_2$ is a superset of this case of divergence.
2. Extraction via recurse succeeds for both sessions, but extracted values are unequal, i.e. $v_1 \neq v_2$. Denote this event by $F_{\neq}$.

By the robust extraction lemma [19] and a union bound, the probability of an extraction failure for the run with Π_1 or Π_2 is at most

$$\Pr[F_1 \vee F_2] \leq 2 \cdot (2^{-\ell+(k+2)\log(M)} + M^2/|\mathcal{C}|).$$

In the following, we consider *modified* outputs out_1, out_2 which always output 0 if $F_1 \vee F_2$ occurred. (For this, they run both Π_1 and Π_2 with the same randomness.) The change in statistical distance is at most $\Pr[F_1 \vee F_2]$. Thus, from now on, we can ignore the failure case $F_1 \vee F_2$.

Next, we show following claim:

Claim 3. $\Pr[F_{\neq}] \leq 2^{-\kappa} + \frac{1}{\text{poly} \cdot T} \cdot \text{Adv}_{\text{COM}',\mathcal{A}_{\text{COM}'}}^{\text{bind}}(\kappa)$.

The lemma then immediately follows. To prove Claim 3, first denote by s^* the first session (on the main thread) where the divergence of Π_1 and Π_2 occurs. Consider the experiment G where after the occurrence of $F_{\neq}$, the corresponding AoK gets extracted, and if extraction is successful, let $(d_{i,j}'')_{i=1}^{\kappa}$ be the extracted decommitments in session s^* slot $j \in \{1, \ldots, \ell\}$. Note already here that, even though the extraction of the AoK uses rewinding, it will never rewind *before* the PRS commitment phase step 1 ended for session s^* (on the main thread).

Observe that $F_{\neq}$ implies that at least one of the following is true.

- If the AoK extraction fails, then for our concrete instantiation, either
  - no two different responses were found (during rewinding), which happens with negligible probability $2^{-\kappa}$.[8] Call this event F_{coll}.
  - or two different responses were found but they were inconsistent, i.e. the decommitments they had in common were not all to the same values. Thus, this yields a binding break.
- If AoK extraction succeeds, then at least one extracted decommitment $d_{i,j}''$ unveils to a different value than recurse extracted for Π_1 or Π_2. Again, this yields a binding break.

We let experiment G output 1 if one of the above happens, and 0 otherwise. Then, by definition, $\Pr[F_{\neq}] \leq \Pr[\text{out}_G = 1]$.

Now, we construct an adversary $\mathcal{A}_{\text{COM}'}$ against the binding property of COM', which essentially runs G. Note that $\mathcal{A}_{\text{COM}'}$ will have to rewind $\mathcal{A}$, but cannot rewind the embedded binding game, so this requires some care. Unsurprisingly, $\mathcal{A}_{\text{COM}'}$ runs Π_1 and Π_2 in lockstep, also simulating $\mathcal{B}$, and then embeds its binding challenge in a random instance of COM' on the main thread. It does so by passing the (external) messages for COM' from $\mathcal{A}$ to the game and returning the challenge receiver's responses. However, $\mathcal{A}_{\text{COM}'}$ must also play the receiver in look-ahead threads, where it cannot embed the binding game anymore. That is, $\mathcal{A}_{\text{COM}'}$ must procure responses for $\mathcal{A}$ whose distribution is identical to that of the receiver of COM' (with the same state as that in the "past" of the thread under consideration). For this, we exploit that COM' has *stateless receiver*: Thus, $\mathcal{A}_{\text{COM}'}$ can simply continue the execution of any COM' receiver. Observe, that since the randomness in all atomic blocks is independent (cf. Remark 4), the

---

[8] Resampling challenges uniformly with replacement, the probability of a collision is $1/n$ if there are n accepting challenges, and $n/2^{\kappa}$ is the probability that the verifier accepted the AoK (and extraction was started). Thus $\max_{n=1}^{2^{\kappa}} 2^{-\kappa} n/n = 2^{-\kappa}$ is an upper bound on failure.

embedding of the COM' challenger in the main thread and computing the state-less receiver responses in look-ahead threads does not affect the distribution (in fact, it is possible to map random tapes from one execution to the other and vice versa). Thus, the probability for $F_{\neq}$ is unchanged. In full, $\mathcal{A}_{\mathsf{COM}'}$ works as follows:

- Pick a random commitment index t^* on the main thread. That is, pick a random session $s^* \leftarrow \{1, \ldots, T\}$ and index $i^* \overset{\$}{\leftarrow} \{1, \ldots, \mathsf{poly}(\kappa)\}$, where $\mathsf{poly}(\kappa) = \mathsf{poly}_{\mathsf{AoK}}(\kappa) + \kappa \cdot \ell(\kappa)$ is an upper bound for the number of COM' commitments in a PRS commitment phase (i.e. both in step 1 and the AoK).
- Run Π_1 and Π_2 in parallel and synchronized on the main thread.
- If $F_{\neq}$ occurs before session s^*, output $\perp$ to the challenger.[9]
- Emulate the rest of the extractor/rewinding schedule essentially unchanged.
- Embed the binding challenge in session s^* and commitment with index i^*.
- After session s^*, extract the AoK (via rewinding) and output a potential binding break for commitment i^* to the challenger, or $\perp$ if none occurred or extraction of the AoK failed. Observe that:
  • The rewinding-based AoK extraction occurs strictly *after* the embedded challenge commitment completed, hence $\mathcal{A}_{\mathsf{COM}'}$ never attempts to rewinding the challenger.
  • The reduction $\mathcal{A}_{\mathsf{COM}'}$ never provides $(\mathsf{End}, s^*, v_{s^*}, \mathsf{view}_{\mathsf{R}_{s^*}})$ to $\mathcal{A}$. Indeed, it could not provide $\mathsf{view}_{\mathsf{R}_{s^*}}$, since in general, $\mathsf{view}_{\mathsf{R}_{s^*}}$ is only known to the binding challenger.

Overall, this yields our adversary $\mathcal{A}_{\mathsf{COM}'}$ against the binding game with the claimed advantage. In more detail: Let B be the event that a binding break is found on the main thread when the AoK for the first diverging session s^* is extracted. We find that

$$\Pr[F_{\neq}] \leq \Pr[F_{\mathsf{coll}}] + \Pr[B] \leq 2^{-\kappa} + \frac{1}{\mathsf{poly} \cdot T} \cdot \mathsf{Adv}^{\mathsf{bind}}_{\mathsf{COM}', \mathcal{A}_{\mathsf{COM}'}}(\kappa).$$

Putting everything together, we find that for all $\kappa \in \mathbb{N}$ and all $z \in \{0,1\}^*$, it holds that

$$\Delta(\mathsf{out}_1(\kappa, x, y, z), \mathsf{out}_2(\kappa, x, y, z)) \leq \Pr[F_1 \vee F_2 \vee F_{\mathsf{coll}} \vee B]$$
$$\leq 2 \cdot (2^{-\ell + (k+2)\log(M)} + M^2/|\mathcal{C}|) + 2^{-\kappa}$$
$$+ \frac{1}{\mathsf{poly} \cdot T} \cdot \mathsf{Adv}^{\mathsf{bind}}_{\mathsf{COM}', \mathcal{A}_{\mathsf{COM}'}}(\kappa, z)$$

This proves the claimed advantage of $\mathcal{A}_{\mathsf{COM}'}$.

Lastly, observe that if $\mathcal{B}$ and $\mathcal{A}$ are PPT, then Π_1 and Π_2 are (overall) PPT algorithms, since $\mathcal{O}_{\mathsf{CCA}}$ is k-robust pseudo-PPT. Since $\mathcal{A}_{\mathsf{COM}'}$ essentially runs Π_1 and Π_2 (with minor modifications for embedding its challenge), it is clear that $\mathcal{A}_{\mathsf{COM}'}$ is PPT until the point the AoK extraction starts. (Indeed, $\mathcal{A}_{\mathsf{COM}'}$ makes at

---

[9] If $F_1 \vee F_2$ occurs before $F_{\neq}$, the modified experiment immediately outputs 0, so $F_{\neq}$ will not occur and this case is irrelevant.

most about M^2S steps up to this point.) By the usual argument, in expectation only 1 rewind happens for AoK extraction. (If p is the probability that an AoK challenge is answered acceptingly, then p^{-1} is the expected number of rewinds to obtain another accepting transcript, hence $(1 - p) \cdot 0 + p \cdot p^{-1} = 1$ rewinds in expectation.) Thus, in expectation, $\mathcal{A}_{\mathsf{COM}'}$ makes at most about $2M^2S$ steps, as claimed.   □

5   Framework and Notion

In order to circumvent the impossibility results of Long-Term Security [24], we modify the UC execution such that rewinding-based extraction of statistically hiding commitment schemes is possible in a way that preserves universal composability. To this end, we take a route similar to [10,31] and provide environment and adversary with an entity called the *helper* $\mathcal{H}$. This *efficient* helper is parameterized with an extractable commitment scheme COM and allows the rewinding-based extraction of instances of COM where the commitment is performed with $\mathcal{H}$ as receiver.

Formally, our notion is cast in the GUC framework [8][10], allowing both the use of the helper $\mathcal{H}$ as well as other global ideal functionalities. We assume that the reader is familiar with the basic concepts of (G)UC security. Due to space constraints, this chapter is a short version only. For the full treatment of framework and notion, see the full version [5].

Extracting (Statistically Hiding) Commitments. $\mathcal{H}$ provides an oracle that allows the extraction of commitments (cf. Sect. 3.2), similar to a CCA oracle. This part is analogous to the helper of [10], with the following differences: The helper of [10] is able to extract statistically binding commitments by inefficient computations. In contrast, we want to consider commitments that are statistically hiding. Such commitments cannot be extracted by brute force, but require different techniques such as an appropriate setup allowing for straight-line extraction (see [24] for an example) or rewinding. More specifically, we adapt the rewinding-based extraction techniques of [19] to our setting, via pseudo-oracles and a suitably adapted analysis in Sects. 3 and 4. We provide the helper with the views of all ITIs that may be affected by a performed rewinding.

While we do not (intend to) achieve composability in the plain model, the resulting security notion has properties and limitations similar to Angel-based security [31] or UC with super-polynomial helpers [10], e.g. with respect to protocol reusability.

As we will later use commitment schemes in the $\mathcal{F}_{\mathsf{CRS}}$-hybrid model, we have adapted the helper accordingly. When a corrupted party starts a new commitment session with $\mathcal{H}$, the committed-value oracle $\mathcal{O}_{\mathsf{CCA}}$ within $\mathcal{H}$ honestly

---

[10] Even though the original work [8] has been superseded by [2], we continue to use the conventions of [8]. We discuss the reasons for this decisions as well as the issues raised (and fixed) in [2] in the full version [5].

executes the CRS generation algorithm of the desired commitment scheme and $\mathcal{H}$ returns the resulting CRS ck to the party initiating the session.

As the commitment key is generated honestly, it is guaranteed to be independent from all other commitment keys. Thus, a corrupted party cannot take a key ck' from another session (e.g. where the sender is honest) and have $\mathcal{H}$ extract commitments relative to ck. A similar policy is enforced in [10] by the use of tags, which we omit as they are not necessary (with different sessions distinguished by their commitment key).

To establish meaningful properties, we require the commitment scheme to feature a committed-value oracle which is *black-box* (Definition 4) and *k-robust composition-order invariant and pseudo-PPT* (Definitions 5 and 6). This allows to a) import protocols with appropriate round complexity into our framework without loss of security due to the committed-value oracle and b) prove the security of protocols within our framework by reducing to security properties with a certain (bounded) round complexity. The robustness property guarantees that we can efficiently simulate the committed-value oracle without having to rewind the challenger in a reduction. In the following, we only consider helpers with pseudo-oracles that have appropriate properties and are, in particular, black-box.

The helper $\mathcal{H}$ is formally defined in Definition 9.

Definition 9 (The Helper $\mathcal{H}$). $\mathcal{H}$ *is parameterized with 1. a security parameter $\kappa \in \mathbb{N}$, 2. auxiliary input z and 3. a commitment scheme* COM *with committed-value (pseudo-)oracle* $\mathcal{O}_{\mathsf{CCA}}$.

- *On input* (corrupt, P_i, sid) *from the environment, record* (corrupt, P_i, sid).
- *On input* (ext-init, P_i, sid, k) *from a corrupted party P_i in the protocol with SID sid: If there is a recorded session (P_i, sid, k), ignore this message. Otherwise, initialize the k-th sub-session of (P_i, sid) with $\mathcal{O}_{\mathsf{CCA}}$ and receive a setup* ck. *Record session (P_i, sid, k) and return* (setup, sid, k, ck) *to P_i.*
- *Upon receiving a message* (ext-mesg, P_i, sid, k, m) *from a corrupted party P_i in the protocol with SID sid: If there is no recorded session (P_i, sid, k), ignore the message. Otherwise, give input (sid, k, m) to $\mathcal{O}_{\mathsf{CCA}}$, possibly obtain a reply m'. If m' is a special message* (End, s, w_s, $\mathrm{view}_{\mathsf{R}_s}$), *return* (ext-val, P_i, sid, k, w_s) *to P_i. Otherwise, return* (ext-mesg, P_i, sid, k, m') *to P_i.*

To allow the helper to perform the rewinding-based extraction, it needs to be provided with the views of the entities to be rewound. This requires slight changes to the framework, which can be found in the full version [5]. Knowledge of these changes is not necessary to understand the following. We call the framework resulting from this modification the *UC Security with Rewinding framework*.

5.1 Protocol Emulation

Before stating long-term protocol emulation, we provide the standard notion of computational protocol emulation adapted to our setting.

Definition 10 (UC Security with Rewinding Protocol Emulation). *Let π and ϕ be PPT protocols and let $\mathcal{H}$ be the helper of Definition 9. We say that π Rewinding-UC-emulates ϕ if for all PPT adversaries $\mathcal{A}$, there exists a PPT simulator $\mathcal{S}$ such that for all $\mathcal{H}$-aided[11] balanced[12] PPT environments $\mathcal{Z}$, there exists a negligible function negl such that for all $\kappa \in \mathbb{N}, z \in \{0,1\}^*$ it holds that*

$$| \Pr[\mathsf{Exec}(\pi, \mathcal{A}, \mathcal{Z})(\kappa, z) = 1] - \Pr[\mathsf{Exec}(\phi, \mathcal{S}, \mathcal{Z})(\kappa, z) = 1]| \le \mathsf{negl}(\kappa)$$

If π Rewinding-UC-emulates ϕ, we write $\pi \ge_R \phi$.

We adapt the notion of long-term protocol emulation in our framework in analogy to the established definition due to [24]. In contrast to standard UC emulation, long-term emulation lets the environment output an arbitrary string of polynomial length and requires statistical indistinguishability of the resulting ensembles. Intuitively, this means that all (even non-polynomial-time) hardness assumptions become invalid after the protocol execution has finished.

To this end, let ExecLT denote the random variable that is identically defined to Exec, except that $\mathcal{Z}$ outputs an arbitrary (polynomial-size) string.

Definition 11 (Long-term UC Protocol Emulation). *Let π and ϕ be PPT protocols and let $\mathcal{H}$ be the helper of Definition 9. We say that π long-term-Rewinding-UC-emulates ϕ if for all PPT adversaries $\mathcal{A}$, there exists a PPT simulator $\mathcal{S}$ such that for all $\mathcal{H}$-aided balanced PPT environments $\mathcal{Z}$, the ensembles $\{\mathsf{ExecLT}(\pi, \mathcal{A}, \mathcal{Z})(\kappa, z)\}_{\kappa \in \mathbb{N}, z \in \{0,1\}^*}$ and $\{\mathsf{ExecLT}(\phi, \mathcal{S}, \mathcal{Z})(\kappa, z)\}_{\kappa \in \mathbb{N}, z \in \{0,1\}^*}$ are statistically indistinguishable.*

If π long-term-Rewinding-UC-emulates ϕ, we write $\pi \ge_R^{lt} \phi$. If π long-term-Rewinding-UC-emulates the ideal protocol of a functionality $\mathcal{F}$, then we say that π long-term-Rewinding-UC-realizes $\mathcal{F}$.

Remark 6. In contrast to the definition of long-term security in [24], the environment of Definition 11 has access to the helper $\mathcal{H}$, which provides a committed-value oracle that does not exist in the original definition.

5.2 Properties

We now discuss the properties of our notion, which are mostly similar to the properties of long-term security and UC security with super-polynomial helpers. In particular, the dummy adversary is complete and both notions of protocol

---

[11] We restate the definition of $\mathcal{H}$-aided environments due to [12]: a) $\mathcal{Z}$ invokes a single instance of $\mathcal{H}$ immediately after invoking the adversary. b) As soon as a party (i.e. an ITI) P is corrupted (i.e. P receives a `corrupted` message), $\mathcal{Z}$ lets $\mathcal{H}$ know of this fact. $\mathcal{H}$ interacts only with the environment, the adversary, and the corrupted parties.

[12] Informally, an environment is *balanced* if it admits a runtime budget to the adversary that is, at any point, at least the sum of the runtime budgets of all other machines. The notion of probabilistic polynomial-time in distributed UC-like systems is of no concern in this paper and we refer the interested reader to [7] for a formal definition.

emulation are transitive. Like UC security with super-polynomial helpers [10] and long-term security [24]), our notion is closed under general concurrent (i.e. universal) composition.

Theorem 2 (Composition Theorem). *Let* ρ, π, ϕ *be PPT protocols where* π *and* ϕ *are subroutine-respecting. If* π *(long-term-) Rewinding-UC-emulates* ϕ *and the pseudo-oracle of* $\mathcal{H}$ *is black-box, then,* $\rho^{\phi \to \pi}$ *(long-term-) Rewinding-UC-emulates* ρ.

For a proof sketch, see the full version [5].

UC Compatibility. When introducing a new security notion that features modular design, a natural question to ask is which existing protocols (that are secure according some other notion) can be reused.

Let π and ϕ be PPT protocols such that $\pi \geq_{\mathrm{UC}} \phi$. Due to the helper $\mathcal{H}$, just as in [10,31], we cannot hope that we can import an arbitrary UC protocol π securely, i.e. that $\pi \geq_{\mathrm{UC}} \phi$ implies that $\pi \geq_{\mathrm{R}} \phi$. This is because a Rewinding UC environment is more powerful than a normal UC environment due to the access to $\mathcal{H}$: The committed-value oracle of $\mathcal{H}$ could invalidate assumptions made in the security proof.

Nevertheless, we can show the compatibility with UC security for large classes of protocols, namely those that have less than or equal to k rounds if the committed-value (pseudo-)oracle provided by $\mathcal{H}$ is black-box (Definition 4) k-robust composition-order invariant (Definition 5) and k-robust pseudo-PPT (Definition 6). This criterion essentially is the same as in [10], except for the additional requirements for the (pseudo-)oracle.

Theorem 3 (UC Compatibility). *Let* $\mathcal{H}$ *be the helper that is parameterized with a commitment scheme* COM *that features an* $O(k)$-*robust black-box composition-order invariant pseudo-PPT committed-value (pseudo-)oracle* $\mathcal{O}_{\mathrm{CCA}}$, *where* $k \in O(\mathrm{poly}(\kappa))$. *Let* ϕ *be a subroutine-respecting PPT protocol and let* π *be a subroutine-respecting PPT protocol with up to* k *rounds such that*

- $\pi \geq_{\mathrm{stat\text{-}UC}} \phi$. *Then,* $\pi \geq_{\mathrm{R}}^{\mathrm{lt}} \phi$.
- $\pi \geq_{\mathrm{ltUC}} \phi$. *Then,* $\pi \geq_{\mathrm{R}}^{\mathrm{lt}} \phi$.
- $\pi \geq_{\mathrm{UC}} \phi$. *Then,* $\pi \geq_{\mathrm{R}} \phi$.

Here, $\geq_{\mathrm{stat\text{-}UC}}$ *denotes statistical UC emulation,* $\geq_{\mathrm{ltUC}}$ *denotes long-term emulation and* $\geq_{\mathrm{UC}}$ *denotes standard UC emulation.*

For the proof, see the full version [5]. Of course, compatibility is not limited to the cases mentioned in Theorem 3 and its variants. However, manual proofs may be necessary.

Meaningfulness. Just like the angel in [31] or the helper in [10], our helper may negatively affect the security guarantees provided by ideal functionalities. To illustrate this, consider a variant $\mathcal{F}'_{\mathrm{COM}}$ of the ideal functionality for commitments $\mathcal{F}_{\mathrm{COM}}$, which we extend to accept a CRS from the adversary. When the honest committer provides its input v, $\mathcal{F}'_{\text{COM}}$ first checks if the CRS is a valid CRS for the statistically hiding commitment scheme COM of $\mathcal{H}^{13}$. Then, it performs the commit phase with the adversary, acting as an honest committer with input v.

In the presence of $\mathcal{H}$, $\mathcal{F}'_{\text{COM}}$ provides no meaningful security for an honest committer. The adversary simply can start a new session with the committed-value oracle provided by $\mathcal{H}$, receiving a valid CRS which it provides to $\mathcal{F}'_{\text{COM}}$. Then, it can forward all commitment-related messages between $\mathcal{H}$ and $\mathcal{F}'_{\text{COM}}$. In the end, the adversary will learn v, i.e. the value committed to by the honest committer, from $\mathcal{H}$. (The argument for [10,31] is analogous.)

Thus, (long-term) Rewinding UC security only guarantees meaningful security for ideal functionalities with at most k rounds if $\mathcal{O}_{\text{CCA}}$ (in $\mathcal{H}$) is black-box, $O(k)$-robust pseudo-PPT and $O(k)$-robust composition-order invariant. Note that very similar limitations with respect to the meaningfulness apply to e.g. [10,31].

Justification. We now discuss under which circumstances our notion implies existing security notions for (composable) multi-party computation. This is helpful to grasp the (intuitive) security guarantees of (long-term) Rewinding UC security. First, we show that Rewinding UC security implies UC security for a large class of protocols.

Proposition 2 (Justification: UC Security). *Let π, ϕ be PPT protocols such that $\pi \geq_{\text{R}} \phi$ (resp. $\pi \geq_{\text{R}}^{\text{lt}} \phi$), let the pseudo-oracle of $\mathcal{H}$ be black-box and let the simulator never interact with $\mathcal{H}$ on the committed-value oracle for the challenge session. Then, $\pi \geq_{\text{UC}} \phi$ (resp. $\pi \geq_{\text{ltUC}} \phi$).*

For the proof, the full version [5]. For the case of ideal functionalities that can be expressed by stand-alone real-ideal security (see e.g. [16]), the following holds regardless of the simulator using the committed-value oracle of $\mathcal{H}$.

Proposition 3 (Justification: Stand-Alone Security for SFE). *Let $\mathcal{H}$ be a helper with a committed-value oracle that is black-box and $O(1)$-robust composition-order invariant and pseudo-PPT. Let π be a N-party PPT protocol in the $\mathcal{F}_{\text{CRS}}$-hybrid model such that π (long-term-) Rewinding-UC-realizes $\mathcal{F}_{\text{SFE}}$ (with $\mathcal{H}$) for some function $f : (\{0,1\}^\kappa)^N \times \{0,1\}^{\text{poly}(\kappa)} \to (\{0,1\}^\kappa)^N$. Then, π securely computes f with abort in the presence of static malicious adversaries.*

In particular, Proposition 3 captures the stand-alone real-ideal security of e.g. zero-knowledge proof systems. The restriction to protocols in the $\mathcal{F}_{\text{CRS}}$-hybrid model can be relaxed to other hybrid functionalities that can be expressed by stand-alone real-ideal security.

---

[13] Here, we assume that a CRS that leads to a statistically hiding commitment scheme is efficiently recognizable.

We omit the proof of Proposition 3, but note that that the distinguisher in the real-ideal security notion is not provided with a committed-value oracle (corresponding to an Rewinding UC environment that never queries the committed-value oracle of $\mathcal{H}$). Thus, the (PPT) simulator may only need to extract commitments for its own simulation, which it can do efficiently via rewinding, regardless of the number of rounds of π.

Environmental Friendliness. Similar to [10], our notion partially fulfills the notion of environmental friendliness [11]. Suppose that the committed-value oracle of $\mathcal{H}$ is $O(k)$-robust pseudo-PPT and $O(k)$-robust composition-order invariant and that a PPT protocol π (long-term-) Rewinding-UC-realizes an ideal functionality $\mathcal{G}$. Then, we can show that for every k-round game-based property of a protocol that is executed concurrently (outside the Rewinding UC execution), the protocol π does not affect this game-based property if it is not already affected by $\mathcal{G}$ (in an execution *without* $\mathcal{H}$). For details, the full version [5].

Impossibility Results. While the addition of the helper $\mathcal{H}$, which allows the extraction of statistically hiding commitments, suffices to "circumvent" the impossibility results of [24], our setting still faces an important impossibility result for *long-term* Rewinding UC security, namely the impossibility of long-term-Rewinding-UC-secure general two-party computation.

Theorem 4 (Impossibility of Oblivious Transfer). *Let $\mathcal{F}$ be a functionality that is long-term revealing for any party. Then, there is no bilateral[14] nontrivial PPT protocol π_{OT} that long-term-Rewinding-UC-realizes $\mathcal{F}_{OT}$ in the $\mathcal{F}$-hybrid model (assuming ideally authenticated communication).*

Theorem 4 is a direct consequence of the folklore impossibility result of *correct* statistically secure oblivious transfer in the plain model (even with passive security only). For the proof, see the full version [5].

6 Long-Term-Secure Composable Commitment Scheme

In this chapter, we present the construction of our long-term-secure commitment scheme π_{COM}. In Sect. 3, we constructed a commitment scheme CCACOM that is both CCA-binding (Definition 7) and trapdoor (Definition 8). The equivocation is performed by embedding a (statistically hidden) trapdoor into the CRS. In contrast, the extraction is performed using rewinding. For the committed-value oracle $\mathcal{O}_{CCA}$, we have been able to establish several important properties such as the *black-box* property (Definition 4) and *k-robust composition-order invariant and pseudo-PPT* (Definitions 5 and 6). In Sect. 5, we embedded the committed-value (pseudo-)oracle $\mathcal{O}_{CCA}$ into a UC-like execution through the helper $\mathcal{H}$.

---

[14] We recall the definition of a bilateral protocol [9]: "[A] protocol π between n parties $P_1, \ldots, P_n$ is *bilateral* if all except two parties stay idle and do not transmit messages."

Thus, the construction is straight-forward: π_{COM} merely wraps an instance of CCACOM, inheriting its properties. In particular, the equivocation by the simulator is done by choosing an appropriate CRS, while the extraction is performed via the helper.

Even though the construction is simple, the proof needs to carefully deal with the pseudo-oracle $\mathcal{O}_{\text{CCA}}$, which is part of the helper. In order for the reductions to properties of CCACOM to go through, we will make heavy use of the aforementioned properties of $\mathcal{O}_{\text{CCA}}$.

Construction 3 (Protocol π_{COM}). *Parameterized by a security parameter κ and a commitment scheme COM with non-interactive unveil phase.*

- *On input* (commit, sid, v) *for C:*
  C and R execute COM with SID ($sid\|$COM) *and input v for the committer. Let d denote the unveil information. If the sub-party of the receiver in COM accepts, R outputs* (committed, sid). *Subsequent* commit *inputs are ignored.*
- *On input* (unveil, sid) *for C:*
  1. *C sends* (unveil, sid, v, d) *to R.*
  2. *R outputs* (unveil, sid, v) *if the commitment opens to v using unveil information d. Otherwise, it halts without output.*

We can now state our main theorem. In the following, we always assume that the protocol under consideration, helper and ideal functionality are consistent, i.e. parameterized with the same commitment scheme COM. The proof of following theorem is in the full version [5].

Theorem 5. *Let $\mathcal{O}_{\text{CCA}}$ be a black-box committed-value pseudo-oracle for the commitment scheme COM. If COM is a CCA-binding and trapdoor commitment scheme w.r.t. $\mathcal{O}_{\text{CCA}}$ and has an appropriate message space, then π_{COM} long-term-Rewinding-UC-realizes $\mathcal{F}_{\text{COM}}$.*

7   Applications

We present several applications of our composable long-term-secure commitment scheme. For a full treatment, see the full version [5].

7.1   Zero-Knowledge and Commit-and-Prove

By plugging our long-term-secure commitment scheme into an appropriate zero-knowledge proof system with statistical UC security in the $\mathcal{F}_{\text{COM}}$-hybrid model (e.g. [9]), we can long-term-Rewinding-UC-realize $\mathcal{F}_{\text{ZK}}$. The resulting protocol thus features composable statistical zero-knowledge and knowledge soundness against computationally bounded provers.

Using a similar approach, we obtain a protocol that long-term-Rewinding-UC-realizes the ideal functionality $\mathcal{F}_{\text{CP}}$ for commit-and-prove for a bounded number of proofs per instance.

7.2 Two-Party Computation with Long-Term Security for One Party

Even given a commitment scheme that is long-term-Rewinding-UC-secure, we cannot hope to achieve long-term secure oblivious transfer from long-term-revealing setups (cf. Theorem 4), which also rules out general secure two-party computation with long-term security for both parties.

By combining $\mathcal{F}_{CP}$ with an appropriate oblivious transfer (OT) protocol that provides statistical security for *one* party, e.g. the dual-mode construction of [29], we obtain a protocol for composable OT where one party is protected with long-term security. Using a very similar approach, we can construct protocols for composable general two-party computation where one party enjoys long-term security. Unfortunately, meaningfully defining security in such a setting is not straight-forward: The simulation of an (honest) party that is only given computational security must depend on this party's secrets, which are (not even indirectly) available for the simulator.

For the constructions and further discussions, see the full version [5].

8   Conclusion

Previous constructions for protocols with composable long-term security required hardware-based setups, often making them impractical due to the necessary distribution of the setup. In particular, natural setups such as common reference strings were shown to be insufficient to achieve long-term security.

We circumvent this impossibility result by enabling a rewinding-based extraction through the introduction of pseudo-oracles. Towards this, we faced and solved many technical hurdles to construct a robust, extractable, and well-behaved CCA-secure commitment scheme. With rewinding-based extraction at hand, we are the first to construct a statistically hiding and composable long-term-secure commitment scheme from standard polynomial-time hardness assumptions solely in the $\mathcal{F}_{CRS}$-hybrid model, i.e. without the use of hardware assumptions.

We give several applications of our commitment scheme, including composable oblivious transfer with long-term security for *one* party in the $\mathcal{F}_{CRS}$-hybrid model and showed how this approach can be extended to general two-party computation with similar guarantees. Due to impossibility results within our security notion, this is the best security one can hope for, unless stronger setups are used.

Acknowledgements. This work has been supported by KASTEL Security Research Labs. Astrid Ottenhues: This work has been supported by funding from the German Federal Ministry of Education and Research (BMBF) under the projects "PQC4MED" (ID 16KIS1044) and "Sec4IoMT" (ID 16KIS1692). Michael Klooß, Jeremias Mechler, Jörn Müller-Quade, Markus Raiber: This work has been supported by funding from the topic Engineering Secure Systems of the Helmholtz Association (HGF). Michael Klooß: This work has been supported by Helsinki Institute for Information Technology HIIT. We thank the reviewers for helpful editorial feedback.

References

1. Asharov, G., Lindell, Y.: A full proof of the BGW protocol for perfectly secure multiparty computation. J. Cryptol. **30**(1), 58–151 (2015). https://doi.org/10.1007/s00145-015-9214-4

2. Badertscher, C., Canetti, R., Hesse, J., Tackmann, B., Zikas, V.: Universal composition with global subroutines: capturing global setup within plain UC. In: Pass, R., Pietrzak, K. (eds.) TCC 2020, Part III. LNCS, vol. 12552, pp. 1–30. Springer, Heidelberg (Nov 2020). https://doi.org/10.1007/978-3-030-64381-2_1

3. Beaver, D.: Commodity-based cryptography (extended abstract). In: 29th ACM STOC, pp. 446–455. ACM Press (May 1997). https://doi.org/10.1145/258533.258637

4. Ben-Or, M., Goldwasser, S., Wigderson, A.: Completeness theorems for non-cryptographic fault-tolerant distributed computation (extended abstract). In: 20th ACM STOC, pp. 1–10. ACM Press (May 1988). https://doi.org/10.1145/62212.62213

5. Berger, R., et al.: Composable long-term security with rewinding. Cryptology ePrint Archive, Report 2023/363 (2023). https://eprint.iacr.org/2023/363

6. Canetti, R.: Universally composable security: a new paradigm for cryptographic protocols. In: 42nd FOCS, pp. 136–145. IEEE Computer Society Press (Oct 2001). https://doi.org/10.1109/SFCS.2001.959888

7. Canetti, R.: Universally composable security. J. ACM **67**(5), 28:1–28:94 (2020). https://doi.org/10.1145/3402457

8. Canetti, R., Dodis, Y., Pass, R., Walfish, S.: Universally composable security with global setup. In: Vadhan, S.P. (ed.) TCC 2007. LNCS, vol. 4392, pp. 61–85. Springer, Heidelberg (Feb 2007). https://doi.org/10.1007/978-3-540-70936-7_4

9. Canetti, R., Fischlin, M.: Universally composable commitments. In: Kilian, J. (ed.) CRYPTO 2001. LNCS, vol. 2139, pp. 19–40. Springer, Heidelberg (Aug 2001). https://doi.org/10.1007/3-540-44647-8_2

10. Canetti, R., Lin, H., Pass, R.: Adaptive hardness and composable security in the plain model from standard assumptions. In: 51st FOCS, pp. 541–550. IEEE Computer Society Press (Oct 2010). https://doi.org/10.1109/FOCS.2010.86

11. Canetti, R., Lin, H., Pass, R.: From unprovability to environmentally friendly protocols. In: 54th FOCS, pp. 70–79. IEEE Computer Society Press (Oct 2013). https://doi.org/10.1109/FOCS.2013.16

12. Canetti, R., Lin, H., Pass, R.: Adaptive hardness and composable security in the plain model from standard assumptions. SIAM J. Comput. **45**(5), 1793–1834 (2016). https://doi.org/10.1137/110847196

13. Canetti, R., Lindell, Y., Ostrovsky, R., Sahai, A.: Universally composable two-party and multi-party secure computation. In: 34th ACM STOC, pp. 494–503. ACM Press (May 2002). https://doi.org/10.1145/509907.509980

14. Damgård, I., Nielsen, J.B.: Perfect hiding and perfect binding universally composable commitment schemes with constant expansion factor. In: Yung, M. (ed.) CRYPTO 2002, LNCS, vol. 2442, pp. 581–596. Springer, Heidelberg (Aug 2002). https://doi.org/10.1007/3-540-45708-9_37

15. Döttling, N., Kraschewski, D., Müller-Quade, J.: Unconditional and composable security using a single stateful tamper-proof hardware token. In: Ishai, Y. (ed.) TCC 2011. LNCS, vol. 6597, pp. 164–181. Springer, Heidelberg (Mar 2011). https://doi.org/10.1007/978-3-642-19571-6_11

16. Goldreich, O.: Foundations of Cryptography: Basic Applications, vol. 2. Cambridge University Press, Cambridge (2004)
17. Goldreich, O., Krawczyk, H.: On the composition of zero-knowledge proof systems. In: Paterson, M.S. (ed.) ICALP 1990. LNCS, vol. 443, pp. 268–282. Springer, Heidelberg (1990). https://doi.org/10.1007/BFb0032038
18. Gorbunov, S., Vaikuntanathan, V., Wichs, D.: Leveled fully homomorphic signatures from standard lattices. In: Servedio, R.A., Rubinfeld, R. (eds.) 47th ACM STOC, pp. 469–477. ACM Press (Jun 2015). https://doi.org/10.1145/2746539.2746576
19. Goyal, V., Lin, H., Pandey, O., Pass, R., Sahai, A.: Round-efficient concurrently composable secure computation via a robust extraction lemma. In: Dodis, Y., Nielsen, J.B. (eds.) TCC 2015, Part I. LNCS, vol. 9014, pp. 260–289. Springer, Heidelberg (Mar 2015). https://doi.org/10.1007/978-3-662-46494-6_12
20. Hohenberger, S., Waters, B.: Short and stateless signatures from the RSA assumption. In: Halevi, S. (ed.) CRYPTO 2009. LNCS, vol. 5677, pp. 654–670. Springer, Heidelberg (Aug 2009). https://doi.org/10.1007/978-3-642-03356-8_38
21. Kiyoshima, S.: Statistical concurrent non-Malleable zero-knowledge from one-way functions. J. Cryptol. **33**(3), 1318–1361 (2020). https://doi.org/10.1007/s00145-020-09348-x
22. Magri, B., Malavolta, G., Schröder, D., Unruh, D.: Everlasting UC commitments from fully malicious PUFs. J. Cryptol. **35**(3), 20 (2022). https://doi.org/10.1007/s00145-022-09432-4
23. Müller-Quade, J., Unruh, D.: Long-term security and universal composability. In: Vadhan, S.P. (ed.) TCC 2007. LNCS, vol. 4392, pp. 41–60. Springer, Heidelberg (Feb 2007). https://doi.org/10.1007/978-3-540-70936-7_3
24. Müller-Quade, J., Unruh, D.: Long-term security and universal composability. J. Cryptol. **23**(4), 594–671 (2010). https://doi.org/10.1007/s00145-010-9068-8
25. Nielsen, J.: On Protocol Security in the Cryptographic Model. Ph.D. thesis, Aarhus Universitet (2003)
26. Orlandi, C., Ostrovsky, R., Rao, V., Sahai, A., Visconti, I.: Statistical concurrent non-malleable zero knowledge. In: Lindell, Y. (ed.) TCC 2014. LNCS, vol. 8349, pp. 167–191. Springer, Heidelberg (Feb 2014). https://doi.org/10.1007/978-3-642-54242-8_8
27. Pass, R., Dustin Tseng, W.-L., Venkitasubramaniam, M.: Concurrent zero knowledge, revisited. J. Cryptol. **27**(1), 45–66 (2012). https://doi.org/10.1007/s00145-012-9137-2
28. Pedersen, T.P.: Non-interactive and information-theoretic secure verifiable secret sharing. In: Feigenbaum, J. (ed.) CRYPTO 1991. LNCS, vol. 576, pp. 129–140. Springer, Heidelberg (Aug 1992). https://doi.org/10.1007/3-540-46766-1_9
29. Peikert, C., Vaikuntanathan, V., Waters, B.: A framework for efficient and composable oblivious transfer. In: Wagner, D. (ed.) CRYPTO 2008. LNCS, vol. 5157, pp. 554–571. Springer, Heidelberg (Aug 2008). https://doi.org/10.1007/978-3-540-85174-5_31
30. Prabhakaran, M., Rosen, A., Sahai, A.: Concurrent zero knowledge with logarithmic round-complexity. In: 43rd FOCS, pp. 366–375. IEEE Computer Society Press (Nov 2002). https://doi.org/10.1109/SFCS.2002.1181961
31. Prabhakaran, M., Sahai, A.: New notions of security: achieving universal composability without trusted setup. In: Babai, L. (ed.) 36th ACM STOC, pp. 242–251. ACM Press (Jun 2004). https://doi.org/10.1145/1007352.1007394

Author Index

G. Rothblum and H. Wee (Eds.): TCC 2023, LNCS 14372, pp. 543–544, 2023.
https://doi.org/10.1007/978-3-031-48624-1

Printed in the United States
by Baker & Taylor Publisher Services